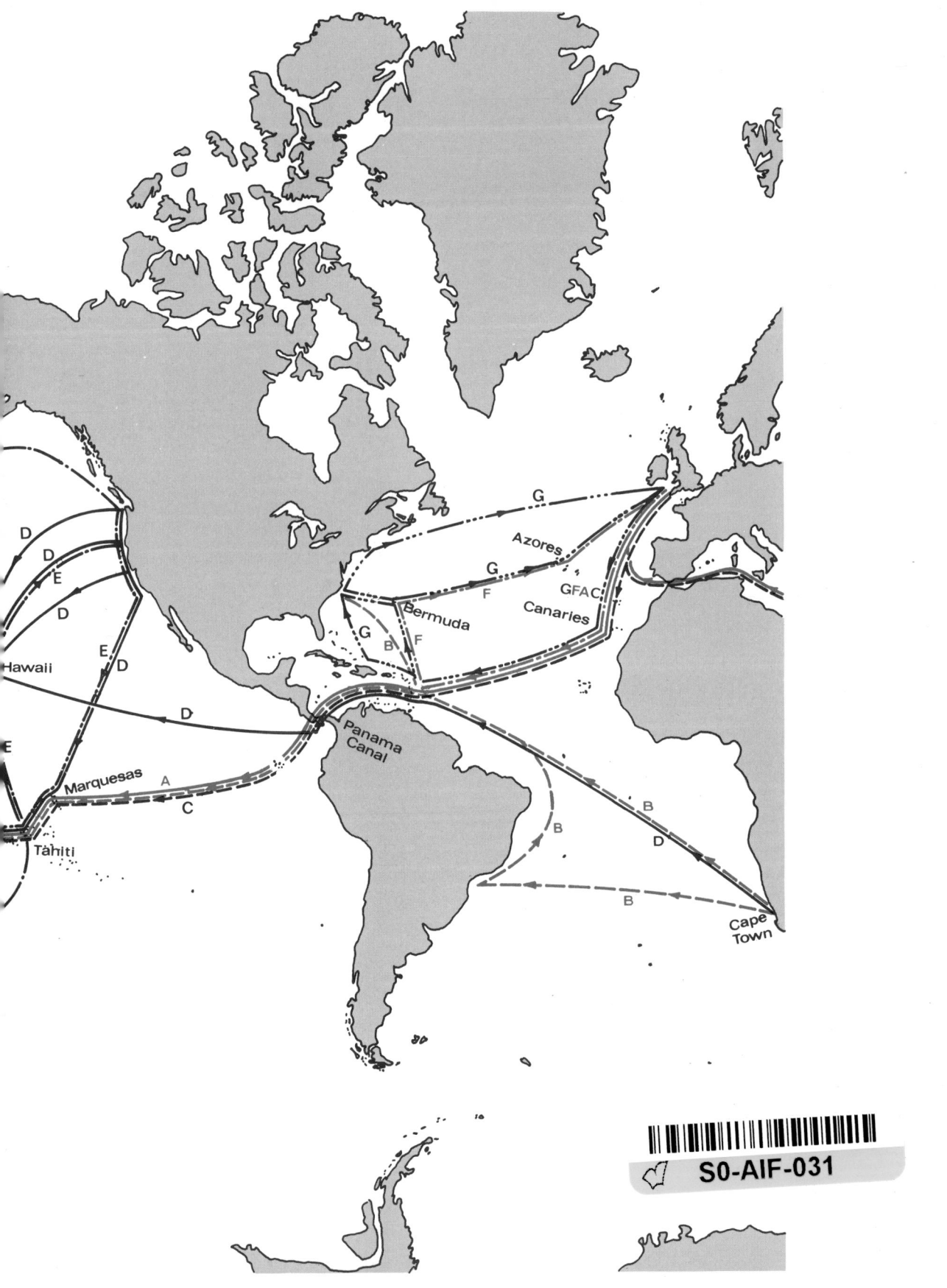

D

D

E

D

E D

Hawaii

E

D

Marquesas A

C

Tahiti

Panama
Canal

G

Azores

G

F

GFAC

Bermuda

Canaries

G

B F

B

B

D

B

Cape
Town

S0-AIF-031

WORLD CRUISING
ROUTES

Other titles of interest

World Cruising Handbook 2nd edition
Jimmy Cornell
Adlard Coles Nautical ISBN 0 7136 4419 2
International Marine ISBN 0 07 013396 4

This companion volume to *World Cruising Routes* deals with all practical matters of interest to long distance cruising sailors. Over 160 countries are covered; ports of entry, customs requirements, clearance procedures, cruising permits, port and medical facilities, health precautions, insurance, hurricane holes, radio and satellite communications, and chart agents worldwide.

Around the World Rally
Jimmy Cornell
Adlard Coles Nautical ISBN 0 7136 3690 4

An analysis of the way in which 36 different cruising boats, their equipment and their crews performed during 16 months and 24,000 miles of tough ocean sailing in the Europa 92 round-the-world rally for cruising boats.

Atlantic Pilot Atlas 2nd edition
James Clarke
Adlard Coles Nautical ISBN 0 7136 4554 7
International Marine ISBN 0 07 011921 X

A complete guide to the weather of the North and South Atlantic, the Mediterranean, and the Caribbean. This is an ideal volume for anyone planning an Atlantic crossing.

The Atlantic Crossing Guide 3rd edition
Ed Anne Hammick/RCC Pilotage Foundation
Adlard Coles Nautical ISBN 0 7136 3599 1
International Marine ISBN 0 07 025911 9

Totally updated and full of practical advice, this book covers the complete Atlantic circuit. An invaluable aid for those planning a crossing or an extended cruise in these waters.

Sell Up and Sail
Bill & Laurel Cooper
Adlard Coles Nautical ISBN 0 7136 3948 2

Now in paperback, this bestselling book is packed with first hand advice for anyone seeking to escape from the rat race and take to a life at sea. Whether your dream is of coral islands or inland waterways, it's all here, told at first hand from the authors' wide experience.

Ocean Cruising on a Budget 2nd edition
Anne Hammick
Adlard Coles Nautical ISBN 0 7136 4069 3
International Marine ISBN 0 07 158012 3

Highly praised as an essential guide for all those planning a blue water voyage, whether on a budget or not. The new updated edition now includes new Appendices on medical matters afloat and a glossary of UK/US terms.

Heavy Weather Sailing 4th edition
K Adlard Coles Nautical and Peter Bruce
Adlard Coles Nautical ISBN 0 7136 3431 6
International Marine ISBN 0 07 011732 2

The unique classic based on years of experience of sailing in the severest conditions. This new edition retains much of the original material and adds recent accounts of wild weather and ways to survive it.

Handbook of Offshore Cruising
Jim Howard
Adlard Coles Nautical ISBN 0 7136 4044 8

Covering every topic of interest to offshore cruisers, this book shows how the dream can become reality.

JIMMY CORNELL

WORLD CRUISING
ROUTES

FOURTH EDITION

*With new cruising routes from the South Seas
to the Arctic and the Antarctic*

INTERNATIONAL MARINE
Camden, Maine

This book is dedicated to my loyal friends
Ruy Moreira and Carlos Ferreira for their unstinting
generosity and their commitment to yachting.

Published by International Marine
A Division of The McGraw-Hill Companies
First published by Adlard Coles Nautical
an imprint of A&C Black (Publishers) Ltd
London

10 9 8 7 6 5 4 3 2 1

Printed in the United States of America by
R.R. Donnelley & Sons, Crawfordsville, Indiana.

Library of Congress Cataloging-in-Publication
Data is available

ISBN 0-07-013406-5

Questions regarding the ordering of this book
should be addressed to:

McGraw Hill
Customer Service Department
P.O. Box 547
Blacklick, OH 43004
Retail Customers: 1-800-262-4729
Bookstores: 1-800-722-4726
www.internationalmarine.com

Contents

FOREWORD

When I made my initial research for this book, in the early 1980s, the number of boats cruising in high latitudes was insignificant and so I decided to limit the scope of the book to the truly popular cruising areas of the world. As a result, the first edition dealt almost exclusively with sailing routes between latitudes 50°N and 50°S. While the warm water routes, and especially the tropics, continue to be the favourite cruising destination for most sailors, the cold waters of the planet are attracting an increasing number of cruising yachts. However, they are certainly no longer a rarity in the cold As (Alaska, Arctic and Antarctic) and even I, after two circumnavigations in lower latitudes, have recently sailed to the Antarctic and plan to include the Arctic and Alaska in my forthcoming cruising plans.

The new cruising routes in the extreme north and south are the main additions to this new edition, although warm water routes continue to form the bulk of the book. My research was greatly helped by my involvement with two round the world sailing events, the Expo '98 Round the World Rally and the Hong Kong Challenge, both breaking new grounds. While the Expo '98 Rally was not only the largest ever round the world event, with over 50 starters, and was the first round the world rally to sail the Cape of Good Hope route, the Hong Kong Challenge was the first round the world race to sail into the North Pacific, which was reached by the Panama Canal – another first for a round the world race. As my World Cruising Club was the organiser of both these events, I had the opportunity to gather much new routing information from their participants and to include these data in this edition. Away from the competitive world of sailing, I continued to monitor the popular cruis-

ing areas and discovered many new destinations in the tropics, all of which were duly added to the ever expanding routing portfolio comprised between the covers of this book.

By far the most important change that has occurred since this book was first published is the almost total dependence on satellite navigation in offshore sailing. Therefore all routes have been thoroughly revised in light of the ascendancy of satellite navigation. To simplify the planning of individual routes essential waypoints are listed. Several new routes have also been added as boats venture further afield and new cruising grounds are being discovered. Landfall information, as well as main ports of entry, are also included to assist the planning of each passage from the beginning to its successful end.

The one major change to affect sailors before the end of the century is the switch over to Global Distress and Safety System (GMDSS) that comes into effect on 1 February 1999. Under this new system, ships and coast stations will cease to monitor traditional distress frequencies, including channel 16. Under GMDSS a fully automatic system will become operational and owners of small boats, although not legally required to adopt the new system, will increasingly find that they have no choice but to fit out their boats with equipment designed for the requirements of the new system.

Sailing routes depend primarily on weather, which changes little over the years. However, possibly as a result of the profound changes that have occurred in the ecological balance of the world environment, there have been several freak weather conditions in recent years. Their most worrying aspect is that they are rarely predicted, occur in the wrong season and often in places where they have not been known before. Violent storms have been recorded recently at times and in places where they had not occurred before. Similarly, the violence of some tropical storms exceeds almost anything that has been experienced before. The depletion of the ozone layer and the gradual warming up of the oceans will undoubtedly affect weather throughout the world and will increase the risk of tropical storms. The unimaginable force of mega-hurricanes Hugo and Andrew should be a warning of worse things to come. All we can do is heed those warnings, make sure that the seaworthiness of our boats is never in doubt and, whenever possible, limit our cruising to the safe seasons. Also, as the sailing community depends so much on the forces of nature, we should be the first in protecting the environment and not contribute to its callous destruction.

As I wrote in the introduction to the first edition, and although since then I have sailed well over 40,000 miles in *La Aventura*, I am basically just as much a dreamer as most of my readers and my favourite pastime continues to be that of studying charts and weather pilots and dreaming of new voyages to exotic destinations. By the time this new edition is published I hope to have sailed the new *Aventura III* beyond the Arctic Circle and then join the Millennium Odyssey to South America, Antarctica, Patagonia and the South Seas – so there will be plenty of first hand material for the next edition. In the meantime I hope your quest for adventure will be satisfied by this book, whether you are actually sailing one of its routes or still at that truly enviable stage of armchair navigation when the entire world is at your feet.

Jimmy Cornell
Provence, May 1998

EXPLANATORY NOTE

The most important change which has occurred in the later editions of this book is the inclusion of individual waypoints for every route. The main aim of these waypoints is to help with the planning of a particular route and, as the original aim of this book was always that of being an aid to route planning, it must be stressed that the inclusion of waypoints must not be regarded as turning this book into a pilot for the world.

In order to organise both routes and waypoints in a logical manner, the world has been divided into three main regions: Atlantic (A), Pacific (P), and Indian (I). Each of the three oceans has been further divided into its two hemispheres, so that sailing routes are grouped in six main regions: North Atlantic (NA), South Atlantic (SA), North Pacific (NP), South Pacific (SP), North Indian (NI), and South Indian (SI). Every route within a region is identified by those two letters and its own number, thus AN46 Madeira to Gibraltar. Because they have certain features in common, transequatorial routes in every ocean have been dealt with separately and are identified by the letter 'T' preceded by the letter identifying the ocean in question, eg PT22 Tahiti to Hawaii. The Red Sea and Mediterranean have been included as separate regions. Because routes in the Red Sea are directional in character, they have been subdivided as northbound (RN) or southbound (RS). As in other parts of the world, Mediterranean routes are dealt with as separate groups and are identified by an 'M'.

Every one of the six main regions has been subdivided into individual groups, the routes included in one of those groups sharing certain common features. The numbering of the group reflects its particular region, thus PS60 groups all routes from New Zealand. Within this particular group there are eight routes, each having an individual identi-fication number, eg PS64 New Zealand to Fiji. The same system of numbering carries on into the numbering of individual waypoints, so that the various waypoints listed for that route PS64 have the following numbers: PS641, PS642, PS643, etc.

The inclusion of waypoints has made it necessary to redesign the table preceding each route. The aim of these tables is to provide at a glance all the essential information pertaining to each individual route: the best time to sail it, the period of tropical storms, US or British passage charts or sailing directions that will be needed, and the relevant cruising guides.

The waypoints themselves are listed in three separate columns: departure, intermediate, and landfall. Also listed are the coordinates of suggested ports of destination, usually those which are also official ports of entry. Departure waypoints are normally located well outside the port of departure and wherever possible clear of land and traffic. Similarly, landfall waypoints are given as close to land as it is normally safe to go before switching over to coastal navigation. Coordinates of the ports of destination are given in italics eg Whangarei *35°44'S, 174°20'E*. The italicised script draws attention to the fact that the particular port cannot be reached directly from the landfall waypoint and therefore its coordinates *should not be used for navigation* and simply fed into the automatic pilot! Indeed, it is rarely possible to sail a direct course from a given landfall point to the nearest port of destination as, for example, above, where the port of Whangarei is located several miles up a winding river. It is therefore hoped that no one will attempt to sail a direct course from PS535 Bream (35°50'S, 174°38'E), the landfall waypoint off Bream Head in the approaches to Whangarei, right into the port of Whangarei itself.

Occasionally italicised coordinates are listed as intermediate waypoints when either a certain detour or an intermediate stop are suggested. For example, such a stop might be considered at Suvorov Atoll by boats on passage from Bora Bora to Pago Pago. Similarly, on a route where individual waypoints cannot be given because of expected weather conditions, such as on route PS44 Samoa to Society Islands, the coordinates of the ports of departure and destination are in italicised script to draw attention to the fact that they are only given for information and that a route cannot be sailed between them.

Just as the number of a route is related to the relevant ocean and hemisphere, so the number of individual waypoints is related to the number of that particular route. Waypoints which are near land also have a name eg PS535 Bream. Intermediate waypoints, especially those which are in mid-ocean, are only identified by their number. Such intermediate waypoints are usually given as a guideline, as in the case of those listed for route PS26 Tahiti to Cape Horn, where the actual route sailed will depend primarily on existing weather conditions. In such situations it is made clear in the text that intermediate waypoints are only hypothetical.

In certain areas the same waypoint is used for several routes, but for the sake of clarity the waypoints are always renumbered to relate to the individual route, although its name will remain the same. Thus, a much used waypoint off Cape Finisterre will appear as AN161 Finisterre on route AN16 Northern Europe to the Mediterranean, and as AN171 Finisterre on route AN17 Northern Europe to Madeira. Occasionally, the same name has had to be used for different waypoints, in which case they have been identified by cardinal points, thus Vincent N, Vincent SW or Vincent S.

On many routes there is a choice of destinations, just as on other routes there is a choice of ports of departure. For instance, boats sailing from Gibraltar to the Azores can clear in at either Ponta Delgada or Horta. Similarly, boats bound from Tonga for the Fijian capital Suva could take their departure from either Tongatapu or Vava'u. On other routes there are two or even three different ways of sailing that particular route, either because of seasonal differences or other considerations. In all such cases, the alternatives are listed separately and are given their own letter eg route PS14A, route PS14B, etc. Waypoints are listed for each alternative route.

Official ports of entry are mentioned at the end of all major routes, and suggestions are made as to which ports are easier to reach or more convenient to use for clearance purposes. Also indicated are the ports where the authorities need to be contacted in advance by radio as well as the recommended procedure on arrival.

Each group of routes is accompanied by a diagram showing a sketch map of that particular region of the world and also the routes crossing it. Every route is identified by its individual number and also lists relevant distances. Distances between the port of departure and that of destination, are also shown in the table accompanying each route.

Author's note

The sketch maps accompanying the text are simple diagrams to show approximate positions of routes only. Since the coordinates of waypoints and any other coordinates listed in this book are only for planning purposes and must not be used for navigation, sailors using this book are strongly advised always to consult the relevant charts and sailing directions for the areas they are sailing through or are planning to cruise. They should also endeavour to obtain the latest corrections to their charts and sailing directions. One must also be aware that there are serious discrepancies between the position of certain reefs, rocks or even entire islands, as depicted on some charts, and their actual coordinates as calculated by GPS.

While every effort has been made to ensure the accuracy of the data included in this volume neither the publishers nor the author can assume any responsibility for possible errors made in these pages.

INTRODUCTION

This book attempts to fill a gap, which existed when I set off on my first circumnavigation, by providing essential information on winds, currents, regional and seasonal weather, as well as details of nearly 600 cruising routes. With the help of the information contained in this book, I hope to make it much easier for anyone who intends to undertake an ocean voyage to do all forward planning from the comfort of their home. Once the voyage has started the book will continue to be useful in suggesting alternatives or detours from the main itinerary.

World Cruising Routes is a guide to sailing routes not a comprehensive pilot for the entire world, and its users are urged to refer to the relevant sailing directions, pilot charts, and regional publications before undertaking a particular passage. Because of the vast area included in the book, only the basic data needed for planning an extensive cruise could be included, as it would have been physically impossible to include in one single volume detailed information about every route. I had to limit myself to giving only general directions on how to get from one destination to the next. These directions mention safe and dangerous seasons, prevailing winds, the kind of weather to be expected, as well as other factors that ought to be known by a small boat voyager. Whenever a particular aspect was debatable or variable, such as the beginning or end of a hurricane season, the strength of a particular current, or the frequency of gales in a specific area, I have preferred to err on the side of caution. For the same reason, I have concentrated on giving details for what is considered to be the safe cruising season and less on weather conditions during unfavourable seasons. I believe that cruising should be a pleasurable activity, and because many unpleasant conditions can be avoided

with a little planning this aspect is emphasised throughout the book. Therefore the book concentrates more on the tropical regions of the world, where most sailors intend to cruise or dream of cruising one day, and less on how to prepare for a gale swept mid-winter crossing of the North Atlantic.

The primary aim of this book is to enable the reader to plan a voyage from beginning to end and the information needed to do this is fourfold: general offshore weather conditions, descriptions of actual routes, dangers to be avoided, and some brief landfall information including recommended ports of entry. Areas which are seldom visited by sailing boats have either been omitted or described briefly. The information concerning weather is only intended as a rough guide to what weather conditions can be expected in certain areas by those planning to sail there.

Every route mentions the best time for a passage to be made along that route and the season when tropical storms affect that particular region. The extent of the hurricane season is given for the entire route, even if the point of departure or that of arrival are not themselves subject to tropical storms, but when the threat of hurricanes does exist in some area along that route. Also given are the great circle distances between principal ports, but as these distances are only meant for guidance, they are approximate, especially when the suggested route is not direct. Also indicated at the beginning of each route are the charts and sailing directions (pilots) relevant to that part of the world. Although the sailing directions deal mainly with pilotage in coastal areas, and their use on ocean passages is limited, it is advisable to have on board pilots of areas adjacent to those that will be sailed through in case an emergency landfall has to be made in an area for which charts are not carried. Both American and British charts and publications are indicated because certain parts of the world are covered better by one or the other hydrographic office. As a general rule, British charts are better for areas which were once part of the former British Empire, whereas American charts tend to be more accurate in areas of prime US interest, such as the North Pacific. Although chart and pilot numbers were correct at the time of going to press, some numbers are changed occasionally and this should be borne in mind especially when ordering charts suggested at the beginning of each route.

For reasons of space, but also because certain well sailed areas of the world are already more than adequately covered by other publications, I have kept to a minimum the information on cruising routes within North America, Northern Europe, and the Mediterranean. The few routes mentioned for those areas are only meant for general guidance for outsiders who plan to cruise in those countries and not as a cruising guide once there. In a similar way, the book gives routes on how to get to a certain area, for example the Bahamas, but it is not a guide to cruising between islands within that area.

I hope to be forgiven if I have missed or overlooked some routes. Several times I have decided to omit a little frequented route when I knew, for instance, that there is rarely more than one cruising boat per year sailing from Tuvalu to the Solomon Islands direct. In such cases I considered that there was sufficient information which could be taken from adjacent routes, where conditions are similar.

There are probably some people who expect a book of this kind to provide precise solutions for all their needs. Obviously this would be impossible, especially when dealing with something as inconsistent as winds and weather. Every so often freak weather occurs which can affect even the normally dependable routes. There is an infinite variety of circumstances which renders it impossible to lay down any fixed rule which can be followed to advantage at all times. Therefore, in those cases in which a certain course is pointed out to be the best to be pursued, but this proves impossible to accomplish, it is always better to follow one's instincts, even if it results in a detour or delay.

As well as drawing on a large variety of sources, much of the material included in the book was provided from my own voyaging. I have also received enormous help from my many sailing friends, particularly those who have ventured where I have not. In those areas, the faculty learnt in my youth of transposing myself to unknown places has served me in good stead. I am still tracing my finger along routes on charts, but this time with a little help from my friends.

1
ROUTE
PLANNING

Some voyages start as a dream, but end as a nightmare, usually due to lack of planning and inadequate preparation. Almost any well found modern sailing boat is able to travel from point A to point B under most conditions, provided the length of time it takes does not matter. Whether this is worth doing or not is highly debatable. Captain Bligh nearly had a mutiny on his hands when he stubbornly tried to round Cape Horn from east to west in the middle of winter. He finally gave up and turned around only to find an even greater challenge in the Tahitian *vahines*. Evidently, even the best forward planning could not have foreseen that kind of danger.

Fortunately the factors that have to be taken into account when planning an extended voyage are more predictable, and most of the dangers that can threaten a cruise are well known. The wise navigator planning an offshore voyage will try to take full advantage of the favourable winds and currents and avoid encountering any extreme weather. An offshore cruising boat should be well enough constructed so as to be able to withstand the average gale, and fortunately along the routes described in this volume the frequency of violent storms is extremely low during the accepted 'safe' cruising season. The main danger to be aware of are tropical revolving storms, whether these are called hurricanes, cyclones, typhoons or willy-willies, but since these affect known areas during certain times of the year, they can be avoided. This is where advance route planning has a major role to play, as it is perfectly possible to plan a voyage to all the popular cruising areas with virtually no risk of encountering a hurricane, cyclone, or typhoon.

Another element that must be taken into account when planning a voyage are the few areas of the world considered to be dangerous because of piracy, drug trafficking, or high criminality. Because of their human nature such dangers are more difficult to predict than natural phenomena, although the areas to be avoided are usually known and the sailing grapevine sounds warnings about areas that should be given a wide berth, be it some of the islands between Indonesia and the Philippines, certain countries in East or West Africa, or parts of the Red Sea. This is where a marine SSB radio or an amateur radio can be very useful since it allows one to obtain information from other sailors cruising in areas which one intends to visit in the immediate future.

Yet in spite of all the information available and the fact that so much more is known about the weather systems of the world, small boats still come to grief every year often because their skippers ignore all warnings and decide to spend the hurricane season in an area known to be hit by these violent storms. Less traumatic, but nevertheless uncomfortable, is the realisation made each year by owners of boats from the west coast of America, who find themselves in some South Pacific island at the end of a pleasant downwind cruise without the slightest idea of how to get back home. Eventually some choose the logical solution and carry on westwards, adding thousands of miles to a cruise, which has turned into an unplanned circumnavigation. A certain degree of advance planning could have made life easier. Such lack of forward planning is the main reason why there are always boats for sale in Caribbean ports, their disenchanted European owners not relishing the return voyage across the Atlantic.

On the other hand, there are obviously instances where either by force or by choice one has to fight the elements to reach a certain point.

After transiting the Panama Canal in *Aventura* we decided to visit Peru and the west coast of South America, before starting our cruise among the islands of the South Pacific. As we were very determined to sail to Peru, the only alternative to a long beat against contrary winds and the Humboldt current would have been an even longer detour around Cape Horn or through the Magellan Straits. Our decision to go against the weather was only taken because of our wish to visit a particular place. When planning a longer voyage, however, the most important thing is to make the best use of favourable winds and to avoid bad weather by choosing a suitable course and, above all, by being in the right place at the right time.

When starting to plan a voyage one of the first requirements in the planning stages is a gnomonic chart for the longer offshore passages one intends to undertake. Although GPS has obviated the need for such charts it is wise to have one on board, and to be familiar with their purpose and how to use them. A gnomonic chart is necessary because the ordinary navigational charts, based on the Mercator projection, cannot be used for planning an offshore passage of more than a few hundred miles. On the Mercator charts all meridians are represented as straight parallel lines that do not converge at the poles, as meridians do in reality. This means that any straight line drawn between two points on one of these charts based on the Mercator projection is not necessarily the shortest distance between those two points, and although a ship that sails such a course will reach its destination, it will not be by the shortest route. To be able to sail more efficiently it is necessary to establish the great circle route, which is the shortest distance between two points on the surface of the earth.

The principles of great circle sailing have been known for a long time and it is believed that great navigators such as Columbus and Magellan were already acquainted with the subject. The advantages of sailing along a great circle route were first mentioned in a work by the Portuguese astronomer Pedro Nuñez in 1537. They were brought to the attention of British seamen in the book *The Arte of Navigation* translated into English by Richard Eden in 1561. Other works also referred to the applications of great circle sailing, but the term itself appears to have been coined by John Davis in a book published in 1594 under the title of *Seaman's Secrets*, which described 'three Kinds of Sayling -Horizontall, Paradoxall and *Sayling upon a Great Circle*'.

It was about the same time that the Dutch mathematician Gerhard Mercator published a universal map on a projection that now bears his name. A course represented by a straight line on a Mercator chart is called a rhumb line and for short voyages sailing along such a line between the port of departure and that of arrival makes a minimal difference. In order to find the shorter route for a longer passage, the same straight line will have to be drawn on a gnomonic chart, which uses a different projection with meridians converging at the poles and parallels of latitude represented by curved lines. Any straight line on a gnomonic chart is part of a great circle and is indeed the shortest distance between the two points joined by that line. Because gnomonic charts cannot be used for navigation, the great circle track drawn on such a chart has to be transferred to a Mercator chart. This is done by making a note of the latitudes at which the great circle route intersects successive meridians which have been selected at convenient intervals, usually at 5°. These positions are transferred to the corresponding Mercator chart and joined by straight lines. This succession of rhumb lines approximates very closely the actual great circle track for that route.

This rather cumbersome method of finding the great circle track for any chosen route can be avoided by solving the problem not graphically but mathematically. All this is taken care of now by GPS, which gives both the great circle course and distance to the next destination with the added advantage of these values being constantly updated. However, GPS only does this when one is already underway. Therefore, for planning purposes one should obtain either a gnomonic chart or a software programme for one's computer.

The purchase of gnomonic charts is therefore no longer absolutely necessary for those who intend to calculate their great circle course by other means, although acquiring the pilot charts for the oceans that will be crossed is essential. These charts are published by the US Department of Defense Hydrographic Center and can be obtained from the usual chart agents. Pilot charts are issued for all oceans of the world and give monthly or quarterly averages of wind direction and strength, currents, percentages of calms and gales, limits of ice, tropical storm tracks, and other kinds of information. The data contained in these charts is based on observations made by ships that have passed through those areas and although they give an accurate overall picture of weather conditions for a certain time of year, they are only *averages* and must be regarded as such.

With the help of the relevant pilot charts for the area to be sailed and the directions contained in this book, planning a voyage can start in earnest. In order to make it simpler to draw up the general outline of a longer cruise, some hypothetical voyages are described in the next chapter. These examples are only meant to show what can be done in a given amount of time. Both short term and long term planning are finally the responsibility of the skipper who knows best what are the capabilities and limitations of his or her crew and boat.

The importance of long term or forward planning can be seen from the following example. Presuming that a cruise of a few months is planned in the Lesser Antilles, the order in which the islands are visited should be determined by subsequent plans. Most people leave from the Canaries concerned only with crossing the Atlantic by the fastest and most convenient route, their landfall in the Caribbean being decided by many factors, but not always by long term considerations. If one is planning to sail to Europe or the USA at the end of the cruising season in the Caribbean, the logical way to cruise through the islands is from south to north, so that the same ground will not be covered twice. On the other hand, if the voyage will continue in the Pacific and a transit of the Panama Canal is planned, it makes more sense to end the transatlantic crossing in one of the islands further north, such as Antigua or Guadeloupe, and then sail down the chain of islands towards Grenada or Venezuela. Such a route would ensure better winds when sailing among the Lesser Antilles and also a shorter passage to Panama when the time arrives. The passage across the Caribbean Sea can be very boisterous at the end of winter and a start from one of the ABC Islands off Venezuela (Aruba, Bonaire, or Curaçao) can make that leg shorter and more pleasant. An additional advantage of this route is the fact that the southernmost part of the Caribbean is very rarely affected by hurricanes, so that if the cruise is delayed for any reason, the boat will be in a relatively safe place.

Equally important when forward planning is to allow certain subjective factors to influence the choice of routes. An order of priorities has to be decided and this is usually the point at which one must be prepared to face up to one's own limitations. All too often people are ashamed to admit to others, and even to themselves, that they are afraid of a certain passage. A good example is the rounding of the Cape of Good Hope, more aptly called the Cape of Storms, which is indeed a very dangerous area, especially if one is not too confident that the boat could take a knockdown or capsize, which is an eventuality that must be faced by all those who take this route. There is absolutely nothing wrong in avoiding such a passage and this can be done easily by choosing the Red Sea route instead. However, this decision must be made well in advance, ideally before going through the Torres Strait and not on the eve of departure from Mauritius.

Reliance on auxiliary engines has become an accepted part of modern cruising and this is the reason why on certain routes skippers are advised to have a good reserve of fuel as this can make a great difference to the length of the passage. The convenience of being able to motor through the doldrums and not be becalmed for days or weeks is one such instance, as is the ability to power against a strong outflowing current to enter a lagoon, which otherwise could not be entered. Filling up one's fuel tanks before a windless passage is part of good forward planning as is choosing a port with good provisioning, refuelling and repair facilities for the start of long offshore passages.

An important element of advance planning is to be aware of official requirements in the countries to be visited and to know where one may need visas, vaccinations, or cruising permits. Much of this practical information is contained in the companion volume to this book, *World Cruising Handbook*. In spite of sailing boats being able to visit more countries than in the past, in many places formalities have not been simplified. The captain must be aware of specific requirements and the location of the official ports of entry; ignorance of local regulations will not be accepted as an excuse. In Australia, for example, any foreign national, except New Zealanders, arriving without a visa will be heavily fined. So as part of forward planning, one may have to plan a detour to a country where there is a diplomatic mission issuing the necessary visa. Choosing the right place, ideally close to an international airport, is equally important when picking up or dropping off crew. Just as important for long term cruisers is to plan regular overhauls in places with good repair facilities. My *World Cruising Guide* was written very much with that objective in mind.

These are some of the factors that can influence planning, both in the short and long term. However, what is needed at all times, and especially once a cruise has started, is a good dose of commonsense, which will help solve most problems. Nowhere is this more true than in the realm of navigation, particularly in view of the current reliance on GPS navigation. For example, if one is not too sure about the position of a certain reef, island, or any other danger, it is generally safer to assume that the latitude stated is more accurate than the longitude. The coordinates of most of these dangers were fixed by navigators before the advent of precise modern instruments, and many charts of remote areas have yet to be corrected. This is why it is still perfectly valid to use the practice of the masters of the sailing ships, who always tried to 'run down' the latitude of a given place, so as to maximise the chances of finding it. On the other hand, if one wishes to avoid a certain danger, the main thing to avoid is its latitude. As many ocean passages along the popular cruising routes are from east to west, this means that it should not be too difficult to choose a safe latitude and stay on it when approaching a known danger.

The influence that such commonsense can have on good seamanship is illustrated by examples in my previous survey books, and one conclusion I drew after talking to a great number of experienced sailors was that one of the most important qualities to have while sailing is patience. A little humility and respect for the powers of nature are undoubtedly just as important and this is probably the explanation why superstitious sailors prefer to say that they are 'bound for' their destination. Many things can happen to stop a ship from reaching its desired destination and careful planning has a major part to play in bringing a ship safely home.

2
PRINCIPAL WORLD CRUISING ROUTES

Planning an offshore voyage is not a simple matter because many factors have to be taken into consideration. The most important factor to be considered is the safety of the vessel and its crew, therefore it is crucial to ensure that the route will avoid areas of known dangers and also that as much as possible of the sailing will be done during favourable seasons. A large proportion of the cruising routes described in this book are in the tropics, which is where world voyagers spend much of their time. However, many tropical areas are only safe for six or seven months of the year, the remaining months being liable to tropical storms. In the following pages I shall try to give some examples of typical world cruises that can be done with maximum safety. The various circumnavigations described are all westabout to take maximum advantage of the prevailing wind systems and to sail as much as possible under trade wind conditions. Because much of the time will be spent in the tropics, the proposed timing will avoid those areas during the tropical storm seasons. The majority of small boat voyages around the world follow the trade wind routes and the number of cruising boats trying to accomplish a circumnavigation against the prevailing winds is so small as not to merit a separate example. Similarly, the following examples all pass through the South Pacific, which continues to be the main attraction for virtually any sailor setting off on a cruise around the world. Routes A to G on the following pages are shown on the endpaper map.

Voyage A: Two year circumnavigation from Europe

The shortest time in which a cruise around the world can be accomplished in a small sailing boat is probably two years. By precise timing and careful choice of favourable seasons, the two EUROPA Round the World Rallies, in 1991–2 and 1994–5, accomplished a circumnavigation in 16 months. However, these are competitive events and the sailors taking part in them were prepared to move at a relatively fast pace. The two year example is still valid for anyone planning to cruise alone.

If the point of departure is Scandinavia, Britain, or Northern Europe, the recommended time for leaving would be early summer when optimum conditions can be expected in the North Sea, English Channel, and across the Bay of Biscay. Departures from Mediterranean ports and Gibraltar can be left as late as October. This is also the time when boats should be on their way to the Canaries, whether sailing direct or via Madeira.

The earliest time for an Atlantic crossing along the NE trade wind route is after the middle of November, as such a departure ensures that landfall is made in one of the Caribbean islands before Christmas at the beginning of the safe cruising season. However, the chances of finding better winds are higher later in winter and some of the fastest passages have been recorded between January and March. Columbus himself left the Canaries in September and had steady trade winds almost all the way across. That first Atlantic crossing along the trade wind route was undertaken at the height of the hurricane season, when such a passage should not even be considered.

After one or two months in the Eastern Caribbean, the Panama Canal should be transited in February or early March. This avoids arriving in the Marquesas before the end of March when the islands of French Polynesia are still subject to tropical cyclones. Because of the limited time available, Tahiti should be left in early June so as to arrive in Fiji by July. As these are the months when the SE trades are at their most constant, these long passages can usually be made at good speeds. Passages from Fiji onwards should be timed to pass through the Torres Strait before the end of August or early in September if taking the Cape of Good Hope route.

The passage across the South Indian Ocean will have to be made in a similar rhythm, with long periods at sea and little time to spend in the islands en route. The start of the cyclone season in December indicates a departure from Mauritius for the passage to South Africa not later than the end of October. The next leg to Cape Town is best made in January or February, when conditions around the tip of Africa are considered to be the most favourable.

Those planning to return to the Mediterranean via the Red Sea have the choice of either calling at Bali and carrying on to Singapore, or making their way to Sri Lanka via Christmas Island. A cruising permit is required for those wishing to pass through Indonesia, which probably dictates the choice of route. The advantage of a passage across the North Indian Ocean is that this can be done in January or February, which allows longer time to be spent earlier in the Pacific, negotiating the Torres Strait only in September or even early October. The end of the year will see the boat somewhere in SE Asia preparing for a winter crossing of the North Indian Ocean, when the NE monsoon normally provides excellent sailing conditions in the first months of the year. The subsequent passage through the Red Sea and the transiting of the Suez Canal in March or April will allow the boat to complete its circumnavigation approximately two years after leaving Europe.

Those returning via the Cape of Good Hope can sail to the Azores, either directly or possibly via Brazil, although the latter may add too much time to the return journey. An arrival in the Azores in April or May would enable a return to the point of departure exactly two years after leaving home.

However, there are so many temptations on the way that often such quick voyages end up by stretching into three and even four years. My first circumnavigation on *Aventura* took all of six years, so it is rather ironic that I should be promoting an event which attempts to encompass the world in less than one quarter of that time. Unfortunately not everyone has that kind of time for a circum-

navigation, nor does everyone wish to be away from home for so long, which is probably one of the reasons for the EUROPA Round the World Rally's ongoing success.

The only purpose of this hypothetical example is to show how it is possible to plan a two year circumnavigation so as to be always in the right place at the right time. Indeed, the points made above were put to good use when planning the itinerary of the first Round the World Rally, some of which I sailed in *La Aventura*. The timing of the first event was so successful that the route of the second one remained almost unchanged. The EUROPA Round the World Rally has now become a regular event to be run every three years, the next one being due to start in January 1997.

Voyage B: Two year circumnavigation from the east coast of North America

For boats leaving on a two year circumnavigation from the east coast of North America and planning to start their voyage at the beginning of winter, the timing of departure is crucial. If some time is to be spent in the Lesser Antilles, an attempt should be made to leave by the first week of November sailing directly to the Virgin Islands or one of the islands in the Eastern Caribbean. The schedule is more relaxed if the departure is planned for the end of spring or early summer. In this case boats normally sail to the Eastern Caribbean via Bermuda in May or June and then make their way south in order to spend the summer in an area with a low risk of hurricanes, such as Venezuela, Colombia, or Panama.

For those leaving later in the year and planning to sail straight to Panama, there are two alternatives: either to go via the Bahamas and the Windward Passage or through the Intracoastal Waterway to Florida and thence to Panama. Boats leaving from Florida can leave later in winter and make their way to Panama eastabout or westabout Cuba, either of which is feasible. Those who leave in November and take the longer route via the Eastern Caribbean arrive at the beginning of winter and thus have at least two months to cruise the islands of the Lesser Antilles before sailing to Panama. Whichever route is sailed to Panama, the Canal should be transited in February or early March. This avoids arriving in the Marquesas before the end of the cyclone season (December to end of March). From Tahiti onwards, the timing is similar to the one described in the previous example. The Society Islands should be left not later than June so as to arrive in Fiji by July. From Fiji onwards, the passages should be timed to pass through the Torres Strait before the end of August or early in September.

The South Indian Ocean will be crossed in a similar rhythm, with long periods at sea and not much time to spend in the islands en route. The start of the cyclone season in December indicates a departure from Mauritius for the passage to South Africa not later than the end of October. The tip of Africa should be weathered in January or February, when conditions in those stormy waters are usually the most favourable. From South Africa boats normally sail to Brazil and thence to the Lesser Antilles. An arrival in the Eastern Caribbean in the spring would enable a return to the point of departure less than two years after leaving home.

A return to America via the North Indian Ocean, the Red Sea, and Mediterranean will certainly make the voyage considerably longer. It is an alternative favoured by many North American sailors who wish to avoid sailing around the Cape of Good Hope. Such an alternative has the attraction of seeing some of SE Asia before the North Indian Ocean is crossed during the NE monsoon of winter. The Red Sea is transited in late winter and the Mediterranean is reached by March. On leaving the Mediterranean, one can either sail home directly, via the Azores and possibly Bermuda, which is best done early in the summer, or take the longer route across the Atlantic via the Canaries, which should not be done before the middle of November.

Voyage C: Three year circumnavigation from Europe or the east coast of North America

The two year circumnavigations described above can be made much more enjoyable if more time is available. Although the additional mileage covered during a three year long circumnavigation would only amount to about 4000 miles, the extra year allows more time to be spent in places en route and makes the entire voyage more enjoyable.

The first part of the voyage either from Europe or North America would be similar to that described in the previous examples. A little more time can be spent in the Caribbean, but the Panama Canal should be transited in March so as to arrive in the Marquesas before the end of April. The following three months can be spent in French Polynesia, allowing one to be there for the unique 14 July celebrations. Leaving the Society Islands before the end of July makes it possible to spend some time in all the island groups en route to Fiji. Because of the approaching cyclone season (late November to March), a decision must be made whether to spend this in Tonga (Vava'u), American Samoa (Pago Pago), New Zealand, or nontropical Australia. Although a number of boats hole up in one of the first two places, these anchorages are in the cyclone area and the vast majority of those cruising the South Pacific make their way to New Zealand, which is outside the cyclone belt. A stay in Fiji is not recommended as the number of safe anchorages is small and they fill up quickly in an emergency.

The passage from Fiji to New Zealand is normally undertaken in November. Most boats spend the entire cyclone season in New Zealand and leave for the Torres Strait and Indian Ocean early in April. Such a departure allows them to visit some of the island groups bordering on the Coral Sea before reaching the Indian Ocean. Another alternative is to sail across the Tasman Sea from New Zealand to Australia in February or March and then sail up the east coast of Australia towards the Torres Strait. An earlier arrival in the Indian Ocean allows more time to be spent en route, whether in Darwin or Indonesia, if a cruising permit has been obtained beforehand. The rest of the voyage is the same as that described in Voyages A and B.

Voyage D: Three year circumnavigation from the west coast of North America

If a circumnavigation is planned from the west coast of North America, either California or the Pacific Northwest including British Columbia, at least three years should be allowed. The primary destination for almost all of those who undertake this voyage is Tahiti, which can be reached either via Hawaii or the Marquesas. A few boats include the Galapagos Islands on their itinerary and although permission to stop there is not given automatically, few boats are actually turned away and most are allowed to spend a few days there. For those taking the Hawaiian route, time of departure is less crucial, while a late March or early April departure is recommended for those intending to sail directly to the Marquesas.

Those making an early departure and arriving in French Polynesia in April or May will be able to follow a similar schedule as that described in Voyages A and B. Later departures will not reach Tahiti before July or August, which means that one will not have much time left to spend in the tropics before sailing to a safe place for the coming cyclone season (December to March). The authorities no longer allow boats to remain in French Polynesia during the cyclone season. This certainly applies to those who leave California in late November and sail direct to the Marquesas, as a number of boats have done in recent years. Although the islands of French Polynesia are not visited by cyclones every year one should not be lulled into a false sense of security, as over the years several boats have been lost in cyclones which have struck Eastern Polynesia. One way to avoid spending the cyclone season in French Polynesia is to leave California in November and spend the winter either in Hawaii, Mexico, or Central America. The voyage to the Marquesas or Tahiti can then be made the following March, allowing one to arrive there at the start of the safe season. The rest of the South Pacific cruise could follow the schedule described in either example A or B.

Those who are in a hurry to return home in the shortest time possible should follow the previously suggested timetable across the South Indian Ocean so as to arrive in Cape Town by Christmas. This would allow them to arrive in the Lesser Antilles by February and in Panama by March or April. Once through the Panama Canal the choice is between a dash along the coast of Central America and Mexico, if one can rely on a powerful engine, or a detour to Hawaii in the hope of finding favourable winds for the return voyage. The timing of one's arrival in Panama is crucial if one is planning to sail to California along the coast, because Cabo San Lucas should be cleared before the onset of the hurricane season in June.

Because of this tight scheduling and other considerations, many west coast sailors are put off by the South African route and choose the Red Sea route instead. As described in Voyage A, the passage across the North Indian Ocean can be done as late as February or even March, which allows a more relaxed pace earlier on. But the main attraction of this alternative route is the chance to spend some time in the Mediterranean. Arriving there through the Suez Canal in April one has about six summer months to sail to Gibraltar and visit interesting places on the way. The passage from Gibraltar to the Canaries can be done in October and the subsequent crossing of the Atlantic will also take place at a good time. Having arrived in the Eastern Caribbean before Christmas, the voyage to Panama and beyond can be undertaken in a more leisurely fashion than if one had arrived there straight from South Africa. With more time in hand even the difficulty of the return passage along the Pacific coast of Central America can be faced with more detachment.

Voyage E: A round Pacific voyage

Probably the greatest disadvantage of the Pacific Ocean from a cruising point of view is that it does not lend itself to a logical circumnavigation, a fact recognised as early as the sixteenth century by the Spanish navigators. Today's voyagers are faced with almost the same dilemma, but at least the improved windward going capability of their craft makes the problem somewhat easier.

The departure point for the suggested Pacific circumnavigation can be either the west coast of North America, which is covered in Voyage D, or Panama, which is described in Voyage A. Because the South Pacific and its myriad islands continue to be the principal attraction of a Pacific cruise, the return voyage to the west coast of North America will be considered from somewhere in the Southwest Pacific, New Zealand being the most likely place for the start of such a voyage. The most logical return itinerary is via Tahiti with the help of westerly winds found below latitude 35°S. This return voyage to Tahiti is best made at the end of the cyclone season, in April or May, before the onset of the southern winter. If a prompt departure is made from New Zealand, there is sufficient time to reach the west coast of North America via Hawaii long before winter also arrives in the northern hemisphere. Such a return trip to Tahiti allows those who had sailed quickly through these islands on their outward voyage to see more of French Polynesia the second time around. The other alternative is to sail from New Zealand to

Hawaii via the Cook Islands by following the same time schedule.

For those who are determined to complete a circumnavigation of the Pacific, there is always the possibility of continuing a South Pacific cruise to the Far East. This is best accomplished by sailing from the Solomon Islands or Papua New Guinea to Guam and thence to Japan, with a possible detour to the Philippines and Hong Kong. The voyage can then be continued via the Aleutian Islands to Alaska, British Columbia, and beyond. Such an itinerary requires careful planning, so as to sail among the islands of the Far East at the most favourable time, but such a northern sweep can be accomplished although it will take longer than the return route via Tahiti and Hawaii.

Other itineraries for a return to the west coast have also been tried out, although far less successfully, because of the high proportion of head winds encountered on the way to Hawaii, particularly in the case of voyages starting from Micronesia. Many of these attempts had to be abandoned and those who managed to complete them vowed never to make such an error of judgement again. This is why the importance of properly planning a return voyage to the west coast cannot be emphasised strongly enough and the various alternatives outlined in these examples should be considered carefully, preferably before leaving home.

Voyage F: A round Atlantic voyage from Europe

Compared to the Pacific Ocean, a circumnavigation of the North Atlantic is much easier to accomplish and it is in fact a voyage undertaken every year by a large number of European sailors, who have time for only a one year offshore cruise or who complete the circle in various stages over several years returning home in between. Christopher Columbus was the first sailor to accomplish such an Atlantic circumnavigation and the following itinerary is largely based on his own voyage of 1492–3. The only significant change is the timing, as on his first transatlantic voyage Columbus sailed west during the hurricane season of summer and returned home too early in winter.

A late spring or summer start is recommended for those leaving from Northern or Western Europe, so as to cross the Bay of Biscay before the middle of August. Such timing allows some time to be spent cruising the coasts of the Iberian peninsula before heading for the Canary Islands, either direct or via Madeira. The crossing of the Atlantic can be made in November or early December along the trade wind route, arriving in the Caribbean before the end of the year. The next four months can be spent cruising the islands of the Eastern Caribbean, preferably from south to north, so as not to cover the same ground twice. The return voyage to Europe should start in April or early May and usually includes a stopover in Bermuda, although a few people sail directly to the Azores. The Azores provide a convenient springboard in mid-Atlantic for a return passage to reach the home port in either Northern Europe or the Mediterranean almost one year after leaving. In fact the Atlantic circle can be accomplished in as little as eight months, especially if the point of departure is in Southern Europe. In such a case one can leave for the Canaries as late as October, cross the Atlantic in the second half of November, and return from the Caribbean the following April. Such timing is followed successfully every year by many boats taking part in the ARC, who incorporate this annual transatlantic event from Gran Canaria to St Lucia into their plans.

A major attraction of such an Atlantic circle for those who cannot take off all the necessary time in one block is the fact that the voyage can be broken up into several stages. The first stage is to sail the boat to a southern port at the beginning of summer. The boat can be left in a marina while the crew returns home by air. This stage can be extended to go as far as the Canaries, which ideally should be reached by August or early September. There are many excellent marinas in the Canaries where a boat can be left in safety and there are also frequent flights to all parts of Europe. If the boat is left for a while in Southern Europe, perhaps in Gibraltar or Lagos, the passage to the Canaries should not be left too late as every year boats miss the start of the ARC because of bad weather encountered on the way to the Canaries in late October or early November. Indeed there is no good reason to leave this section of the voyage to so late in the season.

Once the boat has reached the Caribbean in time for the Christmas holidays, those who have to return home temporarily can do so by leaving the boat in a safe marina, such as Rodney Bay in St Lucia, the finishing point of the ARC. There are frequent flights to Europe from St Lucia,

Martinique, Guadeloupe, Antigua, and Barbados, all of which are convenient places for crew changes. At the completion of the Caribbean cruise, the return passage to Europe must be contemplated. This can be done nonstop to the Azores or via Bermuda. If necessary, the trip can be broken in the Azores where the boat can be left in one of two excellent marinas, either in Horta or Ponta Delgada, both of which have direct flights to Lisbon. From the Azores, the sail back home can be done at any time during the summer.

An extended Atlantic circumnavigation has taken shape in recent years with an increasing number of boats sailing from the Canary Islands to Brazil, either direct or via the Cape Verde Islands and West Africa. Such a detour usually adds another year to the voyage, which from Brazil continues along the coast of South America to the Caribbean where it rejoins one of the routes mentioned above.

A very different return route to Europe has taken shape in recent years by sailors who have visited the eastern seaboard of the USA and decided to continue NE towards Newfoundland. Such a voyage can then continue to Greenland and Iceland, and cross the Atlantic along a route pioneered by the Viking navigators 1000 years ago.

Voyage G: A round Atlantic voyage from North America

A similar circumnavigation of the North Atlantic can also be undertaken from the east coast of either the USA or Canada. The best time for leaving is also late spring or early summer when Europe can be reached either direct or via the Azores. Such timing does not allow too much time to be spent in the more northern parts of Europe as one has to head south before the onset of the autumn gales. However, time can be spent in Portugal, Spain, Gibraltar, or Madeira before joining the other boats preparing the cross to the Caribbean from the Canaries. As described in the previous example, the Atlantic circle can be interrupted at several points should one need to return home for any length of time. The Azores provide a convenient stopover with two good marinas where a boat can be left in total safety and in summer there are direct flights to Boston from the island of Terceira. There are similar places where the voyage can be interrupted in both the Canaries and Caribbean, as mentioned earlier.

The return voyage from the Caribbean to ports on the east coast of North America offers far more choices than those available to European sailors. The quickest way is to sail directly to the east coast at the end of winter (April), either from the Virgins or one of the Lesser Antilles and to make landfall in one of the ports south of Cape Hatteras. Alternatively one can sail to Bermuda from where it might be easier to reach ports lying further north. Yet another possibility is to sail to Florida via the Bahamas and return home through the Intracoastal Waterway.

An alternative way to reach Europe is to sail a more northerly route by heading NE towards Newfoundland. The disadvantage of such a route is that it cannot be sailed too early in the summer, but it has the great attraction that both Greenland and Iceland can be visited before crossing the Atlantic to Northern Europe.

Rallies and races

Just as the wise navigator plans on being in the right place at the right time, so the organisers of various sailing events are timing their events to take place at a time when they can expect to attract the maximum number of cruising boats. The perfect example is the highly successful Antigua Sailing Week, which starts on the last weekend in April at the end of the sailing season in the Caribbean. For nearly three decades hundreds of yachts have congregated in Antigua at this time of year for one week of racing, and a lot of fun besides, before setting off for either Europe or North America.

Races such as the Antigua Sailing Week are now being held regularly in all the popular cruising areas or along the major cruising routes. Also in the Caribbean, the Heineken Regatta is held in St Maarten at the beginning of March every year. Across the world, in Thailand, the annual King's Cup Regatta is held in Phuket at the beginning of December at a time when scores of cruising yachts are congregating there waiting for the northeast monsoon to blow them across the North Indian Ocean. The King's Cup is preceded by the Raja Muda Cup, a cruising rally along the coast of Malaysia timed to bring the boats to Phuket in time for the King's Cup Regatta. The Raja Muda Cup caters mainly for cruising boats on a world voyage and there are now several events aimed at this floating community. One of the oldest established is the Darwin to Ambon Race, starting in July from the capital of Australia's Northern Territory. The main attraction of this annual event is that boats taking part in it automatically obtain the compulsory cruising permit for Indonesia. Many of the participants in the Darwin to Ambon Race will have taken part earlier in two similar events staged in the South Pacific. The annual South Pacific Regatta sets off from Auckland in May and is joined by boats which have spent the cyclone season in New Zealand and are returning to the tropical South Pacific as well as Antipodean sailors at the beginning of their cruises. Later in the season, the Musket Cove to Vila Race is joined by boats sailing from Fiji to Vanuatu.

There are many more examples of such events which are joined by cruising boats to reach a particular popular cruising destination. The various races from Newport, Rhode Island, to Bermuda are often joined by boats on their way to the Caribbean or Europe. Similarly, the Caribbean 1500 Rally is aimed squarely at North American boats sailing in November from the Chesapeake Bay area to the Virgin Islands. The inspiration for this event was the ARC (Atlantic Rally for Cruisers), which has been attracting over one hundred boats every year since it was launched in 1986. The ARC leaves the Canaries at the end of November and is joined by boats planning to reach the Caribbean before

Christmas. The concept of the ARC was applied successfully to the round the world rallies organised by the World Cruising Club and now taking place each year. The circumnavigation has been divided into a number of separate rallies, each covering a certain part of the world. For example, the Pacific Rally sails every February from St Lucia to Panama, Galapagos and French Polynesia, while at the same time the Red Sea Rally leaves Thailand bound for the Red Sea and Mediterranean. The modular concept of the annual World Cruising Rally allows participants to join any of these events and complete a circumnavigation at their own pace.

When planning a voyage it may be worth keeping in mind some of the above events, whether to enjoy a week of racing in a particularly beautiful area or take advantage of the safety in numbers as well as the competitive spirit of such offshore events. Just as attractive can be the help one gets in dealing with local authorities when arriving in some countries as part of such an international event. Keeping track of when and where such events take place can be useful both for those intending to join and to those determined to avoid the crowds!

3

WINDS AND CURRENTS OF THE WORLD

Ever since man first ventured offshore in craft powered by the wind, he has looked for patterns in the wind's behaviour. Such observations may have led the early fishermen to use an offshore breeze to take their canoes to favourite fishing spots in the morning and the onshore breeze to waft them home later in the day. These patterns are still used in some parts of the world where fishermen continue to use sailing craft as their forefathers have done over countless generations. Discovering a similar regularity for offshore voyaging was more difficult and some remote places in the world might have remained unpopulated until much later if early voyagers had been able to find a favourable wind to return home. The fact that there was a regular pattern to the winds was already recognised in ancient times and seasonal sailing routes were a common feature in the ancient world. The Chinese established such routes in the Far East, the Greeks used them in the Aegean, the Polynesians were helped by them to colonise the far flung islands of the Pacific, the Papuans are still following the traditional Kula route with the help of seasonal winds, while Arab traders used the monsoons of the Indian Ocean to establish a regular link between India and East Africa.

This reliance on favourable winds for most offshore voyages lasted until the last century, when the greatly improved windward going capabilities of sailing ships freed their masters of the shackles imposed by having to follow a route governed by the wind alone. However, in spite of being able to sail closer to the wind, neither did the masters of the old clippers nor do the skippers of modern yachts enjoy battling against head winds, and most would still make a detour to pick up a fair wind. Even in a well designed yacht it is often wiser to cover a longer distance with better winds than to stubbornly try to follow the direct route between two points. This is the reason why it is so important to understand the prevailing wind systems of the world, which dictate most of the cruising routes described in the following pages.

The importance of defining the prevailing winds in certain areas of the world was already recognised by the Portuguese and Spanish navigators of the fifteenth and sixteenth centuries, and their findings were kept a closely guarded secret for a long time. The first transatlantic voyage by Christopher Columbus showed his followers that a detour to the south was the best route to the newly discovered islands of the Caribbean, whereas a northerly sweep was to be preferred for the return voyage to Europe. Similarly in the Pacific, Magellan and other early navigators demonstrated that the voyage from east to west across the South Pacific was a relatively easy matter if one stayed within the southeasterly trades. However, a return voyage against the same trades proved impossible until finally the Spanish navigator Urganeta discovered the westerly winds of higher latitudes, which came to be called the anti-trades or passage winds.

This worldwide wind pattern has thus been known for a long time and countless navigators have made use of this knowledge over the centuries. In his *Memoir of the Northern Atlantic Ocean*, published in its 13th edition in 1873, Alexander George Findlay succinctly describes this wind pattern in the following words:

'It has been well observed that the wind systems of our globe naturally govern the tracks of ships crossing the oceans, the trade winds carrying them from East to West within the tropics, while anti-trade or passage winds

Continued on page 24

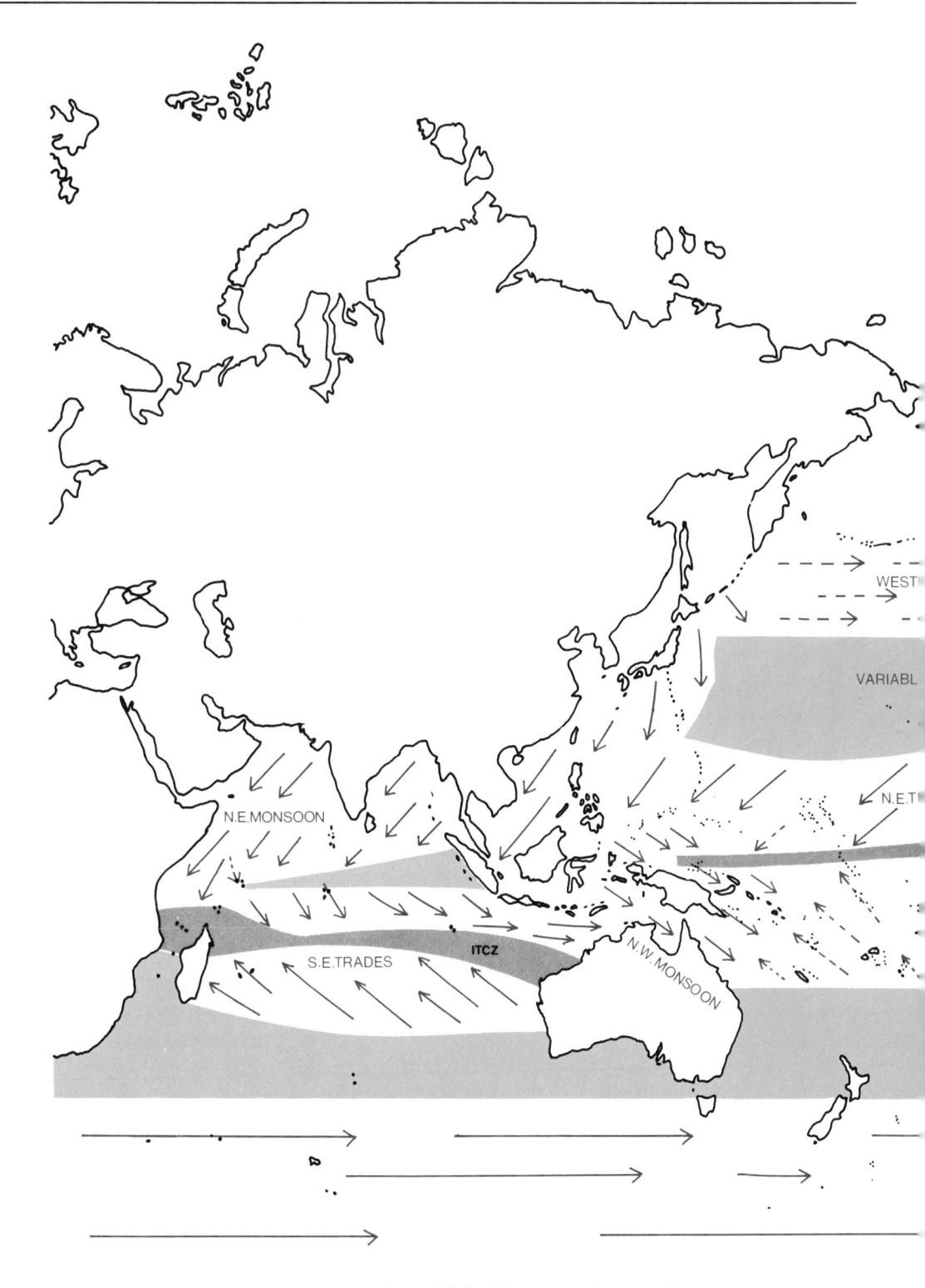

2. PREVAILING WIND SYSTEMS JANUARY TO MARCH

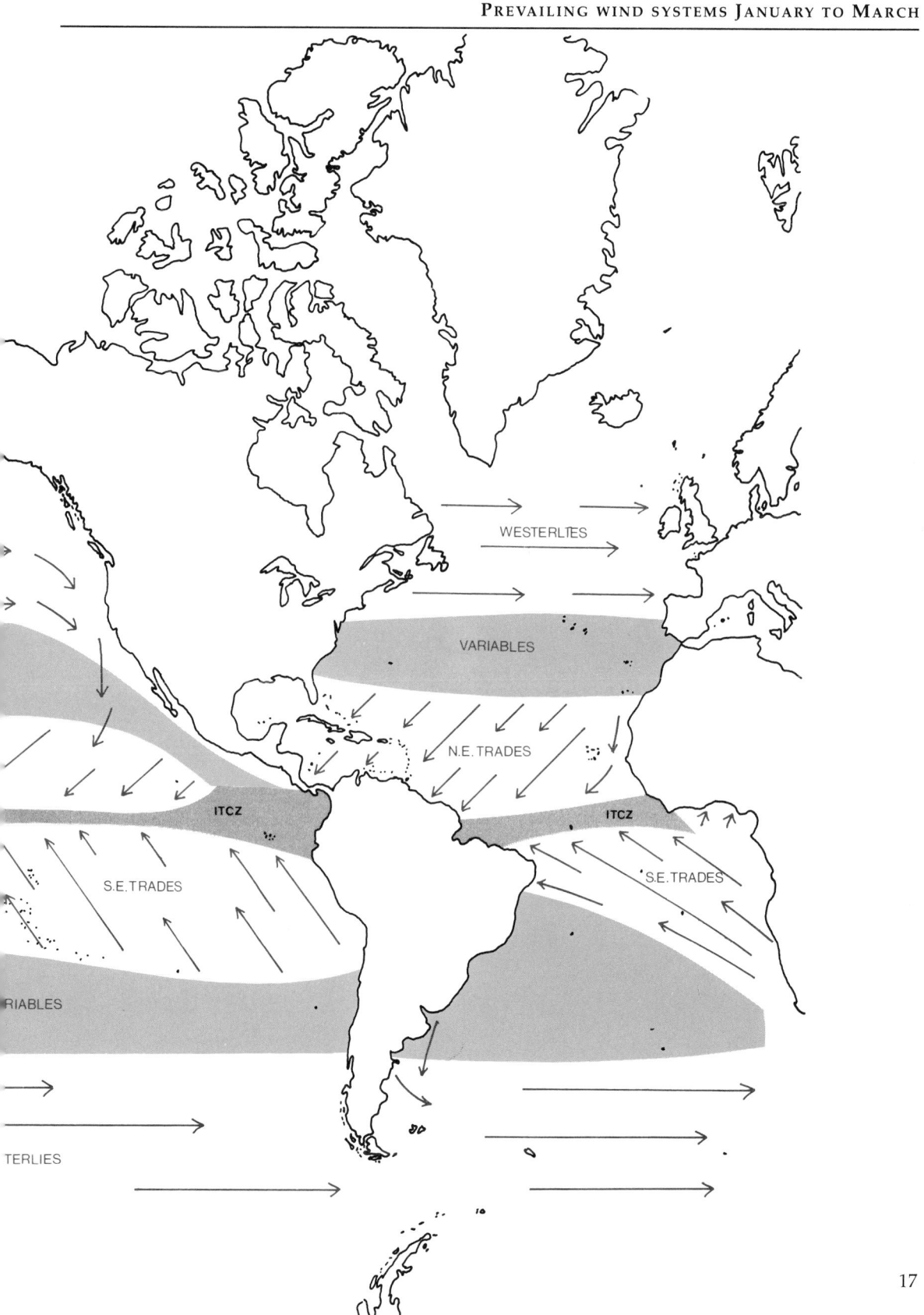

WESTERLIES

VARIABLES

N.E. TRADES

ITCZ

ITCZ

S.E. TRADES

S.E. TRADES

RIABLES

TERLIES

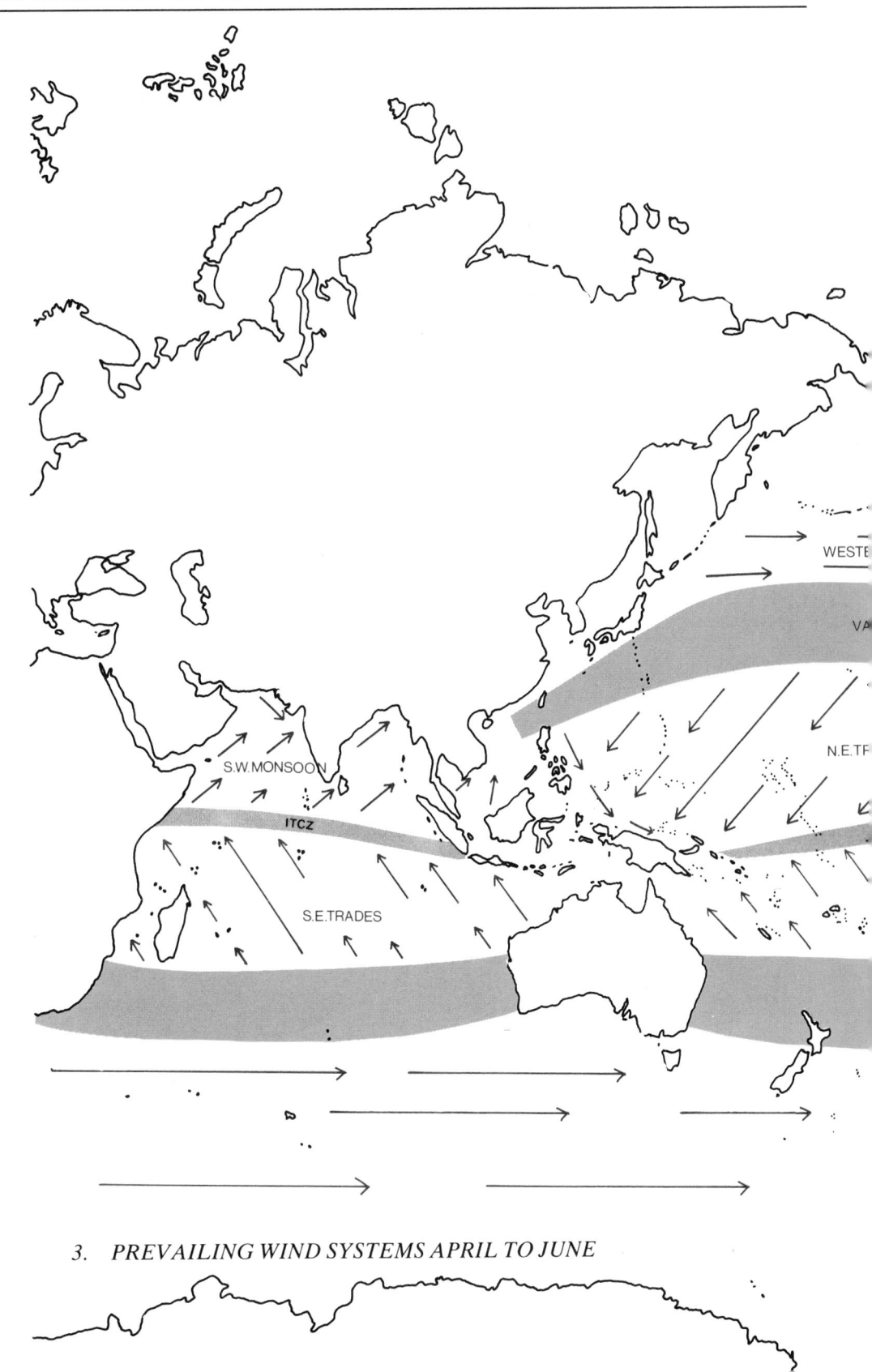

WESTE

VA

N.E.TR

S.W.MONSOON

ITCZ

S.E.TRADES

3. *PREVAILING WIND SYSTEMS APRIL TO JUNE*

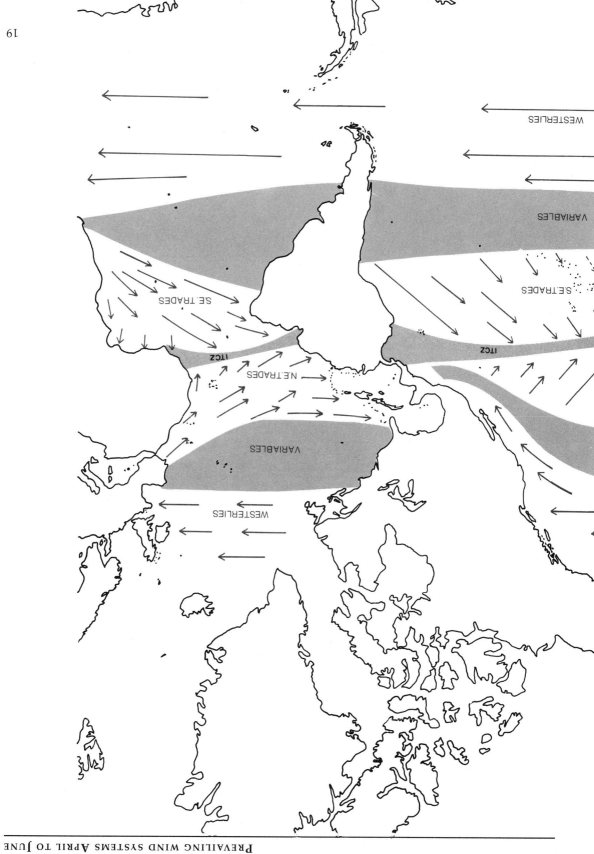

4. PREVAILING WIND SYSTEMS JULY TO SEPTEMBER

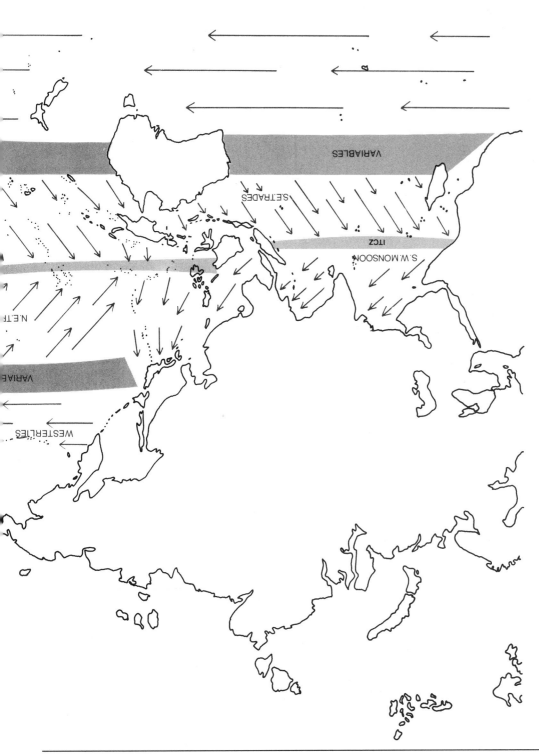

VARIABLES

S.E. TRADES

ITCZ

S.W. MONSOON

N.E. TR

VARIAB

WESTERLIES

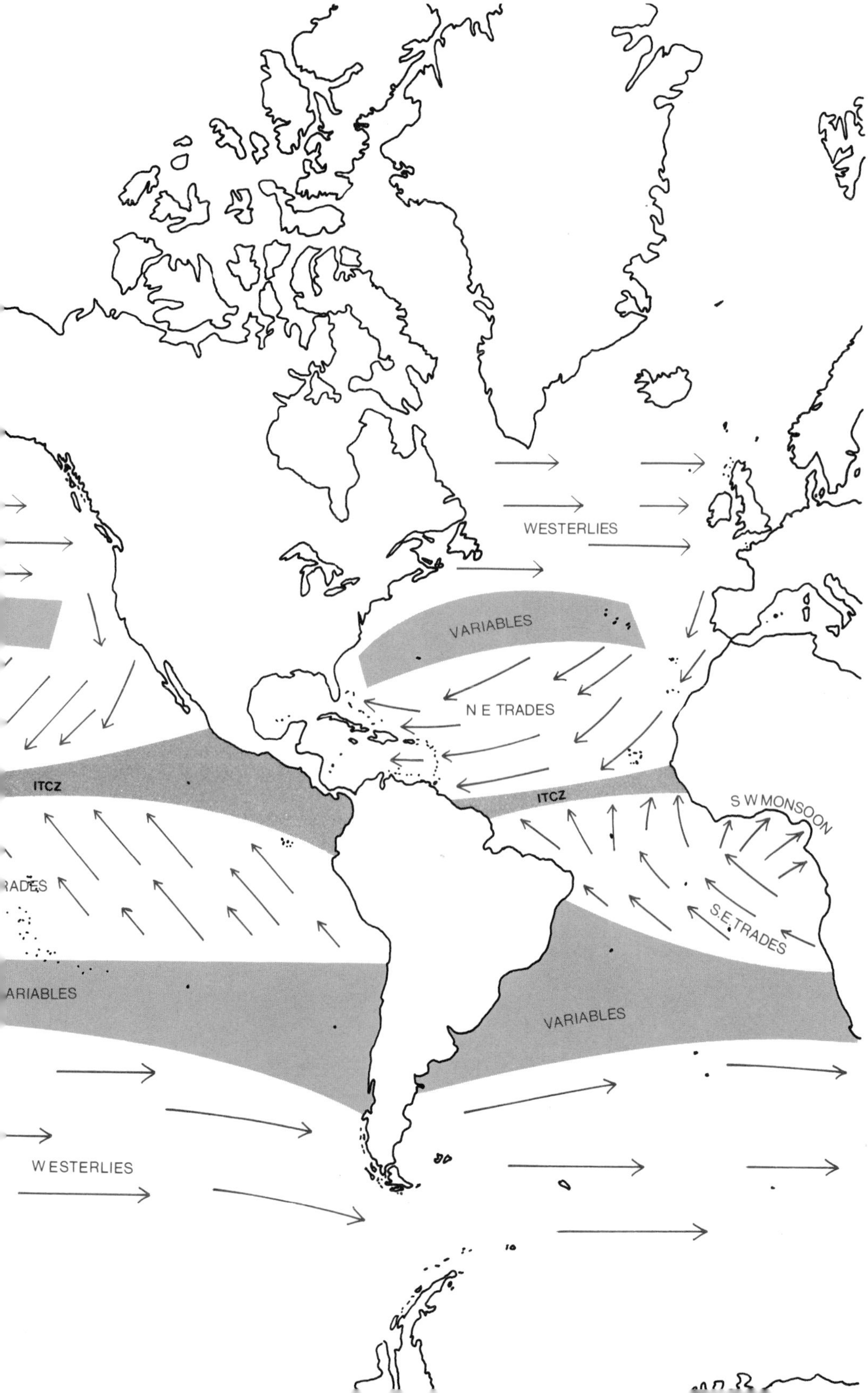

WESTERLIES

VARIABLES

VARIABLES

S E TRADES

SW MONSOON

ITCZ

N E TRADES

VARIABLES

WESTERLIES

TRADES

ITCZ

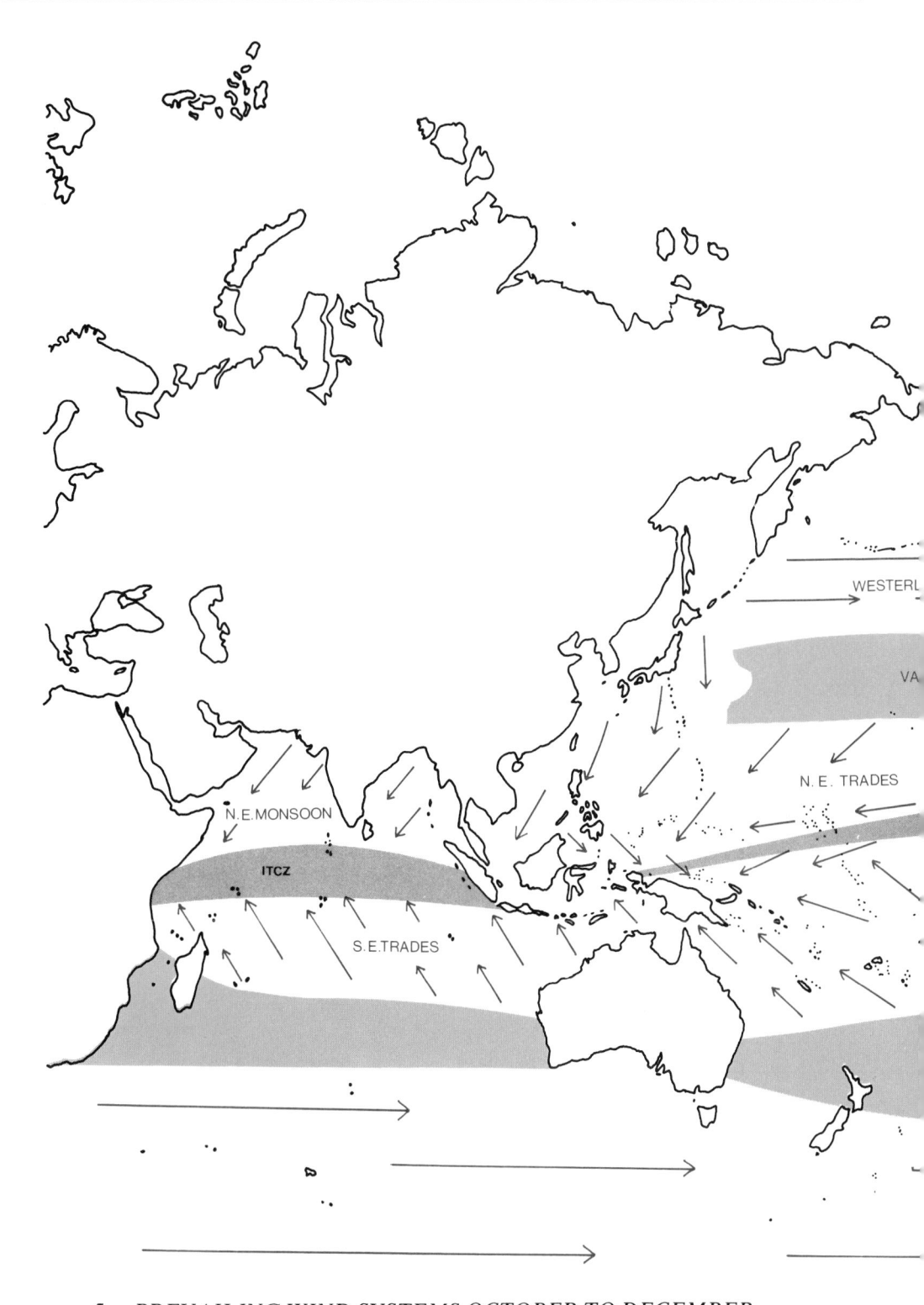

WESTERL

VA

N. E. TRADES

N.E.MONSOON

ITCZ

S.E.TRADES

5. *PREVAILING WIND SYSTEMS OCTOBER TO DECEMBER*

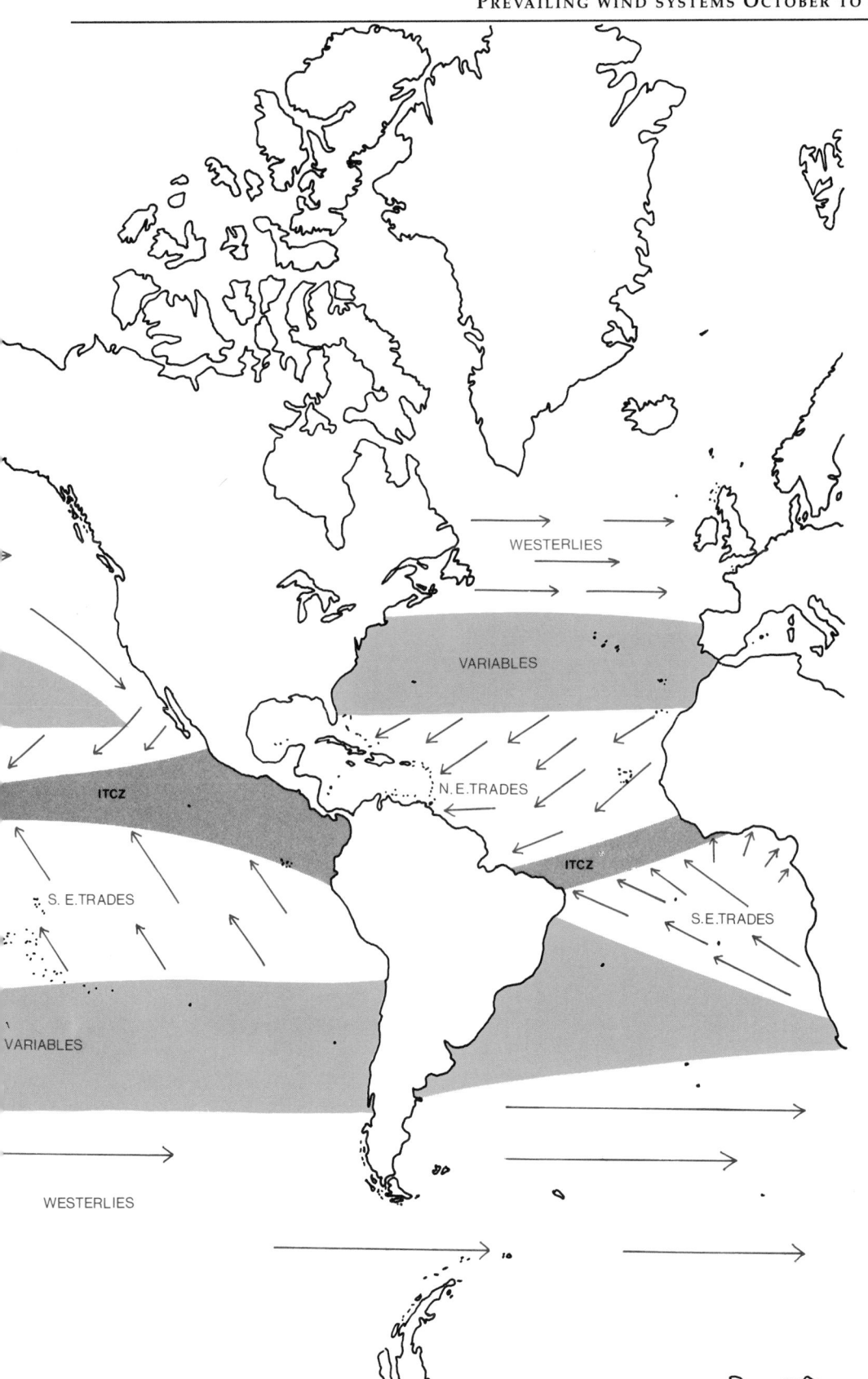

will bring them back again eastward beyond the tropics. If it were not for the intervening belt of calms, sailing directions for vessels going into opposite hemispheres would be of the simplest kind; but the well-known Equatorial embarrassments - "the doldrums" - generally make a very different matter of it, and cause many considerations to enter into the problem of shaping a course.'

The three main factors that influence the formation and direction of the wind are atmospheric pressure, air temperature, and the rotation of the earth. The primary cause of wind is a difference of temperature. This in its turn leads to a difference in atmospheric pressure mainly because of the tendency of warm air to rise, which is then replaced by cold air drawn from elsewhere. Air also tends to flow from an area of high pressure to one of low pressure. Permanent areas of high pressure are situated between approximately the latitudes of 20° and 40°, both north and south of the equator. On either side of these cells of high pressure there are areas of low pressure. If it were not for the rotation of the earth, the wind direction would be either north or south, from an area of high pressure to one of low pressure, but because the earth is rotating on its axis in an easterly direction, air which is drawn towards a centre of low pressure is deflected to the right in the northern hemisphere and to the left in the southern one. The result of this movement in the northern hemisphere is the anti-clockwise circulation of wind around a low pressure area and the clockwise rotation of wind around a high pressure area. The opposite is the case in the southern hemisphere, where the wind circulates in a clockwise direction around a low pressure area and in an anti-clockwise direction around a high pressure area.

Diagrams 2 to 5 show the way in which winds on the equatorial side of the high pressure belts blow towards the equator from a NE direction in the northern hemisphere and from a SE direction in the southern hemisphere. North and south of those areas of high pressure the winds in both hemispheres are predominantly westerly.

In many areas these systems are distorted by land masses, which are subjected to more pronounced differences of temperature and barometric pressure than the oceans. The wind systems are also affected by the seasons, since the annual movement of the sun causes the areas of high pressure to move towards the poles in the summer. Because of this movement, the wind systems associated with these areas of high pressure, particu-larly the trade winds, tend to travel a few degrees south or north with the sun.

Trade winds

These steady winds which blow on either side of the equatorial doldrums were so called because of the assistance they gave to the trade of sailing ships. The early Spanish navigators gave them the more romantic sounding name of *alisios*. These regular winds are usually NE in the northern hemisphere and SE in the southern hemisphere. They rarely reach gale force and on average blow at force 4 to 5. The weather associated with the trade winds is usually pleasant, with blue skies and fluffy cumulus clouds. The barometric pressure within the trade wind belt is steady, interrupted only by a pressure wave, which causes a slight rise and fall of the barometer every 12 hours. If the diurnal movement of the barometer ceases, or if it is very pronounced, a tropical disturbance can be expected. The entire trade wind belt, including the doldrum zone that lies between the two systems, moves north and south during the year. This movement is influenced by the movement of the sun, although there can be a delay of up to two months between the movement of the sun itself and that of the doldrums. The trade winds are less steady in the vicinity of the Intertropical Convergence Zone.

Intertropical Convergence Zone

This area of low barometric pressure lying between the trade wind regions of the two hemispheres is known as the Intertropical Convergence Zone (ITCZ), the equatorial trough, or more commonly as the doldrums. The winds in this area are either light or nonexistent and the weather is sultry and hot. The only interruptions are occasional squalls and thunderstorms, when rain can be very heavy. The extent of the doldrums varies greatly from year to year and season to season. Although the doldrums have earned their bad reputation because of the frequent calms that could delay ships for days on end, doldrum weather can sometimes be particularly unpleasant, with violent squalls and raging thunderstorms. Weather in the doldrums tends to be worse when the trade winds blow at their strongest.

Variable winds

A zone of light and variable winds extends on the

polar sides of the trade winds, corresponding more or less with the high pressure areas of the two hemispheres, between latitudes 25° and 35° approximately. These zones were given the name of Horse Latitudes, because sailing ships that were becalmed in these areas were sometimes forced to kill the animals on board due to the lack of drinking water.

Westerly winds

The higher latitudes of both hemispheres have a large proportion of westerly winds, which prevail north and south of latitude 35°. Westerly winds are stronger and more predominant in the southern ocean, where they often blow with gale force from the same direction for several days. Because of the more extensive land masses in the northern hemisphere, the westerlies of the northern oceans are lighter and less consistent.

Monsoons

Seasonal winds are experienced in several areas of the world, the name monsoon deriving from the Arabic word meaning 'season'. Such winds blow consistently from one direction for one season and after a short interruption blow with equal consistency from the opposite direction. The most important regions affected by such seasonal winds are the Indian Ocean and West Pacific Ocean.

Depressions

A depression is an area of low barometric pressure, which is usually responsible for periods of unsettled weather, although not all depressions are accompanied by strong winds. Depressions occur most frequently in middle and higher latitudes, although the most severe storms encountered at sea are those formed in the low latitudes and of a revolving nature, discussed in the next section.

As stated earlier, winds in the northern hemisphere blow around low pressure areas in an anti-clockwise direction, while in the southern hemisphere the direction is clockwise. Most depressions move in an easterly direction, a few moving in other directions at times. The speed at which they move can vary from very little to 40 knots or more. Usually depressions last about four to five days and their movement gradually slows down as they fill and the pressure rises.

The strength of the wind generated by a depression is dictated by the closeness of the isobars, which can be seen on a synoptic chart as lines joining areas of equal barometric pressure. The closer the isobars lie together the stronger the wind. The approach of a depression is always indicated by a falling barometer and usually by a change in the aspect of the sky and cloud formation. It may be worthwhile studying this aspect of meteorology, so as to be able to predict the kind of wind and weather to expect both on passage and in port.

Tropical squalls

This is a common phenomenon encountered in the tropics, especially below latitude 20°. These linear disturbances travel from east to west at 20–25 knots and are usually perpendicular to the direction of the prevailing wind. They are accompanied by thundery and squally weather. The first indication of an approaching line squall is a heavy band of cumulo-nimbus to the east. The wind is usually light or calm and the atmosphere oppressive. As the cloud approaches it becomes dark and menacing with occasional thunder and lightning. The bottom of the cloud has the appearance of a straight line but it sometimes changes to an arch as it passes overhead. Suddenly there is a blast of wind from an easterly direction, which on average rises to 25 – 30 knots, although occasionally it can be much stronger. Shortly after the blast of wind, it starts to rain heavily. Such squalls last on average about half an hour, although sometimes they may last longer. The barometer does not indicate their approach, therefore they can only be detected visually, although they also show up on radar. As some of these squalls can be quite vicious, it is prudent in squall prone areas to reduce sail at night, when their approach is more difficult to detect. In the North Atlantic, line squalls occur especially at the beginning and end of the rainy season (May to October) and are particularly violent near the African coast. In the South Pacific squalls can occur at all times, although as a rule they are not as violent as the North Atlantic variety. Line squalls are less of a problem during the NE monsoon of the North Indian Ocean, but can be violent during the opposite SW monsoon.

Tornadoes

Tornadoes and waterspouts occur in the same areas and during the same season as tropical storms.

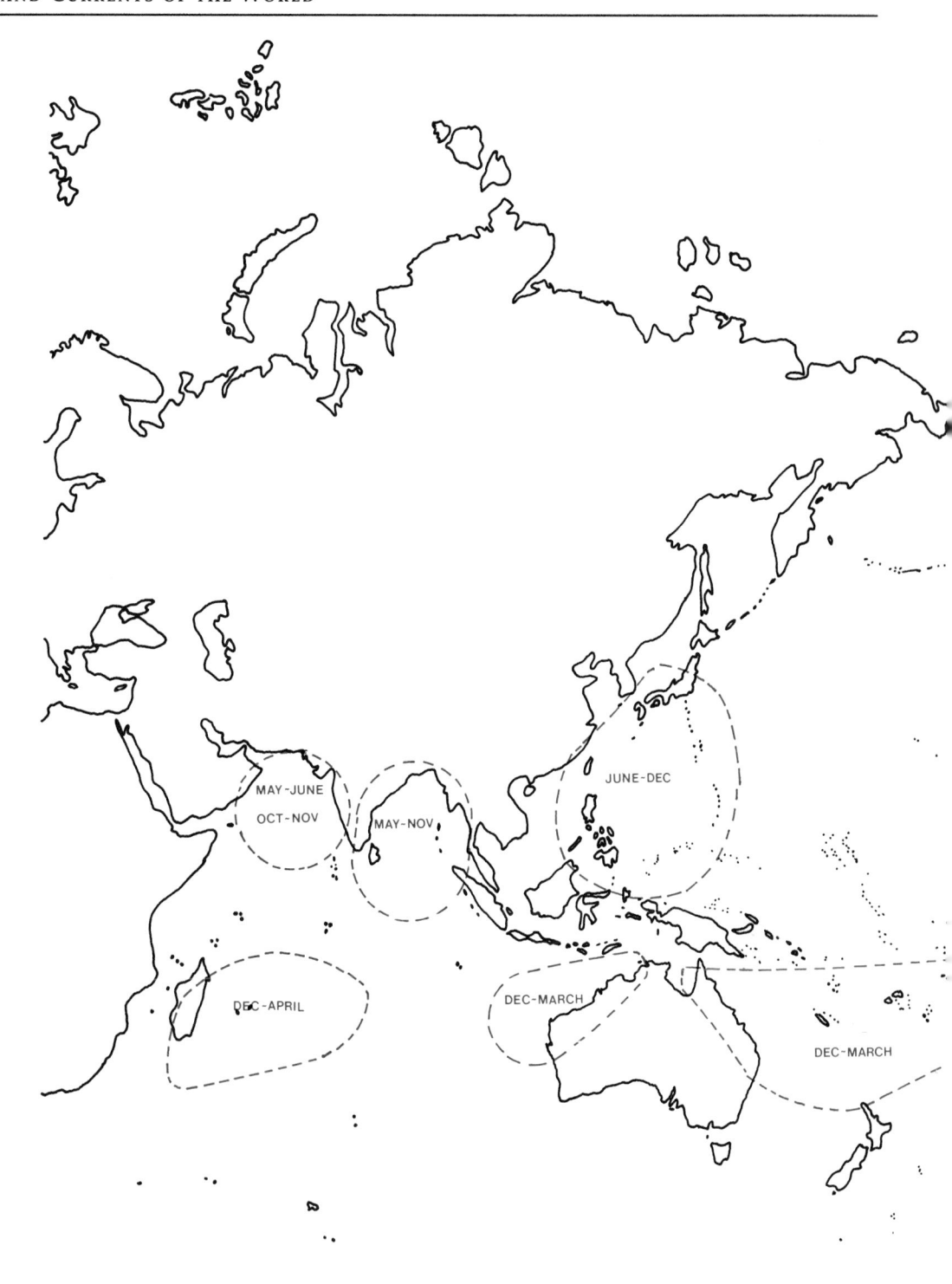

MAY-JUNE
OCT-NOV

MAY-NOV

JUNE-DEC

DEC-APRIL

DEC-MARCH

DEC-MARCH

6.   WORLD DISTRIBUTION OF TROPICAL STORMS

JUNE-NOV

JUNE-OCT

They usually travel in the same direction as the prevailing wind and their approach can normally be seen, especially as they rarely form at night. The wind generated by a tornado can be extremely violent, but as the actual area covered is very small, the likelihood of being hit by such a whirlwind at sea is quite remote. Waterspouts sometimes occur during afternoon thunderstorms in the vicinity of the coast, the ocean side of Chesapeake Bay being particularly vulnerable during the summer months.

Tsunamis

These are large waves caused by an earthquake which can occur thousands of miles from the place where the destructive effects of the gigantic wave will be felt. Tsunamis occur mostly in the Pacific Ocean, and ports both on the continent and islands have been hit by tsunamis during the twentieth century. There have been six destructive tsunamis in Hawaii in the last 50 years. The most recent major tsunami occurred in 1960 causing great destruction in Hilo where over 60 people lost their lives. Boats are better off at sea in deep water, preferably over 100 fathoms, where the effect of a tsunami will pass almost unnoticed.

Tropical revolving storms

Tropical revolving storms are the most violent storms that can be encountered at sea and it is both prudent and wise to try and avoid the areas and seasons where such storms occur. The extremely strong winds generated by these storms and the huge seas they raise can easily overwhelm a small boat. Depending on which part of the world they occur in, these storms are known as hurricanes, cyclones, typhoons, or willy-willies. They blow around an area of low pressure, the rotation being anti-clockwise in the northern hemisphere and clockwise in the southern hemisphere. The wind does not move around the centre in concentric circles but has a spiral movement, being sucked in towards the core of the storm.

Usually these storms occur on the western sides of the oceans, although they are also found in other parts of the world. They usually form between latitudes 7° and 15° on either side of the equator, but there have been many instances when tropical storms formed closer to the equator. The breeding ground of tropical storms is the Intertropical Convergence Zone, where the two opposing trade wind systems converge. Under certain conditions of barometric pressure, temperature, and moisture, the resulting whirlpool of air created at the point of convergence can develop into a severe tropical revolving storm. The most dangerous areas affected by such storms are the western North Atlantic from Grenada to Cape Hatteras, the western North Pacific from Guam to Japan, the South Pacific from the Marquesas to the Coral Sea, the north and northwest coasts of Australia, the southwest Indian Ocean, and the Bay of Bengal. In some of these areas tropical storms occur several times a year, while others are only hit about once every ten years.

In addition to their circular motion, tropical revolving storms also have a forward movement. In the northern hemisphere the movement is initially WNW, storms recurving gradually to the N and NE as they reach higher latitudes. In the southern hemisphere the initial movement is WSW, storms recurving to the SE as they approach latitude 20°S. Sometimes a storm does not recurve but continues in a WNW direction in the northern hemisphere, or a WSW direction in the southern hemisphere, until it hits the continental landmass where it gradually breaks up after causing much damage. Occasionally the storm meanders erratically and its direction is often impossible to predict with certainty. The speed at which a storm is moving is normally about 10 knots in the early stages and accelerates after recurving.

Any boat lying in the path of a storm, particularly its centre, will be in serious danger. The wind remains constant in direction until the eye has passed, then, after a brief calm, the wind returns from the opposite direction, possibly with greater violence, creating rough and confused seas or putting vessels at anchor on a dangerous lee shore. Every storm has two sides, or semicircles, known as the navigable semicircle and the dangerous semicircle. In the northern hemisphere, the dangerous semicircle is the half of the storm lying on the right hand side of the track in the direction in which the storm is moving. In the southern hemisphere, the dangerous semicircle is on the left.

The detection and tracking of tropical storms has greatly improved since the advent of weather satellites. Stations WWV in Fort Collins, Colorado and WWVH in Kauai, Hawaii, broadcast hourly reports of tropical storms, their coordinates, speed of movement and wind strength. Tropical storm warnings for the Atlantic Ocean are broadcast at 8 minutes past each hour by WWV on 2.5, 5, 10, 15, and 20 MHz. Warnings for the Pacific are broadcast by WWVH at 48 minutes past the hour on 2.5, 5, 10, and 15 MHz. From the information obtained from these stations it is possible to plot the course of an approaching storm and take the best avoiding action. The path of the storm in relation to the vessel's latest position will show the degree of danger. If one is at sea, the best course of action is as follows:

Northern hemisphere

When facing the wind, the centre of the storm will be between 90° and 135° on the right of the observer. If the wind veers, i.e. shifts to the right, the boat is in the right hand semicircle which is the dangerous semicircle. A backing wind is associated with the navigable semicircle. If the direction of the wind is constant, its strength increases and the barometer falls, the boat is exactly in the path of the storm. If the direction of the wind is not changing, but its strength decreases while the barometer slowly rises, the boat is directly behind the centre.

The generally accepted tactic for vessels caught in the path of a tropical storm is to run off on the starboard tack by keeping the wind on the starboard quarter. The same tactic should be applied if the boat is in the navigable semicircle when one should try and follow a course at right angles to the assumed track of the storm. Depending on the boat's behaviour in a quartering sea, one should try and either run under bare poles or storm jib. If the boat is in the dangerous semicircle one should heave to on the starboard tack or, if possible, sail close hauled on the same tack, with the object of moving away from the storm centre.

Southern hemisphere

South of the equator, the centre of a tropical storm is between 90° and 135° on the left of the observer. If the wind is backing, the boat is in the dangerous semicircle; if it veers, the boat is in the navigable semicircle. The vessel is directly in the path of the storm if the wind is constant in direction. An increasing velocity combined with a falling barometer means that the boat is in front of the storm, a decreasing wind speed and a rising barometer means that the observer is behind the centre.

The best tactic if one is directly in front of the storm is to run with the wind on the port quarter.

The same tactic should be applied if the boat is in the navigable semicircle, by trying to run away from the storm at right angles to its assumed track, also with the wind on the port quarter. If the boat is in the dangerous semicircle, one should try and sail close hauled on the port tack so as to proceed away from the storm centre. If this is not possible, the boat should heave to on the port tack.

Although these general rules are applicable in most situations, there can be circumstances when they should not be followed without question. Tropical storm strategy depends on many factors, such as the lack of sea room or the behaviour of a particular boat when hove to in strong winds or running before big quartering seas. Such considerations will dictate a different approach to the problem and there is unfortunately no fast rule that can be applied at all times. There is no doubt that the safest course of action is to avoid altogether the areas where tropical storms are likely to occur. Therefore the most important consideration when drawing up plans for a voyage is to make sure that the boat will not be in an area affected by tropical storms during the dangerous season. If one plans to pass through an area which is never entirely free from tropical storms, one should attempt to sail during the months of lowest frequency. Such a strategy is not too complicated to follow and many boats have spent several years cruising in the tropics without ever being in the wrong place at the wrong time, simply by leaving the hurricane zone during the dangerous season and returning at the end of it. The directions given for various cruising routes mention the hurricane prone months, so that these can be avoided when planning a cruise along those routes.

Tropical storms are most frequent during the late summer or early autumn in both hemispheres. The safe season in the northern hemisphere is from mid-November to mid-June, whereas the safe season for the southern hemisphere lasts from about May until mid-November. The only tropical area entirely free of hurricanes is the South Atlantic. In the Western North Pacific no month is considered to be entirely safe, although typhoons are extremely rare in winter. In the Coral Sea, extraseasonal cyclones are not uncommon and have been recorded as late as June and even July. In the Arabian Sea cyclones do not occur in summer, but at the change of the monsoon, either in May–June or in October–November. Diagram 6

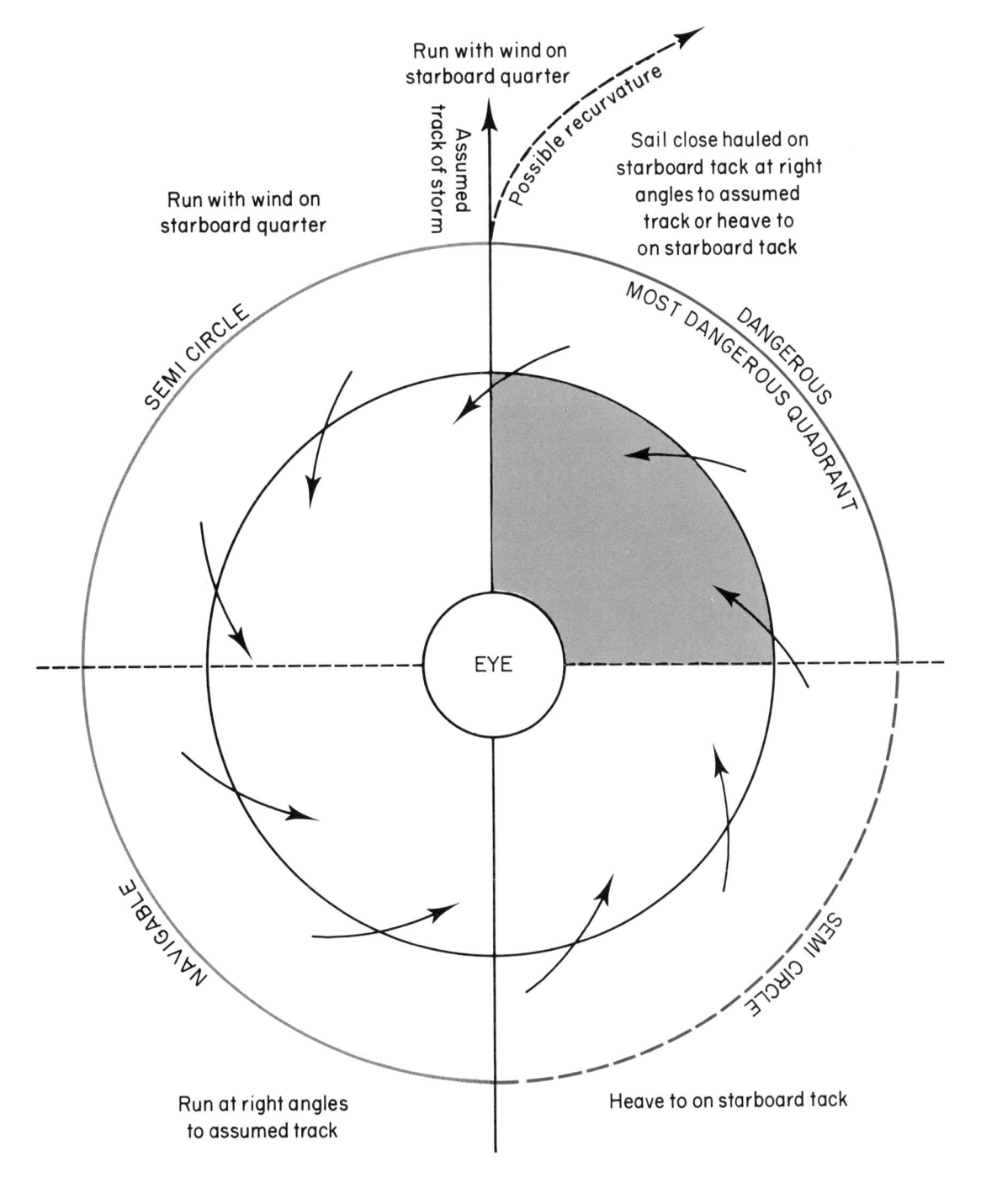

Run with wind on
starboard quarter

Possible recurvature

Sail close hauled on
starboard tack at right
angles to assumed
track or heave to
on starboard tack

Run with wind on
starboard quarter

Assumed
track of storm

SEMI CIRCLE

MOST DANGEROUS QUADRANT

DANGEROUS

EYE

NAVIGABLE

SEMI CIRCLE

Run at right angles
to assumed track

Heave to on starboard tack

7.   *TROPICAL STORM TACTICS*
NORTHERN HEMISPHERE

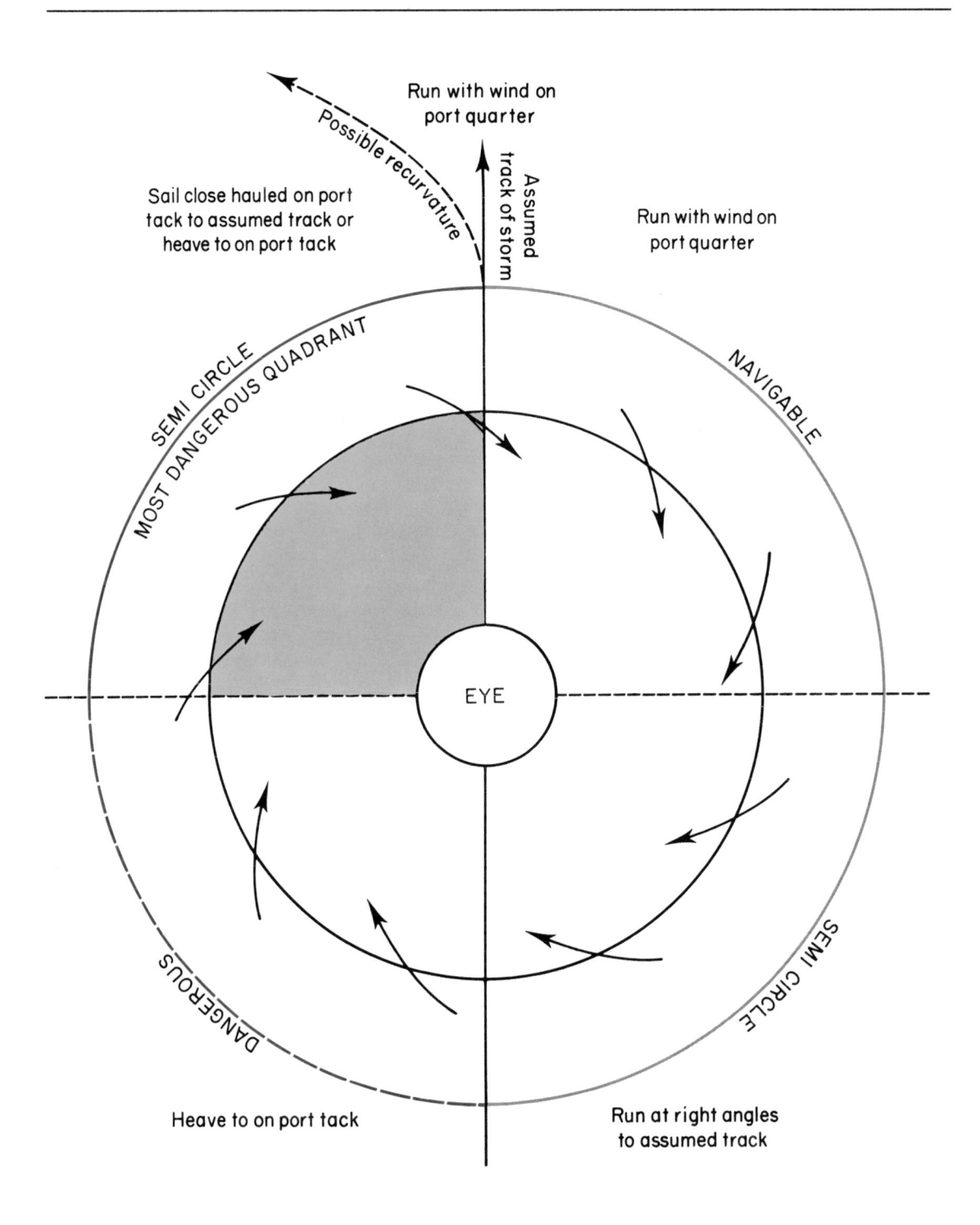

Run with wind on
port quarter

Possible recurvature

Sail close hauled on port
tack to assumed track or
heave to on port tack

Assumed track of storm

Run with wind on
port quarter

SEMI CIRCLE

MOST DANGEROUS QUADRANT

NAVIGABLE

EYE

DANGEROUS

SEMI CIRCLE

Heave to on port tack

Run at right angles
to assumed track

8.   TROPICAL STORM TACTICS
SOUTHERN HEMISPHERE

shows the world distribution of tropical storms and the months when they are most likely to occur.

It is not uncommon for tropical storms to develop outside the official seasons and the early part of the safe season should be treated with caution. World tropical storm seasons follow:

Area	Season	Highest frequency
West Indies	June to November	September
NE Pacific	May to November	July–September
NW Pacific	All year	July–October
Bay of Bengal	May to December	October–November
Arabian Sea	April to December	April–May October–November
S Indian	November to May	December–March
S Pacific	November to April	January–March

Prevailing winds

Prevailing weather conditions will be described in greater detail when dealing with regional routes, but it may be useful to summarise here the wind patterns of the principal six areas of the world as they appear on diagrams 2 to 5.

North Atlantic: The NE trade winds blow roughly between latitudes 2°N and 20°N to 25°N in winter, between 10°N and 30°N in summer. In the northern part of the ocean, the winds are predominantly W becoming SW near the North American coast. Between the trade wind and westerly wind belts there is an area of variable winds.

South Atlantic: The SE trade winds cover a wide belt roughly from the equator to 30°S during the southern summer. They move north during winter (July) when they are found between 3°N to 5°N and 25°S. There are virtually no doldrums south of the equator. Constant westerly winds are to be found in higher latitudes, but they tend to become NW and even N on the South American side of the ocean, especially during summer.

North Pacific: During the summer months the NE trade winds blow between latitudes 12°N and 30°N, but move down to an area comprised between latitudes 4°N or 5°N and 25°N in winter. Between latitudes 35°N and 55°N the winds are W or NW. The doldrums are less well defined.

South Pacific: The SE trades are less constant and reliable than in other oceans. At the height of winter (June to August) they blow in a belt stretching approximately from 5°N to 25°S. During the southern summer the trade winds are even less constant and blow south of the equator as far as latitude 30°S. Westerly winds blow consistently south of 30°S in winter and 40°S in summer.

North Indian: The winds are dominated by the two monsoons, NE in winter (November to March) and SW in summer (May to September). The NE monsoon becomes well established in January and it is most consistent until early March. The winds are much stronger during the SW monsoon, at the height of which in July and August they often blow at over 30 knots.

South Indian: The SE trade winds extend from the equator to latitude 25°S in winter (July). During the southern summer (January), the SE trade winds can be found between about 10°S and 30°S, the NE monsoon also makes itself felt south of the equator possibly as far as 10°S, but is deflected by the rotation of the earth and becomes the NW monsoon. To the south of the SE trade wind belt there is a zone of variable winds. The higher latitudes are known for their strong westerly winds.

Currents of the world

Currents occur at all depths of the oceans, but the only ones of real interest to the small boat voyager are the surface currents. Because the main cause of surface currents is the direction of the wind, there is a close relationship between their direction and that of the prevailing wind. Constant winds, such as the trade winds, create some of the most constant currents, although these do not always follow exactly the direction of the wind that has generated them. As in the case of the winds, the rotation of the earth has an effect on currents too and therefore in the northern hemisphere currents tend to flow to the right of the direction of the wind, in the southern hemisphere to the left. This is the reason why in the northern hemisphere the currents flow in a clockwise direction, while in the southern hemisphere currents generally tend to follow an anti-clockwise direction. Currents will be described in more detail in relevant routes.

El Niño

This current, which occurs in certain years along the west coast of South America, has gained such an international notoriety in recent years that it needs to be treated as a global phenomenon. Its Spanish name derives from the fact that in certain years, around the time of Christmas, the cold north-flowing Humboldt or Peru Current was reversed by a warm south-flowing current and, because of the time of year, was named after the Holy Child. The climate changes brought havoc to the region, but it was not until the devastations caused by the El Niño of 1982–3 – the worst this century – that its global implications were finally established. Based on those findings, the 1991 Niño was accurately predicted, but even so no one could predict how long it would last, as El Niño may be active for only one year, or for two consecutive years as has happened on several occasions. However, the mechanisms that cause the freak weather conditions are no longer a mystery and El Niño is gradually revealing its secrets.

Under normal conditions, the trade winds blowing from east to west displace the warm waters of the equatorial areas towards the West Pacific, thus causing a mass of Southern Ocean cold water to rise along the coasts of Peru and Ecuador. At the same time, the normal area of high precipitations is concentrated in the central and western parts of the Pacific. The appearance of El Niño causes a weakening of the trade winds, which may result in westerly winds in the equatorial area. These westerlies bring warm waters towards continental South America, and displace the area of high precipitation to the west coast of South America. Thus, in 1997, in one particular arid region of Chile more rain fell in 24 hours than in the previous 24 years.

Even more significant among the resulting climatic anomalies is the rise in sea water temperature in the South Pacific, which, in some areas, can be as high as 5°C. A direct consequence of this is an increase in cyclonic activity in the Pacific generally, and especially in its eastern half. The phenomenon that fuels such cyclonic activity is the reversed pressure differential between the eastern and western Pacific regions coupled with the higher than usual sea water temperatures. The British scientist Sir Gilbert Walker was the first to notice a correlation between barometric readings in Tahiti and Darwin. Under normal conditions, the high pressure in the east and the low pressure in the west generate the easterly trade winds. The so-called Southern Oscillation Index (SOI) represents this difference in atmospheric pressure and is a clear indication of the coming of El Niño. In early 1997 the SOI peaked at –26, but dropped to –18 by June 1997. An SOI of less than –10 coincides with an El Niño period. The SOI therefore either creates a low pressure environment, which is favourable to the formation of tropical storms, or an unusually high pressure, which inhibits the formation of such storms.

It is now quite certain that El Niño affects weather far beyond the South Pacific and, in fact, the low cyclonic activity in the Caribbean in 1997 is now seen as a direct consequence of El Niño busily breeding cyclones and typhoons in the Pacific. It is now presumed that the reversal of the currents in the South Pacific may have caused an upwelling of cold water in the South Atlantic with a resultant drop in sea water temperatures in the tropical Atlantic. Indeed, sea water temperatures in 1997 were lower than in normal years and this could well have contributed to the low hurricane activity experienced in the North Atlantic during that year.

Although, for the moment, it is still impossible to predict when a new El Niño will occur, the twentieth century has seen altogether 28 periods, so on average El Niño can be expected to strike every three or four years. Although it is still impossible to predict the year when El Niño will occur, enough is known about what climatic changes we can expect once El Niño is with us, and thus take the necessary avoiding actions. For a start, during an El Niño period sailing during, or close to, the cyclone season should be avoided and, if at all possible, one should attempt to spend the critical period outside the tropical Pacific Ocean.

4
WINDS AND CURRENTS OF THE NORTH ATLANTIC

The Northeast trade winds

The NE trade winds extend in a wide belt north of the equator reaching from the west coast of Africa to the Caribbean Sea. They blow for most of the year on the south side of the anti-cyclone which is situated in about latitude 30°N, commonly known as the Azores high. The northern limit of the trade winds is around latitude 25°N in winter and 30°N in summer, although the constancy of the trade winds cannot be relied on near their northern limits. Therefore when making a transatlantic passage it is advisable to be certain the trade winds are reached before turning west.

The constancy of the trade winds improves during the winter months as does their strength. Although the average strength of these winds is force 3–4, it is not uncommon for them to reach force 6 and even 7 during January to March. The trade winds tend to be lighter and less consistent in summer, which is also the hurricane season. They have more of a northerly component in the eastern part of the ocean and become increasingly easterly in the Caribbean.

The consistency and reliability of the NE trade winds is of particular interest to those who intend to make a transatlantic voyage along the classic route starting in the Canaries. Although the winter months are reputed to have the most consistent winds, there are years in which these winds are found in lower latitudes than normal and it is not unusual for boats to cover almost half the distance to the Caribbean before falling in with steady winds.

Also described as trade winds are the Portuguese Trades which blow from between NE and NW off the western coast of the Iberian peninsula from April to September or October. Another regional variation of the NE trade winds is the *harmattan*. This is a hot and dry wind, created by the NE trade winds blowing over the deserts of Africa and reaching the sea laden with dust. Around latitude 20°N it is encountered only in the vicinity of the African coast, but as one moves further south, the *harmattan* can be experienced farther offshore, covering boats in a fine reddish dust and reducing visibility. This easterly wind normally occurs between November and February.

Another regional phenomenon associated with the area which is normally under the influence of the NE trade winds are northers. During the winter months vast anti-cyclones develop over the North American continent occasionally reaching as far as the Gulf of Mexico. A strong northerly flow of cold air develops ahead of this area of high pressure, and becomes a violent norther which is sometimes felt as far away as the Caribbean. The progress of a norther is usually checked by the higher islands of Hispaniola and Cuba, but to the north of these islands it can be particularly dangerous, mainly because of the steep seas which are created when a strong norther hits the north flowing Gulf Stream. The approach of a norther is usually heralded by a heavy bank of cloud on the N or NW horizon.

Intertropical Convergence Zone

The extent of the trade winds at all times of the

year is influenced by the position of the Intertropical Convergence Zone (ITCZ) or doldrums. The ITCZ stays north of the equator throughout the year, although its position varies greatly, mainly in accordance with the seasonal movement of the sun, but also on a diurnal basis. The width of the doldrums is also variable and averages between 200 and 300 miles, although it tends to be wider near the African coast and narrower near Brazil. The weather inside the doldrum belt is more turbulent in the wider eastern region than in the west, with frequent squalls and thunderstorms occurring.

Southwest monsoon

The heat generated by the landmass of Africa during the summer lowers the barometric pressure over that area and causes the ITCZ to be deflected towards the north. The SE trade wind of the South Atlantic is thus drawn across the equator and arrives off the coast of Africa as the SW monsoon. It lasts from June to October between the equator and latitude 15°N, but in the Gulf of Guinea light SW winds prevail throughout the year.

Variables

A band of variable winds extends across the Atlantic to the north of the NE trade winds. This is the area of high atmospheric pressure which straddles the 30th parallel, being situated slightly to the north of it in summer and to the south in winter. The winds in the eastern half of this area are usually northerly and can be regarded as an extension of the trade winds. In the western part of the ocean the winds are often very light and long periods of calms can be expected. This is the area of the Horse Latitudes and the feared Sargasso Sea where sailing ships used to be becalmed for weeks on end.

Westerlies

Westerly winds predominate in the northern part of the Atlantic Ocean, where the weather is often unsettled, mainly due to the almost continuous passage of depressions that race across the ocean in an easterly direction. The winds in these higher latitudes are less constant in direction than those of the Roaring Forties of the Southern Ocean, although the predominant direction is westerly.

Hurricanes

A large area of the western North Atlantic is affected by tropical revolving storms, which can occur theoretically at any time, as hurricanes have been recorded over the last few centuries in every month of the year, although extremely rarely in some months. The normal hurricane season is from late May until early December, the highest frequency occurring from August to October, with a lower number occurring in the rest of the season. September has the highest frequency, with an average of two hurricanes per month over a period of 100 years, although in some years the number of hurricanes recorded in September was much higher. In fact both the frequency and intensity of hurricanes varies greatly from year to year, some years being extremely bad with up to 15 hurricanes, while other years go by with hardly any being recorded. A West Indian rhyme describes the season as follows:

June too soon,
July standby,
August look out you must,
September remember,
October all over!

Most hurricanes are born in the doldrum area west of the Cape Verde Islands. They usually travel west towards the Caribbean, their tracks moving clockwise around the perimeter of areas of high pressure. The area most affected by hurricanes is the Caribbean Basin, particularly the northern part of the Lesser Antilles, the Virgins, Bahamas, Bermuda, the Gulf of Mexico, and Florida. At the beginning and end of the hurricane season, these storms sometimes develop in the Western Caribbean, from where they move in a northerly direction mainly affecting the southern states of the USA. The later months of the season are particularly dangerous for those sailing in the Caribbean, as September and October hurricanes usually develop locally and warnings are shorter. Therefore if one intends to sail in the Caribbean during the hurricane season, especially among the Lesser Antilles, it is safer to plan to be there at the beginning of the hurricane season (May to June) rather than towards its end (October to early November). The high frequency months of August and particularly September should be avoided altogether. A useful tip concerning West Indian hurricanes is that if during

May, June, and July the wind remains above average strength, the rainfall below average, and the humidity also low, less than two hurricanes can be expected to hit the Eastern Caribbean during August and September.

Currents

The currents of the North Atlantic are part of a vast clockwise moving system that occupies the entire ocean south of latitude 40°N. The NE trade winds create the North Equatorial Current, which sets westward from the Cape Verde Islands to the Caribbean. Running to the north of it is the weaker North Subtropical Current. Part of the North Equatorial Current sets into the Caribbean Sea, while another branch flows northward along the Lesser Antilles and is known as the Antilles Current.

The mainspring of the North Atlantic circulation is the Gulf Stream, which in spite of its name does not originate in the Gulf of Mexico but is a continuation of the North Equatorial Current. The wide band of warm water sweeps along the eastern side of North America until it meets the cold Labrador Current, which forces it to flow in an easterly direction. From about longitude 45°W it ceases to be so strong and continues eastwards as the North Atlantic Current. In the eastern part of the ocean the currents are less well defined, the North Atlantic Current fanning out into different directions to form the south setting Azores Current and further east the Portugal Current. This current sets along the Iberian peninsula, one branch being deflected through the Strait of Gibraltar into the Mediterranean, while the other sets SW along the African coast to become the Canary Current. Ultimately this current turns west to join the North Equatorial Current, thus completing the clockwise system of the North Atlantic currents.

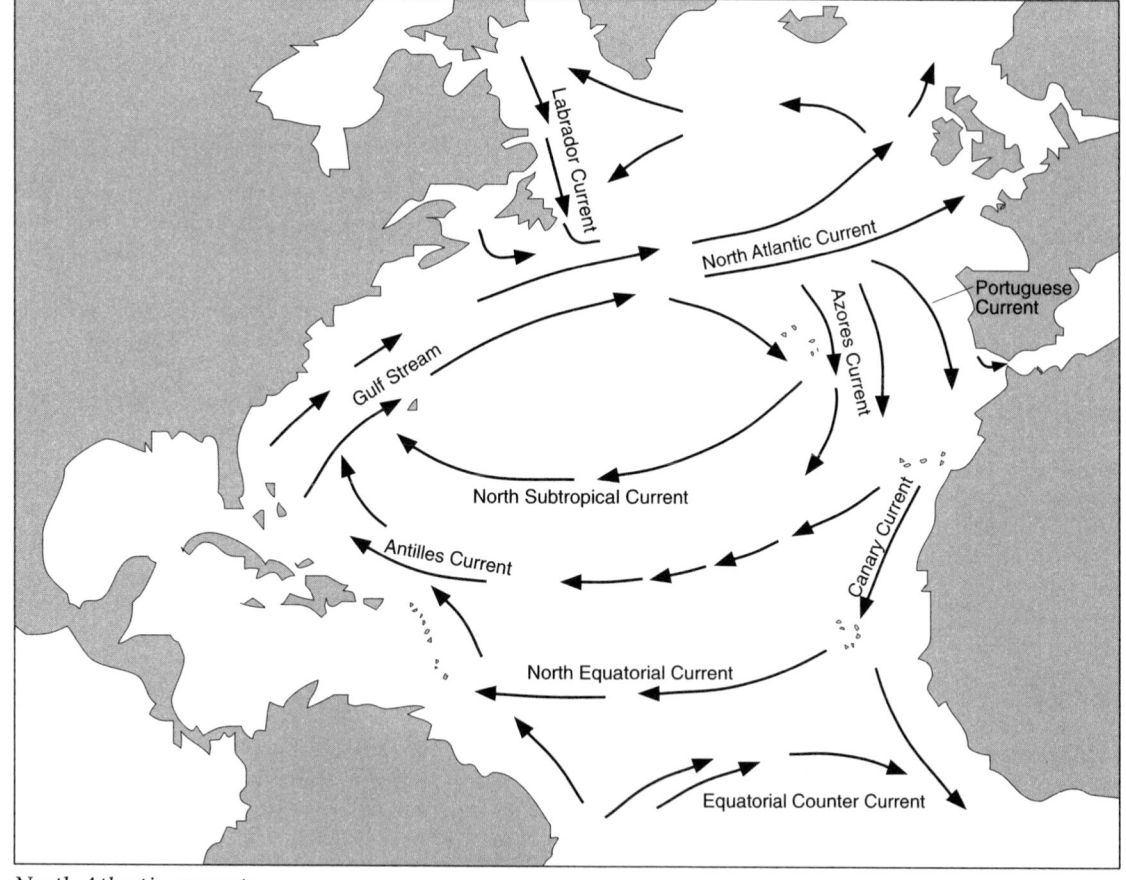

North Atlantic currents

South of latitude 10°N the pattern of the currents is more complex. Between the two westward setting equatorial currents is the Equatorial Countercurrent. In winter this eastward setting countercurrent is most noticeable along latitude 6°N east of about longitude 45°W, but it diminishes in strength towards the South American continent where it disappears altogether. The South Equatorial Current combines in this region with the North Equatorial Current to form a strong westward flowing current which is deflected in a northerly direction along the coast of South America towards the Lesser Antilles.

5
ROUTES IN THE NORTH ATLANTIC

The North Atlantic is crisscrossed by a larger number of sailing routes than any other ocean, and cruising boats have penetrated its furthest reaches from the steaming jungle of the Orinoco to the icy fjords of Greenland. The greatest concentration of cruising boats is in Northern Europe and North America, from which areas most offshore routes originate. To these should be added the routes fanning out from the Mediterranean, another area of great concentration. Although a certain proportion of offshore voyages are two-way and fit into a normal summer vacation, an increasing number of people are undertaking longer voyages lasting several months. Many of them complete a North Atlantic circumnavigation by planning a voyage that takes advantage of the most favourable weather conditions along the entire route.

Christopher Columbus was the first navigator to realise that there was a certain pattern to North Atlantic weather and in his four transatlantic voyages he used the prevailing conditions to best advantage. Ever since Columbus completed the first Atlantic circle in 1493, his example has been followed by countless sailors. The circuit has been increasingly popular with European sailors migrating west with the NE trade winds by reaching the Caribbean islands via the Canaries and returning east with the westerlies of higher latitudes, usually by calling at Bermuda and the Azores. In recent years, the circuit has been joined by sailors from the east coast of North America, who reach the Caribbean by what appears to be a roundabout route. For those who intended to spend a season in the Eastern Caribbean islands the accepted practice was to sail to the Lesser Antilles at the end of the hurricane season, in late October or early November. However, passages from the US east coast at that time of year are seldom easy and therefore the alternative, albeit longer, route is an attractive proposition. Its greatest advantage is that it offers the possibility to cruise in the best seasons throughout the year. By leaving the USA in May, one can cross the Atlantic via Bermuda and the Azores, spend the summer in Europe, recross the Atlantic in November, spend the winter in the Caribbean and return home the following May. This schedule is a perfect example of being in the right place at the right time as it avoids the hurricane season in the Western Atlantic, both Atlantic crossings are undertaken at the most favourable times, the Caribbean islands are visited at the optimum season, and the return home is accomplished before the start of the new hurricane season.

The traditional route from America to Europe, which runs along higher latitudes to take advantage of the prevailing westerlies, is used mostly by American or Canadian sailors crossing to Ireland, Britain or other North European destinations. Boats heading for southern ports in Europe, including the Mediterranean, usually take the warmer route via the Azores.

Most offshore passages from Northern Europe are southbound and there is a very good reason for this. The dream of almost every cold water sailor is to cruise in warmer weather and so, when the time finally comes for that cruise, they invariably point their bows southwards, at least as far as the Mediterranean, but more likely the Canaries and Caribbean. Westbound passages in higher latitudes to America are now very much the exception, as most cruising sailors prefer to reach the other side of the Atlantic by a more roundabout and comfortable route. Even the route to the Azores attracts considerably fewer

North European boats than in the past, when a summer cruise to the Azores was not regarded as out of the ordinary. For most European sailors, the Azores are now mainly a convenient stopover on the way home from the Caribbean.

The opening up of the former Communist countries bordering on the Black and Baltic Seas is attracting boats from both sides of the Atlantic to those areas. Because of the relatively short cruising season in the Baltic, the quickest way to reach that inland sea is via the Kiel Canal.

More ambitious sailors have even been tempted to visit some of the Russian ports on the White Sea and the sight of cruising boats sailing beyond

AN10 ROUTES FROM NORTH EUROPE

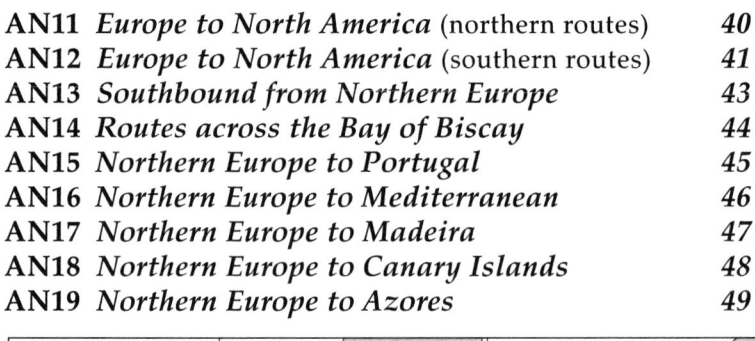

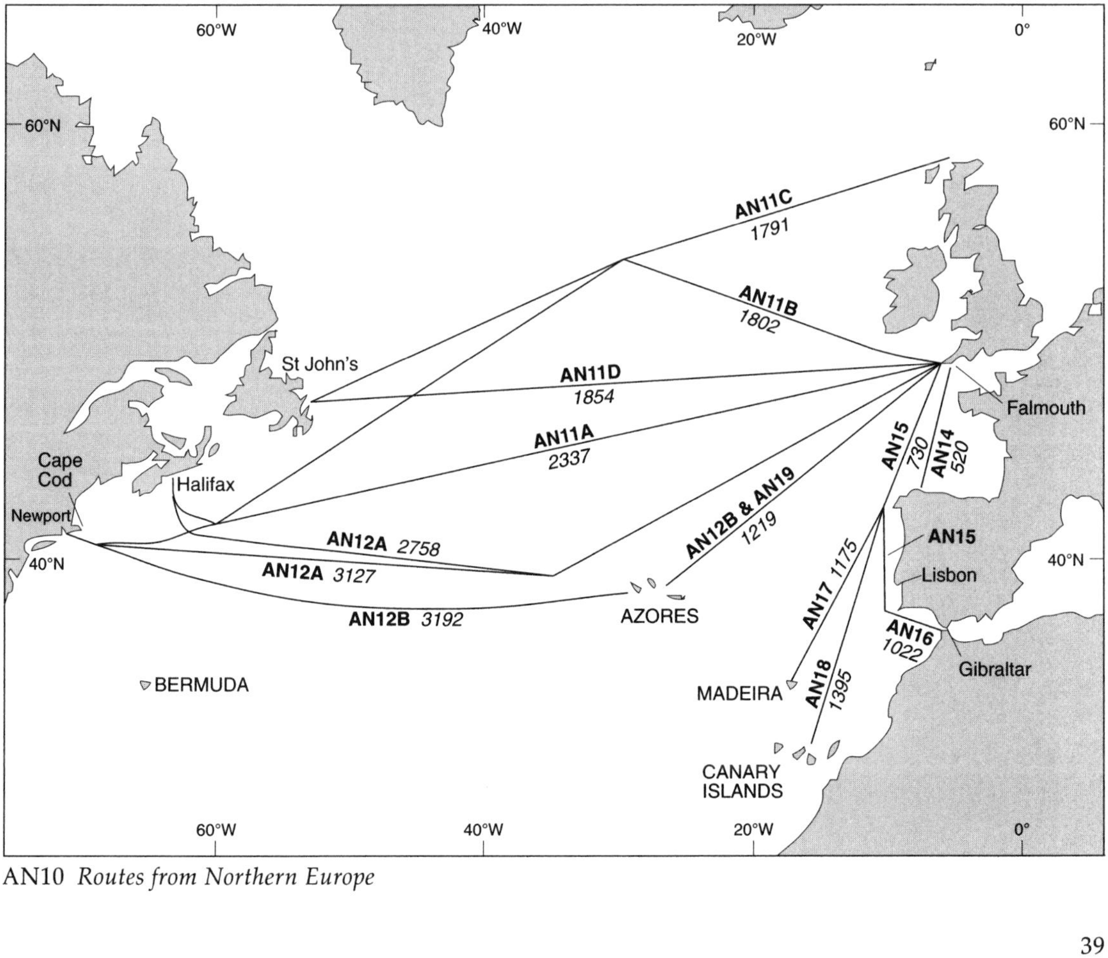

AN10 *Routes from Northern Europe*

the Arctic Circle is no longer a rarity. Two new sections have been added to this edition (AN160 and AN170) to help both those planning to sail from the Nordic countries to warmer seas and those tempted to sail in the opposite direction. For the first time, this book deals with high latitudes in the North Atlantic where cruising boats now sail regularly to Iceland, Greenland and the north of Norway, even as far as Spitsbergen.

Because the sailing season in Northern Europe is limited to only a few months, most offshore passages take place between May and August. Earlier, the weather is still cold and unsettled, although for northbound passages the early part of the season has better chances of favourable, if strong, winds from the SW. With the onset of summer, the likelihood of NE winds is higher. After the end of August the weather becomes more unsettled and at least one violent storm can be expected either side of the autumn equinox.

Anyone sailing from the north has to pass two major hurdles before reaching the more benign southern part of the North Atlantic. Sailing from the North Sea towards the English Channel one has to put up with one of the highest concentrations of shipping in the world, and if the visibility is poor and the wind unfavourable it is better to go into a port and wait for a change. The next hurdle is the Bay of Biscay where even in a moderate gale the seas can become very rough. However, the notorious bay is only about 300 miles across and if one leaves with a favourable forecast from a place like Falmouth, one should be able to cross without being caught out by the weather.

AN11 *Europe to North America* (northern routes)

BEST TIME:	June to August
TROPICAL STORMS:	June to November
CHARTS:	BA: 4011
	US: 121
PILOTS:	BA: 27, 40, 59, 67, 68, 69
	US: 140, 142, 145, 191
CRUISING GUIDES:	*The Atlantic Crossing Guide, Cruising Guide to Newfoundland, Cruising Guide to the Nova Scotia Coast, Yachting Guide to the South Shore of Nova Scotia, Coastal Cruising Guide to the Atlantic Coast, Cruising Guide to the New England Coast.*
WAYPOINTS:	

Departure	Intermediate	Landfall	Destination	Distance (M)
Route AN11A				
AN110 Lizard	AN115 Sable	AN118 off Halifax	Halifax	2337
49°55'N, 5°10'W	43°30'N, 60°00'W	44°25'N, 63°25'W	*44°38'N, 63°34'W*	
	AN116 Nantucket	AN119 Brenton	Newport	2726
	40°30'N, 69°30'W	41°24'N, 71°16'W	*41°29'N, 71°20'W*	
Route AN11B				
AN111 Bishop	AN113 N Atlantic	AN117 off St John's	St John's	1802
49°50'N, 6°35'W	55°00'N, 30°00'W	47°34'N, 52°40'W	*47°34'N, 52°42'W*	
	AN115 Sable	AN118 off Halifax	Halifax	2286
	AN116 Nantucket	AN119 Brenton	Newport	2675
Route AN11C				
AN112 Wrath	AN113 N Atlantic	AN117 off St John's	St John's	1791
58°40'N, 5°10'W	AN115 Sable	AN118 off Halifax	Halifax	2246
	AN116 Nantucket	AN119 Brenton	Newport	2621
Route AN11D				
AN110 Lizard	AN114 Mid-Atlantic	AN117 off St John's	St John's	1854
	51°26'N, 23°24'W			

From the Vikings and the Pilgrim Fathers to participants in singlehanded races, the westbound transatlantic routes of high latitudes have been well sailed over the centuries. The great circle route from the English Channel (AN11A) is probably the most difficult as there is usually a battle against headwinds all the way across. The alternatives are either to make a detour to the north, in the hope of finding more favourable winds (AN11B), a track closer to the great circle route from Scotland (AN11C), or to make a detour to the south, in search of warmer weather, as described in AN12. All of the northern routes can be affected by fog and ice and their timing is therefore crucial. In July, the maximum iceberg limit extends SE from Newfoundland to 39°N, 50°W; in August the ice limit recedes to above latitude 41°N, which limits passages close to those latitudes to a few summer months. As most of the Western Atlantic can be affected by tropical storms, this hazard should be borne in mind also, especially during late summer passages.

The prevailing winds on route AN11A are mostly westerly with the added disadvantage of sailing against the Gulf Stream. It can be counterproductive to try and avoid the contrary current by moving south, as this brings the possibility of straying into the Azores high. To avoid the effect of the Gulf Stream entirely one may have to go further south along one of the routes described in AN12, or take a more northerly track. Timing on these routes is crucial and weather forecasts for as long as a week in advance should be consulted before deciding on the best tactic.

The main object of the more northerly routes (AN11B and AN11C) is to stay north of the lows that move across the Atlantic from west to east. Although the chances of finding entirely favourable winds are only marginally better than on the direct route (AN11A), boats with good windward going capabilities have made speedy passages, as between the lows the winds are most likely to be either NW or SW. These northern routes converge at waypoint AN113 from where a new course is set for the port of destination. As these routes pass through an area with a very high incidence of fog and ice, they should only be attempted later in the summer. There is, however, an even more northerly route that can be sailed in late summer. It originates in Northern Europe and calls at Iceland before sailing to Newfoundland, possibly via Greenland (see also AN178 and AN179).

One of the shortest routes across the Atlantic is the great circle route from the English Channel to St John's in Newfoundland (AN11D). As the course reaches its northernmost latitude at WP AN114, in some years this could be perilously close to the ice limit. Early in the season, or in a year with more ice than usual, it may be worth considering route AN12A which keeps to the south of the ice limit. This limit fluctuates from year to year and month to month. The average iceberg limits for July and August are mentioned above, but a more northerly course can be chanced if up to date ice reports can be obtained by radio.

Boats bound for US ports should use WPs AN115 and AN116 to avoid the shallows off Sable Island and Nantucket Shoal respectively. Only a few intermediate waypoints are suggested as all of these routes should be approached with complete flexibility. Refer also to AN178 and AN179.

AN12 *Europe to North America* (southern routes)

BEST TIME:	June to August
TROPICAL STORMS:	June to November
CHARTS:	BA: 4011
	US: 126
PILOTS:	BA: 27, 40, 59, 67, 68, 69
	US: 140, 142, 145, 191
CRUISING GUIDES:	*The Atlantic Crossing Guide, Azores Cruising Guide, Atlantic Islands, Yachting Guide to Bermuda, Cruising Guide to Newfoundland, Cruising Guide to the Nova Scotia Coast, Yachting Guide to the South Shore of Nova Scotia, Coastal Cruising Guide to the Atlantic Coast, Cruising Guide to the New England Coast.*

WAYPOINTS:				
Departure	*Intermediate*	*Landfall*	*Destination*	*Distance (M)*
Route AN12A				
AN120 Lizard	AN121 Ice			
49°55'N, 5°10'W	39°00'N, 35°00'W			
	AN122 Sable	AN127 off Halifax	Halifax	2758
	43°30'N, 60°00'W	44°25'N, 63°25'W	*44°38'N, 63°34'W*	
	AN123 Nantucket	AN128 Brenton	Newport	3127
	40°30'N, 69°30'W	41°24'N, 71°16'W	*41°29'N, 71°20'W*	
Route AN12B				
AN120 Lizard	AN124 Graciosa			
	39°12'N, 27°50'W			
	AN125 São Jorge			
	38°46'N, 28°20'W			
	AN126 Faial	AN127 off Halifax	Halifax	2811
	38°32.5'N,28°35.5'W			
	AN123 Nantucket	AN128 Brenton	Newport	3192

To avoid the headwinds and cold weather on the more direct transatlantic routes described in AN11, there is a choice of a more southerly course, which can be either direct (AN12A) or via the Azores (AN12B).

The prevailing winds on route AN12A are westerly with the added disadvantage of sailing against the Gulf Stream. It can be counterproductive to try and avoid the contrary current by moving south, as this brings the possibility of straying into the Azores high, so one must be prepared to either put up with the current or move far enough south to avoid it altogether. Fast passages have been recorded on this route, but this has been due mainly to the individual boat's performance as well as access to weather information. Weather forecasts for at least one week in advance should be consulted before departure to be able to decide on the best tactic. Passages in early summer should use WP AN121 to avoid the southern ice limit. West of the Azores waypoints AN122 and AN123 are given to avoid the shallows off Sable Island and Nantucket Shoal respectively.

Route AN12B is a fair weather alternative and also a continuation of route AN19 via the Azores (page 49). Although longer than the other routes, it has the advantage of warmer weather and a mid-Atlantic stop for rest and reprovisioning. The course westward from the Azores will depend both on the final port of destination and the weather encountered. Depending on the winds encountered, one should not move north of about latitude 37°N so as to avoid the southern limit of the Gulf Stream and possibly the Azores high as well. South and southwesterly winds prevail along this route in summer.

This route is likely to be affected by tropical storms after the middle of June, the risk of hurricanes increasing as summer progresses. For the same reason, a stopover in Bermuda is only recommended in an emergency as it involves a detour and also increases the time spent in an area affected by hurricanes. Route AN137 (page 153) should be consulted for details if a stop in Bermuda is envisaged.

AN13 *Southbound from Northern Europe*

BEST TIME:	May to mid-August			
TROPICAL STORMS:	None			
CHARTS:	BA: 4140, 4103			
	US: 126			
PILOTS:	BA: 1, 22, 27, 28, 54, 55, 67			
	US: 143, 191, 192			
CRUISING GUIDES:	*Cruising Association Handbook, Shell Pilot to the English Channel Vols 1 & 2, North Sea Passage Pilot, Atlantic Spain and Portugal.*			
WAYPOINTS:				

Departure	Intermediate	Landfall	Destination	Distance (M)
AN130 Brunsbüttel *53°53'N, 9°08'E*	AN131 Weser *53°55'N, 8°10'E*			
	AN132 Borkum *53°54'N, 6°15'E*			
	AN133 Tersh *53°30'N, 4°40'E*			
	AN134, Strait *51°10'N, 1°46'E*		Dover *51°07'N, 1°19'E*	357
AN135 Crosshaven *51°48.5'N, 8°17'W*	AN136 Cork *51°45'N, 8°16'W*			
	AN137 Brittany *47°30'N, 8°50'W*			
	AN138 Villano *43°10'N, 9°40'W*	AN139 Vigo NW *42°16'N, 8°54'W*	Bayona *42°07'N, 8°50'W*	595

Because of its convenient position, most boats that are heading south with a longer passage in mind use the Kiel Canal at the start of their voyage. Having transited the canal, it is possible to leave straight from Brunsbüttel, at its North Sea end. Waypoint AN131, off the Alte Wester landfall buoy, makes a good point of departure. From there, it is possible to stay inside the shipping separation zone, closer to shore, or take an offshore route. The inshore route has the advantage of being closer to a number of islands where shelter may be sought should the weather deteriorate. To take the offshore route, one needs to cut across the shipping separation zone, so from AN132, a course should be set for AN133. From there, a course may be set for the Dover Strait and waypoint AN134, but as this route will cross, or run close to, a number of oil or gas fields, the area should be approached with great caution. If weather conditions are good, one should resist the temptation to stop in one

of the nearer English ports and try to make it at least as far as England's south coast, where there are several good marinas. See also AN14 and AN161.

For boats heading south from further west, such as Ireland, Crosshaven is probably the best place to depart on a southbound passage as it has the best facilities on the south coast of Ireland. Boats planning to cross the Atlantic to the Caribbean may be tempted to sail nonstop as far as Madeira or even the Canaries (see AN17 and AN18). Those who intend to call on the west coast of the Iberian Peninsula should set a course that passes west of the Brittany weather buoy and make landfall close to Cape Finisterre. AN138 has been given as a landfall waypoint for those who wish to stop in one of the ports in the NW of the peninsula, otherwise it is better to remain well offshore and only close with the land when approaching the port of destination. Bayona and Vigo, in the well protected Vigo estuary, are the nearest Spanish ports after Cape Finisterre. A waypoint NW of the entrance allows boats to use the North Channel, which offers early protection provided by the Bayona islands. Further south is the busy port of Leixoes at the

mouth of the Douro River on whose banks lies the attractive city of Porto. As there are only limited docking facilities in Porto itself, visiting boats are advised to stop first in Leixoes before proceeding upriver.

AN14 *Routes across the Bay of Biscay*

BEST TIME:	May to mid-August			
TROPICAL STORMS:	None			
CHARTS:	BA: 4103			
	US: 126			
PILOTS:	BA: 22, 27, 28, 37			
	US: 143, 191			
CRUISING GUIDES:	*South Biscay Pilot, Atlantic Spain and Portugal.*			
WAYPOINTS:				

Departure	Intermediate	Landfall	Destination	Distance (M)
AN140 Lizard		AN141 Villano		
49°55'N, 5°10'W		43°10'N, 9°40'W		
		AN142 Prior	La Coruña	520
		43°35'N, 8°24'W	*43°21.5, 8°23'W*	
AN140 Lizard		AN141 Villano		
		AN143 Vigo NW	Bayona	519
		42°16'N, 8°54'W	*42°07'N, 8°50'W*	

Whether starting off from an English harbour or any port in continental Europe, it is advisable to make a last stop in Falmouth to wait for a good weather forecast before crossing the Bay of Biscay. This port in the SW of England has good docking and repair facilities and is excellently situated to wait for favourable conditions for the continuation of a voyage. A departure should not be attempted if SW winds are forecast, which are generated by depressions moving across the North Atlantic. As soon as the depression has passed, NW winds can be expected and with a reasonable long term forecast there is usually sufficient time to reach Cape Finisterre before another change in the weather.

Regardless of the forecast and the actual direction of the wind, it is wise to try and make some westing and not follow a rhumb line across the Bay. Taking as a departure point WP AN140, just south of Lizard Point, course is set for WP AN141, 20 miles west of Cape Villano and some 25 miles NW of Cape Finisterre, at the start of the shipping separation zone going around the latter. An alterna-

tive destination, also in NW Spain, but slightly south of Cape Finisterre, is the port of Bayona in the well protected Vigo estuary. Waypoint AN143, NW of the entrance, allows boats to use the North Channel, which offers early protection provided by the Bayona islands. For the continuation of the southbound routes see AN15 and AN16 (pages 45–6).

As a rule, while crossing the Bay of Biscay, if the winds are from the SW and one is sailing on the starboard tack, one should avoid being set too much to the SSE or SE, so as not to be embayed by a SW gale, which is the usual direction of the worst gales. Because of the abrupt change from deep to shallow waters in the Bay of Biscay, seas can become extremely rough even in a moderate storm. The situation is sometimes exacerbated by a high swell generated by a hurricane blowing thousands of miles away.

The best time to make this passage is in early summer, between May and July, when the weather is often settled and the winds favourable, probably from the NE. Towards the end of summer the frequency of gales increases and more attention should be paid to the forecasts from the middle of August to the end of September when some of the most violent storms have been recorded. Although called equinoctial gales these violent storms can occur on either side of the autumn equinox and the seas generated by them in the Bay of Biscay can be extremely rough.

With a good forecast, especially early in the summer, one may be tempted to stop first at one of the Spanish ports, such as La Coruña. The rest of the voyage can then be continued in easy stages along the western coasts of Spain and Portugal. Those planning to stop in Northern Spain can sail a direct route by setting course from WP AN140 to WP AN142, three miles WNW of Cape Prior, in the approaches to La Coruña.

AN15 *Northern Europe to Portugal*

BEST TIME:	May to mid-August			
TROPICAL STORMS:	None			
CHARTS:	BA: 4103			
	US: 126			
PILOTS:	BA: 22, 27, 28, 37, 67			
	US: 143, 191			
CRUISING GUIDES:	*South Biscay Pilot, Atlantic Spain and Portugal.*			
WAYPOINTS:				
Departure	*Intermediate*	*Landfall*	*Destination*	*Distance (M)*
AN150 Lizard	AN151 Villano	AN152 Lima	Viana	540
49°55'N, 5°10'W	43°10'N, 9°40'W	41°42'N, 8°55'W	*41°41'N, 8°55'W*	
	AN153 Berlenga			
	39°30'N, 9°40'W			
	AN154 Raso	AN155 N Channel	Lisbon	730
	38°42'N, 9°33'W	38°40'N, 9°20'W	*38°41.5'N, 9°12'W*	

Boats not intending to stop on the north Spanish coast should skirt the Bay of Biscay and make for waypoint AN151, approximately 25 miles NW of Cape Finisterre. This avoids both the Bay itself and the busy traffic passing close to Cape Finisterre. The best time to make this passage is in early summer, between May and July, when the weather is often settled and the winds favourable. Towards the end of the summer the frequency of gales increases and more attention should be paid to the forecasts from the middle of August to the end of September when some of the most violent storms have been recorded.

Having weathered Cape Finisterre, landfall can be made at WP AN152, off Rio Lima, a tidal river on the north shore of which lies Viana do Castelo, an attractive small town with a marina, which is a convenient place to clear into Portugal. Its main drawback is the bar across the river entrance where seas break in onshore winds. In such a case it is wise to look for an alternative.

If one is short of time, one can sail nonstop to Lisbon. From WP AN151, off Cape Finisterre, a course should be set for WP AN153, west of Berlenga Islands. From there course is altered for WP AN154, off Cabo Raso, in the approaches to Lisbon. Canal Norte (North Channel) leads into the Tagus River, the Portuguese capital being situated about 8 miles upstream on the north shore of the river. Docking facilities for visitors are limited. Boats under 40 ft and drawing less than 6 ft may find a place for a few days at the small marina run by Associaçao Naval de Lisboa at Belem, right by the Discovery Monument on the north shore of the river. The small basin also has fuel. The other alternative is to continue under the large suspension bridge into Alcantara Basin, which is reached through an opening bridge. Further upriver, a new marina has been built on the Expo '98 site with some places being reserved for visiting yachts.

AN16 *Northern Europe to Mediterranean*

BEST TIME:	May to mid-August			
TROPICAL STORMS:	None			
CHARTS:	BA: 4103			
	US: 126			
PILOTS:	BA: 22, 27, 67			
	US: 143, 191, 192			
CRUISING GUIDES:	*Atlantic Spain and Portugal. Yacht Scene, East Spain Pilot, Spanish Mediterranean Yachtsman's Directory.*			
WAYPOINTS:				

Departure	Intermediate	Landfall	Destination	Distance (M)
AN160 Lizard 49°55'N, 5°10'W	AN161 Finisterre W 43°10'N, 10°00'W			
	AN162 Berlenga 39°30'N, 9°40'W			
	AN163 Vincent NW 37°00'N, 9°08'W			
	AN164 Hoyo 36°04'N, 6°20'W			
	AN165 Tarifa 35°59'N, 5°36'W			
	AN166 Carnero 36°03'N, 5°25'W	AN167 Gibraltar 36°08'N, 5°22'W	Marina Bay *36°09'N, 5°21'W*	1022
		AN168 Europa Point 36°04'N, 5°20.5'W		1021

Instructions for crossing the Bay of Biscay are similar to those described in AN15. Boats intending to sail to the Mediterranean nonstop should stay well offshore and pass Cape Finisterre at a safe distance by setting course for WP AN161. During summer the winds along the Portuguese coast are usually favourable northerlies, which will ensure a fast sail all the way to Cape St Vincent. From Cape Finisterre, the course runs along the 10°W meridian and passes close to the west of Berlenga Islands to WP AN162. From there the course will be altered to WP AN163, 7 miles off Cape St Vincent.

From Cape St Vincent the course is altered for the Strait of Gibraltar to WP AN164, off Hoyo Bank, at the SW extremity of the shallows off Cape Trafalgar. The next waypoint to make for is WP AN165, 2 miles south of Tarifa Island and inside the westgoing shipping lane. A course parallel to the Spanish coast will take one into the Bay of Gibraltar to WP AN166 off Punta Carnero and thence to WP AN167 off North Mole and the approaches to Marina Bay. Boats proceeding into the Mediterranean without calling at Gibraltar should make for WP AN168, 3 miles south of Europa Point. At night boats transiting the Strait nonstop may find it easier to cross over to the African coast earlier and stay in the eastgoing shipping lane.

Once past Cape St Vincent, the Portuguese trades are normally lost and winds become more local in character. On summer days, a SW sea breeze occurs on approaching the Bay of Cadiz. This wind comes up around noon and lasts until midnight. If a strong *Levanter* is predicted in the Strait of Gibraltar, it is advisable to wait for a change in one of the ports along the Algarve coast (Lagos or Vilamoura) or Bay of Cadiz (Puerto Sherry). Another convenient port is Barbate, which is not far west of Tarifa and is the closest to the Strait. Alternatively, one can find some shelter in the lee of Tarifa Island itself. Weather information, as well as other shipping news, can be obtained from Tarifa Radio, which operates a 24-hour service in both Spanish and English.

The Strait of Gibraltar separates Europe from Africa and at its nearest point the two continents are only 7.5 miles apart. A traffic separation zone operates along the 35 miles of the Strait, with west-bound traffic using the north lane and eastbound traffic the south lane. Small craft can use the inshore lanes, and boats making for Gibraltar are recommended to keep close to the Spanish shore. However, one should be extremely cautious, par-ticularly at night, as fishing nets are often set with-out any regard for shipping. These nets can stretch for several miles offshore and have even been set in the traffic separation zone between the two ship-ping lanes approaching the Strait from the west. The nets are normally marked by small lights, which are difficult to see from a distance.

Another hazard to watch out for are tidal races and overflows, the most violent occurring on the north side extending SW from Cape Trafalgar. Wind against tide can produce rough seas west of Tarifa with an easterly wind, and east of Tarifa with a westerly wind. The main problem is the strength of the currents and the unpredictability of the tidal streams. There is a permanent east set-ting current of about 2 knots through the Strait,

being strongest at the centre and weakest at the edges. The current is weakest over shallow water where the flow can be reversed by a contrary wind.

Negotiating the Strait from west to east is usu-ally easier because the prevailing current always sets from the Atlantic into the Mediterranean. By entering the Strait at the right time, a boat com-ing from the Atlantic can count on as much as nine hours of favourable current. However, conditions can become extremely rough if a strong *Levanter* blows against the current. Although tidal data in the Strait is not entirely reliable, it has been estab-lished that in the middle of the Strait the east set-ting stream starts approximately at the time of HW Gibraltar and the west going stream six hours later. It can also be assumed that the tidal flow from high to low water is to the east, while the flow from low to high water is to the west. The times of HW Gibraltar can be requested over the VHF radio from Tarifa Radio.

AN17 *Northern Europe to Madeira*

BEST TIME:	May to mid-August
TROPICAL STORMS:	None
CHARTS:	BA: 4014
	US: 120
PILOTS:	BA: 1, 22, 27, 67
	US: 143, 191
CRUISING GUIDES:	*Atlantic Islands, Madeira Cruising Guide.*
WAYPOINTS:	

Departure	Intermediate	Landfall	Destination	Distance (M)
AN170 Lizard 49°55'N, 5°10'W	AN171 Finisterre NW 44°00'N, 10°00'W AN172 off Madeira 33°00'N, 16°32'W AN173 Fora 32°43.5'N, 16°38'W	AN174 Garajau 32°38'N, 16°50'W	Funchal *32°37.5'N, 16°54.5'W*	1175
AN170 Lizard	AN171 Finisterre NW AN175 North Santo 33°10'N, 16°15'W	AN176 Cima SE 33°02'N,16°16'W	Porto Santo *33°03'N, 16°19'W*	1130

As the great circle route from the English Channel to Madeira passes at a safe distance west of Cape Finisterre, similar directions apply for the passage across the Bay of Biscay as for route AN15. As the

intention is not to stop in Northern Spain or con-tinental Portugal, some westing should be made after leaving the English Channel so as to have suf-ficient searoom should a southwesterly gale blow up while crossing the Bay of Biscay. On leaving the English Channel, a course should be set for WP AN171, some 60 miles NW of Cape Finisterre. Such a course avoids the shipping lanes that converge on Cape Finisterre. Having passed the latter, boats going to Funchal should set a direct course to WP AN172, west of Porto Santo Island. The island of Madeira is best approached from the NE by rounding Ilheu de Fora, a small islet on which stands a powerful light. From WP AN173, one mile E of the latter, course can be altered to pass south of Ponta de Garajau (WP AN174) and thence to Funchal.

Because the marina in Funchal, the capital of Madeira, is very crowded in October, when most cruising boats plan to stop there on their way south, a stop in Porto Santo is recommended at this time of year. In such a case, from WP AN171 one should make for WP AN175 and approach the main harbour on Porto Santo from the NE and E. There are a number of dangers along Porto Santo's coasts and these are avoided by keeping well off the coast and

making for WP AN176. From there the course can be altered for the port after Ilheu de Cima, the small islet off the SE extremity of the island, has been left to starboard.

During the summer, winds along this route are mostly favourable with the Portuguese trade winds blowing off the Iberian Peninsula and African coast. Also favourable is the Portugal Current which sets in a SSW direction.

In theory, this passage can be made at any time between April and October but the weather should be watched carefully. If a late start is made as part of a transatlantic passage, particular attention should be paid to the weather forecasts during September and October, as West Indian hurricanes can influence weather conditions even on the east side of the Atlantic. Some of the worst weather on this route has been recorded in September or early October with gale force south-westerlies generated by a passing front.

AN18 *Northern Europe to Canary Islands*

BEST TIME:	May to mid-August				
TROPICAL STORMS:	None				
CHARTS:	BA: 4014				
	US: 120				
PILOTS:	BA: 1, 22, 27, 28, 55, 67				
	US: 143, 191				
CRUISING GUIDES:	*Canary Islands Cruising Guide, Atlantic Islands.*				
WAYPOINTS:					

Departure	Intermediate	Landfall	Destination	Distance (M)
AN180 Lizard	AN181 Finisterre NW	AN182 Isleta	Las Palmas	1395
49°55'N, 5°10'W	44°00'N, 10°00'W	28°09'N, 15°23'W	*28°07.5'N, 15°25.5'W*	
		AN183 Alegranza	Arrecife	1325
		29°25'N, 13°28'W	*28°57'N, 13°32.5'W*	
		AN184 Graciosa	La Sociedad	1313
		29°13'N, 13°34'W	*29°13.8'N, 13°30'W*	

The direct course from the English Channel follows closely the route to Madeira and the same directions apply as for routes AN15 and AN17 to WP AN181 off Cape Finisterre. As such a nonstop passage from Northern Europe to the Canaries is usually attempted late in the season by boats hurrying to join the trade wind route to the Caribbean, the weather can be less favourable and the likelihood of gales is greater than in summer. As suggested when discussing routes across the

Bay of Biscay, such a passage should not be started unless there is a good forecast for at least 72 hours. This nonstop route to the Canaries is only recommended for those who wish to provision there before a transatlantic passage to the Caribbean. If planning to sail on to Cape Town, Brazil, or any other South Atlantic destination, it might be better to keep to the west of the Canaries so as to cross the equator on a meridian where the doldrums are narrower than in the proximity of the African coast. Transequatorial routes are discussed in chapter 6.

South of the Bay of Biscay bad weather is usually associated with depressions moving across the Atlantic to the north of Madeira and generating strong SW winds. In the likelihood of encountering such weather, it is advisable to keep well off the Portuguese coast so as to be able to go on the starboard tack when the SW winds arrive. Once the front has passed, the winds will move rapidly to the NW. A course can then be set for WP AN182, north of La Isleta light in the approaches to Las Palmas. The conspicuous shape of La Isleta makes a perfect landfall. 2.5 miles further south is the entrance to Las Palmas harbour.

Work started in 1998 on a new breakwater to protect the marina from the north.

If the passage is undertaken earlier in the season with the intention of spending some time cruising the Canaries, the first landfall should be in Lanzarote, which lies to windward of all other islands in the archipelago. From WP AN181 course should be set for AN183 off Alegranza. It is also possible to stop first at Graciosa, a small island north of Lanzarote, which has a small but well protected port at La Sociedad, its main settlement situated on the north shore of the narrows separating Graciosa from Lanzarote. In this case landfall is made at AN184 west of Graciosa, from where the south coast of the island is followed around to La Sociedad. Entry formalities can be completed later in Lanzarote itself.

AN19 *Northern Europe to Azores*

BEST TIME:	May to August			
TROPICAL STORMS:	None			
CHARTS:	BA: 4103			
	US: 126			
PILOTS:	BA: 22, 27, 28, 55, 67			
	US: 140, 143			
CRUISING GUIDES:	*Azores Cruising Guide, Atlantic Islands.*			
WAYPOINTS:				

Departure	Intermediate	Landfall	Destination	Distance (M)
AN190 Lizard 49°55'N, 5°10'W		AN191 Arnel 37°50'N, 25°06'W	Ponta Delgada *37°44'N, 25°39.5'W*	1148
	AN192 Graciosa 39°12'N, 27°50'W			
	AN193 Jorge 38°46'N, 28°20'W	AN194 Espalamaca 38°32.5'N, 28°35.5'W	Horta *38°32'N, 28°37.5'W*	1219

The best time to make this passage is in June or July when favourable conditions can usually be expected. Although the likelihood of W and SW winds is quite high at the start of the voyage, the frequency of N winds increases further south during the summer. It pays to wait before leaving the English Channel until N winds are forecast, as they allow a direct course to be set. Arriving from Northern Europe, the most convenient port of entry is the capital Ponta Delgada, which has a new marina. Coming from NE or E landfall will be made at the eastern extremity of São Miguel Island at WP AN191, two miles east of Ponta do Arnel.

Those wishing to sail direct to Horta, on Faial,

should set a course for WP AN192 and make landfall NE of Graciosa, the northernmost island of the archipelago. From there, the course is altered to pass west of São Jorge island (WP AN193) and thence to WP AN194 off Ponta Espalamaca in the approaches to Horta. In strong SW winds, the channel between Pico and Faial, in the approaches to Horta, can be affected by violent gusts. These, and the north setting current, should be taken into account if attempts are made to enter Horta under such conditions.

If W winds persist on leaving the English Channel, or strong SW winds are encountered en route, and a direct course to the Azores does not seem practicable, it might be better to change plans and sail there via Spain or Portugal. Such a route is described in AN15. On the subsequent leg from one of the ports on the Iberian Peninsula one has the benefit of the Portuguese trades, although such a detour can add about 300 miles to the total distance. However, the possibility of encountering westerly winds on the subsequent section to the Azores cannot be discounted and therefore such a detour should not be contemplated unless one has access to reliable weather information.

AN20 ROUTES FROM PORTUGAL

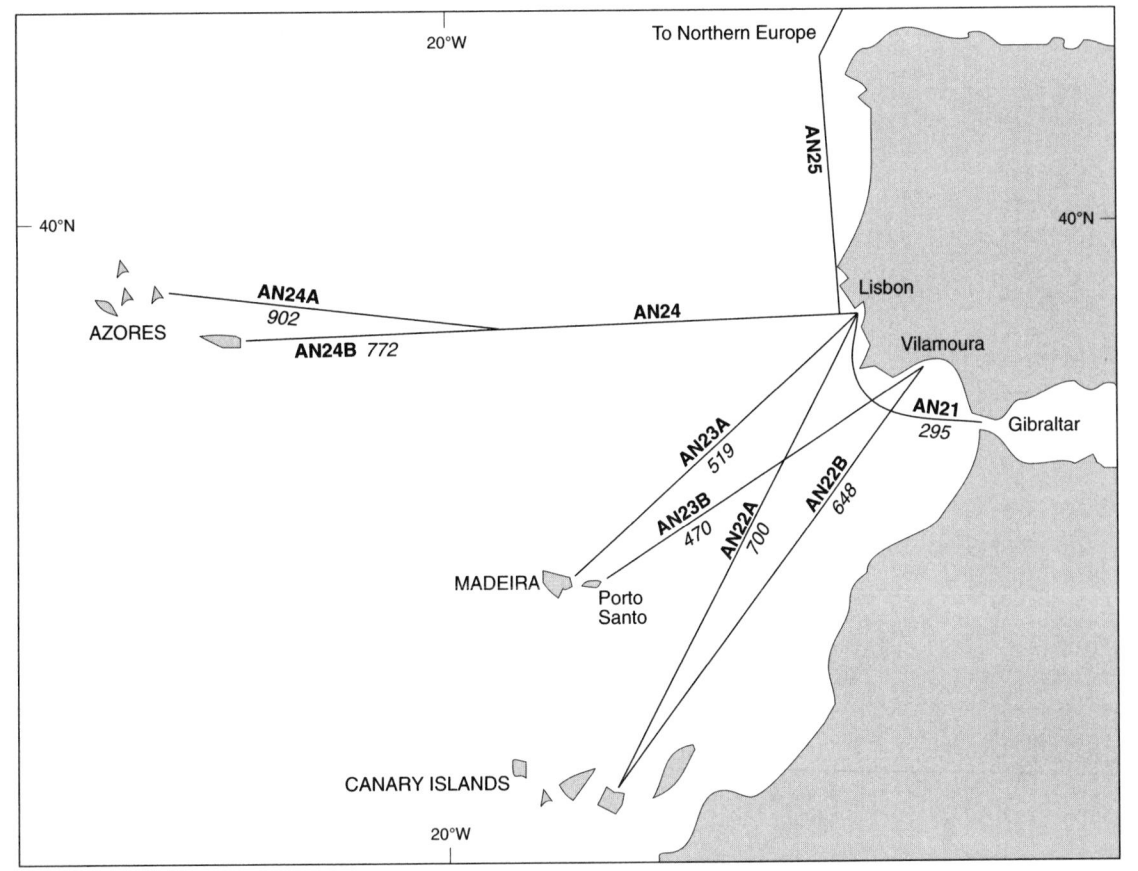

AN20 *Routes from Portugal*

Until recently most sailors associated Portugal with the Algarve coast and the marina at Vilamoura, where many North European sailors left their boats either before venturing further east into the Mediterranean or across the Atlantic. The west coast of Portugal has only recently started attracting cruising boats in any numbers, but things are rapidly changing as sailors discover the many attractions of this small country whose history has always been associated with the sea. The capital Lisbon is a delightful city to explore, although docking facilities for visitors continue to be disappointingly inadequate.

The most significant feature of this area are the Portuguese trades, which blow steadily down the coast during summer months. The prevailing summer winds are northerly. Such winds are common from April to September and in June and July can reach as far as Madeira. The NW shores of the peninsula experience more variable winds, although there is also a northerly component in summer. The prevailing winds make it essential to start a summer cruise as far north as possible. Similarly, during the summer months it is normally easier to sail from mainland Portugal to its outlying islands than vice versa. In fine summer weather there are land and sea breezes along the coast although the northerly trades do modify the sea breezes to some extent. There is also more sea fog in summer near the coast associated with calm or light winds. There is often a remarkable change in weather after Cape St Vincent has been passed. The one potential trouble spot for boats sailing east is the Strait of Gibraltar and the tactics for negotiating it are outlined in route AN16. Sailing from the mainland to Madeira is rarely difficult with the Portuguese trades ensuring fast passages. Occasionally, however, with the passage of a depression, the winds can come from the southwest, when it is better to wait for a change. The same applies to the passage to the Canaries, which also benefits from fair winds most of the time. Passages to the Azores are usually a mixture of good winds for the first half and variable conditions as one approaches the archipelago.

Because mainland Portugal is often the starting point for a cruise in the Azores, a few useful tips are given in route AN24. A cruise in the Azores does not lend itself to a logical sequence and therefore its starting point should be dictated by the subsequent destination. For those heading west across the Atlantic and who have the time to spend at least two weeks in the Azores, the logical landfall, and start of an Azorean cruise, should be either the small island of Santa Maria or the capital Ponta Delgada, on neighbouring São Miguel island. Boats planning to return to Portugal or the Mediterranean, as well as those intending to sail later to Madeira and the Canaries, should consider making their first landfall as far north as Graciosa and start their cruise there by calling at São Jorge, Faial, Pico, and Terceira on their way to São Miguel and Santa Maria. Boats bound for Northern Europe may find better conditions for their voyage to the English Channel by sailing the obverse route to the one described and leave from the Azores at Graciosa.

AN21 *Portugal to Gibraltar*

BEST TIME:	April to October			
TROPICAL STORMS:	None			
CHARTS:	BA: 87			
	US: 51150, 51160			
PILOTS:	BA: 67			
	US: 131, 143			
CRUISING GUIDES:	*Yacht Scene, Atlantic Spain and Portugal.*			
WAYPOINTS:				
Departure	*Intermediate*	*Landfall*	**Destination**	*Distance (M)*
AN211 off Lisbon 38°37'N, 9°20'W	AN212 Vincent NW 37°00'N, 9°08'W AN213 Hoyo 36°04'N, 6°20'W AN214 Tarifa 35°59'N, 5°36'W	AN215 Gibraltar 36°08'N, 5°22'W	Marina Bay *36°09'N, 5°21'W*	295

Along the western coast of Portugal northerly winds can be expected, especially in summer, when the Portuguese trades are the prevailing winds. On leaving Lisbon, or any port further up the coast, Cape Espichel is passed at a safe distance and a course is set for WP AN212, 7 miles off Cape St Vincent. The course is then altered for WP AN213 off Hoyo Bank at the SW extremity of the shallows off Cape Trafalgar. A hazard to be borne in mind along this route are tuna nets, which can stretch for several miles off the Spanish coast and may lay across the above route. The next waypoint to make for is WP AN214, two miles south of Tarifa Island and inshore of the westgoing shipping lane. A course parallel to the Spanish coast leads into the

Bay of Gibraltar. The reporting dock for customs and two of the marinas are easiest found by making for WP AN215 off the North Mole.

After Cape St Vincent has been passed, the winds become variable and the northerlies are usually lost. Closer to the Strait of Gibraltar, the winds change again and usually blow either in or out of the Strait. The current is favourable on this route as there is a constant flow of water from the Atlantic to the Mediterranean. The easterly *Levanter* wind produces a steep sea when blowing against the contrary current, which can make conditions difficult for a small boat when the wind is strong. Additional directions for transiting the Strait are given in route AN16.

AN22 *Portugal to Canary Islands*

BEST TIME:	May to October				
TROPICAL STORMS:	None				
CHARTS:	BA: 4104				
	US: 104				
PILOTS:	BA: 1, 67				
	US: 143				
CRUISING GUIDES:	*Canary Islands Cruising Guide, Atlantic Islands.*				
WAYPOINTS:					
Departure	*Intermediate*	*Landfall*	*Destination*		*Distance (M)*
Route AN22A					
AN221 off Lisbon		AN223 Isleta	Las Palmas		700
38°37'N, 9°20'W		28°09'N, 15°23'W	*28°07.5'N, 15°25.5'W*		
Route AN22B					
AN222 off Vilamoura		AN223 Isleta	Las Palmas		648
37°01'N, 8°08'W					

This is usually a pleasant passage, especially in summer when the Portuguese trades blow consistently and the southbound passage is further aided by the favourable current. Boats leaving from Lisbon (AN22A) can set a course for Gran Canaria as soon as they are safely out of the Tagus estuary through the South Channel. From WP AN221 a course is set for WP AN223 north of La Isleta light in the approaches to Las Palmas. If leaving from Vilamoura (AN22B) the course should stay well off the African coast as steadier winds will be encountered further offshore. From WP AN222 one mile SW of the marina entrance, a course can then be set for the same WP AN223, north of La Isleta. This keeps clear of all dangers, including El Roque rock

off Punta El Nido. The conspicuous shape of La Isleta makes a perfect landfall. 2.5 miles further south is the entrance to Las Palmas harbour. Work started in 1998 on a new breakwater to protect the marina from the north.

From June to September the Portuguese trades usually provide excellent sailing conditions along this route. In May and October the winds are less constant, although their direction continues to be predominantly northerly. November has a higher incidence of winds from other directions, but winds from the northern quarter are still in the majority. The passage to the Canaries should not be left for too late in the season, as strong SW winds with rough seas are often encountered by boats sailing this route after the end of October. Anyone intending to see more of the Canaries should plan on stopping first in Lanzarote, which is the logical island from which to start a cruise in the Canary Islands. See AN18 for further details.

AN23 *Portugal to Madeira*

BEST TIME:	May to October				
TROPICAL STORMS:	None				
CHARTS:	BA: 4104				
	US: 12				
PILOTS:	BA: 1, 67				
	US: 143				
CRUISING GUIDES:	*Atlantic Islands, Madeira Cruising Guide.*				
WAYPOINTS:					
Departure	*Intermediate*	*Landfall*	*Destination*		*Distance (M)*
Route AN23A					
AN231 off Lisbon	AN233 Santo S				
38°37'N, 9°20'W	32°50'N, 16°15'W				
	AN234 Garajau		Funchal		519
	32°38'N, 16°50'W		*32°37.5'N, 16°54.5'W*		
AN232 off Vilamoura	AN233 Santo S				
37°01'N, 8°08'W	AN234 Garajau		Funchal		507
Route AN23B					
AN231 off Lisbon	AN235 Santo N				
	33°10'N, 16°15'W				
	AN236 Cima NE		Porto Santo		478
	33°04'N, 16°15'W		*33°03'N, 16°19'W*		
AN232 off Vilamoura	AN235 Santo N				
	AN236 Cima NE		Porto Santo		470

Throughout the year the predominant winds on this route are from the northerly quarter, but best sailing conditions are usually experienced between June and August when NE winds prevail. Although these Portuguese trades normally reach as far as Madeira, the likelihood of contrary winds increases with the approach of winter. During the summer, winds along this route are mostly favourable when the Portuguese trade winds blow off the Iberian Peninsula and African coast. Also favourable is the Portugal Current which sets in a SSW direction. The weather in the vicinity of Madeira is influenced by the position of the Azores high, light winds and calms occurring when this high moves south of its normal position.

Leaving from either Lisbon (WP AN231) or Vilamoura (WP AN232) boats bound for Funchal

can set a direct course (route AN23A) for WP AN233, south of Porto Santo Island. From there the course is altered for WP AN234, south of Ponta do Garajau, on the south coast of Madeira, and thence to Funchal.

As Porto Santo is on the direct route to Madeira and the marina in Funchal, the capital of Madeira, is often very crowded, a stop in Porto Santo is recommended. If a stop in Porto Santo is intended, the initial course (route AN23B) should be set for WP AN235, NE of Porto Santo. From there make for WP AN236, one mile NE of Ilheu de Cima. There are a number of dangers along Porto Santo's east coast and these are avoided by keeping well off the coast and only altering course for the port after Ilheu de Cima, the small islet off the SE extremity of the island, has been left to starboard.

AN24 *Portugal to Azores*

BEST TIME:	June to August			
TROPICAL STORMS:	None			
CHARTS:	BA: 4103	US: 103		
PILOTS:	BA: 67	US: 143		
CRUISING GUIDES:	*Azores Cruising Guide, Atlantic Islands.*			
WAYPOINTS:				

Departure	Intermediate	Landfall	Destination	Distance (M)
Route AN24A				
AN241 off Lisbon	AN243 Terceira		Horta	902
38°37'N, 9°20'W	38°33'N, 27°00'W		*38°32'N, 28°37.5'W*	
AN242 off Vilamoura	AN245 Sagres			
37°01'N, 8°08'W	36°56'N, 8°57'W			
	AN243 Terceira		Horta	972
Route AN24B				
AN241 off Lisbon		AN244 Garça	Ponta Delgada	772
		37°40'N, 25°23'W	*37°44'N, 25°39.5'W*	
AN242 off Vilamoura	AN245 Sagres	AN244 Garça	Ponta Delgada	836

This route between continental Portugal and its offlying archipelago has the benefit of the Portuguese trades during summer months when northerly winds predominate. If the passage is made in May, strong northerly winds may be encountered for the first days, being replaced by light winds or calms if a ridge of high pressure extending from the Azores high is crossed. The winds on the other side of the ridge normally blow from a SW direction. At the beginning and end of summer the frequency of gales is higher, as are SW winds.

On leaving the mainland with a fair northerly wind, boats using the Azores as a stopover on a transatlantic passage and planning to call at Horta (AN24A) rather than Ponta Delgada (AN24B) should sail a course which passes north of São Miguel. Such a course is recommended because of the difficulty of leaving Ponta Delgada should the winds change later to SW.

From WP AN241 off the South Channel in the approaches to Lisbon, a direct course leads to WP AN243, SE of the island of Terceira. Depending on weather conditions, from that point Horta can be reached by sailing either north or south of the island of Pico. In strong SW winds it is better to stay north of Pico and, if the weather deteriorates, one can seek shelter at Velas (38°40.5'N, 28°12'W), the main port on São Jorge. Terceira itself has a good harbour at Angra do Heroismo (38°39'N, 27°13'W), although it is open to the south and should be avoided in strong winds from that direction. In strong SW winds, the channel between Pico and Faial, in the approaches to Horta, can be affected by violent gusts. These, and the north setting current, should be taken into account if attempting to enter Horta under such conditions.

The direct route to Ponta Delgada (AN24B) leads to WP AN244, 3 miles south of Ponta da Garça, on the south coast of the island of São Miguel. Boats coming from ports south of Lisbon may prefer to make their first Azorean landfall at São Miguel. There is a good new marina at Ponta Delgada, the capital of the Azores, which has the best facilities in the archipelago. Another good starting point for a cruise among the islands is the island of Santa Maria, at the southeastern extremity of the archipelago, from where the other islands can be reached in logical succession. The alternative is to start cruising the Azores from one of the furthest islands, such as Graciosa, and, after visiting islands in the central group, take one's leave from the Azores in Santa Maria. The two westernmost islands of Flores and Corvo are usually visited by boats arriving from the west and their inclusion in a cruise starting from the east is more difficult and less practical.

Some boats sailing from mainland Portugal to the Azores take their leave from Vilamoura, on the Algarve coast. From WP AN242, one mile SW of the marina entrance, a course should be set for WP AN245, 5 miles S of Cape Sagres. From there the course is altered for one of the landfall points mentioned above.

AN25 *Portugal to Northern Europe*

BEST TIME:	April to May
TROPICAL STORMS:	None
CHARTS:	BA: 4103
	US: 103
PILOTS:	BA: 22, 27, 28, 55, 67
	US: 143, 191
CRUISING GUIDES:	*Cruising Association Handbook, The Shell Channel Pilot, North Biscay Pilot.*
WAYPOINTS:	

Departure	Intermediate	Landfall	Destination	Distance (M)
Lisbon 38°41.5'N, 9°12'W	AN251 N. Channel 38°40'N, 9°20'W			
	AN252 Raso 38°42'N, 9°33'W			
	AN253 Berlenga 39°30'N, 9°40'W			
	AN254 Villano 43°10'N, 9°40'W	AN256 Lizard 49°55'N, 5°10'W	Falmouth 50°09.5'N, 5°04'W	745
Viana 41°41'N, 8°55'W	AN255 Lima 41°42'N, 8°55'W			
	AN254 Villano	AN256 Lizard	Falmouth	555

The prevailing northerly winds of summer, which ensure excellent sailing conditions for southbound passages, make the task of reaching northern destinations very difficult throughout the summer months. The easiest solution is to sail up the coast in easy stages by taking advantage of favourable breezes which may blow close inshore. Having reached Northern Portugal, one can wait for favourable conditions to cross the Bay of Biscay.

The other alternative is to take an offshore tack and try to make as much northing as possible until more favourable winds are met. North of latitude 45°N westerly winds become increasingly predominant, but towards the end of summer the frequency of SW gales also increases, so it is better to plan this passage for the first half of summer. The time to avoid, if at all possible, is the period leading up to the autumn equinox as gales which occur around this time can product hazardous conditions in the Bay of Biscay.

Boats leaving from Lisbon should take the Northern Northern Channel so as to reach the open sea at WP AN252, off Cabo Raso. The course then leads west of the Berlenga Islands through WP AN253 and on to WP AN254, some 25 miles NW of Cape Finisterre. From that point a direct course can be set for WP AN256 off Lizard Point in the approaches to Falmouth, a most convenient port of entry into the United Kingdom.

Contrary winds, especially during summer, may force one to break the initial section of this passage into shorter stages. In such a case a good departure point from Northern Portugal is the small port of Viana do Castelo. When leaving from there one should wait for favourable conditions to cross the bar across the entrance. Having reached the open sea, from WP AN255 a course can then be set for AN254 and, provided conditions continue to be right, across the Bay of Biscay into the English Channel.

AN30 ROUTES FROM GIBRALTAR

Gibraltar is described as the gateway to the Mediterranean, although the opposite is equally true as, for westbound boats, the Strait of Gibraltar is the gateway to the Atlantic. One of the most frequented transit ports for yachts in the world, Gibraltar is particularly busy in spring, when boats make their way into the Mediterranean, and autumn, when the end of the sailing season produces a similar movement in the opposite direction. Gibraltar is also a convenient place from which to visit neighbouring ports in North Africa, whether the colourful Tangiers in Morocco or the two remaining Spanish possessions of Mella and Ceuta.

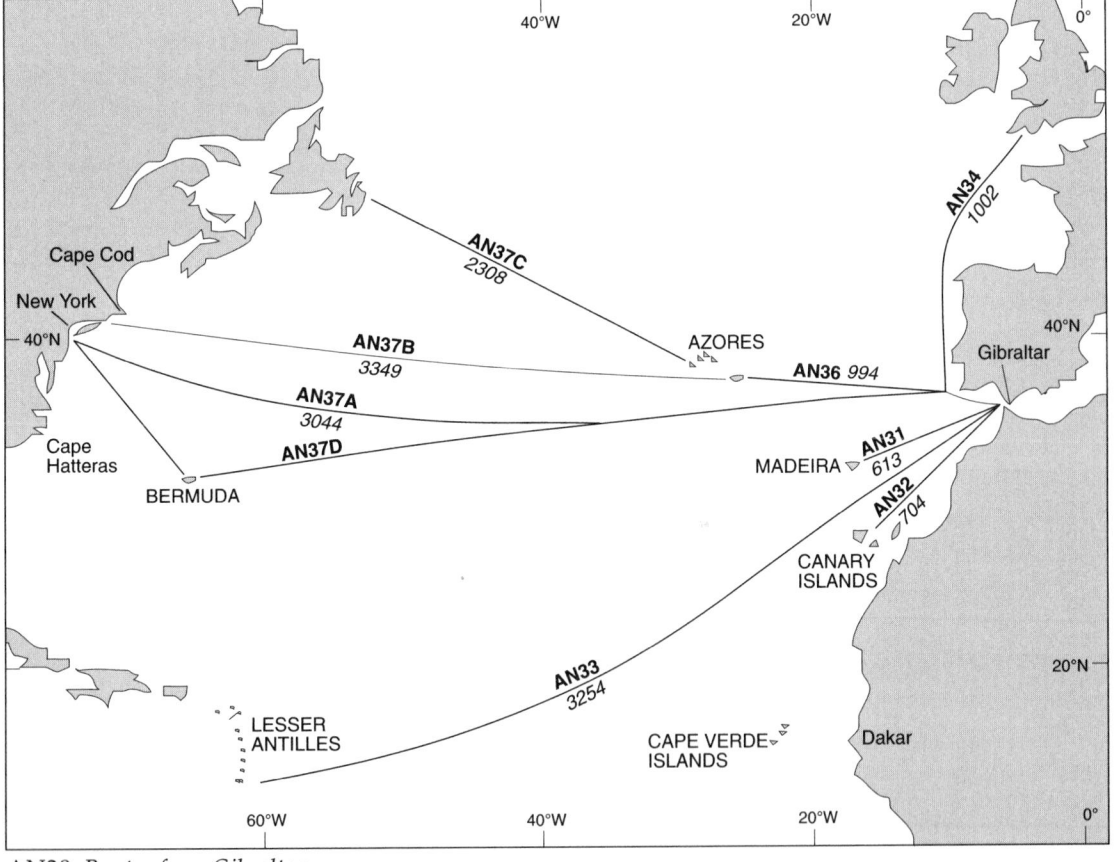

AN30 *Routes from Gibraltar*

As Gibraltar lies at the eastern end of the Strait which bears its name, eastbound boats are less dependent on weather conditions than those intending to sail through the Strait to the Atlantic beyond. A favourable forecast is essential on leaving Gibraltar as the Strait can turn into an insurmountable obstacle if weather conditions are not right. Ideally, westbound boats should wait for a *Levanter* or at least light westerly winds before leaving Gibraltar. Almost as important as the direction of the wind is the state of the tide and this should be played to one's advantage. If one leaves about three hours after HW Gibraltar, the tide will be contrary for only the first hour. After the tide slackens, by keeping to the Spanish side of the Strait, when the tide turns one should have a fair current at least as far as Tarifa. Because of the strong tidal sets, one should avoid sailing too close to the Spanish shore. In strong westerly winds, if one finds it impossible to make headway against them, one can anchor in the lee of Tarifa to wait for a break in the weather and a favourable tide. The situation usually improves significantly once the Strait has been left behind and a course is set for either Madeira or the Canaries. If bound for Northern Europe, a direct course is rarely possible since both winds and current along the Portuguese coast are normally contrary. If the Portuguese trades are still blowing, it is better to head offshore and favour the tack that makes most northing.

Going east from Gibraltar is usually easier, although it pays to wait for a favourable westerly wind. Timing one's departure to take advantage of the tide is less important because the west setting currents along Europa Point are never strong enough to pose serious problems. If not bound for one of the ports along the Spanish Costa del Sol, it is better to stay offshore where the winds are usually steadier. Mediterranean routes from Gibraltar are described in chapter 22.

The weather in the immediate vicinity of Gibraltar can be very different from the weather of the general area. In the southern part of the Iberian peninsula from Cape St Vincent to Gibraltar the winds are more variable in all months. The Portuguese trades are felt less in this area, and in their absence there is an onshore SW or W sea breeze. Sailing conditions close to the Strait of Gibraltar are affected by the geography of the Strait. The wind usually either blows in or out of the Strait and can be quite strong at times. The strong easterly wind is called a *Levanter* and when this blows hard against the prevailing east setting current flowing through the Strait into the Mediterranean, it creates a short sharp sea, which can make it very difficult, and occasionally impossible, to reach Gibraltar from the Atlantic. The opposing *Poniente*, which is a strong W or SW wind, can make it even more difficult to sail in the opposite direction, out of Gibraltar into the Atlantic. The *Levanter* occurs most frequently from July to October and is associated with rain and reduced visibility. Also in summer the occasional small depression moves north from Morocco towards Gibraltar.

AN31 *Gibraltar to Madeira*

BEST TIME:	May to August
TROPICAL STORMS:	None
CHARTS:	BA: 4104
	US: 104
PILOTS:	BA: 1, 67
	US: 131, 143
CRUISING GUIDES:	*Atlantic Islands, Madeira Cruising Guide.*

WAYPOINTS:				
Departure	Intermediate	Landfall	Destination	Distance (M)
AN310 Gibraltar 36°08'N, 5°22'W	AN311 Carnera 36°03'N, 5°25'W AN312 Tarifa 35°59'N, 5°36'W AN313 Paloma 35°59'N, 5°45'W AN314 Espartel 35°50'N, 5°57'W	AN315 Fora 32°44'N, 16°39'W AN316 Cima E 33°03'N, 16°17'W	Funchal 32°37.5'N, 16°54.5'W Porto Santo 33°03'N, 16°19'W	613 576

Gibraltar should not be left in a strong westerly wind as the wind reinforced by the permanent flow of water from the Atlantic into the Mediterranean makes it almost impossible to beat one's way out of the Strait. An equally strong easterly wind blowing against the current does not improve matters much as it creates a short steep sea. Ideally Gibraltar should be left in light or easterly winds, but if this is not possible, it is better to keep to the edges of the Strait where the current is weaker. Detailed tactics for leaving Gibraltar are described at the beginning of this section. In daylight and good visibility one may decide to tack across to the African shore, where the current is weaker. Be aware of the large amount of shipping when crossing the traffic lanes and also to the fast moving ferry from Algeciras to Tangiers.

In favourable wind and tide conditions, the course runs parallel to the Spanish coast. Taking one's departure from WP AN310 an initial course is set for WP AN311 off Punta Carnera. Having left the Bay of Gibraltar, the course is altered for WP AN312 south of Tarifa light. The route continues on this course to keep out of the west going shipping lane. A course of 270° will take one to WP AN313, which clears the shallows off Punta Paloma. From there a direct course can be set for Madeira. As the shipping lanes converging on the Strait of Gibraltar have to be crossed at some point, tacking across should only be done when Cape Espartel can be cleared on that tack. The cape, at the NW point of Africa, should not be approached too closely because of the overfalls in its vicinity. A direct course leads to WP AN315 east of Ilheu de Fora, a rocky islet with a powerful light off the eastern extremity of Madeira. From there the course runs along the south coast of the island to the capital Funchal. The alternative is to call first at Porto Santo and sail to WP AN316 east of Ilheu de Cima. Porto Santo should be approached with care, especially at night, as there are a number of dangers off its eastern coast.

During the summer months the steady Portuguese trades usually ensure favourable sailing conditions all the way to Madeira. At the beginning and end of summer, sailing conditions can be less pleasant and both calms and SW winds may be encountered en route. Passages in May and November are particularly vulnerable to this kind of weather, but between June and early October the prevailing northerly winds should provide a fast sail for most of the way. In strong SW winds, one may be forced to abandon one's intention to call at Madeira and continue to the Canaries without stopping. This course of action is taken every year by boats that have left either Northern Europe or the Mediterranean too late. As the small marina in Funchal gets extremely crowded in October and early November with boats stopping there on their way to the Canaries, bypassing Madeira at this time of year should be considered by anyone short of time.

AN32 *Gibraltar to Canary Islands*

BEST TIME:	May to August
TROPICAL STORMS:	None
CHARTS:	BA: 4104
	US: 104
PILOTS:	BA: 1, 67
	US: 131, 143
CRUISING GUIDES:	*Canary Islands Cruising Guide, Atlantic Islands.*
WAYPOINTS:	

Departure	Intermediate	Landfall	Destination	Distance (M)
AN320 Gibraltar	AN321 Carnera			
36°08'N, 5°22'W	36°03'N, 5°25'W			
	AN322 Tarifa			
	35°59'N, 5°36'W			
	AN323 Paloma			
	35°59'N, 5°45'W			
	AN324 Espartel			
	35°50'N, 5°57'W			
	AN325 Morocco A			
	34°00'N, 8°30'W			
	AN326 Morocco B		La Sociedad	585
	32°40'N, 10°00'W		*29°13.8'N, 13°30'W*	
		AN327 Alegranza	Puerto Calero	608
		29°25'N, 13°28'W	*28°55'N, 13°42'W*	
		AN328 Isleta	Las Palmas	704
		28°09'N, 15°23'W	*28°07.5'N, 15°25.5'W*	

Leaving Gibraltar with a favourable tide, one does not need to go too close to the Spanish coast. Setting course for WP AN321, south of Punta Carnera, avoids any dangers. When leaving the Bay of Gibraltar, one should watch out for the fast ferry plying between Algeciras and Tangiers. As far as Tarifa it is better to stay in the inshore lane and steer for WP AN322 approximately 1 mile south of Tarifa light. This will keep one out of the west-going shipping lane. From there, a course of 270° leads to WP AN323 to clear the shallows off Punta Paloma. As one has to cross the shipping lanes, and if the winds are westerly, one should only tack when one is confident of clearing Cape Espartel on that tack. One should not go too close to this cape as there are overfalls in the area. By setting course for WP AN324 one stays clear of an area of confused seas located off Cape Espartel. Better conditions are usually found farther off the African coast and therefore the course should stay outside the 100 fathom line. This can be done by setting a course which

passes through two intermediate waypoints, AN325 and AN326.

For boats intending to make their first Canarian landfall at Lanzarote, a course should be set for WP AN327 off the small island of Alegranza. The capital and main port on Lanzarote is Arrecife, although better docking facilities will be found at Puerto Calero five miles further down the coast. If time permits, one should consider stopping first at Graciosa, a small island north of Lanzarote, which has a small but well protected port at La Sociedad, on the north shore of the narrows separating Graciosa from Lanzarote.

For boats bound directly for Las Palmas and thus approaching Gran Canaria from the north, the conspicuous hump of La Isleta makes a perfect landfall. WP AN328 clears all dangers, including El Roque rock off Punta El Nido. 2.5 miles further south is the entrance to Las Palmas harbour. Work started in 1998 on a new breakwater to protect the marina from the north.

Sailing conditions to the Canaries are normally

better than those encountered on the way to Madeira. From June to September the prevailing northerlies and a favourable current usually provide excellent sailing conditions along this route. In May and October the winds are less constant, although their direction continues to be predominantly northerly. November has a higher incidence of winds from other directions, but winds from the northern quarter are still predominant. The passage to the Canaries should not be left too late in the season, as strong SW winds with rough seas can be encountered on this route after the end of October. Anyone intending to see more of the Canaries should plan on stopping first in Lanzarote, which is the best island from which to start visiting the Canary Islands in a logical sequence.

AN33 *Gibraltar to Lesser Antilles*

BEST TIME:	May to June
TROPICAL STORMS:	June to November
CHARTS:	BA: 4012
	US: 12
PILOTS:	BA: 1, 67, 71
	US: 131, 140, 143, 147
CRUISING GUIDES:	*The Lesser Antilles, Sailor's Guide to the Windward Islands, Cruising Guide to the Leeward Islands.*
WAYPOINTS:	

Departure	Intermediate	Landfall	Destination	Distance (M)
AN330 Gibraltar 36°08'N, 5°22'W	AN331 Carnera 36°03'N, 5°25'W			
	AN332 Tarifa 35°59'N, 5°36'W			
	AN333 Paloma 35°59'N, 5°45'W			
	AN334 Espartel 35°50'N, 5°57'W	St Lucia 14°03'N, 60°50'W	Rodney Bay 14°04.5'N, 60°58.5'W	3254
		Antigua SE 16°57'N, 61°45'W	English Harbour 17°00'N, 61°46'W	3196

This long passage is only done without calling either at Madeira or one of the Canary Islands by those in a great hurry, as both these island groups lie close enough to the recommended route as to warrant a short stop. Directions as far as Cape Espartel are given in route AN31.

The best time for this passage is in the summer, but an Atlantic crossing during this time, which is the hurricane season, cannot be recommended. Good conditions for a nonstop passage may also be encountered at the end of spring, beginning of summer (May or early June), when the chances of encountering a tropical storm en route are very low. The route at such a time will be close to the great circle course as favourable winds will be found most of the way across. This would be the case also during summer when, however, a crossing carries too many risks, especially at the end of the summer. If this passage is made during the summer months, stations broadcasting early warnings of tropical depressions should be listened to regularly. As the trade wind belt lies further north during the summer months, a more direct course can be sailed across the Atlantic than in winter. Between May and July the frequency of hurricanes is quite low, but it increases after August, reaching a peak in September.

During the winter months, steady NE winds will be found only in lower latitudes, most probably south of latitude 25°N. The route at such a time will pass between the Canaries and Madeira and, depending on weather conditions, the strategy to be employed will be similar to the suggestions given for route AN51 (page 74).

AN34 *Gibraltar to Northern Europe*

BEST TIME:	May to August
TROPICAL STORMS:	None
CHARTS:	BA: 4103
	US: 126
PILOTS:	BA: 1, 22, 27, 28, 55, 67
	US: 143, 191
CRUISING GUIDES:	*Cruising Association Handbook, The Shell Channel Pilot.*
WAYPOINTS:	

Departure	Intermediate	Landfall	Destination	Distance (M)
AN340 Gibraltar	AN341 Carnera			
36°08'N, 5°22'W	36°03'N, 5°25'W			
	AN342 Tarifa			
	35°59'N, 5°36'W			
	AN343 Paloma			
	35°59'N, 5°45'W			
	AN344 Vincent W	Lizard	Falmouth	1002
	37°00'N, 9°05'W	49°55'N, 5°10'W	*50°09.5'N, 5°04'W*	

Directions to sail through the Strait of Gibraltar are given in routes AN31 and AN32. If strong westerly winds are encountered after the Strait has been negotiated, it is better to stay on the port tack and, if conditions deteriorate, one may seek shelter in one of the ports or marinas along the northern shore. The marinas at Lagos and Vilamoura, on the Algarve coast, are convenient places in which to wait for a change of weather. See also route AN35.

After the Strait and the shallows off Cape Trafalgar have been cleared, a course should be set for WP AN344, 5 miles WSW of Cape St Vincent. From there the course runs roughly parallel to the Portuguese coast. During summer the prevailing winds along the western shores of the Iberian peninsula are the Portuguese trades which make the task of reaching any northern destination extremely difficult. For those who are in a hurry it is better to head immediately offshore by sailing on the tack that makes most northing. Otherwise it might be easier to make short hops along the coast until better winds are found or Cape Finisterre is passed. Westerly winds may not be found until latitude 45°N is reached. Occasionally in late summer SW winds reach gale force in the Bay of Biscay when conditions can be very rough, so it is advisable to make this passage before the middle of August.

AN35 *Gibraltar to Portugal*

BEST TIME:	April to May, September
TROPICAL STORMS:	None
CHARTS:	BA: 87
	US: 51150, 51160
PILOTS:	BA: 67
	US: 143
CRUISING GUIDES:	*Atlantic Spain and Portugal.*

WAYPOINTS:				
Departure	*Intermediate*	*Landfall*	*Destination*	*Distance (M)*
AN350 Gibraltar 36°08'N, 5°22'W	AN351 Carnera 36°03'N, 5°25'W			
	AN352 Tarifa 35°59'N, 5°36'W			
	AN353 Paloma 35°59'N, 5°45'W			
	AN354 Hoyo 36°03'N, 6°20'W			
	AN355 Huelva 37°05.5'N, 6°49.5'W	AN356 off Vilamoura 37°01'N, 8°07'W	Vilamoura *37°04.5'N, 8°07'W*	155
		AN357 Vincent W 37°00'N, 9°05'W		
		AN358 S Channel 38°35'N, 9°20'W	Lisbon *38°41.5'N, 9°12'W*	300

Directions for negotiating the Strait of Gibraltar are given in routes AN31 and AN32. From WP AN353, which clears the shallows off Ponta Paloma, set course for WP AN354 so as to stay outside the shallows off Cape Trafalgar. From this point the course becomes NNW and runs across the Bay of Cadiz through shallow waters that rarely exceed 60 feet. A hazard to watch out for along this coast are the large tunny nets, which are supposed to be buoyed and marked by a fishing boat, but often are not. For this reason it is not prudent to sail too close inshore, especially at night. The trip can be broken at Mazagon, at the river entrance into Huelva, from where Columbus left on his historic voyage to the New World in 1492. A new marina is now operating at the river entrance from where it is possible to visit the various sites associated with Columbus in Palos and the surrounding area. The entrance to the river is clearly marked by a light tower and the river is well buoyed. WP AN355 is the landfall buoy one mile SE of the river entrance.

If a strong *Levanter* is blowing in the Strait of Gibraltar, easterly winds will continue into the Bay of Cadiz, although of diminished strength. Otherwise, on summer days, there will be an alternation of breezes, a sea breeze from the SW starting around noon to be followed by a lighter land breeze from the NW.

The Algarve coast has witnessed a huge development in recent years and landmarks can be confusing. The entrance into Vilamoura marina is not easy to spot to those not familiar with the area, but WP AN356, about one mile south of the entrance, should help locate it. Boats bound for the west coast of Portugal should set course for WP AN357, 5 miles WSW of Cape St Vincent. From that point strong northerly winds can be expected during summer, but as there is an abundance of good ports along the entire Portuguese coast this section can be easily covered in short hops.

AN36 *Gibraltar to Azores*

BEST TIME:	May to August
TROPICAL STORMS:	None
CHARTS:	BA: 4012
	US: 12
PILOTS:	BA: 67
	US: 140, 143
CRUISING GUIDES:	*Azores Cruising Guide, Atlantic Islands.*

WAYPOINTS:				
Departure	Intermediate	Landfall	Destination	Distance (M)
AN360 Gibraltar	AN361 Carnera			
36°08'N, 5°22'W	36°03'N, 5°25'W			
	AN362 Tarifa			
	35°59'N, 5°36'W			
	AN363 Paloma			
	35°59'N, 5°45'W			
	AN364 Espartel	AN365 Miguel	Horta	1135
	35°50'N, 5°57'W	38°02'N, 25°10'W	38°32'N, 28°37.5'W	
		AN366 Garça	Ponta Delgada	994
		37°40'N, 25°23'W	37°44'N, 25°40.5'W	

The passage benefits from favourable winds for at least the first half, as the prevailing northerly winds of summer are felt as far as 300 miles off continental Europe and often further than that. At some point an area of light winds or calms will be encountered, after which the winds will probably come from either W or SW. This will depend entirely on the position of the Azores high. The further NW this is situated from its normal position, the higher the likelihood of having favourable NE winds for most, or all, of the passage to the Azores.

Directions for negotiating the Strait of Gibraltar are given in routes AN31 and AN32. If strong SW winds are encountered west of the Strait it is better to put into a port, such as Vilamoura (37°04'N, 8°07'W), and wait there for a change. Directions will then be the same as for route AN35. If strong winds are encountered after passing Cape St Vincent, the area of the Gettysburg and Gorringe Banks (36°30'N, 12°00'W and 36°45'N, 11°10'W) should be avoided as breaking or confused seas have been experienced in that area. Boats intending to sail nonstop to Horta should set a course for WP AN365, 10 miles N of São Miguel. From there the route passes north of Pico. If strong SW winds are encountered among the islands, one can either seek shelter in a port on the north coast of Pico, such as São Roque, or sail towards Terceira, where one can wait for a change of weather at Angra do Heroismo, on that island's south coast.

The direct route to Ponta Delgada leads to WP AN366, 3 miles south of Ponta da Garça, on the south coast of the island of São Miguel. Boats coming from ports south of Lisbon may prefer to make their first landfall there rather than further west. There is a good marina at Ponta Delgada, the capital of the Azores, which has the best facilities in the archipelago. Another good starting point for a cruise among the islands is the island of Santa Maria, at the southeastern extremity of the archipelago, from where the other islands can be visited in logical succession.

AN37 *Gibraltar to North America*

BEST TIME:	May to June
TROPICAL STORMS:	June to November
CHARTS:	BA: 4011
	US: 120
PILOTS:	BA: 67, 69
	US: 140, 143
CRUISING GUIDES:	*Azores Cruising Guide, Yachting Guide to Bermuda, The Atlantic Crossing Guide, Cruising Guide to Newfoundland, Cruising Guide to the Nova Scotia Coast, Yachting Guide to the South Shore of Nova Scotia, Coastal Cruising Guide to the Atlantic Coast, Cruising Guide to the New England Coast.*

WAYPOINTS:				
Departure	Intermediate	Landfall	Destination	Distance (M)
Route AN37A				
AN370 Gibraltar	AN371 Hoyo	AN376 Chesapeake		3323
36°08'N, 5°22'W	36°00'N, 6°20'W	36°45'N, 75°45'W		
		AN377 Brenton	Newport	3044
		41°24'N, 71°16'W	41°29'N, 71°20'W	
		AN378 off Halifax	Halifax	2672
		44°25'N, 63°25'W	44°38'N, 63°34'W	
	AN372 Race	AN379 off St John's	St John's	2290
	46°25'N, 53°10'W	47°30'N, 52°39'W	47°34'N, 52°42'W	
Route AN37B				
AN370 Gibraltar	AN371 Hoyo			
	AN373 Garça			
	37°40'N, 25°23'W			
	Ponta Delgada	AN376 Chesapeake		3349
	37°44'N, 28°40'W	AN377 Brenton	Newport	3110
		AN378 off Halifax	Halifax	2747
		AN379 off St John's	St John's	2331
Route AN37C				
AN370 Gibraltar	AN371 Hoyo			
	AN374 Terceira			
	38°28'N, 27°00'W			
	Horta	AN376 Chesapeake		
	38°32'N, 28°37.5'W	AN377 Brenton	Newport	3097
		AN378 off Halifax	Halifax	2730
		AN379 off St John's	St John's	2308
Route AN37D				
AN370 Gibraltar	AN375 Bermuda E	AN376 Chesapeake		
	32°22'N, 64°38'W	AN377 Brenton	Newport	3544
	St George's	AN378 off Halifax	Halifax	3648
	32°22'N, 64°40'W	AN379 off St John's	St John's	3973

The majority of boats bound for North America from the Mediterranean prefer to take the classic route via the Canaries, which, although considerably longer, has a higher proportion of favourable winds. The direct route (AN37A) has certain attractions, firstly because it can be done at the beginning of summer, and secondly because it can be much speedier. The best time for this passage is at the beginning of summer, but if it is undertaken after July, attention must be paid to the possibility of hurricanes. This applies particularly to those sailing to ports in areas of the USA affected by tropical storms. On the other hand, boats bound for Canadian ports, such as St John's in Newfoundland, should avoid making the passage early in the season because of the danger of ice. Directions and waypoints as far as the western end of the Strait of Gibraltar are the same as for route AN36. Having reached open sea, the direct route across the Atlantic will depend entirely on existing weather conditions, which will dictate whether the Azores are left to port or starboard. A route S of the Azores direct to Bermuda (AN37D) has a certain attraction as the winds will be met at a better angle once the area of prevailing S or SW winds is reached close to Bermuda. Boats bound for Newfoundland and even Nova Scotia will probably peel off this southern route sooner, but those heading for ports S of New York may find a stop in Bermuda too tempting to miss.

As the direct route passes close to the Azores, most boats make at least a brief stop there after the first 1000 miles at sea. Whether a stop in the Azores is intended or not, directions for the route between Gibraltar and that area are given in routes AN24 (page 54) and AN36. If a stop in the Azores is considered, from WP AN371 at the western end of the Strait of Gibraltar, the direct route to Ponta Delgada (AN37B) leads to WP AN373, 3 miles south of Ponta da Garça, on the south coast of the island of São Miguel. Although Ponta Delgada is closer to this route, and there is a good marina there, the traditional port of call remains Horta, on the island of Faial. The latter is probably a better starting off point for the subsequent leg across the Atlantic.

If intending to sail nonstop to Horta (route AN37C), from WP AN371 a course should be set for WP AN374, SE of the island of Terceira. Depending on weather conditions, from that point Horta can be reached by sailing either north or south of the island of Pico. In strong SW winds it is better to stay north of Pico and, if the weather deteriorates, one can seek shelter at São Roque, on the north coast of Pico, or at Velas, the main port on São Jorge. Terceira itself has a good harbour at Angra do Heroismo, although it is open

to the south and should be avoided in strong winds from that direction. In strong SW winds, the channel between Pico and Faial, in the approaches to Horta, can be affected by violent gusts. These, and the north setting current, should be taken into account if attempting to enter Horta under such conditions. A last port in the Azores, where one can seek shelter and wait for an improvement in the weather, is at Lajes, on the SE point of Flores, where a new breakwater has greatly improved the protection of this port. From the Azores the voyage may continue nonstop to one's destination.

Those that have stopped in the Azores should be prepared to wait there until a good long term forecast assures a safe and speedy passage for the continuation of their voyage. Directions for the routes from the Azores to the USA and Canada are given in AN138 and AN139 (page 154). Boats planning to stop in Bermuda may be able to sail a direct course from the Azores to WP AN375, east of the entrance into St George's Harbour. Such a direct route from the Azores to Bermuda has the best chance of favourable winds. This is described in detail in AN137 (page 153). The most likely winds to be encountered on approaching Bermuda are from the SW, but if favourable conditions persist it is best to bypass Bermuda altogether and sail nonstop to one's final destination.

AN38 *Gibraltar to Atlantic Morocco*

BEST TIME:	May to September			
TROPICAL STORMS:	None			
CHARTS:	BA: 4104			
	US: 104			
PILOTS:	BA: 1, 67			
	US: 143			
CRUISING GUIDES:	*North Africa Pilot.*			
WAYPOINTS:				
Departure	*Intermediate*	*Landfall*	*Destination*	*Distance (M)*
AN380 Gibraltar 36°08'N, 5°22'W	AN381 Carnera 36°03'N, 5°25'W		Tangiers *35°17'N, 5°48'W*	55
	AN382 Tarifa 35°59'N, 5°36'W			
	AN383 Paloma 35°59'N, 5°45'W			
	AN384 Espartel 35°50'N, 5°57'W		Casablanca *33°37'N, 7°36'W*	191
			Agadir *30°25'N, 9°38'W*	409

With the exception of Tangiers, which is conveniently located on the south side of the Strait of Gibraltar, most boats avoid Moroccan ports, although those on the Atlantic coast could make convenient stops for boats sailing to the Canaries or West Africa. There are several reasons for this reluctance, the main ones being the complicated formalities, bad pollution in the larger ports, and frequent theft from visiting yachts. Facilities for sailing boats are also lacking, although the few yacht clubs are generally welcoming.

Tangiers, being used to receiving large numbers of visiting boats and thus having relatively easier formalities, is often overcrowded. South of Cape Espartel the predominant features are the large Atlantic swell and the lack of natural harbours, with the notable exception of Mogador. A restricted zone is in force between Rabat and Mohamedia, and any boat straying within 12 miles of the coast may be chased away by Moroccan navy vessels. Casablanca is the largest port along this coast and, for the time being, has the best repair facilities. A fast developing port with adequate facilities is Agadir, which is used as a base by a large number of foreign fishing boats. A marina is under construction in Agadir and, when it is finished, it will be a convenient place to leave a boat while visiting the interior of this interesting country.

AN40 ROUTES FROM MADEIRA

Until not so long ago the only yachts that used to visit Madeira were cruising boats on their way to the Canaries or Caribbean, and occasionally a few racing boats from mainland Portugal. The situation has changed as more boats spend the winter in the Canaries and use Madeira as a convenient stopover on their return voyage to the Mediterranean. The most frequented route, however, remains that to the Canaries, which is at its busiest in October when hundreds of boats make their way south as part of the annual migration to the Caribbean. At this time Madeira is crowded with boats and the marina at Funchal can barely cope with the amount of visitors. Funchal is best avoided at such times and a stop in neighbouring Porto Santo should be considered.

The prevailing summer winds are northeasterly, but because of the height of Madeira, the wind funnels around and can blow from the SW on the southern coast when it is NE offshore. The smaller island of Porto Santo is also high but it does not block the NE wind which accelerates down the mountain blowing in gusts in its lee. In winter the winds are more variable and come from all directions. The North Atlantic fronts that move across the ocean from west to east occasionally take a more southerly track and affect the island, but their effect is less strong than in the Azores. Dust haze, which reduces visibility, can occur when easterly winds blow from the African continent.

A small number of boats choose to start their Atlantic crossing in Madeira rather than take the traditional route via the Canaries. Such a decision makes sense in late winter or spring when the NE trade winds reach further north and the route from Madeira to the Caribbean bypasses the Canaries altogether. Madeira is also a good starting point if one's West Indian destination is one of the more northern islands, such as Antigua or Virgins. The transatlantic route depends very much on access to weather information to be able to know how long one should sail on a SW course before turning west.

Northbound passages from Madeira are seldom easy on account of the prevailing northerly winds. Most boats bound for a port in NW Europe may prefer to make a detour to the Azores and stop in one of the easternmost islands, such as Santa Maria or São Miguel. If bound for mainland Portugal one has little choice and if the winds are from the NE, as is most likely in summer, one must be prepared to beat all the way. The same applies

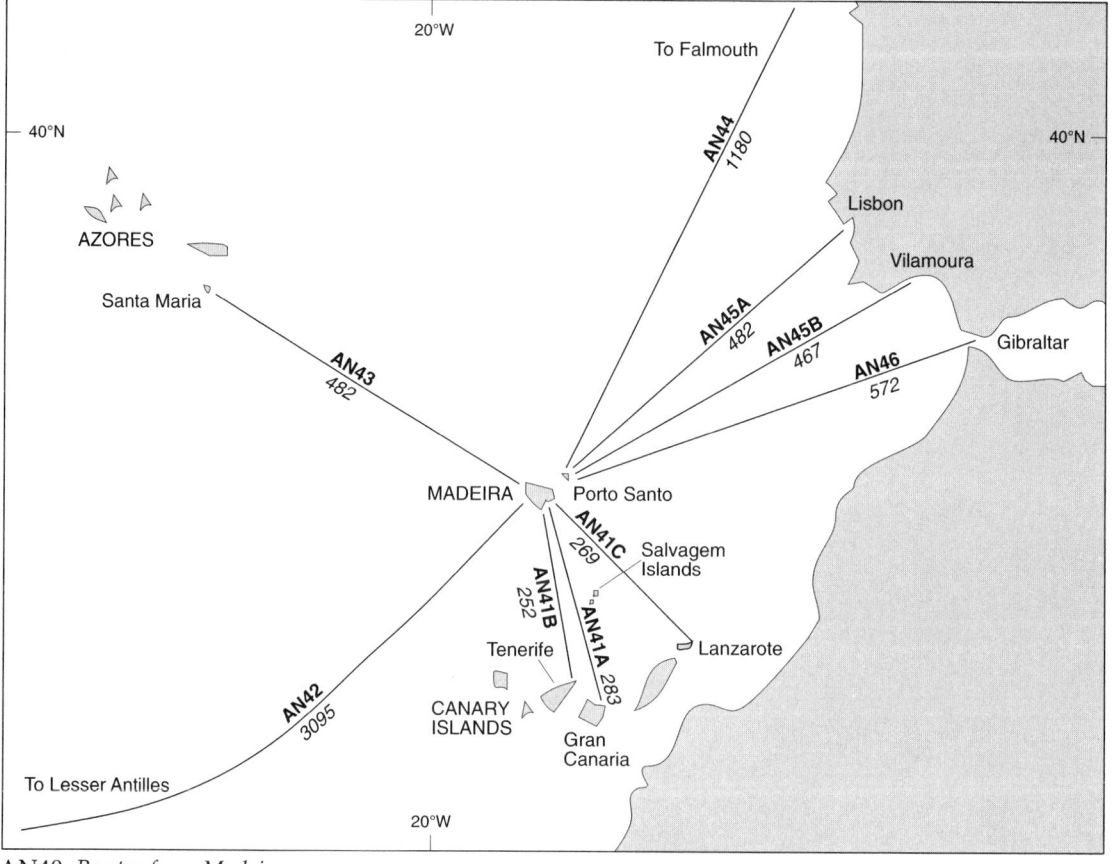

AN40 *Routes from Madeira*

to boats heading for Gibraltar and the Mediterranean with the added complication that the NE winds experienced offshore often turn into easterlies as one approaches the Strait of Gibraltar. If time permits one should wait in Madeira for a spell of SW winds, which normally occur when a depression passes to the north of the island. Such conditions will ensure a fast passage all the way into the Mediterranean.

AN41 *Madeira to Canary Islands*

BEST TIME:	May to October
TROPICAL STORMS:	None
CHARTS:	BA: 3133
	US: 104
PILOTS:	BA: 1
	US: 143
CRUISING GUIDES:	*Canary Islands Cruising Guide, Atlantic Islands, Madeira Cruising Guide.*

WAYPOINTS:				
Departure	*Intermediate*	*Landfall*	*Destination*	*Distance (M)*
Route AN41A				
AN410 Funchal	AN411 Salv. Grande	AN412 Isleta	Las Palmas	283
32°36'N, 16°54'W	30°10'N, 15°45'W	28°09'N, 15°23'W	*28°07.5'N, 15°25.5'W*	
Route AN41B				
AN410 Funchal	AN413 Salv. Pequena	AN414 Anaga	Santa Cruz de Tenerife	252
	30°00'N, 16°15'W	28°36'N, 16°07'W	*28°29.5'N, 16°12.5'W*	
Route AN41C				
AN410 Funchal		AN415 Graciosa	La Sociedad	269
		29°25'N, 13°35'W	*29°13.8'N, 13°30'W*	

This is normally a fast downwind run, particularly during summer. After the beginning of October, although northerly winds are still most common, winds from other directions increase in frequency. From November onwards strong SW winds occur at times and rough seas are encountered between the two island groups. A favourable current of approximately 1/2 knot is normally experienced on this passage.

The direct route passes very close to the Salvagem Islands, a group of uninhabited islands lying halfway to the Canaries and straddling the 30th parallel. The course for Gran Canaria (AN41A) passes between the two islands and, unless sailing by in good light and weather, the course should be altered to pass at a safe distance to the east of Salvagem Grande, such as WP AN411, as there are dangerous rocks close to the islands. From there the route continues towards WP AN412 in the approaches to Las Palmas.

The direct course for Tenerife (AN41B) passes through WP AN413 at a distance of some 10 miles west of Salvagem Pequena. Landfall is made at WP AN414, off Punta de Anaga, the NE point of Tenerife. From there, the course runs parallel to the coast to the newly established marina inside the fishing harbour, some 3 miles north of the capital Santa Cruz.

The course for Lanzarote (AN41C) passes at a safe distance to the NE of the Salvagem Islands. The small island of Alegranza, north of Lanzarote, can be passed on either side by boats going directly to Arrecife. For those who prefer to stop first at Graciosa, landfall should be made on the west side of the latter by setting course for WP AN415 about 5 miles NW of Graciosa, before entering Estrecho del Rio, the channel separating Graciosa from Lanzarote. Although not a port of entry, boats may stop for a short time at La Sociedad, the main port and settlement on Graciosa, before proceeding to Arrecife, the capital of Lanzarote, and clearing in there.

Those intending to stop in one of the Salvagem Islands must obtain a special permit, which is issued in Funchal by the Department of Fisheries within the Autonomous Government of Madeira. In bad weather, yachts are allowed to anchor in Enseada das Cagarras (30°08.3'N, 15°52.2'W) on the SW side of Salvagem Grande, but access ashore is only allowed to those in possession of a landing permit. There are wardens stationed on both islands and they can be contacted on VHF channel 16.

AN42 *Madeira to Lesser Antilles*

BEST TIME:	January to May
TROPICAL STORMS:	June to November
CHARTS:	BA: 4012
	US: 120
PILOTS:	BA: 1, 71
	US: 140, 143, 147
CRUISING GUIDES:	*The Lesser Antilles, Sailor's Guide to the Windward Islands, Cruising Guide to the Leeward Islands.*
WAYPOINTS:	

Departure	Intermediate	Landfall	Destination	Distance (M)
AN420 Funchal 32°36'N, 16°54'W	AN421 27°25'N, 15°30'W AN422 20°00'N, 30°00'W AN423 15°00'N, 40°00'W	AN424 St Lucia 14°03'N, 60°50'W AN425 Antigua SE 16°57'N, 61°45'W	Rodney Bay *14°04'N, 60°58'W* English Harbour *17°00'N, 61°45.5'W*	3095 3139

Because of the strategic location of the Canaries on the route to the Eastern Caribbean, only a small number of boats choose to sail there directly from Madeira. Nevertheless, Madeira can make a good starting point for such a transatlantic passage provided one has access to a good weather picture of the North Atlantic which shows the northern limits of the NE trade winds. If these extend as far as 25°N it is possible to lay a SW course from Madeira to pass to the west of the Canary Islands.

The waypoints suggested above are based on the traditional route which initially has a SW slant into lower latitudes, where the likelihood of finding favourable winds is always higher. At the beginning of winter, however, the trade winds rarely extend beyond latitude 20°N and if this is the case one might as well stop in the Canaries as the course runs virtually through the archipelago. If only a short stop in the Canaries is envisaged, one should choose one of the more westerly ports, such as Santa Cruz de la Palma, which makes a better starting point for the subsequent transatlantic leg. Detailed routeing information for the transatlantic passage is given in route AN51 (page 74).

AN43 *Madeira to Azores*

BEST TIME:	May to August
TROPICAL STORMS:	None
CHARTS:	BA: 4104
	US: 12
PILOTS:	BA: 1, 67
	US: 143
CRUISING GUIDES:	*Azores Cruising Guide, Atlantic Islands.*
WAYPOINTS:	

Departure	Intermediate	Landfall	Destination	Distance (M)
AN430 Funchal *32°37'N, 16°54'W*	AN432 Pargo *32°48'N, 17°20'W*	AN433 Sta Maria 36°55'N, 25°07'W	Vila do Porto *36°56'N, 25°08.5'W*	482
AN431 off Porto Santo 32°58'N, 16°25'W		AN433 Sta Maria	Vila do Porto	490

During summer, when the Portuguese trade winds reach as far south as Madeira, this will be a close hauled passage, although the Azores can normally be reached on one tack. If leaving from Funchal, the high island of Madeira normally blocks northerly winds so that a light westerly breeze will be felt until one reaches the end of the island. From Funchal, the course runs parallel to the coast as far as Ponta do Pargo, the western extremity of the island. From WP AN432, off Ponta do Pargo, a direct course leads to WP AN433 in the SE approaches to Vila do Porto, the main

harbour of Santa Maria, the most southeastern Azorean island. The harbour provides good shelter from all directions except the south.

If time allows it, a visit to Porto Santo will provide a slightly better starting point. In such a case, from WP AN431, off Porto Santo's SW point, the route passes on the weather side of Madeira Grande. This should be passed at a safe distance as in strong northerly winds its north coast is a dangerous lee shore. Landfall will be made at WP AN433, in the approaches to Vila do Porto.

AN44 *Madeira to Northern Europe*

BEST TIME:	March to May				
TROPICAL STORMS:	None				
CHARTS:	BA: 4011				
	US: 120				
PILOTS:	BA: 1, 22, 27, 67				
	US: 140, 143, 191				
CRUISING GUIDES:	*Cruising Association Handbook, The Shell Channel Pilot.*				
WAYPOINTS:					
Departure	*Intermediate*	*Landfall*		*Destination*	*Distance (M)*
AN440 Funchal 32°37'N, 16°54'W	AN441 Garajau 32°38'N, 16°50'W				
	AN442 Fora 32°45'N, 16°38'W	AN443 Lizard 49°55'N, 5°10'W		Falmouth *50°09.5'N, 5°04'W*	1180

A nonstop passage to the English Channel is difficult to accomplish, particularly during the summer months when the Portuguese trades will force one to take a long starboard tack. This will put the boat almost on a heading for the Azores. For this reason, some boats include the latter on their itinerary. In such a case the same directions apply as those for route AN43.

During spring, and occasionally also in summer, a spell of SW winds may allow a direct course to

be sailed to Northern Europe. Having sailed around the eastern extremity of Madeira, a rhumb line course, from WP AN442 off Ilheu de Fora to WP AN443 off Lizard Point in the approaches to the English Channel, passes some 60 miles west of Cape Finisterre. Persistent northerly winds are a feature of summer and so this passage should be planned for middle or late spring when there is a better chance of favourable winds.

AN45 *Madeira to Portugal*

BEST TIME:	April to May
TROPICAL STORMS:	None
CHARTS:	BA: 4104
	US: 104
PILOTS:	BA: 1, 67
	US: 143
CRUISING GUIDES:	*Atlantic Spain and Portugal.*

WAYPOINTS:				
Departure	*Intermediate*	*Landfall*	*Destination*	*Distance (M)*
Route AN45A				
AN451 off Porto Santo		AN452 S Channel	Lisbon	482
33°03'N, 16°15'W		38°35'N, 9°20'W	*38°41.5'N, 9°12'W*	
Route AN45B				
AN451 off Porto Santo		AN453 off Vilamoura	Vilamoura	467
		37°03'N, 8°08'W	*37°04.5'N, 8°07'W*	

Mainland Portugal lies to windward of its offshore dependency for most of the year and therefore this passage is best undertaken before the onset of the NE winds of summer. At the beginning of summer, before they become fully established, these winds blow in spells of a few days at a time, so it is worth waiting for a lull before leaving. A spate of strong NE winds is sometimes followed by one or two days of calms, when it may be possible to gain some useful mileage by motoring. The occasional front, which may generate SW winds, can also be used to one's advantage.

Whether bound for Lisbon (AN45A) or Vilamoura, on the Algarve coast (AN45B), Porto Santo makes a better starting point than Funchal.

From WP AN451, east of Porto Santo, the direct course to Lisbon crosses an area of shallows in the vicinity of the Gettysburg Seamount, which should be avoided in strong winds because of breaking seas. Boats bound for Lisbon should set a course for WP AN452, close to the entrance into South Channel that leads through an area of shallows at the mouth of the Tagus River. The Portuguese capital lies approximately 8 miles upstream on the north shore of the river.

The direct course to Vilamoura also starts off from WP AN451, off the east coast of Porto Santo, and leads to WP AN453, one mile SW of the entrance into the marina.

AN46 *Madeira to Gibraltar*

BEST TIME:	April to May
TROPICAL STORMS:	None
CHARTS:	BA: 4104
	US: 104
PILOTS:	BA: 1, 67
	US: 143
CRUISING GUIDES:	*Yacht Scene.*
WAYPOINTS:	

Departure	*Intermediate*	*Landfall*	*Destination*	*Distance (M)*
AN461 off Funchal	AN463 Espartel			
32°42'N, 16°38'W	35°52'N, 6°00'W			
	AN464 Paloma			
	35°59'N, 5°45'W			
	AN465 Tarifa			
	35°59' N, 5°36'W			
	AN466 Carnera	AN467 Gibraltar	Marina Bay	598
	36°03'N, 5°25'W	36°08'N, 5°22'W	*36°09'N, 5°21'W*	

WAYPOINTS:				
Departure	Intermediate	Landfall	Destination	Distance (M))
AN462 off Porto Santo 33°03'N, 16°15'W	AN463 Espartel AN464 Paloma AN465 Tarifa AN466 Carnera			
		AN467 Gibraltar	Marina Bay	572

Directions for this route are similar to those for AN45 with the added complication that any NE winds, which may have been experienced offshore, will become easterlies on approaching the Strait of Gibraltar. Ideally, this passage should be undertaken in spring when the chances of SW winds are greater than during summer. Occasionally, in summer, when strong NE winds blow offshore, once the longitude of Cape St Vincent has been passed, local weather conditions take over. A SW day breeze can then be expected, which usually springs up around noon and lasts as far as the Strait of Gibraltar.

From WP AN461, east of Madeira, or WP AN462, east of Porto Santo, a direct course leads to WP AN463, some 5 miles NW of Cape Espartel, in the approaches to the Strait of Gibraltar. Directions for negotiating the Strait are given in Routes AN16 and AN21 (pages 46 and 51).

AN50 ROUTES FROM THE CANARY ISLANDS

Sailing to the Canaries has never been considered difficult as the prevailing northerly winds ensure a fast downwind passage from Europe or the Mediterranean at most times of the year. This was the main reason for their popularity in the past as a port of call for ships on the trade routes to Africa, the Orient, and the Americas. The type of ship may have changed with the passing of time but the reasons remain the same for the 1000 or so cruising boats which call at the Canaries every year. They arrive almost without exception from the north, the southbound passages being usually made at the end of summer or during autumn, for most modern sailors treat the Canaries as a mere staging post on their way to the Caribbean, and less commonly to West Africa or South America. However, this situation is gradually changing as more yachts spend longer cruising the Canaries, while others are making their permanent base or chartering there. Every year more boats are seen cruising the islands and the facilities available to them are constantly improving.

For most boats the main destination on leaving the Canaries is the Caribbean. The time of departure from the Canaries is crucial, both for the conditions to be encountered en route and those expected on the other side of the ocean. The hurricane season in the Caribbean in theory lasts about six months, although the really dangerous period is August to October, with September the peak month for hurricanes. Most sailors plan to cruise the West Indian islands between December and April, which is not only the safest time of year but also has the pleasantest weather, with little rain, agreeable temperatures, and the trade winds blowing steadily throughout the winter months. Therefore a late November or early December departure from the Canaries suits most people's

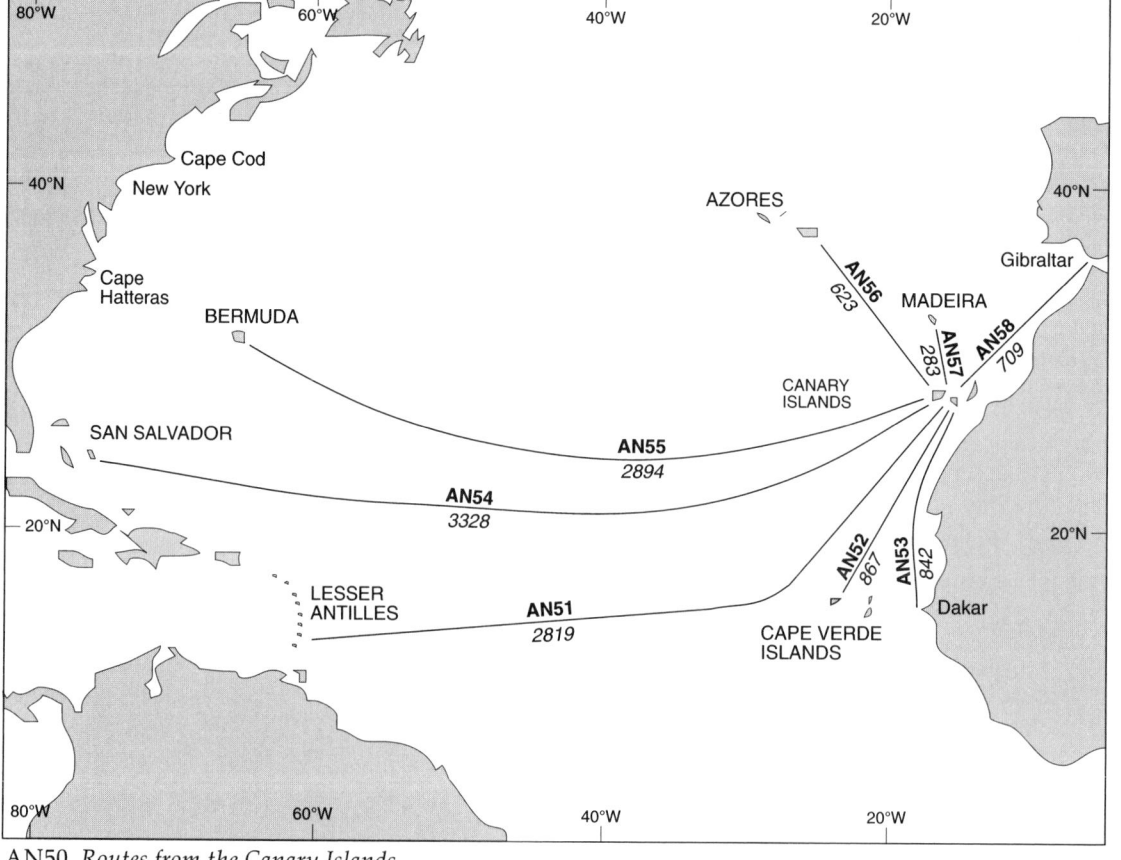

AN50 *Routes from the Canary Islands*

plans and this is the time when the majority of boats leave the Canaries for their transatlantic passage. An earlier departure is not recommended, mainly because of the risk of a late hurricane, but also because the winter trades are seldom established before the second half of November. From the end of November until April the NE trade winds usually blow south of 20°N, their average strength gradually increasing during February and March. Although winds continue to be favourable, summer passages are not recommended for reasons of safety as the risk of hurricanes is too high. As most passages take place in late November or early December, the traditional practice has been to reach lower latitudes as quickly as possible thereby maximising the chances of finding the trade winds. Another good reason to make southing on leaving the Canaries is to be out of the influence of the Atlantic lows. Low pressure systems moving across the Atlantic in winter occasionally deviate from their usual NE

track and reach eastwards as far south as latitude 40°N and even lower. As a consequence, SW or W winds may be generated as far south as latitude 28°N, and occasionally even further south. For those unable to obtain up to date information on the weather systems of the North Atlantic the best tactic is to make most of their crossing on the latitude of their Caribbean destination, or slightly further north in the case of those bound for Antigua or the Virgin Islands.

Although the majority of boats leaving the Canaries are bound for the Caribbean, usually direct or less commonly via the Cape Verdes, there are some who first spend some time cruising West Africa before setting off across the Atlantic. The best time to sail south to either the Cape Verdes or West Africa is winter, when favourable winds will be found all the way to Senegal. The Canaries are also a useful springboard for those sailing to Brazil or other destinations in South America. Sailing from the Canaries to the Mediterranean or

Northern Europe is a more difficult undertaking on account of the prevailing northerlies that make passages in the opposite direction so easy. The best route for a return voyage to Northern Europe is via Madeira and possibly the Azores. A detour to Madeira ought to be considered by those whose destination is Gibraltar or ports on the south coast of the Iberian peninsula. Although the prevailing winds are from NE, winds from SW are not uncommon at the end of spring or beginning of summer, when most boats bound for the Mediterranean make this passage. The suggested stop in Madeira or Porto Santo allows one to wait there for a favourable change of weather.

The prevailing winds in the Canaries are NE throughout the year, being strongest in July and August and lightest in October and November. The high volcanic islands cause some local variations in both wind direction and strength. As a rule there are different winds in the lee of the islands compared to the coasts exposed to the trade winds. When the NE trades are blowing strongly, an opposing wind usually blows on the other side of the island, varying in strength with the strength of the trade wind. A funnelling effect is also felt along the coasts of some of the mountainous islands and the trades can be accelerated by up to 15 knots in places.

The Atlantic lows rarely come as far south as the Canaries, although small lows do develop near the islands themselves and move northeast towards Gibraltar or east towards Africa. Gales are rare, although occasionally these local depressions bring strong S or SW winds. In summer months a strong easterly wind can blow hot from Africa, the air being laden with dust, which reduces visibility considerably.

AN51 *Canary Islands to Lesser Antilles*

BEST TIME:	Mid-November to May			
TROPICAL STORMS:	June to November			
CHARTS:	BA: 4012			
	US: 120			
PILOTS:	BA: 1, 71			
	US: 140, 143, 147			
CRUISING GUIDES:	*Sailor's Guide to the Windward Islands, Cruising Guide to the Leeward Islands.*			

WAYPOINTS:

Departure	Intermediate	Landfall	Destination	Distance (M)
AN510 Las Palmas 28°07'N, 15°24'W	AN511 Canaria S 27°25'N, 15°30'W AN514 20°00'N, 30°00'W AN515 15°00'N, 40°00'W	AN516 St Lucia 14°03'N, 60°50'W	Rodney Bay *14°04.5'N, 60°58.5'W*	2819
		AN517 Martinique 14°22'N, 60°51'W	Fort de France *14°36'N, 61°05'W*	2830
		AN518 Barbados 13°02'N, 59°23'W	Bridgetown *13°06'N, 59°38'W*	2749
		AN519 Antigua SE 16°57'N, 61°45'W	English Harbour *17°00'N, 61°46'W*	2862
AN512 Los Cristianos 28°02'N, 16°43'W	AN513 27°30'N, 18°00'W AN514 AN515	AN516 St Lucia	Rodney Bay	2738
		AN517 Martinique	Fort de France	2748
		AN518 Barbados	Bridgetown	2668
		AN519 Antigua SE	English Harbour	2781

This classic trade wind route has been plied by an enormous variety of vessels in the 500 years since Christopher Columbus himself set sail from the Canary Islands to expand the limits of the known world. Although a lot has been learnt about prevailing winds and weather forecasting in the intervening years, the routeing suggestions made by Columbus as a result of his four voyages to the Caribbean are still valid and can hardly be improved upon. His two fastest passages took 21 days, an excellent time even by today's standards, following a track very close to the optimum route for the time of year. On both those voyages, a SW course was sailed by the fleet until steady trade winds were found in the vicinity of latitude 20°N and only then was the course changed to the west. This essential rule of not setting a course for the desired destination until well inside the trade wind belt has been followed to advantage by all navigators since.

On leaving Las Palmas it is usually best to sail due south before altering course to SW. The only time when it may pay to go around the north of Gran Canaria is in SW winds and then only if it is possible to pass the SE extremity of Tenerife on one tack. The alternative is to stay on the port tack and pass north of Tenerife and then south of La Palma. However, these are unusual conditions since over 90 per cent of the time winds are from the northerly quarter and therefore a southerly course, as recommended, should be taken. Having left Las Palmas at WP AN510, one mile SSE of the harbour, one should not be tempted to turn SW too soon as the wind shadow of the island can extend as far as 20 miles. A convenient point to make for is WP AN511. Depending on weather conditions, from there a course can be set to WP AN514. This was the traditional turning point, from where sailing boats used to set course for the island of destination. With better weather information at their disposal, modern navigators should only use this waypoint as a point of reference and make for it only if such action is justified by existing weather conditions.

Boats leaving from other ports in the Canaries have the choice of passing south or north of El Hierro. If leaving from Los Cristianos, on the south coast of Tenerife, from WP AN512 a course can be set for WP AN513 and thence for WP AN514. Another popular departure port is Santa Cruz on the island of La Palma. On leaving that port, a southerly course should be taken to the southern tip of the island, from where the course should be set for WP AN514.

Every book that has been written on transatlantic voyaging has something to say about the optimum route for a trade wind crossing, although very little can be added to what Columbus found out himself. The first concern is to move as soon as possible out of the region of calms and variable winds which surround the Canary Islands. With a bit of luck a northerly wind may spring up; otherwise one must be prepared to wait or motor. The old advice to make for a point at 25°N 25°W needs some qualification as the winter trades seldom blow consistently as far north as latitude 25°N, so this suggestion should only be followed in summer time. A more valid and often repeated suggestion was to sail SSW for 1000 miles on leaving the Canaries to pass between 200 and 300 miles northwest of the Cape Verde Islands before turning west. This suggestion to pass close to the Cape Verdes still makes sense as steady ENE winds are usually found in their latitude. Nevertheless the added mileage of such a detour must also be taken into account. A more direct route, which crosses latitude 20°N in about 30°W (WP AN514) and latitude 15°N in about 40°W (WP AN515), will probably find the trade winds slightly later but has the advantage of being shorter. Unfortunately there is no hard and fast rule, as weather can vary from one year to another and in some years successful fast passages have been made by boats taking the shortest route across.

The direction of the NE trade winds becomes more easterly as one moves west, and they usually include a southern component as summer approaches. Their strength is not very consistent either and the average force 4 mentioned in some publications is simply an *average* and nothing else. Although gale force winds are rarely experienced in winter, except in squalls, between December and March the trades can blow at force 6 for days on end accompanied by a correspondingly high swell. The swell itself is only regular and steady in direction if the wind has been blowing from the same quarter over a longer period, otherwise a cross swell is not uncommon on this route, with a wind swell being superimposed over another swell generated by some storm many thousands of miles away. In some years the uncomfortable swell has caused more complaints among transatlantic voyagers than the strength of wind, or the lack of it. It would appear that practically no voyage is spared at least one calm period on this run, such calms lasting from a few hours to several days. They are usually followed by a burst of trade winds heralded by a procession of squalls. This route has the benefit of both the Canary Current and North Equatorial Current which set SW and W at an average rate of 1/2 knot. Their constancy, however, is not too reliable, although their direction is.

The above directions apply with small adjustments to all destinations in the Lesser Antilles, from Trinidad in the south to Antigua in the north. After the trade winds have been found the best course can be set for any particular island and the last few hundred miles will probably be sailed on its latitude. The route to the Virgin Islands passes so close to Antigua that it is advisable to make landfall there before proceeding. The same recommendation applies in the case of any islands to leeward of Antigua.

The most popular transatlantic landfalls in the Eastern Caribbean are:

AN516 St Lucia, 4 miles east of Cape Marquis,

on the NE coast of St Lucia. Having sailed along the north coast of St Lucia, the marina in Rodney Bay makes an excellent landfall where entry formalities can be completed.

AN517 Martinique, 3 miles SSE of Martinique. The nearest place to complete formalities is Cul de Sac du Marin, a small port on the SE tip of the island. This is more convenient than the capital Fort de France, which is another 25 miles up the coast.

AN518 Barbados, 9 miles east of South Point, the southern extremity of Barbados. The Shallows, lying SE of that point, should be avoided in heavy weather as the seas break over them. Formalities are completed in the commercial port of Bridgetown, north of Carlisle Bay, the recommended anchorage.

AN519 Antigua SE, 2 miles SSE of English Harbour on the SE coast of Antigua. Formalities can be completed in the nearby historic port of English Harbour.

AN52 *Canary Islands to Cape Verde Islands*

BEST TIME:	October to May			
TROPICAL STORMS:	None			
CHARTS:	BA: 4104			
	US: 120			
PILOTS:	BA: 1			
	US: 143			
CRUISING GUIDES:	*Atlantic Islands.*			
WAYPOINTS:				
Departure	*Intermediate*	*Landfall*	*Destination*	*Distance (M)*
AN520 Las Palmas	AN521 Canaria S	AN522 São Vicente	Mindelo	867
28°07'N, 15°24'W	27°25'N, 15°30'W	17°00'N, 25°00'W	*16°53'N, 25°00'W*	

This route is sailed by boats using the Cape Verde Islands as an intermediate stage either in their transatlantic voyage or en route to West Africa. As one of the recommended routes from the Canaries to the Lesser Antilles passes NW of these islands, a detour is easily accomplished. Although only basic provisions are available in Mindelo, on São Vicente, the main island of the group, the Cape Verde Islands make a good starting point for the transatlantic voyage because they lie in the trade wind belt and fast passages have been made along their latitude. Most boats which break their Atlantic crossing there do

so to refill their fuel tanks. Unless one is dangerously low on fuel, or determined to visit the islands, such a stop in the Cape Verdes makes little sense as much less fuel will be needed to reach the Caribbean than will have been used up to get from the Canaries to the latitude of the Cape Verdes. Rather than burn up additional fuel to reach them, it is better to ration one's consumption earlier and sail the most fuel efficient course from the Canaries.

Those who intend to stop in one of the Cape Verde Islands should set a direct course from WP AN521, south of Gran Canaria, to WP AN522, north of São

Vicente. During the winter months, from the middle of December or early January to April, the NE trades blow strongly between the Canary and Cape Verde Islands. Fast passages are aided by the SW setting Canary Current which merges with the North Equatorial Current in the vicinity of the islands. The visibility near the islands is often poor, either because of haze or the dust-laden *harmattan* which blows here in winter. In October and November, winds between the two island groups are less constant in direction, although the NE trades gradually become established as one approaches the Cape Verde Islands. The area south of the Cape Verde Islands is subject to the SW monsoon from June to October, although the frequency of southerly winds is very low north of latitude

15°N, even at the height of the SW monsoon. The strongest and most consistent north winds between the two island groups have been recorded in summer, between July and September, when as much as 90 per cent of the winds are from the north.

There are three official ports of entry: Mindelo (16°53'N, 25°00'W), Praia (14°54'N, 23°31'W), and Sal (16°45'N, 23°00'W). The first two ports have better provisions and facilities, whereas Sal has an international airport, which is its main attraction for those needing to make a crew change or fly home in an emergency. To visit any place in the Cape Verde Islands outside of the above ports, one needs special written permission from immigration obtainable when clearing in at one of those ports.

AN53 *Canary Islands to West Africa*

BEST TIME:	October to May			
TROPICAL STORMS:	None			
CHARTS:	BA: 4104			
	US: 120			
PILOTS:	BA: 1			
	US: 143			
CRUISING GUIDES:	*Cruising Guide to West Africa.*			
WAYPOINTS:				

Departure	Intermediate	Landfall	Destination	Distance (M)
AN530 Las Palmas 28°07'N, 15°24'W	AN531 Canaria S 27°25'N, 15°30'W			
	AN532 Blanc 20°50'N, 18°15'W		Nouadhibou 20°54'N, 17°03'W	533
AN530 Las Palmas	AN531 Canaria S			
	AN532 Blanc			
	AN533 Vert 14°45'N, 17°35'W		Dakar 14°42.7'N, 17°25.5'W	842
AN530 Las Palmas	AN531 Canaria S			
	AN532 Blanc			
	AN534 Bald 13°35'N, 16°55'W		Banjul 13°26.5'N, 16°34.5'W	929

An increasing number of boats sail to West Africa, some of them en route to Brazil, others just making a detour before crossing the Atlantic to the Caribbean. The situation for cruising boats is gradually improving in this region which has many attractions, as both officials and local people are getting used to the influx of foreign sailors.

The best time to make the passage south is in winter, when favourable winds will be found all along

the coasts of Mauritania and Senegal. The NE trade winds blow consistently as far as the latitude of Dakar, but south of latitude 13°N they become increasingly light, and below latitude 10°N may become variable. South of the latitude of Dakar, the winds are affected by the SW monsoon of summer when SW and W winds predominate. The current along the African coast, as far as Dakar, always sets to the south. Further south, a contrary current may be experienced during the SW monsoon.

Boats leaving from Las Palmas should make for WP AN531 south of Gran Canaria, from where a course should be set for WP AN532, 60 miles off Cap Blanc. If not intending to stop in Mauritania, it is recommended to stay well offshore to avoid not only the shallow waters and large number of fishing boats but also the risk of being stopped and possibly boarded by a Mauritanian naval vessel patrolling the disputed area of former Spanish Sahara. Those who intend to call at Nouadhibou, the main port of Mauritania, should approach the coast with great caution and attempt to make landfall NW of Cap Blanc at daybreak so as to reach port in daylight. If continuing to Senegal, St Louis, at the extreme north of that country, on the border with Mauritania, has been used as a port of entry into Senegal, but the entrance has a dangerous breaking bar and is therefore difficult to enter in a sailing yacht.

Boats bound for Dakar should sail the same route as far as WP AN532 from where the next WP AN533 is about 10 miles off Cap Vert, north of Dakar. The area should be approached with caution on account of the heavy traffic. Cap Vert, a traditional ships' graveyard, should be given a wide berth. Boats entering Dakar must pass S and E of Goree Island. The recommended anchorage for yachts is in position 14°42.7'N, 17°25.5'W.

If sailing from Dakar to Banjul, the time of arrival at the entrance into the river Gambia should be planned to coincide with a rising tide. Boats not stopping at Dakar bound for Banjul should stay well off Cap Vert and, having passed it, set a course for WP AN534 NW off Bald Cape in the approaches to Banjul, the capital and only port of entry into Gambia. As the harbour entrance is encumbered by shoals, entering the harbour at night is not recommended. The anchorage used by visiting yachts is in position 13°26.5'N, 16°34.5'W, but as there have been many reports of theft from yachts one should either take adequate safety measures or find another anchorage. Permission to take the boat up the river Gambia, which is navigable for about 200 miles, can be obtained from the harbour master in Banjul.

All rivers in this area are navigable and even keeled boats can travel far inland. A popular river with visiting yachts is the Casamance, which belongs to Senegal and lies south of the Gambian enclave. The main town on the Casamance is Ziguinchor (12°35'N, 16°16.5'W), located some 50 miles upriver. Boats must clear in first at Dakar and, at the time of writing, could not clear into Senegal at Ziguinchor. Officials occasionally check papers at Elinkine, some 30 miles downstream of Ziguinchor and a main tourist centre (12°30'N, 16°40'W). Also navigable is the river Saloum, with many cruising attractions in its lower reaches. French charts for these West African countries are reported to be better than the British or American charts.

AN54 *Canary Islands to Bahamas*

BEST TIME:	March to May
TROPICAL STORMS:	June to November
CHARTS:	BA: 4012
	US: 120
PILOTS:	BA: 1, 70
	US: 140, 143, 147
CRUISING GUIDES:	*Yachtsman's Guide to the Bahamas, The Bahamas Cruising Guide..*
WAYPOINTS:	

Departure	Intermediate	Landfall	Destination	Distance (M)
AN540 Las Palmas	AN541	AN542 Salvador	Cockburn Town	3328
28°07'N, 15°24'W	20°00'N, 60°00'W	23°54'N, 74°32'W	*24°03'N, 74°31.5'W*	

With the exception of Christopher Columbus, who sailed this route in 1492 and thereby established a permanent link between the Old and New Worlds, few modern boats attempt to sail nonstop to the Bahamas. In 1992, on the occasion of the quincentenary of that historic voyage, this traditional route was sailed by many boats, their crews commemorating in this way the deeds of one of the greatest navigators in history. The route can be useful for boats intending to sail to the southern USA directly from the Canaries.

Being unaware of the hurricane season in the yet to be discovered lands he was heading for, Columbus made his passage from the Canaries in September and was extremely fortunate in having good weather throughout, or the history of the world might have been very different. Armed with modern knowledge about the behaviour of West Indian hurricanes, the passage should not be attempted before the end of November. For the transatlantic section of the voyage directions are similar to those detailed in route AN51. However, depending on weather conditions, it may not be necessary to dip as far south as do the boats going to islands in the Southern Caribbean. If the trade winds extend as far north as 20°N, or even further, it should

be possible to lay a fairly direct course across.

Whichever course is chosen for the Atlantic crossing, on approaching the Eastern Caribbean islands, one should try not to sail below WP AN541 so as to stay well clear of such islands as Anguila and Sombrero, which have claimed too many ships in the past. From there, the course should stay well offshore to pass the Turks and Caicos group at a safe distance before closing with San Salvador, marked by a powerful light. After landfall is made at WP AN542, 5 miles SE of Sandy Point, the SW extremity of San Salvador, the W of the island should be passed at a safe distance before approaching the main settlement at Cockburn Town. Entry formalities can be completed there or one mile further north at Riding Rock Marina, which has a difficult entrance with a maximum depth of 7 ft at high tide.

AN55 *Canary Islands to Bermuda*

BEST TIME:	April to May				
TROPICAL STORMS:	June to November				
CHARTS:	BA: 4012				
	US: 120				
PILOTS:	BA: 1, 70, 71				
	US: 140, 143, 147				
CRUISING GUIDES:	*Yachting Guide to Bermuda.*				
WAYPOINTS:					
Departure	*Intermediate*	*Landfall*		*Destination*	*Distance (M)*
AN550 Las Palmas 28°07'N, 15°24'W	AN551 25°00'N, 60°00'W	AN552 Bermuda E 32°22'N, 64°38'W		St George's *32°22'N, 64°40'W*	2894

The number of boats sailing nonstop from the Canaries to Bermuda is relatively small, probably because the best sailing conditions on this route coincide with the start of the hurricane season in the Western Atlantic. The greatest frequency of hurricanes in Bermuda itself has been recorded from mid-August to mid-October, June and July being considered relatively safe months.

For anyone in a hurry to return to the USA, this direct route has much to recommend it and fast passages have been recorded. If the voyage is made during the safe season, from November to April, the winter trades are so far south that a detour to find them would take the track so close to the Lesser Antilles that it would be just as easy to make a stop there. As the sun changes its declination and

starts moving north, the trade wind belt does the same and, in spring or early summer, a passage to Bermuda can be done between latitudes 20° and 25°N. Constant NE and later E winds will be found along these latitudes for most of the transatlantic voyage. The temptation should be resisted to alter course for Bermuda too soon as this leads into an area of variable winds. One should therefore aim for WP AN551 so that Bermuda is approached from the SSE. For the remaining distance the winds should be from the SW, which are the prevailing winds in Bermuda during summer. Landfall should be made at WP AN552 east of St David's Head, in the approaches to the Town Cut which leads into St George's Harbour, where entry formalities are completed.

AN56 *Canary Islands to Azores*

BEST TIME:	May to August
TROPICAL STORMS:	None
CHARTS:	BA: 4104
	US: 12
PILOTS:	BA: 1, 67
	US: 143
CRUISING GUIDES:	*Azores Cruising Guide, Atlantic Islands.*
WAYPOINTS:	

Departure	Intermediate	Landfall	Destination	Distance (M)
AN560 Santa Cruz	AN561 La Palma	AN562 Santa Maria	Vila do Porto	623
28°40.5'N, 17°45.5'W	28°52'N, 17°45'W	36°54'N, 25°09'W	*36°56'N, 25°08.5'W*	
AN560 Santa Cruz	AN561 La Palma	AN563 Faial	Horta	811
		38°30'N, 28°36'W	*38°32'N, 28°37.5'W*	

The most likely winds in summer will be from the NE making this a close hauled passage, especially if one leaves from one of the more western islands such as La Palma. A contrary current of up to 1/2 knot may also be experienced. Although the Azores are considered to be outside the tropical storms area, very rarely such storms have reached the archipelago. Such occurrences are well forecast so that adequate precautions can be taken.

Taking as a departure point WP AN561 NE of La Palma, the direct course to Ponta Delgada, the capital of the Azores, leads so close to the island of Santa Maria, that one may decide to stop first at its main port of Vila do Porto. In such a case, course should be set for WP AN562, 2 miles south of that harbour. An alternative destination is Horta, on the island of Faial. In this case, landfall can be made at WP AN563, 3 miles SE of the port of Horta.

If leaving the Canaries from one of the islands east of Tenerife, the voyage can be interrupted in Madeira from where the same directions apply as for route AN43 (page 69).

AN57 *Canary Islands to Madeira*

BEST TIME:	April to June, October
TROPICAL STORMS:	None
CHARTS:	BA: 4104
	US: 104
PILOTS:	BA: 1
	US: 143
CRUISING GUIDES:	*Atlantic Islands, Madeira Cruising Guide.*
WAYPOINTS:	

Departure	Intermediate	Landfall	Destination	Distance (M)
AN571 Graciosa		AN572 Madeira	Funchal	269
29°13'N, 13°33'W		32°38'N, 16°54'W	*32°37.5'N, 16°54.5'W*	
AN573 Las Palmas	AN574 Isleta			
28°08'N, 15°24'W	28°09'N, 15°23'W			
	AN575 Salvagem	AN572	Funchal	283
	30°10'N, 15°45'W			

As the prevailing winds of summer are from the northern quarter, this passage is best undertaken either in the spring or autumn. Ideally, one should wait for a spell of southerly winds before leaving the Canaries. At any time, but particularly during summer, it may be easier to sail first to Lanzarote from where the winds will be at a better angle for the subsequent leg to Madeira. In such a case, the best departure point from the Canaries is the small island of Graciosa, north of Lanzarote.

The direct route from both Tenerife and Gran Canaria passes close to the Salvagem Islands, which lie approximately halfway between the two island groups. As landing in these islands is prohibited without a permit and the area surrounding them has many dangers, it is best to pass them at a safe distance. In an emergency it is possible to seek shelter in the anchorage at Cagarras Bay (30°08.3'N, 15°52.2'W), on the SW side of Salvagem Grande, where the resident caretaker is based. From Salvagem Grande the route for Madeira must avoid dangers north of the island before a direct course can be set for Funchal.

AN58 *Canary Islands to Gibraltar*

BEST TIME:	April to May			
TROPICAL STORMS:	None			
CHARTS:	BA: 4104			
	US: 104			
PILOTS:	BA: 1, 67			
	US: 143			
CRUISING GUIDES:	*Yacht Scene.*			
WAYPOINTS:				

Departure	Intermediate	Landfall	Destination	Distance (M)
AN580 Las Palmas 28°08'N, 15°24'W	AN581 Isleta 28°09'N, 15°23'W			
	AN582 33°00'N, 11°00'W			
	AN583 Espartel 35°52'N, 6°00'W			
	AN584 Hoyo 36°04'N, 6°20'W			
	AN585 Tarifa 35°59'N, 5°36'W			
	AN586 Carnera 36°03'N, 5°25'W	AN587 Gibraltar 36°08'N, 5°22'W	Marina Bay *36°09'N, 5°21'W*	709

The recommended time to make this passage is in late spring before the onset of the NE winds of summer. If persistent northerly winds are met after leaving the Canaries, it may be necessary to break the voyage in Madeira and stop at Funchal or Porto Santo and wait for the weather to change. One may also wait for such a change at the anchorage on Salvagem Grande (see route AN57).

If weather conditions allow a relatively direct route to be sailed from Las Palmas, a course should be set for an intermediate WP AN582. From there a new course should be set to WP AN583, some 5 miles NW of Cape Espartel, in the approaches to the Strait of Gibraltar. Directions for negotiating the Strait are given in routes AN16 and AN21 (pages 46 and 51).

AN60 ROUTES FROM THE CAPE VERDE ISLANDS AND WEST AFRICA

The former Portuguese colony of the Cape Verde Islands is a group of small islands 200 miles off the coast of West Africa which used to be a busy coaling station frequented by intercontinental steamers. They have been rediscovered as a convenient stopover for those wishing to shorten their transatlantic passage to the Caribbean or intending to make their landfall in Brazil. As the Cape Verdes lie in the NE trade wind belt, the prevailing wind is NE most of the year, being stronger from February to June, when winds of 25 knots or more blow most of the time. As the convergence zone moves to its most northerly position in summer months there are more variable winds, with fresh southerlies in August and September, the time of the SW monsoon.

In neighbouring West Africa, the strong NE trades blowing across continental Africa between December and February can produce *harmattan* winds. These often create a dust haze and cover the boat and sails in reddish dust. Distinguished by a yellow sky and a blurred horizon, this haze

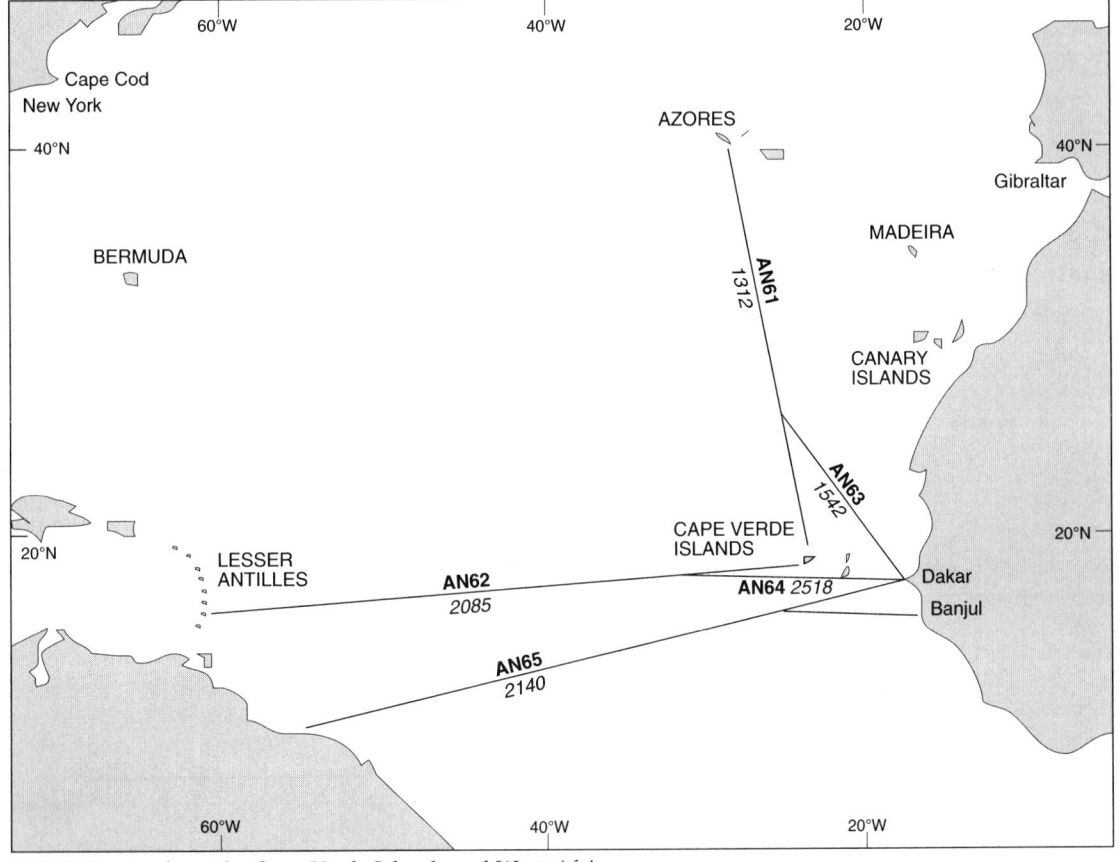

AN60 *Routes from the Cape Verde Islands and West Africa*

not only reduces visibility to a few hundred yards, but even when the visibility is several miles it makes it very difficult to estimate distances at sea until land or an object is seen. Therefore great care must be taken when approaching the Cape Verde Islands during these conditions.

For a taste of Africa, some of the best cruising on that continent is to be found in Senegal and Gambia with the possibility of navigating the larger rivers in this area. Although cruising in West Africa is usually incorporated into a longer voyage by those making a more southerly Atlantic crossing to Brazil, the number of cruising boats is steadily increasing. As in some other parts of the world, the first to discover these new cruising grounds were French sailors, who were aided by the fact that some of the countries are former French colonies and French is widely spoken. The best time to visit the area is during the winter months, from December to April, when temperatures are pleasant and there is little rain. The summer months are hot, humid, and wet.

Transatlantic passages starting from either West Africa or the Cape Verdes do not present major problems as the winds are usually favourable. More difficulties are experienced by boats intending to return to Europe; they have to beat against the prevailing NE winds and most break the trip in the Azores.

AN61 *Cape Verde Islands to Azores*

BEST TIME:	June to August
TROPICAL STORMS:	None
CHARTS:	BA: 4012
	US: 12
PILOTS:	BA: 1, 71
	US: 140, 143
CRUISING GUIDES:	*Azores Cruising Guide, Atlantic Islands.*
WAYPOINTS:	

Departure	Intermediate	Landfall	Destination	Distance (M)
AN610 São Vicente 16°54'N, 25°01'W			Vila do Porto 36°56'N, 25°09'W	1202
			Ponta Delgada 37°44'N, 25°40'W	1251
			Horta 38°32'N, 28°37.5'W	1312
			Lajes 39°23'N, 31°10'W	1387

Northerly winds blow on average 80 per cent of the time on the route between these island groups. Therefore the optimum time for this passage is late spring or early summer when the proportion of NE winds is higher than at other times and, depending on the type of boat, one may be able to lay the Azores on one tack. An additional bonus may be provided by a depression intersecting one's track in higher latitudes, and although the resulting SW winds may cause uncomfortable conditions at least they will be blowing from a favourable direction. SW winds are quite rare in the latitude of the Cape Verdes, although they do occur during summer so it may be worth waiting for a spell of SW winds before leaving the Cape Verdes. Winds in the latter part of the passage are greatly influenced by the position of the Azores high. Being able to obtain up to date weather information can be a great bonus here as it helps one choose the more favourable tack.

There are several destinations in the Azores, such as Ponta Delgada, the capital of the archipelago. The route passes so closely to the island of Santa Maria, that one may decide to stop first at its main port of Vila do Porto. Because of the NE winds, which will have been encountered en route, a more likely landfall will be further west, such as at Horta on the island of Faial, or even Lajes on the westernmost island of Flores.

AN62 *Cape Verde Islands to Lesser Antilles*

BEST TIME:	December to April
TROPICAL STORMS:	June to November
CHARTS:	BA: 4012
	US: 12
PILOTS:	BA: 1, 71
	US: 140, 143, 147
CRUISING GUIDES:	*Sailor's Guide to the Windward Islands, Cruising Guide to the Leeward Islands.*
WAYPOINTS:	

Departure	Intermediate	Landfall	Destination	Distance (M)
AN620 São Vicente 16°53'N, 25°00'W		AN621 St Lucia 14°03'N, 60°50'W	Rodney Bay *14°04.5'N, 60°58.5'W*	2085
		AN622 Martinique 14°22'N, 60°51'W	Fort de France *14°36'N, 61°05'W*	2094
		AN623 Barbados 13°02'N, 59°23'W	Bridgetown *13°06'N, 59°38'W*	2019
		AN624 Antigua SE 16°57'N, 61°45'W	English Harbour *17°00'N, 61°46'W*	2110

Columbus was first to see the attraction of these islands as a better springboard for a trade wind passage across the Atlantic than the Canaries and he set off on his third voyage to the Caribbean from here. The advantage of this route is not only that the actual transatlantic passage is shorter but also that the Cape Verdes are situated for most of the year in the heart of the NE trades. Fast passages are usually logged by boats starting off from the Cape Verdes provided their course does not dip too far south into an area where the trade winds become less constant. A great circle course is usually the best route to take across. More detailed directions for the transatlantic passage are given in route AN51 (page 74).

AN63 *West Africa to Azores*

BEST TIME:	April to August
TROPICAL STORMS:	None
CHARTS:	BA: 4012
	US: 12
PILOTS:	BA: 1, 67
	US: 140, 143
CRUISING GUIDES:	*Azores Cruising Guide, Atlantic Islands.*
WAYPOINTS:	

Departure	Intermediate	Landfall	Destination	Distance (M)
AN631 Vert 14°45'N, 17°35'W			Vila do Porto *36°56'N, 25°09'W*	1391
			Ponta Delgada *37°44'N, 25°40'W*	1444
			Horta *38°32'N, 28°37.5'W*	1542

As explained in route AN61, NE winds predominate in the area south of the Azores and passages should therefore be timed for a period when the proportion of such winds is lowest. Starting off from one of the West African ports, as opposed to the Cape Verdes, has the advantage of a better angle in relation to the prevailing winds, so unless one has a very good reason to stop in the Cape Verdes, the valuable easting should not be lost.

If leaving from Dakar, the recommended route passes east of the Cape Verdes, and should the need arise, the island of Sal (16°45'N, 23°00'W) is in the most convenient position for a landfall. It can be assumed that the trade winds will be lost around 25°N from where it should be easier to make the necessary northing. North of latitude 30°N the winds and weather are very much dependent on the position of the Azores high. If this lies further south than its usual seasonal position, light winds can be expected in the vicinity of the Azores. There are several destinations in the Azores, such as Ponta Delgada, the capital of the archipelago. As the route passes closely to the island of Santa Maria, a first stop could be made at its main port of Vila do Porto. Because of the NE winds earlier in the passage, a more likely landfall will be further west, such as at Horta on the island of Faial.

The timing of this passage may also depend on the destination after the Azores. It is not advisable to attempt this passage before April to give the strong NE winds of winter a chance to diminish in strength. South of latitude 15°N they are replaced in summer by the SW monsoon, which blows between Senegal and the Cape Verde Islands from June to October. The start of the SW monsoon is therefore the best time to leave West Africa for the Azores as it would ensure good winds at least for the early part of the voyage.

AN64 *West Africa to Lesser Antilles*

BEST TIME:	December to May
TROPICAL STORMS:	June to November
CHARTS:	BA: 4012
	US: 12
PILOTS:	BA: 1, 71
	US: 140, 143, 147
CRUISING GUIDES:	*Sailor's Guide to the Windward Islands, Cruising Guide to the Leeward Islands.*
WAYPOINTS:	

Departure	Intermediate	Landfall	Destination	Distance (M)
AN641 Vert 14°45'N, 17°35'W		AN643 St Lucia 14°03'N, 60°50'W	Rodney Bay *14°04.5'N, 60°58.5'W*	2518
		AN644 Martinique 14°22'N, 60°51'W	Fort de France *14°36'N, 61°05'W*	2528
		AN645 Barbados 13°02'N, 59°23'W	Bridgetown *13°06'N, 59°38'W*	2449
		AN646 Antigua SE 16°57'N, 61°45'W	English Harbour *17°00'N, 61°46'W*	2551
AN642 Banjul 13°35'N, 16°55'W		AN643 St Lucia	Rodney Bay	2564
		AN644 Martinique	Fort de France	2574
		AN645 Barbados	Bridgetown	2492
		AN646 Antigua SE	English Harbour	2601

Whether leaving from a port in Senegal or the Gambia, steady favourable winds will be encountered on this route throughout the winter months. If winds are westerly on leaving continental Africa, which is not unusual during the summer months, it is recommended to stay on the starboard tack. As one moves offshore, the winds will veer, allowing one to pass the Cape Verdes without tacking.

From the Cape Verdes onwards this route is similar to route AN62. As the Cape Verdes are so close to the direct route it may be convenient to stop there before proceeding west. If leaving from mainland Africa direct, especially from more southern ports, attention must be paid to the currents both in the vicinity of the coast and during the transatlantic passage. Sailing too close to the southern limit of the NE trades should be avoided as there is a danger of being pushed by a branch of the North Equatorial Current towards the doldrums and an area of less steady winds. More details concerning the Atlantic crossing are given in route AN51 (page 74).

AN65 *West Africa to Northern Brazil and Guyanas*

BEST TIME:	November to May
TROPICAL STORMS:	None
CHARTS:	BA: 4012
	US: 106, 107
PILOTS:	BA: 1, 7A
	US: 124, 143
WAYPOINTS:	

Departure	Intermediate	Landfall	Destination	Distance (M)
AN651 Vert 14°45'N, 17°35'W	AN653 10°00'N, 40°00'W		Degrad des Cannes 4°51'N, 52°16'W	2140
			Paramaribo 5°50'N, 55°10'W	2284
			Georgetown 6°49'N, 58°11'W	2447
AN652 Banjul 13°35'N, 16°55'W	AN653		Degrad des Cannes	2169
			Paramaribo	2313
			Georgetown	2475

This passage is best undertaken during winter when the NE trade winds reach further south. If leaving from a port south of the river Gambia, a NW course should be sailed first to avoid an area of light and variable winds close to the equator. If leaving from Senegal, the recommended route passes south of the Cape Verde Islands. In both cases, a course should be set for WP AN653. This intermediate waypoint is suggested to avoid the effects of a contrary current which has been observed south of 10°N. If the port of destination lies south of this latitude, the course can be set for it once the recommended waypoint has been passed. The North Equatorial Current will give a boost to passage along most of this route. A strong current sets northwards along the coast of South America and this current must be taken into account when making landfall. Dangerous shallow areas extend off the coast, especially near river mouths. If entering any of these rivers, attention must be paid to the strong tides.

This route is often sailed by boats heading for Belem and the Amazon River. Although such a destination would make this into a transequatorial route, in order to ensure better conditions during the crossing the latter should be done north of the equator. Knowing the position of the ITCZ, shown on satellite pictures obtained by weatherfax, is essential in such a case so as to minimise the time spent under its influence. Very slow passages with violent squalls and a contrary current have been recorded during summer. The main reason for crossing at such a time is to arrive in Amazonia at the start of the dry season (July).

The three former Guyanas, French (Cayenne), Dutch (Suriname), and British Guyana attract a small number of cruising boats. Entry formalities in French Guyana are completed at Degrad des Cannes. The port of entry for Suriname is Paramaribo, approximately 13 miles up the Suriname River, where boats now clear in at the new harbour, Nieu Haffen. The least visited of the three is Guyana itself, where the only official port of entry is its capital Georgetown.

AN70 ROUTES FROM THE LESSER ANTILLES

The Windward and Leeward Islands continue to be the most popular cruising destination in the North Atlantic and, although commonly referred to as the Caribbean, their correct name is the Lesser Antilles. The majority of sailors, whether coming from Europe or North America, usually spend a season cruising the islands before embarking on the return voyage home. The greatest exodus takes place between the middle of April and the end of May, when most boats leave either for Bermuda or directly for the Azores. The route to Bermuda is used both by boats sailing to the east coast of North America and by Europeans returning home. The direct route to the Azores, without calling at Bermuda, has been gaining in popularity in recent years as it shortens the distance by several hundred miles, even if favourable winds are the exception rather than the rule on this direct route which crosses both the Horse Latitudes and the infamous Sargasso Sea.

Much more wind is experienced by those heading across the Caribbean Sea proper, most of whom are bound for the Panama Canal. If this passage is made in winter, when the trade winds are at their strongest, large seas can be expected on the way to Panama. The situation improves with the approach of summer and passages in April and May are more comfortable. Rather than sail directly to Panama, many boats now cross the Caribbean Sea in shorter stages by calling at the offshore islands of Venezuela, the Dutch islands of Aruba, Bonaire and Curaçao, and also Colombia. In Panama itself, the islands of San Blas continue to be one of the most fascinating destinations in the area. The main advantage of cruising along the northern coast of South America in easy stages is that the area is rarely affected by tropical storms. Occasionally, however, a hurricane does reach Venezuela or the SW part of the Caribbean, so if possible even this area should be avoided during summer, from the end of July until the end of October.

Although most sailors bound for the US east coast take their leave from the Eastern Caribbean in one of the northern islands, such as Antigua, St Martin, or one of the Virgins, a less frequented route to the USA is one which crosses the Caribbean Sea. Such a southern route has certain attractions for anyone bound for Florida or one of the southern states. Leaving from one of the southern islands in the Eastern Caribbean, such as St Lucia, the route stays south of Puerto Rico as far as the Mona Passage from where it continues north of Hispaniola and on to the Bahamas. The other, probably more attractive, alternative is to take the offshore route south of all the Greater Antilles, with possible stops in Jamaica, Grand Cayman, or Cuba. Such a route is described in detail in AN83, and although it originates in the Virgins, conditions would be similar if one left from one of the islands to the south.

One of the main attractions of the Lesser Antilles is their weather. During winter months the NE trades blow with regularity and both day and night temperatures are pleasantly warm. The average temperature rarely varies from 26–28°C throughout the year. In late summer and autumn, when the trades ease up, the threat of hurricanes spoils this perfection. The number of boats that carry on cruising during this period is relatively small because of the fear of being caught out by a hurricane. Although not recommended, it is possible to cruise, provided some basic precautions are observed.

From the middle of December until the end of April, the trade winds blow between NE and ENE,

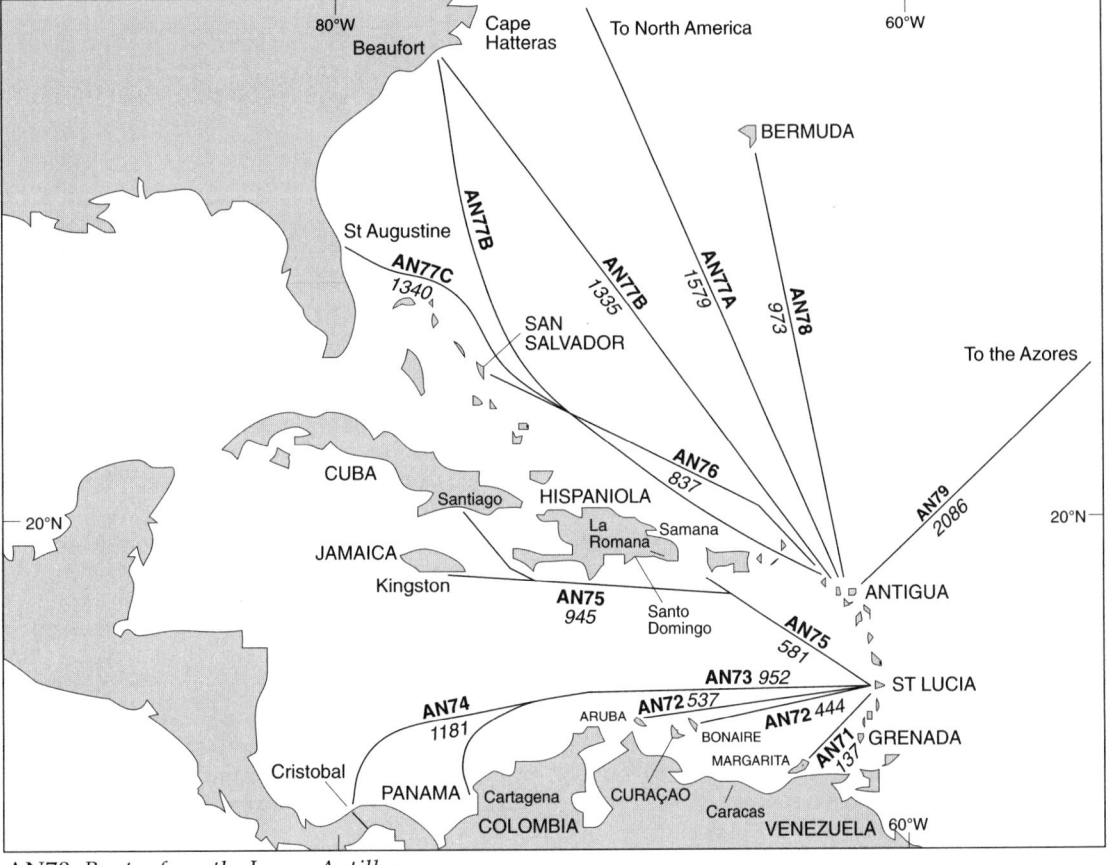

AN70 *Routes from the Lesser Antilles*

usually at a constant 15–20 knots. Occasionally these increase to 25–30 knots for a few days and can have stronger gusts, especially in late January and early February. As summer approaches the wind tends to veer SE and even S, gradually returning to the E and NE towards the end of the year. In summer months the winds are lighter, from 12–15 knots in June through to September. This is the rainy season, particularly from August into November.

Occasionally the weather is interrupted by an Easterly Wave, a low pressure trough, which moves westward and can develop into a hurricane. Whenever the wind shifts to the north during the summer months, a stiff blow can be expected. West Indian hurricanes usually form about 800 miles to the east of Barbados and track north and west. Hurricanes are more frequent in the more northern Leeward Islands than in the Windward Islands lying further south, and rarely strike the most southerly islands such as Grenada. The likelihood of experiencing such a storm is less the further south and east one is at the height of the hurricane season. A common path is for hurricanes to pass about the latitude of Guadeloupe or further north and then move along the Leeward Islands before turning north. The hurricane season is from June to November, with the greatest number occurring in September. Very rarely a hurricane strikes in May or December.

AN71 *Lesser Antilles to Venezuela*

BEST TIME:	December to May
TROPICAL STORMS:	June to November
CHARTS:	BA: 4402
	US: 400
PILOTS:	BA: 7A, 71
	US: 147, 148
CRUISING GUIDES:	*Cruising Guide to Trinidad and Tobago, Venezuela and Bonaire, Street's Cruising Guide to the Eastern Caribbean - Venezuela.*
WAYPOINTS:	

Departure	Intermediate	Landfall	Destination	Distance (M)
AN710 Grenada 12°02.5'N, 61°46'W	AN711 Testigos 11°30'N, 63°00'W	AN712 Margarita 11°00'N, 63°35'W	Pampatar *11°00'N, 63°47'W*	137

This short passage benefits from favourable winds throughout the year. Sometimes in winter, between January and March, when the trade winds blow strongly, conditions can be rough. Better conditions are found at the change of seasons when winds continue to be favourable, but are usually lighter than in winter. On all westbound passages allowance should be made for the strong Equatorial Current which can set westward at rates of up to 2 knots.

Boats leaving from Grenada normally sail directly to Pampatar, on the SE coast of Margarita Island, the nearest official port of entry. The route passes dangerously close to Los Testigos, a group of low islands surrounded by shallows and reefs, which should be given a wide berth unless planning to stop there. More dangers will be passed on the way to Margarita, such as the low island of La Sola. So this passage, although short, should be treated with due caution.

AN72 *Lesser Antilles to ABC Islands*

BEST TIME:	December to May
TROPICAL STORMS:	June to November
CHARTS:	BA: 4402
	US: 400
PILOTS:	BA: 7A, 71
	US: 147, 148
CRUISING GUIDES:	*Cruising Guide to Trinidad and Tobago, Venezuela and Bonaire, Yachting Guide to the ABC Islands.*
WAYPOINTS:	

Departure	Intermediate	Landfall	Destination	Distance (M)
AN721 Grenada 12°02.5'N, 61°46'W	AN722 Roques 12°10'N, 66°40'W		Kralendijk *12°09'N, 68°17'W*	382
			Willemstad *12°07'N, 68°56'W*	421
			Oranjestad *12°30'N, 70°02'W*	487

The former Dutch colonies off the coast of Venezuela are easily reached from any of the Lesser Antilles as both wind and current are in one's favour virtually throughout the year. If coming from Grenada, from WP AN721, outside St George, a course should be set for WP AN722 to pass at a safe distance north of Los Roques islands off Venezuela. A strong current may be experienced when sailing among the ABC Islands, so this should be monitored constantly.

Approaching Bonaire from the north, Bonaire can be passed on either side. Although sailing down the west side will save a few miles, the strong contrary current will cancel any advantage. Boats coming from the east should stay south of the island and go straight to Kralendijk to complete formalities. The customs dock is the northernmost dock in the commercial harbour. It is also possible to clear Customs at Bonaire Marina. Bonaire has a Venezuelan Consulate where visas for crew visiting that country can be obtained.

Formalities in Curaçao can be completed in the capital Willemstad. Contact the Port Authority on arrival on VHF channel 12 or 14 for docking instructions. Yachts may also clear at the marina in Spanish Water (12°09'N, 68°17'W). However, as the Customs dock in Willemstad is very busy and dirty, it is advisable to go directly to Spanish Water, and clear there.

Aruba Port Control should be contacted on VHF channel 16 when entering for berthing and clearance instructions.

AN73 *Lesser Antilles to Colombia*

BEST TIME:	December to May			
TROPICAL STORMS:	June to November			
CHARTS:	BA: 4402			
	US: 400			
PILOTS:	BA: 7A, 71			
	US: 147, 148			
CRUISING GUIDES:	Cruising Guide to the Caribbean.			
WAYPOINTS:				
Departure	Intermediate	Landfall	Destination	Distance (M)
AN730 St Lucia W 14°04'N, 61°00'W	AN732 Gallinas 12°55'N, 71°38'W AN733 12°23'N, 73°12'W AN734 11°10'N, 75°25'W	AN735 off Cartagena 10°25'N, 75°38'W	Cartagena *10°25'N, 75°32'W*	952
AN731 Antigua S 16°58'N, 61°47'W	AN732 Gallinas AN733 AN734	AN735 off Cartagena	Cartagena	906

A successful anti-drug campaign in the early 1990s has made it possible once again to include Colombia in one's cruising plans, and a large number of visiting boats are stopping in Colombia, especially in the attractive city of Cartagena. Directions for sailing to Colombia are similar to routes AN71 and AN74. From WP AN732, 28 miles north of Punta Gallinas on Guajira Peninsula, the recommended route leads to WPs AN733 and AN734. Both points are just outside the 1000 metre line where there are relatively less rough seas, although both strong winds and high seas are a rule on all Caribbean routes, especially during the winter months. From AN734 the course can be altered to WP AN735 in the approaches to the port of Cartagena. The area should be approached with caution because of the dangers in the approaches to Cartagena. The entrance through Boca Grande should not be attempted as it is badly silted. The dredged entrance is now Boca Chica, identified by a landfall buoy, close to the end of Isla de Tierra Bomba. An 8 mile long channel leads northward through the shallow Bahia de Cartagena to the commercial port and two marinas. The port lies on the banks of the River Magdalena and approaches are very difficult. Arriving yachts are advised to contact Club Nautico on channel 16 for clearance and docking information. The GPS position of the orange and white entrance buoy has been reported at 10°18.97'N, 75°35.98'W.

AN74 *Lesser Antilles to Panama*

BEST TIME:	April to May, November to December			
TROPICAL STORMS:	June to November			
CHARTS:	BA: 4402			
	US: 400			
PILOTS:	BA: 7A, 71			
	US: 147, 148			
CRUISING GUIDES:	*Cruising Guide to Panama, The Panama Guide.*			
WAYPOINTS:				

Departure	Intermediate	Landfall	Destination	Distance (M)
AN740 St Lucia W 14°04'N, 61°00'W	AN742 Gallinas 12°55'N, 71°38'W			
	AN743 Manzanillo 9°47'N, 79°32'W	AN744 off Panama 9°26.25'N, 79°55'W	Cristobal *9°21'N, 79°55'W*	1181
AN741 Antigua S 16°58'N, 61°45'W	AN742 Gallinas AN743 Manzanillo	AN744 off Panama	Cristobal	1162

This can be a very rough passage, confirmed by the fact that many experienced sailors describe their passage across the Caribbean Sea perhaps as the roughest part of their voyage around the world. This is usually the case at the height of the trade wind season, when the constant easterly winds pile up the water in the western part of the Caribbean making sea conditions hazardous. Many boats have been knocked down or pooped by the steep following seas, while others have been lost on the coast of Colombia after having been set off course by the strong current.

Although direct passages to Panama cross an area which is rarely affected by hurricanes, this passage should not be done between July and October when the risk of tropical storms is highest. The best times are either in November–December, when the trades are not yet blowing at full strength, or in April–May, when the strength of the winter trades starts to diminish. The months of January to March, although free of hurricanes, are also the period of the strongest trades, when conditions in the western part of the Caribbean can become uncomfortable, or occasionally even dangerous, for small boats. Best conditions can therefore be expected at either the beginning or the end of the winter season.

Boats sailing to Panama nonstop should keep at a safe distance from the Colombian coast to avoid the rougher seas associated with those shallow waters. Whether stopping in Aruba, as many boats

do, or sailing nonstop to Panama, WP AN742, 28 miles north of Punta Gallinas on Guajira Peninsula allows the course to be set just outside the 1000 metre line where relatively less rough seas can be expected. From there, a direct course leads to WP AN743, about 10 miles N of Punta Manzanillo and 30 miles from the Panama Canal entrance. The latter is reached by altering course for WP AN744 which is the landfall buoy, approximately 3 miles N of the entrance into the port of Cristobal. Traffic Control should be contacted on VHF channel 12, although small boats may enter if they proceed carefully. Traffic lights control the entrance through the breakwaters and small boats are advised to keep as close as possible to the sides. See page 583 for detailed instructions concerning Panama entry and transit procedure.

When planning this passage across the Caribbean Sea it is well worth considering a stop in either Venezuela or the offlying ABC islands, most of which are situated outside the hurricane belt. The advantage of such a stop is that the voyage towards Panama can be continued at any time of the year, and with sufficient care even during the hurricane season, as the route from Aruba to Panama lies to the south of the area affected by tropical storms. Another suggested stop is in the San Blas Islands, which belong to Panama. The port of entry is Porvenir (9°34'N, 78°57'W). As described in AN73, the voyage can also be interrupted at Cartagena, in Colombia.

AN75 *Lesser Antilles to Greater Antilles*

BEST TIME:	December to May			
TROPICAL STORMS:	June to November			
CHARTS:	BA: 4402			
	US: 400			
PILOTS:	BA: 70, 71			
	US: 148			
CRUISING GUIDES:	*Cruising Guide to the Caribbean, Cruising Guide to Cuba, The Yachtsman's Guide to Jamaica.*			
WAYPOINTS:				

Departure	Intermediate	Landfall	Destination	Distance (M)
Route AN75A				
AN750 St Lucia W	AN751 Rojo			
14°04'N, 61°00'W	17°45'N, 67°12'W			
	AN752 Engano		Samana	581
	18°38'N, 67°51'W		*19°12'N, 69°26'W*	
Route AN75B				
AN750 St Lucia W	AN753 Saona		La Romana	533
	18°00'N, 68°45'W		*18°25'N, 68°57'W*	
			Santo Domingo	586
			18°28'N, 69°53'W	
Route AN75C				
AN750 St Lucia W	AN754 Alta Vela			
	17°20'N, 71°40'W			
	AN755 Plumb		Kingston	945
	17°50'N, 76°40'W		*17°58'N, 76°48'W*	
	AN756 Northeast		Port Antonio	926
	18°15'N, 76°15'W		*18°11'N, 76°27'W*	
			Montego Bay	1010
			18°28'N, 77°56'W	
Route AN75D				
AN750 St Lucia W	AN754 Alta Vela			
	AN757 Tiburon		Santiago de Cuba	954
	18°10'N, 74°40'W		*19°59'N, 75°53'W*	

Not such a popular cruising destination as the Lesser Antilles, the large islands of Cuba, Hispaniola, Puerto Rico, and Jamaica are mainly visited by yachts en route to other places. From islands south of Antigua, direct offshore routes lead across the Caribbean Sea to the south coasts of all the Greater Antilles. Ports on the north coasts of all these islands can be reached in easy stages if setting off from the Virgin Islands. The north coast of Hispaniola, islands in the Turks and Caicos, as well as some of the Bahamas, are best reached through the Mona Passage.

While experiencing the typical Caribbean weather pattern of winters dominated by the NE trades, punctuated by northers, and summers threatened by hurricanes, these large islands affect local weather conditions considerably due to their height and position. Normally the winds along the coasts moderate at night as cooled air flows off the hills and out to sea. This land breeze can be quite strong at night off all the islands, so as to counteract the trade winds completely and give calm conditions. In winter the prevailing NE trades can become more easterly along northern coasts. During this period the islands are affected by northers, which bring strong N or more often NW winds and cold temperatures to the north and west coasts of the islands. These winds come without much warning and often out of a clear sky, although some indication may be the wind veering gradually to S and SW. In summer the trade winds have a more southerly component and winds tend to be much lighter, the sea and land breezes being prominent. Thundery squalls are common over the whole area, especially in the late afternoon close to land. Some of the most violent squalls in the Caribbean, short but sharp with lightning and heavy rain, occur off the south coast of Cuba. Because the high islands block the passage of N winds, line squalls are more associated with the northern coasts of Hispaniola and Cuba. Jamaica is more sheltered than the other islands and has less seasonal change, the winds being generally lighter and more variable. The Greater Antilles are in the middle of the hurricane belt and hurricanes accelerating through the Caribbean frequently hit the shores of these islands on their curved path northward. Their eastern shores are more frequently affected than the western shores.

When coming from any of the islands in the Eastern Caribbean, set course for WP AN751, 10 miles south of Cabo Rojo, the SW extremity of Puerto Rico. To pass through the Mona Passage (Route AN75A), alter course for WP AN752 so as to stay clear of the shallows, and rough seas associated with them, east of Cape Engano on Hispaniola. Boats intending to stop on the west coast of Puerto Rico are warned that the official port of entry is Mayaguez (18°12'N, 67°07'W) and not Boqueron. All boats, including those flying the US flag, must stop at the former to clear in. A convenient port of entry into the Dominican Republic is Samana, on the north coast of Hispaniola. Another port of entry on the north coast is Luperon (Puerto Blanco), 19°55'N, 70°56'W.

Favourable conditions are experienced on westbound routes, which stay south of the islands, at almost any time of the year. Boats sailing route AN75B should set a course for WP AN753, off Saona island, at the SE point of Hispaniola, and then alter course for either La Romana or Santo Domingo.

Boats bound for Jamaica and beyond (AN75C) should make for WP AN754, off the small island of Alta Vela, south of Hispaniola, where those intending to call at the Jamaican capital Kingston should alter course for WP AN755. Boats bound for ports on the north coast of Jamaica should steer for WP AN756, off Northeast Point, and then make for their port of destination. Finally, boats bound for Cuba (AN75D) should alter course from AN754 for WP AN757, off Cape Tiburon, from where it is a clear run to Santiago de Cuba, the nearest Cuban port of entry to this route.

AN76 *Lesser Antilles to Bahamas*

BEST TIME:	December to May
TROPICAL STORMS:	June to November
CHARTS:	BA: 4400 US: 400
PILOTS:	BA: 70, 71 US: 147
CRUISING GUIDES:	*Yachtsman's Guide to the Bahamas, The Bahamas Cruising Guide.*
WAYPOINTS:	

Departure	Intermediate	Landfall	Destination	Distance (M)
AN761 Antigua W 17°00'N, 61°56'W	AN762 17°45'N, 63°00'W AN763 18°55'N, 64°08'W AN764 Caicos 22°20'N, 72°10'W AN765 Samana 23°10'N, 73°20'W	AN766 Salvador 23°54'N, 74°32'W	Cockburn Town 24°03'N, 74°31.5'W	837

In winter, this route benefits from both favourable winds and current. The offshore passage can be made at any time outside of the hurricane season. Between December and April, at the height of the winter trades, fair, if strong, winds can be expected as well as the favourable Antilles Current. Light winds and occasional calms can be expected at the change of seasons, especially in

May. The route can be affected by depressions passing to the north with resulting NW winds. As both the Virgin Islands and Puerto Rico are situated on or very close to the direct route from the Eastern Caribbean to the Bahamas, most boats stop there before continuing their voyage. If stopping in the Virgin Islands, directions for the onward passage are given in route AN85 (page 103).

For boats leaving Antigua on a nonstop passage to the Bahamas, from WP AN761, off the SW of Antigua the initial course passes NE of Nevis, St Kitts, and St Eustatius to WP AN762, halfway between St Barts and Saba. From there a new course should be set for WP AN763 to stay clear of Anegada and the many dangers surrounding it. The course then stays well offshore to pass outside all dangers. The Southern Bahamas can be reached via several deep water passes, all of which are subject to strong currents as indeed is the entire area of the Bahamas. The route follows a NW direction to WP AN764 off Caicos Passage. The nearest island to clear into the Bahamas is Mayaguana, whose eastern point should be given a wide berth

to avoid the reefs surrounding it. Although Abrams Bay, the main settlement on the south coast of the island, is not an official port of entry, boats are allowed to stop there provided they complete formalities in the first official port of entry. The nearest is Cockburn Town on the island of San Salvador. If continuing on the offshore route, course for the latter should not be set until one is well clear of Samana Cay, a low unlit island lying between Mayaguana and San Salvador. From WP AN764 the course should be altered for WP AN765 east of Samana then for WP AN766.

After landfall is made at WP AN766, 5 miles SE of Sandy Point, the SW extremity of San Salvador, the west of the island should be passed at a safe distance before approaching the main settlement at Cockburn Town. Entry formalities can be completed there or one mile further north at Riding Rock Marina, which has a difficult entrance with a maximum depth of 7 ft at high tide. The GPS latitude of the entrance channel into the small marina has been reported as 24°03.4'N. The marina management will answer calls on VHF channel 6.

AN77 Lesser Antilles to North America

BEST TIME:	Late April to June
TROPICAL STORMS:	June to November
CHARTS:	BA: 4403 US: 108
PILOTS:	BA: 59, 68, 69, 70, 71 US: 140, 145, 147
CRUISING GUIDES:	Coastal Cruising Guide to the Atlantic Coast.
WAYPOINTS:	

Departure	Intermediate	Landfall	Destination	Distance (M)
Route AN77A				
AN770 Antigua S	AN771 Antigua W			
16°58'N, 61°45'W	17°00'N, 61°56'W			
	AN772			
	17°08'N, 62°00'W			
	AN773			
	18°25'N, 62°20'W			
	AN774 David		Chesapeake	1553
	32°21'N, 64°38'W		36°45'N, 75°45'W	
		AN 775 Brenton	Newport	1579
		41°24'N, 71°16'W	41°29'N, 71°20'W	
			Halifax	1683
			44°38'N, 63°34'W	

| WAYPOINTS: | | | | |
Departure	Intermediate	Landfall	Destination	Distance (M)
Route AN77B				
AN770 Antigua S	AN773		Beaufort *34°43'N, 76°40'W*	1335
Route AN77C				
AN770 Antigua S	AN773 AN774 Abaco *26°50'N, 76°30'W* AN775 Bahama *27°30'N, 78°00'W*		St Augustine *29°55'N, 81°16'W*	1340

The recommended time for this passage is at the end of the winter sailing season in the Caribbean. At such times the winds usually have a southern component. If a direct course is sailed to ports south of Cape Hatteras, favourable winds can be expected as far as the northern limit of the trade winds. Occasionally southerly winds last right through the zone of calms that extends between latitudes 25°N and 30°N. North of this zone the winds are variable, with a predominance of S and SW winds. The danger of a blustery winter norther is minimal after the middle of April. The temptation of a ride in the Gulf Stream should be resisted if this passage is made early in the season to avoid being caught by a late norther. This route is not recommended after the end of June because of the increased likelihood of hurricanes. Summer passages should be avoided as the tracks of past hurricanes almost coincide with the direct northbound route.

For destinations north of Cape Hatteras as far as Nova Scotia (AN77A), a stopover in Bermuda has certain attractions. In fact very few boats sail nonstop from the Eastern Caribbean to ports east of New York without stopping in Bermuda. Details for such a route are given in AN78 and AN121 (pages 96 and 140). Boats leaving from English Harbour can leave Antigua either to port or starboard. The second alternative is more comfortable for the start of the voyage and so a course should be set to sail west parallel to Antigua's south coast to WP AN771 before altering course for WP AN772. The course can then be set for WP AN773 to pass west of Barbuda and stay well clear of Anguilla and associated dangers. From there a direct course leads to WP AN774, one mile east of St David's Head in the approaches to the Town Cut which leads into St George's Harbour. This is

Bermuda's only port of entry. The entrance is difficult to negotiate in the dark and those unfamiliar with it should avoid arriving or at least using it at night.

For boats bound for ports south of Cape Hatteras a detour via Bermuda makes little sense. There are two routes which can be sailed to reach any of those ports, either by a direct offshore route (AN77B) or an indirect route passing close to the Bahamas (AN77C). Although the direct route (AN77B) appears to be shorter, it is not necessarily the faster as it cuts diagonally across the zone of calms that will be found north of latitude 25°. Such a direct offshore route should only be attempted if favourable weather conditions are likely to be encountered. In this case, from WP AN773 a course may be set for the port of destination. The suggested alternative (AN77C) is to follow a NW course to windward of both Turks and Caicos and the Bahamas. From Great Abaco the route turns north and picks up the Gulf Stream. Both winds and current are favourable along most of this route. Boats bound for ports in Northern Florida should continue to WP 775 before altering course for their destination.

A direct passage along any of the above routes should not be attempted during the winter months when a slower cruise through the Bahamas to Florida is to be preferred and the US can be reached in a more leisurely way. For boats bound for South Florida there are three alternatives. Between April and June the most direct route passes outside Turks and Caicos as well as the Southern Bahamas as far as Great Abaco. From there the route goes through the NE and NW Providence Channels and crosses the Gulf Stream to Florida. The other two alternatives can be used at any time between November and June, although they cannot be regarded as offshore passages because both consist of island hopping, either right through the Turks and Caicos as well as the Bahamas, or along the northern shores of Puerto Rico, Hispaniola, and Cuba. The high risk of hurricanes must be taken into account if any of these inshore routes is sailed in summer.

AN78 *Lesser Antilles to Bermuda*

BEST TIME:	Mid-April to June
TROPICAL STORMS:	June to November
CHARTS:	BA: 4400
	US: 108
PILOTS:	BA: 70, 71
	US: 140, 147
CRUISING GUIDES:	*Yachting Guide to Bermuda.*
WAYPOINTS:	

Departure	Intermediate	Landfall	Destination	Distance (M)
AN780 Antigua S 16°58'N, 61°45'W	AN781 Antigua West 17°00'N, 61°56'W AN782 17°08'N, 62°00'W AN783 18°25'N, 62°20'W	AN784 David 32°21'N, 64°38'W	St George's *32°22'N, 64°40'W*	973

The favoured point of departure for this route is Antigua's English Harbour, where boats take their leave from the Lesser Antilles and head north for Bermuda as part of a return trip either to Europe or North America. This normally happens at the end of the winter season, when most boats that have been cruising the Eastern Caribbean congregate in or around English Harbour for the annual Antigua Sailing Week.

A departure from Antigua to Bermuda puts a boat more to windward than a departure from the Virgin Islands or Puerto Rico, as described in route AN88 (page 107). The better slant puts one onto a close reach as far as the northern limit of the trade winds, which at the optimum time for this passage can be carried to latitude 26°N or even 28°N. The winds from late April to the middle of June are mostly E to SE for the first half of this passage, becoming lighter farther north. Light southerly winds are sometimes carried right through the Horse Latitudes, but calms are the rule not the exception in the region of the Sargasso Sea. If constant SE winds are carried through, the weather remains clear, otherwise it is cloudy and overcast.

Boats leaving from English Harbour can leave Antigua either to port or starboard. The second alternative is more comfortable for the start of the voyage and so a course should be set to sail west parallel to Antigua's south coast to WP AN781 before altering course for WP AN782. The course can then be set for WP AN783 to pass west of Barbuda and stay well clear of Anguilla and associated dangers. From there, a direct course leads to WP AN784, one mile east of St David's Head in the approaches to the Town Cut which leads into St George's Harbour. This is Bermuda's only port of entry. The entrance is difficult to negotiate in the dark and those unfamiliar with it should avoid arriving or at least using it at night.

For those who are determined to make good time to Bermuda there is no alternative but to motor through the calms that may be encountered and this is definitely advisable later in the season because of the risk of hurricanes. This route is not recommended after the end of June because of the increased likelihood of hurricanes. Passages along this route are definitely discouraged after July as the tracks of past hurricanes almost coincide with the direct course to Bermuda, passing north of the Virgin Islands and running between the US east coast and Bermuda. Tropical depressions become more frequent after the beginning of July and even if they do not generate strong winds, the weather in their vicinity is very unsettled with heavy rain. If such a depression forms close to the northern extremity of the Lesser Antilles, contrary winds can be expected on the way to Bermuda.

This passage can also be done towards the end of the hurricane season, when the frequency of S and SW winds on the way to Bermuda is higher, but so also is the risk of a late hurricane. Fortunately the best time for this route is also the most convenient as it coincides with the end of the safe cruising season in the Caribbean, Antigua Week, and optimum weather for a subsequent passage to either Europe or North America.

AN79 *Lesser Antilles to Azores*

BEST TIME:	May to June				
TROPICAL STORMS:	June to November				
CHARTS:	BA: 4011				
	US: 120				
PILOTS:	BA: 67, 71				
	US: 140, 143, 147				
CRUISING GUIDES:	*Azores Cruising Guide, Atlantic Islands.*				
WAYPOINTS:					
Departure	*Intermediate*	*Landfall*	*Destination*		*Distance (M)*
AN790 Antigua S	AN791 Antigua E	AN792 Faial	Horta		2167
16°58'N, 61°45'W	17°00'N, 61°40'W	38°30'N, 28°47'W	*38°32'N, 28°37.5'W*		
		AN793 Flores	Lajes		2086
		39°20'N, 31°18'W	*39°23'N, 31°10'W*		

For many years yacht captains were not prepared to challenge the accepted wisdom that a return voyage from the Caribbean to Europe should only be attempted along the classic route that passes through Bermuda and the Azores. What started as a devil-may-care route used mostly by delivery crews and skippers of charter boats in a hurry to return to the Mediterranean at the end of the season in the Caribbean, is now attracting cruising boats as well. As the route via Bermuda is at least 500 miles longer than the great circle route from Antigua to Horta, and one cannot even be sure of fair winds for half that voyage via Bermuda, many prefer to stay in warmer weather and hope for the best.

On leaving Antigua, or any other of the Lesser Antilles, a NE course is set, which should be possible to achieve because the trade winds are mostly south of east when this passage is usually made, in May or June. The chances of SE winds increases as one moves north until the belt of calms and light winds is reached which separates the trade winds from the westerlies of higher latitudes. This is the time when a powerful engine and a good reserve of fuel make up for the lack of wind and this is the tactic preferred by those who take this route. With luck, winds on the other side of the Horse Latitudes may be favourable. If this occurs, some people are tempted to bypass the Azores altogether and carry on nonstop to Gibraltar, if bound for the Mediterranean.

The optimum time for this passage is between May and July, although most boats sail this route in May. April is a little too early since the frequency of gales in the Atlantic is still high. After July the frequency of hurricanes increases, making all passages to or from the Caribbean a hazardous affair. If a summer passage is considered, the Caribbean should only be left with a reasonable long term forecast. If no tropical depression is seen to be forming, there is a fairly good chance of not being overtaken by the resulting storm. Taking as a departure point WP AN791, 5 miles east of Antigua's English Harbour, the great circle route is joined immediately unless one has good reason to believe that a different course may have a better chance of favourable winds. If NE winds make it impossible to sail the great circle course, initially one should favour the tack which makes most northing.

The most popular landfall in the Azores continues to be Horta, on the island of Faial, where there is a good marina and entry formalities can be completed. To reach Horta, make landfall at WP AN792, 3 miles SW of Faial and then sail along the south coast of the island before turning north at the conspicuous Mount Guia.

The recently improved port of Lajes, on the westernmost island of Flores, offers the possibility of clearing into the Azores at a point from where it is easier to visit most other islands. Having made landfall at WP AN793, 3 miles SW of Flores, the island's south coast is followed to Lajes.

AN80 ROUTES FROM THE VIRGIN ISLANDS

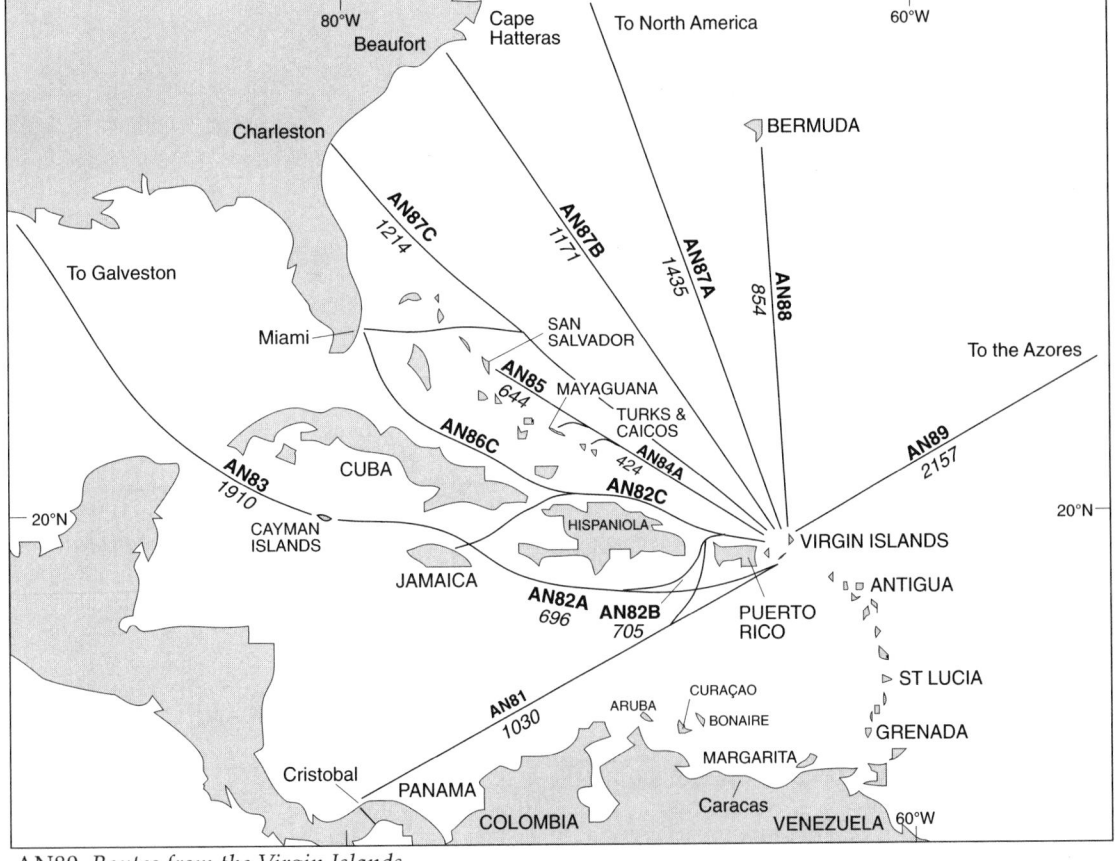

AN80 *Routes from the Virgin Islands*

There are several routes fanning out from the Virgin Islands, particularly from St Thomas, whose excellent facilities are a great attraction to anyone planning to set off on a long ocean passage. The main exodus occurs at the end of the winter season as boats make their way north, usually to Bermuda, either on their way home to North America or back to Europe. Because of their strategic position at the point where the Greater Antilles give way to their lesser sisters, the Virgins are also a favourite starting point for cruises in the area. Most US boats bound for the Eastern Caribbean make their first landfall in the Virgins, from where they start making their way south through the chain of the Lesser Antilles. Some come back for their return passage home, but most carry on their clockwise circuit of the Caribbean rim. In contrast, most European boats arrive in the Virgins at the end of their Caribbean cruise and use the Virgins as a convenient springboard for the continuation of their voyage, most commonly to Bermuda and home, and occasionally to the Bahamas and Florida.

These small islands to the east of Puerto Rico are an extremely popular cruising ground, enjoying very similar weather conditions to the Lesser Antilles. The prevailing wind tends to be easterly, the trade winds being north of east in winter and south of east in summer. The trades are stronger in winter months, around 20 knots, gusting occasionally to over 30 knots. Northers can also affect the islands in winter, although not so frequently nor so strongly as in other areas, such as the Bahamas. The Virgin Islands lie in the hurricane area and they can be affected by tropical storms every year.

AN81 *Virgin Islands to Panama*

BEST TIME:	April to May, November to December				
TROPICAL STORMS:	June to November				
CHARTS:	BA: 4402				
	US: 400				
PILOTS:	BA: 7A, 71				
	US: 147, 148				
CRUISING GUIDES:	*Cruising Guide to Panama, The Panama Guide.*				
WAYPOINTS:					

Departure	Intermediate	Landfall	Destination	Distance (M)
AN810 St Thomas *18°20'N, 64°56'W*	AN811 Vieques 18°00'N, 65°13'W			
	AN814 Manzanillo 9°47'N, 79°32'W	AN815 Panama 9°26.25'N, 79°55'W	Cristobal *9°21'N, 79°55'W*	1030
AN810 St Thomas	AN812 Borinquen 18°35'N, 67°10'W			
	AN813 Mona 18°00'N, 67°40'W			
	AN814 Manzanillo	AN815 Panama	Cristobal	1058

A downwind trip at all times, this passage diagonally across the Caribbean Sea should not be undertaken during the peak months of the hurricane season, between July and October. Another period to be avoided is at the height of the winter trades, between January and the middle of March, when strong winds and high seas are the rule in the Caribbean Sea. Reference should be made to route AN74 (page 91) as directions are similar, with the exception that for those who start off from the Virgin Islands, the recommended stop in the ABC Islands or Venezuela is not applicable unless one wishes to spend some time cruising there.

Boats setting off from St Thomas on the direct route to Panama leave Vieques Island to starboard and take their departure from the Virgins at WP AN811, 10 miles SE of Vieques. Those who prefer to call first at San Juan, Puerto Rico, take a route along the north coast of Puerto Rico to its western extremity and reach the Caribbean Sea through the Mona Passage. From WP AN812, 5 miles NNW of Cape Borinquen, a course can be set through the Mona Passage to WP AN813, ESE of Mona Island. Unless stopping in San Juan, the detour around the north of Puerto Rico should be avoided as it can be windless at the end of winter when the island blocks the winds.

Whichever route is chosen, be it south or north of Puerto Rico, from those waypoints AN811 or AN813 a clear course leads right across the Caribbean Sea to WP AN814 about 10 miles N of Punta Manzanillo and 30 miles from the Panama Canal entrance. The latter is reached by altering course for WP AN815 which is the landfall buoy 3 miles N of the entrance into the port of Cristobal. Traffic Control should be contacted on VHF channel 12, although small boats may enter

if they proceed carefully. Traffic lights control the entrance through the breakwaters and small boats are advised to keep as close as possible to the sides. See page 583 for detailed instructions concerning entry and transit procedure.

Most boats leave the Virgins for Panama in winter and all those who have done this passage in February complain about the rough conditions in the Caribbean Sea. A later start, when the winter trades have lost some of their power, might be preferable, although this may be too late for those planning to continue their voyage along the Pacific coast of Central America and Mexico. For those who are bound for the islands of the South Pacific an early start from the Virgins is not essential, as the seasons there are the opposite to what they are in the Caribbean and a later passage to Panama in April or early May is acceptable.

AN82 *Virgin Islands to Jamaica*

BEST TIME:	April to May, November
TROPICAL STORMS:	June to November
CHARTS:	BA: 4402
	US: 400
PILOTS:	BA: 70, 71
	US: 147
CRUISING GUIDES:	*The Yachtsman's Guide to Jamaica.*
WAYPOINTS:	

Departure	Intermediate	Landfall	Destination	Distance (M)
Route AN82A				
AN820 St Thomas	AN821 Vieques			
18°20'N, 64°56'W	*18°00'N, 65°13'W*			
	AN822 Investigator			
	17°45'N, 66°15'W			
	AN825 Alta Vela			
	17°20'N, 71°40'W			
	AN826 Plumb		Kingston	696
	17°50'N, 76°40'W		*17°58'N, 76°48'W*	
AN820 St Thomas	AN821 Vieques			
	AN822 Investigator			
	AN825 Alta Vela			
	AN827 Northeast		Port Antonio	677
	18°15'N, 76°15'W		*18°11'N, 76°27'W*	
			Montego Bay	761
			18°28'N, 77°56'W'	

WAYPOINTS:				
Departure	*Intermediate*	*Landfall*	*Destination*	*Distance (M)*
Route AN82B				
AN820 St Thomas	AN823 Borinquen			
	18°35'N, 67°10'W			
	AN824 Mona			
	18°00'N, 67°40'W			
	AN825 Alta Vela			
	AN826 Plumb		Kingston	705
AN820 St Thomas	AN823 Borinquen			
	AN824 Mona			
	AN825 Alta Vela			
	AN827 Northeast		Port Antonio	686
			Montego Bay	770

The direct route from St Thomas (AN82A) leaves Vieques Island to starboard, and takes its departure from WP AN821, 10 miles SE of Vieques. Course is then set for WP AN822 to stay well clear of Puerto Rico. Those who prefer to call first at San Juan, Puerto Rico, will reach Mona Passage by sailing along the north coast of Puerto Rico to its western extremity (AN82B). From WP AN823, 5 miles NNW of Cape Borinquen, a course can be set through the Mona Passage to WP AN824, ESE of Mona Island. Both routes will then set course for WP AN825, 10 miles south of Isla Alta Vela, off the southern tip of Hispaniola. From WP AN825 those intending to call at the Jamaican capital Kingston should alter course for WP AN826 off Plumb Point in the approaches to Kingston. Boats bound for ports on the north coast of Jamaica should steer for WP AN827, off Northeast Point, and then make for their port of destination. If bound for the Gulf of Mexico, one of the ports on the north coast of Jamaica will probably be preferable. From WP AN827 a course can be set for either Port Antonio or Ocho Rios, both of which are official ports of entry. At the western extremity of Jamaica lies Montego Bay (18°28'N, 77°56'W), also a port of entry and a convenient port of departure for westbound boats.

An alternative route (AN82C) stays north of both Puerto Rico and Hispaniola and uses the Windward Passage to regain the Caribbean Sea. No waypoints are listed as this route entails mainly coastal cruising. The advantage of the direct routes described earlier is the certainty of better winds, whereas by keeping to the north of the large islands, the trade winds are blocked and one may have to rely on coastal breezes. This is particularly the case in late spring and early summer when the trade winds have a southerly component and therefore Caribbean passages have a much better chance of favourable winds.

As with most trans-Caribbean passages, the best time is the transition months of April–May, before the start of the hurricane season, or November, at the start of the safe sailing season. Generally, favourable winds and currents can be expected along the offshore routes described above.

AN83 *Virgin Islands to the Gulf of Mexico*

BEST TIME:	April to May, November	
TROPICAL STORMS:	June to November	
CHARTS:	BA: 4400	US: 400
PILOTS:	BA: 69A, 70, 71	US: 147
CRUISING GUIDES:	*Cruising Guide to the Caribbean, Cruising Guide to Belize and Mexico's Caribbean Coast, Cruising Guide to the Northwest Caribbean.*	

WAYPOINTS: Departure	Intermediate	Landfall	Destination	Distance (M)
Route AN83A				
AN830 St Thomas	AN831 Vieques			
18°20'N, 64°56'W	18°00'N, 65°13'W			
	AN832 Investigator			
	17°45'N, 66°15'W			
	AN835 Alta Vela			
	17°20'N, 71°40'W			
	AN836 Northeast			
	18°15'N, 76°15'W			
	AN837 Galina			
	18°40'N, 77°00'W			
	AN838 Cayman		Georgetown	978
	19°30'N, 81°20'W		*19°18'N, 81°23'W*	
	AN839 Yucatan		Galveston	1902
	21°45'N, 85°15'W		*29°18'N, 94°48'W*	
Route AN83B				
AN830 St Thomas	AN833 Borinquen			
	18°35'N, 67°10'W			
	AN834 Mona			
	18°00'N, 67°40'W			
	AN835 Alta Vela			
	AN836 Northeast			
	AN837 Galina			
	AN838 Cayman		Georgetown	974
	AN839 Yucatan		Galveston	1910

This is a convenient route for boats sailing to the southern states bordering on the Gulf of Mexico as it is more direct and less difficult than a crossing of the Bahamas. The route between the Virgins and Jamaica is similar to route AN82 and runs parallel to the south coasts of Puerto Rico and Hispaniola. The route then continues north of Jamaica. If a stop in Jamaica is not intended, from WP AN836, off Jamaica's northeast point, a course is set for WP AN837, N of Galina Point. The route then continues in a NW direction and passes between Little and Grand Cayman to WP AN838.

The route passes so close to Grand Cayman that a stop in Georgetown may be considered. If stopping in Georgetown, contact Port Security on VHF channel 16, which is monitored permanently. From Grand Cayman, the route continues towards the Yucatan Channel and WP AN839, off Cuba's Cape San Antonio. Route AN83B lists the waypoints for those preferring to sail along the north coast of

Puerto Rico and the Mona Passage and join the offshore route at WP835 south of Hispaniola.

Boats bound for ports on the north side of the Gulf of Mexico, such as New Orleans, may prefer a route which stays north of all the Greater Antilles. The one distinct disadvantage of this route is the contrary Gulf Stream that will have to be faced north of Cuba. From the navigational point of view, the southern route across the Caribbean Sea, as described above, is easier and also benefits from both better winds and a favourable current for almost its entire length.

The best time for a passage along either route is the transition months of April–May, before the hurricane season, or November before the onset of winter northers which may be felt west of Jamaica and can seriously affect weather in the Gulf of Mexico. Northbound boats occasionally wait for favourable conditions to cross the Gulf of Mexico at Isla Mujeres (21°15'N, 86°45.5'W).

AN84 *Virgin Islands to Turks & Caicos*

BEST TIME:	April to May, November			
TROPICAL STORMS:	June to November			
CHARTS:	BA: 4402			
	US: 400			
PILOTS:	BA: 70, 71			
	US: 147			
CRUISING GUIDES:	*Yachtsman's Guide to the Bahamas, Turks and Caicos Charts.*			
WAYPOINTS:				

Departure	*Intermediate*	*Landfall*	*Destination*	*Distance (M)*
Route AN84A				
AN840 St Thomas	AN841 Culebrita	AN842 Turk	Cockburn Town	404
18°20'N, 64°56'W	18°22'N, 65°08'W	21°35'N, 71°00'W	*21°28'N, 71°06'W*	
			Cockburn Harbour	424
			21°30'N, 71°31'W	
Route AN84B				
AN840 St Thomas	AN841 Culebrita			
	AN843 Borinquen			
	18°35'N, 67°10'W			
	AN844 Mouchoir			
	20°35'N, 71°00'W		Cockburn Town	429
			Cockburn Harbour	438

There is a choice of two routes for this passage. The offshore route AN84A leaves all banks (Navidad, Silver, and Mouchoir) to port and keeps well clear of all dangers. Route AN84B stays south of the banks and runs closer to Puerto Rico. The offshore route is both easier to navigate and benefits more from the favourable current. The best time for passages on either route is at the change of seasons, but even at the height of the winter trades, the only inconvenience will be the occasional strong wind.

On leaving St Thomas, and having cleared Savana Island, off its western extremity, make for WP AN841. From this waypoint, just north of the light on Culebrita Island, route AN84A makes for WP

AN842, 12 miles NE of Grand Turk. The course is altered there to enter Turks Passage and make for Cockburn Town, the main settlement and port of entry on Grand Turk. Alternatively, one may prefer to cross over to Cockburn Harbour, on South Caicos.

The southern route (AN84B) also takes its departure from WP AN841 from where the course leads to WP AN843 off Cape Borinquen. The route then runs in a NW direction south of Navidad and Silver Banks to WP AN844, SW of Mouchoir Bank. From there the course is altered to pass at a safe distance SW of Sandy Cay, at the southern entrance into Turks Passage.

AN85 *Virgin Islands to Bahamas*

BEST TIME:	December to May
TROPICAL STORMS:	June to November
CHARTS:	BA: 4400
	US: 403
PILOTS:	BA: 70, 71
	US: 147
CRUISING GUIDES:	*Yachtsman's Guide to the Bahamas, The Bahamas Cruising Guide.*

WAYPOINTS:				
Departure	*Intermediate*	*Landfall*	*Destination*	*Distance (M)*
Route AN85A				
AN850 St Thomas	AN851 Culebrita			
18°20'N, 64°56'W	18°22'N, 65°08'W			
	AN852 Silver			
	21°10'N, 70°00'W			
	AN853 Caicos			
	22°20'N, 72°10'W			
	AN854 Samana	AN855 Salvador	Cockburn Town	644
	23°10'N, 73°20'W	23°54'N, 74°32'W	*24°03'N, 74°31.5'W*	

To reach the Bahamas from the Virgin Islands one can take either an inshore route, along the north coasts of Puerto Rico and Hispaniola (AN85B), or an offshore route staying outside all islands (AN85A). As the inshore route requires mostly coastal cruising, no waypoints are given. The offshore route (AN85A) is both shorter and faster especially if the destination is in the Northern Bahamas. It follows a NW course parallel to the chain of islands as far as the NE Providence Channel. Whether going offshore immediately on leaving St Thomas, or stopping first in San Juan, Puerto Rico, the course should pass Navidad, Silver, and Mouchoir Banks at a safe distance. The offshore passage can be made at any time outside of the hurricane season. Between December and April, at the height of the winter trades, fair, if strong winds, can be expected as well as the favourable NW setting Antilles Current. Light winds and even calms can be expected at the change of seasons, especially in May. The route can be affected by depressions passing to the north with resulting NW winds.

On leaving St Thomas, and having cleared Savana Island, off its western extremity, from Savana Passage and WP AN851 a course is set for WP AN852, north of Silver Bank. The route continues in a NW direction to WP AN853 off Caicos Passage. The Southern Bahamas can be reached via several deep water passes, all of which are subject to strong currents, as indeed is the entire area of the Bahamas. The nearest island to clear into the Bahamas is Mayaguana, whose eastern point should be given a wide berth to avoid the reefs surrounding it. Although Abrams Bay, the main settlement on the south coast of the island, is not an official port of entry, boats are allowed to stop there provided they complete formalities in the first official port of entry. The nearest is Cockburn Town on the island of San Salvador. If continuing on the offshore route, course for the latter should not be set until one is well clear of Samana Cay, a low unlit island lying between Mayaguana and San Salvador. From WP AN853 the course should be altered for WP AN854 east of Samana. From there a course can be set for WP AN855.

After landfall is made at WP AN855, 5 miles SE of Sandy Point, the SW extremity of San Salvador, the west of the island should be passed at a safe distance before approaching the main settlement at Cockburn Town. Entry formalities can be completed there, or at the airport, where the officials are based. There is an anchorage off the settlement or a small marina one mile further north. Riding Rock Marina has a difficult entrance with a maximum depth of 7 ft at high tide. The GPS latitude of the entrance channel into the small marina has been reported as 24°03.4'N. The marina can be contacted on VHF channel 6.

AN86 *Virgin Islands to Florida*

BEST TIME:	November to May			
TROPICAL STORMS:	June to November			
CHARTS:	BA: 4400			
	US: 403			
PILOTS:	BA: 69, 70, 71			
	US: 140,147			
CRUISING GUIDES:	*Cruising Guide to Eastern Florida.*			
Departure	*Intermediate*	*Landfall*	*Destination*	*Distance (M)*
Route AN86A				
AN860 St Thomas	AN861 Culebrita			
18°20'N, 64°56'W	18°22'N, 65°08'W			
	AN863 Abaco			
	26°50'N, 76°30'W			
	AN864 Bahama		St Augustine	1134
	27°30'N, 78°00'W		*29°55'N, 81°16'W*	
Route AN86B				
AN860 St Thomas	AN861 Culebrita			
	AN862 Providence		Fort Lauderdale	974
	25°40'N, 76°50'W		*26°05.5'N, 80°06'W*	

For boats bound for Florida there are several alternative routes to choose from. Between April and June, the most direct route runs in a NW direction parallel to the Turks and Caicos Islands as well as the Bahamas as far as Great Abaco (AN86A). This offshore route benefits from strong winds throughout the winter months and also the favourable Antilles Current. More benign conditions will be experienced at the change of seasons, in April and May. Directions for this route are similar to those for both AN85 and AN87C to which reference should be made. Boats bound for ports in South Florida can follow route AN86A as far as Great Abaco island where route AN86B branches off through the NE and NW Providence Channels and crosses the Gulf Stream to Florida.

The other alternatives consist of island hopping, either right through Turks and Caicos and the Bahamas, or along the northern shores of Puerto Rico, Hispaniola, and Cuba (AN86C). In the latter case, Florida is reached through the Old Bahama Channel, south of the Great Bahama Bank. Both these routes can be used at any time from November to June, but as they cannot be regarded as offshore passages they are not described in detail, nor are there any waypoints listed.

AN87 *Virgin Islands to North America*

BEST TIME:	Late April to June (offshore)
	December to May (via Bahamas)
TROPICAL STORMS:	June to November
CHARTS:	BA: 4403
	US: 403
PILOTS:	BA: 69, 70, 71
	US: 140, 147
CRUISING GUIDES:	*Coastal Cruising Guide to the Atlantic Coast.*

WAYPOINTS:

Departure	Intermediate	Landfall	Destination	Distance (M)
Route AN87A				
AN870 St Thomas	AN871 Culebrita	AN872 Brenton	Newport	1435
18°20'N, 64°56'W	18°22'N, 65°08'W	41°24'N, 71°16'W	*41°29'N, 71°20'W*	
		AN873 Chesapeake		1249
		36°45'N, 75°45'W		
Route AN87B				
AN870 St Thomas	AN871 Culebrita	AN874 off Beaufort	Beaufort	1171
		34°30'N, 76°40'W	*34°43'N, 76°40'W*	
Route AN87C				
AN870 St Thomas	AN871 Culebrita			
	AN875 Abaco		Charleston	1214
	26°50'N, 76°30'W		*32°44'N, 79°50'W*	

The end of the winter sailing season in the Eastern Caribbean is the time when most boats set off on this passage, which is also the time when best conditions can be expected for most of the way. On the direct route (AN87A), which does not call at Bermuda, favourable winds can be expected as far as the northern limit of the trade winds. Southerly winds occasionally last right through the zone of calms that extends between latitudes 25°N and 30°N. The temptation to ride the Gulf Stream should be resisted if this passage is made early in the season to avoid being caught by a late norther. For boats bound for ports to the north of Cape Hatteras similar directions apply as for route AN88 and in fact many people prefer to break the voyage in Bermuda and reach the more distant ports on the US east coast or even Canada that way.

For boats bound for ports south of Cape Hatteras a detour via Bermuda is not justified. They have a choice of either a slightly indirect route (AN87C) or the direct route AN87B, which follows a rhumb line from the Virgins to the US east coast.

Although this route is undoubtedly the shortest, as it is the most direct, it may not be the quickest as it cuts diagonally across the zone of calms that will be found north of latitude 25°.

Boats taking route AN87C will sail on a NW course parallel to the Turks and Caicos and Bahamas as far as the Abacos before heading for their destination. On leaving St Thomas, and having cleared Savana Island, off its western extremity, from WP AN871 a direct course, which keeps well outside all dangers, can be set for WP AN875, north of Great Abaco. From there the route turns north and enters the Gulf Stream. Both winds and current are favourable along most of this route.

Whichever alternative is chosen, the optimum time for leaving the Virgins also coincides with the end of the safe cruising season in the Eastern Caribbean. A direct passage along any of the above routes should not be attempted during the winter months when a slower cruise through the Bahamas to Florida is to be preferred and US ports can be reached in a more leisurely way.

AN88 *Virgin Islands and Puerto Rico to Bermuda*

BEST TIME:	Late April to June
TROPICAL STORMS:	June to November
CHARTS:	BA: 4403
	US: 108
PILOTS:	BA: 70, 71
	US: 140, 147
CRUISING GUIDES:	*Yachting Guide to Bermuda.*
WAYPOINTS:	

Departure	Intermediate	Landfall	Destination	Distance (M)
AN880 St Thomas 18°20'N, 64°56'W	AN881 Culebrita 18°22'N, 65°08'W	AN883 David 32°21'N, 64°38'W	St George's *32°22'N, 64°40'W*	854
AN882 Puerto Rico 18°29'N, 66°07'W		AN883 David	St George's	865

Bermuda provides an attractive stop for boats sailing from the Virgins or Puerto Rico to either Europe or the US east coast. Best conditions on this route, which crosses the Horse Latitudes, will be found in late spring or early summer. At this time of year the trade winds are more E or SE in direction than in winter. Even if the winds blow from the NE, it does not matter if one is pushed slightly to the west of the desired course, because the further north one goes, the greater likelihood there is of a shift of wind to the SE or even S. If favourable winds are not found the ground lost to the west can be regained, by motoring through the calms. North of the zone of calms, the winds become variable, with a predominance of S or SW winds and only rarely N winds. The danger of a winter norther is minimal after the middle of April when most passages are made on this route. Generally, the best conditions are encountered in May. This route is not recommended after the end of June because of the increased frequency of hurricanes. Those who are determined to make good time to Bermuda should be prepared to motor if they encounter any calms. This advice should be followed especially later in the season when there is a higher risk of being caught by a hurricane and one should not dally too long in this area. Summer passages along this route are definitely discouraged as the tracks of past hurricanes almost coincide with the direct course to Bermuda. Tropical depressions become more frequent after the beginning of July and even if they do not generate strong winds, the weather in their vicinity is very unsettled with heavy rain. If such a depression forms close to the Virgin Islands, contrary winds can be expected on the way to Bermuda.

Boats leaving from St Thomas usually reach the open sea through Savana Passage, west of the island. From WP AN881 a direct course leads all the way to Bermuda where landfall is made at WP AN883. If leaving from Puerto Rico, from WP AN882 a course can be set for the same WP AN883, one mile east of St David's Head in the approaches to the Town Cut. This leads into St George's Harbour, which is Bermuda's only port of entry. The entrance through Town Cut is difficult to negotiate in the dark and those unfamiliar with it should avoid using it at night.

AN89 *Virgin Islands to Azores*

BEST TIME:	May to June			
TROPICAL STORMS:	June to November			
CHARTS:	BA: 4012			
	US: 120			
PILOTS:	BA: 67, 71			
	US: 140, 143, 147			
CRUISING GUIDES:	*Azores Cruising Guide, Atlantic Islands.*			
WAYPOINTS:				

Departure	Intermediate	Landfall	Destination	Distance (M)
AN890 St Thomas		AN891 Faial	Horta	2245
18°20'N, 64°56'W		38°30'N, 28°50'W	*38°32'N, 28°37.5'W*	
		AN892 Flores	Lajes	2157
		39°20'N, 31°18'W	*39°23'N, 31°10'W*	

Because of the extensive area of variable winds that lies across the direct route to the Azores, the recommended route across the Atlantic leads first in a NE direction into an area of prevailing westerly winds. As such a route passes close to Bermuda, most boats taking it usually stop there before continuing the voyage to the Azores. Directions for those routes are found on pages 107 and 143 (routes AN88 and AN125).

Although considerably shorter, the great circle route can seldom be sailed for its entire length and a good supply of fuel should be carried so as to motor through the almost unavoidable areas of calms. In spring and early summer, the winds as far as latitude 26°N or 28°N will be south of east. Further north they will become light and variable, with prolonged calms a strong possibility. The optimum time for a direct passage is between May and July. April is probably too early as the frequency of gales in the Atlantic is still high. After July the frequency of hurricanes increases and if a summer passage is considered, the Caribbean should only be left with a reasonable long term forecast. If no tropical depression is seen to be forming in the area, there is a fairly good chance of not being overtaken by the resulting storm.

Intermediate waypoints cannot be given as the route sailed will depend entirely on the winds encountered. The most popular landfall in the Azores continues to be Horta, on the island of Faial, where there is a good marina and entry formalities can be completed. To reach Horta, landfall is made at WP AN891, 3 miles SW of Faial. The island's south coast is followed before turning north at the conspicuous Mount Guia.

The recently improved port of Lajes, on the westernmost island of Flores, offers the possibility of clearing into the Azores earlier. Having made landfall at WP AN892, 3 miles SW of Flores, the island's south coast is followed to Lajes.

AN90 CARIBBEAN ROUTES FROM PANAMA

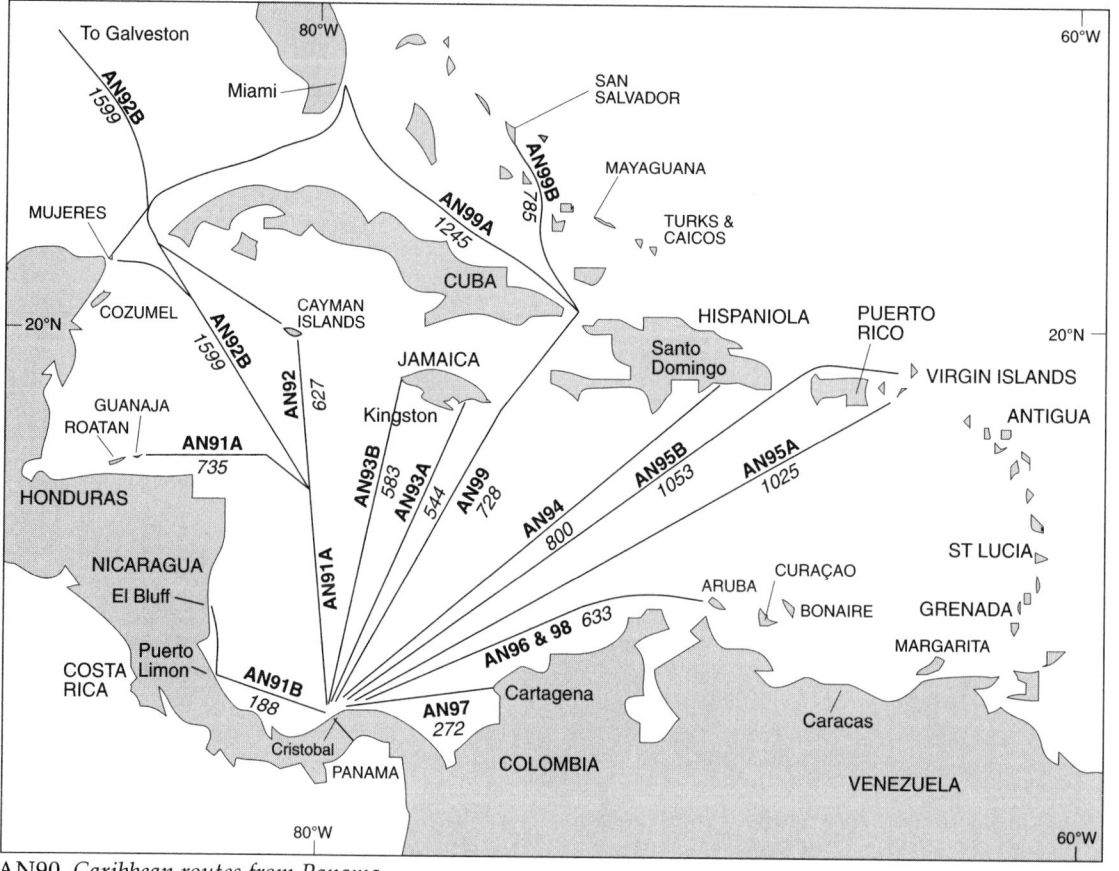

AN90 *Caribbean routes from Panama*

Most routes in the Caribbean Sea either start or end in Panama, and because they have many features in common it is worth considering them together. Because of the multitude of destinations, the routes are difficult to define, although there are certain considerations that have to be taken into account whichever route is contemplated. Most of these considerations are closely related to weather, and passages through the Caribbean are discouraged during the hurricane season, especially during the months of highest frequency, from August to October. Some of the late hurricanes actually form in the Caribbean and warnings are therefore shorter than when the depression has been tracked across the Atlantic. Rough weather can also be experienced in the Western Caribbean at the height of the winter trades, whereas in the Gulf of Mexico winter is associated with violent northerly storms. Another concern in the Gulf of Mexico are the strong currents whose direction is often different to that depicted on charts.

The entire area is affected by winter northers, although these winter storms gradually decrease in intensity further south and are not so strong south of Honduras. However, these northers, combined with strong NE trade winds can result in very strong winds described as intensified trades in the most southerly portion of the Caribbean Sea. From November to March the winds off the coast of Central America tend to be more northerly than the northeasterlies which prevail at other times of the year. This coast is particularly affected by land and sea breezes. The sea breeze commences from the NE in mid-morning and gradually increases, drawing around to the E between mid-afternoon and sunset. The breeze carries on moving around clockwise until in the night it blows moderately from the SE. In the more southern coastal areas this land breeze can become W and SW. The summer rainy season is characterised by squally weather especially in the late afternoon. It is rarely calm and a similar pattern of land and sea breezes prevails as in the winter.

Eastbound passages from Panama can be very difficult at most times of the year, because of the prevailing direction of the winds and current. Many people are tempted to make this passage late in the year so as to arrive in the Lesser Antilles during the hurricane-free season. In such a case, the eastward passage must be made before the onset of the strong winter trades. Better and more comfortable passages have been made in late spring or early summer, although this has the disadvantage of arriving in the Lesser Antilles at the beginning of the hurricane season. In order to make this passage at the best time, and also avoid the hurricane season, there are two options. If the Panama Canal cannot be transited before winter it is better to wait until April or May and then head for Venezuela and the islands to the north of it. As this area is mostly outside the hurricane zone it is safe to cruise there until November when the voyage can be continued to the Lesser Antilles. If the Canal is transited in late October or early November and the trade winds are already too strong to attempt a direct passage, it may be worth approaching the Lesser Antilles from the north, by sailing first to the Virgin Islands via Puerto Rico. This latter course of action will depend greatly on the windward performance of the boat, as most of the passage will be hard on the wind. An easier option would be to reach the Eastern Caribbean in shorter stages, either by following the north coast of South America via the San Blas Islands, Colombia, the ABC islands, and Venezuela, or to take a northern sweep via the Dominican Republic and Puerto Rico. Whichever alternative is chosen, the onward passage from Panama should be carefully planned to avoid being immobilised in Panama while waiting for the trade winds to subside.

AN91 *Panama to Central America*

BEST TIME:	November, mid-April to June			
TROPICAL STORMS:	June to November			
CHARTS:	BA: 4402			
	US: 402			
PILOTS:	BA: 7A, 69A			
	US: 148			
CRUISING GUIDES:	*Cruising Guide to the Northwest Caribbean, Cruising Guide to Belize and Mexico's Caribbean Coast, Cruising Guide to the Caribbean, Cruising Guide to the Rio Dulce.*			
WAYPOINTS:				

Departure	Intermediate	Landfall	Destination	Distance (M)
Route AN91A				
AN910 Panama	AN911 Roncador			
9°26'N, 79°55'W	13°30'N, 79°40'W			
	AN912 Serrana			
	14°25'N, 79°47'W			
	AN913			
	15°35'N, 81°30'W			
	AN914 Gorda			
	16°00'N, 82°05'W			
	AN915 Hobbies		Guanaja	735
	16°10'N, 83°10'W		*16°28'N, 85°54'W*	
			Coxen Hole	773
			16°18'N, 86°35'W	
			Livingston	898
			15°50.5'N, 88°43.5'W	
			Belize City	875
			17°30'N, 88°10'W	

WAYPOINTS:				
Departure	*Intermediate*	*Landfall*	*Destination*	*Distance (M)*
Route AN91B				
AN910 Panama			Puerto Limon	188
			10°00'N, 83°03'W	
			El Bluff	273
			12°01'N, 83°44'W	

On leaving the Panama Canal area there are two alternatives, either a direct offshore route to the north of Honduras (AN91A), or an indirect route for those who intend to cruise on their way through Honduras, Belize, or other parts of Central America (AN91B).

The more direct offshore route requires careful navigation, especially at the beginning, because of the numerous banks and cays that lie off the coast of Central America. From WP AN910, off the entrance into the Panama Canal, the course goes due north to WP AN911, 20 miles east of Roncador Bank. A northerly course will be maintained to the next WP AN912 to pass at a safe distance east of Serrana Bank. From there, a NW course for WP AN913 follows a relatively deeper channel. Boats bound for the Bay Islands of Honduras or beyond, from WP AN913 should set a course for WP AN914, 20 miles ENE of Gorda Cay. As this course leads over some shallow spots it should only be taken if the weather is not too rough, otherwise the seas breaking over the banks can make conditions hazardous. The course from Gorda Cay passes north of Hobbies Cays through WP AN915, from where a clear course leads to the islands of Guanaja or Roatan (Coxen Hole), both of which have ports where entry formalities into Honduras can be completed.

Boats bound for Guatemala's Rio Dulce can clear into that country at Livingston. From the Bay Islands, the route continues into the Gulf of Honduras. A shallow bar at the river entrance has to be negotiated to reach Livingston, and this is best done at high tide. The landfall buoy has been reported in position 15°50.5'N, 88°43.5'W.

The extensive cruising grounds of Belize are easily reached from the Bay Islands. Boats normally clear into Belize at Belize City.

The alternative inshore route (AN91B) follows the Mosquito Coast of Nicaragua and Honduras. On leaving the Panama Canal, a first stop can be made in Costa Rica's Puerto Limon. If continuing along the coast to Nicaragua, the official port of entry there is El Bluff.

Those who take the offshore route on leaving Panama can stop at either San Andres or Providencia, two islands just north of Panama which belong to Colombia. The GPS coordinates of the landfall buoy off Puerto Isabel, on Providencia, have been reported as 13°24'N, 81°23.6'W. However, if conditions are unfavourable or visibility poor, it is strongly recommended to take the offshore route described earlier and stay well clear of all dangers.

The cruising grounds of Honduras, Guatemala, and Belize can be explored before rejoining the offshore route which continues to the Gulf of Mexico as described in AN92.

AN92 *Panama to the Gulf of Mexico and Florida*

BEST TIME:	November, mid-April to June
TROPICAL STORMS:	June to November
CHARTS:	BA: 4400
	US: 400, 401
PILOTS:	BA: 7A, 69A, 70
	US: 147, 148
CRUISING GUIDES:	*Cruising Guide to the Northwest Caribbean, Cruising Guide to Belize and Mexico's Caribbean Coast, Cruising Guide to the Florida Keys.*

WAYPOINTS:				
Departure	Intermediate	Landfall	Destination	Distance (M)
Route AN92A				
AN920 Panama	AN921 Roncador			
9°26'N, 79°55'W	13°30'N, 79°40'W			
	AN922 Serrana			
	14°25'N, 79°47'W			
	AN923 Cayman		Georgetown	627
	19°23'N, 81°27'W		19°18'N, 81°23'W	
Route AN92B				
AN920 Panama	AN924 Sueno			
	14°20'N, 80°45'W			
	AN923 Cayman		Georgetown	610
	19°23'N, 81°27'W			
AN920 Panama	AN924 Sueno	AN925 Swan		
		17°25'N, 85°50'W		
		AN926 Sur	Isla Mujeres	881
		21°10'N, 86°42'W	21°15'N, 86°45.5'W	
		AN927 Yucatan	Galveston	1599
		21°50'N, 85°10'W	29°18'N, 94°48'W	

As the direct route from Panama to the Gulf of Mexico passes close to a number of attractive cruising grounds, the voyage can be interrupted in any of these Central American destinations, as described in AN91. Northbound passages to the Yucatan Channel can be made either nonstop, albeit through an area encumbered by dangers, or can be interrupted at either Grand Cayman or Swan Island.

As in the case of all Caribbean passages, the timing for this route is crucial. Apart from the risk of being caught by a hurricane, especially from July to October, many boats have got into difficulty when hit by a strong norther in the Gulf of Mexico. The whole area is affected by northers from November until the beginning of April and their effect can be felt as far south as Panama, although their strength is greatly diminished by the time the winds reach those latitudes. The violent conditions produced by the northerly wind blowing against the strong currents in the Gulf have caused boats to capsize or even founder. The best time to make this passage is from the middle of April to the end of June, when there is a reasonable chance of winds with a southerly component. Northbound passages can also be made from late October to early December, but the weather must be watched more carefully. Both periods avoid the worst of the winter northers and fall outside the months with a high frequency of hurricanes. If the passage is made in winter, it is recommended to wait until immediately after a norther, when light conditions may be expected for a few days.

In the summer the prevailing winds are from the SE and the weather is rainy with heavy squalls and calm periods. From April to July land and sea breezes alternate along the south coast of the USA. The Gulf is one of the areas most affected by hurricanes between June and November, being threatened both by tropical storms that form in the Gulf itself and those travelling from other areas of the Caribbean. From September to November hurricanes spawned in the Western Caribbean are most likely to pass through the Yucatan Channel and then curve around north and east towards Cuba and Florida. Tornadoes, waterspouts, and arched squalls are also a feature of the hurricane season.

The prevailing winds in the Western Caribbean are NE to E, with a southern component making itself felt north of Yucatan. The currents along this route set in a NW direction attaining their strongest rate in the Yucatan Channel. The sets in the Gulf of Mexico are complex and difficult to predict, particularly in the area of the Dry Tortugas where extreme caution should be exercised.

Northbound boats have a choice of two routes, one which stays well offshore of all dangers and is more attractive to those intending to stop at Grand Cayman (AN92A), and a slightly shorter route taking a more direct course to the Yucatan Channel (AN92B). From WP AN920, north of the Panama Canal entrance, route AN92A goes due north to WP AN921, 20 miles east of Roncador Bank. The northerly course will be maintained to the next WP AN922 east of Serrana Bank. From there, a course is set for WP AN923 off Grand Cayman. On arrival off Georgetown contact Port Security on VHF channel 16, which is monitored permanently.

Boats taking route AN92B, from WP AN920 should set a course for WP AN924, halfway between Sueno and Serrana Banks, both of which have lights. From there, boats that have decided to stop at Grand Cayman should alter course almost due north over a shallow bank to WP AN923, off the NW extremity of Grand Cayman. From there, the course turns east to reach the capital Georgetown. Rather than stop in Grand Cayman, another convenient stop on the way to the Yucatan Channel is at Swan Island. If such a stop is considered, from WP AN924 the course is altered to pass over Gorda Bank to WP AN925 off Swan Island's eastern point. Going north from Swan Island, one can either head straight for the Yucatan Channel or make another stop at Isla Mujeres, which is a favourite place at which to wait for favourable conditions to cross the Gulf of Mexico. To call at Isla Mujeres, set a course for WP AN926, SE of Punta Sur, at the island's SE extremity. Isla Mujeres is an official port of entry into Mexico. If no stops are intended anywhere en route, from WP AN924, a course should be set for WP AN927 off Cuba's Cape San Antonio, which marks the eastern side of the Yucatan Channel.

Whether sailing nonstop or planning to visit some places on the way, this route has many attractions for boats bound for US ports in the Gulf of Mexico as well as on both coasts of Florida. Other routes, such as AN93, should be considered for more northern destinations on the east coast of the USA.

AN93 *Panama to Jamaica*

BEST TIME:	April to June, November			
TROPICAL STORMS:	June to November			
CHARTS:	BA: 4012			
	US: 124			
PILOTS:	BA: 7A, 70			
	US: 140, 147, 148			
CRUISING GUIDES:	*The Yachtsman's Guide to Jamaica.*			
WAYPOINTS:				
Departure	*Intermediate*	*Landfall*	*Destination*	*Distance (M)*
Route AN93A				
AN930 Panama	AN931 Plumb		Kingston	544
9°26'N, 79°55'W	17°45'N, 76°50'W		*17°58'N, 76°48'W*	
Route AN93B				
AN930 Panama	AN932 Serranilla			
	I5°50'N, 79°17'W			
	AN933 Pedro	AN934 Negril NW	Montego Bay	583
	17°20'N, 79°05'W	18°25'N, 78°30'W	*18°28'N, 77°56'W*	

Navigation in the central Caribbean Sea is made difficult by the large number of banks, reefs, and shoals, aggravated by the strong west-setting current. Because of this current, a direct course for Jamaica leads dangerously close to the New Bank and Pedro Bank and adequate allowance should be made for leeway when setting a course to windward of them. Both these banks can be very dangerous in heavy weather and their vicinity should be avoided. From Panama and WP AN930 the direct route (AN93A) passes east of the various banks to WP AN931 south of Plumb Point, in the approaches to the Jamaican capital Kingston.

Boats bound for the NW coast of Jamaica, such as Montego Bay, should sail a more western route that stays east of Roncador, Serrana and Serranilla Banks (AN93B) before course is altered to pass to the west of the extensive shallows of Pedro Bank to make landfall off Negril Point at Jamaica's western extremity. Montego Bay has the best facilities and most active sailing community in Jamaica. The local yacht club is the host to a number of international races and visiting boats are always welcome.

AN94 *Panama to Hispaniola*

BEST TIME:	May to June, November				
TROPICAL STORMS:	June to November				
CHARTS:	BA: 4402				
	US: 402				
PILOTS:	BA: 7A, 70				
	US: 147, 148				
CRUISING GUIDES:	*Cruising Guide to the Caribbean.*				
WAYPOINTS:					
Departure	*Intermediate*	*Landfall*		*Destination*	*Distance (M)*
AN940 Panama	AN941 Palenque	AN942 Domingo		Santo Domingo	800
9°26'N, 79°55'W	18°05'N, 70°00'W	18°23'N, 69°54'W		*18°28'N, 69°53'W*	

Because the prevailing winds in the Caribbean Sea are NE or E, all destinations on this route are to windward of Panama for most of the year. Unless there is a shift of wind to the south, it would be better to follow directions as for route AN93B and then work one's way eastward along the south coast of Hispaniola with the help of land breezes. Close inshore there is sometimes an east-setting current. Boats bound for the north coast of Haiti and Dominican Republic should follow the same directions as for route AN93B as far as the Windward Passage.

From WP AN940 outside the entrance to the Panama Canal, a direct course leads right across the Caribbean Sea to WP AN941, 10 miles SSE of Punta Palenque. The course is altered there for WP AN942 in the approaches to Santo Domingo, the Dominican capital.

AN95 *Panama to Virgin Islands*

BEST TIME:	May to June, November
TROPICAL STORMS:	June to November
CHARTS:	BA: 4402
	US: 402
PILOTS:	BA: 7A, 70
	US: 147, 148
CRUISING GUIDES:	*Cruising Guide to the Virgin Islands, Yachtsman's Guide to the Virgin Islands.*
WAYPOINTS:	

Departure	Intermediate	Landfall	Destination	Distance (M)
Route AN95A				
AN950 Panama	AN951 Manzanillo	AN952 Vieques	Charlotte Amalie	1025
9°26'N, 79°55'W	9°47'N, 79°32'W	18°00'N, 65°13'W	*18°20'N, 64°56'W*	
Route AN95B				
AN950 Panama	AN951 Manzanillo			
	AN953 Mona			
	18°00'N, 67°40'W			
	AN954 Borinquen		Charlotte Amalie	1053
	18°35'N, 67°10'W			

This is a difficult route throughout the year on account of the prevailing winds and the west-setting current. The direct route offers two alternatives, either south of Puerto Rico (AN95A), or via the Mona Passage and north of Puerto Rico (AN95B). On both those routes the initial course has to clear Manzanillo Point at WP AN951 before a clear course can be set diagonally across the Caribbean Sea. Boats bound directly for St Thomas will make their landfall at WP AN952, off Vieques Island, east of Puerto Rico. Boats preferring to sail around the north coast of Puerto Rico will make their landfall at WP AN953 at the entrance into the Mona Passage. The route then swings around the NW point of Puerto Rico at WP AN954 from where it runs parallel to the north coast as far as St Thomas.

These two direct routes have a better chance of favourable conditions in early summer, when SE winds are not uncommon. Lighter winds may be experienced at the change of seasons, another time when this passage can be attempted. At all other times two radically different routes offer more attractive alternatives. Depending on the time of year, it might be better to sail route AN93 through the Windward Passage and then turn east along the north coasts of Hispaniola and Puerto Rico. Another possibility is to sail as close to the wind as possible to the south coast of Hispaniola and then continue to the Virgins by either staying south of Puerto Rico or going north of the island through the Mona Passage. See also route AN94.

As none of the above alternatives should be attempted during the hurricane season, a more drastic alternative may have to be contemplated entailing a lengthy detour through the Southern Caribbean. Such a route has the attraction that it can be sailed at almost any time of the year. This entails a detour to Venezuela and the islands off the Venezuelan coast and offers the possibility of spending the summer in this safer area before heading north at the end of the hurricane season. Routes AN97 and AN98 have more details.

AN96 *Panama to Lesser Antilles*

BEST TIME:	April to May, November
TROPICAL STORMS:	June to November
CHARTS:	BA: 4402
	US: 402
PILOTS:	BA: 7A, 70
	US: 147, 148
CRUISING GUIDES:	*The Lesser Antilles, Cruising Guide to the Caribbean, Sailor's Guide to the Windward Islands, Cruising Guide to the Leeward Islands.*

This can be a very rough trip as the direct passage is to windward all the way. It is a challenge that is faced by all those who intend to head east after transiting the Panama Canal. Because of the sheer difficulty of reaching the Eastern Caribbean nonstop, most boats break up the voyage into shorter stages by stopping at some places on the way. Some call in first at the San Blas Islands, for which the compulsory cruising permit should be obtained before leaving Cristobal. An additional permit must be obtained on arrival in Porvenir, which is an obligatory stop for those wishing to cruise the San Blas Islands. Whether calling at the San Blas Islands or not, a further stop can be made in Colombia. The next stop could be the island of Aruba, unless one is prepared to sail nonstop to the Lesser Antilles, a task which is not easily accomplished because of the contrary wind and current along the Venezuelan coast.

The best time for a passage along a southern route is between June and August, when the trade winds are less consistent in both strength and direction than in winter. October and November, the other two months when one can expect lighter winds, are still in the hurricane season, and although Venezuela and the offlying islands are mostly outside the hurricane belt, conditions in the Western Caribbean can become extremely uncomfortable if a hurricane is passing farther to the east or north. The worst time to do this passage is at the height of the winter trades, from January to early April.

The eastbound passage through Venezuelan waters should be made as close inshore as possible to take advantage of both land and sea breezes and a favourable current that runs close to the coast. At night the trade winds usually die away and this is the time to sail inshore to use the land breeze. A boat which sails well to windward can take an offshore tack during the day and head for the shore before nightfall. In this way Grenada can be reached in short hops and from there any of the other islands in the Eastern Caribbean. The first stage of an eastbound voyage is described in detail in route AN97. An alternative way of reaching islands in the NE Caribbean is described in route AN95.

AN97 *Panama to Colombia*

BEST TIME:	April to June, November
TROPICAL STORMS:	June to November
CHARTS:	BA: 4402
	US: 402
PILOTS:	BA: 7A
	US: 148
CRUISING GUIDES:	*Cruising Guide to the Caribbean.*
WAYPOINTS:	

Departure	Intermediate	Landfall	Destination	Distance (M)
AN970 Panama 9°26'N, 79°55'W	AN971 Manzanillo W 9°48'N, 79°35'W	AN972 off Cartagena 10°20'N, 75°45'W	Cartagena *10°25'N, 75°32'W*	272

Reaching the Atlantic coast of Colombia from neighbouring Panama is not easily accomplished at any time of the year on account of the contrary wind and strong current. A convenient stop en route is the San Blas Islands, which belong to Panama. The route then cuts across the Gulf of Darien to Cartagena, an attractive historic town, which has become the most popular port of call among cruising boats visiting Colombia. From WP AN970, at the entrance to the Panama Canal, a first course should be set for WP AN971, 10 miles N of Punta Manzanillo. The course is then altered for WP AN972 in the approaches to the port of Cartagena. The area should be approached with cau-

tion because of the dangers in the approaches to Cartagena. Also avoided should be the silted Boca Grande as the dredged entrance is Boca Chica, identified by a landfall buoy, close to the end of Isla de Tierra Bomba. An 8 mile long channel leads northward through the shallow Bahia de Cartagena to the commercial port and two marinas. The port lies on the banks of the River Magdalena and approaches are very difficult. Arriving yachts are advised to contact Club Nautico on channel 16 for clearance and docking information. The GPS position of the orange and white entrance buoy has been reported at 10°18.97'N, 75°35.98'W.

AN98 *Panama to Venezuela and the ABC Islands*

BEST TIME:	April to June, November
TROPICAL STORMS:	June to November
CHARTS:	BA: 4402
	US: 402
PILOTS:	BA: 7A, 71
	US: 148
CRUISING GUIDES:	*Cruising Guide to the Caribbean, Cruising Guide to Venezuela and Bonaire.*
WAYPOINTS:	

Departure	Intermediate	Landfall	Destination	Distance (M)
AN980 Panama	AN981 Gallinas	AN982 Aruba	Oranjestad	633
9°26'N, 79°55'W	13°00'N, 71°40'W	12°35'N, 70°05'W	*12°30'N, 70°02'W*	

Those who do not intend to stop in Colombia are faced with a long offshore tack to WP AN981, 30 miles north of Punta de Gallinas. Having reached that point, a first stop can be made in Aruba, where Port Control should be contacted on VHF channel 16 for berthing and clearance instructions before entering Oranjestad.

The above course is difficult, if not impossible, to hold against the prevailing NE or E winds of winter and this passage is better attempted at the change of seasons. Light winds and even calms occur sometimes in November, and if one is prepared to use the engine good progress can be made while favourable conditions last. Better conditions may be encountered early in summer, when a southern component in the trade winds may provide some help in one's tacking efforts.

At all other times there is unfortunately no alternative to a hard beat to windward and the undisputed difficulty of this route must be seriously considered before including it in one's overall cruising plans. A direct nonstop route eastwards

from Panama is extremely difficult because of both adverse winds and current, which can set westwards at up to 2 knots. At the height of the trade wind season the winds themselves often blow at force 7 or even 8 and this combined with the current makes progress almost impossible. The logical solution is to cover this section in short cruising stages by sailing first to the San Blas Islands, then Cartagena in Colombia (see route AN97), where to wait for a favourable change in the weather. Occasionally the predominantly easterly winds will have enough north in them to allow some short tacks along the Colombian coast. Such tacks should be very short so as to keep out of the strength of the main west-setting current and also benefit from some shelter from the swell. Detailed coastal charts will be needed as well as both a boat capable of beating to windward and a crew prepared to put up with the hard going.

A different way for boats to reach Venezuela and the ABC Islands is to reserve them for the end of a Caribbean cruise. In such a case, it is both easier and more comfortable to sail north on leaving Panama by following the directions for one of the northbound routes and eventually reach Venezuela from the north and Lesser Antilles. See routes AN94 and AN95 for more details.

AN99 *Panama to Bahamas and USA*

BEST TIME:	April to June, November
TROPICAL STORMS:	June to November
CHARTS:	BA: 4012
	US: 124
PILOTS:	BA: 7A, 70
	US: 140, 147, 148
CRUISING GUIDES:	*The Yachtsman's Guide to Jamaica.*
WAYPOINTS:	

Departure	Intermediate	Landfall	Destination	Distance (M)
Route AN99A				
AN990 Panama	AN991 Morant			
9°26'N, 79°55'W	17°15'N, 75°32'W			
	AN992 Navassa W			
	18°25'N, 75°16'W			
	AN993 Maisi			
	20°12'N, 73°55'W			
	AN994 Diamond			
	22°07'N, 77°18'W			
	AN995 Santaren SE	AN996 Coral	Miami	1245
	22°58'N, 78°48'W	25°44'N, 80°02'W	*25°47'N, 80°10'W*	
Route AN99B				
AN990 Panama	AN991 Morant			
	AN992 Navassa			
	AN993 Maisi		Matthew Town	785
			20°57'N, 73°41'W	
			Cockburn Town	980
			24°03'N, 74°31.5'W	
Route AN99C				
AN997 Matthew	AN998 Mira			
	22°08'N, 74°25'W			
	AN999 Salvador			
	24°10'N, 74°35'W			
	AN9991 Abaco			
	26°50'N, 76°30'W			
	AN9992 Bahama		Beaufort	924
	27°30'N, 78°00'W		*34°43'N, 76°40'W*	
			Charlestown	814
			32°44'N, 79°50'W	

This northbound route through the Windward Passage is favoured by those who wish to reach ports along the east coast of the USA, although the times when this route can be sailed comfortably are relatively short. The best periods are either between April and June, when the trades have lost their winter strength and winds have a southerly element in them, or November, before the onset of the strong winter trades. When sailing this route late in the year, there is also the danger of encountering a norther. Passages during the hurricane season should be avoided, especially during the months of highest frequency (August to October). During all other summer months the weather should be observed closely.

Because of the traffic separation zone off Cape Maisi, at Cuba's eastern extremity, it is advisable to stay in the northgoing lane until level with Punta Maisi. At that point the course can be altered so as to cut across the soutbound lane and sail parallel to Cuba's north coast towards the Old Bahama Channel. A traffic separation zone is here in operation also, but by sailing close to the bank itself one will stay out of the NW going lane as far as AN994. From there the course will be altered to pass through Santaren Channel into the Straits of Florida. A direct course can be steered to make landfall off Fowey Rocks light, SE of the entrance into Miami Harbour. As one approaches the Florida coast the effects of the Gulf Stream will become increasingly pronounced, and this should be kept in mind if there is a threat of a norther. If this is the case it is better to stay close to the Great Bahama Bank, where the Gulf Stream is weaker, and, if necessary, seek shelter at one of the anchorages inside the bank. On arrival in Miami, Government Cut leads to the city itself, but the nearer marinas are at Miami Beach, close by the ocean entrance.

If a stopover in Jamaica is not intended, on leaving Panama from WP AN990, the course should be set for WP AN991 about 20 miles SE of Morant Cays, SE of Jamaica. This offshore route (AN99B) leads well clear of all dangers. From AN991 the course can pass either to the west of Navassa Island, or between this island and Cape Tiburon, the SW extremity of Hispaniola. In strong winds it is safer to take the westerly route to WP AN992, 10 miles west of Navassa Island, to avoid the breaking seas on the shallow banks lying close to the Haitian coast. The course then leads through the Windward Passage to WP AN993, SE of Cape Maisi, at Cuba's eastern extremity. A traffic separation zone is in operation off this point.

Having reached the Windward Passage boats bound for South Florida should take the route which runs along the north of Cuba and passes through the Old Bahama and Santaren Channels (AN99A). The route to northern ports on the US east coast (AN99C) cuts right across the Outer Bahamas. Initially the route passes west of Great Inagua and those who wish to stop in the Bahamas can clear in at Matthew Town, the main settlement on that island. The route continues northwards through the Mira-Por-Vos Passage, west of Acklins and Crooked Islands and also west of San Salvador Island before gaining the open ocean. From San Salvador, a direct route can be set to ports north of Cape Hatteras, whereas for ports to the south of Cape Hatteras, the route turns NW and runs parallel to the chain of islands. Attention should be paid to the current setting strongly to the NW along the Northern Bahamas, which is a continuation of the Antilles Current. From WP AN9991, north of Great Abaco, the route turns north and enters the Gulf Stream. For ports in Northern Florida or South Carolina, it may be necessary to continue to WP AN9992, north of Grand Bahama, before the course is altered for the port of destination. To take full advantage of the Gulf Stream, especially if one's destination is in North Florida or South Carolina, that initial course may have to continue in a NW direction so as to reach the area of the strongest current closer to the Florida coast.

The Windward Passage is clear of dangers but attention is drawn to those continuing their voyage northwards through Caicos Passage, between Mayaguana Island and the Caicos Bank. Strong currents have been recorded in the Caicos Passage, which have caused many ships and yachts to be lost on the reefs surrounding Mayaguana Island. The currents appear to be much stronger than stated and are difficult to detect, especially if one sails through the area by night.

AN100 ROUTES IN THE CARIBBEAN SEA

The fact that Venezuela and the offshore islands lie to the south of the hurricane belt, while still being in the trade wind zone, is the main attraction of this area for those who wish to continue cruising during the summer months when the risk of hurricanes hangs over the rest of the Caribbean. Although most of the area is outside the hurricane area, very rarely a rogue storm has been known to head that way and heavy swells can be experienced when a hurricane is passing further north. The offshore islands of Venezuela and the former Dutch territories of Aruba, Bonaire, and Curaçao are all under the influence of the NE trade winds for most of the year and enjoy similar weather conditions to the more southern islands of the Lesser Antilles. A strong current may be experienced when sailing among the ABC Islands, so this should be monitored constantly.

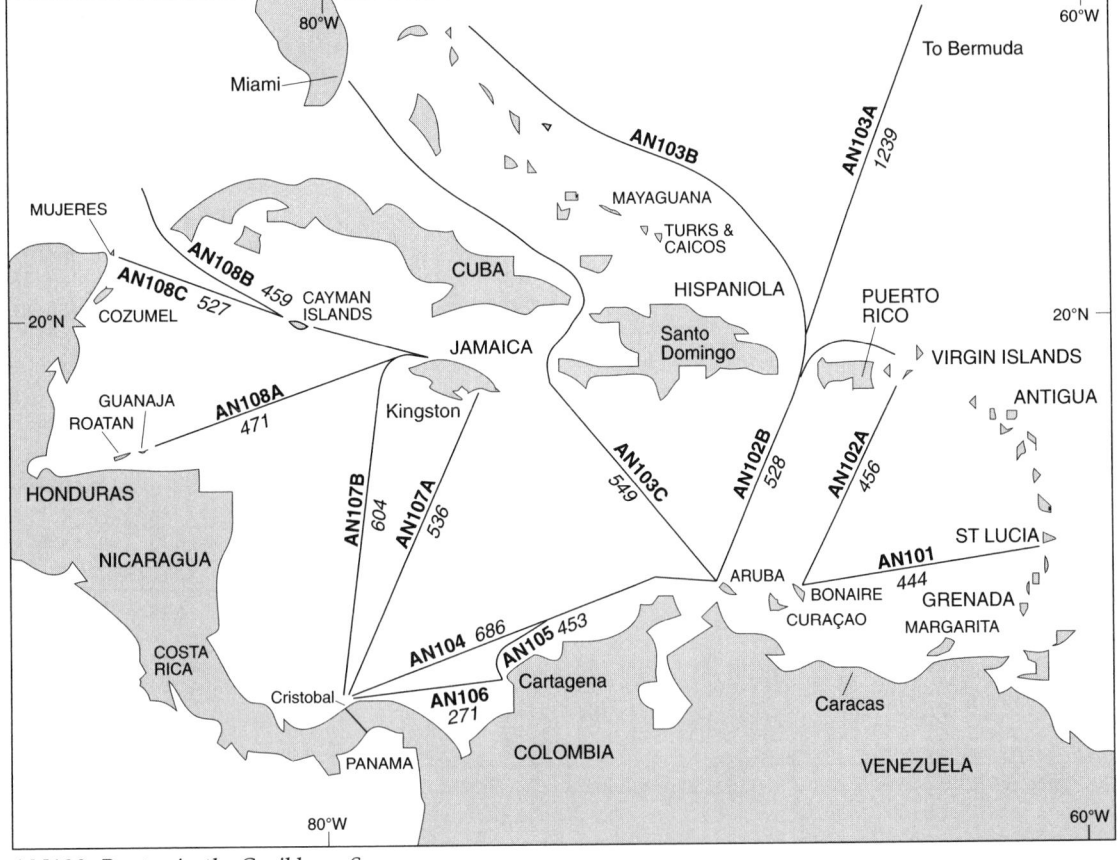

AN100 *Routes in the Caribbean Sea*

The weather along continental Venezuela is influenced by the land mass of the South American continent. The NE trade winds have a pronounced easterly component along this coast, particularly from March to June. The season of the strongest winds is December to April when the trades blow NE to E. From June to September, when most people choose to cruise this area, the winds are lighter and more variable. The land mass causes easterly breezes which usually blow in the daytime and die out at night, it often being quite calm at dawn.

The day breeze picks up during the morning and by mid-afternoon can blow quite strongly. From May to November, there are strong southerly squalls which lose their intensity as they head offshore. In the Maracaibo area local afternoon squalls called *chubascos* can blow with up to 50 knots of wind. In the same area strong winds build up in the winter due to the desert heating up and drawing the wind inland off the water. In the autumn hot short blasts called *calderatas* occasionally blow down the mountains.

AN101 *ABC Islands and Venezuela to Lesser Antilles*

BEST TIME:	April to May, November
TROPICAL STORMS:	June to November
CHARTS:	BA: 4402
	US: 402
PILOTS:	BA: 7A, 71
	US: 147, 148
CRUISING GUIDES:	*The Lesser Antilles, Sailor's Guide to the Windward Islands, Cruising Guide to the Leeward Islands.*
WAYPOINTS:	

Departure	Intermediate	Landfall	Destination	Distance (M)
AN1010 Curaçao 12°09'N, 68°17'W		St Lucia W 14°04'N, 61°00'N	Rodney Bay *14°04.5'N, 60°50.5'W*	450

Because of the direction of the prevailing wind it is usually better to work one's way east between the coast and the offlying islands before setting course for one of the Lesser Antilles. The distance between Venezuela's Margarita Island and Grenada, the most southerly of the Lesser Antilles, is only 140 miles. However, rather than beat against the strong wind and equally strong current, it is better to sail as close to the wind as possible and make for one of the islands further to the north. The other alternative is to stay close to the Venezuelan coast and do the entire trip in short stages. Trinidad can be reached in this way and, although longer in both time and distance, it will be easier on gear and crew. From Trinidad it is then easier to wait for a good weather window to sail to Grenada and beyond. Towards spring, with a better chance of SE winds, direct passages to more northerly islands are easier to accomplish, but even then it is better to start off from as far east as possible. This is normally easier at the change of seasons when lighter winds make it possible to gain some easting with the help of the engine.

AN102 *ABC Islands and Venezuela to Virgin Islands*

BEST TIME:	Mid-April to May, November
TROPICAL STORMS:	June to November
CHARTS:	BA: 4402
	US: 402
PILOTS:	BA: 7A, 71
	US: 147, 148
CRUISING GUIDES:	*Cruising Guide to the Virgin Islands, Yachtsman's Guide to the Virgin Islands.*

WAYPOINTS:				
Departure	*Intermediate*	*Landfall*	*Destination*	*Distance (M)*
Route AN102A				
AN1020 Aruba		AN1021 Vieques	Charlotte Amalie	456
12°35'N, 70°05'W		18°00'N, 65°10'W	*18°20'N, 64°56'W*	
Route AN102B				
AN1020 Aruba	AN1022 Mona			
	18°00'N, 67°40'W			
	AN1023 Borinquen		Charlotte Amalie	528
	18°35'N, 67°10'W			

This is a difficult passage during the winter months when the trade winds may have too much north in them. From December to April it is usually easier to reach the Virgins by following the suggestion in AN101 and then sail north in short hops along the chain of Lesser Antilles. For a direct passage (AN102A), it is better to wait until the second half of April, when there is a better chance of having the wind from a more favourable direction. Taking one's departure from WP AN1020 off Aruba's NW point, the direct offshore route leads to WP AN1021 SE of Vieques Island, off Puerto Rico's east coast. If it proves too difficult to lay such a direct course for the Virgins, it is better to use the Mona Passage by setting course for WP AN1022 and reach the Virgin Islands by sailing along the north coast of Puerto Rico (AN102B). However, should it be impossible to lay a course even for the Mona Passage because of unfavourable winds, landfall can be made further west, along the coast of Hispaniola, from where it should be possible to work one's way east along the coast with the help of a fair inshore current and land breezes. The same can be done along the south coast of Puerto Rico if a detour via Mona Passage is not attractive.

AN103 *Northbound from Venezuela and the ABC Islands*

BEST TIME:	April to May, November			
TROPICAL STORMS:	June to November			
CHARTS:	BA: 4402			
	US: 400			
PILOTS:	BA: 7A, 70, 71			
	US: 147, 148			
WAYPOINTS:				
Departure	*Intermediate*	*Landfall*	*Destination*	*Distance (M)*
Route AN103A				
AN1030 Aruba	AN1031 Mona			
12°35'N, 70°05'W	18°00'N, 67°40'W			
	AN1023 Borinquen	AN1033 David	St George's	1239
	18°35'N, 67°10'W	32°21'N, 64°38'W	*32°22'N, 64°40'W*	
Route AN103B				
AN1030 Aruba	AN1031 Mona	AN1036 off Beaufort	Beaufort	1493
	AN1032 Borinquen	34°30'N, 76°40'W	*34°43'N, 76°40'W*	
		AN1037 Abaco	Charleston	1509
		26°50'N, 76°30'W	*32°44'N, 79°50'W*	

Departure	Intermediate	Landfall	Destination	Distance (M)
Route AN103C				
AN1030 Aruba	AN1034 Navassa			
	18°20'N, 74°45' W			
	AN1038 Maisi			
	20°12'N, 73°55'W			
	AN1039 Diamond			
	22°07'N, 77°18'W			
	AN10311 Santaren SE	AN10312 Coral	Miami	
	22°58'N, 78°48'W	25°44'N, 80°02'W	25°47'N, 80°10'W	1067

For those who have cruised in this area and do not plan to continue their voyage towards Panama and possibly the Pacific Ocean, but intend to sail either to the USA or Europe, the best season for the northbound passage is spring, when the winds usually start shifting to the SE. It is best to start this passage from as far east as possible, both Bonaire and Curaçao being good points of departure. If heading for the Mona Passage allowance should be made for the west-setting current during the crossing of the Caribbean Sea. In case one cannot lay Mona Passage and one is swept to the west, it is possible to break the trip on the south coast of Hispaniola and then work one's way east with the help of an easterly current that sets close inshore. As there is a good deal of north in the trades during the early part of winter, the passage should not be attempted too early in the year. The best time to attempt the direct route (AN103A) across the Caribbean Sea is April or May, when there is less of a chance of the winds swinging to the north. If one plans to carry on towards Europe, from Mona Passage a direct course can be set for Bermuda. Boats bound for ports east of New York may also consider such a stop in Bermuda. For the continuation of the route north of Mona Passage see also routes AN87, AN88, and AN102.

For those sailing to ports on the east coast of the USA, and not interested in a detour to Bermuda, the alternative on leaving Mona Passage is to take a NW route parallel to the Bahamas and reach ports south of Cape Hatteras by staying offshore (AN103B). Alternatively it is possible to take a route which goes to Florida via the Bahamas and then use the Intracoastal Waterway to reach more northern ports (AN103C). If this latter alternative is being considered, it would hardly be worth fighting the elements to reach the Mona Passage when a route through the Windward Passage would be considerably easier to accomplish. In this case from AN1030 a course should be set for WP AN1034 east of Navassa Island, off Hispaniola's SW extremity. From there the route turns north towards the Windward Passage and continues either right through the Bahamas or turns NW through the Old Bahama Channel. Boats taking this route to ports in Southern Florida should remain in the northbound lane of the traffic separation zone that operates off Cape Maisi, at Cuba's eastern extremity. When level with Punta Maisi the course can be altered so as to cut across the southbound lane and sail parallel to Cuba's north coast towards the Old Bahama Channel. A traffic separation zone is here in operation also, so by sailing close to the bank itself one will stay out of the NW going lane as far as AN10311. From there the course will be altered to pass through Santaren Channel into the Straits of Florida. A direct course can be steered across the straits to make landfall off Fowey Rocks light, SE of the entrance into Miami Harbour. As one approaches the Florida coast the effects of the Gulf Stream will become increasingly pronounced, and this should be kept in mind if there is a threat of a norther. If this is the case it is better to stay close to the Great Bahama Bank, where the Gulf Stream is weaker and, if necessary, seek shelter at one of the anchorages inside the bank. On arrival in Miami, Government Cut leads to the city itself, but the nearer marinas are at Miami Beach, close to the entrance. Boats bound for more northerly ports should refer to route AN93 (page 113) which describes the continuation of this route through the Outer Bahamas and beyond.

Another way to reach Southern Florida is to cross the entire Caribbean and reach the Gulf of Mexico through the Yucatan Channel. Directions for the later part of the passage are given in AN83.

AN104 *ABC Islands and Venezuela to Panama*

BEST TIME:	April to May, November to December
TROPICAL STORMS:	June to November
CHARTS:	BA: 4402
	US: 402
PILOTS:	BA: 7A
	US: 148
CRUISING GUIDES:	*Cruising Guide to the Caribbean, Panama Canal Pilot's Handbook.*
WAYPOINTS:	

Departure	Intermediate	Landfall	Destination	Distance (M)
AN1040 Aruba 12°35'N, 70°05'W	AN1041 Gallinas 12°55'N, 71°38'W AN1042 Manzanillo 9°47'N, 79°32'W	AN1043 Panama 9°26.25'N, 79°55'W	Cristobal *9°21'N, 79°55'W*	630

A large number of westbound boats stop in Venezuela or the offlying islands before continuing the voyage towards Panama. Although this route is just outside the region affected by hurricanes, it is better to plan this passage for the intermediate seasons when more pleasant conditions can be expected.

The best point of departure for Panama is Aruba, from where a course should be steered to pass rapidly into deeper waters. On leaving Aruba, the shallow bank to its west should be avoided as the west-setting offshore current combined with an east-setting inshore current can produce rough and confused seas. The recommended course is outside the 1000 fathom line, which avoids the rough seas that occur in the shallower waters closer to land.

From WP AN1040 outside Oranjestad, the course should be set for WP AN1041 28 miles north of Punta Gallinas on Guajira Peninsula just outside the 1000 fathom line. From there, a direct course can be set for WP AN1042 10 miles N of Punta Manzanillo and 30 miles from the Panama Canal entrance. Then the course should be altered for WP AN1043 at the landfall buoy off the entrance into the port of Cristobal Colon. Traffic Control should be contacted on VHF channel 12. Traffic lights control the passage through the breakwaters and small boats are advised to keep as close as possible to the sides. See page 583 for detailed instructions concerning entry and transit procedure for the Panama Canal.

AN105 ABC *Islands and Venezuela to Colombia*

BEST TIME:	April to May, November to December
TROPICAL STORMS:	June to November
CHARTS:	BA: 4402
	US: 402
PILOTS:	BA: 7A
	US: 148
CRUISING GUIDES:	*Cruising Guide to the Caribbean.*

WAYPOINTS:				
Departure	*Intermediate*	*Landfall*	*Destination*	*Distance (M)*
AN1050 Aruba 12°35'N, 70°05'W	AN1051 Gallinas 12°55'N, 71°38'W AN1052 12°23'N, 73°12'W AN1053	AN1054 off Cartagena 10°25'N, 75°38'W	Cartagena *10°25'N, 75°32'W*	392
	11°10'N, 75°25'W			

After being avoided for many years by cruising boats, Colombia is again being included in cruising plans and a large number of visiting boats are stopping in Colombia, especially in the historic city of Cartagena. Directions for sailing to Colombia are similar to routes AN73 and AN74 (pages 90–1). Boats leaving from Aruba should set an initial course for WP AN1051 28 miles north of Punta Gallinas on Guajira Peninsula. From there the recommended route leads to WPs AN1052 and AN1053. Both points are just outside the 1000 fathom line, although strong winds and high seas can be expected on this route, especially during the winter months. From waypoint AN1053 the course can be altered for WP AN1054 in the approaches to the port of Cartagena. The area should be approached with caution because of the dangers in the approaches. Also avoid the silted Boca Grande as the dredged entrance is Boca Chica, identified by a landfall buoy, close to the end of Isla de Tierra Bomba. An 8 mile long channel leads northward through the shallow Bahia de Cartagena to the commercial port and two marinas. The port lies on the banks of the River Magdalena and approaches are very difficult. Arriving yachts are advised to contact Club Nautico on channel 16 for clearance and docking information. The GPS position of the orange and white entrance buoy has been reported at 10°18.97'N, 75°35.98'W.

As on most other routes in the Caribbean Sea, best conditions are encountered in either April–May, or November. Because the route crosses an area known for its rough seas, Aruba should not be left in winds over 30 knots, or if there is a forecast of strong winds to come. The current will be in one's favour almost all the way to Cartagena, with sets of 1.5 to 2 knots, although a counter-current may make itself felt in the last 20–30 miles to Cartagena. The area around Cartagena is affected by a violent southerly wind called *chocosono*, which can attain speeds of 50 or even 60 knots.

AN106 *Colombia to Panama*

BEST TIME:	April to May, November to December			
TROPICAL STORMS:	June to November			
CHARTS:	BA: 4402			
	US: 402			
PILOTS:	BA: 7A			
	US: 148			
CRUISING GUIDES:	*Cruising Guide to Panama, The Panama Guide.*			
WAYPOINTS:				
Departure	*Intermediate*	*Landfall*	*Destination*	*Distance (M)*
AN1060 off Cartagena 10°25'N, 75°38'W	AN1061 Manzanillo W 9°48'N, 79°35'W	AN1062 Panama 9°26.25'N, 79°55'W	Cristobal *9°21'N, 79°55'W*	271

Most boats take their leave from Colombia in Cartagena, from where a direct course leads across the Gulf of Darien to the Panama Canal entrance. From outside Cartagena, at WP AN1060 a course can be set for WP AN1061, 10 miles N of Punta Manzanillo. The course can then be altered for WP AN1062, the landfall buoy at the entrance to the Panama Canal. The above course passes outside the San Blas Islands and stays in deeper water to avoid the rougher seas further inshore. The

voyage can be interrupted in the San Blas Islands, which belong to Panama and where one can clear and obtain the compulsory cruising permit at Porvenir (9°34'N, 78°57'W).

The area to be crossed is not subjected to tropical storms, although the effect will be felt if a hurricane occurs further north. During winter months passages along this route will be affected by the large swell caused by the strong trade winds piling up the water in this corner of the Caribbean.

AN107 *Jamaica to Panama*

BEST TIME:	April to May, November to December			
TROPICAL STORMS:	June to November			
CHARTS:	BA: 4402			
	US: 402			
PILOTS:	BA: 7A, 70			
	US: 147, 148			
CRUISING GUIDES:	*Cruising Guide to Panama, The Panama Guide.*			
WAYPOINTS:				
Departure	*Intermediate*	*Landfall*	*Destination*	*Distance (M)*
Route AN107A				
AN1071 Plumb	AN1072 Pedro	AN1073 Panama	Cristobal	536
17°45'N, 76°50'W	16°20'N, 77°10'W	9°26.25'N, 79°55'W	*9°21'N, 79°55'W*	
Route AN107B				
AN1074 Negril	AN1075 Rosalind			
18°18'N, 78°30'W	16°00'N, 80°10'W			
	AN1076 Sueno			
	14°20'N, 80°45'W			
	AN1077 Roncador	AN1073 Panama	Cristobal	604
	13°30'N, 79°40'W			

A direct route (AN107A) leads to Panama from ports in the eastern part of Jamaica. The winds will be light while in the lee of the island, but outside Jamaica's wind shadow they will rapidly become strong with large seas. The strong winds and high seas experienced on this route for most of the year, combined with a strong west-setting current, call for accurate navigation as the route passes dangerously close to a number of offshore banks. As the direct route to Panama leads close to the New and Pedro Banks, sufficient allowance for leeway should be made when setting a course to windward of them. The area should also be avoided because of the breaking seas that occur over the shallows. Both these banks can be very dangerous

in heavy weather and their vicinity should be avoided. Another hazard is the many fishing boats, some of which do not show lights, as well as the buoyed nets set on the banks.

From WP AN1071 south of Plumb Point, in the approaches to Kingston, a course should be set for WP AN1072 to pass well to the east of the various banks. If leaving from one of the ports on the NE coast of Jamaica, a course should be shaped around the east of the island and you should make for the same waypoint AN1072. From there it is a clear run to WP AN1073, the landfall buoy in the approaches to the Panama Canal.

For boats leaving from ports in the west of Jamaica, the route has to avoid a series of dangers, and as some of their positions, as depicted on the charts, are not entirely accurate, the area should be approached with great caution. Having passed Point Negril, at the western extremity of Jamaica, from WP AN1074 set course for WP AN1075 to pass between Rosalind and Serranilla Banks. The course is then altered for WP AN1076 halfway between Sueno and Serrana Banks, both of which have lights. The next WP AN1077 is 20 miles east of Roncador Bank, from where the course can be altered for WP AN1073 at the entrance into the port of Cristobal. Boats approaching the breakwaters

at the entrance into the Panama Canal should call Traffic Control on VHF channel 12. Traffic lights regulate the passage between the breakwaters, but small boats may pass if they keep close to the side, both when passing through the breakwaters and in the shipping channels.

Boats going straight to the San Blas Islands should be aware of the poor visibility in their vicinity as low cloud often obscures the mainland and land may not become visible until a few miles away. The official port of entry is Porvenir (9°34'N, 78°57'W).

AN108 *Jamaica to Central America and Mexico*

BEST TIME:	April to May, November to December				
TROPICAL STORMS:	June to November				
CHARTS:	BA: 4400 US: 400				
PILOTS:	BA: 69A, 70 US: 147, 148				
CRUISING GUIDES:	*Cruising Guide to the Northwest Caribbean, Cruising Guide to Belize and Mexico's Caribbean Coast.*				
WAYPOINTS:					
Departure	*Intermediate*	*Landfall*		*Destination*	*Distance (M)*
Route AN108A					
Montego Bay *18°28'N, 77°56'W*	AN1081 Swan 16°55'N, 84°00'W			Guanaja *16°28'N, 85°54'W*	471
				Belize City *17°30'N, 88°10'W*	600
Route AN108B					
Montego Bay	AN1082 Grand Cayman 19°25'N, 81°05'W			AN1083 Yucatan SE *21°50'N, 85°10'W*	459
Route AN108C Montego Bay	AN1084 Sur 21°10'N, 86°42'W			Mujeres *21°15'N, 86°45.5'W*	527

Westbound routes from Jamaica benefit from both good winds and a favourable current during most of the year. The best time for passages along these routes is the transition months of April–May, before the hurricane season, or November before the onset of winter northers, which may be felt west of Jamaica and can seriously affect weather in the Gulf of Mexico and, to a smaller extent, further south.

Boats leaving from ports on either side of Jamaica and bound for the Bay of Islands in Honduras (AN108A) should set course for WP AN1081 south of Swan Island. A convenient place to clear into Honduras is at Guanaja. The route to Belize also passes right by Swan Island. To reach

Belize City one has to use one of several passes through the reefs, Eastern Channel being the main shipping channel.

The route to the Gulf of Mexico passes close to the Cayman Islands, where the voyage may be interrupted at the capital Georgetown on Grand Cayman. From there the route continues towards the Yucatan Channel and WP AN1083 off Cuba's Cape San Antonio. Boats bound for ports in the Gulf of Mexico can wait for favourable conditions to cross the Gulf at Isla Mujeres, an official port of entry into Mexico, in which case a course should be set for WP AN1084, off that island's south point, Punta Sur.

AN110 ROUTES FROM THE BAHAMAS AND FLORIDA

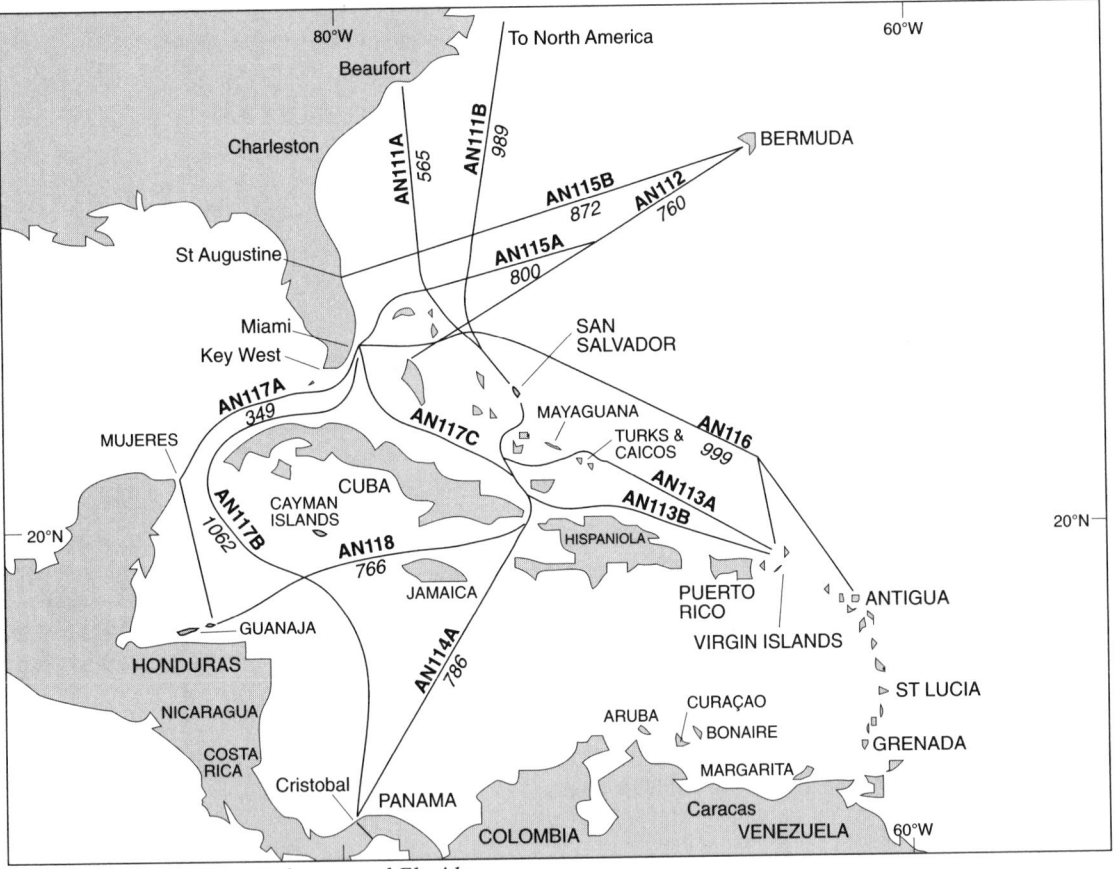

AN110 *Routes from the Bahamas and Florida*

The low lying islands of the Bahamas and their associated banks and reef areas offer a wide choice of anchorages, especially to shallow drafted craft. Although cruised by a large number of boats, few arrive in the Bahamas at the end of a long offshore passage since most boats reach the islands in short hops, mostly from Florida.

The prevailing winds are from NE to SE with the most northern islands lying on the edge of the trade wind belt. As the islands are low there is no regular land breeze. Northers interrupt the NE trades with regularity during the winter and typically start with the wind veering to the S and SW. When the cold front arrives, the wind suddenly shifts to the NW then N and usually blows itself out in the NE. After a while, the normal winds take over from more or less their usual direction. In mid-winter, the cycle can take several days, in spring only 24 hours. Most northers are dry, although on occasions they can be accompanied by rain and thunder squalls. However, they very rarely bring winds over 30 knots and mainly the more northerly Bahamas are the most affected by these northers.

Summer weather starts around May, after the last norther has blown itself out, and lasts until November. The trades are more SE in the summer and most winds during these months are from E or SE. During August and September there can be periods of calms, especially at night. The balmy summer weather can be interrupted occasionally by an Easterly Wave, a trough of low pressure found in the trade wind belt. This is usually accompanied by showers and high humidity. Sometimes Easterly Waves can degenerate into tropical depressions and even hurricanes. May to October are the wettest months and rainy squalls occur during this season.

In Florida the prevailing winds are E and SE, but they become more variable higher up the coast, tending to be more SW. Thunderstorms are more common in summer, although there are few gales. However, in this season hurricanes can affect the eastern seaboard over the whole region, those arising in the Atlantic usually approaching from the E and SE. Tropical storms generated in the Caribbean Sea come from the south and are more frequent in the months of September and October. The whole area is affected by weather conditions on the North American land mass and the semipermanent anticyclone stationed there. As the pressure rises, it develops into a norther, a N and NW flow of cold air that blows hard for several days. During the winter, gales occur, as depressions move across the southern states eastward into the Atlantic. North of Florida these fronts bring strong SW gales, the wind veering W or NW behind the depression.

The hurricane season is from June to November, although usually in June and July hurricanes pass to the south of the Bahamas. The most dangerous months are August to October, but hurricanes have been recorded as early as May and as late as December. The Bahamas have one of the highest frequencies of hurricanes in the North Atlantic, as they are in the path of hurricanes generated in both the Atlantic and the Caribbean.

AN111 *Northbound from the Bahamas and Florida*

BEST TIME:	May to June
TROPICAL STORMS:	June to November
CHARTS:	BA: 4403
	US: 403
PILOTS:	BA: 68, 69, 70
	US: 140, 147
CRUISING GUIDES:	*Coastal Cruising Guide to the Atlantic Coast.*
WAYPOINTS:	

Departure	Intermediate	Landfall	Destination	Distance (M)
Route AN111A				
AN1111 Providence 25°50'N, 76°50'W	AN1112 Abaco NE 27°00'N, 76°50'W	AN1113 off Beaufort 34°30'N, 76°40'W	Beaufort *34°43'N, 76°40'W*	533
		AN1114 Chesapeake 36°45'N, 75°45'W		658
		AN1115 Brenton 41°24'N, 71°16'W	Newport *41°29'N, 71°20'W*	982
Route AN111B				
AN1111 Providence	AN1112 Abaco NE	AN1116 off Charleston 32°40'N, 79°40'W	Charleston *32°44'N, 79°50'W*	450

Although there is a steady movement of boats between the Bahamas and Florida virtually throughout the year, offshore passages to more northern states are restricted to spring and early summer. This is the time when boats, which have passed the winter in the tropics, return home. However, even at the best of times, some people prefer to forgo the attractions of a quick offshore passage and instead take the Intracoastal Waterway.

The best time for an offshore passage, especially for ports north of the Chesapeake Bay, is in spring and early summer, when the chances of favourable winds are highest and there is little or no danger of either late northers or early hurricanes. The latter danger increases with the approach of summer, but even then offshore passages are feasible provided one leaves with a favourable long term forecast. A stop in Bermuda is not really recommended, except for boats bound for Canadian ports.

Because of the favourable set of the Gulf Stream, the route should use this advantage to the maximum. However, if there is a likelihood of strong northerly winds, it is better to forgo it and wait for better conditions, if leaving from a port in South Florida, or sail a more offshore route, if leaving from the Bahamas or Northern Florida.

For destinations south of Cape Hatteras, boats leaving from Florida have little choice but to sail a course roughly parallel to the coast. Boats taking an offshore route from the Bahamas, from WP AN1111, in the NE Providence Channel, should set an initial course for WP AN1112, NE of Great Abaco Island. From that point, boats bound for more northern destinations can sail a direct offshore route (AN111A). Boats bound for southern ports may continue in a NW direction before altering course for the port of destination (AN111B). To take full advantage of the Gulf Stream, especially if one's destination is in North Florida or South Carolina, that initial course may have to continue in a NW direction so as to reach the area of the strongest current closer to the Florida coast. Latest information on the location and strength of the Gulf Stream can be obtained from NOAA Miami, who issue regular Gulf Stream flow charts, and can be contacted on Tel. (305) 665 4707.

AN112 *Bahamas to Bermuda*

BEST TIME:	May to June				
TROPICAL STORMS:	June to November				
CHARTS:	BA: 4403				
	US: 403				
PILOTS:	BA: 70				
	US: 140, 147				
CRUISING GUIDES:	*Yachting Guide to Bermuda.*				
WAYPOINTS:					
Departure	*Intermediate*	*Landfall*		*Destination*	*Distance (M)*
AN1121 Providence 25°50'N, 76°50'W	AN1122 Bermuda SW 32°12'N, 64°50'W	AN1123 David 32°21'N, 64°38'W		St George's *32°22'N, 64°40'W*	760

Similar directions apply as for route AN115, which is used by boats sailing from Florida to Bermuda. The recommended time for a passage from the Bahamas is late spring or early summer, when weather conditions on this route will be better than at any other time. If leaving from the Northern Bahamas a NNE course can be easily followed with the help of the prevailing winds and the north setting Gulf Stream. During the summer months the winds north of the Bahamas are usually from the SE, so it is sometimes possible to sail a direct course from the Bahamas to Bermuda right through the Horse Latitudes. Light winds are sometimes experienced along this route and gales are very rare at the recommended time of year. Although the hurricane season officially starts in Bermuda on 1st June, hurricanes rarely pass that way before the end of July and even when they do, their path is to the west of Bermuda nearer to the American mainland.

If the NE Providence Channel is used as a point of departure from the Bahamas, from WP AN1121 a direct course can be set for WP AN1122 south of Gibbs Hill, at the SW point of Bermuda. From there the course runs parallel to the island to WP AN1123 off St David's Head. Town Cut leads into

St George's Harbour, the official port of entry into Bermuda. The narrow cut, although well buoyed and lit, should not be attempted at night by those unfamiliar with the area.

AN113 *Bahamas to the Eastern Caribbean*

BEST TIME:	Mid-April to June, November to mid-December
TROPICAL STORMS:	June to November
CHARTS:	BA: 4400
	US: 400
PILOTS:	BA: 70, 71
	US: 147
CRUISING GUIDES:	*Gentleman's Guide to Passages South, Yachtsman's Guide to the Bahamas, Cruising Guide to the Leeward Islands.*

Having reached the Southern Bahamas either by one of the offshore routes or through the islands, the subsequent leg to the Virgins will be to windward for most of the way and also for most of the year. The route has been called the 'thorny path', and for very good reason. The best time to undertake it is at the change of seasons, when the trade winds are lighter and the risk of hurricanes not so great. Another matter of concern, apart from the contrary winds, are the strong currents that occur in this area. These, combined with the numerous reefs, low islands, and few lights call for accurate navigation at all times.

Those who are determined to sail offshore to either the Virgins or Lesser Antilles, and are confident that their boat is capable of it, should gain the open ocean by the quickest way and set an easterly course as soon as possible. This avoids the strong NW current setting parallel to the Bahamas. If the winds allow it, the due east course should be held until the longitude of the port of destination is reached and course is altered to the south.

An offshore passage from the Southern Bahamas to the Virgins, either direct (AN113A) or via Puerto Rico, can regain the ocean through the Crooked Island, Mayaguana, Caicos, or Turks Passages. The initial course should lead well clear of all dangers, including the banks east of Grand Turk. A variation of such an offshore route is described in AN116. Because of contrary wind and current, such a passage would be very difficult; unless the winds are northerly or light, an alternative route (AN113B) may have to be considered. This means staying south of Caicos and sailing along the north coasts of Hispaniola and Puerto Rico. Even

when the trade winds are strong these high islands provide some lee and light coastal breezes.

Directions for boats sailing to one of the northern islands in the Lesser Antilles are very similar. However, those whose destination lies further south, should consider taking an offshore route from the Mona Passage onwards. Having sailed along the north coast of Hispaniola as far as Samana, at Mona Passage the route enters the Caribbean Sea. At the beginning of winter, NE winds ought to make it possible to reach some of the more southern islands, such as Grenada or Trinidad, on one tack. This route is not recommended towards spring when the winds become SE.

An alternative chosen every year by numerous sailors is to sail the distance in short stages. The best tactics to be deployed are described in *The Gentleman's Guide to Passages South*, which is dedicated to this very route. The advice given in that book, and also by others who have sailed that difficult route, is to take one's time and watch the weather carefully. Even in winter, when strong easterlies are the norm, the frequent fronts provide a respite of calms and light winds. The recommended tactic is to sail ahead of such fronts and then run for shelter as the front approaches. The weather is usually uncomfortable for 12 hours before a frontal passage and for about 24 hours afterwards.

As the voyage may be interrupted in the Turks and Caicos Islands, entry formalities in those islands can be completed at the following ports: Sapodilla Bay (Providenciales, 21°44'N, 72°17'W), Cockburn Harbour (South Caicos, 21°30'N, 71°31'W), and Cockburn Town (Grand Turk, 21°28'N, 71°06'W). Convenient ports of entry on the north coast of the Dominican Republic are Puerto Plata (19°49'N, 70°42'W), Manzanillo Bay (19°43'N, 71°45'W), and Samana (19°12'N, 69°26'W). The official port of entry on Puerto Rico's west coast is Mayaguez (18°12'N, 67°07'W) and not Boqueron. Although a US territory, US boats must clear into Mayaguez like everyone else. An additional suggestion for those sailing along the south coast of Puerto Rico, especially at night, is to avoid the numerous fish traps.

AN114 *Bahamas to Panama*

BEST TIME:	April to May, November to December			
TROPICAL STORMS:	June to November			
CHARTS:	BA: 4400			
	US: 400			
PILOTS:	BA: 7A, 70			
	US: 147, 148			
CRUISING GUIDES:	*Cruising Guide to Panama, The Panama Guide.*			
WAYPOINTS:				
Departure	*Intermediate*	*Landfall*	*Destination*	*Distance (M)*
Route AN114				
AN1140 Matthew Town	AN1141 Maisi N			
20°56'N, 73°42'W	*20°23'N, 74°05'W*			
	AN1142 Navassa			
	18°25'N, 75°16'W			
	AN1143 Morant	AN1144 Panama	Cristobal	786
	17°15'N, 75°32'W	*9°26.25'N, 79°55'W*	*9°21'N, 79°55'W*	

Regardless of the Bahamian port of departure, all variations of this route converge on the Windward Passage. Matthew Town, the main settlement on Great Inagua Island, is a good place to stop before negotiating the Windward Passage and is used as a hypothetical departure point. A course for WP AN1141, eight miles NE of Cuba's Cape Maisi, takes one into the southbound lane of the traffic separation zone which operates off that cape. Having negotiated the Windward Passage, the route to Panama can pass on either side of Navassa Island, but its western side is to be preferred in strong winds as seas break on the shallows off the SW extremity of Hispaniola. A course should be set for WP AN1142, 10 miles west of Navassa Island. If a stop in Jamaica is not intended, the course leads to WP AN1143 about 20 miles SE of Morant Cays. From there, the course should be altered for WP AN1144, the seabuoy off the Panama Canal entrance. The recommended route across the Caribbean Sea stays clear of the various banks and shallows.

Allowance should be made for leeway if passing close to Pedro and New Banks as the current sets towards them.

The winds are favourable along this route throughout the year, although both the hurricane season and the strong trade winds of winter should be avoided. In the latter case boisterous sailing conditions can be predicted with certainty from January to March when the trades are at their strongest. The extent of the hurricane season is less precisely defined and the actual months when there is no danger of hurricanes are the same winter months from January to April. The intermediate months have a much lower frequency of tropical storms, but hurricanes have been recorded even as late as December, making passages through the Caribbean more dangerous at the end than at the beginning of the season. This is the reason why southbound passages should be planned for late winter or early spring.

AN115 *Florida to Bermuda*

BEST TIME:	May to June
TROPICAL STORMS:	June to November
CHARTS:	BA: 4400
	US: 400
PILOTS:	BA: 71
	US: 140, 147
CRUISING GUIDES:	*Yachtsman's Guide to Bermuda.*
WAYPOINTS:	

Departure	Intermediate	Landfall	Destination	Distance (M)
AN1150 Lauderdale 26°05.5'N, 80°06'W	AN1151 Bahama 27°40'N, 79°00'W			
	AN1152 Bermuda SW 32°12'N, 64°50'W	AN1153 David 32°21'N, 64°38'W	St George's *32°22'N, 64°40'W*	800
AN1154 St Augustine *29°55'N, 81°16'W*	AN1155 Comachee 29°53'N, 81°12'W			
	AN1152 Bermuda SW	AN1153 David	St George's	872

This passage is made mostly in May and June, when the chances of favourable conditions are better than at any other time of the year. The timing suits most people's plans as this route is sailed mostly by boats that have spent the winter in Florida and are using Bermuda as a convenient point before continuing towards the Azores, Northern Europe, or the Mediterranean. The prevailing winds in early summer are SW which, added to the favourable Gulf Stream, can make for a speedy start to the passage. The Miami office of NOAA issues regular Gulf Stream flow charts and the latest information on this can be obtained by telephoning (305) 665 4707. Provided there is no forecast of a late norther, the Gulf Stream can be ridden for a while, but sooner rather than later the direct course for Bermuda must take priority. If leaving from ports in Southern Florida, Grand Bahama Island and the reefs and islets to the north of it should be passed at a safe distance before the course is altered for Bermuda. Having reached WP AN1151 off Grand Bahama a direct course can be set for WP AN1152, south of Gibbs Hill, at the SW point of Bermuda. From there the course runs parallel to the island to WP AN1153 off St David's Head. Town Cut leads into St George's Harbour, the official port of entry into Bermuda. The narrow cut, although well buoyed and lit, should not be attempted at night by those unfamiliar with the area.

The oldest Spanish settlement in North America, located just south of Jacksonville, makes an excellent departure port in North Florida and is in fact the starting point of at least one annual race to Bermuda. This is a picturesque town with a thriving sailing community and as it is also the home of Hunter yachts, repair facilities are very good. As the city is located on the west shore of the Intracoastal Waterway, at least one opening bridge will have to be negotiated before the sea is reached through a well marked channel. From a waypoint just east of the channel a direct course can be set for the south coast of Bermuda. On such a course the Gulf Stream will be traversed at a right angle. A considerable advantage of leaving for Bermuda from a more northern port is that in case of bad weather offshore, such as a norther, one has plenty of sea room to deal with it.

The SW winds experienced at the start of this passage may become SE further offshore and occasionally these can last as far as Bermuda. Weather forecasts should be listened to regularly during this passage as weather systems can change rapidly in the areas crossed by this route. If the passage is made early in the season, there is a real possibility of encountering strong northerly winds, in which case one should try to move out of the Gulf Stream as quickly as possible. Later in the season there is the danger of tropical storms and, even if they do not develop into fully fledged hurricanes, depressions which form over the Bahamas usually bring squally weather and rough seas.

AN116 *Florida to the Eastern Caribbean*

BEST TIME:	May, November			
TROPICAL STORMS:	June to November			
CHARTS:	BA: 4400			
	US: 400			
PILOTS:	BA: 71			
	US: 140, 147			
CRUISING GUIDES:	*The Lesser Antilles, Cruising Guide to the Leeward Islands, Sailor's Guide to the Windward Islands.*			
WAYPOINTS:				

Departure	Intermediate	Landfall	Destination	Distance (M)
AN1161 Providence 25°50'N, 76°50'W	AN1162 Optimist 25°00'N, 65°00'W	AN1164 Culebrita 18°26'N, 65°10'W	Charlotte Amalie *18°23'N, 64°56'W*	999
AN1161 Providence	AN1163 Ideal 25°00'N, 61°30'W			
	AN1165 Barbuda 17°30'N, 61°30'W	AN1166 Antigua E 17°00'N, 61°38'W	English Harbour *17°00'N, 61°45'W*	1320

The timing for a direct passage from Florida to the Eastern Caribbean is critical as a summer voyage carries the risk of hurricanes and a winter voyage that of contrary easterly winds as well as northerly storms. Therefore the best time appears to be November, when the danger of hurricanes is low and winter gales are still rare.

The offshore route has the advantage that it can also be sailed in winter, although it has the distinct disadvantage of strong contrary winds once the trade winds are met. The offshore route is more attractive to boats starting from Northern Florida as they can set a direct course, which stays clear of the Bahamas. Boats leaving from ports in Southern Florida can join that same offshore route by taking the NW and NE Providence Channels. In both cases the recommended practice is to make one's easting along latitude 25°N and only turn south after meridian 65°N has been crossed. In November and December the trade winds are moderate NE, but become E and stronger after January, so even this offshore route should not be

sailed too late in winter. Having reached the open sea through the NE Providence Channel, from WP AN1161, the tack will be sailed which makes best easting to WP AN1162, if bound for the Virgin Islands, or AN1163, if bound for one of the ports in the Lesser Antilles. From WP AN1162, the course is altered for WP AN1164, so as to make landfall close to the island of Culebrita and approach St Thomas from the north and west. An alternative way of approaching the Virgin Islands from the NE is described in route AN127 (page 146). Boats bound for Antigua should set a course from AN1163 for AN1165, so as to approach the island from windward. Landfall will be made at WP AN1166, east of English Harbour.

An alternative way to reach the Eastern Caribbean is by the inter-island route that threads its way through the Bahamas, Turks and Caicos, Puerto Rico and beyond, an intricate and time consuming route that still does not avoid the strong headwinds which await one at the end. This alternative is discussed in detail in route AN113.

AN117 *Southbound from Florida*

BEST TIME:	December to May			
TROPICAL STORMS:	June to November			
CHARTS:	BA: 4400			
	US: 400			
PILOTS:	BA: 71			
	US: 140, 147, 148			
CRUISING GUIDES:	*Cruising Guide to the Caribbean.*			
WAYPOINTS:				

Departure	Intermediate	Landfall	Destination	Distance (M)
Route AN117A				
AN1170 Key West	AN1171 Tortuga	AN1172 Yucatan NW	Mujeres	349
24°33'N, 81°48'W	24°25'N, 83°00'W	21°18'N, 86°46'W	*21°15'N, 86°45.5'W*	
			Belize City	588
			17°30'N, 88°10'W	
			Livingston	696
			15°50.5'N, 88°43.5'W	
			Guanaja	640
			16°28'N, 85°54'W	
Route AN117B				
AN1170 Key West	AN1173 Antonio			
	21°50'N, 85°05'W			
	AN1174 Serrana	AN1175 Panama	Cristobal	1062
	14°20'N, 80°40'W	9°26.25'N, 79°55'W	*9°21'N, 79°55'W*	
Route AN117C				
AN1176 Augustine	AN1177			
29°55'N, 81°16'W	25°00'N, 74°40'W			
		AN1178 Mira		
		22°05'N, 74°24'W		
		AN1179 Maisi N		
		20°23'N, 74°05'W		739

Many American sailors use Florida as a convenient springboard to reach destinations south and while this may work out well for some, for others it may prove to be counterproductive. Mainly for those sailing from northern states, who are bound for Central America, getting there via the Bahamas and Windward Passage makes more sense than fighting one's way past Florida and across the Gulf of Mexico.

In the summer the prevailing winds in Florida are from the SE and the weather is rainy with heavy squalls and calm periods. The Gulf of Mexico is one of the areas most affected by hurricanes between June and November, not only by those forming in the Gulf itself but also by those trav-

elling from other areas of the Caribbean. From September to November hurricanes spawned in the Western Caribbean are most likely to pass through the Yucatan Channel and then curve around north and east towards Cuba and Florida. Tornadoes, waterspouts, and squalls are also a feature of the hurricane season.

The greatest dilemma faced by anyone planning a voyage from Florida to any of the countries bordering on the Caribbean Sea is whether to sail east or west of Cuba. The situation will undoubtedly change once that country's doors are fully opened to cruising boats and visiting sailors will be able to enjoy its many attractions. In the meantime, boats setting off from Northern Florida are probably better off sailing through the Bahamas and Windward Passage to reach Central America. The answer is not so simple for boats leaving from Southern Florida, for which both alternatives have certain attractions. Although Mexico itself is more easily reached by a direct route through the Yucatan Channel, a voyage to Belize, Guatemala, or Honduras by the same route is shorter but tougher, mainly because of the contrary current. In contrast, the roundabout route via the Bahamas and Windward Passage is considerably longer, but benefits from mostly favourable winds and current, and also offers the chance of several interesting stops en route.

The time of year when the passage is made will have a major bearing on the choice of route. In winter, when strong E and NE winds can be expected, a direct route through the Yucatan Channel is to be preferred, not just for destinations in Guatemala, Belize, or Honduras, but even as far as Panama. However, this may mean waiting until favourable conditions set in. In winter, the recommended time to leave is immediately after a norther has blown itself out. The best time for a southbound passage, at least as far south as the Yucatan Peninsula, is from mid-April to the end of June. At this time, winds may be light and one has to be prepared to motor. To avoid the full strength of the current, which can be as high as 2.5 knots, it is recommended to either sail a route which stays close to the Dry Tortugas, or cross over towards Cuba and follow that country's NW coast, but making sure one does not stray into its territorial waters. A good departure point from the US is Key West. The northern route (AN117A) stays just outside the 100 fathom line to WP AN1171, 14 miles south of the Dry Tortugas. From there a direct course can be set to pass through the Yucatan Channel to WP AN1172, two miles north of Isla Mujeres, a convenient place to clear into Mexico. From there one is in easy reach of the best cruising grounds in Central America, whether in Belize, Guatemala, or Honduras.

If not intending to stop in Mexico or carry on to Belize and Guatemala, it is probably better to cross over from Key West to the Cuban side (AN117B)

and sail along its coast to WP AN1173, eight miles off Cape San Antonio. A weak but favourable countercurrent may be experienced along Cuba's north coast. Having passed through the Yucatan Channel, a direct course leads to WP AN1174 between Sueno and Serrana Banks, both of which have lights. From there, course is altered for WP AN1175, the landfall buoy marking the entrance into the Panama Canal.

Increasingly boats stop in Cuba and a convenient place to clear into that country is Marina Hemingway, west of Havana. The marina is sometimes confusingly referred to as Barlovento and the easiest way to find the entrance through the reef is to identify the outer marker, whose GPS coordinates are reported as 23°05.3'N, 82°29.3'W. The entrance should not be attempted in strong onshore winds when big rollers break all around the narrow pass through the reef. Guarda Frontera should be contacted on VHF channel 16 when entering Cuban territorial waters. Hemingway Marina monitors channel 72. Contact the marina on channel 16 when 12 miles out and the control tower will acknowledge. The marina monitors channels 16, 72 and also SSB 7462 kHz. It is essential to line up well for the entry into the channel, which is flanked by reefs on both sides.

At the change of seasons, or in early summer, a route via the Windward Passage (AN117C) may be more attractive than the one through the Yucatan Channel described above. From a port in North Florida, such as St Augustine (AN1176), the Windward Passage is best reached by sailing on a SE course which avoids the Abacos to WP AN1177. There the route turns south to pass west of San Salvador, Crooked and Acklins Island to WP AN1178, in Mira-Por-Vos Passage. A slight course alteration will be needed to reach WP AN1179, eight miles NE of Cuba's Cape Maisi. From there on, the route south of the Windward Passage is described in AN114. The southbound route across the Caribbean Sea is also joined in the Windward Passage by boats coming from ports in South Florida, either via the Bahamas or through the Old Bahama Channel.

AN118 *Southern Bahamas to the Western Caribbean*

BEST TIME:	December to May
TROPICAL STORMS:	June to November
CHARTS:	BA: 1220, 2579
	US: 400
PILOTS:	BA: 69A, 70
	US: 147, 148
CRUISING GUIDES:	*Yachtsman's Guide to the Bahamas, Cruising Guide to the Northwest Caribbean, Cruising Guide to Belize and Mexico's Caribbean Coast, The Insider's Cruising Guide to the Rio Dulce.*
WAYPOINTS:	

Departure	Intermediate	Landfall	Destination	Distance (M)
AN1180 Matthew *20°56'N, 73°42'W*	AN1181 Caleta *19°50'N, 74°20'W* AN1182 Guantanamo *19°45'N, 75°00'W* AN1183 Swan *16°55'N, 84°00'W*		Guanaja *16°28'N, 85°54'W* Livingston *15°50.5'N, 88°43.5'W*	766 933
AN1180 Matthew	AN1181 Caleta AN1182 Guantanamo	AN1184 Mauger *17°40'N, 87°43'W*	Belize City *17°30'N, 88°10'W*	874

Destinations in the Western Caribbean are best reached by sailing through the Windward Passage and continuing south of Cuba. Matthew Town, on Great Inagua, is the largest settlement in the Southern Bahamas and, although facilities are basic, it has regular air links with Nassau so that any essential supplies can be flown in. The initial route heads south past Cape Maisi, then course is altered to the west to pass south of Guantanamo. In an emergency one may be able to stop here, provided one obtains permission by radio before approaching the harbour, otherwise the nearest port in Cuba is Santiago de Cuba (19°59'N, 75°53'W), where cruising boats have stopped without any problems.

For boats bound for Honduras, the route leads to a point off Swan Island, and thence to the port of destination, Guanaja being one of the official ports of entry. The coordinates listed for Livingston is the reported GPS position of the buoy marking the river entrance. The direct route to Belize passes south of Grand Cayman and makes landfall close to Mauger Cay, which has a light and is passed at a safe distance to the north. The reef strewn approaches to Belize City should be approached only in daylight and preferably before noon, so as to have the sun from behind. Eastern Channel is the main pass that leads into Belize City.

Winds, especially in winter, are normally favourable on this route and one should also have a slight current in one's favour when sailing along the south coast of Cuba. On the route to Belize, a number of shoals will be passed as one crosses meridian 84°, where rough seas may be experienced – especially during a period of sustained trade winds. If this is the case, the course should be altered to avoid sailing through this area.

AN120 ROUTES FROM BERMUDA

Bermuda occupies such a strategic position in the Western Atlantic that even those planning not to stop there find it difficult to bypass this attractive island. Although good protection is assured in its well sheltered harbours, the approaches to Bermuda are dangerous and a brief look at the chart will explain why this cluster of islands surrounded by reefs was first settled by shipwrecked Englishmen on their way to America. In more recent times a shipping exclusion zone has been declared around Bermuda's shores, and ships are warned to keep their distance unless they intend to call there. However, with reliable lights and clearly marked channels, the approaches are not too difficult, unless one attempts to make landfall at night or in a southwesterly blow, neither of which are recommended.

Bermuda is in the Horse Latitudes, the region of variables north of the trade wind zone and south of the westerlies. There is no prevailing wind and the weather of the island is affected by two main systems, the position of the Azores high and the flow of weather systems over the eastern seaboard of the United States into the Atlantic. In summer the Azores high is the dominating feature and produces SW winds of around 15 knots. The Gulf Stream also influences the climate, making the water around Bermuda warmer and keeping the winters mild. Hurricanes cannot be ignored, although most of these tropical storms which form in the North Atlantic curve to pass to the west of Bermuda, very few storms passing directly over the island. The hurricane season is officially 1 June to 30 November, the greatest frequency occurring from August until October. In winter high winds and gales strike the island, February being the worst month with an average of 8 gales.

Around 1000 cruising boats call at Bermuda every year, most of them spending only a few days there before setting off for new destinations.

Bermuda is the finishing point of various races from the US east coast, the biannual race from Newport being one of the longest established off-shore races in the world. Most people, however, use Bermuda as a convenient springboard either to the Caribbean or to the Azores and Europe. The routes radiating from Bermuda are very seasonal, the spring, from April to June, being busy with boats returning home either to North America or Europe. At such time, European boats are in the majority and in Bermuda they are joined by US or Canadian boats also bound for Europe. The summer sees mainly a two-way traffic from the USA as the hurricane season keeps most people away from the Caribbean, while the autumn brings a new influx of North American boats on their way south.

Those starting their transatlantic voyage in Bermuda are confronted with a serious challenge and there are few routes described in this book on which access to up-to-date weather information is of such paramount importance as the route to the Azores. The position of the North Atlantic high or anticyclone, commonly referred to as the Azores high, ought to be known at all times and a course chosen accordingly. Occasionally, uncommon easterly winds slow down the boats making their way to the Azores in spring. This is due to the Azores high being situated much farther north than its normal position for an unusually long time, allowing easterly winds to make themselves felt as far north as 40°N. Under such circumstances, even the accepted practice of heading north to pick up the prevailing westerlies would make no difference.

Passages to the United States are very much a matter of luck as they can be fast and comfortable with southerly winds, or a hard beat if northwesterly winds are generated by a depression passing to the north. Because of the north-setting Gulf Stream, passages to ports south of Cape

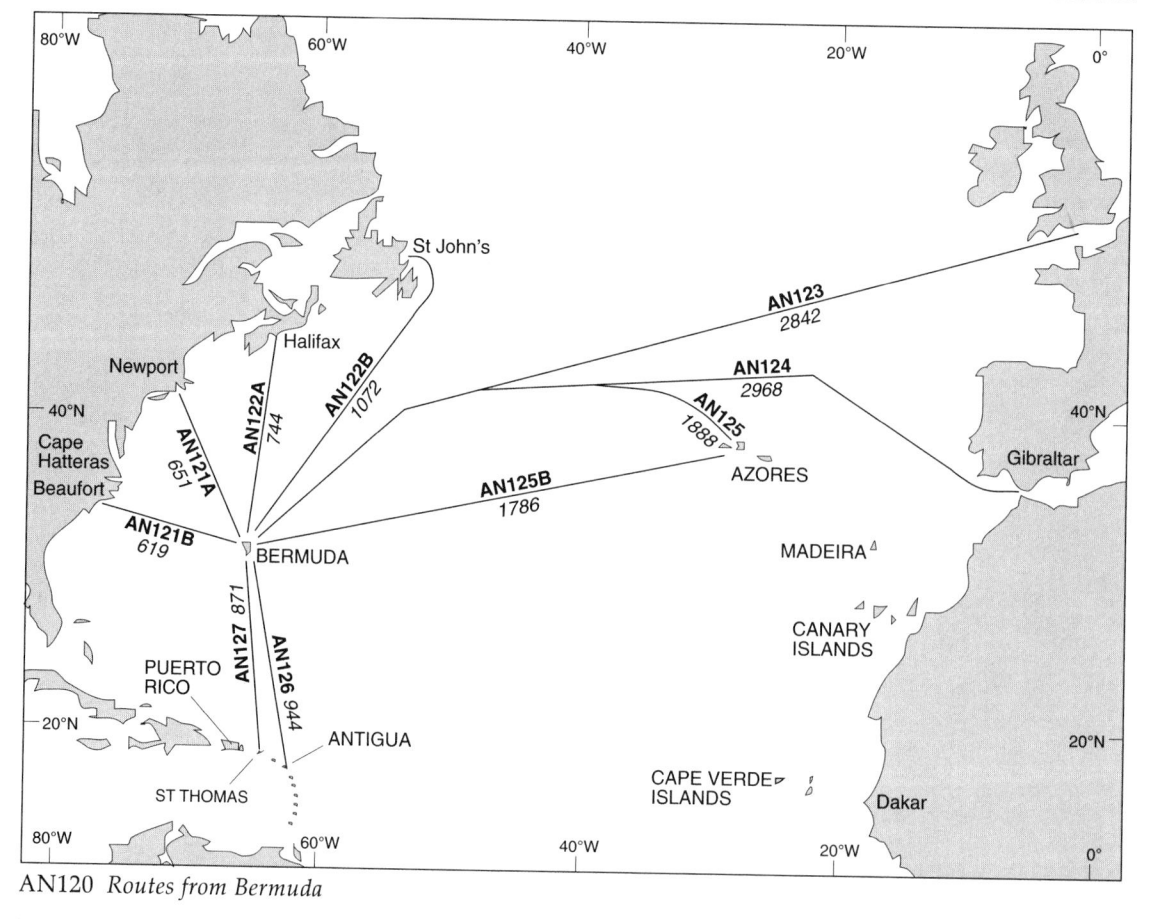

AN120 *Routes from Bermuda*

Hatteras are a difficult undertaking. However, the Gulf Stream does not affect passages to the Eastern Caribbean, which are best undertaken at the change of seasons, betweeen the middle of November and early December.

AN121 *Bermuda to USA*

BEST TIME:	May to June
TROPICAL STORMS:	June to November
CHARTS:	BA: 4403
	US: 403
PILOTS:	BA: 69, 70
	US: 140, 147
CRUISING GUIDES:	*Cruising Guide to the Atlantic Coast, Cruising Guide to the New England Coast.*

WAYPOINTS:

Departure	Intermediate	Landfall	Destination	Distance (M)
Route AN121A				
AN1210 St George's	AN1211 Bermuda W	AN1213 Brenton	Newport	651
32°22'N, 64°40'W	32°12'N, 64°50'W	41°24'N, 71°16'W	*41°29'N, 71°20'W*	
		AN1214 Chesapeake		615
		36°45'N, 75°45'W		
Route AN121B				
AN1210 St George's	AN1212 North Rock	AN1213 Brenton	Newport	634
	32°30'N, 64°50'W	AN1214 Chesapeake		607

Summer passages to most ports on the US east coast normally benefit from pleasant weather and the only thing to spoil the picture is the risk of tropical storms whose tracks pass too close to Bermuda for comfort. Such storms, however, are kept under such close observation from the moment they start forming that warnings are usually given long before they are likely to strike. Nevertheless, passages during the months with the highest frequency of hurricanes, from August to the end of October, should be avoided. Safer passages, in both directions, can be made in late spring and early summer. The high frequency of SW winds in summer should provide good sailing conditions to most ports lying north of Cape Hatteras, but this is rarely the case. Even in May and June, the weather can often turn quite rough and the worst conditions have been recorded in the area of the Gulf Stream. The passage of cold fronts from continental America produces unsettled weather, which is often accompanied by violent rain squalls. This can be particularly dangerous in the Gulf Stream, when a strong wind blows against the equally strong current and therefore the Gulf Stream

should always be crossed at right angles to minimise the time spent in it. A ride in the Gulf Stream should only be attempted if the weather is settled.

Depending on weather conditions on leaving Bermuda, the island can be left either to port or starboard before course is set for one's port of destination. If a SW course can be sailed after leaving the island, the point of departure will be WP AN1211, SW of the island and well clear of all dangers. Boats going around the north of Bermuda and leaving the island to port will take their departure at WP AN1212 off North Rock. Because of the multitude of destinations and resulting routes, only landfall waypoints for the main destination have been given, AN1213 SE off Brenton Reef, for boats bound for Newport, or AN1214 at the entrance into the south channel leading into the Chesapeake Bay. For those not familiar with the USA, who are sailing there at the beginning of the summer season, a useful tip is to start their cruising as far north and east as possible, so as to benefit most from the warm weather and also the reduced risk of hurricanes, and then work their way gradually to the south.

AN122 *Bermuda to Canada*

BEST TIME:	Mid-June to July			
TROPICAL STORMS:	June to November			
CHARTS:	BA: 4011			
	US: 121			
PILOTS:	BA: 59, 65, 70			
	US: 140, 145, 146, 147			
CRUISING GUIDES:	*Cruising Guide to the Nova Scotia Coast, Cruising Guide to Newfoundland.*			
WAYPOINTS:				

Departure	*Intermediate*	*Landfall*	*Destination*	*Distance (M)*
Route AN122A				
AN1220 St George's	AN1221 North Rock	AN1222 off Halifax	Halifax	744
32°22'N, 64°40'W	32°30'N, 64°50'W	44°25'N, 63°25'W	*44°38'N, 63°34'W*	
Route AN122B				
AN1220 St George's	AN1221 North Rock			
	AN1223 Race	AN1224 Spear	St John's	1077
	46°25'N, 53°10'W	47°30'N, 52°39'W	*47°34'N, 52°42'W*	

Weather conditions for this route are similar to AN121, although the optimum time for sailing it is somewhat later. One added complication is that at the beginning of summer passages to ports in Newfoundland can be affected by ice. Fog is yet another consideration on these routes and these factors limit northbound passages to the high summer. Favourable conditions can be expected at this time because of a high proportion of SW winds. Earlier passages, at the end of May or in June, may also benefit from favourable winds, but a careful eye should be kept on the weather and should there be a gale warning, the course should be altered to avoid being caught on one of the banks where the strong wind will generate very rough seas. Similar action should be taken if there is a threat of a northerly gale while riding the Gulf Stream.

Taking WP AN1221 north of Bermuda as a departure point, a direct course (AN122A) leads to WP AN1222 in the approaches to Halifax, Nova Scotia. Leaving from the same waypoint AN1221, the course for St John's, Newfoundland (AN122B), uses WP AN1223 SE of Cape Race, as an intermediate point before course is altered for WP AN1224 off Cape Spear in the approaches to St John's.

AN123 *Bermuda to Northern Europe*

BEST TIME:	May to July			
TROPICAL STORMS:	June to November			
CHARTS:	BA: 4011			
	US: 120, 121			
PILOTS:	BA: 27, 40, 67, 70			
	US: 140, 147, 191			
CRUISING GUIDES:	*The Shell Channel Pilot.*			
WAYPOINTS:				
Departure	**Intermediate**	**Landfall**	**Destination**	**Distance (M)**
AN1230 Bermuda	AN1231			
32°22'N, 64°38'W	39°00'N, 55°00'W			
	AN1232	AN1233 Lizard		2842
	39°00'N, 50°00'W	49°55'N, 5°10'W		

The nonstop route to Northern Europe is far less popular than AN125, as most sailors prefer to stop in the Azores, conveniently placed about halfway between Bermuda and Europe. However, the direct route has the advantage over route AN125 that once the prevailing westerly winds have been found they can usually be held for most of the crossing. On leaving Bermuda, from WP AN1230 it is recommended to sail a NNE course to WP AN1231 before altering course for WP AN1232. Having reached that point, the great circle route to the English Channel can be joined. It must be stressed that both are highly hypothetical points, as the main objective of the exercise is to reach as quickly as possible the area of prevailing westerly winds. To avoid the southern limit of ice, in early summer it is recommended that the latitude of WP AN1232 is not passed. If one has access to either weather or ice information, and knows what to expect in the immediate future, or if favourable SW winds are found right from the start, the great circle route can be joined directly. Occasionally it

may be necessary to go to 40°N or even further north to reach the area of prevailing westerlies.

While the frequency of gales is lower to the south of the recommended route, the temptation to turn east too soon should be resisted because of the danger of losing the westerlies as one enters the Azores high which extends further north in summer. The Gulf Stream runs along most of this route and a favourable rate of at least 1/2 knot can be expected. Boats that have tried to follow the great circle route all the way from Bermuda to the English Channel have experienced prolonged calms as the route crosses the area of high pressure, hence the two recommended waypoints. In the absence of reliable weather information it is therefore recommended to make the crossing in higher, rather than lower, latitudes. Hurricanes rarely affect this route outside the immediate vicinity of Bermuda, but late summer passages are nevertheless discouraged because of the violent storms that occasionally occur in the Eastern Atlantic after the middle of August.

AN124 *Bermuda to Gibraltar*

BEST TIME:	May to July
TROPICAL STORMS:	June to November
CHARTS:	BA: 4011
	US: 120
PILOTS:	BA: 67, 70
	US: 140, 143, 147
CRUISING GUIDES:	*Yacht Scene, East Spain Pilot.*

WAYPOINTS:

Departure	Intermediate	Landfall	Destination	Distance (M)
AN1240 Bermuda 32°22'N, 64°38'W	AN1241 39°00'N, 55°00'W AN1242 40°00'N, 20°00'W AN1243 Vincent NW 37°00'N, 9°08'W AN1244 Hoyo 36°04'N, 6°20'W AN1245 Tarifa 35°59'N, 5°36'W AN1246 Carnero 36°03'N, 5°25'W	AN1247 Gibraltar 36°08'N, 5°22'W	Marina Bay *36°09'N, 5°21'W*	2968

Boats bound for the Mediterranean have the choice of sailing nonstop from Bermuda or the more popular alternative of breaking the voyage in the Azores. The direct route should follow similar instructions as AN123 so as to make most of the Atlantic crossing with the help of the prevailing westerly winds and east setting current. Taking one's leave from WP AN1240 NE of Bermuda, a course should be set for WP AN1241. Depending on weather conditions, the crossing should be made as close as feasible to latitude 40°N, or even higher if conditions warrant it. From WP AN1242 the course can be altered for WP AN1243, seven

miles west of Cape St Vincent. It is unlikely that westerly winds will continue beyond WP AN1242, as the prevailing winds of summer in the vicinity of the Portuguese coast are northerly. Instructions for the section between Cape St Vincent and Gibraltar are described in detail in route AN16 (page 46).

A stop in the Azores will provide an interesting interlude, but will add considerably to the passage. Allowance should also be made for a slower passage from the Azores to continental Europe. For more details see routes AN125 and AN134 (below and page 151).

AN125 *Bermuda to Azores*

BEST TIME:	May to June
TROPICAL STORMS:	June to November
CHARTS:	BA: 4011
	US: 120
PILOTS:	BA: 67, 70
	US: 140, 143, 147
CRUISING GUIDES:	*Azores Cruising Guide, Atlantic Islands.*
WAYPOINTS:	

Departure	Intermediate	Landfall	Destination	Distance (M)
Route AN125A AN1250 Bermuda 32°22'N, 64°38'W	AN1251 40°00'N, 55°00'W AN1252 40°00'N, 50°00'W AN1253 Azores 40°00'N, 32°30'W	AN1254 Flores 39°20'N, 31°18'W AN1255 Faial 38°30'N, 28°50'W	Lajes *39°23'N, 31°10'W* Horta *38°32'N, 28°37.5'W*	1761 1888

WAYPOINTS:				
Departure	*Intermediate*	*Landfall*	*Destination*	*Distance (M)*
Route AN125B				
AN1250 Bermuda		AN1254 Flores	Lajes	1670
		AN1255 Faial	Horta	1786

The Azores are situated in such a convenient position in mid-Atlantic that very few boats choose to sail nonstop from Bermuda to Europe. Because Bermuda lies to the south of the region of prevailing westerlies, the recommended strategy is to make as much northing as possible after leaving Bermuda in the hope of picking up favourable winds around latitude 40°N. The advantages of this somewhat indirect route (AN125A), which goes north of 40°N, are a greater certainty of W or SW winds and a favourable current. The disadvantages are a higher frequency of gales and a colder and wetter passage than along a more southerly route which does not go beyond latitude 38°N. Opinions are divided as to which is the best course to follow and in fact some people prefer to forgo the chance of favourable winds and, in their attempts to find the most pleasant alternative, follow a rhumb line to the Azores (AN125B). This option may indeed ensure warmer weather, but is often bedevilled by calms and headwinds. If the northern route is sailed in late spring or even early summer, it is advisable not to sail beyond 40°N before WP AN1252 is reached, because of the danger of ice in the early part of summer.

May and June are the best months to make this passage, a later start being preferable if the northern route is chosen. If this decision is taken, it is best to commit oneself fully to that route and sail almost NNE on leaving Bermuda so as to enter the region of westerlies as soon as possible. After the beginning of July, the risk of hurricanes becomes increasingly higher in the area around Bermuda and this passage should only be made at such time if absolutely necessary. The risk of hurricanes recedes as one moves east across the Atlantic, although the effects of a hurricane can be felt as far east as the Bay of Biscay.

Looking at the records of passages made over a number of years, it soon becomes obvious that the slowest passages were made by those who were not prepared to go far enough north in search of westerlies. Most of those boats who stayed south of latitude 38°N encountered calms as they entered the ridge of high pressure that extends between Bermuda and the Azores much earlier than if they had kept further north. Sooner or later the Azores high will slow down any boat making this passage, but by approaching the Azores from the NW rather than the west, the ridge of high pressure will be crossed at right angles and the time needed to cross it will be shorter. At such times the use of the engine is recommended and, particularly if taking a southern route, a good supply of fuel should be taken on board before leaving Bermuda.

Taking WP AN1250 as a departure point from Bermuda, boats sailing on route AN125A are recommended to set a course for WP AN1251 and remain on that latitude to WP AN1252. In late spring, the course should not go above latitude 39°N because of the risk of ice. If weather conditions are favourable, the same latitude should be maintained as far as WP AN1253, 60 miles NW from Corvo and Flores, the westernmost islands in the Azores. From this point, course can be altered for one's port of destination.

Boats bound for Lajes, on the SE coast of Flores, should make landfall at WP AN1254, off Ponta do Ilheus, the SW extremity of Flores and then follow the south coast of the island to Lajes. The recent improvements to Lajes have made it an attractive first port of call into the Azores. If bound directly for Horta, which continues to be the favourite Azorean destination, from WP AN1253 course should be set for WP AN1255, five miles SW of Ponta do Castello Branco, and then sail along Faial's south coast, which is the recommended way to approach Horta. In strong SW winds, if Horta is approached from the north, allowance should be made for a strong contrary current in the channel between Faial and Pico.

Boats following a rhumb line from Bermuda (AN125B), can set a direct course from WP AN1250 for AN1254, if bound for Lajes das Flores, or for WP AN1255, if bound for Horta.

AN126 *Bermuda to Lesser Antilles*

BEST TIME:	November to mid-December			
TROPICAL STORMS:	June to November			
CHARTS:	BA: 4400			
	US: 400			
PILOTS:	BA: 70, 71			
	US: 140, 147			
CRUISING GUIDES:	*The Lesser Antilles, Cruising Guide to the Leeward Islands.*			
WAYPOINTS:				

Departure	Intermediate	Landfall	Destination	Distance (M)
AN1260 Bermuda 32°22'N, 64°38'W	AN1261 Barbuda 17°30'N, 61°30'W	AN1262 Antigua E 17°00'N, 61°40'W	English Harbour *17°00'N, 61°45'W*	944
AN1260 Bermuda	AN1263 Sombrero 18°40'N, 63°30'W			
	AN1264 Martin 17°55'N, 63°22'W	AN1265 Antigua NW 17°10'N, 61°55'W	St Johns *17°07'N, 61°52'W*	968

It is difficult to suggest an optimum time for this passage as the summer carries the danger of tropical storms and the winter that of northerly gales. The best time to make this passage is at the change of seasons, when the risk of hurricanes has abated and the frequency of winter storms is acceptably low. Most boats making this passage actually do it at the best time which fortunately coincides with most people's cruising plans. North American boats passing through Bermuda in November are all on their way to the Eastern Caribbean for the start of the winter sailing season.

In November or early December, the winds on leaving Bermuda can be from any direction, and if they are light it is advisable to motor so as to make the necessary southing. Having passed through the belt of variables, the NE trade winds should be found between latitudes 22°N and 25°N. As the northern approaches to the Lesser Antilles are quite dangerous because of the many unlit reefs, as much easting as possible should be made in the early part of the passage so as to pass well to windward of all dangers and approach Antigua from the NE. If this proves to be too difficult, it is better to choose an easier landfall and continue to Antigua, or any other island, in shorter stages.

Taking as a departure point WP AN1260 just out-side Town Cut, a direct course leads to WP AN1261, 15 miles east of Barbuda. The course is then altered for WP AN1262, off Antigua's SE coast. Entry formalities can be completed at English Harbour. If, as suggested above, it is impossible to make sufficient easting to approach the Antilles from windward, a course should be set for WP AN1263, 5 miles north of Sombrero light at the entrance into Anegada Passage. From there course is altered for WP AN1264 NW of St Martin and finally for WP AN1265 off Antigua's west coast. From there the south coast is followed to English Harbour, unless one prefers to complete formalities in the capital St Johns, in which case the course for the latter should be changed earlier.

Although a passage along this route during the hurricane season cannot be recommended, fair weather can be expected at the beginning of summer when the risk of hurricanes is not very high. If southerly winds are encountered on leaving Bermuda, which is quite likely, these should be used to make some easting before the trades are found near latitude 25°N. Occasionally the summer trades do not have a southerly component and then it may be possible to sail a direct course to the Leeward Islands, Antigua being one of the easiest to approach. Otherwise it may be necessary to make landfall in the Virgins as mentioned above.

AN127 *Bermuda to Virgin Islands*

BEST TIME:	November to mid-December			
TROPICAL STORMS:	June to November			
CHARTS:	BA: 4400			
	US: 400			
PILOTS:	BA: 70, 71			
	US: 140, 147			
CRUISING GUIDES:	*Cruising Guide to the Virgin Islands, Yachtsman's Guide to the Virgin Islands.*			
WAYPOINTS:				

Departure	*Intermediate*	*Landfall*	*Destination*	*Distance (M)*
AN1270 Bermuda	AN1271 Culebrita		Charlotte Amalie	850
32°22'N, 64°38'W	18°26'N, 65°10'W		*18°23'N, 64°56'W*	
AN1270 Bermuda	AN1272 Anegada		Virgin Gorda	871
	18°45'N, 63°35'W		*18°27'N, 64°26'W*	

The same directions apply as for route AN126 until the area of trade winds has been reached. Taking as a departure point WP AN1270 just outside Town Cut, a direct course leads to WP AN1271, eight miles NE of the light on Culebrita Island. Keeping at a safe distance to avoid the dangers off the western point of St Thomas, that island's south coast is followed along to its main port of Charlotte Amalie.

Approaching the Virgin Islands from the north, as suggested above, may present some difficulties as most dangers are unlit. As an alternative, it might be advisable to make a landfall on Sombrero Island, which has a powerful light, and approach the Virgins from windward rather than try and make landfall directly on St Thomas. In such a case a course should be set for WP AN1272, 15 miles NW of Sombrero light at the entrance into Anegada Passage. The latter course is in any case recommended for destinations in the British Virgins. Arriving from a NE direction, the nearest port of entry is at Virgin Gorda. However, extreme attention should be paid to the numerous dangers surrounding the Virgin Islands.

AN130 ROUTES FROM THE AZORES

AN131 *Azores to Ireland*	*148*
AN132 *Azores to English Channel*	*148*
AN133 *Azores to Portugal*	*150*
AN134 *Azores to Gibraltar*	*151*
AN135 *Azores to Madeira*	*152*
AN136 *Azores to Canary Islands*	*152*
AN137 *Azores to Bermuda*	*153*
AN138 *Azores to USA*	*154*
AN139 *Azores to Canada*	*154*

Approximately 1000 boats pass through the Azores every year, the majority arriving there from the Caribbean, either direct or via Bermuda. During July a few boats arrive from North America and Northern Europe, but the traffic is confined mainly to the months of May and June, when most boats are on their way to either Northern Europe or the Mediterranean. These are the two main routes taking boats away from the Azores. Boats bound for the English Channel and beyond are usually faced with a tougher passage as the prevailing winds in early summer, when most of these passages are made, are from the NE. Those same winds make the passage through to the Mediterranean an easier affair.

The weather in the Azores themselves is very changeable and this is probably the main reason why most people do not cruise the islands and instead confine themselves to only one stop, usually the marina in Horta. The opening of a second marina in Ponta Delgada and improvements to several ports, notably Lajes on the island of Flores, may well change matters.

The Azores boast an Atlantic climate, of which the dominant feature is the area of high pressure named after them. The position of the Azores high varies with the season, being more to the north in October and furthest south in February. It usually lies to the S or SW of the islands and in summer is often stationary, when prolonged periods of calm can be expected. At other times the winds are very variable in both strength and direction, although those from the western sector are slightly more frequent. Close to land the wind is deflected, especially where the coastline is steep and the direction of the wind varies from island to island and place to place. The weather in the Azores is also affected by the lows which pass across the Atlantic from west to east. These usually pass to the north, except in winter when they can pass directly over the islands. When one of these fronts passes, the winds change quickly, veering from SW to NW and bringing rain. Rain occurs in all months, although more falls in winter, especially associated with the Atlantic lows. Although not in the hurricane belt, extremely rarely a rogue hurricane has taken an abnormal path to pass near the Azores, but is generally weakened by the time it reaches that far. There is a moderate frequency of gales over the Azores, of which more occur in winter months.

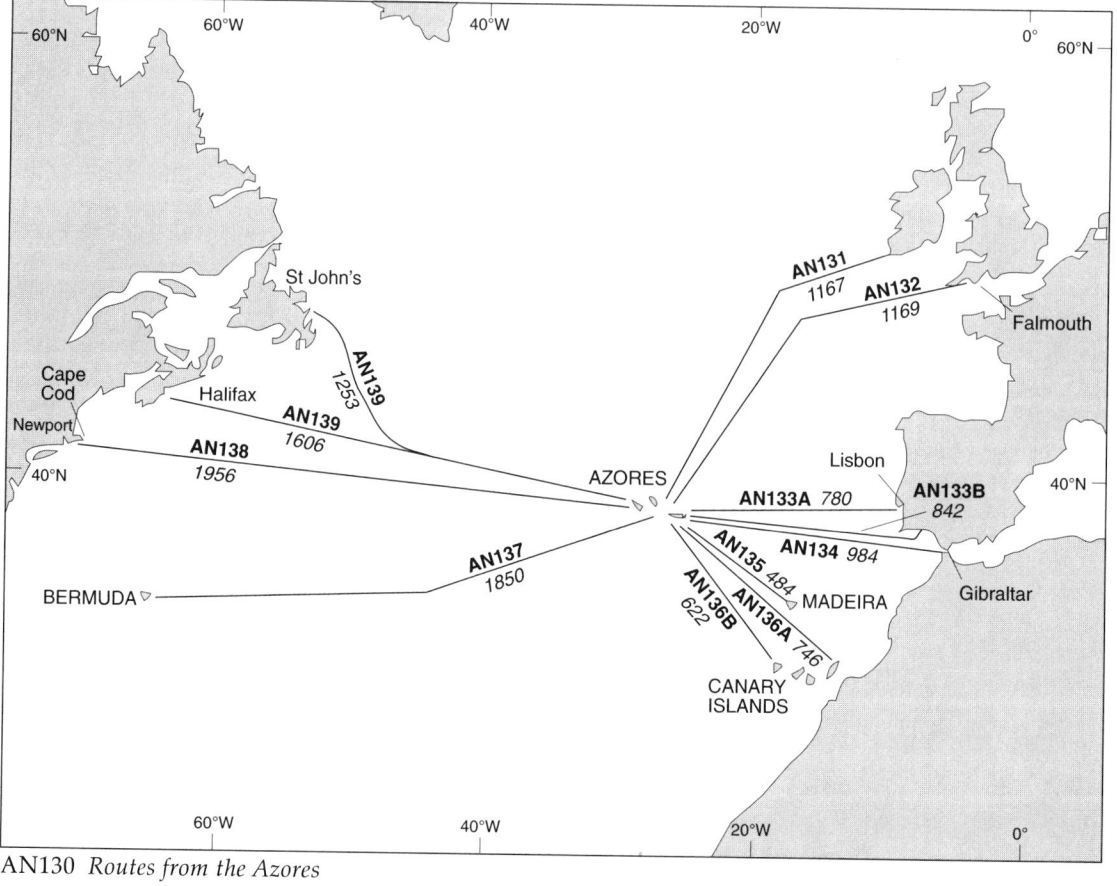

AN130 *Routes from the Azores*

AN131 *Azores to Ireland*

BEST TIME:	June to July			
TROPICAL STORMS:	None			
CHARTS:	BA: 4011			
	US: 126			
PILOTS:	BA: 22, 27, 40, 67			
	US: 140, 142, 143			
CRUISING GUIDES:	Cruising Association Handbook, South and West Coast of Ireland.			
WAYPOINTS:				

Departure	Intermediate	Landfall	Destination	Distance (M)
AN1310 Horta *38°32'N, 28°37'W*	AN1311 Graciosa *39°00'N, 27°55'W*	AN1315 Cork *51°45'N, 8°17'W*	Crosshaven *51°48.5'N, 8°17.5'W*	1167
AN1312 Delgada *37°44'N, 25°40'W*	AN1313 Arnel *37°50'N, 25°05'W*	AN1315 Cork	Crosshaven	1126
AN1312 Delgada	AN1314 Ferraria *37°52'N, 25°52'W*	AN1315 Cork	Crosshaven	1130

The same general directions apply as for route AN132, but as destinations in Ireland are more westerly than those in the English Channel, the suggestion to sail due north on leaving the Azores does not have to be followed slavishly as it does not matter too much if some leeway is made to the west. This can be corrected later with the help of the westerlies that normally prevail in higher latitudes. Calms are sometimes experienced in the vicinity of the Azores, particularly in July and August, when the Azores high reaches its maximum pressure of the year. Calms and light variable winds might also be encountered en route, so one should leave with a good supply of fuel. With the exception of the odd sunny day at the start, the weather along this route is invariably grey, wet, and cold.

Boats leaving from Horta should pass close to the western extremity of São Jorge and then set course for WP AN1311 one mile SE of Ilheu de Baixo, a small islet off Graciosa's SE extremity. A northerly course can then be set to pass east of Graciosa. In strong SW winds, shelter can be sought at the well protected port of Praia (39°03'N, 27°58'W), on Graciosa's east coast, although such winds should really be used to advantage.

If leaving from Ponta Delgada, São Miguel's south coast should be followed as far as Ponta do Arnel, its easternmost headland, to WP AN1313 from where a course can be set for one's destination. In strong NE winds, it is better to sail west on leaving Ponta Delgada and take one's leave from the Azores at WP AN1314 off Ponta da Ferraria at the NW extremity of São Miguel. Landfall is made at WP AN1315, in the approaches to Cork Harbour, one of the best protected ports on the south coast of Ireland. Entry formalities are completed in Crosshaven.

AN132 *Azores to English Channel*

BEST TIME:	June to July
TROPICAL STORMS:	None
CHARTS:	BA: 4103
	US: 126
PILOTS:	BA: 22, 27, 67
	US: 140, 143, 191
CRUISING GUIDES:	Cruising Association Handbook, The Shell Channel Pilot.

WAYPOINTS:				
Departure	*Intermediate*	*Landfall*	*Destination*	*Distance (M)*
AN1320 Horta *38°32'N, 28°37'W*	AN1322 Graciosa *39°00'N, 27°55'W* AN1325 *43°00'N, 20°00'W* AN1326 *47°50'N, 10°00'W*	AN1327 Lizard *49°55'N, 5°10'W*	Falmouth *50°09'N, 5°04'W*	1227
AN1321 Delgada *37°44'N, 25°40'W*	AN1323 Arnel *37°50'N, 25°05'W* AN1325 AN1326	AN1327 Lizard	Falmouth	1169
AN1321 Delgada	AN1324 Ferraria *37°52'N, 25°52'W* AN1325 AN1326	AN1327 Lizard	Falmouth	1174

The prevailing winds of summer are NE and therefore all passages from the Azores to Northern Europe are usually close hauled. A direct course for the English Channel is rarely possible, nor is it advisable, as the westerly winds and east-setting current that prevail in higher latitudes will set the boat into the Bay of Biscay. The usual tactic for this route is to sail due north until steady westerly winds are encountered, but not to join the great circle route to the English Channel before latitude 45°N has been reached.

In the area immediately to the north of the Azores calms are frequent, their extent depending on the position of the Azores high and the ridge of high pressure that normally extends from it towards Europe during summer. If such calm spots are encountered one should be prepared to motor through them and make the desired northing. Even if there is no wind, the weather will be fine and sunny before it gives way to westerly winds, overcast skies, and generally wet and cold weather. Summer weather for the English Channel is difficult to predict and the winds can come from any direction and at any strength. Visibility can become poor in the approaches to the Channel and both this fact and the presence of strong tidal currents, as well as the large amount of shipping, must all be borne in mind when making a landfall on the English coast.

Boats leaving from Horta should pass close to the western extremity of São Jorge and on to WP AN1322 one mile SE of Ilheu de Baixo, an islet off Graciosa's SE point. From there, a northerly course is set to reach the area of prevailing westerly winds at which point the course can be altered for WP AN1327.

If leaving from Ponta Delgada, São Miguel's south coast should be followed as far as Ponta do Arnel, its easternmost headland, to WP AN1323. In strong NE winds, it is better to sail west on leaving Ponta Delgada and take one's leave from the Azores at WP AN1324 off Ponta da Ferraria, São Miguel's NW extremity. A course should then be set for WPs AN1325 and AN1326 on the rhumb line to the English Channel, where landfall will be made at WP AN1327 10 miles south of Lizard Point. A convenient place to clear into the United Kingdom is the port of Falmouth (50°09'N, 5°04'W).

AN133 *Azores to Portugal*

BEST TIME:	May to September			
TROPICAL STORMS:	None			
CHARTS:	BA: 4103			
	US: 126			
PILOTS:	BA: 67			
	US: 140, 143			
CRUISING GUIDES:	*Atlantic Spain and Portugal.*			
WAYPOINTS:				

Departure	Intermediate	Landfall	Destination	Distance (M)
Route AN133A				
AN1330 Delgada	AN1331 Garça	AN1333 S Channel	Lisbon	780
37°44'N, 25°40'W	*37°42'N, 25°22'W*	*38°37'N, 9°20'W*	*38°41.5'N, 9°12'W*	
AN1332 Sta Maria		AN1333 S Channel	Lisbon	757
36°56'N, 25°00'W				
Route AN133B				
AN1330 Delgada	AN1331 Garça			
	AN1334 Vincent SW	AN1335 off Vilamoura	Vilamoura	842
	36°55'N, 9°00'W	*37°03'N, 8°06'W*	*37°04.5'N, 8°07'W*	
AN1332 Sta Maria	AN1334 Vincent SW	AN1335 off Vilamoura	Vilamoura	812

Favourable winds can be expected for most of the way if this passage is made at the beginning of summer. The winds in the vicinity of the islands are variable, with a predominance of SW winds. In May and early June a belt of calms is usually crossed somewhere between the Azores and the mainland before entering the area of prevailing northerly winds. At times the calms can be quite extensive and one should be prepared to motor. Steadier winds can be expected towards the middle of summer. During July and August the strong Portuguese trades, blowing at a steady 15–20 knots, make this a fast and exhilarating trip. Such northerly winds will be encountered from about 300 miles off the Portuguese coast. Occasionally, if the Azores high is located north of the islands, NE winds may be experienced all the way across to Portugal. Because of the prevailing winds, northern ports on the Portuguese coast will be to windward if a rhumb line is sailed from the Azores. This should be taken into account, and also the south setting Portugal Current, when final course

adjustments are made for the port of destination so as to approach the coast slightly to windward of the intended port.

Boats that have cruised the Azores from NW to SE will find it more convenient to take their departure either at Ponta Delgada on São Miguel, or Vila do Porto, on Santa Maria. In the former case, a direct course for the Portuguese mainland can be set from WP AN1331 south of Ponta da Garça, on São Miguel's south coast. If leaving from Santa Maria, the departure point is WP AN1332 off that island's Ponta do Castelo, on Santa Maria's SE extremity. Boats bound for Lisbon (AN133A) should make their landfall at WP AN1333. From there the South Channel leads into the Tagus River on whose north shore lies the Portuguese capital.

The route to Vilamoura, on the Algarve coast (AN133B), leads due east to WP AN1334, 6 miles S of Cape St Vincent. Avoiding the heavy traffic passing through the area, the course should be altered for WP AN1335, one mile SW of Vilamoura. The marina monitors VHF channels 16 and 20.

AN134 *Azores to Gibraltar*

BEST TIME:	May to September			
TROPICAL STORMS:	None			
CHARTS:	BA: 4103			
	US: 126			
PILOTS:	BA: 67			
	US: 131, 140, 143			
CRUISING GUIDES:	*Yacht Scene, East Spain Pilot.*			
WAYPOINTS:				

Departure	Intermediate	Landfall	Destination	Distance (M)
AN1340 Delgada *37°44'N, 25°40'W*	AN1341 Garça *37°42'N, 25°22'W* AN1343 Strait *36°00'N, 6°00'W* AN1344 Tarifa *35°59'N, 5°36'W*	AN1345 Gibraltar *36°08.5'N, 5°22'W*	Marina Bay *36°09'N, 5°21'W*	984
AN1342 Sta Maria *36°56'N, 25°00'W*	AN1343 Strait AN1344 Tarifa	AN1345 Gibraltar	Marina Bay	952

Directions as far as Cape St Vincent are the same as those for AN133 and similar weather conditions can be expected until the route comes under the influence of continental weather. East of Cape St Vincent, the Portuguese trades are normally lost and winds become more local in character. On summer days, a SW sea breeze occurs on approaching the Bay of Cadiz. This wind comes up around noon and lasts until midnight. If a strong *Levanter* is predicted in the Strait of Gibraltar, it is advisable to wait for a change in one of the ports along the Algarve coast (Vilamoura), Costa de la Luz (Mazagon, near Huelva), or Bay of Cadiz (Puerto Sherry). Another convenient port is Barbate, which is not far west of Tarifa and is the closest to the Strait. Alternatively, one can find some shelter in the lee of Tarifa Island itself. The latest weather information, as well as other shipping news, can be obtained from Tarifa Radio, which operates a 24-hour service in both Spanish and English.

Two convenient ports from where to depart the Azores are Ponta Delgada, on São Miguel, or Vila do Porto, on Santa Maria. In the former case, a direct course for the Strait of Gibraltar can be set from WP AN1341 south of Ponta da Garça, on São Miguel's south coast. If leaving from Santa Maria, take your departure from WP AN1342 off that island's Ponta do Castelo. A direct course should be set to WP AN1343 in the approaches to the Strait of Gibraltar. From there, sail due east to WP AN1344, two miles south of Tarifa Island by staying inshore of the westgoing shipping lane. A course parallel to the Spanish coast will take one into the Bay of Gibraltar. The reporting dock for customs and two of the marinas are easiest found by making for WP AN1345 off the North Mole. Detailed directions for negotiating the Strait of Gibraltar are given in route AN16 (page 46).

AN135 *Azores to Madeira*

BEST TIME:	May to August			
TROPICAL STORMS:	None			
CHARTS:	BA: 4104			
	US: 126			
PILOTS:	BA: 1, 67			
	US: 143			
CRUISING GUIDES:	*Atlantic Islands, Madeira Cruising Guide.*			
WAYPOINTS:				

Departure	Intermediate	Landfall	Destination	Distance (M)
AN1350 Vila		AN1351 Pargo	Funchal	484
36°57'N, 25°07'W		32°38'N, 17°20'W	*32°37.5'N, 16°54.5'W*	

The winds between these two Portuguese outposts are usually favourable and the likelihood of NE winds increases as one approaches Madeira. A good departure port from the Azores is Vila do Porto on the island of Santa Maria as it is the nearest to Madeira. From WP AN1350 south of Vila do Porto, a direct course can be set for WP AN1351 off Ponta do Pargo at Madeira's western end. From there the course runs parallel to Madeira's SW coast to the capital and main port Funchal. Funchal marina monitors VHF channel 16 during office hours.

AN136 *Azores to Canary Islands*

BEST TIME:	June to August			
TROPICAL STORMS:	None			
CHARTS:	BA: 4104			
	US: 126			
PILOTS:	BA: 1, 67			
	US: 143			
CRUISING GUIDES:	*Canary Islands Cruising Guide, Atlantic Islands.*			
WAYPOINTS:				

Departure	Intermediate	Landfall	Destination	Distance (M)
Route AN136A				
AN1360 Delgada		AN1363 Graciosa	La Sociedad	794
37°44'N, 25°40'W		29°25'N, 13°35'W	*29°13.8'N, 13°30'W*	
AN1362 Vila		AN1363 Graciosa	La Sociedad	746
36°57'N, 25°07'W				
Route AN136B				
AN1360 Delgada		AN1364 Palma	Santa Cruz	675
		28°52'N, 17°45'W	*28°40.5'N, 17°45.5'W*	
AN1362 Vila		AN1364 Palma	Santa Cruz	622

Both winds and current are usually favourable on this passage. If the intention is to cruise the Canaries it is best to sail first to one of the eastern islands of the Canarian archipelago, such as Lanzarote. This will ensure favourable winds during the subsequent cruise and also allows the islands to be visited in logical order. The direct route from the Azores to Lanzarote (AN136A) passes so close to Madeira as to make a stop there almost unavoidable. Directions for the route to Madeira are described in AN135. The subsequent section from Madeira to the Canaries is dealt with in route AN41 (page 67).

The direct route from Ponta Delgada or Santa Maria to Lanzarote (AN136A) bypasses Madeira and goes NE of the Salvagem Islands. Landfall is made at WP AN1363, about 5 miles NW of Graciosa, before entering Estrecho del Rio, the channel separating Graciosa from Lanzarote. Although not a port of entry, boats may stop for a short time at La Sociedad, the main port and settlement on Graciosa, before proceeding to Lanzarote and clearing in there.

If the Canaries are only used as an intermediate stop to prepare for a transatlantic passage, it may be more convenient to only call at one of the western islands, such as La Palma (AN136B). Course should be set for WP AN1364 NE of the island's capital, Santa Cruz de la Palma. This is an excellent place for reprovisioning the boat for the onward passage.

AN137 *Azores to Bermuda*

BEST TIME:	June to July
TROPICAL STORMS:	June to November
CHARTS:	BA: 4012
	US: 120
PILOTS:	BA: 67, 70
	US: 140, 143, 147
CRUISING GUIDES:	*Yachting Guide to Bermuda.*
WAYPOINTS:	

Departure	Intermediate	Landfall	Destination	Distance (M)
AN1371 Faial 38°30'N, 28°37'W	AN1373 35°00'N, 35°00'W	AN1374 Bermuda 32°22'N, 64°38'W	St George's *32°22'N, 64°40'W*	1850
AN1372 Flores 39°22'N, 31°10'W	AN1373	AN1374 Bermuda	St George's	1804

For most sailors contemplating this passage, the Azores are only a convenient stop on a longer voyage, and so is the stop in Bermuda. Horta used to be the traditional starting point for the passage to Bermuda, but the improvements to the port of Lajes, on Flores, now makes it possible to start one's voyage at the western extremity of the Azorean archipelago. However, as the recommended tactic is to reach the latitude of Bermuda as soon as possible, the advantage of starting from Lajes is minimal. From whichever port one leaves, it is essential to obtain a long term weather forecast. If westerly winds are forecast it is best to wait for a change rather than try to beat one's way westward. The recommended time, in June or July, is not necessarily the one with the most favourable winds, but with the best chance of good weather.

In summer the predominant winds on the direct route, and especially north of latitude 35°N, are SW and there is also a contrary current, so it is recommended to sail as much as possible on Bermuda's own latitude. This may even entail going further south, to be assured of favourable winds. If westerly winds are encountered in the early part of the voyage, one should stay on the starboard tack even if it means going as far south as latitude 30°N. In summer, the further south one sails, the higher the proportion of easterly winds. The one disadvantage of a late summer passage is the increased risk of hurricanes in or around Bermuda.

If leaving from Horta, from WP AN1371 set a first course to WP AN1373. Boats leaving from Lajes at WP AN1372 should follow the same directions and also set course for the same intermediate waypoint. From that point, the route should follow closely the latitude of Bermuda, as described above. Landfall is made at WP AN1374, two miles from Town Cut at the entrance into St George's Harbour.

AN138 *Azores to USA*

BEST TIME:	June to July
TROPICAL STORMS:	June to November
CHARTS:	BA: 4011
	US: 120
PILOTS:	BA: 67, 68, 69
	US: 140, 143
CRUISING GUIDES:	*Coastal Cruising Guide to the Atlantic Coast, Cruising Guide to the New England Coast.*
WAYPOINTS:	

Departure	Intermediate	Landfall	Destination	Distance (M)
AN1381 Faial 38°30'N, 28°37'W		AN1382 Brenton 41°24'N, 71°16'W	Newport *41°29'N, 71°20'W*	1956
		AN1383 Chesapeake 36°45'N, 75°45'W		2218

A difficult decision to be taken on leaving the Azores is whether or not to call at Bermuda. If a stop in Bermuda is envisaged, the same directions apply as for route AN137. Otherwise, it is probably better to wait and see what the weather does, then sail a course which does not take one too far away from the recommended route to Bermuda, so as to be able to stop there if necessary. The chances of finding favourable winds above latitude 35°N are quite low, which only reinforces the argument for making the passage close to, or even below, the latitude of Bermuda. Therefore, a stop there becomes almost unavoidable, especially for boats bound for ports south of New York. Those sailing to ports lying further NE may find it possible to alter course from about longitude 55°W for their port of destination. Because of the multitude of destinations and resulting routes, only landfall waypoints for the main destinations have been given, AN1382 SE of Brenton Reef in the approaches to Newport, for boats heading for that port, or AN1383 at the entrance into the south channel leading into Chesapeake Bay.

If this passage is made after the middle of June, the risk of an early tropical storm should be borne in mind as the tracks of previous hurricanes pass through the area between Bermuda and continental USA.

AN139 *Azores to Canada*

BEST TIME:	July to August
TROPICAL STORMS:	June to November
CHARTS:	BA: 4011
	US: 120
PILOTS:	BA: 67, 68, 69
	US: 140, 143
CRUISING GUIDES:	*Cruising Guide to the Nova Scotia Coast, Cruising Guide to Newfoundland.*
WAYPOINTS:	

Departure	Intermediate	Landfall	Destination	Distance (M)
AN1391 Faial 38°30'N, 28°37'W		AN1392 off Halifax 44°25'N, 63°25'W	Halifax *44°38'N, 63°34'W*	1606
AN1391 Faial	AN1393 Race 46°25'N, 53°10'W	AN1394 Spear 47°30'N, 52°39'W	St John's *47°34'N, 52°42'W*	1253

Directions are similar to those for route AN138 and similar tactics are suggested if westerly winds are encountered after leaving the Azores. Going on to a port tack too early in the voyage carries the risk of making too much northing and entering an area of steady westerlies and also a contrary current. Particularly in the case of boats with modest windward performance, a southerly route, as described above, has certain attractions. Further west, one may find that SW winds, which predominate in summer west of meridian 50°W, will allow them to go on to the port tack around that point. Boats setting off on a southern route

should take their departure from Horta at WP AN1391. The landfall point for Halifax, in Nova Scotia, is WP AN1392. Boats bound for St John's, in Newfoundland, should make their landfall at WP AN1393 SE of Cape Race, before altering course for WP AN1394 off Cape Spear in the approaches to St John's.

The recommended time for this passage coincides with the start of the hurricane season in the Western Atlantic, so the weather patterns should be observed carefully, especially as one approaches Bermuda, or if a stop there is being considered.

AN140 ATLANTIC ROUTES FROM NORTH AMERICA

The number of boats sailing nonstop to Europe along the higher latitudes has decreased considerably in recent years and most North American boats reach Europe via Bermuda and the Azores. For anyone planning a long offshore voyage from one of the ports north of Chesapeake Bay, whether to the Caribbean or Europe, the first landfall is usually Bermuda. Those heading for the Virgins or Lesser Antilles have a choice of an offshore passage, either via Bermuda or direct. If the port of departure is north of Cape Hatteras, a stop in Bermuda would not add too many miles, but from ports situated further south a direct course makes more sense. Beaufort in North Carolina is a favourite point of departure for the annual southbound exodus and the most common landfall is St Thomas in the US Virgins. Those who leave from ports south of the Carolinas are often tempted to beat their way through the Bahamas, which may not be a solution to everyone's taste as strong easterly winds are likely to be encountered most of the way. All the above passages to the Caribbean should be made after the beginning of November

when the hurricane season has come to an end. An alternative way of reaching the Caribbean by a longer but more attractive route is described at the beginning of this chapter, when routes in the North Atlantic are discussed (see page 38). Routes from Florida are described in AN110 (page 128).

Eastbound passages from North America are undertaken mostly in late spring or early summer, from May until July, when best conditions can be expected. Regardless of the destination, the Gulf Stream will have to be crossed at some point, and because of the difficulties associated with this it is advisable to obtain the latest information concerning the strength and direction of the Gulf Stream. The best sources are the Gulf Stream flow charts issued regularly by NOAA. Anyone leaving on a direct passage to the Caribbean must take into account the strength of the Gulf Stream as well as the possibility of strong northerly winds blowing against the current, a combination which can turn the passage into an extremely uncomfortable experience. If adverse conditions persist it is probably better to make for the nearest continental port

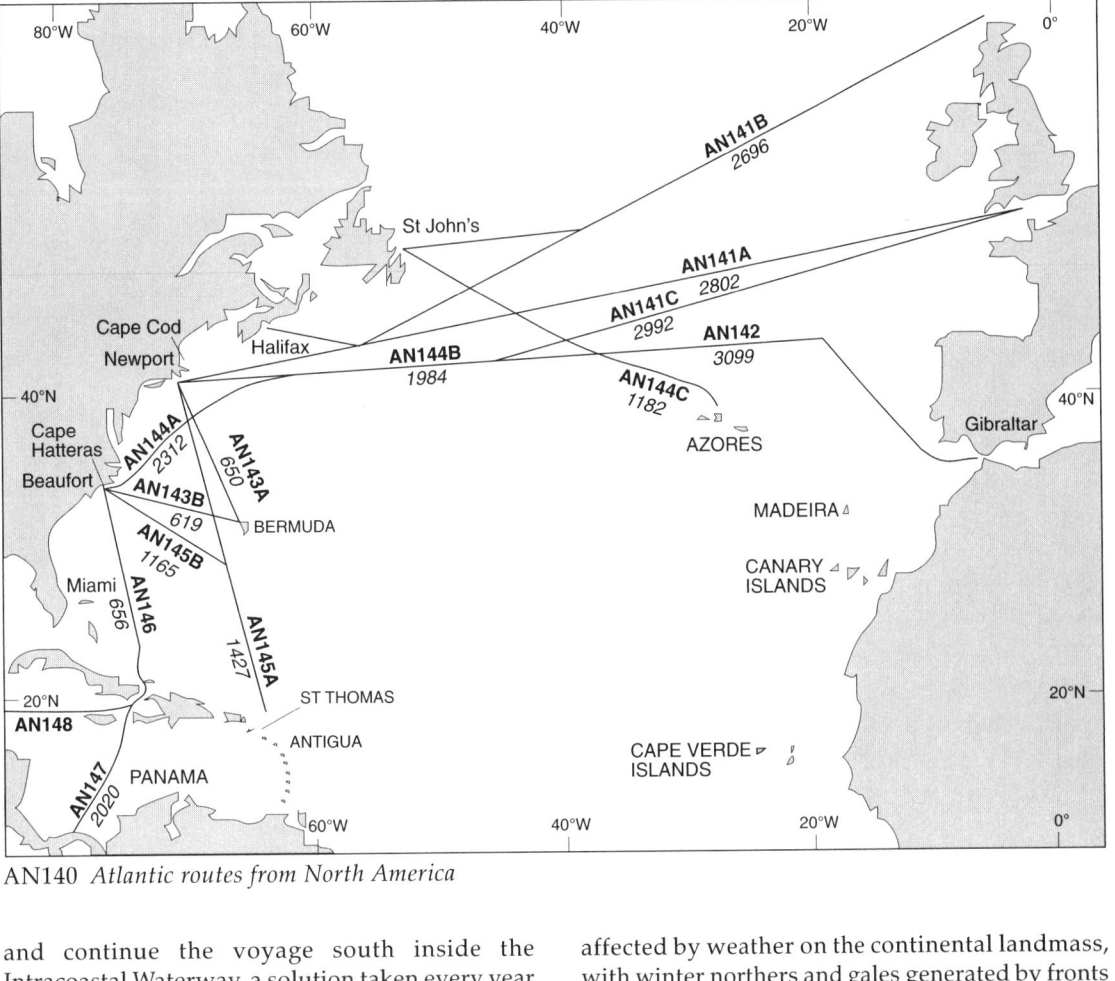

AN140 *Atlantic routes from North America*

and continue the voyage south inside the Intracoastal Waterway, a solution taken every year by those who have either left the passage to the Caribbean too late or were not fortunate enough to meet the right conditions for this offshore passage. The problem is often compounded by the fact that, for many sailors, the passage to the Caribbean may be their first serious offshore passage. Naturally they regard this test with certain apprehension and, equally naturally, tend to wait for a perfect weather window to set off. Unfortunately the optimum time for southbound passages is relatively short and that hoped for perfect window may not occur, so the opportunity is missed and other alternatives need to be considered to reach their distant goal. Some of these alternatives are described in the section AN116 describing routes starting from Florida (page 134).

The area from Cape Hatteras to Cape Cod is in the region of variable winds and is also strongly affected by weather on the continental landmass, with winter northers and gales generated by fronts moving from west to east. Hurricanes can reach up to 40°N, which is the region of New York, and their tails may affect areas even further north, particularly in late summer and autumn. Between Cape Hatteras and Cape Cod, summer weather is determined very much by the North Atlantic high and although winds are variable, there is a high proportion of SW winds. East of Cape Cod coastal weather is influenced by the landmass more than by the ocean, the weather systems moving generally in a west to east direction. Rainy thunderstorms occur in June, July, and August and often there is coastal fog, especially in the mornings. A lot of local variations occur in this area with sea breezes on some coasts and frequent wind shifts.

The prevailing winds in the Cape Cod to Newfoundland area are SW or S, which veer to NW as depressions pass over. In summer there are few gales and the wind is lighter inshore than at sea. The area from Maine to Newfoundland and over the Grand Banks is affected by fog, particularly in the spring and summer. This is caused by a S or SW wind bringing warm moist air over the sea, which is kept cool by the Labrador Current. A careful lookout for the many fishing boats and lobster pots in this area must be kept when visibility is poor. A northerly wind tends to clear the fog. Also in spring and summer up to July, when the polar ice

is breaking up, icebergs are sometimes carried south into the area off Newfoundland. The US coast and Nova Scotia are normally out of the iceberg zone. Refer also to the routes described in AN170, which deals with high latitudes in the NW Atlantic and contains information that may be useful to anyone interested in sailing a near-Arctic route to Northern Europe or at least visit Greenland and Iceland.

AN141 *North America to Northern Europe*

BEST TIME:	June to August			
TROPICAL STORMS:	June to November			
CHARTS:	BA: 4011			
	US: 121			
PILOTS:	BA: 27, 40, 59, 67, 68, 69			
	US: 140, 142, 145, 191			
CRUISING GUIDES:	*Cruising Association Handbook, Shell Pilot to the English Channel Vol. 1.*			
WAYPOINTS:				

Departure	Intermediate	Landfall	Destination	Distance (M)
Route AN141A				
AN1411 Brenton 41°24'N, 71°16'W	AN1412 Nantucket 40°30'N, 69°30'W (AN1413) (39°00'N, 50°00'W)	AN1417 Lizard 49°55'N, 5°10'W	Falmouth *50°0.9'N, 5°04'W*	2802
AN1414 off Halifax 44°25'N, 63°25'W	AN1415 Sable 43°30'N, 60°00'W AN1416 43°00'N, 50°00'W (AN1413)	AN1417 Lizard	Falmouth	2480
AN1418 off St John's 47°34'N, 53°40'W		AN1417 Lizard	Falmouth	1905
Route AN141B				
AN1411 Brenton	AN1415 Sable	AN1419 Wrath 58°40'N, 5°10'W		2696
AN1414 off Halifax	AN1415 Sable	AN1419 Wrath		2340
AN1418 off St John's		AN1419 Wrath		1821
Route AN141C				
AN1411 Brenton	AN1413	AN1417 Lizard	Falmouth	2992

A cold, wet, and foggy route at the best of times, at least it has the advantage of both favourable winds and current. The great circle route is the obvious choice for a fast passage to Northern Europe, but for destinations south of the Bay of Biscay some of the alternatives ought to be considered. These are described in routes AN123, AN124 (pages 142), AN143 and AN144.

Having chosen the great circle route, some of the problems which affect this northernmost route must be considered first. There are two main causes of concern for those who undertake this passage: fog and ice. Both of them are linked to the Labrador Current, a cold current that flows along the coasts of Newfoundland and Nova Scotia. Fog is caused by warm air blowing over the cold waters brought down from the Arctic by the Labrador Current which also carries icebergs south during the summer. As the North Atlantic warms up with the advance of summer, fog becomes less frequent and the icebergs also start melting, although they sometimes drift as far south as latitude 40°N. Therefore the latter part of summer appears to be safer and the recommended time for this passage is August. This might be too late for those who intend to do some cruising in Northern Europe during the same summer and the alternative is either to leave earlier and brave the dangers or take a more southerly route (AN141C).

The great circle route from US ports passes south of Nova Scotia and Newfoundland from where it splits into a northern branch, going round the north of Scotland towards Scandinavia (AN141B), and a southern branch to the English Channel (AN141A). The most difficult parts of the voyage are the first few hundred miles until the concentration of fishing boats on the Grand Banks has been left behind and also the area with the highest risk of fog and icebergs, close to Newfoundland. For all the above reasons, but also because better sailing conditions will be found further south, the great circle course should not be joined before meridian 55°W is passed. Naturally, if conditions warrant it, the great circle course to the port of destination can be joined earlier, but in the absence of reliable weather information, it is safer to follow the above advice. In this case, boats leaving from Newport, and using as a departure point WP AN1411 off Brenton Reef, should sail first to WP AN1412 off Nantucket Shoal, to stay well clear of the various shoals. This suggestion also applies to boats leaving from New York. In late spring, or even early summer, the course may have to dip south to WP AN1413 and stay on this latitude until longitude 55°W is reached, as suggested earlier.

The initial course for boats leaving from Halifax, Nova Scotia, bound for the English Channel leads to WP AN1415 south of Sable Island. Only if there are no reports of ice on that latitude can the course be altered for the next WP AN1416. Otherwise it may be advisable to sail to WP AN1413, as suggested above. Boats leaving from St John's, Newfoundland, and also bound for the English Channel, are so far within the ice zone that passages

early in the season should not be attempted unless one is confident that there is no such danger. Eastbound passages from St John's can join a great circle course directly.

The winds in late spring and early summer will be westerly around 15–20 knots, occasionally higher. The frequency of gales in August is low for these latitudes and calms are rare. As the route passes well to the north of the Azores high, the weather should be outside of its direct influence, but there might be an effect if the high does move north. If the Azores high is located in its usual position, the weather is more likely to be affected by one of the lows moving eastwards across the Atlantic from North America to Europe. In higher latitudes, such lows can produce gale force NE or E winds. The favourable effect of the Gulf Stream becomes less noticeable eastwards of about longitude 40°W, where it changes its name to the North Atlantic Current.

Route AN141B, which is the great circle route passing north of Scotland, uses the same waypoints to WP AN1415, south of Sable Island. From there, if there are no reports of ice en route, a course can be set for WP AN1419 off Scotland's Cape Wrath. Boats leaving from Halifax should also use WP AN1415 before joining the great circle route to WP AN1419, whereas boats leaving from St John's can join that route directly.

Boats from the US east coast sailing the southern route (AN141C), should set an initial course for WP AN1413. The main objective of this is to avoid the southern limit of ice and, in early summer, it is recommended that the latitude of this waypoint is not passed. Occasionally, provided there is no danger of ice, it may be necessary to go to 40°N or even further north to reach an area of prevailing westerlies. The frequency of gales is lower to the south of the recommended route, but one should not be tempted to turn east too soon because of the danger of losing the westerlies as one enters the Azores high which extends furthest north in summer. The Gulf Stream runs along most of this route at a favourable rate of at least 1/2 knot. In the absence of reliable weather information it is therefore recommended to make the crossing in higher, rather than lower, latitudes. Hurricanes rarely affect this route east of Bermuda, but late summer passages are nevertheless discouraged because of the violent storms that occasionally occur in the eastern Atlantic after the middle of August.

AN142 *North America to Mediterranean*

BEST TIME:	June to July			
TROPICAL STORMS:	June to November			
CHARTS:	BA: 4011			
	US: 121			
PILOTS:	BA: 27, 40, 59, 67, 68, 69			
	US: 140, 142, 145, 131			
CRUISING GUIDES:	*Yacht Scene, East Spain Pilot, Mediterranean Cruising Handbook.*			
WAYPOINTS:				

Departure	*Intermediate*	*Landfall*	*Destination*	*Distance (M)*
AN1421 Brenton 41°24'N, 71°16'W	AN1422 Nantucket 40°30'N, 69°30'W			
	AN1423 40°00'N, 55°00'W			
	AN1424 40°00'N, 20°00'W			
	AN1425 Vincent NW 37°00'N, 9°08'W			
	AN1426 Hoyo 36°04'N, 6°20'W			
	AN1427 Tarifa 35°59'N, 5°36'W			
	AN1428 Carnero 36°03'N, 5°25'W	AN1429 Gibraltar 36°08'N, 5°22'W	Marina Bay *36°09'N, 5°21'W*	3099

Most of the suggestions made in route AN141 are also valid for passages to the Mediterranean. However, as better conditions can be expected around latitude 40°N, the route should stay as close as possible to this latitude. From the point of departure, such as AN1421 off Brenton Reef, a course should be set to pass through waypoints AN1422 and AN1423. In late spring or early summer the initial course should not go above 39°N. Depending on weather conditions, the crossing should be made on or close to this latitude to WP AN1424. Having reached that point, the course can be altered for WP AN1425, 7 miles WSW of Cape St Vincent. For the rest of the passage, detailed instructions are given in routes AN124 (page 142) and AN16 (page 46). The latter should be consulted for details on tactics for negotiating the Strait of Gibraltar. Boats bound for the Mediterranean should also consult route M11 (page 536).

AN143 *North America to Bermuda*

BEST TIME:	May to June, November
TROPICAL STORMS:	June to November
CHARTS:	BA: 4403
	US: 124
PILOTS:	BA: 68, 69, 70
	US: 140, 147
CRUISING GUIDES:	*Yachting Guide to Bermuda.*

WAYPOINTS:				
Departure	Intermediate	Landfall	Destination	Distance (M)
AN1431 Brenton 41°24'N, 71°16'W	AN1434 Gibbs 32°12'N, 64°55'W	AN1436 Bermuda 32°22'N, 64°38'W	St George's 32°22'N, 64°40'W	650
AN1432 Chesapeake 36°45'N, 75°45'W		AN1436 Bermuda	St George's	610
AN1433 off Beaufort 34°40'N, 76°40'W		AN1436 Bermuda	St George's	619
AN1431 Brenton	AN1435 Bermuda N 32°35'N, 64°50'W		St George's	627

Early summer passages from any port on the US east coast should not be too difficult as the prevailing SW winds are favourable, even if it may entail a close hauled passage for boats sailing out of ports north of New York. Provided that a favourable forecast has been obtained before leaving, the crossing of the Gulf Stream should present no problems.

In the early summer the weather is usually pleasant and even if the winds are light, at least the weather is warm. The occasional depression forming over the Bahamas and then following a NE track can produce squalls and rough seas, but, at the recommended time, they are the exception rather than the rule. Later in the summer particular attention must be paid to hurricanes developing in the Caribbean as their tracks usually pass between Bermuda and the mainland. Because of this risk passages to Bermuda after the end of July are discouraged. September and October are the months with the highest incidence of hurricanes. Although the danger of hurricanes diminishes after the end of October, from early November onwards

there is an increasing risk of encountering an early winter norther which can produce extremely rough conditions when blowing against the Gulf Stream. Therefore passages in November should be carefully timed and the weather developing over continental USA watched closely.

Regardless of the port of departure, the Gulf Stream should be crossed at right angles and once clear of its influence, a course can be set for WP AN1434, five miles SW of Gibbs Hill at Bermuda's SW point. As it is easier to approach the island from the SW, the course runs parallel to the island as far as WP AN1436 to reach Town Cut leading into St George's Harbour. Boats approaching Bermuda from the NW may find it more convenient to make landfall at WP AN1435. Approaching the island from the north is more difficult as several dangers have to be left to starboard to reach that same WP AN1436, close to the Town Cut. The narrow channel, although well buoyed and lit, should not be used at night by anyone not familiar with the area. Bermuda Harbour Radio should be contacted on VHF channel 16 for pilotage information.

AN144 *North America to Azores*

BEST TIME:	May to July
TROPICAL STORMS:	June to November
CHARTS:	BA: 4011
	US: 120
PILOTS:	BA: 59, 67, 68, 69
	US: 140, 143
CRUISING GUIDES:	*Azores Cruising Guide, Atlantic Islands.*

WAYPOINTS:

Departure	Intermediate	Landfall	Destination	Distance (M)
Route AN144A				
AN1440 off Beaufort	AN1441 Azores	AN1448 Flores	Lajes	2183
34°40'N, 76°40'W	40°00'N, 32°30'W	39°20'N, 31°18'W	*39°23'N, 31°10'W*	
		AN1449 Faial	Horta	2312
		38°30'N, 28°50'W	*38°32'N, 28°37.5'W*	
Route AN144B				
AN1442 Brenton	AN1443 Nantucket			
41°24'N, 71°16'W	40°30'N, 69°30'W			
	AN1444			
	40°00'N, 50°00'W			
	AN1441 Azores	AN1448 Flores	Lajes	1857
		AN1449 Faial	Horta	1984
		AN1448 Flores	Lajes	1857
		AN1449 Faial	Horta	1984
Route AN144C				
AN1445 off Halifax	AN1446 Sable	AN1448 Flores	Lajes	1472
44°25'N, 63°25'W	43°30'N, 60°00'W	AN1449 Faial	Horta	1602
Route AN144D				
AN1447 off St John's		AN1448 Flores	Lajes	1054
47°34'N, 52°40'W		AN1449 Faial	Horta	1182

The advantage of this direct route to the Azores over route AN125, which originates in Bermuda, is that the latitudes of prevailing westerly winds can be reached sooner. Directions for the initial course are similar to those given for routes AN141 and AN142. Having reached WP AN1444, the same directions apply for the continuation of the passage as for route AN125 from Bermuda (page 143). Boats leaving from ports to the south of Cape Hatteras (route AN144A) normally ride the Gulf Stream to latitude 40°N before turning east once steady westerly winds have been found. Although latitude 38°N has been mentioned as the recommended turning point, during the summer, when the Azores high extends farther north, consistent westerly winds will only be found in higher latitudes so one has to be prepared to go as far north as 40°N. For boats leaving from ports east of New York (AN144B), the area of prevailing westerlies can be reached sooner, although one should stay clear of the Nantucket Shoals, as suggested in route AN141, by using WP AN1443 as an intermediate point of reference. If weather conditions are favourable, the same latitude should be maintained as far as WP AN1441, 60 miles NW from

Corvo and Flores, the westernmost islands in the Azores. From this point, course can be altered for one's port of destination.

Boats bound for Lajes, on the SE coast of Flores, should make landfall at WP AN1448, off Ponta do Ilheus, the SW extremity of Flores and then follow the south coast of the island to Lajes. The recent improvements to Lajes have made it an attractive first port of call into the Azores. If bound directly for Horta, which continues to be the favourite Azorean destination, from WP AN1441 course should be set for WP AN1449, five miles SW of Ponta do Castello Branco, and then sail along Faial's south coast, which is the recommended way to approach Horta. In strong SW winds, if Horta is approached from the north, allowance should be made for a strong contrary current in the channel between Faial and Pico.

From May to July, mostly SW winds can be expected for the first part of the passage. The danger of early hurricanes should be borne in mind especially if leaving from southern ports, but up to the middle of July the risk is reasonably low. A rhumb line course along a southerly route is only recommended if one is prepared to motor through the area of calms and variable winds that may be encountered in those latitudes. Directions for such a direct route are similar to those for the route from the Lesser Antilles to the Azores (route AN79 page 97). For boats leaving from Canadian ports, whether in Nova Scotia (AN144C) or Newfoundland (AN144D), a late spring or early summer start is not very attractive and for this reason most boats set off on a passage to the Azores and Europe in July or even August. The one risk to watch out for is a hurricane, because even if one can avoid the direct path of such a storm, one would still be affected by the strong winds and swell. Therefore one should avoid leaving if there is any likelihood of a hurricane developing during the first week or ten days. This should be possible by consulting the weather charts for the entire North Atlantic, as the depressions which develop into tropical storms usually take a long time to reach maturity and are usually carefully tracked. In the eventuality of being caught out by a hurricane on the way to the Azores, it is safer to stay offshore and run with the wind and swell.

AN145 *North America to the Eastern Caribbean*

BEST TIME:	November (offshore) November to May (via Bahamas)			
TROPICAL STORMS:	May to November			
CHARTS:	BA: 4403, 4402 US: 124			
PILOTS:	BA: 68, 69, 70, 71 US: 140, 147			
CRUISING GUIDES:	*Cruising Guide to the Virgin Islands, Cruising Guide to the Leeward Islands, Sailor's Guide to the Windward Islands.*			

WAYPOINTS:

Departure	Intermediate	Landfall	Destination	Distance (M)
Route AN145A				
AN1450 Brenton 41°24'N, 71°16'W	AN1453 Culebrita 18°26'N, 65°10'W		Charlotte Amalie *18°23'N, 64°56'W*	1427
AN1451 Chesapeake 36°45'N, 75°45'W	AN1453 Culebrita		Charlotte Amalie	1246
AN1452 off Beaufort 34°40'N, 76°40'W	AN1453 Culebrita		Charlotte Amalie	1165
Route AN145B				
AN1450 Brenton	AN1454 Anegada 18°45'N, 63°35'W		Virgin Gorda *18°27'N, 64°26'W*	1467
AN1451 Chesapeake	AN1454 Anegada		Virgin Gorda	1308
AN1452 off Beaufort	AN1454 Anegada		Virgin Gorda	1234
Route AN145C				
AN1450 Brenton	AN1455 Barbuda 17°30'N, 61°30'W	AN1456 Antigua E 17°00'N, 61°40'W	English Harbour *17°00'N, 61°45'W*	1556
AN1451 Chesapeake	AN1455 Barbuda	AN1456 Antigua E	English Harbour	1416
AN1452 off Beaufort	AN1455 Barbuda	AN1456 Antigua E	English Harbour	1348

Departure	Intermediate	Landfall	Destination	Distance (M)
Route AN145D				
AN1450 Brenton	AN1457 Sombrero 18°40'N, 63°30'W			
	AN1458 Martin 17°55'N, 63°22'W	AN1459 Antigua NW 17°10'N, 61°55'W	St John *17°07'N, 61°52'W*	1565
AN1451 Chesapeake	AN1457 Sombrero			
	AN1458 Martin	AN1459 Antigua NW	St John	1407
AN1452 off Beaufort	AN1457 Sombrero			
	AN1458 Martin	AN1459 Antigua NW	St John	1334

There are several alternatives to reach either the Virgin Islands or Lesser Antilles from ports on the east coast of the USA and Canada, and the ultimate choice depends mainly on the type of boat and the experience of the crew. The most direct route leads well offshore and should be attempted only with a thoroughly tested boat and crew. If the voyage starts from any port east of New York, a stop in Bermuda can be contemplated as it does not greatly lengthen the distance. However, as the frequency of gales in November around Bermuda is rather high, such a detour may not be necessarily the wisest choice. One solution is to make the passage to Bermuda earlier in the summer, spending some time there and carrying on to the Virgins or Lesser Antilles later in the year, although it must be stressed that the threat of hurricanes in Bermuda is very real in summer. Directions for southbound passages from Bermuda are described in routes AN126 and AN127 (page 145–6).

The timing for a direct passage to the Virgins (AN145A) is critical as a summer voyage carries the risk of hurricanes and a winter voyage that of northerly storms. Therefore the best time appears to be after the middle of October when the danger of hurricanes is on the wane and it is too early for winter gales. However, gale force NW winds, not necessarily the dreaded northers of winter, can strike at any time and cause very rough conditions when they collide with the Gulf Stream. Recently, an annual race sailing to the Virgins ran into just such an unpredicted storm in late October which caused major damage to a number of boats and forced some to return to the Chesapeake. The winds down to about latitude 30°N are normally NW and especially when these are strong the Gulf Stream should be crossed as quickly as possible. If the winds are from SW, the starboard tack should be

preferred as any ground lost to the east will be easily recuperated when the NE trade winds are found somewhere between latitude 22°N and 25°N. If this passage is made at the end of spring, easting should be made in the early part of the voyage to compensate for the SE slant of the trades later on. Making easting is less important in November when the predominant direction of the trade winds is NE.

Having passed through the area of variable winds, boats bound for the US Virgins should alter course for WP AN1453, 8 miles NE of the light on Culebrita Island. Keeping at a safe distance to avoid the dangers off the western point of St Thomas, that island's south coast is followed to its main port of Charlotte Amalie. However, making landfall in the Virgin Islands from the northerly direction may be difficult as most dangers are unlit. The alternative (AN145B) is to make landfall on Sombrero Island, which has a powerful light, and approach the Virgins from NE rather than try and make landfall directly on St Thomas, as suggested above. In such a case a course should be set for WP AN1454, 15 miles NW of Sombrero light at the entrance into Anegada Passage. Arriving from this direction, the nearest port of entry in the British Virgins is at Virgin Gorda. Utmost caution should be exercised in this area because of the numerous dangers surrounding the Virgin Islands.

For boats bound for Antigua on a direct offshore route (AN145C), a direct course should be set for WP AN1455, 15 miles east of Barbuda, so as to approach Antigua well from windward and clear of any dangers. The course is then altered for WP AN1456 off Antigua's SE coast. Entry formalities can be completed at English Harbour. If, as suggested above, it is impossible to make sufficient easting to approach Antigua from windward, a course should be set for WP AN1457, 5 miles N of

Sombrero Island (AN145D). From there course is altered for WP AN1458 SW of St Martin and finally for WP AN1459 off Antigua's SW coast. From there the south coast is followed to English Harbour, unless one prefers to complete formalities in the capital St John, in which case course for the latter should be changed earlier.

Rather than take one of the offshore routes described above, some people prefer to make the southbound voyage through the Intracoastal Waterway. This can be done during the summer so that one is ready to go offshore as soon as the hurricane season has come to an end. Having reached a port south of Cape Hatteras, such as Beaufort, it is strongly recommended to go offshore immediately. Leaving with a favourable forecast from a port such as Beaufort (AN145B) an easterly course should be steered to cross the Gulf Stream as quick-

ly as possible after which a course can be set for the Virgins. To avoid beating against the trade winds it is best to set a course that intersects the meridian of the port of destination in about latitude 25°N. This means that the islands are approached from a better angle in relation to the prevailing wind.

Whereas a direct offshore route to the Eastern Caribbean from more northern ports, such as Beaufort, is feasible, trying to do the same from ports in Florida will entail a lot of windward work as the winds become more easterly as latitudes become lower. This is the reason why those intending to reach the Eastern Caribbean by an offshore route are urged not to leave on such a passage from ports south of North Carolina. Alternative routes from Florida to the Eastern Caribbean are described in AN116 (page 134).

AN146 *North America to Bahamas*

BEST TIME:	November (direct)			
	November to April (from Florida)			
TROPICAL STORMS:	June to November			
CHARTS:	BA: 4403			
	US: 108, 124			
PILOTS:	BA: 68, 69, 70			
	US: 140,147			
CRUISING GUIDES:	*Yachtsman's Guide to the Bahamas, The Bahamas Cruising Guide.*			
WAYPOINTS:				

Departure	Intermediate	Landfall	Destination	Distance (M)
AN1461 Brenton 41°24'N, 71°16'W		AN1464 Salvador 24°10'N, 74°35'W	Cockburn Town *24°03'N, 74°51.5'W*	1064
AN1462 Chesapeake 36°45'N, 75°45'W		AN1464 Salvador	Cockburn Town	774
AN1463 off Beaufort 34°40'N, 76°40'W		AN1464 Salvador	Cockburn Town	656

A direct route to the Bahamas from ports north of Cape Hatteras should only be considered if the destination is in the Southern Bahamas because the route has to go a fair distance to the east to avoid the strength of the Gulf Stream. Mainly for this reason, many boats reach the Bahamas by covering at least part of the distance in the Intracoastal Waterway. The offshore section of the voyage is only attempted from one of the ports south of Cape Hatteras, such as Beaufort, Morehead City, or Charleston. There is a fairly narrow window for

such a passage and the recommended time is November. An earlier start carries the risk of hurricanes, whereas a later start runs the risk of the winter northers which can produce dangerous conditions in the Gulf Stream. The frequency of hurricanes after the beginning of November is reasonably low and a good forecast obtained before departure should warn both of existing tropical depressions and of impending northers.

The course on leaving the coast should lead in a ESE direction so as to cross the Gulf Stream at right angles. One should proceed for at least 100 miles in this direction before changing course for the Bahamas. In light winds or calms, it is advisable to use the engine to move away quickly from the coast and the Gulf Stream. Perhaps the easiest landfall in the Bahamas is the island of San Salvador, which stands clear of all dangers and has a powerful light on its NE extremity, although a more convenient landfall is NW of the island, at WP AN1464. Entry formalities can be completed at Cockburn Town, the main settlement on the west side of the island, although the officials are often

to be found at the airport. There is an anchorage off the settlement or a small marina one mile further north. Riding Rock Marina has a difficult entrance with a maximum depth of 7 ft at high tide. The GPS latitude of the entrance channel into the small marina has been reported as 24°03.4'N. The marina can be contacted on VHF channel 6.

Although Bermuda is nowhere near the direct route, some people prefer to make the detour to that island and reach the Bahamas in this way. Southbound routes from Bermuda are described in AN127.

AN147 *North America to Panama*

BEST TIME:	May to June, November			
TROPICAL STORMS:	June to November			
CHARTS:	BA: 4012			
	US: 120			
PILOTS:	BA: 68, 69, 70, 7A			
	US: 140, 147, 148			
CRUISING GUIDES:	*Cruising Guide to Panama, The Panama Guide.*			
WAYPOINTS:				

Departure	Intermediate	Landfall	Destination	Distance (M)
Route AN147A				
AN1471 Brenton	AN1474 Salvador			
41°24'N, 71°16'W	24°10'N, 74°35'W			
	AN1475 Mira-Por-Vos			
	22°08'N, 74°25'W			
	AN1476 Maisi N			
	20°23'N, 74°05'W			
	AN1477 Navassa	AN1478 Panama	Cristobal	2020
	18°25'N, 75°16'W	9°26.25'N, 79°55'W	*9°21'N, 79°55'W*	
Route AN147B				
AN1472 Chesapeake	AN1475 Mira-Por-Vos			
36°45'N, 75°45'W	AN1476 Maisi N			
	AN1477 Navassa	AN1478 Panama	Cristobal	1730
Route AN147C				
AN1473 off Beaufort	AN1475 Mira-Por-Vos			
34°40'N, 76°40'W	AN1476 Maisi N			
	AN1477 Navassa	AN1478 Panama	Cristobal	1612

As the direct route from ports in North America to Panama has to pass through the Bahamas, few boats do it without stopping there. The best times are at the change of seasons and the recommended routes are described in AN146. The difficult part of a nonstop passage is the crossing of the Bahamas, where shallow banks, extensive reefs, and unpredictable currents call for accurate navigation. As suggested in AN146, it is best to sail directly to the Southern Bahamas (AN147A) and make landfall on San Salvador at WP AN1474. The route from there crosses the Southern Bahamas through the Crooked Passage, passing west of Acklins Island and through the Mira-Por-Vos Passage and WP AN1475. The route reaches the Windward Passage at WP AN1476, off Cuba's Cape Maisi. An alternative landfall in the Bahamas is at Mayaguana, but as its main settlement Abrams Town is not a port of entry, San Salvador is preferable.

The trade winds are usually lost in the lee of Hispaniola and winds are often light in the Windward Passage but they are picked up again as one moves south. The remaining waypoints mark the route across the Caribbean Sea, which stays east of Jamaica and the reefs south of that island. Landfall in Panama is made at WP AN1478, at the entrance into the Panama Canal. Boats approaching the breakwaters at the entrance into Cristobal should call Traffic Control on VHF channel 12. Traffic lights regulate the passage between the breakwaters, but small boats may pass if they keep close to the side, both when passing through the breakwaters and in the shipping channels. Further details about the Panama Canal are given on page 583.

The best months for the passage south are May–June and November, when favourable winds can be expected for most of the way and both the danger of hurricanes and winter northers is acceptably low. The second half of May and the first half of November are considered the best times for a nonstop passage to Panama. If leaving from one of the ports in North Carolina (AN147C), a favourable forecast is essential for the first leg across the Gulf Stream, after which winds should be E or SE for most of the way to the Bahamas. For the passage through the Caribbean, favourable winds will also be found in winter, from December to April, although the strong trade winds can make sailing in the Western Caribbean uncomfortable. The route south of the Bahamas is described in detail in AN114 (page 132).

AN148 *North America to the Western Caribbean*

BEST TIME:	Mid-October to mid-November, May
TROPICAL STORMS:	June to November
CHARTS:	BA: 2710, 2579, 1220
	US: 108, 124, 401
PILOTS:	BA: 69, 70, 69A
	US: 140, 147, 148
CRUISING GUIDES:	*Yachtsman's Guide to the Bahamas, Cruising Guide to Belize and Mexico's Caribbean Coast, Cruising Guide to the Northwest Caribbean.*

WAYPOINTS:

Departure	Intermediate	Landfall	Destination	Distance (M)
AN1480 Brenton 41°24'N, 71°16'W	AN1481 Salvador 24°10'N, 74°35'W AN1482 Mira 22°08'N, 74°25'W AN1483 Maisi N 20°23'N, 74°05'W AN1483 Caleta 19°50'N, 74°20'W AN1484 Guantanamo 19°45'N, 75°00'W AN1485 Swan 16°55'N, 84°00'W		Guanaja 16°28'N, 85°54'W Livingston 15°50.5'N, 88°43.5'W	2002 2174
AN1480 Brenton	AN1481 Salvador AN1482 Mira AN1483 Caleta AN1484 Guantanamo	AN1486 Mauger 17°40'N, 87°43'W	Belize City 17°30'N, 88°10'W	2115
AN1487 Chesapeake 36°45'N, 75°45'W	AN1481 Salvador AN1482 Mira AN1483 Caleta AN1484 Guantanamo AN1485 Swan		Guanaja Livingston	1713 1837
AN1488 off Beaufort 34°40'N, 76°40'W	AN1481 Salvador AN1482 Mira AN1483 Caleta AN1484 Guantanamo AN1485 Swan		Guanaja Livingston	1595 1794

Boats leaving from any port north of Florida will probably find it easier to reach destinations in the Western Caribbean, or even in Jamaica and the Cayman Islands, by sailing through the Windward Passage and continuing south of Cuba. In effect, this is a detour from route AN147, whose directions should be followed as far as the Southern Bahamas. Matthew Town, on Great Inagua, is the largest settlement in the Southern Bahamas and makes a good port where the voyage may be interrupted if necessary. Although facilities are limited, there are regular flights to Nassau.

Having sailed through the Windward Passage past Cape Maisi, the course is altered to the west and runs parallel to the coast of Cuba passing close to Guantanamo. In an emergency one may be able to stop here, provided one obtains permission by radio before approaching the harbour, otherwise the nearest port in Cuba is Santiago de Cuba (19°59'N, 75°53'W). Waypoints are not repeated for the various route options as from Salvador to Guantanamo they are the same for all routes.

For boats bound for Honduras, the route leads to a point off Swan Island, and thence to the port of destination, Guanaja being one of the official ports of entry into Honduras. Boats bound for

Guatemala's Rio Dulce should proceed to the river entrance where the GPS coordinates of the buoy marking the entrance channel are those listed under Livingston. The direct route to Belize passes south of Grand Cayman and makes landfall close to Mauger Cay, which has a light and is passed at a safe distance to the north. The reef strewn approaches to Belize City should be approached only in daylight and preferably

before noon, so as to have the sun from behind. Eastern Channel is the main pass into Belize City.

Winds, especially in winter, are normally favourable on this route and one should also have a slight current in one's favour when sailing along the south coast of Cuba. On the route to Belize, some shoals will be passed as one crosses meridian 84°, when rough seas may be experienced – especially during a period of sustained trade winds.

AN150 NORTHERN ROUTES FROM THE BRITISH ISLES

Cold, ice and a short sailing season no longer deter cruising boats from reaching the furthest reaches of the North Atlantic. Better boats, better aids to navigation and also better clothing have resulted in ever larger numbers of cruising boats visiting Iceland, Greenland and even Spitsbergen, all of which now receive a steady stream of boats during the short summer months, from June to August. These are the old sailing grounds of the Vikings, who were crossing the North Atlantic long before Columbus had even been born, and some incredible voyages were achieved in those open boats while in other parts of Europe ships rarely ventured out of sight of land. When considering a voyage to this area one should bear in mind that it is now 1000 years since the legendary Eric the Red sailed from Norway first to Iceland and then to Greenland, a remarkable achievement even by today's standards.

Nearer to hand, the reunification of Germany, the disintegration of the Soviet Union and the collapse of the communist regimes in the former Soviet satellite countries have made the Baltic Sea a more interesting cruising destination than ever before. A new section has therefore been added to this edition that caters both for those attracted

to the traditional Viking sailing grounds as well as to their home waters.

As in the old days, when planning a longer offshore passage, one should try to sail from east to west with the prevailing easterlies of higher latitudes and generally watch the weather so as to attempt to stay north of the depressions tracking eastwards. The reverse is the case when sailing east and it should not be too difficult to hitch a ride on the back of one of those depressions as it makes its way east. Further south, the prevailing winds are westerlies for most of the time, and eastbound passages are therefore easier to plan.

The one major hazard in the higher latitudes covered by these routes is ice, which, even at the height of summer, can be encountered further south in the area near Greenland than near Norway. When sailing in the western part of the North Atlantic in early summer, it is essential to keep south of latitude 58°30'N until on the meridian of Greenland's Cape Farvel. On the eastern side, ice recedes much further north in summer and only poses a hazard in the area around Spitsbergen. Up-to-date information on ice can be obtained by VHF, HF or fax from the various meteorological offices in the area. Generally, ice should be avoided by small boats. The larger ice-bergs show up well on radar, and can easily be avoided, but the smaller bergy-bits or growlers, which break off all the time, do not show up on radar, and can be a real danger in poor visibility or on dark nights.

The weather, for a well prepared boat, should present no problems while sailing even in the higher latitudes in summer, when often it is warm and, occasionally, windless. While the usual temperatures are in single figures Celsius, it can get as high as 20°C on a nice summer day. However, this can change instantly with temperatures dropping to freezing, snow and the wind-chill factor making things even more uncomfortable than the actual air temperature. So good protective clothing is essential, and also some way of heating the boat.

Conditions are not nearly as bad for those sailing only as far as the Baltic or South Norway, which are reached by routes also included in this section.

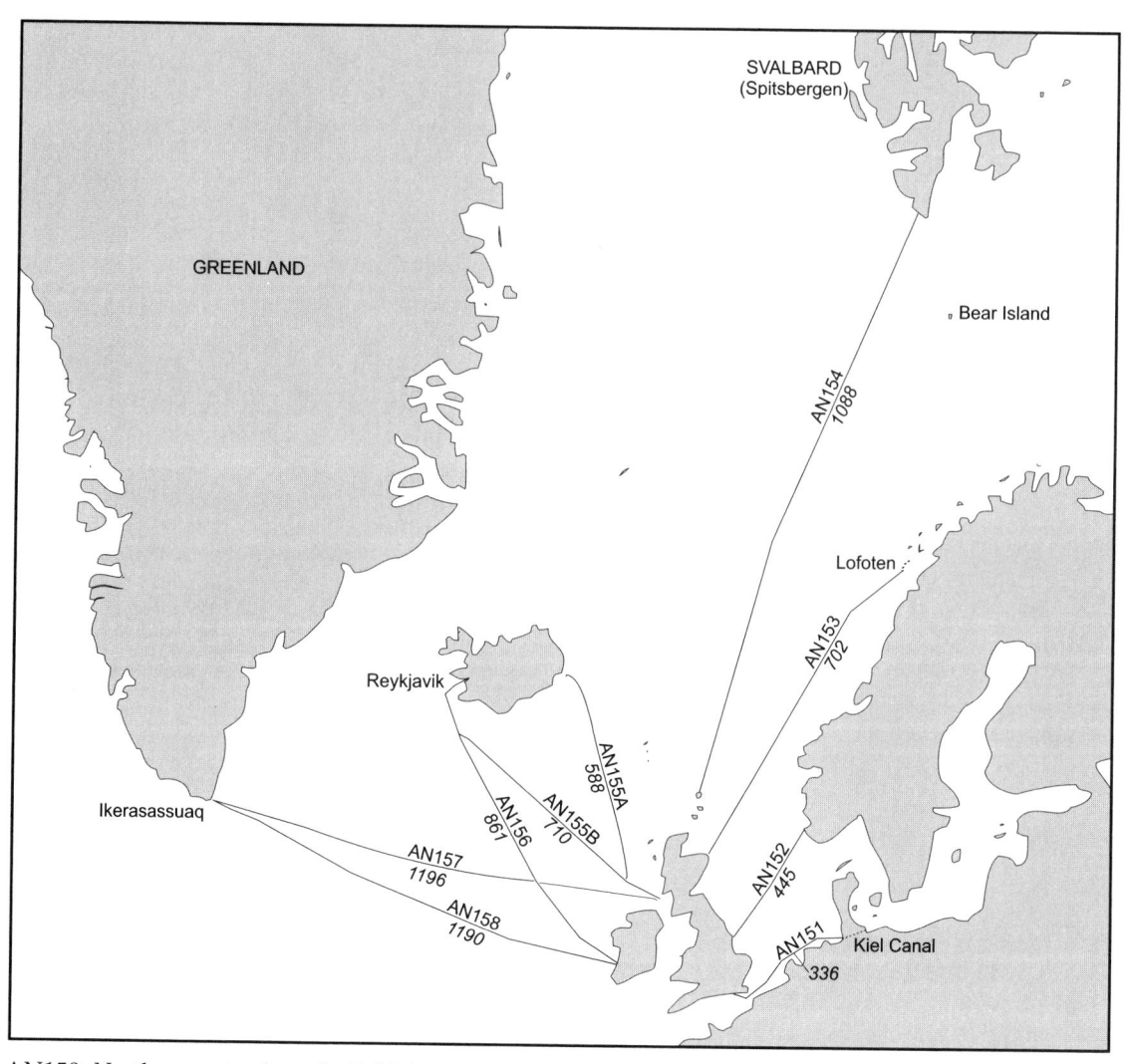

AN150 *Northern routes from the British Isles*

The Baltic Sea

CRUISING GUIDES: *The Baltic Sea,*
Cruising Association Handbook.

Because most sailing is coastal and offshore passages are quite short, the Baltic Sea falls outside the scope of this book. However, as an increasing number of cruising boats migrate to the Baltic from all over the world every year, the following notes have been added to assist when planning a voyage to that area.

The sailing season is relatively short and lasts only from June to September. The best months are July and August, when the days are long and the sea has had time to get warm. The winds in summer tend to be from south to west and are of moderate strength. As weather conditions are quite stable, steady winds from one direction may last for a few days before changing.

Most boats arriving from outside the Baltic reach it by way of the Kiel Canal and only a minority do so by sailing around the top of Denmark and through the Kattegat. Although some of the best cruising grounds are concentrated in that very SW corner, where a summer can easily be spent without ever going offshore, for those who wish to experience more of the variety that the Baltic and the nine countries that border on it have to offer, a circumnavigation of the entire sea is a temptation not easy to resist. This can be done either clockwise or anti-clockwise, and most visitors seem to prefer the latter. This means that the former communist countries are visited first, where facilities are among the worst in the area, and also some of the longer passages are done at the beginning of the voyage as the distances between suitable ports on the east coast can be as much as 100 miles. Wind conditions should also be more favourable with the added advantage that, if one starts running out of time towards the end of summer, there will be better facilities at one's disposal, should they be needed. Finally, such an anti-clockwise circumnavigation can end on a high note by reaching the North Sea via the Gotha Canal, a system of locks, rivers and canals that cut right across Southern Sweden, and is regarded as one of the highlights of a Baltic cruise.

AN151 *English Channel to the Baltic*

BEST TIME:	May to August			
TROPICAL STORMS:	None			
CHARTS:	BA: 4140			
	US: 126			
PILOTS:	BA: 28, 55			
	US: 190, 191			
CRUISING GUIDES:	*Cruising Association Handbook, The Baltic Sea.*			
WAYPOINTS:				
Departure	*Intermediate*	*Landfall*	*Destination*	*Distance (M)*
AN1510 Dover	AN1511 Strait			
51°07'N, 1°19'E	*51°10'N, 1°46'E*			
	AN1512 Helder			
	52°55'N, 4°25'E			
	AN1513 Vlieland N	AN1514 Weser	Cuxhaven	336
	53°26'N, 4°54'E	*53°55'N, 8°10'E*	*53°52.5'N, 8°42.5'E*	
			Brunsbüttel	351
			53°53'N, 9°08'E	

Most boats heading NE bound for the Kiel Canal and the Baltic will probably attempt to pass through the Dover Strait without stopping. Indeed, this is a good tactic and therefore, regardless of where one comes from, whether nonstop, or from an English or French port, the passage through the busy strait should be timed for daylight and, ideally, with a fair tide and wind. Dover itself makes a good port of departure, although the inner harbour being tidal makes the time of departure more difficult to control. Having left Dover, or arriving from the SW, waypoint AN1511 makes a good point of departure into the North Sea. It is now for the skipper to decide whether to continue in the main northbound shipping lane, or sail over closer to the Belgian coast to avoid some of the heavy traffic. As one enters Dutch waters, and having crossed the busy lanes going in and out of Rotterdam's Europoort, the situation is exacerbated by the large number of oil rigs and platforms. An intermediate waypoint has been suggested off Den Helder, which, in any case, is probably the best place to stop for those not attracted by the idea of sailing in one go all the way to the Kiel Canal. Den Helder is also a good place to shelter in bad weather, or to wait for a change. The harbour entrance should be approached with caution as landmarks are difficult to identify along this low, dune-fringed coast. Harbour Control should be contacted on channel 14 if in any doubt about entry procedure.

Whether stopping in Den Helder or not, the next waypoint marks the turn towards the German coast. Landfall is made north of the Alte Weser landfall buoy, where a decision needs to be made whether to proceed directly to Brunsbüttel, at the entrance of the Kiel Canal, or stop at Cuxhaven. The latter has excellent yachting facilities and is a convenient stop not just for those intending to transit the Kiel Canal, but also to visit this part of Germany. For those short of time, it is probably advisable to make directly for Brunsbüttel, where there is a small yacht harbour to spend the night if one arrives too late to commence the transit. The Elbe is a busy river, with strong currents, which should be borne in mind if crossing from Cuxhaven to Brunsbüttel, or attempting to reach Hamburg, a rewarding experience for those who have the time to do so.

The Kiel Canal was built in 1895 and its correct name, in German, is Nord-Ostsee Kanal (Baltic-North Sea Canal). Small craft are only allowed to use the Canal in daylight, and in good visibility, so ideally one should attempt to leave at first light so as to negotiate the 54 miles in one go. However, there are places where a sailing boat may spend the night, such as at Rendsburg, in the Gieselau Canal, or behind the dolphins at the various passing places. 'Canal Pilot' should be contacted on channel 12. The transit fees are payable at Holtenau, at the Baltic Sea end.

Traffic in the Canal is controlled by lights: three red vertical lights forbid all movements; a single white light permits a yacht to enter a lock; a yellow flashing light means that the police have a message for the yacht being signalled.

AN152 *England to Scandinavia*

BEST TIME:	June to August
TROPICAL STORMS:	None
CHARTS:	BA: 4140
	US: 126
PILOTS:	BA: 54, 55, 56
	US: 192
CRUISING GUIDES:	*Norwegian Cruising Guide, Cruising Association Handbook, The Baltic Sea.*

WAYPOINTS:				
Departure	*Intermediate*	*Landfall*	*Destination*	*Distance (M)*
AN1520 Dover *51°07'N, 1°19'E*	AN1521 Strait *51°10'N, 1°46'E* AN1522 Helder *52°55'N, 4°25'E* AN1523 Vlieland *53°26'N, 4°54'E*	AN1524 Gradyb *55°25.5'N, 8°14'E*	Esbjerg *55°28'N, 8°26'E*	371
AN1520 Dover	AN1521 Strait AN1522 Helder AN1523 Vlieland	AN1524 *58°00'N, 8°00'E*	Kristiansand *58°08.5'N, 8°00'E*	498
AN1525 Harwich *51°55.5'N, 1°23'E*	AN1526 Davy *53°00'N, 3°00'E* AN1527 Markham *54°00'N, 3°20'E*	AN1524 Gradyb	Esbjerg	347
AN1525 Harwich	AN1526 Davy *54°00'N, 3°20'N* AN1528 Dan *55°30'N, 5°30'E*	AN1524	Kristiansand	446
AN1520 Harwich	AN1521 Davy AN1522 Markham	AN1529 *58°54'N, 5°28'E*	Tananger *58°56'N, 5°35'E*	445
AN1520 Harwich	AN1521 Davy AN1522 Markham AN15211 Odin *60°00'N, 2°30'E* AN15212 Arctic S *62°00'N, 3°20'E*	AN1528 Lofoten S *67°20'N, 11°50'E*	Skomvaer *67°24'N, 11°52'E*	1023

The Baltic shores of Scandinavia are probably best reached via the Kiel Canal, as described in AN151. For a direct route to Scandinavia, the options increase as one moves north and Norway offers almost unlimited destinations, whether sailing from a port in England or Scotland. The closest port to make for in Scandinavia proper is Esbjerg, on the east coast of Denmark. It has the advantage of being linked by ferry to Harwich, in the east of England, making crew changes easy, and has excellent rail links with the rest of Denmark.

The west coast of Sweden can also be reached directly, but as either Denmark or Southern Norway will be most probably visited on the way, it was felt that Esbjerg and Kristiansand would suffice as suggested ports of arrival. The choice of a Norwegian destination will depend greatly on one's preference for a direct, albeit longer, offshore passage, or the shortest possible crossing. The choice of landfalls is abundant and will depend primarily on one's subsequent cruising plans. For those sailing through the Strait of Dover, a direct passage to Southern Norway, without any further intermediate ports, is an attractive option as sailing to and from any ports on England's east coast may only complicate matters. The offshore passage may be reduced in length by stopping in a port in Holland, such as Den Helder. Setting off from Scotland (AN153) does reduce the length of the offshore passage, which may be an important factor for those who are not too keen on long passages, especially through such a busy shipping area as the North Sea. The decision for those leaving from the west coasts of England or Scotland, or those coming from Ireland, is much easier as the logical way is to reach the North Sea via the Caledonian Canal (see AN153).

The worst weather one can expect is a NW gale, so this should be borne in mind when choosing a route, and should be a factor if an intermediate stop in Holland is considered. However, long term weather forecasts are so much more reliable that one should be able to obtain a fairly accurate prediction for at least the next 72 hours before setting off on such a passage.

Two major hazards on any of these routes are the high density of shipping and the large number of offshore oil rigs, platforms and ancillary services. Both need a good lookout at all times and, in the case of oil rigs, they should be given as wide a berth as possible. The situation is often exacerbated by poor visibility, so radar is highly recommended. Shipping separation zones operate in some areas and these should be strictly observed.

Sailing conditions in summer are generally good and, provided one has access to weather information, it should not be too difficult to find a good weather window for the offshore passage, although one may have to wait a few days for a change in the weather. Prevailing winds on offshore passages are generally W or SW south of approximately latitude 60°N, becoming more variable in more northerly latitudes.

A number of Norwegian landfall options are listed as the choice will depend on one's cruising plans. For those planning to cruise the south coast, Kristiansand is indeed a good landfall. For those who plan to visit first the west coast, Tananger, near the larger city of Stavanger, makes a good departure point. For those heading for the Arctic, but needing a stop en route, the scenic Lofoten should be the logical choice. Sailing north from Tananger, one has the choice of taking the sheltered inside route, which covers most of the distance with only a few places exposed to the open ocean. With a large yachting population of its own,

Norway has good facilities in all major ports.

The route from the Dover Strait to Esbjerg follows the same directions as AN151 as far as Vlieland, from where the course is altered for the NE. Esbjerg should be approached in good visibility as the low land and sandbanks demand careful navigation. Landfall should be made at the Gradyb Bar buoy. The Gradyb channel has a bar, which is dredged. However, the seas break in strong W or SW winds, so the area should be avoided in this kind of weather.

The direct route from Harwich to Kristiansand passes through, or close by, several oil or gas drilling fields, so the waypoints listed outline a hypothetical route which should avoid all major hazards. However, all these areas should be approached with great caution and, if visibility is poor, a more prudent route should be sailed. Landfall is made well to the south of the harbour entrance. The main harbour of Kristiansand is divided by a low bridge connecting the island of Odderoya with the city, so visiting yachts should make for the eastern harbour, where there are several marinas.

A similar initial route is recommended if sailing directly from Harwich to Tananger and the same waypoints are listed so as to avoid the Broken Bank and surrounding area. Undoubtedly the best landfall on the west coast is at Tananger, which has a well protected harbour and is close to Stavanger airport, making it an ideal place for crew changes.

Those heading for Norway's far north or even Spitsbergen may wish to sail offshore as far as Lofoten. Two intermediate waypoints are recommended so as to avoid some of the Norwegian offshore rigs. From there, the route runs parallel to the mainland, but at a safe distance offshore. Landfall will be made at Skomvaer lighthouse, at the SW tip of Lofoten chain. The small island of Skomvaer offers only limited protection, but there are plenty of excellent harbours in the inner Lofoten, which form a barrier between the Atlantic and the mainland along the spectacular Vestfjorden.

AN153 *Scotland to Norway*

BEST TIME:	June to August
TROPICAL STORMS:	None
CHARTS:	BA: 2182b, 2128c
	US: 14
PILOTS:	BA: 52, 54, 57A
	US: 141, 182, 193
CRUISING GUIDES:	*Norwegian Cruising Guide, Cruising Association Handbook.*
WAYPOINTS:	

Departure	Intermediate	Landfall	Destination	Distance (M)
AN1530 Inverness *57°30'N, 4°13'W*	AN1531 Moray *57°44'N, 3°45'W*	AN1532 Naze *58°00'N, 6°56'E*	Korshamn *58°01'N, 7°00'E*	362
AN1533 Peterhead *57°29.8'N, 1°45.5'W*		AN1534 *58°54'N, 5°28'E*	Tananger *58°56'N, 5°35'E*	248
AN1533 Peterhead	AN1535 Arctic S *62°00'N, 3°20'E*	AN1536 Lofoten S *67°20'N, 11°50'E*	Skomvaer *67°24'N, 11°52'E*	702
AN1537 Lerwick *60°09.3'N, 1°08.5'W*	AN1538 Bressay *60°06'N, 1°00'W*	AN1359 Fedje SW *60°42'N, 4°40'E*	Fedje *60°46.5'N, 4°44'E*	182
AN156 Lerwick	AN1538 Bressay AN15311 Tampen E *61°00'N, 3°00'E*	AN1536 Lofoten S	Skomvaer	584

Setting off from Scotland reduces the length of the offshore passage considerably, which may be an important factor for those who are not too keen on long passages, especially through such a busy shipping area as the North Sea. The decision for those setting off from the west coast of England or Scotland, or those coming from Ireland, is much easier as the logical way is to reach the North Sea via the Caledonian Canal. A departure point in the Moray Firth is therefore given for those who have just left the Caledonian Canal at Inverness. Another good departure port from Scotland is Peterhead.

The predominant winds in the North Sea are SW or W, their average strength increasing as one moves north. However, in higher latitudes, summer winds tend to be variable. Summer gales, when they occur, are mostly from NW, and, usually, are of short duration.

A number of landfall options are listed as the choice will depend on one's cruising plans. For those planning to cruise the south coast of Norway, the port of Korshamn, NW of the Naze, is a good landfall. For those who plan to stop first

on the west coast, Tananger, near the city of Stavanger, makes a good place to start a cruise, either to the north or to the south-east. For those heading for the Arctic, but needing a stop en route, the scenic Lofoten make a logical choice. Sailing north from Tananger, one has the choice of taking the sheltered inside route, which covers most of the distance with only a few places exposed to the open ocean. With a large yachting population of its own, Norway has good facilities in all major ports.

Those heading for Norway's far north or even Spitsbergen may wish to sail offshore as far as Lofoten. Two intermediate waypoints are recommended so as to avoid some of the Norwegian offshore rigs. From there, the route runs parallel to the mainland, but at a safe distance offshore. Landfall will be made at Skomvaer lighthouse, at the SW tip of Lofoten chain. The small island of Skomvaer offers only limited protection, but there are plenty of excellent harbours in the inner Lofoten, which form a barrier between the Atlantic and the mainland along the spectacular Vestfjorden.

Sailing from Scotland, one has a wide choice of both departure and landfall ports. Peterhead was chosen because of its convenient position, as was Tananger. The recommended route avoids all known dangers, but if the Norwegian coast is approached in strong westerly winds, this should be done with utmost caution as the coast is completely exposed, and staying well offshore until the weather has abated will be better than seeking shelter.

Lerwick, the capital of the Shetlands, is the closest departure port for most of Norway. A good landfall in the approaches to Bergen is Fedje, a small offshore island that offers excellent protection in one of its two harbours. Lerwick is also a good departure point for Lofoten, not only because it shortens considerably the length of the passage, but also because the offshore route avoids the NE winds that prevail along the west coast of Norway in early summer.

AN154 *Scotland to Spitsbergen*

BEST TIME:	June to August			
TROPICAL STORMS:	None			
CHARTS:	BA: 4010			
	US: 10			
PILOTS:	BA: 11, 52			
	US: 141, 182			
CRUISING GUIDES:	*Norwegian Cruising Guide, Norwegian Arctic Pilot.*			
WAYPOINTS:				

Departure	Intermediate	Landfall	Destination	Distance (M)
AN1540 Peterhead 57°29.8'N, 1°45.5'W	AN1541 Arctic SE 62°00'N, 3°30'E	AN1542 Sorkapp S 76°26'N, 16°20'E	Hornsund 77°00'N, 15°34'E	1254
AN1543 Lerwick *60°09.3'N, 1°08.5'W*	AN1544 Bressay N 60°11.5'N, 1°07'W			
	AN1545 Tampen W 62°00'N, 1°30'E	AN1542 Sorkapp S	Hornsund	1088

A voyage to Spitsbergen, or, to give its correct Norwegian name, the Svalbard archipelago, is a unique experience. Sailing conditions in summer are relatively moderate and poor visibility may be more of a hazard than strong winds. At the height of summer in a normal year, ice does not pose a serious problem and the west coast of Spitsbergen is usually free of pack ice from June until November. However, weather conditions deteriorate rapidly after the middle of August, so early summer is to be preferred. The coast of Spitsbergen is indented by deep fjords offering good shelter. Large glaciers slope off into the sea, fronted by high ice cliffs. Ice conditions on the passage from mainland Norway are usually good in early summer, when the Gulf Stream assures a mostly ice free passage after the middle of June.

Because of the relatively short summer season, one may be tempted to sail the entire distance from Scotland to Spitsbergen offshore. This would also avoid the possibility of running into NE winds, which prevail along the Norwegian coast in early summer. If one wishes to visit the mainland coast of Norway, this can be better done on the return voyage. As in the case of passages to the Norwegian mainland, the ports of Peterhead, in mainland Scotland, or Lerwick, in the Shetlands, make good departure ports.

From waypoint AN1540, off Peterhead, the initial route stays east of an agglomeration of oil rigs, before a direct course may be steered for Sorkappoya, a small island south of Spitsbergen. From Lerwick, which is left through the north channel, a course is first laid to waypoint AN1545, so as to pass well clear of the Tampen oil field. A direct course can be sailed from there all the way to Spitsbergen.

Most boats intending to sail to Spitsbergen cruise along the Norwegian coast possibly as far as Tromsö before heading offshore. Tromsö is the traditional port of departure for Arctic expeditions, with excellent repair facilities, provisioning and weather information. An easy inside passage leads to Torsvag, a good harbour at the NW tip of Vannoya. This is a good jumping off point for the offshore passage, but all provisioning, including diesel, should have been done in Tromsö as local supplies are limited and diesel is not available.

Another option is to leave the mainland north of Lofoten as the distance will not be shortened considerably by continuing ENE towards North Cape. A direct route leads to Sorkapp, a small island off Spitsbergen proper.

Bear Island (Bjornoya) lies roughly halfway to Spitsbergen and offers the possibility of some shelter if the weather deteriorates. Although the island does not have an all-weather harbour, there are anchorages on all of its sides so, depending on wind direction, one should be able to find some shelter. The best anchorage is at Sorhamna (74°22'N, 19°10'E), two miles NE of the southern tip of the island. It offers good shelter from winds with a northerly component. Kvalrossbukta (74°23'N, 19°10.5'E), close to NE of Sorhamna, offers better shelter from the westerly swell.

Although the weather charts show a higher incidence of SW winds in summer, variable winds are usually the order of the day along this route. Fog is frequent, especially near Bear Island and in the southern approaches to Spitsbergen. Because of the relatively short distance to the magnetic pole, as one approaches Spitsbergen the compass reacts slower and, sailing north along the coast of Spitsbergen, magnetic compasses become less and less reliable. A serious hazard in the Barents Sea are large floating logs, which are partly submerged and almost impossible to see.

Sorkapp, at the southern extremity of Sorkappoya, makes a good landfall as it is visible from far away on a clear day. In poor visibility the area should be approached with great caution as the low land and shoals extend 10 miles south of the high ground. Ice may be present in early summer, both offshore and closer to land. Both winds and the swell are augmented in the immediate vicinity of Sorkapp. In strong easterly winds, good shelter can be found at Stormbukta, 14 miles NNW of Sorkappoya. However, the nearest sheltered anchorage is at Hornsund (77°00'N, 15°36'E), the site of a Polish polar station. Nearby is a well protected lagoon, created by the Hansbreen glacier. The area should be entered with great caution as it has not been fully charted. The name Antonio Pigafettahamna has been conferred to the harbour in honour of Magellan's officer, Antonio Pigafetta, who reported on the first circumnavigation. Although no special permit is required to visit Spitsbergen, the office of the District Governor, who is in charge of the rescue services, must be informed of one's movements. Visiting yachts are required to have insurance cover for SAR operations. For details, write in advance to: Sysselmannen pa Svalbard, N-9170 Longyearbyen, Norway. Longyearbyen (78°13.5'N, 15°37'E), located in Isfjorden, on the west coast of Spitsbergen, is the administrative centre and has the best facilities; there are also frequent flights to Oslo and Tromsö.

Severe restrictions apply to nature reserves and, from 15 May to 15 August, it is prohibited to move within 300 metres of a bird sanctuary. Most animals are protected and, in the case of polar bears, may be killed only in self defence. As bears pose a major risk in all areas, visitors are advised to carry arms for self protection. These can be hired locally from Svalbard Arctic Sport, N-9070 Longyearbyen, Norway, who also arrange SAR insurance, although at higher rates than obtainable elsewhere.

AN155 *Scotland to Iceland*

BEST TIME:	June to August			
TROPICAL STORMS:	None			
CHARTS:	BA: 4011			
	US: 11			
PILOTS:	BA: 11, 52			
	US: 141, 181			
CRUISING GUIDES:	*Cruising Association Handbook; Faeroe, Iceland and Greenland Cruising Notes.*			
WAYPOINTS:				

Departure	Intermediate	Landfall	Destination	Distance (M)
AN1550 Oban *56°25'N, 5°29'W*	AN1551 Barra S *56°45'N, 7°40'W*	AN1552 Djupivogur *64°37'N, 14°12'W*	Berufjordur *64°39'N, 14°18'W*	588
AN1550 Oban	AN1551 Barra S	AN1553 Reykjanes S *63°48'N, 22°48'W*		
		AN1554 Reykjanes N *64°08'N, 22°50'W*	Reykjavik *64°09'N, 21°56'W*	710

A direct passage to Iceland from almost any port in England or Scotland is almost impossible to achieve without first doing some coastal navigation to reach the open sea. Boats from the east coast may have to sail first to Scotland and either go over the top, or use the Caledonian Canal to reach Oban. A hypothetical point of departure, clear of all dangers, has been chosen just south of Barra Head. This also has the advantage of being close to the excellent harbour at Castlebay, at the southern end of the Outer Hebrides, where there are adequate facilities and also a ferry link to Oban on the mainland. In strong SW winds it may be better to reach the open sea through the Minch channel by leaving the Hebrides to port.

Depending on the overall weather conditions in the North Atlantic, summer depressions may pass either to the north or south of Iceland. Generally, winds around Iceland follow a certain pattern, with those north of Iceland having an easterly component and those south of Iceland having a westerly component. This means that for boats approaching Iceland from the E or SE, it makes more sense to make a tour of the island in an anticlockwise direction. In this case, landfall should be made on the SE coast. Boats arriving from the W should head straight for Reykjavik, which has the best facilities, and then cruise clockwise. If the forecast is for the north coast to be encumbered by ice, the only alternative is to make for the west

coast, which offers the best cruising opportunities. According to the locals, good sailing conditions prevail from early May to September, and in some years the first half of October is also pleasant.

Bearing in mind the above points, boats coming from the SE can make landfall on either the SE coast of Iceland, such as Hornafjordur or Djupivogur, or at the SW point of the island, off Reykjanes. Hornafjordur (64°15'N, 15°12'W) is a busy, well sheltered, fishing harbour, with a rather difficult entrance. Its main attraction is the proximity to the Vatnajokull glaciers. Djupivogur is the most southerly fjord on the east coast. It is a well sheltered natural harbour with a good range of facilities and the best starting point for a cruise around Iceland.

If sailing first to the west coast, landfall will be made off the south coast of Iceland, close to Surtsey, a newly formed volcanic island. Nearby Vestmannaeyjar, off the south coast, is a spectacular volcanic archipelago, where recent eruptions have created new islands and mountains. A stop here should not be missed. The offshore route continues towards Reykjanes peninsula, at the SW extremity of Iceland, then runs north, parallel to the coast, to waypoint AN1554 before turning east towards Reykjavik.

The capital Reykjavik is not necessarily the best place to find a good berth for cruising boats and Hafnarfjordur (64°04'N, 21°58'W), 5 miles south of

Reykjavik, is a favourite port among visiting sailors. The port is always busy, but visitors are never turned away. All facilities are available in the nearby town, which also boasts a highly popular Viking Festival held every two years (the next one is planned for July 1999).

AN156 *Ireland to Iceland*

BEST TIME:	June to August
TROPICAL STORMS:	None
CHARTS:	BA: 4011
	US: 11
PILOTS:	BA: 11, 40
	US: 142, 181
CRUISING GUIDES:	*Cruising Association Handbook; Faeroe, Iceland and Greenland Cruising Notes.*
WAYPOINTS:	

Departure	Intermediate	Landfall	Destination	Distance (M)
AN1560 Valentia NW 51°6.5'N, 10°00'W	AN1561 Inish 52°02'N, 10°45'W	AN1562 Djupivogur 64°37'N, 14°12'W	Berufjordur *64°39'N, 14°18'W*	783
AN1560 Valentia NW	AN1561 Inish AN1563 Reykjanes S 63°48'N, 22°48'W	AN1564 Reykjanes N 64°08'N, 22°50'W	Reykjavik *64°09'N, 21°56'W*	861

An Irish port is probably the best point of departure for yachts bound for Iceland from ports in SW Europe or England. Having sailed around Land's End, boats from the south of England have a choice of Irish ports to provision before taking the offshore route. Yachts leaving from the west coast of England or from Northern Ireland may find it more convenient to sail through the North Channel and follow directions as in AN155.

There are several convenient final departure points in SW Ireland and the harbour of Valentia is recommended as it affords shelter in all winds. The harbour can be entered from SW through Portmagee Channel, where there is an opening bridge. The NW channel is more convenient when leaving. To avoid any dangers before altering course for Iceland, a waypoint (AN1561) has been set SW of Inishtrahull light. From there a direct course may be sailed to SE Iceland passing east of Rockall and making landfall at Djupivogur. This is the most southerly fjord on the east coast. It is a well sheltered natural harbour with a good range of facilities and the best starting point for a cruise

around Iceland. Weather and other considerations will have a bearing on one's cruising plans in Iceland, all of which are described in detail in AN155.

Those who prefer to sail directly to Reykjavik should set course for waypoint AN1563, off Reykjanes Point at the SW extremity of Iceland. From there the course leads north parallel to the coast to waypoint AN1564 before turning east towards Reykjavik.

The capital Reykjavik is not necessarily the best place to find a good berth for cruising boats and Hafnarfjordur (64°04'N, 21°58'W), 5 miles south of Reykjavik, is the favourite port among visiting sailors. The port is always busy, but visitors are never turned away. All facilities are available in the nearby town, which also boasts a highly popular Viking Festival held every two years (the next one is planned for July 1999).

Vestmannaeyjar, off the south coast, is a spectacular volcanic archipelago, where recent eruptions have created new islands and mountains. A stop here should not be missed.

AN157 *Scotland to Greenland*

BEST TIME:	June to August
TROPICAL STORMS:	None
CHARTS:	BA: 4011
	US: 11
PILOTS:	BA: 11, 66
	US: 142, 181
CRUISING GUIDES:	*Faeroe, Iceland and Greenland Cruising Notes.*
WAYPOINTS:	

Departure	Intermediate	Landfall	Destination	Distance (M)
AN1570 Oban	AN1571 Barra S	AN1572 Farvel NE	Ikerasassuaq	1196
56°25'N, 5°29'W	*56°45'N, 7°40'W*	*60°00'N, 43°05'W*	*60°03'N, 43°10'W*	

These northern routes were sailed by the Vikings just over one thousand years ago; and while the vessels have changed almost beyond recognition, the weather has not and conditions in Greenland are often far from favourable. The main difficulty is posed by ice, which only eases its grip on this enormous island during a short period at the height of summer. Along the east coast there is an ice free strip, but offshore pack ice makes it impossible, or very dangerous, for a sailing boat to cruise through that area. In a good year, the whole of Davis Strait and Baffin Bay can be free of pack ice, but not of icebergs, which are never absent. The west coast is mountainous with deep fjords, similar to Norway. There is an ice free area in the SW which also includes some of the offshore islands. In an average summer winds tend to be variable, with a northerly component. On land, summer temperatures vary between 2°C and 20°C, but sea temperatures very rarely rise above 4°C. This means that fog can be quite frequent in summer, especially around Ivgut. The Nuuk area is relatively free of fog.

Cruising anywhere in Greenland needs careful planning. Because the west coast between 63°N and 69°N is usually clear of ice by early June, thanks to the warm West Greenland Current, the area may be entered from the west by giving Cape Farvel a wide berth. This can be as much as 120 miles, depending on existing conditions. Long days, reasonable weather and acceptable temperatures make cruising possible until shorter days and deteriorating conditions signal the end of a rather too short sailing season. The south-setting East Greenland Current, which brings down ice from the Arctic, makes the east coast inhospitable throughout the year, and although by August it may be possible to reach that coast, the danger of being trapped inshore deters most sailors from visiting it.

Because of the difficulties associated with making landfall on the east coast, but mainly because the best cruising grounds are on the west side, probably the best landfall for boats arriving from the east is at Prince Christian Sound, NE of Cape Farvel. Taking one's departure from a point south of Barra Head, the course passes south of Skeryvore light and then runs offshore to make landfall close to the southern tip of Greenland. Ikerasassuaq (Prince Christian Sound) is a spectacular sound, which provides a narrow passage north of Cape Farvel. There is always a large amount of ice in the sound, but by August most of it should have cleared. Strong winds funnel through the narrow passage and, in some years, the eastern entrance to the sound may be blocked by ice, thus making access impossible. Advice should be sought from Ice Central at Narssarssuaq, either by VHF via a coastal station, or, further offshore, on MF via Jualianehab Radio. If the eastern entrance into Prince Christian Sound is not open, one may be able to enter Torsukattak from the west near Frederiksdal (59°59'N, 44°40'W).

There are international flights from the capital Nuuk (Godthab) and also from the airfield at Narssarssuaq. Best repair facilities are in Nuuk, where there is also good provisioning.

AN158 *Ireland to Greenland*

BEST TIME:	June to August			
TROPICAL STORMS:	None			
CHARTS:	BA: 4011			
	US: 11			
PILOTS:	BA: 11, 40			
	US: 142, 181			
CRUISING GUIDES:	*Faeroe, Iceland and Greenland Cruising Notes.*			
WAYPOINTS:				

Departure	Intermediate	Landfall	Destination	Distance (M)
AN1580 Valentia NW		AN1581 Farvel NE	Ikerasassuaq	1190
51°56.5'N, 10°20'W		60°00'N, 43°05'W	*60°03'N, 43°10'W*	

A stop in SW Ireland makes much sense for any yacht bound for Greenland from ports in SW Europe or England as it makes it possible to wait for a good weather window before setting off on the long offshore passage. Having sailed around Land's End, boats from the south of England have a choice of Irish ports where they can provision before continuing their voyage. Yachts leaving from the west coast of England or from Northern Ireland may find it more convenient to sail through the North Channel and follow directions as in AN157, although, as the prevailing winds are from the W or SW, leaving Ireland to starboard may ensure a better sailing angle.

The harbour of Valentia is recommended as it affords shelter in all winds and is therefore a good final port of departure. The harbour can be entered from SW through Portmagee Channel, where there is an opening bridge. The NW channel is more convenient when leaving.

Weather and cruising conditions in Greenland are described in detail in route AN157, to which reference should be made. Because of the difficulties associated with making landfall on the east coast, but mainly the fact that the best cruising grounds are on the west side, probably the best landfall for boats arriving from the east is at Prince Christian Sound, NE of Cape Farvel. The recommended route runs clear of all dangers from the west coast of Ireland to the southern tip of Greenland. Landfall is made close to Ikerasassuaq, a spectacular sound, which provides a narrow passage north of Cape Farvel. There is always a large amount of ice in the sound, but by August most of it should have cleared. Strong winds funnel through the narrow passage and, in some years, the eastern entrance to the sound may be blocked by ice, making access impossible. Advice should be sought from Ice Central at Narssarssuaq, either by VHF via a coastal station, or, further offshore, on MF via Jualianehab Radio. If the eastern entrance into Prince Christian Sound is not open, one may be able to enter Torsukattak from the west near Frederiksdal (59°59'N, 44°40'W).

There are international flights from the capital Nuuk (Godthab) and also from the airfield at Narssarssuaq. Best repair facilities are in Nuuk, where there is also good provisioning.

AN160 ROUTES FROM SCANDINAVIA

There is a profound historical dimension to the routes described in this section, which covers the waters of the North Sea and Atlantic – once the undisputed fief of Viking sailors. Those outstanding navigators were the first in Europe to understand, and put to good use, the prevailing ocean winds and currents. In so doing they discovered new lands and pioneered ocean routes in daring voyages through waters that are held in awe by even today's sailors. It is indeed a great satisfaction for any sailor to sail in the wake of those outstanding men, and to feel the same excitement as they did as one makes landfall in Iceland, Greenland or faraway Spitsbergen.

Weather conditions, as far as we know, have changed little in the thousand years since Eric the Red sailed across to Iceland and Greenland, nor have the tactics used for such long passages. With the prevailing westerlies making west to east passages relatively easy, it is the westbound passages that need careful planning and it is here that we have a clear advantage over our forebears as we are able to observe the developing weather systems and choose the right weather window in order to benefit from favourable conditions.

Weather conditions in summer are rarely bad enough to cause any serious difficulties to a well prepared boat, and gale force winds show a low percentage during the recommended period from mid-June to mid-August. Ice poses a problem at all times in the vicinity of Greenland, and should be treated with great caution, whereas in the east, it is only in the proximity of Spitsbergen that one is likely to encounter pack ice in summer. However, the occasional iceberg may drift into lower latitudes whatever the season, a hazard that small boats must heed to avoid sharing the fate of the *Titanic*. One other hazard that needs to be taken into account are the strong tidal races among the smaller island groups, such as the Shetlands or Faeroes, which are compounded by the presence of submerged rocks – a good reason to plot courses that avoid these areas when planning a longer offshore passage.

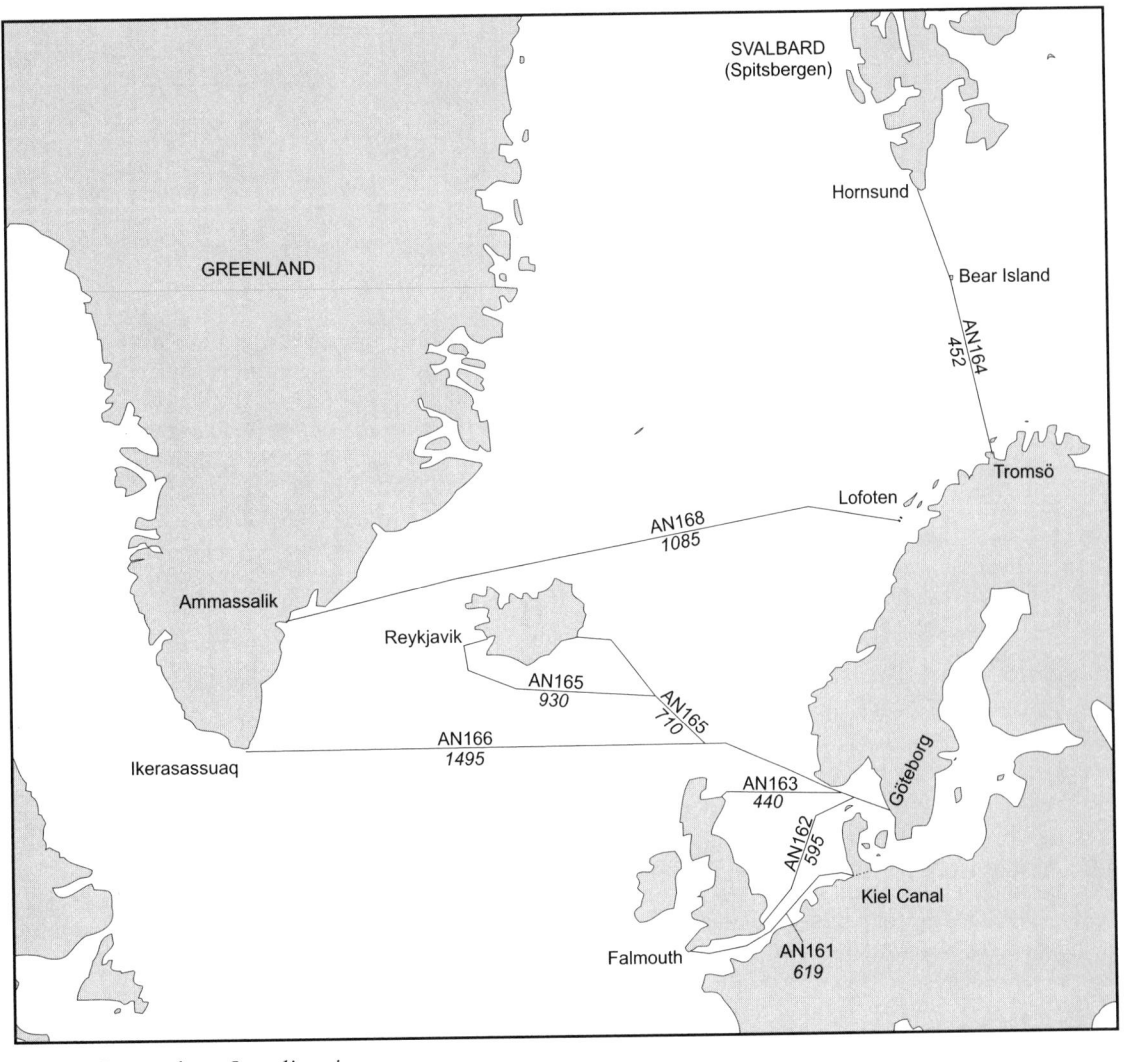

AN160 *Routes from Scandinavia*

AN161 *Southbound from the Baltic*

BEST TIME:	June to August			
TROPICAL STORMS:	None			
CHARTS:	BA: 4140			
	US: 126			
PILOTS:	BA: 28, 55			
	US: 192			
CRUISING GUIDES:	*The Baltic Sea, Norwegian Cruising Guide, Cruising Association Handbook.*			
WAYPOINTS:				

Departure	Intermediate	Landfall	Destination	Distance (M)
AN1610 Brunsbüttel	AN1612 Weser			
53°53'N, 9°08'E	*53°55'N, 8°10'E*			
	AN1613 Borkum			
	53°54'N, 6°15'E			
	AN1614 Tersh			
	53°30'N, 4°40'E			
	AN1615 Strait			
	51°10'N, 1°46'E			
	AN1616 Beachy	AN1617 Lizard E	Falmouth	619
	50°22'N, 0°10'W	*50°05'N, 5°00'W*	*50°09'N, 5°04'W*	

Because of its convenient position, most boats that are heading south with a longer passage in mind use the Kiel Canal at the start of their voyage. Having transited the Canal, it is perfectly possible to leave straight from Brunsbüttel, at its North Sea end. The alternative is to sail across the Elbe into Cuxhaven, where yachting facilities are much better and one can prepare for the voyage under better conditions. In either case, one needs then to make some offing to reach the open sea. Waypoint AN1612, off the Alte Weser landfall buoy, makes a good point of departure. From there, it is possible to stay inside the shipping separation zone, closer to shore, or take an offshore route. The inshore route has the advantage of being closer to a number of islands where shelter may be sought should the weather deteriorate.

To take the offshore route, one needs to cut across the shipping separation zone, so from AN1612 a course should be set first for AN1613 and then AN1614. From there, a course may be set for Dover Strait and waypoint AN1615, although as this route will cross, or run close to, a number of oil or gas fields, the area should be approached with great caution. The high density of shipping will only exacerbate the situation, so if weather conditions are not favourable the voyage may have to be interrupted. A convenient place to do so is at Den

Helder, where facilities are good. Den Helder Harbour Control monitors channel 14.

If weather conditions are good, one should resist the temptation to stop in one of the nearer English ports and try to make it at least as far as England's south coast, where there are several good marinas. The last, and best, place to wait for a good weather window to cross the Bay of Biscay is the port of Falmouth in the SW extremity of England. The other alternative is to sail closer to the French coast and possibly stop in the Channel Islands. However, for the subsequent crossing of Biscay, Falmouth makes a better starting point than the Channel Islands as the latter route would pass too close to the Ushant, whereas from Falmouth a clear course can be set right across the Bay of Biscay. In Falmouth visiting yachts may anchor off Customs House quay, pick up a mooring buoy or proceed to Falmouth Marina, about 2 miles up Penryn River.

Nordic and German sailors following the sun may be tempted to join a rally leaving every year from Wilhelmshaven, about 50 miles SW of the Kiel Canal. The Nor'South Rally is open to cruising boats heading south, either to the Mediterranean or, more likely, the Canaries and Caribbean.

AN162 *Scandinavia to England*

BEST TIME:	June to August
TROPICAL STORMS:	None
CHARTS:	BA: 4140
	US: 126
PILOTS:	BA: 54, 55, 56
	US: 192
CRUISING GUIDES:	*The Baltic Sea, Norwegian Cruising Guide, Cruising Association Handbook.*
WAYPOINTS:	

Departure	Intermediate	Landfall	Destination	Distance (M)
AN1620 Göteborg *57°40'N, 11°50'E*	AN1621 Vinga *57°40'N, 11°33'E* AN1622 Skagen *57°50'N, 10°30'E* AN1623 Jammer *57°30'N, 8°54'E* AN1624 Dan *55°30'N, 5°30'E* AN1625 Markham *54°00'N, 3°20'E* AN1626 Davy *53°00'N, 3°00'E* AN1627 Strait *51°10'N, 1°46'E* AN1628 Beachy *50°22'N, 0°10'W*	AN16293 Thames *51°44'N, 1°20'E*	London *51°30'N, 0°04'W*	595 650
AN1629 Kristiansand *58°08.5'N, 8°00'E*	AN16291 *58°00'N, 8°00'E* AN1624 Dan AN1625 Markham AN1626 Davy AN1627 Strait AN1628 Beachy	AN16293 Thames	London	510 565
AN16292 Thyborön *56°43'N, 8°14'E*	AN1625 Markham AN1626 Davy AN1627 Strait AN1628 Beachy	AN16293 Thames	London	447 502

Boats sailing from southern Sweden and Denmark may well use the Kiel Canal to reach the North Sea, but for anyone leaving from a more northern port, the open sea will be reached through the Skagerrak. One alternative is the Limfjord channel, which cuts across the top of Denmark and reaches the North Sea at Thyborön. From a multitude of departure points, the three most obvious ones have been chosen: Kristiansand, in southern Norway, Gothenberg, in western Sweden, and Thyborön, on the west coast of Denmark's Jutland. Yachts that use the Kiel Canal should refer to AN161.

The choice of destinations in England is not easy so the premise was used that visiting sailors to England may wish to stop in London or, more likely, head for one of the ports on the south coast. London is indeed an interesting destination, and sailing up the Thames, with the right tide, can be an exhilarating experience. Visiting boats will find good berthing at St Katharine's Yacht Haven, right by Tower Bridge, or at Limehouse Basin, where the Cruising Association is now based. The former is close to the City, whereas the latter is a more economic option. Having made landfall at waypoint AN16293, in the Thames estuary, an attempt should be made to arrive off Southend at low tide so as to catch a favourable current as the tide turns. The river is very well marked and easy to negotiate and,

by maintaining a speed of 6 knots, plus the favourable tide, London should be reached on one tide.

Boats headed for one of the ports on the south coast should use the same waypoints as far as AN1626, then set a course for Dover Strait at AN1627. The last waypoint is set SW of Beachy Head. Those planning to continue across the Bay of Biscay should also refer to AN13 and AN14.

AN163 *Scandinavia to Scotland*

BEST TIME:	June to August
TROPICAL STORMS:	None
CHARTS:	BA: 2182c
	US: 14
PILOTS:	BA: 52, 54, 55, 57A
	US: 141, 192, 193
CRUISING GUIDES:	*The Baltic Sea, Norwegian Cruising Guide, Cruising Association Handbook.*
WAYPOINTS:	

Departure	Intermediate	Landfall	Destination	Distance (M)
AN1630 Thyborön *56°43'N, 8°14'E*		AN1631 Bass *56°07'N, 3°22'E*	Granton *55°29.3'N, 3°13'E*	204
AN1632 Göteborg *57°40'N, 11°50'E*	AN1633 Vinga *57°40'N, 11°33'N* AN1634 Skagen *57°50N, 10°30'E*	AN1635 Head *57°29.5'N, 1°45'W*	Peterhead *57°30'N, 1°46.5'W*	440
AN1636 Korshamn *58°01'N, 7°00'E*	AN1637 Naze *58°00'N, 6°56'E*	AN1638 Moray *57°44'N, 3°45'W*	Inverness *57°30'N, 4°13'W*	365
AN1636 Korshamn	AN1637 Naze	AN1639 Pentland *58°43'N, 2°50'W*	Scapa Flow *58°54'N, 3°05'W*	327
AN16391 Tananger *58°56'N, 5°35'E*	AN16392 *58°54'N, 5°28'E*	AN163 Moray	Inverness	324
AN16391 Tananger	AN16392	AN1639 Pentland	Scapa Flow	276

For Scandinavian sailors Scotland is much more easily reached than any other place in the British Isles, and this is demonstrated by the large number of Scandinavian yachts that cross the North Sea to Scotland every year. From northern Denmark the most convenient port of departure is Thyborön, at the western end of Limfjorden. A southerly route leads straight across the North Sea to the Firth of Forth and Edinburgh, passing almost too close for comfort to the Eldfisk oil and gas

fields. Landfall is made close to Bass Rock. The closest port to Edinburgh, where a visiting yacht may find a berth, is Granton, although better facilities will be found further west at Port Edgar.

Boats leaving from a port in southern Sweden, such as Göteborg, may wish to stop first in Peterhead, even if their intended Scottish destination is further away. Those who wish to reach the west coast may do so either by using the Caledonian Canal or sailing around the top of

Scotland. However, because of the hazards associated with passing through Pentland Firth, it may be advisable, if the Orkneys route is used, to sail through Scapa Flow. In this case landfall will be made NE of Pentland Skerries. Scapa Flow is then entered by passing south of South Ronaldsay. Tides and currents in Scapa Flow are nowhere as fierce as in Pentland Firth and the west coast can be reached by this easier route. In both cases a point of departure has been suggested just to the west of the Naze, near the port of Korshamn. Another good point of departure on the west coast of Norway, both for boats bound for Inverness and the Orkneys, is Tananger, near Stavanger.

AN164 *Norway to Spitsbergen*

BEST TIME:	June to August				
TROPICAL STORMS:	None				
CHARTS:	BA: 4010				
	US: 10				
PILOTS:	BA: 11, 58A, 58B				
	US: 182				
CRUISING GUIDES:	*Norwegian Cruising Guide, Norwegian Arctic Pilot.*				
WAYPOINTS:					
Departure	*Intermediate*	*Landfall*	*Destination*		*Distance (M)*
AN1640 Tromsö	AN1641 Torsvag				
69°39'N, 18°58'E	*70°14'N, 19°30'E*				
	AN1642 Bear S	AN1642 Sorkapp S	Hornsund		452
	74°20'N, 19°10'E	*76°26'W, 16°20'E*	*77°00'N, 15°34'E*		
AN1644 Lofoten N		AN1645 Sorkapp S	Hornsund		472
69°10'N, 15°28'E					

A voyage to Spitsbergen, or, to give its correct Norwegian name, the Svalbard archipelago, is a unique experience. Sailing conditions in summer are relatively moderate and poor visibility may be more of a hazard than strong winds. At the height of summer in a normal year, ice does not pose a serious problem and the west coast of Spitsbergen is usually free of pack ice from June until November. However, weather conditions deteriorate rapidly after the middle of August, so early summer is to be preferred. The coast of Spitsbergen is indented by deep fjords offering good shelter. Large glaciers slope off into the sea, fronted by high ice cliffs. Ice conditions on the passage from mainland Norway are usually good in early summer, when the Gulf Stream assures a mostly ice free passage after the middle of June.

Most boats heading for Spitsbergen cruise along the Norwegian coast possibly as far as Tromsö before heading offshore. Tromsö is the tra-ditional port of departure for Arctic expeditions, with excellent repair facilities, provisioning and weather information. An easy inside passage leads to Torsvag, a good harbour at the NW tip of Vannoya. This is a good jumping off point for the offshore passage, but all provisioning, including diesel, should have been done in Tromsö as local supplies are limited and diesel is not available. Also in Tromsö one can obtain weather and ice charts from the meteorological office.

Another option is to leave the mainland north of Lofoten as the distance will not be shortened considerably by continuing ENE towards North Cape. A direct route leads to Sorkapp, a small island off Spitsbergen proper.

Bear Island (Bjornoya) lies roughly halfway to Spitsbergen and offers the possibility of some shelter if the weather deteriorates. Although the island does not have an all-weather harbour, there are anchorages on all its sides so, depending on wind direction, one should be able to find some shelter. The best anchorage is at Sorhamna (74°22'N, 19°10'E), two miles NE of the southern tip of the island. It offers good shelter from winds with a northerly component. Kvalrossbukta (74°23'N, 19°10.5'E), close to NE of Sorhamna, offers better shelter from the westerly swell.

Although the weather charts show a higher incidence of SW winds in summer, variable winds are usually the order of the day along this route. Fog is frequent, especially near Bear Island and in the southern approaches to Spitsbergen. Because of the relatively short distance to the magnetic pole, as one approaches Spitsbergen the compass reacts slower and, sailing north along the coast of Spitsbergen, magnetic compasses become less and less reliable. A serious hazard in the Barents Sea are large floating logs, which are partly submerged and almost impossible to see.

Sorkapp, at the southern extremity of Sorkappoya, makes a good landfall as it is visible from far away on a clear day. In poor visibility the area should be approached with great caution as the low land and shoals extend 10 miles south of the high ground. Both winds and the swell are augmented in the immediate vicinity of Sorkapp. In strong easterly winds, good shelter can be found at Stormbukta, 14 miles NNW of Sorkappoya. However, the nearest sheltered anchorage is at Hornsund (77°00'N, 15°36'E), the site of a Polish polar station.

Occasionally the entrance is blocked by ice and one may not be able to stop. Nearby is a well protected lagoon (Antonio Pigafettahamna), created by the Hansbreen glacier. The area should be entered with great caution as it has not been fully charted and there are many submerged rocks.

In a bad ice year, Sorkapp may be surrounded by ice and one then has to sail well to the west, possibly as much as 40 miles, before being able to close with the west coast of Spitsbergen. Although no special permit is required to visit Spitsbergen, the office of the District Governor, who is in charge of the rescue services, must be informed of one's movements. Visiting yachts are required to have insurance cover for SAR operations. For details, write in advance to: Sysselmannen pa Svalbard, N-9170 Longyearbyen, Norway. Longyearbyen (78°13.5'N, 15°37'E), located in Isfjorden, on the west coast of Spitsbergen, is the administrative centre and has the best facilities; there are frequent flights to Oslo and Tromsö.

Severe restrictions apply to nature reserves and, from 15 May to 15 August, it is prohibited to move within 300 metres of a bird sanctuary. Most animals are protected and, in the case of polar bears, may be killed only in self defence. As bears pose a major risk in all areas, visitors are advised to carry arms for self protection. These can be hired locally.

AN165 *Norway to Iceland*

BEST TIME:	June to August			
TROPICAL STORMS:	None			
CHARTS:	BA: 4011			
	US: 11			
PILOTS:	BA: 11, 52, 57A			
	US: 141, 181, 182			
CRUISING GUIDES:	*Cruising Association Handbook; Faeroe, Iceland and Greenland Cruising Notes.*			
WAYPOINTS:				
Departure	*Intermediate*	*Landfall*	*Destination*	*Distance (M)*
AN1651 Eigeroy 58°27'N, 5°50'E	AN1652 Hole 59°42'N, 1°20'E			
	AN1653 Suduroy 61°16'N, 6°55'W	AN1654 Djupivogur 64°37'N, 14°12'W	Berufjordur *64°39'N, 14°18'W*	710
AN1651 Eigeroy	AN1655 Surtsey 63°10'N, 20°20'W			
	AN1656 Reykjanes S 63°48'N, 22°48'W	AN1657 Reykjanes N 64°08'N, 22°50'W	Reykjavik *64°09'N, 21°56'W*	930

This is the traditional Viking route that was plyed regularly in the Middle Ages following the legendary voyage of Eric the Red to Iceland and Greenland, towards the end of the tenth century. It was the knowledge gained by those sailing this route that led the first Vikings to Vinland, as they called North America, several centuries before Columbus stumbled upon a continent which, right up to his death, he was convinced was part of the continent of Asia.

The prevailing easterly winds that are common in higher latitudes ought to provide good sailing conditions, especially if the point of departure is far enough to the north to avoid the effect of the depressions moving east across the North Atlantic. Occasionally, one may have to make a detour to the north in search of those easterlies, so it is essential not to leave on this passage if a depression is approaching from the west on or close to one's latitude. If such a depression passes far enough to the south, it ought to produce the wished for easterlies.

A convenient departure port, perfectly located for boats coming from Denmark, Sweden or southern Norway, is Egersund. It is a well sheltered harbour with two entrances, which makes it accessible in almost any weather. It also has adequate facilities to prepare for the forthcoming passage.

From waypoint AN1651, NW of Eigeroy light-house, a course should be set which passes through the aptly called Hole separating the Shetlands from Fair Isle (waypoint AN1652). The safest course passes well to the south of Sumburgh Head, the southern extremity of main-land Shetland. Violent currents are experienced in this area, so a course should be steered that pass-es at least 3 miles clear of Sumburgh Head. Course is then altered to pass south of the Faeroes. A slightly more northerly route is taken if the in-tention is to make landfall in SE Iceland. If, how-ever, one intends to sail directly to Reykjavik, on the west coast, from waypoint AN1652, a course is set for AN1665, which will pass close to the Foinaven oil field so this area should be approached with caution. Landfall will be made off the south coast of Iceland, close to Surtsey, a newly formed volcanic island. Nearby Vest-mannaeyjar, off Iceland's south coast, is a spect-acular volcanic archipelago, where recent eruptions have created new islands and mountains. A stop here should not be missed. The subsequent waypoints lead around the SW of the island into Reykjavik Harbour.

Lying almost astride the direct route to Iceland, both the Shetlands and Faeroes make tempting stopping points. In the case of the Shetlands, the strong tides and other hazards associated with navigating in those difficult waters may be a powerful deterrent from stopping there.

Strong tides and difficult navigation also apply to the Faeroes. The capital and main harbour is Torhavn on the island of Streymoy. Because it lies almost in the centre of the small archipelago, and thus intricate coastal navigation is required, fur-ther instructions are beyond the scope of this book. Those who decide to stop there may consider reach-ing the NW side of the Faeroes by negotiating the Sundini channel between the islands of Streymoy and Eysturoy. The channel is spanned by a bridge with a height of approximately 16 metres and as the maximum spring rate can be as much as 12 knots, it is essential to plan the passage around slack water.

Further details on weather and yachting facil-ities in Iceland are given in route AN155.

AN166 *Norway to Greenland*

BEST TIME:	June to August
TROPICAL STORMS:	None
CHARTS:	BA: 4010
	US: 10
PILOTS:	BA: 11, 52, 57A
	US: 141, 181, 182
CRUISING GUIDES:	*Faeroe, Iceland and Greenland Cruising Notes.*
WAYPOINTS:	

Departure	Intermediate	Landfall	Destination	Distance (M)
AN1661 Eigeroy 58°27'N, 5°50'E	AN1662 Hole 59°42'N, 1°20'W	AN1663 Farvel NE 60°00'N, 43°05'W	Ikerasassuaq *60°03'N, 43°10'W*	1495
AN1664 Lofoten S 62°00'N, 3°20'E		AN1665 Dan 65°36'N, 34°00'W	Ammassalik *65°37'N, 37°30'W*	1085

Sailed for the first time just over one thousand years ago, the southern route is slightly more benign, while the northern route only attracts those in search of adventure. While the passage on either route should present no major problems to a well found boat, conditions in Greenland itself are often far from favourable. The main difficulty is posed by ice, which only eases its grip on this enormous island during a short period at the height of summer. Along the east coast there is an ice free strip, but offshore pack ice makes it impossible, or very dangerous, for a sailing boat to cruise through that area. In a good year, the whole of Davis Strait and Baffin Bay can be free of pack ice, but not of icebergs, which are never absent. The west coast is mountainous with deep fjords and in the south there is an ice free area which also includes some of the offshore islands. In an average summer, winds tend to be variable, with a northerly component. On land, summer temperatures vary between 2°C and 20°C, but sea temperatures very rarely rise above 4°C. This means that fog can be quite frequent in summer, especially around Ivgut. The Nuuk area is relatively free of fog.

Cruising anywhere in Greenland needs careful planning. Because the west coast between 63°N and 69°N is usually clear of ice by early June, thanks to the warm West Greenland Current, the area may be entered from the west by giving Cape Farvel a wide berth. Depending on existing conditions, this can be as much as 120 miles. Long days, reason-able weather and acceptable temperatures make cruising possible until shorter days and deteriorating conditions signal the end of a rather too short sailing season. The East Greenland Current, which brings down ice from the Arctic, makes the east coast inhospitable throughout the year, and although by August it may be possible to reach that particular coast, the danger of being trapped inshore deters most sailors from visiting this area.

There are two route options open to boats sailing from Norway: a southern route from southern Norway to the west coast of Greenland, and a northern route that passes to the north of Iceland and makes landfall at Ammassalik, on Greenland's east coast.

The southern route passes close to the Shetlands and Faeroes, which provide convenient stops if necessary. This can also be said of Iceland, which is not too far off the direct route; in fact, it is indeed doubtful that anyone will sail the entire route nonstop. For those who do, the suggested waypoints outline the simplest route. The best landfall for boats coming this way is at Prince Christian Sound, NE of Cap Farvel, close to the southern tip of Greenland. Ikerasassuaq is a spectacular sound, which provides a narrow passage north of Cape Farvel. There is always a large amount of ice in the sound, but by August most of it should have cleared. Strong winds funnel through the narrow passage and, in some years, the eastern entrance to the sound may be blocked by ice, thus making access impossible. Advice should be sought from Ice Central at Narssarssuaq, either by VHF via a coastal station, of, further offshore, on MF via Jualianehab Radio. If the eastern entrance into Prince Christian Sound is not open, one may be able to enter Torsukattak from the west near Frederiksdal (59°59'N, 44°40'W). There are international flights from the capital Nuuk (Godthab) and also from the airfield at Narssarssuaq. Best repair facilities are in Nuuk, where there is also good provisioning.

For those planning to sail a more northerly route,

a good point of departure would be Skomvaer light at the southern extremity of Lofoten. Route B, across the Norwegian Sea, makes landfall near Cape Dan, which should be approached with great caution as there are dangerous rocks SW of that cape. Advice should be sought by MF radio from Ice Central at Narssarssuaq, via Jualianehab (Qaqortoq) Radio, when well offshore. Ammassalik is a small town, and the main settlement on Greenland's east coast. Facilities are adequate and there are regular flights to Reykjavik and Nuuk.

AN170 HIGH LATITUDE ROUTES IN THE NW ATLANTIC

Once considered only suitable for expeditions by the foolhardy, the far North Atlantic is now visited by increasing numbers of ordinary cruising boats, their owners undeterred by the hardships associated with sailing in high latitudes. Their efforts are more than rewarded by some of the most stunning scenery anywhere in the world, from the mighty glaciers of Greenland to the live volcanic landscape of Iceland and the spectacular fjords of Norway. Sailing conditions are far from perfect, but at least – in summer – they are rarely outright dangerous, and pose no real problems for a well prepared boat and crew.

Most of these routes are above the area of prevailing westerlies, but the eastbound movement of summer depressions should be monitored carefully as one may be able to put to good advantage the winds generated by them. An important part in one's routing should be the existing currents,

which played a major part in the routes sailed by the early Vikings. After all, this used to be their playground and, amazingly, among the best sources for information on these routes are the Icelandic sagas. Written in the twelfth century, the sagas describe the routes sailed by the early Viking seafarers from Iceland and Greenland to Vinland.

The routes described in this section, read in conjunction with sections AN150 and AN160, should make it easier to plan a passage to any of these destinations, or even an Atlantic crossing in high latitudes, following closely the routes originated by those intrepid Viking navigators. For the real adventurer, even destinations above the Arctic Circle should be achievable and, with careful planning, a round trip from North America even as far as Spitsbergen, with stops in Greenland and Iceland, could be completed in one summer season.

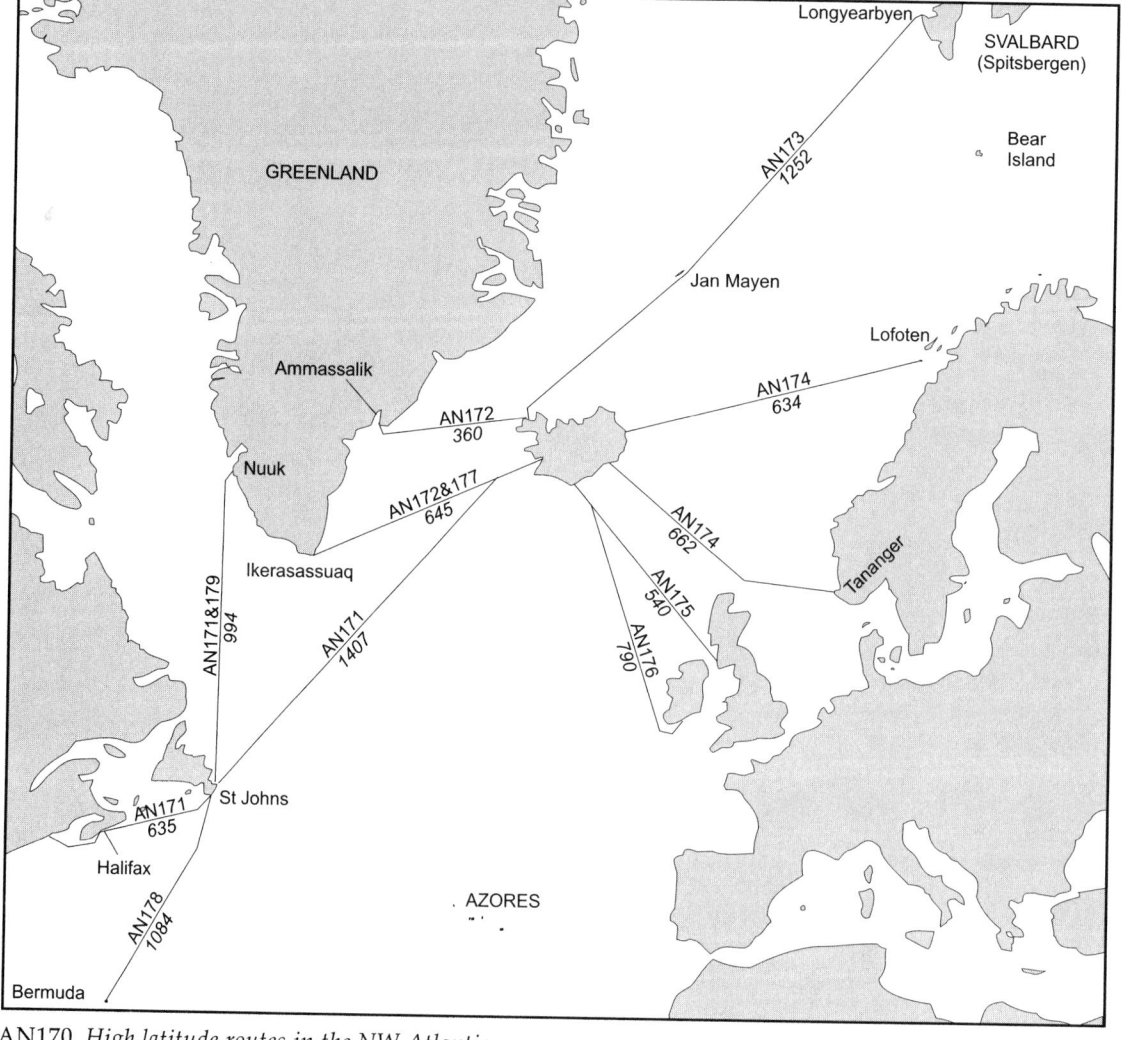

AN170 *High latitude routes in the NW Atlantic*

AN171 *Northbound from North America*

BEST TIME:	June to August
TROPICAL STORMS:	None
CHARTS:	BA: 4011
	US: 121
PILOTS:	BA: 11, 50, 65
	US: 145, 146, 181
CRUISING GUIDES:	*Cruising Guide to Nova Scotia, Cruising Guide to Newfoundland, Faeroe, Iceland and Greenland Cruising Notes.*

WAYPOINTS:

Departure	Intermediate	Landfall	Destination	Distance (M)
AN1710 Maine 43°00'N, 65°00'W		AN1711 Sambro 44°20'N, 63°25'W	Halifax *44°38'N, 63°34'W*	130
AN1712 Scotia 44°30'N, 63°28'W	AN1713 Race 46°35'N, 53°00'W	AN1714 Terra SE 47°30'N, 52°35'W	St John's *47°34'N, 52°42'W*	635
AN1715 Terra N 47°40'N, 52°30'W		AN1716 Frederik 61°53'N, 49°55'W	Frederikshab *62°00'N, 49°40'W*	868
		AN1717 Green 63°55'N, 52°10'W	Nuuk *64°10'N, 51°44'W*	994
AN1718 Terra E 47°36'N, 52°30'W		AN1718 Reykjanes N 64°08'N, 22°50'W	Reykjavik *64°09'N, 21°56'W*	1407

Whereas the routes described in AN141 were meant primarily for those planning to make a non-stop voyage to Northern Europe by taking advantage of the prevailing westerlies, the route options described here are for those tempted to sail towards the Arctic Circle and beyond. The routes described in this section may also be combined to provide a high latitude crossing to Northern Europe, something that is now being done mainly by European boats returning home by this less frequented route. Indeed, some of the boats that had crossed the Atlantic to the Caribbean by the trade wind route, and then sailed up the US east coast as far as Canada, found themselves so far north that it made more sense to continue in that direction. The one major problem for these boats is that normally a cruise up the east coast takes place in mid-summer, by which time it is almost too late in the season to commence a voyage to Europe along such a route. Ideally such a high latitude passage should start late in June, or even early July, which, for Europeans at least, means either leaving the boat in New England during the previous winter, or starting the American cruise earlier so as to be able to leave towards Nova Scotia and

Newfoundland as soon as weather conditions are right.

Indeed, Nova Scotia and Newfoundland make excellent stopping places and, as they are virtually on the direct route, calling at Halifax and St John's does not amount to much of a detour. Because of the almost infinite numbers of ports of departure, a hypothetical point has been chosen just off Cape Sable, at the southern extremity of Nova Scotia.

North of Newfoundland, one has the choice of sailing directly to Iceland, or stopping first in Greenland. The direct route would most probably lead to Reykjavik, the Icelandic capital, which is a good place from where to start a cruise around that scenic island. A compromise solution is to interrupt the voyage at the southern tip of Greenland, but this should only be attempted if one has reliable information that the area around Cape Farvel is indeed free of ice, which, early in the season, is not often the case. If so, this area should be given a wide berth of at least 120 miles. The best cruising area of Greenland is the west coast, which not only has the advantage of being free of ice earlier than the rest, but also because the area around the capital Nuuk (Gothab) is the most attractive cruising ground. Here, the West Greenland Current will be in one's favour. In a good year, the whole of Davis Strait and Baffin Bay can be free of pack ice, but not of icebergs, which are never absent. The west coast is mountainous with deep fjords, similar to Norway. There is an ice free area in the SW which also includes some of the offshore islands. In an average summer, winds tend to be variable, with a northerly component. On land, summer temperatures vary between 2° and 20°C, but sea temperatures very rarely rise above 4°C. This means that fog can be quite frequent in summer, although the Nuuk area is relatively free of fog.

Sailing north from Newfoundland, if ice permits, a good first stop on Greenland's west coast is at Frederikshab (Paamiut). An inner route leads north from this small and well sheltered harbour. However, in some summers, the coast is blocked by ice as far as here, so one may have to continue offshore to Nuuk, whose approaches are well marked; however, very careful navigation is still required because of the many dangerous rocks.

Cruising anywhere in Greenland needs careful planning. Because the west coast between 63°N and 69°N is usually clear of ice by early June, thanks to the warm West Greenland Current, the area may be entered from the west by giving Cape Farvel a wide berth. This can be as much as 120 miles, depending on existing conditions. Long days, reasonable weather and acceptable temperatures make cruising possible until shorter days and deteriorating conditions signal the end of a short sailing season. The East Greenland Current, which brings down ice from the Arctic, makes the east coast inhospitable throughout the year and although by August it may be possible to reach that coast, the danger of being trapped inshore deters most sailors from visiting that area.

Boats leaving Newfoundland directly for Iceland will have to cross the adverse Labrador Current, although closer to Iceland the north-setting Irminger Current should make up for the ground lost earlier on.

Depending on the overall weather conditions in the North Atlantic, summer depressions may pass either to the north or south of Iceland. Generally, winds around Iceland follow a certain pattern, with those north of Iceland having an easterly component, and those south of Iceland, a westerly one. Therefore boats approaching Iceland from SW should head for Reykjavik, which has the best facilities, and then cruise anti-clockwise around the island. For more details on Iceland see AN155. The following routes described in this section give details of how to continue the voyage towards Northern Europe, or perhaps to Spitsbergen.

AN172 *Greenland to Iceland*

BEST TIME:	June to August			
TROPICAL STORMS:	None			
CHARTS:	BA: 4112			
	US: 112			
PILOTS:	BA: 11			
	US: 181			
CRUISING GUIDES:	Faeroe, Iceland and Greenland Cruising Notes.			
WAYPOINTS:				
Departure	**Intermediate**	**Landfall**	**Destination**	**Distance (M)**
AN1720 Ikerasassuaq	AN1721 Farvel NE	AN1722 Reykjanes N	Reykjavik	645
60°03'N, 43°10'W	60°00'N, 43°05'W	64°08'N, 22°50'W	64°09'N, 21°56'W	
AN1723 Ammassalik	AN1724 Dan	AN1725 Vestfir	Isafjördur	360
65°37'N, 37°30'W	65°36'N, 34°00'W	66°13'N, 23°30'W	66°04'N, 23°07'W	

Winds for this passage should be favourable, and should make up for the contrary East Greenland Current. One major concern are icebergs, which are brought southward by that same current, so a permanent watch must be kept, especially in the area closer to Greenland. For boats coming from the west coast of Greenland, a good departure point is Prince Christian Sound, as it offers good shelter if one needs to wait for better weather. From a point off Cape Farvel, a direct course leads to a point north of Reykjanes Peninsula in the approaches to Reykjavik. Berthing facilities for visitors are limited in Reykjavik and a good alternative is Hafnarfjordur (64°04'N, 21°58'W), 5 miles south of Reykjavik. This is a favourite port among visiting sailors and, although the port is always busy, visitors usually find a place. All facilities are available in the nearby town, which also boasts a highly popular Viking Festival held every two years (the next one is planned for July 1999).

Boats leaving from Ammassalik, having cleared the dangers close to Cape Dan, should set a course that will take them across the Denmark Strait to AN1725. For boats coming from Greenland's east coast, or from further north, such as Spitsbergen, the most convenient landfall port is Isafjördur, occupying a sheltered position in a fjord on the NW side of Vestfirdir. This is the large peninsula that forms the NW of Iceland, a remarkable area indented by deep fjords. Because of the proximity of the East Greenland Current, which sweeps through the Denmark Strait, this is the coldest part of Iceland and snow lingers on into the summer. Isafjördur is the main settlement on the south side of the fjord of that name. It has good facilities and communications, and is an excellent base from which to explore the surrounding area, whether by boat or land. Refer to AN155 for further cruising information on Iceland.

AN173 *Iceland to Spitsbergen*

BEST TIME:	June to August				
TROPICAL STORMS:	None				
CHARTS:	BA: 4010				
	US: 10				
PILOTS:	BA: 11				
	US: 181, 182				
CRUISING GUIDES:	*Faeroe, Iceland and Greenland; Norwegian Arctic Pilot.*				
WAYPOINTS:					
Departure	*Intermediate*	*Landfall*	*Destination*		*Distance (M)*
AN1730 Isafjördur	AN1731 Straumnes				
66°04'N, 23°07'W	*66°30'N, 23°10'W*				
	AN1732 Mayen S				
	70°47'N, 8°58'E				
	AN1733 Mayen N	AN1734 Linné	Longyearbyen		1252
	71°11'N, 7°58'E	*78°02'N, 13°35'E*	*78°13.5'N, 15°37'E*		

With a higher percentage of SW winds during the short summer than from any other direction, passages from Iceland to Spitsbergen (Svalbard) usually benefit from better conditions than in the opposite direction. Conveniently located almost at the halfway mark, the island of Jan Mayen provides an interesting stop, although it lacks an all weather anchorage. It is interesting to note that whereas the relatively lower latitudes were sailed by the Vikings around the turn of the first millennium, the Irish monk Brendan actually set foot on Jan Mayen in the seventh century, and his description of the 'black and scorched island' is the first written record of any Arctic exploration!

Because of the relatively short distance to the magnetic pole, as one approaches Spitsbergen the compass is slower to react and, sailing north along the coast of Spitsbergen, magnetic compasses become less and less reliable. A serious hazard in the Barents Sea are large floating logs, which are partly submerged and almost impossible to see. Fog is frequent in summer, especially as one approaches Spitsbergen.

Boats heading NE from Iceland will most probably leave from the west coast, where facilities are best to prepare for this passage. The small port of Isafjördur provides an excellent jumping off point, with good provisioning and links to the capital of Reykjavik. Sailing north out of the fjord, a good departure point is off NW Vestfirdir, from where a direct course can be steered for Sorkapp (70°49.6'N, 8°59.1'W), the southern extremity of Jan Mayen. Because of the submerged rocks that virtually surround this island, it should be given a berth of at least 1.5 miles. The only inhabited place is at Olonkinbyen, where there is a manned Loran and radio station. Nearby Batvika is a small bay offering good shelter in W winds, while Kvalrossbukta, across the island, gives good shelter in E winds. A good anchorage in S winds is at Nordbukta, just west of Nordkapp (71°09.6'N, 7°58'W), the northern extremity of the island. This is a good departure point for the continuation of the voyage.

Boats approaching Spitsbergen from the SW should make for the main settlement and capital at Longyearbyen, located in Isfjorden, on the west coast of Spitsbergen. Landfall will be made off Cape Linné, at the entrance into Isfjorden, before proceeding into the deep fjord.

Although no special permit is required to visit Spitsbergen, the office of the District Governor, who is in charge of the rescue services, must be informed of one's movements. Visiting yachts are required to have insurance cover for SAR operations. For details, write in advance to: Sysselmannen pa Svalbard, N-9170 Longyearbyen, Norway. Longyearbyen is the administrative centre and has the best facilities, and also frequent flights to Oslo and Tromsö. For more details on Spitsbergen, refer to AN154 and AN164.

AN174 *Iceland to Norway*

BEST TIME:	June to August
TROPICAL STORMS:	None
CHARTS:	BA: 4011
	US: 11
PILOTS:	BA: 11, 52, 57A
	US: 141, 181, 182
CRUISING GUIDES:	*Cruising Association Handbook; Faeroe, Iceland and Greenland Cruising Notes.*
WAYPOINTS:	

Departure	Intermediate	Landfall	Destination	Distance (M)
AN1740 Berufjordur *64°39'N, 14°18'W*	AN1741 Djupivogur *64°37'N, 14°12'W*	AN1742 *58°52'N, 5°32'E*	Tananger *58°56'N, 5°35'E*	662
AN1743 Surtsey *63°10'N, 20°20'W*	AN1744 Hole *59°42'N, 1°20'E*	AN1745 Eigeroy *58°27'N, 5°50'E*	Egersund *58°27'N, 6°00'E*	823
AN1743 Surtsey	AN1744 Hole	AN1746 Jutland *56°44'N, 8°11'E*	Thyborön *56°43'N, 8°14'E*	935
AN1747 Seydhisfjördur *65°16'N, 13°59'W*	AN1748 *65°20'N, 13°36'W*	AN1749 Lofoten S *67°20'N, 11°50'E*	Skomvaer *67°24'N, 11°52'E*	634

A direct route to ports in southern Norway or Denmark should benefit from the westerlies that prevail in the latitudes south of Ireland. Lying astride the direct route, both the Faeroes and Shetlands make convenient stops, even if the difficult navigation in their vicinity might prove to be a deterrent. Generally, it makes more sense to visit first the rest of Iceland and then take one's departure from the east coast. A good port of departure on that coast is Berufjordur. From there, the route leads close to the north of the Faeroes and Shetlands to make landfall off Tananger. This small port close to the town of Stavanger is a good place to start a cruise along the south coast of Norway.

The alternative is to leave until last a visit to the newly formed volcanic islands at Vestmann-aeyjar, and bid Iceland farewell from there. The route passes far enough to the south of Sumburgh Head in the Shetlands to avoid the rough seas associated with it. From there, one route leads to Eigeroy, in southern Norway, while the other carries on to the Danish port of Thyborön. The latter is at the western end of Limfjorden, a beautiful cruising ground of lakes and channels that cuts across the Jutland peninsula and thus provides a scenic route to the Baltic. Because winds along the west coast of Norway are predominantly NE in summer, it makes more sense to cruise that coast from north to south, in which case a route that goes from Iceland to one of the northern ports in Norway ought to be preferred. This may also be the route preferred by those bound for Spitsbergen, who may wish to take their departure for that Arctic possession of Norway from a mainland port such as Tromsö. A good place to leave Iceland for this route is Seydhisfjördur, as it is the ferry terminal from Norway, Denmark and the Shetlands. There are good repair facilities and good provisioning. The route across the Norwegian Sea leads to Lofoten, where landfall is made at Skomvaer lighthouse, at the SW extremity of Lofoten chain. Going north from here, one can sail in the sheltered waters of Vestfjorden as Lofoten form a barrier between the Atlantic and mainland.

AN175 *Iceland to Scotland*

BEST TIME:	June to August			
TROPICAL STORMS:	None			
CHARTS:	BA: 4011			
	US: 11			
PILOTS:	BA: 11, 52			
	US: 141, 181			
CRUISING GUIDES:	*Cruising Association Handbook; Faeroe, Iceland and Greenland Cruising Notes.*			
WAYPOINTS:				
Departure	*Intermediate*	*Landfall*	*Destination*	*Distance (M)*
AN1750 Berufjordur *64°39'N, 14°18'W*	AN1751 Djupivogur *64°37'N, 14°12'W*	AN1752 Barra S *56°45'N, 7°40'W*	Oban *56°25'N, 5°29'W*	588
AN1750 Berufjordur	AN1751 Djupivogur	AN1753 Lewis *58°35'N, 6°00'W*		434
AN1754 Surtsey *63°10'N, 20°20'W*		AN1752 Barra S		540
AN1754 Surtsey		AN1753 Lewis		500

As most of those who visit Iceland attempt to circumnavigate it, the point of departure will depend primarily on where that circumnavigation is completed. A good port of departure on the east coast is off Djupivogur fjord, whereas those coming from the west coast can take their departure off Surtsey, a recently formed volcanic island. Close to the north is Vestmannaeyjar, a recently formed archipelago born out of the eruptions that shook Iceland in the 1970s. It is a good place to conclude a summer cruise to Iceland.

From Surtsey, the direct route leads to Barra Head, in the approaches to the North Channel. If weather or other considerations require another landfall, one should sail north of the Hebrides and use the shelter provided by the Minch to reach destinations in either Scotland or England. Ports on the east coast can be reached via the Caledonian Canal, but if an offshore route is preferred, it is safer to sail either north of the Orkneys or through the sheltered waters of Scapa Flow.

Summer winds along this route should be mostly favourable as the predominant direction is from W or SW.

AN176 *Iceland to Ireland*

BEST TIME:	June to August
TROPICAL STORMS:	None
CHARTS:	BA: 4011
	US: 11
PILOTS:	BA: 11, 40
	US: 142, 181
CRUISING GUIDES:	*Cruising Association Handbook; Faeroe, Iceland and Greenland Cruising Notes.*
WAYPOINTS:	

Departure	Intermediate	Landfall	Destination	Distance (M)
AN1761 Surtsey 63°10'N, 20°20'W		AN1762 Fair 55°25'N, 7°25'W	Coleraine *55°09'N, 6°41'W*	638
AN1761 Surtsey	AN1763 Inish 52°02'N, 10°45'W AN1764 Mizen 51°26'N, 9°56'W		Crosshaven *51°28.2'N, 9°43'W*	790

Weather conditions on this passage should be favourable as even strong winds normally blow from the right direction. Boats leaving from Iceland's west coast can take their departure off Surtsey, a recently formed volcanic island at the southern extremity of Vestmannaeyjar, the recently formed archipelago born out of the eruptions that shook Iceland in the 1970s.

The north and west coasts of Ireland offer so many cruising attractions that recommending a suitable landfall is almost impossible. For those wishing to see as much as possible and then end on the more sheltered SW coast, it is probably better to head for a port on the north coast. A hypothetical waypoint has been given off Fair Head but it is stressed that landfall should only be made

in fair weather as this is a distinctly dangerous stretch. In deteriorating weather one should make for Bann River (55°10.4'N, 6°46.5'W) where Coleraine Marina offers the best facilities in the area. Inishtrahull Sound should not be used if there is a large swell, and in bad weather one should pass as much as 3 miles north of Torr Rocks.

When making landfall, the coast should be approached with great caution as in onshore winds many ports cannot be entered because of breaking swell. This is true for all of Ireland's west coast. Another hazard to avoid are the salmon nets and lobster pots that are found along the entire coast.

Boats heading for the SW coast should make landfall off Mizen Head, at the SW extremity of

Ireland. The nearest shelter is at Crookhaven, where only basic facilities are available. Proper facilities will not be found until much further east at Kinsale (51°42'N, 8°30.5'W), or even further at Crosshaven (51°48.2'N, 8°17.7'N) in Cork Harbour. This is the best marina on Ireland's south coast and is close to the city of Cork.

AN177 *Iceland to Greenland*

BEST TIME:	June to August			
TROPICAL STORMS:	None			
CHARTS:	BA: 4112			
	US: 112			
PILOTS:	BA: 11			
	US: 181			
CRUISING GUIDES:	*Faeroe, Iceland and Greenland Cruising Notes.*			
WAYPOINTS:				
Departure	*Intermediate*	*Landfall*	*Destination*	*Distance (M)*
AN1770 Reykjavik	AN1771 Reykjanes N	AN1772 Farvel NE	Ikerasassuaq	645
64°09'N, 21°56'W	*64°08'N, 22°50'W*	*60°00'N, 43°05'W*	*60°03'N, 43°10'W*	
AN1773 Isafjördur	AN1774 Vestfir	AN1775 Dan	Ammassalik	360
66°04'N, 23°07'W	*66°13'N, 23°30'W*	*65°36'N, 34°00'W*	*65°37'N, 37°30'W*	

There are not many destinations to choose from in Greenland and, in some years, the entire east coast may still be closed off by ice in early summer. The one area that becomes accessible earlier in the season is on the west coast, in the proximity of Nuuk. If this is the only accessible destination, boats leaving from Iceland will have to sail well to the south of Cape Farvel – possibly as much as 120 miles – before being able to turn NW. The best destination, if free of ice, is Prince Christian Sound, at the southern tip of Greenland. This is a narrow sound that joins Ilua and Torsukattak and provides a convenient and highly scenic inshore passage just north of Cape Farvel. Ice information may be obtained from Narssarssuaq and, if the eastern entrance to the sound is encumbered by ice, it is possible to use the western entrance at Frederiksdal.

The closest port in Greenland is Ammassalik, just across the Denmark Strait. A good departure port is Isafjördur, on the NW side of Vestfirdir peninsula. Extra care should be taken when sailing this more northern route because of the danger posed by the icebergs carried south by the East Greenland Current. When approaching land, the rocks lying SW of Cape Dan should be given a wide berth before heading for the channel leading into Ammassalik harbour. This has the best facilities on Greenland's east coast, and also regular flights to Nuuk and Reykjavik.

AN178 *Iceland to Canada and Bermuda*

BEST TIME:	June to August
TROPICAL STORMS:	July to October
CHARTS:	BA: 4011
	US: 121
PILOTS:	BA: 11, 50, 59, 65, 70
	US: 140, 145, 146, 181
CRUISING GUIDES:	*Faeroe, Iceland and Greenland, Cruising Guide to Newfoundland, Yachting Guide to Bermuda.*
WAYPOINTS:	

Departure	Intermediate	Landfall	Destination	Distance (M)
AN1780 Reykjavik *64°09'N, 21°56'W*	AN1781 Reykjanes *64°08'N, 22°50'W*	AN1782 Terra E *47°36'N, 52°30'W*	St John's *47°34'N, 52°42'W*	1416
AN1784 St John's *47°34'N, 52°42'W*	AN1785 Terra SE *47°30'N, 52°35'W*			
	AN1786 Race *46°35'N, 53°00'W*	AN1787 Scotia *44°30'N, 63°28'W*	Halifax *44°38'N, 63°34'W*	532
AN1784 St John's	AN1785 Terra SE			
	AN1786 Race			
	AN1787 Bermuda N *32°35'N, 64°50'W*	AN1788 Bermuda *32°22'N, 64°38'W*	St George's *32°22'N, 64°40'W*	1084

A direct route preferred by those who do not have the time to stop in Greenland, which in this case should be avoided by sailing as much as 200 miles south of Cape Farvel to reduce the chance of encountering ice brought south by the East Greenland Current. Even so, one should be alert as icebergs can drift much further south than one may expect. Poor visibility calls for even greater watchfulness. In summer, winds along this route are mostly SW, and usually light, with strong winds being the exception. The likelihood of gales increases as one moves south and enters the area of prevailing westerlies.

Reykjavik, or a port in its vicinity, where Iceland's top yachting facilities are concentrated, is the best place to leave from on this passage. The effects of the various currents that one will encounter should be taken into account – first the contrary Irminger Current, and later the favourable East Greenland and Labrador Currents. A stop in St John's is highly recommended before continuing towards a port in the Gulf of Main or northern New England. As this is an area of prevailing westerly winds, southbound boats will be better off by sailing directly to Bermuda. One major consideration to be borne in mind is that Bermuda is affected by hurricanes, which may strike the island any time between June and November, although July to October is the more dangerous period, with September being the worst month. Therefore an early summer passage to Bermuda will be safer than one later in the season, when weather conditions further south should be monitored very carefully.

Boats approaching Bermuda from the N should approach the island with great caution as its worst dangers extend in that direction. Two waypoints have been listed to assist in approaching St George's Harbour from the N and NE, which is reached through the Town Cut. See AN143.

AN179 *Southbound from Greenland*

BEST TIME:	June to August			
TROPICAL STORMS:	None			
CHARTS:	BA: 4011			
	US: 121			
PILOTS:	BA: 11, 50, 65, 70			
	US: 145, 146, 181			
CRUISING GUIDES:	*Faeroe, Iceland and Greenland, Cruising Guide Newfoundland.*			
WAYPOINTS:				

Departure	Intermediate	Landfall	Destination	Distance (M)
AN1790 Nuuk	AN1791 Green	AN1792 Terra N	St John's	1004
64°10'N, 51°44'W	*63°55'N, 52°10'W*	*47°40'N, 52°30'W*	*47°34'N, 52°42'W*	
AN1793 Frederiksdal	AN1794 Frederik	AN1795 Terra N	St John's	800
59°59'N, 44°40'W	*59°56'N, 44°40'W*			
AN1796 St John's	AN1797 Terra SE			
47°34'N, 52°42'W	*47°30'N, 52°35'W*			
	AN1798 Race	AN1799 Scotia	Halifax	541
	46°35'N, 53°00'W	*44°30'N, 63°28'W*	*44°38'N, 63°34'W*	

This is a route strictly for late summer when, hopefully, the West Greenland Current has cleared enough ice to make it possible to cross the Labrador Sea to Newfoundland. As the area around Nuuk is usually free of ice earlier in the season than in other parts of Greenland, and the best facilities are also available in Nuuk, this should make a good port of departure. Because of the concentration of ice around Cape Farvel, if sailing on a direct course for the east coast of Newfoundland, careful watch should be kept for icebergs until at least 200 miles from Cape Farvel.

Those who have cruised the west coast of Greenland as far as Prince Christian Sound will make their departure off Frederiksdal. The entrance to the sound is encumbered by rocks and islets, calling for extremely careful navigation until the open sea is reached. Limited facilities are available in St John's but there are good air links to many destinations, both national and international. For the continuation of the voyage southwards see AN178.

6

TRANSEQUATORIAL ROUTES IN THE ATLANTIC

The best way to sail from one hemisphere to the other has preoccupied mariners ever since early explorers discovered the zone of calms that separates the trade wind systems of the two oceans. 'The well known equatorial embarrassments' is how Alexander George Findlay refers to the doldrums in his *Memoir of the Northern Atlantic Ocean* published last century, a comprehensive book in which he tries to bring together all that was known at the time about the wind systems of the North Atlantic. The best strategy for tackling the doldrums is discussed in great detail, because fast passages across the equator were still of utmost importance to the masters of sailing ships linking Europe and North America with the rest of the world before the opening of the two great canals and the proliferation of powered vessels.

The first meteorologist who tried to put wind and weather observations on a proper scientific basis was an officer in the US Navy, Captain Matthew Fontaine Maury, who started collecting weather information in a methodical way in the early part of the nineteenth century and originated the pilot charts. Although primarily concerned with the weather of the North Atlantic and the best ways to speed up passages between the United States and Northern Europe, Captain Maury's research also dealt with passages across the equator. The main dilemma faced by ships plying between the two hemispheres was where to cross the doldrum belt. It had been known for a long time that the Atlantic doldrums have a triangular shape with their base lying along the African coast, between the Cape Verdes and the equator, and

becoming narrower to the west. Therefore by crossing the doldrums well to the west they may be traversed in a shorter distance.

As a result of Captain Maury's work, based on thousands of observations obtained from the mariners whom he had persuaded to fill in special logbooks provided by him, it was suggested that the equator should be crossed between the meridians of 30°W and 31°W. As these recommendations were primarily directed at vessels sailing from North America to either Cape Horn or the Cape of Good Hope, the directions were later modified for transequatorial voyages originating in Europe so as to take full advantage of the seasonal changes of weather which affect the doldrums. Specific directions for each month are necessary not only because of the seasonal movement of the ITCZ but also because the direction of the SE trade winds tends to be more southerly when the sun is north of the equator than when it is south.

Another debate between masters of southbound sailing vessels was the best way to sail around the Cape Verde Islands, whether to westward or between the archipelago and the African coast. Taking up the challenge of Captain Maury's arguments in favour of a westerly crossing of the equator at all times of the year, the Royal Netherlands Meteorological Institute published a comparative study of the routes followed by a number of Dutch sailing ships, both inside and outside of the Cape Verde Islands. The passage times of the 455 Dutch vessels were then compared with the times taken by 144 American vessels, many of them clippers, which had also chosen either the inside or outside route on their voyages across the equator. The results of the combined experience of 599 vessels makes fascinating reading, even if the conclusions are not as clear cut as expected. Many more ships (340 Dutch, 111 American) decided to stay west of the islands than east (114 Dutch, 34 American), but the mean times showed only one day in favour of those that went outside. It does appear that the western track is to be preferred and the only time when the inside passage might be advantageous is between December and February, but the advantage is so small that the final decision as to which route to pursue should be determined by other considerations, which will be discussed in connection with the relevant routes.

The controversies caused by the Atlantic dol-drums continue to this day and the dilemma has still to be resolved. The optimum strategy for southbound transequatorial routes is a major consideration for the skippers and navigators of the various round the world races, who rack their brains over which route will give them the best run to either the Cape of Good Hope or the Horn just as the masters of yesterday's clippers did before them. However, with ever improving satellite observations, the doldrums might finally give up their secrets and land based weather routeing services can now advise even small sailing boats on the best way to go. Much of the fun and excitement will be taken out of route planning, but at least those 'equatorial embarrassments' will cease to be a nuisance.

AT10 SOUTHBOUND ROUTES

The best longitude to cross the equator depends very much on the position of the Intertropical Convergence Zone at the time of the passage. Fortunately satellite pictures show its exact position, which can help those with access to this data to decide on the best strategy. The ITCZ changes not only its location but also its shape, being narrower in one area and wider in another. Being able to cross it at, or near, its narrowest part can be a great advantage and the results of several recent races were decided on the equator.

Whereas racing boats usually sail nonstop over long distances, their requirements are very different from those of cruising sailors whose passages are influenced by many considerations, of which speed is not necessarily the most important. Immediate cruising plans, proximity of convenient provisioning ports, and a host of other factors may have to be weighed before a final decision is made as to the best course of action.

As the great circle route from Europe to the South Atlantic passes close to the Cape Verde Islands, between January and April one should try and pass close to the west of the islands by keeping along meridian 26°W. The alternative route inside the Cape Verde Islands will be discussed later. At this time of year southerly winds will be met around latitude 4°N and the equator should be crossed between longitudes 26°W and 28°W. Between May and July the same directions apply, but an attempt should be made to make some easting below the Cape Verde Islands so as to cross the equator at 25°W or 26°W.

The transequatorial routes are influenced from the middle of July onwards by the SW monsoon, which blows on the African side of the Atlantic between the equator and the Cape Verde Islands. During these months easting can be made with the help of the SW winds south of latitude 10°N and the equator should be crossed along meridian 23°W. After August the crossing points move gradually west, being 25°W in September and 27°W or 28°W in October. During these months southerly winds may be met between 7°N and 8°N. In November and December it is advisable to make some easting south of the Cape Verde Islands, so as to cross

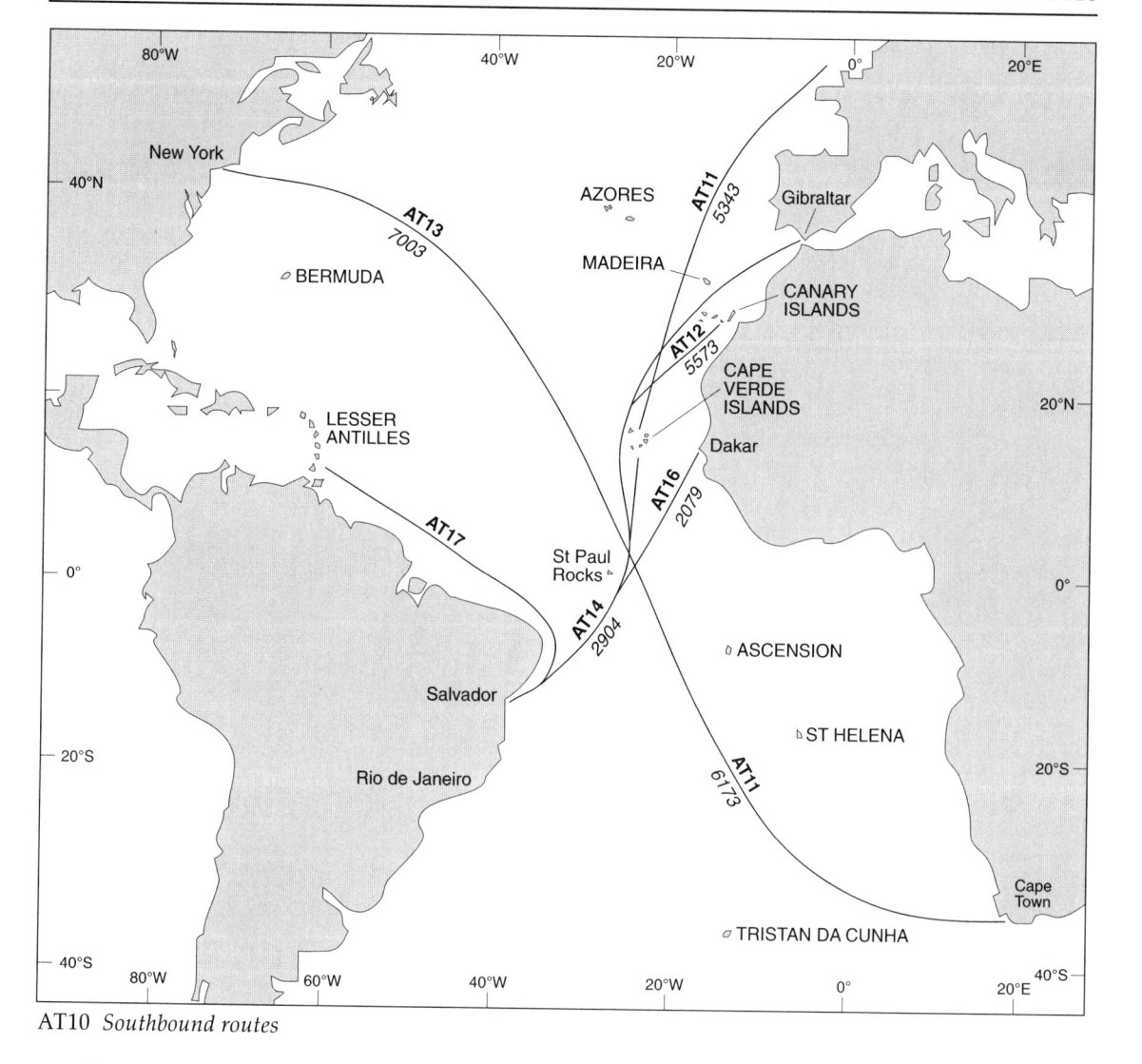

AT10 *Southbound routes*

meridian 25°W in about 6°N, from where the tack giving most southing should be taken to enable the equator to be crossed not further west than 29°W.

These instructions are only guidelines, because conditions vary from year to year and a different strategy might have to be applied if the SE trades are met further north. For a southbound voyage across the equator the most convenient place to cross the doldrums is not the only consideration,

for it is also important to have sufficient easting in hand to be able to keep the SE trades on the port tack past the bulge of South America.

Because on some routes intermediate waypoints cannot be given, only departure and destination waypoints are indicated. Therefore the distances shown are great circle distances unless otherwise indicated.

AT11 *Europe to South Africa*

BEST TIME:	October to January			
TROPICAL STORMS:	None			
CHARTS:	BA: 2127			
	US: 22, 120			
PILOTS:	BA: 1, 2, 5, 22, 27, 67			
	US: 121, 123, 140, 143, 191			
CRUISING GUIDES:	*South Africa Nautical Almanac.*			
WAYPOINTS:				
Departure	*Intermediate*	*Landfall*	*Destination*	*Distance (M)*
AT110 Lizard 49°55'N, 5°10'W	AT111 Finisterre 44°00'N, 10°00'W	AT116 Table S 34°00'S, 18°20'E	Cape Town *33°55'S,18°26'E*	6173
AT112 Gibraltar 36°08'N, 5°22'W	AT113 Espartel 35°50'N, 5°57'W AT115 20°00'N, 26°00'W	AT116 Table S	Cape Town	5573
AT114 Vilamoura 37°01'N, 8°08'W	AT115	AT116 Table S	Cape Town	5503

The optimum time to round the Cape of Good Hope limits the departure from Europe to one or two months. Most favourable conditions around the tip of Africa can be expected between December and February and therefore boats bound for Cape Town should plan to arrive off the Cape of Good Hope during that period. Therefore, the best time indicated above refers to passing the actual Cape and not to the entire passage. Because a winter departure from Northern Europe could hardly be recommended, it is presumed that boats setting off on this passage would either arrange to leave earlier and stop somewhere en route, or leave from a place in Southern Europe, such as Gibraltar or Vilamoura, from where a winter departure should pose less of a problem.

Directions for boats leaving the English Channel are similar to those described in AN13 (page 43). Having crossed the Bay of Biscay, skippers of southbound boats are faced with the dilemma of whether to take an easterly or westerly route. The winner of the first leg of the Whitbread Round the World Race in 1993 was decided by the choice of route and therefore the strategy should be based on the latest weather prognosis available. An easterly route will pass east of the Canaries and, depending on the time of year and expected weather conditions, either east or west of the Cape Verde Islands. See also routes AN18 and AN 52 (pages 48 and 76).

Those who have decided on a westerly route should make some westing on leaving the English Channel and set a course to pass west of Madeira. A decision will have to be taken at that point whether to go inside or outside the Cape Verde Islands and the various alternatives are described in AT10. Steadier winds are usually found on the west side of the Cape Verdes, and if such a route is taken some easting must be made south of the islands so as to arrive in the SE trades at a better angle.

Boats leaving from ports in Southern Europe should follow directions as for AN32 as far as the Canary Islands from where the same directions apply as for AT12. If a nonstop passage is preferred, the route from Gibraltar passes between Madeira and the Canaries and joins the route from Northern Europe in longitude 20°W (WP AT115). Normally the SE trades will have been found by the time the equator is crossed and in November–December they usually extend to latitude 5°N. At this time of year the recommended longitude for crossing the equator is between 27°W and 29°W. Although such a crossing normally benefits both from better winds and a narrower belt of doldrums, some people prefer to make more easting north of the equator and carry this advantage through into the SE trades. The risk of such an action is the risk of having to cross a wider band of doldrums.

South of the equator the object is to make as much easting as possible while still in the SE trades, which usually reach as far south as 23°S. Beyond the southern limit of the trades the winds are variable. Between 25°S and Cape Town the predominant direction of the winds during summer is northerly so that it should not be too difficult to make easting in these latitudes. However, because there is a much higher proportion of easterly winds in the eastern half of the South Atlantic, such easting should not be made too early. Having lost the trade winds, the route loops towards the Cape of Good Hope crossing meridian 20°W in about 30°S, 10°W in 32°S, and 0° in 35°S. The rest of the voyage will be made on the latitude of Cape Town. On nearing the South African coast, care must be taken not to be swept northward by the strong current. Ideally Cape Town should be approached from the SW.

Occasionally the SE trades extend further south and make it difficult to make sufficient easting above latitude 30°S. In such a case the route might have to take a more southerly dip and pass close to Tristan da Cunha. A stop in this remote and windswept island is well worth a small detour and the warm welcome from its lonely inhabitants will make up for the rough anchorage. As the main anchorage is exposed, it must be left if the weather deteriorates. See also routes AS21, AS22, and AS23 (pages 228 and 230).

AT12 *Canary Islands to South Africa*

BEST TIME:	October to January			
TROPICAL STORMS:	None			
CHARTS:	BA: 2127			
	US: 22, 120			
PILOTS:	BA: 1, 2, 5			
	US: 121, 123, 140, 143			
CRUISING GUIDES:	*South Africa Nautical Almanac.*			
WAYPOINTS:				
Departure	*Intermediate*	*Landfall*	*Destination*	*Distance (M)*
AT120 Las Palmas 28°07'N, 15°24'W	AT121 Canaria S 27°25'N, 15°30'W			
	AT122 20°00'N, 26°00'W	AT123 Table S 34°00'S, 18°20'E	Cape Town *33°55'S, 18°26'E*	4889

As the route from Europe to Cape Town passes close to the Canaries, most boats which are not actually racing stop in these islands on their way south. Such a stop allows a departure from Europe during the autumn and the subsequent passage to South Africa can be made when the time is right. For those who are already underway, a stop in either the Canaries or the Cape Verdes is not always justified, particularly in winter when it is better to cross the equator further west. See also routes AN52 and AN53 if planning to stop in either the Cape Verdes or West Africa (pages 76 and 77).

On leaving the Canaries the direct route runs SSW and passes close to the NW of the Cape Verde Islands. This route to the west of the Cape Verdes is to be preferred between October and January, when steadier winds are found west of those islands. Directions concerning the longitudes in which the equator should be crossed are given in AT10. South of the equator similar directions apply as for route AT11.

Although the route crosses a potential breeding ground for hurricanes to the west of the Cape Verde Islands, these storms rarely reach hurricane force while they are still developing, so the passage can be made at any time of the year.

AT13 *North America to South Africa*

BEST TIME:	November			
TROPICAL STORMS:	June to November			
CHARTS:	BA: 2127			
	US: 22, 120			
PILOTS:	BA: 1, 2, 5, 69, 70			
	US: 121, 123, 124, 140			
CRUISING GUIDES:	*South Africa Nautical Almanac.*			
WAYPOINTS:				
Departure	*Intermediate*	*Landfall*	*Destination*	*Distance (M)*
AT131 Chesapeake	AT132			
36°45'N, 75°45'W	35°00'N, 45°00'W			
	AT133			
	5°00'N, 25°00'W			
	AT134	AT135 Table S	Cape Town	7003
	30°00'S, 30°00'W	34°00'S, 18°20'E	*33°55'S, 18°26'E*	
AT130 Brenton	AT132			
41°24'N, 71°16'W				
	AT133			
	AT134	AT135 Table S	Cape Town	7980

As in the case of boats leaving from Europe, the time of departure from the US east coast is dictated by the best time for rounding the Cape of Good Hope, which is between January and March. If the voyage is to terminate in Cape Town, the time of arrival is less crucial and the passage can be made at almost any time, although the winter months in the Cape area, from May to September, are best avoided.

A good departure time from any port on the US east coast is the beginning of November. Such a departure should avoid both the first of the winter northers and the risk of a late hurricane. As the NE trade wind belt will have to be traversed across its entire width, it is preferable to make as much easting as possible along latitude 35°N, where NW winds prevail in November. After meridian 45°W has been crossed (WP AT132), the route turns gradually SE to pass close to the west of the Cape Verde Islands. Some easting should be made south of the Cape Verdes so that latitude 5°N is crossed in the vicinity of the 25°W meridian (WP AT133). The SE trades will be met at about this latitude and the recommended easting allows the equator to be crossed on the port tack. The point where the equator is crossed is governed by the width and position of the ITCZ and AT10 describes the optimum longitudes in which the narrowest band of doldrums can be expected at different times of year. On a passage to Cape Town, however, the skipper may decide to carry his easting across the equator, even if a wider doldrum belt has to be crossed and make use of the engine if necessary. Arriving in the South Atlantic further east will ensure that the SE winds will be taken at a better angle. Otherwise, for the recommended time of year, the equator should be crossed between longitudes 27°W and 29°W.

The SE trades are crossed at the best angle that the windward performance of the boat will permit. The southern limit of these trades extends normally to a line joining the Cape of Good Hope to the Brazilian island of Trinidade. The route continues SE into an area of variables to WP AT134. Roughly the same course should be maintained until latitude 35°S is reached. The rest of the passage to Cape Town should be sailed along this latitude. See also routes AT11, AS22, and AS23 (pages 204 and 230).

AT14 *Canary Islands to Brazil*

BEST TIME:	September to February			
TROPICAL STORMS:	None			
CHARTS:	BA: 4012, 4022			
	US: 22, 120			
PILOTS:	BA: 1, 5			
	US: 121, 124, 140, 143			
CRUISING GUIDES:	*South Atlantic Coasts of South America.*			
WAYPOINTS:				

Departure	Intermediate	Landfall	Destination	Distance (M)
AT140 Las Palmas 28°07'N, 15°24'W	AT141 Canaria S 27°25'N, 15°30'W AT142 20°00'N, 26°00'W AT143 Noronha N 3°40'S, 32°28'W		Fortaleza *3°43'S, 38°29'W*	2601
AT140 Las Palmas	AT141 Canaria S AT142 AT143 Noronha N	AN144 Bahia 12°55'S, 38°25'W	Salvador *12°58'S, 38°30'W*	2904
AT140 Las Palmas	AT141 Canaria S AT142 AT143 Noronha N	AN145 Rio 22°50'S, 43°05'W	Rio de Janeiro *22°55'S, 43°12'W*	3554

The timing of this passage is dictated primarily by the preferred time of arrival in Brazil, rather than by sailing conditions expected en route. The majority of those who make this passage attempt to be in Brazil for Carnival, which means arriving in Salvador (Bahia) or Rio de Janeiro before the beginning of February.

The passage across the doldrums presents a major dilemma, with opinions divided over the best place to cross the equator. The first decision, however, is whether to sail inside or outside the Cape Verde Islands after leaving the Canaries. If a stop in either the Cape Verde Islands or in West Africa is not being considered, it is probably better to keep slightly to the west of the Cape Verde Islands (WP AT142). Depending on the time of year, the NE trades will be lost somewhere between 10°N (September) and 4°N (December). As the Atlantic doldrum belt narrows towards the west, it is more logical to try and cross it nearer the Brazilian coast. Boats crossing the doldrums near the African coast normally have to go much farther in search of the

SE trade winds than those which cross further west. The width of the doldrums fluctuates greatly according to season and longitude, being anything from 100 to 400 miles wide. Southbound vessels normally find the SE trade winds between the equator (July) and latitude 3°S (January), although winds with a southerly component may be encountered anywhere south of 10°N.

A popular stop for boats en route to Brazil is Fernando de Noronha, a small island off the coast of Brazil. Those intending to stop there can make landfall NE of the island at WP AT143, which has been listed as an intermediate waypoint. Although not an official port of entry, boats are allowed to make a short stop there in a real emergency, but otherwise cruising boats are no longer allowed to stop there. A convenient port of entry into Brazil, just south of the equator, is Fortaleza. Other landfalls and possible destinations listed are Salvador and Rio de Janeiro. It should be pointed out that between October and February NE winds prevail along the Brazilian coast between Cape São Roque and Cape Frio, making southbound passages easy, also helped by the SW setting current. Sailors are reminded that most foreign nationals visiting Brazil must arrive with a valid visa.

AT15 *Cape Verde Islands to Brazil*

BEST TIME:	October to February
TROPICAL STORMS:	None
CHARTS:	BA: 4215, 4202
	US: 22, 106
PILOTS:	BA: 1, 5
	US: 124, 143
CRUISING GUIDES:	*South Atlantic Coasts of South America.*
WAYPOINTS:	

Departure	Intermediate	Landfall	Destination	Distance (M)
AT150 Vicente 16°53'N, 25°00'W	AT151 Noronha N 3°40'S, 32°28'W	AT152 off Fortaleza 3°40'S, 38°27'W	Fortaleza *3°43'S, 38°29'W*	1672
AT150 Vicente	AT151 Noronha N	AT153 off Recife 8°00'S, 34°49'W	Recife *8°04'S, 34°52'W*	1610
AT150 Vicente	AT151 Noronha N	AN154 Bahia 12°55'S, 38°25'W	Salvador *12°58'S, 38°30'W*	1973

Suggestions regarding the optimum point for crossing the equator are given in AT10. If the destination in Brazil is between Cape São Roque and Cape Frio, the equator can be crossed further west than the recommended crossing points for routes which continue towards South Africa. However, the equator should not be crossed further west than 30°W, as this might mean beating against the SE trades south of the equator unless this passage is made between October and February, when NE winds prevail between Cape São Roque and Cape Frio.

During the favourable season, the winds along the Brazilian coast are NE and the current sets SW, making it easy to reach any port along this stretch of coast. Between March and September the winds are predominantly SE and the current sets NE. This makes it necessary to make southing well off the coast and attempt to make landfall to windward of the port of destination. Coming from the north it is advisable to plan to arrive in the more southern ports between October and February, when the winds are NE, and sail up the coast during the rest of the year, when the SE trades take over.

The rocks of St Peter and St Paul should be approached with extreme caution as they are often difficult to see until very close to them. Depending at which point the Brazilian coast is approached, a possible first stop is Fernando de Noronha, a small island off Cape São Roque. Those planning to stop there should make landfall NE of the island at WP AT151. Although not an official port of entry, boats are only allowed to make a short stop there in a real emergency. A convenient port of entry, just south of the equator, is Fortaleza. Other landfalls and possible destinations listed are Recife and Salvador.

AT16 *West Africa to Brazil*

BEST TIME:	October to February
TROPICAL STORMS:	None
CHARTS:	BA: 4215, 4202
	US: 22, 106
PILOTS:	BA: 1, 5
	US: 124, 143
CRUISING GUIDES:	*South Atlantic Coasts of South America.*

WAYPOINTS:				
Departure	Intermediate	Landfall	Destination	Distance (M)
AT161 Cap Vert 14°45'N, 17°35'W				
AT162 Banjul 13°35'N, 16°55'W	AT163 Noronha N 3°40'S, 32°28'W	AT164 off Fortaleza 3°40'S, 38°27'W	Fortaleza 3°43'S, 38°29'W	1778 1751
AT161 Cap Vert AT162 Banjul	AT163 Noronha N	AT165 off Recife 8°00'S, 34°49'W	Recife 8°04'S, 34°52'W	1716 1689
AT161 Cap Vert AT162 Banjul	AT163 Noronha N	AN166 Bahia 12°55'S, 38°25'W	Salvador 12°58'S, 38°30'W	2079 2052

West Africa is becoming a more popular destination and many boats that cruise there continue their voyage to Brazil before sailing on to the Caribbean. The transequatorial passage requires careful planning as the doldrum belt in the proximity of the African coast can be 400–500 miles wide. Even if one is prepared to try and motor through it, a power assisted passage through the doldrums can be very uncomfortable because of the confused swell generated by the trade wind systems meet-

ing at that point. It is therefore recommended to try and stay with the NE trades north of the equator and only cross it in longitude 29°W or 30°W. A more westerly crossing point is not advisable if making for Salvador because of the risk of headwinds south of the equator. As a result of hosting a number of international sailing events, Salvador da Bahia now has the best yachting facilities in northern Brazil. See also AT10 and AT15.

AT17 Lesser Antilles to Brazil

BEST TIME:	November to February
TROPICAL STORMS:	None
CHARTS:	BA: 4216, 4202
	US: 22, 108
PILOTS:	BA: 5, 7A, 71
	US: 124, 147, 148
CRUISING GUIDES:	South Atlantic Coasts of South America.

The strong NW setting Guyana current dissuades most people from undertaking this direct passage, and those who have attempted it in the past have preferred to take an offshore route. However, by staying close inshore, it is possible to avoid the worst of the current. By staying in relatively shallow water (30 to 50 metres), one avoids most or even all of the strong NW-setting Guyana current. If sailing very close inshore, GPS can be a great help in assessing the strength and direction of the current. The continental shelf extends a long way offshore, with the 50 metre depth contour as far as 40 to 80 miles from the Brazilian coast. The best time to sail south is between October and March when the prevailing winds are easterlies and NE trade winds become more pronounced.

The best place to start this voyage is in Trinidad

from where the coast of South America should be followed by staying close to or even inside the 10 fathom line. Because of the extensive continental shelf, shallow waters reach far offshore making it possible to sail relatively long tacks. Occasionally a favourable countercurrent will also be found. Naturally, the help of a powerful engine will come in useful and also the full range of coastal charts. As one approaches the mouth of the Amazon, it is advisable to move offshore to avoid the worst of the river currents.

Past Cape São Roque, conditions during the recommended season improve dramatically as the winds along the Brazilian coast are NE between October and February. The current is also favourable as it sets SW, making it easy to reach any port along this stretch of the coast. Between March and September the winds are predominantly SE and the current sets NE. For southbound boats during this period it thus becomes necessary to sail well off the coast where the chances of finding favourable winds are better.

The logical departure point for the southbound passage is Trinidad. Although enjoying NE trade winds for most of the year, the more southerly position of Trinidad and its proximity to the mainland coast does lessen their effect in the summer months from June to November, which is also the rainy season. A SE wind sweeps across the plains bordering the Gulf of Paria, building up a sea every afternoon in the gulf. Sea conditions are generally rough near the island due to the clashing of winds and currents setting strongly out of the Gulf of Paria and around the north coast of the island. The current in the Dragon's Mouth can have northerly sets of 5 knots and seldom sets south. Being south of the hurricane area, Trinidad rarely suffers any serious storms and this century only one tropical storm has affected the island.

The three former Guyanas, British (Guyana), Dutch (Suriname), and French (Cayenne) will be passed on the way south. This region of the South American continent lies mainly in the belt of the NE trades, although the SE trade winds do penetrate into the area from August to October when the ITCZ moves north. May to July is the wettest season, September and October the driest months. The NE trade winds are strongest from January to March with a more northerly component earlier in the season and more easterly later on. From May through to July there are more calms and frequent squalls as the winds gradually change through ENE to ESE. When established, the SE trade winds are not very strong and the change back to the NE in late October or early November occurs more suddenly and without the squalls that characterise the other change of season. Near to the coast the winds decrease at night and pick up again in the morning, usually the earlier in the day this occurs the stronger the wind will be that day. Land breezes from SW to NW can occur close to the coast, especially towards the latter part of the year, but they do not last long. The only official port of entry into Guyana is its capital Georgetown (6°49'N, 58°11'W). For Suriname, the port of entry is the capital Paramaribo (5°50'N, 55°10'W), approximately 13 miles up the Suriname River. Entry formalities in Cayenne are completed at Degrad des Cannes (4°51'N, 52°16'W), although southbound boats may be able to stop without clearing in at the Iles du Salut (5°15'N, 52°35'W), just inside the border between Suriname and Cayenne as one comes south. The first official port of entry into Brazil, just south of the equator, is São Luis Maranhao (2°30'S, 44°20'W).

AT20 NORTHBOUND ROUTES

The transequatorial strategy for northbound vessels is somewhat less daunting than the one applied by boats heading south and the point where the equator should be crossed is dictated by the locations of the ports of departure and destination. As most boats sailing north from Cape Town call at St Helena, the best course from there is to sail west of Ascension Island so as to cross the equator between longitudes 25°W and 30°W. In July and August, the equator should be crossed further east, between longitudes 20°W and 25°W, to ensure better winds north of the equator. The longitude of crossing depends greatly on the route that will be pursued in the North Atlantic, as a more easterly crossing will ensure a better slant in the NE trade winds on the subsequent leg to the Azores. However, for boats bound for the Caribbean, Bermuda, or the US east coast, a more westerly crossing of the equator is recommended to take advantage of the favourable current.

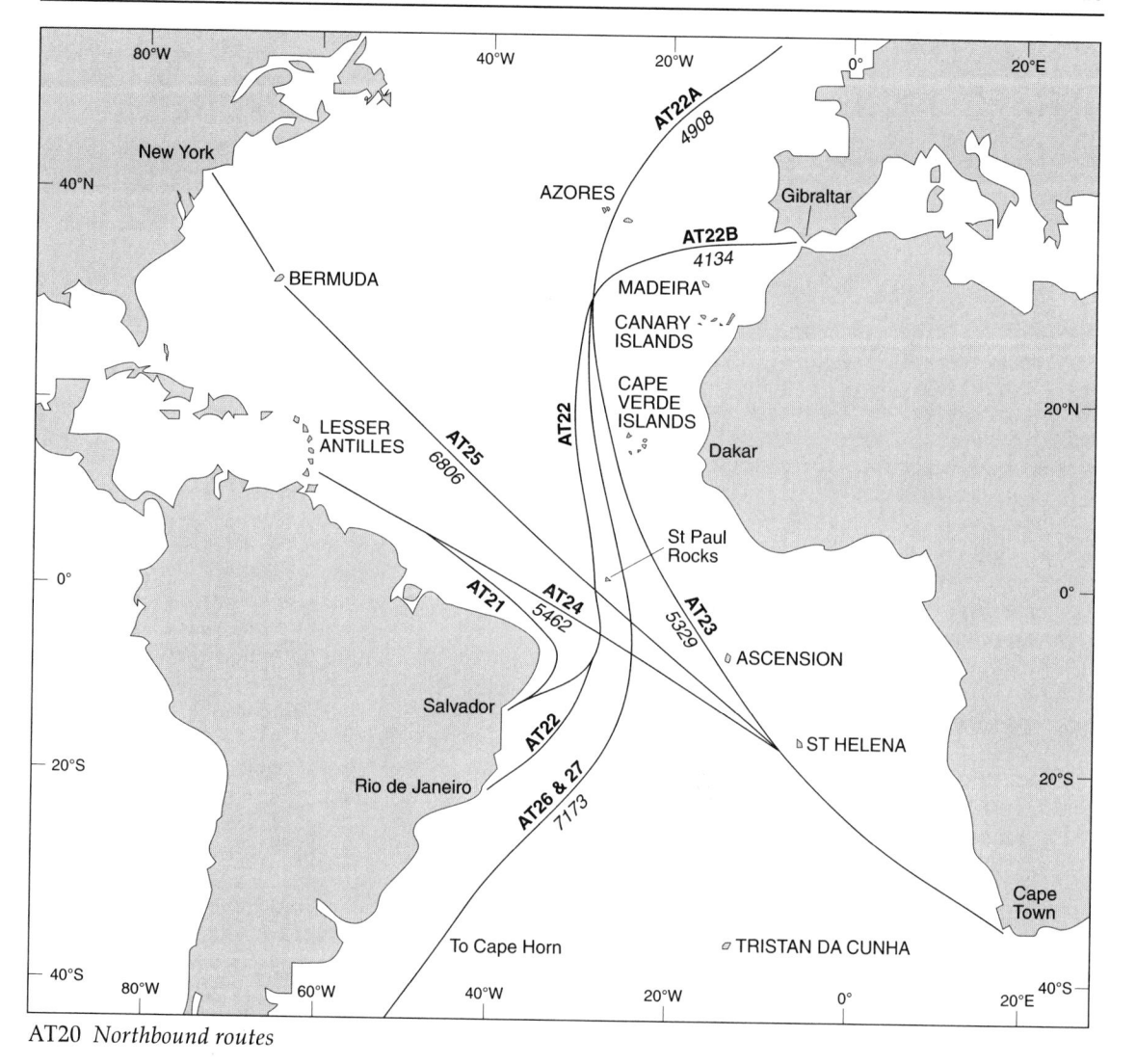

AT20 *Northbound routes*

From recent reports it appears that boats bound for the Caribbean from the South Atlantic made better times by crossing the equator further west, between longitudes 37°W and 39°W. A countercurrent was reported north of the equator in approximately 6°00'N, 49°00'W and the favourable NW setting current was found around 8°00'N, 55°00'W. The favourable current can be found earlier by closing with the Brazilian coast, but this means sailing through shallow waters and calls for very careful navigation. Therefore it may be preferable to stay offshore.

AT21 *Brazil to Lesser Antilles*

BEST TIME:	March to June
TROPICAL STORMS:	June to November
CHARTS:	BA: 4216, 4202
	US: 22, 108
PILOTS:	BA: 5, 7A, 71
	US: 124, 147, 148
CRUISING GUIDES:	*The Lesser Antilles, Sailor's Guide to the Windward Islands, Cruising Guide to Trinidad and Tobago.*

Northbound passages from ports in Southern Brazil are hampered by the strong NE winds and SW current, which occur between October and February. Passages during this time from ports south of Recife are best avoided. If the passage cannot be undertaken at a better time, the only solution is to stand well offshore until the SE trades are found and then make northing with their help. Boats coming from ports south of Rio de Janeiro will find better conditions between March and September when the prevailing winds are from the SE. If an inshore passage from southern ports is preferred, care must be taken when passing between the Abrolhos Islands and the mainland as the charts are inaccurate and the reefs more extensive than charted. If the islands are passed offshore, caution must also be exercised as the reefs extend about 35 miles offshore.

From ports north of Recife (Pernambuco), the passage to the West Indies can be made at any time of the year, although arriving there during the hurricane season should be avoided. Winds along the north coast of Brazil are always favourable and the current sets strongly to the northwest. The Guyana current runs between 70 to 100 miles off the Brazilian coast and will give a boost of at least 1 knot to boats heading NW from the Amazon Delta. Winds are E or NE and become more steady as one moves north. Local fishing boats without lights at night are a hazard that needs to be taken into account. The waters along this coast of Brazil are often very muddy from the Amazon, and as depths are shallow a good distance offshore must be kept as the colour of water gives no indication of its depth. The extent of the doldrums varies with the time of year, being wider during the northern summer. An area of variable winds, calms, and squalls normally extends from the equator in longitude

30°W to about latitude 3°N–5°N in longitude 38°W. Weather conditions along the coasts of Guyana and Trinidad are described in route AT17.

Northbound boats seldom sail nonstop all the way to the Caribbean and there are several interesting places worth visiting en route in one of the three former Guyanas, French (Cayenne), Dutch (Suriname), and British (Guyana). Entry formalities in Cayenne are completed at Degrad des Cannes (4°51'N, 52°16'W). Formalities can also be completed at Kourou. To enter the river on which Kourou is located, landfall should be made at the first leading buoy. Its GPS position has been reported as 5°12.9'N, 52°36.4'W. Interesting places to visit nearby are the Iles du Salut and the old French penal colony. The recommended anchorage is located at 5°17'N, 52°35'W.

The port of entry for Suriname is Paramaribo (5°50'N, 55°10'W), approximately 13 miles up the Suriname River, where boats now clear in at the new harbour, Nieu Haffen. The least visited of the three countries is Guyana itself, where the only official port of entry is its capital Georgetown (6°49'N, 58°11'W). One should attempt to arrive during working hours (0700–1500) and contact Lighthouse Service on channel 16. Visiting boats may tie up at the customs dock, near the clock tower, to complete formalities. Boats bound for Trinidad will have to negotiate the Serpent's Mouth, the narrows separating the island from the mainland, to reach one of the ports of entry, of which perhaps the most convenient is Point Fortin (10°11'N, 61°41'W). Trinidad Coast Guard should be contacted on VHF channel 16 as soon as territorial waters are entered. Boats not intending to stop in Trinidad itself will find a more convenient port of entry at Scarborough (11°11'N, 60°44'W), the capital of Tobago.

AT22 *Brazil to Europe*

BEST TIME:	April to September			
TROPICAL STORMS:	None			
CHARTS:	BA: 2059, 4202			
	US: 22, 120			
PILOTS:	BA: 1, 5, 22, 27, 67			
	US: 124, 140, 143, 191			
CRUISING GUIDES:	*Cruising Association Handbook, The Shell Channel Pilot, Yacht Scene, East Spain Pilot.*			
WAYPOINTS:				

Departure	Intermediate	Landfall	Destination	Distance (M)
Route AT22A				
AT220 Rio	AT221 Horta			
22°50'S, 43°05'W	*38°32'N,28°37'W*			
	AT222 Pta Delgada	AT223 Lizard		4908
	37°44'W, 25°40'W	49°55'N, 5°10'W		
Route AT22B				
AT220 Rio			AT224 Gibraltar	4134
			36°08'N, 5°22'W	

Northbound passages from Brazilian ports south of Cape Frio should avoid the period October to February, when NE winds prevail along the coast. During this time, the normal practice is to take a long tack offshore until well inside the SE trades. This will then make it possible to weather Cape São Roque, at the eastern extremity of Brazil. After sufficient easting has been made, the course can be altered to northward so that the equator is crossed between longitudes 28°W and 30°W.

From April to September northbound passages are much easier and the equator should be crossed as far east as possible so as to enter the NE trades at the most favourable slant. North of the equator the route runs close to the west of the Cape Verdes and on to the Azores, which should be always passed to the west if the vessel is bound for Northern Europe (route AT22A). Depending on the winds encountered in the vicinity of the Azores, the recommended practice is to stay on the tack which gives most northing as westerly winds will be found in higher latitudes and the course can then be altered to NE. For the rest of the passage to Northern Europe see route AN132 (page 148).

For vessels bound for the Mediterranean (route AT22B), the route north of the equator should stay as far east as the NE trade winds will allow. If too much leeway is made to the west and the Azores cannot be avoided, Horta or Ponta Delgada provide convenient stops from where route AN134 gives details for the continuation of the voyage to the Mediterranean (page 151).

AT23 *South Africa to Azores*

BEST TIME:	January to April			
TROPICAL STORMS:	None			
CHARTS:	BA: 4022, 2127			
	US: 22, 120			
PILOTS:	BA: 1, 2, 67			
	US: 121, 123, 140, 143			
CRUISING GUIDES:	*Azores Cruising Guide, Atlantic Islands.*			
WAYPOINTS:				
Departure	*Intermediate*	*Landfall*	*Destination*	*Distance (M)*
AT230 Table N	AT231 Helena			
33°55'S, 18°23'E	*15°55'S, 5°43'W*			
	AT232 Ascension			
	7°56'S, 14°25'W			
	AT233 Verde		Horta	5329
	16°30'N, 26°00'W		*38°32'N, 28°38'W*	
			Pta Delgada	5284
			37°44'N, 25°40'W	

The great circle route from Cape Town to the Azores runs close to both St Helena (route AS11) and Ascension (route AS12) and few boats pass those islands without stopping briefly. If no stop is intended, the great circle route should be taken from Cape Town to one of the longitudes recommended in AT10 where the equator should be crossed. As most of the passage in the South Atlantic is made in the SE trades, steady winds can be expected almost all the way to the equator. From Ascension, the route continues in a NW direction towards the equator which is crossed further west during the northern winter and further east in summer. The recommended longitudes are between 26°W and 28°W in December to February, 22°W to 25°W between June and September. The latter period coincides with the SW monsoon, when it may be better to cross the equator more to the east and take a route between the Cape Verde Islands and the African coast to take advantage of the SW

winds. This would mean that the NE trades would be entered at a better angle north of the Cape Verdes. Such an alternative route could also include a detour to West Africa.

The route inside of the Cape Verdes is not recommended in winter when the islands should be passed as closely as possible on their west side. To be able to do this, sufficient easting must be made while still in the SE trades. Otherwise the easting will have to be made with the help of the engine before the NE trade winds are met in the vicinity of 5°N. A route which passes close to the Cape Verdes, or is even interrupted there, is essential as it increases the chances of reaching the Azores on one tack. Official ports of entry in the Cape Verdes are Mindelo (16°53'N, 25°00'W), Praia (14°54'N, 23°31'W), and Sal (16°45'N, 23°00'W). Directions for the continuation of the route to the Azores are given in AN61 (page 83).

AT24 *South Africa to Lesser Antilles*

BEST TIME:	November to March
TROPICAL STORMS:	June to November
CHARTS:	BA: 4022, 4400
	US: 22, 124
PILOTS:	BA: 2, 5, 71
	US: 121, 123, 124, 147
CRUISING GUIDES:	*The Lesser Antilles, Sailor's Guide to the Windward Islands, Cruising Guide to Trinidad and Tobago.*
WAYPOINTS:	

Departure	Intermediate	Landfall	Destination	Distance (M)
AT240 Table N 33°55'S, 18°23'E	AT241 Helena *15°55'S, 5°43'W* AT242 Ascension *7°56'S, 14°25'W* AT243 Equator *0°00', 32°30'W*			
		AT244 Tobago 11°08'N, 60°40'W	Scarborough *11°11'N, 60°44'W*	5384
		AT245 Barbados 13°00'N, 59°37'W	Bridgetown *13°05'N, 59°38'W*	5369
		AT246 St Lucia 14°03'N, 60°50'W	Rodney Bay *14°04.5'N, 60°58.5'W*	5462
		AT247 Martinique 14°22'N, 60°51'W	Fort de France *14°36'N, 61°05'W*	5482
		AT248 Antigua SE 16°57'N, 61°45'W	English Harbour *17°00'N, 61°46'W*	5514

As an alternative to AT25, this route has the advantage that it can leave South Africa earlier so as to arrive in the Caribbean after the middle of November and the start of the safe cruising season there. As the route passes close to St Helena, most boats make a brief call there before continuing towards the equator. Another favoured stop en route to the Caribbean is the island of Fernando de Noronha, off the coast of Brazil. Directions for the above routes are given in AS11 and AS13 (pages 223 and 225).

The direct route from South Africa to the Caribbean crosses the equator in about longitude 32°30' (WP AT243), where the doldrums are very narrow at the recommended time of year (December to February). The SE trades are normally lost soon after the equator has been crossed and the NE trades are picked up 100 to 150 miles further on. The route continues parallel to the coast of Brazil, where a very strong current setting NW at rates of 1 1/2 to 2 knots gives an excellent boost. Route AT21 describes some of the possible stops along the northern coast of South America.

As the NE trade winds are normally found in about latitude 5°N and their initial direction is sometimes NNE, boats that are bound for the Leeward or Virgin Islands are advised not to cross the equator too far west so as to have a better slant through the trades. In such a case, the recommended longitude for crossing the equator is between 30°W and 32°W.

For boats arriving from the south, the most convenient landfalls in the Caribbean are:

AT244, five miles SE of Scarborough, the capital of Tobago, where entry formalities into Trinidad and Tobago can be completed.
AT245, five miles SW of South Point, the southern extremity of Barbados. Formalities are completed in the commercial port of Bridgetown, north of Carlisle Bay, which is the recommended anchorage.
AT246, four miles east of Cape Marquis, on the NE coast of St Lucia. Having sailed along the north coast of St Lucia, the marina in Rodney Bay makes an excellent landfall where entry formalities can be completed. St Lucia can be also approached from

the south, in which case the port of entry at Vieux Fort (13°44'N, 60°57') can be used.

AT247, three miles SSE of Martinique. The nearest place to complete formalities is Cul de Sac du Marin, a small port on the SE tip of the island. This is more convenient than the capital Fort de France, which is another 25 miles up the coast.

AT248, two miles SSE of English Harbour on the SE coast of Antigua. Formalities can be completed in the nearby historic port of English Harbour.

AT25 *South Africa to North America*

BEST TIME:	January to April				
TROPICAL STORMS:	June to November				
CHARTS:	BA: 2127				
	US: 22, 120				
PILOTS:	BA: 2, 5, 69, 70, 71				
	US: 121, 123, 140, 147				
CRUISING GUIDES:	*Coastal Cruising Guide to the Atlantic Coast, Yachting Guide to Bermuda.*				
WAYPOINTS:					
Departure	*Intermediate*	*Landfall*	*Destination*		*Distance (M)*
AT250 Table N	AT251 Helena				
33°55'S, 18°23'E	*15°55'S, 5°43'W*				
	AT252 Ascension				
	7°56'S, 14°25'W				
	AT253 West				
	0°00', 28°00'W				
	AT254 St George's		Newport		6806
	32°23'N, 64°40'W		*41°29'N, 71°20'W*		

Similar directions apply as far as the equator as for route AT23, although a more westerly crossing of the equator may be preferable for boats bound for the USA. A convenient stop south of the equator is the small Brazilian island Fernando de Noronha in which case the equator will be crossed further west than WP AT253. Because the optimum departure time from Cape Town (January to March), brings boats too early into the North Atlantic, few people sail the entire route nonstop and usually make a detour to the Caribbean. This is easily accomplished as the route runs quite close to the Lesser Antilles.

Route AN77 describes the subsequent leg from the islands to the USA (page 94).

Having crossed the equator, the direct route runs NW through the NE trades to Bermuda from where route AN121 gives directions for the continuation of the voyage to the USA (page 140). If a nonstop passage is planned from Cape Town, an arrival in Bermuda is not recommended before the middle of April. In this case, a departure from Cape Town at the end of February or beginning of March is not too late as favourable sailing conditions still prevail in the South Atlantic.

AT26 *Cape Horn to Europe*

BEST TIME:	December to March			
TROPICAL STORMS:	None			
CHARTS:	BA: 2127			
	US: 20, 120			
PILOTS:	BA: 1, 5, 6, 22, 27, 67			
	US: 121, 124, 140, 143, 191			
WAYPOINTS:				

Departure	Intermediate	Landfall	Destination	Distance (M)
AT260 Horn 56°02'S, 67°15'W	AT261 55°55'S, 66°53'W AT262 Le Maire 55°00'S, 65°00'W			
		AT263 Falkland 53°00'S, 58°30'W AT264 Pembroke 51°45'S, 57°35'W	Stanley *51°39'S, 57°43'W*	447
	AT265 45°00'S, 48°00'W AT266 40°00'S, 42°00'W AT267 30°00'S, 34°00'W AT268 Equator *00°00', 26°00'W*	Lizard 49°55'N, 5°10'W Espartel 35°50'N, 5°57'W	Falmouth *50°09'N, 5°04'W* Gibraltar *36°08'N, 5°22'W*	7173 6435

This busy route in the heyday of the clipper ships is used nowadays mainly by participants in round the world races and only a few cruising boats, which choose this tough way of reaching Europe from the antipodes. After rounding Cape Horn, from WP AT260, five miles south of Cape Horn, the course is altered for WP AT261. From here, the route can pass either east or west of Staten Island. If this island is passed to seaward, a wide berth should be given to Cape St John, as a dangerous tide rip extends offshore for about six miles making conditions hazardous when the wind blows against the tide. Alternatively, the route through Le Maire Strait can be taken, especially if the intention is to pass to the west of the Falkland Islands. In this case a course should be set for WP AT262 at the entrance into the Strait. Going north through Le Maire Strait it is essential to wait for a fair tide and, if at all possible, a fair wind as well. The choice must be made whether to lay a course which will pass between the mainland and the Falklands or

choose an offshore course. In the latter case a stop in the Falklands should be considered. WP AT263 keeps well clear of Beauchene Island and Mintay Rock, south of the Falklands, from where the course is altered for WP AT264, off Cape Pembroke in the approaches to Stanley Harbour.

Regardless of whether one stops in the Falklands or not, there is a choice of either an inshore or offshore route to the equator. The inshore route along the coast of Argentina is the more cautious one as it benefits from the favourable current, the seas are not as rough as offshore, and the danger of encountering icebergs is also greatly reduced. The latter are usually seen well offshore and occasionally can reach as far north as the latitude of the River Plate. Winds from the southerly quarter are most likely on this stretch during summer months. As the effect of the Falklands Current peters out, the route should move offshore so as not to get caught by the contrary Brazil Current. See AS29 for northbound routes from Argentina and Brazil.

If the offshore route is taken from the Falklands, the route runs in a general NE direction through an area of prevailing westerly winds. It is advisable to make some easting in these latitudes before reaching the SE trades so that the subsequent route to the equator will intersect them at a better angle. From the Falkland Islands the route passes through waypoints AT265, AT266, and AT267, so that the SE trades will be found somewhere along meridian 30°W. The SE trades normally extend to latitude 25°S and near their southern limit their

direction becomes more easterly. Once in the trades, the course becomes northerly so that the equator is crossed between longitudes 26°W and 30°W, depending on the time of year (see AT20). During the southern summer, from May to September, it is usually possible to stay closer to the Brazilian coast and sail between Cape Frio and the offlying islands. After the equator is crossed, the NE trade winds will be found between latitudes 3°N and 5°N. For the continuation of the passage to Europe see routes AT22 and AT23.

AT27 *Cape Horn to North America*

BEST TIME:	December to March
TROPICAL STORMS:	June to November
CHARTS:	BA: 2127
	US: 20, 120
PILOTS:	BA: 5, 6, 69, 70, 71
	US: 121, 124, 140, 147

WAYPOINTS:

Departure	Intermediate	Landfall	Destination	Distance (M)
AT270 Horn 56°02'S, 67°15'W	AT271 55°55'S, 66°53'W AT272 Le Maire 55°00'S, 65°00'W			
		AT273 Falkland 53°00'S, 58°30'W AT274 Pembroke 51°45'S, 57°35'W	Stanley *51°39'S, 57°43'W*	447
	AT275 45°00'S, 48°00'W AT276 40°00'S, 42°00'W AT277 30°00'S, 34°00'W AT278 *00°00', 30°00'W*	David 32°22'N, 64°38'W Brenton 41°24'N, 71°16'W	St George's *32°22'N, 64°40'W* Newport *41°29'N, 71°20'W*	6903 7472

This route follows the same track as route AT26 until the SE trade winds are found, from where a more westerly route can be taken to the equator passing close to Fernando de Noronha island. As far as the equator, the same waypoints can be used as in AT26 with the same option of making an intermediate stop in the Falklands. The equator is

crossed in about longitude 30°W (WP AT278) and the great circle route is taken from there either to Bermuda or direct to the port of destination. This route is not recommended during the North Atlantic hurricane season, but as Cape Horn will have been doubled probably during the most favourable months, which are the southern summer months of December to February, this passage will reach the North Atlantic at the end of winter. As the optimum time for rounding Cape Horn does not fit in with the best arrival time in North America, some alternatives may have to be considered to avoid a winter arrival in the USA. This can be accomplished by spending some time en route in Brazil, Lesser Antilles, or Bermuda. See also routes AT21, AS28, AS29, AN77, and AN78 (pages 221, 235, 94 and 96). The direct route north of the equator passes through the NE trades which normally last as far as latitude 25°N from where the Horse Latitudes will have to be crossed.

7
WINDS AND CURRENTS OF THE SOUTH ATLANTIC

The Southeast trade winds

Because the Intertropical Convergence Zone is situated north of the equator throughout the year, it may be said that the South Atlantic Ocean does not have a doldrums zone. The SE trade winds are more constant than their North Atlantic counterpart, the NE trades. They form the equatorial side of the air circulation around the oceanic anticyclone, which is situated between latitudes 22°S and 30°S and has a direct bearing on the winds and weather of the entire tropical South Atlantic.

The SE trade winds extend as far as the equator during the southern winter and their northern limit retreats by a few degrees to the south in the summer after December. Their southern limit extends normally to a line joining the Cape of Good Hope to the Brazilian island of Trinidade. Their direction varies from being SE or SSE on the eastern side of the ocean to become almost easterly in the western part. The average strength of the SE trades is 15 knots, but they diminish in strength towards the equator.

Variables

A zone of light variable winds extends to the south of the SE trade wind belt and is similar to the Horse Latitudes of the North Atlantic. This region of variable winds coincides with the areas of oceanic high pressure which are located between latitudes 25°S and 32°S approximately. Their position is influenced by the seasonal movement of the sun, reaching their southern limit in January and their

northern limit in July. To the east of the 0° meridian the winds tend to be mostly southerly and can be regarded as an extension of the trades. The summer winds in the western half of this region are mostly NE.

Westerlies

The winds in the higher latitudes of the South Atlantic are predominantly westerly. This is the region of the Roaring Forties where the continuous passage of depressions from west to east generate winds which often blow with gale force. The strong westerlies are a normal feature of southern waters where they blow unhindered south of the three great capes.

Tropical storms

Tropical revolving storms do not occur in the South Atlantic Ocean.

Currents

The currents of the South Atlantic Ocean are part of a well defined anti-clockwise circulation. The South Equatorial Current flows in a broad belt from east to west with its axis roughly along latitude 6°S. The part of this current which is between the equator and latitude 6°S is reputed to be one of the most constant currents in the world. The set is always in a westerly direction, usually between WNW and WSW, the average rate being about 1 knot. Further south, to about latitude 20°S, there is the weaker

South Subtropical Current also setting to the west. The South Equatorial Current extends across the equator to about latitude 4°N and one branch of it combines with the North Equatorial Current to form a strong current setting towards the West Indies. The other branch is deflected to the south by the South American continent and combines with the South Subtropical Current to form the Brazil Current. This current sets strongly parallel to the coast until it reaches latitude 25°S, where part of it turns east. The remainder carries on as far as latitude 35°S, where it also turns east to join the vast body of water which sets eastward and is generated by the Southern Ocean Current. This broad belt of cold water sets eastward in the southern hemisphere to the south of all continents. After passing Cape Horn, a branch of this current turns to the northeast into the South Atlantic and forms the Falklands Current.

On the African side the main ocean circulation of the South Atlantic is completed by the Benguela Current. This current sets north along the coast of Africa and is a continuation of the Agulhas Current after the latter has passed the Cape of Good Hope. The Benguela Current is reinforced by some of the Southern Ocean Current. North of latitude 20°S the Benguela Current sets away from the African coast fanning out into the Subtropical and South Equatorial Currents. Near the African coast, however, the set of the current is always northerly and from February to April it reaches as far as the equator.

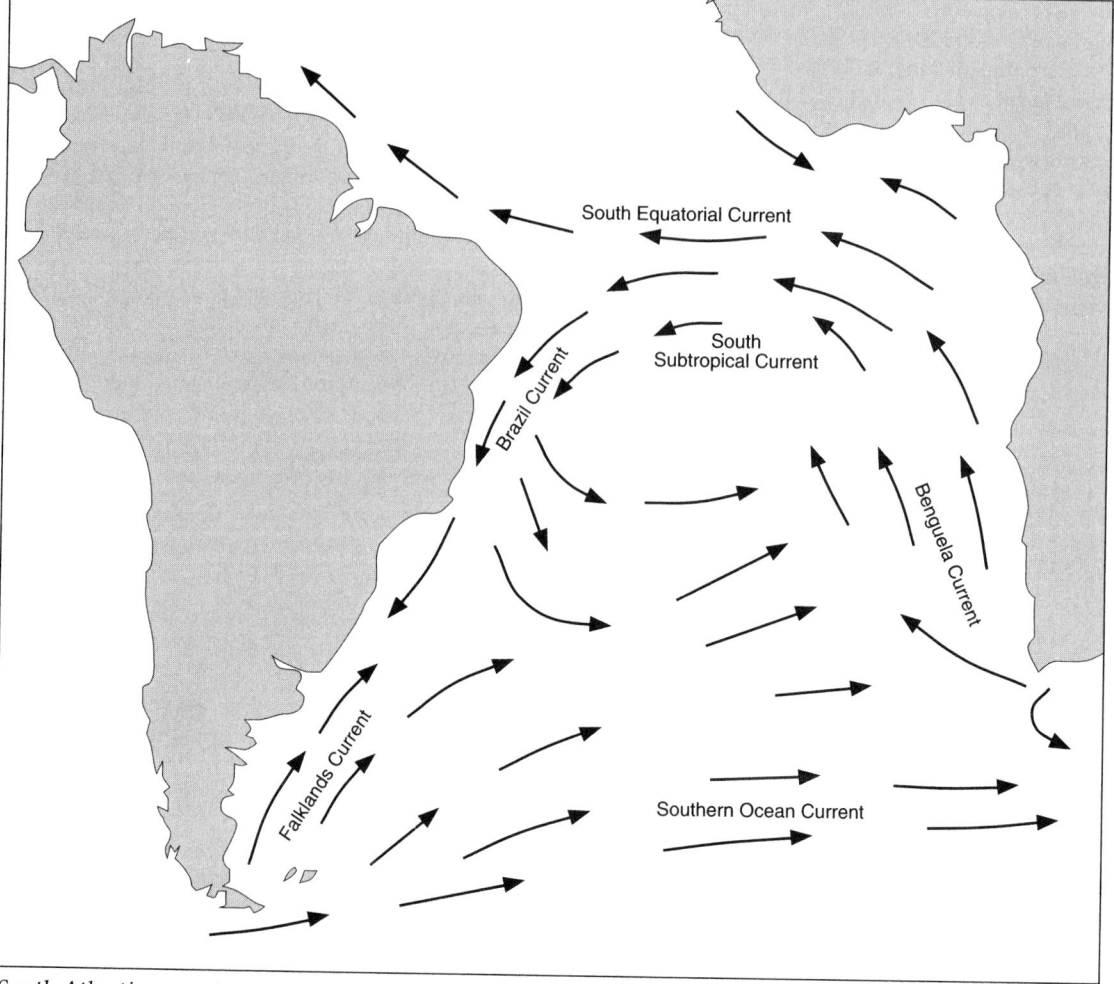

South Atlantic currents

8

ROUTES IN THE SOUTH ATLANTIC

Compared to the North Atlantic, the South Atlantic is intersected by only a handful of routes and the number of cruising boats sailing them is relatively small. The classic route from the Cape of Good Hope to St Helena is used nowadays by a smaller number of boats than in the past as more yachts sail to Europe via the Red Sea and Suez Canal. One area, however, which has seen an increase in recent years is Brazil, particularly the northeastern coast, which is visited by boats making a detour on their way from Europe to the Caribbean. Otherwise, much of South America is still undiscovered by cruising boats , although every year an increasing number of yachts brave the elements and sail down to the Strait of Magellan.

A few yachts reach the Atlantic by sailing from the South Pacific to Chile eastabout through the Magellan Strait. The traditional circumnavigating route around the Cape of Good Hope is used mainly by racing boats taking part in round the world races. On their return voyage, these boats pass again through the South Atlantic after having weathered Cape Horn. Even if few cruising boats sail those offshore routes in the Southern Ocean, more of them are now venturing south to Patagonia, Tierra del Fuego or even Antarctica. For those not deterred by the cold and ice, a new section has been added to cover routes in the Southern Ocean.

The weather in the South Atlantic is dictated by the powerful South Atlantic high and as its position has a direct bearing on the winds encountered on most of these routes, an attempt should be made to obtain its approximate coordinates before leaving on an offshore passage.

AS10 ROUTES FROM SOUTH AFRICA

The routes leading into the South Atlantic from South Africa are used mainly by circumnavigating boats on their way to Europe or North America. South African yachts, themselves leaving on a longer cruise, also join these routes. The Cape to Rio Race, which has been reinstated after an interruption of several years, is used by many South Africans as a convenient start to their own voyage to the tropics. After many years of isolation, South Africa is now firmly back on the cruising circuit and the number of boats sailing the Cape of Good Hope route is growing every year.

With the hot mass of Africa to the north and the cold Antarctic ice to the south, the high coastline presents an obstacle to opposing air currents from those regions. The main feature of weather conditions in this area is the high proportion of gale force winds, which come from almost any direction and with little warning, quickly raising high and dangerous seas. The weather forecasts here rarely give a prognosis for longer than 12 hours. Often winds build up to gale force in the day and fall at night, but this is not a rule, nor can it be relied on.

Another local phenomenon is to have gales from different directions, NE followed by SW on succeeding days. The strong currents in this area are part of the reason why seas build up so high and so rapidly, especially when the gales are opposing the current. A typical sequence of weather is for a NE gale to blow hard, followed by a lull, and then SW winds setting in with gale force. In summer depressions come up from the south giving a cold change similar to the southerly busters experienced in SE Australia.

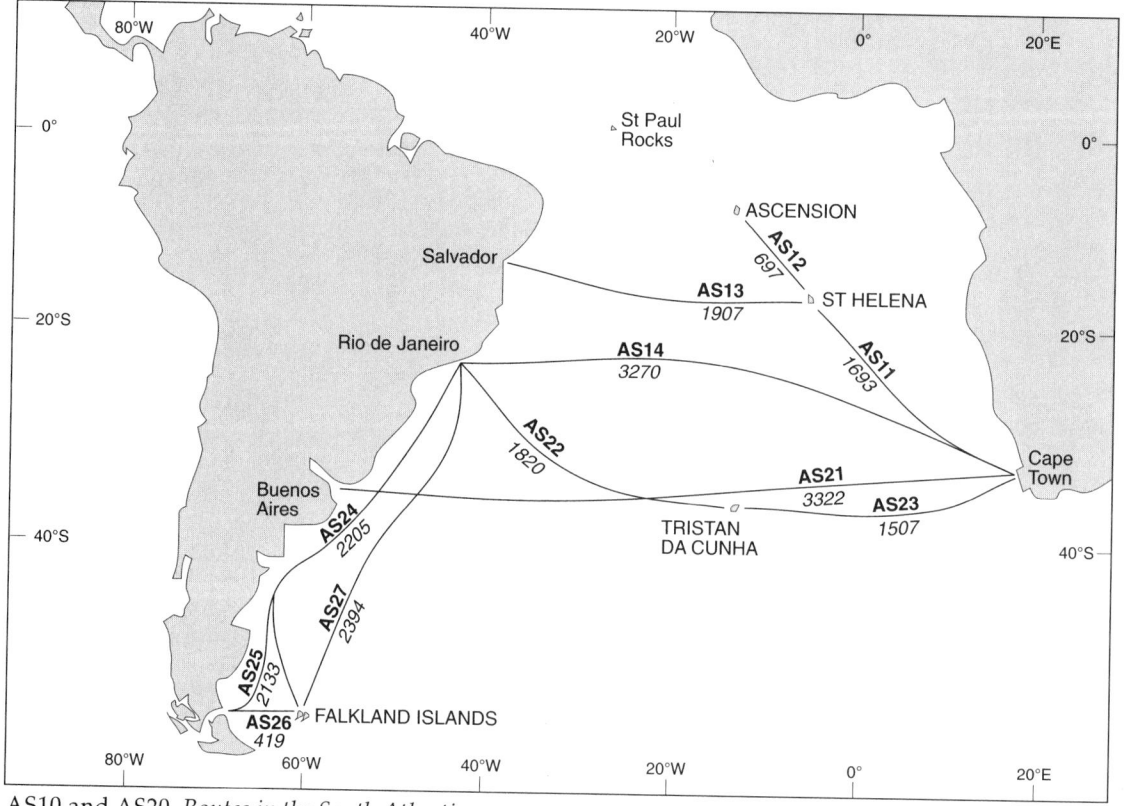

AS10 and AS20 *Routes in the South Atlantic*

AS11 *Cape Town to St Helena*

BEST TIME:	November to March
TROPICAL STORMS:	None
CHARTS:	BA: 4022
	US: 22
PILOTS:	BA: 2
	US: 121, 123
WAYPOINTS:	

Departure	Intermediate	Landfall	Destination	Distance (M)
AS110 Table N	AS111	AS112	Jamestown	1693
33°55'S, 18°23'E	33°50'S, 18°20'E	15°55'S, 5°38'W	*15°55'S, 5°43'W*	

Because of the consistency of the SE trade winds and the absence of tropical storms in the South Atlantic, this passage can be made throughout the year. However, most sailors plan on leaving the Cape area before the onset of the winter gales and therefore the best time for this passage are the summer months, from November to April. Such timing fits most forward plans, whether it is to arrive in Brazil for Carnival, the Caribbean for the winter cruising season, or the USA and Europe in late spring or early summer.

It is generally advisable to wait in Cape Town for a favourable forecast, or at least until any existing lows have passed over. Strong SW winds sometimes give a welcome boost at the start of this passage, although they occasionally reach gale force. If the African coast is followed northward, the strong Benguela current will be in one's favour, although fog is often associated with this area and is caused by the warm wind blowing over the cold waters of the current. The suggestion to follow the African coast, in order to take advantage of the favourable current and possible land breezes, runs contrary to the recommendation made in the past when the masters of sailing ships leaving Cape Town were urged to make a good offing to the NW to avoid being caught on a lee shore by W or NW squalls. This advice is still valid and during unsettled weather it is indeed better to keep a safe distance off the coast. Violent onshore squalls have been recorded in both seasons, so a prudent distance should be kept off the coast to be able to take an offshore tack should a squall strike unexpectedly.

During summer, the southern limit of the SE trades reaches as far as Cape Town, but because of the peculiar nature of the weather in this area, true trade wind conditions are usually met only north of latitude 25°S. Violent gales of short duration are not uncommon even during January and February, which are the best months for this passage, although the gales occur mainly south of 30°S. As the position of the South Atlantic high has such a major bearing on the winds to be experienced on this route, its location should be obtained before leaving Cape Town. One tactic used by past participants in the Cape to Rio Race is to stay well to the east of the high. This may mean staying east of the rhumb line, but the course can be altered for St Helena once steady winds have been found. Boats sailing north along the coast of SW Africa will find some facilities in the two Namibian ports, Luderitz (26°38'S, 15°09'E) and Walvis Bay (22°57'S, 14°30'E), both used extensively by fishing boats.

Having left Table Bay, from WP AS111, the great circle route leads to WP AS112, east of St Helena. This rather forbidding island, place of exile for Napoleon, often stands out like a fortress, visible from 60 miles away, due to the excellent clear visibility that prevails in this region. The island's only harbour is called the Anchorage, which gives reasonable shelter from the prevailing SE winds. The main settlement is Jamestown, where formalities are completed. Port Control should be contacted on VHF channel 16 for mooring instructions.

There are various sea mounts on this route and they should be approached with caution as occasionally large freak waves have been reported in their vicinity. Unnaturally high breaking waves have been reported also in the area of the Valdivia Bank and it is presumed that these are caused when a strong wind is blowing in the same direction as the Benguela current.

AS12 *St Helena to Ascension*

BEST TIME:	All year			
TROPICAL STORMS:	None			
CHARTS:	BA: 4022			
	US: 22			
PILOTS:	BA: 2			
	US: 123			
WAYPOINTS:				
Departure	Intermediate	Landfall	Destination	Distance (M)
AS121 Helena 15°50'S, 5°50'W		AS122 Ascension 7°52'S, 14°20'W	Clarence 7°56'S, 14°25'W	697

As a continuation of a northbound passage from South Africa, the subsequent leg from St Helena to Ascension benefits from favourable winds throughout the year. The direction of the wind is predominantly SE, although its strength varies and sometimes can be light, especially in the summer months January to March. From WP AS121, NW of St Helena, a course should be set for WP AS122, SE of Ascension.

A bustling military base, this outpost in mid-Atlantic is another welcome stop for those on long Atlantic voyages. The SE trades have often spent some of their force by the time they reach Ascension and can be as light as 5 knots. Heavy rollers and swell from the NW can be experienced when the NE trade is at its height in the North Atlantic, which can make landing difficult. Ascension Island is a British military base and yachts are discouraged from calling there unless they have an emergency. Because of its military nature, yachts may only stop in Ascension for 48 hours. Formalities are completed in Georgetown and the anchorage is at Clarence Bay. Yachts are supposed to anchor in the area north of Pierhead, in Clarence Bay.

AS13 *St Helena to Brazil*

BEST TIME:	All year				
TROPICAL STORMS:	None				
CHARTS:	BA: 4022				
	US: 22				
PILOTS:	BA: 2, 5				
	US: 123, 124				
CRUISING GUIDES:	*South Atlantic Coasts of South America.*				
WAYPOINTS:					
Departure	*Intermediate*		*Landfall*	*Destination*	*Distance (M)*
AS131 Helena			AS132 Bahia	Salvador	1907
15°50'S, 5°50'W			13°05'S, 38°25'W	*12°58'S, 38°30'W*	
AS131 Helena			AS133 off Recife	Recife	1768
			8°00'S, 34°49'W	*8°04'S, 34°52'W*	
AS131 Helena	AS134 Noronha S			Fortaleza	2088
	3°50'S, 32°28'W			*3°43'S, 38°29'W*	

Rather than take the direct route from St Helena to the Eastern Caribbean, many boats make a detour to Brazil before rejoining their NW route. One of the main attractions on Brazil's NE coast is Salvador, commonly referred to as Bahia, whose annual Carnival is a keen rival of the more famous Carnival of Rio. Landfall is made at WP AS132 off Cape Santo Antonio in the approaches to the perfectly sheltered natural harbour. With several yacht clubs and a number of international sailing events stopping there, Salvador now has the best yachting facilities in northern Brazil, including a new marina. Further up the Brazilian coast, another convenient port of entry is Recife. Landfall can be made at WP AS133, 3 miles outside the harbour.

Boats not intending to stop in mainland Brazil often use the island of Fernando de Noronha, off Cape São Roque, as a convenient stop on the way to the Caribbean. Landfall can be made SE of the island at WP AS134. However, as this is not an official port of entry, boats may not be allowed to stop there. A convenient port of entry into Brazil, just south of the equator, is Fortaleza. Those intending to stop in mainland Brazil must arrive with a valid visa which is required of most nationalities. Route AT21 gives details of the rest of the route to the Eastern Caribbean (page 212).

The weather on this route is mostly pleasant, with consistent E and SE winds that very rarely reach gale force. Between March and September the winds along the Brazilian coast are predominantly SE and the current sets NE. Between October and February the prevailing winds are NE and the current sets to SW, a combination making northbound passages very difficult. During this period it is recommended to either keep well offshore or plan one's arrival for the favourable season.

AS14 *Cape Town to Brazil*

BEST TIME:	December to March			
TROPICAL STORMS:	None			
CHARTS:	BA: 4022			
	US: 22			
PILOTS:	BA: 2, 5			
	US: 123, 124			
CRUISING GUIDES:	*South Atlantic Coasts of South America.*			
WAYPOINTS:				

Departure	Intermediate	Landfall	Destination	Distance (M)
AS140 Table N 33°55'S,18°23'E		AS141 Rio 23°05'S, 43°05'W	Rio de Janeiro *22°55'S, 43°12'W*	3270
AS140 Table N		AS142 Bahia 13°05'S, 38°25'W	Salvador *12°58'S, 38°30'W*	3328
AS140 Table N		AS143 off Recife 8°00'S, 34°49'W	Recife *8°04'S, 34°52'W*	3320
AS140 Table N	AS144 Noronha S 3°50'S, 32°28'W	AS145 off Fortaleza 3°43'S, 38°27'W	Fortaleza *3°43'S, 38°29'W*	3717

The great circle route to Rio de Janeiro and ports south of Cape Frio is well outside the southern limit of the SE trade winds, so it is advisable to make this passage between latitudes 20°S and 23°S where the chances of having favourable winds is much greater. The SE trade winds have their southern limit along a diagonal line that runs from Trinidade Island to the Cape of Good Hope. The initial route from Cape Town to Rio de Janeiro runs NW for about 1200 miles until steady SE trades are found. It then goes west as far as longitude 30°W, from where a course is shaped for the coast. A similar tactic, taking full advantage of the SE trade winds, should also be used if sailing to ports lying further south along the coast of Brazil.

A more direct route from Cape Town can be steered to ports lying north of Cape Frio. As the ports on the Brazilian coast between Cape São Roque and Cape Frio are under the influence of steady NE winds between October and February and the current along the coast also sets SW, a subsequent passage from Rio de Janeiro northward should be planned for the SE season, from March to September.

Although intermediate waypoints cannot be given as the route across will depend entirely on weather conditions at the time the passage is made, landfall waypoints only are listed to ease planning: WP AS141 in the approaches to Rio de Janeiro, WP AS142 off Cape Santo Antonio in the approaches to Salvador (Bahia), WP AS143, three miles outside Recife. The island of Fernando de Noronha, off Cape São Roque, is not an official port of entry and boats are allowed to stop there only in genuine emergencies. A convenient port of entry into Brazil, just south of the equator, is Fortaleza.

AS20 ROUTES FROM SOUTH AMERICA

The small number of routes in the South Atlantic is not due to a paucity of destinations as there are many interesting places to visit in South America. Nor is the weather itself an impediment as, particularly in the tropics, weather conditions can be very pleasant throughout the year with the added advantage that the area is not affected by tropical storms. In the past, most cruising boats reached South America as part of a longer voyage that, in most cases, had taken them through the Indian Ocean and South Africa or, less commonly, around Cape Horn. Nowadays, many circumnavigators prefer the Red Sea route and so the boats that reach South America, and particularly Brazil, arrive from the North Atlantic, either from the Canaries direct or by way of a detour to West Africa. Not

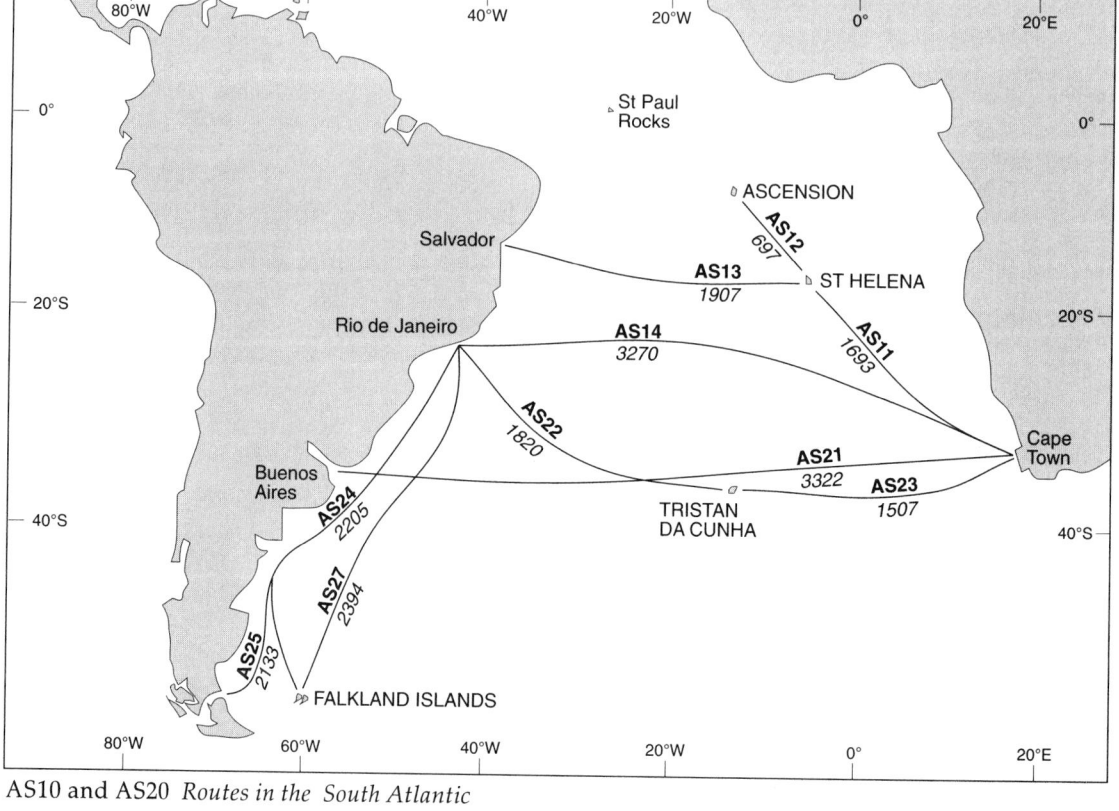

AS10 and AS20 *Routes in the South Atlantic*

many boats sail further south than Rio de Janeiro before turning around and heading for the Caribbean. The southern half of South America is still to be discovered by cruising boats in any numbers and, although every year more boats venture to the Straits of Magellan, Falklands, Cape Horn, and even Antarctica, they are still the exception. Whereas passages in the northern half of the South Atlantic can be undertaken at any time of the year, the weather in the southern part is not conducive to cruising during the winter months from April to November.

In the River Plate estuary in the summer months from September through to March, the prevailing wind is from an easterly direction. The rest of the year a W to SW wind prevails in the entrance reaches, becoming more northerly in the river. The weather is usually fine when the wind is settled in the north. During June to October, strong SW squalls called *pamperos* can occur with little warning. Named because they blow across the pampas, these squalls bring rain and cold temperatures that can even change the rain to hail. Most frequent in the winter months, the *pamperos* can last two or three days, occasionally longer. In other months they are less frequent and do not last so long, but may pack a more violent wind. Although centred on the Rio de la Plata, the *pamperos* affect the surrounding coastal area between latitudes 31° and 40°S and as far out to sea as 48°W.

The southern coast of Brazil from Rio de Janeiro to Rio de la Plata has very variable winds with seasonal variations. From October through to April, winds from a NE direction predominate, which when strong are usually followed by calms and a SW wind. In April NW and SW winds blow in equal proportion to the NE winds, which after a few SE to SW gales give way to SW winds in May.

These SW winds prevail until October. From July to September, westerly winds bring bad weather on rare occasions. NW squalls lasting several hours occur at this time near Rio de Janeiro.

Above Rio de Janeiro the lower east coast of Brazil enjoys NE winds, fine weather, and a clear sky for most of the year, the winds being strongest close to the coast from December to February. Off the capes of Frio and São Tomé the combination of fresh NE winds and strong currents can create rough seas. The NE winds are not felt so strongly west of Cape Frio as the mountains check their force. Higher up the coast the SE trade wind is felt from March to August as far south as Salvador (Bahia), although the rest of the year it reaches only as far as Recife (Pernambuco). Both the SE and NE winds sometimes give way to squally SW weather lasting a few days and bringing clouds and rain. This SW weather occurs particularly from April to August when the winds are usually lighter and more variable. The barometer usually falls 24 hours before the onset of SW winds. Although there are land and sea breezes all along the coast, the land breeze is normally short-lived and weak unless the sea breeze is strong.

On the north coast of Brazil towards the Amazon, the movement of the Intertropical Convergence Zone influences the weather bringing the SE trade wind, accompanied by fine weather, from August to October and the NE trade wind from November to March. This latter period is the wet season along this coast. Both of these winds have a more easterly component tending to be ESE and ENE. Between April and the onset of the SE trades in August, the wind first moves into the ESE and then gives way to a couple of months of doldrum weather giving calms, squalls, and variables.

AS21 *South America to South Africa*

BEST TIME:	November to March
TROPICAL STORMS:	None
CHARTS:	BA: 4022
	US: 22
PILOTS:	BA: 2, 5
	US: 121, 123, 124
CRUISING GUIDES:	*South Africa Nautical Almanac.*

WAYPOINTS:

Departure	Intermediate	Landfall	Destination	Distance (M)
AS210 Rio 23°05'S, 43°05'W	AS211 30°00'S, 35°00'W AS212 34°30'S, 13°00'W [AS213 36°00'S, 13°00'W] AS214 36°00'S, 5°00'E	AS216 Table S 34°00'S, 18°20'E	Cape Town *33°55'S, 18°26'E*	3322
AS215 Plata 35°00'S, 57°00'W	AS213	AS216 Table S	Cape Town	3705

A direct route to the Cape of Good Hope cannot be sailed from any of the northern ports in South America on account of the SE trade winds which blow consistently in the tropical South Atlantic virtually throughout the year. The one exception is the area south of Cape São Roque, below the bulge of South America, where NE winds prevail between October and February. During the same period, a favourable SW current also sets parallel to the coast. Boats leaving from one of the ports in Northern Brazil should take advantage of winds and current to make the necessary southing before heading offshore.

If leaving from one of the ports in Southern Brazil, the most favourable tack should be sailed to reach the area of westerly winds, the northern limit of which depends on the time of year. An area of variable winds will have to be crossed between latitudes 25°S and 33°S, its width being dependent on the time of year. At the beginning of summer, W or N winds will be found around latitude 33°S, but as the summer progresses the northern limit of the westerlies retracts, and it may be necessary to sail to 37°S and even 38°S to find steady westerly winds.

Taking WP AS210 as a departure point from Rio de Janeiro, a course should be set slightly south of the great circle route to reach the area of favourable winds as soon as possible. Having reached WP AS211 the recommended route continues to WP AS212. To increase the chances of finding good winds it may be necessary to dip even further south of the great circle route to WP AS213, 60 miles north of Tristan da Cunha. It is at this point that one may decide to stop at that island (see also route AS22). Having reached this point, the temptation should be resisted to join the shortest route for the rest of the voyage to Cape Town as staying on a higher latitude increases the chances of having better winds as one approaches the tip of Africa, especially if met by strong southerly winds. Therefore the great circle route for Cape Town should not be joined before WP AS214 is passed.

Boats leaving from ports in Uruguay or Argentina benefit from better winds and can sail the great circle route to South Africa. Leaving from WP AS215, at the mouth of Rio de la Plata, a rhumb line to WP AN213 has better chances of favourable winds than a great circle route. As described above, a stop in Tristan da Cunha may be considered as the island lies very close to the recommended route to Cape Town. Directions for the rest of the passage are the same as those described above. Landfall will be made at WP AS216, in the approaches to Cape Town. Cape Town is South Africa's premier yachting centre with excellent repair facilities.

AS22 *Brazil to Tristan da Cunha*

BEST TIME:	November to March			
TROPICAL STORMS:	None			
CHARTS:	BA: 4022			
	US: 22			
PILOTS:	BA: 2, 5			
	US: 121, 123, 124			
WAYPOINTS:				

Departure	Intermediate	Landfall	Destination	Distance (M)
AS220 Rio	AS221	AS222	Edinburgh	1820
23°0'S, 43°05'W	30°00'S, 35°00'W	36°55'S, 12°25'W	*37°03'S, 12°18'W*	

As the great circle route from Rio de Janeiro to Cape Town passes through an area of variable winds, navigators are advised to set a more SW course on leaving Rio de Janeiro so as to reach the area of prevailing NW and W winds sooner. Such a route passes close to Tristan da Cunha. From WP AS220, SE of Rio de Janeiro, a course should be set for WP AS221. From there the course can be altered for WP AS222, some eight miles NW of Tristan da Cunha. If this passage is made at the beginning of summer, in October or November, westerly winds are usually found in latitude 33°S or 34°S and it may not be necessary to go south in search of steady winds. As the summer progresses, the belt of variables moves south and in February or March it may be necessary to go as far as 37°S to find steady westerlies. The winds in these latitudes are usually 20 to 25 knots, occasionally reaching 40 knots.

The island's port of entry is Edinburgh. The small harbour is only suitable for the small local boats, but an anchorage can usually be found in the lee of the island.

AS23 *Tristan da Cunha to Cape Town*

BEST TIME:	December to March			
TROPICAL STORMS:	None			
CHARTS:	BA: 4022			
	US: 22			
PILOTS:	BA: 2			
	US: 121, 123			
CRUISING GUIDES:	*South Africa Nautical Almanac.*			
WAYPOINTS:				

Departure	Intermediate	Landfall	Destination	Distance (M)
AS230 Cunha	AS231	AS232 Table S	Cape Town	1507
36°55'S, 12°10'W	36°00'S, 5°00'E	34°00'S, 18°20'E	*33°55'S, 18°26'E*	

The winds below latitude 35°S are much more favourable for the passage to Cape Town than those blowing further north and so a more southerly route is recommended. Near Tristan da Cunha the winds are mostly from between N and W in summer becoming more westerly as one moves east. From WP AS230 the recommended route runs due east along the latitude of Tristan da Cunha. From WP AS231 a direct course can be set for WP AS232 in the approaches to Cape Town. As the prevailing summer winds in the Cape Town area are SE and gales from that direction are frequent, the coast should be approached from the SW to avoid being set to leeward by the wind and current setting strongly northward. Cape Town is South Africa's premier yachting centre with excellent repair facilities.

AS24 *South America to Falkland Islands*

BEST TIME:	December to February
TROPICAL STORMS:	None
CHARTS:	BA: 4200, 4201
	US: 20
PILOTS:	BA: 5, 6
	US: 121, 124
CRUISING GUIDES:	*Falklands Islands Shores.*
WAYPOINTS:	

Departure	Intermediate	Landfall	Destination	Distance (M)
AS240 Rio 23°05'S, 43°05'W	AS241 36°00'S, 54°30'W		Mar del Plata *37°57'S, 57°32'W*	1163
	AS242 43°00'S, 62°00'W		Puerto Madryn *42°46'S, 65°03'W*	1656
			Puerto Deseado *47°45'S, 65°54'W*	1850
	AS243 47°00'S, 65°00'W			
	AS244 51°25'S, 57°30'W	AS245 Pembroke N 51°37'S, 57°40'W	Port Stanley *51°39'S, 57°43'W*	2205

The route from Rio de Janeiro southward runs close to the coast, and if not calling at ports in the Rio de la Plata estuary, the direct offshore route is to be preferred, certainly as far south as latitude 35°S. The winds between Rio de Janeiro and this latitude are mostly NE in summer. South of latitude 35°S, winds become increasingly westerly and it is advisable to stay well to the west of the direct route to the Falklands to avoid being blown off course by a westerly gale. The weather is generally better inshore than further offshore. Another reason why an inshore route is preferable is to avoid the strong north setting Falklands Current which can reach as much as 2 knots offshore. For these reasons, south of the River Plate estuary the route should run parallel and very close to the Argentinian coast.

From Rio de Janeiro and WP AS240, the course follows the coast closely to take advantage of the favourable wind and current. The course is altered at WP AS241, in the Rio de la Plata estuary, for WP AS242. The recommended route runs parallel to the Argentinian coast, at 60 to 100 miles offshore. There are several ports in Argentina where it is possible to stop in an emergency, such as Mar del Plata, Puerto Madryn, or Puerto Deseado. Having run closely to the Argentinian shore, at WP AS243 the route swings offshore and a course can be set for WP AS244, seven miles NE of Volunteer Point on East Falkland. The course can then be altered for WP AS245, off Cape Pembroke in the approaches to Port Stanley.

The prevailing wind direction in the Falklands is westerly and these truly windy islands have an average yearly wind speed of 17 knots with a slight rise in the summer months of December to March. The winds can drop to calm at sunset with a tendency to increase to 10–15 knots during the night, calming again at dawn. The winds tend to increase during the day and can reach gale force by the afternoon.

Gales usually begin in the NW and quickly draw around to the SW. The worst gales tend to be those from the N and NE, which are not easily predicted and often occur without warning. They are caused by depressions moving north between the islands and the Patagonian coast. Northerly winds, which are common in the summer months from December to April, often produce fog along the north coast. When strong westerlies are blowing, the islands are prone to willywaws, which can be extremely dangerous to small craft. These occur mostly in the lee of the islands and in some of the narrow passages between islands in the west.

Those who plan to cruise among the islands should obtain the 'mine maps' which are given free of charge at the Secretariat Building in Port Stanley and contain details of the areas which were mined during the 1982 war.

AS25 *South America to Tierra del Fuego*

BEST TIME:	November to February			
TROPICAL STORMS:	None			
CHARTS:	BA: 4200			
	US: 20			
PILOTS:	BA: 5, 6			
	US: 121, 124			
WAYPOINTS:				

Departure	Intermediate	Landfall	Destination	Distance (M)
AS250 Rio 23°05'S, 43°05'W	AS251 36°00'S, 54°30'W AS252 43°00'S, 62°00'W		Punta Arenas *53°10'S, 70°54'W*	2245
	AS253 Deseado 48°00'S, 65°00'W	AS254 Virgins 52°20'S, 68°10'W		2133
AS250 Rio	AS251 AS252 AS253 Deseado AS255 Le Maire N 54°36'S, 64°56'W			
	AS256 Le Maire S 54°55'S, 65°12'W	AS257 Pio 55°08'S, 66°32'W	Puerto Williams *54°56'S, 67°37'W*	2350
AS258 Mar del Plata *37°57'S, 57°32'W*	AS259 Corientes 38°00'S, 57°27'W AS252			
	AS253 Deseado	AS254 Virgins	Punta Arenas	1095
AS258 Mar del Plata	AS259 Corientes AS252 AS253 Deseado AS255 Le Maire N			
	AS256 Le Maire S	AS257 Pio	Puerto Williams	1200

The southbound route from Rio de Janeiro runs parallel to the coast and, as far as the latitude of the Falkland Islands, directions are similar to those described for route AS24. A place with good facilities at which to prepare for the southbound passage is Mar del Plata, which is also the base of the whale watching boats going to the Valdez Peninsula.

Caution must be exercised when sailing close to the land because of the danger of onshore currents. From Rio de la Plata southward, the route runs very close to the coast to stay in sheltered waters and also to avoid the strong north setting Falklands Current. The winds in this region are predominantly westerly so that the risk of being caught on a lee shore is remote. Gales from the east are extremely rare and when they occur, there is always sufficient warning.

From September through to June one can get SE gales accompanied by rain and heavy seas. These winds can also bring fog. A very dense fog can also occur with NW winds along the southerly portions of this coast in the months from February to October. When the wind shifts more to the south of west the fog usually clears. In warmer weather thunder and lightning can occur with N and W winds.

Northerly gales are preceded by overcast skies, haze, lots of small cloud very high up, and some lightning. The wind increases gradually to gale force. On the other hand southerly winds increase to gale force much more suddenly and are more violent. A sign of impending bad weather from the south is large masses of heavy cloud on the southern horizon. If a very low barometer starts rising, this may also be a sign of a wind shift to the south.

From WP AS253, off Puerto Deseado, the course can be altered for WP AS254, NE of Cape Virgins, at the entrance into the Strait of Magellan. The strait must be approached with extreme caution as the tidal range is great and the tidal streams set strongly towards Sarmiento Bank and the dangers extending from Cape Virgins.

The time of arrival at the strait should coincide with the start of the favourable tide and it must be remembered that the times of high and low water get later as one proceeds westward, until Royal Road is passed. This fact greatly assists passages from east to west and a vessel that catches the beginning of the west setting stream in the First Narrows has a good chance to ride the favourable tide for 9 hours, possibly as far as Punta Arenas. The tidal stream runs through the First Narrows from 5 to 7 knots and through the Second Narrows

from 3 to 6 knots. The tidal range itself varies from about 40 feet at the east end of the strait to only 5 feet at its western end.

The usual route from the Atlantic runs through the following channels: Smyth, Sarmiento, Inocentes, Concepcion, Largo, Messier and out through the Gulf of Peñas into the Pacific Ocean. A shorter route reaches the Pacific through Cockburn Channel.

Yachts bound for the Beagle Channel or Cape Horn should sail due south from WP AS253 to WP AS255, north of Cape San Diego, at the entrance into Le Maire Strait. This southern route enters the Beagle Channel and leads to Puerto Williams, a small Chilean port on the north coast of Navarino Island. Formalities must be completed here for anyone planning to cruise in Chilean waters, call at Cape Horn or sail on to the Antarctic Peninsula. Facilities at Puerto Williams are very basic, and for any repairs or long term provisioning one needs to continue along the Beagle Channel to Ushuaia, in Argentina. Ushuaia has the best facilities in the area and also regular flights to Buenos Aires.

AS26 *Southbound from Brazil*

BEST TIME:	December to April			
TROPICAL STORMS:	None			
CHARTS:	BA: 4201			
	US: 200, 201			
PILOTS:	BA: 5			
	US: 124			
CRUISING GUIDES:	*Cruising Notes of South America.*			
WAYPOINTS:				

Departure	Intermediate	Landfall	Destination	Distance (M)
Salvador da Bahia *12°58'S, 38°30'W*	AS260 Bahia *13°03'S, 38°20'W* AS261 Portocel *20°00'S, 37°30'W* AS262 Frio *23°04'S, 41°55'W*	AS263 Rio *23°05'S, 43°08'W*	Rio de Janeiro *22°55'S, 43°12'W*	825
Rio de Janeiro *22°55'S, 43°12'W*	AS2363 Rio AS264 Marta *28°40'S, 48°40'W* AS265 Tramandai *30°10'S, 49°40'W* AS266 Plata *35°00'S, 54°00'W* AS267 Lobos *35°10'S, 54°45'W*		Buenos Aires *34°36'S, 58°22'W*	1150

WAYPOINTS:				
Departure	*Intermediate*	*Landfall*	*Destination*	*Distance (M)*
Rio de Janeiro	AS263 Rio AS264 Marta AS265 Tramandai AS266 Plata	AS268 Mar 38°00'S, 57°30'W	Mar del Plata *37°57'S, 57°32'W*	1180

Southbound routes benefit from both the Brazilian Current, which sets SW at rates between 1 and 2 knots and, between December and April, from predominantly NE winds. Further south, a countercurrent setting northwards along the shore should be taken into account and, on any longer legs, going offshore is recommended.

As most boats coming south across the equator now make Salvador da Bahia their first destination, this is indeed a good point of departure for southbound passages. A good time to be in Salvador is Carnival, which usually ends in early March, which is the ideal time to head south. The inshore route, as far as Cape Sao Tomé, offers a variety of cruising opportunities, although for planning purposes only offshore waypoints are listed. Another hypothetical point of departure is Rio de Janeiro, although boats heading south may be tempted to explore more of the Brazilian coast south of Rio before heading offshore. Yachting facilities improve as one moves south and are best in the area between Rio de Janeiro and Santos, which includes Sao Sebastian, now a thriving sailing centre as a result of having been chosen as a stop on the Volvo round the world race.

AS27 *Northbound from Falkland Islands*

BEST TIME:	December to March
TROPICAL STORMS:	None
CHARTS:	BA: 4201, 4207
	US: 20
PILOTS:	BA: 5, 6
	US: 124
CRUISING GUIDES:	*Cruising Notes of South America.*

WAYPOINTS:				
Departure	*Intermediate*	*Landfall*	*Destination*	*Distance (M)*
Port Stanley *51°51'S, 57°50'W*	AS271 Pembroke *51°40'S, 57°42'W*	AS272 Corientes *38°00'S, 57°27'W*	Mar del Plata *37°57'S, 57°32'W*	837
Port Stanley	AS271 Pembroke AS273 *40°00'S, 54°00'W*	AS274 Rio *23°05'S, 43°08'W*	Rio de Janeiro *22°55'S, 43°12'W*	1902

The northbound passage as far as Rio de la Plata can be done throughout the summer months and the direct route benefits both from the strong north setting Falklands Current and the prevailing W winds. North of Rio de la Plata, the prevailing winds in summer (October to March) are NE and therefore this passage should not be attempted before April. Ideally the passage from the Falklands to Rio de la Plata should be done between December and February, with the subsequent leg to Rio de Janeiro and beyond only being undertaken later, between May and September, when favourable winds prevail along the entire Brazilian coast.

From WP AS271 off Volunteer Point on East Falkland, the course for the River Plate estuary runs almost due north, on a rhumb line, to WP AS272. Boats bound for Rio de Janeiro should join the great circle route which passes through WP AS273 and thence to WP AS274 in the approaches to Rio de Janeiro.

A passage from the Falklands to Europe or the US east coast can either incorporate the above alternative or it can join the direct routes from Cape Horn to those destinations as described in routes AT26 and AT27 (pages 217 and 218).

AS28 *Northbound from Tierra del Fuego*

BEST TIME:	December to March			
TROPICAL STORMS:	None			
CHARTS:	BA: 4200, 4201			
	US: 200, 201			
PILOTS:	BA: 5			
	US: 124			
CRUISING GUIDES:	*Cruising Notes of South America.*			
WAYPOINTS:				

Departure	Intermediate	Landfall	Destination	Distance (M)
Punta Arenas 53°10'S, 70°54'W	AS281 Magellan 52°25'S, 68°25'W			
	AS282 Virgins 52°20'S, 68°10'W	AS283 Corientes 38°00'S, 57°27'W	Mar del Plata 37°57'S, 57°32'W	1086
Puerto Williams 54°56'S, 67°37'W	AS284 Pio 55°08'S, 66°32'W			
	AS285 Le Maire S 54°55'S, 65°12'W			
	AS286 Le Maire N 54°36'S, 64°56'W	AS283 Corientes	Mar del Plata	1155

Heading north from Tierra del Fuego, the large island that makes up most of the southern tip of South America, one can use either the Strait of Magellan or the Beagle Channel to reach the open sea. Especially for boats coming from the south and not intending to stop in Argentina, the Falklands provide a convenient interruption before heading north into the South Atlantic (see AS35).

Having left the Strait of Magellan at Cape Virgenes, the route runs parallel to the Argentinean coast. Because none of the ports along this stretch of coast hold any real attraction for a cruising boat, a direct offshore route is highly recommended. If, for any reason, one needs to stop along the coast of Patagonia, the ports of Comodoro Rivadavia and Puerto Madryn offer basic facilities and fuel. However, inshore weather conditions and the favourable Falklands Current are strong arguments in favour of an offshore route. Landfall will be made close to Cape Corientes from where the course should be altered to NW and Mar del Plata. Similar directions apply to boats coming from Cape Horn or the Beagle Channel, who will have passed through the Le Maire Strait before altering course to the north. Weather conditions prevailing along the east coast of Argentina are described in AS25. Mar del Plata is Argentina's main seaside resort and has good yachting facilities.

AS29 *Northbound from Argentina and Brazil*

BEST TIME:	May to July
TROPICAL STORMS:	None
CHARTS:	BA: 4201
	US: 201
PILOTS:	BA: 5
	US: 124
CRUISING GUIDES:	*South Atlantic Coasts of South America.*
WAYPOINTS:	

Departure	Intermediate	Landfall	Destination	Distance (M)
Mar del Plata 37°57'S, 57°32'W	AS290 Mar 38°00'S, 57°30'W AS292 Plata N 35°00'S, 54°00'W AS283 Tramandai 30°10'S, 49°40'W AS294 Marta 28°40'S, 48°40'W	AS295 Rio 23°05'S, 43°08'W	Rio de Janeiro 22°55'S, 43°12'W	1180
Punta del Este 34°58'S, 54°57'W	AS291 Lobos 35°05'S, 54°45'W AS292 Plata N AS293 Tramandai AS294 Marta	AS295 Rio	Rio de Janeiro	1150
Rio de Janeiro 22°55'S, 43°12'W	AS296 Frio 23°04'S, 41°55'W AS297 Portocel 20°00'S, 37°30'W	AS298 Bahia 13°03'S, 38°20'W	Salvador da Bahia 12°58'S, 38°30'W	825

Sailing NE along the coast of South America is not an easy undertaking as there are a number of considerations to be taken into account, such as the Brazilian Current, which sets SW at a rate of around 1 knot and covers a belt that reaches between 200 and 400 miles off the coast. Between May and July, a countercurrent sets northward close inshore and may give a boost to boats heading in that direction. NE winds predominate along almost the entire coast from October to April, and are strongest between December and February. Beyond Cape Frio, the SE trade winds prevail between March and August, which is the time when one should plan sailing north along this coast as at other times NE winds make passages difficult. At all times of the year offshore passages are to be preferred, especially in the section south of Cape Frio where, with a few exceptions, attractions for cruising boats are limited.

Boats heading north from the Plate River area, whether coming from Buenos Aires, one of the ports in Uruguay or Mar del Plata, will sail a route parallel to the Brazilian coast, keeping within the effects of the countercurrent but at a safe distance offshore. Punta del Este, at the very mouth of the River Plate estuary, is a busy sailing centre and a good port of departure. The same can be said of Mar del Plata, Argentina's summer sailing capital. There are a number of possible ports of call along the Brazilian coast between Capes Santa Marta Grande and Frio, although only Rio de Janeiro has been listed here as a destination as the choice is far too wide. If stopping in Rio, one will find a better reception among the sailing clubs in Niteroi, such as the Brazilian Navy Club, although the most convenient marina is Gloria marina near the centre of the city.

Those sailing an inshore route should be aware of the vagaries of weather close to land as in some places sudden violent gusts can hit without any warning out of a clear sky. One also needs to be aware of the possibility of a strong onshore setting current that can be experienced all along the coast but is most evident in the vicinity of capes, especially in shallow waters. One such area is over the Sao Tomé bank, close to the cape of the same name. One more hazard in inshore waters is the large number of fishing boats that are out at night in coastal waters, sometimes anchoring in deep water and showing no lights. Most are wooden, so will not show up on radar. Seasonal considerations become even more important for boats sailing north from Rio de Janeiro, unless one is prepared to move well offshore to avoid coastal influences. The inshore route passes close to the Abrolhos Islands and heads for Salvador da Bahia. Both are recommended stops, the former for the excellent cruising opportunities, the latter as a city with a vibrant culture. Salvador is now the finishing point of a number of international sailing events, and as a result its yachting facilities are steadily improving. Northbound routes are described in further detail in AT21 (page 212).

AS30 ROUTES IN THE SOUTHERN OCEAN

Cape Horn and the stormy seas that surround it enjoy such a bad reputation in maritime lore that until not very long ago cruising boats would not dare go anywhere near that area. A few did sail past Cape Horn on their way to Europe, but sailing south of Cape Horn was simply not done. It is only in the last decade that cruising boats have actually crossed the Drake Passage and cruised the western side of the Antarctic Peninsula during the short summer season. One or two even spent the winter there. Suddenly the awe that surrounded the sixth continent was broken as more sailors braved the elements and headed for the frozen south. The number of cruising boats that sail there annually is still counted in single figures and it will be some time before it gets really crowded down there, but the trend has undoubtedly started.

Nevertheless, sailing south into the 50s and 60s should not be taken too lightly, as these are still the stormiest waters in the world and being caught by a storm while crossing the Drake Passage, with a huge swell rolling in from the west, uninterrupted by any landmass, the wind screaming in the rigging and a lonely albatross gliding like a phantom in the clear sky, will fill even the most phlegmatic sailor with awe. These are wild seas, and you'd better be prepared for them!

Westerly winds predominate over the entire area and extend from about 40°S to 55°S for most of the year and to 60°S in summer. These are the well known 'Roaring Forties', which aptly describes the constancy and strength of these winds. Wind directions alter with the approach of fronts, and may vary from SW to NW, as they do during the passage of depressions. Further south, between 55°S and 65°S, in a region dominated by the movement of depressions, there is an almost equal distribution between W and E winds. The direction of these winds is dictated by the northern limit of the depression tracks. Even further south, in the vicinity of the Antarctic coast, easterly winds prevail throughout the year. Average summer tempera-

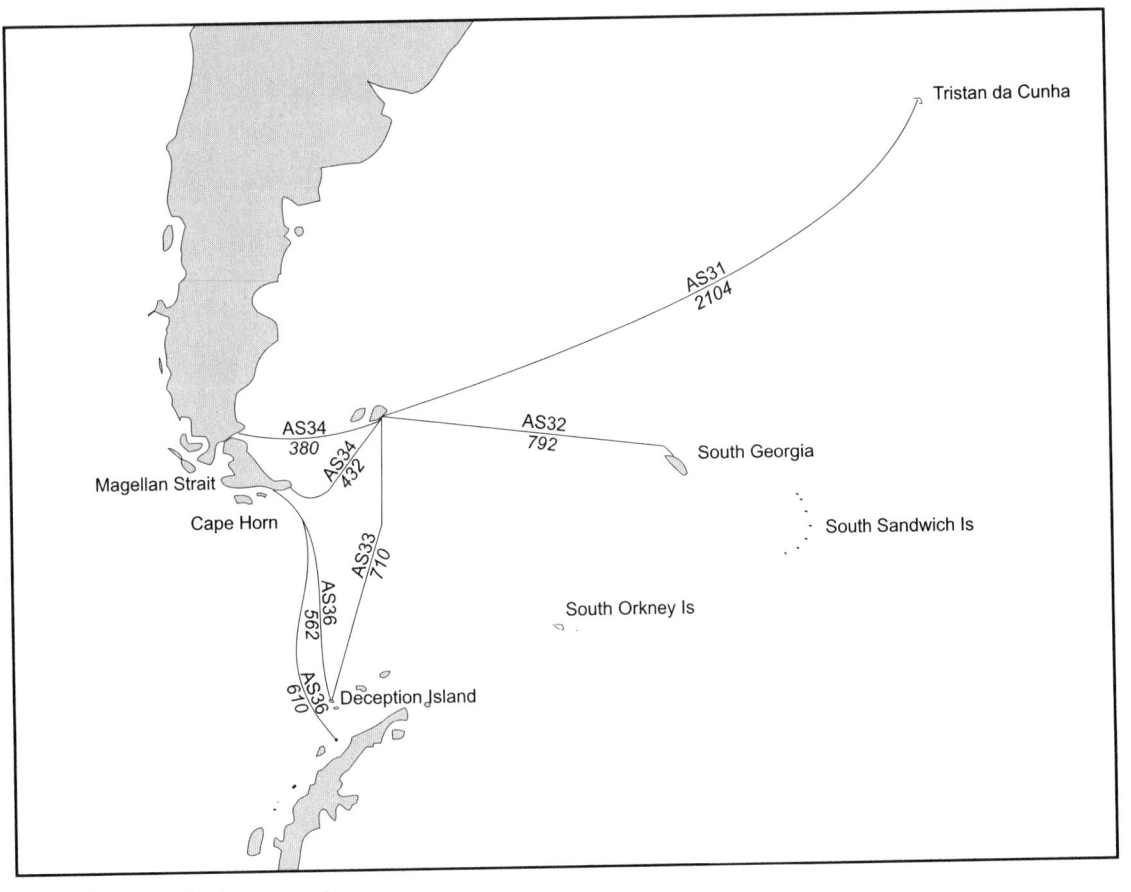

AS30 *Routes in the Southern Ocean*

tures, near land, are around 0°C, although the wind-chill factor must be taken into account.

Although sea ice extends to a considerable distance from the Antarctic coastline in winter, most of this ice melts in summer – thus making some parts of the coastline accessible from December to March. In a good summer most of the Antarctic Peninsula and much of the Bellinghausen Sea are free of pack ice. Icebergs occasionally drift north of 50°S in an area east of the Falklands as far as 30°W. In Drake Passage, the northern limit of icebergs coincides with the Antarctic Convergence Zone, although occasionally icebergs have been seen as far north as the latitude of Rio de Janeiro.

Sailing any of the routes described in this section is a real challenge and will give the crew a well deserved sense of satisfaction, but nothing will match the thrill and fulfilment felt by those

fortunate enough to have sailed to and from the Antarctic. Although one or two yachts have reached the Antarctic in recent years from Australia, the great majority of cruising yachts that visit the Antarctic come from South America, not only because of the shorter distances involved but also because the Antarctic Peninsula, as well as the Shetland Islands to the north, provide the best cruising grounds.

When planning a voyage to these waters it is well worth reading the accounts of those who have sailed here before. Outstanding among these are the adventures of the Shackleton expedition of 1914–1916, not only for their experiences on the Antarctic continent itself but, from a sailor's point of view, the amazing feat of the survivors who sailed the 20 ft whaleboat *James Caird* to Elephant Island and on to South Georgia after the *Endurance* was crushed by ice in the Weddel Sea. When reading about those experiences in a small open boat, a very different perspective is added to a voyage into the Southern Ocean, even in a well found modern sailing yacht.

Antarctica and islands south of 60°S are covered by an International Treaty signed in 1961, and reinforced by a Protocol signed in 1991, whose main objective is to preserve this wonderful region for future generations. Strict regulations apply to any person or vessel entering this area and mariners should therefore familiarise themselves with the provisions of the Antarctic Treaty and Protocol before arrival. For more details consult *World Cruising Handbook*.

AS31 *Falklands to Tristan da Cunha*

BEST TIME:	January to April
TROPICAL STORMS:	None
CHARTS:	BA: 4206, 4213
	US: 211
PILOTS:	BA: 2, 6
	US: 123, 124
CRUISING GUIDES:	*Falkland Islands Shores.*
WAYPOINTS:	

Departure	Intermediate	Landfall	Destination	Distance (M)
AS310 Stanley 51°41'S, 57°50'W	AS311 Pembroke 51°40'S, 57°40'W	AS312 Inaccess 37°15'S, 12°50'W	Edinburg *37°03'S, 12°18'W*	2104

The passage between these two British dependencies should benefit from the prevailing westerlies for most of the way, although as one approaches Tristan da Cunha winds do become more variable. Depending on weather conditions, a great circle route is perhaps the way to go, but if one wishes to be sure of staying with westerly winds as far as possible, it may pay to stay south of the rhumb line and only alter course for Tristan as one crosses meridian 30°W. In summer, the belt of steady westerlies is further south than normal and lies below the latitude of the island, so this should be assessed when deciding which route to sail.

Approaching Tristan from SW one will pass first the two uninhabited islands of Inaccessible and Nightingale before altering course for the north coast of Tristan. None of the islands may be visited before clearing in at Tristan. The port of entry is Edinburg and the harbour master should be contacted on channel 16 for advice on the best place to anchor. The boat will be inspected on arrival by customs. Repair facilities are adequate and provisioning, depending on the season, is good but visitors pay a 40 per cent surcharge on supplies. Provisioning should be done at the first opportunity as one may be forced to leave at short notice should the weather deteriorate.

AS32 *Falklands to South Georgia*

BEST TIME:	January to April				
TROPICAL STORMS:	None				
CHARTS:	BA: 4213				
	US: 20				
PILOTS:	BA: 6, 9				
	US: 124				
CRUISING GUIDES:	*Falkland Islands Shores, Southern Ocean Cruising.*				
WAYPOINTS:					
Departure	*Intermediate*	*Landfall*	*Destination*		*Distance (M)*
AS320 Stanley	AS321 Pembroke				
51°41'S, 57°50'W	*51°40'S, 57°40'W*				
	AS322 Shag	AS323 North	Grytviken		792
	53°28'S, 42°00'W	*53°55'S, 37°45'W*	*54°16'S, 36°30'W*		

Prevailing westerly winds and the favourable Southern Ocean Current should ensure a fast passage across the Scotia Sea. A danger to be avoided are the Shag Rocks which lie exactly on the direct route. The main group (53°33'S, 42°02'W) has one rock 70 metres (200 feet) high. Ten miles SE is the 3 metre (10 feet) high Black Rock and half a mile east of Black Rock is an unnamed rock, over which the seas break heavily.

Landfall will be made off Cape North from where the east coast will be followed as far as Grytviken, which used to be a thriving settlement but is now almost abandoned. Best anchorages will be found along this east coast, which is indented by several fjords. Bird and sea life is prolific throughout this wind-swept island.

The Marine Officer should be contacted on arrival in Grytviken and there will be a charge, which is payable by all vessels visiting South Georgia. The main settlement is at King Edward Point Station (54°17'S, 36°30'W), the headquarters of the British Antarctic Survey. No supplies are available, but mail may be sent out via BAS.

As part of Britain's South Atlantic dependencies, South Georgia may only be visited with permission from the Commissioner for South Georgia and the South Sandwich Islands, who should be contacted at Government House, Stanley, Falkland Islands, Tel. +500 27433, Fax +500 27434. All islands to be visited should be listed.

AS33 *Falklands to Antarctica*

BEST TIME:	January to March			
TROPICAL STORMS:	None			
CHARTS:	BA: 3200			
	US: 211			
PILOTS:	BA: 6, 9			
	US: 124, 200			
CRUISING GUIDES:	*Falkland Islands Shores, Southern Ocean Cruising.*			
WAYPOINTS:				

Departure	Intermediate	Landfall	Destination	Distance (M)
AS330 Stanley *51°41'S, 57°50'W*	AS331 Pembroke *51°40'S, 57°40'W*	AS332 Seal *60°55'S, 55°25'W*	Minstrel Cove *61°04'S, 55°26'W*	575
AS330 Stanley	AS331 Pembroke AS332 Nelson *62°15'S, 59°15'W* AS333 Robert *62°30'S, 59°15'W*	AS334 Neptune *63°00'S, 60°30'W*	Deception Island *62°56'S, 60°37'W*	710

Boats bound for the Antarctic may interrupt their voyage at Elephant Island, where the survivors of the *Endurance* expedition led by Sir Ernest Shackleton spent several months in 1916 before being rescued. For the passage from the Falklands it is advisable to wait for a spell of NE winds and then make some westing before closing with Elephant Island. The Antarctic Convergence Zone will be passed on the way, an area rich in sealife, as countless birds, fish, dolphins and whales are attracted to these feeding grounds created by an ocean upwelling. The first icebergs will also be seen in this area, and they will remain a constant companion throughout one's stay in the Antarctic.

Boats coming from the north should make landfall to the east of Seal Islands and then approach the north coast of Elephant Island from that direction. Depending on weather conditions, temporary shelter may be found on that coast and there are two recommended inlets providing reasonable shelter at Emma Cove on the west coast, and at Minstrel Cove on the north coast. All of these anchorages must be vacated in onshore winds. The SE coast is largely occupied by the Endurance Glacier. Because the island offers no all-weather anchorage, the weather should be monitored carefully.

If weather conditions do not permit a stop at Elephant Island it is advisable to sail directly to Deception Island. In this case, landfall should be made north of Nelson Island so as to approach Deception Island from NE. Deception Island is a partly collapsed volcanic cone which provides excellent shelter, and it was a major whaling station in the past. Port Foster is entered through Neptune's Bellows, the aptly called narrow entrance that leads into the enclosed anchorage. Deception makes a good starting point for an Antarctic cruise. The best cruising area is along the west coast of the Antarctic Peninsula as far as Marguerite Bay, although the latter may only be reached in a summer when the pack ice limit has receded further south. There are a number of research stations in the area, some of which welcome visiting yachts.

AS34 *Falklands to Tierra del Fuego*

BEST TIME:	December to March			
TROPICAL STORMS:	None			
CHARTS:	BA: 539			
	US: 200			
PILOTS:	BA: 6			
	US: 124			
CRUISING GUIDES:	*Falkland Islands Shores, Southern Ocean Cruising.*			
WAYPOINTS:				

Departure	Intermediate	Landfall	Destination	Distance (M)
AS340 West 52°12'S, 60°53'W		AS341 Magellan 52°25'S, 68°25'W	Punta Arenas *53°10'S, 70°54'W*	380
AS342 Stanley *51°41'S, 57°50'W*	AS343 Pembroke 51°42'S, 57°40'W AS344 Lion 52°28'S, 58°48'W AS345 Estados 54°52'S, 63°48'W	AS346 Pio 55°08'S, 66°32'W	Puerto Williams *54°56'S, 67°37'W*	432

The Falklands make a convenient starting point for boats sailing to Tierra del Fuego from the east, whether bound for the Strait of Magellan, Beagle Channel or even Cape Horn. The one drawback is that the passage will be mostly on the wind as the prevailing winds between the Falklands and the mainland are westerlies. To shorten the passage, and also to await a break in the weather, it is preferable to leave the Falklands from as far west as possible. This is certainly the case for those heading for the Strait of Magellan, for whom a good point of departure is one of the anchorages on the west side of East Falkland. Landfall will be made south of Dungeness Point at the entrance into the Strait of Magellan. Refer to AS26 for more details. The Argentinean port of Punta Arenas is the main settlement in the area, having a range of facilities and flights to Buenos Aires and other destinations.

Boats taking the south route may also wish to make some westing before heading offshore. The decision as to whether to use Le Maire Strait or go south of Isla de Los Estados will depend on existing weather conditions, but because of the fierce currents that sweep through Le Maire, it is probably better to sail south of Isla de Los Estados. The Beagle Channel is entered north of Isla Nueva and leads to Puerto Williams. This small port is located on Navarino Island, where the Chilean military maintain a small base. Although facilities are limited, and better facilities and provisioning will be found at Ushuaia, in Argentina, Puerto Williams is a convenient place from which to explore the surrounding area, or to set off on the passage to the Antarctic.

AS35 *Tierra del Fuego to Falkland Islands*

BEST TIME:	December to March
TROPICAL STORMS:	None
CHARTS:	BA: 539
	US: 200
PILOTS:	BA: 6
	US: 124
CRUISING GUIDES:	*Falklands Islands Shores.*
WAYPOINTS:	

Departure	Intermediate	Landfall	Destination	Distance (M)
AS260 Magellan 52°25'S , 68°25'W	AS261 East 52°28'S , 59°30'W	AS262 Pembroke S 51°42'S , 57°40'W	Port Stanley *51°39'S , 57°43'W*	419
AS353 Puerto Williams *54°56'S, 67°37'W*	AS354 Pio 55°08'S, 66°32'W			
	AS355 Estados 54°52'S, 63°48'W			
	AS356 Lion 52°28'S, 58°48'W	AS357 Pembroke S 51°42'S, 57°40'W	Port Stanley	432

The Falkland Islands are best visited after sailing eastwards through the Strait of Magellan as the prevailing westerly winds make this a relatively easy passage. Caution must be exercised when leaving the strait as the strong tidal stream often sets towards the rocks extending offshore from Cape Virgins. From Dungeness Point and WP AS260 at the entrance into the Strait of Magellan, a course can be set almost due east to WP AS261, SW of East Falkland. The route follows the south and east coasts of that island passing between it and Sea Lion Island and avoiding several dangers, such as Shag Rock. Having rounded Cape Pembroke at WP AS262, the course can be altered for Port Stanley.

The alternative route, south of Tierra del Fuego, uses the Beagle Channel to reach the open sea. A departure point is listed south of Cape San Pio from where the offshore route heads east. Depending on weather conditions, the Le Maire Strait may be used to get some shelter from SW winds by sailing north of Isla de los Estados, but because of the difficult navigation through that strait, and the fierce currents that sweep through it, it is probably better to carry on south of Isla de los Estados. From a waypoint just SE of the island, a course is set for the Falklands. Landfall will be made close to the Sea Lion Islands, which should be left well to port, and then the east coast is followed to Pembroke Point and Port Stanley.

AS36 *Tierra del Fuego to Antarctica*

BEST TIME:	January to February			
TROPICAL STORMS:	None			
CHARTS:	BA: 3200			
	US: 29002			
PILOTS:	BA: 6, 9			
	US: 124, 200			
CRUISING GUIDES:	*Southern Ocean Cruising.*			
WAYPOINTS:				

Departure	Intermediate	Landfall	Destination	Distance (M)
AS360 Pto Williams *54°56'S, 67°37'W*	AS361 Barne *55°50'S, 66°22'W*	AS312 Boyd *62°50'S, 62°00'W*	Deception Island *62°56'S, 60°37'W*	562
AS360 Pto Williams	AS361 Barne	AS313 Anvers *64°10'S, 62°52'W*	Melchior Harbour *64°19'S, 62°59'W*	610

Because Chile controls a wedge of land and sea that comprises most of the very south of the South American continent, including the disputed Beagle Channel, as well as the Antarctic Peninsula, vessels that pass through this area, and certainly any that intend to stop in the Antarctic Peninsula, must complete formalities in Puerto Williams. Located on the north shore of Navarino Island, and facing the Beagle Channel, this colourful little settlement has the distinction of being the most southerly town in the world. The Chilean Navy has a base here, provisioning is adequate, and there is also a small airfield. Better facilities as well as a larger airport will be found at Ushuaia, in Argentina, about 30 miles west along that same Beagle Channel. Ushuaia is in fact used as a transit port by all charter boats based in the area as it has the best facilities in the region and regular flights to Buenos Aires.

Weather forecasts can be obtained from the Chilean naval station in Puerto Williams before setting off across the Drake Passage. The first 30 miles lead through the protected waters of the Beagle Channel and the open sea is reached through Richmond Pass, although in strong easterly winds it is better to stay west of Lennox Island, making sure one avoids the rocks in mid-channel. A direct course across Drake Passage can be set when level with the Barnevelt Islands. The Antarctic Convergence Zone will be passed on the way to Antarctica, an area rich in sealife, as countless birds, fish, dolphins and whales are attracted to these feeding grounds created by an ocean upwelling. The first icebergs will also be seen in

this area, and they will remain a constant companion throughout one's stay in the Antarctic.

There are several points where landfall can be made on the Antarctic Peninsula, and they will dictate the route across Drake Passage. There is also the consideration as to which order to cruise the peninsula, as it makes more sense to finish such a cruise as far south and west as possible so as to benefit from the best wind angle for the return passage. The disadvantage of this is that the further south one starts, the longer the distance to sail in the open sea. Generally, it is felt that making landfall in one of the South Shetlands, then to cruise south and leave from the Melchior Islands, is the best solution.

An ideal first stop is Deception Island, a partly collapsed volcanic cone which provides excellent shelter and was a major whaling station in the past. Those who take this route will make landfall north of Smith Island and approach Deception from the west through Boyd Channel. Port Foster is entered through Neptune's Bellows, the aptly called narrow entrance that leads into the enclosed anchorage.

An alternative route is to sail further south and make landfall at the Melchior Islands, entering the scenic Gerlache Strait from the west, whereas those who stop in Deception will do so from the north. In either case, the best cruising area is between here and Marguerite Bay, although the latter may only be reached in a summer when the pack ice limit has receded further south. There are a number of research stations in the area, some of which welcome visiting yachts.

AS37 *Antarctica to Tierra del Fuego*

BEST TIME:	January to March			
TROPICAL STORMS:	None			
CHARTS:	BA: 3200			
	US: 29002			
PILOTS:	BA: 6, 9			
	US: 124, 200			
CRUISING GUIDES:	*Southern Ocean Cruising.*			
WAYPOINTS:				

Departure	Intermediate	Landfall	Destination	Distance (M)
AS370 Melchior *64°19'S, 62°59'W*	AS371 Anvers *64°10'S, 62°52'W*	AS373 Horn *56°02'S, 67°10'W*	Puerto Williams *54°56'S, 67°37'W*	600
AS373 Deception *62°56'S, 60°37'W*	AS374 Boyd *62°50'S, 62°00'W*	AS373 Horn	Puerto Williams	560

When the time comes for the return passage from the Antarctic to the South American mainland, probably the best place to wait for a good weather window is in the shelter of the Melchior Islands. Melchior Harbour offers all round protection and is just a short distance from the open sea. An Argentine station is located close by, but it is only open and manned at the height of the summer season.

As the course across Drake Passage is west of north and some of the worst gales are also from NW, it pays to make some westing while still in lower latitudes. One must also reckon with the Southern Ocean Current, which sets east at about 1 knot. A combination of all these could make it very difficult to get back to one's point of departure, close to Cape Horn, so every effort should be made not to be swept eastwards. If everything works according to plan, landfall will be made off Cape Horn Island, which can be visited in settled weather. There is a beach on the NE side where a dinghy can be landed if there is not too much swell,

just below a small building housing some Chilean army personnel.

Woolaston Islands, north of Cape Horn, have a number of sheltered anchorages if one cannot proceed immediately to Puerto Williams. It must be stressed that the channel on the west side of Navarino Island, which would provide a short cut to Ushuaia, is closed by the Chilean military for strategic reasons and vessels are strictly forbidden to use this channel. They must proceed east of Navarino Island and enter the Beagle Channel from the east. Just before Puerto Williams, the small fishing port of Puerto Toro (55°05'S, 67°05'W) provides good shelter and the chance to buy some fresh seafood when the local fishing boats bring in their catch. No other provisions are available.

On arrival in Puerto Williams, visiting boats tie up alongside a half sunken ship, acting now as the local yacht club, in a creek on the west side of the settlement. Arriving yachts must complete clearance formalities, even if technically they have not left Chilean waters.

AS38 *Antarctica to Falkland Islands*

BEST TIME:	January to March			
TROPICAL STORMS:	None			
CHARTS:	BA: 3200			
	US: 211			
PILOTS:	BA: 6, 9			
	US: 124, 200			
CRUISING GUIDES:	*Falkland Islands Shores, Southern Ocean Cruising.*			
WAYPOINTS:				

Departure	Intermediate	Landfall	Destination	Distance (M)
AS383 Deception *62°56'S, 60°37'W*	AS384 Neptune *63°00'S, 60°30'W* AS385 Robert *62°30'S, 59°15'W* AS386 Nelson *62°15'S, 59°15'W*	AS382 Pembroke S *51°42'S, 57°40'W*	Port Stanley *51°41'S, 57°50'W*	710
AS387 George *61°55'S, 57°25'W*		AS382 Pembroke S	Port Stanley	742
AS380 Melchior *64°19'S, 62°59'W*	AS381 Smith *62°50'S, 62°15'W*	AS382 Pembroke S	Port Stanley	783

Passages from the Antarctic Peninsula to the South American mainland are always difficult because of wind and current, so a destination further east, such as the Falklands, may be preferable. Because of the difficulties associated with a return to Cape Horn, it may be advisable to plan the voyage in such a way that Tierra del Fuego will be visited before the Antarctic so that on completion of the Antarctic cruise one can sail directly to the Falklands. This is a considerably easier route and also benefits from the shelter provided by the South Shetland Islands before a course is set across the open sea.

There are various points from where to depart, such as Deception Island or perhaps King George Island, where there are a number of research stations as well as a military airfield. One will find here the best facilities in the area, including a small hospital. For this latter route, a departure point was chosen NE of King George Island. Landfall will be made off Cape Pembroke, in the approaches to Port Stanley.

Those who wish to depart from a point further west may do so from the Melchior Islands where Melchior Harbour offers all round protection and is just a short distance from the open sea. An Argentine research station is located close by, but it is only opened and manned at the height of the summer season. The route passes between Low and Smith Islands before a course can be set across Drake Passage.

Although neither the Antarctic Peninsula nor the South Shetland Islands any longer fall under the direct jurisdiction of the British authorities, those planning to complete their voyage in the Falklands would be well advised to write in advance about their cruising plans to the Commissioner for South Georgia and the South Sandwich Islands, Government House, Stanley, Falkland Islands, Tel. +500 27433, Fax +500 27434.

9

WINDS AND CURRENTS OF THE NORTH PACIFIC

The Northeast trade winds

These winds blow on the southern side of the area of high pressure, which is normally located around latitude 30°N. During the summer months this high is usually situated farther north than in winter and the NE trades can be found as far north as latitude 32°. During the summer the trade winds are predominant to the east of the 150°E meridian, being replaced to the west of this meridian by the SW monsoon of the Western Pacific Ocean.

The NE trade winds of the North Pacific Ocean are particularly consistent in both direction and strength over large areas. Their direction is more N and even NW near the American coast, becoming increasingly E towards the west. Their strength is about 10–15 knots, although they can become fresher at times and at the height of the trade wind season stronger winds of 30 knots are not uncommon. The strongest winds are likely to be encountered in winter, between November and March, but they diminish in strength as one moves south towards the equator.

The entire trade wind belt moves north and south throughout the year in accordance with the declination of the sun. However, their northern and southern limits do not run in a straight line from east to west, but in a curve which reaches its highest point in summer in about latitude 35°N about 200 miles from the American coast, the corresponding southern limit being in latitude 8°N. The northern limit of the trade winds in winter is 29°N, in about longitude 150°W, with the southern limit for the same period being the equator.

Intertropical Convergence Zone

The NE trade winds are bound to the south by the ITCZ, which remains north of the equator throughout the year east of meridian 160°W. To the west of that longitude it moves south of the equator during the northern winter, from about December to April or early May. During the summer of the northern hemisphere, when the SE trade winds are at their strongest in the South Pacific, the ITCZ disappears altogether west of about 150°W, where the two trade wind systems almost run into each other and the belt of doldrums is virtually nonexistent. In the western part of the North Pacific, the ITCZ is only present during the changeover periods of the monsoons, either from mid-April to mid-May or from mid-September to mid-November.

The weather inside the zone is typical doldrums weather, with calms or very light winds alternating with squalls, heavy rain, and thunderstorms. However, as one moves west, the frequency of calms and light variable winds becomes less and the prevailing winds, even inside the doldrums, are easterlies. This is a fact worth bearing in mind if planning transequatorial passages especially west of the meridian of the Marquesas.

The Northeast monsoon

The intense cold of the winter months over the land mass of Asia creates an area of high pressure over parts of the Far East. The resulting wind circulation around this winter high produces a flow of NE winds which prevail during the winter months in

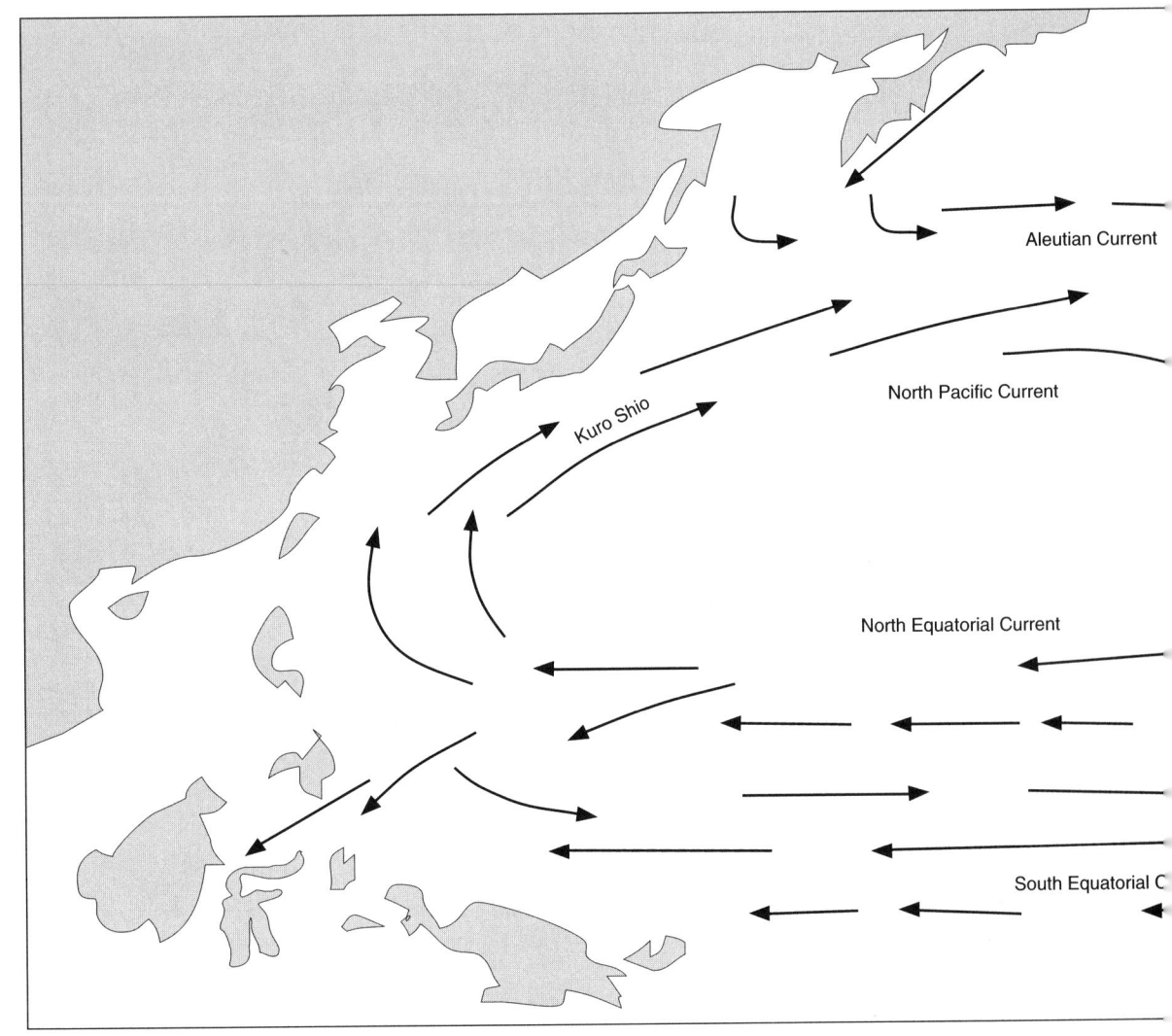

North Pacific Currents

the China Sea and adjacent waters. The NE monsoon of the Western North Pacific is particularly noticeable between latitudes 5°N and 30°N. Its eastern limits are more difficult to define as it merges with the NE trade winds of the North Pacific. Although the monsoons of the China Sea can be regarded as an extension of the monsoon system of the Indian Ocean, there is a certain difference between them. In the China Sea, it is the NE monsoon of the winter months which is the stronger and more consistent wind, whereas in the Indian Ocean, the SW monsoon of summer is the stronger constant wind. At its height, the NE monsoon of the China Sea forms a continuous wind system with the NE trade wind of the North Pacific, so that in December and January particularly, there is a belt of strong NE winds right across the ocean from California to China.

The arrival of the monsoon depends on latitude and it starts earlier in the north and later further south. Although it commences around September at its northern limit, the NE monsoon is only fully established in the area by late November and lasts until March. During the changeover periods with the SW monsoon, in April–May and August–September, there are calms and variable winds.

The strength of the wind is also influenced by latitude, the monsoon being strongest in the north,

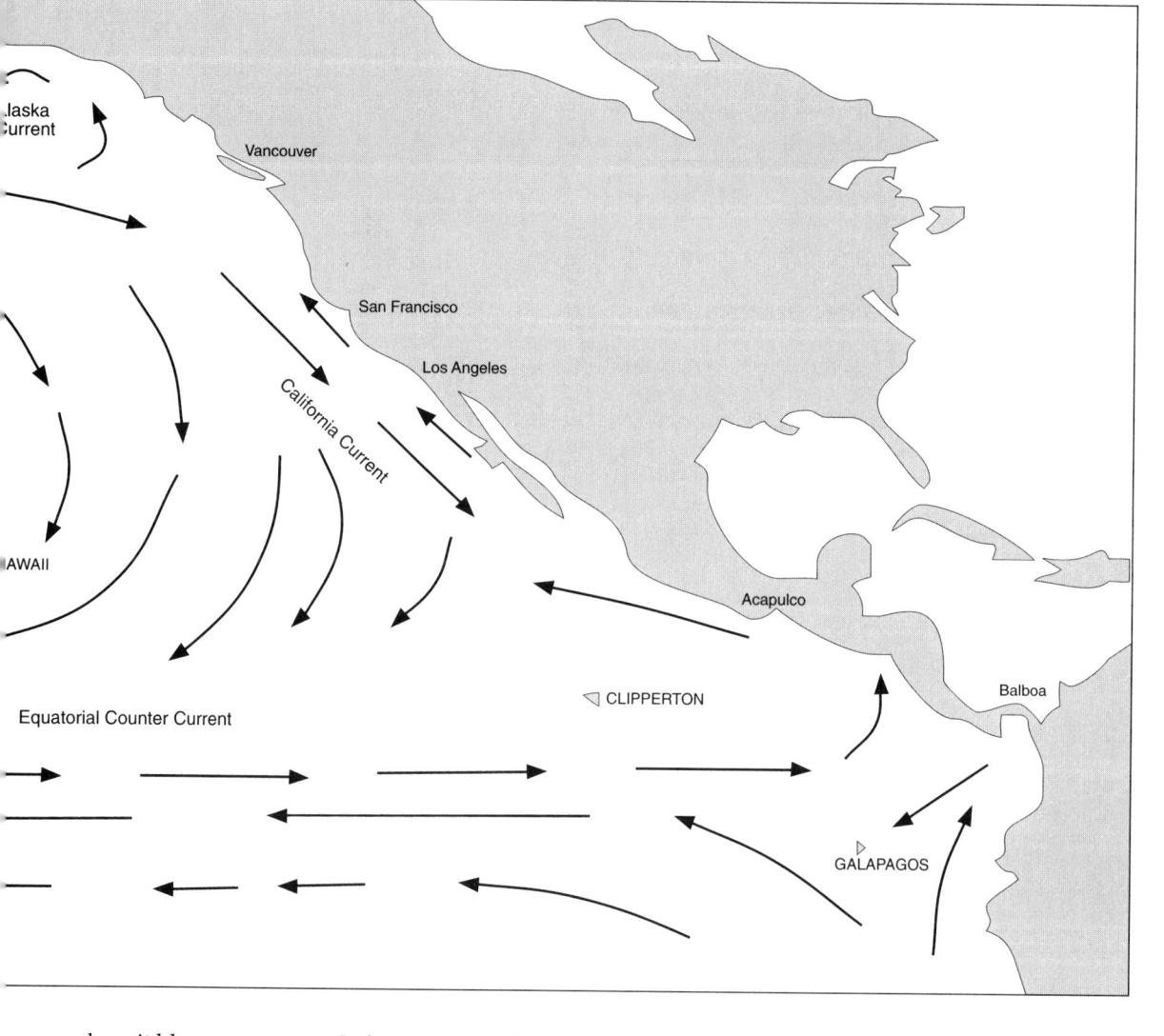

where it blows an average 25 knots, decreasing to 15 knots and less among the islands of the Philippines and Northern Indonesia. However, at the height of winter, in December and January, the monsoon can blow with gale force for many days, the stormiest area being the open waters between the Philippines, Taiwan, and Japan.

The Southwest monsoon

A reversal of the NE monsoon occurs during the summer when the heating up of Asia creates a large area of low pressure over the eastern part of the continent. As a result of this, the SE trade winds of the Indian and Pacific Oceans are drawn across the equator. Because of the rotation of the earth, the SE winds are deflected to the right becoming the SW monsoon in the western part of the Pacific Ocean. In the China Sea the winds are predominantly S and SW, whereas towards Japan they are either S or SE. The area affected by the SW monsoon is generally situated west of the 140°E meridian and south of latitude 40°N. Steady SW winds are experienced in the China Sea during July, but further north the monsoon is felt less and less and variable winds become increasingly common. The weather during the SW monsoon is often unsettled and there is a high frequency of squalls, in which the wind reaches gale force.

Variables

The two monsoons and the NE trade winds are replaced on the polar side of the North Pacific by a belt of variable winds. Although it corresponds to the Horse Latitudes of the Atlantic Ocean, the variable belt of the North Pacific is much narrower and rarely exceeds 300 miles in width. The variable zone is influenced by the position of the high pressure area, which moves north in summer, when light and variable winds can be expected between latitudes 35°N and 40°N. The high moves south in summer, when it stretches from about 25°N to 30°N. The movement of air around the North Pacific high has a direct bearing on the winds of the variable zone. In the eastern half of the ocean, winds tend to be northerly in summer and merge with the NE trades. In the western part of the ocean, the direction of the winds is more southerly so that they form an extension of the SW monsoon.

Westerlies

The zone of variable winds is gradually replaced by an area of prevailing westerlies north of about latitude 35°N. These are not so boisterous as the westerlies of the Southern Ocean and the northern limit of the variables is more difficult to define. Westerly winds are more reliable both in direction and strength during the winter months, but this is hardly the time when anyone would consider cruising in the higher latitudes of the North Pacific, where the weather is very rough. In summer the weather is more benign, when fewer depressions race across the North Pacific between Japan and Alaska. The best weather can be expected in July, when light to moderate westerly winds predominate north of latitude 40°N.

Tropical storms

There are two areas of the North Pacific Ocean that are subject to tropical revolving storms: the typhoons of the Far East and the hurricanes of the eastern part of the North Pacific.

The region affected by hurricanes lies in the vicinity of the American coast, south of latitude 30°N to about latitude 10°N and west to longitude 140°W. This area includes the Pacific coasts of Mexico and Central America and extends as far offshore as longitude 140°W, an aspect that must be borne in mind by those planning to cross this area during the dangerous season. Theoretically the hurricane season lasts from May to November, although most hurricanes have been recorded between June and October, the month with the highest frequency being September. The only four months considered to be safe are January to April, as hurricanes have occurred in December on a few occasions. As a general rule only the earlier hurricanes travel to the western limit, whereas later in the season hurricanes are more likely to stay close to the coast. Therefore if a passage through this area is undertaken towards the end of the hurricane season, it is advisable to move offshore as quickly as possible.

The region affected by typhoons covers a much larger area stretching all the way from the Caroline Islands to Japan. To the east the area is bounded by Guam and the Mariana Islands, to the west by the Philippines, Taiwan and the northern part of the South China Sea. The typhoon season is less well defined than the hurricanes of the Eastern Pacific and no month can be regarded as completely safe. However, most typhoons occur between May and December, and during this period over half the typhoons have been recorded between July and October. September is the most dangerous month, with an average of over four typhoons. The period with the least likelihood of typhoons is January to April. As no typhoons have been recorded from December to April in the area between the northern part of the China Sea and the western side of the Eastern Sea, this is considered to be the safest time for passages to and from Japan, although this coincides with the winter weather.

Currents

The surface circulation of the North Pacific Ocean resembles a huge merry-go-round in which various currents move in a clockwise direction around a cell located slightly offcentre in the northern hemisphere. The main spring of this circular movement is the North Equatorial Current which flows westward with its axis at about latitude 12°N. To the south of this current is the eastward flowing Equatorial Countercurrent, which has its southern limits between latitudes 2°N and 4°N where it is bounded by the South Equatorial Current.

The North Equatorial Current is fed mainly by the California Current and the northern branch of the Equatorial Countercurrent. Further west it is reinforced by the North Pacific Current and further still it divides in two, the southern branch reversing its direction to become the Equatorial Countercurrent, while the northern branch carries on towards Taiwan and Japan. This is the main source of the Kuro Shio, a flow of warm water similar to the Gulf Stream of the North Atlantic. The main difference is that the direction of the Kuro Shio is seasonal, setting to the NE during the SW monsoon, but reversing its direction in winter, at the height of the NE monsoon.

The main direction of the Kuro Shio is NE along the southern coast of Japan. It subsequently fans out in about latitude 35°N to form the North Pacific Current. This current, reinforced by the Aleutian Current, flows in a broad band across the North Pacific towards America. East of latitude 160°E this current starts fanning out, part of it turning south, while the main body continues eastwards towards the North American continent where it turns SE.

This southerly drift changes its name to the California Current which flows into the North Equatorial Current thus completing the clockwise circulation round the North Pacific basin.

The surface circulation along the Pacific coast of Central America and Gulf of Panama is more erratic, with great seasonal variations that make predictions impossible. The Equatorial Countercurrent flows into this area and normally is deflected to the north west along the coast of Central America to join the California Current and eventually the North Equatorial Current. In the first months of the year a branch of the Equatorial Countercurrent turns south and flows into the South Pacific. In the Gulf of Panama the movement of water is more complicated, with an inflow of water at both extremes and an outflow in the centre that finally joins the South Equatorial Current.

10

ROUTES IN THE NORTH PACIFIC

In spite of the great concentration of sailing boats on the west coast of North America, particularly in California, the number of offshore routes in the North Pacific is relatively small. By far the most popular offshore destination is Hawaii; otherwise cruising boats from the USA or Canada looking for an offshore challenge have to sail either to the South Pacific or down the coast of Mexico to the Sea of Cortez and beyond to Central America. One cruising destination which is gaining in popularity is Alaska, which is usually reached by Californian boats via Hawaii. In spite of the longer distances involved, a detour via Hawaii has the attraction of better winds, as a direct route from California or the Pacific Northwest would have contrary winds much of the way. For those who are not attracted by the long detour to Hawaii, but are equally undeterred by the prospect of being hard on the wind and relying heavily on their engine to make progress, then the more direct route along the Mexican coast may provide the answer (see PN21 and PN22). For the sake of simplicity, the west coast of North America has been divided into two large groups, with routes starting from either California or the Pacific Northwest, the latter including British Columbia.

Because of the paucity of offshore destinations, most cruising is coastal. Inshore passages along the coast of California and beyond are therefore beyond the scope of this book. However, because of the strength of the prevailing winds many people who might prefer to sail offshore are forced to choose the inshore tactic. The one point to remember by those heading north is to keep moving and make the best of calm weather, which rarely lasts long. It is also worth remembering that November has the lighter winds, especially along the coast of Baja California, whereas May, the other month when many boats make their way along this coast, has stronger winds. In conclusion, it is better to use November to move in both directions, and to avoid May if at all possible for making northbound passages.

The islands of Micronesia are yet to be discovered as a major cruising ground and the relatively small number of boats visiting them does not bear comparison with the continuing popularity of the South Pacific. A few of those cruising the latter eventually cross the equator, usually on their way to the Far East. On the whole, however, very few boats are seen cruising the countries of the Far East either. The situation may change in the future, as the number of locally owned boats is steadily increasing.

PN10 ROUTES FROM THE WEST COAST OF NORTH AMERICA

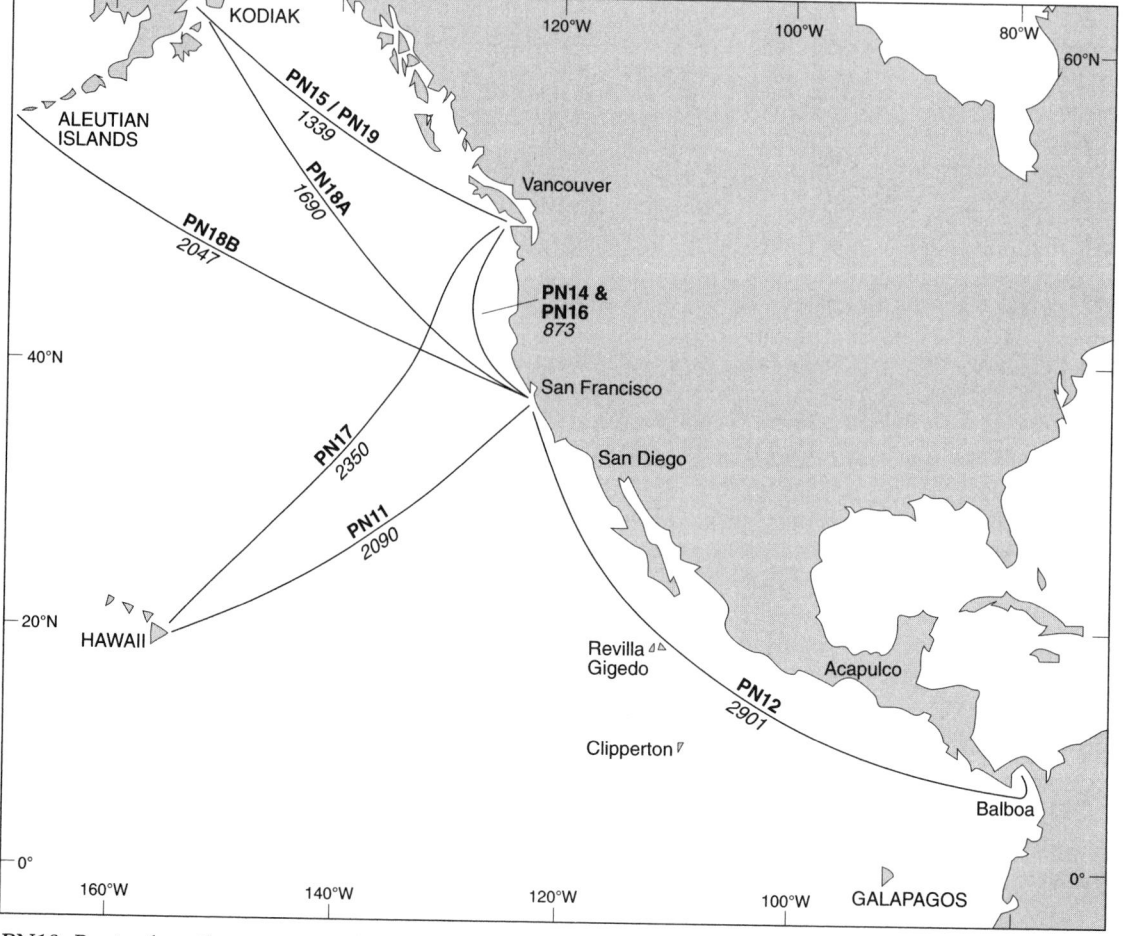

PN10 *Routes from the west coast of North America*

The Pacific coast of North America is a more hostile area than its Atlantic counterpart, the weather is harsher, there are fewer all-weather harbours, and the chilly California Current is exactly the opposite to the warm Gulf Stream. The coast, in particular the Pacific Northwest, is therefore a real challenge, not only for the sailors setting off from that area, but also for those, undaunted by its reputation, who have decided to visit this beautiful region. The Pacific Northwest has indeed a well earned reputation for gales, rain, and poor visibility. The prevailing winds are either from the northwest or less frequently from the southeast. In summer, from May to September, northwest winds predominate, although some northeast winds also occur. In winter, as well as the prevailing northwesterlies, southeast winds, often of gale force, are more common. Further south, the hurricane season is from June to October, when the tropical areas should be avoided. Mexico and Baja California are hit by an average of six hurricanes every year, so this part of Mexico should be avoided during summer and early autumn.

The premier destination for anyone contemplating an offshore cruise from California, the Pacific Northwest or British Columbia is undoubtedly Hawaii. For those who lack the time for a longer cruise to the South Pacific, Hawaii offers the chance of a Polynesian landfall which can be reached during an extended summer vacation. For those who do not wish to return straight away, Hawaii is an excellent springboard for voyages west, to Micronesia and the Far East, or south, to Tahiti and the rest of Polynesia.

The major meteorological feature affecting routes between the mainland and Hawaii is the North Pacific high. In summer it reaches its most northwesterly position in about 38°N, 150°W, while in winter it moves southeast to approximately 30°N, 130°W. The high is particularly stable between June and August, which is the best time for return passages to the mainland, although one should stay north of the tropics to avoid any hurricane forming farther south.

Those who are heading south from California bound for some distant destination, be it Panama, Galapagos, Marquesas, or Tahiti, are faced with two choices: either to head offshore and sail direct, or hug the coast and cruise in shorter stages. Both alternatives have certain advantages, but as this book deals with ocean routes only, the second alternative will not be dealt with in detail. Some people have successfully combined these two alternatives by cruising along the coast for some distance and then setting off for distant destinations either from Mexico or Costa Rica. This has the advantage of shaking down both boat and crew while still within a short distance of stateside facilities.

The advantage of an offshore passage south from California is that the prevailing NW winds will put the boat on a broad reach or run, as soon as the coast has been safely left behind. Because of the dependability of these prevailing winds, it is preferable to wait for a period of settled weather with a long term forecast of N or NW winds before setting off on a long passage. Regardless of the final destination it is advisable to head offshore immediately after leaving the coast, as the winds tend to be steadier about one hundred miles from the mainland.

PN11 *California to Hawaii*

BEST TIME:	April to May, October to November
TROPICAL STORMS:	June to October
CHARTS:	BA: 4807
	US: 51, 520
PILOTS:	BA: 8, 62
	US: 152
CRUISING GUIDES:	*Charlie's Charts of the Hawaiian Islands, Landfalls of Paradise.*

WAYPOINTS:				
Departure	*Intermediate*	*Landfall*	*Destination*	*Distance (M)*
PN111 Angeles 33°45'N, 118°20'W	PN112 30°00'N, 130°00'W PN113 26°00'N, 140°00'W PN114 22°00'N, 150°00'W	PN116 Hawaii NE 19°48'N, 155°00'W	Hilo *19°44'N, 155°04'W*	2133
PN115 Francisco 37°40'N, 122°30'W	PN112 PN113 PN114	PN116 Hawaii NE	Hilo	2090

This route enjoys favourable winds throughout the year, although few boats attempt to make the passage in winter, both on account of the cold and the high proportion of strong winds. On the other hand, summer months carry the risk of tropical storms, August and September being considered the most dangerous months. Although very few of these storms reach as far west as Hawaii, their tracks sometimes swing to the NW and thereby cross the sailing routes from the mainland. Between the two extremes, the threat of winter gales or summer hurricanes, there are some months when sailing conditions along this route can be perfect, May and November fulfilling most of these criteria. Good weather can also be found in April, although an early start is usually associated with colder temperatures. Even when the winds are fair, the sky is sometimes overcast making life difficult for those who are keen to try their hand at celestial navigation on this long offshore passage.

The winds for the first few hundred miles are N or NW becoming NE and finally E closer to Hawaii. As the great circle route goes too far north it may be better to sail a rhumb line. However, this will depend on the position of the North Pacific high and the extent of the NE trades, the northern limit of which moves in relation to the high. If it is felt that the course may pass too close to the position of the high, it is better to detour slightly to the south into an area with less pressure than towards the centre of the high.

Boats leaving from Los Angeles take their departure at WP PN111, from where the route goes south of the great circle course to WP PN112. From there, the route runs through WPs PN113 and PN114 before the course can be altered for the Hawaiian port of destination. Boats starting from San Francisco should follow the same advice and set a course which will take them sooner into the area of NE trade winds. From WP PN115, off the main shipping channel, the course should be set for WP PN112 and thence along a similar route as the one recommended for boats leaving from Los Angeles. The above intermediate points are only guidelines and the actual route should be dictated by the weather conditions prevailing at the time of departure.

When making landfall, because of increased wind strengths in channels separating the Hawaiian islands, it is usually better to gain the lee of the islands rather than approach them from windward. The best landfall in Hawaii for boats arriving from the continent is Hilo, as it is to windward of all other ports in the archipelago and therefore a perfect starting point for a cruise among the islands. Honolulu (21°18'N, 157°52'W), because of its position, is better left for the end of a Hawaiian cruise.

PN12 *Southbound from California*

BEST TIME:	November to May			
TROPICAL STORMS:	June to October			
CHARTS:	BA: 4051			
	US: 51			
PILOTS:	BA: 7A, 8			
	US: 152, 153			
CRUISING GUIDES:	*Charlie's Charts of the Western Coast of Mexico, Cruising Guide to the Sea of Cortez, Cruising Guide Acapulco to the Panama Canal, The Forgotten Middle.*			
WAYPOINTS:				

Departure	*Intermediate*	*Landfall*	*Destination*	*Distance (M)*
PN121 Diego 32°40'N, 117°20'W	PN122 31°50'N, 117°10'W			
	PN123 28°00'N, 116°20'W			
	PN124 21°30'N, 111°25'W			
	PN125 16°30'N, 102°00'W			
	PN126 Coiba 7°10'N, 82°00'W			
	PN127 Frailes 7°10'N, 80°00'W	PN128 Panama S 8°50'N, 79°30'W	Balboa *8°57'N, 79°34'W*	2901

The best time to make this passage is during the winter months, when the prevailing winds off the Mexican coast are northerly. There is a favourable current along the coast of Mexico, but a contrary current further south along the coast of Central America. Boats sailing nonstop along this route should stay at least 100 miles off the coast to avoid the influence of land breezes and also the many ships that ply the coast closer inshore. The route runs parallel to the coast of Central America and gradually curves in to enter the Gulf of Panama at Cabo Mala.

Taking its leave of the USA at WP PN121, south of San Diego, the route runs parallel to the coast of Baja California to WPs PN122, PN123, and PN124. The course is then altered at WP PN125 to WP PN126 before entering the Gulf of Panama at WP

PN127 off Cabo Mala in the approaches to the Panama Canal. Boats intending to transit the Canal should go straight to the Balboa Yacht Club. See page 583 for further instructions.

The other alternative, favoured by many, is to sail the entire distance in easy stages by calling at the different ports en route. If this option is chosen, more attention should be paid to local weather conditions, particularly during the winter months January to March when very strong winds occur in the gulfs of Tehuantepec and Papagayo. These are described in detail in PN20 (page 262). The inshore route is not recommended during the summer, when there is a risk of hurricanes in the area and the winds are less consistent, with long periods of calms. More details on destinations in Central America are given in route PN27 (page 272).

PN13 *Northbound from California*

BEST TIME:	April
TROPICAL STORMS:	None
CHARTS:	BA: 4050
	US: 501, 520
PILOTS:	BA: 8, 25, 26
	US: 152
CRUISING GUIDES:	*Charlie's Charts of the US Pacific Coast.*

Northbound passages from California are difficult to plan as it is quite rare that one can be certain of favourable winds. Therefore most people plan their cruise to include as many coastal stops as possible. In this way it is possible to take advantage of early morning breezes. One suggestion for an easier passage north is to leave in April with one of the last southerly gales. At this time of year they are usually milder than those of the winter months. Although it may be tempting to ride one of these storms, one should be very careful when running along the coast before such a storm as most ports are on a dangerous lee shore.

During the summer one has to be prepared for a lot of beating, often into strong winds. If one is planning to motor it is usually better to do this at night when the winds are lighter. Especially along the north coast of California the trip can be very tough because of the strong northerly winds which blow throughout the summer. However, those who have time to make the best of the adverse weather will be rewarded for their efforts. The coast of Northern California is replete with beautiful harbours providing shelter from the prevailing summer winds. Among them Tomales Bay and Mendocino should not be missed.

PN14 *California to British Columbia*

BEST TIME:	May to June
TROPICAL STORMS:	None
CHARTS:	BA: 4801
	US: 501
PILOTS:	BA: 8, 25, 26
	US: 152, 154
CRUISING GUIDES:	*Charlie's Charts North to Alaska, Cruising Guide to British Columbia.*
WAYPOINTS:	

Departure	Intermediate	Landfall	Destination	Distance (M)
PN141 Reyes	PN142	PN143 Flattery	Victoria	873
37°55'N, 123°00'W	40°00'N, 128°30'W	48°25'N, 124°50'W	*48°25'N, 123°24'W*	

Both in winter and summer NW winds predominate along the North American coast, which makes a direct offshore passage very difficult if not impossible. There are various ways of dealing with these headwinds and the most radical suggestion is that the coast should be left immediately on a route heading offshore for about 200 miles before it turns north. The most favourable tack should then be taken until the latitude of the port of destination is reached. A new course can then be set to approach the coast on the tack that would put the boat to windward of the

destination. An inshore route can also be followed by sailing in shorter hops along the coast and going into a port for shelter as soon as the weather becomes threatening. Yet another alternative is to try and sail parallel to the coast about 30 miles offshore so as to be within range of VHF weather broadcasts and shelter if necessary. In the case of choosing one of the inshore alternatives, great care must be paid not only to the weather but also the difficulty of crossing river bars or entering some of the harbours if the winds blow onshore. If the offshore alternative is chosen, from Reyes Point an initial course should be sailed to a point about 200 miles offshore. Whether such a relatively direct route can be sailed will depend entirely on the windward performance of the boat. The recommended landfall is off Cape Flattery, in the approaches to Juan de Fuca Strait.

Extreme caution is necessary in the approaches to the Juan de Fuca Strait because of heavy shipping and strong currents. Shipping separation zones are in operation, with the southern lane being used by arriving ships and the northern lane reserved for outgoing traffic. The lanes diverge at designated points so as to allow ships to turn either

north towards Vancouver or south towards Seattle. To complicate matters, there is often a large number of fishing boats around the Swiftsure Bank, east of the entrance to the strait. Traffic in the area is controlled by Tofino Radio (VHF channels 16 and 74). Incoming vessels are requested to report when due south of Amphitrite Point. The station operates a regular roll call, every ship reporting their position, speed, and course. In bad visibility the station will advise ships that are in the vicinity of a small boat's position. The station will also assist yachts with directions and may even track such vessels on radar.

PN15 *Alaska to British Columbia*

BEST TIME:	June to August			
TROPICAL STORMS:	None			
CHARTS:	BA: 4050			
	US: 531			
PILOTS:	BA: 4, 25, 26			
	US: 152, 154			
CRUISING GUIDES:	*Cruising Guide to Prince William Sound, Cruising Guide to British Columbia, Charlie's Charts North to Alaska.*			
WAYPOINTS:				
Departure	*Intermediate*	*Landfall*	*Destination*	*Distance (M)*
PN151 Kodiak E 57°45'N, 152°00'W	PN152 53°00'N, 150°00'W	PN153 Flattery 48°25'N,124°50'W	Victoria *48°25'N, 123°24'W*	1339
		PN154 Scott 51°00'N,129°00'W	Victoria	1075
PN155 Sedanka 53°50'N, 165°55'W	PN156 51°00'N, 165°00'W	PN153 Flattery	Victoria	1777
		PN154 Scott	Victoria	1519

The winds in the Gulf of Alaska are variable in direction during the summer months, with a slight predominance of westerly winds. Later in the season, SE winds are not uncommon making eastbound passages across the Gulf difficult. Also contrary is the Aleutian Current, which sets westward across the Gulf. Fog can be another hazard during the crossing, but gales are rare in summer. Prince Rupert harbour, where entry formalities into Canada can be completed, is reached through Dixon Strait, between Prince of Wales and Graham Islands.

Because the sailing season in Alaska is so brief, most people are in a hurry when the time comes to move south. Although a faster passage can be made on an offshore route, few people choose to miss the

unsurpassed beauty of the inshore route that threads its way past countless islets and inlets along British Columbia's fragmented coast. A recommended alternative is to cruise the area in reverse order by sailing from British Columbia to Alaska in short stages, cross the Gulf of Alaska in summer and sail back to British Columbia at the end of the summer cruising season. The sailing season is very short and lasts from May to the middle of September. In July, the North Pacific high may reach as far as the Prince William Sound, ensuring light winds and pleasant weather.

Boats setting off on the offshore route from either Dutch Harbour or Kodiak should sail due south for 200–300 miles to avoid the area affected by the lows tracking across the Pacific and then pick up the direct course with the help of the prevailing westerlies. Boats leaving from Kodiak, from WP PN151 should set a course for WP PN152. From there the course can be altered to reach Victoria by going south of Vancouver Island through the Juan de Fuca Strait, making landfall off Cape Flattery at WP PN153. An alternative is to approach Vancouver Island through Queen Charlotte Sound by making landfall north of Cape Scott at WP PN154. Similar directions apply for those leaving from Dutch Harbour on Unalaska Island. From WP PN155 the initial course leads to WP PN156 before the course is altered for one of the landfalls suggested above.

PN16 *British Columbia to California*

BEST TIME:	May to October			
TROPICAL STORMS:	None			
CHARTS:	BA: 4801			
	US: 501, 530			
PILOTS:	BA: 8, 25			
	US: 152, 154			
CRUISING GUIDES:	*Charlie's Charts of the US Pacific Coast, Cruising Guide to California's Offshore Islands.*			
WAYPOINTS:				
Departure	*Intermediate*	*Landfall*	*Destination*	*Distance (M)*
PN161 Flattery 48°25'N,124°50'W	PN162 46°30'N,126°30'W			
	PN163 40°00'N, 126°30'W	PN164 Reyes 37°55'N, 123°00'W	San Francisco *37°50'N, 122°15'W*	766
PN161 Flattery	PN162			
	PN163	PN165 Conception 34°20'N, 120°30'W	Los Angeles *33°45'N, 118°20'W*	1075

Winds along this route are always favourable and the south-setting California Current provides an added bonus. The offshore route is to be preferred for most southbound passages and, once chosen, one should stay at least 100 miles off the coast. Because of the pressure gradient between the offshore high and the continental low pressure system, winds tend to be stronger and seas higher more than 60 miles from land than closer inshore. However, because of the drawbacks of the inshore route, which are described below, the offshore route is to be preferred. From WP PN161, off Cape Flattery, the initial course goes to WP PN162. From there the route goes due south to the latitude of Cape Mendacino before the course is altered at WP PN163 for the port of destination. If the destination is San Francisco, landfall is made at WP PN164 off Reyes Point, from where Bonita Channel leads into San Francisco Bay. Directions for boats bound for destinations in the Los Angeles area are similar as far as Cape Mendacino from where the course is altered for PN165, off Cape Conception. Occasionally referred to as the Cape Horn of North America, the strong winds that blow here frequently create rough seas, which should be borne in mind if closing with the point during a NW gale. From there, the route turns east and goes inshore of the Catalina Islands.

Because of the stronger winds and bigger swell further offshore, some people prefer the inshore route. This is an attractive alternative when sailing in the other direction, but is less attractive to southbound boats determined to cover the distance in the shortest time possible. Because several harbours have bars and are difficult or dangerous to enter when there is a heavy swell, extreme caution is needed if sailing the inshore route. Another hazard along this coast is fog, which often reduces visibility drastically and can be extremely dangerous because of the high amount of shipping.

PN17 *Pacific Northwest to Hawaii*

BEST TIME:	May to June, October
TROPICAL STORMS:	None
CHARTS:	BA: 4050
	US: 50, 520
PILOTS:	BA: 25, 62
	US: 152, 154
CRUISING GUIDES:	*Landfalls of Paradise, Charlie's Charts of the Hawaiian Islands.*
WAYPOINTS:	

Departure	Intermediate	Landfall	Destination	Distance (M)
PN171 Flattery 48°25'N,124°50'W	PN172 40°00'N,130°00'W PN173 30°00'N, 140°00'W	PN174 Hawaii NE 19°48'N, 155°00'W	Hilo *19°44'N, 155°04'W*	2350

Good weather conditions prevail throughout the summer months, but in order to avoid the hurricane season, the passage should be planned for late spring or early summer. Although the route crosses an area where tropical cyclones have occurred in the past, the danger of encountering such a storm at the recommended time is fairly remote. However, weather forecasts should be listened to regularly during the summer to avoid any tropical storms which may be heading that way. To avoid westerly winds or straying into the North Pacific high at the beginning of the voyage, setting a direct course to Hawaii on departure is not recommended. Better conditions will be found by taking a southerly course, which will benefit both from northerly winds and the favourable current. It is generally recommended that the course should not be altered for Hawaii until the latitude of San Francisco is reached. Although a great circle route can be taken to Hawaii from about 40°N, it is usually better to stay slightly south of the rhumb line. The NE trades will be met somewhere between latitudes 28° and 30°N, from where the winds should remain favourable all the way to Hawaii.

Leaving from WP PN171 the route passes through two intermediate waypoints PN172 and PN173 before the course can be altered for the Hawaiian port of destination. For boats arriving from the NE the most convenient port of entry is Hilo on Hawaii Island. Landfall can be made at WP PN174 NE of the Big Island and some five miles from Hilo itself.

PN18 *California to Alaska*

BEST TIME:	June to August
TROPICAL STORMS:	June to October
CHARTS:	BA: 4050
	US: 520
PILOTS:	BA: 4, 8, 25, 26
	US: 152
CRUISING GUIDES:	*Charlie's Charts of the US Pacific Coast, Charlie's Charts North to Alaska.*

WAYPOINTS:				
Departure	*Intermediate*	*Landfall*	*Destination*	*Distance (M)*
Route PN18A				
PN180 Francisco 37°40'N, 122°30'W	PN181 Reyes W 37°55'N, 123°20'W	PN182 off Kodiak 57°45'N, 152°15'W	Kodiak *57°47'N, 152°25'W*	1690
PN183 Angeles 33°45'N, 118°20'W	PN184 Conception 34°20'N, 120°30'W	PN182 off Kodiak	Kodiak	2016
Route PN18B				
PN180 Francisco	PN181 Reyes W	PN185 Sedanka 53°50'N, 165°55'W	Dutch Harbour *53°54'N, 166°32'W*	2047
PN183 Angeles	PN184 Conception	PN185 Sedanka	Dutch Harbour	2346

There are three basic options for this route and every one has major disadvantages. Trying to sail along the coast, with or without stopping, is not going to be easy because of contrary winds, heavy shipping, river bars and other difficulties. The recommended tactic of using Hawaii as an intermediate stop adds a lot of miles to what is already a long passage. This leaves only one other option and that is a direct, nonstop offshore route. Because of the Pacific high, which dictates weather conditions throughout the region, the logical solution is to sail at the best angle possible to the prevailing NW winds to make sufficient westing and, as NE winds are found further offshore, sail a course that passes to the west of the high. The other alternative is to leave with full tanks and motor through the high and the light winds that one is bound to encounter before falling in with the prevailing westerlies of higher latitudes. Staying east of the high may not be feasible if one is deter-

mined to sail, but, depending on existing conditions, may be attempted in a boat that can make good progress under power. A good reserve of fuel should be carried as light winds and calms, as well as fog, are notorious in Alaskan waters in summer time.

There are two major destinations in Alaska and both have their attractions. Kodiak is nearer and has the better facilities, whereas Dutch Harbour probably makes a better starting point for a summer cruise. Boats bound for Kodiak will make landfall at PN182 east of Kodiak Island. The east coast is then followed to the approaches into Kodiak Harbour. This well protected harbour is reached from NE through a dredged channel. The old town is located on the NW shore of the harbour and island of the same name.

Boats bound for Dutch Harbour will make landfall off Sedanka Island from where they will sail through Akutan Pass into Unalaska Bay.

PN19 *Pacific Northwest to Alaska*

BEST TIME:	June to August
TROPICAL STORMS:	July to October
CHARTS:	BA: 4050
	US: 531
PILOTS:	BA: 4, 25, 26
	US: 152, 154
CRUISING GUIDES:	*Charlie's Charts North to Alaska.*

WAYPOINTS:				
Departure	*Intermediate*	*Landfall*	*Destination*	*Distance (M)*
PN190 Flattery 48°25'N, 124°50'W	PN191 53°00'N, 150°00'W	PN192 off Kodiak 57°45'N, 152°15'W	Kodiak *57°47'N, 152°25'W*	1298
PN190 Flattery		PN193 Sedanka 53°50'N, 165°55'W	Dutch Harbour *53°54'N, 166°32'W*	1563
PN194 Scott 51°00'N, 129°00'W		PN192 off Kodiak	Kodiak	908
PN194 Scott		PN193 Sedanka	Dutch Harbour	1351

Although more boats choose to take the inside route, which follows the scenic route through the sheltered waters off the coast of British Columbia, there are certain advantages in going offshore, mainly to gain time. As the recommended route passes through an area of prevailing westerly winds, boats that go reasonably well to windward will be at a distinct advantage. To benefit from the short Alaskan season, which extends from early June to the middle of August, passages should be planned for this period – although the chances of favourable SE winds are higher later in the summer. Although tropical storms rarely affect this area, occasionally typhoons generated in the Western North Pacific have recurved NE and reached Alaska, as happened in 1984 when typhoon Holly brought 100 knot winds to Seward.

Boats leaving from Seattle or southern ports in British Columbia will reach the open sea through the Juan de Fuca Strait and join the offshore route at WP PN190, off Cape Flattery. The alternative is to stay in the sheltered waters east of Vancouver Island and reach the open sea at Cape Scott. From either place, a direct course will then be sailed to a waypoint off Kodiak Island, unless one is bound for Dutch Harbour. Although the latter is further west, if one has the time Dutch Harbour makes a better starting point for a summer cruise in Alaskan waters.

PN20 PACIFIC ROUTES FROM CENTRAL AMERICA AND MEXICO

For boats which have transited the Panama Canal there is a rather limited choice of routes heading out into the Pacific. Basically, there are two options: either to stay in the North Pacific, where there is a narrow range of initial destinations, or to head towards the South Pacific, where the choices multiply constantly as one moves west. Similarly a considerable proportion of offshore routes from Central America are also southbound and transequatorial. These transequatorial routes and routes in the South Pacific are described in chapters 11 and 13.

Sailing directly from Panama to the west coast of North America is a difficult undertaking. An alternative preferred by many as the best way to reach California, and especially ports further north, is to sail first to Hawaii. Panama is a good starting point

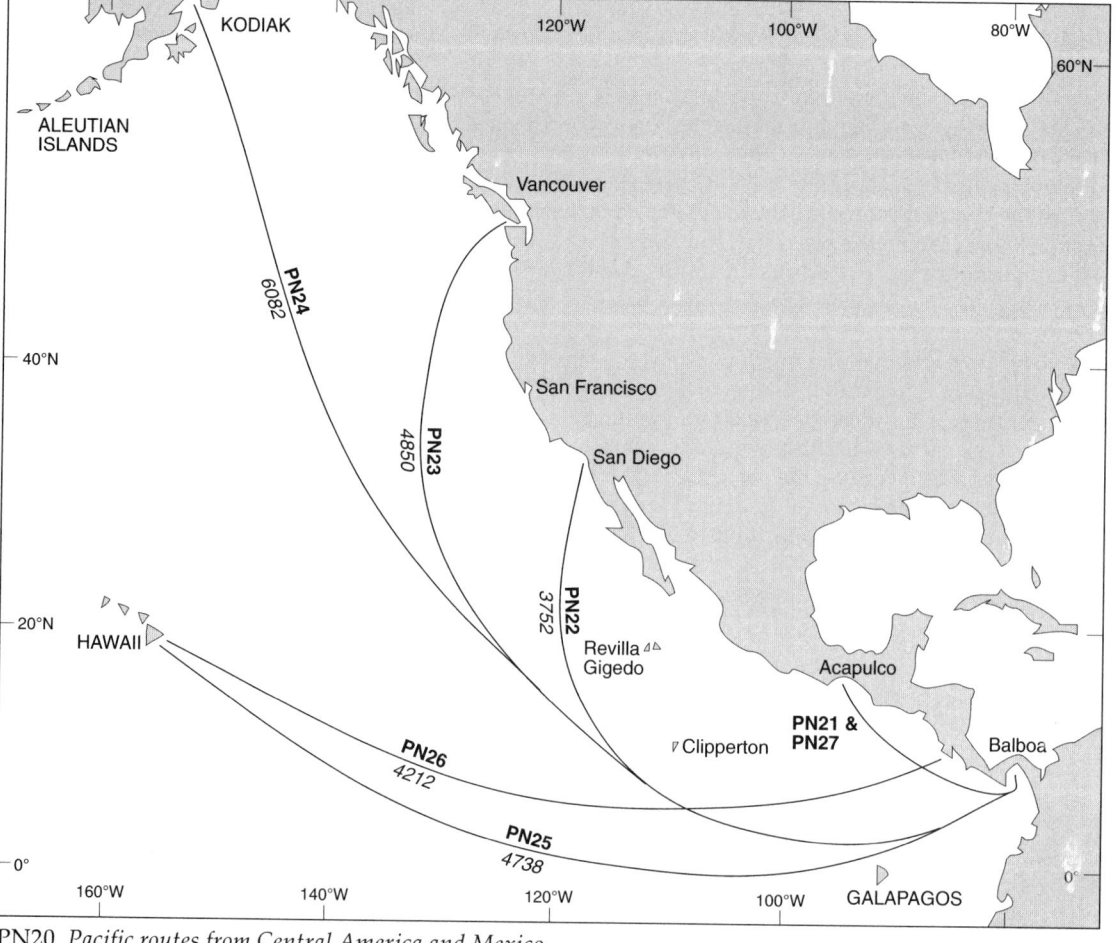

PN20 *Pacific routes from Central America and Mexico*

for sailing to ports on the west coast of Central America and as the distances involved are relatively short, even if unfavourable conditions are encountered at least they do not have to be endured for too long. Because the hurricane season affects most of this area between June and October, sailing to Mexico or California during these months should be avoided. Therefore if heading north from Panama it is best to plan to transit the Canal between November and April, so as to avoid the danger of being caught by a hurricane off the coast of Central America.

Before sailing out of the Gulf of Panama, some boats stop at the Las Perlas Islands, which have some excellent anchorages. They belong to Panama and one is not allowed to stop there after having cleared out in Balboa, without having obtained a cruising permit.

The most popular route leaving from Panama is that to the Galapagos Islands (route PT12). Most boats bound for the South Pacific take advantage of the conveniently placed Galapagos Islands to make at least a brief stop in these islands made famous by Charles Darwin. It is no longer permitted to cruise around the islands, which are a protected nature reserve, but a 72 hour stop can be made at the discretion of the port captain at either of the two ports of entry, Baquerizo Moreno (Wreck Bay) on San Cristobal Island and Puerto Ayora (Academy Bay) on Santa Cruz Island. Because of these restrictions, some boats avoid the Galapagos Islands altogether and head straight for the Marquesas and French Polynesia (PT13).

Those who want to visit ports along the west coast of South America are faced with a tough voyage against wind and current (PT11). A few boats make this trip every year showing that, in spite of all difficulties, it can be done. The alternative is to postpone visiting South America until one is farther west in the Pacific when Chile can be easier reached with the help of favourable westerly winds of higher latitudes. However, this is a long and tough trip which may be less attractive than a beat against the Humboldt current. The major attraction of such a foray down the coast of South America is the opportunity to visit Ecuador and Peru as well as some rarely frequented islands such as Easter, Pitcairn or Gambier.

Apart from the occasional norther, rare westerly, or summer hurricane, the west coasts of Central America could be described as having a truly Pacific weather with little wind and smooth seas. Local conditions along the coast do vary very much with the topography of the land. Two local weather phenomena, which affect particularly the inshore routes, are the very strong winds which take their name from the gulfs where they occur,

Papagayo and Tehuantepec. The worst period is from October to April, with the highest frequency between the end of November and the end of January. The effect of these winds can be felt as far as 150 miles offshore.

Papagayos are caused by an intensification of the NE trade winds on the Caribbean side of the isthmus. The winds reach the Pacific through a gap in the Cordillera where they blow with great force. Further north, the *Tehuantepecers* are caused by a build up of atmospheric pressure over the Gulf of Mexico, the resulting winds blowing over the continental divide and being felt most strongly in the Gulf of Tehuantepec. Both winds reach gale force 8 and even 9, and are very difficult to predict locally. However, by following weather forecasts for the Gulf of Mexico and Caribbean area it is usually possible to predict when changes in weather conditions on the Atlantic side of Central America or Mexico will affect its Pacific shores.

PN21 *Panama to Central America and Mexico*

BEST TIME:	April to May, November
TROPICAL STORMS:	June to October
CHARTS:	BA: 4051
	US: 51
PILOTS:	BA: 7, 8
	US: 153
CRUISING GUIDES:	*Cruising Guide Acapulco to the Panama Canal, Charlie's Charts of Costa Rica, Charlie's Charts of the Western Coast of Mexico, The Forgotten Middle.*

WAYPOINTS:

Departure	Intermediate	Landfall	Destination	Distance (M)
PN210 Balboa 8°57'N, 79°34'W	PN211 Panama S 8°50'N, 79°30'W PN212 Frailes 7°10'N, 80°00'W PN213 Coiba 7°10'N, 82°00'W PN214 Ten 10°00'N, 95°00'W PN215 Fifteen 15°00'N, 93°30'W	PN216 Diamante 16°45'N, 99°55'W	Acapulco 16°50'N, 99°58'W	1535

Northbound passages to ports on the Pacific coast of Central America are always difficult due either to contrary winds or prolonged periods of calms. Although a favourable current can be expected as far as the Gulf of Fonseca, from there onwards the current is mostly contrary. One should be prepared to take advantage of every shift of wind and also to use the engine when necessary in order to counter the unfavourable current. The area is prone to thunderstorms with intense lightning.

While an inshore route may be the answer for boats bound for the more southern ports in Central America, a direct offshore passage is more appealing for anyone in a hurry to reach Mexico. The recommended offshore route lists a number of waypoints, which are set far enough offshore to avoid the influence of land and localised weather patterns associated with certain areas. Those who are not keen on a long offshore voyage may prefer to treat this difficult route as a coastal hopping exercise. Stops can be made in all Central American countries, Costa Rica, Nicaragua, Honduras, El Salvador, Guatemala, and there are several attractive cruising areas on the way. The reception extended to visiting yachts by the various Central American countries depends very much on the political situation at the time, and occasionally also on the nationality of the yacht in question.

One of the most attractive stops on the coast is Golfito, in Costa Rica (8°36'N, 83°12'W). In Nicaragua the ports of Corinto (12°28'N, 87°11'W) and San Juan del Sur (11°15'N, 85°53'W) have attracted mixed comments, while the Honduran port of San Lorenzo (13°25'N, 87°27'W) has been recommended as an emergency stop. In El Salvador the situation has improved dramatically with the cessation of hostilities and a good place to stop is Acajutla (13°36'N, 89°50'W), which is one of El Salvador's official ports of entry, the other being Cutuco (13°19'N, 87°49'W). On entering the Gulf of Fonseca, the Salvadorean Coast Guard should be contacted on VHF channel 16. Stopping at one of the ports on the Pacific coast of Guatemala has little attraction, but beyond that stretches the long coast of Mexico, its main cruising attraction being located in its northern part – Baja California and the Sea of Cortez.

Detailed directions for this inshore route, which consists mostly of coastal cruising, are beyond the scope of this book. However, attention must be drawn to the two areas where the weather can seriously affect the inshore route. These are the gulfs of Tehuantepec and Papagayo, where the strong local winds described in the introduction to this section can occur. Both north and southbound inshore passages should attempt to transit the Gulf of Tehauntepec at the change of seasons, either around the middle of May or early in November. January and February are the months to avoid because of the high frequency of these gale force winds. Because the strong winds in the Gulf of Tehuantepec are caused by the trade winds building up the pressure on the opposite side of Mexico, according to local wisdom one should monitor the pressure in the Gulf of Campeche. If the pressure there is high, or a high pressure system is approaching, strong winds can be expected at Tehuantepec, and the same rules also apply to Papagayo. Usually the strongest winds will be experienced east of Salina Cruz, which will generate rough seas offshore. This is why it is strongly recommended to stay as close to the shore as possible, where the seas will be calm and it is easier to deal with just the strength of the wind.

PN22 *Central America and Mexico to California*

BEST TIME:	March to May, October to mid-November (offshore)
	February to May, mid-October to mid-November (inshore)
TROPICAL STORMS:	June to October
CHARTS:	BA: 4051
	US: 51
PILOTS:	BA: 7, 8
	US: 152, 153
CRUISING GUIDES:	*Charlie's Charts of the US Pacific Coast, Cruising Guide to the Sea of Cortez, The Forgotten Middle.*

WAYPOINTS:				
Departure	*Intermediate*	*Landfall*	*Destination*	*Distance (M)*
Route PN22A				
PN220 Panama S	PN221 Mala			
8°50'N, 79°30'W	7°30'N, 79°30'W			
	PN222			
	3°00'N, 105°00'W			
	PN223 Clipperton W			
	10°00'N, 110°00'W			
	PN224		San Diego	3752
	20°00'N, 120°00'W		32°42.5'N, 117°14'W	
			Los Angeles	3803
			33°43'N, 118°16'W	
PN220 Panama S	PN221 Mala			
	PN222			
	PN223 Clipperton W			
	PN225		San Francisco	4096
	30°00'N, 125°00'W		*37°50'N, 122°15'W*	
Route PN22B				
PN220 Panama S	PN221 Mala			
	PN226			
	0°00', 105°00'W			
	PN227		San Diego	4219
	20°00'N, 125°00'W		Los Angeles	4248
			San Francisco	4230
Route PN22C				
PN220 Panama S	PN228 Frailes			
	7°10'N, 80°00'W			
	PN229 Coiba			
	7°10'N, 82°00'W			
	PN2210 Costa Rica N			
	10°00'N, 86°20'W			
	PN2211 Clipperton N		San Diego	3278
	10°30'N, 109°00'W		Los Angeles	3353
			San Francisco	3659

For boats leaving from Panama, this can be a long and arduous trip. For this reason it has been suggested that it is easier to sail from Panama to Hawaii and thence to the west coast of North America, rather than direct to California, especially for those who like long offshore passages and are not pressed for time. If a detour to Hawaii is considered, details for that passage are given in route PN25.

A nonstop passage from Panama to California should be undertaken well offshore where better winds can be expected, even if a longer distance has to be covered. After leaving the Gulf of Panama, one should attempt to reach the SE trade wind area as soon as possible to take full advantage of both the SE winds and favourable current. From June to January, the recommended route PN22A runs between the Galapagos Islands and latitude 5°N as far as meridian 105°W. At WP PN222 the course is altered to pass west of Clipperton Island at WP PN223. For southern Californian ports (Los Angeles, San Diego) the most favourable tack should be taken after WP PN224 has been passed. After picking up the NE trade winds and if the destination is San Francisco, course is altered for WP PN225 from where the course sailed depends entirely on the winds that are encountered.

From February to May after leaving the Gulf of Panama the recommended route (AN22B) passes south of the Galapagos Islands. It then heads west as far as WP PN226 and then to WP PN227 before altering course to the NW into the NE trade wind zone. However, if winds are favourable after passing Cabo Mala, a more direct route can be sailed to California. The initial course on this route (PN 22C) runs parallel to the coast of Central America as far as Costa Rica, keeping only about 20 miles off the coast. From northern Costa Rica at WP PN2210, the route heads due west for about 1000 miles to WP PN2211, just north of Clipperton Island. The route then runs parallel to the mainland coast in a NW direction gradually curving towards the port of destination by using the existing winds to best advantage. If taking this route one must be prepared to motorsail when necessary, especially during the first leg from Panama northwards. This route is often preferred by delivery skippers, who recommend its use particularly during the first months of the year.

Another alternative is to stay relatively close to the coast all the way, the advantage of this course of action being that one can find shelter in some of the ports en route such as Puerto Madero or Salina Cruz. The first part of this coastal route is described in PN21. Two local weather phenomena must be taken into account if taking this inshore route during winter and they are the strong winds in the gulfs of Papagayo and Tehuantepec. The worst period is from October to April, with the highest frequency between the end of November and the end of January. The effect of the winds can be felt as much as 150 miles offshore. The advice given by captains of boats plying this coast regularly is to stay as close inshore as safety will permit. There are several ports en route where shelter can be sought, although by sailing close to the shore one should be able to handle even the strongest winds.

Because the strong winds in the Gulf of Tehuantepec are caused by the trade winds building up the pressure on the opposite side of Mexico, according to local wisdom one should monitor the pressure in the Gulf of Campeche. If the pressure there is high, or a high pressure system is approaching, strong winds can be expected at Tehuantepec, and the same rules also apply to Papagayo. Usually the strongest winds will be experienced east of Salina Cruz, which will generate rough seas offshore. This is why it is strongly recommended to stay as close to the shore as safely possible, where the seas will be calm and it is easier to deal with just the strength of the wind.

When sailing north from Panama one should plan to be north of Cabo San Lucas by 1st June, especially as some insurance companies make this provision in their policies in view of the hurricane season in Central America. This consideration, coupled with weather conditions in the Caribbean, make it advisable to plan on transiting the Panama Canal early in the year, so as to have plenty of time either to reach the west coast before the onset of the hurricane season or to make alternative arrangements.

The northbound routes from Mexico are never easy, but if the weather is watched carefully, the occasional window will provide favourable conditions. Often in November, and occasionally December, the approach of a cold front in the North Pacific will stop the prevailing NW winds and bring calms or light winds. In late spring, when there are strong headwinds offshore, close inshore it is often possible to make good progress with the help of the diurnal land and sea breezes. The recommended tactic is to stay near the shore during the calm night and morning hours and then tack offshore in the afternoon. Being close to shore, it is then possible to find an anchorage when conditions are not favourable.

Boats taking the offshore route from Panama or Costa Rica can break the trip at offshore islands, such as Cocos Island (5°30'N, 87°00'W), 285 miles off Costa Rica. The island is a nature reserve and has some resident wardens, but boats are allowed to stop. Even more remote is the French possession, Clipperton Island (10°17'N, 109°15'W), which is uninhabited, although occasionally it is visited by meteorologists and other scientists.

PN23 *Panama to British Columbia*

BEST TIME:	April to May, November			
TROPICAL STORMS:	June to October			
CHARTS:	BA: 4050, 4051			
	US: 51, 50			
PILOTS:	BA: 7, 8, 25			
	US: 152, 153, 154			
CRUISING GUIDES:	*Cruising Guide to British Columbia.*			
WAYPOINTS:				
Departure	*Intermediate*	*Landfall*	*Destination*	*Distance (M)*
PN230 Panama S	PN231 Frailes			
8°50'N, 79°30'W	7°10'N, 80°00'W			
	PN232 Coiba			
	7°10'N, 82°00'W			
	PN233	PN234 Flattery	Victoria	4896
	20°00'N, 130°00'W	48°25'N, 124°50'W	*48°25'N, 123°24'W*	

Directions for this route are similar to those for route PN22 and in fact skippers are faced with exactly the same dilemma whether they intend to sail from Panama to California or all the way to British Columbia. The choice is between a relatively direct route along the coast of Central America, an indirect offshore route or a grand detour via Hawaii. If the prospect of such a long detour via Hawaii is not acceptable, the choice is between the other two routes, both of which have advantages and also some serious disadvantages. The choice of route should depend primarily on the windward performance of the boat itself as much of the voyage will be hard on the wind, and for this reason those who are not prepared to face a beat of several thousand miles, or whose boat may not be up to the challenge, should perhaps reconsider their plans.

The offshore route offers a greater certainty of favourable winds for the first half of the voyage but then becomes a hard beat against the prevailing winds. A route that runs parallel to the coast is shorter but depends more on the use of the engine. In both cases the final leg north of latitude 30°N may prove to be the toughest because of the high pro-portion of N and NW winds during the summer months. No waypoints are given for the second route as the best way to go should be decided by the weather conditions at the time.

If the offshore route is sailed in April or May, from WP PN232, off Coiba Island, the shortest route should be sailed to WP PN233. From there, the route continues due north following as closely as possible meridian 130°W before the course is altered for the coast. Much will depend on the position of the North Pacific high, and one may either have to go further west to avoid it altogether, or power through it, if one is so inclined. In the first instance, depending on the season, it may be necessary to go as far north as latitude 43°N before turning towards the coast of British Columbia (see also route PN32, page 275). If the passage is undertaken in November, the time of arrival in British Columbia will be so late that one should consider spending the winter in Hawaii. At that time of year, a great circle route can be sailed from Panama across to Hawaii and one can count on both favourable winds and currents for almost the entire distance.

PN24 *Panama to Alaska*

BEST TIME:	May
TROPICAL STORMS:	June to October
CHARTS:	BA: 4050, 4051
	US: 51, 50
PILOTS:	BA: 4, 7, 8
	US: 152, 153
CRUISING GUIDES:	*Charlie's Charts North to Alaska.*
WAYPOINTS:	

Departure	Intermediate	Landfall	Destination	Distance (M)
PN240 Panama S	PN241 Frailes			
8°50'N, 79°30'W	7°10'N, 80°00'W			
	PN242 Coiba			
	7°10'N, 82°00'W			
	PN243			
	22°00'N, 140°00'W			
	PN244			
	30°00'N, 150°00'W			
	PN245 Kodiak SE	PN246 off Kodiak	Kodiak	6082
	57°23'N, 152°00'W	57°45'N, 152°15'W	*57°47'N, 152°25'W*	

A detour via Hawaii (see route PN25) has certain advantages over a nonstop passage to Alaska, especially between September and March when it would be either too late or too early to head for Alaska. From April to August the more direct route should be considered, the best month for a northbound passage probably being May as it means arriving in Alaska at the beginning of the summer sailing season. This also means that the area affected by tropical storms will have been sailed through during the safe season.

Directions as far as latitude 30°N are similar to those given for route PN23. A first recommended intermediate waypoint is PN243, but whether one can sail a direct course for this point will depend entirely on the performance of the boat, as much of the passage will be close on the wind. From PN243 a new course is set for WP PN244, from where the route should arc northwards by trying to keep west of the North Pacific high. North of latitude 40°N favourable winds can be expected for most of the way, as above 40°N an average of 70 per cent of the winds are from between S and W. The weather gets increasingly cold as higher latitudes are reached and north of latitude 40°N there is also a high proportion of fog.

From WP PN244 the best course is sailed for WP PN245, southeast of Kodiak Island. From that point the route runs along the east coast of that island to WP PN246 from where it enters Kodiak Harbour.

PN25 *Panama to Hawaii*

BEST TIME:	March to May, November			
TROPICAL STORMS:	June to October			
CHARTS:	BA: 4051			
	US: 51			
PILOTS:	BA: 7, 62			
	US: 152, 153			
CRUISING GUIDES:	*Charlie's Charts of the Hawaiian Islands, Landfalls of Paradise.*			
WAYPOINTS:				

Departure	Intermediate	Landfall	Destination	Distance (M)
Route PN25A				
PN250 Panama S	PN251 Frailes			
8°50'N, 79°30'W	7°10'N, 80°00'W			
	PN252	PN257 Hawaii SE	Hilo	4880
	3°00'N, 130°00'W	19°30'N,154°45'W	*19°44'N,155°04'W*	
Route PN25B				
PN250 Panama S	PN253 Mala			
	7°30'N, 79°30'W			
	PN254			
	2°00'S, 85°00'W			
	PN255	PN257 Hawaii SE	Hilo	5331
	0°00', 130°00'W			
Route PN25C				
PN250 Panama S	PN251 Frailes			
	PN256 Coiba	PN257 Hawaii SE	Hilo	4530
	7°10'N, 82°00'W			

The painful dilemma faced by all those who plan to sail from Panama to Hawaii is whether to follow the traditional sailing route and make a detour of some 800 miles or take the great circle route and hope for the best. The great circle route skirts an area of calms and light winds between longitudes 80°W and 110°W, which can be avoided by following the directions given to the masters of sailing ships who were advised to always try and make their westing with the help of the SE trade winds (route PN25A). The tactic is to make as much westing as possible south of the ITCZ, so it is imperative to be able to assess its location. Generally one will find SE trade winds somewhere between 2°N and 4°N, and therefore once favourable winds have been found the course should not be altered too soon for Hawaii. Usually this means not before 130°W has been reached from where the great circle route can be sailed to Hawaii. This southerly route is strongly recommended during the hurricane season (June to October), when the great circle route from Panama

passes through an area of tropical storms west of Mexico. Boats sailing this longer route and leaving Panama at WP PN250 should stay west of Las Perlas Islands and continue south to WP PN251. From there a course is set for WP PN252 by sailing north of the Galapagos Islands to take advantage of both favourable wind and current. From WP PN252 the great circle course can be joined to Hawaii.

From February to May after leaving the Gulf of Panama the recommended route (PN25B) heads south and passes south of the Galapagos Islands. Westing is made close to the equator, to take full advantage of the prevailing SE winds and favourable current. From WP PN255, the great circle course is joined for Hawaii.

For the rest of the year, between November and February, the direct route from Panama (PN25C) is to be preferred as it takes less time to reach the NE trade wind belt, which extends further south in winter. If the passage is undertaken in November, favourable winds and current can be expected for almost the entire distance. Having left the Gulf of Panama, from WP PN256, a great circle course can be set for WP PN257, off Cape Kumuhaki, at the eastern extremity of Hawaii Island. A convenient port of entry, for boats arriving from the east, is Hilo.

For those who prefer to break up this passage into shorter stages, it is possible to sail first to Costa Rica, either in one offshore leg, or in short hops along the coast. From there similar directions apply for the rest of the voyage to Hawaii as for route PN26.

The above recommendation was put to the test in December 1996 when the yachts racing in the Hong Kong Challenge sailed from Panama to Hawaii. It was interesting to note that while one yacht took route PN256A, and thus crossed the ITCZ twice, all the others opted for the direct route PN25C. Although the former sailed over 500 miles more, he arrived first, but only beat the nearest rival by less than one day after 35 days at sea! However, sailing conditions on route PN25C were described as generally better, although it was pointed out that if the yachts that had taken the shorter route had been able to motor through some of the calms, which under racing rules they were not permitted to do, they would have reached the NE trade winds sooner and the entire passage would have been that much shorter.

PN26 *Central America and Mexico to Hawaii*

BEST TIME:	March to May, November			
TROPICAL STORMS:	June to October			
CHARTS:	BA: 4051			
	US: 51			
PILOTS:	BA: 8, 62			
	US: 152, 153			
CRUISING GUIDES:	*Charlie's Charts of the Hawaiian Islands, Landfalls of Paradise.*			
WAYPOINTS:				
Departure	*Intermediate*	*Landfall*	*Destination*	*Distance (M)*
PN261 Golfito *8°36'N, 83°12'W*		PN263 Hawaii SE *19°30'N,154°45'W*	Hilo *19°44'N, 155°04'W*	4212
PN262 Acapulco *16°50'N, 99°58'W*		PN263 Hawaii SE	Hilo	3140

Tropical storms affect this route throughout the summer, although boats leaving from Mexico are at greater risk than those setting off from Costa Rica, where the route can be easily shaped to stay south of the danger area. Mainly because of the threat of these storms, most passages on this route are made either before June or after October. At all times it is essential to move offshore as quickly as possible to escape the influence of the land and find the prevailing NE trades. In April and early May, the weather in the vicinity of the coast is often unsettled, with thunderstorms and variable winds. The winds offshore are very steady during the early summer, especially west of longitude 120°W. In November and December the trade winds are much stronger and there is often a big swell, the result of gales further north.

A direct course can be normally sailed at the recommended times. Landfall will be made at WP PN263, off Cape Kumuhaki, at the eastern extremity of Hawaii Island. A convenient port of entry is Hilo, on the east coast of that same island.

PN27 Central America and Mexico to Panama

BEST TIME:	November, May
TROPICAL STORMS:	June to October
CHARTS:	BA: 4051
	US: 51
PILOTS:	BA: 8, 62
	US: 152, 153
CRUISING GUIDES:	*Cruising Guide Acapulco to Panama Canal, The Forgotten Middle.*
WAYPOINTS:	

Departure	Intermediate	Landfall	Destination	Distance (M)
PN271 Acapulco 16°50'N, 99°58'W	PN272 15°00'N, 99°30'W PN273 10°00'N, 95°00'W PN274 Coiba 7°10'N, 82°00'W PN275 Frailes 7°10'N, 80°00'W	PN276 Panama S 8°50'N, 79°30'W	Balboa *8°57'N, 79°34'W*	1533

Because of the lack of protected harbours in Guatemala and the political situation in El Salvador and Nicaragua, until recently most boats preferred to sail nonstop from Mexico to Costa Rica. In spring and autumn, the winds are often light and there are frequent calms. The situation is very different in winter, when gale force winds make the crossing of the gulfs of Tehuantepec and Papagayo a daunting experience. Because the strong winds in the Gulf of Tehuantepec are caused by the trade winds building up the pressure on the opposite side of Mexico, according to local wisdom one should monitor the pressure in the Gulf of Campeche. If the pressure there is high, or a high pressure system is approaching, strong winds can be expected at Tehuantepec, and the same rules also apply to Papagayo. Usually the strongest winds will be experienced east of Salina Cruz, which will generate rough seas offshore. This is why it is strongly recommended to stay as close to the shore as safely possible, where the seas will be calm and you should find it easier to deal with just the strength of the wind.

When sailing relatively close to the coast, the strong NW setting current has caused problems for those closing with the coast thinking that they were already in Costa Rican waters but were in fact still in Nicaragua. The topography along the south coast of Nicaragua is very similar to the north of Costa Rica, so it is easy to make such a mistake. It

is therefore advisable to keep well offshore and only approach the coast when absolutely sure of the position.

The reception extended to visiting yachts by the various Central American countries depends very much on the political situation at the time, and occasionally also on the nationality of the yacht in question. Stopping at one of the ports on the Pacific coast of Guatemala has little attraction, whereas in El Salvador the situation has improved dramatically with the coming of peace. A good place to stop is Acajutla (13°36'N, 89°50'W), which is one of El Salvador's official ports of entry, the other being Cutuco (13°19'N, 87°49'W). On entering the Gulf of Fonseca, the Salvadorean Coast Guard should be contacted on VHF channel 16. The Honduran port of San Lorenzo (13°25'N, 87°27'W) has been recommended as an emergency stop, while in Nicaragua the ports of Corinto (12°28'N, 87°11'W) and San Juan del Sur (11°15'N, 85°53'W) have attracted mixed comments. One of the most attractive stops on the Costa Rica coast is Golfito (8°36'N, 83°12'W).

The alternative to the inshore route is to sail well off the coast thereby avoiding the effect of the local strong winds described earlier. This makes sense, especially if leaving from northern Mexico, so that the entire passage is made well off the coast and the Gulf of Tehuantepec is passed at some 400–500 miles offshore. The route then curves towards

Cocos Island (5°33'N, 87°02'W), where a stop is recommended, before entering the Gulf of Panama at Cabo Mala. Directions for transiting the Panama Canal are given on page 583.

PN30 ROUTES FROM HAWAII

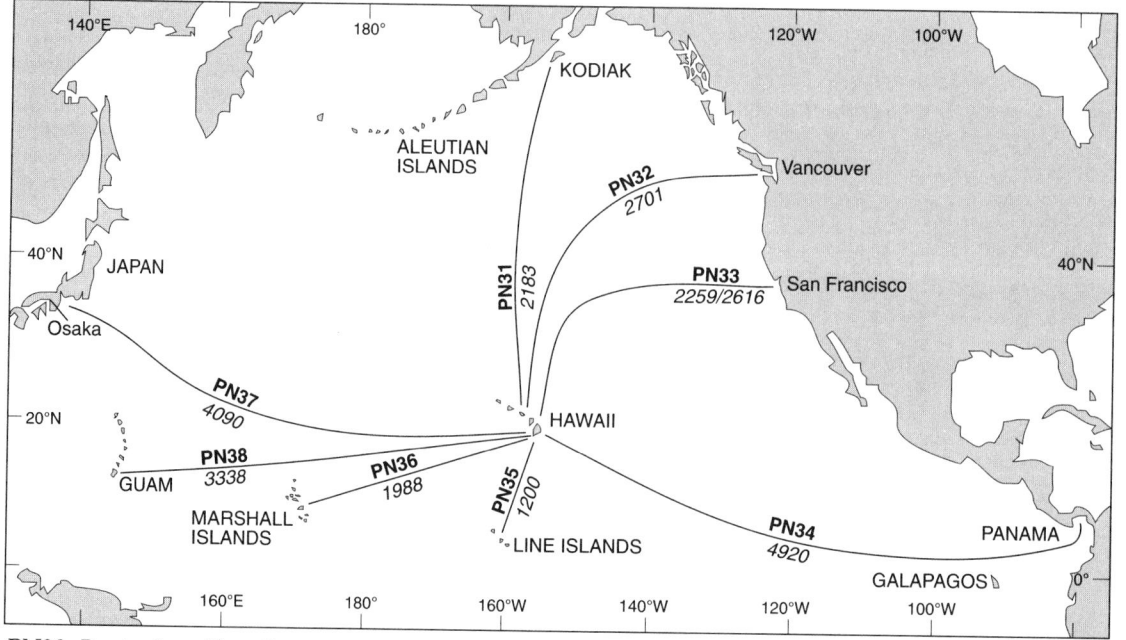

PN30 *Routes from Hawaii*

The main attraction of America's outpost in the North Pacific are the NE trade winds which ensure a fast downwind passage from ports on the west coast of America, especially from those in California. Hawaii's main disadvantage is the same trade winds, which make a return voyage to those ports a more difficult undertaking. The logical solution for a return passage with fair winds is to make a big sweep to northward hoping to find in higher latitudes the favourable winds needed for the passage home. The prevailing NE winds also make a return to Hawaii very difficult from any of the Micronesian islands to the west, and forward planning should be the main concern for anyone planning a voyage to or from Hawaii. Most routes in or out of Hawaii are under the direct influence of the North Pacific high, which generates the NW winds that prevail along the Pacific coasts of Canada and the USA as well as the NE trade winds mentioned above. Boats returning to continental America are faced with a difficult obstacle by the same high which must be bypassed to avoid the calms and light winds associated with it. Although the Hawaiian islands are rarely affected by tropical storms, some have occurred there in recent years and this should be borne in mind by those who are there in summer.

The NE trade winds prevail around Hawaii for most of the year. The winds tend to be northerly in March, becoming more easterly later on. The NE trade winds are stronger near these islands than anywhere else in the Pacific. Lighter winds and calms can be experienced in October, while in November and December southerly winds can interrupt the trades. The worst months are January and February, when S and SW gales called *konas* strike, lasting from a few hours to 2–3 days and bringing rain.

The high volcanic islands do affect winds locally and gentle land and sea breezes flow on and off the land. The trades also divide and flow around the coast to the north and south of Molokai and Maui especially. Because of the height of most islands, there is a considerable wind shadow in their lee and the trade winds are sometimes blocked altogether. On the other hand, in the channels between the islands the wind is accelerated, particularly strong gusts and rough seas being experienced in the Alenuihaha Channel separating Maui from the Big Island. Winds tend to be lighter in the morning before the trades strengthen for the day.

Of all the routes originating in Hawaii, only the route across the equator to Tahiti (PT25) offers a chance of good passages in both directions, although this is not the main reason for the popularity of this route. Ever since the South Pacific was put on the world cruising map in the early 30s, Hawaii has been used as a convenient stepping stone by boats on their way to other Polynesian destinations. Modern sailing boats have given back to Hawaii its important position at the apex of the triangle linking the far flung corners of Polynesia, from Aotearoa (New Zealand) in the west to Rapa Nui (Easter Island) in the east. For a foray into the South Seas, the islands of Hawaii offer an excellent starting point. For those who are not afraid of sailing a little farther in search of better winds, Hawaii is in just as convenient a position, whether the destination is in Japan, Alaska, or the Pacific Northwest.

The eastern part of the North Pacific lends itself to a circular route, which can be easily accomplished in as little as six months. By sailing to Hawaii in late winter or early spring, preferably from a port in California, one benefits from the best sailing conditions across. The early summer is then spent exploring the Hawaiian islands before the return voyage is undertaken, ideally not later than July. That would allow sufficient time for a short cruise in British Columbia before sailing back to California in the autumn.

PN31 *Hawaii to Alaska*

BEST TIME:	Mid-June to August			
TROPICAL STORMS:	None			
CHARTS:	BA: 4050			
	US: 530			
PILOTS:	BA: 4, 62	US: 152		
CRUISING GUIDES:	*Charlie's Charts North to Alaska.*			
WAYPOINTS:				
Departure	*Intermediate*	*Landfall*	*Destination*	*Distance (M)*
Route PN31A				
PN311 Hanalei	PN312			
22°15'N, 159°31'W	40°00'N, 160°00'W			
	PN313	PN314 off Kodiak	Kodiak	2183
	57°23'N, 152°00'W	57°45'N, 152°15'W	*57°47'N, 152°25'W*	
Route PN31B				
PN311 Hanalei	PN312	PN315 Sedanka	Dutch Harbour	1952
		53°50'N, 165°55'W	*53°54'N, 166°32'W*	

Summer is undoubtedly the best time to make this passage and most boats which take this north-bound route normally leave Hawaii in the second half of June. Such a departure ensures longer and warmer days in higher latitudes and at least one month of cruising in Alaska before heading south again.

The course from Hawaii is almost due north and skirts the western edge of the North Pacific high. In summer (June to August), the high is normally centred around 38°N, 150°W. NE winds normally persist at least as far as latitude 30°N before being replaced by variable winds. In some years the shift to westerlies can be quite abrupt, in other years steady westerly winds are almost nonexistent and light winds and calms persist all the way to Alaska. Generally, however, favourable winds can be expected for most of the way, as above latitude 40°N an average of 70 per cent of the winds are from between S and W. The weather gets increasingly cold as higher latitudes are reached and north of latitude 40°N there is also a high proportion of fog. This can be a cause of concern because of the large amount of shipping, both cargo and fishing boats. Yet another problem is the overcast sky, which is a feature of higher latitudes in summer.

The permanent cloud cover makes it impossible to take sun sights, which makes satellite navigation almost indispensable.

A favourite starting point from Hawaii is Hanalei Bay on Kauai Island. From WP311, outside Hanalei Bay, the course is almost due north along meridian 160°W, so as to keep west of the Pacific high. From WP PN312 the course is altered for WP PN313, east of Kodiak Island. From that point the route runs along the east coast of that island to WP PN314 in the approaches to Kodiak Harbour. The well protected harbour is best entered from NE through a dredged channel, which leads N of Near Island to Kodiak, an old town on the NW shore of Kodiak Harbour.

Boats bound for Dutch Harbour will follow similar directions and, from WP PN312, will set course for WP315 off Sedanka Island. The course can then be altered to sail through Akutan Pass to reach Dutch Harbour in Unalaska Bay on the north coast of Unalaska Island. Dutch Harbour is a better starting point than Kodiak for a cruise along the northern shore of the Gulf of Alaska. However, if time is short and one wishes to spend some time cruising on the way south, Kodiak is probably a better choice.

PN32 *Hawaii to the Pacific Northwest*

BEST TIME:	May to August			
TROPICAL STORMS:	June to October			
CHARTS:	BA: 4806, 4807			
	US: 530			
PILOTS:	BA: 25, 62			
	US: 152, 154			
CRUISING GUIDES:	*Cruising Guide to British Columbia, Charlie's Charts of the US Pacific Coast.*			
WAYPOINTS:				

Departure	Intermediate	Landfall	Destination	Distance (M)
PN321 Hanalei 22°15'N, 159°31'W	PN322 40°00'N, 160°00'W	PN323 Flattery 48°25'N, 124°50'W	Victoria 48°25'N, 123°24'W	2701
			Seattle 47°37'N, 122°21'W	2755

The summer months are to be preferred for this passage, not so much because they ensure better winds, but because the weather is warmer. Indeed, faster passages have been made in February, when a higher proportion of southerly winds have made it possible to sail almost a great circle course to Juan de Fuca. At all other times the recommendation is to sail due north on leaving Hawaii and only start turning east when steady westerly winds are met. This normally happens above latitude 40°N and the point where the route takes on that easterly curve is furthest north in August and furthest south in December. In summer it might be necessary to go as far north as 45°N before being able to turn east. With the approach of autumn, the North Pacific high starts moving south, which means that the swing to the north need not be so great. However, such an advantage has to be weighed against the increase in gale force winds.

This route depends very much on the position of the North Pacific high, which in summer is centred on 38°N, 150°W. The recommended route follows its western edge and then curves around its northern fringe trying to avoid the calms that are met if the area of high pressure is crossed. Undeterred by this prospect, some people who are prepared to use their engines try to steer the shortest course across and are occasionally rewarded by a faster, if windless, passage. In recent years, the most common strategy has been to sail north to the limit of the NE trade winds and then use the engine to reach the area of prevailing westerlies. For those who prefer to sail all or most of the way, there is less choice, and their reward for a longer and colder passage into higher latitudes is a fast reach in steady westerlies. As the route skirts the fringes of the high, the skies are often overcast and celestial navigation is usually impossible.

Because of the needed northing, boats usually leave from Hanalei Bay on Kauai and take their departure from Hawaii at WP PN321. Intermediate waypoints cannot be given for the reasons described above, but in summer, one may have to head as far north as WP PN322 before altering course for the mainland coast. Landfall will be made at WP PN323, NW of Cape Flattery in the approaches to Juan de Fuca Strait.

Besides the weather, there are several hazards to watch out for on this route, such as the large fishing nets, which are often left unattended and even unlit. Such nets have been reported anywhere between 35°N and 45°N and as far west as 145°W. Another hazard, especially north of 40°N is dense fog. Extreme caution is necessary in the approaches to Juan de Fuca Strait because of heavy shipping and strong currents. Shipping separation zones are in operation, with the southern lane being used by arriving ships and the northern lane reserved for outgoing traffic. The lanes diverge at designated points so as to allow ships to turn either north towards Vancouver or south towards Seattle. To complicate matters, there is often a large number of fishing boats around the Swiftsure Bank, east of the entrance to the strait. Traffic in the area is controlled by Tofino Radio (VHF channels 16 and 74). Incoming vessels are requested to report when due south of Amphitrite Point. The station operates a regular roll call, every ship reporting their position, speed, and course. In bad visibility the station will advise ships that are in the vicinity of a small boat's position. They will also assist yachts with directions and may even track such vessels on radar.

PN33 *Hawaii to California*

BEST TIME:	March to May, September to October			
TROPICAL STORMS:	June to October			
CHARTS:	BA: 4807			
	US: 530			
PILOTS:	BA: 8, 62			
	US: 152			
CRUISING GUIDES:	*Charlie's Charts of the US Pacific Coast.*			
WAYPOINTS:				

Departure	Intermediate	Landfall	Destination	Distance (M)
PN331 Hanalei 22°15'N, 159°31'W	PN332 February 30°00'N, 150°00'W	PN335 Reyes 37°55'N, 123°00'W	San Francisco *37°50'N, 122°15'W*	2147
PN331 Hanalei	PN333 May 35°00'N, 150°00'W	PN335 Reyes	San Francisco	2259
PN331 Hanalei	PN334 August 40°00'N, 155°00'W	PN335 Reyes	San Francisco	2616

Directions for this route are almost the same as for PN32 as sailing a direct course from Hawaii to California is seldom possible due to the prevailing NE winds. The recommended sailing route from Hawaii runs almost due north before turning east once the area of steady westerly winds has been reached. The turning point varies in latitude throughout the year, being as far north as 40°N in summer and 32°N in winter. The recommended summer route turns quite sharply at the point where steady westerlies are met, whereas at other times the route follows a curve that turns gradually NE and then E towards the port of destination. If the passage is made at the end of winter, in February or March, the route should start turning NE at about latitude 30°N (WP PN332) when the best course should be set for the port of destination. The NE turning point in May is somewhere around WP PN333, and in August WP PN334. From these hypothetical waypoints the route curves gradually northeast and then east for one's destination. The August turning point is the most northerly in latitude 40°N, or even higher. Because the recommended summer routes make destinations in the Pacific Northwest closer than those in California, boats from South California often take advantage of this by cruising some of that area before heading for home.

Boats sailing nonstop to San Francisco should make landfall at WP PN335 off Point Reyes, at the entrance into the traffic separation zone. In poor visibility one should contact the US Coastguard Vessel Traffic Service (CVTS) on VHF Channel 16 to obtain information on shipping traffic.

As described in PN32, all these routes are greatly influenced by the position of the North Pacific high, as they attempt to follow the contour of this area of high pressure. Boats with a good windward performance can often take a more direct route than the recommended one, as can those whose skippers are prepared to make their easting with help from the engine. Some fast passages have been made in May by boats taking the great circle route and motorsailing to windward in light winds. At other times, boats heading for Southern California have tried to beat their way across by keeping south of the high, something that can be done especially if one is able to keep track of the weather. Otherwise it is better to follow the old practice of making northing while under the influence of the NE trade winds and sail east with the westerlies of high latitudes. In between the two systems one may not have much choice except to use the engine. However, as the position of the North Pacific high has such a bearing on all routes to the mainland, it is essential to obtain a long term forecast before leaving Hawaii so as to be able to plot the best course in relation to the existing weather conditions.

PN34 *Hawaii to Central America and Mexico*

BEST TIME:	November			
TROPICAL STORMS:	June to October			
CHARTS:	BA: 4051			
	US: 51			
PILOTS:	BA: 8, 62			
	US: 152, 153			
CRUISING GUIDES:	*Charlie's Charts of Costa Rica, Charlie's Charts of the Western Coast of Mexico, Cruising Guide Acapulco to the Panama Canal.*			

WAYPOINTS:

Departure	Intermediate	Landfall	Destination	Distance (M)
PN341 Hilo	PN342	PN343 Mala S	Balboa	4920
19°45'N, 155°00'W	5°00'N, 140°00'W	7°00'N, 80°40'W	*8°57'N, 79°34'W*	
PN341 Hilo	PN344 Cocos	PN345 Dulce	Golfito	4338
	5°34'N, 87°05'W	8°36'N, 83°14'W	*8°38'N, 83°11'W*	

Because of the prevailing northeasterly winds, which blow throughout the year on the direct route to continental America, directions for passages to ports in Northern Mexico are similar to those described in PN33. Reaching Mexico from Hawaii by such a roundabout route is so time consuming that one should think seriously before committing oneself to such a passage. The alternative is only marginally more attractive, as it entails a similar detour to the south. Ports in Central America, and especially Panama, can be reached by such a southern route, which is best sailed in late October or November. Recommended waypoints are only listed for such a southern route.

A good starting point from Hawaii is Hilo. From WP PN341, outside Hilo, existing weather conditions should be used to best advantage to reach WP PN342. An area of prevailing SE and S winds extends eastwards from this point and also the east-setting Equatorial Countercurrent. The route passes north of the Galapagos Islands with the winds becoming increasingly S and SW so that the route can gradually curve to NE and the Gulf of Panama, where landfall will be made at WP PN343 off Cabo Mala.

Boats bound for Costa Rica may be able to alter course earlier for WP344 north of Cocos Island. The island belongs to Costa Rica and has a good anchorage in Chatham Bay (5°33'N, 87°02'W). The voyage can then be continued to mainland Costa Rica to WP345, at the entrance to Golfo Dulce and the port of Golfito.

Even in a month when the best conditions can be expected along these routes, such as November, this will be a tough passage and should only be undertaken *in extremis* after all other alternatives have been considered. It is also essential that the voyage is made in a boat that goes well to windward as much of the passage will be hard on the wind.

PN35 *Hawaii to Line Islands*

BEST TIME:	April to May			
TROPICAL STORMS:	None			
CHARTS:	BA: 782			
	US: 504			
PILOTS:	BA: 62			
	US: 126, 152			
CRUISING GUIDES:	*Landfalls of Paradise, Charlie's Charts of Polynesia.*			
WAYPOINTS:				

Departure	Intermediate	Landfall	Destination	Distance (M)
PN351 Oahu S 21°16'N, 157°51'W	PN352 10°00'N, 155°00'W	PN353 2°05'N, 157°30'W	Christmas *1°59'N, 157°28'W*	1200
PN351 Oahu S	PN352	PN354 4°00'N, 159°25'W	Fanning *3°51'N, 159°22'W*	1152

The route running due south to these islands lying close to the equator has the benefit of the NE trade winds throughout the year. These winds are particularly strong and steady in winter, but tend to get lighter as the islands are approached. The NE winds are usually lost somewhere between latitudes 8°N and 2°N. The doldrums rarely exceed 2° in width in these longitudes and the switch to the SE trade winds of the South Pacific can be quite sudden, especially between May and August. South of latitude 8°N the proportion of southerly winds is always higher. The area is under the influence of all three equatorial currents, their direction, rate, and steadiness varying throughout the year. Sometimes in winter a very strong west-setting current makes itself felt between Christmas and Fanning islands, whereas in summer the countercurrent can be just as strong in its easterly set. Generally, the west-setting North Equatorial Current will be experienced down to about 10°N. The east-setting North Equatorial Countercurrent has been observed between latitudes 5°N and 8°N. South of 3°N to just below the equator, the current is again setting west. The latter is the South Equatorial Current.

From WP PN351, off Honolulu, course is set for WP PN352. Because winds will be NE as far as 5°N, and from there E and SE winds will prevail, some easting should be made in the early part of the voyage so as to approach the islands from windward. If possible, one should attempt to start off from one of the most eastern ports in Hawaii, in which case leaving from Honolulu is perhaps not such a good idea. If bound for Christmas Island, from WP PN352 the course should be altered for WP PN353, NW of that island. The island's well protected natural harbour is entered through Cook Island Passage (1°58'N, 157°29'W). Boats bound for Fanning, also known as Teraina, should set course for WP PN354, so as to approach that island from the north. However, it must be pointed out that because of the prevailing SE winds, sailing from Fanning to Christmas Island may not be easy, so one may have to choose between one or the other. The Northern Line Islands belong to Kiribati, and there are official entry procedures only at Christmas and Fanning (Teraina) Island. Otherwise, the comings and goings of cruising boats appear to be tolerated without formalities.

PN36 *Hawaii to Marshall Islands*

BEST TIME:	All year			
TROPICAL STORMS:	None			
CHARTS:	BA: 781, 782			
	US: 521			
PILOTS:	BA: 61, 62			
	US: 126, 152			
CRUISING GUIDES:	*Landfalls of Paradise.*			
WAYPOINTS:				

Departure	Intermediate	Landfall	Destination	Distance (M)
PN361 Oahu S	PN362 Johnston S	PN363 Majuro N	Majuro	1988
21°16'N, 157°51'W	16°30'N, 169°00'W	7°11'N, 171°09'E	*7°08'N, 171°22'E*	
			Ebeye	2197
			8°46'N, 167°44'E	

This is a downwind run all the way pushed along by the NE trades, which become more easterly in the proximity of the islands. Winds are less constant among the islands themselves and in summer the weather can be squally although the direction of the winds remains predominantly easterly. The unsettled summer weather is caused by the ITCZ moving north over the islands.

The North Equatorial Current and Equatorial Countercurrent set strongly through the archipelago producing a complex pattern. The set among the northern islands is mostly west while in the southern islands it is east. Because of the complexity of the currents and also because the islands are all low lying atolls, it is advisable to only sail among them in daylight and avoid night passages.

From WP PN361, off Honolulu, a direct route for Majuro passes close to the south of Johnston Atoll (16°50'N, 169°30'W). As navigation within 3 miles of this atoll is prohibited, course should be set for WP PN362, to pass well to the south of it. The route then continues north of Majuro Atoll to WP PN363. The large lagoon is entered through Calalin Pass on its western side (7°10'N, 171°10'E). The two mile wide pass is located between Eroj and Calalin Island and has a shallow area in the centre which divides it into two channels. The Port Authority should be contacted on VHF channel 16 as one approaches the atoll. Boats should proceed to Uliga dock where formalities are completed. The only ports of entry in the Marshalls are the capital Majuro and Ebeye, in Kwajalein Atoll. The latter should not be approached until radio contact has been established with Kwajalein Atoll Control as the area is used for missile testing by the US military. Boats arriving from overseas are strongly recommended to make their first entry at Majuro. Cruising in all islands is only allowed with a special permit which can be obtained in Majuro.

PN37 *Hawaii to Japan*

BEST TIME:	April to May, November
TROPICAL STORMS:	May to December
CHARTS:	BA: 4053
	US: 53
PILOTS:	BA: 42A, 42B, 62
	US: 152, 158, 159

WAYPOINTS:				
Departure	Intermediate	Landfall	Destination	Distance (M)
PN371 Oahu S 21°16'N, 157°51'W	PN372 18°00'N, 160°00'E PN373 26°00'N, 150°00'E PN374 30°00'N, 143°00'E	PN375 Shikoku 33°30'N, 135°00'E	Osaka 34°39'N, 135°24'E	4090

Favourable winds prevail along most of this route throughout the year, although the time of arrival in Japan must take into account the typhoon season in that part of the world. A passage in winter, when there is little or no danger of typhoons, is not recommended as the weather can be cold and stormy in Japan. A better time is late spring towards the end of the NE monsoon and before the start of the typhoon season. If planning to cruise in Japan, the best time to leave Hawaii is towards the end of March so as to arrive in Japan by late April or early May. Another alternative is to make the passage just before the onset of winter, late October or November being a good time in which both winds and current are favourable.

On leaving Hawaii the route runs due west along the Tropic of Cancer if the passage is made between April and September. Although conditions for a westbound passage appear to be the best in summer, the risk of encountering a typhoon in the Western Pacific makes summer passages far less attractive. Later in the year and during winter, the NE trades are steadier further south which makes it necessary to possibly go as far south as 16°N to be sure of favourable winds. The recommended route for November runs along latitude 18°N, although better winds might be found even further south. The North Equatorial Current sets west along this route throughout the year. The routes recommended for various times of the year start curving NW after meridian 160°E has been crossed. It is at that point that a decision has to be made whether to pass to the east or west of Ogasawara Gunto, the chain of islands stretching south of Japan. The recommended route for boats bound for ports east of Tokyo stays east of these islands. For ports in the west of Japan, better conditions will be found if the route passes to the west of the islands in Ogasawara Gunto. An interesting and convenient island in the latter group, in which an emergency stop can be made, is Chichishima (27°05'N, 142°11'E). The main settlement Omura is in the well sheltered Futami Ko Bay, which may become untenable in strong SW winds.

Leaving from Honolulu and WP PN371, depending on the time of year, the route will pass either south or north of Johnston Atoll. The route will have to avoid a number of dangers west of that atoll before passing through WP PN372. From there, the route turns NW towards WP PN373. It then carries on to WP PN374 from where it passes between the islands of Hahashima and Chichishima to make landfall at WP PN375, in the approaches to Osaka. Visiting yachts must clear in at one of the official ports of entry. One of the most conveniently located is Osaka, especially for those planning to cruise the Inland Sea.

PN38 *Hawaii to Guam*

BEST TIME:	January to March			
TROPICAL STORMS:	All year			
CHARTS:	BA: 4053			
	US: 526			
PILOTS:	BA: 42A, 62			
	US: 152, 158			
CRUISING GUIDES:	*Landfalls of Paradise.*			
WAYPOINTS:				
Departure	*Intermediate*	*Landfall*	*Destination*	*Distance (M)*
PN380 Honolulu	PN381 Oahu SW			
21°18'N, 157°52'W	21°15'N, 157°55'W			
	PN382 Rional	PN383 Guam N	Apra	3338
	18°00'N, 177°20'E	13°50'N, 144°55'E	*13°27'N, 144°37'E*	

The steady NE trade winds of winter should ensure a fast passage all the way. Although in theory typhoons can affect Guam at any time of the year, the highest risk is from May to December. East Pacific hurricanes rarely reach as far as Hawaii before August, so the early part of the year can be considered safe. Nevertheless, as one approaches the Marianas, the weather should be monitored constantly so as to be able to take evading action should a typhoon head that way. Because of the good facilities available in Honolulu, this is a good port of departure. The initial route passes to the north of a group of reefs, of which Rional Reef is the nothernmost. Landfall is made NE of Guam, from where the course is altered to the SW and the approaches to Apra Harbour. On arrival, visiting boats need to contact Apra Port Control on channels 12, 13 and 16. Normally cruising boats are directed to the commercial pier for clearance.

ROUTES IN THE FAR EAST

Compared to other parts of the world, cruising routes in the Far East do not fall into a logical pattern, because the area is off the beaten track and the weather is unpredictable. The western part of the North Pacific is far from major cruising routes and Far Eastern countries can only by reached by a lengthy detour. However, many more cruising boats might venture to explore its remoteness were it not for the often appalling weather. Virtually the entire area is subject to violent typhoons, which limit the safe sailing season to only a few months per year. As most distances involved are very long, it usually means that one must be prepared to remain there between seasons and spend the typhoon season in or near a safe anchorage, of which fortunately there are many. Although tropical storms have been recorded in every month of the year, May to December is regarded as the typhoon season.

The three main cruising areas are the Philippines, Japan, and Micronesia. The attraction of the Philippines is the generally pleasant climate and the great number of islands, inlets, and bays to explore. Although typhoons strike the archipelago with regularity, there are many good anchorages where shelter can be sought. The Inland Sea of Japan and the great number of small fishing harbours make Japan an attractive cruising destination, although the safe sailing season is very short. The scattered islands of Micronesia are much closer in character to the islands of the South Pacific and are in fact convenient stepping stones between the South Pacific and the Far East.

The main drawback of the Far East remains, however, the difficulty of getting there. In spite of the favourable NE trade winds that blow across the North Pacific ensuring a fast and pleasant sail from the west coast of America, the number of North American yachts that embark on such a transpacific voyage is very small. They are much more likely to be tempted by the lure of the South Seas and sail to the South Pacific instead, although some venture into the North West Pacific at a later stage, most reaching the Far East via Papua New Guinea and Micronesia. Another route sailed by cruising boats to reach the Far East through the Philippines and Hong Kong is the route originating in Singapore. The reports of piracy in the South China Sea in the 1980s had dissuaded many sailors from using that route. The situation has greatly improved as a result of the gradual liberalisation of Vietnam and the region surrounding it may soon become an attractive cruising destination. For the time being, the best solution for boats starting off from Singapore is to follow the north coast of Borneo, where stops can be made in the small states of Sarawak, Brunei, or Sabah. The other alternative is to arrive in the Far East via Papua New Guinea at the end of a cruise in the South Pacific. Yet another possibility is to sail nonstop to Japan from the west coast of North America or Hawaii and either continue the voyage towards Singapore and the Indian Ocean, or sail south through Papua New Guinea to Australia, across to New Zealand and along the southern route to Tahiti.

PN40 PACIFIC ROUTES FROM SINGAPORE

The majority of cruising boats arrive in Singapore either from the south, through Indonesia, or the NW through the Malacca Strait, and most leave by the same routes. Very few venture eastward from Singapore, although there is an increasing traffic of locally owned yachts, some of which commute between the various regional yacht races, such as the annual King's Cup Regatta in Phuket or the Hong Kong to Manila Race. The gradual opening of Vietnam to foreign tourism will undoubtedly attract more cruising boats to that area. An equally interesting cruising area is the north coast of Borneo. The Philippines are another area waiting to be visited by more cruising boats. The compulsory cruising permit for Indonesia discourages short cruises between Singapore and its southern neighbour, but an easing of restrictions is already underway and a few Indonesian islands close to Singapore can now be visited without a cruising permit.

PN40 *Pacific routes from Singapore*

PN41 *Singapore to the Gulf of Siam*

BEST TIME:	May to October			
TROPICAL STORMS:	May to December			
CHARTS:	BA: 4508 US: 632			
PILOTS:	BA: 30 US: 160, 161			
WAYPOINTS:				
Departure	*Intermediate*	*Landfall*	*Destination*	*Distance (M)*
PN411 Channel N 1°30'N, 104°20'E	PN412 2°45'N, 104°15'E			
	PN413 6°00'N, 104°00'E	PN414 13°00'N,100°35'E	Bangkok *13°23'N,100°36'E*	763

The best time to sail this route, which runs parallel to the east coast of continental Malaysia, is during the SW monsoon. On leaving the Strait of Singapore through the North Channel, from WP PN411 a course is set for WP PN412. The route passes west of Pulau Pemanggil, one of the smaller Tioman Islands, an attractive archipelago belonging to Malaysia, where a stop should be considered. From WP PN412, the route runs due north parallel to the Malaysian coast to WP PN413, close to the point where the route enters Thai waters.

From there the course can be altered for WP PN414, near Ko Phai light and Bangkok Pilot Station, in the approaches to Bangkok (Krung Thep) at the entrance to the buoyed channel leading across Bangkok Bar. The busy port of Bangkok has spread on both shores of the Chao Phraya river and can hardly be recommended as a cruising destination in itself. Visiting boats should head for Pattaya, where the Royal Varuna Yacht Club is based, and complete entry formalities with the help of the Yacht Club.

PN42 *Singapore to Vietnam*

BEST TIME:	April–May, November				
TROPICAL STORMS:	May to December				
CHARTS:	BA: 4508				
	US: 632				
PILOTS:	BA: 30				
	US: 160, 161				
WAYPOINTS:					

Departure	Intermediate	Landfall	Destination	Distance (M)
PN421 Channel N 1°30'N, 104°20'E		PN422 Mekong 10°35'N, 106°30'E	Ho Chi Minh *10°47'N, 106°42'E*	577
PN421 Channel N	PN423 Chadwick 10°00'N, 108°45'E			
	PN424 Dao 10°35'N, 109°00'E	PN425 Mui 12°10'N, 109°22'E	Nha Trang *12°16'N, 109°12'E*	725

Similar directions apply as for route PN41 as far as the Tioman Islands, if a stop there is intended. The best time to sail to Vietnam is the same as for the Gulf of Siam as sailing anywhere in this area should be timed to take full advantage of the two monsoons: NE monsoon in winter (December to April) and SW monsoon in summer (May to October).

Boats intending to sail direct to Vietnam, on leaving the Strait of Singapore through the North Channel, from WP PN421 course is set for WP PN422, W of Con Son Island, in the approaches to the channel leading through the shallow waters of the Mekong Delta. Ho Chi Minh City, the former Saigon, stands on the west bank of the Song Sai Gon river. The former South Vietnamese capital is about 40 miles from the sea and access to it is by one of two dredged channels. Anchorage in the river is prohibited except well away from the city.

A more convenient destination on the east coast is the port of Nha Trang, the seaport of the provincial capital Dien Khanh and now the finish of a regular race from Hong Kong. The recommended route passes to the west of Mangkai Island and also the Udang oil field, which should be approached with caution. The course leads to WP PN423 just to the west of the Chadwick Islands. From there the course is altered to pass east of Dao Phu Qui. This is an area of shallows frequented by Vietnamese fishing boats, so due care should be exercised when navigating in these waters. Landfall will be made close to Mui Rach Trang at the entrance into Nha Trang Bay, but attention is drawn to the dangerous rocks that extend to seaward from the eastern extremity of Hontre Island. The port of Nha Trang, which lies on the south bank of the Song Cai river, can be reached by either leaving Hontre Island to port and using the main shipping channel that leads into Nha Trang, or through the scenic channel between the mainland and the islets south of Hontre. Facilities in Nha Trang are limited and visiting boats usually anchor approximately one mile offshore. Entry formalities are long and time consuming.

Because foreign cruising boats are still subject to certain restrictions, before the start of the voyage permission to visit Nha Trang, or any other

Vietnamese port, should be sought from one of the Vietnamese diplomatic missions in the region. Permission to visit must be obtained from several government departments and the cost can be several thousand US dollars. Other official ports of entry are Pan Thiet (10°55.4'N, 108°06.3'E) and Qui Non (13°45.7'N, 119°15'E).

PN43 *Singapore to Hong Kong*

BEST TIME:	May to June			
TROPICAL STORMS:	May to December			
CHARTS:	BA: 4508			
	US: 632			
PILOTS:	BA: 30, 31			
	US: 157, 160, 161, 162			
WAYPOINTS:				
Departure	*Intermediate*	*Landfall*	*Destination*	*Distance (M)*
Route PN43A				
PN430 Channel N	PN431 Chadwick			
1°30'N, 104°20'E	10°00'N, 109°43'E			
	PN432 Paracel W	PN433		
	17°05'N, 111°20'E	Hong Kong SW	Hong Kong	1390
		22°00'N, 114°04'E	*22°18'N, 114°10'E*	
Route PN43B				
PN434 Channel M	PN435 Natuna			
1°25'N, 104°25'E	3°30'N, 108°25'E			
	PN436 Luconia			
	4°20'N, 112°30'E			
	PN437 Balabac			
	7°35'N, 117°00'E			
	PN438 Palawan	PN439		
	10°30'N, 118°00'E	Hong Kong SE	Hong Kong	1784
		22°10'N, 114°22'E		

Direct passages through the South China Sea must avoid a large area of reefs and associated dangers north of Borneo. In the past the recommended route passed between the north coast of Borneo and this reef area and re-entered the South China Sea through the Palawan Passage. As described in route PN42, the recent changes in Vietnam have made it possible to sail close to the shores of that country and this has considerably shortened the distance to Hong Kong for those who prefer to sail this shorter route (PN43A). Those who intend to stop in North Borneo or the Philippines will con-

tinue to use the traditional route through Palawan Passage (PN43B).

The most favourable winds on either of these routes will be found at the start of the SW monsoon and although more consistent winds can be expected in July and August, the increased likelihood of typhoons in the area around Hong Kong makes passages in late summer too risky. Winter passages are not threatened by typhoons but are very difficult to accomplish as this is the time of the NE monsoon when strong NE winds and an equally strong south flowing current occur north of Borneo. A winter passage is best undertaken in short stages with stops along the north coast of Borneo, as described in routes PN44 and PN45.

Boats sailing route PN43A to Hong Kong should leave the Strait of Singapore through the North Channel. From WP PN430 the route passes W of Mangkai Island to WP PN431, 30 miles E of the Chadwick Islands, off Vietnam's SE coast. The route continues in a northerly direction parallel to the Vietnamese coast to WP PN432, 15 miles W of North Reef, the westernmost reef in the Paracel Islands. From there a course can be set for WP PN433, in the SW approaches to Hong Kong.

Route PN43B leaves the Strait of Singapore through the Middle Channel. From WP PN434 the route runs between South Natuna and Subi Kechil islands to WP PN435. From there, a course is set for WP PN436, south of Luconia Shoals. From WP PN436 a straight course can be steered for WP PN437, 12 miles S of Melville Island at the entrance into Balabac Strait. From there the route

to Hong Kong continues through Palawan Passage. The narrowest part of this passage is 28 miles wide, where it is bound on the west by Captain Royal Shoal and on the east by Balabac Island. As the currents set strongly eastward through the Balabac Strait, Balabac Island should not be approached in bad weather. In the area between Borneo and Palawan, the currents often behave erratically and many vessels have come to grief on either side of Palawan passage when going through in poor visibility. From WP PN438, at the northern entrance into Palawan Passage, a direct course, which passes east of Macclesfield Bank, can be set for WP PN439, in the SE approaches to Hong Kong. Visiting yachts are welcome at the Royal Hong Kong Club, located in Victoria Harbour, on the N side of Hong Kong Island. Arriving yachts should contact Port Operation Service on VHF channel 12 and proceed to the western quarantine anchorage. Because of the heavy amount of shipping, it is essential to time one's arrival for daylight hours.

PN44 *Singapore to the Philippines*

BEST TIME:	May to July
TROPICAL STORMS:	May to December
CHARTS:	BA: 4508
	US: 632
PILOTS:	BA: 30, 31, 33
	US: 160, 161, 163, 166
WAYPOINTS:	

Departure	Intermediate	Landfall	Destination	Distance (M)
Route PN44A				
PN441 Channel M 1°25'N, 104°25'E	PN442 Natuna 3°30'N, 108°25'E			
	PN443 Luconia 4°20'N, 112°30'E	PN445 Balabac 7°35'N, 117°00'E		855
PN441 Channel M	PN442 Natuna PN443 Luconia PN446 Saracen 6°10'N, 115°00'E			
	PN447 Palawan 10°40'N, 118°00'E	PN448 Luzon 14°25'N, 120°15'E	Manila *14°35'N,120°58'E*	1336
Route PN44B				
PN441 Channel M	PN444 Api 1°35'N, 108°35'E			
	PN443 Luconia PN446 Saracen	PN445 Balabac		872
	PN447 Palawan	PN448 Luzon	Manila	1353

Few boats attempt to make this passage without stopping as there are a number of convenient ports on the north coast of Borneo. A passage during the SW monsoon offers the best chance of favourable winds, but such a summer passage also carries the risk of typhoons as one approaches the Philippines. Typhoons, however, are less frequent in the southern half of that archipelago so one should plan on restricting one's cruising to that area during the critical period. There would be less risks from typhoons if the passage is made during the NE monsoon, but then the winds will be mostly contrary. As the route runs along the coast of Borneo, the voyage can be interrupted in any one of the three states bordering on the South China Sea and there are several ports in Sarawak, Brunei and Sabah where yachts can find good shelter.

There are two variants which can be sailed on this route. Having left the Strait of Singapore through the Middle Channel, from WP PN441, the more northern route (PN44A) runs between South Natuna and Subi Kechil islands to WP PN442. From there, a course is set for WP PN443, south of Luconia Shoals.

The alternative route (PN44B), also leaving the Strait of Singapore at WP PN441, goes first to WP PN444 by passing south of a group of small islands, the closest of which is Pulau Kajuara. From WP PN444, the course turns NE and goes through Api Passage, NW of Borneo, to join the other route at WP PN443, south of Luconia Shoals. In all these

passes attention must be paid to the currents, which can be very strong at times. Another hazard along the north coast of Borneo are the various oil platforms, most of which are lit.

From WP PN443 boats bound for the Southern Philippines can set a straight course for WP PN445, 12 miles S of Melville Island at the entrance into Balabac Strait. From Balabac Strait the route enters the Sulu Sea, where conditions can be quite rough during the NE monsoon. This is one of the reasons why the inside route through the Sulu Sea is not necessarily the best if bound for Luzon and Manila. Ports in the Northern Philippines are better reached through the Palawan Passage, as described below.

Boats bound for ports in the Northern Philippines and intending to use the Palawan Passage, should alter course at WP PN443, off Luconia Shoals, for WP PN446, west of Saracen Bank. From there a direct course can be set which leads through the Palawan Passage to WP PN447. From there, the same course is maintained to WP PN448, off Luzon Point in the approaches to Manila.

The alternative to the above routes is to break up the passage into shorter stages by calling at ports in the Natuna Islands, Sarawak and Brunei. A convenient stop on the NE corner of Borneo is Kota Kinabalu, the capital of Sabah, one of the states belonging to the Federation of Malaysia. Details of these stops are described in route PN45.

PN45 *Singapore to North Borneo*

BEST TIME:	May to July			
TROPICAL STORMS:	May to December			
CHARTS:	BA: 4508			
	US: 632			
PILOTS:	BA: 31			
	US: 160, 161, 163			
WAYPOINTS:				
Departure	*Intermediate*	*Landfall*	*Destination*	*Distance (M)*
PN451 Channel M	PN454 Api		Kuching	357
1°25'N, 104°25'E	1°35'N, 108°35'E		*1°34'N, 110°21'E*	
			Muara	692
			5°02'N, 115°04'E	
			Kota Kinabalu	772
			5°59'N, 116°03'E	

Most boats bound for the Philippines and beyond take advantage of the conveniently placed ports on the north coast of Borneo to break the voyage in one of the states belonging to the Federation of Malaysia. From the Strait of Singapore and WP PN451, the route leads to WP PN452, close to the Api Passage, passing south of a group of small islands, the closest of which is Pulau Kajuara. A first stop can be made in Natuna Besar, a group of islands belonging to Indonesia. The main port is Genting, on Sedanau Island (3°45'N, 108°00'E). As there is a dispute over the islands between Indonesia and Malaysia, only emergency stops are allowed.

From Api Passage the route follows closely the coast of Sarawak, one of the states in the Malaysian Federation. Its capital Kuching is 22 miles up the river Sarawak. There are sand bars across the river entrance, but they only cause problems to deep drafted boats.

The next country on Borneo's north coast is Brunei. The main port of this oil rich state is Muara, at the mouth of the river on which is also the capital of Brunei, Bandar Seri Bagawan. Further east, on the NE corner of Borneo, is the state of Sabah, whose capital is Kota Kinabalu.

The area is rarely affected by typhoons and the effect of the monsoons is also less noticeable than further north. Especially during the early part of the SW monsoon, winds are often light, there are frequent calms and, if sailing close to the coast, land and sea breezes are more reliable than seasonal winds. A good reserve of fuel should be carried as much of the distance may have to be covered under power. The SW monsoon becomes stronger towards the end of summer.

PN50 ROUTES FROM THE PHILIPPINES

Rumours of piracy in the notorious Sulu Sea, difficulties with the officials, and the threat of typhoons have all combined to keep most cruising boats away from this beautiful and interesting country. As in other parts of the world, some of these points may have been exaggerated and reports from cruising boats which have visited the Philippines recently paint a brighter picture.

Over 7,000 islands make up this large archipelago and with so many in such a large area it is obvious that local weather conditions will vary considerably. Prevailing winds blowing over the islands are influenced mainly by monsoons in the China Sea, the Philippines forming a border between this sea and the Pacific Ocean. The NE monsoon blows from mid-October until mid-May and this is regarded as the fine season, with dry, clear weather.

The SW monsoon only becomes well established from July and lasts until October. During the latter part of this period the weather becomes squally with violent gales, which can last for several days. These gales usually begin from the N or NW and back to SW or S, blowing strongly with heavy rain. September to November are the worst months for this kind of weather. This is also the period during which typhoons strike these waters. These storms usually originate to the SE of the islands and move across them into the China Sea, some reaching the China coast, while others curve up towards Japan. The Philippines have one of the highest incidence of typhoons and although the main season is from June to October they can possibly occur at any time between May and December.

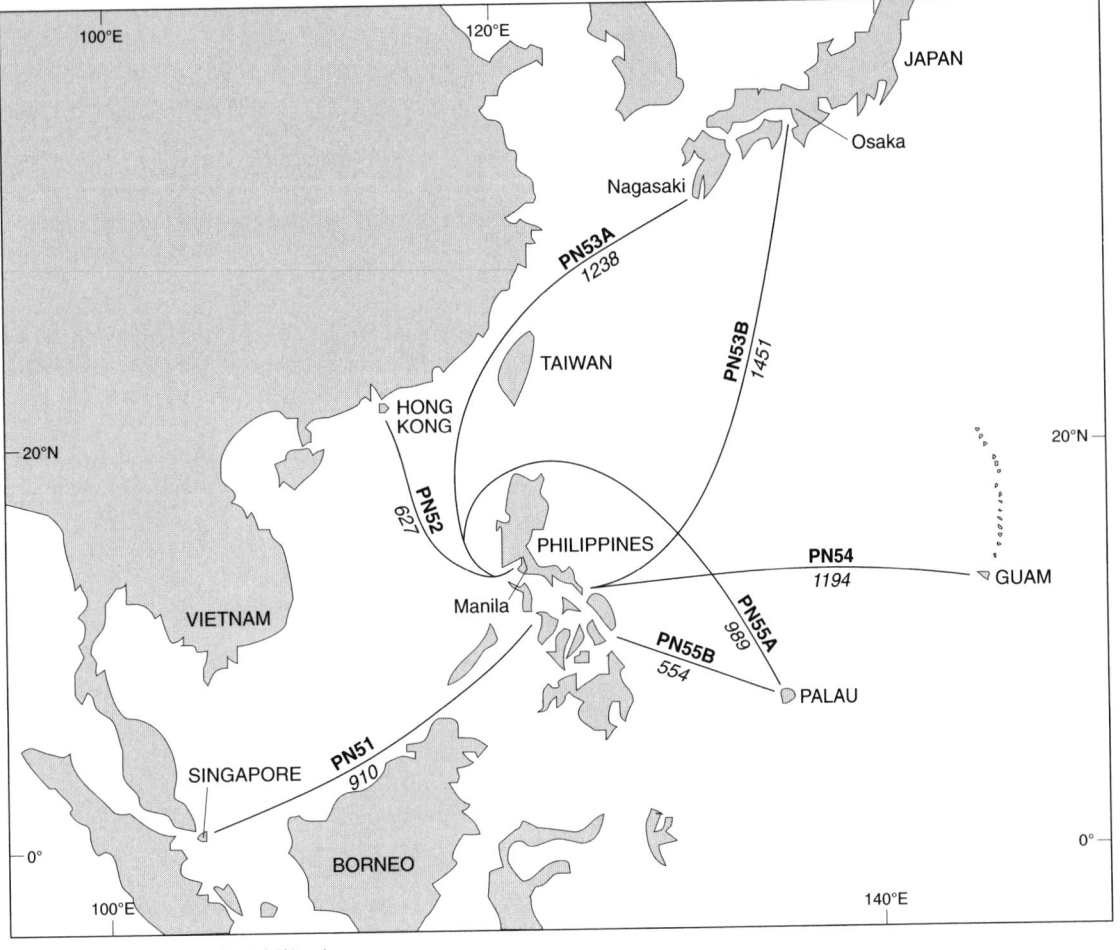

PN50 *Routes from the Philippines*

PN51 *Philippines to Singapore*

BEST TIME:	January to March			
TROPICAL STORMS:	May to December			
CHARTS:	BA: 4508			
	US: 524			
PILOTS:	BA: 30, 31, 33, 44			
	US: 157, 160, 161			
WAYPOINTS:				
Departure	*Intermediate*	*Landfall*	*Destination*	*Distance (M)*
Route PN51A				
PN511 Melville	PN512 Luconia			
7°35'N, 117°00'E	4°20'N, 112°30'E			
	PN513	PN514 Channel M	Singapore	893
	3°30'N, 108°25'E	1°25'N, 104°25'E	*1°16'N, 103°50'E*	
Route PN51B				
PN511 Melville	PN512 Luconia			
	PN515 Api	PN514 Channel M	Singapore	910
	1°35'N, 108°35'E			

Because of the low incidence of tropical storms in the areas traversed by this route, southbound passages can be made at any time of the year, although more favourable sailing conditions occur during the months in which the NE monsoon is well established. During summer and the SW monsoon, typhoons occasionally pass through the Philippines and therefore offshore passages are best avoided, particularly during the peak months of August and September. As these are also the months when the SW monsoon is blowing at its strongest, passages should indeed be left for another time.

After leaving the Sulu Sea through Balabac Strait, from WP PN511, 12 miles south of Melville Island, the route runs parallel to the north coast of Borneo to WP PN512, south of Luconia Shoals. From there, Singapore can be reached either through Api Passage, close to the NW extremity of Borneo, or by an offshore route that goes through the pass separating Subi Kechil Island and the Natuna Islands. To take the offshore route (PN51A), from WP PN512 a course is set for WP PN513 before altering course for WP PN514 to negotiate the Strait of

Singapore through the Middle Channel.

The more southern route (PN51B) splits from WP PN512 in a SW direction and passes through Api Passage to WP PN515. From there a course is set for WP PN514 and the Strait of Singapore passing south of a group of small islands, the closest of which is Pulau Kajuara. Boats arriving in Singapore from the east may find it easier to go to the anchorage off the Changi Yacht Club, NE of Singapore Island, and complete entry formalities from there. The alternative is the new Raffles Marina (1°20.53'N, 103°38.22'E), on the west coast of Singapore Island.

Few boats sail this route without stopping in one of the three small states in North Borneo, all of which have excellent harbours, Kota Kinabalu (5°59'N, 116°03'E) in Sabah, Muara in Brunei (5°02'N, 115°04'E), and Kuching in Sarawak (1°34'N, 110°21'E). A stop in any of these ports is particularly welcome during the SW monsoon when contrary winds and currents make this passage slow and tedious. All those ports are described in more detail in route PN45 (page 288).

PN52 *Philippines to Hong Kong*

BEST TIME:	Mid-December to mid-March			
TROPICAL STORMS:	May to December			
CHARTS:	BA: 4508			
	US: 524			
PILOTS:	BA: 30, 31, 33			
	US: 157, 162			
WAYPOINTS:				

Departure	*Intermediate*	*Landfall*	*Destination*	*Distance (M)*
Manila *14°35'N, 120°58'E*	PN521 Luzon *14°25'N, 120°22'E*	PN523 Hong Kong SE 22°00'N, 114°22'E	Hong Kong *22°18'N, 114°10'E*	627
San Fernando *16°37'N, 120°19'E*	PN522 Lingayen *16°40'N, 120°15'E*	PN523 Hong Kong SE	Hong Kong	488

This passage is usually made either direct from Manila Bay or from one of the ports further north along the west coast of Luzon. Whichever point of departure is chosen, the passage presents no problems during the NE monsoon, when favourable conditions can be expected for the entire passage, although the winds can be quite strong. The best time to do this passage is from mid-December to mid-March. During the remainder of the year, particular attention must be paid to tropical depressions forming in the South China Sea or even further afield, as these can develop into fully fledged typhoons before a safe harbour can be reached.

Pratas Reef should be given a wide berth, and unless the weather is clear and settled it should not be passed too close on its windward side. During the NE monsoon, when strong winds and overcast skies can last for several days, vessels approaching Pratas Reef from the S or SE should check their position frequently, as many vessels have been lost on this reef due to a doubtful position.

The busy port of Manila attracts fewer cruising boats than in the past. Boats leaving from there take their leave at WP PN521, off Luzon Point. A direct course can be set from there for Hong Kong and WP PN523. A more popular port, and a better point of departure from the Philippines, is San Fernando, north of Manila. To leave from there, a direct course for Hong Kong can be set from WP PN522 for WP PN523, in the approaches to Hong Kong. Visiting yachts are welcome at the Royal Hong Kong Yacht Club, located in Victoria Harbour, on the N side of Hong Kong Island. Arriving yachts should contact Port Operation Service on VHF channel 12 and proceed to the western quarantine anchorage. Because of the heavy amount of shipping, it is essential to time one's arrival for daylight hours.

PN53 *Philippines to Japan*

BEST TIME:	May			
TROPICAL STORMS:	May to December			
CHARTS:	BA: 4509			
	US: 522			
PILOTS:	BA: 33, 42A, 42B			
	US: 158, 159, 162			

WAYPOINTS:				
Departure	*Intermediate*	*Landfall*	*Destination*	*Distance (M)*
Route PN53A				
San Fernando	PN531 Lingayen			
16°37'N, 120°19'E	*16°40'N, 120°15'E*			
	PN532 Taiwan N			
	23°00'N, 118°30'E			
	PN533 East China	PN534 Kyushu	Nagasaki	1238
	27°30'N, 123°00'E	*32°45'N, 129°45'E*	*32°43'N, 129°50'E*	
Route PN53B				
PN535 Bernardino		PN536 Murato	Osaka	1451
12°40'N, 124°20'E		*33°10'N, 134°50'E*	*34°39'N, 135°24'E*	
Route PN53C				
PN535 Bernardino		PN537 Okinawa	Naha	835
		26°08'N, 127°37'E	*26°13'N, 127°40'E*	

The best time to make this passage is in May, at the beginning of the SW monsoon, when the danger of being overtaken by an early typhoon is minimal. The winds are generally favourable for most of the passage, although calms can be expected when approaching the Japanese coast. The offshore route follows the Kuro Shio current, which sets NE at a considerable rate especially during the SW monsoon. Occasionally the weather can be quite rough as one passes from one wind system to the next and attention should be paid to the movement of frontal systems. An equally alert watch must be kept for the large amount of shipping in this area, both commercial and fishing.

Depending on the port of destination, the route can stay either east or west of Nansei Shoto (Ryukyu), the chain of islands which stretch between Japan and Taiwan. The western route (PN53A) enters the East China Sea through Taiwan Strait and then heads for the SW coast of Kyushu, where a convenient port of entry into Japan is Nagasaki. From San Fernando and WP PN531, the initial route goes almost due north towards Taiwan Strait and WP PN532. The route crosses the shallow Taiwan Bank, where rough seas may be encountered in strong winds and which also has a

high concentration of fishing boats. Having passed through Taiwan Strait, the route runs parallel to the mainland coast across the East China Sea and makes landfall at WP PN534.

At the change of seasons, or perhaps right at the beginning of the SW monsoon, a direct offshore passage (PN53B) can be feasible. In such a case, the most convenient place to leave the Philippines is through the Bernardino Strait. From WP PN535 the offshore route leads to WP PN536 off Murato Saki in the approaches to Osaka. The latter is a convenient port of entry and also a good starting point for those wishing to enter the Inland Sea (Seto Naikai) from the east.

If one cannot avoid sailing to Japan during the NE monsoon of winter, very strong NW winds can be expected for the best part of the passage. The main advantage of a passage during that season is the absence of typhoons. Early in the year, in February or March, an alternative to beating into the wind by sailing the offshore route nonstop, is to head for Okinawa and start cruising among the Japanese islands from there. Starting from the SW extremity of the Japanese archipelago, it is then easier to move NE along the chain of islands. The port of entry on Okinawa is Naha.

PN54 *Philippines to Guam*

BEST TIME:	July to September			
TROPICAL STORMS:	May to December			
CHARTS:	BA: 781			
	US: 524			
PILOTS:	BA: 33, 60			
	US: 126, 162			
CRUISING GUIDES:	*Landfalls of Paradise.*			
WAYPOINTS:				

Departure	Intermediate	Landfall	Destination	Distance (M)
Route PN54A				
PN541 Bernardino	PN542	PN543 Guam	Apra	1194
12°40'N, 124°20'E	13°00'N, 140°00'E	13°27'N, 144°34'E	*13°27'N, 144°37'E*	
Route PN54B				
PN544 Babuyan		PN543 Guam	Apra	1322
18°45'N, 122°20'E				

The steadiness of the NE trade winds and the west-setting current during winter, when the risk of typhoons is lowest, precludes the possibility of making this passage during the safe season. The only time when a reasonable proportion of fair winds can be expected is during the SW monsoon (PN54A). At this time the proportion of easterly winds is indeed much lower, but the risk of typhoons is very high. Leaving from San Bernardino Strait at WP PN541 the route goes almost due east to WP PN542. From there course is altered to make landfall at WP PN543, off Guam, where formalities are completed in Apra Harbour.

Harbour Control should be contacted on arrival on VHF channels 12, 13, or 16. Cruising boats are normally directed to the commercial pier for clearance.

If this passage is considered during the NE monsoon (PN54B), a better slant should be achieved by sailing around the north of Luzon passing through the Babuyan Islands. From WP PN544 a direct course can be set for Guam and WP PN543.

Because of the difficulty of making easting at almost any time along this route, and also the risk of typhoons during most months, an alternative is to make a detour via Palau (7°20'N, 134°27'E) and Yap (9°30'N, 138°08'E) as described in route PN55.

PN55 *Philippines to Palau*

BEST TIME:	January to March			
TROPICAL STORMS:	May to December			
CHARTS:	BA: 781			
	US: 524			
PILOTS:	BA: 33, 60			
	US: 126, 162			
CRUISING GUIDES:	*Landfalls of Paradise.*			
WAYPOINTS:				

Departure	Intermediate	Landfall	Destination	Distance (M)
Route PN55A				
PN551 Babuyan		PN552 Palau W	Malakal	989
18°45'N, 122°20'E		7°32'N, 134°28'E	*7°20'N, 134°27'E*	

Departure	Intermediate	Landfall	Destination	Distance (M)
Route PN55B PN553 Surigao 10°30'N, 125°50'E		PN552 Palau W	Malakal	554

Most boats normally sail this route as part of a longer trip to the South Pacific. The best time for making this passage is during the winter months when there is little danger of being caught out by a typhoon. The first part of the passage is under the influence of the NE monsoon, which from December to March can blow quite strongly, although the NE winds gradually become lighter in the vicinity of Palau. The North Equatorial Current has a strong westerly set in this region and this should be taken into account.

Because of the high proportion of NE and E winds in the latitude of San Bernardino Strait, an attempt should be made to leave the Philippines as far north as possible to benefit from a better angle across the prevailing winds. During the NE monsoon, a better sailing angle can be achieved by sailing around the north of Luzon (PN55A) to WP PN551 and setting course from there for WP PN552, off Palau. Boats arriving from the west use Toagel Mlungui Pass (7°32'N, 134°29'E) to reach Komebail

lagoon, on the west side of Babeltuap Island, before entering Malakal Harbour. This is the official port of entry into Palau. Yachts must not stop anywhere before Malakal and the Port Authority must be informed in advance of a yacht's ETA. Yachts arriving without a permit, which must be obtained in advance, may only be allowed to stay for a maximum three days.

If the passage is made outside the NE monsoon, the argument in favour of a better sailing angle is less important and the Philippines may be left from further south. During the transition period, or at the very start of the SW monsoon, it is then possible to leave the Philippines through the Surigao Strait (PN55B), east of Leyte Island, and set a direct course for Palau from WP PN553. This is a shorter route than the one described previously, but as it cannot be sailed during the relatively safe winter months, the risk of being caught by a tropical storm must be weighed up against it.

PN60 ROUTES FROM HONG KONG

In spite of a large and active local sailing community, Hong Kong is visited by few cruising boats. This is probably explained by Hong Kong's remoteness from the most popular cruising routes, but also because of the relative shortness of the safe sailing season. Although sailing in the immediate vicinity of Hong Kong is safe throughout the year because of the proximity of several typhoon shelters, there are hardly any cruising areas in the vicinity to tempt foreign sailors. The situation may change now that Hong Kong has reverted to China and it is hoped that more of China will be accessible to visiting

boats. For the time being cruising in mainland China is severely limited and foreign yachts may only stop at a number of designated ports.

On the edge of the tropics, Hong Kong has a seasonal climate with well marked seasons. The winter from November to April is the time of the NE monsoon, with cooler temperatures and a lower humidity. The summer, from May to October, is hot and steamy with plenty of rain. This is the time of the SW monsoon. During this period bad depressions from the SE and SSE affect Hong Kong and these can build up into typhoons. These storms usually start in the Pacific east of the Philippines and then move NW. Typhoons are most frequent between May and October, but they can occur at the beginning of the NE season as well.

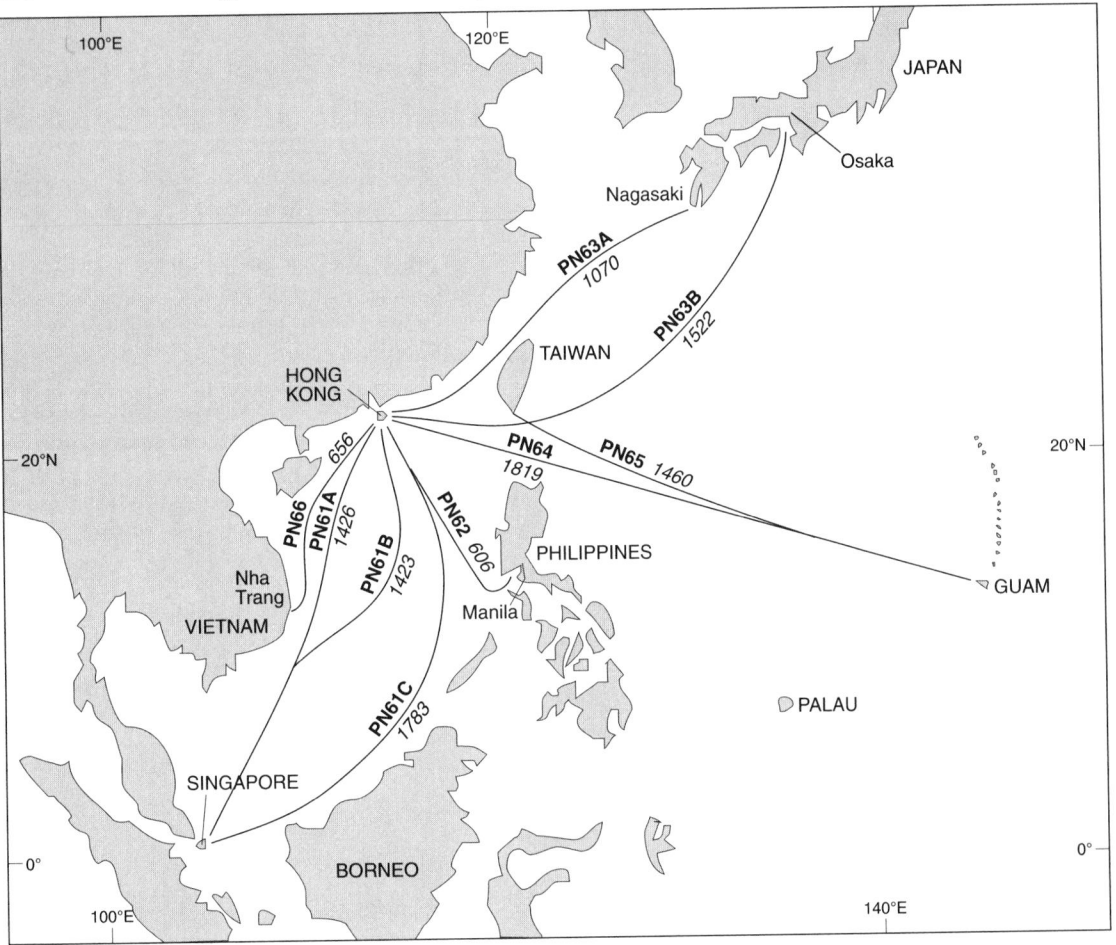

PN60 *Routes from Hong Kong*

PN61 *Hong Kong to Singapore*

BEST TIME:	January to March			
TROPICAL STORMS:	May to December			
CHARTS:	BA: 4508	US: 632		
PILOTS:	BA: 30, 31	US: 157, 160, 161, 162, 163		
WAYPOINTS:				
Departure	*Intermediate*	*Landfall*	*Destination*	*Distance (M)*
Route PN61A				
PN610 Hong Kong SW	PN612 Paracel W			
22°00'N, 114°05'E	15°00'N, 110°00'E			
	PN613 Chadwick	PN619 Channel M	Singapore	1426
	10°30'N, 110°00'E	1°25'N, 104°25'E	*1°16'N, 103°50'E*	

Departure	Intermediate	Landfall	Destination	Distance (M)
Route PN61B				
PN610 Hong Kong SW	PN614 Paracel E 15°00'N, 113°00'E			
	PN613 Chadwick	PN619 Channel M	Singapore	1423
Route PN61C				
PN611 Hong Kong SW 22°00'N, 114°22'E	PN615 Palawan N 9°40'N, 117°30'E			
	PN616 Melville 7°35'N, 117°00'E			
	PN617 Luconia 4°20'N, 112°30'E			
	PN618 3°30'N, 108°25'E	PN619 Channel M	Singapore	1783

Most favourable conditions on this route occur at the height of the NE monsoon, when steady winds and a south flowing current ensure a fast passage. The route can be sailed for the entire duration of the NE monsoon, from October to April, although less consistent winds and squally weather can be expected during the transitional period. During the winter months the risk of typhoons in the Hong Kong area is slight, whereas in the southern part of the South China Sea, the Gulf of Siam, and all of Northern Indonesia, tropical storms are extremely rare in all seasons.

Because the more direct route (PN61A) passes close to Vietnam, that route should only be sailed if one can keep out of that country's territorial waters. The gradual opening of Vietnam to foreign visitors has resulted in an easing of restrictions imposed on cruising yachts. The latest situation should be ascertained before setting off on this passage as it may be possible to stop at one of the Vietnamese ports en route (see PN66). The alternative is to use a more easterly route, which cuts right across the centre of the South China Sea (PN61B). Yet another alternative is to sail a route passing close to the Philippines and Borneo (PN61C).

Taking one's departure from Hong Kong at WP PN610 route PN61A crosses the Gulf of Tonkin to WP PN612. This route passes some 15 miles west of North Reef, the westernmost danger in the Paracel Islands. From WP PN612, the route runs due south along meridian 110°E parallel to the Vietnamese coast and passes some 30 miles east of Cape Varella to WP PN613, NE of the Chadwick

Islands. From there, the route passes NW of Natuna Islands and close to the west of Mangkai Island, the westernmost island in the Anambas Group. The route enters the Strait of Singapore through the Middle Channel at WP PN619.

The alternative route (PN61B), which also leaves from WP PN610, avoids the vicinity of Vietnam and passes east of the Paracel Islands to WP PN614. From there course is altered to join route PN61A at WP PN613. Route PN61C takes its leave from Hong Kong at WP PN611. The route runs east of Macclesfield Bank to WP PN615, in the northern approaches to Palawan Passage. Throughout this area extreme caution is necessary when sailing past the various dangers which are difficult to see in poor visibility, the situation being compounded by the complexity of the currents. The most dangerous area is in the southern part of Palawan Passage, close to Balabac Strait, where strong currents make navigation hazardous. Having negotiated Palawan Passage, from WP PN616, 12 miles south of Melville Island, the route runs parallel to the north coast of Borneo to WP PN617, south of Luconia Shoals. The course is then altered for WP PN618 and finally WP PN619 at the entrance into the Middle Channel in the Strait of Singapore.

As described in routes PN45 (page 288) and PN51 (page 290), the voyage along the north coast of Borneo can be interrupted in Sabah, Brunei, or Sarawak, all of which have good harbours. Boats arriving in Singapore from this direction may find it more convenient to go to the anchorage off the Changi Yacht Club, on the NE side of Singapore

Island, and complete entry formalities from there. The alternative is the new Raffles Marina, on the west side of Singapore Island (1°20.53'N, 103°38.22'E).

Cruising boats are not normally inspected by the authorities and the captain has to visit the various offices himself.

PN62 *Hong Kong to Philippines*

BEST TIME:	February to April			
TROPICAL STORMS:	May to December			
CHARTS:	BA: 4508			
	US: 632			
PILOTS:	BA: 30, 31, 33			
	US: 157, 160, 162			
WAYPOINTS:				
Departure	*Intermediate*	*Landfall*	*Destination*	*Distance (M)*
PN621 Hong Kong SE 22°00'N, 114°22'E		PN622 Luzon 14°25'N, 120°20'E	Manila *14°35'N, 120°58'E*	606
PN621 Hong Kong SE		PN623 Lingayen 16°40'N, 120°15'E	San Fernando *16°37'N, 120°19'E*	467

Best passages on this route are made in spring towards the end of the NE monsoon, which lasts from early November until April or sometimes early May. Earlier passages in the NE monsoon can be unpleasant, as in early December the South China Sea can be quite rough, especially when a cold front passes through from the north. A good time to leave Hong Kong is soon after one of these fronts has passed. Good weather forecasts can be obtained from the Royal Observatory, which also gives advance warnings of the movement of any tropical storms within 400 miles of Hong Kong. In some years the arrival of the NE monsoon is accompanied by gale force winds in the northern part of the South China Sea, resulting in very rough passages in either direction. As an additional discomfort lower temperatures are usually associat-

ed with this kind of weather.

Southbound passages during the typhoon season, especially between June and October, can be quite risky, although reliable long term forecasts usually ensure a safe start to this passage. The peak of the typhoon season coincides with the SW monsoon, when light winds can be expected during settled weather.

Taking one's leave from Hong Kong at WP PN621 a direct course is set for WP PN622 off Luzon Point in the approaches to Manila. A more popular port of entry into the Philippines is San Fernando, which is also the destination of the annual yacht race from Hong Kong. A direct route can also be sailed from Hong Kong to San Fernando and landfall is made at WP PN623 off Cape Lingayen.

PN63 *Hong Kong to Japan*

BEST TIME:	May
TROPICAL STORMS:	May to December
CHARTS:	BA: 4508, 4509
	US: 523
PILOTS:	BA: 30, 32, 42A, 42B
	US: 157, 158, 159, 160

WAYPOINTS:

Departure	Intermediate	Landfall	Destination	Distance (M)
Route PN63A				
PN631 Hong Kong E	PN632 Strait			
22°10'N, 114°20'E	23°00'N, 118°00'E			
	PN633 East China	PN634 Kyushu	Nagasaki	1070
	27°30'N, 123°00'E	32°45'N, 129°45'E	*32°43'N, 129°50'E*	
Route PN63B				
PN631 Hong Kong E	PN635 Taiwan SE			
	21°30'N, 121°00'E			
	PN636	PN637 Murato	Osaka	1522
	26°20'N, 130°00'E	33°10'N, 134°50'E	*34°39'N, 135°24'E*	
Route PN63C				
PN631 Hong Kong E	PN635 Taiwan SE	PN638 Okinawa	Naha	839
		26°08'N, 127°37'E	*26°13'N, 127°40'E*	

If this passage is undertaken in May, at the beginning of the SW monsoon, it is possible to have both favourable winds and avoid the worst of the typhoon season. The route to Japan can pass either east or west of Nansei Shoto (Ryukyu Islands). If one intends to sail to Nagasaki and the NW coast of Japan (PN63A), it is best to sail through the Taiwan Strait from where the route runs parallel to the coast of China across the East China Sea. For boats bound for the west of Japan, a convenient port of entry into Japan is Nagasaki, on the SW coast of Kyushu.

Sailing the same route during the NE monsoon is much more difficult as the wind will be blowing strongly from ahead, although the high proportion of strong NW winds may make an offshore passage more attractive. During the NE monsoon, by sailing parallel to the Chinese coast it might be possible to profit from the fact that the wind shifts slightly to the N at night and the E by day. With the help of the favourable current it is possible to make progress to the NNE by keeping to the west of the Nansei Shoto Islands. The south coast of Japan can then be reached through one of the channels south of Osumi Kaikyo.

An alternative route on leaving Hong Kong (PN63B) is to head east through the Bashi Channel, south of Taiwan, and then sail NE with the help of the Kuro Shio current. This route can only be sailed during the SW monsoon when the danger of being caught by a typhoon or even a depression in the Bashi Channel makes this alternative rather hazardous unless the weather is perfectly settled. The

best time to sail this offshore route is towards the end of the NE monsoon, when it may be possible to sail from Hong Kong to the Bashi Channel without tacking, as the trade winds tend to be more SE than in winter. Indeed, if the passage is made in late spring and the winds are SE, it may be preferable to stay west of Taiwan and reach Japan by crossing the East China Sea. If the passage is made at the change of seasons, and certainly during the SW monsoon, Hong Kong should not be left if there is any likelihood of a tropical depression moving northwards and developing into a typhoon.

The direct offshore route (PN63B) for boats bound for Central Japan leaves Hong Kong at WP PN631. From there the route runs almost due east to WP PN635, south of Taiwan. The course can then be altered for WP PN636, from where the route continues parallel to the Nansei Shoto Islands to WP PN637 off Murato Saki in the approaches to Osaka. Osaka is a convenient port of entry and also a good starting point for those wishing to reach the Inland Sea (Seto Naikai) from the east.

If one cannot avoid sailing to Japan during the NE monsoon, strong N or NW winds can be expected for the best part of the passage. The main advantage of a winter passage is the absence of typhoons. Early in the year, in February or March, an alternative to beating into the wind is to stop at Okinawa and start cruising among the Japanese islands from there (PN63C). Starting from the SW extremity of the Japanese archipelago, it is then easier to move NE along the chain of islands. The port of entry on Okinawa is Naha.

PN64 *Hong Kong to Guam*

BEST TIME:	December to March			
TROPICAL STORMS:	May to December			
CHARTS:	BA: 781, 4508			
	US: 524			
PILOTS:	BA: 30, 32, 60			
	US: 126, 160, 161			
CRUISING GUIDES:	*Landfalls of Paradise.*			
WAYPOINTS:				
Departure	**Intermediate**	**Landfall**	**Destination**	**Distance (M)**
PN641 Hong Kong E	PN642 Babuyan	PN643 Guam	Apra	1819
22°10'N, 114°20'E	18°45'N, 122°20'E	13°27'N, 144°34'E	*13°27'N, 144°37'E*	

This passage is best made in winter, when the risk of typhoons is low, the disadvantage being the strong NE winds. As the winds tend to become more easterly in lower latitudes, it is advisable to make some easting while still in higher latitudes, which would also compensate for the west-setting current.

The direct route runs through Luzon Strait into the Philippine Sea. From WP PN641, the direct route passes between the Babuyan Islands and the north coast of Luzon to WP PN642. Depending on weather conditions, a direct course can be set from there for WP PN643, off Guam, where formalities are completed in Apra Harbour. Harbour Control should be contacted on arrival on VHF channels 12, 13, or 16. Cruising boats are normally directed to the commercial pier for clearance.

If the passage is undertaken either at the start of or during the SW monsoon, a more sheltered course can be taken through the Philippine archipelago and out through the San Bernardino Channel, or even through Surigao Strait, as described in routes PN54 (page 294) and PN62 (page 298). This alternative may be more attractive, although it must be stressed that typhoons are not uncommon near Guam in April and therefore winter passages are considerably safer.

PN65 *Taiwan to Guam*

BEST TIME:	December to March			
TROPICAL STORMS:	May to December			
CHARTS:	BA: 781			
	US: 524			
PILOTS:	BA: 32, 60			
	US: 126, 157, 162			
CRUISING GUIDES:	*Landfalls of Paradise.*			
WAYPOINTS:				
Departure	**Intermediate**	**Landfall**	**Destination**	**Distance (M)**
PN651 Taiwan S	PN652	PN653 Guam	Apra	1460
21°50'N, 120°50'E	21°50'N, 125°00'E	13°27'N, 144°34'E	*13°27'N, 144°37'E*	

December to March are the safest months to undertake this passage as the danger of being caught by a typhoon is quite remote. The only serious drawback is the strength of the NE trade winds, which can make the entire passage hard on the wind. As most boats would probably find it difficult, if not impossible, to reach Guam on one tack, it might be advisable to make as much easting as possible after leaving Taiwan before setting a direct course for Guam. Taking one's leave from Taiwan at WP

PN651, SE of that island's southern extremity, the route goes first due east to WP PN652, from where a direct course is set for Guam and WP PN653. Formalities are completed in Apra Harbour.

Although this passage can also be made during the summer months, it is not recommended to cross the Philippine Sea in the middle of the typhoon season. Even if there is no typhoon, the weather in July and August is often stormy with overcast skies and rough seas. An alternative route through the Philippines is described in PN54 (page 294).

PN66 *Hong Kong to Vietnam*

BEST TIME:	January to March			
TROPICAL STORMS:	May to December			
CHARTS:	BA: 4508			
	US: 508			
PILOTS:	BA: 30, 32			
	US: 151, 161			
WAYPOINTS:				
Departure	*Intermediate*	*Landfall*	*Destination*	*Distance (M)*
PN660 Hong Kong SW 22°00'N, 114°05'E	PN661 Paracel W 15°00'N, 110°00'E	PN662 Honcha 12°22'N, 109°24'E	Nha Trang *12°16'N, 109°12'E*	656
PN660 Hong Kong SW	PN661 Paracel W	PN663 Mekong 10°35'N, 106°30'E	Ho Chi Minh *10°47'N, 106°42'E*	842

This route can be sailed at any time during the NE monsoon, although better conditions normally prevail after the winter monsoon has had time to establish itself. The recommended route crosses the Gulf of Tonkin and passes at a good distance to the west of North Reef, the westernmost danger in the Paracel Islands. NE winds at an average of 20 knots are normally experienced during the winter monsoon, with occasional squalls in excess of 40 knots.

With the gradual opening of Vietnam to foreign tourists, the number of cruising boats is also increasing and the fact that the Royal Hong Kong Club is now organising regular races to Vietnam, which started before Hong Kong had even reverted to China, is the best indication that sailing to Vietnam may now be included in one's cruising plans. While foreign vessels are still subject to a number of restrictions, the latest situation should be ascertained at a Vietnamese diplomatic mission before commencing the voyage. Permission to visit must be obtained from several government departments and the cost can be several thousand US dollars.

For southbound boats the port of Nha Trang in the bay of the same name is the most convenient port of call, and it is also the destination of an annual race from Hong Kong. Nha Trang is the seaport of the provincial capital of Dien Khanh, located some 7 miles up the River Song Cai, on whose south bank lies Nha Trang. Boats arriving from the north will make landfall off Honcha islet and then turn SW into the large Nha Trang Bay, avoiding the shallows of Grand Bank located in the northern part of the bay. Facilities in Nha Trang are limited and visiting boats usually anchor approximately one mile offshore.

Further south, the former South Vietnamese capital Saigon (now Ho Chi Minh City) is still one of the most attractive destinations in SE Asia. Having made landfall off Con Son Island, the port is reached through a channel that leads through the shallow waters of the Mekong Delta. The port is 40 miles from the sea. The recommended route then leads to PN663, west of Con Island and the approaches to the channel leading through the shallow waters of the Mekong Delta. The former South Vietnamese capital is located about 40 miles from the sea and is reached by one of two dredged channels.

PN70 ROUTES FROM JAPAN

Because of the short sailing season and rarely pleasant sailing conditions, only a few cruising boats venture to Japan, although the difficulties of getting there are more than made up for by the warm reception extended everywhere. The choice of routes on leaving Japan encompasses the entire North Pacific, although most boats that have visited Japan favour either a southbound route to Micronesia and beyond, or an eastbound route, either direct to Hawaii, or to the Pacific Northwest, possibly via Alaska. Whereas passages to Alaska or the Pacific Northwest should be planned for the early summer, the time of departure for Hawaii is more flexible. The same is true if one intends to visit the islands of Micronesia, although in all cases the risk of typhoons must be borne in mind, particularly during the most dangerous period between August and October. Unfortunately, passages from Japan to Hong Kong, the Philippines, and Singapore are even more under threat of typhoons and should be planned either for the end of spring or late autumn, early winter.

As Japan is situated in the belt of variables, the wind can blow from almost any direction in the summer. This summer period also bears the risk of typhoons from May through to October as these storms move NW out of their breeding grounds further south. Another hazard of sailing in

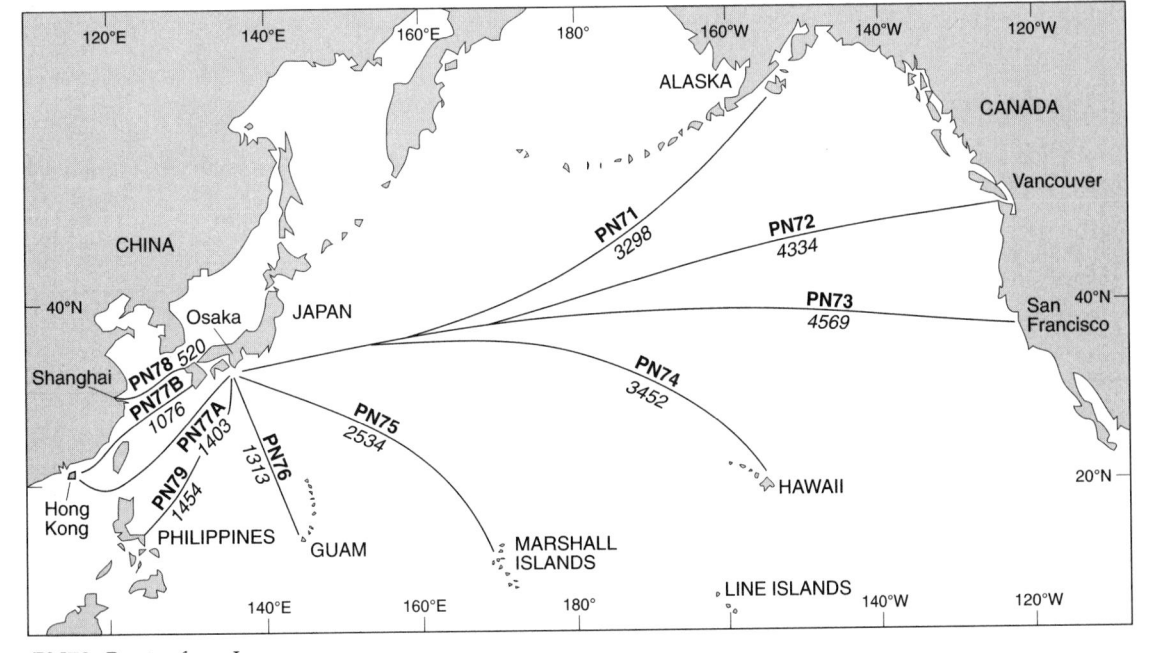

PN70 *Routes from Japan*

Japanese waters is the high proportion of foggy days. This is due to the cold current coming down from the north meeting the warmer Kuro Shio current and producing a similar effect to that found at Grand Banks and Newfoundland area in the Atlantic.

PN71 *Japan to Alaska*

BEST TIME:	June to July			
TROPICAL STORMS:	May to December			
CHARTS:	BA: 4053			
	US: 523			
PILOTS:	BA: 4, 23, 41, 42A			
	US: 152, 158			
CRUISING GUIDES:	*Charlie's Charts North to Alaska.*			
WAYPOINTS:				

Departure	Intermediate	Landfall	Destination	Distance (M)
PN711 Japan E 34°45'N, 140°00'E	PN712 35°00'N, 160°00'E	PN713 Sedanka 53°50'N, 165°55'W	Dutch Harbour *53°54'N, 166°32'W*	2847
PN711 Japan E	PN714 35°00'N, 165°00'E			
	PN715 Kodiak S 57°23'N, 152°10'W	PN716 Kodiak E 57°45'N, 152°15'W	Kodiak *57°47'N, 152°25'W*	3469

The few boats which take this route across the top of the North Pacific sometimes break the passage in the Aleutian Islands. The only reasonable time to make this passage is in summer, between late June and early August, when the weather is warmer and the days are long. During the summer months there are sometimes prolonged periods of calms or light winds when it may be necessary to motor. On the other hand there is an equal chance that one may experience rough weather all the way. The route coincides with the track of east moving depressions, which form either in the Sea of Japan or off the Kamchatka Peninsula. They usually move along the chain of the Aleutians and then across the Gulf of Alaska. Occasionally the lows stall above the Gulf of Alaska, causing gale force winds from E or SE and very rough seas.

Taking WP PN711 as a point of departure from Japan, the great circle route should be sailed to WP PN712 to make as much easting as possible and to take full advantage of the favourable winds and current. Because the weather closer to the Aleutians is often unsettled, as much easting as possible should be made while sailing in the area of prevailing westerlies and one should stay longer on a lower latitude before altering course for WP PN712. If existing weather conditions warrant it, easting should be made along 35°N, or even south of that latitude. During summer a convergence zone runs from east to west close to 35°N. East moving low pressure systems, which form over the Asian landmass, track north of this line as far as 155°E or 160°E where they curve NE. Because winds generated by such depressions will be S or SW south of this convergence, while to the north they will be SE or E, it is recommended that one sails as long as possible close to 35°N. Only once longitude 160°E or even 165°E has been reached should a direct course be set for one's port of destination. PN712 is a hypothetical waypoint from where boats bound for Dutch Harbour on Unalaska Island should alter course for WP PN713 off Sedanka Island. From there the course is altered to sail through Akutan Pass to reach Dutch Harbour in Unalaska Bay, on the NE coast of Unalaska Island. Dutch Harbour is a good starting point for a cruise along the northern shore of the Gulf of Alaska. If the intention is to sail straight to Kodiak, the initial great circle route should continue to WP PN714 so as to stay under the influence of favourable westerly winds as long as possible. The course can then be altered for WP PN715, east of Kodiak Island. From that point the route runs along the east coast of the island to WP PN716 in the approaches to Kodiak Harbour. The well protected harbour is best entered from NE through a dredged channel, which leads N of Near Island to Kodiak, an old town on the NW shore of Kodiak Harbour. On this route, even more important than the prevailing westerlies is the activity of the frontal systems that may affect this entire route, so developing systems should be monitored constantly and also the location of the North Pacific high, which has a major bearing on conditions to be experienced. Boats that plan to make landfall at one of the nearer Aleutian Islands, such as Attu, will leave the area of prevailing westerlies sooner and experience mixed weather conditions with occasional strong contrary winds, or calms and fog. Although one may stop for shelter, technically one is supposed to clear in at an official port of entry before landing anywhere.

The timing for this passage will be influenced by future plans as September is the latest time for heading south from Alaska. However, if one intends to leave the boat in Alaska for the winter, an earlier arrival time is not so crucial. Because of the short cruising season, both in Alaska itself and in British Columbia, this solution is taken by many as it allows them to start sailing again as soon as summer returns the following year.

PN72 *Japan to Pacific Northwest*

BEST TIME:	July to August			
TROPICAL STORMS:	May to December			
CHARTS:	BA: 4050, 4053			
	US: 520, 523			
PILOTS:	BA: 25, 42A, 62			
	US: 152, 154, 158			
CRUISING GUIDES:	*Cruising Guide to British Columbia, Charlie's Charts of the US Pacific Coast.*			
WAYPOINTS:				
Departure	*Intermediate*	*Landfall*	*Destination*	*Distance (M)*
PN721 Japan E 34°45'N, 140°00'E	PN722 35°00'N, 165°00'E			
	PN723 45°00'N, 160°00'W	PN724 Flattery 48°25'N, 124°50'W	Victoria *48°25'N, 123°24'W*	4434
			Seattle *47°37'N, 122°21'W*	4488

Fair winds can be expected right across the North Pacific on this long passage, if it is planned for the high summer. The most favourable conditions are in the summer months, from mid-June to August, when winds are mostly between S and W and some help can also be expected from the Aleutian Current. The percentage of gales in the summer months is low, although the occasional depression can pass over bringing stronger winds. Fog is quite frequent during these summer months and a careful watch should be kept when visibility is poor, as some of the fishing boats that work in this area are often left on automatic pilot with no one on watch. The one serious disadvantage is leaving Japan during a period when the frequency of typhoons is high.

The recommended summer route, if leaving from one of the ports in Central Japan, is to make most of the crossing between latitudes 35°N and 42°N, where there are better chances of finding favourable winds. Taking one's leave from Japan at WP PN721, easting should be made along 35°N, or even south of this latitude, if weather conditions warrant this. During summer a convergence zone runs eastward close to 35°N. East moving low pressure systems, which form over the Asian landmass, track north of this line as far as 155°E or 160°E where they curve NE. South of the line of such depressions the winds will be S or SW, whereas north of it they will be SE or E. To take advantage of favourable conditions generated by such systems, it is recommended to sail an easterly course, depending on existing conditions, as far as 160°E or even 165°E. From there a direct course can be set for one's port of destination, provided it does not cut across the North Pacific high. To avoid being becalmed inside the latter, the course should follow its northern extremity. The imaginary line along 35°N also forms a fog boundary, with little fog reported south of it.

Waypoints PN722 and PN723 are entirely hypothetical, as their coordinates will be decided entirely by the position of the North Pacific high. Having reached that point, a direct course can be taken from there to Juan de Fuca Strait, where landfall is made at WP PN724, NW of Cape Flattery in the approaches to Juan de Fuca Strait.

Extreme caution should be exercised in the approaches to the Strait of Juan de Fuca because of heavy shipping and strong currents. Shipping separation zones are in operation, with the southern lane being used by arriving ships and the northern lane reserved for outgoing traffic. The lanes diverge at designated points so as to allow ships to turn either north towards Vancouver or south towards Seattle. There is often a large number of fishing boats around the Swiftsure Bank, east of the entrance to the Strait, so this area should be avoided if at all possible. Traffic in the area is controlled by Tofino Radio (VHF channels 16 and 74). Incoming vessels are requested to report when due south of Amphitrite Point. The station operates a regular roll call, every ship reporting their position, speed, and course. In bad visibility the station will advise ships that are in the vicinity of a small boat's position. They will also assist yachts with directions and may even track such vessels on radar.

PN73 *Japan to California*

BEST TIME:	July to August			
TROPICAL STORMS:	May to December			
CHARTS:	BA: 4050, 4053			
	US: 520, 523			
PILOTS:	BA: 8, 42A, 62			
	US: 152, 158			
CRUISING GUIDES:	*Charlie's Charts of the US Pacific Coast.*			
WAYPOINTS:				
Departure	*Intermediate*	*Landfall*	*Destination*	*Distance (M)*
PN731 Japan E	PN732			
34°45'N, 140°00'E	42°00'N, 170°00'W			
	PN733			
	42°00'N, 160°00'W			
	PN734	PN735 Reyes	San Francisco	4569
	40°00'N, 150°00'W	37°55'N, 123°00'W	*37°50'N, 122°15'W*	

Directions are similar to those given for route PN72 but a direct course for California should be shaped only after meridian 150°W has been crossed. If this passage is made either earlier or later in the year than the recommended time, the route should follow a more southerly course as it may not be necessary to go above 40°N in search of favourable winds. In the eastern part of the North Pacific, this route depends very much on the position of the North Pacific high, which in summer is centred on 38°N, 150°W. The route should therefore follow the contour of the high around its northern fringe in order to avoid the calms that are met if the area of high pressure is crossed.

Because the recommended route passes close to British Columbia, boats bound for California often take advantage of this by cruising some of that area before continuing the voyage south. For further details see also routes PN33 (page 277) and PN72 (page 304).

PN74 *Japan to Hawaii*

BEST TIME:	June to September, February to March			
TROPICAL STORMS:	May to December (Japan)			
	June to October (Hawaii)			
CHARTS:	BA: 4053			
	US: 523			
PILOTS:	BA: 42A, 62			
	US: 152, 158			
CRUISING GUIDES:	*Charlie's Charts of the Hawaiian Islands, Landfalls of Paradise.*			
WAYPOINTS:				

Departure	Intermediate	Landfall	Destination	Distance (M)
Summer				
PN741 Japan E	PN742			
34°45'N, 140°00'E	35°00'N, 180°00'W			
	PN743			
	35°00'N, 170°00'W			
	PN744	PN747 Kauai	Nawiliwili	3452
	33°00'N, 165°00'W	22°20'N, 159°20'W	*21°57.5'N, 159°21'W*	
Winter				
PN741 Japan E	PN745			
	30°00'N, 150°00'E			
	PN746	PN747 Kauai	Nawiliwili	3478
	30°00'N, 165°00'W			

The Kuro Shio will give a considerable boost at the start of this passage, which should also benefit from the S and SW winds that are common in summer. Because of this high proportion of southerly winds, on leaving Japan it may not be necessary to go too far north in search of favourable winds and, weather permitting, easting will be made along latitude 35°N. The northern limit of the route depends on the winds encountered up to the point where meridian 180° is crossed. Taking WP PN741 as a departure point from Japan, an initial course should be set for WP PN742. A great circle course can be sailed to this hypothetical point, which, as explained above, may have to be placed further north. Because of the high proportion of easterly winds in lower latitudes east of the 180° meridian, it may be necessary to carry on making easting in higher latitudes by sailing to WP PN743 before the course is finally altered for Hawaii. This decision will depend entirely on existing winds and on the location of the North Pacific high. Normally, it should be possible to change course for Hawaii by the time WP PN744 has been passed.

Although the start of the passage is during the typhoon season, as the route moves away from Japan the risk of being overtaken by one of these storms decreases. As one approaches Hawaii there is the slight danger of running into a hurricane, which have the highest frequency between August and October. A winter departure from Japan, although much colder, would eliminate both these risks with the added advantage of favourable winds in lower latitudes. If Japan were left in February, the belt of prevailing easterly winds would be much further south than in summer and most of the easting could be made along latitude 30°N, considerably shortening the passage. For a winter crossing of the Pacific, on leaving Japan course would be set for WP PN745. The route continues due east to WP PN746 before the course is altered for WP PN747, NE of Kauai island. A convenient port for boats arriving from the NW is Nawiliwili Harbour, which is an official port of entry.

An attractive place for a short stop after leaving Japan on a southern route, as described above, is Chichishima (27°05'N, 142°11'E) in Ogasawara

Gunto, an excellent harbour close to the top of the arc of islands stretching south from Japan. The main settlement is Omura, in Futami Ko Bay, which is only vulnerable to the swell created by strong NW winds.

For boats bound for the South Pacific after Hawaii, a late winter departure from Japan also has the advantage of allowing one to arrive in the South Pacific in April at the start of the safe sailing season south of the equator.

PN75 *Japan to Marshall Islands*

BEST TIME:	January to March				
TROPICAL STORMS:	May to December				
CHARTS:	BA: 781				
	US: 523				
PILOTS:	BA: 42A, 61				
	US: 126, 127				
CRUISING GUIDES:	*Landfalls of Paradise.*				
WAYPOINTS:					

Departure	Intermediate	Landfall	Destination	Distance (M)
PN751 Japan S 33°30'N, 135°00'E	PN752 27°10'N, 142°10'E			
	PN753 Ewenetak 12°30'N, 162°10'E	PN754 Kwajalein 9°10'N, 166°40'E	Ebeye *8°46'N, 167°44'E*	2296
			Majuro *7°08'N, 171°22'E*	2534

Making easting in the North Pacific against the prevailing easterly winds of lower latitudes is never easy. Because of the risk of typhoons at other times of the year, this passage is best done in late winter. A boat, which goes reasonably well to windward, will be able to sail the entire route on port tack. For most of the way the North Equatorial Current will set westward at an average 1/2 knot.

Taking one's departure from Japan in Osaka Bay, from WP PN751 a course is set for WP PN752. As this direct route passes close to the north of Chichishima (27°05'N, 142°11'E) in Ogasawara Gunto, a stop should be considered before a new course is set for WP PN753, north of Ewenetak.

From there the route enters the Marshall archipelago and, if a stop in Kwajalein Atoll is intended, a course should be set for WP PN754. Ebeye, in Kwajalein Atoll, is one of two official ports of entry into the Marshalls. Kwajalein Atoll should not be approached until radio contact has been established with Kwajalein Atoll Control as the area is used for missile testing by the US military.

The other port of entry is the capital Majuro. Cruising in any of the Marshall Islands is only allowed with a special permit which can be obtained in Majuro, and boats should not stop at any of the islands before having cleared at one of the above ports. See also route PN36, page 280.

PN76 *Japan to Guam*

BEST TIME:	November, February to April
TROPICAL STORMS:	All year
CHARTS:	BA: 781
	US: 522
PILOTS:	BA: 42A, 60
	US: 126, 158
CRUISING GUIDES:	*Landfalls of Paradise.*

WAYPOINTS:				
Departure	*Intermediate*	*Landfall*	*Destination*	*Distance (M)*
PN761 Japan E 34°45'N, 140°00'E		PN763 Guam W 13°30'N, 144°35'E	Apra *13°27'N, 144°37'E*	1303
PN762 Japan S 33°30'N, 135°00'E		PM763 Guam W	Apra	1313

This passage is best made either late in November, when the worst of the typhoon season is over, or in late winter, before the onset of the new typhoon season and after the worst winter gales are over. If leaving from one of the ports in eastern Japan, such as Tokyo (WP PN761), some easting should be made while still in an area of prevailing westerlies. The route then stays east of the Mariana Islands and approaches Guam from the NE. The direct route for boats leaving from ports further west, such as Osaka (WP PN762), will probably stay west of the Mariana Islands and will be much harder on the wind once the area of prevailing NE trade winds is reached. Landfall will be made at WP PN763, NW of the entrance into Apra Harbour.

A popular alternative is to break the trip by stopping in Chichishima (27°05'N, 142°11'E) in the Ogasawara Gunto group, which is also recommended as a place to seek shelter if a typhoon does threaten during the passage to Guam. The main settlement on Chichishima is Omura, in Futami Ko, a well protected bay. The port of entry into Guam is Apra Harbour. Port Control should be contacted on VHF channel 16. Cruising boats are normally directed to the commercial dock in the NE part of the large harbour.

PN77 *Japan to Hong Kong*

BEST TIME:	February to March, November			
TROPICAL STORMS:	May to December			
CHARTS:	BA: 4508, 4509 US: 522			
PILOTS:	BA: 30, 32, 42A US: 157, 158, 159, 160			
WAYPOINTS:				
Departure	*Intermediate*	*Landfall*	*Destination*	*Distance (M)*
Route PN77A PN771 Murato 33°10'N, 134°50'E	PN772 Taiwan SE 21°30'N, 121°00'E	PN773 Hong Kong E 22°10'N, 114°20'E	Hong Kong *22°18'N, 114°10'E*	1403
Route PN77B PN774 Kyushu 32°45'N, 129°45'E	PN775 East China 27°30'N, 123°00'E PN776 Strait 23°00'N, 118°00'E	PN773 Hong Kong E	Hong Kong	1076

The best time for this passage is either towards the end of the NE monsoon in February or March or at its start in November. Passages during the SW monsoon are not recommended, both because of the contrary southerly winds and the risk of typhoons. There are various routes that can be taken, depending on the time of year and also the port of departure. From ports on the north coast of Japan or the west coast of Kyushu (PN77A), the route sets SW parallel to the Chinese coast and through the Taiwan Strait. The offshore route, leaving from the south coast of Honshu, has to contend with the strong Kuro Shio current, although its rate is greatly diminished during the NE monsoon.

Boats setting off from ports on the south coast have two alternatives: either to stay close inshore and pass into the East China Sea through one of the channels south of Kyushu, or to stand offshore and reach Hong Kong through the Bashi Channel south of Taiwan (PN77B). Boats sailing the latter route may break the voyage at Okinawa (26°13'N, 127°40'E).

Because of the generally stronger winds, the offshore route is not recommended for winter passages, when the route through the East China Sea may be more attractive. In February, a favourable current sets southward along the mainland coast of China and so it is recommended to set a course which runs parallel to this coast at about 60 miles and down the middle of the Taiwan Strait. From Nagasaki and WP PN774, a course is set down the centre of the East China Sea for WP PN775. From that point, the route runs parallel to the Chinese mainland through Taiwan Strait to WP PN776 and thence to WP PN773, at the entrance into Lema Channel. Arriving yachts should contact Port Operation Service on VHF channel 12 and proceed to the western quarantine anchorage.

PN78 *Japan to China*

BEST TIME:	April to June			
TROPICAL STORMS:	May to December			
CHARTS:	BA: 3480			
	US: 509			
PILOTS:	BA: 32, 42A			
	US: 157, 159			
WAYPOINTS:				
Departure	*Intermediate*	*Landfall*	*Destination*	*Distance (M)*
PN780 Fukuoka *33°37'N, 130°23'E*	PN781 Hakata *33°42'N, 130°13'E*			
	PN782 Iki *33°35'N, 129°40'E*	PN783 Chang *31°05'N, 122°30'E*	Shanghai *31°15'N, 121°30'E*	520

Although the number of cruising boats visiting mainland China is still small, every year some Japanese yachts venture across the China Sea, usually as part of a race or organised event. Because of the many restrictions imposed on the movement for foreign vessels in Chinese waters, the usual destination is Shanghai, where the authorities are slightly more accommodating than in other ports. Facilities for pleasure boats are almost non-existent, although the fact that Shanghai is now visited by a number of international races means that facilities can only get better. As the fastest developing city in China, Shanghai is a dynamic city with direct air links to many Asian destinations outside of mainland China. One major disadvantage of finishing a passage in Shanghai is that the port is a long way up the Huangpu river, which itself is a tributary of the Yangtze. There are three deep channels into the Yangtze but only Nan Shuidao is navigable. The Chinese authorities insist that all vessels, including sailing boats, are met at the mouth of the Yangtze and then guided the 38 miles to the mouth of the Huangpu river and on to Shanghai by a pilot, which can be a very costly affair.

Probably the best port of departure from Japan is Hakata, in Western Kyushu. Hakata is the port of Fukuoka, which has the distinction of being the closest Japanese city to mainland Asia. Fukuoka has a thriving sailing community, good facilities and two marinas. The newer of these, at Marinoa, is a good place to prepare for the passage.

Having left the busy port of Hakata, the initial route passes south of Iki Shima island from where a direct course can be sailed across the Korea Strait to make landfall at the mouth of the Yangtze River. Landfall will be made at WP783, north of a cardinal buoy marking a wreck; arriving boats must proceed west to the recommended area (31°03.5'N, 122°12'E) where the pilot vessel is stationed. Any foreign vessel intending to sail to Shanghai must give an ETA in advance of leaving its port of departure. The ETA must be updated and reported every 48 hours and also 24 hours before arrival.

Although the most pleasant conditions will be experienced during the summer months, the high risk of typhoons after the beginning of July makes an early summer passage more attractive.

PN79 *Japan to Philippines*

BEST TIME:	January to April			
TROPICAL STORMS:	May to December			
CHARTS:	BA: 4509			
	US: 509			
PILOTS:	BA: 33, 42A			
	US: 159, 162			
WAYPOINTS:				
Departure	*Intermediate*	*Landfall*	*Destination*	*Distance (M)*
PN790 Osaka	PN791 Murato	PN792 Cat	PN793 Bernardino	1454
34°39'N, 135°24'E	*33°10'N, 134°50'E*	*13°50'N, 124°30'E*	*12°40'N, 124°20'E*	
PN794 Naha	PN795 Okinawa	PN792 Cat	PN793 Bernardino	835
26°13'N, 127°40'E	*26°08'N, 127°37'E*			

The NE monsoon of winter provides the best sailing conditions, and even though it can be quite cold at the start of the passage, temperatures rise significantly as one approaches the Philippines. In the first three months of the year the strongest winds will be from NW and the Kuro Shio current will also give a considerable boost to southbound passages. Boats sailing from Osaka should sail the offshore route, which passes west of Kita Daito Shima and makes landfall off the east coast of Catanduanes Island in the approaches to the Bernardino Strait.

A shorter alternative is the route from Okinawa, whose capital Naha makes a convenient departure port and also offers good shelter if the passage is made during the typhoon season. For both routes the Bernardino Strait has been recommended as a landfall so as to enter the Philippines archipelago from the east and then sail through sheltered waters to one of the ports of entry. The alternative is to stop first and clear in at Legaspi (13°09'N, 123°45'E) before negotiating the Bernardino Strait.

PN80 ROUTES IN WESTERN MICRONESIA

PN81 *Guam to Palau*	312
PN82 *Guam to Carolines*	312
PN83 *Guam to Japan*	313
PN84 *Palau to Guam*	314
PN85 *Guam to Philippines*	314
PN86 *Palau to Philippines*	315

The islands of Micronesia cover a vast area of the tropical North Pacific but their remoteness has kept their isolation almost intact. Only a handful of cruising boats venture west of Hawaii, their numbers augmented by the few that pass through Micronesia on their way to or from the South Pacific and the Far East. The remoteness of these islands is only one reason why more cruising boats do not visit Micronesia. Another reason is the difficult navigation among the low unlit islands, most of which are encumbered by reefs. Satellite navigation and the proliferation of radar will probably bring an increase in the number of visiting boats, but it is doubtful whether they will ever reach the numbers seen in the South Pacific.

The NE trade wind blows freshly over the area from October to May. In some years the arrival of the trades can be delayed or advanced by up to one month. At Ponape, in the eastern part of the archipelago, the arrival of the NE trades can sometimes be delayed as late as January. In the early part of the season the trades are strong, accompanied by violent squalls and rain. By June, the trades are replaced by calms and variable winds, which continue for the rest of the year. In June, July, and August the SW monsoon takes over, and this is interrupted sometimes by periods of calm or even short spells of easterly winds. Towards the end of the SW monsoon, late in August or September, strong SW gales can occur. These appear to be linked with the typhoons which have their breeding ground in this region. Although these usually move NW away from the islands, North Pacific typhoons do reach full strength very quickly and the few that affect the Carolines can do so with

great force, such as one which passed over Ulithi Atoll in 1960 with winds of 125 knots.

A series of recent typhoons has affected the islands of Micronesia during the off season period between late November and January. Those who are cruising the islands should listen regularly for typhoon warnings *whatever the time of the year*. Most tropical depressions that may develop into typhoons are predicted several days in advance, which provides sufficient time either to find a safe anchorage or even to sail south into an area not affected by such storms.

All Micronesian islands apply strict rules to visiting boats and some insist on obtaining a cruising permit in advance of one's arrival. As the issuing of such permits normally takes several months, the necessary procedure needs to be started long before one is due to arrive in the area. With the exception of Guam, which is the most developed island in the area, facilities in most islands are basic. Better provisioning and repair facilities are available in Palau.

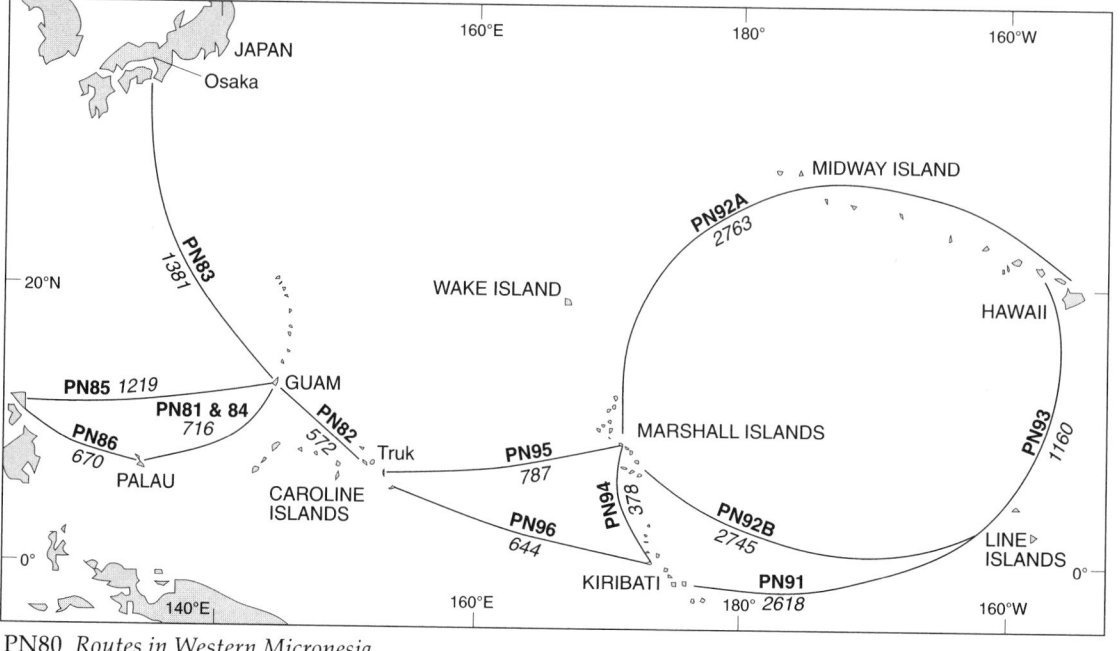

PN80 *Routes in Western Micronesia*

PN81 *Guam to Palau*

BEST TIME:	December to March			
TROPICAL STORMS:	All year			
CHARTS:	BA: 781			
	US: 525			
PILOTS:	BA: 60			
	US: 126			
CRUISING GUIDES:	*Landfalls of Paradise.*			
WAYPOINTS:				
Departure	Intermediate	Landfall	Destination	Distance (M)
PN811 Guam SW 13°27'N, 144°35'E	PN812 Yap 9°30'N, 138°20'E	PN813 Palau E 7°20'N, 134°34'E	Malakal 7°20'N, 134°29'E	716

Unfortunately no month is completely free of tropical storms and one or more of these have passed through the area crossed by this route in every month of the year in recent history. This does not necessarily mean that typhoons occur in every month, only that such a possibility cannot and should not be discounted. During the NE trade wind season NE and E winds make this a fast downwind passage.

From WP PN811 outside Apra Harbour, the direct route runs west of Ulithi Atoll and east of Yap Island. An initial course is set for WP PN812, east of Yap. From there the course is altered for WP PN813, east of Babeltuap, Palau's largest island.

The official port of entry into Palau is Malakal Harbour on Koror Island and yachts must not stop anywhere before Malakal. Boats coming from the east should use Malakal Passage, but this should be done at slack water because of the strong tidal streams.

In principle boats are not allowed to enter the Republic of Palau without a cruising permit, which must be obtained in advance, as well as entry visas for all the crew members, including the captain. Cruising permits may be obtained on arrival, but at a higher cost than normal. The vessel's ETA must be brought to the attention of the authorities by radio.

PN82 *Guam to Carolines*

BEST TIME:	January to April			
TROPICAL STORMS:	All year			
CHARTS:	BA: 781			
	US: 525			
PILOTS:	BA: 60			
	US: 126			
CRUISING GUIDES:	*Landfalls of Paradise.*			
WAYPOINTS:				
Departure	Intermediate	Landfall	Destination	Distance (M)
PN821 Guam S 13°10'N, 144°40'E	PN822 Namonuito 9°30'W, 150°30'E	PN823 Truk 7°25'N, 151°24'E	Moen 7°27'N, 151°50'E	572

Better winds may be encountered on this passage to the Carolines during the summer months, when there is a higher proportion of SW winds, but as this is also the typhoon season, winter passages are to be preferred. Easterly winds predominate throughout the Carolines, so most of this passage will be on the wind. The North Equatorial Current sets westward and its effect is particularly noticeable between latitudes 8°N and 12°N. As this route is normally sailed as part of a voyage to the South Pacific, it is more convenient to plan on completing formalities at one of the central islands, such as Moen in Truk Lagoon (7°27'N, 151°50'E) or Kolonia (6°59'N, 158°13'E), in Pohnpei. The Carolines are divided into four separate states, all of which belong to the Federated States of Micronesia. Different entry requirements apply in each state, but it is normally tolerated if yachts stop en route before having actually cleared in.

Having left Apra Harbour and sailed down the west coast of Guam, from WP PN821 boats bound for Truk should set a course for WP PN822, NE of Namonuito Atoll. From there, the route turns south for WP PN823. Truk lagoon is entered through Piaanu Pass, on the west side of the large lagoon. Formalities are completed at either Moen or Weno Island.

An interesting place to make a subsequent stop by boats bound for the South Pacific is Kapingamarangi (1°04'N, 154°45'E), an isolated community where visiting yachts are always welcome. The island belongs to the state of Pohnpei. Greenwich Passage, on the south side of the atoll, leads into the large lagoon. Extreme caution should be exercised when approaching this atoll as it is reported to be 5 miles east of its charted position.

PN83 *Guam to Japan*

BEST TIME:	March to April			
TROPICAL STORMS:	May to December			
CHARTS:	BA: 781			
	US: 522			
PILOTS:	BA: 42A, 60			
	US: 126, 158			
WAYPOINTS:				
Departure	*Intermediate*	*Landfall*	*Destination*	*Distance (M)*
PN831 Guam W 13°30'N, 144°35'E		PN832 Shikoku 33°30'N, 135°00'E	Osaka *34°39'N, 135°24'E*	1381

The best time to do this passage is in March or April, when the weather starts to become warmer further north and the typhoon season has not started in earnest. However, typhoons can form just north of the equator at any time of the year in the Western Pacific, although with a good forecast from the US Navy's Typhoon Warning Center in Apra Harbour, it is possible to depart from Guam knowing that good weather can be expected for at least the first few days.

Up to latitude 25°N the prevailing winds are the NE trades, which can be quite boisterous in the late winter months. Because of the high proportion of strong NW winds north of 30°N, the passage should not be attempted before March. If it is found that the trade winds have too much north in them, one can ease the sheets and head for Okinawa (26°13'N, 127°40'E), from where it may be easier to start cruising the many islands of the Japanese archipelago.

Boats bound for Central Japan should try to sail the direct route that stays west of both the Marianas and Ogasawara Gunto islands, where one can stop at Chichishima (27°05'N, 142°11'E) before the final dash to the Japanese coast. From WP PN831, outside Apra Harbour, a direct course leads to WP PN832, in the approaches to Osaka. This is a port with good facilities and is convenient both for clearing into Japan and for starting a cruise in Japan's Inland Sea.

PN84 *Palau to Guam*

BEST TIME:	July to October			
TROPICAL STORMS:	All year			
CHARTS:	BA: 781			
	US: 525			
PILOTS:	BA: 60			
	US: 126			
CRUISING GUIDES:	*Landfalls of Paradise.*			
WAYPOINTS:				
Departure	*Intermediate*	*Landfall*	*Destination*	*Distance (M)*
PN841 Palau E	WP842 Yap	WP843 Guam SW	Apra	700
7°20'N, 134°34'E	9°30'N, 138°20'E	13°27'N, 144°35'E	*13°27'N, 144°37'E*	

As stated in directions for the reciprocal route (PN81), the risk of typhoons cannot be ignored in any month, although their highest frequency is during August and September. Unfortunately this is also the time when favourable winds can be expected on this route, which for most of the year is under the influence of the NE trade winds. The prevailing NE winds are reversed during the summer months by the SW monsoon, although this is never as steady as its NE counterpart and easterly winds can never be discounted on this route. If contrary winds persist, the voyage can be broken in Yap, which lies on the direct route to Guam. The port of entry into Yap is Kolonia (9°30'N, 138°08'E). It is also possible to stop at Ulithi Atoll (9°55'N, 139°30'E), but only if the boat has obtained a cruising permit in advance, otherwise one should stop first at Kolonia. Boats arriving without a permit will be allowed to stay a maximum three days.

The North Equatorial Current sets to the west along this route although its direction may be deflected to the south by the SW monsoon. If NE winds are encountered on leaving Palau, it is better to make easting in the latitude of Palau, where at least there is the chance of getting some help from the east-setting Equatorial Countercurrent.

From WP PN841, SE of Babeltuap Island, the route passes east of Yap to WP PN842. The route continues in a NE direction past Ulithi Atoll and reaches Guam at WP PN843, outside Apra Harbour. This is the official port of entry into Guam. Port Control should be contacted on VHF channel 16. Cruising boats are normally directed to the commercial dock in the NE part of the large harbour.

PN85 *Guam to Philippines*

BEST TIME:	January to March			
TROPICAL STORMS:	All year			
CHARTS:	BA: 4507			
	US: 507			
PILOTS:	BA: 33, 60			
	US: 126, 162			
WAYPOINTS:				
Departure	*Intermediate*	*Landfall*	*Destination*	*Distance (M)*
PN850 Apra		PN851 Bernardino E	Legaspi	1219
13°27'N, 144°37'E		13°05'N, 124°20'E	*13°09'N, 123°45'E*	

Best weather conditions will be experienced during the winter months when the NE trade winds prevail over the entire area and the North Equatorial Current will give an additional boost of between 10 and 25 miles per day. As there is a risk of typhoons in the Guam area even in the first months of the year, this passage should only be started if the long term forecast does not indicate the existence of any tropical depressions that may develop into a storm.

With Guam being on almost the same latitude as the Bernardino Strait, this shortest route across is recommended. Landfall will be made in the approaches to the Bernardino Strait from where one may proceed to Legaspi, the nearest port of entry into the Philippines.

PN86 *Palau to Philippines*

BEST TIME:	January to March			
TROPICAL STORMS:	All year			
CHARTS:	BA: 4507			
	US: 507			
PILOTS:	BA: 33, 60			
	US: 126, 162			
WAYPOINTS:				

Departure	Intermediate	Landfall	Destination	Distance (M)
PN860 Malakal *7°20'N, 134°27'E*	PN861 Palau W *7°32'N, 134°38'E*	PN861 Surigao *10°30'N, 125°50'E*	Cebu City *10°18'N, 123°54'E*	670
PN860 Malakal		PN851 Bernardino E *13°05'N, 124°20'E*	Legaspi *13°09'N, 123°45'E*	724

The NE trade winds of winter usually ensure a fast passage, which is also aided by the favourable west-setting North Equatorial Current. Having reached the open ocean through Toagel Mlungui Pass, the nearest destination in the Philippines is Cebu City, which can be reached through Surigao Strait. Boats bound for ports in the Northern Philippines should use the San Bernardino Strait, where Legaspi is the nearest port of entry. Passages during the summer months should be avoided both on account of the contrary winds and the high risk of typhoons.

PN90 ROUTES FROM EASTERN MICRONESIA

PN91 *Kiribati to Hawaii* 317
PN92 *Marshall Islands to Hawaii* 317
PN93 *Line Islands to Hawaii* 319
PN94 *Marshall Islands to Kiribati* 319
PN95 *Marshall Islands to the Carolines* 320
PN96 *Kiribati to the Carolines* 321

The islands of Eastern Micronesia have a much lower risk of tropical storms than the western group and this is one of the reasons why they are visited by more cruising boats. The other reason is that they are closer both to Hawaii and to the popular cruising destinations in the South Pacific. Weather conditions generally are better than in Western Micronesia and although the islands can be visited at virtually any time of the year, the best sailing season is in winter when the NE trade winds make themselves felt over most of the islands. From February to June the NE winds blow over the entire archipelago and winds from that direction also prevail during the summer months, although they are lighter and not so consistent. Typhoons do affect the Marshall Islands, but only very rarely Kiribati. However, contrary to a widespread belief, it is not the actual winter months when the Marshalls are really safe, but rather the period from late March to July when typhoons normally affect Western Micronesia. The Marshalls are more likely to be hit by a hurricane between August and early April, and in recent years no typhoons have been recorded between mid-May and mid-July, while they have occurred in all other months. Weather conditions in all

of Micronesia are described in PN80 on page 311.

Whereas in Kiribati facilities in the outer islands are virtually non-existent and only in the capital Tarawa can facilities be described as adequate, the opposite is true of Majuro, the capital of the Marshalls. Due to the American influence both repair facilities and provisioning are good, although this is not the case in any of the outer islands. As in Western Micronesia, cruising yachts are subject to various restrictions when visiting the Marshall Islands, especially those with a traditional lifestyle. Regulations are not so strict in Kiribati, although here too boats must clear in at Tarawa before visiting any of the outer islands.

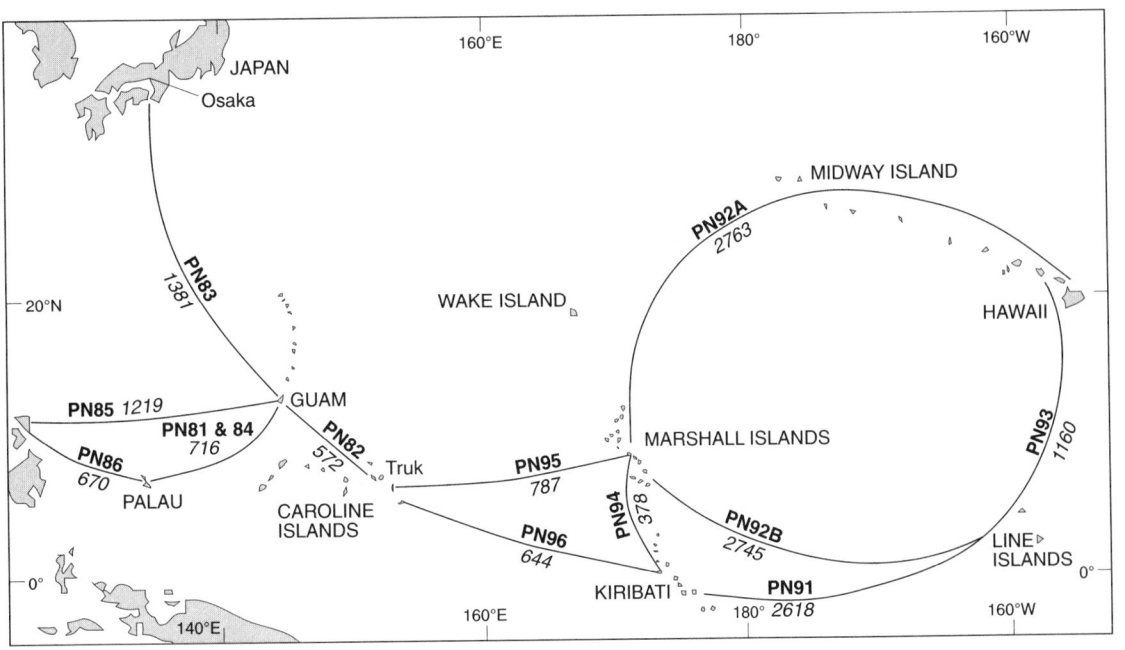

PN90 *Routes from Eastern Micronesia*

PN91 *Kiribati to Hawaii*

BEST TIME:	October to April
TROPICAL STORMS:	June to October
CHARTS:	BA: 4052
	US: 526
PILOTS:	BA: 61, 62
	US: 126, 152
CRUISING GUIDES:	Charlie's Charts of the Hawaiian Islands, Landfalls of Paradise.
WAYPOINTS:	

Departure	Intermediate	Landfall	Destination	Distance (M)
PN911 Tarawa S 1°18'N, 173°00'E	PN912 5°00'N, 160°00'W	PN913 Oahu S 21°15'N, 157°55'W	Honolulu 21°17'N, 157°53'W	2618

Because of the prevailing NE winds, this route is best sailed in winter, and although a high proportion of headwinds cannot be avoided, the weather is more settled and pleasant. The route runs east between latitudes 5°N and 8°N trying to take advantage of the east-setting Equatorial Countercurrent. A stop can be made in the Northern Line Islands, which belong to Kiribati and from where it should be possible to reach Hawaii on the starboard tack (see also route PN93). Kingsman Reef (6°25'N, 162°20'W), lies immediately to the north of the Line Islands. It is a prohibited area and must not be approached within 3 miles.

If SE winds are encountered between Kiribati and the Line Islands, the latter should be bypassed altogether and an attempt made to reach Hawaii without stopping. The difficulties associated with a return to Hawaii from either the Marshalls or Kiribati cannot be avoided and often the only way is to hope for a lull in the strong trade winds, when the engine can be used to gain ground to windward.

Having left Tarawa through the western pass into the lagoon, from WP PN911, south of Tarawa, the recommended route goes eastwards as far as WP PN912 along parallel 5°N to take advantage of the east-setting current. From there the route runs due north and will be helped at least as far as latitude 10°N by the higher proportion of SE and E winds. The risk of tropical storms should be borne in mind if the Hawaiian islands are reached during the hurricane season.

For boats arriving from the S or SW, probably the most convenient port of arrival is Honolulu and therefore landfall should be made at WP PN913, which is two miles SW of that harbour on Oahu's south coast.

PN92 *Marshall Islands to Hawaii*

BEST TIME:	April, October
TROPICAL STORMS:	June to October
CHARTS:	BA: 4052
	US: 526
PILOTS:	BA: 61, 62
	US: 126, 152
CRUISING GUIDES:	Charlie's Charts of the Hawaiian Islands, Landfalls of Paradise.

WAYPOINTS:				
Departure	*Intermediate*	*Landfall*	*Destination*	*Distance (M)*
Route PN92A				
PN920 Majuro N	PN921			
7°28'N, 171°20'E	10°00'N, 170°30'E			
	PN922			
	20°00'N, 170°00'E			
	PN923			
	25°00'N, 180°00'			
	PN924	Kauai	Nawiliwili	2763
	30°00'N, 170°00'W	22°20'N, 159°15'W	*21°57.5'N, 159°21'W*	
Route PN92B				
PN925 Majuro W	PN926			
7°10'N, 171°10'E	6°00'N, 172°00'E			
	PN927	PN928 Oahu SW	Honolulu	2745
	5°00'N, 160°00'W	21°15'N, 157°55'W	*21°17'N, 157°52'W*	

This is an extremely difficult passage at all times as the direct route is against the prevailing winds all the way. Very few boats can make it direct to Hawaii unless the captain is prepared to power his way through the NE trades. In such a case the lighter winds at the beginning and end of summer would be preferable, but even then the trip would be upwind most of the way. The alternative to constant tacking is to make a detour, either to the north, possibly via Wake and Midway islands, or south via Kiribati and possibly the Line Islands.

During summer, when the trades have more E and S in them in these latitudes, the northern alternative (PN92A) may be preferable, although it must be stressed that if the idea of a nonstop passage to Hawaii is not attractive, both Wake and Midway are restricted islands used by the US military and only emergency stops are allowed there. Even so, this does at least give the peace of mind that there is a place to get help in a real emergency. A feature of this northerly route at the beginning of summer are northerly gales, which can be quite violent.

Boats taking the northern route from Majuro (PN92A) should set an initial course that stays in the lee of Maloelap Atoll to WP PN921. From there the route from the Marshalls runs almost due north to latitude 20°N from where it curves NE, staying on the tack that makes most easting, but never below the latitude of Hawaii. In fact, it might become necessary to go way above latitude 25°N to be able to make the required easting. The route passes close to Laysan, the most northwestern of the Hawaiian islands, which is a bird sanctuary and has no safe anchorage. The only good anchorage close to this route is further south, at French Frigate Shoals, but permission to call there must be obtained beforehand.

The alternative southern route via Kiribati (PN92B) is best undertaken in winter when the trade winds are NE and E in direction and the weather is also more settled. From Majuro the route passes close to the west of Mili Atoll to WP PN926. A course is set there to stay to the east of the Northern Kiribati Islands and make as much easting as possible along latitude 5°N. Having reached WP PN927, the course is altered for Hawaii. See also the previous route from Kiribati to Hawaii, PN91.

PN93 *Line Islands to Hawaii*

BEST TIME:	June to October			
TROPICAL STORMS:	June to October			
CHARTS:	BA: 4052 US: 541			
PILOTS:	BA: 62 US: 126, 152			
CRUISING GUIDES:	*Charlie's Charts of the Hawaiian Islands, Landfalls of Paradise.*			
WAYPOINTS:				

Departure	Intermediate	Landfall	Destination	Distance (M)
PN931 Christmas *1°59'N, 157°30'W*		PN932 Oahu SW *21°15'N, 157°55'W*	Honolulu *21°17'N, 157°52'W*	1160

The area separating these two island groups is always under the influence of the NE trade winds and, particularly in winter, when the trade winds blow strongly, the northbound passage is on the wind all the way. The winds are usually more easterly in summer and as they are also lighter, passages are best made at that time. The immediate vicinity of the Line Islands is in the doldrum belt which extends to about latitude 8°N. The Equatorial Countercurrent normally sets strongly to the east close to the islands and can be used to ad-

vantage to make some easting before heading into the NE trades. The risk of tropical storms should be borne in mind if the Hawaiian islands are reached during the hurricane season. Kingsman Reef (6°25'N, 162°20'W), lies immediately to the north of the Line Islands. It is a prohibited area and must not be approached within 3 miles.

From WP PN931, NW of Christmas Island, the route runs almost due north to WP PN932, south of Oahu. For boats arriving from the south, Honolulu is probably the most convenient port of entry.

PN94 *Marshall Islands to Kiribati*

BEST TIME:	January to March			
TROPICAL STORMS:	All year			
CHARTS:	BA: 4507			
	US: 507			
PILOTS:	BA: 33, 60			
	US: 126, 162			
CRUISING GUIDES:	*Landfalls of Paradise, South Pacific Anchorages.*			
WAYPOINTS:				

Departure	Intermediate	Landfall	Destination	Distance (M)
PN940 Majuro *7°08'N, 171°22'E*	PN941 Catalin *7°10'N, 171°09'E*	PN942 Tarawa N *1°23'N, 172°54'E*	Betio *1°21'N, 172°55'E*	378

Although, in theory, the Marshall Islands may be visited by typhoons in any month of the year, tropical storms are very rare between the middle of May and the middle of July. The risk of tropical storms decreases as one moves south, so the passage to the former Gilbert Islands can be undertaken at any time, although best sailing conditions will probably prevail during the NE trade winds of winter.

The large Majuro lagoon is left through Catalin Pass, from where the southbound route passes a number of atolls. These may be visited only if permission to do so was obtained before leaving the capital. The first Kiribati island to be passed is Butaritari, but stopping there is prohibited before having cleared in at Tarawa. Arriving boats must make their way to Betio, in the SW corner of Tarawa lagoon. As there is only a depth of 6 ft in the channel leading into the inner harbour at Betio, deep drafted vessels should either anchor or tie up at the commercial dock. Tarawa Radio should be contacted on channel 16 before the lagoon is entered to give an ETA.

PN95 *Marshall Islands to the Carolines*

BEST TIME:	December to April			
TROPICAL STORMS:	All year			
CHARTS:	BA: 4506			
	US: 506			
PILOTS:	BA: 60, 61			
	US: 126			
CRUISING GUIDES:	*Landfalls of Paradise, South Pacific Anchorages.*			
WAYPOINTS:				
Departure	*Intermediate*	*Landfall*	*Destination*	*Distance (M)*
PN950 Majuro	PN951 Catalin	PN952 Kosrae	Lelu	511
7°08'N, 171°22'E	*7°10'N, 171°09'E*	*5°20'N, 163°03'E*	*5°20'N, 163°01'E*	
PN90 Majuro	PN951 Catalin	PN953 Pohnpei N	Takatik	
		7°05'N, 158°15'E	*6°59.5'N, 158°14'E*	787

Because much of Micronesia is subject to tropical storms in any month of the year, westbound passages from the Marshalls have the choice of doing this when best winds can be expected, such as in winter, or when the chances of typhoons are lowest. In Eastern Micronesia, such as Kosrae, tropical storms are relatively rare but their frequency increases as one moves west. On leaving Majuro lagoon through Catalin Pass, a direct course can be set for Kosrae, the easternmost island in the Carolines. The mountainous island is surrounded by a barrier reef, which gives access to two ports: Lelu on the east side and Okat on the west. For boats coming from the east Lelu is more convenient and this is also the main settlement, although marine facilities at Okat are improving due to the proximity of the airport. Before entering Lelu, Marine Resources should be called on channel 16 to arrange clearance. Facilities in Lelu can be described as adequate.

The alternative is to sail directly to Pohnpei (Ponape) and make landfall north of the atoll at PN953. Approaching from the NW, two passes lead through the reef, and one can take either Pohnpei or Sokehs Passage to reach the commercial port close to Takatik Island. One may tie up to the commercial pier to complete formalities. A causeway links the small island to the administrative centre at Kolonia where facilities are somewhat better than at Kosrae.

PN96 *Kiribati to the Carolines*

BEST TIME:	December to April
TROPICAL STORMS:	All year
CHARTS:	BA: 4506
	US: 506
PILOTS:	BA: 60, 61
	US: 126
CRUISING GUIDES:	*Landfalls of Paradise, South Pacific Anchorages.*
WAYPOINTS:	

Departure	Intermediate	Landfall	Destination	Distance (M)
PN960 Betio	PN961 Tarawa	PN962 Kosrae	Lelu	644
1°21'N, 172°55'E	*1°23'N, 172°54'E*	*5°20'N, 163°03'E*	*5°20'N, 163°01'E*	

The nearest destination is Kosrae, a mountainous island surrounded by a barrier reef, which gives access to two ports: Lelu on the east side and Okat on the west. For boats coming from the east Lelu is more convenient as it is also the main settlement. On arrival, contact Marine Resources on channel 16 to arrange clearance. Facilities in Lelu are adequate.

Best sailing conditions will be experienced during the winter months when the NE trade winds are most constant. Although the incidence of trop-ical storms is lower in winter, in recent years the islands of Eastern Micronesia have been affected by typhoons even during the relatively safe period of January to March, so, as one moves west, the weather should be monitored constantly. Kosrae is the ideal place to start a cruise in the little frequented Carolines, most of whose isolated island communities continue to have a traditional lifestyle. The only drawback are the strict regulations that are applied to cruising boats throughout the island states of Micronesia.

11

TRANSEQUATORIAL ROUTES IN THE PACIFIC

Unlike the Atlantic, where most cruising routes keep to the northern hemisphere and only a minority cross the equator, the equatorial region of the Pacific is crisscrossed by a multitude of routes. The busiest area is in the east, where boats starting off from Panama or the west coast of North America have to cross the equator to reach their destinations in the South Pacific. Although the Intertropical Convergence Zone is widest at its eastern end, the crossing of the doldrums is seldom a major problem and the zone itself is usually transited in a relatively short time. The doldrums only become a problem when their position and extent have not been assessed accurately and a course stays in the doldrums too long. The main objective is to intersect the ITCZ at right angles and the course should be always altered to achieve this whenever a route crosses the doldrums.

West of about longitude 150°W, which is the longitude of Tahiti, the doldrums are very narrow and it is often possible to sail from one trade wind system into the next almost without interruption. Further west, transequatorial routes linking the two hemispheres seldom encounter true doldrum conditions, although the weather can be squally and unsettled where the two trade wind systems meet. Doldrum weather is also associated with the period between monsoons, especially in Papua New Guinea, where the arrival of the NW monsoon is always heralded by this kind of weather, particularly evident on routes to Micronesia.

Another feature of the equatorial region of the Pacific, is the complexity and unpredictability of the three main currents. All transequatorial routes are affected by them to a greater or lesser extent and even if their behaviour cannot be predicted with accuracy, being aware of their existence can avoid unpleasant surprises.

PT10 TRANSEQUATORIAL ROUTES IN THE EASTERN PACIFIC

PT11 *Southbound from Panama*

BEST TIME:	November to March			
TROPICAL STORMS:	None			
CHARTS:	BA: 4062			
	US: 62			
PILOTS:	BA: 7			
	US: 125, 153			
WAYPOINTS:				

Departure	Intermediate	Landfall	Destination	Distance (M)
PT111 Panama S 8°50'N, 79°30'W	PT112 Mala 7°30'N, 79°30'W PT113 Galera 1°00'N, 81°00'W PT114 Elena 2°15'S, 81°40'W		Salinas 2°13'S, 80°55'W	725
PT111 Panama S	PT112 Mala PT113 Galera PT114 Elena PT115 Parinas 4°40'S, 81°25'W		Paita 5°05'S, 81°07'W	859
			Callao 12°03'S, 77°09'W	1137

All passages southward from Panama, along the west coast of South America, are very difficult because of the persistent southerly winds and the contrary Peru or Humboldt current, which sets north throughout the year. Sailing ships which did not have the advantage of an auxiliary engine used to be advised to try and beat along the coast only if bound for ports north of Callao, in Peru. For ports further south, it was recommended they work their way offshore into the SE trade winds and then reach the coast with the help of the prevailing westerlies which are to be found south of latitude 30°S. As far as Chilean ports are concerned, this suggestion continues to be valid for modern yachts also (see also PS18 on page 362). Ports lying to the north of Callao can be reached from Panama without such a lengthy detour, provided one is prepared to make the most of every shift of wind and use the engine when necessary.

From WP PT111 south of Panama City, an initial course is sailed that passes west of the Las Perlas islands and then due south to WP PT112 so as to pass clear of Cabo Mala. From WP PT112 a course is set for WP PT113 so as to pass at least 50 miles to the west of Punta Galera, at the southern extremity of

the Gulf of Panama. The currents are very complex and variable in the Gulf of Panama, a combination of the Humboldt and Equatorial Countercurrent, which can reach up to 2 1/2 knots at times, setting eastward into the bay. It is therefore very easy to be swept into the bay while crossing it, which is avoided by giving Punta Galera a wide berth.

South of the Gulf of Panama, the winds blow from between S and SW for most of the year, so it is a matter of choosing the best tack to make as much southing as possible. As far as the Gulf of Guayaquil, it does not matter if the course is well offshore, as better conditions will be found 50 to 100 miles from the coast. Southward from Guayaquil it is better to keep in with the coast to take advantage of the daily land and sea breezes. During periods of calm or light winds, it will be necessary to motor to counteract the strong north-setting current.

It is not uncommon to have favourable winds when crossing the Gulf of Panama, and during the northern winter, especially between February and April, the NE trade winds are sometimes felt as far south as the equator. From December to March, the doldrum belt is furthest south and can extend west of Ecuador as far as the Galapagos

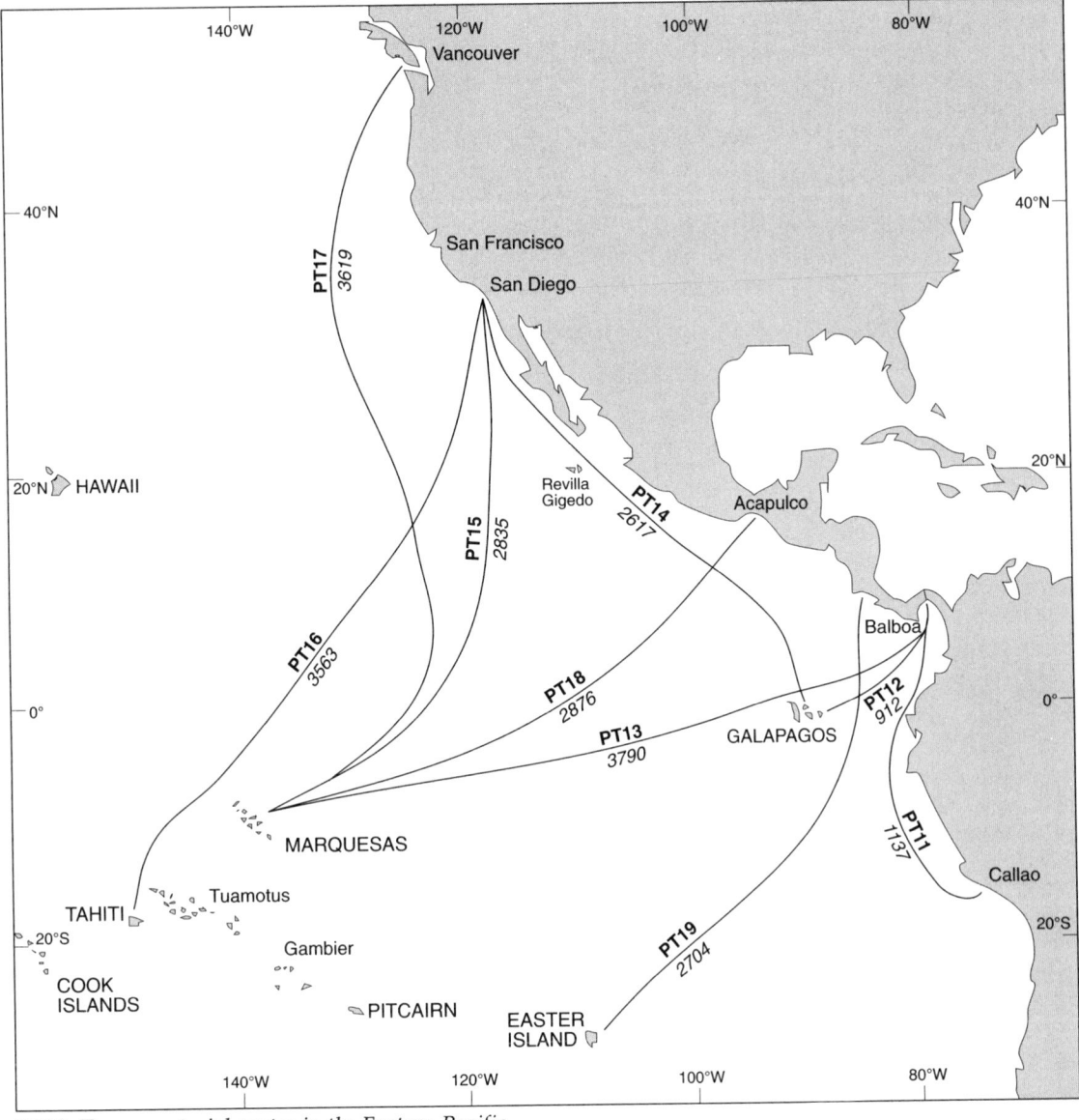

PT10 *Transequatorial routes in the Eastern Pacific*

Islands. Further south, along the Peruvian coast, the SE trade winds prevail for most of the year, although close to the coast the wind has more S than E in it. Gales are very rare in Peruvian waters and cyclones unheard of. Due to the cold Humboldt current, fog, mist, and poor visibility are common close to the land. Another danger for small boats is the unusually big swell that sometimes occurs without warning along this coast. Its origin is probably submarine seismic activity, a known phenomenon in the region. The high swell can cause considerable damage to boats moored alongside wharves or docks.

There are several convenient ports along the coast where to stop for provisions or fuel, one of the best being the Ecuadorian port of Salinas, which has an excellent yacht club where visiting yachts are always welcome and is a good place to leave the boat to visit the interior. In Peru, the port of Paita is the northernmost port of entry, while Callao is the port of the capital Lima, with good repair facilities and a welcoming yacht club. See also PS18.

PT12 *Panama to Galapagos*

BEST TIME:	February to June			
TROPICAL STORMS:	None			
CHARTS:	BA: 4051			
	US: 51			
PILOTS:	BA: 7			
	US: 125, 153			
CRUISING GUIDES:	*Landfalls of Paradise, South Pacific Anchorages.*			
WAYPOINTS:				

Departure	Intermediate	Landfall	Destination	Distance (M)
PT121 Panama S 8°50'N, 79°30'W	PT122 Mala 7°30'N, 79°30'W			
	PT123 Malpelo 3°50'N, 81°00'W	PT124 Cristobal 0°45'S, 89°37'W	Baquerizo Moreno *0°53.7'S, 89°37'W*	912
		PT125 Cruz E 0°35'S, 90°00'W	Puerto Ayora *0°44.9'S, 90°18.3'W*	940

Weather conditions on this route are very varied, and regardless of the time of year when the passage is made an area of calms will probably be met on the way. It is therefore recommended to leave Panama with a good reserve of fuel to cope with the calms and also possible headwinds, for S or SW winds are common between the mainland and the Galapagos Islands. Because the area to be crossed is under the direct influence of the Intertropical Convergence Zone, it is worth finding out its location before leaving Panama. If time permits, waiting for the ITCZ to move north will ensure good sailing conditions to the Galapagos.

In the Gulf of Panama the winds blow mostly from the north between October and April. From May to September, the winds are either westerly or variable. If SW winds are encountered after Cabo Mala, it is preferable to stay on the starboard tack and pass east of Malpelo Island. By heading south parallel to the mainland coast, possibly as far south as latitude 3°S, the chances of finding favourable winds are normally better. In this way, one will spend a shorter time in the doldrums than by sailing along the rhumb line. The north-setting current along the coast of South America can be very strong as it gradually turns NW and then W. Currents can be very strong in this area and this should be borne in mind when closing with the Galapagos Islands, as poor visibility in their vicinity and stronger currents than anticipated have caused the loss of several yachts. Those planning to make their landfall on Tower Island should exercise due care when approaching this low island, especially in squally weather. If the weather is particularly bad with poor visibility when approaching the Galapagos Islands, care must be taken if heaving to for the night in the proximity of the islands, both on account of the strong currents and the absence of reliable lights.

Boats sailing from ports in Central America to the Galapagos may encounter steady SW winds south of 5°N. They may find that by staying on the starboard tack they have been pushed too far east, but this can be corrected south of the equator, even if it means sailing a longer route. Otherwise, by staying too long on the port tack, the strong west-setting current will push the boat too far NW and one will have to fight one's way back against wind and current to gain one of the two ports of entry. This recommendation has also some validity for boats leaving from Panama.

For boats leaving from Panama and WP PT121 the course passes west of the Las Perlas islands and continues due south to pass well clear of Cabo Mala to WP PT122. From there a direct course can be set for the Galapagos, although it may pay to stay east of Isla Malpelo (WP PT123) to take advantage of the south-setting current in the Bay of Panama. From there, the course can be altered for the port of destination. If calling first at Baquerizo Moreno, which is the administrative centre of the archipelago, one should sail first to WP PT124 before altering course for Baquerizo Moreno. The island of San Cristobal is better left to port and Baquerizo Moreno approached from the NE. Because the lights in the approaches are not always working, the port should not be entered at night.

If the destination is Puerto Ayora, a course should be set from WP PT123 for WP PT125 between the islands of Santa Fé and Santa Cruz, before altering course for Puerto Ayora on the latter island.

In theory, unless they have obtained permission beforehand from the Ecuadorian authorities, cruising yachts are not allowed to stop in the Galapagos, except in an emergency, when a maximum stay of 72 hours can be granted at the discretion of the Port Captain. As the authorities in Puerto Ayora appear to be more tolerant, and there is also a larger number of local excursion boats based at that island, boats without a permit usually fare better if they sail directly to Puerto Ayora and plead an emergency. During the permitted stop, some of the surrounding islands can be visited with the local excursion boats to gain at least a fleeting impression of their unique wildlife. The various port dues, immigration fees, landing fees, and National Park entrance fee can amount to several hundred dollars for a 72 hour stay.

PT13 *Panama to Marquesas*

BEST TIME:	February to June			
TROPICAL STORMS:	December to March			
CHARTS:	BA: 4051			
	US: 51			
PILOTS:	BA: 7, 62			
	US: 122, 125, 126, 153			
CRUISING GUIDES:	*Landfalls of Paradise, Charlie's Charts of Polynesia, South Pacific Anchorages.*			
WAYPOINTS:				

Departure	Intermediate	Landfall	Destination	Distance (M)
Route PT13A (South)				
PT131 Panama S	PT132 Mala			
8°50'N, 79°30'W	7°30'N, 79°30'W			
	PT133			
	3°00'S, 85°00'W			
	PT134	PT136 Hiva Oa E	Atuona	4051
	3°00'S, 100°00'W	9°45'S, 138°45'W	*9°48'S, 139°02'W*	
		PT137 Nuku Hiva SE	Taiohae	4107
		8°55'S, 139°55'W	*8°56'S, 140°06'W*	
Route PT13B (North)				
PT131 Panama S	PT132 Mala			
	PT135			
	0°00', 100°00'W	PT136 Hiva Oa E	Atuona	3790
		PT137 Nuku Hiva SE	Taiohae	3842

The difficulty of obtaining a cruising permit for the Galapagos Islands, or even permission to stop for long in one of the two official ports, is the main reason why some boats make this passage nonstop and avoid the Galapagos altogether. When sailing to the Marquesas direct, on leaving the Gulf of Panama the decision has to be made whether to pass north or south of the Galapagos Islands. Whichever way the Galapagos are passed, they should be given a wide berth as poor visibility and very strong currents can make navigation in their vicinity hazardous.

From June to January it is advisable to pass north of the Galapagos, so as to avoid beating into the SW winds which can be expected after leaving the Gulf of Panama. This route (PT 13B) also takes advantage of the westerly set of the North Equatorial Current, which can be considerable. By crossing the equator in longitude 100°W, the route passes clear of all dangers. If unfavourable winds are encountered after the longitude of the Galapagos Islands has been passed, it is better to continue to make westing with the wind and current and only cross the equator when the winds have the desired slant.

From February to May it is better to pass south of the Galapagos Islands, and once the islands have been left safely behind a direct course for the Marquesas can be set (PT13A). West of the Galapagos Islands, the best conditions are experienced during the SE trade wind season, between May and August. Reasonable conditions can also be expected earlier, in the second half of March and April, when most of the passages along this route are made as boats time their arrival in French Polynesia for the first half of April to coincide with the end of the cyclone season (December to March).

From WP PT131, south of Panama City, an initial course is sailed that passes west of the Las Perlas islands and then due south to pass well clear of Cabo Mala. From WP PT132 the route stays east of Isla Malpelo to take advantage of the south-setting current in the Gulf of Panama. Depending on weather conditions encountered up to that point, a course will be set for WP PT133 to cross the equator at some point east of the Galapagos. When this new course is set an area to be avoided by boats passing south of the Galapagos is between longitudes 90°W and 95°W and latitudes 3°S and 8°S

where several yachts have reported unpleasant weather conditions. The area appears to be an extension of the doldrums with little or no wind, thundery squalls, and a heavy swell which makes conditions very uncomfortable. Most of this area can be avoided if from WP PT133 a new course is set to pass south of the Galapagos to WP PT134, but avoiding going south of latitude 3°S before that new waypoint is reached. From there, depending on weather conditions, a great circle course can be sailed to WP PT136, three miles east of Cape Matafenua, the eastern extremity of Hiva Oa. The route follows the coast into Taaoa Bay, in the NW corner of which is located the small port of Atuona. The harbour is protected by a short breakwater, but this does not offer much protection from the southerly swell. The entrance into the port is not easily identified at night so it is strongly recommended to arrive in daytime.

Boats sailing straight to Nuku Hiva should stay well clear of Clark Bank (8°05'S, 139°35'W), where seas break over shallow water, and make for WP PT137, five miles east of Nuku Hiva. From there the coast is followed around Cape Tikapo towards Taiohae, the main port and capital of the Marquesas. Because of the prevailing winds and also the layout of the islands, it is better to stop first at Atuona and visit the islands in its vicinity before continuing to Nuku Hiva.

PT14 *California and Mexico to Galapagos*

BEST TIME:	March to April
TROPICAL STORMS:	June to October
CHARTS:	BA: 4051
	US: 51
PILOTS:	BA: 7, 8
	US: 125, 153
CRUISING GUIDES:	*Landfalls of Paradise, South Pacific Anchorages.*

WAYPOINTS:				
Departure	*Intermediate*	*Landfall*	*Destination*	*Distance (M)*
PT141 Diego 32°40'N, 117°20'W	PT142 20°00'N, 110°00'W PT143 10°00'N, 95°00'W	PT144 Plazas 0°35'S, 90°06'W	Puerto Ayora *0°46'S, 90°18W*	2617
		PT145 Five Fingers 0°50'S, 89°40'W	Baquerizo Moreno *0°54'S, 89°37'W*	2631
PT146 Acapulco *16°50'N, 99°58'W*	PT147 Diamante 16°45'N, 99°55'W PT148 Marchena 0°25'N, 90°20'W	PT144 Plazas	Puerto Ayora	1216
PT146 Acapulco	PT147 Diamante PT148 Marchena	PT145 Five Fingers	Baquerizo Moreno	1230

The optimum season when favourable weather conditions may be encountered on this route is only one of several considerations that will decide the time when this passage should be undertaken. Because the Galapagos Islands are only visited on the way to somewhere else, the first thing to consider is the time when one wishes to arrive at that final destination. If such a destination is in the South Pacific, where most islands are affected by tropical storms between December and March, one should not arrive there before the beginning of April. Therefore the optimum time of departure from California is the end of February. As this route crosses the hurricane zone off the coast of Mexico, this passage should not be made between May and October. In fact better conditions will be experienced at the end of winter, with the possibility of strong winds right at the start. For this reason, boats are often sailed earlier in the year from northern ports to a marina in Southern California, as the southbound passage can start at almost any time from a port such as San Diego.

Depending on the time of year when this passage is undertaken, one may have to sail through both the NE and some of the SE trade wind systems to reach the Galapagos, which requires making good some 30 degrees of easting. As the winds in the vicinity of the islands blow from the southerly quarter for most parts of the year, it is advisable to try and make as much easting as possible further north. This means sailing an initial course that runs parallel to the continental coast. Boats setting off from places further south, such as Mexico, will ex-

perience better conditions and may have northerly winds almost as far as the equator. Depending on the time of year, the ITCZ will be encountered somewhere between 3°N and 8°N. Having crossed that area the winds will gradually become southerly.

Taking as a point of departure WP PT141, south of San Diego, the initial route runs parallel to the coast of Baja California to WP PT142. The course can then be altered for WP PT143 so that the Galapagos are approached almost from the north. From WP PT143 a course is set to pass east of Pinta and Marchena islands and make landfall at WP PT144 east of Santa Cruz Island. From there the course runs parallel to the coast to Academy Bay, where Puerto Ayora is located.

Boats intending to call at Baquerizo Moreno should set a course from WP PT143 to pass west of Genovesa Island to WP PT145, NW of Five Fingers Rock in the approaches to Baquerizo Moreno, the administrative centre of the Galapagos. For boats leaving from Acapulco, a direct course can be sailed to make landfall close to Marchena, one of the smaller Galapagos Islands just north of the equator. From there one has the choice of two ports of entry at Baquerizo Moreno or Puerto Ayora.

In order to reach as soon as possible an area of steady winds, boats leaving from Mexico should move immediately offshore so as to get away from the influence of the continental landmass.

Visiting boats are subjected to severe restrictions in the Galapagos, which is a National Park, where cruising is strictly prohibited. Occasionally a cruising permit may be obtained from the Ecuadorian Government, but as a rule boats are only permitted a 72 hour emergency stop in one of the two official ports, Baquerizo Moreno on San Cristobal Island and Puerto Ayora on Santa Cruz Island.

PT15 *California to Marquesas*

BEST TIME:	March to May
TROPICAL STORMS:	June to October(North Pacific)
	December to March(South Pacific)
CHARTS:	BA: 4051
	US: 51
PILOTS:	BA: 8, 62
	US: 122, 126, 152
CRUISING GUIDES:	*Charlie's Charts of Polynesia, Landfalls of Paradise, South Pacific Anchorages.*
WAYPOINTS:	

Departure	Intermediate	Landfall	Destination	Distance (M)
PT151 Diego	PT152	PT153 Hiva Oa E	Atuona	2890
32°40'N, 117°20'W	0°00', 130°00'W	9°45'S, 138°45'W	*9°48'S, 139°02'W*	
		PT154 Nuku Hiva SE	Taiohae	2888
		8°55'S, 139°55'W	*8°56'S, 140°06'W*	

The majority of people undertaking this passage prefer to call at ports in Baja California or even further south before setting off on this long ocean passage, although this tactic does not necessarily ensure better sailing conditions. Therefore, unless one wishes to cruise along the Mexican coast, it might be better to make straight for the Marquesas. The time of arrival in the Marquesas should be considered before leaving, as a departure in November usually means an arrival in the Marquesas in the middle of summer, which is the cyclone season there. A better time of departure is between March and May, which ensures a winter arrival in the Marquesas at the most pleasant time of the year. On average, the slowest passages are those made in the early part of the year, when light winds and calms are common. In some years no real trade wind conditions are experienced until May, although throughout the year the currents are favourable. Winds are stronger and steadier in the later part of the year, but that is the wrong time to arrive in Polynesia.

The great circle route crosses the doldrums at a slant and, if a great circle course is being sailed, this should be altered as soon as the doldrums are encountered so as to cut across them at right angles. If steady NE trade winds are experienced while sailing north of the equator, it might be better to stay with them and make as much westing as possible before crossing the equator. However, no advantage will be gained by crossing the equator further west than 130°W (WP PT152). During winter, NE winds will be experienced until close to the ITCZ and as the length of this passage will depend greatly on how quickly one has crossed that zone, it is essential to find out its location. This can be done either from satellite pictures, or by keeping in touch with other boats that are further ahead. The ITCZ will be encountered anywhere between 3°N and 10°N, and will be characterised by light winds and frequent squalls, some quite violent. Once through the ITCZ and also across the equator, one should rapidly fall in with the SE trades and when this happens it pays not to be too close hauled, so the advice is not to cross the equator further west than 128°W or 130°W.

One hazard that has been reported on or close to this route is a number of weather buoys at 0°, 2°N and 5°N – all at 125°W. The buoys are unlit and large enough to show up on radar.

Taking WP PT151 as a point of departure from San Diego, and presuming that the equator has been crossed at WP PT152, from there a new course can be set for WP PT153, three miles east of Cape Matafenua on the eastern extremity of Hiva Oa. The south coast of Hiva Oa is followed around into Taaoa Bay, in the NW corner of which is located the small port of Atuona. The harbour is protected by a short breakwater, but this does not offer much protection from the southerly swell. The entrance is difficult to identify at night and so it is advisable to arrive in daytime.

Boats going straight to Nuku Hiva should stay well clear of Clark Bank (8°05'S, 139°35'W), where seas break over shallow water, and make for WP PT154, five miles off the east coast of Nuku Hiva.

From there the coast is followed around Cape Tikapo towards Taiohae, the main port and capital of the Marquesas. Because of the prevailing winds and the layout of the islands, it is better to clear at Atuona, visit the islands in its vicinity, and leave Nuku Hiva for the end of a Marquesan cruise.

PT16 *California to Tahiti*

Best time:	November to May				
Tropical storms:	June to October (North Pacific)				
	December to March (South Pacific)				
Charts:	BA: 4051, 4061				
	US: 51				
Pilots:	BA: 8, 62				
	US: 122, 126, 152				
Cruising guides:	*Charlie's Charts of Polynesia, Landfalls of Paradise, South Pacific Anchorages.*				
Waypoints:					
Departure	*Intermediate*	*Landfall*	*Destination*		*Distance (M)*
PT161 Diego	PT162				
32°40'N, 117°20'W	0°00', 140°00'W				
	PT163 Manihi				
	14°24'S, 145°29'W				
	PT164 Rangiroa E	PT165 Tahiti	Papeete		3563
	15°13'S, 147°02'W	17°30'S, 149°34'W	*17°32.5'S, 149°34.5'W*		

This less frequented route is taken by those who are in a hurry to get to Tahiti and are prepared to sail nonstop rather than call at the Marquesas or sail the longer route via Hawaii. The recommended route crosses the equator above the Marquesas in about 140°W, where the doldrums are narrower than farther east. The width of the doldrums varies from year to year and there are times when no doldrums are encountered, the NE trade winds giving way to the SE trade winds almost without a break.

Taking WP PT161 as a point of departure from San Diego, the great circle route can be sailed to the recommended point where the equator is crossed at WP PT162. From there, the route passes west of the Marquesas and through the Western Tuamotus to pass between the atolls of Takaroa and Manihi at WP PT163. From there the course should be altered to pass east of Rangiroa through WP PT164. Approaching Tahiti from the NE, landfall is made NNE of the entrance into Papeete at WP PT165. The pass through the reef leading into the harbour is at 17°32.18'S, 149°35.1'W.

PT17 *Pacific Northwest to Marquesas*

BEST TIME:	May to June			
TROPICAL STORMS:	June to October (North Pacific)			
	December to March (South Pacific)			
CHARTS:	BA: 4051, 4801			
	US: 520, 526			
PILOTS:	BA: 8, 25, 62			
	US: 122, 126, 152, 154			
CRUISING GUIDES:	*Charlie's Charts of Polynesia, Landfalls of Paradise, South Pacific Anchorages.*			
WAYPOINTS:				

Departure	Intermediate	Landfall	Destination	Distance (M)
PT171 Flattery 48°20'N, 124°50'W	PT172 46°00'N, 128°00'W			
	PT173 0°00', 135°00'W	PT174 Hiva Oa E 9°45'S, 138°45'W	Atuona *9°48'S, 139°02'W*	3619
		PT175 Nuku Hiva SE 8°55'S, 139°55'W	Taiohae *8°56'S, 140°06'W*	3597

For those who intend to start their South Pacific cruising in the Marquesas and the Tuamotus, a direct route from the Pacific Northwest to the Marquesas is both the most logical and convenient. A detour via Hawaii cannot be recommended as it would then entail a lot of windward work to reach the Marquesas. The best time to leave is in May or early June, when the winter storms are usually over off the coasts of Washington and Oregon and there is enough time to get south of 10°N before the start of the hurricane season. An earlier start is also possible, if the long term weather forecast is good. A later start is more risky as most of the hurricanes that form off the coast of Mexico follow a track that intersects this route.

On leaving the coast it is essential to sail off the continental shelf as quickly as possible, as the seas are always rougher there. Taking one's leave from WP PT171 off Cape Flattery, an initial SW course is sailed to WP PT172 to move as quickly as possible off the continental shelf and into steadier offshore conditions. From there a direct course can be set for the Marquesas. If one sails the great circle course, one should keep east of 135°W until south of the equator, to avoid having to beat into the SE trade winds. During the first part of the passage the winds are likely to be NW or W and the current is also favourable. In May and June, the NE trade winds reach as far north as latitude 25°N, although in some years they may only be found a few degrees further south. The doldrums are not too wide at this time of year, but if one is planning to motor through them, it is recommended to head slightly east of south, both to counteract the westerly set of the South Equatorial Current and also to be in a better position when the SE trade winds are met.

Having crossed the equator at WP PT173, a new course can be set for WP PT174, three miles east of Cape Matafeuna at the eastern extremity of Hiva Oa. From there, the route runs parallel to the coast to make landfall at Atuona, one of the official ports of entry into French Polynesia. Boats sailing straight to Nuku Hiva should stay well clear of Clark Bank (8°05'S, 139°35'W), where seas break over shallow water, and make for WP PT175, five miles off the east coast of Nuku Hiva. From there the coast is followed around Cape Tikapo towards Taiohae, the main port and capital of the Marquesas. Because of the prevailing winds and also the layout of the islands, it is better to stop first at Atuona and visit the islands in its vicinity before continuing to Nuku Hiva.

PT18 *Mexico and Central America to Marquesas*

BEST TIME:	March to May
TROPICAL STORMS:	June to October (North Pacific)
	December to March (South Pacific)
CHARTS:	BA: 4051
	US: 51
PILOTS:	BA: 8, 62
	US: 122, 126, 153
CRUISING GUIDES:	*Charlie's Charts of Polynesia, Landfalls of Paradise, South Pacific Anchorages.*
WAYPOINTS:	

Departure	Intermediate	Landfall	Destination	Distance (M)
PT181 Acapulco 16°50'N, 99°58'W	PT183 0°00', 128°00'W	PT184 Hiva Oa E 9°45'S, 138°45'W	Atuona *9°48'S, 139°02'W*	2826
		PT185 Nuku Hiva SE 8°55'S, 139°55'W	Taiohae *8°56'S, 140°06'W*	2842
PT182 Golfito 8°36'N, 83°12'W	PT183	PT184 Hiva Oa E	Atuona	3612
		PT185 Nuku Hiva SE	Taiohae	3628

The length of this passage, which can take as long as four weeks, depends very much on the extent of the doldrums. As mentioned in route PT15, it is advisable to try and stay with the NE trade winds as long as possible. This tactic is particularly recommended in the early part of the year, before the SE trade winds are fully established south of the equator. In other months, a great circle route should be followed until the doldrums are reached. Normally NE winds will be experienced until close to the ITCZ, which will be encountered anywhere between 3°N and 10°N. If one manages to cross the ITCZ and also the equator without too much delay, the SE trade winds will ensure a fast passage for the rest of the voyage. As these winds can have a lot of south in them, in order not to be too close hauled it is recommended not to cross the equator further west than 128°W or, at the most, 130°W. If the departure is made after the beginning of June, it is best to head immediately offshore to avoid the *chabascos*, strong winds which occur off the coast of Central America. A summer passage is usually associated with thunderstorms, light and variable winds N of the equator, but consistent SE trade winds S of it. Summer departures from Mexico should be aware of the danger of hurricanes. Similarly, winter departures should move away from the coast quickly to avoid the strong winds associated with some areas, as described in PN20.

The route from Mexico passes close to Clipperton Island (10°17'N, 109°15'W), an uninhabited French possession occasionally visited by meteorologists or other scientists. Yachts on passage to the South Pacific sometimes make an unscheduled stop there.

If this passage is made at the recommended time, which is also the optimum time to arrive in French Polynesia, a great circle route can be joined as soon as the coast has been left safely behind. A course can then be set for WP PT183 at the recommended point for crossing the equator. This is a hypothetical point as its position will depend both on the time of year but mainly on the weather conditions prevailing south of the equator. From WP PT183 the course is altered for PT184 three miles east of Cape Matafeuna at the eastern extremity of Hiva Oa. From there, the route runs parallel to the coast to make landfall at Atuona, one of the official ports of entry into French Polynesia. Boats sailing straight to Nuku Hiva should stay well clear of Clark Bank (8°05'S, 139°35'W), where seas break over shallow water, and make for WP PT185, five miles off the east coast of Nuku Hiva. From there the coast is followed around Cape Tikapo towards Taiohae, the main port and capital of the Marquesas. Because of the prevailing winds and also the layout of the islands, it is better to stop first at Atuona and visit the islands in its vicinity before continuing to Nuku Hiva.

PT19 *Central America to Galapagos and Easter Island*

BEST TIME:	December to February
TROPICAL STORMS:	June to October (North Pacific)
CHARTS:	BA: 4062
	US: 62
PILOTS:	BA: 8, 62
	US: 122, 125, 153
CRUISING GUIDES:	*Landfalls of Paradise, South Pacific Anchorages.*
WAYPOINTS:	

Departure	Intermediate	Landfall	Destination	Distance (M)
PT191 Golfito 8°36'N, 83°12'W	PT193 0°00', 95°00'W	PT196 Easter N 27°00'S, 109°25'W	Hanga Roa *27°09'S, 109°26'W*	2704
PT192 Panama S 8°50'N, 79°30'W	PT194 Mala 7°30'N, 79°30'W PT195 0°00', 85°00'W	PT196 Easter N	Hanga Roa	2793
PT191 Golfito		PT197 Five Fingers 0°50'S, 89°40'W	Baquerizo Moreno *0°54'S, 89°37'W*	691
PT191 Golfito		PT198 Plazas 0°35'S, 90°06'W	Puerto Ayora *0°46'S, 90°18'W*	705

This is a long haul southward for those who do not wish to make the detour via the Galapagos Islands, mainly to avoid the formalities and costs that cruising boats face there. Boats leaving from northern ports in Central America or from Mexico should sail an initial course that runs due south, passing west of the Galapagos, so that the equator is crossed around longitude 95°W (PT193). This gives an acceptable slant across the SE trades which become more easterly as the route goes further south. If the winds south of the equator have too much south in them, any ground which may be lost to the west will be made up later as winds become more easterly south of 20°S. Favourable winds should be found most of the way and even the doldrums should not be too wide if this route is sailed at the recommended time.

Boats leaving from Panama or Costa Rica should attempt to sail a course which stays east of the Galapagos, where better conditions should be found so that the equator is crossed near WP PT195. If leaving from Panama, from WP PT192, the initial course passes west of the Las Perlas islands and then due south to pass well clear of Cabo Mala. From WP PT194, the course stays east of Isla Malpelo to take advantage of the south-setting current in the Gulf of Panama. Depending on weather conditions encountered up to that point, the equator will be crossed somewhere around longitude 85°W (WP PT195). See also route PS12 (page 357).

Having crossed the equator, a new course can be set so as to make landfall at Easter Island at WP PT196, north of the island's North Cape. The NW coast should be followed to the main settlement at Hanga Roa, where a few keeled boats can find shelter at the small port of Hanga Piko.

As the route to Easter Island passes so close to the Galapagos, a stop there should be considered. Cruising boats are now allowed to spend a few days there provided they stop at one of two approved ports. These are Baquerizo Moreno on Santa Cruz Island and Puerto Ayora on San Cristobal. Some of the other islands can be visited from one of these two ports on local excursion boats. Although the administrative centre of the archipelago is at Baquerizo Moreno, cruising boats normally encounter fewer formalities at Puerto Ayora, which is also a better place from which to visit other islands. More details are given in PT12 on page 325.

PT20 TRANSEQUATORIAL ROUTES IN THE CENTRAL PACIFIC

Most transequatorial routes in the Central Pacific either originate or finish in Hawaii. Compared to the eastern part of the equatorial area, the doldrums affecting these routes are much narrower and winds can be carried through from one trade wind system to the other almost without interruption.

PT21 *Marquesas to Hawaii*

BEST TIME:	April to May, November			
TROPICAL STORMS:	December to March (South Pacific)			
	June to October (North Pacific)			
CHARTS:	BA: 4051			
	US: 526			
PILOTS:	BA: 62			
	US: 126, 152			
CRUISING GUIDES:	*Charlie's Charts of the Hawaiian Islands, Landfalls of Paradise.*			
WAYPOINTS:				
Departure	*Intermediate*	*Landfall*	*Destination*	*Distance (M)*
PT211 Nuku Hiva NW 8°55'S, 140°15'W	PT212 Motu One 7°54'S, 140°20'W PT213 0°00', 140°20'W PT214 10°00'N, 143°00'W	PT215 Hawaii E 19°30'N, 154°45'W	Hilo *19°44'N, 155°04'W*	2067

This is a fast and pleasant passage at almost any time of the year, although because of the opposing tropical storm seasons, the two areas should be avoided during the critical periods and passages between the island groups should be made at, or close to, the change of seasons.

On leaving the Marquesas it is best to head straight north so as to arrive north of the equator with as much easting in hand as possible. As the logical point of departure is Nuku Hiva, from WP PT211, west of the island, the route sets due north to WP PT212 to pass 5 miles east of Motu One, a low cay lying dangerously close to the recommended course. The same course will be maintained to cross the equator at WP PT213. The northerly course should be maintained until the NE trade winds are met. From that point, a direct course can be set for Hawaii, or, depending on weather conditions, for WP PT214. The initial northerly course will also ensure that the area with a contrary current below 8°N will be crossed at right angles. Having reached WP PT214 one will start feeling the effects of the west-setting North Equatorial Current. From there the course can be set for WP PT215 off Cape Kumukahi, at the eastern extremity of Hawaii Island. The best port of entry into Hawaii is Hilo, as it is to windward of all other ports in the archipelago and therefore a perfect starting point for a cruise among the islands. Honolulu (21°18'N, 157°52'W), because of its position, is better left for the end of a Hawaiian cruise.

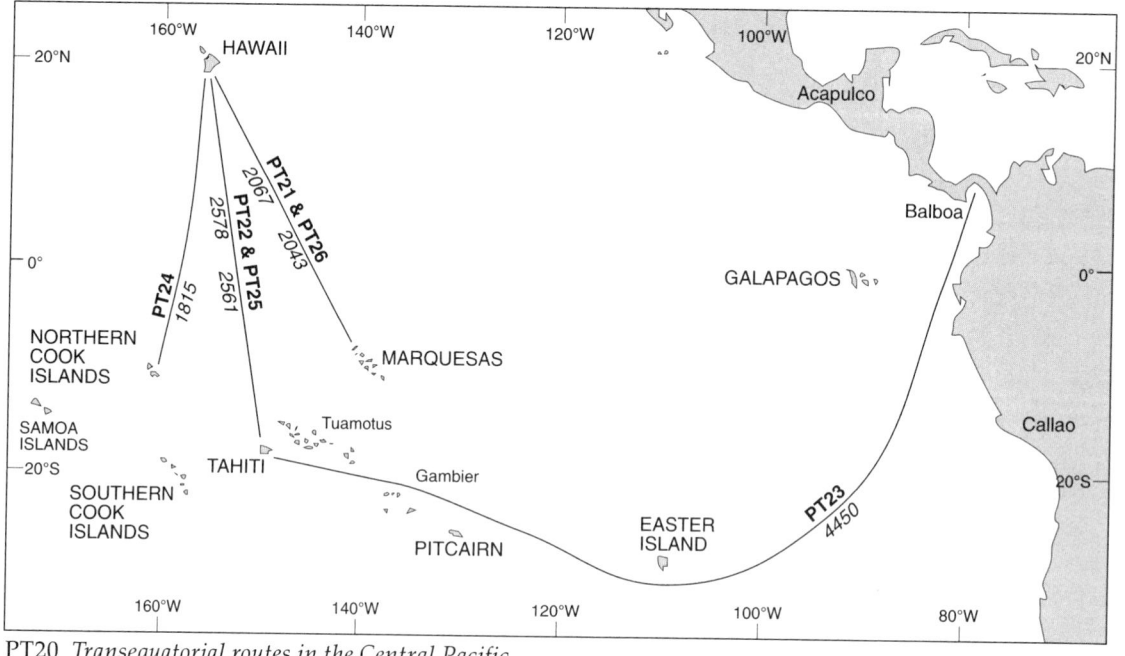

PT20 *Transequatorial routes in the Central Pacific*

PT22 *Tahiti to Hawaii*

BEST TIME:	April to June, October to November			
TROPICAL STORMS:	December to March (South Pacific)			
	June to October (North Pacific)			
CHARTS:	BA: 782, 4061			
	US: 541			
PILOTS:	BA: 62			
	US: 126, 152			
CRUISING GUIDES:	*Charlie's Charts of the Hawaiian Islands, Landfalls of Paradise.*			
WAYPOINTS:				

Departure	Intermediate	Landfall	Destination	Distance (M)
PT221 Tahiti 17°32'S, 149°35'W	PT222 Tetiaroa 17°00'S, 149°22'W			
	PT223 15°00'S, 149°30'W			
	PT224 0°00', 145°00'W	PT225 Oahu SE 21°15'N, 157°52'W	Honolulu *21°18'N, 157°52'W*	2578

This passage is best made during the winter months of the South Pacific, when there is no danger of cyclones in the Society Islands or the Tuamotus. During most of this period consistent trade winds are found south of the equator. The optimum time to leave Tahiti, or any other port in the Society Islands, is between April and July, when favourable conditions are usually encountered on both sides of the equator. If Tahiti is left after the end of May, one would arrive in Hawaii during the hurricane season there, so attention should be paid to weather forecasts as one enters the area north of the Line Islands.

On leaving Tahiti, from WP PT221, outside

335

Papeete Harbour, a course is set first to WP PT222, 10 miles east of Tetiaroa Atoll. The course continues due north to pass to the west of all islands in the Tuamotus. From WP PT223, a new course should be set to cross the equator at WP PT224. Any easting made at this stage will be an advantage later on.

From Tahiti to about latitude 10°S the SE trades often blow from E or even NE, but after latitude 10°S is passed the trade winds are SE, so that it becomes possible to choose the best point for crossing the equator. In these longitudes the SE trades extend beyond the equator for most of the year and the doldrum belt rarely exceeds a width of 100 miles. Sometimes the doldrums are virtually nonexistent, the transit from one trade wind system to the next being quite sudden. The NE trades are normally found around latitude 10°N. The course should continue to be slightly to the east of the desired destination, both to allow for the west-setting current and to arrive to windward of one's chosen landfall.

However tempting it might be to break the voyage in one of the Line Islands, as suggested on the reciprocal route from Hawaii to Tahiti, doing so on the way north might be a mistake as too much easting would be lost and the subsequent leg to Hawaii would most probably be hard on the wind. One way of ensuring an easier passage north of the equator is to leave from an island further east than Tahiti, such as Rangiroa, in the Tuamotus, or even further east. For boats arriving from the south, probably the most convenient port of arrival in Hawaii is Honolulu and therefore landfall should be made at WP PT225, two miles south of that harbour on Oahu's south coast.

PT23 *Tahiti to Panama*

BEST TIME:	Mid-October to mid-December
TROPICAL STORMS:	December to March
CHARTS:	BA: 4051, 4061
	US: 62, 621
PILOTS:	BA: 7, 7A, 62
	US: 122, 125, 126, 153
CRUISING GUIDES:	*Cruising Guide Acapulco to the Panama Canal.*

This rarely used route is sailed by those who do not wish to reach the Atlantic either via Cape Horn or the westbound trade wind route. Depending on the time of year, those who wish to reach Panama from Tahiti either have to make their easting with the help of westerly winds of higher latitudes, or cut diagonally across the SE trade winds on a more direct but also more difficult route.

The roundabout route with the help of westerly winds can be taken at all times of the year. From Tahiti the course leads SSE through the Austral Islands until the area of prevailing westerly winds is reached. During the winter months, when the limit of the SE trade winds is furthest north, easting should be made between latitudes 28°S and 32°S. During the summer months it might be necessary to go as far south as latitude 35°S to find consistent W winds. On reaching the meridian of 100°W, the course becomes gradually NE until the SE trades are found again. The route then runs parallel to the South American coast taking advantage of the north-setting Humboldt Current.

The more direct route can be taken when the SE trades are not so fully established, the best time being the southern summer from mid-October to mid-March. As this is the cyclone season in Tahiti, the weather should be carefully watched until one is out of the danger area. On leaving Tahiti a SE course should be sailed so as to pass to the south of the Tuamotu Archipelago. Having passed the Gambier Islands the route leads past Pitcairn Island, from where the great circle route is taken to Panama. Having closed with the South American coast, both wind and current become favourable.

PT24 Cook Islands to Hawaii

Best time:	April to June, November			
Tropical storms:	December to March (South Pacific)			
	June to October (North Pacific)			
Charts:	BA: 780, 782			
	US: 541			
Pilots:	BA: 62			
	US: 126, 152			
Cruising guides:	Charlie's Charts of Polynesia, Charlie's Charts of the Hawaiian Islands, Landfalls of Paradise.			
Waypoints:				

Departure	Intermediate	Landfall	Destination	Distance (M)
PT241 Penrhyn 8°57'S, 157°55'W	PT242 Christmas 1°58'N, 157°32'W			655
	PT243 0°00', 157°45'W	PT244 Oahu S 21°15'N, 157°52'W	Honolulu 21°18'N, 157°52'W	1815

Most boats which take this route through the Northern Cooks (Pukapuka, Manihiki, Penrhyn, and Rakahanga) stop at one of these islands before heading north across the equator. As the Line Islands also lie on the direct route to Hawaii, it may be convenient to stop there too, Fanning and Palmyra having the best anchorages. The passage can be made in any month outside of the cyclone season, which should be avoided as the Northern Cooks have been hit by cyclones in the past. Weather conditions encountered to the north of the Cook Islands is typical doldrum weather and is often squally, with thunderstorms followed by calms. Particularly unpleasant conditions have been encountered north of the equator during the North Pacific hurricane season, as the route passes through a breeding area for tropical depressions. The last leg, from the Line Islands to Hawaii, is mostly hard on the wind, especially north of latitude 10°N where the NE trade winds are usually found. To avoid such headwinds, as much easting as possible should be made in the earlier stages of the voyage.

A good departure point for this passage is Penrhyn Atoll, in the Northern Cooks. From WP PT241, outside its Northeast Pass, the direct route passes so close to Christmas Island that a stop there becomes almost unavoidable. In this case a course can be set for WP PT242, west of the Cook Island Passage, which leads into that island's lagoon. Christmas Island belongs to Kiribati and clearance formalities are completed at the main settlement called London. If a stop is not intended, from WP PT241 a course is set to cross the equator at WP PT243. The route then passes west of Christmas Island and heads for WP PT244 south of Oahu. Entry formalities will be completed in Honolulu Harbour.

PT25 *Hawaii to Tahiti*

BEST TIME:	April to October			
TROPICAL STORMS:	June to October (North Pacific)			
	December to March (South Pacific)			
CHARTS:	BA: 782, 4061			
	US: 541			
PILOTS:	BA: 62			
	US: 122, 126, 152			
CRUISING GUIDES:	*Charlie's Charts of Polynesia, Landfalls of Paradise.*			
WAYPOINTS:				

Departure	Intermediate	Landfall	Destination	Distance (M)
Route PT25A				
PT251 Oahu S	PT252			
21°15'N, 157°52'W	0°00', 145°00'W			
	PT253 Manihi			
	14°24'S, 145°29'W			
	PT254 Rangiroa E	PT255 Tahiti	Papeete	2561
	15°13'S, 147°02'W	17°30'S, 149°34'W	*17°32'S, 149°35'W*	
Route PT25B				
PT251 Oahu S	PT256 Christmas			
	1°58'N, 157°32'W			
	PT257			
	l5°00'S, l49°30'W			
	PT258 Tetiaroa	PT255 Tahiti	Papeete	2436
	17°00'S, 149°22'W			

The first part of this passage can sometimes be unpleasant, particularly in winter, when strong easterly winds and high seas can occur. The weather improves as one moves south and winds become lighter. The width of the doldrums depends on the time of year, some boats having crossed them in a matter of hours, while others have had to battle with light winds and squalls for several days. Although the passage can be done at any time of the year, it is advisable to plan the arrival in Tahiti outside of the cyclone season. April or May are considered to be the best months for the passage south, as the SE trade winds are not yet fully established south of the equator and the favourable season in the Society Islands, and the rest of the South Pacific, is just beginning.

The direct route (PT25A) passes close to the Line Islands where it may be convenient to break the journey, although a price may have to be paid for the stop by having to sail the rest of the voyage hard on the wind. Although NE trade winds will ensure fair winds to about latitude 5°N, once the SE trades are encountered, headwinds are almost

a certainty. This can be avoided by taking a more SE course after leaving Hawaii so as to cross the equator at WP PT252. By that time one has gone so far east that a stop in the Marquesas may be considered (see also PT26).

From WP PT252, boats bound for Tahiti should sail a route that crosses the Western Tuamotus to pass between Takaroa and Manihi atolls at WP PT253. From there the course is altered to pass east of Rangiroa through WP PT254. Approaching Tahiti from NE, landfall is made NNE of the entrance into Papeete at WP PT255. The pass through the reef leading into the harbour is at 17°32.18'S, 149°35.1'W.

Boats that have not made sufficient easting north of the equator, or have stopped at Christmas Island (route PT25B), from WP PT256 should set a course for WP PT257. From that point the course for Tahiti is almost due south and passes west of all the Tuamotus. From WP PT257 the route goes to WP PT258, 10 miles east of Tetiaroa Atoll and finally to WP PT255, at the entrance into Papeete Harbour.

PT26 *Hawaii to Marquesas*

BEST TIME:	April to September			
TROPICAL STORMS:	June to October (North Pacific)			
	December to March (South Pacific)			
CHARTS:	BA: 4051			
	US: 526			
PILOTS:	BA: 62			
	US: 122, 126, 152			
CRUISING GUIDES:	*Charlie's Charts of Polynesia, Landfalls of Paradise.*			
WAYPOINTS:				

Departure	Intermediate	Landfall	Destination	Distance (M)
PT261 Hawaii S	PT262	PT263 Nuku Hiva NE	Taiohae	2043
19°50'N, 155°40'W	0°00', 140°00'W	8°48'S, 139°59'W	*8°56'S, 140°06'W*	

Similar directions apply as for route PT25, although an even more southeasterly course will have to be sailed on leaving Hawaii so as to cross the equator more or less on the meridian of the Marquesas (140°W). The route crosses all three equatorial currents and their combined sets will probably have a westerly resultant, which can make it even more difficult to cross the equator in longitude 140°W. Therefore it is essential to make as much easting as possible while still in the NE trades. One way to overcome this difficulty is to use the Equatorial Countercurrent to make the required easting and only head south towards the equator after the meridian of Nuku Hiva has been crossed.

Because having sufficient easting in hand is so important on this route, one should attempt to leave from one of the most eastern ports in Hawaii, such as Kealakekua. Hilo itself would probably be too much to windward. From WP PT261, off Ka Lae, the southern point of Hawaii Island, a direct course should be set for WP PT262. Having crossed the equator, a direct course can be set for Nuku Hiva and WP PT263, off the island's NE point. From here the south coast of Nuku Hiva is followed into the perfectly protected bay of Taiohae, the capital of the Marquesas. There are two official ports of entry into the Marquesas, Taiohae and Atuona (9°51'S, 139°02'W), on the island of Hiva Oa. Because of the layout of the islands in relation to the prevailing winds, it is usually better to clear in at Atuona, cruise the various islands from SE to NW, and visit Nuku Hiva at the end of the cruise. However, this means making even more easting on the passage from Hawaii, but it could be an early sacrifice which would be highly appreciated later on.

PT30 TRANSEQUATORIAL ROUTES IN THE WESTERN PACIFIC

The few routes which cross the equator in the Western Pacific are heavily influenced by the opposing tropical storm seasons and in fact many of those who cross the equator in one or the other direction do so to escape the threat of cyclones or typhoons in their own hemisphere. Whereas south of the equator the northern limit of tropical storms is fairly reliable, and cyclones only very rarely occur north of 10°S, north of the equator typhoons have formed in or around the Carolines at almost any time of the year making it much more important to watch the weather carefully at all times.

The crossing of the equator itself presents little problems as the doldrums in the Western Pacific are quite narrow and passages through the ITCZ, and from one wind system to the next, are quickly accomplished. The currents in the Western Pacific have a very complex pattern. The South Equatorial Current sets westward in a wide belt south of latitudes 4°N to 5°N. At the northern limit of this belt there is an abrupt reversal in the direction of the current.

The east-setting Equatorial Countercurrent is relatively narrow and gives way to the North Equatorial Current. The latter sets to the west and, depending on the season, can affect an area between latitudes 7°N or 8°N to 15°N. Occasionally it can extend as far north as 20°N. The strength of these currents is about 1 to 1½ knots, so when sailing any of these routes particular attention should be paid to the complex character of these phenomena.

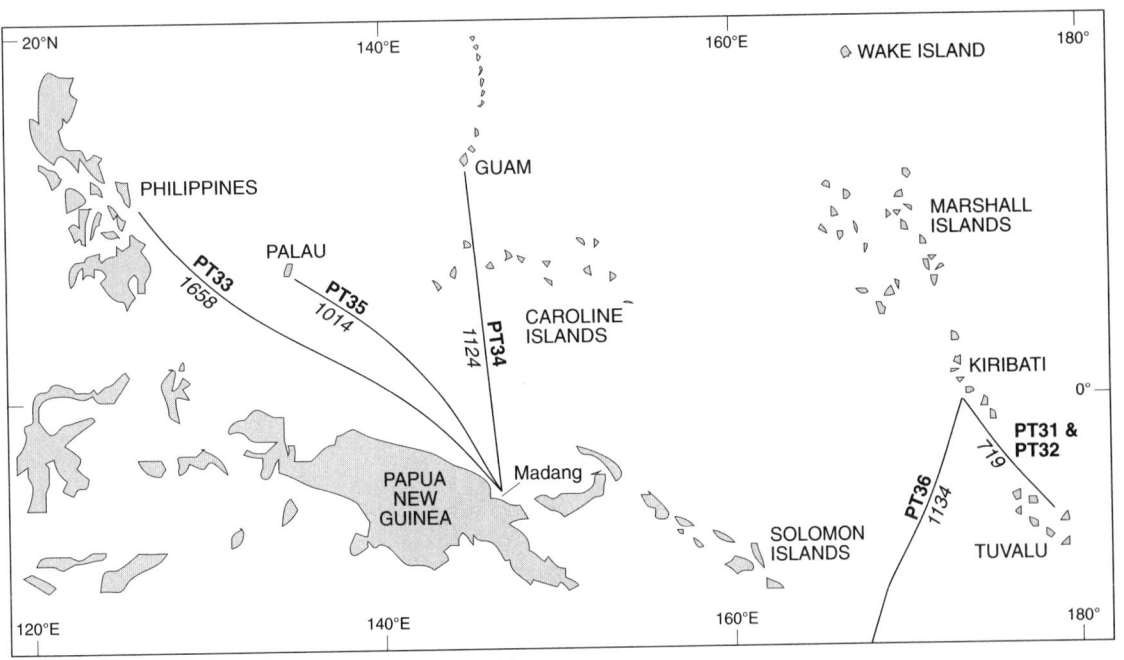

PT30 *Transequatorial routes in the Western Pacific*

PT31 *Tuvalu to Kiribati*

BEST TIME:	April to October			
TROPICAL STORMS:	November to March			
CHARTS:	BA: 4052			
	US: 526			
PILOTS:	BA: 61			
	US: 126			
CRUISING GUIDES:	*Landfalls of Paradise.*			
WAYPOINTS:				

Departure	Intermediate	Landfall	Destination	Distance (M)
PT311 Funafuti N 8°25'S, 179°07'E	PT312 5°00'S, 176°00'E			
	PT313 0°00', I72°50'E	PT314 Tarawa S 1°24'N, 172°53'E	Betio *1°21'N, 172°55'E*	719

The passage between these two former partners in the Gilbert and Ellice Islands colony can be made throughout the year, although the best sailing conditions can be expected from April to October, when winds are mostly from the easterly quarter. November to February is the rainy season in the islands when strong westerly gales are common. This is also the cyclone season in the South Pacific and Tuvalu has been occasionally struck by cyclones in the past. Especially during the westerly season, the currents among the islands are very irregular and their set impossible to predict. Generally the currents among the islands of both Tuvalu and Kiribati behave in an erratic way throughout the year and this should be borne in mind when sailing in these waters.

The direct course from Funafuti to Tarawa, the capitals of these two countries, passes close to several islands, at some of which it is possible to stop. The best protected lagoon is at Nukufetau, the nearest atoll north of Funafuti. Having left Funafuti lagoon through its northern pass Te Ava i de Lape, from WP PT311, outside the pass, boats intending to sail nonstop to Kiribati should set a course for WP PT312 to pass on the windward side of Nukufetau. From there, the course can be altered to cross the equator at WP PT313. As the direct route passes very close to several islands and reefs, such as Niutao, slight course adjustments will not only be unavoidable but essential on account of the

strong currents which are occasionally experienced in this area. Having crossed the equator, the course becomes almost due north and passes to the west of Maiana to make landfall at WP PT314, on the SW side of Tarawa lagoon close to the pass leading into it. Arriving boats should make their way into the small port at Betio, in the SW corner of Tarawa lagoon. There is a depth of only 6 ft in the channel leading into Betio, so one may have to come alongside the commercial wharf on the way in or anchor in the lagoon. Tarawa Radio should be contacted on VHF channel 16 when approaching the island to give an ETA.

The islands of Kiribati straddle the equator and although one is supposed to clear in first at Tarawa, in an emergency one can stop briefly at one of the southern islands, the safest anchorages being found in the lagoons of Onotoa, Tabiteua, and Abemama. When approaching Tarawa from the south, the island of Maiana should be treated with caution as it is wrongly depicted on the charts and the reef extending to the SW of the island is more extensive than indicated. In fact, the charted position of all islands in this area should be treated with a degree of suspicion as many are surrounded by dangerous reefs, the positions of which are often poorly charted, as the charts have not been updated for many years. This hazard is compounded by the fact that many of these reefs cannot be seen at night or in poor visibility.

PT32 *Kiribati to Tuvalu*

BEST TIME:	March to October			
TROPICAL STORMS:	November to March			
CHARTS:	BA: 4052			
	US: 526			
PILOTS:	BA: 61			
	US: 126			
CRUISING GUIDES:	*Landfalls of Paradise.*			
WAYPOINTS:				

Departure	Intermediate	Landfall	Destination	Distance (M)
PT321 Tarawa SW 1°24'N, 172°53'E	PT322 0°00', 172°50'E PT323 5°00'S, 176°00'E	PT324 Funafuti N 8°25'S, 179°07'E	Fongafale *8°31'S, 179°12'E*	723

The directions for this route are similar to those for the opposite route PT31. If planning to stop at any of the southern islands of Kiribati, permission to do so should be obtained before leaving Tarawa. The route south of Tarawa passes close to Maiana, which should not be approached too closely as its position does not agree with the charts. From WP PT321, SW of Tarawa lagoon, a course is set to cross the equator at WP PT322. Most islands in Southern Kiribati have well protected lagoons and a stop en route is highly recommended. The islands of Tuvalu provide fewer protected anchorages, with the notable exceptions of Nanumea and Nukufetau. After landfall is made at WP PT324, Funafuti lagoon is entered through Te Ava i de Lape Pass. Yachts should make their way to the commercial wharf, on the east side of the lagoon, to complete formalities. Funafuti is Tuvalu's only port of entry and boats are not supposed to stop at any of the islands before having cleared in.

The period between the middle of October and the end of March should be avoided if one intends to stop in Tuvalu for any length of time as most anchorages there are unsafe in strong westerly winds, which are common during this time. Although Tuvalu is normally considered to lie outside the cyclone zone, on rare occasions tropical storms have hit the islands. The worst of these in recent times occurred in October 1952 and devastated Funafuti. Considerable damage was also caused by cyclone Ofa in February 1990.

PT33 *New Guinea to Philippines*

BEST TIME:	December to March			
TROPICAL STORMS:	April to December (North Pacific)			
CHARTS:	BA: 4507			
	US: 524			
PILOTS:	BA: 33, 60			
	US: 162,164			
WAYPOINTS:				

Departure	Intermediate	Landfall	Destination	Distance (M)
PT331 Madang 5°12'S, 145°52'E	PT332 4°10'S, 145°45'E PT333 0°00', 140°00'E	PT334 Surigao 10°30'N, 125°50'E	Cebu City *10°18'N, 123°54'E*	1658

This route is sailed mainly by those who are looking for a change of scenery from the islands of the South Pacific and intend to sail on to Hong Kong and possibly Japan. This passage is normally sailed during the NW monsoon, between November and March, so as to arrive in the Philippines before the onset of the typhoon season. Although this season is less well defined in the North West Pacific than the tropical storm seasons in other parts of the world, the most dangerous months are considered to be the summer months, from July to October, with the highest frequency of typhoons in September. Passages north of the equator should be avoided during this period.

Boats leaving from Rabaul on the island of New Britain should follow a route to pass east of the Admiralty Islands, whereas for those leaving from Madang, or other ports on the main island of New Guinea, a NW course passing west of the Admiralty group is more logical. Although this westerly route also allows a stop at the Hermit Islands, at the height of the NW monsoon, the wind can blow strongly from the north in the slot between New Guinea and the Admiralty Islands, making it a difficult and rough passage. The monsoon loses its strength as the equator is approached and the doldrum region entered. The width of the doldrums varies with the time of year, but it is seldom wider than 100 miles, and can be crossed quickly by motoring through. It is indeed recommended that yachts pass through this area as quickly as possible as the currents have a very complex pattern.

The South Equatorial Current sets westward in a wide belt south of latitudes 4°N to 5°N. At the northern limit of this belt there is an abrupt reversal in the direction of the current. The east-setting Equatorial Countercurrent is relatively narrow and gives way to the west-setting North Equatorial Current. The latter can extend from latitude 7°N or 8°N to 15°N or even 20°N, depending on the season. The strength of these currents is about 1 to 1½ knots, so when sailing this route particular attention should be paid to the complex character of these currents.

North of the doldrums light northerly winds can be expected until about latitude 5°N where the NE trade winds should be encountered. During the winter months, from December to March, the trade winds are stronger and more consistent in these lower latitudes, but they tend to become lighter and more variable with the approach of summer. The weather forecasts broadcast from Guam cover this entire region and can be very helpful during the typhoon season.

Madang is perhaps the best starting point for this passage. From WP PT331 the initial course runs due north passing west of Karkar Island to WP PT332. After a course alteration at that point the route sets off in a NW direction, parallel to the north coast of New Guinea, passing several islands on the way to cross the equator at WP PT333. The route then passes close to Sonsorol Island and makes landfall at WP PT334 from where Surigao Channel is used to reach Cebu City, the nearest port of entry into the Philippines.

Most boats en route to the Philippines stop in Palau. The official port of entry is Malakal Harbour (7°20'N, 134°29'E). Yachts must not stop anywhere before Malakal and the Port Authority must be informed in advance of a yacht's ETA. Yachts arriving without a permit, which must be obtained in advance, may only be allowed to stay for a maximum of three days.

PT34 *New Guinea to Micronesia*

BEST TIME:	December to March
TROPICAL STORMS:	All year
CHARTS:	BA: 4506, 4507
	US: 524
PILOTS:	BA: 60
	US: 126, 164
CRUISING GUIDES:	*Landfalls of Paradise.*

WAYPOINTS:				
Departure	*Intermediate*	*Landfall*	*Destination*	*Distance (M)*
Route PT34A				
PT341 Madang	PT342	PT343 Guam W	Apra	1124
5°12'S, 145°52'E	0°00', 145°40'E	13°27'N, 144°35'E	*13°27'N, 144°37'E*	
Route PT34B				
Rabaul	PT344			
4°12'S, 152°11'E	4°50'S, 153°00'E			
	PT345	PT346 Pohnpei	Kolonia	843
	0°00', 155°10'E	7°02'N,158°10'E	*6°59'N, 158°13'E*	

Because of the high incidence of typhoons that either hit Guam or form between the island and the equator, passages to Guam are usually timed during the northern winter. This is the time of the NW monsoon in New Guinea when the weather in the Bismarck Sea and northern islands of Papua New Guinea is less settled than during the rest of the year. Few boats attempt to sail this passage nonstop and there are various islands which can be visited en route. However, a series of recent typhoons which have affected the islands of Micronesia during the supposedly safe period of November and December, provide a strong argument in favour of avoiding an arrival in this area before January.

If the northbound passage is made at the change of monsoons, in November or early December, calms will be frequent south of the equator. By the middle of December steady NE winds become prevalent north of the equator and rather than beat all the way to Guam, some people prefer to break the trip in Truk, where it is possible to reprovision and also refuel. A good port of departure for a direct passage from New Guinea to Guam is Madang. From WP PT341, outside Madang Harbour, the initial course runs due north passing west of Karkar Island and close to the east of Kaniet Island to cross the equator at WP PT342. The route passes a number of reefs and atolls in Micronesia and makes landfall off the west coast of Guam at WP PT343, outside Apra Harbour. On arrival at Apra, Harbour Control must be contacted on VHF channel 16 for berthing and clearance instructions.

Few boats attempt to make this passage nonstop and a convenient place to stop on the way is Truk. The main harbour is Moen (7°20'N, 151°50'E), in Truk Lagoon. An earlier stop can be made at Kapingamarangi (1°04'N, 154°45'E), although few provisions will be available in that isolated community. Greenwich Passage, on the south side of the atoll, leads into the large lagoon. The passage is divided into two channels by a shallow patch. Tidal streams are very strong in the pass which should be entered at or near slack water. Extreme caution should be exercised when approaching this atoll as it is reported to be 5 miles east of its charted position.

Pohnpei, which is reported to be the best place for reprovisioning in this area outside of Guam, is usually difficult to reach because of constant easterly winds. If a stop at Pohnpei is intended, it is probably better to leave on this passage from further east in Papua New Guinea from a port such as Rabaul. In this case, the point of departure will be south of the island of New Ireland at WP PT344 from where a direct course can be set for Pohnpei. The equator is crossed at WP PT345 and landfall is made at WP PT346, from where Sokehns Passage is used to enter Pohnpei Harbour. The port of entry is Kolonia.

Like everywhere else in the Federated States of Micronesia a cruising permit is required and this should be obtained in advance.

PT35 *Palau to New Guinea*

BEST TIME:	October to March			
TROPICAL STORMS:	April to December (North Pacific)			
CHARTS:	BA: 780, 781			
	US: 524			
PILOTS:	BA: 60			
	US: 126, 164			
CRUISING GUIDES:	*Landfalls of Paradise.*			
WAYPOINTS:				
Departure	**Intermediate**	**Landfall**	**Destination**	**Distance (M)**
Route PT35A				
PT351 Palau SE	PT352		Vanimo	720
7°20'N, 134°45'E	0°00', 140°00'E		2°41'S, 141°18'E	
			Wewak	848
			3°35'S, 143°40'E	
Route PT35B				
PT351 Palau SE	PT353		Lorengau	1218
	0°00', 150°00'E		2°00'S, 147°15'E	
			Kavieng	1174
			2°34'S, 150°48'E	

The best time to make this passage is from October to March, so as to arrive in the vicinity of New Guinea either after or before the SE monsoon (April to mid-October), thus avoiding contrary winds and the strong current which sets NW along the coast of New Guinea. During October and November little wind can be expected in the Bismarck Sea as the monsoon shifts from SE to NW, so one should be prepared to motor. From December to March favourable winds and current can be expected in the vicinity of New Guinea and the passage should present no problems.

After leaving Palau, from WP PT351, SE of Babeltuap Island, one should stand to the SE to cross the equator in about longitude 140°E (WP PT352), if wishing to call at ports on the main island of New Guinea (PT35A) or further east if bound for islands in the Bismarck Sea (PT35B). Attention should be paid to the complex character of the currents in this region, as described at the beginning of this section.

If the passage is made in September, when the SW monsoon is still in force north of the equator, winds from that direction can be expected between Palau and latitude 5°N. From there, the doldrums may extend as far south as latitude 1°S. As SE winds are still strong further south at this time, the change of seasons (November) can be awaited either in the Ninigo or Hermit Islands, a convenient stopping point for boats making this passage in either direction.

If one has no choice but to make this passage after April and the start of the SE monsoon south of the equator, it is recommended to make as much easting as possible while still north of the equator, taking advantage of the easterly set of the Equatorial Countercurrent. The equator should be crossed in about longitude 150°E (PT353), and allowance be made for the west-setting South Equatorial Current, so as to enter the Bismarck Sea to the east of the Admiralty Islands.

For boats coming from this direction, the most convenient ports of entry into Papua New Guinea are Vanimo and Wewak, both on the north coast of New Guinea, Lorengau on Manus (Admiralty) Island, and Kavieng on New Ireland.

PT36 *Micronesia to Southern Melanesia*

BEST TIME:	April, November			
TROPICAL STORMS:	December to March			
CHARTS:	BA: 4506, 4604			
	US: 506, 604			
PILOTS:	BA: 60, 61			
	US: 126			
CRUISING GUIDES:	*Landfalls of Paradise, South Pacific Anchorages.*			
WAYPOINTS:				
Departure	*Intermediate*	*Landfall*	*Destination*	*Distance (M)*
PT360 Betio	PT361 Tarawa W			
1°21'N, 172°55'E	*1°18'N, 172°52'E*			
	PT362 Banks			
	13°00'S, 168°00'E			
	PT363 Santo NE	PT364 Santo	Luganville	1134
	15°00'S, 167°22'E	*15°33'S, 167°20'E*	*15°31'S, 167°10'E*	

By planning to arrive south of the equator at the start of the safe sailing season in the South Pacific (April to November), favourable NE winds will be experienced virtually all the way to the equator. This is true especially for those starting off from the Marshalls or Kiribati who should try to cross the equator not further west than 165°E, so as to ensure a better angle across the SE trade winds. Boats sailing from the Carolines will find it quite difficult to make the required easting north of the equator, unless they manage to do this by making short hops through the archipelago and setting off from an island such as Kapingamarangi.

Heading south across the equator, one has a choice of destination in the Solomons, Vanuatu, and even Fiji, although in the latter case, because of the risk of having to sail straight into the SE trade winds, some easting should be made north of the equator. Generally it is advisable to make as much easting as possible while still north of the equator,

where the North Equatorial Countercurrent will give an additional boost. Ideally one should attempt to start this passage as far east as possible, and in this case Tarawa in Kiribati is probably the best choice. There are many alternatives if one starts from the Carolines and, if so, an interesting stop could be made at Kapingamarangi. This isolated Polynesian island is administered by Pohnpei (Ponape), but because of its isolation, visitors are always welcome. The large lagoon provides good shelter and is entered by a pass through the reef.

For boats heading for islands in the South Pacific a good destination is Northern Vanuatu, where the official port of entry is at Luganville on Espiritu Santo Island (Santo). The route passes to the east of the Banks Islands, from where the course is set for the SE side of Santo. Facilities in Luganville are adequate and a good place for cruising boats to find a safe mooring is at Aore Resort, on neighbouring Aore Island.

PT37 *Melanesia to Micronesia*

BEST TIME:	April, November			
TROPICAL STORMS:	All year			
CHARTS:	BA: 4506, 4604			
	US: 506, 604			
PILOTS:	BA: 60, 61			
	US: 126			
CRUISING GUIDES:	*Landfalls of Paradise, South Pacific Anchorages.*			
WAYPOINTS:				

Departure	Intermediate	Landfall	Destination	Distance (M)
PT370 Graciosa Bay *10°44'S, 165°49'E*	PT371 Duff *10°00'S, 167°20'E*			
	PT372 *0°00', 172°45'E*	PT373 Tarawa S *1°24'N, 172°53'E*	Betio *1°21'N, 172°55'E*	870
PT370 Graciosa Bay	PT371 Duff			
	PT374 Nauru *0°31'S, 166°56'E*	PT375 Kosrae *5°20'N, 163°03'E*	Lelu *5°20'N, 163°01'E*	1094

Starting from the premise that the majority of those crossing the equator wish to start visiting the islands of Micronesia as far east as possible, two destinations are recommended: Tarawa, the capital of Kiribati, or Kosrae, in the Federated States of Micronesia. As making easting will not be easy, either south or north of the equator, it is suggested that the furthest point of departure should be Graciosa Bay, a port of entry in the Santa Cruz Islands, which belong to the Solomons. This small group of islands, lying east of the main Solomons archipelago, is easily reached from most other island groups in the South Pacific.

One of the difficulties associated with this route is to match the opposing cyclone seasons on the two sides of the equator. Whereas the austral winter (May to September) is the safe season in Melanesia, this is the worst period for typhoons north of the equator. Therefore a good time to cross the equator is either around the beginning or end of the typhoon season, and even at those times the weather should be monitored carefully, especially north of the equator where tropical storms can occur in any month.

As NE winds may be expected north of the equator as much easting as possible should be made while south of the line, which should not be too difficult as one will be helped in this by the east-setting Equatorial Counter Current. Boats bound for Tarawa should attempt to cross the equator almost due south of their destination. The route passes west of Maiana, which should be approached with caution as it is erroneously depicted even on current charts. The port of Betio is in the SW corner of the large Tarawa lagoon and is reached by a dredged channel. The channel leading into the inner harbour has a charted depth of only 6 ft.

Boats bound for Kosrae may be tempted to stop at Nauru, the once phosphate-rich island nation which lies close to the direct route. Facilities at the port of Aiwo, Nauru's main port, are for large ships only but visiting yachts may use a ship's mooring if available. North of the equator, NE winds will be experienced on the way to Kosrae, a mountainous island surrounded by a barrier reef. The main settlement is on the east coast and boats will find a sheltered anchorage at Lelu.

12

WINDS AND
CURRENTS OF THE
SOUTH PACIFIC

The Southeast trade winds

The majority of cruising routes in the South Pacific are dependent on these winds which blow over a large area of this ocean. The SE trade winds blow on the equatorial side of the high pressure area situated in about 30°S. In the vicinity of the coast of South America the trade winds blow from between S and SE, but their direction becomes increasingly E towards the west of the ocean. In the vicinity of Australia the winds become SE again, especially during the winter months. During the summer months, from November to April, the trade wind is less steady over large parts of the ocean. West of about 140°W, there are frequently winds from other directions, although the prevailing direction remains between NE and SE.

The average strength of the SE trade wind is 15 knots, although in some areas it can increase to 20 or even 25 knots. The strongest winds are experienced in the Coral Sea, where they reach 30 knots on occasion. However, the SE trade winds of the South Pacific are neither as steady nor as constant as the trade winds of other oceans. A continuous belt of SE wind blowing steadily across the entire ocean exists only during the months of June, July, and August. During the rest of the year there is an area 600 miles wide, in which the force of the trade winds is not so constant. In this large area, stretching diagonally across the trade wind belt, extending SE from the Phoenix Islands through the Tuamotus as far as Easter Island, the direction of the wind often changes to the NE to be succeeded by calms. After a while the winds revert to blow-

ing strongly from the SE and are frequently accompanied by heavy rain squalls.

Reinforced trade winds often bring stronger than expected winds. This phenomenon occurs mostly south of 10°S and depends on both the location and intensity of the South Pacific high. On a weather-fax chart this will show up as a closer spacing of the isobars and also a more northern location of the high itself. Even stronger winds, usually from S, are generated by the passage of a front. Ahead of such a front, the SE winds get lighter as they back to E and NE. Often they cease altogether as the front passes to the south of the area. As the front passes, strong winds blow from SW and then gradually back to S and SE, often to be followed by a period of reinforced trades as the high fills in.

The belt of trade winds moves considerably during the year. The southern limit moves almost 300 hundred miles, while the northern limit moves less, about 150 miles, and is situated north of the equator throughout the year except in the east of the ocean. The northern limit of the SE trade winds forms a gentle curve with its highest point reaching 5°N in January and as far as 9°N in July. The lower boundary curves similarly in July with its higher limit being about 18°S , whereas in January the trade winds deepen toward the South American coast reaching as far south as 30°S.

Intertropical Convergence Zone

The northern limit of the SE trade winds is determined by the position of the Intertropical Convergence Zone (ITCZ), which stays north of the equator throughout the year east of about longitude 160°W. In the western half of the ocean, it moves to the southern hemisphere from about November to April, reaching furthest south in February, at the peak of the southern summer. The movement of the ITCZ is most pronounced in the vicinity of Australia and Papua New Guinea, where the width of the doldrum belt can be greatest. On average it has a width of about 150 miles, but in some places it can be twice as wide, whereas in other areas it can be entirely absent. Weather conditions inside the zone are typical of doldrums everywhere, with calms or light variable winds alternating with rain squalls and thunderstorms. These conditions are more extreme in the doldrums of the Western Pacific than elsewhere because of the wide angle at which the SE trade winds and NW monsoon meet in that area.

South Pacific Convergence Zone

One special feature of South Pacific weather is the South Pacific Convergence Zone (SPCZ), which occurs during winter and stretches roughly ESE from 5°S, 155°E to 20°S, 150°W, affecting the area between the Solomons and Tahiti. The SPCZ, which must not be confused with the ITCZ, moves along the above area and affects weather conditions when it is active or when a front passes through it. The winds usually shift rapidly from NE to S and can reach storm and even hurricane force. The location of this zone and whether it is active or not is indicated in some local weather forecasts.

Northwest monsoon

During the summer months, west of meridian 180 and between the equator and the ITCZ, which is situated over Northern Australia, a prevailing NW wind blows over the western part of the South Pacific. The NW monsoon normally lasts from December to March, but its constancy depends on the latitude of the area concerned. The areas mostly affected by the NW monsoon are the Solomon Islands, Papua New Guinea, and Northern Australia. The direction of the wind is mainly N or NE near the equator, becoming NW or even W in more southerly latitudes. The NW monsoon is not very consistent either in strength or direction, but in spite of that, at the height of the season, winds from between S and E are quite rare. The strength of the monsoon is light or moderate, although it can

reach gale force in squalls, which are quite frequent. The weather is generally cloudy and overcast, with heavy rainfall. Close to the direction of the wind can be greatly affected by local conditions.

Variables

Between the southern limit of the SE trade winds and the northern limit of the westerlies, there is an area of variable winds of moderate strength. This belt of variable winds extends from 25°S to 40°S during the summer months and from 20°S to 30°S during winter. The belt does not extend across the entire ocean and its position also varies from year to year. East of about 85°W, the prevailing winds are S or SE, being an extension of the SE trade winds. The strength and direction of these variable winds can vary considerably, although they tend to become stronger in higher latitudes.

Westerlies

The prevailing westerly winds or Roaring Forties predominate south of the South Pacific high, which is situated in about latitude 30°S. In the west, these winds are influenced by the movement of anticyclones tracking east from the vicinity of Australia. The almost continuous passage of depressions from west to east causes the wind to vary greatly in both direction and strength. The westerlies are most consistent between latitudes 40° and 50°S. Gales are common in winter, although strong winds can be experienced at any time of the year.

Tropical storms

A large area of the South Pacific is affected by cyclones between December and April. The greatest frequency has been recorded from January to March. The area mainly affected lies to the south of about 8° to 10°S and to the west of 140°W, in a wide belt stretching all the way from the Marquesas in the east to Torres Strait in the west. In some areas, such as the Coral Sea, tropical storms have occurred on rare occasions at other times outside of the accepted cyclone season. The most dangerous months are December to March, when tropical depressions which develop over the Coral Sea or Gulf of Carpentaria can turn into a cyclone.

The number of tropical storms varies greatly from year to year as do their paths, although the central area of the South Pacific does experience more cyclones than the fringe areas. In some areas with-

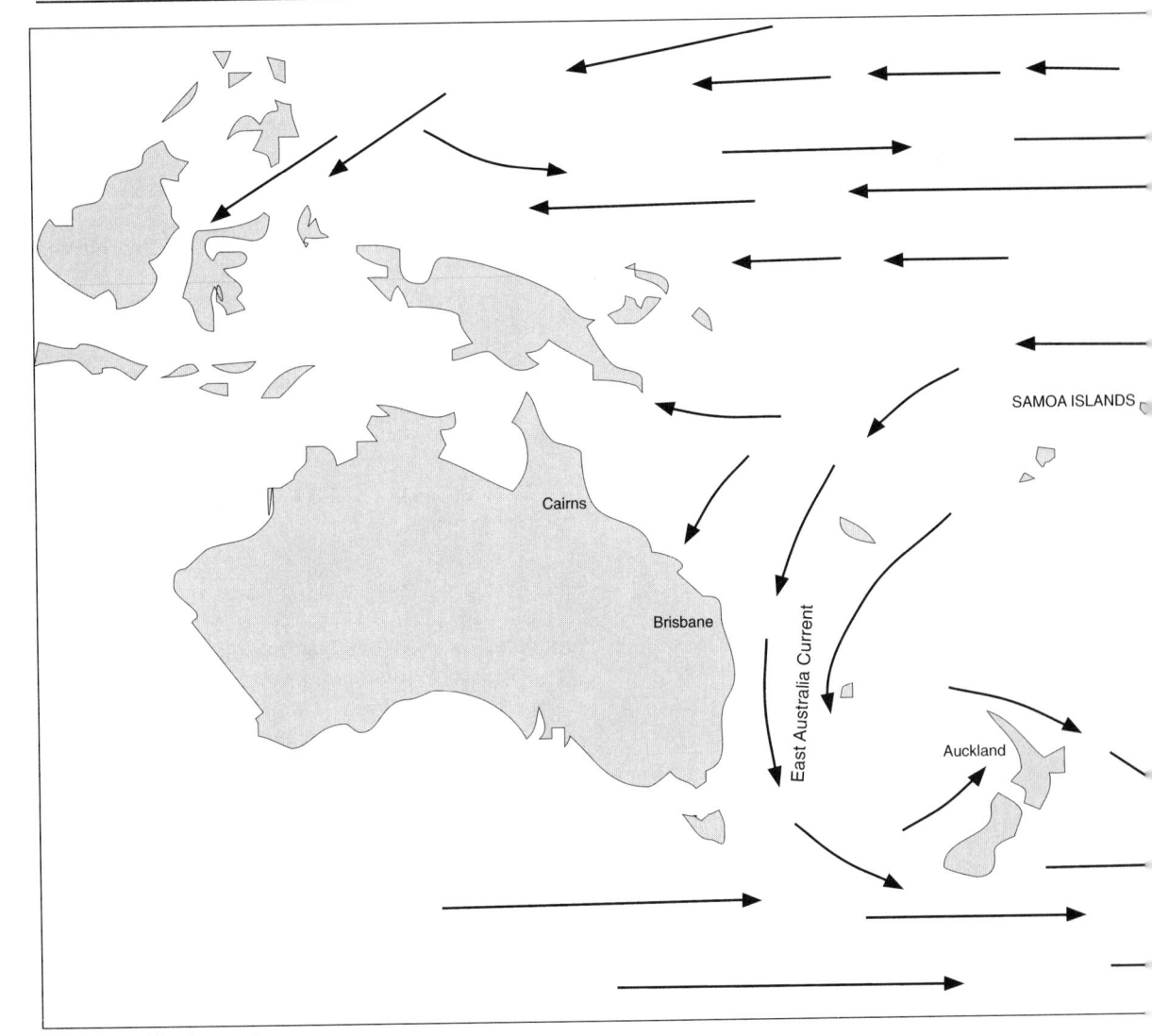

South Pacific Currents

in the cyclone belt, such as Tahiti, cyclones may not occur for many years, which has lulled people into erroneously regarding these areas as cyclone free.

Currents

The main surface circulation of the South Pacific Ocean is counterclockwise, although less is known about these currents than those of other oceans. Around the edges of the South Pacific, the four components of this counterclockwise movement are the west-setting South Equatorial Current, the south-setting East Australia Current, the east-setting Southern Ocean Current, and finally the north-setting Peru or Humboldt Current.

Many cruising routes are affected by the South Equatorial Current which has its northern limit from 1° to 4°N or even 5°N depending both on season and longitude. The axis of this current lies furthest north of the equator in the southern summer and just north of the equator in winter. The South Equatorial Current decreases in strength south of latitude 6°S, although it maintains its westerly direction. Between latitudes 6°S and 20°S, this weaker current is known as the South Subtropical Current.

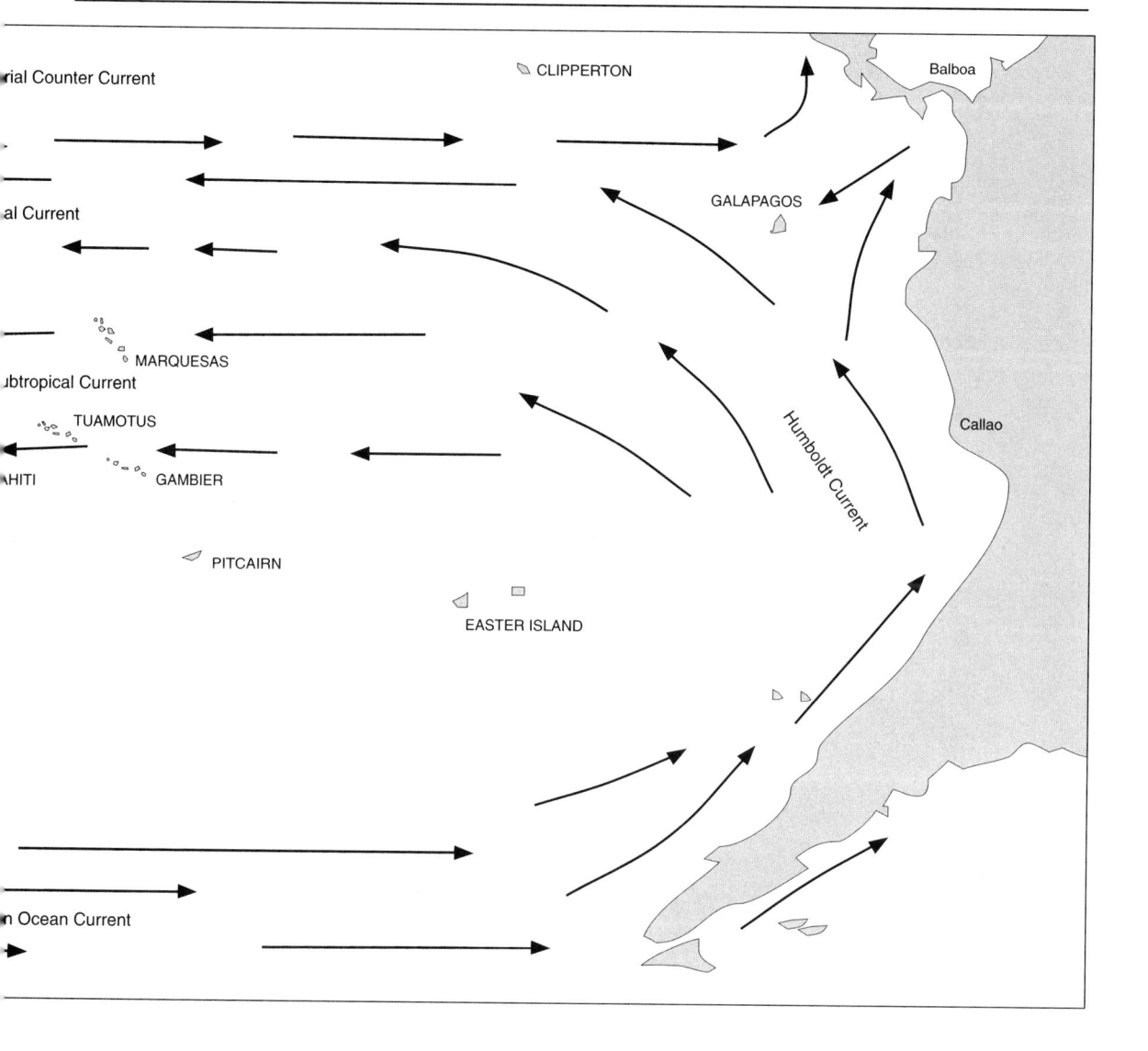

In the western part of the South Pacific, the direction of the current varies seasonally. Between June and August the current follows the coast of New Guinea in a NW direction. In September to November and also in March to May, there is a reversal of the Equatorial Countercurrent, which during those periods flows along the coast of New Guinea in a SE direction.

There is a SW flow from the South Subtropical Current past the islands of Tuvalu, Vanuatu, and New Caledonia, but the currents in this region show considerable variation. The same can be said about currents among the islands of the Tuamotu archi-

pelago and also between Tonga and Fiji, as well as among the islands of Fiji's Lau Group. When sailing in any of these areas utmost attention should be paid to the unpredictability of local currents.

The currents of the Coral Sea are also little known, except that in the northern part the current sets strongly towards Torres Strait, whereas in the southern part the current is S or SW. This current eventually joins the stronger East Australia Current which flows south along the coast of Australia and can be of great help to those bound for ports in New South Wales. In the Tasman Sea, between Australia and New Zealand, the current is mostly variable, although it tends to set east.

The Southern Ocean Current sets E or NE in higher latitudes. Most of this current flows into the Atlantic Ocean south of Cape Horn, but one part of it turns north along the west coast of South America to become the Peru or Humboldt Current. This cold current flows north towards the equator and eventually feeds into the South Equatorial Current. The flow of the Humboldt Current is sometimes reversed by the Equatorial Counter-current, which extends further south during the southern hemisphere summer than at other times.

A branch of this current sometimes turns south along the coast of Ecuador and on rare occasions can reach as far south as the latitude of Callao. Because this warm southgoing current sometimes appears around Christmas, it has been called El Niño or the Holy Child Current. In years when it is fully established this warm current can greatly influence weather conditions in the eastern half of the South Pacific. The freak conditions of 1983 have been attributed to El Niño, which raised the surface temperature of the sea by several degrees causing an unprecedented weather pattern. (See page 33.)

13
ROUTES IN THE SOUTH PACIFIC

No other region of the world exerts such a lasting fascination on sailors and nonsailors alike as the South Pacific. From the *Bounty* mutineers to Bernard Moitessier, many a sailor has succumbed to the irresistible temptation of the South Seas. This phenomenon is by no means limited to the past as every year other people fall in love with the South Pacific. Although jet travel and better inter-island communications have brought much of the South Pacific within reach of the outside world, there are still countless places which can only be reached by boat. For those travelling in this way, the South Pacific offers an unspoilt face, especially to those who are prepared to deviate from the well trodden track. This vast expanse of water covering one third of the earth's surface is dotted with a myriad of tiny islands on which live some of the most remote and isolated communities in the world. Communications between most of the islands are usually by boat, although only in a few places are traditional sailing craft still in use. The small boat voyager is therefore at a great advantage and one of the greatest satisfactions experienced while sailing in the South Pacific is the warm welcome extended by islanders to those arriving from the sea.

Sailing conditions in the South Pacific are unfortunately not always as idyllic as people expect and the vagaries of the weather must be treated with as much caution as elsewhere in the world. Although the seasons are fairly well defined and there are few storms apart from tropical cyclones, which only occur in certain months and certain areas, the wind systems are less consistent than in other parts of the world. The SE trade winds, which affect most of the cruising routes across the South Pacific, are renowned for their fickleness and are often disappointing, especially to those who come from the Caribbean. There are years when the

trades blow with surprising consistency, just as there are years when they come in spurts, either blowing at near gale force for weeks on end or being replaced by calms and squally weather.

One feature of South Pacific weather that many are not aware of is the South Pacific Convergence Zone (SPCZ). This unusual phenomenon, which occurs during winter, affects weather both on passage and while at anchor, so boats must be very much aware of it when anchoring in places where there is no protection from the SW, as this is the direction where the strongest and also unexpected winds will come from, whether generated by a passing front or the SPCZ itself. The location of the zone is indicated in some of the local forecasts.

Generally, however, the weather encountered by the majority of those who cruise in the South Pacific is usually pleasant and only rarely uncomfortable or outright dangerous. The worst conditions are often encountered not on passage, but in port, usually by those who have either picked an unsafe anchorage or have decided to spend the cyclone season in the tropics. Both these dangers can be avoided, as there are sufficient safe anchorages available and the cyclone season can easily be spent outside the area affected by tropical storms.

Unfortunately weather is not the only hazard faced by those who sail in the South Pacific and in fact a much higher proportion of boats are lost every year because of other causes. The most obvious danger are the coral reefs which extend to windward of many low, unlit islands, making navigation throughout the South Pacific a very difficult operation. This problem is often compounded by the presence of strong currents among some island groups. Every year the reefs of various archipelagos cause the loss of several cruising boats, as do the cyclones that sweep through some of the same areas. Modern navigational equipment, a good dose of common sense, and some advance planning can reduce such risks to an acceptable minimum, making a cruise in the South Pacific as safe as anywhere else.

The main cruising route across the South Pacific runs in a gigantic arc linking Panama with the Torres Strait. It has been affectionately nick-named the 'Milk Run', an apt description especially in the case of those who stick to it and avoid the cyclone seasons. The Germans call it more pro-saically the 'Barefoot Route', underlining one of its greatest attractions for those who are used to sail-ing in colder climates. There are countless varia-tions to this trunk route, with secondary routes branching off and rejoining it along its entire length. At its eastern end, the route is fed by a sub-stantial influx of American and Canadian boats, most arriving directly in the Marquesas from the USA or British Columbia. At its western end, the route is joined by boats from New Zealand or Australia setting off on their world voyages. This truly international trunk road of the oceans con-tinues then into the Indian Ocean where it splits into two branches, one leading towards the Red Sea and Mediterranean, the other towards the Cape of Good Hope and the Atlantic Ocean.

The prime destination for practically any boat arriving in the South Pacific is French Polynesia and its main island Tahiti. Most people take the direct route there by way of the Marquesas, espe-cially those who have reached the Pacific Ocean by way of the Panama Canal or whose home ports are on the west coast of North America. Some of the lat-ter arrive in Tahiti via Hawaii. There is also the pos-sibility of reaching Polynesia by a more roundabout way, via South America and Easter Island, a route which offers the chance to visit some of the remotest communities in the eastern South Pacific, Pitcairn Island being perhaps the most famous among them. By this southern route it is also pos-sible to visit some of the outer islands of French Polynesia before joining the main route in Tahiti. Finally, a number of boats make their way to Tahiti from New Zealand, their skippers undaunted by the tougher conditions associated with sailing in higher latitudes.

Lying at the centre of a network of routes, Tahiti offers several possibilities for the continuation of the voyage, although most people prefer to stick to the main trade wind route. A secondary route leaves from Tahiti across the equator to Hawaii, which is also the route taken by some of the boats returning to the west coast of North America. Several secondary routes branch off later on, the northbound routes leading mostly across the equator towards Micronesia. Having passed through the Cooks, Tonga, or Samoa, the main route finally reaches Fiji, another major cruising centre. Fiji is at the centre of a number of routes, the pattern in the SW Pacific becoming more complex. This area offers a great choice of destinations, with the added advantage of shorter distances between them. Undoubtedly the most popular destination in the SW Pacific is New Zealand, where a large number of cruising boats spend the cyclone season in the safety of North Island's protected harbours. At the same time, many put their prolonged stay in New Zealand to good use by carrying out essen-tial repair and maintenance work on their boats by taking advantage of the excellent facilities avail-able. Such a stop, whether in New Zealand or in Australia, where facilities are equally good, should be included in their plans by all those who intend to spend longer than a year in the South Pacific.

Many people seem to reach a turning point in their voyages during their cruise in the South Pacific. A decision has to be made about the future and the solutions are not always obvious. North American and European yachts now sail the South Pacific in almost equal numbers, but when a return home has to be considered the choice for the Europeans is fairly simple. The obvious way is to carry on westabout around the world taking advantage of favourable weather systems. This is probably also the most logical solution for those whose homeports are on the US east coast. However, for those who hail from the west coast of North America and wish to restrict their cruising to the Pacific, the choices are less obvious. Every year boats arrive in the Western Pacific with their skippers at a loss as to the best way of getting back home. Some of these alternatives are described in chapter 2 and also in PS60 routes from New Zealand.

These are only some of the aspects that should be considered before planning a cruise among the islands of the South Pacific. Apart from wind and weather, the human side should also be considered. Since the arrival of the first Europeans two cen-turies ago, Pacific islanders have often been sub-jected to cruel treatment by outsiders, from blackbirding to nuclear testing and dumping. That they still receive us with open arms is a sign of their generosity and forgiveness. The South Pacific continues to be one of the most peaceful, non-polluted regions of the world and it is in our best interest to help keep it that way.

PS10 Routes in the Eastern South Pacific

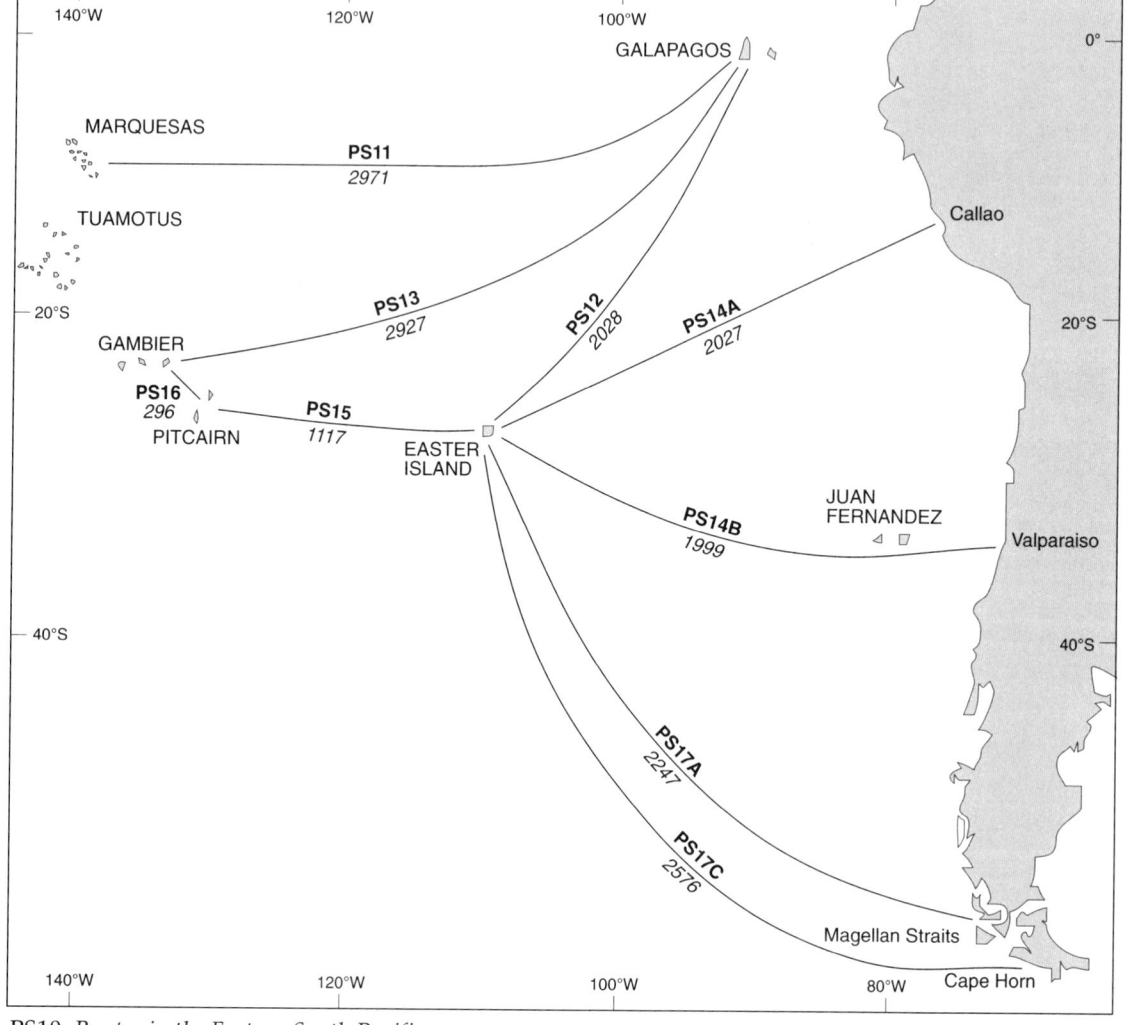

PS10 *Routes in the Eastern South Pacific*

The trunk route from Panama to Tahiti draws most of the boats that pass through this area, as very few boats venture south either to South America or towards such islands as Pitcairn or Easter Island. So a decision must be reached in Panama or Galapagos whether to stick to the direct route and sail to the Marquesas, or make a detour south. The eastern part of the South Pacific is not affected by tropical storms, which means that it can be sailed at any time of the year. However, this unaffected area does not include the islands of French Polynesia, which should be avoided during the cyclone season between December and early April. One good reason for a detour to the south is to avoid this critical period and the rewards of such a detour will make up for the longer passages, which should also benefit from favourable winds. The notable exception is the trip down the coast of South America, where both wind and current will be contrary. Undeterred by this, a small number of boats sail down the west coast of South America – attracted by the grandeur of southern Chile.

PS11 *Galapagos to Marquesas*

Best time:	April to September			
Tropical storms:	December to March			
Charts:	BA: 4051			
	US: 51			
Pilots:	BA: 7, 62			
	US: 122, 125, 126			
Cruising guides:	*Charlie's Charts of Polynesia, Landfalls of Paradise.*			
Waypoints:				
Departure	*Intermediate*	*Landfall*	*Destination*	*Distance (M)*
PS111 Cruz	PS112			
0°46.5'S, 90°18'W	2°00'S, 92°00'W			
	PS113	PS114 Hiva Oa E	Atuona	2971
	3°00'S, 100°00'W	9°45'S, 138°45'W	*9°48'S, 139°02'W*	
		PS115 Nuku Hiva SE	Taiohae	3027
		8°55'S, 139°55'W	*8°56'S, 140°06'W*	

For many cruising boats the passage from the Galapagos Islands to the Marquesas is their longest offshore passage and, if one is lucky with the weather, it can also be one of the most pleasant. Although the area lies under the influence of the SE trade winds for the best part of the year, weather conditions can differ drastically from one year to the next and the presence or absence of the El Niño current can exert a great influence on weather conditions in the eastern half of the South Pacific.

Good passages have been made at all times of the year, but the most favourable period appears to be from April to August when the trade winds usually blow steadily from the E or SE and the favourable west-setting current is at its strongest (1–1½ knots). However, some people are tempted to make this passage early in the year in order to make a good start to their sailing season in the South Pacific and arrive in the Marquesas before the end of March. In some years this can be a mis-take as a cyclone can either be met on the way or after one's arrival in the Marquesas. In February 1983 cyclone William reached a point nearly 1000 miles to the east of the Marquesas, its effects being felt by several boats sailing along this route at that time. Two cyclones were recorded in the islands in that year, although the frequency of cyclones in the Marquesas is relatively low and years can go by without the islands being hit by a fully fledged cyclone. On the occasions when they do occur, trees and other debris washed out to sea create additional hazards to small craft and caution should be exercised, especially at night. This route runs through an area where collisions with whales and attacks by whales have been reported, so it pays to treat whales with suspicion and not approach or make them feel threatened unnecessarily.

An area to be avoided if passing south of the Galapagos is between longitudes 90°W and 95°W and latitudes 3°S and 8°S where several yachts have reported unpleasant weather conditions. The area appears to be an extension of the doldrums with little or no wind, thundery squalls, and a heavy swell which makes conditions very uncomfortable. Most of this area can be avoided by boats leaving from Puerto Ayora (Academy Bay), if from WP PS111, south of Punta Estrada, a course is set for WP PS112 and thence to WP PS113. This tactic conflicts with the experience of participants in one of the round the world rallies who found better conditions by staying closer to the equator and only going south of 5°S further west. In that area they also experienced a stronger current, occasionally at 2 knots, which over the entire passage gave them a boost of 300 miles. Those boats that followed this route were greatly helped by daily updates on weatherfax. Otherwise, it is probably just as well to use the recommended waypoints and, from PS113, set a great circle course for WP PS114, three miles east of Cape Matafenua at the eastern extremity of Hiva Oa. From that point the south coast of Hiva Oa is followed around into Taaoa Bay, in the NW corner of which is located the small port of Atuona. The harbour is protected by a short breakwater, but this does not offer much protection from the southerly swell. The entrance into the port is not easily identified at night so it is strongly recommended to arrive in daytime.

Boats sailing straight to Nuku Hiva should stay well clear of Clark Bank (8°05'S, 139°35'W), where seas break over shallow water, and make for WP PS115, five miles off the east coast of Nuku Hiva. From there one sails around Cape Tikapo towards Taiohae, the main port and capital of the Marquesas.

The average length of this passage is from 15 to 30 days, the longest times being recorded by those who were not prepared to motor in calm or light weather conditions. In the vicinity of both the Galapagos Islands and the Marquesas the winds can turn light even at the height of the trade wind season. On average, the slowest passages appear to be those made in the early part of the year, when light winds and calms are most common on this route. In some years no real trade wind conditions are experienced until May, although throughout the year the currents along this route are favourable. Winds are stronger and steadier in the later part of the year and for those making this passage in October or even November it may be worth laying a course to the north of the rhumb line, as both winds and current can be more favourable nearer to the equator.

There are two official ports of entry into the Marquesas, at Atuona, on the island of Hiva Oa, and Taiohae on Nuku Hiva. Because of the layout of the islands, it is better to clear in at the former, cruise the various islands, and leave Nuku Hiva for the end of a Marquesan cruise.

PS12 *Galapagos to Easter Island*

BEST TIME:	November to March			
TROPICAL STORMS:	None			
CHARTS:	BA: 4062			
	US: 62			
PILOTS:	BA: 7, 62			
	US: 122, 125			
CRUISING GUIDES:	*Landfalls of Paradise.*			
WAYPOINTS:				
Departure	*Intermediate*	*Landfall*	*Destination*	*Distance (M)*
PS121 Cruz S	PS122	PS123 Easter N	Hanga Roa	2028
0°46.5'S, 90°18'W	0°00', 90°00'W	27°00'S, 109°25'W	*27°09'S, 109°26'W*	

The few boats that take this route to the island of giant statues are usually rewarded by a fast passage with the SE trade winds on the beam. The best period is between December and May when the trade winds extend furthest to the south, although at such times it may take longer to reach the trade winds on leaving the Galapagos. This must be weighed up against the fact that the weather around Easter Island is more settled in the earlier months of the year. If sailing direct to Easter Island from Panama or other ports in Central America, similar directions apply for the first part of the voyage as for the routes to the Galapagos Islands. See also routes PT12 and PT19 (pages 325 and 333). If S or SW winds are encountered south of the Galapagos Islands, one should stay on the starboard tack as far as latitude 3°S before going on the other tack. South of that latitude SW winds are rarely encountered as winds gradually back to the south and eventually SE. Having gone on to the port tack, if one finds that winds south of the equator have too much south in them, and in the early part of the year they are usually SSE, any ground which may be lost to the west can be made up later as the winds become more easterly south of 20°S. Favourable winds will be found along most of the way and even the doldrums should not be too wide at the recommended time of year.

Boats leaving from Puerto Ayora, on Santa Cruz Island, from WP PS121, east of Punta Estrada, should sail a course due south which passes east of Floreana Island. On this course, depending on existing weather conditions, the equator will be crossed at WP PS122. As mentioned earlier, an area

to be avoided if passing south of the Galapagos is between longitudes 90°W and 95°W and latitudes 3°S and 8°S where several yachts have reported unpleasant weather conditions. The area appears to be an extension of the doldrums with little or no wind, thundery squalls, and a heavy swell which makes conditions very uncomfortable. To avoid this area, if SW winds are encountered on leaving the Galapagos, it would be better to stay on the starboard tack and keep east of meridian 90°W, even if it means temporarily diverting from the direct route. Depending on weather conditions, a course can then be set to make landfall at Easter Island at WP PS123 north of the island's North Cape.

The NW coast should be followed to the main settlement of Hanga Roa. The small port at nearby Hanga Piko, south of Hanga Roa, has been improved recently allowing a few keeled boats to find shelter. The Port Captain should be contacted on VHF channel 16 on arrival and he will meet the boat outside the port. Because of the rapidly changing weather, boats at anchor should never be left unattended at Easter Island.

PS13 *Galapagos to Gambier Islands*

BEST TIME:	April to October				
TROPICAL STORMS:	December to March				
CHARTS:	BA: 4061, 4062				
	US: 62, 621				
PILOTS:	BA: 7, 62				
	US: 122, 125, 126				
CRUISING GUIDES:	*Landfalls of Paradise, Charlie's Charts of Polynesia.*				
WAYPOINTS:					
Departure	*Intermediate*	*Landfall*	*Destination*		*Distance (M)*
PS131 Cruz S	PS132				
0°46.5'S, 90°18'W	2°00'S, 92°00'W				
	PS133	PS134 Mangareva SE	Rikitea		2927
	3°00'S, 94°00'W	23°20'S, 134°50'W	*23°07'S, 134°58'W*		

This route eschews the well sailed route to the Marquesas and allows one to reach French Polynesia from the SE rather than the NE. Instructions are similar to those for the route from Galapagos to Easter Island, with the added advantage that as the Gambier Islands lie so much further to the west, the SE trades provide an even better slant for this route which crosses one of the most deserted areas of the world. A great circle course can be set as soon as steady SE trade winds

are found. During the southern winter (May to September), they often reach as far north as the Galapagos themselves.

In order to avoid an area of confused seas and little wind south of the Galapagos Islands, lying between longitudes 90°W and 95°W and latitudes 3°S and 8°S, boats leaving from Puerto Ayora (Academy Bay), from WP PS131, east of Punta Estrada, should set an initial course for WP PS132 and thence to WP PS133. From there, a great circle course can be set for WP PS134, SE of Mangareva lagoon. Because of the reefs extending to windward on the east side of the large lagoon, Mangareva should not be approached from the east, but from the SE. From WP PS134 the course goes west roughly parallel to the line of reefs and enters the lagoon through Southwest Pass. Entry formalities in the

Gambier can be completed at Rikitea, the settlement on Mangareva, the main island of the group.

A tempting stop on the way and close to the recommended route is the island of Pitcairn (25°04'S, 130°06'W), whose isolated community is always happy to welcome passing yachts.

PS14 *South America to Easter Island*

BEST TIME:	November to March
TROPICAL STORMS:	None
CHARTS:	BA: 4062
	US: 62
PILOTS:	BA: 7, 62
	US: 122, 125
CRUISING GUIDES:	*Landfalls of Paradise, South Pacific Anchorages.*
WAYPOINTS:	

Departure	Intermediate	Landfall	Destination	Distance (M)
Route PS14A				
PS141 Callao		PS142 Easter SE	Hanga Roa	2028
12°00'S, 77°18'W		*27°08'S, 109°12'W*	*27°09'S, 109°27'W*	
Route PS14B				
PS143 Valparaiso	PS144 Robinson Crusoe	PS145 Easter SW	Hanga Roa	1990
33°01'S, 71°38'W	*33°38'S, 78°50'W*	*27°12'S, 109°27'W*		
PS146 Valdivia		PS145 Easter SW	Hanga Roa	1950
39°48'S, 73°14'W				

Whichever point of departure is chosen, a passage to Easter Island from any port on the west coast of South America should present no great problem as favourable winds can be expected for most of the way. From ports lying to the north of Callao, a direct course can be steered immediately on leaving the mainland as favourable winds are prevalent in this area during most of the year. Although, according to the pilot charts, Easter Island lies slightly outside the SE trade wind belt, the winds between the island and the continent tend to blow between E and S most of the time. A direct course can also be sailed from ports lying further south, but if westerly winds are encountered, a NW course should be sailed until the SE trade winds are found. Those sailing along the coast of Chile with a favourable wind and current (route PS14B) should not set a course for Easter Island before the latitude of Valparaiso has been crossed. The same should be done if intending to call first at Juan Fernandez

Islands (Robinson Crusoe, Alexander Selkirk, and Santa Clara). They are dependencies of Chile and the main settlement is on Robinson Crusoe in Cumberland Bay. Those who have cruised the Chilean canals of Patagonia should continue to cruise along the coast at least as far as Valdivia before going offshore. Valdivia has the best facilities in the area and is also a safe place to leave the boat to visit the interior.

Taking as a point of departure the Peruvian port of Callao, from WP PS141, north of San Lorenzo Island in Callao Bay, a great circle course is set for WP PS142, off Cape Roggeven, on the SE side of Easter Island. The island's south and SW coast is followed around to the main settlement at Hanga Roa, where officials are based and should be contacted on VHF channel 16. There is now a small port at Hanga Piko, south of Hanga Roa, with room for a few keeled boats, but the harbour cannot be entered or left during periods of heavy surge.

PS15 *Easter Island to Pitcairn*

BEST TIME:	November to March			
TROPICAL STORMS:	None			
CHARTS:	BA: 4061			
	US: 607			
PILOTS:	BA: 62			
	US: 122, 125, 126			
CRUISING GUIDES:	*Landfalls of Paradise.*			
WAYPOINTS:				

Departure	Intermediate	Landfall	Destination	Distance (M)
PS151 Easter W		PS152 Pitcairn E	Adamstown	1117
27°08'S, 109°28'W		25°04'S, 130°04'W	*25°04'S, 130°05.5'W*	

Fair winds can be expected along this route during the best part of the year. The most settled weather is in summer, from December to May, when the SE trade winds extend furthest south. However, even during these months the trade wind pattern can be interrupted by spells of squally weather, rain, and variable winds. A direct course from Easter to Pitcairn Island leads well to the south of Ducie and Henderson islands, both of which are uninhabited. As they are nature reserves, landing is prohibited.

From WP PS151, off Hanga Roa, a direct route can be set for WP PS152, so as to approach Pitcairn from the east. The nearest anchorage to the settlement of Adamstown is in Bounty Bay, off Pitcairn's NE coast. The small community monitors VHF channel 16 and a boat will be sent out to meet arriving yachts. The main anchorage is at Bounty Bay, but it is only tenable in very settled weather. Sometimes it may be possible to anchor at Tedside, on the west side of the island. All anchorages should be treated with suspicion as several boats have been lost on Pitcairn as the weather changed unexpectedly while the crew were ashore.

PS16 *Pitcairn to Gambier Islands*

BEST TIME:	March to June			
TROPICAL STORMS:	December to March			
CHARTS:	BA: 4061			
	US: 607			
PILOTS:	BA: 62			
	US: 122, 126			
CRUISING GUIDES:	*Landfalls of Paradise, Charlie's Charts of Polynesia.*			
WAYPOINTS:				

Departure	Intermediate	Landfall	Destination	Distance (M)
PS161 Pitcairn NW		PS162 Mangareva SE	Rikitea	296
25°03'S, 130°07'W		23°20'S, 134°50'W	*23°07'S, 134°58'W*	

This passage can be made at all times of the year as both Pitcairn and the Gambier group are very rarely threatened by cyclones. However, the first months of the year should be avoided so as not to arrive in French Polynesia during the cyclone season there. Best sailing conditions can be expected either at the beginning or the end of the southern winter. As this route skirts the southern extremity of the SE trades, weather conditions can be variable during winter months and westerly gales are not uncommon. The Gambier Islands should be approached with caution in thick weather as they can be hidden by low cloud and currents in their vicinity can be strong at times.

From WP PS161, NW of Pitcairn a direct course can be set for WP PS162, SE of Mangareva lagoon. Because of the reefs extending to windward of the large lagoon, Mangareva should be approached with caution. From WP PS162 the course follows roughly the line of the reefs and enters the lagoon through Southwest Pass. In poor visibility it may be advisable to use the Western Pass, between the islands of Taravai and Mangareva, as it has the best markings and is normally used by the supply ship from Tahiti. Entry formalities in the Gambier Islands are completed at Rikitea, the main settlement on Mangareva, the largest island of the group.

PS17 *Easter Island to Magellan Strait or Cape Horn*

BEST TIME:	December to February			
TROPICAL STORMS:	None			
CHARTS:	BA: 4062			
	US: 62			
PILOTS:	BA: 6, 62			
	US: 122, 124, 125			
WAYPOINTS:				
Departure	*Intermediate*	*Landfall*	*Destination*	*Distance (M)*
Route PS17A				
PS171 Easter SW	PS172	PS173 Pillar		2247
27°13'S, 109°27'W	45°00'S, 100°00'W	52°40'S, 74°50'W		
Route PS17B				
PS171 Easter SW	PS172	PS174 Chacao		2296
		41°40'S, 74°15'W		
Route PS17C				
PS171 Easter SW	PS175	PS176 Horn		2576
	50°00'S, 95°00'W	56°02'S, 67°15'W		

Although the number of boats that make Easter Island the starting point for a voyage to the stormy Southern Ocean is relatively small, the same route is used for much of its length by boats heading for the south of Chile. Just as Cape Horn or the Straits of Magellan are best reached from Easter Island with the help of the prevailing westerly winds of higher latitudes, so is the south of Chile. The main objective after leaving Easter Island is to reach the region of prevailing westerly winds as quickly as possible. By taking advantage of every shift of wind it ought to be possible to make some easting even before the Roaring Forties are reached, from where fair, if strong, winds can be expected. The proportion of gale force winds is highest in the vicinity of the southern tip of the American continent, the worst period being the winter months of June, July, and August and passages during these months should be avoided. The recommended time not only has the benefit of better winds en route, but also ensures arriving in Tierra del Fuego and Patagonia at the best time, which is at the height of the southern summer.

Taking WP PS171 as a departure point from Easter Island, the initial course will head in a SSE direction. As so much depends on weather conditions encountered at the time, WP PS172 has been given only as a guideline. Boats bound for the Magellan Strait (route PS17A) should set course for PS173 as soon as the area of prevailing westerly winds has been reached. Landfall will be made at PS173 off Cape Pillar. Entering the Strait in heavy weather should be avoided, because strong currents create rough seas at the entrance to the Strait. Those wishing to visit the south of Chile and explore the Chilean channels on their way to the Magellan Strait, should make landfall further north in the approaches to Chacao Channel (route PS17B). The same suggestion applies as above and the latter channel should only be entered in settled weather and with a fair tide. To obtain this information, contact the Corona Lighthouse on VHF channel 16 to request information on the state of the tide.

Boats bound for Cape Horn (route PS17C) will make most of their easting with the prevailing westerly winds, so that latitude 50°S is only crossed in about longitude 95°W (WP PS175). The course is then altered for PS176 to pass close to the south of Cape Horn. In recent years, most boats sailing this route have stopped in Tierra del Fuego, either by entering Beagle Channel immediately after having weathered Cape Horn, or by reaching Cape Horn itself through the relatively more sheltered channels to NW of it by choosing one of the landfalls described above.

After rounding Cape Horn, the route can pass either east or west of Staten Island. If the island is passed to seaward, a wide berth should be given to Cape St John, as a dangerous tide rip extends offshore for about six miles making conditions hazardous when the wind blows against the tide. Alternatively, the route can pass through Le Maire Strait, especially if the intention is to pass to the west of the Falkland Islands. Going north through Le Maire Strait it is essential to wait for a fair tide and, if at all possible, a fair wind as well. Further directions for boats heading north into the Atlantic Ocean are given in routes AT26, AT27 and AS26 (pages 217, 218 and 233).

PS18 *Ecuador and Peru to Chile*

BEST TIME:	December to March			
TROPICAL STORMS:	None			
CHARTS:	BA: 4062			
	US: 62			
PILOTS:	BA: 7			
	US: 125			
CRUISING GUIDES:	*Yachtsman's Navigator Guide to the Chilean Channels.*			
WAYPOINTS:				

Departure	Intermediate	Landfall	Destination	Distance (M)
PS180 Salinas *2°13'S, 80°55'W*	PS181 Carnera *2°15'S, 80°58'W*	PS182 Parinas *4°40'S, 81°25'W*	Paita *5°05'S, 81°07'W*	182
PS180 Salinas	PS181 Carnera PS183 Aguja *6°00'S, 81°20'W*	PS184 Anson *12°00'S, 72°12'W*	Callao *12°03'S, 77°09'W*	883
PS180 Salinas	PS186 Pacific *35°00'S, 92°00'W*	PS187 Crusoe *33°38'S, 78°50'W*	Valdivia *39°48'S, 73°14'W*	3180

Southbound passages along the west coast of South America are never easy, primarily because of the contrary Peru or Humboldt Current. However, in certain years, when the now notorious El Niño Current plays havoc with weather conditions throughout the Pacific, southbound boats at least have the compensation that the north-setting current will be either totally absent or even replaced by a weak current in the opposite direction. In normal years, though, one has little choice if bound for ports in Peru than to fight one's way south, probably motorsailing against the current and light SE winds. Boats bound for ports in

Chile may follow the advice given to the masters of sailing ships to take a long port tack until well offshore in the hope of finding the prevailing westerlies of higher latitudes. Once those winds are found, the coast can be approached with a favourable wind. One interesting stop on such an offshore route is the island of Robinson Crusoe, which belongs to Chile. From there, one has a wide choice of mainland ports. However, boats bound for the Pacific entrance into the Magellan Strait should remain offshore to take advantage of westerly winds. The various options are described in detail in PS17.

The best port of departure in Ecuador, because of its good facilities centred on the Salinas Yacht Club, is Salinas. The inshore route is quite unattractive as it follows the arid Peruvian coast where there are few ports and even stopping for fuel is not easy. Two ports where yachts have stopped in the past for refuelling are Manta, in Ecuador, and Paita, in Peru. Manta is a busy fishing port and, as a result, has good repair facilities. The first Peruvian port where one can stop for refuelling or provisioning is Paita, although it has no other attraction. Those who do not need to stop should make for the port of Callao, serving the Peruvian capital Lima, which has good facilities and a welcoming yacht club. It is also a good place to leave the yacht to visit Peru's interior, which can be said also of Salinas for those interested in visiting the interior

of Ecuador. See also PT11 page 323.

Suggestions for southbound passages from Callao are similar, but, as distances to ports in Northern Chile are shorter, taking an offshore route has little attraction, unless one is bound for the south of Chile when an offshore route is recommended. There are many good ports along the Chilean coast; facilities are adequate in most of them so following the coast in stages presents no real problems. However, those who prefer to take a nonstop offshore route may have to go as far as 35°S and 92°W before being out of the influence of the SE winds and thus able to close with the coast. A recommended port, with a small marina and good facilities, is Valdivia. Further south, Puerto Montt is the best place to start exploring the Chilean fjordland as it has a new marina and good facilities.

PS20 Routes in Eastern Polynesia

Whether arriving from the north (Hawaii), northeast (California or Panama), east (Galapagos), southeast (Easter or Pitcairn Island), or southwest (New Zealand), one should plan to arrive in French Polynesia not earlier than the beginning of April, when the cyclone season is on the wane and the SE trade wind season is about to begin. Such a timing will ensure several months of carefree cruising before the onset of the next cyclone season. Those with only a limited amount of time can spend about two months in French Polynesia, provided they arrive there in June. If one leaves the Society Islands only after the 14th July celebrations, which is an occasion few wish to miss, the safe cruising season in the rest of the tropics is well advanced and one has to be prepared to push on and probably spend the coming cyclone season in New Zealand, or some other safe place outside the tropics. The other alternative is to remain in the tropics during the summer, by staying close to one of the relatively

safe harbours downwind from Tahiti, such as Pago Pago (American Samoa), Vava'u (Tonga), or Suva (Fiji). For those who decide to stay in the Society Islands, there are several harbours, both in the Windward and the Leeward Islands, that are reputed to be safe in a cyclone, although the authorities are increasingly reluctant to allow cruising boats to remain there during the cyclone season. Indeed, many sailors plan to spend the cyclone season there, not heeding the lessons of 1983, when several cyclones swept through French Polynesia. It is true that several years can go by without a cyclone hitting these islands, but when a cyclone comes this way it can wreak havoc. If one is prepared to take this risk and stay in French Polynesia between December and March, one should try to be near one of the recommended ports. It must be pointed out, however, that in recent years the authorities in Papeete have occasionally forbidden crews to remain on board their boats during the cyclone season, although the boats themselves may be left unattended in a safe place, such as the marina at Raiatea.

Even without the danger of cyclones, summers ought to be avoided as the weather is much less pleasant than in winter, when from May to October the SE trade winds are normally in full force in these latitudes, although occasionally they can be interrupted by squalls and short periods of light winds and calms. During the summer months, from December to March, winds are less predictable and the weather can be hot and sultry. The Tuamotus should be avoided during the cyclone season as no anchorage can be regarded as really safe. Because of the revolving nature of these storms, even a relatively protected anchorage can quickly turn into a lee shore and the long fetch in most lagoons can create highly dangerous conditions for boats at anchor.

Satellite navigation has undoubtedly played a major part in opening the more remote islands, and especially the Tuamotus, to cruising boats, many of whose owners would not have dared pass through those waters without GPS. Although most of these dangers are now easier to avoid, it must be remembered that most charts of the area were drawn during the last century and many are quite inaccurate. Therefore positions obtained by GPS will rarely agree completely with those taken off from a chart. This calls for extreme caution when in the vicinity of reefs or when sailing at night or in bad visibility. Nor should the strong currents that sweep through the area be ignored, which makes it essential to update one's position as frequently as possible. As many of the anchorages in the Tuamotus are in large lagoons, the long fetch will cause uncomfortable, and occasionally dangerous, conditions in strong winds. Finally, being so heavily dependent on satellite navigation when navigating in the South Pacific, and particularly in

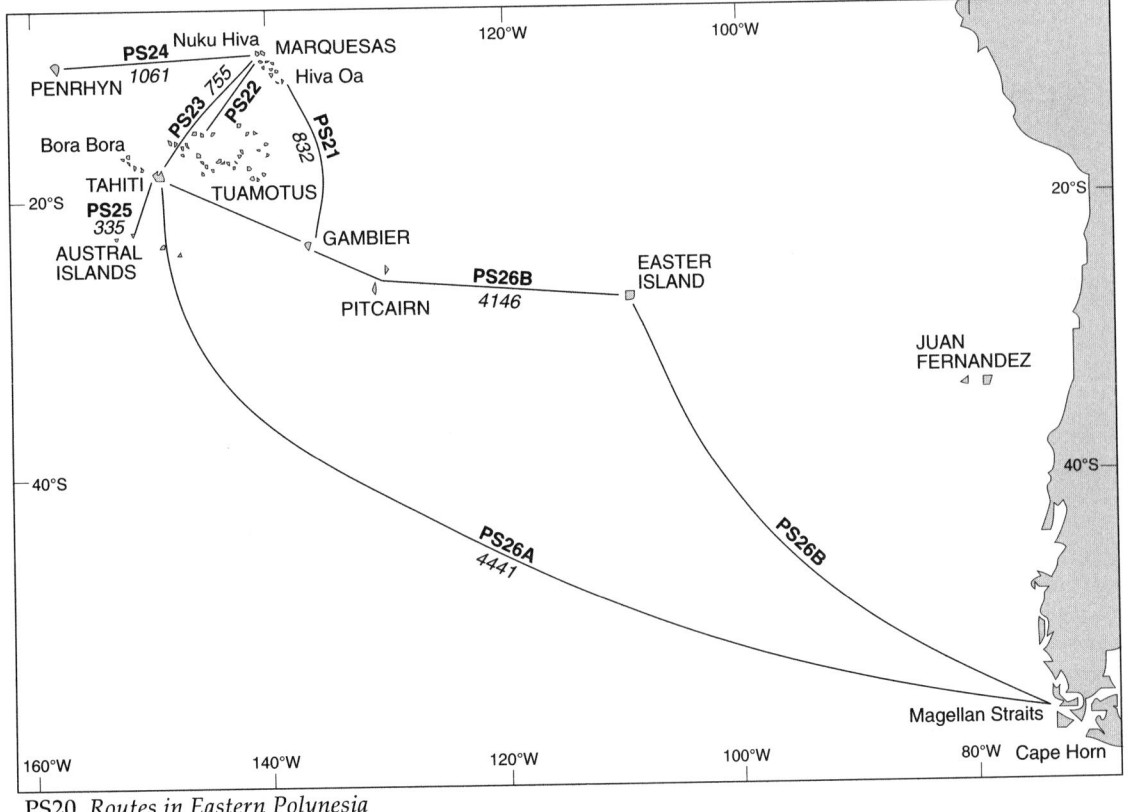

PS20 *Routes in Eastern Polynesia*

such a difficult area as the Tuamotus, a second backup GPS, possibly portable, would be a wise investment. Just as useful will be tide tables as well as detailed charts. In the case of the Tuamotus, French charts are preferable as they are the most recent and are being updated regularly.

PS21 *Gambier to Marquesas*

BEST TIME:	April to September			
TROPICAL STORMS:	December to March			
CHARTS:	BA: 4607			
	US: 607			
PILOTS:	BA: 62			
	US: 126			
CRUISING GUIDES:	*Charlie's Charts of Polynesia, Landfalls of Paradise.*			
WAYPOINTS:				

Departure	Intermediate	Landfall	Destination	Distance(M)
PS211 Mangareva W 23°05'S, 135°05'W	PS212 21°30'S, 135°15'W			
	PS213 20°00'S, 135°30'W	PS214 Fatu Hiva 10°33'S, 138°40'W	Omoa *10°29.9'S, 138°40.6'W*	786
PS211 Mangareva W	PS212			
	PS213	PS215 Hiva Oa S 9°51'S, 139°01'W	Atuona *9°48'S, 139°02'W*	832

The direct course between these two island groups in French Polynesia skirts the eastern extremity of the Tuamotus and passes dangerously close to South Marutea (21°32'S, 135°28'W) and Reao (18°32'S, 136°17'W). Having left Mangareva through the West Pass, from WP PS211, a course should be set for WP PS212 and thence to WP PS213 to pass east of those two atolls. As one has already cleared into French Polynesia, it is possible to stop at one of these atolls or at Pukapuka further along the route. If not stopping anywhere en route, a course can be set for Fatu Hiva, the southernmost of the Marquesas. Approaching the Marquesas from the south, it is indeed most convenient to stop first at Fatu Hiva, where one can anchor at Omoa. The gendarmerie is located in this village and one should report there on arrival. Boats arriving from outside French Polynesia cannot clear in at Fatu Hiva and will have to complete formalities at one of the official ports of entry such as Atuona. One of the most spectacular anchorages in the Marquesas is at Hanavave (10°27'S, 138°39.25'W), on the west coast of Fatu Hiva.

Boats bound directly for Atuona, on Hiva Oa, from WP PS213 should set a course to WP PS215, at the entrance into Taaoa Bay. The small port of Atuona is in the NW corner of the bay. The other port of entry in the Marquesas is Taiohae (8°56'S, 140°06'W) on Nuku Hiva. However, because of the layout of the islands it is better to clear in at Atuona, cruise the various islands, and take one's departure from the Marquesas at Taiohae.

PS22 *Marquesas to Tuamotus*

BEST TIME:	May to September			
TROPICAL STORMS:	December to March			
CHARTS:	BA: 4607			
	US: 607			
PILOTS:	BA: 62			
	US: 126			
CRUISING GUIDES:	*Charlie's Charts of Polynesia, Landfalls of Paradise.*			
WAYPOINTS:				

Departure	Intermediate	Landfall	Destination	Distance(M)
PS221 Nuku Hiva S 9°00'S, 140°10'W		PS222 Takaroa N 14°20'S, 144°55'W	Teavaroa 14°29'S, 145°02.5W	436

There are various routes that can be taken to or through the Tuamotus and the choice depends on how many islands one intends to visit before sailing on to Tahiti. The atolls of Takaroa and Manihi are the easiest option as there are no dangers en route from the Marquesas. Having stopped at one or both, the route to Tahiti passes close to Ahe and Rangiroa. The alternative is to start further east at Takume or Raroia and then thread one's way through the islands. One of the easiest landfalls is at Takaroa, which has a clear pass which can be easily negotiated in good visibility. As there is a clear run between Nuku Hiva and Takaroa, the latter makes a good starting point for a Tuamotu cruise. From PS221, south of Nuku Hiva, a direct course can be sailed to PS222, north of Takaroa. Pass Teavaroa leading into the lagoon is on the SW side of the atoll. A wide pass without obstructions also leads into Kauehi, which is centrally located on the route to the Society Islands.

PS23 *Marquesas to Tahiti*

BEST TIME:	May to October			
TROPICAL STORMS:	December to March			
CHARTS:	BA: 4606			
	US: 607			
PILOTS:	BA: 62			
	US: 122, 126			
CRUISING GUIDES:	*Charlie's Charts of Polynesia, Landfalls of Paradise.*			
WAYPOINTS:				

Departure	Intermediate	Landfall	Destination	Distance(M)
Route PS23A PS231 Nuku Hiva S 9°00'S, 140°10'W	PS232 Ahe 14°00'S, 146°10'W PS233 Rangiroa W 15°15'S, 147°05'W	PS236 Tahiti 17°30'S, 149°34'W	Papeete *17°32.5'S, 149°34.5'W*	755
Route PS23B PS231 Nuku Hiva S	PS234 Manihi 14°24'S, 145°29'W PS235 Rangiroa E 15°13'S, 147°02'W	PS236 Tahiti	Papeete	752

The direct route leads right through the Tuamotu Archipelago, also known in the past as the Dangerous Archipelago on account of its reefs, low lying islands, and very strong currents. Until recently many yachts preferred to bypass this area altogether rather than risk its many dangers. However, satellite navigation and the proliferation of radar on small boats have made it possible for many more to cruise among these delightful atolls. For those who do not intend to stop en route to Tahiti, it is still recommended to lay a safe course outside all dangers. The recommended practice in the past has been to wait and leave the Marquesas with a full moon, both for improved visibility at night and to be able to use a wider selection of celestial bodies in navigation.

The easiest route (PS23A) from Nuku Hiva to Tahiti passes close to Ahe. From WP PS231, SW of Nuku Hiva, a course should be set for WP PS232, north of Ahe, from where the course is altered to pass west of that atoll. The next course alteration, for WP PS233, will lead through the 20 mile gap between Arutua and Rangiroa. The latter has a powerful light on its NW corner, which can be a help especially if a more western route is sailed to the one described above so as to pass through the 20 mile wide pass between Mataiva and Tikehau. Those who wish to play it totally safe can leave the entire Tuamotus to port and pass west of Mataiva. However, this latter course has the great disadvantage of being almost certainly hard on the wind for the rest of the passage to Tahiti.

At full moon, one can sail the most direct route (PS23B) and thread a cautious course through the Tuamotus, possibly between Takaroa and Manihi (WP PS234) and then east of Rangiroa (WP PS235). Approaching Tahiti from NE, landfall is made NNE of the entrance into Papeete at WP PS236. The pass through the reef leading into the harbour is at 17°32.18'S, 149°35.1'W. Arriving boats should proceed to the quay on the south side of the harbour. Boats are not normally boarded and the captain is expected to visit the various offices, located close to the main cruise ship quay, during office hours.

PS24 *Marquesas to Northern Cooks*

Best time:	April to September			
Tropical storms:	December to March			
Charts:	BA: 4061			
	US: 526			
Pilots:	BA: 62			
	US: 122, 126			
Cruising guides:	*Charlie's Charts of Polynesia, Landfalls of Paradise.*			
Waypoints:				
Departure	*Intermediate*	*Landfall*	*Destination*	*Distance(M)*
PS241 Nuku Hiva S 9°00'S, 140°10'W		PS242 Penrhyn E 9°00'S, 157°53'W	Omoka *9°00'S, 158°04'W*	1061

To avoid formalities in Papeete, as well as one of the busiest cities in the South Pacific, a number of boats bypass both the Tuamotu and Society Islands and sail directly from the Marquesas to the Northern Cooks or even Samoa. From a purely practical point of view, such a decision makes sense, as it greatly simplifies navigation by sailing a route which stays well to the north of the Tuamotus, aptly called the Dangerous Archipelago. Such a decision makes even more sense late in the season for boats in a hurry to reach a distant destination, such as New Zealand. On the other hand, it also means missing the Society Islands, undoubt-edly some of the most beautiful islands not just in the Pacific, but in the entire world.

The route to Penrhyn, the northernmost of the Cook Islands, passes close to the Southern Line Islands of Caroline and Vostok. From WP PS241, SW of Nuku Hiva, a direct course, due west, can be set for WP PS242 east of Penrhyn. Its lagoon is entered through Northeast Pass. Penrhyn, also known as Tongareva, is an official port of entry into the Cooks and the main settlement is at Omoka. The other two Northern Cook islands, Rakahanga and Manihiki, can be visited next. The route then continues due west towards Tokelau, one of the least visited island groups in the South Pacific. The nearest island is Fakaofo (9°23'S, 171°15'W), which is the capital of this small group of coral atolls administered by New Zealand.

PS25 *Tahiti to Austral Islands*

BEST TIME:	April to May, October to November			
TROPICAL STORMS:	December to March			
CHARTS:	BA: 4061			
	US: 607			
PILOTS:	BA: 62			
	US: 126			
CRUISING GUIDES:	*Charlie's Charts of Polynesia, Landfalls of Paradise.*			
WAYPOINTS:				
Departure	*Intermediate*	*Landfall*	*Destination*	*Distance(M)*
PS251 Tahiti SW		PS252 Tubuai	Mataura	335
17°47'S, 149°38'W		23°20'S, 149°31'W	*23°21'S, 149°29'W*	

This group of islands, of which the nearest, Rurutu, lies 300 miles south of Tahiti, attracts only a few visitors every year. During the winter months, from May to September, when the SE trade winds blow strongly between Tahiti and the islands, it is sometimes difficult to reach some of the windward Australs. When the wind has too much south in it, it is probably better to call first at Tubuai, which has a pass into the lagoon, and then work one's way gradually to the other islands. Sailing to the islands is better done at the start of the SE season, in April, when the trade winds are not so strong. If easting can be made on leaving Tahiti, and the necessary permission has been obtained to call at Rapa, the island should be visited first before calling at the others. However, if the SE winds make this impossible, one should alter course for Tubuai, which is almost due south from Tahiti and should be easier to reach.

Having sailed around the west coast of Tahiti, from WP PS251, a direct course can be set for WP PS252, NW of Tubuai. Tubuai's lagoon is entered through the Main Pass, on the NW side. The main settlement is at Mataura. The other ports of entry in the Australs are Moerai, on Rurutu (22°28'S, 151°20'W) and Rairua, on Raivavae (23°52'S, 147°44'W). Both Raivavae and Rapa have good anchorages, but permission to visit Rapa must be obtained before leaving Tahiti.

Because of the difficulty of reaching the Australs from Tahiti, those intending to sail from New Zealand to Tahiti at a later stage may visit the Australs on that occasion as they are close to the recommended route (PS67 page 408). The alternative is to reach the Australs from the east, possibly from the Gambier Islands, when much better conditions would be encountered as both winds and current would be in one's favour. This option should be considered by boats arriving in French Polynesia from the east, possibly via Easter Island, who could visit the Gambier and Australs first before continuing to Tahiti.

PS26 *Tahiti to Cape Horn or Magellan Strait*

BEST TIME:	November to December
TROPICAL STORMS:	December to March
CHARTS:	BA: 4061, 4062
	US: 607, 621
PILOTS:	BA: 6, 62
	US: 122, 125, 126

WAYPOINTS:				
Departure	*Intermediate*	*Landfall*	*Destination*	*Distance (M)*
Route PS26A				
PS261 Tahiti SW	PS262			
17°47'S, 149°38'W	30°00'S, 150°00'W			
	PS263			
	40°00'S, 140°00'W			
	PS264	PS265 Cape Horn S		4441
	50°00'S, 115°00'W	56°15'S, 67°15'W		
Route PS26B				
Papeete	Mangareva			
17°32.5'S, 149°34.5'W	*23°07'S, 134°58'W*			
	Pitcairn	PS266 Pillar		4146
	25°04'S, 130°05.5'W	52°40'S, 74°50'W		
		PS267 Chacao		4093
		41°40'S, 74°15'W		

Bernard Moitessier described this as the logical route for a return voyage to Europe. Opinions on this are certainly divided as most cruising boat sailors regard a westbound voyage along the trade wind routes as the more attractive, even if not logical, alternative. Although a passage through the Roaring Forties may not promise ideal sailing conditions, those who sail this route do so not just to double the famous Cape, but also to reach the increasingly popular cruising grounds of Patagonia.

The time of departure on this passage is crucial so as to reach Cape Horn at the height of the southern summer, which is the optimum time. The recommended time to leave Tahiti is during November or December as such a departure would ensure a rounding of the Cape between January and February. The course on leaving Tahiti leads due south through the Austral Islands. Depending on the direction and strength of the SE trade winds, the course should be slightly to the east of south. There is a south going current setting strongly through this area. The winds at the beginning of the southern summer (early December) are usually light with frequent calms down to latitude 50°S. The recommended time for the alternative route, via the islands, is after the end of the SE trade wind season, in November. Such a departure time from the tropics has the added attraction of also avoiding the cyclone season there, which starts in December.

If taking the direct route (PS26A), from Tahiti and

WP PS261 the initial course goes almost due south and therefore it may be tempting to stop at Tubuai, or one of the other Austral Islands, as described in route PS25. Whether stopping in the Australs or not, latitude 30°S should be crossed in about longitude 150°W (WP PS262) and latitude 40°S in longitude 140°W (WP PS263). When the area of prevailing westerly winds is reached, the course becomes more easterly, so that latitude 50°S is only crossed in about longitude 115°W (WP PS264). A course is then sailed to pass some 12 miles south of Cape Horn through WP PS265. This route is seldom sailed nowadays without stopping on the way, either in the Australs, as mentioned above, or in Tierra del Fuego itself. This can be done either by entering Beagle Channel immediately after having weathered Cape Horn, or by reaching Cape Horn through the relatively more sheltered channels in Southern Chile. For the continuation of this route into the South Atlantic see AT26 and AT27 (pages 217 and 218).

An alternative to the offshore route described above, is one with several stops (PS26B). On leaving Tahiti, one would sail first to the Gambier Islands, from where it is only a relatively short hop to Pitcairn Island. Yet another stop, although not entirely en route, is at Easter Island. As so much depends on weather conditions encountered on the way, precise intermediate waypoints cannot be given. Boats bound for the Magellan Strait, which is entered at Cape Pillar, should eventually set a course for WP PS266. Making landfall there in heavy weather should be avoided as the strong currents create rough seas at the entrance to the Strait. Those wishing to visit the south of Chile and explore the Chilean channels on their way to the Magellan Strait should make landfall at WP PS267, in the approaches to Chacao Channel. The

same suggestion applies as above and the latter channel should only be entered in settled weather and with a fair tide. To obtain the latest information on tides and weather, the Corona Lighthouse should be contacted on VHF channel 16. See also route PS17 (page 361).

PS30 ROUTES IN CENTRAL POLYNESIA

Tahiti and the Society Islands are one of the most enticing cruising destinations in the world and their continuing popularity is assured in spite of several shortcomings. The most obvious among these are the compulsory bond for all visiting yachts, the relatively high cost of living, and the fact that most of French Polynesia's islands are in the cyclone belt. While the first two aspects are virtually unavoidable, the same cannot be said about the last point. The cyclone season in this part of the world lasts from December to March, with the worst months being February and March. It coincides with the southern summer, when the SE trade winds are absent and the weather is often muggy and overcast. It is not the kind of weather to entice anyone to stay, when one could easily be elsewhere. It is all a matter of timing and a little advance planning can make it possible to be in Tahiti at the best of times and avoid the worst.

In spite of several routes terminating in Tahiti, the number of routes originating from there is quite small. The main ones are PS31 and PS32, the trunk routes to the west, the 'milk run', which name is something of a misnomer, as ideal trade wind conditions are seldom present along the entire length of this route. Although it is possible to leave on a westbound voyage at any time from April to October, when reasonable sailing conditions can be expected, it would be wrong to set off without some idea of where to spend the following cyclone sea-

son. This would then dictate both the timing of one's departure from French Polynesia and also the amount of time that could be spent visiting the islands en route.

Occasionally, weather conditions in the South Pacific fail to conform to the norm and results can be very different to what is expected. Such a year was 1991 when unusual conditions prevailed throughout the South Pacific. Some experts blamed the El Niño Current, and indeed the sea water temperature was one and even two degrees higher than usual, which was sufficient to severely disturb the finely balanced ecosystem, especially in some lagoons. That year the SE trade winds were very late, and on the passage from Bora Bora to Tonga in June the winds were 50 per cent from the westerly quarter. By contrast, earlier in the year, in April and May, on a passage from New Zealand to Tahiti there were easterly winds as far as 40°S, where westerly winds are the norm. This example is given to draw attention to the importance of never taking anything for granted, certainly not 'normal' weather.

Westerly winds on westbound passages from the Society Islands are not uncommon even at the height of the winter trade wind season. They are generated by the passage of a low and associated fronts south of the area. In such a case the winds will back from NW to W and SW. After the front has passed, the winds will return to SSE and final-

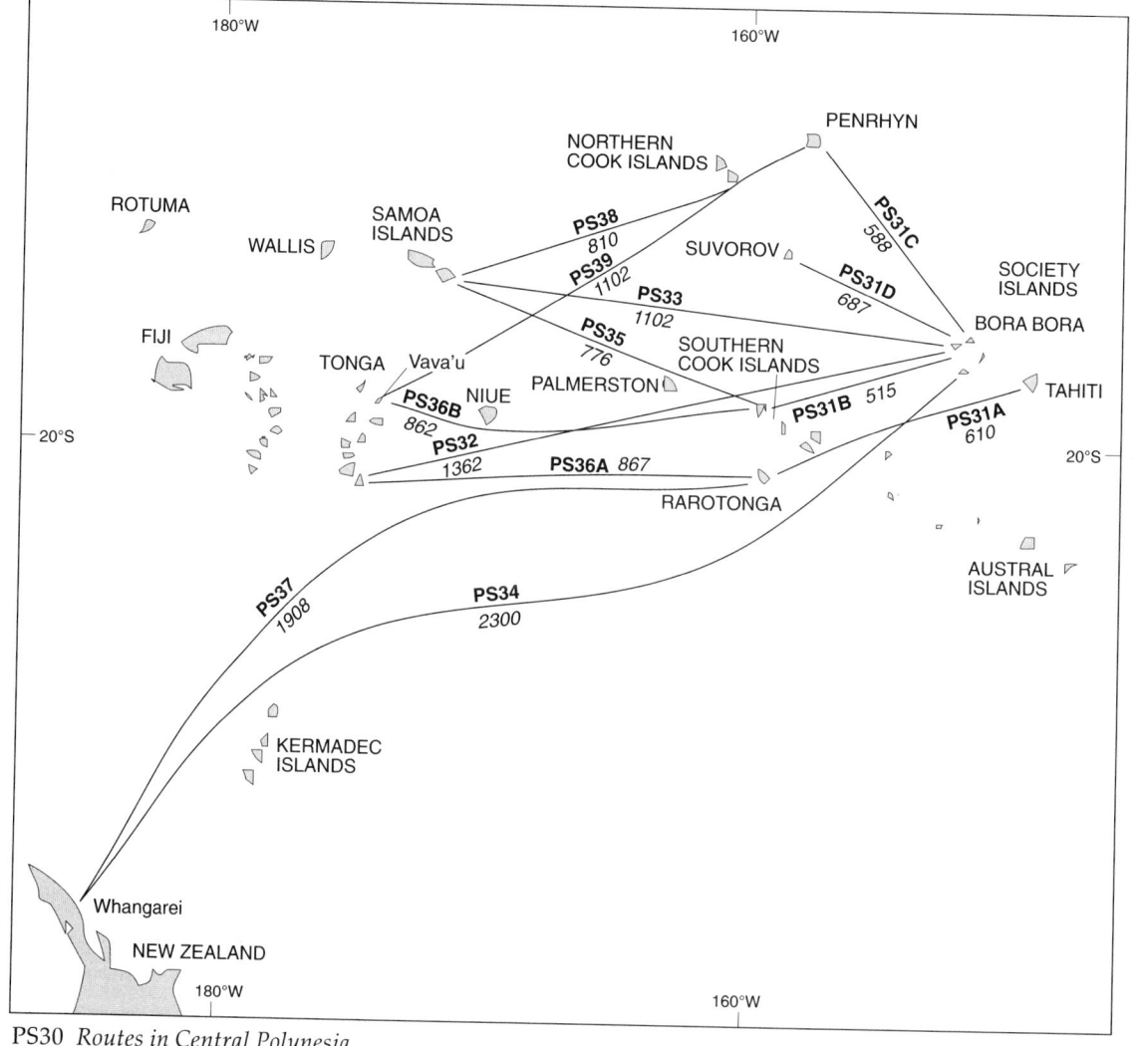

PS30 *Routes in Central Polynesia*

ly SE. After a spell of SE winds, which can last from two to five days and occasionally longer, the pattern may repeat itself.

For those for whom Tahiti is a point of return, either to the west coast of North America, or to Europe and the US east coast, there are a limited number of alternatives to choose from. The usual route taken by those who plan to return to the Atlantic is to continue westabout around the world along the trade wind routes of the three oceans. As mentioned in the previous section, the alternative is to take what Bernard Moitessier called 'the logical route' and reach the Atlantic via Cape Horn (PS26 page 368). Although shorter than the trade wind route, the Cape Horn route offers the prospect of a much tougher voyage. Another possibility is to reach the Atlantic via the Panama Canal (PT23 page 336). In this case the coast of South America can be reached from Tahiti with the help of westerly winds in higher latitudes. From there, the SE trade winds and north-setting Humboldt Current should make the rest of the trip to Panama fairly easy.

A return from Tahiti to the Pacific coast of North America is more straightforward. The most convenient route leads from Tahiti to Hawaii (PT22 page 335) and this route should also be sailed by those who hail from other parts of the world and wish to visit Alaska, British Columbia, or California.

PS31 *Society Islands to Cook Islands*

BEST TIME:	May to September			
TROPICAL STORMS:	December to March			
CHARTS:	BA: 4061			
	US: 606			
PILOTS:	BA: 62			
	US: 122, 126			
CRUISING GUIDES:	*Landfalls of Paradise, Charlie's Charts of Polynesia.*			
WAYPOINTS:				

Departure	Intermediate	Landfall	Destination	Distance (M)
Route PS31A				
PS311 Tahiti W		PS312 Rarotonga N	Avatiu	610
17°35'S, 149°42'W		21°11'S, 159°46'W	*21°11.5'S, 159°46.5'W*	
Route PS31B				
PS313 Bora Bora		PS314 Aitutaki N	Aratunga	515
16°29.5'S, 151°47'W		18°48'S, 159°45'W	*18°52'S,159°48'W*	
Route PS31C				
PS313 Bora Bora		PS315 Penrhyn E	Omoka	588
		9°00'S, 157°53'W	*9°00'S, 158°04'W*	
Route PS31D				
PS313 Bora Bora		PS316 off Suvorov	Suvorov	687
		13°10'S, 163°00'W	*13°14'S, 163°06'W*	

Most westbound boats take their leave from the Society Islands in Bora Bora, where departure formalities can be completed, the monies deposited for the compulsory bond collected, and the boat can be provisioned for the forthcoming passage. During the SE trade wind season, favourable conditions prevail for most of the passage, although during July and August the trade winds reach their peak and sailing conditions can be boisterous with large seas. During the summer months, from November to the end of March, the greater proportion of winds are still from the SE or E, but W and NW winds are not uncommon and are usually accompanied by squally weather. This is also the cyclone season when the area is best avoided as none of the islands can be considered entirely safe.

Boats heading west have a number of alternatives at their disposal as the routes fan out to visit islands either in the Southern or Northern Cooks, the two groups being separated by some 500 miles of ocean. The majority of boats head for Aitutaki (PS31B) or the capital Rarotonga (PS31A), with only a few making the detour to Penrhyn in the Northern Cooks (PS31C), which is one of three ports of entry into that country. If intending to visit the Northern Cooks and then continue westwards, it is better to call first at Penrhyn and then sail to neighbouring Rakahanga and Manihiki, lying approximately 200 miles to the southwest. If intending to visit the Southern Cooks, it is best to sail first to the capital Rarotonga and afterwards to Aitutaki as this will use the prevailing winds to better advantage.

On route PS31A, a direct course, which keeps outside all dangers, can be sailed from Tahiti to Rarotonga. From WP PS311 off Tahiti's west coast, a course is set which passes south of Moorea to WP PS312 off Rarotonga's north coast. The route passes right by Mauke, but as this is not a port of entry it is not permitted to stop there. It is sometimes possible to stop at nearby Atiu (19°59'S, 158°08'W), but one may be charged the transportation costs of the officials from Rarotonga. The official port of entry is Avatiu, the commercial harbour of Rarotonga, where the captain should report to the Port Captain, who monitors VHF channel 16 during office hours. It is also possible to stop ½ mile east of Avatiu, at Avarua, an anchorage in front of the capital.

Boats intending to stop at Aitutaki, and certainly any of those bound for the Northern Cooks, should leave French Polynesia from one of the more western islands, such as Bora Bora. From WP PS313, outside Te Ava Nui Pass, the route to Aitutaki (PS31B) passes south of Maupiti and makes landfall at WP PS314, north of Aitutaki. From there the course follows the NW side of the lagoon to the main pass, off Aratunga village. The pass is rather difficult to negotiate because of the strong outflowing current and limited depth (6 ft). Larger boats or those with deeper drafts may have to anchor outside the reef. Aitutaki is an official port of entry.

Boats bound for Penrhyn, in the Northern Cooks, should also take their departure from Bora Bora at WP PS313. The direct route passes right by Motu Iti, a small uninhabited island belonging to French Polynesia. Landfall is made at WP PS315 east of Penrhyn. The large lagoon is entered by the Northeast Pass and then one can make one's way to the main settlement Omoka, where entry formalities are completed.

Many boats do not stop in any of the Cooks at all and make straight for Suvorov, an atoll lying close to the direct route to Samoa. Suvorov has a good anchorage in settled weather, but becomes untenable in squally weather, and because of the large fetch the lagoon can become very rough. Yachts have been lost after breaking free from their anchors and driven onto the reef, so in threatening weather it is safer to put to sea immediately. The pass into the lagoon is on the NE side of the atoll, between Anchorage Island and Northeast Reef. Access is very difficult when there is a swell running.

The direct route from Bora Bora to Suvorov (PS31D) also has its starting point at WP PS313, from where a direct course can be sailed to WP PS316. The outline of the atoll is followed around to its NE side where a pass enters the lagoon between Northeast Reef and Anchorage Island. The entrance should not be attempted if there is a big swell running. The best anchorage is in the lee of Anchorage Island. Suvorov has been declared a national park by the Cook Islands government and a warden now resides there. Boats that have not cleared into the Cooks are allowed to spend a limited time at Suvorov, without any formalities except to register with the warden, who makes sure that sailors do not overstay their welcome. Suvorov has been reported to lie 1 mile east of its charted position.

PS32 *Society Islands to Tonga*

Best time:	May to September
Tropical storms:	December to March
Charts:	BA: 4061
	US: 606
Pilots:	BA: 61, 62
	US: 122, 126
Cruising guides:	*Landfalls of Paradise, Cruising Guide to the Vava'u Island Group.*

WAYPOINTS:				
Departure	*Intermediate*	*Landfall*	*Destination*	*Distance (M)*
Route PS32A				
PS321 Bora Bora	PS322			
16°29.5'S, 151°47'W	16°44'S, 152°13'W			
	PS323			
	17°00'S, 153°55'W			
	PS324			
	18°12'S, 159°48'W			
	PS325	PS326 Tongatapu E	Nuku'alofa	1362
	19°37'S, 167°45'W	20°57'S, 175°00'W	*21°08'S, 175°11'W*	
		PS327 Eua Iki	Nuku'alofa	1359
		21°05'S, 174°57'W		
Route PS32B				
PS321 Bora Bora	Palmerston			662
	18°03'S, 163°13'W			
	Niue	PS328 Vava'u N	Neiafu	1284
	19°03'S, 169°55'W	18°32'S, 173°54'W	*18°39'S, 173°59'W*	

Few of the boats sailing the trade wind route fail to call at one of the Cook Islands as the route passes them so closely. Indeed, sailing by some of those islands without stopping makes little sense and, if time permits, a stop in the Cooks should be allowed for, in which case route PS31 should be consulted first. The direct route from Bora Bora to the Tongan capital Nuku'alofa (PS32A) takes its departure outside Te Ava Nui Pass, at WP PS321. The route passes 15 miles south of Maupiti Island through WP PS322 and also south of Maupihaa Island through WP PS323. It then passes 40 miles north of Aitutaki through WP PS324.

The weather in the area between the Cooks and Tonga is rarely consistently good and this, combined with the various dangers, calls for constant alertness. Two reefs, Beveridge (20°02'S, 167°46'W) and Albert Meyer (20°54'S, 172°18'W), are close to the direct route from Bora Bora to Tongatapu. Further details on these and other dangers in the area will be found in PS36. To avoid them, from WP PS324 the course is altered for WP PS325. From that point, a new course can be set for WP PS326, three miles due north of Eastern Reef, in the outer approaches to Tongatapu lagoon. From that point it is a clear run to buoy no. 1 (21°00'S, 175°10.25'W), at the start of the Ava Lahi Pass, which is the shipping channel leading to Nuku'alofa. The buoyed channel leads across the lagoon to the small boat harbour at Faua, one mile east of the capital Nuku'alofa. Boats drawing under 8 ft (2.40 m) can

use this small harbour. The channel through the lagoon is not easy to use at night and therefore one should attempt to arrive in daytime. Boats may proceed directly into Faua harbour, from where the captain should make his way to the nearby port and to the customs offices. Because of Sunday observance, arriving at weekends should also be avoided.

In daylight and good visibility it is also possible to use Piha Passage, which is shorter and easier to negotiate and leads directly to Nuku'alofa. In this case, landfall should be made at WP PS327, two miles NE of Eua Iki Island, from where Piha Passage is taken into the lagoon.

The route from Bora Bora to Vava'u (PS32B), in Tonga's northern group, passes close to Palmerston Atoll, which belongs to the Cooks and whose isolated community is always pleased to greet visiting yachts. There is an anchorage on the SW side of the atoll, close to a number of small boat passages through the reef, of which the deepest is only 4 ft (1.20 m). Close to the direct route to Vava'u is also Niue, a small island nation. Boats stopping there clear in at Alofi, the main settlement.

Boats bound for Vava'u should make landfall at WP PS328, NE of the island. From there the north coast is followed around to Faihava Pass, on the west side of the island. This leads into Neiafu, located in one of the best sheltered bays in the South Pacific and considered one of the few cyclone shelters in the area.

PS33 *Society Islands to Samoa*

BEST TIME:	May to September			
TROPICAL STORMS:	December to March			
CHARTS:	BA: 4606			
	US: 606			
PILOTS:	BA: 61, 62			
	US: 122, 126			
CRUISING GUIDES:	*Landfalls of Paradise.*			
WAYPOINTS:				

Departure	Intermediate	Landfall	Destination	Distance (M)
Route PS33A				
PS331 Bora Bora	PS332 Maupiti	PS333 Tutuila SE	Pago Pago	1102
16°29.5'S, 151°47'W	16°33'S, 152°15'W	14°20'S, 170°38'W	*14°17'S, 170°41'W*	
Route PS33B				
PS331 Bora Bora	PS332 Maupiti			
	PS334 Tau N	PS335 Upolu N	Apia	1170
	14°00'S, 169°30'W	13°46'S, 171°44'W	*13°48'S, 171°46'W*	

Weather conditions on this route are usually better than those on the more southern route to Tonga, mainly because the area crossed by this route is less affected by the fronts passing in higher latitudes. From Bora Bora, the route to American Samoa (PS33A) passes south of Maupiti (WP PS332) from where it carries on uninterrupted as far as WP PS333, off the south coast of Tutuila in the approaches to Pago Pago. The capital of American Samoa is a popular stop primarily among American sailors, who are attracted by the opportunity to reprovision their boats with US products. On arrival at Pago Pago yachts must go directly to the customs dock. The excellently sheltered natural harbour, one of the safest hurricane holes in the South Pacific, has few attractions besides its American type supermarkets.

Boats intending to sail nonstop from Bora Bora to Western Samoa (PS33B) should use the same intermediate waypoint PS332 and then set a course to WP PS334 so as to pass north of Tau Island. From there the course is altered for WP PS335 to make landfall north of Upolu Island in the approaches to Apia, the capital of Western Samoa. Arriving boats must contact Harbour Control on VHF channel 16 when within 40 miles of Apia.

This route is the nearest to pass Suvorov Atoll and most boats sailing it make the detour to stop in that idyllic place. Suvorov belongs to the Cook Islands and a resident caretaker is based there to ensure that the crews of visiting yachts do not overstay their welcome. The caretaker deals with the necessary formalities, which are minimal. More details are given in PS31.

PS34 *Society Islands to New Zealand*

BEST TIME:	Mid-October to mid-November			
TROPICAL STORMS:	December to March			
CHARTS:	BA: 4061			
	US: 621, 622			
PILOTS:	BA: 51, 62, 126			
	US: 122, 127			
CRUISING GUIDES:	*Coastal Cruising Handbook of the Royal Arakana Yacht Club, Pickmere's Atlas of Northland's East Coast.*			
WAYPOINTS:				

Departure	Intermediate	Landfall	Destination	Distance (M)
PS341 Tahiti W 17°35'S, 149°42'W	PS342 20°00'S, 160°00'W PS343 Raoul 30°00'S, 180°00W	PS344 Kerikeri 35°10'S, 174°10'E	Opua *35°19'S, 174°07'E*	2279
PS345 Tahiti W	PS342 PS343 Raoul	PS345 Bream 35°50'S, 174°38'E	Whangarei *35°44'S, 174°20'E*	2300

The recommended time for this passage is just before summer comes to the tropics and with it the threat of cyclones, which is the main reason why most cruising boats leave the tropics in the first place. Fortunately this is also the start of the sailing season in New Zealand, when the worst of the winter gales are over. If the passage is made earlier in winter, when the SE trade winds are still blowing strongly in the tropics, it is probably better to sail west at least as far as longitude 165°W before altering course for New Zealand. The reason for this is to have some westing in hand should a SW gale blow up while approaching the top of New Zealand. Whether this tactic is justified or not depends very much on the weather encountered. Some people are of the opinion that if the weather conditions are favourable one might as well stick to the shortest route to New Zealand and hope for the best.

The direct route from Tahiti, as recommended at the change of seasons, passes so close to Rarotonga that a stop there should be considered (see route PS31). This would also provide the opportunity to obtain a long term weather forecast and thus plan the subsequent leg accordingly. One feature, which can seriously affect weather on this passage, is the South Pacific Convergence Zone. The SPCZ moves south during summer and is the main reason why the weather south of latitude 20°S can be very changeable making access to the latest weather information more useful than in many other parts of the world. The SPCZ is described in more detail at the beginning of this chapter.

If a stop in Rarotonga, or anywhere else in the Cook Islands, is not envisaged, from WP PS341, west of Tahiti, the route passes south of Maiao to WP PS342. From there, the route passes close to the north of Raoul island in the Kermadecs to another intermediate waypoint (PS343) before the course is altered for PS344, off Cape Kerikeri in the approaches to the Bay of Islands, where entry formalities can be completed at Opua.

Boats bound for Whangarei, further down North Island's east coast, should set a direct course from WP PS343 for WP PS345, off Bream Head, in the approaches to Whangarei. From there a long but well buoyed river channel leads to the port of Whangarei.

PS35 *Southern Cook Islands to Samoa*

BEST TIME:	May to September
TROPICAL STORMS:	December to March
CHARTS:	BA: 4061
	US: 541
PILOTS:	BA: 606
	US: 122, 126
CRUISING GUIDES:	*Landfalls of Paradise.*
WAYPOINTS:	

Departure	Intermediate	Landfall	Destination	Distance (M)
PS351 Aitutaki W 18°52'S, 158°50'W		PS352 Tutuila SE 14°20'S, 170°38'W	Pago Pago *14°17'S, 170°41'W*	776
PS351 Aitutaki W	PS353 Tau S 14°25'S, 169°30'W	PS354 Upolu N 13°46'S, 171°44'W	Apia *13°48'S, 171°46'W*	848

Many of the boats heading for the Samoan islands do so in order to reprovision in Pago Pago, in American Samoa, where a good selection of US goods is available. During the SE trade wind season favourable winds can be expected for most of this passage, although there are occasions when the trades do not blow with the hoped for consistency. In the area between the Cook Islands and Samoa, the trade winds follow a cyclic pattern, with several days of consistent winds followed by a short period of calms or variable winds, followed in turn by another spell of steady E or SE winds. In some years the SE trade winds are not established until late in the season and boats making this passage in April and even May can have a mixed weather pattern, with calms at night and squally weather during the day. The fastest passages are usually made in July and August, although during those months the trade winds may be almost too strong for some people's taste.

From Aitutaki and WP PS351 a direct course can be sailed to Samoa, but as the route passes close to Palmerston, a typical South Seas atoll, a stop there should be considered in settled weather. Boats bound for American Samoa should set a course for WP PS352 to make landfall south of Tutuila, in the approaches to the perfectly sheltered natural harbour of Pago Pago.

Boats bound nonstop for Western Samoa should set a course for WP PS353, south of Tau Island, from where the course should be altered to pass N of Tutuila and make landfall at WP PS354, off Upolu's north coast, in the approaches to Apia, Western Samoa's capital. Arriving boats must contact Harbour Control on VHF channel 16 when within 40 miles of Apia.

PS36 *Southern Cook Islands to Tonga*

BEST TIME:	May to September
TROPICAL STORMS:	December to March
CHARTS:	BA: 4061
	US: 606
PILOTS:	BA: 61, 62
	US: 122, 126
CRUISING GUIDES:	*Landfalls of Paradise, Cruising Guide to the Vava'u Island Group.*

WAYPOINTS:				
Departure	*Intermediate*	*Landfall*	*Destination*	*Distance (M)*
Route PS36A				
PS361 Rarotonga W	PS362	PS363 Tongatapu E	Nuku'alofa	867
21°10'S, 159°47'W	21°20'S, 164°00'W	20°57'S, 175°00'W	*21°08'S, 175°11'W*	
		PS364 Eua Iki	Nuku'alofa	
		21°05'S, 174°57'W		
Route PS36B				
PS365 Aitutaki W		PS366 Vava'u N	Neiafu	862
18°52'S, 159°50'W		18°32'S, 173°54'W	*18°39'S, 173°59'W*	

Although at first sight this appears to be a simple passage in the trade wind belt, there are some factors that should be considered in association with this route. In the winter months, from June to August, when most passages are made, the southern limit of the SE trades is slightly to the north of this area and, especially from Rarotonga to Tongatapu, one cannot be sure of encountering true trade wind sailing conditions. Although the majority of winds still blow from an easterly direction, periods of settled weather never last long and it is usual to encounter rough weather somewhere along this route. Although this route crosses an area affected by cyclones, these are not frequent and rarely occur before Christmas or after the end of March. Caution must be exercised between January and March, especially in Tonga, where the incidence of cyclones during these months is much higher than in the Cooks.

A hazard on this route are various reefs, the most dangerous being Beveridge Reef (20°02'S, 167°55'W), which has claimed at least one yacht. It lies only slightly to the south of the rhumb line between Rarotonga and Tongatapu and as the charts are not entirely accurate and there have been reports of unpredictable currents in the area, both this reef and all others should be given a wide berth. The breakers marked on the charts in position 21°05'S, 164°05'W, first reported in 1945, should be taken seriously, as a yacht on passage to Tonga was swamped by two abnormally large waves in exactly this area during a gale. The route from Rarotonga to Tongatapu passes very close to two other dangers, whose exact position is still considered doubtful and therefore should be given a wide berth. The first is in position 21°43'S, 167°46'W and is suspected to have caused the loss

of a yacht which reported striking an unidentified object at night and sinking almost immediately. The crew took to the liferaft, but did not have the chance to establish accurately the location of the incident. Several years later the remains of a yacht were found in the vicinity of this unnamed reef when another yacht stopped there and its crew went diving. The second danger is Harrans Reef, lying about 66 miles further west at 21°32.5'S, 168°57'W. Yet another reef, which will be passed closely on this route, is Albert Meyer Reef (20°54'S, 172°18'W).

The direct route from Rarotonga to the Tongan capital Nuku'alofa (PS36A) passes close to some of the dangers described above. From WP PS361, outside Avatiu, on Rarotonga's north coast, an initial course is set for WP PS362, to avoid the danger mentioned earlier (21°05'S, 164°05'W). From there, a direct course can be set for WP PS363, three miles due north of Eastern Reef, in the outer approaches to Tongatapu. From that point it is a clear run to buoy no. 1 (21°00.15'S, 175°10.25'W), at the start of Ava Lahi Pass, which is the shipping channel into Nuku'alofa. The channel winds its way through the lagoon to Faua. Boats drawing under 8 ft (2.40 m) can use the small boat harbour at Faua, one mile east of Nuku'alofa.

In daylight and in good visibility it is possible to use Piha Passage, which is shorter and leads directly into Nuku'alofa. In this case landfall should be made slightly further south at WP PS364, 2 miles NE of Eua Iki Island.

The route from Aitutaki to Vava'u (PS36B) passes close to Palmerston, where yachts are always welcome, especially if the crew had the foresight to bring the islanders' mail as the supply ship does not call there frequently. Another stop en route is at Niue, where boats stop at Alofi, the main settlement on the island (19°03'S, 169°55'W). Whether any of those stops is made or not, a course should be set for WP PS366, NE of Vava'u. From there the north coast is followed around to Faihava Pass, on the west side of the island. This leads into Neiafu, located in one of the best sheltered bays in the South Pacific and one of the best hurricane holes in the region.

PS37 *Cook Islands to New Zealand*

BEST TIME:	Mid-October to mid-November			
TROPICAL STORMS:	December to March			
CHARTS:	BA: 4061			
	US: 622			
PILOTS:	BA: 51, 62			
	US: 122, 126, 127			
CRUISING GUIDES:	*Coastal Cruising Handbook of the Royal Arakana Yacht Club, Pickmere's Atlas of Northland's East Coast.*			
WAYPOINTS:				

Departure	Intermediate	Landfall	Destination	Distance (M)
PS371 Rarotonga W 21°10'S, 159°47'W	PS372 24°00'S, 178°00'W			
	PS373 30°00'S, 175°00'E	PS374 Kerikeri 35°10'S, 174°10'E	Opua *35°19'S, 174°07'E*	1864
PS371 Rarotonga W	PS372			
	PS373	PS375 Bream 35°50'S, 174°38'E	Whangarei *35°44'S, 174°20'E*	1908

Directions for this passage are very similar to those described in PS34, which should be consulted also. Because of the risk of encountering a late winter gale while approaching New Zealand, or running the risk of being caught by an early cyclone, if leaving the tropics too late, the optimum time for this passage is rather limited. Although the direct route from Rarotonga leads east of the Kermadec Islands, if this passage is made before November it is advisable to make some westing while still under the influence of the SE trade winds, and therefore pass to the north and west of the Kermadecs. This means that North Island will be approached from the north, which is the accepted practice for this time of year so as to ensure a better sailing angle in case a gale comes up from the W or SW. This tactic is normally used by boats sailing to New Zealand from Fiji, when making the required westing is not much of a problem. Boats sailing from the Cooks may find it too much of a burden to make so much westing and may be tempted to sail a more direct route. Such action should only be taken if it is supported by reliable weather information. After the beginning of December the likelihood of SW gales is more remote, so the advice to make some westing can be ignored and a more direct route sailed, possibly east of the Kermadecs.

Presuming that this passage is made at the recommended time, and bearing in mind the comments made above, if the point of departure is Rarotonga an initial course should be set for WP PS372. Such a route would avoid all the dangers mentioned in PS36 and also allow New Zealand to be approached from the north, rather than east. A direct course can be set from there for the port of destination, but if it is felt that this may be too early, the course should be altered for WP PS373 so that meridian 175°E is crossed in latitude 30°S and North Island is approached from the north. The course is then set for WP PS374, off Cape Kerikeri at the entrance into the Bay of Islands, where entry formalities can be completed at Opua.

Boats bound for Whangarei, further down

North Island's east coast, should set a direct course from WP PS373 for WP PS375, off Bream Head, in the approaches to Whangarei. From there a long but well buoyed river channel leads to the port of Whangarei.

PS38 *Northern Cook Islands to Samoa*

BEST TIME:	May to September			
TROPICAL STORMS:	December to March			
CHARTS:	BA: 4606			
	US: 606			
PILOTS:	BA: 61			
	US: 122, 126			
CRUISING GUIDES:	*Landfalls of Paradise, South Pacific Anchorages.*			
WAYPOINTS:				
Departure	*Intermediate*	*Landfall*	*Destination*	*Distance (M)*
PS380 Omoka	PS381 Mani	PS382 Tutuila NE	Pago Pago	810
9°00'S, 158°04'W	*10°15'S, 161°00'W*	*14°16'S, 170°38'W*	*14°17'S, 170°41'W*	
PS380 Omoka	PS381 Mani	PS383 Upolu N	Apia	860
		13°46'S, 171°44'W	*13°48'S, 171°46'W*	

Because of the large distance separating the two groups that make up the Cook Islands, some sailors prefer to take a northern route from the Society Islands to the rest of Polynesia. This is indeed a less frequented part of the world and the route to Samoa has the added advantage that it benefits from favourable winds throughout the Austral winter.

Among the three main islands in the Northern Cooks, Penrhyn provides the best shelter in its large lagoon and therefore has been recommended as a point of departure. The other two Northern Cook Islands, Rakahanga and Manihiki, will be passed quite closely, but as neither has a safe anchorage stopping there should only be attempted in settled weather. Slightly off the direct route is Suvorov, which also belongs to the Cooks, and is a favourite stop for westbound boats (see PS31).

Boats arriving in Pago Pago must proceed to the customs dock to complete formalities. The authorities in Western Samoa require all boats to contact Harbour Control when within 40 miles of Apia.

PS39 *Northern Cook Islands to Tonga*

BEST TIME:	May to September
TROPICAL STORMS:	December to March
CHARTS:	BA: 4606
	US: 606
PILOTS:	BA: 61
	US: 122, 126
CRUISING GUIDES:	*Landfalls of Paradise, South Pacific Anchorages.*

WAYPOINTS:				
Departure	*Intermediate*	*Landfall*	*Destination*	*Distance (M)*
PS390 Omoka *9°00'S, 158°04'W*	PS391 Suvorov N *13°12'S, 163°03'W*	PS391 Vava'u *18°32'S, 173°54'W*	Neiafu *18°39'S, 173°59'W*	1102
PS392 Suvorov *13°14'S, 163°06'W*		PS391 Vava'u	Neiafu	712
PS390 Omoka		PS393 Tongatapu E *20°57'S, 175°00'W*	Nuku'alofa *21°08'S, 175°11'W*	1229

As mentioned in route PS38, among the Northern Cooks only Penrhyn has a good anchorage, and for this reason it has been chosen as a point of departure. Almost astride the direct route lies one of the most enticing destinations in the South Pacific: the uninhabited Suvorov atoll. The Cook Islands Government has declared the atoll a nature reserve and is represented by a caretaker, who usually grants visiting boats a four-day stay. The pass through the reef is between Northeast Reef and Anchorage Island, the latter providing reasonable shelter in its lee. The pass should not be attempted if there is a big swell running. Also, mariners are advised that Suvorov has been reported to lie 1 mile east of its charted position.

Whether sailing direct, or stopping in Suvorov, boats bound for Tonga will find detailed information on the ports of Neiafu and Nuku'alofa in PS32.

PS40 ROUTES IN WESTERN POLYNESIA

This area of the South Pacific offers some of the best cruising in the world, although navigation among the various island groups can be very difficult on account of reefs and strong currents. The triangular stretch of water between Samoa, Tonga, and Fiji can be quite stormy at times and some boats have reported their worst South Pacific weather in this area. Although the area appears to be right in the path of the SE trade winds, these are sometimes absent and cannot be relied upon. The explanation for such conditions, which are quite different from what people expect South Seas weather to be like, could be the movement of the South Pacific Convergence Zone which moves north and south with the seasons and can produce similar conditions to its equatorial counterpart, the better known Intertropical Convergence Zone.

Passages between Tonga and Fiji used to have the reputation of being the most hazardous in the South Pacific, and the number of cruising boats which were lost in these waters confirmed this assumption. The route passes through an area infested with reefs, where only few of the dangers are marked by lights. The 180 mile wide stretch of water between Tonga and Fiji has strong currents and because of the distance involved it is impossible to pass all dangers in daylight. Often this meant that the most dangerous area was reached with an unreliable position and the loss of most boats occurred usually at night and was always blamed on an inaccurate position.

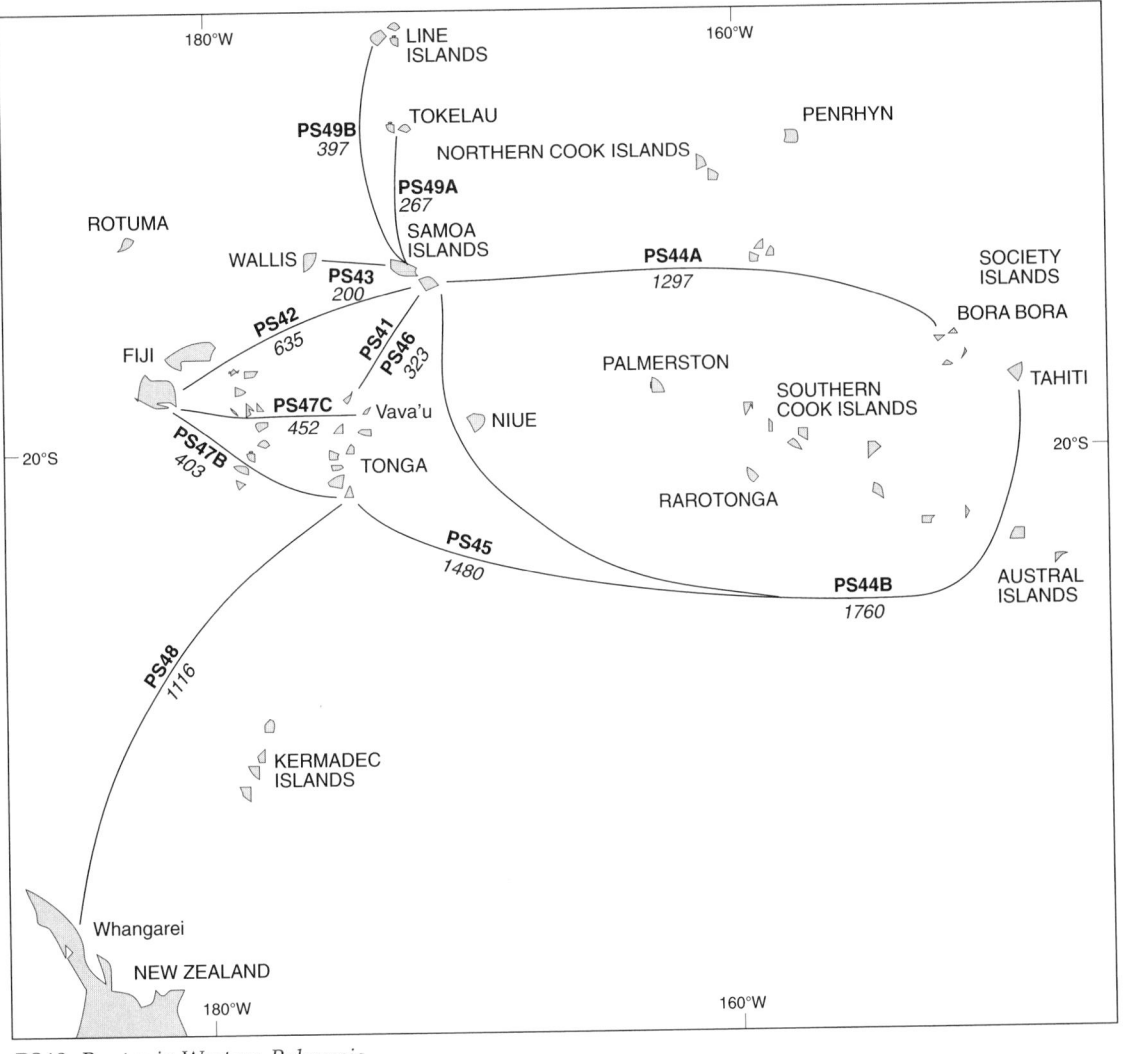

PS40 *Routes in Western Polynesia*

These navigational difficulties may have been compounded by Tonga's decision to keep the same date as Fiji, although lying well to the east of the 180° meridian. As a result of this decision, local time in Tonga is GMT + 13, rather than GMT – 11 as it should be. This means that the date in Tonga is one day ahead of the actual GMT day. Arriving from the east, most people change their time and date to the local standard after their first visit ashore and often do not give the matter another thought. The real problem starts on the next leg of the voyage when some navigators forget to set back their time by 24 hours. Working out a sextant sight by using the wrong day entry in the Nautical Almanac can result in an error serious enough to

have grave consequences in an area strewn with reefs, where passes between islands are only a few miles wide. All of these problems should have been eliminated by satellite navigation and yet, although virtually all yachts passing through the area are equipped with GPS, the number of boats lost on reefs is only marginally lower than two decades ago. The obvious explanation for this rather surprising state of affairs is the navigators' absolute trust in satellite navigation and their overreliance on the accuracy of charts, many of which were compiled over a century ago and have not been resurveyed.

Another major disadvantage of the Central Pacific is that the entire area is subject to cyclones, which occur mostly in the first three months of the year. Although the majority of boats leave the area during the dangerous season, every year a number of boats spend the summer in or near one of the ports where shelter can be sought should a cyclone come that way. One of the safest places is Pago Pago, in American Samoa, while another favourite hurricane anchorage is Neiafu, in Tonga's Vava'u group, although boats did suffer damage during a recent cyclone that passed through there. In Fiji most boats remain in the vicinity of Suva, where the Trade Winds anchorage and surrounding inlets offer the best shelter. The decision to spend the summer in the tropics is a matter of personal choice, but the number of boats lost or damaged in recent years has persuaded most skippers to plan their South Pacific cruise so as to leave the area before the start of the cyclone season.

PS41 *Samoa to Tonga*

BEST TIME:	April to October
TROPICAL STORMS:	December to March
CHARTS:	BA: 1829
	US: 83039
PILOTS:	BA: 61
	US: 126
CRUISING GUIDES:	*Landfalls of Paradise, Cruising Guide to the Vava'u Island Group.*
WAYPOINTS:	

Departure	Intermediate	Landfall	Destination	Distance (M)
Route PS41A				
PS411 Apolima		PS413 Vava'u NW	Neiafu	312
13°50'S, 172°10'W		18°32'S, 174°05'W	*18°39'S, 173°59'W*	
Route PS41B				
PS412 Tutuila SW		PS413 Vava'u NW	Neiafu	323
14°25'S, 170°43'W				

The weather on this route can be very variable and even at the height of the SE trade wind season one can never be sure what conditions to expect. Violent squalls are sometimes experienced in this area and also electric storms with tremendous sheets of lightning and thunder. These conditions can occur throughout the year. Passages during the cyclone season should be avoided as the area is sometimes crossed by tropical storms.

Because of the direction of the prevailing winds, boats leaving from Apia (PS41A) fare better by sailing west along the north coast of Upolu and reaching the open sea via Apolima Strait between Upolu and Savai'i. From WP PS411, SW of Apolima Island, a direct course can be set for WP PS413, off the NE coast of the main island of Vava'u. Faihava Pass, on the west side of the island, leads into Neiafu, one of the best protected anchorages in the South Pacific. Neiafu is the capital of Tonga's northern group and an official port of entry into the kingdom.

Boats sailing from American Samoa directly to Vava'u (PS41B) can set a course from WP PS412, SW of Pago Pago for the same WP PS413, in the approaches to Neiafu. Southbound boats can now clear into Tonga at Niuatoputapu (15°58'S, 173°44'W), but a stop at this island, conveniently placed halfway between Samoa and Vava'u, should only be attempted in settled weather. The island has a protected lagoon, which can be entered through a pass on the NW of the island. The pass is easier to identify at low tide when the reef becomes visible. Range markers, which must be brought in line, indicate the break in the reef. If the weather is unsettled, it is safer to proceed directly to Neiafu, on Vava'u, which can be entered under most conditions.

PS42 *Samoa to Fiji*

BEST TIME:	April to October			
TROPICAL STORMS:	December to March			
CHARTS:	BA: 1829			
	US: 83039			
PILOTS:	BA: 61			
	US: 126			
CRUISING GUIDES:	*Yachtsman's Fiji.*			
WAYPOINTS:				
Departure	*Intermediate*	*Landfall*	*Destination*	*Distance (M)*
Route PS42A				
PS421 Tutuila SW		PS422 Nanuku	Levuka	635
14°25'S, 170°43'W		16°40'S, 179°05'W	*17°41'S, 178°52'E*	
Route PS42B				
PS423 Apolima		PS422 Nanuku	Levuka	567
13°50'S, 172°10'W				
Route PS42C				
PS424 Savai'i W		PS425 Nggelelevu	Levuka	549
13°28'S, 172°48'W		16°05'S, 179°05'W		

Boats leaving Pago Pago bound for Fiji (PS42A) should make their way to the SW of Tutuila and from WP PS421 set a direct course for Nanuku Passage, on the NE side of the Fijian archipelago. The route passes slightly to the south of the Tongan island of Niua Fo'ou (15°36'S, 175°38'W). In settled weather it is possible to stop briefly at this high volcanic island. There is an anchorage in an open roadstead off the main settlement Angala, on the north side of the island. Whether stopping there or not, it is then a clear run to WP PS422, five miles north of the light on Welangilala, marking the eastern side of Nanuku Passage. As only this eastern side of the pass is marked by a light it should be favoured, as there is no light on the southern extremity of Nanuku Reef, on the west side of the passage. Great care should be exercised when approaching Nanuku Passage as the currents in this area can be very strong and the light on Welangilala is not always operational.

From Nanuku, the course runs down the middle of the Koro Sea, where all dangers are marked by lights. If wishing to stop before the capital Suva, there is a port of entry at Levuka on Ovalau Island. The more conveniently placed port of Savusavu, on the SE side of Vanua Levu Island (16°47'S, 179°21'E) will become a port of entry in the future, but this has not been confirmed and the latest situation should be ascertained before going there.

Boats sailing to Fiji from Western Samoa can either sail through Apolima Strait, between the Samoan islands of Upolu and Savai'i (PS42B), and then head for Nanuku Passage, or cruise the north coast of Savai'i before making for Fiji and enter the latter through the Somosomo Strait (PS42C). Permission to stop in Savai'i after having cleared out at Apia can be obtained from the Ministry of Foreign Affairs in Apia.

Boats sailing from Apia along the north coast of Upolu and using Apolima Strait to reach the open sea can set a direct course from WP PS423, SW of Apolima Island, for the Nanuku Passage. From there similar directions apply as described above.

Boats that have cruised along the north coast of Savai'i can reach the Fijian archipelago either through the same Nanuku Passage, or approach the Fijian islands from a more northerly direction and reach the Koro Sea through the Somosomo Strait separating Taveuni and Vanua Levu islands. From WP PS424, off Cape Mulinuu, at the western extremity of Savai'i, a direct course can be set for WP PS425, off Nggelelevu in the Ringgold Islands, from where the route winds its way SW towards the Somosomo Strait and the Koro Sea.

PS43 *Samoa to Wallis*

BEST TIME:	April to October
TROPICAL STORMS:	December to March
CHARTS:	BA: 1829
	US: 83039
PILOTS:	BA: 61
	US: 126
CRUISING GUIDES:	*Landfalls of Paradise.*
WAYPOINTS:	

Departure	Intermediate	Landfall	Destination	Distance (M)
PS431 Savai'i W *13°28'S, 172°48'W*		PS432 Wallis SE *13°25'S, 176°05'W*	Mata Utu *13°17'S, 176°08'W*	200

This route lies within the SE trade wind belt and for the best part of the year winds tend to have an easterly component. From Apia the route follows the north coast of Savai'i to its western extremity. From WP PS431, off Cape Mulinuu, a course is set for WP PS432, SW of Faioa Island, which marks the SE extremity of the large lagoon at Wallis. Care should be exercised when approaching Wallis from the east as the island's position is incorrectly charted and in fact the island lies about two miles further east than its charted position. The danger is compounded by the fact that the reef surrounding the lagoon is sometimes difficult to see. The entrance into the lagoon, Honikulu Pass, is on the south side of the lagoon in the reported GPS position 13°23.5'S, 176°13'W. There is a strong current at ebb tide, so it is better to negotiate the pass at flood tide or at slack water, especially when the sea is rough. At ebb tide the outflowing current can set at 6 knots and there are dangerous overflows outside the pass. The passes and reefs inside the lagoon are well marked. Formalities are completed at Mata Utu, the main settlement on Uvea. If conditions at this anchorage are uncomfortable, visiting yachts are allowed to anchor in Gahi Bay, on the SE corner of the main island of Uvea.

Although lying to the east of the 180° meridian, both Wallis and Futuna have decided to keep the same date as New Caledonia, the nearest French territory. This means that Wallis is one day ahead of Samoa.

Warning: Check your GMT time and date on leaving Wallis.

PS44 *Samoa to Society Islands*

BEST TIME:	November, April
TROPICAL STORMS:	December to March
CHARTS:	BA: 4606
	US: 526
PILOTS:	BA: 61, 62
	US: 122, 126
CRUISING GUIDES:	*Landfalls of Paradise, Charlie's Charts of Polynesia.*
WAYPOINTS:	

Departure	Intermediate	Landfall	Destination	Distance (M)
Pago Pago *14°17'S, 170°41'W*	Suvorov *13°14'S, 163°06'W* Aitutaki *18°52'S, 159°48'W*		Bora Bora *16°30'S, 151°46'W*	1297

Only a few boats attempt to make this passage against the prevailing winds and the advice is to avoid it if at all possible. The only months when there is at least a chance of some favourable winds are the summer months, December to early April. This is the time when the SE trade winds are at their weakest and least consistent, and there is a reasonable chance of occasional westerly winds on the direct route. Unfortunately it is also the cyclone season, with February and March being the most likely months for cyclones. Therefore the only time when this passage should be attempted is at the change of seasons, when the risk of cyclones is acceptably low, either in the second half of November or the first half of April. If a direct route

can be sailed, a useful stop is at Suvorov or another of the Cook Islands, such as Aitutaki, which lies close to this route (PS44A).

The risk of cyclones can be minimised by sailing a northern route and possibly calling at Penrhyn in the Northern Cooks. On such a northern route the winds at the change of seasons would be light, so one could cover at least part of the distance under power. A safer, if considerably longer route, can be sailed during the winter months, from May to October (PS44B). This entails sailing south in search of westerly winds (see route PS67) and make easting between latitudes 30°S and 35°S, before turning north for Tahiti.

PS45 *Tonga to Society Islands*

BEST TIME:	April to May				
TROPICAL STORMS:	December to March				
CHARTS:	BA: 4606				
	US: 606				
PILOTS:	BA: 61, 62				
	US: 122, 126				
CRUISING GUIDES:	*Landfalls of Paradise, Charlie's Charts of Polynesia.*				
WAYPOINTS:					
Departure	*Intermediate*	*Landfall*	*Destination*	*Distance (M)*
Vava'u NW	Alofi		Bora Bora	1287
18°32'S, 174°05'W	*19°03'S, 169°55'W*		*16°30'S, 151°46'W*	

Although boats have attempted to sail this route along the rhumb line by calling at the Cook Islands, the passage can be very difficult even at the best time, which is the change of seasons when the SE trade winds are not yet fully established. The feasibility of this passage depends very much on the type of yacht attempting it, as a boat which goes well to windward will probably achieve it without too much hardship. It is also important to wait both at the start, and in the Cooks, if a stop is made there, for favourable weather conditions for the subsequent passage. Throughout the year, and especially

at the change of seasons, westerly winds are not uncommon in this area. They are usually generated by passing fronts, which are the kind of conditions one should wait for to make the necessary easting.

If a direct route is sailed from Vava'u, such a route passes close to the island of Niue, where a stop can be made at Alofi. In summer, when the risk of cyclones is too high, it is better to follow the same directions as those given for route PS44 and make this passage in higher latitudes with the help of westerly winds (see also route PS67 page 408).

PS46 *Tonga to Samoa*

BEST TIME:	April to October			
TROPICAL STORMS:	December to March			
CHARTS:	BA: 1829			
	US: 83039			
PILOTS:	BA: 61			
	US: 126			
CRUISING GUIDES:	*Landfalls of Paradise.*			
WAYPOINTS:				

Departure	Intermediate	Landfall	Destination	Distance (M)
PS461 Vava'u NW 18°32'S, 174°05'W		PS462 Upolu SE 14°05'S, 171°20'W	Apia *13°48'S, 171°46'W*	346
PS461 Vava'u NW		PS463 Tutuila SW 14°25'S, 170°43'W	Pago Pago *14°17'S, 170°41'W*	327

The weather on this route can be very variable and even at the height of the SE trade wind season one can never be sure what conditions to expect. Violent squalls are sometimes experienced in this area and also electric storms with tremendous sheets of lightning and thunder. These conditions can occur throughout the year. The cyclone-prone months of January to March should be avoided as cyclones have crossed through this area in the past without hitting either Tonga or Samoa.

Most boats take their leave from Tonga in Vava'u from where there is a relatively clear run to both Samoas. After leaving Vava'u through Faihava Pass, from WP PS461 a direct course can be set for WP PS462 SE of Upolu. The recommended route passes to the east of both Toku and Fonualei islands, both of which belong to Tonga. The same course leads well to the east of Niuatoputapu and its surrounding dangers. If bound for Apia, the island of Upolu should be rounded from the east.

The official port of entry into Western Samoa is the capital Apia. Arriving yachts must contact Harbour Control on VHF channel 16 when within 40 miles of Apia.

Boats bound for American Samoa should set a course for WP PS463, off the south coast of Tutuila, in the approaches to Pago Pago. This is the only official port of entry in American Samoa, where on arrival yachts should go directly to the clearance dock.

PS47 *Tonga to Fiji*

BEST TIME:	April to October
TROPICAL STORMS:	December to March
CHARTS:	BA: 1829
	US: 83039
PILOTS:	BA: 61
	US: 126
CRUISING GUIDES:	*Yachtsman's Fiji.*

WAYPOINTS:				
Departure	Intermediate	Landfall	Destination	Distance (M)
Route PS47A				
PS471 Tongatapu W	PS472 Vatua			
21°02'S, 175°18'W	19°30'S, 178°13'W			
	PS473 Totoya	PS474 Ovalau	Levuka	400
	19°06.5'S, 179°55'W	17°41'S, 178°52'E	*17°41'S, 178°52'E*	
Route PS47B				
PS471 Tongatapu W	PS472 Vatua			
	PS473 Totoya			
	PS475 Rewa	PS476 Daveta	Suva	403
	18°15'S, 178°35'E	18°12'S, 178°23.5'E	*18°09'S, 178°26'E*	
Route PS47C				
PS477 Vava'u W	PS478 Late			
18°39'S, 174°05'W	18°40'S, 174°40'W			
	PS472 Vatua			
	PS473 Totoya	PS474 Ovalau	Levuka	452

This passage between the two neighbouring island groups can be made at any time of the year, although the cyclone season should be avoided, especially the period January to March when both the islands and the waters between them are crossed by cyclones. During July and August, when the SE trade winds are at their strongest, the passage can be rough. At the beginning and end of the winter season the winds are lighter, but the sky is often overcast which can make navigation through these dangerous waters quite difficult.

Because of the risks involved in passing through Fiji's Lau Group, boats leaving from Vava'u should avoid the more direct Oneata Passage and sail instead through the wider passage between Ongea Levu and Vatua islands (route PS47C). The latter passage is also used by boats leaving from Tongatapu. If using Oneata Passage, one should be aware of the dangers of sailing at night through the area west of Oneata, where none of the islands have lights. For similar reasons, Lakemba Passage should also be used with great caution.

The southern passage, between Vatua and Ongea Levu, is marked by lights both on Vatua Island and the southern extremity of Totoya Island and is therefore the easiest to use. Having left Tongatapu through Egeria Channel (route PS47A), from WP PS471 a course is set for WP PS472, 10 miles due north of the light on Vatua. From there the course is altered for WP PS473, approximately 5 miles south of Totoya. From that point a direct course can be set for WP PS474, one mile east of Balavu Reef, at the southern entrance into Levuka, on the island of Ovalau, an official port of entry into Fiji.

Boats bound for Suva direct (route PS47B), from WP PS473, south of Totoya Island, should set a course for WP PS475, in the approaches to Suva. For the last few miles, the course runs parallel to the reef as far as WP PS476, at the entrance into Daveta Levu Passage, which leads into Suva Harbour. The approaches are well buoyed and lit and there are clear range markers making it easy to enter this harbour even at night if necessary. Arriving boats should go straight to the quarantine anchorage and wait to be cleared by a health officer. After that they can proceed to King's Wharf to complete the rest of the entry formalities.

Boats leaving from Vava'u and using the same southern passage (PS47C), from WP PS477, outside Faihava Passage, should set an initial course for WP PS478, to pass north of Late Island. From there the course should be altered for WP PS472, north of Vatua Island, and subsequently the same direction can be followed to pass through the recommended waypoints and clear in at either Levuka or Suva. The route from Ha'apai to Fiji passes very close to Metis Shoal (19°11.4'S, 174°51'W), where an active volcano is erupting and has created a cone standing at least 50 m (150 ft) above sea level.

Although spectacular, the area should be approached with caution.

Stopping and going ashore anywhere in Fiji before clearing in first at one of the ports of entry is strictly prohibited. Special permission is necessary to cruise in the Lau Group and must be obtained in Suva. For boats arriving from the east,

these are the only two ports of entry, at Levuka and Suva, but it is expected that Savusavu (16°47'S, 179°21'E), on the SE coast of Vanua Levu, will become an official port of entry as well.

Warning: Check your GMT date on leaving Tonga.

PS48 *Tonga to New Zealand*

BEST TIME:	October to November
TROPICAL STORMS:	December to March
CHARTS:	BA: 780
	US: 622
PILOTS:	BA: 51, 61
	US: 126, 127
CRUISING GUIDES:	*Coastal Cruising Handbook of the Royal Arakana Yacht Club, Pickmere's Atlas of Northland's East Coast.*
WAYPOINTS:	

Departure	Intermediate	Landfall	Destination	Distance (M)
PS481 Tongatapu SW 21°05'S, 175°23'W	PS482 24°00'S, 177°30'W			
	PS483 30°00'S, 175°00'E	PS484 Kerikeri 35°10'S, 174°10'E	Opua *35°19'S, 174°07'E*	1071
PS481 Tongatapu SW	PS482			
	PS483	PS485 Bream 35°50'S, 174°38'E	Whangarei *35°44'S, 174°20'E*	1116

This passage is normally made just before the onset of the cyclone season, which officially starts in November, although tropical storms have very rarely been recorded in this month. Those who are tempted to leave on this passage too early risk encountering wintry weather further south. The direct course from Tongatapu leads close to the Minerva Reefs, which can be visited in settled weather. Yachts have anchored inside North Minerva Reef, which can be reached through a pass on its NW side and offers adequate protection, especially at low tide, when the reef dries. However, if one does not intend to stop at Minerva it is wiser to give it a wide berth as many vessels have come to grief on this dangerous reef lurking in mid-ocean.

Having left Tongatapu though Egeria Channel, from WP PS481, the course passes close to the west of Ata Island to WP PS482. From there, the route stays well to the east of North Minerva Reef. Depending on the direction of the wind after having passed Minerva Reef, it is advisable to steer a

course which would intersect the meridian of New Zealand's North Cape well to the north of it. The reason for making sufficient westing early in the passage is to counteract the possibility of a SW gale later on. This precaution is worth taking especially if this passage is made during the winter months (May to October), but from November onwards it is probably just as well to steer the shortest course for the desired destination.

A compromise solution is to set a course for WP PS483 so that meridian 175°E is crossed in latitude 30°S and North Island is approached from the north. A course is then set for WP PS484, off Cape Kerikeri, at the entrance into the Bay of Islands, where entry formalities into New Zealand are completed at Opua.

Boats bound for Whangarei, further down North Island's east coast, should set a direct course from WP PS483 for WP PS485, off Bream Head, in the approaches to Whangarei. From there a long but well buoyed river channel leads to the port of Whangarei.

PS49 *Northbound from Samoa*

BEST TIME:	April to October			
TROPICAL STORMS:	December to March			
CHARTS:	BA: 4052			
	US: 505			
PILOTS:	BA: 61			
	US: 126			
CRUISING GUIDES:	*Landfalls of Paradise, South Pacific Anchorages.*			
WAYPOINTS:				

Departure	*Intermediate*	*Landfall*	*Destination*	*Distance (M)*
PS490 Apia	PS492 Upolu N	Fakaofu	Fenuafala	267
13°48'S, 171°46'W	*13°45'N, 171°46'W*	*9°24'S, 171°25'W*	*9°23'S, 171°16'W*	
PS493 Fakaofu		Phoenix SW	Canton	397
		2°52'S, 171°45'W	*2°49'S, 171°43'W*	

Samoa is a good starting point for a voyage to one of the least visited island groups in the Pacific: the Tokelaus. Although the Tokelaus have a special status and are administered by New Zealand, there is an office of Tokelau Affairs in Apia, which must be visited to obtain permission to call at these isolated islands. Although they are New Zealand dependencies, the local chiefs have total jurisdiction over their internal affairs and do not appear too keen to encourage contacts with the outside world. However, cruising yachts have obtained permission to stop in the Tokelaus provided they follow the correct procedure.

None of the three islands – Fakaofu, Nukunonu and Atafu – has a safe anchorage, although there are day anchorages in the lee of each atoll and all have had passes blasted through the reef to provide access by small boat. There is a ship's buoy on the SW side of Nukunonu which is used by the supply ship. There is a relatively well sheltered anchorage in the lee of Fenuafala Island, on the SW side of Fakaofu atoll. As this is also the main settlement, formalities will have to be completed here. Approaching boats may contact the local authorities on 9088 kHz.

The Tokelaus are an interesting stop for boats heading north towards the Phoenix group, where the best shelter will be found at Canton Island, once a thriving military base but now home for a number of families from Kiribati, to whom it belongs. There is an anchorage on the west side of the island, and also a channel that leads inside, but this should only be attempted at slack water as tidal streams are very strong. A sheltered basin has been blasted out of the reef on the west side of the lagoon. There is a depth of only 6 ft into the small basin.

It has been reported that the island's position differs from the way it is depicted on current charts (BA 1451 and US 83105), and also that it is slightly off its charted coordinates. Canton monitors SSB 6230 kHz.

PS50 ROUTES IN THE CENTRAL PACIFIC

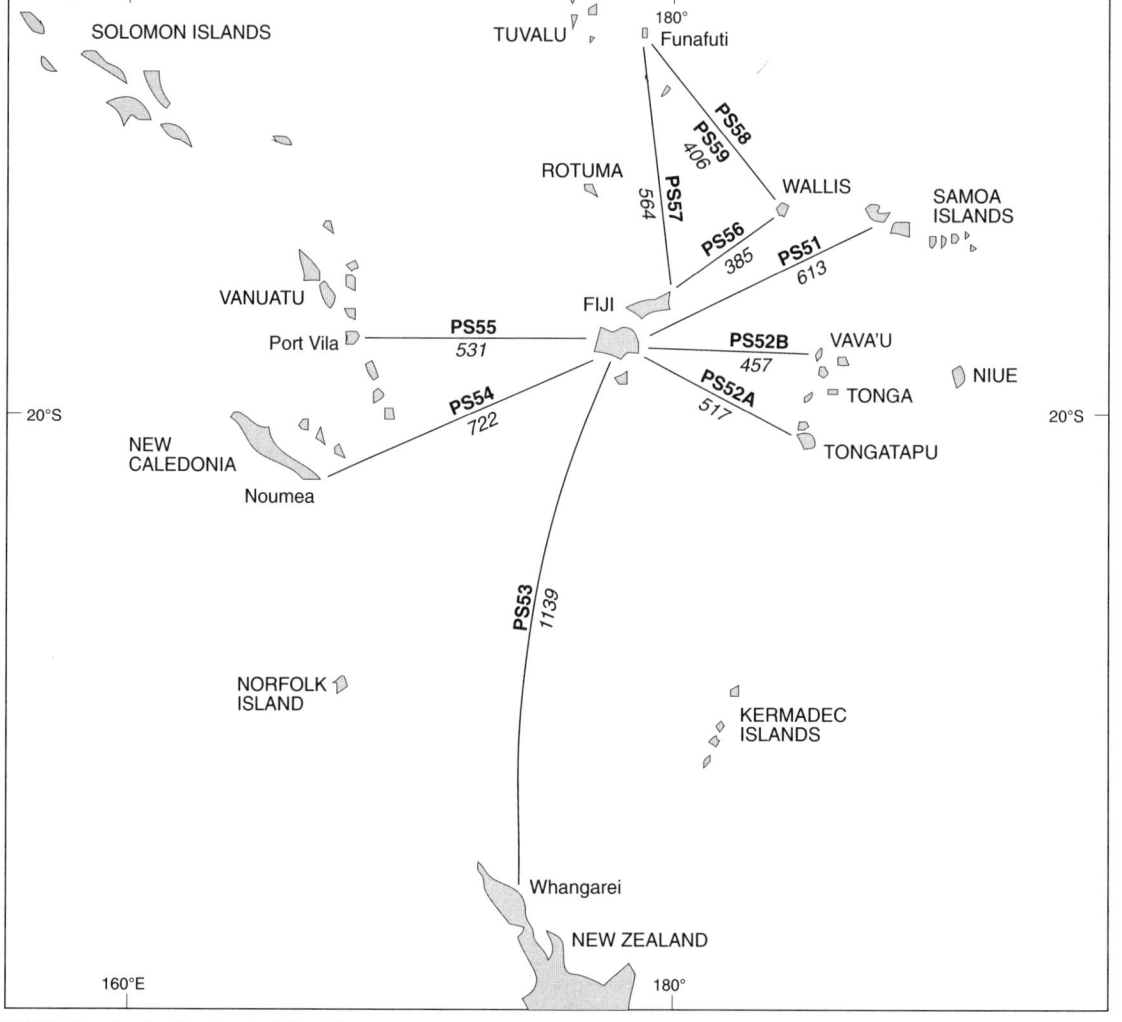

PS50 *Routes in the Central Pacific*

Because of its strategic position astride the main sailing route of the South Pacific, as well as its many cruising attractions, Fiji plays a special role among those who cruise in this area. The capital Suva, in particular, has been a favourite port of call for anyone passing through, partly because repair facilities are better than in any of the neighbouring islands and its yacht club is one of the most welcoming in the South Pacific.

With the exception of Melanesian Vanuatu and New Caledonia, Fiji is surrounded by Polynesian islands. Popular routes link Fiji with all its neighbours, although the northbound routes to Wallis, Futuna, and Tuvalu are less frequented. For most New Zealand sailors, Fiji is the natural tropical destination. Many of them who do not have the time for a longer cruise among the islands of the South Pacific manage to squeeze into their sailing plans a return trip to Fiji, often in the form of a race, such as the annual Auckland to Suva race. There is therefore a considerable traffic between the two countries, the busiest time being November, when cruising boats that do not wish to spend the cyclone season in the tropics make their way south to New Zealand.

A great exodus takes place every year as cruising boats head out of the tropics to spend the summer in a safer area, New Zealand being the favourite destination. The best time to make this passage, is on the eve of the cyclone season, late in October or early in November. Such a timing allows a stay in the tropics to the end of the safe season and a passage to New Zealand without much danger of encountering a late winter gale. The chance of a gale does not seem to worry the skippers of New Zealand boats returning home, who often make this passage earlier than other nationalities.

Although passages to New Zealand have been made at all times of year, it would be dangerous to set off during the cyclone season without a reliable forecast, as the tracks of some storms that have hit Fiji in the past almost coincide with the route to New Zealand. The central area of the South Pacific is hit by at least one tropical cyclone every year, so this must be taken into account when drawing up cruising plans, and the area is best avoided between December and the end of March. Although there are supposedly hurricane-proof harbours, such as at Pago Pago in American Samoa and Neiafu in Tongan Vava'u, in Fiji itself no place is considered absolutely secure, especially as the few safe places are usually taken up by local boats as soon as a hurricane warning is issued. Such a place is the Trade Winds anchorage and surrounding area, which gets extremely crowded due to its proximity to Suva. During the remaining part of the year, particularly from June to September, the SE trade winds ensure good sailing conditions.

PS51 *Fiji to Samoa*

BEST TIME:	April to October			
TROPICAL STORMS:	December to March			
CHARTS:	BA: 1829			
	US: 83039			
PILOTS:	BA: 61			
	US: 126			
CRUISING GUIDES:	*Landfalls of Paradise.*			
WAYPOINTS:				
Departure	*Intermediate*	*Landfall*	*Destination*	*Distance(M)*
PS511 Ovalau 17°41'S, 178°52'E	PS512 Thakaumomo 17°43'S, 179°12'E			
	PS513 Nanuku 16°40'S, 179°05'W	PS514 Savai'i W 13°28'S, 172°48'W	Apia *13°49'S, 171°45.5'W*	613
			Pago Pago *14°17'S, 170°41'W*	682

For this passage it is best to leave Fiji through the Nanuku Pass. As this means crossing the entire Koro Sea, it is more convenient to clear out at Levuka. However, as Fijian officials are less strict about boats stopping en route after having cleared out, than on their way into Fiji, boats may stop at various islands on their way NE through the Fijian archipelago. The one area where boats should not stop without prior permission is the Lau Group. As these little visited islands are close to the route to Samoa, an effort should be made while in Suva to obtain the compulsory official permission for a stop there.

At the height of the SE trade winds, in July and August, this can be a rough windward passage, when the ability to stop en route will be greatly appreciated. However, there are times when the trade winds betray their name and are less consistent than expected, which makes for easier sailing conditions. The weather between Fiji and Samoa can be quite stormy at times, as pointed out in directions for route PS46 (page 387).

The most convenient place to clear out of Fiji is Levuka, on the island of Ovalau. From PS511, outside the reef, an initial course is set for WP PS512 so as to pass south of Wakaya and also clear Thakaumomo Reef. From that point, the route runs right across the Koro Sea to WP PS513 and leaves Fijian waters through Nanuku Passage. If bound for Pago Pago, in American Samoa, but unable to lay that port on account of the weather, it is better to make for the lee of Savai'i, in Western Samoa, by making landfall at WP PS514. From there the route continues eastwards under the protection of the high islands of Savai'i and Upolu. The gap between Upolu and Tutuila can be crossed in settled weather. In strong SE winds one can continue around the north side of Tutuila and reach Pago Pago from the east.

The official port of entry into Western Samoa is the capital Apia. Arriving yachts must contact Harbour Control on VHF channel 16 when within 40 miles of Apia. The only official port of entry in American Samoa is Pago Pago, where on arrival yachts should always go directly to the clearance dock.

PS52 *Fiji to Tonga*

BEST TIME:	April, October to November			
TROPICAL STORMS:	Mid-November to March			
CHARTS:	BA: 1829			
	US: 83039			
PILOTS:	BA: 61			
	US: 126			
CRUISING GUIDES:	*Landfalls of Paradise, Cruising Guide to the Vava'u Island Group.*			
WAYPOINTS:				

Departure	Intermediate	Landfall	Destination	Distance(M)
Route PS52A				
Suva	PS521 Daveta			
18˚09'S, 178˚26'E	*18˚12'S, 178˚ 23.5'E*			
	PS522 Rewa			
	18˚15'S, 178˚35'E			
	PS523 Totoya			
	19˚06.5'S, 179˚55'W			
	PS524 Vatua	PS525 Tongatapu W	Nuku'alofa	517
	19˚30'S, 178˚13'W	*21˚02'S, 175˚18'W*	*21˚08'S, 175˚11'W*	
Route PS52B				
Levuka	PS526 Ovalau			
17˚41'S, 178˚51'E	*17˚41'S, 178˚52'E*			
	PS523 Totoya			
	PS524 Vatua			
	PS527 Late	PS528 Vava'u W	Neiafu	457
	18˚40'S, 174˚40'W	*18˚39'S, 174˚05'W*	*18˚39'S, 173˚59'W*	

Regardless of whether one is heading for Tongatapu (PS52A), at the southern extremity of the Tongan archipelago, or Vava'u (PS52B), at its northern end, this passage will be mostly hard on the wind. Most of those who make this passage do so either at the end or before the onset of the cyclone season. If Fiji is left before the start of the SE trade winds in April, the chances of encountering a late cyclone are remote and sailing conditions are less strenuous than later in the year. Similarly, for a departure in late October or early November the chance of an early cyclone is minimal. By this time the SE winds would also be less strong and consistent than earlier.

After having cleared out of Fiji at either Suva or Levuka, and provided one has obtained the compulsory permit to stop at some of the islands on the way, the route threads its way through the islands of the Lau Group before heading for the open sea through the Lakemba or Oneata passes. If one has failed to obtain the necessary permission, or conditions are unfavourable when leaving Suva, it is strongly recommended to use the southern route and on leaving Suva to steer a SE course that passes between Matuku and Totoya islands (PS52A). From Suva the initial course runs parallel to the reef to WP PS522 from where the course is altered to pass south of Totoya through WP PS523. From there the route goes to WP PS524 to pass safely through the gap separating Vatua and Ongea Levu islands. Boats bound for the Tongan capital Nuku'alofa should make landfall at WP PS525 and use Egeria Pass to enter the lagoon. Boats drawing under 8 ft (2.40 m) may use the small boat harbour at Faua. See also directions for the opposite route PS47 (page 387).

Boats leaving from Levuka join the above route at PS523 from where the same directions apply as described. Boats bound for Vava'u will follow the same directions as far as WP PS524. Having cleared the passage north of Vatua Island, a course can then be set for WP PS527, north of Late Island, a small island west of Vava'u. From that point, the course is altered for WP PS528 so that the port of Neiafu is reached through Faihava Passage.

Warning: Although the 180° meridian will be crossed on this passage, the official date in Tonga is the same as in Fiji.

PS53 *Fiji to New Zealand*

BEST TIME:	Mid-October to mid-November
TROPICAL STORMS:	Mid-November to March
CHARTS:	BA: 4605
	US: 605
PILOTS:	BA: 51, 61
	US: 120, 126, 127
CRUISING GUIDES:	*Coastal Cruising Handbook of the Royal Arakana Yacht Club, Pickmere's Atlas of Northland's East Coast.*
WAYPOINTS:	

Departure	Intermediate	Landfall	Destination	Distance(M)
Suva 18°09'S, 178°26'E	PS531 Daveta 18°12'S, 178°23.5'E PS532 Kandavu 19°05'S, 177°48'E PS533 26°00'S, 174°00'E	PS534 Kerikeri 35°10'S, 174°10'E	Opua 35°19'S, 174°07'E	1091
		PS535 Bream 35°50'S, 174°38'E	Whangarei 35°44'S, 174°20'E	1139

Favourable winds can be expected for at least the first half of this passage, but south of latitude 30°S it is very much a matter of luck, regardless of the time of year. Weather conditions on this route can be extremely variable and the reports from several yachts which have made this passage in recent years show that one can expect anything, from motoring in a flat calm for several days, to gale force winds from ahead, or a pleasant reach all the way.

Depending on weather conditions when leaving Suva, Astrolabe Reef and Kadavu Island can be passed on either side, although staying in their lee is probably easier by passing between Beqa (Mbengga) and Kadavu islands. Having left Suva Harbour through Daveta Passage, from WP PS531, a course can be set for WP PS532, off Kandavu's Cape Washington, from where a direct course can be sailed to New Zealand. The alternative is to take a SE course on leaving Suva and pass E of Kadavu and all dangers. Having reached the open sea, the course passes well to the W of the Minerva Reefs, where yachts on passage to or from New Zealand often stop as there is an anchorage which offers some protection even in strong winds. The anchorage is inside North Minerva Reef and can be reached through a pass on its NW side. As the Minerva Reefs are not on the direct route it is debatable whether such a detour is justified.

As the greatest risk on this passage is encountering a SW gale when approaching New Zealand, a suggested tactic is to make some westing soon after leaving Fiji, in which case a detour via the Minerva Reefs makes even less sense. Ideally the meridian of New Zealand's Cape North should be intersected about 500 miles north of that Cape and this meridian followed south before altering course for the port of destination. This course of action is particularly recommended if the passage is made between June and September, when the probability of encountering a SW gale is much higher than later in the year. Receiving information about weather conditions in the Tasman Sea can be a great help, as this allows the best course to be sailed. How far west the route will go and implicitly the longitude of WP PS533, will depend on expected weather conditions, and therefore the coordinates of WP PS533 are only tentative.

From WP PS533, boats bound for Opua should set a course for WP PS534, off Cape Kerikeri, at the entrance into the Bay of Islands. From that point one should proceed to the wharf in Opua where entry formalities into New Zealand are completed.

Boats bound for Whangarei, further down North Island's east coast, should set a direct course from WP PS533 for WP PS535, off Bream Head, in the approaches to Whangarei. From there a long but well buoyed river channel leads to the port of Whangarei.

PS54 *Fiji to New Caledonia*

BEST TIME:	Mid-April to October
TROPICAL STORMS:	Mid-November to March
CHARTS:	BA: 4602
	US: 602
PILOTS:	BA: 61
	US: 126
CRUISING GUIDES:	*Cruising in New Caledonia, Landfalls of Paradise.*
WAYPOINTS:	

Departure	Intermediate	Landfall	Destination	Distance(M)
Suva *18°09'S, 178°26'E*	PS541 Vatulele W *18°25'S, 177°35'E*	PS543 Havannah *22°15'S, 167°10'E*	Noumea *22°16'S, 166°26'E*	722
Lautoka *17°36'S, 177°27'E*	PS542 Malolo *17°52'S, 177°11'E*	PS543 Havannah	Noumea	686

During the SE trade wind season, winds along this route are mostly fair and there is also a favourable current. Boats leaving from Suva should keep close to the south coast of Viti Levu and go through the Mbengga Channel to avoid the reefs surrounding the island of that name (Beqa or Mbengga). Having passed Vatulele Island, from WP PS541 a course can be set for the NE extremity of New Caledonia Island if the intention is to sail direct to Noumea. If leaving from Lautoka it is best to reach the open sea through Malolo Passage before setting a course for New Caledonia from WP PS542. A direct course leads to WP PS543, in the approaches to Havannah Pass. This pass should be negotiated on a flood tide. Due to the prevailing SE winds the tide sets very strongly through the pass creating large waves when the ebb tide runs against a strong wind. Because of the large landmass, the SE winds become southerly as they are deflected around the main island of New Caledonia.

Noumea is New Caledonia's only port of entry and all boats must clear in there. Approaches into Noumea are difficult at night and should not be attempted. If coming from either Boulari or Havannah Pass, and Noumea cannot be reached in daylight it is recommended to anchor for the night and enter the port the following morning. Noumea Harbour is entered through Petite Passe. Arriving boats should contact Port Moselle on channel 67 to arrange a berth at the visitor's dock. The marina will contact customs and immigration for clearance. Although New Caledonia is a French overseas territory, a bond is not required from cruising boats as in the case of French Polynesia.

PS55 *Fiji to Vanuatu*

BEST TIME:	Mid-April to October			
TROPICAL STORMS:	Mid-November to March			
CHARTS:	BA: 4602			
	US: 604			
PILOTS:	BA: 61			
	US: 126			
CRUISING GUIDES:	*Landfalls of Paradise.*			
WAYPOINTS:				
Departure	*Intermediate*	*Landfall*	*Destination*	*Distance(M)*
Suva 18°09'S, 178°26'E	PS551 Vatulele N 18°20'S, 177°40'E	PS553 Efate 17°52'S, 168°35'E	Vila 17°44'S, 168°18'E	582
Lautoka 17°36'S, 177°27'E	PS552 Malolo 17°52'S, 177°11'E	PS553 Efate	Vila	531

The route leaving from Suva follows the south coast of Viti Levu closely to avoid the reefs surrounding Mbengga (Beqa) Island. North of Vatulele Island, at WP PS551 a course can be set for the southern extremity of Efate Island. Boats leaving from Lautoka will find it easier to reach the open sea through the Malolo Pass and set course for Vanuatu from WP PS552. Alternatively, one can sail due west from Lautoka and thread one's way through the islands and reefs of the Mamanuca Islands. The open sea is then reached through one of the many passes in the Mamanuca Reefs.

A direct course can be set for WP PS553, SE of Efate. From there the route stays parallel to the south coast of Efate to Pango Point before turning into Mele Bay and finally into Port Vila Bay.

Favourable winds can be expected on this route during the SE trade wind season. The currents in this area set to the SW and this should be allowed for. The visibility in the vicinity of Efate is sometimes very poor and, although a high island, it can remain obscured until close to land. A regular feature of this route is the annual Musket Cove to Vila Race, a fun event joined by most cruising boats planning to sail west during that period (September). The race leaves from Musket Cove on Malololailai Island.

Port Vila is one of two official ports of entry into Vanuatu. The other one is Luganville, on Espiritu Santo Island (15°31'S, 167°10'E). On arrival at Port

Vila, boats should tie up to the quarantine buoy and wait to be cleared. Port Vila Radio should be contacted on VHF channel 16 to request that the relevant officials are informed. Those who intend to spend the cyclone season in Port Vila must make arrangements to have their boats hauled out as the authorities do not allow cruising boats to stay in the water from December until March.

PS56 *Wallis to Fiji*

BEST TIME:	April to October				
TROPICAL STORMS:	Mid-November to March				
CHARTS:	BA: 1829				
	US: 83039				
PILOTS:	BA: 61				
	US: 126				
CRUISING GUIDES:	*Yachtsman's Fiji, Landfalls of Paradise.*				
WAYPOINTS:					
Departure	*Intermediate*	*Landfall*	**Destination**		**Distance(M)**
Route PS56A					
PS561 Wallis S	Futuna				126
13°24'S, 176°13'W	*14°18'S, 178°10'W*				
	PS562 Nanuku		Levuka		411
	16°40'S, 179°05'W		*17°41'S, 178°51'E*		
Route PS56B					
PS561 Wallis S	PS563 Nggelelevu		Levuka		385
	16°05'S, 179°05'W				
Route PS56C					
PS561 Wallis S	PS564 Vatauia		Levuka		385
	15°55'S, 179°17'W				

Favourable winds are most likely on this route during the SE trade wind season. The passage can be broken at Futuna, the sister territory of Wallis, which is also a French overseas possession. There is an anchorage at Singave Bay on the west coast of Futuna. Continuing towards Fiji, one can gain access to the islands either through Nanuku Passage, on the NE side of the archipelago, or through Somosomo Strait.

Whether a stop is made at Futuna or not, on route PS56A it is a clear run to WP PS562, five miles north of the light on Welangilala, which marks the eastern side of Nanuku Passage. As only the east side of the passage is marked by a light, it should be favoured, as there is no light on the southern extremity of Nanuku Reef, on the west side of the passage. Great care should be exercised when approaching Nanuku Passage as the currents in this area can be very strong and the light on Welangilala is not always operational.

If the intention is to reach the Koro Sea through Somosomo Strait (route PS56B), a direct course can be set for WP PS563, off Nggelelevu atoll in the Ringgold Islands, from where the route winds its way SW towards the Somosomo Strait. As there is a light at the eastern extremity of Nggelelevu Reef, this route should be preferred if landfall is made at night, although generally it is strongly recommended to attempt a daylight arrival, and too much faith should not be put in the lights working. An alternative daylight landfall (PS56C), from where it is easier to reach Somosomo Strait, can be made by using Vatauia Channel, west of Nggelelevu. In this case the course should be set for WP PS564, NE of Vatauia Island.

All the above routes lead into the Koro Sea, where there is a port of entry at Levuka, on Ovalau Island. All dangers in the Koro Sea are well buoyed and lit and, if necessary, it is not difficult to carry on as far as Suva, even at night.

PS57 *Tuvalu to Fiji*

BEST TIME:	April to October			
TROPICAL STORMS:	Mid-November to March			
CHARTS:	BA: 780			
	US: 526			
PILOTS:	BA: 61			
	US: 126			
CRUISING GUIDES:	*Yachtsman's Fiji, Landfalls of Paradise.*			
WAYPOINTS:				

Departure	Intermediate	Landfall	Destination	Distance(M)
PS571 Funafuti SE 8°40'S, 179°10'E		PS572 Undu 16°00'S, 180°00	Levuka *17°41'S, 178°51'E*	564

During the SE trade wind season the winds on this route are generally favourable and calms quite rare, occurring usually at night. At the change of seasons, in October, westerly winds become more frequent and are accompanied by squalls. Although the islands of Tuvalu are rarely visited by tropical storms, some years ago a cyclone devastated the main island of Funafuti in the month of October, its earliness in the season taking everyone by surprise. As Tuvalu lies close to the breeding ground of the cyclones, it is very unlikely that adequate warning would be given if a storm heads in this direction.

Leaving Funafuti through the SE pass, from WP PS571 the direct route passes close to the west of Niurakita, the smallest of Tuvalu's islands. Some easting should be made early on even if it means going over the banks SSE of Niurakita Island. Such easting will be made easier early in the passage, when winds are more easterly, than in the vicinity of Fiji, where there is a greater likelihood of SE winds. The route passes close to the west of the island of

Thikombia before making landfall at WP572, north of Cape Undu, the NE extremity of Vanua Levu Island. From there the Koro Sea is reached through the Somosomo Strait. Entry formalities can be completed at Levuka, on Ovalau.

An alternative route is to leave the entire Fijian archipelago to port and arrive in Suva from the west. Both alternatives have advantages and disadvantages, and the final choice will probably depend on the direction of the wind, as with a strong SE wind it may be too difficult to lay Cape Undu. In this case one can use one of the passes into Bligh Water west of Vanua Levu, such as Round Island Passage, and enter Fiji at Lautoka, on Viti Levu's NW coast (17°36'S, 177°26'E). An even more radical alternative is to stay west of the Yasawa Group. This westabout route avoids the reefs to the west of Viti Levu and continues along its south coast to Suva. The disadvantage of this route is the certainty of encountering strong headwinds and a contrary current after turning the SW corner of Viti Levu on the way to Suva.

PS58 *Tuvalu to Wallis*

BEST TIME:	October, April			
TROPICAL STORMS:	Mid-November to March			
CHARTS:	BA: 780			
	US: 526			
PILOTS:	BA: 61			
	US: 126			
CRUISING GUIDES:	*Landfalls of Paradise.*			
WAYPOINTS:				

Departure	Intermediate	Landfall	Destination	Distance(M)
PS581 Funafuti SE 8°40'S, 179°10'E	PS582 Nukulaelae E 9°10'S, 180°00	PS583 Wallis SW 13°25'S, 176°16'W	Mata Utu *13°17'S, 176°08'W*	406

This passage is difficult to accomplish during the SE trade wind season from April to October, when the probability of encountering strong winds is very high. The alternative to beating all the way to Wallis, coupled with the disadvantage of a contrary current, is to make this passage at the change of seasons when westerly winds are more common. The passage can also be made during the summer, from December to March, although the danger of sailing in the cyclone season must be realised when making this decision. If this passage is made at the height of the winter trades, from June to September, the winds at Funafuti are sometimes NE. If this is the case, as much easting as possible should be made on leaving Funafuti because the winds are bound to become more SE further south.

Having left Funafuti lagoon through one of its SE passes, from WP PS581 the direct route to Wallis passes very close to Nukulaelae, which has no pass into its lagoon, so yachts wishing to stop there must anchor in the lee of the reef. If a stop in Nukulaelae is not intended, from WP PS581 an initial course is set for WP PS582, so as to pass to the east of that island. The course is then altered for WP PS583, SW of Wallis. This route passes over a number of shallow banks before closing with Wallis, which is entered through Honikulu Pass, on the south side of the island in the reported GPS position 13°23.5'S, 176°13'W. There is a strong current at ebb tide, so it is better to negotiate the pass at flood tide or at slack water, especially when the sea is rough. At ebb tide the outflowing current can set at 6 knots and there are dangerous overflows outside the pass. The passes and reefs inside the lagoon are well marked. Formalities are completed at Mata Utu, the main settlement on Uvea.

Although meridian 180° will be crossed on this passage, the date should not be changed as Wallis keeps the same date as its neighbours to the west. Attention must also be paid to the fact that the position of Wallis, as depicted on the charts, is incorrect and does not agree with GPS observations which put the island 2 miles to the east of its charted position.

PS59 *Wallis to Tuvalu*

BEST TIME:	May to September				
TROPICAL STORMS:	Mid-November to March				
CHARTS:	BA: 780				
	US: 526				
PILOTS:	BA: 61				
	US: 126				
CRUISING GUIDES:	*Landfalls of Paradise.*				
WAYPOINTS:					
Departure	**Intermediate**	**Landfall**	**Destination**		**Distance(M)**
PS591 Wallis W	PS592 Nukulaelae W	PS593 Funafuti SE	Fongafale		402
13°25'S, 176°15'W	9°10'S, 179°45'E	8°40'S, 179°10'E	*8°31'S, 179°12'E*		

During the SE trade wind season the winds along this route are mostly favourable. Both Wallis and Tuvalu are in the cyclone area and, although relatively rare, at least one has devastated Tuvalu in October. Because Tuvalu lies close to the hurricane breeding ground south of the equator tropical storm warnings are less reliable than in other parts of the world.

The direct course for Funafuti passes over several banks, but these present no danger to yachts as there is sufficient depth over them. They should only be avoided during strong winds when seas break, but in fair weather it is worth sailing over them as fishing is excellent. On the direct course to Funafuti, the first island to be passed will be Nukulaelae. There is no pass into its lagoon, but in settled weather it is possible to anchor outside the reef off the main settlement on the west side of the atoll. However, as one is supposed to clear in first at Funafuti before visiting any other islands, from WP PS591, off Wallis, the recommended course is set for WP PS592, west of Nukulaelae. From there, the course is altered for WP PS593 so that Funafuti lagoon is entered through one of the passes on its SE side.

The official port of entry for Tuvalu is Fongafale,

the main settlement on Funafuti, and the capital of this small nation. There are several passes into Funafuti lagoon, but none of them should be attempted at night or when the visibility is not good.

PS60 ROUTES FROM NEW ZEALAND

Several cruising routes start out from New Zealand, fanning out in all directions like the fingers of an outstretched hand. Although the number of local boats that go cruising in foreign waters is impressively high for a small nation, many of the boats that set sail from New Zealand fly the flags of distant nations. In recent years New Zealand has become a major cruising destination and few yachts sail through the South Pacific without making a detour to New Zealand. The majority come to New Zealand to spend the cyclone season in the safety of North Island's protected harbours.

This stay in New Zealand is often a time of decision making about the future direction of a voyage, as the many routes leaving from New Zealand offer a wide choice. For those with time on their hands, a return to cruising in the tropics is a possibility, either by sailing back to Tahiti or by making one of the easier passages to Tonga or Fiji. Those for whom time is a commodity in short supply are probably mulling over the most pleasant way of getting back home. For voyagers from Europe or the east coast of North America the choice is quite simple, as the logical way is to carry on around the world and reach the Atlantic either via the Cape of Good Hope or the Red Sea and Mediterranean. The other possibility is to make the return voyage using the prevailing westerly winds of higher latitudes and reach the Atlantic via Cape Horn, an alternative shunned by most blue water sailors, few of whom are concerned about joining the elite rank of Cape Horners.

The most difficult decision is faced by those hailing from the west coast of North America, both American and Canadian, who do not fancy the prospect of a circumnavigation of the world, with a hard leg from Panama to their home port at the very end of it. Unfortunately there is no easy solution and the prospect of a return voyage of several thousand miles, most of it to windward, is a matter of great concern. There are several routes that can be taken from New Zealand to the west coast of America and probably the simplest is the route via Tahiti and Hawaii (PS67, PT22, and PN33). Those who are in a great hurry can complete this voyage in about four months, provided the boat goes reasonably well to windward. The course resembles a gigantic letter 'Z', with the horizontal bars representing the two legs in the westerlies of higher latitudes and the diagonal bar the slant across the SE and NE trade wind systems.

Although the route from New Zealand to Hawaii via Tahiti is the logical one, there are a number of other routes using different intermediate points. All of them probably would take more time than the Tahiti route, although they do offer, by way of compensation, the chance to visit less frequented places in the Pacific. The first of these alternative routes leads from New Zealand to Rarotonga or Aitutaki in the Southern Cooks (PS66). It then passes through the Line Islands after having touched some of the Northern Cooks. This route to Hawaii has the advantage of less windward work after leaving New Zealand, a good enough reason perhaps to give Tahiti a miss. Unfortunately, as this route approaches Hawaii from the south the last leg will be against the prevailing NE winds. It must also be remembered that unlike Tahiti, there are few repair or servicing facilities in the Cooks, which might make them less

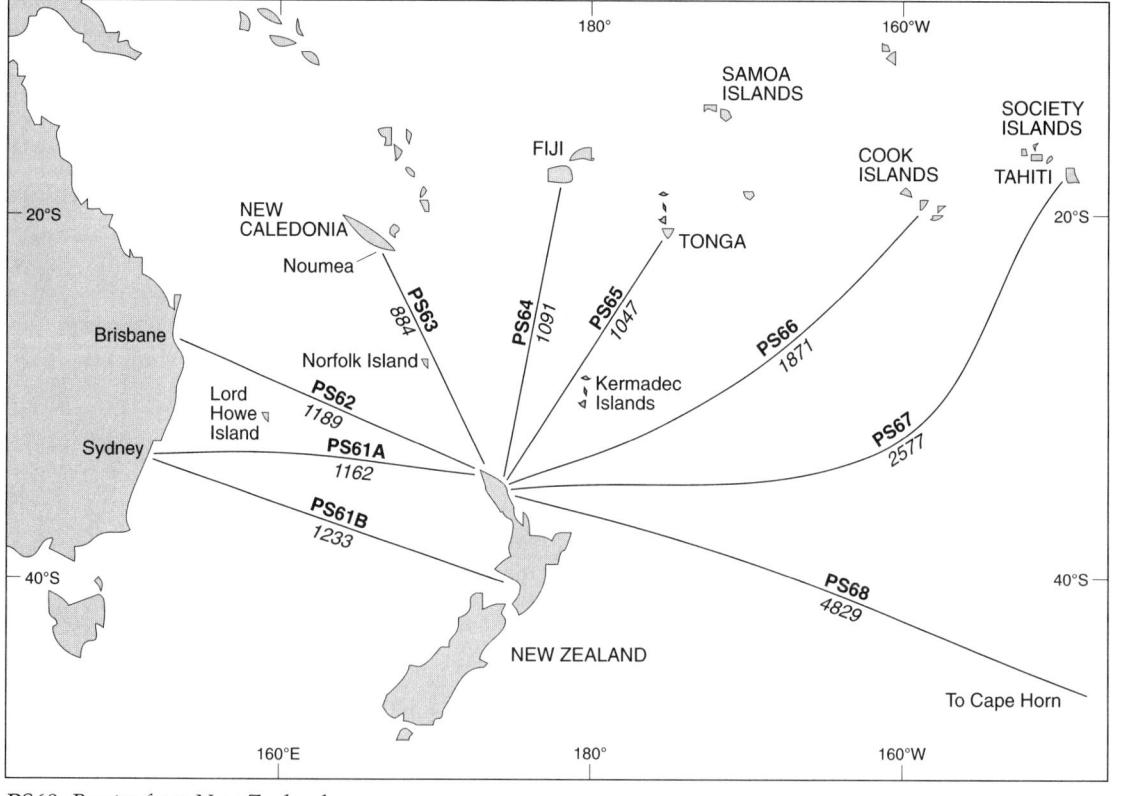

PS60 *Routes from New Zealand*

attractive as an intermediate port on such a long passage.

All other alternative routes lie further to the west and, although they might make the first leg from New Zealand to the tropics less tiresome, it must be remembered that the further west one moves, the more contrary will be the NE trade winds on the leg to Hawaii. Yet another acceptable alternative to the Tahiti route is the one that leads from New Zealand to Tonga, Samoa, and the Phoenix Islands and on to the Line Islands and Hawaii. Taking an even more westerly track via Fiji, Tuvalu, Kiribati, and possibly the Marshalls cannot be recommended as it carries the guarantee of a prolonged and tough windward leg north of the equator.

One major route from New Zealand leads across the Coral Sea towards the Torres Strait and beyond. Depending on the time available, the choice is between a route via New Caledonia (PS63) or one via Australia and the Great Barrier Reef (PS62). The timing for the start of this passage is essential, not only for the first part of the voyage

but also for later on. For those who wish to cruise en route but do not wish to be caught by the cyclone season in the South Indian Ocean (November to March), an early April departure from New Zealand is imperative. The more southerly route across the Tasman Sea to ports in New South Wales (PS61) is generally taken by those who wish to cruise along the east coast of Australia and do not mind the time it takes. There are also some who take a look at Australia and return to New Zealand for another quiet summer and an inexhaustible choice of new cruising destinations.

Regardless of their destination, most cruising boats leave New Zealand at the end of summer, when the cyclone season has come to an end in the tropical South Pacific. This is also the time when, with winter approaching, the best sailing season is coming to an end in New Zealand itself. By early April it is therefore time to head north. Usually it is possible to obtain a long term forecast which will ensure favourable weather for most of the forthcoming passage. There is, of course, always the risk of bad weather and one should leave New Zealand well prepared to be able to deal with any contingency. The violent storm that hit boats heading for Tonga in early June 1994 will be remembered for a long time, especially as it was totally unexpected. A depression forming NW of the fleet taking part in the annual regatta from Auckland to Nuku'alofa started moving SE. Because of an unseasonally strong high the depression was compressed, and struck several boats with winds of hurricane force. Those in its path had little chance and tragically one New Zealand yacht was lost with all hands, their half inflated liferaft being found empty not far from the place where the boat was last reported, in approximately 29°S, 179°E, which was very close to the storm centre. Another three yachts were abandoned by their crews, fortunately all being saved by passing freighters. Boats sailing within 50–60 miles from the storm centre experienced winds of up to 70 knots. Based on the weather patterns of the last 20 years, the only conclusion that can be drawn is that every year is different and that while in one year it is safe to leave for the tropics as early as the beginning of April, in other years the end of May or even early June may be safer. The best tactic is to get ready to leave when it is deemed to be safe, but if the latest weather chart shows a depression or front threatening to cross one's route, the wise thing to do is wait and let it pass.

PS61 *New Zealand to New South Wales*

Best time:	April to May			
Tropical storms:	December to March			
Charts:	BA: 4601			
	US: 601			
Pilots:	BA: 14, 15, 51			
	US: 127			
Cruising guides:	*Circumnavigating Australia's Coastline.*			
Waypoints:				
Departure	*Intermediate*	*Landfall*	*Destination*	*Distance (M)*
Route PS61A				
Opua	PS611 North Cape			
35°19'S, 174°07'E	*34°20'S, 173°05'E*			
	PS612 Kings	PS615 Jackson	Sydney	1162
	34°20'S, 171°50'E	*33°50'S, 151°20'E*	*33°50'S, 151°15'E*	
Opua	PS611 North Cape			
	PS612 Kings			
	Lord Howe		Coffs Harbour	1117
	31°32'S, 159°05'E		*30°18'S, 153°09'E*	
Route PS61B				
Wellington	PS613 Cook			
41°17'S, 174°46'E	*41°20'S, 174°30'E*			
	PS614 Stephens	PS615 Jackson	Sydney	1233
	40°30'S, 174°20'E			

Most people prefer to make this passage either before or after the cyclone season, although the Tasman Sea is only marginally affected by these storms which originate in the tropics. Conditions encountered across the Tasman Sea can be extremely varied, from flat calms to violent SW gales. The general consensus is that May offers the best chance of decent weather, although prolonged periods of calms can be expected during this month. Several days of calm or light variable winds often occur after a SW gale has passed.

Good sailing conditions occur when a stationary high over the southern part of the Tasman Sea generates easterly winds further north. Such conditions can last up to a week and are sometimes followed by another high creating similar weather conditions. Unfortunately these are most common during the summer, which is also the cyclone season in the South West Pacific. Only a few of these tropical storms find their way into the Tasman Sea, and usually by the time they get there most of their fury is spent. Provided a favourable long term forecast has been obtained, it is possible to leave New Zealand during the cyclone season, as cyclones generated further north would take several days to reach this route. During the winter months both lows and highs move to the north reducing the chances of E winds in the Tasman Sea. Lows are usually accompanied by strong SW winds and it is very rare that a winter passage can be made without encountering at least one gale.

When sailing around the top of North Island, Cape North and Cape Reinga should be approached with caution not only because of the confused currents that set around the two capes, but also the dangerous area in the vicinity of the Three Kings, a group of rocky islets to the NW of Cape Reinga. Having reached North Cape and WP

PS611, the course should be altered for WP PS612, SW of the above dangers. This is a good departure point for westbound boats, from where a direct course can be set across the Tasman Sea for Sydney at WP PS615.

Although the majority of boats setting off across the Tasman take the route around North Cape, for those leaving from further south it might be more advantageous to reach the Tasman Sea via Cook Strait (PS61B). From WP PS613, at the southern entrance into the Cook Strait, an initial course is set for WP PS614, NE of Stephens Island. From there, a direct course can be sailed to WP PS615, in the approaches to Port Jackson and Sydney.

Some boats break the trip across the Tasman by calling at Lord Howe Island (31°32'S, 159°05'E), which is an official port of entry for Australia. The anchorage is not well protected and can become dangerous in strong westerly winds, especially at high tide. As Lord Howe Island lies north of the direct route to Sydney, a stop there is only attractive for boats bound for more northern ports in New South Wales, such as Coffs Harbour.

PS62 *New Zealand to Queensland*

BEST TIME:	Mid-April to June			
TROPICAL STORMS:	December to March			
CHARTS:	BA: 4602			
	US: 602			
PILOTS:	BA: 15, 51			
	US: 127			
CRUISING GUIDES:	*Cruising the Coral Coast, Circumnavigating Australia's Coastline.*			
WAYPOINTS:				
Departure	*Intermediate*	*Landfall*	*Destination*	*Distance (M)*
Opua	PS621 North Cape			
35°19'S, 174°07'E	*34°20'S, 173°05'E*			
	PS622 Kings			
	34°20'S, 171°50'E			
	PS623 Middleton	PS624 Stradbroke	Brisbane	1189
	29°40'S, 159°20'E	*27°25'S, 153°35'E*	*27°19'S, 153°10'E*	

As all ports of destination on this route lie within the cyclone belt, an early departure during the summer months is not recommended. The best time to leave New Zealand is either in the second half of April or in May before the frequency of winter gales increases in the Tasman Sea. However, not all boats that have made this passage in later months

have encountered totally unfavourable conditions. Although this route lies further to the north than the route to ports in New South Wales (PS61), weather conditions up to latitude 30°S and even beyond are influenced by the high and low pressure systems lying over the Tasman Sea. With a favourable weather forecast from New Zealand it is therefore possible to make a good start on this route which offers several options. A NW course can be taken after leaving New Zealand and a stop made in Norfolk Island. Another alternative is to take a more westerly course and stop at Lord Howe Island, Australia's lonely outpost in the Tasman Sea. As both Elizabeth Reef (29°28'S, 159°02'E) and Middleton Reef (29°40'S, 159°20'E) lie virtually on the rhumb line from North Cape to Brisbane, some people cannot resist the temptation of anchoring behind a reef in mid-ocean. In unsettled weather the temptation should be resisted and the reefs given a wide berth. Both reefs have an anchorage, the one in the lee of Elizabeth Reef is on its NE side, whereas Middleton has the access on the NW side to an anchorage called the Sound.

Whichever route is chosen across the Tasman Sea, it should not reach the Australian coast too far south of the desired port because of the strong current setting south along the coast. The prevailing winds south of Sandy Cape are westerly from May to September. From October to April the winds are mostly NE. The area north of Sandy Cape is under the influence of the SE trade winds and during the winter months, from May to October, the winds are either SE or E.

In the case of boats bound for ports to the north of Sandy Cape, these may be best reached by going inside the Great Barrier Reef. Although there is also an offshore route, for small boats the inner route is more convenient. Those who are in a hurry and wish to get to the Torres Strait as soon as possible, should sail from New Zealand to New Caledonia direct and from there take the recommended route across the Coral Sea (PS75).

Having reached North Cape and WP PS621, the course should be altered for WP PS622, SW of the Three Kings. From there, if sailing to Brisbane, the direct route goes to WP PS623, east of Elizabeth and Middleton Reefs. This intermediate waypoint, and especially the reefs west of it, should be approached with great caution. From there, a course can be set for WP PS624, NE of Stradbroke Island, in the approaches to Brisbane, one of several official ports of entry into Queensland. Generally in Australia, the Port Authority of the intended port of destination should be notified on 2182 kHz or VHF channel 16 at least three hours in advance of a vessel's impending arrival. There are severe penalties for stopping anywhere before having cleared in and, with the exception of New Zealand citizens, all foreign visitors must arrive with a valid Australian visa.

PS63 *New Zealand to New Caledonia*

BEST TIME:	April to June			
TROPICAL STORMS:	December to March			
CHARTS:	BA: 4602			
	US: 602			
PILOTS:	BA: 51, 61			
	US: 126, 127			
CRUISING GUIDES:	*Cruising in New Caledonia.*			
WAYPOINTS:				
Departure	*Intermediate*	*Landfall*	*Destination*	*Distance (M)*
Opua	PS631 North Cape			
35°19'S, 174°07'E	*34°20'S, 173°05'E*			
	PS632 Norfolk E		Kingston	541
	29°00'S, 170°00'E		*29°01'S,167°59'E*	
		PS633 Boulari	Noumea	884
		22°31'S, 166°24'E	*22°16'S, 166°27'E*	

The end of summer is the best time to make this passage when favourable sailing conditions can be expected. A departure in April or early May reduces the chance of encountering winter gales in the first half of the passage, although if a gale is encountered it only speeds progress to the north. The incidence of gales after June is higher and the weather colder, two factors which dissuade most people from making this passage too late in the season. For some boats the passage to New Caledonia is the first leg of a longer voyage to the Torres Strait and beyond, which makes an early start from New Zealand essential if the intention is to cross the Indian Ocean during the best season (May to October).

Having passed Cape North, from WP PS631 a direct course can be set for New Caledonia. The direct route passes through WP PS632, some 100 miles east of Norfolk Island, and many boats make the detour to stop there briefly, but the anchorage off Kingston provides limited shelter and should

be left in impending bad weather. Either from WP PS632, or from Norfolk itself, a course can be set for WP PS633, off Boulari Pass (22°30'S, 166°26'E) in the southern approaches to Noumea, New Caledonia's capital and only port of entry. Because of the many reefs, entering Noumea at night is difficult and should not be attempted. Arriving boats should contact Port Moselle on VHF channel 67 to arrange a berth at the visitor's dock. The marina will contact customs and immigration for clearance. Although New Caledonia is a French overseas territory a bond is not required from cruising boats, as in the case of French Polynesia.

New Caledonia should be approached with care both on account of the reefs extending to the south of the main island and the currents reported in this area. If strong westerly winds are encountered below latitude 25°S it does not matter if only a northerly course can be steered. The lost ground can be made up later in an area where SE and E winds are more prevalent, usually north of latitude 25°S.

PS64 *New Zealand to Fiji*

BEST TIME:	April to July			
TROPICAL STORMS:	December to March			
CHARTS:	BA: 4605			
	US: 605			
PILOTS:	BA: 51, 61			
	US: 126, 127			
CRUISING GUIDES:	*Yachtsman's Fiji, Landfalls of Paradise.*			
WAYPOINTS:				

Departure	*Intermediate*	*Landfall*	*Destination*	*Distance (M)*
PS641 Bream *35°50'S, 174°38'E*	PS642 Astrolabe *18°45'S, 178°45'E*	PS644 Daveta *18°12'S, 178°23.5'E*	Suva *18°09'S, 178°26'E*	1091
PS641 Bream	PS643 Kandavu *19°06'S, 177°54'E*	PS644 Daveta	Suva	1084
PS641 Bream	PS645 Vatulele SW *18°35'S, 177°10'E*	PS646 Navula *17°55'S, 177°10'E*	Lautoka *17°36'S, 177°26'E*	1108

As for all other passages from New Zealand to the tropics, this route is not recommended during the cyclone prone months from December to the end of March. Even at the beginning of April the weather should be carefully watched, because the direct course from New Zealand to Fiji intersects the tracks of some of the late cyclones recorded in the recent past.

Most boats make this passage after the first week in April, when the cyclone season further north has drawn to a close as has the summer season in New Zealand. For those who have spent this season in New Zealand such a timing is perfect as it offers the prospect of at least six months of safe cruising in the tropics. A later departure has the disadvantage of colder weather and a higher probability of SW gales. Regardless of the time of departure, a direct course leads clear of all dangers. Should strong westerly winds be encountered in the early part of the passage, it does not matter if one is pushed to the east of the rhumb line as the loss can be made up later with the help of the SE trades which blow north of latitude 25°S. If sailing to the east of the rhumb line, the route should avoid passing too close to the two Minerva Reefs, which have claimed many boats in the past. Those who wish to stop there may do so in settled weather as there is an anchorage inside North Minerva Reef, which can be reached through a pass on its NW side and provides adequate protection, especially at low tide, when the reef dries.

Boats leaving from Whangarei, once they are off Bream Head (PS641) can set a direct course for Fiji. Boats bound for Suva should approach the port from the south passing to the east of Kandavu Island and giving Astrolabe Reef a wide berth. WP PS642 keeps clear of all these dangers.

Alternatively, Suva may be reached easier by sailing in the lee of Kandavu in which case landfall is made at WP PS643, off Cape Washington. From there, the course is altered for WP PS644 and the Daveta Levu Pass is used to enter Suva Harbour. Arriving yachts must anchor close to the quarantine buoy and await a health officer for clearance before proceeding to King's Wharf to complete the remaining formalities.

Those intending to sail to Lautoka, on the west coast of Viti Levu, should sail a direct course for WP PS645, SW of Vatulele Island, from where the course is altered for WP PS646, outside Navula Passage, which is then used to reach Lautoka. Attention should be paid to the strong currents when sailing in the vicinity of the reefs off the SW coast of Viti Levu. Boats are not supposed to stop anywhere after having entered Fijian waters before having cleared at one of the official ports of entry. Because of strict Sunday observance laws, arriving at weekends should be avoided.

PS65 *New Zealand to Tonga*

BEST TIME:	April to May			
TROPICAL STORMS:	December to March			
CHARTS:	BA: 4605			
	US: 622			
PILOTS:	BA: 51, 61			
	US: 126, 127			
CRUISING GUIDES:	*Landfalls of Paradise.*			
WAYPOINTS:				
Departure	*Intermediate*	*Landfall*	*Destination*	*Distance (M)*
PS651 Bream 35°50'S, 174°38'E	PS652 24°00'S, 178°00'W	PS653 Eua SW 21°20'S, 175°24'W PS654 Tongatapu SE 21°09'S, 175°00'W	Nuku'alofa *21°08'S, 175°11'W*	1047
PS651 Bream	PS652	PS655 Tongatapu SW 21°06'S, 175°23'W	Nuku'alofa	1044

With the exception of the cyclone season, this passage can be made in any month. The best time to leave New Zealand is between the beginning of April and the middle of May when winter has not yet established itself in southern latitudes and the danger of encountering a cyclone either en route or on arrival is minimal. A later departure would probably run the risk of strong W or SW winds at

the beginning and also colder weather. Regardless of the time of year when this passage is made, it will be a close hauled affair most of the way. It is essential to leave New Zealand with a reasonable long term weather forecast to avoid being overtaken by a front. In order to benefit from a better sailing angle once the SE trade winds are met somewhere around latitude 25°S, it may be advisable to make some easting while in lower latitudes and possibly pass east of the Kermadecs. Rather than go that far east, some people set a course to pass right by these islands, which belong to New Zealand and where stopping without permission is not permitted. In an emergency, however, there are several bays which offer reasonable protection but because of the islands' exposed nature and the rapidly changing weather, one should be prepared to put to sea at very short notice.

If a direct course is to be sailed for Tonga, from WP PS651, off Bream Head in the approaches to Whangarei, a course can be set for WP PS652, NW of the Kermadecs. This rhumb line from North Island to Tongatapu leads well to the west of the Kermadec Islands and also misses the two Minerva Reefs by a safe margin. Indeed, this is the course taken by those who have access to weather information, and also by those sailing at the recommended time (early April), when the strong easterly winds of winter are rarely fully established in the tropics. The direct course passes close to Ata

Island, a high island lying some 90 miles SW of Tongatapu, the main island of the kingdom. Landfall will be made at WP PS653, SW of Eua. From there, the course should be altered for WP PS654, south of Eua Iki, in the channel separating Tongatapu and Eua islands.

There are passes into Tongatapu's lagoon both from the east and the west. In strong SE winds it is better to gain the lee of Eua Island and enter the lagoon from the east through Piha Passage. This is the most direct pass into the lagoon, but as it has no lights it can only be used in daylight. At all other times, Egeria Channel, the main shipping channel leading into the lagoon from the west, is an easier option. To reach it, landfall should be made at WP PS655, SW of the light on Niu Aunofo, the NW extremity of Tongatapu. From there a course can be sailed to pass between the latter and Duff Reef (21°03.9'S, 175°22.6'W) to reach Egeria channel leading into Nuku'alofa. Yachts drawing less than 8 ft (2.40 m) may use the small boat harbour at Faua, one mile east of Nuku'alofa.

PS66 *New Zealand to Cook Islands*

BEST TIME:	April to June				
TROPICAL STORMS:	December to March				
CHARTS:	BA: 4061				
	US: 622, 526				
PILOTS:	BA: 51, 62				
	US: 126, 127				
CRUISING GUIDES:	*Landfalls of Paradise, Charlie's Charts of Polynesia.*				
WAYPOINTS:					

Departure	*Intermediate*	*Landfall*	*Destination*	*Distance (M)*
PS661 Bream 35°50'S, 174°38'E	PS662 April 35°00'S, 165°00'W	PS664 Rarotonga NW 21°12'S, 159°51'W	Avatiu *21°11'S, 159°47'W*	1871
			Aitutaki *18°52'S, 159°48'W*	2014
PS661 Bream	PS663 June 33°00'S, 170°00'W	PS664 Rarotonga NW	Avatiu	1673
			Aitutaki	1816

As a return passage to the tropics, this route is easier and more pleasant than the route to Tahiti. However, on no account should this route be taken as a first leg to Tahiti, as the subsequent beat from the Cooks to Tahiti has put off most of those who have tried to sail it direct. If, for whatever reason, the voyage has to continue from the Cooks to the Society Islands, the best way is to sail south from

the Cooks into the area of prevailing westerlies and curve north through the Austral Islands. See also route PS67 (page 408).

Those who take the direct route from New Zealand to the Cooks have the choice of an early start, with the advantage of warmer weather when leaving New Zealand, or a later start, when the probability of westerly winds is higher. If an early departure date is chosen this should not be before the middle of March as the cyclone season has not come to an end in the tropics and it is not wise to arrive in the Cooks before the end of March, or preferably in early April. For a passage in April, easting should be made in the latitude of the port of departure and a northerly course set only near meridian 165°W. In the case of a later departure, in May or even June, easting should be made between latitudes 35°S and 30°S. Latitude 30°S should not be crossed before reaching longitude 170°W after which, depending on the wind, a direct course can be set for the desired destination. The same directions also apply for the remaining winter months when the SE trade wind belt lies furthest

north and better winds can be expected to make the required easting, although the weather on leaving New Zealand would be very cold. The chances of winter gales would also be much higher, which would be sufficient argument in favour of making this passage before June.

Boats leaving from Whangarei or Auckland will sail an initial course along the latitude of departure. Depending on existing weather conditions and also the time of year, the route will start swinging to the NE after meridian 165°W has been crossed. Landfall should be made at WP PS664, NW of Rarotonga, from where the island's north coast is followed to the main port of Avatiu.

PS67 *New Zealand to Tahiti*

BEST TIME:	Mid-March to May			
TROPICAL STORMS:	December to March			
CHARTS:	BA: 4061			
	US: 621, 622			
PILOTS:	BA: 51, 62			
	US: 122, 126, 127			
CRUISING GUIDES:	*Landfalls of Paradise, Charlie's Charts of Polynesia.*			
WAYPOINTS:				

Departure	Intermediate	Landfall	Destination	Distance (M)
PS671 Bream 35°50'S, 174°38'E	PS672 35°00'S, 155°00'W			
	PS673 30°00'S, 152°00'W	PS674 Tubuai 23°21'S, 149°33'W	Mataura *23°21'S, 149°29'W*	2240
		PS675 Tahiti W 17°35'S, 149°40'W	Papeete *17°32'S, 149°35'W*	2577

The recommended tactic for this route is to stay south of, or close to, latitude 40°S in order to take full advantage of the westerly winds prevailing in higher latitudes, although this means rather cold weather, especially if New Zealand is left after April. Most people prefer to compromise and attempt to make their easting between latitudes 35°S and 30°S, where the weather is indeed warmer. This is an area of variable winds that lie between the trade winds and prevailing westerlies, although weather conditions differ from year to year and in some winters consistent westerly winds have been encountered as far north as 32°S. Similarly there are years when even keeping south of latitude 40°S is no guarantee of consistent westerlies. This passage to Tahiti is usually a tough

windward passage with a high proportion of SE winds. From the reports of those who have sailed this route in recent years, everyone reports encountering at least one gale on the way. Often such gales are from the east and the best solution is to heave to and wait for them to blow over. In spite of the temptation to head NE early in the passage, this should not be done before meridian 155°W is crossed. Meridian 152°W should be crossed in latitude 30°S, from where a course is shaped to pass close to the Austral Islands. In April the SE trade winds are normally found around latitude 25°S.

This passage can also be done at the end of winter, in October or November, when the winds are often light making it a slow passage. The disadvantage of a summer passage is the risk of arriving in Tahiti in the midst of the cyclone season.

Whatever time is chosen for this passage, on no account should one attempt to reach Tahiti via Rarotonga, because the subsequent leg from the Cooks to Tahiti, against the full force of the trade winds, will be very rough.

Some boats stop in the Austral Islands as they are close to the recommended route to Tahiti and provide a convenient break. If the intention is to stop there, a course should be set for WP PS674, west of Tubuai. That island's lagoon is entered through the Main Pass, on the NW side. The main settlement is at Mataura. Other ports of entry in the Australs are Moerai, on Rurutu (22°28'S, 151°20'W) and Rairua, on Raivavae (23°52'S, 147°44'W). Whether stopping in the Australs or not, boats coming from the south or SW should make landfall on the west coast of Tahiti at WP PS675, from where the NW coast of the island will be followed to the entrance into Papeete Harbour. The pass through the reef is at 17°32.18'S, 149°35.1'W. Arriving boats should proceed to the quay on the south side of the harbour. Boats are not normally boarded and the captain is expected to visit the various offices, located close to the main cruise ship quay, during office hours.

PS68 *New Zealand to Cape Horn or Magellan Strait*

BEST TIME:	January to March
TROPICAL STORMS:	None
CHARTS:	BA: 4061, 4062
	US: 621, 625
PILOTS:	BA: 6, 51, 62
	US: 122, 124, 125, 127
WAYPOINTS:	

Departure	Intermediate	Landfall	Destination	Distance (M)
Auckland *36°50'S, 174°47'E*	PS681 *48°00'S, 120°00'W*	PS682 Horn S 56°15'S, 67°15'W		4829
		PS683 Pillar 52°40'S, 74°50'W		4599
		PS684 Chacao 41°40'S, 74°15'W		4830

Only a handful of cruising boats attempt to take this classic route across the Southern Ocean. Most of this passage is made in the Roaring Forties where there is usually a high proportion of westerly winds. On leaving New Zealand the route heads SE so as to reach the area of westerly winds as soon as possible. However, as mentioned in route PS67, there is no guarantee of encountering consistent westerly winds even in latitude 40°S and therefore it may be necessary to continue into higher latitudes. During the summer months, when the limit of the ice lies furthest to the south, the route runs between latitudes 47°S and 50°S. From longitude 120°W the course becomes gradually more southerly and passes south of Cape Horn. The continuation of the route into the Atlantic is described in AT26 and AT27 (pages 217 and 218).

A more southerly course is recommended for the summer months from December to February when the passage should be made in about latitude 55°S. Westerly winds in this latitude are more consistent, although the danger of encountering ice discourages most skippers from sailing in such high latitudes. But even in higher latitudes westerly winds can be absent in summer as happened in March 1986 during the Whitbread Round the World Race. During that year even on the great circle route which dips down to 62°S, there was an unusually high proportion of NE winds. Icebergs were sighted as far north as latitude 54°S showing that an extreme southerly route is both risky and hard to justify. Those who would rather avoid the Roaring Forties may sail an easier route by staying just to the south of the band of SE trade winds without moving too far south into the area of strong westerlies. By watching the weather carefully it may be possible to make most of one's easting between 35°S and 38°S. There is also the option of breaking the voyage in Tahiti; and although this is a considerably longer route, it is probably much less demanding on both crew and gear.

This route is seldom sailed nowadays without stopping in Tierra del Fuego itself. This can be done either by entering Beagle Channel immediately after having weathered Cape Horn, or by reaching Cape Horn through the relatively more sheltered channels in Southern Chile. Boats bound for the Magellan Strait, which is entered at Cape Pillar, should eventually set a course for WP PS683.

Making landfall there in heavy weather should be avoided as the strong currents create rough seas at the entrance to the Strait. Those wishing to visit the south of Chile and explore the Chilean channels on their way to the Magellan Strait should make landfall at WP PS684, in the approaches to Chacao Channel. The same suggestion applies as above and the latter channel should only be entered in settled weather and with a fair tide. To obtain the latest information on tides and weather, the Corona Lighthouse should be contacted on VHF channel 16.

PS70 ROUTES FROM SOUTHERN MELANESIA

The routes grouped in this section and the following section PS80 all originate in one of the four Melanesian countries bordering on the Coral Sea. Routes from the other Melanesian country, Fiji, have been dealt with earlier. The western part of the South Pacific attracts significantly fewer cruising boats than its eastern part, although there is just as much to see. One of the main reasons is that by the time most cruising boats get to this part of the Pacific they are in a hurry to catch the favourable season in the Indian Ocean and therefore only have time to stop briefly in the main ports. As in so many other parts of the world, the delights of these islands can only be savoured if one reaches the more isolated and less frequented places and to do that one needs time. So it is worth bearing this in mind and allowing sufficient time for cruising when planning a voyage through these waters.

Tropical cyclones affect the entire region with the exception of Papua New Guinea north of approximately latitude 10°S. The critical period is December to the end of March when anyone would be ill advised to be cruising in this region. From April onwards the weather is good, although the SE trade winds tend to get almost too strong for

some people's liking at the height of the southern winter in July and August, when consistent winds of around 25 knots are not uncommon. This is why it is best to plan to cruise the area either from south to north or from east to west. Fortunately this fits in with most people's plans as the two main routes originate in either New Zealand or Fiji. The northbound route from New Zealand is used by people who have spent the cyclone season there, while those coming westward from Fiji usually sail later in the season, in August and September, both routes converging towards the Torres Strait and Indian Ocean.

Although the majority of routes are westbound, those who intend to sail east across the Coral Sea should plan to do so either before or after the onset of the SE trade winds which blow most consistently between May and September. Usually in early April the trade winds are not yet fully established and eastbound passages can be accomplished without great difficulty. However, there is a better chance of finding favourable winds in late October or early November at the start of the NW monsoon, although this must be weighed up against the risk of being caught out by an early cyclone. The period

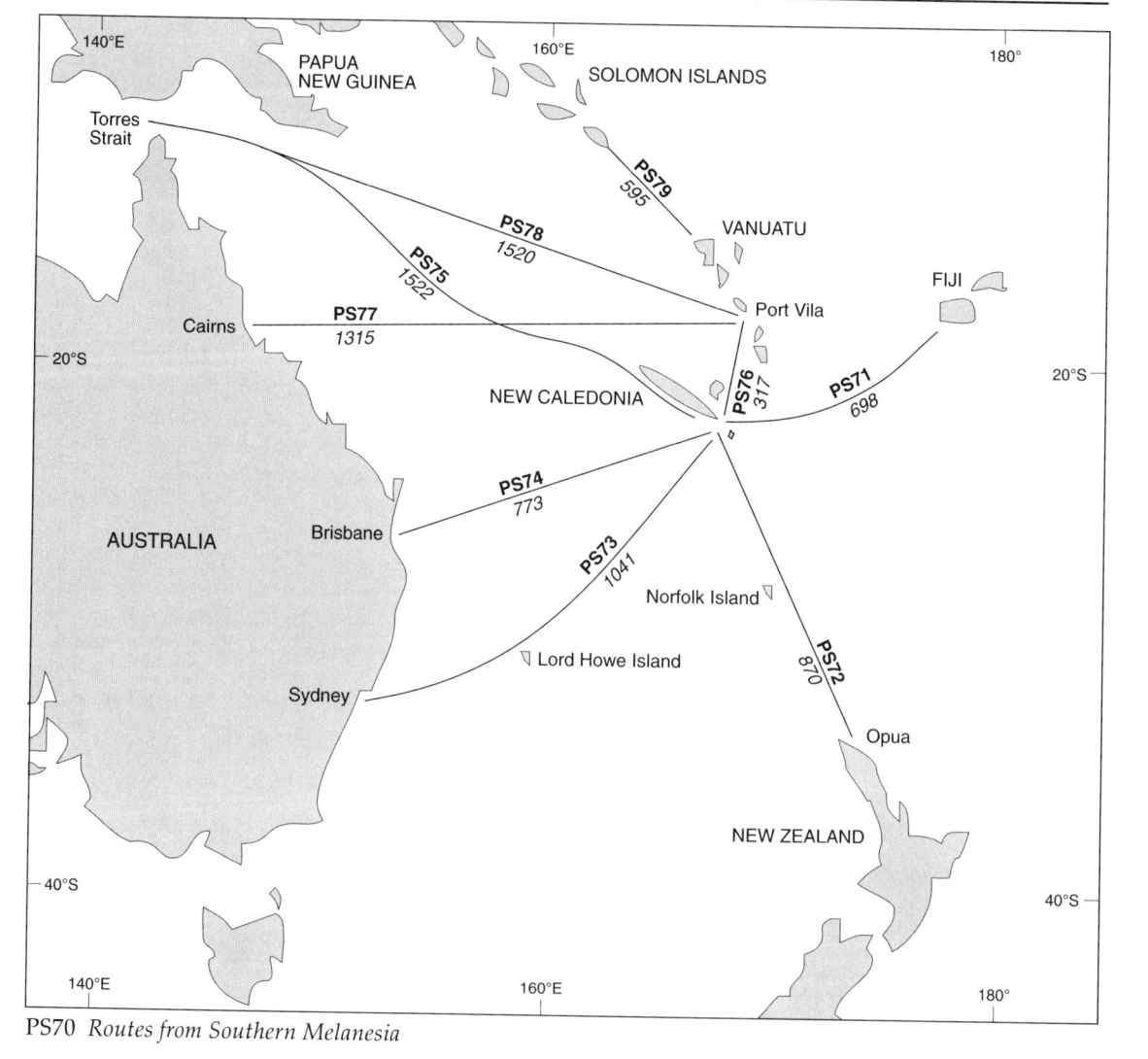

PS70 *Routes from Southern Melanesia*

when these tropical storms occur in the Coral Sea should be treated with great suspicion as very few months are entirely free and cyclones have been recorded in both the accepted transitional months of June and November.

PS71 *New Caledonia to Fiji*

BEST TIME:	April
TROPICAL STORMS:	December to March
CHARTS:	BA: 4602
	US: 602
PILOTS:	BA: 61
	US: 126
CRUISING GUIDES:	*Yachtsman's Fiji, Landfalls of Paradise.*

WAYPOINTS:				
Departure	*Intermediate*	*Landfall*	*Destination*	*Distance (M)*
PS711 Havannah 22°20'S, 167°05'E	PS712 Vatulele N 18°25'S, 177°35'E	PS713 Daveta 18°12'S, 178°23.5'E	Suva *18°09'S, 178°26'E*	667
PS711 Havannah		PS714 Navula 17°55'S, 177°10'E	Lautoka *17°36'S, 177°26'E*	698

Because of prevailing E and SE winds this passage is mostly on the wind. A good time to sail this route is early in April, when the danger of a late cyclone is not great and the SE trades have not yet fully established themselves. Leaving either from the main island of New Caledonia or from one of the Loyalty Islands, as much easting as possible should be made at the beginning of the passage. Having sailed through Havannah Passage, from WP PS711, SE of the main island of New Caledonia, the direct route passes between Maré Island and Durand Reef. The course leads to WP PS712, north of Vatulele Island from where the route continues to Suva through the Mbengga Channel, where strong contrary currents can be expected, to WP PS713. Having entered Suva Harbour through

Daveta Passage, boats must proceed to the quarantine anchorage for clearance.

If such a direct course for Fiji cannot be sailed on account of the wind, and easting has to be made on a more southerly route, several dangers will be passed closely. The first two islands, Matthew (22°21'S, 171°21'E) and Hunter (22°24'S, 172°05'E), are easily visible as they are quite high. Much more dangerous is the low reef Theva-i-Ra (21°44'S, 174°38'E), which should be given a wide berth. The name of this reef is sometimes spelt Ceva-i-Ra and is also known by its previous name Conway Reef.

Boats bound for Lautoka, on the west coast of Viti Levu, which is also a port of entry, should set course for WP PS714, at the entrance into Navula Passage.

PS72 *New Caledonia to New Zealand*

BEST TIME:	October to November
TROPICAL STORMS:	December to March
CHARTS:	BA: 4602
	US: 602
PILOTS:	BA: 51, 61
	US: 126, 127
CRUISING GUIDES:	*Coastal Cruising Handbook of the Royal Arakana Yacht Club, Pickmere's Atlas of Northland's East Coast.*

WAYPOINTS:				
Departure	*Intermediate*	*Landfall*	*Destination*	*Distance (M)*
PS721 Boulari 22°31' S, 166°24'E	PS722 Norfolk E 29°00'S, 170°00'E	PS723 North Cape 34°20'S, 173°05'E		
		PS724 Kerikeri 34°40'S, 173°30'E	Opua *35°19'S, 174°07'E*	870
		PS 725 Bream 35°50'S, 174°38'E	Whangarei *35°44'S, 174°21'E*	925

Similar directions apply for this route as those given for route PS53 from Fiji to New Zealand. Boats starting off from New Caledonia have a better chance of encountering favourable winds as

they are more to the west. Yet from the reports of boats that have made this passage in recent years it does appear that the proportion of headwinds were just as high, if not higher than those encountered by boats sailing direct from Fiji. Although this passage has been made at all times of the year November is considered to be the safest month as the danger of either an early hurricane or a late winter gale is not too great.

After leaving Noumea through the Boulari Pass, from WP PS721, the direct course passes some 100 miles east of Norfolk Island (WP PS722). As such a direct course can rarely be sailed and the SE winds likely to be encountered at the start of the passage will probably set the boat to the west, many boats stop at Norfolk Island briefly. The anchorage off Kingston (29°01'S, 167°59'E) is only safe in settled weather and should be left if con-

ditions deteriorate. Because from this latitude onwards the main danger is to be caught out by a SW gale, any ground lost to the west, whether by calling at Norfolk Island or staying on the port tack, can be made up nearer to New Zealand. Landfall will be made at WP PS723, off North Cape. The route then continues along the coast to WP PS724, off Cape Kerikeri at the entrance into the Bay of Islands. The most convenient ports of entry are Opua, in the Bay of Islands, or Whangarei, further down North Island's east coast. To reach the latter, the course should be set for PS725 in the approaches to Whangarei.

PS73 *New Caledonia to New South Wales*

BEST TIME:	April to May, September to mid-November			
TROPICAL STORMS:	December to March			
CHARTS:	BA: 4602			
	US: 602			
PILOTS:	BA: 14, 15, 61			
	US: 126, 127			
CRUISING GUIDES:	*Circumnavigating Australia's Coastline.*			
WAYPOINTS:				
Departure	*Intermediate*	*Landfall*	*Destination*	*Distance (M)*
WP731 Dumbea 22°22'S, 166°14'E		PS732 Solitary 30°12'S, 153°20'E	Coffs Harbour *30°18'S, 153°09'E*	844

The only conclusion to be drawn from the large number of people who have made this passage is that one can never be sure of the kind of weather to expect along this route. Favourable winds should be expected down to about latitude 30°S, as the proportion of easterly winds is generally higher, especially during the winter SE trade wind season. Further south, the frequency of SW gales increases as winter approaches. From this point of view the transitional months between summer and winter are preferable for this passage.

If it is not possible to lay a course for the desired port because of consistent headwinds, it may be better to try and reach the Australian coast by the shortest route and use the south-setting current to reach ports further south. South of Sandy Cape the prevailing winds off the coast are westerly from

May to September and NE from October to April. The south going current is generally strongest around the 100 fathom line.

Having left Noumea through Dumbea Pass, from WP PS731 a direct course can be sailed for Coffs Harbour and landfall made at WP PS732, off Solitary Island. Coffs Harbour is the northernmost port of entry into New South Wales, and because of the favourable south-setting current it is a convenient place to clear into Australia. From there it is easy to sail to more southern ports along the coast. Boats taking the direct route from New Caledonia to Sydney occasionally stop at Middleton (29°28'S, 159°04'E) and Elizabeth Reefs (29°55'S, 159°02'E). If not stopping or in unsettled weather, these reefs should be passed at a safe distance.

PS74 *New Caledonia to Queensland*

BEST TIME:	April to October			
TROPICAL STORMS:	December to March			
CHARTS:	BA: 4602			
	US: 602			
PILOTS:	BA: 15, 61			
	US: 126, 127			
CRUISING GUIDES:	*Cruising the Coral Coast.*			
WAYPOINTS:				

Departure	Intermediate	Landfall	Destination	Distance (M)
PS741 Dumbea 22°22'S, 166°14'E		PS742 Moreton 27°20'S, 153°30'E	Brisbane *27°19'S, 153°10'E*	773
PS741 Dumbea		PS743 Curtis 24°15'S, 153°00'E	Bundaberg *24°46'S, 152°23'E*	784
PS741 Dumbea		PS744 Capricorn 22°50'S, 152°00'E	Mackay *21°06'S, 149°13'E*	977

Favourable winds can be expected between New Caledonia and the Queensland coast throughout the SE trade wind season, although westerly winds can sometimes be encountered on routes that lead to ports in South Queensland, mainly in winter. If persistent headwinds make it difficult to lay a direct course for ports lying south of Sandy Cape, it is better to stay on the port tack, make landfall further up the coast and use the strong south-setting current to reach the desired port. Because of the large number of reefs dotted about the southern part of the Coral Sea, to reach ports lying north of Sandy Cape it is normally easier to sail inside the Great Barrier Reef, which can be entered through several passes. Curtis Channel should be used for Bundaberg and Gladstone, while Capricorn Channel is convenient for ports lying further north.

Having left Noumea and reached the open sea through Dumbea Pass, from WP PS741, a direct course can be set for various destinations in South Queensland. Boats bound for Brisbane should set a course for WP PS742, east of Moreton Island, in the approaches to the Queensland capital. If bound for Bundaberg, landfall will be made at WP PS743, off Lady Elliot Island, whereas for ports reached through the Capricorn Channel, such as Mackay, a course should be steered for WP PS744. For routes to ports in North Queensland see PS77.

PS75 *New Caledonia to Torres Strait*

BEST TIME:	May to October			
TROPICAL STORMS:	December to April			
CHARTS:	BA: 780			
	US: 526			
PILOTS:	BA: 15, 61			
	US: 126, 127, 164			
CRUISING GUIDES:	*Cruising the Coral Coast.*			
WAYPOINTS:				

Departure	Intermediate	Landfall	Destination	Distance (M)
PS751 Dumbea 22°22'S, 166°14'E	PS752 21°40'S, 165°00'E			
	PS753 17°30'S, 160°00'E	PS754 Eastern 9°40'S, 145°50'E	PS755 Bligh 9°15'S, 144°00'E	1522

This route across the Coral Sea lies within the SE trade wind belt and favourable winds can be expected throughout the winter months. However, cyclones can occur in the Coral Sea both during the summer and autumn months and, although in most years this passage can be made at any time after the middle of April, it is safer not to attempt it before the middle of June.

After leaving Noumea through Dumbea Pass, from WP PS751 a parallel course to the coast should be steered to pass between the main island and the various dangers lying to the west of New Caledonia. From WP PS752, a new course can be set for WP PS753 to stay clear of all dangers. This direct route to the Torres Strait has the great advantage that it avoids all known dangers right up to the entrance into Torres Strait. The route runs parallel to the Papuan coast to WP PS754 to pass NE of Eastern Fields, the first dangerous reefs in the eastern approaches to Torres Strait. The course should then be altered to pass clear of Goldie Reef and enter the Great NE Channel, which goes west of Bramble Cay. If WP PS754 is reached in good light, it may be possible to use Bligh Channel and stay south of Bramble Cay. Whichever route is taken, great care must be taken both in the approaches to the Torres Strait and in the channels leading through it as the numerous reefs make navigation extremely difficult and dangerous. More detailed directions on the approaches to the Torres Strait are given in route PS85 (page 423). The continuation of the route to Darwin, in Northern Australia, is described in IS11 (page 480).

PS76 *Vanuatu to New Caledonia*

BEST TIME:	April to November			
TROPICAL STORMS:	December to March			
CHARTS:	BA: 4602			
	US: 602			
PILOTS:	BA: 61			
	US: 126			
CRUISING GUIDES:	*Cruising in New Caledonia.*			
WAYPOINTS:				
Departure	*Intermediate*	*Landfall*	*Destination*	*Distance (M)*
PS761 Efate S 17°46'S, 168°12'E	PS762 Lifou 21°00'S, 167°32'E	PS763 Havannah 22°20'S, 167°05'E	Noumea *22°16'S, 166°27'E*	317

This passage is rarely made nonstop as most of those who sail this route try to visit some of the southern islands of Vanuatu on the way. Permission to do this should be sought before leaving Vila. It is also possible to stop at some of New Caledonia's Loyalty Islands before continuing to Noumea via Havannah Pass, although in principle one should have cleared into New Caledonia first. From WP PS761, SW of Efate, the direct course for Havannah Pass, at the SE extremity of New Caledonia, goes right past Lifou Island, at WP PS762. If not stopping at Lifou Island, the pass between it and Maré should be negotiated in good light before making for WP PS763, in the approaches to Havannah Pass. This pass should be negotiated on a flood tide. Due to the prevailing SE winds the tide sets very strongly through the pass creating large waves when the ebb tide runs against a strong wind.

The other alternative, that of sailing west from Vila and reaching New Caledonia through Grand Passage, is not recommended because of the near certainty of encountering strong headwinds when sailing along the west side of New Caledonia. Because the trade winds are deflected by the large landmass, SE winds tend to become southerly on the west side of New Caledonia.

Noumea is New Caledonia's only port of entry and all boats must clear in there. Approaches into Noumea are difficult at night and should not be attempted. If coming from either Boulari or Havannah Pass and if Noumea cannot be reached in daylight it is recommended to anchor for the night and enter the port the following morning. Arriving boats should contact Port Moselle on channel 67 to arrange a berth at the visitor's dock. The marina will contact customs and immigration for clearance. Although New Caledonia is a French overseas territory, a bond is not required from cruising boats as in the case of French Polynesia.

PS77 *Vanuatu to North Queensland*

BEST TIME:	May to September			
TROPICAL STORMS:	December to April			
CHARTS:	BA: 780			
	US: 526			
PILOTS:	BA: 15, 61			
	US: 126, 127			
CRUISING GUIDES:	*Cruising the Coral Coast.*			
WAYPOINTS:				
Departure	*Intermediate*	*Landfall*	*Destination*	*Distance (M)*
Route PS77A				
PS771 Efate W	PS772 Entrecasteaux			
17°46'S, 168°08'E	17°30'S, 163°00'E			
	PS773 Mellish			
	18°00'S, 156°00'E			
	PS774 Marion	PS775 Flinders	Townsville	1229
	18°20'S, 152°00'E	18°35'S, 148°20'E	*19°15'S, 146°50'E*	
Route PS77B				
PS771 Efate W	PS776 Sand	PS777 Grafton	Cairns	1315
	15°25'S, 149°38'E	16°38'S, 146°15'E	*16°56'S, 145°47'E*	
Route PS77C				
Luganville	PS778 Santo W			
15°31'S, 167°10'E	15°40'S, 166°45'E			
	PS776 Sand	PS777 Grafton	Cairns	1257

Steady winds and a favourable current usually ensure a fast passage across the Coral Sea although there are many reefs waiting to strike the unwary. Thanks to satellite navigation passages are now much safer, but utmost attention is still required when navigating through this area.

An almost direct route can be sailed from Efate to North Queensland (PS77A) by sailing a middle course between the various dangers. From WP PS771, SW of Efate Island, an initial course is set for WP PS772, north of the d'Entrecasteaux Reefs. A slight course alteration is needed to reach WP PS773 to pass south of Mellish Reef. The route then goes to WP PS774 to pass halfway between Lihou and Marion Reefs. Finally, a course is set for WP PS775 from where Flinders Passage can be taken to reach Townsville, which is the nearest port of entry into Australia. This route is also joined by boats coming from Noumea and bound

for the North Queensland coast.

Boats bound for ports lying further north should stay outside the Great Barrier Reef on a parallel course to it and use one of the other passes to reach the coast. Because of its convenient position at the heart of the Great Barrier Reef, Cairns in North Queensland is a popular destination for cruising boats. There are extensive reefs on the direct route from Port Vila to Cairns (PS77B) and the safest route is to leave them all to port by setting a course for the light on Bougainville Reef (15°32'S, 147°08'E). From WP PS771, SW of Efate, a course is set for WP PS776, 12 miles north of Sand Cay on Diane Bank. From that point, the course can be altered for WP PS777, two miles north of Euston Reef light at the entrance into Grafton Passage. Because of the various dangers, and also strong currents in the area, the course should not be altered for Grafton Pass until confident that one is well past the northernmost of Moore Reefs (15°52'S, 149°10'E). Grafton Pass is recommended as it is used by commercial shipping and is well buoyed and lit. Cairns is the official port of entry for that area and has a good range of yachting facilities.

An easier course across the Coral Sea can be sailed by those who clear out of Vanuatu at Luganville, on Espiritu Santo Island, from where the direct route to Bougainville Light (PS77C) passes clear of all dangers. Having reached the open sea, from WP PS778, SW of Espiritu Santo, a course is set for WP PS776, north of Sand Cay. From there similar directions apply as described above to reach Grafton Pass at WP PS777.

PS78 *Vanuatu to Torres Strait*

BEST TIME:	May to October				
TROPICAL STORMS:	December to April				
CHARTS:	BA: 780				
	US: 526				
PILOTS:	BA: 15, 61				
	US: 126, 127, 164				
CRUISING GUIDES:	*Cruising the Coral Coast.*				
WAYPOINTS:					
Departure	**Intermediate**	**Landfall**		**Destination**	**Distance (M)**
PS781 Efate W	PS782 Papua				
17°46'S, 168°08'E	11°30'S, 149°00'E				
	PS783 Eastern	PS784 Bligh		Thursday Island	1130
	9°40'S, 145°50'E	9°15'S, 144°00'E		*10°35'S, 142°13'E*	

This is a long passage across the entire breadth of the Coral Sea but good winds can be expected throughout the SE trade wind season. During the winter months the SE trade winds blow strongly and consistently along this route and fast passages have been accomplished, especially between July and early September. Although December to March are the months with the highest incidence of cyclones in the Coral Sea, it must be stressed that these can occur as late as June and this should be borne in mind when planning passages across the Coral Sea.

From WP PS781, SW of Matao Tiupeniu Point, on Efate Island, a direct course can be set for WP PS782. From there, the route runs parallel to the Papuan coast to WP PS783 to pass NE of Eastern Fields, the first dangerous reefs in the eastern approaches to Torres Strait. Course is then altered to pass clear of Goldie Reef and enter the Great NE Channel. If WP PS783 is reached in good light it may be possible to use Bligh Channel and stay south of Bramble Cay. Whichever route is taken, great care must be taken both in the approaches to the Torres Strait and in the channels leading through it as the numerous reefs make navigation extremely difficult and dangerous. More detailed directions on the approaches to the Torres Strait are given in route PS85 (page 423). The continuation of the route to Darwin, in Northern Australia, is described in IS11 (page 480).

PS79 *Vanuatu to Solomon Islands*

BEST TIME:	May to October			
TROPICAL STORMS:	December to April			
CHARTS:	BA: 4604			
	US: 604			
PILOTS:	BA: 60, 61			
	US: 126			
CRUISING GUIDES:	*Landfalls of Paradise.*			
WAYPOINTS:				
Departure	*Intermediate*	*Landfall*	*Destination*	*Distance (M)*
Luganville	PS791 Santo E			
15°31'S, 167°10'E	*15°33'S, 167°20'E*			
	PS792 Santo NE	PS793 Santa Ana	Honiara	595
	15°00'S, 167°22'E	*10°50'S, 162°35'E*	*9°25'S, 159°58'E*	

Having sailed through the island chain of Vanuatu, the 300 mile passage to the Solomon Islands is straightforward, especially as the winds tend to be favourable throughout the SE trade wind season. During July and August the trades blow strongly, making this a fast but rough passage. Both at the beginning and towards the end of the winter season the trade winds are less consistent and days with calms or westerly winds are common.

From Luganville the south coast of Espiritu Santo is followed to WP PS791. From there a course is set for WP PS792. The course runs almost due north parallel to the coast before course is altered for WP PS793 to make landfall SE of Santa Ana Island, a small island lying close to the east of San Cristobal Island. During strong SE winds, if bound for Honiara, it is better to stay in the lee of San Cristobal, which offers good shelter along its north coast. Entry formalities can be completed at the capital Honiara, on the north coast of Guadalcanal.

A more convenient port of entry into the Solomons may be Graciosa Bay (10°44'S, 165°49'E), on Ndende Island in the Santa Cruz group, lying almost due north of Vanuatu.

PS80 ROUTES FROM NORTHERN MELANESIA

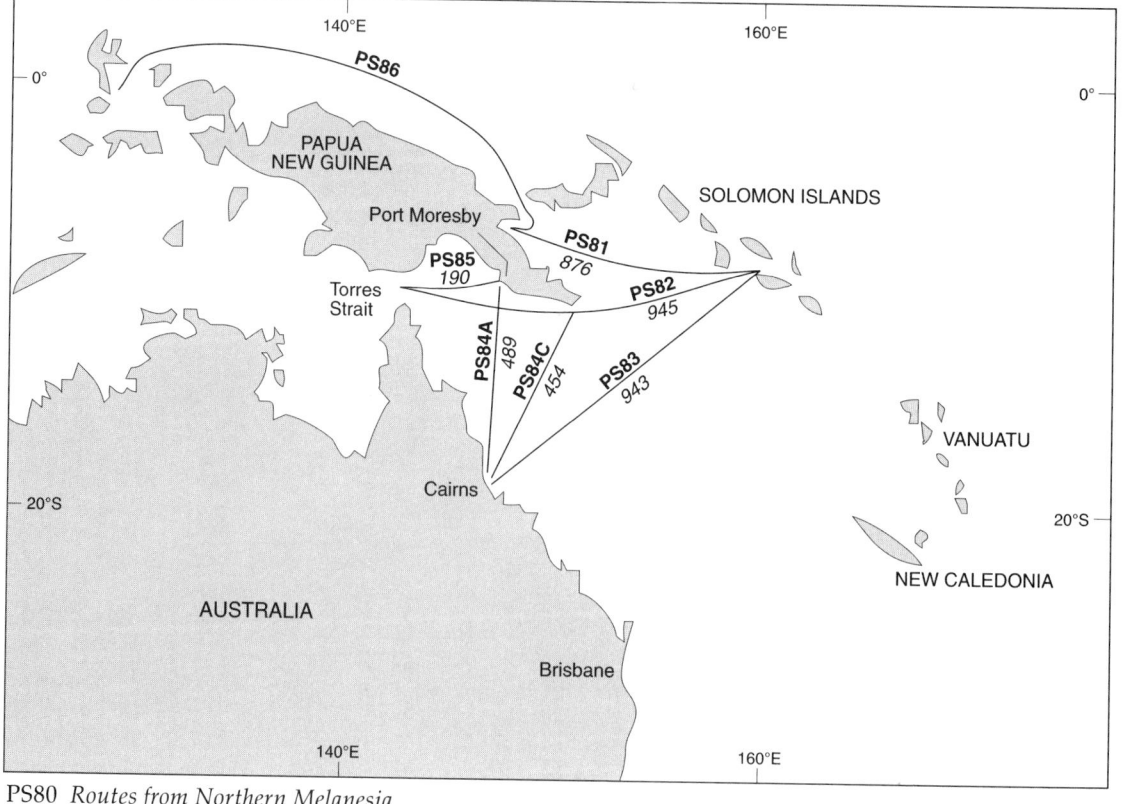

PS80 *Routes from Northern Melanesia*

PS81 *Solomon Islands to Papua New Guinea*

Best time:	April to November
Tropical storms:	December to April
Charts:	BA: 780
	US: 604
Pilots:	BA: 60
	US: 126, 164
Cruising guides:	*Landfalls of Paradise, Cruising Guide to Southeast Asia (2).*

The cyclone season in the Solomon Islands coincides with the NW monsoon which affects most of Papua New Guinea and the northwestern half of the Solomons. Most people try to leave the Solomons by early December not only to avoid the approaching cyclone season, but also the headwinds that can be expected on this route during the NW monsoon. As the majority of those who sail between these two countries have usually cruised along the Solomon Islands chain, the crossing to Papua New Guinea is hardly an ocean passage. The best point of departure is Korovou, on Shortland

Island (7°04'S, 155°52'E), where departure formalities can be completed.

Bougainville Island, the nearest island in Papua New Guinea, has been involved in a dispute with the Port Moresby government and while hostilities last yachts should keep well away from the island. The most popular destination in the area is Rabaul (4°12'S, 152°11'E), on New Britain Island, 260 miles across the Solomon Sea. This well protected harbour is also a port of entry for Papua New Guinea, its main disadvantage being the fact that it lies in the proximity of an active volcano,

419

which has erupted recently. Volcanic activity in the area is being carefully monitored, but the area should be avoided until life returns to normal. Arriving boats should proceed to the main wharf in the northern part of Simpson Harbour to complete entry formalities. Cruising yachts normally anchor off the yacht club on the east side of the harbour but the club was badly damaged by the latest eruption.

From April to October the winds in the Solomon Sea blow mostly from the SE. During the transition period between the SE trade wind season and the NW monsoon, the winds are variable and there are also prolonged periods of calm. When negotiating St George's Channel between the islands of New Britain and New Ireland, attention should be paid to the currents, which set to the south during the NW monsoon and to the north during the SE trade wind season.

PS82 *Solomon Islands to Torres Strait*

BEST TIME:	May to September			
TROPICAL STORMS:	December to April			
CHARTS:	BA: 780			
	US: 526			
PILOTS:	BA: 15, 60			
	US: 126, 164			
WAYPOINTS:				
Departure	*Intermediate*	*Landfall*	*Destination*	*Distance (M)*
PS821 Guadalcanal 9°18'S, 159°30'E	PS822 12°00'S, 153°55'E PS823 12°00'S, 150°00'E PS824 Portlock 9°15'S, 145°00'E	PS825 Bligh 9°15'S, 144°00'E	Thursday Island *10°35'S, 142°13'E*	1130

The chances of a fast passage to the Torres Strait are best when the SE trade winds are still in force. This timing will also ensure favourable winds west of the Strait. With the approach of the NW monsoon, the SE trade winds become less reliable and by the end of September the onward leg from the Torres Strait will have light winds. The currents on this route set strongly NW and this should be taken into account if the course passes too closely to the reefs off Papua New Guinea.

Boats leaving from Honiara will have an easier route to sail and also a better wind angle than boats leaving from ports further west. The route from Honiara leaves Guadalcanal to port and from WP PS821, off the NW point of that island, a course can be set to WP PS822 to pass well clear of Pockington Reef and Adele Island. The route then continues along the same latitude south of the Louisiade Islands to WP PS823 from where a new course is set for WP PS824, north of Portlock Reef. Another course alteration is then made for WP PS825, in Bligh entrance, 10 miles SE of Bramble Cay. From Bramble Cay the route enters North East Channel. This well marked channel runs in a SW direction for some 130 miles to the Prince of Wales Channel that finally opens into the Arafura Sea. Additional details on approaches to the Torres Strait are given in route PS85 (page 423). The continuation of the route to Darwin is described in IS11 (page 480). Thursday Island is an official port of entry into Australia.

PS83 *Solomon Islands to Queensland*

BEST TIME:	May to September			
TROPICAL STORMS:	December to April			
CHARTS:	BA: 780			
	US: 526			
PILOTS:	BA: 15, 60			
	US: 126, 127			
CRUISING GUIDES:	*Cruising the Coral Coast, Circumnavigating Australia's Coastline.*			
WAYPOINTS:				

Departure	Intermediate	Landfall	Destination	Distance (M)
PS831 Guadalcanal 9°18'S, 159°30'E	PS832 Mellish 17°30'S, 156°45'E			
	PS833 Kenn 21°20'S, 155°00'E	PS834 Moreton NW 26°50'S, 153°20'E	Brisbane *27°19'S, 153°10'E*	1141

The approach of the cyclone season brings an exodus of cruising boats from the Solomons, either north to Papua New Guinea (route PS81) or south to Australia. A popular place to spend the summer is the Queensland capital Brisbane. The route across the Coral Sea has good winds at least until September. Those who leave too late can expect anything, including the possibility of a tropical depression, which may or may not develop into a fully fledged cyclone. Extremely strong winds have been encountered in the Coral Sea in November when a depression moves over the area.

From WP PS831, off the NW tip of Guadalcanal, a course can be set for WP PS832 to pass east of Mellish Reef. The route continues to WP PS833 to pass between Saumarez and Wreck Reefs. Landfall is made at WP PS834 in the northern approaches to Brisbane. There are several reefs en route where one may be tempted to stop in good weather, the largest being Chesterfield Reef which has several anchorages where yachts have stopped in the past. The reef belongs nominally to France and is administered as part of its New Caledonia territory. There is an unattended meteorological station on one of the cays. There are several passes through the reef, the widest being Long Island Pass, but it is affected by the swell, strong currents, and overfalls. The narrower Passage Pass is calmer and easier to negotiate. There is a protected anchorage off Loop Islet in the southern part of the large lagoon. The entire area is an important breeding ground for birds and turtles.

PS84 *Papua New Guinea to Queensland*

BEST TIME:	April to October			
TROPICAL STORMS:	December to April			
CHARTS:	BA: 780			
	US: 526			
PILOTS:	BA: 15, 60			
	US: 127, 164			
CRUISING GUIDES:	*Cruising the Coral Coast, Circumnavigating Australia's Coastline.*			
WAYPOINTS:				

Departure	Intermediate	Landfall	Destination	Distance (M)
Route PS84A				
PS841 Basilisk SE 9°34'S, 147°07'E	PS842 Bougainville 15°30'S, 147°30'E	PS843 Grafton 16°35'S, 146°25'E	Cairns *16°56'S, 145°47'E*	489

Departure	Intermediate	Landfall	Destination	Distance (M)
Route PS84B PS841 Basilisk SE		PS844 One Half 14°20'S, 145°30'E		301
Route PS84C PS845 Brumer 10°52'S, 150°15'E	PS842 Bougainville	PS843 Grafton	Cairns	454

The attraction of a sheltered sail in smooth waters tempts most people to go behind the Great Barrier Reef as soon as they have the Coral Sea behind them. If coming from Port Moresby, the choice is large as there are several passes that lead through the reef, from Flinders Entrance in the north to Cook's Pass in the south, a distance of some 250 miles. Coming from other parts of Papua New Guinea, probably the most convenient pass is Grafton Passage that leads into Cairns, the nearest port of entry in Northern Queensland. Thursday Island, in Torres Strait, is also a port of entry, but only a few boats take this roundabout way from Port Moresby to Queensland.

The winds in the Coral Sea blow mostly from the E or SE between April and October so that a more easterly departure point in Papua New Guinea normally ensures a better slant across the prevailing winds. Between May and August the trade winds can sometimes be very strong, but during the transitional months they are often light and the weather can be squally. NW winds predominate in summer, which is also the cyclone season. Because of the west-setting current and the many reefs lying to leeward, navigation in the Coral Sea must be very accurate and finding the passes through the Great Barrier Reef can be often difficult.

Having left Port Moresby through Basilisk Pass, from WP PS841, the safest offshore route (PS84A) leads to the east of Osprey and Shark Reefs to WP PS842, east of Bougainville Reef, which has a powerful light and provides a convenient point of reference. A slight course alteration is then made for WP PS843 outside Grafton Passage. A well buoyed and lit channel leads into Cairns.

A slightly shorter offshore route (PS84B) can be taken from Port Moresby to WP PS844 from where the One and a Half Mile Opening (14°25'S, 145°26'E) is used to reach the sheltered waters behind the Great Barrier Reef on the way to Cairns, the nearest official port of entry into Australia. Although entry formalities must be completed in Cairns itself, the best docking facilities for visiting boats are now at Halfmoon Bay Marina in Yorkeys Know, a small resort a few miles north of Cairns.

For boats that have cruised the eastern part of Papua New Guinea, a departure from Samarai through the China Strait has the advantage of a virtually clear run across the Coral Sea (PS84C). Having passed Brumer Island and gained the open sea, from WP PS845, a direct course can be set for WP PS842. The course can then be altered for WP PS843 outside Grafton Passage.

The Australian authorities must be contacted at least three hours before arrival in a port of entry on 2182 kHz or VHF channel 16 to request clearance. Stopping anywhere before having cleared in is strictly prohibited and everyone on board, including the captain, must have a visa for Australia.

PS85 *Papua New Guinea to Torres Strait*

BEST TIME:	April to September
TROPICAL STORMS:	December to April
CHARTS:	BA: 1039
	US: 603
PILOTS:	BA: 15, 60
	US: 164
CRUISING GUIDES:	*Cruising the Coral Coast.*
WAYPOINTS:	

Departure	Intermediate	Landfall	Destination	Distance (M)
PS851 Basilisk SW 9°34'S, 147°05'E	PS852 Portlock 9°15'S, 145°00'E	PS853 Bligh 9°15'S, 144°00'E	Thursday Island *10°35'S, 142°13'E*	319

In the days before satellite navigation, Port Moresby was the preferred port of departure for the passage to the Torres Strait. This was a logical choice as the various difficulties associated with navigation through the Torres Strait made it essential to plan the time of arrival in the eastern approaches to the Strait so as to minimise the risk of passing close to some of the reefs at night. Although satellite navigation has greatly simplified matters, a start from Port Moresby still makes it easier to time one's arrival more accurately than if one leaves from a more distant port.

The first danger en route is Portlock Reef, at a distance of 130 miles from Port Moresby. Goldie Reef is 20 miles NNW of Portlock. Ideally one should try to arrive off Portlock Reef in late afternoon, so as to pass between it and Goldie Reef during daylight. The next point to make for is Bramble Cay, lying some 65 miles further west. The distance between Portlock and Bramble Cay can be covered during the hours of darkness, and as there is a light with 14 miles visibility on Bramble Cay this should be sighted before dawn. Such a timing would mean that Bramble Cay is passed in the early morning and that most of the subsequent reefs and islets will also be negotiated in daylight. The other alternative, especially for faster boats, is to arrive off Portlock Reef in the morning so that the remaining distance to Bramble Cay is covered in daylight. The disadvantage of the latter alternative is that Portlock Reef has no light, thus making it very dangerous to arrive in its vicinity at night.

Leaving Port Moresby through Basilisk Pass, from WP PS851 a course can be set for WP PS852, north of Portlock Reef. The course is then altered for WP PS853, in Bligh entrance, 10 miles SE of Bramble Cay. From Bramble Cay the route enters

North East Channel. This well marked channel runs in a SW direction for some 130 miles to the Prince of Wales Channel that finally opens into the Arafura Sea. The continuation of this route is described in IS11 and IS12 (page 480).

The winds on this passage are predominantly easterly and between June and August they are often strong. The currents running through the Strait have a strong westerly set at the height of the SE trades, but their rates are unpredictable. The currents are also tidal and in the Strait itself they run WSW on the flood and NE on the ebb tide. The strongest sets have been recorded in the Prince of Wales Channel, where 5 and 6 knot currents are the order of the day. Another hazard in the eastern approaches is the shallow water that extends far offshore so that the depth sounder cannot give a reliable indication of one's position. Yet another cause of confusion are the murky waters met far offshore caused by a muddy discharge from the Fly River. The colour of the water gives no indication of its depth.

Although navigation through this reef strewn area is not difficult after landfall on Bramble Cay, it is easier to sail in daylight and spend the nights at anchor behind one of the many cays. It must be pointed out, however, that landing on any of the islands is not allowed, as these belong to Australia and legally one should clear in first at Thursday Island. This is impossible for boats coming from the east, so one should heed the above advice and only anchor if absolutely necessary and neither go ashore nor have contact with any other vessel. Australian Coast Guard helicopters regularly overfly the area to ensure that these regulations are not violated and those who ignore them are severely punished.

PS86 *Papua New Guinea to Indonesia*

BEST TIME:	May to September
TROPICAL STORMS:	None
CHARTS:	BA: 4507
	US: 524
PILOTS:	BA: 35, 60
	US: 164
CRUISING GUIDES:	*Cruising Guide to Southeast Asia (2).*

The difficulties associated with the passage through the Torres Strait and the long detour to Port Moresby, persuades some people to reach Indonesia by sailing along the north coast of New Guinea. This northern route is used mostly by boats that have spent the cyclone season in the eastern part of Papua New Guinea or have been cruising in that area and are therefore better poised for this route. It also gives the opportunity to visit the Hermit and Ninigo Islands before clearing out of Papua New Guinea at Vanimo (2°41'S, 141°18'E).

This is a passage that can be done only during the SE trade wind season, as during the NW monsoon, from November to March, both winds and current are contrary. The transitional period is difficult to define, as in some years the NW monsoon comes early, while in others the SE trade winds do not establish themselves until May. Normally this passage should not be attempted after the middle of November or before the middle of April. Although the weather along this route is governed by the two monsoons, the winds are rarely steady in either direction or strength and there are many days when they are light or nonexistent. Calms are particularly frequent during the transitional period. The most constant SE winds usually occur in July and August when there is also a very strong NW setting current, with rates that can exceed 2 knots.

Jayapura, the capital of the Indonesian province of Irian Jaya (Western Irian), is the official port of entry (2°32'S, 140°43'E). The town has changed its name to Sukarnapura, while in the colonial past it used to be known as Hollandia. Yachts without a cruising permit should enquire at the Indonesian Embassy in Port Moresby whether they would be allowed to make a emergency stop in Jayapura before committing themselves to this route.

PS90 ROUTES FROM NEW SOUTH WALES

PS91 *New South Wales to New Zealand*	*425*
PS92 *New South Wales to New Caledonia*	*426*
PS93 *New South Wales to Fiji*	*427*
PS94 *New South Wales to Vanuatu*	*428*

Australian sailors have the entire South Pacific on their doorstep, yet reaching most of the Pacific islands is seldom easy, as the winds between the east coast of Australia and the island groups to the east are usually contrary. For this reason most Australians setting off on a world voyage prefer to leave the South Pacific until the end of their trip when most of the sailing will be downwind. For those whose plans are less ambitious than a circumnavigation of the world, the accepted practice is to sail first to New Zealand, which makes a much better stepping off point for a cruise among the South Sea islands than Australia itself. Shorter cruises from Australia's east coast lead across the Coral Sea, the more southern destinations, such as New Caledonia, being reached directly, whereas for destinations in Papua New Guinea it is usually better to stay for a while inside the Great Barrier Reef before taking an offshore route.

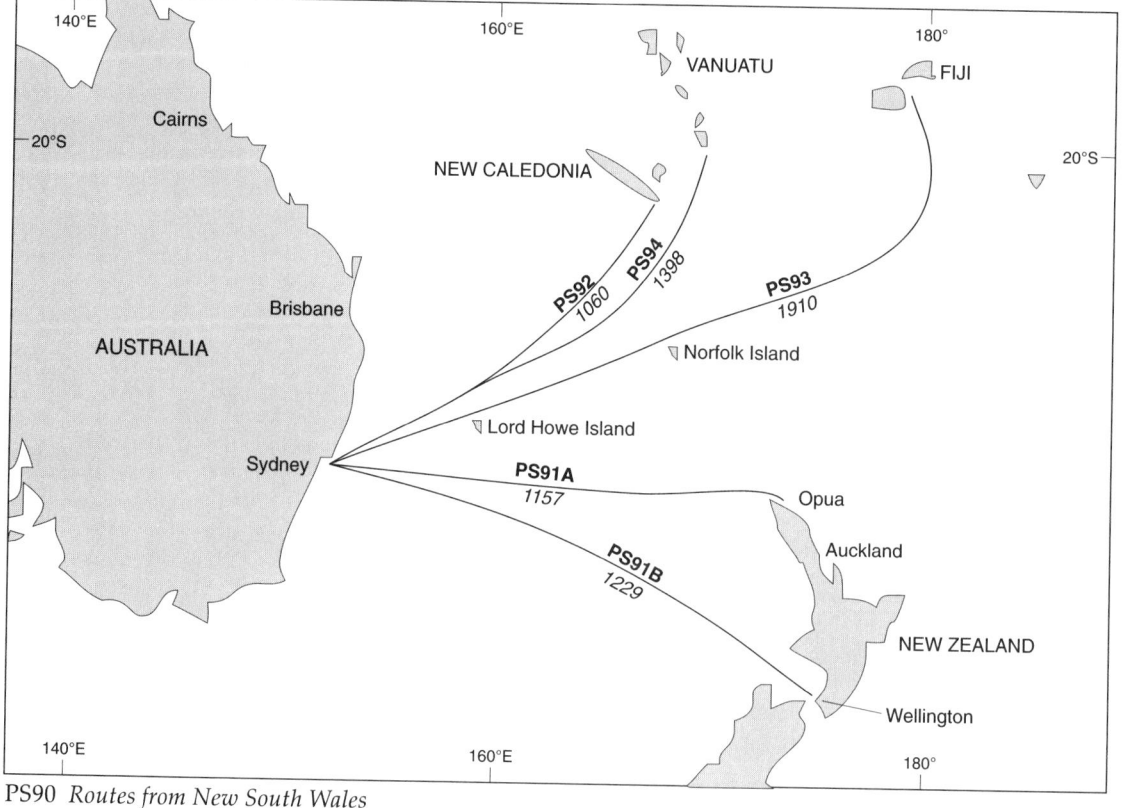

PS90 *Routes from New South Wales*

PS91 *New South Wales to New Zealand*

BEST TIME:	November to March
TROPICAL STORMS:	December to March
CHARTS:	BA: 780, 4061
	US: 622
PILOTS:	BA: 14, 15, 51
	US: 127
CRUISING GUIDES:	*Coastal Cruising Handbook of the Royal Arakana Yacht Club, Pickmere's Atlas of Northland's East Coast.*
WAYPOINTS:	

Departure	Intermediate	Landfall	Destination	Distance (M)
Route PS91A				
PS911 Jackson	PS912 Kings	PS913 North Cape	Opua	1157
33°50'S, 151°20'E	34°20'S, 171°50'E	34°20'S, 173°05'E	*35°18'S, 174°08'E*	
		PS914 Bream	Whangarei	1213
		35°50'S, 174°38'E	*35°44'S, 174°21'E*	
Route PS91B				
PS911 Jackson	PS915 Stephens	PS916 Cook	Wellington	1229
	40°30'S, 174°20'E	41°20'S, 174°30'E	*41°17'S, 174°46'E*	

This passage across the Tasman Sea can occasionally be very rough and it pays to wait for a favourable forecast before leaving. Lows moving across the Tasman Sea are accompanied by strong SW winds, often of gale force, and it may be worth leaving on the tail of such a gale, which will usually ensure several days of favourable winds. Although the proportion of westerly winds is higher in winter, a passage between June and September is not recommended because of the likelihood of encountering at least one severe gale. The best months are January and February when conditions are often settled and winds are light. Although these months coincide with the cyclone season in the South Pacific, tropical cyclones rarely find their way to these latitudes, and even when they do their force is usually spent. The Tasman Sea is affected more by extratropical cyclones, although these normally only touch its southern part and have a higher frequency in winter; another good reason to avoid a passage during that time.

The route from southern ports is direct, but a stop at Lord Howe Island might be considered by those leaving from northerly ports. Boats leaving from Sydney on a direct passage to North Island (route PS91A), from WP PS911 outside Port Jackson, can set a course for WP PS912 south of the Three Kings, a group of rocks NW of Cape Reinga. Having made landfall at PS913, off North Cape, the nearest ports of entry are Opua, in the Bay of Islands, or Whangarei.

From ports south of Sydney, a more direct route (PS91B) leads through Cook Strait to Wellington, this more southerly route having a better chance of westerly winds. From WP PS911 outside Sydney, a course can be set for PS915 off D'Urville island in the approaches to Cook Strait. From there the course is altered for WP PS916 in the Cook Strait before proceeding into Wellington. Wellington Radio should be contacted on 2182 or 4125 kHz, or VHF channel 16, not later than 12 hours before arrival to arrange clearance.

PS92 *New South Wales to New Caledonia*

BEST TIME:	April to June				
TROPICAL STORMS:	December to March				
CHARTS:	BA: 4602				
	US: 602				
PILOTS:	BA: 15, 61				
	US: 126, 127				
CRUISING GUIDES:	*Cruising in New Caledonia.*				
WAYPOINTS:					
Departure	*Intermediate*	*Landfall*	*Destination*		*Distance (M)*
PS921 Jackson		PS922 Dumbea	Noumea		1060
33°50'S, 151°20'E		22°22'S, 166°14'E	*22°16'S, 166°26'E*		

Because of the danger posed by cyclones during the summer, this passage should not be undertaken before the end of March. There is always a high proportion of easterly winds on this route, but more favourable conditions may be found during the transition period, in April and early May, before the onset of the strong easterlies of winter.

The initial course should lead straight offshore to pass quickly through the current that sets strongly south along the Australian coast. As the route from southern ports in New South Wales passes close to Lord Howe Island, a stop there may be considered. Most routes also pass close to Minerva and Elizabeth Reefs, which are best avoided, although it is possible to anchor there in settled weather.

From WP PS921, outside Port Jackson, a direct course can be set for New Caledonia where landfall is made at WP PS922 outside Dumbea Pass. Noumea is New Caledonia's only port of entry and all boats must clear there. Approaches into Noumea are difficult and should not be attempted at night. Arriving boats should contact Port Moselle on VHF channel 67 to arrange a berth at the visitor's dock, where they will be cleared in.

PS93 *New South Wales to Fiji*

BEST TIME:	April to June
TROPICAL STORMS:	December to March
CHARTS:	BA: 4602
	US: 602
PILOTS:	BA: 15, 61
	US: 126, 127
CRUISING GUIDES:	*Yachtsman's Fiji, Landfalls of Paradise.*
WAYPOINTS:	

Departure	Intermediate	Landfall	Destination	Distance (M)
Route PS93A				
PS931 Jackson	PS932			
33°50'S, 151°20'E	32°00'S, 170°00'E			
	PS934 Vatulele N	PS936 Daveta	Suva	
	18°25'S, 177°35'E	18°12'S,178°23.5'E	*18°09'S, 178°26'E*	1910
Route PS93B				
PS931 Jackson	PS933 Kune			
	22°52'S, 167°37'E			
	PS934 Vatulele N	PS936 Daveta	Suva	1752
PS931 Jackson	PS933 Kune			
	PS935 Kandavu	PS936 Daveta	Suva	
	19°06'S, 177°54'E			1764
Route PS39C				
PS931 Jackson	PS933 Kune	PS937 Navula	Lautoka	
		17°55'S, 177°10'E	*17°36'S, 177°26'E*	1718

The near certainty of encountering contrary winds on the great circle route rules out a direct passage to Fiji from any port in New South Wales. The recommended route (PS93A) stays south of latitude 32°S until longitude 170°E is crossed from where it gradually curves NE so that the islands are approached from the south. The initial course should stay slightly north of east, so as to pass well to the south of Minerva and Elizabeth Reefs and close to Norfolk Island. A stop at either Norfolk or Lord Howe Island can be convenient to await the easing of strong easterly winds. WP PS932 is only a guideline as the course that will be sailed will depend on existing weather conditions and the windward performance of the boat in question. In fact, a boat that goes well to windward may be able to sail an almost direct course (PS93B). In such a case, the initial course should be set to pass close to the SE of New Caledonia, to WP PS933. From that point, SE of Kune Island, the direct route to Fiji passes close to a number of dangers south of Durand Reef. If such a direct course for Fiji cannot

be sailed on account of the wind, and easting has to be made on a more southerly route, several dangers will be passed closely. The first two islands, Matthew (22°21'S, 171°21'E) and Hunter (22°24'S, 172°05'E), are easily visible as they are quite high. Much more dangerous is the low reef Theva-i-Ra (21°44'S, 174°38'E), which should be given a wide berth.

Regardless of the route sailed, boats bound for Suva can make landfall at WP PS934, north of Vatulele Island from where the route continues to Suva through the Mbengga Channel, where strong contrary currents can be expected. If sufficient easting has been made to approach Suva from the south, landfall can be made at WP PS935, SW of Kandavu. The course can then be altered for WP PS936 so that Suva Harbour is entered through Daveta Passage. Arriving vessels must either tie to the quarantine buoy or anchor in this area and await clearance.

Boats bound for Lautoka (PS93C), on the west coast of Viti Levu, from WP PS933 should set course for WP PS937, at the entrance into Navula Passage.

From there the route crosses Nadi waters to Lautoka, an official port of entry into Fiji.

Because a passage to Fiji should be avoided during the cyclone season, the alternative to a direct passage is to sail first to New Zealand, which can be done earlier in the year (see route PS91) and continue to Fiji in April. This detour has the prospect of better winds on the passage to New Zealand and a better slant through the SE trades on the subsequent leg to Fiji. See also route PS64 (page 405).

PS94 *New South Wales to Vanuatu*

BEST TIME:	April to June			
TROPICAL STORMS:	December to March			
CHARTS:	BA: 4602			
	US: 602			
PILOTS:	BA: 15, 61			
	US: 126, 127			
CRUISING GUIDES:	*Landfalls of Paradise.*			
WAYPOINTS:				
Departure	*Intermediate*	*Landfall*	*Destination*	*Distance (M)*
Route PS94A				
PS941 Jackson	PS942 Fairway			
33°50'S, 151°20'E	21°00'S, 162°30'E			
	PS943 Grand			
	19°00'S, 162°30'E			
	PS944	PS945 Efate SW	Vila	1436
	18°10'S, 164°30'E	17°46'S, 168°12'E	*17°44'S, 168°18'E*	
Route PS94B				
PS941 Jackson	PS946 Kune			
	22°52'S, 167°37'E			
	PS947 Maré	PS945 Efate SW	Vila	1398
	21°35'S, 168°10'E			

Because the islands of New Caledonia straddle most direct routes to Vanuatu, a stop in Noumea is included in most passage plans. This is probably the easier way to reach Vanuatu and directions for it are similar to those for route PS92.

A direct route from Sydney (PS94A), which bypasses New Caledonia, leads west of Lord Howe Island, Elizabeth and Minerva Reefs. The route heads in the direction of New Caledonia to WP PS942 to pass clear of Fairway Reef and avoid the other dangers to the west of New Caledonia. The route then goes due north to WP PS943 and enters Grand Passage. This is sailed in a NE direction to WP PS944 before the course can be altered for Port Vila. Great caution is necessary when navigating west and north of New Caledonia where the positions of some reefs are doubtful and others have not been accurately charted. Approaching the island of Efate from the west, landfall should be made at WP PS945, SW of Efate. The route then enters Mele Bay to reach Port Vila, the capital of Vanuatu. On arrival in Port Vila boats should tie up to the quarantine buoy and wait to be cleared in. Port Vila Radio should be contacted on VHF channel 16 to request that the relevant officials are informed.

Because of the near certainty of encountering strong easterly winds between Grand Passage and Efate, an alternative route (PS94B) may be considered which passes south of New Caledonia. In this case, the initial course leads to WP PS946, SE of Kune Island. From there, the course is altered to pass to windward of the Loyalty Islands to WP PS947, SE of Maré Island. From that point, the course can be altered for WP PS945, in the approaches to Port Vila.

PS100 ROUTES FROM QUEENSLAND

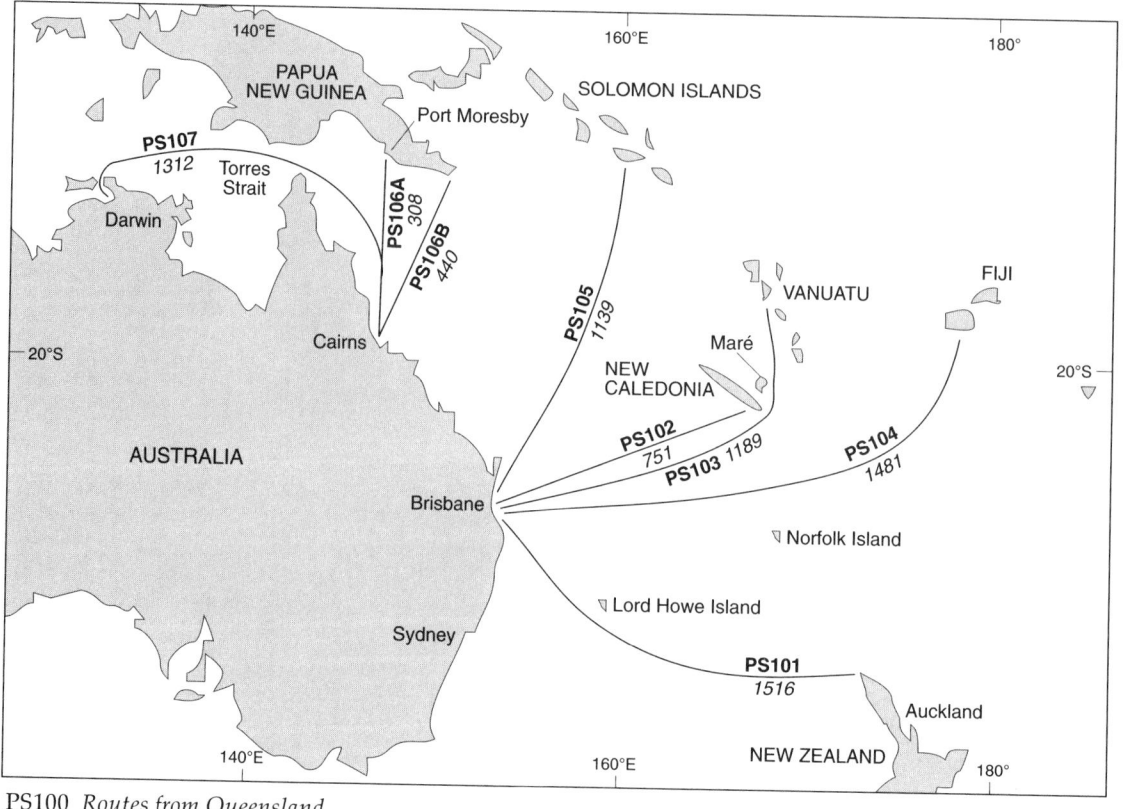

PS100 *Routes from Queensland*

A tropical climate, the Great Barrier Reef, and almost unlimited cruising opportunities have turned Queensland into a favourite destination not only among foreign sailors but also Australian ones. The one major disadvantage are the tropical cyclones which affect both Queensland and the surrounding region, with the exception of Papua New Guinea north of approximately latitude 10°S. The critical period is December to the end of March when cruising should be kept to a minimum and one should always be within easy reach of a safe harbour. From April onwards the weather is good, with strong and steady SE trade winds. In July and August particularly, the winds can be quite strong and so it is recommended that, especially in winter, the Queensland coast should be cruised from south to north.

Although the main routes are northbound and thus benefit from the prevailing winds, those who intend to sail east across the Coral Sea should plan to do so either before or after the onset of the SE trade winds which blow most consistently between

May and September. Usually in early April the trade winds are not yet fully established and eastbound passages are easier to accomplish. Passages after the end of October should be avoided because of the danger of early cyclones. The period when these tropical storms occur in the Coral Sea should be treated with great suspicion as very few months are known to be entirely free and cyclones have been recorded in both the transitional months of June and November.

PS101 *Queensland to New Zealand*

BEST TIME:	April to May, October to November				
TROPICAL STORMS:	December to March				
CHARTS:	BA: 780				
	US: 602				
PILOTS:	BA: 15, 51				
	US: 127				
CRUISING GUIDES:	*Coastal Cruising Handbook of the Royal Arakana Yacht Club.*				
WAYPOINTS:					
Departure	Intermediate	Landfall		Destination	Distance (M)
PS1011 Stradbroke 27°25'S, 153°35'E	PS1012 Elizabeth 29°40'S, 159°00'E PS1013 Kings 34°20'S, 171°50'E PS1014 North Cape 34°20'S, 173°05'E			Opua *35°19'S, 174°07'E*	1516

As a passage during the cyclone season is not recommended and one in the middle of winter has few attractions, the best time should be between those two seasons. In April or May, the danger of cyclones is acceptably low, the weather is not yet cold, and the SE trade winds have not reached their mid-winter strength. The passage can be just as pleasant at the end of winter, in late October or early November, when SW gales are also less frequent.

The route from ports north of Sandy Cape should pass well to the north of Middleton Reef.

The direct route from Brisbane takes its leave at PS1011, off Stradbroke Island. From there a course is set for WP PS1012, halfway between Middleton (29°28'S, 159°04'E) and Elizabeth Reef (29°55'S, 159°02'E), both of which have anchorages which have been used by yachts in settled weather. The route continues to WP PS1013, south of the Three Kings, a group of rocks off New Zealand's Cape Reinga. Having rounded North Cape, the nearest ports of entry are Opua, in the Bay of Islands, or Whangarei (35°44'S, 174°21'E).

PS102 *Queensland to New Caledonia*

BEST TIME:	April to May, mid-September to October
TROPICAL STORMS:	December to March
CHARTS:	BA: 4602
	US: 602
PILOTS:	BA: 15, 61
	US: 126, 127
CRUISING GUIDES:	*Cruising in New Caledonia, Landfalls of Paradise.*

WAYPOINTS:				
Departure	Intermediate	Landfall	Destination	Distance (M)
PS1021 Capricorn 22°50'S, 152°00'E	PS1022 Wreck 22°45'S, 155°00'E	PS1025 Dumbea 22°22'S, 166°14'E	Noumea 22°16'S, 166°26'E	802
PS1023 Curtis 24°15'S, 153°00'E	PS1024 Cato 23°55'S, 155°00'E	PS1025 Dumbea	Noumea	751

This can be a difficult passage at all times because of the certainty of encountering contrary winds for at least part of the voyage, if not the whole of it. It is therefore important to wait for a forecast for westerly winds, which at least will ensure a speedy start. Such winds are normally generated by fronts moving up from the south and the weather associated with them is rarely pleasant. Because of the high proportion of easterly winds in winter it is better to plan this passage for the intermediate season. Similarly, because of the risk of cyclones in the Coral Sea, this passage should not be undertaken after the middle of November or before the end of March.

A direct offshore route can be sailed from ports in South Queensland, but from ports north of Sandy Cape, either Capricorn or Curtis Channels should be used to reach the open sea before laying a course for Dumbea Pass, at the SW extremity of New Caledonia. The route for boats leaving through Capricorn Channel goes to WP PS1022 halfway between Wreck and Cato Reefs. Boats leaving through Curtis Channel should stay south of Cato Reef by setting course for WP PS1024. The routes converge at WP PS1025 outside Dumbea Pass. This leads into Noumea, New Caledonia's capital and only port of entry. Approaches into Noumea are difficult at night and should not be attempted. Arriving boats should contact Port Moselle on channel 67 to arrange a berth at the visitor's dock. The marina will contact customs and immigration for clearance.

PS103 Queensland to Vanuatu

BEST TIME:	April to May, mid-September to October			
TROPICAL STORMS:	December to March			
CHARTS:	BA: 4602			
	US: 602			
PILOTS:	BA: 15, 61			
	US: 126, 127			
CRUISING GUIDES:	Landfalls of Paradise.			
WAYPOINTS:				
Departure	Intermediate	Landfall	Destination	Distance (M)
PS1031 Capricorn 22°50'S, 152°00'E	PS1032 Wreck 22°45'S, 155°00'E PS1033 23°10'S, 166°50'E PS1034 Kune 22°52'S, 167°37'E PS1035 Maré 21°35'S, 168°10'E	PS1036 Efate SW 17°46'S, 168°12'E	Port Vila 17°44'S, 168°18'E	1189

Prevailing easterly winds, contrary currents, and the many dangers dotted about the southern part of the Coral Sea make this one of the most diffi- cult routes in the South Pacific. Direct passages from ports in Northern Queensland should not even be considered and an alternative route chosen to reach the islands of Vanuatu without having to fight the elements all the way. The best tactic is to make a detour to the south, inside the Great Barrier Reef. Having reached the open sea via the Capricorn Channel, the route joins route PS94, if a nonstop passage to Vanuatu is intended.

An easier alternative is to join route PS102 and follow directions as far as Noumea from where Vanuatu can be reached via the islands spread out among the two groups. Such an approach has certain attractions as it avoids the dangerous reefs to the west of New Caledonia and offers the possibility of breaking up the voyage in some of the islands of New Caledonia or Southern Vanuatu, if the winds prove too much to cope with.

The suggested direct route takes its leave from Australia through the Capricorn Channel, from where a course is set to pass south of the various reefs and round the island of New Caledonia from the south. From a point SE of Kune Island (WP PS1034), the course is altered to pass to windward of the Loyalty Islands to WP PS1035, SE of Maré Island. From that point, the course can be altered for WP PS1036, SW of Efate, in the approaches to Port Vila. The route then enters Mele Bay to reach Port Vila, the capital of Vanuatu. On arrival in Port Vila, boats should tie up to the quarantine buoy and wait to be inspected by a health officer. Port Vila Radio should be contacted on VHF channel 16 to request that the relevant officials are informed.

Another alternative is to take a route which goes through Grand Passage, north of New Caledonia, as described in route PS94. On that route, a better wind angle may make it possible to stay on the starboard tack NE of Grand Passage and sail to Espiritu Santo Island, where it is possible to clear into Vanuatu at Luganville (15°31'S, 167°10'E).

PS104 *Queensland to Fiji*

BEST TIME:	April to June			
TROPICAL STORMS:	December to March			
CHARTS:	BA: 4602			
	US: 602			
PILOTS:	BA: 15, 61			
	US: 126, 127			
CRUISING GUIDES:	*Yachtsman's Fiji, Landfalls of Paradise.*			
WAYPOINTS:				

Departure	Intermediate	Landfall	Destination	Distance (M)
Route PS104A PS1041 Stradbroke 27°25'S, 153°35'E	PS1042 Norfolk S 30°00'S, 168°00'E	PS1045 Navula 17°55'S, 177°10'E	Lautoka *17°36'S, 177°26'E*	1681
Route PS104B PS1041 Stradbroke	PS1043 23°10'S, 166°50'E PS1044 Kune 22°52'S, 167°37'E	PS1045 Navula	Lautoka	1447
PS1041 Stradbroke	PS1043 PS1044 Kune PS1046 Vatulele N 18°25'S, 177°35'E	PS1047 Daveta 18°12'S, 178°23.5'E	Suva *18°09'S, 178°26'E*	1481

Because of both contrary winds and current sailing a direct route from Queensland to Fiji would be a very difficult undertaking. The most feasible way to reach Fiji is by a detour to the south where better winds might be found to make the required easting (route PS104A). Although the recommended tactic is to sail south of latitude 32°S, where the chances of finding favourable winds are higher, a slightly more northerly route can be taken should the winds permit this. Ideally one should wait for a forecast of westerly winds before leaving. Even with favourable winds, the route should remain south of the latitude of Norfolk Island until past that island. If consistent headwinds are met while in the vicinity of Norfolk, a stop can be made there. The anchorage at Kingston (29°01'S, 167°59'E) is not considered safe and should be left if the weather threatens to deteriorate.

Preferably one of the ports in South Queensland should be taken as a departure port. From WP PS1041, off Stradbroke Island, the initial course goes to WP PS1042, south of Norfolk Island. From there, the course should start curving NE. If a direct course can be sailed from WP PS1042 to Fiji, attention must be paid to Theva-i-ra Reef, also known as Conway Reef (21°44'S, 174°38'E), which will be passed closely. Having made landfall off Navula Passage, at WP PS1045, that pass will be taken through the reef into Nadi Waters and on to Lautoka to complete entry formalities into Fiji.

Depending on weather conditions and the windward performance of the boat in question, a more direct route (PS104B) passing close to New Caledonia may be sailed. Although shorter, such a route may not be necessarily easier as there is a higher chance of encountering contrary winds on the subsequent leg between New Caledonia and Fiji. From WP PS1041, an initial course will be sailed to WPs PS1043 and PS1044, SE of the main island of New Caledonia. From there, the route passes close to a number of dangers south of Durand Reef, before a course can be set for WP PS1045, if the intention is to make for Lautoka. The alternative, if the necessary easting can be made, is to head for Suva, in which case landfall should be made at WP PS1046, north of Vatulele Island. From that point, the Fijian capital will be reached through Beqa Channel, separating the island of that name from Viti Levu. Daveta Passage leads into Suva Harbour where arriving boats should go to the quarantine anchorage and wait to be cleared.

PS105 *Queensland to Solomon Islands*

BEST TIME:	April to October
TROPICAL STORMS:	December to March
CHARTS:	BA: 780
	US: 622
PILOTS:	BA: 15, 60
	US: 126, 127
CRUISING GUIDES:	*Landfalls of Paradise.*
WAYPOINTS:	

Departure	Intermediate	Landfall	Destination	Distance (M)
PS1051 Moreton NW 26°50'S, 153°20'E	PS1053 Saumarez 21°20'S, 155°00'E			
	PS1054 Mellish 17°30'S, 156°45'E	PS1055 Guadalcanal 9°18'S, 159°30'E	Honiara 9°25'S, 159°58'E	1139
PS1052 Capricorn 22°50'S, 152°00'E	PS1053 Saumarez PS1054 Mellish	PS1055 Guadalcanal	Honiara	986

Although this passage can be made at any time outside of the cyclone season, the months of July and August ought also to be avoided as it is the time when the SE trade winds attain their peak and sailing conditions can be quite rough. Because of the numerous reefs that have to be avoided in the Coral Sea, there are various routes that leave from the Australian coast. Boats leaving from Brisbane should set a course for WP PS1053 to pass safely between Wreck and Saumarez Reefs. The route then passes between Kenn and Frederick Reefs to reach WP PS1054, east of Mellish Reef.

Boats which have reached the open seas through Capricorn Channel from WP PS1052 should set a course for the same waypoint PS1053. The course can then be altered for WP PS1054 to pass east of Mellish Reef. From there a clear route leads to WP PS1055, off the NW tip of Guadalcanal. The capital Honiara is on the west side of the same island. Boats should proceed to the anchorage off Point Cruz Yacht Club and contact Honiara Radio on VHF channel 16 and request clearance.

PS106 *Queensland to Papua New Guinea*

BEST TIME:	April to October
TROPICAL STORMS:	December to March
CHARTS:	BA: 780
	US: 623
PILOTS:	BA: 15, 60
	US: 127, 164
CRUISING GUIDES:	*Landfalls of Paradise, Cruising Guide to Southeast Asia (2).*

WAYPOINTS:

Departure	Intermediate	Landfall	Destination	Distance (M)
Route PS106A				
PS1061 One Half		PS1062 Basilisk SW	Port Moresby	308
14°20'S, 145°30'E		9°33'S, 147°05'E	*9°28'S, 147°09'E*	
Route PS106B				
PS1063 Grafton	PS1064 Bougainville	PS1065 Brumer	Samarai	440
16°35'S, 146°25'E	15°30'S, 147°30'E	10°52'S, 150°15'E	*10°36'S, 150°39'E*	

There are two main routes crossing the Coral Sea from Queensland to Papua New Guinea, one that goes direct to the capital Port Moresby (PS106A), the other to Samarai (PS106B), a small island off the SE extremity of New Guinea. The latter route is taken by those who wish to cruise in the outer islands before heading for Port Moresby and beyond. Because Port Moresby is downwind of all other possible destinations, it is a mistake to go there first as it can be very tough sailing against the boisterous SE trades to reach the smaller islands east of New Guinea. If the destination is one of those islands, Samarai provides a most convenient port of entry.

For the direct passage to Port Moresby from ports in North Queensland it is better to stay inside the Great Barrier Reef until almost due south of Port Moresby. Cairns is the last port in Queensland where exit formalities can be completed and although boats are allowed to day sail inside the Great Barrier Reef after having cleared out of Australia, landing either along the coast or on one of the offlying islands is prohibited.

From Cairns, one has the choice of either taking the inshore route as far as Lizard Island and reaching the open sea through the One and a Half Mile Opening, or going outside the Great Barrier Reef through Grafton or Trinity Passage. In good light the latter can be easily negotiated and is more convenient than Grafton.

The course from the One and a Half Mile Opening (14°25'S, 145°26'E) is free of any dangers all the way to Port Moresby. From WP PS1061 outside of that passage a course can be set for WP PS1062 at the entrance into Basilisk Pass, which leads into Port Moresby. Boats should proceed to the Royal Papua Yacht Club where visiting yachts sometimes find docking space. The captain should then visit the various offices to complete the formalities.

The alternative route to Samarai can leave the Great Barrier Reef by a multitude of passes, Grafton Passage just outside Cairns being one of the best. Because of the direction of the prevailing winds, the more northerly the starting point of this passage, the closer it will be to the wind. As winter passages across the Coral Sea can be quite rough, this is an aspect that should be considered when planning this route. The strong winds coupled with the west-setting current make it necessary to do some easting whenever the winds permit this.

Having left Cairns and gained the open sea through Grafton Passage, from WP PS1063, outside that passage, an initial course is set for WP PS1064, east of Bougainville Island. The route then crosses the Coral Sea to make landfall at WP PS1065, SW of Brumer Island, off the Papuan coast. Sufficient time should be allowed to be able to cover the remaining 30 miles to Samarai in daylight, where entry formalities into Papua New Guinea can be completed. If there is not enough time to reach Samarai in daylight, it is safer to anchor off the mainland coast for the night. A good anchorage can be found behind Deirina Island, close to the Strait.

PS107 *North Queensland to Darwin*

BEST TIME:	May to September			
TROPICAL STORMS:	December to April			
CHARTS:	BA: 4603			
	US: 603			
PILOTS:	BA: 15, 17			
	US: 127, 175			
CRUISING GUIDES:	*Cruising the Coral Coast, Northern Territory Coast.*			
WAYPOINTS:				

Departure	Intermediate	Landfall	Destination	Distance (M)
PS1071 One Half 14°20'S, 145°30'E	PS1072 Ashmore 10°00'S, 145°08'E PS1073 9°23'S, 145°00'E PS1074 Bligh 9°15'S, 144°00'E PS1075 Thursday *10°34'S, 142°06.5'E* PS1076 Arafura 10°30'S, 132°20'E PS1077 Bathurst 11°10'S, 130°00'E		 Darwin *12°30'S, 130°51'E*	 1312

There are two alternatives to reach Australia's Northern Territory from its east coast, either by an inshore route that keeps close to the coast and stays inside the Great Barrier Reef or an offshore route that goes through the Torres Strait using the main shipping channels. The inside route is well buoyed, so it can be done nonstop and night sailing, although difficult, is not impossible. However, most yachts sail this route in day hops as there are plenty of anchorages or small ports in which to stop for the night. Having passed the top of Australia at Cape York, the Sea of Arafura is reached through the intricate Endeavour Strait.

Those who wish to sail offshore will have to use one of the passes through the Great Barrier Reef to reach the open sea. The safest, but also longest, way through the Torres Strait is through the main shipping channel, which is well lit and buoyed. To join this channel, from WP PS1071 outside the One and a Half Mile Opening north of Lizard Island the route leads almost due north to WP PS1072 passing halfway between Eastern Fields and Ashmore

Reef. Maintaining a northerly heading to WP PS1073, the course is then altered for WP PS1074, SE of Bramble Cay in Bligh Entrance, the gateway into Torres Strait. From there, the main shipping channel should be followed to reach the Arafura Sea. The well marked channel runs in a SW direction for 130 miles to the Prince of Wales Channel. From there, the rest of the route to Darwin is the same as that for boats having taken the inshore route. From PS1075, west of Thursday Island, a westerly course leads clear of all dangers to WP PS1076. From there the course can be altered to pass through Dundas and Clarence Straits, although the longer route around both Melville and Bathurst Islands is recommended. From WP PS1077, NW of Bathurst Island, a southerly course leads past Cape Fourcroy in the approaches to Darwin, from where a buoyed channel leads into the harbour. Arriving boats should contact Darwin Port Authority on VHF channel 16 or HF 2182 kHz and then proceed to Fishermen's Wharf for clearance.

14
WINDS AND CURRENTS OF THE NORTH INDIAN OCEAN

The winds and weather of the entire Indian Ocean are dominated by the monsoons, which although affecting primarily the northern half of the ocean also have a bearing on the weather pattern of the tropical South Indian Ocean. The NE monsoon prevails when the sun has a southern declination and the SW monsoon when the sun's declination is north.

Northeast monsoon

A predominantly NE wind blows during the winter months in the North Indian Ocean, Bay of Bengal, and the Arabian Sea. The wind is very steady and constant over most parts of the North Indian Ocean, blowing with an average 10–15 knots, its strength diminishing towards the equator. On rare occasions the monsoon can reach gale force, but for most of the time sailing conditions can be described as near perfect as possible. There are two areas in which the monsoon is less reliable and the winds more variable. In the Arabian Sea, north of latitude 20°N, the weather pattern is sometimes affected by the passage of depressions to the north of the area. The other area lies to the SE of Sri Lanka, between latitude 5°N and the equator, where winds are less constant in strength and direction, the normal direction of the wind being northerly. Further east, in the Malacca Strait, the monsoon is also less pronounced than elsewhere.

The NE monsoon lasts from November to March, beginning earlier in the northern part of the region where it is well established by the middle of November. Towards the equator it does not arrive in full strength until December. The winter monsoon is preceded and followed by a transitional period as it is replaced by the SW monsoon and vice versa. This transitional period coincides with the movement across the region of the Intertropical Convergence Zone which separates the air masses of the northern and southern hemispheres. The ITCZ is most active in April–May and October–November, which are also the months when most cyclonic storms occur over the North Indian Ocean. During this transitional period the weather is often squally and the winds can reach gale force in these squalls. Otherwise this period can be compared to the doldrums of other oceans, with light winds and calms, which are gradually replaced by the coming monsoon. This doldrum belt is not so distinctly defined as in the Atlantic and Pacific Oceans.

Southwest monsoon

The heating of the Asian land mass during the summer months creates a large area of low pressure over the NW part of the Indian subcontinent. This causes the SE trade wind of the South Indian Ocean to be drawn across the equator where it joins the general movement of air that flows in a anticlockwise direction around the area of low pressure lying over India. This is the SW monsoon which is felt from June to September in the same areas as its NE counterpart. The SW monsoon is a consistent wind blowing at an average 20 knots for long periods and frequently reaching gale force. An area lying about 200 miles to the east of Socotra Island is reputed to be the windiest spot in the Indian Ocean with a frequency of gales in July similar to that of Cape Horn in summer! The winds diminish gradually in strength during August, and by September both the strength of the wind and its direction become less constant. In October and November, the winds are often light until the arrival of the NE monsoon. The weather during the SW monsoon is overcast and often unsettled with heavy rainfall.

Tropical storms

Tropical storms or cyclones occur in the Arabian Sea and the Bay of Bengal. The two periods of the year when their frequency reaches a maximum coincide with the transitional period between the two monsoons. The first period of cyclonic activity is at the beginning of the SW monsoon from late May to the middle of June. The second period coincides with the onset of the NE monsoon and lasts from the end of October to the second half of November. Most of these storms form in the vicinity of the ITCZ when it is situated between latitudes 5°N and 15°N.

Most of the storms that occur in May and June are bred in the Arabian Sea from where they move either in a NW and W direction, or in a N direction recurving towards the NE and the coast. Some of the cyclones that form in October and November in the Bay of Bengal move westward across South India into the Arabian Sea. Both in the Arabian Sea and Bay of Bengal, October has the highest frequency of cyclones. Their frequency decreases in November and they are rare in December and January, none having been recorded in February and March. After the middle of April the likelihood of a cyclone begins to increase.

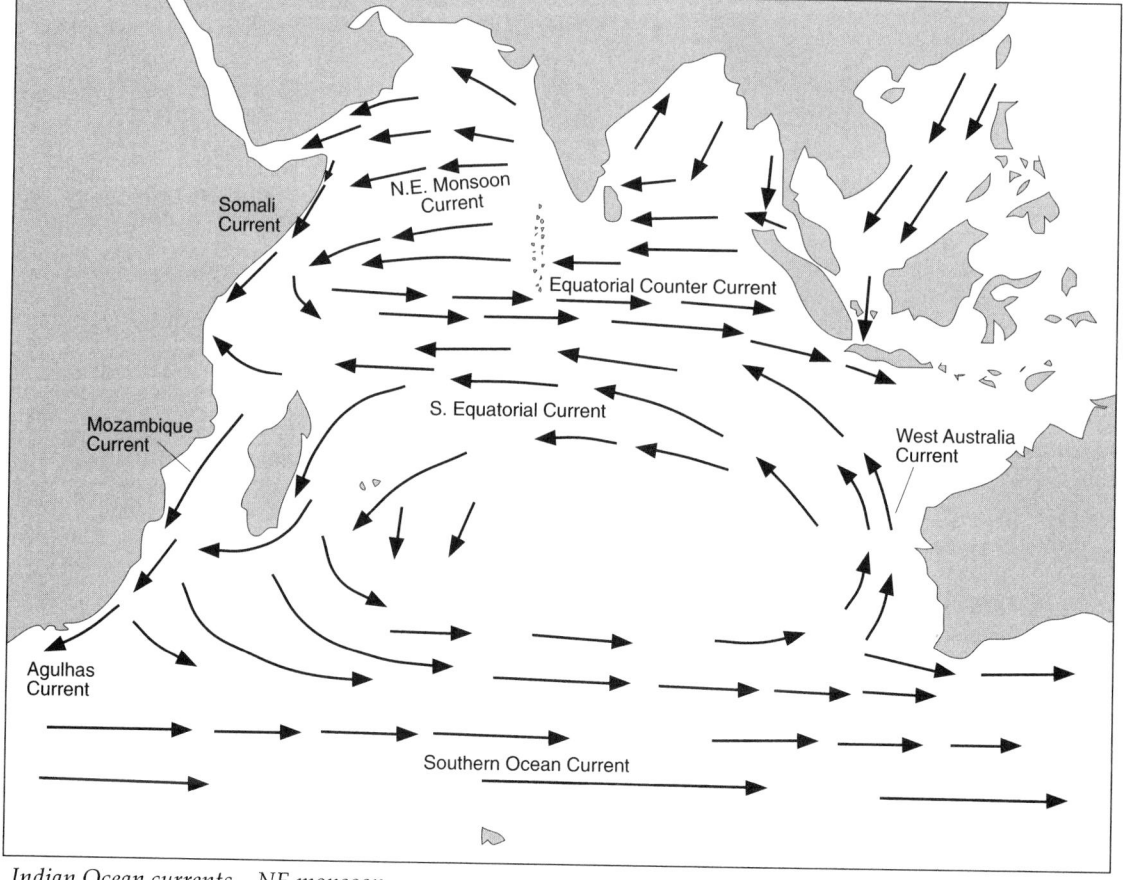

Indian Ocean currents – NE monsoon

Currents

The currents of the North Indian Ocean follow a seasonal pattern because of the monsoons and reverse their direction under their influence. The Northeast Monsoon Current occurs during the NE monsoon and reaches its peak in February. It is located between the equator and latitude 6°N and has a westward set. Its counterpart is the Southwest Monsoon Current which occurs from May to September and can be considered to be a continuation of the Somali Current. This current can attain very high rates, especially off the coast of Somalia and in the vicinity of Socotra, where some of the strongest sets in the world have been recorded, with rates of up to 7 knots. Although the initial set is NE, the current becomes east in the open waters of the Arabian Sea until it reaches the landmass of India and turns SE.

At the time of the NE monsoon, the Somali Current flows SW along the African coast as far as the equator where it meets the north flowing East Africa Coast Current. In December and January, the current turns east and becomes the Equatorial Countercurrent.

The Equatorial Countercurrent is the only current of the North Indian Ocean which does not reverse its direction as a result of the monsoons. However, its strength is reinforced during the transitional periods between the two monsoons in April–May and October–November. It sets east throughout the year and lies to the north of the west-setting Equatorial Current. The Equatorial Countercurrent reaches its southern limit in February, at the height of the NE monsoon, when it sometimes flows very close to the Northeast Monsoon Current. This means that by moving slightly to the north or south, it is possible to shift from a west-setting to an east-setting current. The southern limit of the Countercurrent is always south of the equator, regardless of season.

15

ROUTES IN THE NORTH INDIAN OCEAN

Compared to the other two great oceans of the world, the Indian Ocean is crisscrossed by a relatively small number of cruising routes. One reason for this is the smaller number of sailing boats that spend any length of time cruising as opposed to crossing this ocean as part of a world voyage. The routes are governed by the predictability of the weather, the seasons being much better defined than anywhere else. The regularity of the monsoons was recognised by early navigators who knew how to take full advantage of the seasonal wind patterns. Because of this regularity it is very easy to plan a voyage well in advance so as to make a particular passage at the optimum time. This applies both to the northern half of the ocean, which is dominated by the NE and SW monsoons, and to its southern half which is under the influence of the SE trade winds.

There are two major routes crossing the Indian Ocean, both of which start from the Torres Strait. For those who wish to cruise in the Mediterranean or intend to reach southern Europe by the shortest route, the logical way leads through the North Indian Ocean and Red Sea. For those who wish to reach the Atlantic by way of the Cape of Good Hope, the direct route leads across the South Indian Ocean to South Africa.

Most other routes in the Indian Ocean are variations of the above two. For boats sailing in the North Indian Ocean, the harbour of Galle in Sri Lanka continues to be a popular port of call which does not seem to have been affected by political troubles in that country. Most boats arrive in Galle from Thailand or Malaysia. They are mostly bound for the Red Sea and have waited in SE Asia to make the crossing of the North Indian Ocean at the optimum time.

In spite of India's many attractions, most cruising boats continue to bypass this great country,

mostly because of the complicated and lengthy formalities to which visiting yachts are submitted by Indian officials. For similar reasons, few boats venture into any of the Gulf states.

The favourable season for a passage across the North Indian Ocean is during the NE monsoon, when almost perfect sailing conditions can be expected. Although this season lasts from December to March, passages made in January and February have the advantage that the Mediterranean is reached after the coldest weather is over and the cruising season is beginning.

The Bay of Bengal has typical monsoon weather. The NE monsoon begins in October in northern areas and is established only in November further south. It blows steadily with fine dry weather until April, when the weather becomes hot, still, and oppressive. The SW monsoon only establishes itself around the middle of June, but quickly becomes strong, around 20–25 knots and blows steadily until August when it starts to decrease, disappearing in October. Cyclones are more numerous in the Bay of Bengal than in any other area of the Indian Ocean, although they are sometimes shorter and less severe. They can occur from April through to December, but are most frequent in July and October at the change of monsoons.

Weather conditions are very similar in the Arabian Sea and it is the seasonal winds of this sea which gave rise to the word 'monsoon' meaning season. As in other parts of the North Indian Ocean, the NE monsoon has the better weather. The wet season coincides with the SW monsoon, which commences in May in the south and spreads over the whole area by June. There is usually squally weather at the monsoon changeover. On the Indian coast the SW monsoon arrives with a sudden burst of wind from the east, heavy rain and thunder for several hours before the SW winds take over. This burst of the monsoon is preceded by a week of vivid lightning which disappears every day when the sun sets. The SW winds in the Arabian Sea are very strong and can blow at 30 knots for several days. There is a very high frequency of gale force winds especially near the island of Socotra during the month of July. In September the winds start weakening and the monsoon breaks up and disappears by October.

Cyclones occur at two periods of the year which coincide with the monsoon changeover. April to July is one period, with the highest frequency in June, while October has the highest frequency in the other period, although cyclones can occur from September through until December. Most cyclones curve NW to strike the shores of the Arabian Peninsula or else tend to recurve to the NE towards India and Pakistan.

The NE monsoon lasts from October to April, although the winds are diverted to blow more easterly into the Gulf of Aden, blowing SE or S through the Bab el Mandeb Strait into the Red Sea. From June until August the SW monsoon takes over, blowing strongest in July with frequent winds around 30 knots. During the SW monsoon, a strong local land breeze called the *kharif* blows for up to 30 miles off the African coast. Reinforcing the SW wind, it can reach gale force during the night and is very dry, full of dust and sand off Africa. In a similar fashion a strong N or NW wind called the *belat* blows off the Arabian coast from December to March. Again it starts at night, is full of dust and sand, and can reach 30 knots in some coastal areas. There is sometimes poor visibility due to haze or mist, especially along the Arabian coast during the SW monsoon. Very rarely cyclones stray with little warning from the Arabian Sea into the Gulf of Aden. The dangerous months are June and October.

Note: Navigators are warned that the position of the Maldive Islands do not agree with current GPS observations and therefore the islands should be approached with utmost care. It is stressed that any waypoints are only given as guidelines and should not be relied upon when making landfall.

IN10 ROUTES FROM SOUTHEAST ASIA

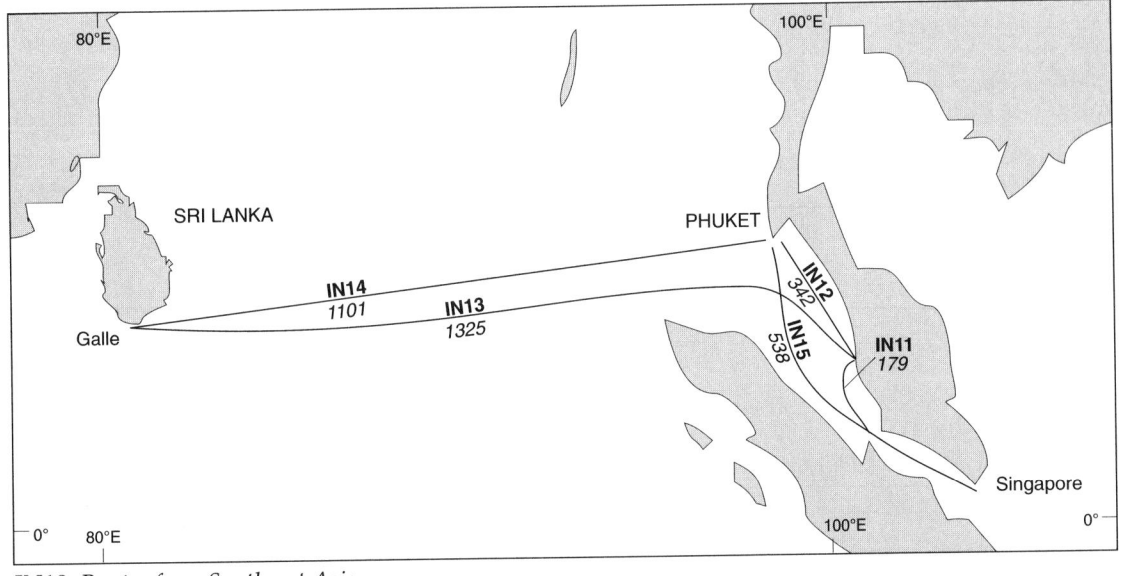

IN10 *Routes from Southeast Asia*

The main cruising route leads from Singapore through the Malacca Strait into the Bay of Bengal. It is used mostly by boats on a world voyage from the South Pacific to the North Indian Ocean and the Red Sea. They are joined in Singapore by boats coming from the countries of the Far East, mostly from Hong Kong and the Philippines. The number of boats sailing through Southeast Asia in the opposite direction is much smaller. Pacific routes from Singapore are described on page 283.

Being so close to the equator, Singapore has a hot and humid climate, which varies little throughout the year. Calms and light winds occur throughout the year. The NE monsoon begins in November, although the NE winds are deflected and appear at the beginning of this period as a NW monsoon. By January NE winds are established but they do not blow as strongly or as steadily as over the South China Sea. From April onwards the SE trade winds penetrate from south of the equator, the winds often having a southerly component. Between April and November the area is affected by *sumatras*, thundery storms with strong winds, which blow across from Sumatra and last for several hours.

Although within the monsoon areas of the Indian Ocean, the weather in the Malacca Strait is highly influenced by local conditions, and variable winds with regular land and sea breezes occur at all times of the year. The SW monsoon is blocked by the high island of Sumatra, while the Malaysian peninsula does the same to the NE monsoon. January to March normally has the best weather, fewer squalls, and less rain as the NE monsoon penetrates into the area. Even in this season it is possible to get NW or W winds for some days. March and April are variable and the SW monsoon starts early in May, being strongest in July and August. The SW winds are strongest in the northern portions of the Malacca Strait, variable from SE to SW with calms in the centre and more SE in southern areas towards Singapore.

Sea and land breezes occur on both shores of the Malacca Strait and up to 20 miles offshore. The sea breeze begins about mid-morning and reaches a maximum in the afternoon, dying away at sunset. The strength of the breeze can be augmented to 20 knots if it combines with the prevailing monsoon or can remain light and variable if the monsoon opposes the breeze. Conditions vary greatly from place to place. On the Malaysian coast the night land breeze can be very strong, starting in the evening and sometimes blowing hard all night. Further up the coast towards Thailand, the SW monsoon blows more steadily and strongly than in the Malacca Strait, lacking the shielding effect of the large island of Sumatra. SW winds dominate from May to September with their maximum steadiness in July and August. On the other hand the high landmass of Thailand shelters this coast from the NE monsoon, which tends to have a more northerly component than elsewhere. Very rarely, about once every fifty years, tropical storms come across from the Bay of Bengal and reach the Gulf of Siam.

IN11 *Singapore to Western Malaysia*

BEST TIME:	October to November, April			
TROPICAL STORMS:	None			
CHARTS:	BA: 1355			
	US: 707			
PILOTS:	BA: 21, 44			
	US: 174			
CRUISING GUIDES:	*Phuket and Malacca Straits Guide.*			
WAYPOINTS:				
Departure	*Intermediate*	*Landfall*	*Destination*	*Distance (M)*
Route IN11A				
IN111 Channel W	IN112 Muar			
1°14'N, 103°30'E	1°57'N, 102°30'E			
	IN113 Panjang N	IN114 Klang S	Port Klang	179
	2°09'N, 102°15'E	2°50'N, 101°15'E	*3°00'N, 101°23'E*	

Departure	Intermediate	Landfall	Destination	Distance (M)
Route IN11B IN115 Klang N 3°20'N, 101°00'E	IN116 Sembilan 4°00'N, 100°27'E IN117 Penang S 5°09'N, 100°10'E	IN118 Langkawi S 6°08'N, 99°45'E	Bass Harbour *6°18'N, 99°50'E*	198

Although a passage through Malacca Strait can be undertaken throughout the year, the most settled weather is during the NE monsoon, when the frequency of squalls is much lower than during the opposite season. The notorious *sumatras* are more frequent during the SW monsoon, and because they are accompanied by heavy rain and gale force winds they can make navigation difficult, the situation being also complicated by the large amount of shipping.

Another feature of navigation in Malacca Strait are the strong tidal currents which, combined with the normally light winds, make it more convenient to anchor between tides than to try and sail against the current. This can be easily done as there are anchoring depths all along the sides of the strait and there are sufficient protected places where one can stop for a few hours. The Malaysian side is preferable if this passage is done in shorter stages. Light winds and calms are more frequent during the day, so it is better to sail at night when breezes are steadier and the weather is generally more pleasant. One hazard, however, that is almost impossible to avoid at night are the numerous fish traps that line the two sides of the strait, so it is a good idea to keep out of shallow water during the hours of darkness.

Very few, if any, voyages along the west coast of Malaysia are made without stopping and for this reason this route has been divided into two, with a break at Port Klang where most northbound boats usually interrupt their journey. There are several ports between Malacca and Penang that can be visited by northbound boats from Singapore. Entry formalities for Malaysia can be completed at Malacca, where it is possible to come alongside other boats moored on the banks of the river. Taking WP IN111, at the entrance into the Malacca Strait, as a point of departure, the route runs parallel to the Malaysian coast to WP IN112. A first stop can be made at Muar (2°02'N, 102°34'E), which is an official port of entry into Malaysia. Alternatively, one may continue to WP IN113, off Panjang Island, in the approaches to Malacca (2°15'N, 102°35'E). WP IN114 brings one to the south entrance to the channel leading into Port Klang, Malaysia's main port serving the capital Kuala Lumpur. South Klang Strait leads into the port, where the Royal Selangor Yacht Club is located on its eastern side (3°00.3'N, 101°23.5'E). Visiting boats may use the facilities of the yacht club, whose office will also assist with the clearance formalities.

Northbound boats will leave the port through North Klang Strait and pick up the offshore route at WP IN115. The route continues parallel to the Malaysian coast to WP IN116 west of the Sembilan Islands. Ten miles further north, the island of Pangkor hides the entrance into Dindings river and the small town of Lumut. If a stop in Penang is not intended, the route continues offshore of that island. Otherwise, WP IN117 marks the entrance into South Channel, which leads to the narrows separating Penang from the mainland. Access under the bridge joining Penang to the mainland is prohibited without written permission, so if one does not have such permission, one should either anchor south of the bridge or use North Channel. To clear into Malaysia at Penang, one has to visit Customs in Georgetown, whereas the Immigration Office is in Butterworth on the mainland. For most northbound boats, the last stop in Malaysia will be the island of Langkawi, whose main attraction is that it is a duty-free area. WP IN118 is off Tyson Strait leading into the perfectly protected Bass Harbour.

IN12 *Western Malaysia to Thailand*

BEST TIME:	October to November, April
TROPICAL STORMS:	None
CHARTS:	BA: 4707
	US: 707
PILOTS:	BA: 21, 44
	US: 173, 174
CRUISING GUIDES:	*Sail Thailand, Phuket and Malacca Straits Guide.*
WAYPOINTS:	

Departure	Intermediate	Landfall	Destination	Distance (M)
IN121 Penang N 5°30'N, 100°15'E	IN122 Langkawi SW 6°08'N, 99°45'E		Bass Harbour *6°18'N, 99°50'E*	54
IN121 Penang N	IN123 Langkawi W 6°15'N, 99°40'E			
	IN124 Butang 6°34'N, 99°24'E	IN125 Phuket S 7°47'N, 98°25'E	Ao Chalong *7°49'N, 98°21.5'E*	180

The best season for this route is during the NE monsoon, when the weather is most settled, although winds for this northbound passage are not always favourable. The main cruising attraction on Thailand's west coast is the island of Phuket and the surrounding area.

Boats leaving from Georgetown, Penang's main town and harbour, should use North Channel to reach the open sea. As most northbound boats stop in Langkawi on their way to Thailand, from Penang and WP IN121 the course leads to WP IN122 off Tyson Strait, which opens into Bass Harbour. Whether stopping in Langkawi or continuing directly to Phuket, from WP IN123, west of Langkawi, a course can be set for WP IN124, halfway between Besi and Tenga islands in the Butang group, which belong to Thailand. From there the route continues in a NW direction past several offlying islets and rocks to WP IN125, off Ao Chalong and Phuket harbour. Boats can anchor in the well protected bay at Ao Chalong, from where the captain has to make his own way into Phuket Town to complete entry formalities. Alternatively one can continue north for another five miles into Ban Nit Marina, which is reached via a one mile long channel.

IN13 *Western Malaysia to Sri Lanka*

BEST TIME:	January to March
TROPICAL STORMS:	May to June, October to November
CHARTS:	BA: 4707
	US: 707
PILOTS:	BA: 38, 44
	US: 170, 173, 174
WAYPOINTS:	

Departure	Intermediate	Landfall	Destination	Distance (M)
Route IN13A IN131 Penang N 5°30'N, 100°15'E	IN133 Rondo 6°15'N, 95°10'E			
	IN134 Dondra 5°50'N, 80°35'E	IN135 Galle E 5°59'N, 80°15'E	Magalle *6°01.9'N, 80°13.7'E*	1210

443

Departure	Intermediate	Landfall	Destination	Distance (M)
Route IN13B IN132 Langkawi SW 6°10'N, 99°45'E	IN133 Rondo IN134 Dondra	IN135 Galle E	Magalle	1177

The best passages along this route are made between January and March, when the NE monsoon blows consistently over the North Indian Ocean. The passage should not be undertaken too early before the monsoon has had time to establish itself, as steady winds can rarely be relied upon before the middle of December. A start from Singapore or Malaysia in early January has the best chance of excellent winds both on the leg to Sri Lanka and on to the Red Sea. Much less favourable conditions will be encountered during the transitional period, in April and October–November, when westerly winds are quite common and there is a high risk of cyclones in the Bay of Bengal.

This passage is not recommended during the SW monsoon, both on account of the contrary winds and the danger of cyclones in the Bay of Bengal. Although boats have tried to reach Sri Lanka during the SW monsoon by sailing on a southerly course after passing the northern extremity of Sumatra, in the hope of making their westing south of the equator, this is an extremely difficult passage and should be avoided if at all possible. A more logical alternative is to reach the Indian Ocean from Singapore via Sunda Strait and then follow directions as for route IT12 (page 462).

During the NE monsoon boats leaving from ports in the south of the Malacca Strait or even Singapore should sail on the Malaysian side until the north of Sumatra can be fetched on the starboard tack. There are two convenient ports from which boats

normally set off on this passage, both of them being located on islands off the Malaysian coast. Boats leaving from Penang (route IN13A) will reach the open sea through North Channel and take their departure from WP IN131. Another popular departure point is Langkawi (route IN13B), in which case the passage will start from WP IN132, in Tyson Strait. The direct route to the southern tip of Sri Lanka passes between Rondo and Great Nicobar Island. From either of those departure points a course should be set for WP IN133. It is normally possible to call at Sabang, a small port on the island of Wé (5°53'N, 95°19'E), off the northern coast of Sumatra, where yachts have been allowed to stop briefly even if they were not in the possession of an Indonesian cruising permit. Having passed Sumatra, from WP IN133 the course is altered for WP IN134, off Dondra Head, the southern tip of Sri Lanka. The island's south coast is then followed to Galle, which is entered through the Eastern Channel. The town of Galle is on the west side of the large bay, whereas the small port is in the NE corner of the bay in a part of the town called Magalle. The entrance into the port is difficult to find in the dark, so arrivals should be either timed for daylight or one can anchor for the night in the NE corner of the bay and enter the port the following morning. The services of a local agent are required to complete the necessary fomalities and such an agent will normally visit the boat soon after arrival.

IN14 *Thailand to Sri Lanka*

BEST TIME:	January to March
TROPICAL STORMS:	May to November
CHARTS:	BA: 4707
	US: 707
PILOTS:	BA: 21, 38
	US: 170, 173

WAYPOINTS:				
Departure	Intermediate	Landfall	Destination	Distance (M)
Route IN14A				
IN141 Phuket SW	IN142 Nicobar			
7°44'N, 98°19'E	6°30'N, 93°50'E			
	IN144 Dondra	IN145 Galle E	Magalle	1101
	5°50'N, 80°35'E	5°59'N, 80°15'E	*6°01.9'N, 80°13.7'E*	
Route IN14B				
IN141 Phuket SW	IN143 Sombrero			
	7°38'N, 93°35'E			
	IN144 Dondra	IN145 Galle E	Magalle	1096

At the height of the NE monsoon, between January and March, the winds along this route can be perfect and some of the most pleasant passages have been experienced on this route. Directions are very similar to those given for route IN13.

Taking one's departure from Phuket at WP IN141, east of Ko Keonoi, there is a choice of routes to pass either to one side or the other of the Nicobar Islands. WP IN142, south of Great Nicobar, offers the easier option and is the recommended route (IN14A). The alternative (IN14B) is to set course for WP IN143, north of Little Nicobar, and pass through Sombrero Channel. The disadvantage of the latter is that there will be more dangers to avoid and also more small boat traffic, especially at night.

The Nicobars belong to India and cruising boats have not been allowed to stop there in the past.

Having passed the Nicobars, the course can be altered for WP IN144, off Dondra Head, the southern tip of Sri Lanka. From there, the route runs parallel to the island's south coast to Galle Harbour, which is entered through Eastern Channel. Approaching Galle from the east, especially at night, Goda Gala rocks, SE of the harbour, should be given a wide berth and the bay approached from the south. The town of Galle is on the west side of the large bay, whereas the small port is in the NE corner of the bay in Magalle. Boats are normally met by an agent whose services are needed to complete entry formalities.

IN15 *Thailand to Singapore*

BEST TIME:	December to April			
TROPICAL STORMS:	None			
CHARTS:	BA: 1355	US: 707		
PILOTS:	BA: 21, 44	US: 173, 174		
CRUISING GUIDES:	*Cruising Guide to Southeast Asia.*			
WAYPOINTS:				

Departure	Intermediate	Landfall	Destination	Distance (M)
Route IN15A				
IN151 Phuket S	IN152	IN156 Penang N	Georgetown	201
7°47'N, 98°25'E	6°00'N, 99°00'E	5°30'N, 100°15'E	*5°25'N, 100°20.5'E*	
	IN155			
	4°00'N, 100°00'E			
	IN157	IN158 Channel W	Singapore	538
	2°55'N, 100°55'E	1°14'N, 103°30'E	*1°16'N, 103°50'E*	
Route IN15B				
IN151 Phuket S	IN153 Butang	IN154 Langkawi	Bass Harbour	129
	6°34'N, 99°24'E	6°15'N, 99°40'E	*6°18'N, 99°50'E*	

The west coast of Thailand south of Phuket can be cruised throughout the year as it is not affected by the cyclones that originate in the Bay of Bengal, although the more pleasant weather occurs during the NE monsoon. During the SW monsoon the weather is sultry and hot and the frequency of squalls is higher. Sailing conditions along the Malaysian coast and in the Malacca Strait are also better during the NE monsoon. In both seasons the main current has a northerly set.

Although a passage through Malacca Strait can be undertaken throughout the year, the best weather conditions will be experienced during the NE monsoon, when the frequency of squalls is much lower than during the opposite season. Also less frequent are the notorious *sumatras*, which can make navigation very difficult in these busy waters as the squalls are accompanied by heavy rain and gale force winds. As mentioned earlier, another feature of navigation in Malacca Strait is the strong tidal currents which, combined with the normally light winds, make it more convenient to anchor between tides. This can easily be done as there are anchoring depths all along the Malaysian shore and there are sufficient protected places where one can stop for a few hours. The Malaysian side is preferable if this passage is done in shorter stages. Light winds and calms are more frequent during the day, so it is better to sail at night when breezes are steadier. One hazard which is almost impossible to avoid at night are the numerous fish traps that line the two shores. It is therefore recommended to sail in deeper waters during the hours of darkness.

On leaving Phuket, southbound boats have the choice of either taking an inshore route (IN15B) and stopping in a number of conveniently placed ports along the Malaysian shore, or staying offshore (IN15A). Leaving from WP IN151, south of Phuket, the offshore route goes to WP IN152. If planning to stop in Langkawi, the nearest port of entry into Malaysia, the inshore route is taken to WP IN153, halfway between Besi and Tenga islands in the Butang group. From there the course can be altered for WP IN154, off the west coast of Langkawi. While the offshore route continues to WP IN155, those wishing to stop at Penang should set course for WP IN156, at the entrance into North Channel leading to Georgetown.

The density of shipping traffic increases as one moves towards Singapore, and by the time the offshore route has reached WP IN157 one should be prepared for a lot of shipping. The route continues to WP IN158, at the entrance into the Singapore Channel. The new Raffles Marina, on the west shore of Singapore Island, is the best place to make for in this, the busiest port in the world.

Although most cruising boats prefer the west coasts of Malaysia and Thailand, a number of yachts have ventured recently along the east coasts of these two countries which face the South China Sea. There are many attractive fishing harbours along the coast from Singapore to the Gulf of Siam. Because that coast is exposed to easterly winds, it is better to sail there during the SW monsoon. See route PN41 (page 284) for more details.

IN20 ROUTES FROM SRI LANKA AND THE MALDIVES

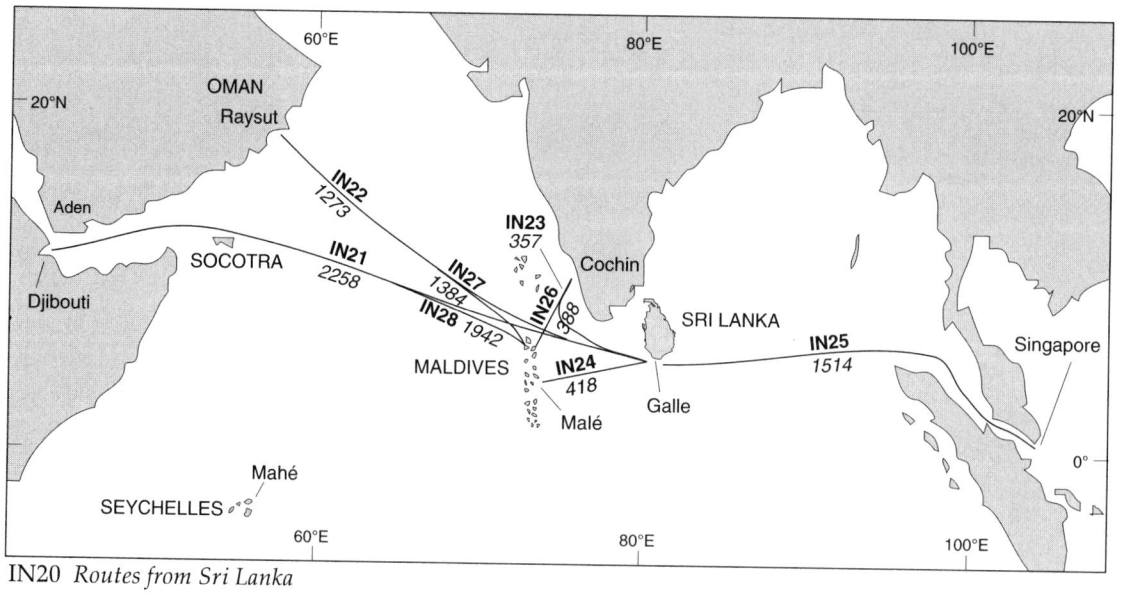

IN20 *Routes from Sri Lanka*

Sri Lanka occupies such a strategic position at the crossroads of the North Indian Ocean that few boats pass it by without stopping. Because the capital Colombo is a busy commercial harbour, all cruising boats call at Galle, on the southern tip of the island. The usual time to arrive is at the height of the NE monsoon, in January and February, when the small port is full to capacity. Because most world voyagers are westbound towards the Red Sea and Suez Canal, eastbound passages are rather rare although there are a few boats arriving in Sri Lanka from the Red Sea or East Africa. Those who plan to sail eastwards across the North Indian Ocean must wait for the SW monsoon, which provides excellent sailing conditions even if at times the winds might be too strong for some people's liking. Although most boats passing through Sri Lanka are in a hurry to reach the Red Sea, some use the island as a convenient starting point for a cruise among the islands scattered around the centre of the Indian Ocean. Because of their position, the Maldives fulfil this role even better, although they suffer from a general absence of yachting facilities. As the Maldives are attracting increasingly more cruising boats, this is now being put right by the creation of a yacht base at Giraavaru. This is a small island inside North Malé Atoll, where a passage has been cleared through the reef to give access to the deep Giraavaru lagoon, where there are moorings, fuel and some facilities for cruising yachts.

The NE monsoon only sets in at the end of November or even in December, arriving with squally weather and rain. The moderate NE winds prevail with fine dry weather until March or April. The SW monsoon lasts longer than elsewhere, beginning in May and lasting right through until December. The SW monsoon often commences with a 'monsoon burst', a blast of east wind that arrives with rain, thunder and lightning after a week of large clouds and vivid lightning which disappear after sunset. The SW winds are fairly constant in direction, usually strengthening to 20–35 knots by mid-morning and slackening off in the late afternoon, dropping to around 10 knots during the night. Heavy rain occurs on the SW coast from May to September. The south coast is affected by heavy swell during the SW monsoon. Although rarely hit by cyclones originating in the Arabian Sea, which move to the NW, those which originate in the Bay of Bengal can strike Sri Lanka, most frequently in the months of November and December.

IN21 *Sri Lanka to Red Sea*

BEST TIME:	January to March			
TROPICAL STORMS:	April to May, October to November			
CHARTS:	BA: 4071			
	US: 71			
PILOTS:	BA: 38, 64			
	US: 170, 172, 173			
CRUISING GUIDES:	*Red Sea Pilot.*			
WAYPOINTS:				

Departure	Intermediate	Landfall	Destination	Distance (M)
Route IN21A				
IN211 Galle W	IN212 Eight			
6°01'N, 80°13'E	7°50'N, 73°00'E			
	IN213 Socotra NE	IN214 Tadjoura	Djibouti	2258
	13°20'N, 54°30'E	11°40'N, 43°13'E	*11°36.5'N, 43°07.5'E*	
Route IN21B				
IN211 Galle W	IN212 Eight			
	IN213 Socotra NE	IN215 Yemen SE	Aden	2146
		12°44'N, 45°00'E	*12°48'N, 44°58'E*	

At the height of the NE monsoon, when the average wind strength is between 10 and 15 knots, this passage can be truly delightful. There is also a favourable current and the frequency of gales in the North Indian Ocean is nil. Winds become lighter towards March and at such times it is advisable to leave Sri Lanka with a good reserve of fuel. The one problem to worry about is the large amount of shipping, either converging into the Gulf of Aden, or crossing to and from the Persian Gulf.

Having left Galle Harbour through the Western Channel, boats bound for Djibouti (route IN21A) from WP IN211 can set an initial course for WP IN212 to pass through the Eight Degree Channel, 20 miles south of Minicoy Island. The route then crosses the Arabian Sea to WP IN213, 30 miles NE of Socotra Island. If the winds allow it, Socotra should be passed to the north and at least 30 miles off, due to the apparent unfriendliness of its inhabitants. After the middle of March, if SW winds are experienced near the island, it may be necessary to pass south of Socotra and between it and the African coast.

From WP IN213 a course can be set for WP IN214, in the Gulf of Tadjoura. The route passes south of the Musha islands and then turns SW towards the port of Djibouti avoiding the various dangers, all of which are marked by buoys. The recommended anchorage (11°36.1'N, 43°08.1'E) is off the Djibouti Yacht Club whose facilities may be used by visiting boats. The various authorities are in the nearby commercial harbour and must be visited to complete entry formalities.

From WP IN123, boats bound for Aden (route IN21B) should set a course for WP IN125, at the entrance into the port of Aden. A marked channel leads into the Inner Harbour, where yachts anchor off the customs dock. Boats are normally met on arrival by a port control launch and directed to the anchorage.

This passage is not normally undertaken during the SW monsoon and it should not even be considered. The only alternative is to cross the equator and make one's westing with the help of the SE trade winds, possibly south of the Chagos Archipelago, before recrossing the equator. As such a route runs close to the Seychelles, directions would be similar to those for route IT16 (page 466).

IN22 *Sri Lanka to Oman*

BEST TIME:	January to March			
TROPICAL STORMS:	May to June, October to November			
CHARTS:	BA: 4071			
	US: 71			
PILOTS:	BA: 38, 64			
	US: 170, 172, 173			
WAYPOINTS:				

Departure	Intermediate	Landfall	Destination	Distance (M)
PN221 Galle W 6°01'N, 80°13'E	IN222 Nine S 9°00'N, 73°00'E	IN223 Oman SE 16°52'N, 54°05'E	Raysut *16°56'N, 54°00'E*	1273

Rather than sail nonstop to the Red Sea, a few boats break the voyage on the way, Oman providing one of the few places where this is possible. The course after leaving Galle at WP IN221 leads to WP IN222, south of the Laccadive Islands in the middle of the Nine Degree Channel. Occasionally boats have stopped at Sueli Par, an atoll on the north side of the channel. A course can then be set for WP IN223, five miles SE of the entrance into Raysut harbour.

The weather during the NE monsoon is very pleasant and the passage from Sri Lanka usually enjoys excellent winds. The passage should not be made before the end of the year to allow the monsoon to establish itself.

Although the Sultanate of Oman does not encourage tourism, cruising boats that make the detour to stop there are treated courteously. Foreign boats are only allowed to stop in Raysut (Mina Razute), an excellently protected harbour. Those who have had the foresight to arrive with visas may move around the country freely, those without have to observe a curfew and are only allowed outside the port area during daylight hours on working days (Saturday to Wednesday).

IN23 *Sri Lanka to India*

BEST TIME:	December to February			
TROPICAL STORMS:	May to June, October to November			
CHARTS:	BA: 4706			
	US: 706			
PILOTS:	BA: 38			
	US: 173			
WAYPOINTS:				

Departure	Intermediate	Landfall	Destination	Distance (M)
IN231 Galle W 6°01'N, 80°13'E	IN232 Comorin 7°45'N, 77°20'E			
	IN233 Tangaserri 8°50'N, 76°25'E	IN234 Cochin SW 9°55'N, 76°12'E	Cochin *9°58'N, 76°15'E*	357

Mainly because of considerable bureaucratic hurdles, only a small number of yachts include India in their cruising plans. Although the NE monsoon has more settled weather, the high proportion of NW winds make it difficult to reach most ports on the west coast of the Indian subcontinent during this monsoon. Coastal navigation is made somewhat easier between December and February by alternating land and sea breezes which make it possible to take long tacks along the coast. When sailing along the coast at night it is almost impossible to avoid the numerous fishing nets and small boats without lights that are a feature of this coast. During the hours of darkness it is safer to stay a few miles offshore.

The northbound passage is not easier during the SW monsoon when the weather is often unsettled. One alternative is to reach NW India towards the end of the SW monsoon, in September, and sail down the coast with the help of the NW winds and south-setting current that occur at the change of seasons. During the NE monsoon constant, light northerly winds will be experienced as far north as Cochin. For this reason few boats venture further north than Cochin, where it is possible to leave the boat under guard and travel inland.

Having left Galle Harbour through the Western Channel, from WP IN231, a course can be set for WP IN232, 20 miles south of Cape Comorin, the southern tip of India. In strong winds and big seas,

this point should be rounded further offshore as the seas tend to get very rough in its vicinity. The route then swings north parallel to the coast to WP IN233, off Tangaserri Point. Another course alteration is made for WP IN234, SW of the entrance into Cochin harbour. Entering the well protected port at night is possible, although the lights on several buoys have been reported as not working. Arriving yachts should contact Cochin Port Authority on VHF channel 16 and anchor off the north tip of Willingdon Island, where a customs launch will come to start entry formalities. The Port Authority should be contacted from the entrance buoy into Cochin channel, reported at approximately 9°57.7'N, 76°10'E. The quarantine anchorage (9°58.2'N, 76°15.4'E) is off the Malabar Hotel.

IN24 *Sri Lanka to Maldives*

BEST TIME:	January to March				
TROPICAL STORMS:	None				
CHARTS:	BA: 4707 US: 707				
PILOTS:	BA: 38 US: 173				
WAYPOINTS:					
Departure	*Intermediate*	*Landfall*	*Destination*		*Distance (M)*
IN241 Galle W	IN242 North Malé	IN243 Malé E	Malé		418
6°01'N, 80°13'E	4°18'N, 73°40'E	4°10'N, 73°33'E	*4°10'N, 73°30'E*		

This passage is best made during the NE monsoon when winds are mostly favourable. Contrary winds and a strong east-setting current are the order of the day for a passage during the SW monsoon, and even during the transitional months the winds are often westerly. Tropical storms very rarely touch the Northern Maldives and the danger of encountering a cyclone along this route is remote. The Maldives should be approached with great caution both because they are all low lying islands and because of the strong currents.

From WP IN241 outside Galle harbour a direct course leads to North Malé Atoll. If heading

straight for the capital Malé (the only port of entry), landfall should be made at WP IN242, south of Mirufenfushi and Diffushi, two low islets marking the easternmost point of North Malé Atoll. The course can then be altered for WP IN243, 2.5 miles east of Malé Passage that leads into the large lagoon. Port Control should be contacted on arrival on VHF channel 16. Entry formalities may now be completed at Giraavaru, a small island inside North Malé Atoll, where a passage has been cleared through the reef to give access to the deep Giraavaru lagoon. Moorings, fuel and some facilities are now available there for visiting yachts.

IN25 Sri Lanka to Singapore

BEST TIME:	July to September			
TROPICAL STORMS:	May to November			
CHARTS:	BA: 4707 US: 707			
PILOTS:	BA: 38, 44 US: 170, 173, 174			
CRUISING GUIDES:	*Cruising Guide to Southeast Asia.*			
WAYPOINTS:				

Departure	Intermediate	Landfall	Destination	Distance (M)
Route IN25A				
IN251 Galle SE	IN252 Dondra			
5°58'N, 80°15'E	5°50'N, 80°35'E			
	IN253 Nicobar			
	6°15'N, 95°10'E			
	IN254 Malacca N			
	5°00'N, 99°10'E			
	IN255	IN256 Channel W	Singapore	1514
	2°55'N, 100°55'E	1°13'N, 103°20'E	*1°16'N, 103°50'E*	
Route IN25B				
IN251 Galle SE	IN252 Dondra			
	IN253 Nicobar	IN257 Penang N	Georgetown	1206
		5°30'N, 100°15'E	*5°25'N, 100°20.5'E*	
Route IN25C				
IN251 Galle SE	IN252 Dondra			
	IN253 Nicobar			
	IN254 Malacca N	IN258 Klang N	Port Klang	1323
		3°20'N, 101°00'E	*3°00'N, 101°24'E*	

The recommended time for this passage is during the SW monsoon, although at its height the winds may be rather too strong. The transition months may provide better sailing conditions, but they also carry the higher risk of cyclones. Although the cyclone season in the Bay of Bengal extends over the entire SW monsoon period, at the height of the monsoon the development of tropical storms is opposed by the strong monsoon; the few cyclones between July and September normally stay well to the north of the area crossed by this route.

In the Malacca Strait the SW monsoon is usually blocked by the land mass of Sumatra and better winds are therefore found on the Malaysian side of the strait. Sailing along that shore is in any case recommended as one can clear into Malaysia at a number of ports, whereas a stop in Sumatra necessitates the compulsory Indonesian cruising permit. The one notable exception is Sabang, on Pulau Wé, a small island off the northern tip of Sumatra

where boats have been allowed to stop briefly even without a permit. Because of the strong tidal currents in Malacca Strait, it is usually better to anchor between tides. The SW winds are strongest in the northern portions of the Malacca Strait, variable from SE to SW with calms in the centre, and more SE in southern areas towards Singapore.

Sea and land breezes occur on either coast and up to 20 miles offshore. The sea breeze begins about mid-morning and reaches a maximum in the afternoon, dying away at sunset. The strength of the breeze can be augmented to 20 knots if it combines with the prevailing monsoon. On the Malaysian coast the night land breeze can be very strong, starting in the evening and sometimes blowing hard all night. Between April and November the area is affected by *sumatras*, thundery storms with gale force winds, which blow across from Sumatra and last for several hours.

Having left Galle harbour through the Eastern

Channel, from WP IN251 the route follows Sri Lanka's south coast to WP IN252, off Dondra Head, the southern tip of the island. The route then crosses the Bay of Bengal to WP IN253, south of Great Nicobar Island. If the intention is to sail nonstop to Singapore, the course should be altered for WP IN254 at the entrance into Malacca Strait. The offshore route (IN25A) continues to WPs IN255 and IN256, at the entrance into the Singapore Channel. The new Raffles Marina, on the west shore of Singapore Island, is the best place to stop in this extremely busy port.

Boats intending to visit some of Malaysia before reaching Singapore can clear in at Penang (IN25B). From WP IN253, the course should be altered for

WP IN257, at the entrance into North Channel leading to Georgetown, the main town on the island. The customs office is in Georgetown, whereas the immigration office is on the mainland, at Butterworth. When leaving Penang, boats must not pass under the bridge joining Penang to the mainland without written permission.

Alternatively, boats intending to sail direct to Port Klang (IN25C) from WP IN254 should alter course for WP IN258, at the northern entrance into Klang Strait. This leads into Port Klang, which serves Malaysia's capital Kuala Lumpur. Visiting boats may use the facilities of the Royal Selangor Yacht Club in Port Klang, located on the eastern shore of the harbour.

IN26 *Maldives to India*

BEST TIME:	December April–May			
TROPICAL STORMS:	May to June, October to November			
CHARTS:	BA: 4703			
	US: 703			
PILOTS:	BA: 38			
	US: 173			
CRUISING GUIDES:	*Indian Ocean Handbook.*			
WAYPOINTS:				
Departure	*Intermediate*	*Landfall*	*Destination*	*Distance (M)*
IN260 Malé	IN261 Malé E			
4°10'N, 73°30'E	*4°10'N, 73°33'E*			
	IN262 North Malé	IN262 Cochin SW	Cochin	388
	4°18'N, 73°40'E	*9°55'N, 76°12'E*	*9°58'N, 76°15'E*	

Although best sailing conditions in the North Indian Ocean coincide with the NE monsoon of winter, on this route strong head winds make it imperative to sail at a time when the monsoon is not yet fully established. Better winds will be found during the SW monsoon, but one should be careful not to sail into the Arabian Sea during the local cyclone season. A simpler solution is to choose a port of departure closer to India among the Northern Maldives.

As none of these are official ports of entry, this needs to be cleared with the authorities in the capital, Malé. If leaving from the latter, during the NE monsoon it is probably better to stay east

of the islands, so as to benefit from a better sailing angle.

Although not an official port of entry, northbound cruising boats have been able to make a brief stop at Turakunu Island (7°06'N, 72°54'E) inside Ihavandiffulu Atoll. The local authorities will request permission by radio from Malé, or this should be arranged before leaving the capital. On arrival in Cochin, the Port Authority should be contacted on channel 16 from the entrance buoy into Cochin channel, reported at approximately 9°57.7'N, 76°10'E. Boats are directed to the quarantine anchorage (9°58.2'N, 76°15.4'E) off the Malabar Hotel, north of Willingdon Island.

IN27 *Maldives to Oman*

BEST TIME:	January to March			
TROPICAL STORMS:	May to June, October to November			
CHARTS:	BA: 4705			
	US: 705			
PILOTS:	BA: 38, 64			
	US: 172, 173			
CRUISING GUIDES:	*Indian Ocean Handbook.*			
WAYPOINTS:				

Departure	Intermediate	Landfall	Destination	Distance (M)
IN270 Malé *4°10'N, 73°30'E*	IN271 Wadu *4°09'N, 73°20'E* IN272 Toddu *4°40'N, 73°00'E* IN273 Ari *4°40'N, 72°30'E*	IN274 Oman SE *16°52'N, 54°05'E*	Raysut *16°56'N, 54°00'E*	1384

Excellent weather conditions will be experienced during the NE monsoon of winter and the only hazard on this route is the large amount of shipping, especially where the lanes converge on to the entrance into the Perisan Gulf.

During the NE monsoon, boats leaving from Malé should make their way north of Toddu and Ari atolls. From there a clear course leads across the Arabian Sea to make landfall off the Omani coast. Visiting boats must proceed into the well protected Raysut harbour. Those who arrive with visas will be free to visit the country, while those without will be confined to the port area during nights and local weekends (Thursday to Saturday). As the number of local yachts is increasing, repair facilities are better than expected.

IN28 *Maldives to Red Sea*

BEST TIME:	January to March			
TROPICAL STORMS:	May to June, October to November			
CHARTS:	BA: 4703, 4704			
	US: 703, 704			
PILOTS:	BA: 38, 64			
	US: 172, 173			
CRUISING GUIDES:	*Indian Ocean Handbook, Red Sea Pilot.*			
WAYPOINTS:				

Departure	Intermediate	Landfall	Destination	Distance (M)
IN270 Malé *4°10'N, 73°30'E*	IN271 Wadu *4°09'N, 73°20'E* IN272 Toddu *4°40'N, 73°00'E* IN273 Ari *4°40'N, 72°30'E* IN274 Socotra NE *13°20'N, 54°30'E*	IN275 Tadjoura *11°40'N, 43°13'E*	Djibouti *11°36.5'N, 43°07.5'E*	1942
		IN276 Yemen SE *12°44'N, 45°00'E*	Aden *12°48'N, 44°58'E*	1823

Best sailing conditions on this route prevail during the winter months, when the NE monsoon ensures a most pleasurable passage. On leaving the Maldives one needs to decide whether to pass north or south of Socotra. The recommended route leaves the island to port and passes some 30 miles to the north, although, depending on weather conditions, passing between Socotra and the African mainland is an acceptable alternative. However, one should try to stay well away both from Socotra and the Somali coast.

Most cruising boats prefer nowadays to use Djibouti as an intermediate port to prepare for the passage through the Red Sea. Indeed, facilities in Djibouti are better, there is a welcoming yacht club and formalities are also simpler. Djibouti also has the advantage of regular flights to Paris, thus making crew changes easier. Stopping in Aden is also feasible – and although repair facilities are very basic, one will be able to provision here for the onward passage.

IN30 ROUTES IN THE ARABIAN SEA

Most small boat traffic in the Arabian Sea is westbound and the busiest routes are those sailed by boats using the NE monsoon to reach the Red Sea from Sri Lanka or the Maldives. Eastbound voyages are far less common and, outside the months of January and February, sailing boats are quite a rarity. The mostly unpleasant weather encountered during the SW monsoon is not the only reason why most sailors avoid the North Indian Ocean in summer. The other reason is the less than friendly

reception extended to cruising yachts in many of the countries bordering on the Arabian Sea.

The seasonal winds of this sea gave us the word 'monsoon' and both the NE and SW monsoons blow with great strength and constancy over this area. The NE monsoon begins in November and is the time of fair weather. In the northern areas it can be more N than NE and even NW. It blows at an average 10 to 15 knots at the beginning of the season. The winds increase to 15 to 20 knots in

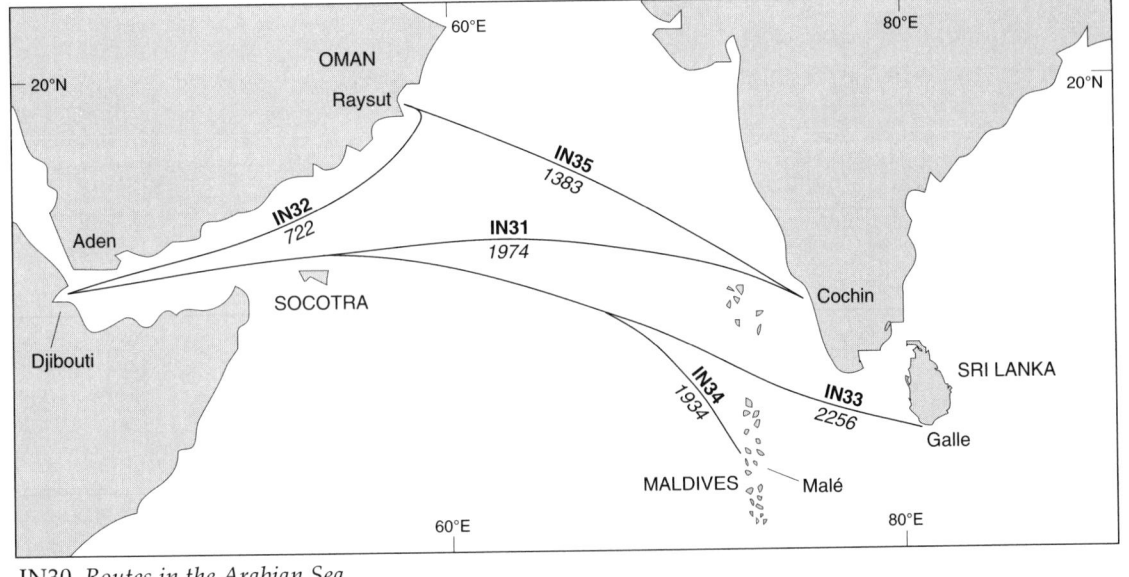

IN30 *Routes in the Arabian Sea*

December and can be even stronger in the north. The wet season coincides with the SW monsoon, which commences in May in the south and spreads over the whole area by June. The weather can be very squally at the monsoon changeover. On the Indian coast, the SW monsoon arrives with a sudden burst of wind from the east, heavy rain, and thunder for several hours before the SW winds take over. This burst of the monsoon is preceded by a week of vivid lightning which disappears every day at sunset. The SW winds in the Arabian Sea are very strong and can blow at gale force for several days. There is a high frequency of gales near

the island of Socotra in July. In September the winds start weakening and the monsoon breaks up and disappears by October.

Cyclones occur at two periods of the year which coincide with the monsoon changeover. April to July is one period with a high frequency, with June having the highest incidence of cyclones. October has the highest frequency in the other period, although cyclones can occur from September through until December. Most cyclones curve NW to strike the shores of the Arabian Peninsula or else tend to recurve to the NE towards India and Pakistan.

IN31 *India to Red Sea*

BEST TIME:	December to February
TROPICAL STORMS:	May to June, October to November
CHARTS:	BA: 4705
	US: 705
PILOTS:	BA: 38, 64
	US: 172, 173
CRUISING GUIDES:	*Red Sea Pilot.*
WAYPOINTS:	

Departure	Intermediate	Landfall	Destination	Distance (M)
IN311 Cochin W 9°55'N, 76°12'E	IN312 Nine N 9°50'N, 72°00'E			
	IN313 Socotra NE 13°20'N, 54°30'E	IN316 Tadjoura 11°40'N, 43°13'E	Djibouti *11°36.5'N, 43°07.5'E*	1974
IN311 Cochin W	IN312 Nine N IN314 Socotra S 11°30'N, 53°40'E			
	IN315 12°30'N, 50°00'E	IN316 Tadjoura	Djibouti	1968
IN311 Cochin W	IN312 Nine N IN313 Socotra NE	IN317 Yemen SE 12°44'N, 45°00'E	Aden *12°48'N, 44°58'E*	1860

A direct route to the Red Sea can be sailed from anywhere on the west coast of India at the height of the NE monsoon, from December to the beginning of March. After the middle of March the winds are less constant and there is a higher percentage of calms in the Arabian Sea. Towards the end of the NE monsoon choosing the best route through this area becomes crucial as there is an increased chance of contrary winds close to Socotra Island. In April it is advisable to steer for a point 50 miles south of Socotra so as to be able to clear the Horn

of Africa comfortably as the current is also setting north towards Socotra at this time.

From WP IN311, outside Cochin Harbour, the route runs due west through the Nine Degree Channel staying south of Kalpeni and Suheli Par. Occasionally boats have been able to stop briefly in the latter, which is an atoll with a well protected lagoon. From WP IN312 a course can be set for IN313, 30 miles NE of Socotra Island. After the middle of March, if SW winds are experienced near the island, it may be necessary to pass south of

Socotra and between it and the African coast. In such a case, from WP IN312 a course should be set for WP IN314 south of Socotra. Having sailed past Cape Guardafui, at WP IN315 the northern route is rejoined for the port of destination, as described below.

From WP IN313, if the intention is to sail to Djibouti, course should be set for WP IN316, in the Gulf of Tadjoura. The route goes south of the Musha Islands and then turns SW towards the port of Djibouti. The recommended anchorage is off the Djibouti Yacht Club whose facilities may be used by visiting boats. Entry formalities are completed in the nearby commercial harbour.

From WP IN313, boats bound for Aden should sail for WP IN317, at the entrance into the port of Aden. A marked channel leads into the Inner Harbour, where yachts anchor off the customs dock. Boats are normally met on arrival by a port control launch and directed to the anchorage.

A direct passage across the North Indian Ocean is virtually impossible during the SW monsoon, from May to September, when the only alternative is to make a long detour south of the equator via the Chagos Archipelago. This route passes NE of the Seychelles and recrosses the equator in about longitude 53°00'E. See also route IT16 Seychelles to Red Sea (page 466).

IN32 *Oman to Red Sea*

BEST TIME:	January to March			
TROPICAL STORMS:	May to June, October to November			
CHARTS:	BA: 4705			
	US: 705			
PILOTS:	BA: 64			
	US: 172			
CRUISING GUIDES:	*Red Sea Pilot.*			
WAYPOINTS:				
Departure	*Intermediate*	*Landfall*	*Destination*	*Distance (M)*
IN321 Raysut SW	IN322 Fartak	IN323 Yemen SE	Aden	611
16°53'N, 53°58'E	15°00'N, 52°20'E	12°44'N, 45°00'E	*12°48'N, 44°58'E*	
IN321 Raysut SW	IN322 Fartak	IN324 Tadjoura	Djibouti	722
		11°40'N, 43°13'E	*11°36.5'N, 43°07.5'E*	

Excellent sailing conditions prevail during the NE monsoon, January and February being the best months to head for the Red Sea. Because of a higher percentage of calms near land, the initial course from Raysut should lead offshore. The proportion of SW winds increases towards the end of March when a contrary current also starts making itself felt parallel to the Arabian coast. The passage should not be undertaken during the SW monsoon, when strong headwinds make it almost impossible to reach the Red Sea along this route. During the

transitional period between monsoons, the area is subject to tropical storms.

From WP IN321, three miles SW of Raysut, an initial course is set for WP IN322, south of Ras Fartak. The route runs parallel to the coast all the way to Aden as far as WP IN323 in the approaches to Aden. Boats bound for Djibouti will continue to WP IN324 south of the Musha Islands in the Gulf of Tadjoura, in the approaches to the port of Djibouti. See IN31 for further details on both Aden and Djibouti.

IN33 *Red Sea to Sri Lanka*

BEST TIME:	September				
TROPICAL STORMS:	May to June, October to November				
CHARTS:	BA: 4071				
	US: 71				
PILOTS:	BA: 38, 64				
	US: 172, 173				
WAYPOINTS:					

Departure	Intermediate	Landfall	Destination	Distance (M)
IN331 Tadjoura 11°40'N, 43°13'E	IN333 Socotra N 13°30'N, 54°00'E			
	IN334 Eight 7°50'N, 73°00'E	IN336 Galle W 6°01'N, 80°13'E	Magalle 6°01.9'N, 80°13.7'E	2256
IN332 Yemen SE 12°44'N, 45°00'E	IN333 Socotra N			
	IN335 Nine N 9°50'N, 72°00'E	IN336 Galle W	Magalle	2148

Choosing the time for this passage presents a major dilemma, as the cyclone free months of July and August also have the highest frequency of gales. In fact the frequency of gales in July just to the east of Socotra is similar to that off Cape Horn in summer. As passages across the Arabian Sea can be extremely rough at the height of the SW monsoon, only September offers the prospect of a reasonably comfortable voyage. The transition periods between the two monsoons cannot be recommended either because of the risk of cyclones, although an April passage has a good chance of fair winds and a lower risk factor.

The course from either Djibouti or Aden passes well to the north of Socotra to avoid the strong west-setting current along the African coast in the Gulf of Aden. From WP IN331 south of the Musha Islands in the Gulf of Tadjoura, a course can be set for WP IN333 north of Socotra. Boats leaving from Aden take their departure from WP IN332 and use the same intermediate WP IN333 north of Socotra. Sri Lanka can be reached through either the Nine or Eight Degree Channels, which are separated by Minicoy Island. Whichever channel is used it should be approached with caution, especially at night or in the thick weather which is sometimes associated with the SW monsoon.

Landfall will be made at WP IN336, just outside Galle Harbour, from where Western Channel leads to the small port in the NE part of the bay. Boats are usually met by a local agent whose services are necessary to complete entry formalities.

IN34 *Red Sea to Maldives*

BEST TIME:	September
TROPICAL STORMS:	May to June, October to November
CHARTS:	BA: 4071
	US: 71
PILOTS:	BA: 38, 64
	US: 172, 173
CRUISING GUIDES:	*Indian Ocean Handbook.*

WAYPOINTS:				
Departure	Intermediate	Landfall	Destination	Distance (M)
IN341 Tadjoura 11°40'N, 43°13'E	IN342 Socotra N 13°30'N, 54°00'E IN343 Ari 4°40'N, 72°30'E IN344 Toddu 4°40'N, 73°00'E	IN345 Wadu 4°09'N, 73°20'E	Malé 4°10'N, 73°30'E	1934

Directions are very similar to those for route IN33 and a course for Malé, the capital and port of entry for the Maldives, should only be set after having passed well to the north of Socotra. The low lying Maldives should be approached with extreme caution because of the strong current that sets on to the islands during the SW monsoon. It is indeed crucial that WP IN344 is reached in the morning so that the remaining distance to Malé can be covered during daylight hours.

From WP IN342 north of Socotra, the route leads to WP IN343, north of Ari Atoll. To reach the capital Malé, the route continues east to pass north of Toddu Atoll. At WP IN344, it turns SE towards WP

IN345 at the entrance into Wadu Channel. This leads to Malé, which is reached through Malé Passage. In good light it may be possible to reach Malé by entering North Malé Atoll through one of its western passes. The Port Authority should be contacted on VHF channel 16 on arrival. As Malé is the only official port of entry, boats are not allowed to stop anywhere before having cleared in there. Entry formalities may now be completed at Giraavaru, a small island inside North Malé Atoll, where a passage has been cleared through the reef to give access to the deep Giraavaru lagoon. Moorings, fuel and some facilities are now available there for visiting yachts.

IN35 *India to Oman*

BEST TIME:	January to March			
TROPICAL STORMS:	May to June, October to November			
CHARTS:	BA: 4705 US: 705			
PILOTS:	BA: 38, 64 US: 172, 173			
CRUISING GUIDES:	*Indian Ocean Handbook.*			
WAYPOINTS:				
Departure	Intermediate	Landfall	Destination	Distance (M)
IN350 Cochin 9°58'N, 76°15'E	IN351 Cochin W 9°58'N, 76°12'E IN352 Suheli 9°55'N, 72°15'E	IN352 Oman SE 16°52'N, 54°05'E	Raysut 16°56'N, 54°00'E	1383

With the NE monsoon ensuring good sailing conditions throughout the winter months, Cochin, or any other port on the west coast of India, will make a good point of departure. The direct route from Cochin passes right through the low islands and shallows of the Lakhadweep Archipelago, so the recommended route heads initially due west

before the course is altered for Raysut, once all dangers have been cleared.

On arrival in Oman, visiting boats must proceed to Raysut (Mina Razute) to complete formalities. Although visas are not compulsory for those arriving by yacht, one's movements are restricted to the port area for those arriving without a visa.

16
TRANSEQUATORIAL ROUTES IN THE INDIAN OCEAN

From Indonesia in the east to Kenya in the west, the equator is crossed by a variety of routes used mostly by northbound boats. Because of the finely matched seasons in the two hemispheres of the Indian Ocean, with careful planning it is possible to cruise throughout the year, always having the benefit of favourable weather. Over the centuries the Arab dhows set a perfect example of how to use the prevailing weather conditions to best advantage. Although their trading routes do not always coincide with those used by modern cruising yachts, today's sailors have much to learn from those skilled mariners, some of whom are still plying the coasts of Arabia and East Africa.

IT10 NORTHBOUND ROUTES

For centuries Arab dhows have sailed from the Persian Gulf to the East African coast to trade, sailing down on one monsoon and back on the other, although in present day Kenya and Tanzania they are becoming a rare sight. The SE trade winds blow steadily from April to October and rarely exceed 20 knots. The wide band of the northbound current runs close to the shore and can be augmented by these SE trade winds so as to reach 4 knots. Therefore it makes sense to plan any northbound passages to coincide with this season. During the NE monsoon, when winds from the NE and E prevail, this current is slacker. Along the Tanzanian coast it is possible to take an inshore route that stops inside the reefs and various offshore islands.

Boats intending to set off on a northbound transequatorial passage should time this to take best advantage of the monsoons on either side of the equator. From December to March, when the ITCZ moves south, the NE monsoon is deflected across the equator to give a NW flow of wind. This NW monsoon is not so reliable and brings rain. It blows most strongly in January and February. This period is also the cyclone season in the South Indian Ocean, but these storms normally form south of Chagos and move in a southerly direction. They almost never track north towards the equator.

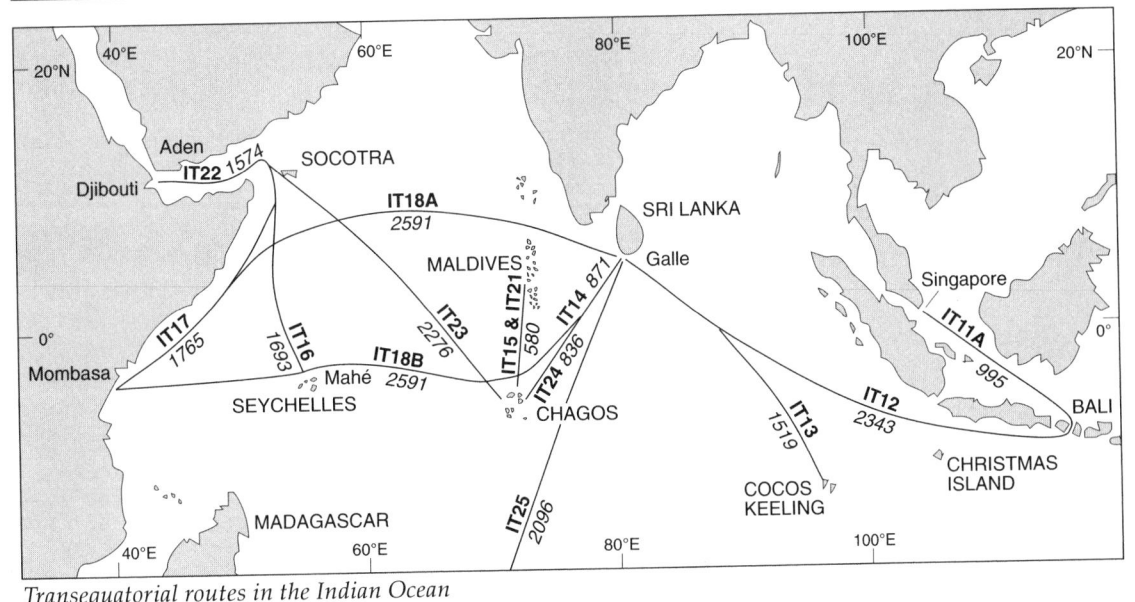

Transequatorial routes in the Indian Ocean

IT11 *Bali to Singapore*

BEST TIME:	May to September			
TROPICAL STORMS:	None			
CHARTS:	BA: 4508			
	US: 508			
PILOTS:	BA: 34, 36, 44			
	US: 163, 174			
CRUISING GUIDES:	*Cruising Guide to Southeast Asia.*			
WAYPOINTS:				

Departure	Intermediate	Landfall	Destination	Distance (M)
Route IT11A				
IT110 Bali E	IT111 Lombok			
8°43'S, 115°11.5'E	8°24'S, 115°47'E			
	IT112 Karang			
	7°03'S, 114°53'E			
	IT113 Bawean E			
	5°45'S, 113°00'E			
	IT114 Karimata			
	3°30'S, 109°30'E			
	IT115 Mombarang			
	2°30'S, 109°10'E			
	IT116 Ontario			
	2°07'S, 108°38'E			
	IT117 Lingga			
	0°00', 106°00'E			
	IT118 Mapor	IT119 Channel S	Singapore	995
	1°00'N, 105°00'E	1°20'N, 104°40'E	*1°16'N, 103°50'E*	

Departure	Intermediate	Landfall	Destination	Distance (M)
Route IT11B				
IT110 Bali E	IT111 Lombok			
	IT112 Karang			
	IT1110 Bawean SE			
	6°00'S, 112°30'E			
	IT1111 Bangka		Singapore	1010
	3°50'S, 107°00'E			

There are two main routes that can be sailed from Bali to Singapore, either direct through the Karimata Strait (IT11A) or by the more indirect route via Bangka and Riouw Straits (IT11B). The first route is faster and can be done nonstop as it is mostly offshore, the second route is slower and offers the possibility of overnight stops if the winds are not favourable. The second route is not recommended for those who do not possess an Indonesian cruising permit. For both routes the best time is during the South Indian SE monsoon and the North Indian SW monsoon, between May and September. During the transitional months of April, October, and early November, winds are more variable and calms frequent. During these months there is also a high frequency of rain squalls, often of torrential proportions, that make it difficult to anchor every night in safety and make the offshore route more attractive.

On leaving Benoa the course leads NE through the Lombok Strait where extremely strong currents can be experienced. During the SE monsoon the main direction of the currents is southerly, although at certain times a favourable current sets NE along the east coast of Bali. This current occurs approximately at the time of the moon's transit and lasts for two or three hours so it is worth timing a departure for two hours before the transit and leave Benoa at slack water.

From WP IT110, outside Benoa Harbour, the offshore route (IT11A) sets off in a NE direction through Selat Badung (Badung Channel), NW of Nusa Lembongan, as far as WP IT111, off Bali's easternmost point. From there the route turns NW to cross the Bali Sea to pass through the 10 mile wide gap between Goagoa island and Karang Takat Reef at WP IT112. As neither of these dangers are lit, one should attempt to pass through this area during daylight. Bearing in mind the distances involved, a good tactic is to leave Benoa around noon so as to pass WP IT111 before nightfall, cross

the Bali Sea at night and arrive at WP IT112 the following morning. An alternative way to reach the Java Sea, especially at night, is to use Sapudi Strait, east of Madura Island, which has lights on Sapudi island itself.

Having reached the Java Sea the route continues in a NW direction and passes east of Bawean Island through WP IT113 to WP IT114 at the entrance into Karimata Strait, east of Borneo (Kalimantan), a wide body of water encumbered by many unlit reefs. The position of some of these do not necessarily agree with GPS observations, so the area should be treated with great caution. Strong currents of up to 2 knots have been reported, their direction depending on the monsoon and setting predominantly N or NW from May to September and S or SE from November to March. The route goes to WP IT115 before the course is altered for WP IT116 halfway between Ontario and Flying Fish reefs. The route continues in a NW direction and crosses the equator at WP IT117. Bintan Island is passed to the east by making for WP IT118 before the course can be altered for Singapore Strait. The area E and NE of Bintan should be passed in daytime as there are often fishing nets set up in those waters. At night it is therefore advisable to stay further offshore.

There is a choice of channels at the eastern entrance into the Singapore Strait. Coming from the SE, the most convenient is South Channel, between the north coast of Bintan and Horsburgh Reef. To reach it, from WP IT118 the course should be altered for WP IT119. From this point, it is equally easy to pass through either South or Middle Channel.

Route IT11B leads through Bangka Strait, the narrows between Sumatra and Bangka islands. Directions for reaching the Java Sea are similar to those given above. Once the Java Sea has been reached, from WP IT112 a course can be set for WP IT1110, SE of Bawean Island. The route continues in a NE direction to WP IT1111, in the approaches to Bangka Strait. The direction of the wind in the strait is usually parallel to the coast, although strong SW winds can be experienced towards the end of the SE monsoon. Because of the nature of the tidal currents in the strait, it is better to stay close to the coast of Sumatra during the SE monsoon.

North of Bangka Strait it is possible to follow either a direct or an indirect route to Singapore. The former leads outside Lingga island to Riouw Strait and because it is easily navigable it is used by most boats. The indirect route follows the coast of

Sumatra through Berhala and Pengelap Straits and joins the direct route for the final approach to Singapore through Riouw Strait. A slightly more indirect route leads to Singapore from SW through Durian Strait and Phillip Channel.

Boats arriving in Singapore from the SE may find it easier to anchor off the Changi Yacht Club, NE of Singapore Island, and complete entry formalities from there. The alternative is the new Raffles Marina (1°20.53'N, 103°38.22'E), on the W coast of Singapore Island. Yet another option is to go only as far as the new Nongsa Marina on Bintan Island.

IT12 *Bali to Sri Lanka*

BEST TIME:	September to mid-October				
TROPICAL STORMS:	May to July, October to November (Bay of Bengal)				
CHARTS:	BA: 4071				
	US: 71				
PILOTS:	BA: 34, 38, 44				
	US: 163, 173, 174				
CRUISING GUIDES:	*Indian Ocean Handbook.*				
WAYPOINTS:					
Departure	*Intermediate*	*Landfall*	*Destination*		*Distance (M)*
Route IT12A					
IT121 Bali S	IT122 Java SW				
8°55'S, 115°12'E	7°30'S, 105°00'E				
	IT123				
	5°00'S, 95°00'E				
	IT124	IT125 Galle S	Magalle		2358
	0°00'N, 85°00'E	6°00'N, 80°14'E	*6°01.9'N, 80°13.7'E*		
Route IT12B					
IT121 Bali S	IT122 Java SW				
	IT126 Sumatra SW				
	4°30'S, 100°00'E				
	IT127				
	0°00', 96°30'E				
	IT128 Dondra	IT129 Galle E	Magalle		2343
	5°50'N, 80°35'E	5°59'N, 80°15'E			

This is a more direct route to reach the North Indian Ocean than route IT11 and is used mainly by those who are on their way to the Red Sea and wish to avoid sailing via Singapore and the Malacca Strait. If the port of departure is Bali it is best to head immediately offshore and sail south of Java. In September or early October the SE trade winds will provide favourable winds to about latitude 5°S, but because winds tend to be more consistent further south it is advisable not to set a direct course for Sri Lanka until

longitude 95°E has been reached, as both contrary winds and currents are more likely to be encountered closer to Sumatra. The transitional period from the SW to the NE monsoon provides the best conditions for this route. If the passage is made at the height of the SW monsoon, all necessary westing should be made south of latitude 5°S, as strong westerly winds will make it very difficult to reach Sri Lanka on a direct course. During the SW monsoon route IT12A should be sailed.

From WP IT121, south of Benoa harbour, the route runs south of both Bali and Java to WP IT122. If SE winds persist, one should continue in the same direction to WP IT123. Depending on weather conditions, the equator should be crossed as far west as possible and in any case not sooner than meridian 85°E has been reached (WP IT124). From this point a direct course can be set for Galle and WP IT125, south of Galle harbour which is entered through the Central Channel. The town of Galle is on the west side of the large bay, whereas the small port, where entry formalities are completed, is in the NE corner in Magalle.

This passage is not recommended during the NE monsoon when mostly contrary winds will be met, especially south of the equator. If such a passage during the NE monsoon cannot be avoided (route IT12B), northing should be made in the lee of Sumatra by sailing not more than 50 miles west of the offlying islands. From WP IT122 SW of Java, the course should be altered for WP IT126 so as to follow a course parallel to the west coast of Sumatra. The NW course parallel to Sumatra may be continued after the equator has been crossed at WP IT127. The course should be changed for Sri Lanka only after favourable conditions have been found north of the equator. Directions for route IT13 should also be consulted as they refer to the same area of the Indian Ocean.

IT13 *Cocos Keeling to Sri Lanka*

BEST TIME:	September			
TROPICAL STORMS:	May to July, October to November (Bay of Bengal)			
CHARTS:	BA: 4707			
	US: 707			
PILOTS:	BA: 34, 44			
	US: 170, 173			
CRUISING GUIDES:	*Indian Ocean Handbook.*			
WAYPOINTS:				

Departure	Intermediate	Landfall	Destination	Distance (M)
Route IT13A				
IT131 Keeling	IT132			
12°04'S, 96°50'E	4°00'S, 80°00'E			
	IT133	IT134 Galle S	Magalle	1712
	0°00', 80°00'E	6°00'N, 80°14'E	*6°01.9'N, 80°13.7'E*	
Route IT13B				
IT131 Keeling	IT135			
	0°00', 90°00'E			
	IT136 Dondra	IT137 Galle E	Magalle	1519
	5°50'N, 80°35'E	5°59'N, 80°15'E		

Although this passage can be made at any time of the year, most people who undertake it intend to continue their voyage towards the Red Sea and therefore plan to arrive in Sri Lanka on the eve of the NE monsoon. For this reason the timing of this passage should be carefully calculated, because passages later in the year risk encountering northerly winds north of the equator. It is therefore advisable to make this passage while the SW monsoon is still in force in the North Indian Ocean, September probably being the best month. Boats that have made this passage in the second half of October encountered light variable winds and erratic currents between latitude 3°S and the equator. Similar conditions were experienced north of the equator all the way to Sri Lanka.

The most difficult aspect of this route is the fact that it crosses three different currents, none of which can be predicted with complete accuracy. The route runs first through the west-setting South Equatorial Current, its effect being probably cancelled out on nearing the equator by the east-setting Equatorial Countercurrent. The currents north of the equator depend on the state of the monsoon, setting east during the SW monsoon, west during the NE monsoon. However, it does appear that the combined set of the currents is usually to the east and all boats making this passage have found themselves further east than expected. Yet another factor to be borne in mind on this route is that it crosses the doldrums, although the belt of calms or light winds between the SE trade winds and the monsoon prevailing north of the equator is not too wide and sometimes the wind systems merge into each other almost without a break. During August and September the SE trade winds reach as far north as latitude 5°S. Leaving South Cocos Keeling from WP IT131 the recommended procedure at this time of year (route IT13A) is to make for WP IT132, then sail north along the 80°E meridian until the equator is crossed at WP IT133. From this point a course can be set for WP IT134 south of Galle harbour.

If this passage is made during the NE monsoon, from December to March (route IT13B), as much northing as possible should be made soon after leaving Cocos Keeling so as to cross the equator in about longitude 90°E (WP IT135) and approach Sri Lanka from a better angle. Having crossed the equator, a direct course for Sri Lanka should only be set when favourable winds have been encountered.

IT14 *Chagos to Sri Lanka*

BEST TIME:	May to September			
TROPICAL STORMS:	November to December			
CHARTS:	BA: 4071			
	US: 71			
PILOTS:	BA: 38, 39			
	US: 170, 171, 173			
CRUISING GUIDES:	*Indian Ocean Handbook.*			
WAYPOINTS:				
Departure	*Intermediate*	*Landfall*	*Destination*	*Distance (M)*
Route IT14A				
IT141 Peros N	IT142	IT143 Galle S	Magalle	871
5°00'S, 72°00'E	0°00', 73°00'E	6°00'N, 80°14'E	*6°01.9'N, 80°13.7'E*	
Route IT14B				
IT141 Peros N	IT144	IT143 Galle S	Magalle	1047
	0°00', 82°00'E			

The strategy for this passage depends entirely on the state of the monsoon north of the equator. During the SW monsoon, from May to Sepember, it is probably best to try and sail a direct course for Sri Lanka and only compensate for the set of the current after having crossed the equator (route IT14A). Attention should be paid to the strong currents that set around the northern part of the Chagos Archipelago. Although the winds can be expected to be light at the beginning of the passage, the effect of the monsoon should make itself felt on nearing the equator with winds veering gradually from south to SW and finally west.

Taking as departure point WP IT141 NE of Peros Banhos, the course stays east of the Maldives and crosses the equator at WP IT142. The course can then be altered for WP IT143 south of Galle from where the harbour is entered through Central Channel.

During the NE monsoon (route IT14B) it is essential to make as much easting as possible south of the equator which should be crossed in about longitude 82°E (WP IT144), so as to approach Sri Lanka from slightly east of south.

IT15 *Chagos to Maldives*

BEST TIME:	May to September			
TROPICAL STORMS:	None			
CHARTS:	BA: 4703			
	US: 703			
PILOTS:	BA: 38, 39			
	US: 171, 173			
CRUISING GUIDES:	*Indian Ocean Handbook.*			
WAYPOINTS:				

Departure	Intermediate	Landfall	Destination	Distance (M)
Route IT15A				
IT151 Peros N	IT152			
5°00'S, 72°00'E	0°00', 74°00'E			
	IT153 Felidhe	IT154 North Malé	Malé	584
	3°30'N, 74°00'E	4°09'N, 73°34'E	*4°10'N, 73°30'E*	
Route IT15B				
IT151 Peros N	IT155			
	0°00', 72°30'E			
	IT156 Nilandhe	IT157 Wadu	Malé	567
	3°20'N, 73°20'E	4°09'N, 73°20'E		

The most favourable sailing conditions for this route can be expected during the SW monsoon when southerly winds predominate south of the equator. During the changeover period winds are much lighter and there are long periods of calms. During the NE monsoon the winds south of the equator are mostly NW. Currents in this region can be very strong and their set is difficult to predict, particularly in the transitional period between monsoons. The strongest current during the SW monsoon is the Indian Monsoon Current, which sets strongly east on both sides of the equator.

From WP IT151 NE of Peros Banhos, the course is almost due north and there are no dangers en route until the Maldives archipelago is approached. The capital Malé is at the southern extremity of North Malé Atoll and as this is the only port of entry, all vessels must complete entry formalities there. This considerably complicates matters as most of the archipelago has to be crossed to reach Malé. For this reason, boats occasionally stop at Addu Atoll, the southernmost of the Maldives and the only one south of the equator.

Depending on the monsoon, to reach Malé the course should pass east or west of the islands. As the currents set towards the islands, it is probably safer to sail in their lee, west during the NE mon-soon and east during the SW monsoon. At all times, allowance should be made for the currents and also the fact that their set does not necessarily agree with the direction of the monsoon.

To pass east of the islands (route IT15A), the equator should be crossed at WP IT152. The route continues due north to WP IT153 east of Felidhe Atoll. It then swings NW to WP IT154, at the entrance into Malé Passage that leads into North Malé Atoll and the capital itself.

During the NE monsoon, the islands should be passed on their west side (route IT15B) by setting an initial course to cross the equator at WP IT155. The course turns almost due north to WP IT156 from where the channel is taken between North Nilandhe and Ari Atolls. The route continues in a NE direction to WP IT157 at the entrance into Wadu Channel between South and North Malé Atolls. The capital Malé is at the southern end of North Malé Atoll and is reached through one of the passes leading through the reef. Entry formalities may now be completed at Giraavaru, which is a small island inside North Malé Atoll, where a passage has been cleared through the reef to give access to the deep Giraavaru lagoon. Moorings, fuel and some facilities are now available there for visiting yachts.

IT16 *Seychelles to Red Sea*

BEST TIME:	September to mid-October			
TROPICAL STORMS:	May to June, October to November (North Indian)			
CHARTS:	BA: 4071			
	US: 71			
PILOTS:	BA: 3, 39, 64			
	US: 170, 171, 172			
CRUISING GUIDES:	*Red Sea Pilot.*			
WAYPOINTS:				

Departure	Intermediate	Landfall	Destination	Distance (M)
Route IT16A				
IT60 Mahé N	IT161			
4°34'S, 55°27'E	0°00', 51°00'E			
	IT162			
	3°30'N, 49°00'E			
	IT163 Hafun			
	10°30'N, 52°00'E			
	IT164 Guardafui			
	12°00'N, 51°50'E			
	IT165	IT166 Tadjoura	Djibouti	1693
	12°30'N, 50°45'E	11°40'N, 43°13'E	*11°36.5'N, 43°07.5'E*	
		IT167 Yemen S	Aden	1584
		12°44'N, 45°00'E	*12°48'N, 44°58'E*	
Route IT16B				
IT160 Mahé N	IT168			
	0°00', 63°00'E			
	IT169 Socotra NE			
	13°20'N, 54°30'E			
	[IT164 Guardafui]			
	IT165	IT166 Tadjoura	Djibouti	2153

The best time to make this passage is towards the end of the SW monsoon, in September or early October, when the strength of the winds begins to subside in the NW part of the Indian Ocean. At this time of year the SE trade winds reach as far north as the equator. From there the winds become gradually SW and blow with increasing force as one approaches Socotra Island. This area is notorious for its high frequency of gales during the SW monsoon and this is the reason why an earlier passage, during July or August, is not recommended. Even towards the end of the SW monsoon winds can be very strong and this fact combined with the strong currents usually produce rough seas around the Horn of Africa.

Taking one's departure from WP IT160, off North Point on Mahé Island, boats sailing during the rec-

ommended period (route IT16A) should follow a NW course on leaving the Seychelles so as to cross the equator at WP IT161. If conditions allow it, more westing should be made while south, before the equator is crossed. This avoids the strong current that sets SE during the transitional period between monsoons. From the equator the course can be altered for WP IT162 from where the route runs parallel to the African coast. Along this coast the Somali Current sets strongly to the north and can reach rates as high as 170 miles per day in the area south of Socotra Island. During the transitional period, the SE trade winds blow as far as the equator and favourable winds can be held into the Gulf of Aden. In October winds in that area will be SW or S. However, the passage must not be left too late, because NE winds start to predominate north of the equator after the second half of October. Thick haze and poor visibility make navigation hazardous along the African coast and a safe distance should be kept off the coast both at night and in day time.

From WP IT162 a course can be set for WP IT163, off Ras Hafun. From there the course turns almost due north to WP IT164, NE of Cape Guardafui. Having reached the Horn of Africa, the route passes SW of Socotra towards WP IT165, in the Gulf of Aden. If the intention is to call at Djibouti, from WP IT165 a course can be set for WP IT166, in the Gulf of Tadjoura. The route passes south of the Musha Islands and then turns SW towards the port of Djibouti avoiding the various dangers, all of which are marked by buoys. The recommended anchorage (11°36.1'N, 43°08.1'E) is off the Djibouti Yacht Club whose facilities may be used by visiting boats. The various authorities are in the nearby commercial harbour and must be visited to complete entry formalities.

From WP IT165, boats bound for Aden should alter course for WP IT167, at the entrance into the port of Aden. A marked channel leads into the Inner Harbour, where yachts anchor off the customs dock. Boats are normally met on arrival by a port control launch and directed to the anchorage.

Although better conditions may be experienced during the SW monsoon, the time of arrival in the Red Sea may not agree with most people's plans, unless one is prepared to spend the coming winter in the Red Sea and only reach the Mediterranean the following spring. Mainly for these reasons,

most boats tend to make this passage in the early part of the year (route IT16B). If the passage is attempted during the NE monsoon, sufficient easting should be made south of the equator so that the NE winds will be met at a better angle. Because of the strong N or NW winds that will be met on leaving the Seychelles, a NE course should be sailed so that the equator is crossed as far east as longitude 66°E or even 68°E. The ground lost to the east will be made up later when a better sailing angle will ensure good speeds once under the full influence of the NE monsoon. However, it may not be always necessary to make so much easting south of the equator and boats that have made the passage towards the end of the NE monsoon, in late February or March, have been able to sail a more northerly course after leaving the Seychelles and have crossed the equator around longitude 63°E (WP IT168). From the equator the course turns NW to pass, if conditions allow it, on the windward side of Socotra. During the NE monsoon winds in the Gulf of Aden are mostly easterly.

After the equator has been crossed, and if sufficient easting has been made, it should be possible to set a course that passes east of Socotra through WP IT169. If this proves impossible to achieve, or not convenient if the equator had been crossed too far to the west, a course should then be set for WP IT164, NE of Cape Guardafui, to pass between Socotra and the Horn of Africa. From there similar directions apply as for the alternative route described above.

IT17 *Kenya to Red Sea*

BEST TIME:	April to May, September				
TROPICAL STORMS:	June, October				
CHARTS:	BA: 4071				
	US: 71				
PILOTS:	BA: 3, 64				
	US: 170, 171, 172				
CRUISING GUIDES:	*Red Sea Pilot.*				
WAYPOINTS:					
Departure	**Intermediate**	**Landfall**	**Destination**		**Distance (M)**
IT171 Mombasa 4°00'S, 39°45'E	IT172 0°00', 43°00'E IT173 5°00'N, 49°00'E IT174 Hafun 10°30'N, 52°00'E				

Departure	Intermediate	Landfall	Destination	Distance (M)
	IT175 Guardafui 12°00'N, 51°50'E IT176 12°30'N, 50°45'E	IT177 Tadjoura 11°40'N, 43°13'E IT178 Yemen S 12°44'N, 45°00'E	Djibouti 11°36.5'N, 43°07.5'E Aden 12°48'N, 44°58'E	1765 1656

This classic route of the Arab traders benefits from favourable winds throughout the SW monsoon, from May to September. However, as the winds often attain gale force during the months of July and August in the vicinity of Socotra and the Horn of Africa, the voyage is more comfortable either at the beginning or at the end of the SW monsoon. Good passages on this route have been made in September, when the winds are favourable both south and north of the equator and the strong Somali Current also gives a considerable boost to daily runs. The course runs parallel to the African coast, but because of the thick haze and poor visibility associated with the SW monsoon, particular attention must be paid to navigation. The most dangerous area is when approaching Ras Hafun, which has claimed several boats whose navigators had wrongly identified this headland.

The time of departure is critical, as the transitional period is very short and the NE monsoon can sometimes arrive before the middle of October, when both winds and current change direction. Alternatively, the passage can be made at the beginning of the SW monsoon, when winds might be lighter. If the passage is made at the height of the SW monsoon, in July or August, one must be prepared to put up with very strong winds and rough seas. Although strong, the winds will be favourable as far as the Horn of Africa, but in the Gulf of Aden strong westerly winds will make it very difficult to reach Bab el Mandeb.

If this passage is made during the NE monsoon it is better to wait until the end of March, so as to arrive north of the equator at the change of monsoons. On leaving Mombasa, easting should be made south of the equator, which should be crossed in about longitude 53°E. The best tack should be sailed from there northwards so as to pass between Socotra and Cape Guardafui.

Boats making this passage at the optimum time, in late April or early May, on leaving Mombasa at WP IT171 should sail a course parallel to the coast and cross the equator at WP IT172. Continuing parallel to the coast, the route then passes through WP IT173 to WP IT174, off Ras Hafun. From here the course turns almost due north to WP IT175, NE of Cape Guardafui, to pass between Socotra and the Horn of Africa. Having passed the Horn of Africa, the route enters the Gulf of Aden and makes for WP IT176. From that point, boats bound for Djibouti should set a course for WP IT177 in the Bay of Tadjoura. Those planning to stop in Aden should alter course for WP IT178. See route IT16 for details on Djibouti and Aden.

IT18 *Kenya to Sri Lanka*

BEST TIME:	July to September
TROPICAL STORMS:	May to June, October to November
CHARTS:	BA: 4071
	US: 71
PILOTS:	BA: 3, 38
	US: 171, 173
CRUISING GUIDES:	*Indian Ocean Handbook.*

WAYPOINTS:				
Departure	*Intermediate*	*Landfall*	*Destination*	*Distance (M)*
Route IT18A				
IT181 Mombasa	IT182			
4°00'S, 39°45'E	0°00', 44°00'E			
	IT183			
	4°00'N, 55°00'E			
	IT184 Maldives	IT185 Galle W	Magalle	2591
	7°30'N, 73°00'E	6°01'N, 80°13'E	*6°01.9'N, 80°13.7'E*	
Route IT18B				
IT181 Mombasa	IT186 Seychelles			
	2°00'S, 55°00'E			
	IT187 Equatorial	IT185 Galle W	Magalle	2591
	0°00', 73°15'E			

This is a route strictly for the SW monsoon, when both winds and current will be favourable. On leaving Mombasa at WP IT181, the route runs parallel to the African coast to take full advantage of the favourable current. After the equator is crossed at WP IT182, the course can be altered for WP IT183. From there, a course can be set for WP IT184, north of Ihavandifullu Atoll, in the Eight Degree Channel north of the Maldives. Having cleared the Eight Degree Channel, the course can be altered for WP IT185 at the entrance into Western Channel that leads into Galle harbour.

A shorter, but not necessarily faster, alternative is to take a more southerly route (IT18B) and stay south of the equator longer by passing close to the north of the Seychelles. The favourable east-setting Equatorial Countercurrent will give a welcome boost of between 1/2 and 2 knots, although the SW monsoon will not be so noticeable as north of the equator. The recommended route passes through the Equatorial Channel, south of Huvadhoo Atoll in the Maldives, from where the course is altered for Galle. One advantage of this southerly route is that it avoids the strong winds and rough seas associated with the SW monsoon. The same conditions make Galle a far less comfortable port than during the NE monsoon.

During the recommended period there is no danger of cyclones in the southern part of the Arabian Sea. Route IN25 (page 451) gives directions for the continuation of the route to Malaysia and Singapore.

IT20 SOUTHBOUND ROUTES

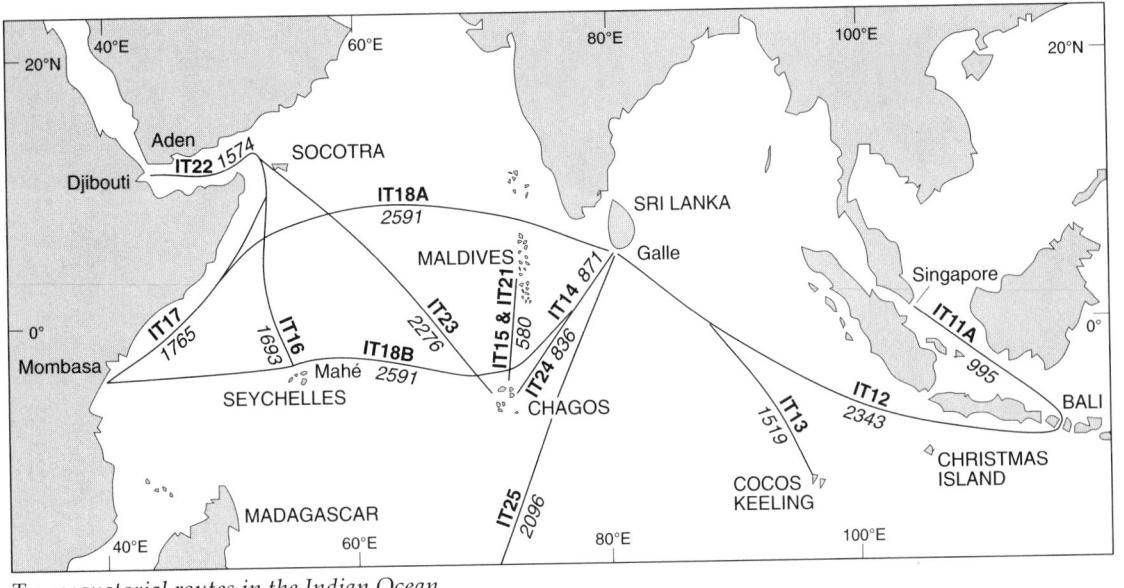

Transequatorial routes in the Indian Ocean

IT21 *Maldives to Chagos*

BEST TIME:	May to September			
TROPICAL STORMS:	December to March			
CHARTS:	BA: 4707			
	US: 707			
PILOTS:	BA: 38, 39			
	US: 170, 171			
WAYPOINTS:				

Departure	*Intermediate*	*Landfall*	*Destination*	*Distance (M)*
IT211 Wadu 4°09'N, 73°20'E	IT212 Nilandhe 3°20'N, 72°20'E			
	IT213 0°00', 72°30'E	IT214 Peros W 5°13'S, 71°45'E	Fouquet 5°26.6'S, 71°48.5'E	607

The best time to make this passage is during the NE monsoon when favourable winds will be found both north and south of the equator. From May to November the predominant direction of the winds is southerly and even during the transitional period boats have experienced a high proportion of southerly winds, so the only time when one can be sure of fair winds is at the height of the NE monsoon. Permission must be obtained from the authorities in Malé if one wishes to visit the southern Maldives and possibly clear out at Addu, the southernmost atoll of the group.

Depending on the monsoon, the Maldives will be passed to the east or west. Because all islands are low and there are only a few navigational lights, navigation in the area is very difficult, the situation being compounded by the strong currents that sweep through the archipelago. For this reason, it is probably safer to sail in the lee of the islands. As it is assumed that the passage to Chagos will be made during the NE monsoon, the recommended route passes to the west of the islands.

Having left Malé through Wadu Channel, from WP IT211, the course turns SW to pass through the channel between North Nilandhe and Ari Atolls. From WP IT212 the course turns S and crosses the equator in WP IT213. From there, the course continues almost due south to WP IT214, north of Peros Banhos in the Chagos Archipelago.

Diego Garcia, the main island of the group, is a military base leased by the British government to the USA and a stop in that island is only permitted in an emergency. However, boats can stop in most

other islands of the Chagos Archipelago, Peros Banhos and the Salomon Islands being the most convenient stops for those arriving from the north. The recommended anchorage at Peros Banhos is in the lee of Fouquet Island, on the south side of the large lagoon.

IT22 *Red Sea to East Africa*

Best time:	November to March
Tropical storms:	May to June, October
Charts:	BA: 4071
	US: 71
Pilots:	BA: 3, 64
	US: 170, 171, 172
Cruising guides:	*East Africa Pilot.*
Waypoints:	

Departure	Intermediate	Landfall	Destination	Distance (M)
IT221 Mandeb 12°20'N, 43°40'E	IT222 Asir 12°10'N, 50°45'E			
	IT223 Guardafui 12°00'N, 51°30'N			
	IT224 Hafun 10°30'N, 51°50'E			
	IT225 5°00'N, 49°00'E			
	IT226 0°00', 43°45'E	IT227 Kenya N 2°15'S, 41°00'E	Lamu *2°18'S, 40°55'E*	1574

Because Kenya and other points along the east coast of Africa are easier to reach during the NE monsoon, passages to that area should be planned for that time. The major difficulty usually occurs soon after the Red Sea has been left behind, when consistent easterly winds make it difficult to get out of the Gulf of Aden. Once the Horn of Africa has been weathered, favourable winds and current ensure a fast sail along the east coast of Africa. For this reason, southbound passages through the Red Sea should take place in the autumn, so that the Gulf of Aden is crossed at the change of seasons, in late October or early November. However, arriving too early off the Horn of Africa carries the risk of the NE monsoon not yet being established. It is therefore a matter of weighing up the disadvantages of contrary winds in the Gulf of Aden against the advantages of favourable winds and current along

the coast of East Africa. The favourable south-setting current has been reported as being about 20 miles off the coast.

Having passed through Bab el Mandeb, from WP IT221, a direct course leads to WP IT222, off the Horn of Africa, which is rounded by setting course for WP IT223, off Cape Guardafui. From there the course goes due south to WP IT224 off Ras Hafun and then runs parallel to the African coast passing through WP IT225 and crossing the equator at WP IT226. A first port of entry into Kenya is at Lamu. The other two official ports of entry are Malindi (3°13'S, 40°07'E) and Mombasa (4°04'S, 39°41'E).

During the SW monsoon the coast of Africa can only be reached by taking a roundabout route via the Seychelles. Having passed north of Socotra, the course leads SE and crosses the equator as far west as the winds will permit. Having met the SE trade winds between latitudes 2°S and 4°S, the course can be shaped to pass north of the Seychelles and on to Kenya. Alternatively a stop can be made in the Seychelles and East Africa reached later. See also routes IS42 and IS43 (pages 497 and 498).

IT23 *Red Sea to South Indian Ocean*

BEST TIME:	November to December
TROPICAL STORMS:	May to June, October (North Indian)
	November to March (South Indian)
CHARTS:	BA: 4071
	US: 71
PILOTS:	BA: 3, 39, 64
	US: 170, 171, 172
CRUISING GUIDES:	*Indian Ocean Handbook, East Africa Pilot.*
WAYPOINTS:	

Departure	Intermediate	Landfall	Destination	Distance (M)
Route IT23A				
IT231 Mandeb	IT232 Asir			
12°20'N, 43°40'E	12°10'N, 50°45'E			
	IT233 Guardafui			
	12°00'N, 51°30'N			
	IT234			
	0°00', 54°15'E			
	IT235 Bird	IT236 Mahé N	Victoria	1487
	3°40'S, 55°25'E	4°32'S, 55°28'E	*4°36.5'S, 55°28'E*	
Route IT23B				
IT231 Mandeb	IT237 Socotra NE			
	13°20'N, 54°30'E			
	IT238	IT239 Peros W	Fouquet	2276
	0°00', 72°00'E	5°13'S, 71°45'E	*5°26.6'S, 71°48.5'E*	

Although most yacht traffic in the Red Sea is from south to north, every year a number of boats sail to various destinations in the South Indian Ocean by this more direct route from Europe and the Mediterranean.

Similar considerations apply for the first part of the voyage as far as the Horn of Africa as described in route IT22. Passages to the Seychelles during the NE monsoon (route IT23A) benefit from favourable conditions once the Horn of Africa has been left behind. Therefore the early part of the voyage should coincide with the transition period to avoid contrary winds in the Gulf of Aden. From WP IT233, off Cape Guardafui, the direct route crosses the equator at WP IT234. The next WP IT235 lies halfway between Bird and Denis, the northernmost Seychelles Islands. From there, a course can be set for WP IT236, three miles north of the entrance into Port Victoria. Port Control should be contacted on VHF channel 16. Arriving yachts must anchor 3 cables north of Victoria lighthouse.

The SW monsoon provides better conditions for reaching the further island groups in the South Indian Ocean, such as Chagos. On the route from the Red Sea to Chagos and Mauritius (route IT23B), easting is made north of the equator, which is crossed between longitudes 70°E and 72°E. Landfall in Chagos is made at WP IT239, north of Peros Banhos. Southbound from Chagos the same directions apply as for route IS36 (page 494). A September passage from the Red Sea would also benefit from more favourable sailing conditions for the next leg to Mauritius, provided it takes place before the start of the cyclone season in the South Indian Ocean. For boats which have reached the

South Indian Ocean towards the end of the year, the next leg of the voyage from either the Seychelles or Chagos to destinations further south should be postponed until after the end of the cyclone season in the South Indian Ocean. See also route IS41 (page 496).

IT24 *Sri Lanka to Chagos*

BEST TIME:	April				
TROPICAL STORMS:	November, December to March				
CHARTS:	BA: 4071				
	US: 71				
PILOTS:	BA: 38, 39				
	US: 173				
CRUISING GUIDES:	*Indian Ocean Handbook.*				
WAYPOINTS:					

Departure	*Intermediate*	*Landfall*	*Destination*	*Distance (M)*
IT240 Magalle *6°01.9'N, 80°13.7'E*	IT241 Galle S 6°00'N, 80°14'E			
	IT242 Speaker 4°50'S, 72°40'E	IT243 Salomon 5°17.5'S, 72°15'E	Takamaka *5°20'S, 72°16'E*	836

Although the NE monsoon will ensure better sailing conditions, at least as far as the equator, south of the line the winds will be less reliable. The risk of tropical storms is slight, especially south of the equator where cyclones very rarely affect the islands of the Chagos Archipelago. Nonetheless, if at all possible, the periods of cyclonic activity should be avoided on both sides of the equator and for this reason April has been recommended, as by then the cyclone season in the South Indian Ocean is nearly over.

Although the Chagos Archipelago is under British administration, Diego Garcia is a restricted military area and the access of cruising yachts is prohibited. Their presence is tolerated in the uninhabited islands of the archipelago, such as Peros Banhos, Egmont and Salomon Islands. The most popular anchorage is in the Salomon lagoon, off Takamaka Island.

Having cross the equator, landfall will be made east of the Speaker Bank where the course will be altered to pass north of Blenheim Reef. Waypoint IT243 is close to the NW pass into the lagoon and the recommended anchorage is on its SE side.

IT25 *Sri Lanka to Mauritius*

BEST TIME:	May–June, September				
TROPICAL STORMS:	November to April				
CHARTS:	BA: 4071				
	US: 71				
PILOTS:	BA: 38, 39				
	US: 173				
CRUISING GUIDES:	*Indian Ocean Handbook.*				
WAYPOINTS:					

Departure	*Intermediate*	*Landfall*	*Destination*	*Distance (M)*
IT250 Magalle *6°01.9'N, 80°13.7'E*	IT251 Galle S 6°00'N, 80°14'E			
	IT252 Chagos SE 7°00'S, 73°00'E	IT253 Mauritius N 19°48'S, 57°37'E	Port Louis *20°09'S, 57°29'E*	2096

The risks of two cyclone seasons, north and south of the equator, will have to be balanced before a time is chosen as to when to make this passage. As the risk of encountering a cyclone is higher in the South Indian Ocean, it is recommended to avoid this route after the beginning of December and before the middle of April. This is also the period with a low risk of cyclones north of the equator.

The recommended route stays east of the Maldives and, during the SE trade wind season (May to October), should also stay east of the Chagos Archipelago to benefit from a better sailing angle to Mauritius. As the route passes quite close to Chagos, a stop there may be tempting (see IT24). On the recommended route landfall will be made north of Mauritius, close to North Island, from where the coast will be followed into Port Louis. The Port Authority must be contacted on channel 16 to obtain permission to enter the harbour.

17

WINDS AND CURRENTS OF THE SOUTH INDIAN OCEAN

The weather in the tropical zone of the South Indian Ocean is greatly influenced by the advance of the North Indian monsoon south of the equator during the northern winter and its corresponding retreat during summer. Outside of the tropics the weather follows a normal pattern.

The Southeast trade winds

These winds blow on the equatorial side of the counterclockwise circulation of air that exists around the area of high pressure situated in about latitude 30°S. Compared to the other oceans, the South Indian high rarely consists of a single cell and often contains a succession of east moving anticyclonic systems. The trade winds blow on their north side and form a wide belt that stretches across the ocean from Western Australia to Madagascar and the coast of Africa. Between July and September this belt spreads over a very large area and becomes continuous with the SE trade winds of the South Pacific. The entire belt moves north and south throughout the year, its northern limit varying from latitude 2°S in August to latitude 12°S in January. The fluctuation of the southern limit is less pronounced, from 24°S in August to 30°S in January.

The average strength of these trade winds is between 10 and 15 knots in summer and 15 to 20 knots in winter. Over the central region, the wind blows steadily from SE or ESE, especially from May to September when the SW monsoon is in force north of the equator.

The Northwest monsoon

From November to March, when the ITCZ is situated south of the equator, the NE monsoon of the North Indian Ocean is drawn into the southern hemisphere. Because of the rotation of the earth it is deflected to the left and becomes a NW wind in the northern part of the South Indian Ocean. Winds are generally light and vary considerably both in direction and strength during this period. The weather is often squally and unsettled.

Monsoons of the Indonesian Archipelago

The weather pattern of the Indonesian Archipelago is more seasonal than that of the adjacent areas, which are dominated by the two monsoons. The SE monsoon generally lasts from April to September and is replaced by a NW monsoon from October till March. Though neither of them is very strong, the SE monsoon is the more consistent both in strength and in direction, particularly during July and August when it becomes continuous with the SE trade winds of the South Pacific and Indian Oceans. During the NW monsoon, the direction of the winds is predominantly NW, although their strength and consistency diminish further south. South of latitude 4°S the weather is often squally alternating with calms, variable winds and rain.

Variables

On the polar side of the SE trade wind belt there is

an area of light variable winds which coincides with the high pressure region. The axis of this high is situated in about latitude 30°S in winter, moving further south towards latitude 35°S during the summer. The weather varies greatly within this zone, which has similar characteristics to the Horse Latitudes of the Atlantic Ocean.

Westerlies

Westerly winds prevail on the polar side of the South Indian Ocean high pressure region. The almost continuous passage of depressions from west to east causes the wind to vary considerably in direction and strength. Particularly in the higher latitudes of the Roaring Forties and further south, the frequency of gales is high, the weather cold, and the seas rough.

Tropical storms

The cyclone season of the South Indian Ocean lasts from November to May, although December to April are considered to be the dangerous months, as cyclones occur only rarely in November and May. The month with the highest frequency of storms is January.

The willy-willies that affect the coasts of W and NW Australia occur mostly between December and April. They can extend as far as the Timor Sea and Arafura Sea, the latter being also subject to South Pacific cyclones that occasionally hit Northern Australia. Their season is from December to March.

Currents

The main surface circulation of the South Indian Ocean is counterclockwise but because of the mon-

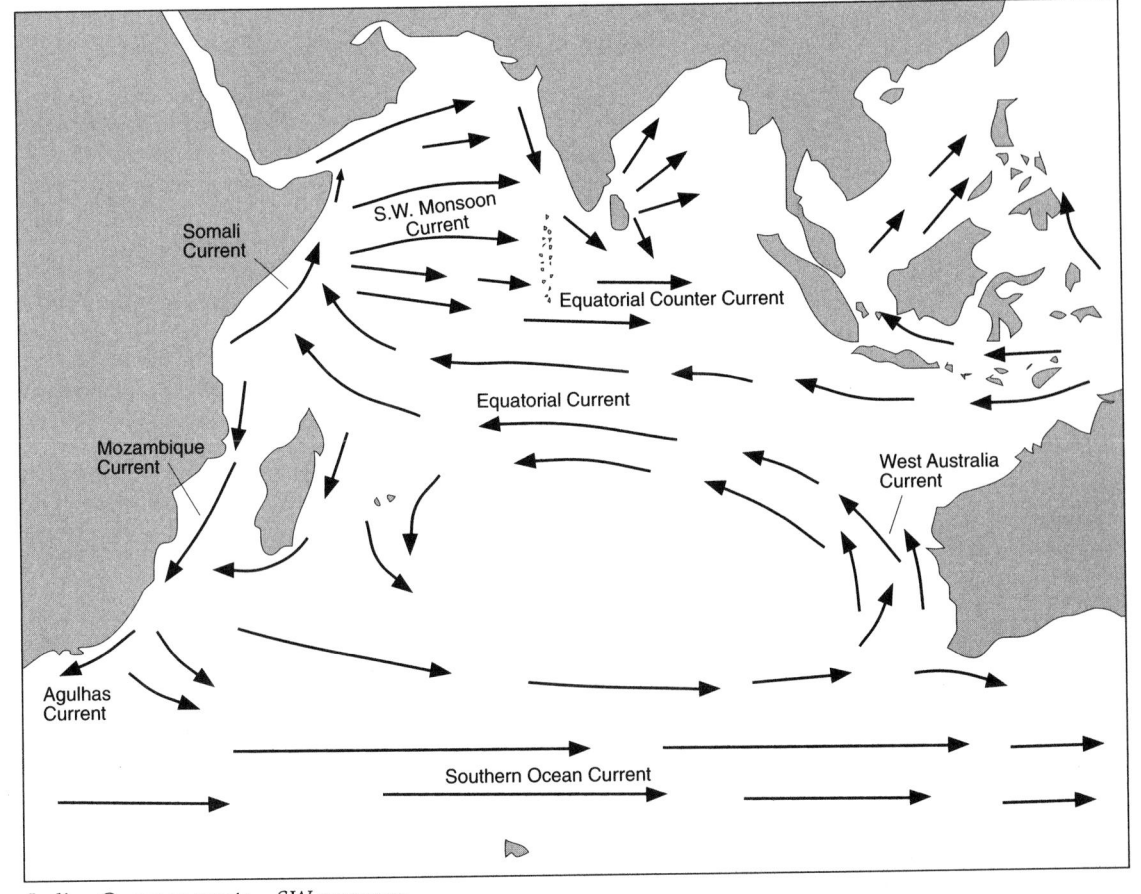

Indian Ocean currents – SW monsoon

soons of the North Indian Ocean there is only one Equatorial Current. The west flowing Equatorial Current always lies south of the equator, its northern limit varying between latitudes 6°S and 10°S depending on longitude and season. The limit is nearer the equator during the SW monsoon of the North Indian Ocean. On the western side of the ocean, the northern part of the current flows past Madagascar until it reaches the coast of Africa. The current splits in two, one branch following the coast in a northerly direction, the other setting south into the Mozambique Channel. This becomes the Mozambique Current which further south alters its name to that of the Agulhas Current.

The Agulhas Current contains not just the waters of the Mozambique Current but also those of the southern branch of the Equatorial Current. The two currents meet off the coast of Africa in about latitude 28°S from where the combined current sets strongly SW before it passes the Cape of Good Hope into the South Atlantic. One part of the Agulhas Current branches off to the SE where it joins the Southern Ocean Current. The south side of the main circulation of the South Indian Ocean is formed by this current which sets in an E and NE direction. The eastern side of this counterclockwise movement is formed by the West Australian Current, which sets in a NW direction along the west coast of Australia. Eventually it passes into the Equatorial Current, thus completing this giant cycle.

18

ROUTES IN THE SOUTH INDIAN OCEAN

Before the Red Sea route became the more popular way to complete a circumnavigation, most boats used to sail around the Cape of Good Hope on their way to the Atlantic. Nowadays the majority of cruising boats use the northern route and this has resulted in a considerable drop in the number of boats sailing through the South Indian Ocean. Occasionally, boats sailing south through the Red Sea make their way into the South Indian Ocean, but very few go further than Kenya or the Seychelles.

For those who are on a world voyage and plan to take the southern route, there are various factors to be taken into account at the planning stages. The most important factor is to make the passage around the Cape of Good Hope at the most favourable time, which is during the summer months, from December to March. Such a timing means that the crossing of the South Indian Ocean takes place during the safe season, when no cyclones can be expected south of the equator. The cyclone season in the South Indian Ocean lasts from November to April and passages during this time should be avoided. Although cyclones have been recorded in other months too, notably the cyclone of July 1871, which originated south of Sumatra, it is generally agreed that May to October is a perfectly safe time to cross the South Indian Ocean. As

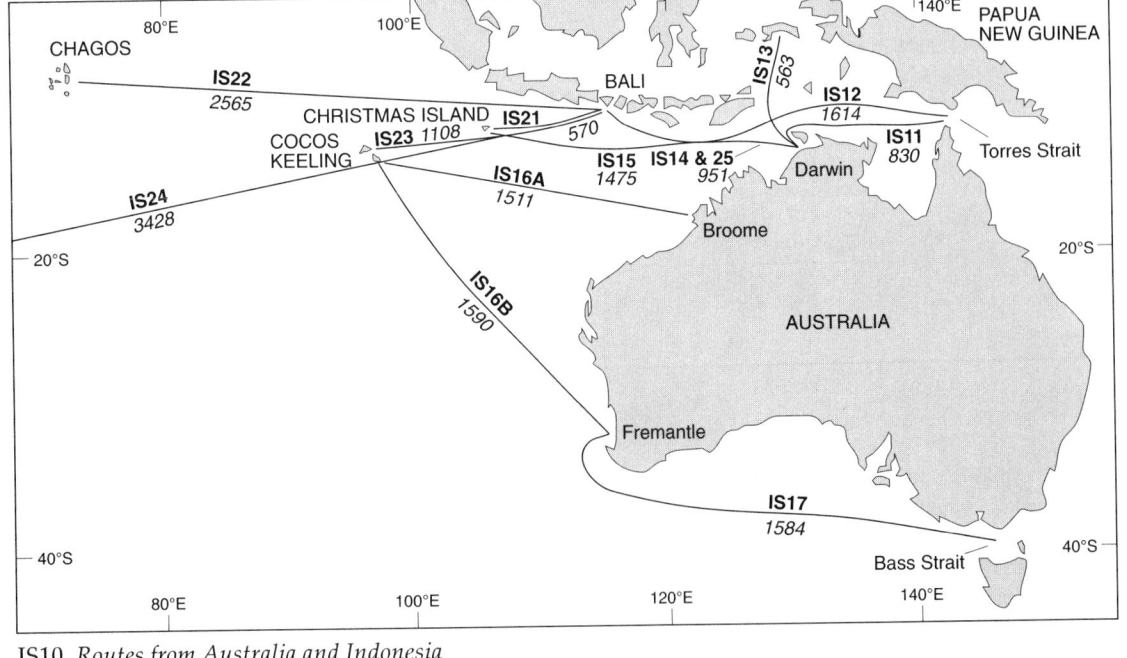

IS10 *Routes from Australia and Indonesia*

the South Atlantic is free of cyclones, the onward voyage can start off from Cape Town at practically any time of the year although, as stated earlier, better weather will be found in summer, from December to March. Because of the conveniently placed island groups in the South Indian Ocean, most boats that sail this route do it in stages by calling at Christmas Island, Cocos Keeling, Mauritius, Réunion, and finally Durban. If more time is available a worthwhile detour can be made to the Chagos Archipelago.

A warning has to be given regarding the leg around South Africa. Several circumnavigators have encountered the worst weather of their voyage along this route where a sudden SW gale can create extremely dangerous conditions when it hits the south flowing Agulhas current. Boats have been knocked down, pooped, and even lost on this stretch, so it is well worth considering the alternatives before becoming committed to this route. Nevertheless, with due care and access to weather information, any well found boat should be able to pass even this hurdle. Some useful tips are given in the relevant sections, mainly in routes IS52 and IS63 (pages 502 and 509).

The island groups scattered across the centre of the Indian Ocean continue to attract a number of cruising boats every year, although their number does not appear to be increasing. On the other hand, more boats are visiting the east coast of Africa, cruising boats being now welcomed or at least tolerated in most African countries bordering on the Indian Ocean.

IS10 ROUTES FROM AUSTRALIA

IS11	*Torres Strait to Darwin*	*480*
IS12	*Torres Strait to Bali*	*480*
IS13	*Darwin to Ambon*	*482*
IS14	*Darwin to Bali*	*482*
IS15	*Darwin to Christmas Island*	*483*
IS16	*West Australia to Cocos Keeling*	*484*
IS17	*West Australia to Bass Strait*	*485*

Most boats on a world voyage only touch Northern Australia briefly before sailing on to Bali and beyond. Although a cruising permit is required for those wishing to visit the Indonesian archipelago, it is usually possible to make a stop in Benoa on the island of Bali, where the authorities appear to be more tolerant, although some people have had to pay a fine for stopping there without a permit. Benoa is therefore a favourite destination for most boats heading west, both those intending to continue their voyage through the North Indian Ocean and those taking the southern route via the Cape of Good Hope. The routes starting off from Northern Australia are under the influence of the two monsoons. The SE monsoon, lasting from May until September, has the more pleasant weather as well as favourable winds. The NW monsoon coincides with the cyclone season in the tropical part of the South Indian Ocean, and for this reason few cruising boats stay in the areas affected by tropical storms between late November and March. During that time it may be tempting to sail to the southern part of Australia, which is under the influence of westerly winds for most of the year, but very few cruising boats venture that way.

IS11 *Torres Strait to Darwin*

BEST TIME:	May to September			
TROPICAL STORMS:	December to March			
CHARTS:	BA: 4603			
	US: 603			
PILOTS:	BA: 15, 17			
	US: 164, 175			
CRUISING GUIDES:	*Northern Territory Coast.*			
WAYPOINTS:				
Departure	*Intermediate*	*Landfall*	*Destination*	*Distance (M)*
IS111 Thursday 10°34'S, 142°06.5'E	IS112 Coburg 10°30'S, 132°20'E	[IS113 Dundas] 11°11'S, 131°38'E		635
	IS114 Bathurst 11°10'S, 130°00'E			
	IS115 Fourcroy 11°55'S, 129°55'E	IS116 Charles 12°21'S, 130°42'E	Darwin *12°28'S, 130°51'E*	830

During the SE monsoon, from the middle of April to the end of September or early October, winds on this route are mostly favourable. To reach Darwin there is a choice of either taking a short cut through the Van Diemen Gulf or by sailing around the west of Bathurst Island. Because of the strong tidal streams in Dundas and Clarence Straits, and the difficult navigation in the approaches to Darwin, the roundabout route is often quicker, although it is longer. Those who have more time might prefer to cover the entire distance from the Torres Strait to Darwin in daily stages as there are plenty of good anchorages from Cape Arnhem onward.

Having reached the Arafura Sea, the route to Darwin is the same as that for boats which have followed the inshore route from North Queensland. From WP IS111, west of Thursday Island, at the western end of the Prince of Wales Channel, a westerly course is set which passes close to the north of Booby Island. By setting a course for WP IS112 the route avoids all dangers off the north coast of Australia. From that point the course can be altered for WP IS113 to pass through Dundas and Clarence Straits. Because of the strong tidal sets and near impossibility of clearing the straits in one daylight period, this route is not recommended. Those who are taking it must allow for the strong currents, which usually set either north or south.

The route around both Melville and Bathurst Islands, although longer, is recommended and is the route most commonly used. If this offshore route is taken, from WP IS112 a course can be set for WP IS114, NW of Bathurst Island. The course should be changed again for WP IS115, off Cape Fourcroy, and finally altered for WP IS116 at the start of the main shipping channel into Darwin. If arriving from outside Australia, boats are required to give at least three hours' notice by contacting Darwin Port Authority on VHF channel 16 or HF 2182 kHz. Because of the large tidal range, the easiest place to come alongside is Fishermen's Wharf and this should be requested when arranging clearance.

IS12 *Torres Strait to Bali*

BEST TIME:	May to September
TROPICAL STORMS:	December to April
CHARTS:	BA: 4603
	US: 603
PILOTS:	BA: 15, 34, 35
	US: 163, 164
CRUISING GUIDES:	*Cruising Guide to Southeast Asia*

WAYPOINTS:				
Departure	*Intermediate*	*Landfall*	*Destination*	*Distance (M)*
IS121 Thursday 10°34'S, 142°06.5'E	IS122 Melville 10°30'S, 130°00'E IS123 Roti 11°15'S, 123°00'E IS124 Dana 11°00'S, 121°20'E	IS125 Bali E 8°50'S, 115°20'E	Benoa *8°45'S, 115°15'E*	1614

For most people the timing of this passage is crucial for the later stages of their voyage. Most boats bound for the South Indian Ocean pass through the Torres Strait between June and August when the best sailing conditions can be expected on this route. After the Arafura Sea has been crossed, the same directions apply as for those setting off from Darwin (route IS14). If one is too late in the season, the best way to avoid encountering a cyclone en route is by sailing along the north coast of the southern Indonesian islands where cyclones are not known to occur. Boats bound for Singapore and the North Indian Ocean have more time at their disposal than those intending to sail around the Cape of Good Hope, so they tend to pass through the Torres Strait later, in September or even early October. This means that they will have missed the best time for the passage to Bali and should be prepared for light winds and calms on that section.

The direct route from Torres Strait to Bali crosses both the Arafura and Timor Seas, where the weather is dominated by the SE and NW monsoons. The trade winds blow strongly from May till August from between SE and SSE and there is a considerable sea. At the start and end of the season the wind is often E backing to ENE. The SE monsoon lasts until the end of October or even November, although SE winds are both lighter and less consistent after the middle of September. It is then followed by variable winds and calms. As the NW monsoon coincides with the cyclone season, passages during this time are best avoided. The seasons in the Timor Sea follow almost the same pattern. Sometimes during the SE monsoon the air is laden with dust brought from the Australian desert and visibility can be poor. In the vicinity of land the winds are generally influenced by the contour of the islands, while in the channels between the islands the winds often blow with great force.

The effect of the tidal streams is felt particularly in the area between Darwin and the Ashmore Reef. For westgoing boats it is mostly favourable both east and west of Ashmore Reef. West of Ashmore Reef the westerly set can reach 2 knots. A weaker countercurrent, of up to half a knot, may make itself felt for a few hours every day. Further west, the currents in the Lombok Strait run at considerable rates and can produce dangerous conditions in the approaches to Benoa harbour when a strong wind is blowing against the current. During the SE monsoon, the main direction of the current is southerly.

From WP IS121, west of Thursday Island, at the western end of the Prince of Wales Channel, a westerly course can be set which passes close to the north of Booby Island. By setting a course for WP IS122 the route avoids all dangers off the north coast of Australia. From there, the course should be altered for WP IS123, 20 miles south of Roti Island, SW of Timor. This course stays well to the north of the oil drilling area around 12°00'S, 125°00'E and also avoids the Hibernia and Ashmore reefs. Karmt Shoals will be crossed en route, but the area presents no known dangers. Making a detour through Roti Channel, between Roti and Timor, is not recommended as currents are very strong.

From WP IS123 the route then goes to WP IS124, south of Dana Island. The course can then be altered for WP IS125, SW of Nusa Penida, in the approaches to Benoa harbour, Bali's main port. A buoyed channel leads through the reef, which is clearly visible in daylight. Entering at night is not recommended as often the lights are not working and the leading lights can be confusing. Because of the strong currents it is preferable to spend the night out at sea, although with care it may be possible to anchor for the night near the landfall buoy if there is not too much swell.

The opening of the new Bali International Marina in 1994 has considerably improved docking facilities in Benoa harbour. The marina is located in the NE of the harbour. Anchoring space is rather limited and is restricted to the area south of the main wharf. Entry formalities are completed at the various offices lining the causeway leading into Denpasar.

IS13 *Darwin to Ambon*

BEST TIME:	May to September				
TROPICAL STORMS:	December to April				
CHARTS:	BA: 4603				
	US: 603				
PILOTS:	BA: 17, 35				
	US: 164, 175				
WAYPOINTS:					
Departure	*Intermediate*	*Landfall*	*Destination*		*Distance (M)*
IS131 Charles 12°21'S, 130°42'E	IS132 Fourcroy 11°55'S, 129°50'E				
	IS133 Babar 8°10'S, 129°20'E	IS134 Nusanive 3°50'S, 128°07'E	Ambon *3°42'S, 128°10'E*		563

This route is used mainly by boats taking part in the annual Darwin to Ambon Race. Participants in this event, which is organised by the Darwin Sailing Club, automatically obtain the compulsory cruising permit for Indonesia. For those in possession of a cruising permit, this route allows one to start exploring that vast archipelago in one of its most interesting parts. The best time to head north is at the height of the SE monsoon, when the weather is settled and favourable winds can be expected for most of the way.

Taking as a departure point WP IS131 at the start of the main shipping channel into Darwin, a course can be set for WP IS132 off Point Fourcroy. The course then runs almost due north to WP IS133 in Selat Babar, the passage between Babar and Sermata Islands. From there, the route across the Banda Sea avoids all dangers by setting course for WP IS134 off Nusanive, at the entrance into Ambon (Yos Sudarso).

IS14 *Darwin to Bali*

BEST TIME:	May to September				
TROPICAL STORMS:	December to April				
CHARTS:	BA: 4603				
	US: 603				
PILOTS:	BA: 17, 34				
	US: 163, 175				
CRUISING GUIDES:	*Cruising Guide to Southeast Asia.*				
WAYPOINTS:					
Departure	*Intermediate*	*Landfall*	*Destination*		*Distance (M)*
Route IS14A IS141 Charles 12°21'S, 130°42'E	IS142 Challis 12°15'S, 125°00'E				
	IS143 Hibernia 12°07'S, 123°23'E	IS145 Bali E 8°50'S, 115°20'E	Benoa *8°45'S, 115°15'E*		951
Route IS14B IS141 Charles	IS144 11°30'S, 124°30'E	IS145 Bali E	Benoa		939

This route leads south of all Indonesian islands. The only dangers on the direct route are the Hibernia and Ashmore reefs to the south of Timor Island. The passage can be broken at Ashmore Reef, especially if the winds are light. The green reflection or blink of the shallow water can often be seen in the sky long before the actual reef is sighted. Currents in the area are usually strong (see also route IS12). The best anchorage is in the NW corner of the reef, off a small cay. In good visibility it is fairly easy to thread one's way among the coral heads. The reef is often visited by Indonesian fishermen.

From WP IS141, outside the entrance into the main shipping channel into Darwin, the direct route (IS14A) leads to WP IS142. There are oil platforms in the area 12°00'S, 125°00'E, which should be avoided if possible. The course should then be altered for WP IS143 to pass halfway between Hibernia and Ashmore Reefs. The alternative is to take a more northerly course on leaving Darwin so as to pass to the north of both the oilfields and the above two reefs (route IS14B). In this case from WP IS141 the course should be set for WP IS144. Although the oil platforms are easily seen, both in daytime and at night, one should not pass too close to them so as not to get entangled in the anchoring cables which stretch a long way away from the platform and are not easily seen. From either of the above waypoints IS143 or IS144 it is then a clear run to WP IS145, SW of Nusa Penida, in the approaches to Benoa Harbour.

During the SE monsoon the prevailing winds both in the Arafura and Timor Seas are from the SE or E. The only difficulty likely to be encountered are the very strong currents in the Lombok Strait in the approaches to Benoa harbour. Because of the currents and the meandering entrance channel to Benoa, this port should only be entered in daylight. A strong current will be encountered SW of Lombok where the ocean current setting along the southern coasts of the islands meets the outflow-ing current from the Lombok Channel, separating the islands of Lombok and Bali. The area abounds with overfalls and rough breaking seas and can be quite dangerous in strong winds, which fortunately do not occur too often. Also one should be prepared for ghost readings on the depth sounder with sudden shallow readings caused by the different layers of water.

The best passages on this route are made during July and August, when the SE winds are most regular. At the beginning and especially at the end of the SE monsoon the winds become irregular, SSW winds sometimes being encountered in the Timor Sea in October. The south side of the Indonesian islands should not be approached until close to Bali on account of contrary currents. During April, and also in November and December, winds on this route are often light and there are prolonged periods of calms.

From outside Benoa, a buoyed channel leads through the reef, which is clearly visible in daylight. Entering the harbour at night is not recommended as often the lights are not working and the leading lights can be confusing. Because of the strong currents it is preferable to spend the night out at sea, although with care it may be possible to anchor for the night near the landfall buoy if there is not too much swell. The opening of the new Bali International Marina in 1994 has considerably improved docking facilities in Benoa harbour. The marina is located in the NE part of the harbour. Anchoring space is rather limited and is restricted to the area south of the main wharf. Clearance formalities are completed at the various offices lining the causeway leading to Denpasar. The marina office may help with the clearance formalities. A cruising permit is required for all sailing boats wishing to visit Indonesia. However, on some occasions boats arriving in Benoa without a permit have been allowed by the Harbour Master to stay a few days for reprovisioning.

IS15 *Darwin to Christmas Island*

Best time:	May to September
Tropical storms:	December to April
Charts:	BA: 4603, 4070
	US: 524
Pilots:	BA: 17, 34
	US: 163, 175

WAYPOINTS:				
Departure	Intermediate	Landfall	Destination	Distance (M)
IS151 Charles 12°21'S, 130°42'E	IS152 Challis 12°15'S, 125°00'E IS153 Hibernia 12°07'S, 123°23'E	IS154 Christmas 10°28'S, 105°46'E	Flying Fish 10°25'S, 105°43'E	1475

This is normally a fast sail in 15–25 knot SE winds if the passage is timed for July or August. If it is left later than the first half of September, the trade winds can be less reliable and there is a greater chance of calms and light variable winds. As far as Ashmore reef, the same directions apply as those for route IS14. In strong winds or poor visibility it might be safer to avoid both the oil platforms in approximately 12°00'S, 125°00'E and the two reefs to the west of them by taking a route which passes well to the south or north of the area. From WP IS153 between Ashmore and Hibernia reefs, a direct course leads outside all dangers to WP IS154, two miles east of Christmas Island. The best anchorage is at Flying Fish Cove. Boats should fly the Q flag on arrival and will be visited by customs. The rest of entry formalities will be completed ashore. As the island is an Australian territory, similar visa requirements apply as in Australia itself and those crew members arriving without a visa may not be allowed to stay. The strict Australian food quarantine regulations are not applied as rigorously as on the mainland.

At Christmas Island the SE trade winds blow almost continuously from May until December, but in the first months of the year, when the NW monsoon is established in the area to the north of the island, the NW monsoon makes itself felt with occasional heavy rains, strong winds, and thunderstorms. In January and February winds can blow strongly from the west or north. The island is normally spared the cyclones which affect the area between it and North West Australia.

The anchorage at Christmas Island can become uncomfortable when the trade winds are at their strongest, a good incentive to up anchor and sail the 500 miles to Cocos Keeling, where there is a choice of safe and beautiful anchorages.

IS16 West Australia to Cocos Keeling

BEST TIME:	May to October			
TROPICAL STORMS:	November to April			
CHARTS:	BA: 4070			
	US: 70			
PILOTS:	BA: 17, 44			
	US: 174, 175			
WAYPOINTS:				
Departure	Intermediate	Landfall	Destination	Distance (M)
IS161 Broome 18°00'S, 122°05'E	IS162 Mermaid 16°45'S, 119°40'E	IS163 Keeling E 12°05'S, 97°00'E	Direction 12°05.5'S, 96°52.5'E	1511
IS164 Fremantle 32°00'S, 115°45'E	IS165 West 32°00'S, 115°40'E	IS163 Keeling E	Direction	1590

Tropical storms affect the area crossed by this route during the summer months, from the middle of November to April, and a passage during this period is therefore not recommended. Better sailing conditions usually occur in May–June and September–October, when the SE trade winds either have not reached their full strength or have started to diminish. Occasionally strong squalls have been encountered on this run, with sudden winds of up to 50 knots.

A good port of departure from Western Australia is Broome. On leaving the port one should move immediately offshore as the reefs north of Gantheaume Point are reported to be more extensive than charted. Better yachting facilities are available at Fremantle, from where a direct route can also be sailed to Cocos Keeling, although one cannot be as certain of favourable SE winds as in the case of boats leaving from ports further north, such as Broome. In the latter case, from WP IS161 a course can be set for WP IS162, north of Mermaid Reef, so that all dangers south of that reef are left to port. The direct route leads to WP IS163, six miles east of Direction Island on South Cocos.

As the only powerful light is at the airport, on the SW side of the lagoon, the atoll should be approached carefully at night. The entrance into the lagoon at South Cocos is between Horsburgh and Direction Island. The recommended anchorage for yachts is south of Direction Island and is reached by leaving Direction Island 1/4 mile to port. A marker shows where to turn to port to reach the yellow quarantine buoy. Flight Services should be called on VHF channel 16 and customs, immigration, and quarantine officers will come to the boat. Strict food quarantine regulations apply here and only Australian food products, labelled as such, will be allowed. Australian visas are compulsory.

IS17 *West Australia to Bass Strait*

BEST TIME:	December to March			
TROPICAL STORMS:	None			
CHARTS:	BA: 4709, 4601			
	US: 709, 601			
PILOTS:	BA: 13, 14, 17			
	US: 127, 175			
CRUISING GUIDES:	*Circumnavigating Australia's Coastline.*			
WAYPOINTS:				
Departure	*Intermediate*	*Landfall*	*Destination*	*Distance (M)*
IS171 Garden 32°06'S, 115°38'E	IS172 Naturaliste 33°40'S, 114°35'E			
	IS173 Leeuwin 34°40'S, 115°00'E			
	IS174 35°30'S, 117°00'E	IS175 King 39°25'S, 144°00'E		1584

Sailing along the south of Australia can be done either in one long leg to Bass Strait or in easy coastal stages by stopping at various places en route. The offshore route has the advantage of more constant winds as the Great Australian Bight is renowned for its baffling winds in summer. If the transocean route from South Africa has been left for a detour to Western Australia, it is advisable to regain that route after rounding Cape Leeuwin. Extreme caution must be exercised when approaching Bass Strait from westward, especially at night or in bad visibility, because of the strong currents that sweep through the strait.

Leaving Fremantle at WP IS171, NW of Garden Island, the course runs down the west coast of Australia to WP IS172, off Cape Naturaliste. The next course alteration, to WP IS173, takes the route south of Cape Leeuwin. From WP IS174 a direct course can be set across the Australian Bight to WP IS175, north of King Island, in the western approaches to Bass Strait.

For vessels bound for Sydney direct from either Western Australia or even Cape Town, the passage through Bass Strait is only recommended in winter. During the summer better conditions are met by keeping south of Tasmania. After passing Tasmania, the course should only turn north after longitude 155°E has been passed, so as to avoid the full effect of the south-setting Australian current and to approach Sydney from offshore where the current is much weaker and the winds are steadier.

IS20 ROUTES FROM INDONESIA

Bali occupies a unique position on the world sailing routes because of its convenient position astride the main cruising route around the world. Since it is also a very attractive island with lots to see and do, Bali is rarely bypassed by anyone sailing through the area. There are only three main routes out of Bali, one destined for the islands of the South Indian Ocean, a direct route to Sri Lanka south of Sumatra, and one heading across the equator to Singapore. The first of these routes is used by boats bound for South Africa as well as those bound for the Red Sea by a more indirect route via the Seychelles and possibly East Africa. A small number of boats also use Bali as a departure point for ports in Northern and Western Australia. Because of the prevailing winds these routes are best sailed at the change of seasons, in April or October. At the present time the most frequented route out of Bali is the transequatorial route to Singapore IT11 (page 460).

The area around Bali is under the influence of the NW and SE monsoons, although the high mountains and irregular coastline cause significant modifications to local weather conditions and the high Indonesian islands often block the monsoons completely. Strong winds are quite rare, although some squalls can be violent, and as these often develop suddenly they can be quite dangerous to those caught unaware. Tropical cyclones are also very rare, the only area affected being near Timor and Flores Islands, with less than one storm per year, in the period from January to April.

Although conditions may vary locally as the Indonesian archipelago stretches over a considerable portion of the ocean, generally the SE monsoon lasts from April to October and the NW monsoon from November to March. Among the islands to the east of Java, which includes Bali, the SE monsoon blows strongly from the ESE, being at its height during June, July, and August. The NW monsoon sets in about December and attains its maximum strength in January. The NW monsoon is the wet season, with the highest rainfall in December and January, when squalls are most frequent.

Along the northern shores of the higher islands, winds in both seasons are steadier during the night hours, being influenced by land and sea breezes. For this reason most Indonesian sailing craft tend to make their passages at night, keeping close to the shore. Land and sea breezes are very important for those planning to sail in these waters and are very evident along the coasts of larger islands, although weaker on smaller islands. These breezes are at their strongest when the monsoons are weak. The change from land to sea breeze occurs in the middle of the morning, while that from sea to land breeze occurs shortly after sunset near mountainous coasts and later in the night near flat country. The force of the breeze decreases with distance from the shore but can be felt up to 20 miles offshore. The breezes are strongest near mountainous country sloping gradually to the sea and are also stronger on clear days.

IS21 *Bali to Christmas Island*

BEST TIME:	May to October
TROPICAL STORMS:	December to April
CHARTS:	BA: 4071
	US: 70
PILOTS:	BA: 34
	US: 163, 170

| WAYPOINTS: | | | | |
Departure	Intermediate	Landfall	Destination	Distance (M)
IS211 Bali S 8°55'S, 115°12'E		IS212 Christmas 10°28'S, 105°46'E	Flying Fish 10°25'S, 105°43'E	570

Generally pleasant sailing conditions can be expected during the months when the majority of boats make this passage, which is August and September. The trade winds blow strongly in July and August, but sometimes there are years when the trade winds fail to be established and winds are either very light or can blow at gale force for several days. At Christmas Island the SE trade winds blow almost continuously from May until December, but in the first months of the year, when the NW monsoon is established in the area to the north of the island, the NW monsoon makes itself felt with occasional heavy rains, strong winds, and thunderstorms. In January and February winds can

blow strongly from the west or north. The island is normally spared the cyclones which affect the area between it and North West Australia.

From WP IS211, south of Benoa harbour, a direct route runs south of Java and Sumatra to WP IS212, two miles east of Christmas Island. The best anchorage is at Flying Fish Cove. Boats should fly the Q flag on arrival and will be visited by customs. The rest of the entry formalities will be completed ashore. As the island is an Australian territory, similar visa requirements apply as in Australia itself and those arriving without a visa may not be allowed to stay. The strict Australian food quarantine regulations may also apply.

IS22 Bali to Chagos

BEST TIME:	May to October			
TROPICAL STORMS:	December to April			
CHARTS:	BA: 4071			
	US: 70			
PILOTS:	BA: 34, 39			
	US: 163, 170, 171			
WAYPOINTS:				
Departure	Intermediate	Landfall	Destination	Distance (M)
IS221 Bali S 8°55'S, 115°12'E	IS222 Blenheim 5°20'S, 72°35'E	IS223 Salomon 5°17.5'S, 72°15'E	Takamaka 5°20'S, 72°16'E	2565

This more direct route is preferred by those who are not tempted by the usual detour via Christmas and Cocos Keeling Islands. The route from Bali runs slightly north of latitude 10°S where good sailing conditions can be expected throughout the SE monsoon and the risk of cyclones is almost nonexistent. The route is joined south of Sumatra by boats that have reached the Indian Ocean through the Sunda Strait. Although the route from Bali is under the general influence of the SE trade winds, strong winds from the southern quarter are not unusual during the winter months and they are often accompanied by a big swell. Rough seas have been encountered especially around longitude 90°E, the ocean disturbance being apparently

caused by a submarine mountain ridge.

Chagos enjoys South Indian Ocean weather with SE trade winds from April to November, but as the islands are close to the upper limit of the trade winds, they can be light and more variable. From December to March, when the ITCZ moves south, the NE monsoon is deflected south of the equator to give a NW flow of wind. The NW monsoon is not so reliable, brings rain, and blows most strongly in January and February. The period of the NW monsoon is also the cyclone season, but these storms normally form south of Chagos and move in a southerly direction. They almost never track north towards the equator.

From WP IS221, south of Benoa harbour, a direct

route runs south of Java and Sumatra to WP IS222, 10 miles SE of Blenheim Reef. From there a course can be set for WP IS223 close to the NW pass leading into the lagoon at Salomon Island. The lagoon is entered through the NW pass and the recommended anchorage is off Takamaka Island, on the east side of the lagoon. Because of the extensive reefs and absence of lights, except at Diego Garcia itself, the area should be approached with great care. Special regulations apply to visitors to Diego Garcia, which is a military base leased by the UK to the USA. Only genuine emergency stops at Diego Garcia are allowed, although the presence of cruising boats is tolerated in the other islands.

IS23 *Bali to Cocos Keeling*

BEST TIME:	May to October				
TROPICAL STORMS:	November to April				
CHARTS:	BA: 4071				
	US: 70				
PILOTS:	BA: 34, 44				
	US: 163, 175				
CRUISING GUIDES:	*Indian Ocean Handbook.*				
WAYPOINTS:					
Departure	**Intermediate**	**Landfall**		**Destination**	**Distance (M)**
IS230 Benoa	IS231 Bali S	IS232 Keeling E		Direction	1108
8°45'S, 115°15'E	*8°55'S, 115°12'E*	*12°05'S, 97°00'E*		*12°05.5'S, 96°52.5'E*	

The SE trade winds are normally found once a boat has left the influence of the Indonesian archipelago, so it is recommended to head offshore as soon as possible. At the height of the SE trade wind season, the winds on this route, and especially closer to Cocos Keeling, can be quite strong. Combined with a large swell from the south, this can produce rather uncomfortable conditions. Better conditions will be experienced at the beginning of the winter season, in May and June.

Landfall will be made east of Direction Island on South Cocos. The entrance into the large and well protected lagoon is west of Direction Island. To reach the recommended anchorage, Direction Island is left 1/4 mile to port. A marker shows where to turn to port to reach a yellow quarantine buoy. Arriving yachts must anchor in its vicinity and wait to be cleared by calling Flight Services on channel 16.

Strict food quarantine regulations apply and any fresh produce may be confiscated. Tinned food that is not of Australian origin may also be seized. Australian visas are compulsory for all crew members, including the captain. In spite of all difficulties, mainly caused by rigid Australian bureaucracy, this is a recommended stop.

IS24 *Bali to Mauritius*

BEST TIME:	May–June, October
TROPICAL STORMS:	November to April
CHARTS:	BA: 4070
	US: 70
PILOTS:	BA: 34, 39
	US: 163, 170, 171

| WAYPOINTS: | | | | |
Departure	Intermediate	Landfall	Destination	Distance (M)
IS240 Benoa *8°45'S, 115°15'E*	IS241 Bali S *8°55'S, 115°12'E*	IS242 Mauritius N *19°48'S, 57°37'E*	Port Louis *20°09'S, 57°29'E*	3428
IS240 Benoa	IS241 Bali S	IS243 Rodriguez *19°37'S, 63°25'E*	Port Mathurin *19°41'S, 63°25'E*	3082

As sailing conditions at the height of the SE trade wind season can be quite boisterous, the recommended time is outside the period when the trade winds are in full force. Between July and September, the winds often blow at 25 knots, or even more, and occasionally reach gale force. There is also often a cross swell, which makes for uncomfortable passages. Better conditions are experienced at the beginning and end of the Austral winter. Conditions generally improve as one approaches Mauritius where landfall will be made close to North Island. Port Control should be contacted on channel 16 before entering the harbour. Facilities for cruising boats have been improving in Port Louis since it became the destination of a round the world rally.

Some boats break the voyage at Rodriguez, where formalities are completed at Port Mathurin. The clearance is only valid locally and must be renewed on arrival in Mauritius. The winds between the two sister islands are very strong at the height of the SE trades in July and August when gale force winds are common.

Although a nonstop passage is quite feasible, the voyage could easily be interrupted at Cocos Keeling (see IS23). Slightly off the direct route, the islands of the Chagos Archipelago provide another interesting diversion.

IS25 Bali to Darwin

BEST TIME:	November, May
TROPICAL STORMS:	December to April
CHARTS:	BA: 4603
	US: 603
PILOTS:	BA: 17, 34
	US: 163, 175
CRUISING GUIDES:	*Cruising Guide to Southeast Asia (2).*
WAYPOINTS:	

Departure	Intermediate	Landfall	Destination	Distance (M)
IS250 Benoa *8°45'S, 115°15'E*	IS251 Bali E *8°50'S, 115°20'E*			
	IS252 *11°30'S, 124°30'E*	IS253 Charles *12°21'S, 130°42'E*	Darwin *12°28'S, 130°51'E*	956

There are basically only two options for anyone intending to sail east from Bali: to sail short legs along the chain of Indonesian islands, or to take the offshore route. The first option is feasible at practically any time of the year and, by sailing along the north coast of the islands, one will be able to take advantage of the diurnal alternation between land and sea breezes. The second option can only be recommended at the change of seasons, from the SE to the NW monsoon. It is stressed, however, that the eastbound passage ought to be completed before the onset of the cyclone season in December, or after the risk of cyclones has decreased to an acceptable level, such as in May.

The recommended offshore route stays south of all Indonesian islands and is also clear of an agglomeration of oil platforms (12°00'S, 125°00'E) as well as the reefs of Ashmore and Hibernia.

Currents in the area south of Timor are often strong, so it should be approached with caution. The passage may be interrupted at Ashmore Reef, where there is a good anchorage in the lee of a small cay close to the NW corner of the reef. The reef is often visited by Indonesian fishermen. A well buoyed channel leads into Darwin Harbour, where visiting boats should proceed to Fishermen's Wharf. Darwin Port Authority needs to be contacted three hours in advance on VHF channel 16 or HF 2182 kHz to give an ETA. All persons arrriving in Australia must have a valid visa. Yachting facilities in Darwin are among the best in Australia. There is now a marina at Cullen Bay, but as the entrance is tidal, directions should be requested before entering.

IS30 ROUTES IN THE CENTRAL INDIAN OCEAN

The islands of the South Indian Ocean provide one of the most attractive cruising grounds in the world, yet the number of boats that visit them is very small. There are several reasons for this: the remoteness of the islands from the major cruising routes, the restrictions imposed on the movement of cruising boats in some of the islands, either by civil or military authorities, and the fact that by the time they have reached the Indian Ocean most sailors seem to have run out of time.

The routes linking the islands with each other, as well as with neighbouring Africa, are mostly under the influence of the SE trade winds, which last from April until November. The best sailing season is the

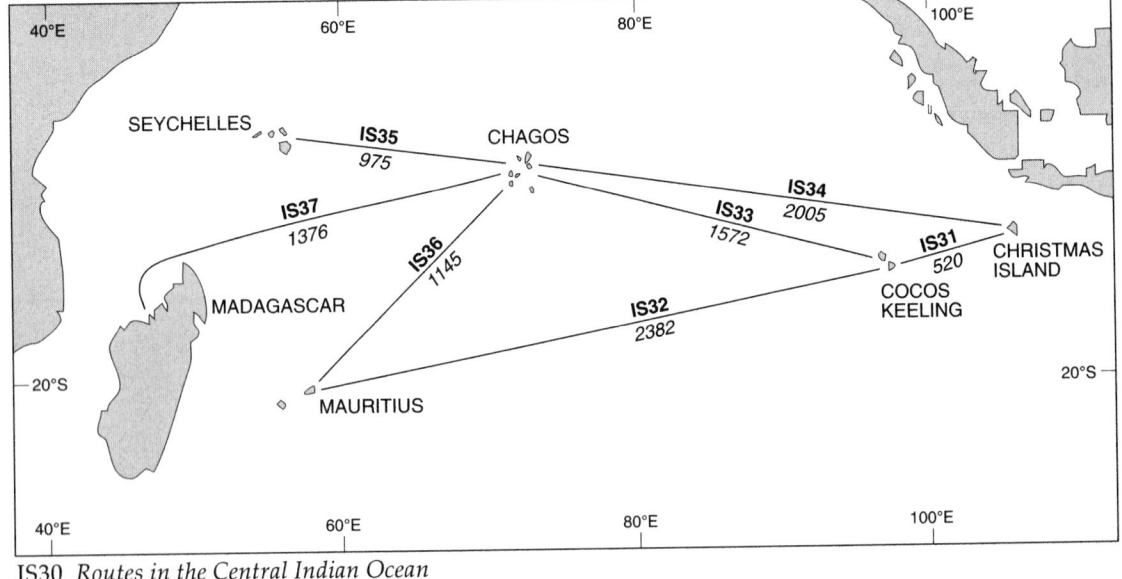

IS30 *Routes in the Central Indian Ocean*

southern winter, from June to September. In some of the islands in lower latitudes, such as Chagos or the Seychelles, the SE trade winds can be light and more variable, especially outside the peak winter months. From December to March, when the ITCZ moves south, the NE monsoon in the North Indian Ocean is deflected south of the equator and provides a flow of NW winds. The weather in summer is less attractive, a hot and humid NW monsoon and the danger of tropical cyclones in the south.

IS31 *Christmas Island to Cocos Keeling*

BEST TIME:	May to October
TROPICAL STORMS:	November to April
CHARTS:	BA: 4070
	US: 70
PILOTS:	BA: 34, 44
	US: 163, 174
WAYPOINTS:	

Departure	Intermediate	Landfall	Destination	Distance (M)
IS311 Christmas W 10°25'S, 105°33'E		IS312 Keeling E 12°05'S, 97°00'E	Direction *12°05.5'S, 96°52.5'E*	520

During the SE trade wind season the winds on this route are almost always favourable. Occasionally the trades cease to blow for a day, but periods of calms or light winds are usually short lived. The one unpleasant feature of this route is the large swell from the south or southwest. Because the wind blows from the SE and the swell is almost at right angles to the direction of the wind, the motion can be very uncomfortable and it can also be tough on selfsteering gears, which have sometimes broken under the strain of the violent motion.

A direct route links these two Australian possessions. From WP IS311, west of Christmas Island, a course should be set for WP IS312, six miles east of Direction Island on South Cocos. As the only powerful light is at the airport, on the SW side of the lagoon, the atoll should be approached carefully at night. The entrance into the large lagoon is west of Direction Island and the recommended anchorage is in its lee. To reach the anchorage, Direction Island is left 1/4 mile to port. A marker shows where to turn to port to reach the yellow quarantine buoy where arriving yachts should anchor and wait for clearance. The Q flag must be flown until cleared. Flight Services should be called on VHF channel 16 and customs, immigration, and quarantine officers will come to the boat.

Strict food quarantine regulations apply and only Australian food products, labelled as such, will be allowed. Occasionally, fresh produce taken on board at Christmas Island has been confiscated at Cocos Keeling. Australian visas are compulsory.

IS32 *Cocos Keeling to Mauritius*

BEST TIME:	May to June, September to October
TROPICAL STORMS:	November to April
CHARTS:	BA: 4070
	US: 70
PILOTS:	BA: 39, 44
	US: 170, 171, 174

WAYPOINTS:				
Departure	Intermediate	Landfall	Destination	Distance (M)
Route IS32A				
IS321 Keeling W		IS322 Mauritius N	Port Louis	2382
12°04'S, 96°49'E		19°48'S, 57°37'E	20°09'S, 57°29'E	
Route IS32B				
IS321 Keeling W		IS323 Rodriguez	Port Mathurin	2037
		19°37'S, 63°25'E	19°41'S, 63°25'E	

This long haul across the width of the South Indian Ocean has the full benefit of the SE trade winds during the southern winter months, from May to October. These winds often blow at 20 to 25 knots for days on end and sometimes reach gale force. The pleasure of a fast passage is often marred by an uncomfortable cross swell which rolls in relentlessly from the Southern Ocean. The weather is generally rougher in the proximity of Cocos Keeling and both winds and seas usually moderate after the halfway mark to Mauritius has been passed. The trade winds continue to blow consistently in October, but the weather becomes more squally and the chances of encountering gale force winds are greater. Although it would appear that by making a sweep to the north it would be possible to avoid the area with the highest frequency of gale force winds, this does not seem to be the case. Boats that have arrived in Mauritius by a more roundabout way have encountered equally rough conditions as those which sailed a direct course.

Boats normally leave the lagoon at South Cocos by the Northern Entrance, although in good light and if there is not a large swell, it is possible to thread one's way SW across the lagoon and leave by the Western Entrance. The Northern Entrance, however, is easier and therefore safer. Having left Horsburgh Island to port, from WP IS321, NW of that island, a direct course (route IS32A) can be set for WP IS322, three miles north of Round Island north of Mauritius. From there the course should be altered to sail along the NW coast to Port Louis, the island's main harbour. The Port Authority must be contacted on VHF channel 16 to obtain permission to enter the port. Arriving yachts are normally directed to the customs dock.

Some boats break the journey to Mauritius by calling in at Rodriguez (route IS32B), where cruising boats are welcome and local boats sometimes sail out to guide the visitors in. If a stop there is intended, from Cocos Keeling the course should be set for WP IS323, off the north point of the island. The main harbour is at Port Mathurin, where boats have to clear in. Although the island belongs to Mauritius, the clearance is only valid locally and one must clear in again on arrival in Mauritius. The winds between the two islands are often very strong, especially at the peak of the SE trade winds, in July and August, when winds of up to 50 knots have been reported.

IS33 *Cocos Keeling to Chagos*

BEST TIME:	May to June, September to October			
TROPICAL STORMS:	November to April			
CHARTS:	BA: 4070			
	US: 70			
PILOTS:	BA: 39, 44			
	US: 170, 171, 174			
WAYPOINTS:				
Departure	Intermediate	Landfall	Destination	Distance (M)
IS331 Keeling W	IS332 Blenheim	IS333 Salomon	Takamaka	1572
12°04'S, 96°49'E	5°20'S, 72°35'E	5°17.5'S, 72°15'E	5°20'S, 72°16'E	

For the duration of the SE monsoon both winds and current are favourable along this route. Occasionally in July and August the trade winds blow very strongly south of latitude 10°S, but these conditions are less common further north. Better sailing conditions are often encountered at the beginning and end of the SE monsoon, September being considered to be the best month. During the NE monsoon of the North Indian Ocean, the influence of this monsoon makes itself felt as far south as latitude 10°S. Between January and April winds are less constant in direction and usually have a northerly component. The weather in the transition period between monsoons is often unsettled, with overcast skies and rain squalls, often accompanied by violent winds.

Because of the restrictions that apply to boats arriving in Diego Garcia it is better to make straight for the islands on the north side of the archipelago, such as Salomon or Peros Banhos, unless an emergency call at Diego Garcia can be justified.

Having left the lagoon at Cocos Keeling through the North Entrance, from WP IS331, NW of Horsburgh Island, a direct course can be set for WP IS332, 10 miles SE of Blenheim Reef. From there the course can be altered for WP IS333 close to the NW pass leading into the lagoon at Salomon Island. Because of the extensive reefs and absence of lights, except at Diego Garcia itself, the area should be approached with great care.

IS34 *Christmas Island to Chagos*

BEST TIME:	May to September
TROPICAL STORMS:	November to April
CHARTS:	BA: 4070
	US: 70
PILOTS:	BA: 34, 44
	US: 163, 170, 171
WAYPOINTS:	

Departure	Intermediate	Landfall	Destination	Distance (M)
IS341 Christmas W 10°25'S, 105°33'E	IS342 Blenheim 5°20'S, 72°35'E	IS343 Salomon 5°17.5'S, 72°15'E	Takamaka *5°20'S, 72°16'E*	2005

There are few boats which bypass Cocos Keeling Island and sail direct from Christmas Island to Chagos. However, in unsettled weather it might be preferable to sail a direct course, rather than make the detour to the south. The winter months of May to September provide both favourable winds and current. The weather on this route is similar to that on routes IS31 and IS33 to which reference should be made. It should also be noted that Diego Garcia is a restricted military island and anchorage must be sought elsewhere in the Chagos Archipelago.

From WP IS341, west of Christmas Island, a direct course leads to WP IS342, 10 miles SE of Blenheim Reef. From there the course can be altered for any of the islands and atolls in this uninhabited archipelago. The Salomon Islands, Peros Banhos, and Egmont Islands are all popular with cruising boats. The most convenient anchorage is in Salomon lagoon. To reach it, from WP IS342 the course should be altered for WP IS343, close to the pass leading into the lagoon.

IS35 *Chagos to Seychelles*

BEST TIME:	May to September
TROPICAL STORMS:	None
CHARTS:	BA: 4702
	US: 702
PILOTS:	BA: 39
	US: 170, 171
CRUISING GUIDES:	*Indian Ocean Handbook.*

WAYPOINTS:				
Departure	*Intermediate*	*Landfall*	*Destination*	*Distance (M)*
IS351 Peros W 5°13'S, 71°45'E	IS352 Frigate 4°38'S, 56°00'E	IS353 Mahé E 4°35'S, 55°30'E	Victoria *4°36.6'S, 55°28'E*	975

The SE monsoon should be favoured for this route which has the best weather between May and September, when both winds and current are favourable. Near perfect sailing conditions have been encountered by boats making this passage in May and June. Later in the year the NE monsoon starts making itself felt in the South Indian Ocean, the transitional months of October and November being associated with light winds, calm seas, and the occasional violent rain squall.

A good place to leave from Chagos is Peros Banhos. Having left the large lagoon through the NW Pass, from WP IS351, north of Diamond Island, the route runs due west along parallel 5°S. The route

is clear of dangers, but the Seychelles should be approached with caution because of the rocks and reefs that surround them. The safest approach is to make landfall at Frigate Island by setting course for WP IS352, five miles SE of that island. From there the course can be altered for WP IS353, north of St Anne Island in the approaches to Port Victoria, the capital located on Mahé, the main island of the group. Beacons lead through the reefs into the harbour. Having contacted the Port Authority on VHF channel 16, arriving yachts must anchor in the quarantine area north of Victoria lighthouse where they will be boarded for clearance.

IS36 *Chagos to Mauritius*

BEST TIME:	May to June, September to October			
TROPICAL STORMS:	November to April			
CHARTS:	BA: 4702			
	US: 702			
PILOTS:	BA: 39			
	US: 170, 171			
WAYPOINTS:				
Departure	*Intermediate*	*Landfall*	*Destination*	*Distance (M)*
IS361 Egmont 6°38'S, 71°19'E		IS362 Mauritius N 19°48'S, 57°37'E	Port Louis *20°09'S, 57°29'E*	1145

A windward passage during most of the SE trade wind season, this route can benefit from better winds at the beginning and end of winter, when the trade winds do not have too much south in them. It has been noticed that the stronger the SE trade winds, the more south there is in them and vice versa. Therefore it may be worth avoiding this route in July and August when the trade winds are known to be quite blustery. Boats that have made this passage in October have reported pleasant sailing conditions. If the winds are easterly, it is possible to call first at Rodriguez Island before continuing to Mauritius (see route IS32).

A good point of departure are the Egmont

Islands, in the SE part of the Chagos archipelago. From WP IS361, a direct course may be set for Mauritius. The route passes well to the east of Cargados Carajos Reef, which belongs to Mauritius. Boats which have not yet cleared into Mauritius are not allowed to stop there without prior permission. The route leads to WP IS362, three miles north of Round Island north of Mauritius. From there the course should be altered to sail along the NW coast to Port Louis, the island's main harbour. The Port Authority must be contacted on VHF channel 16 for permission to enter the port. Arriving yachts are normally directed to the customs dock.

IS37 *Chagos to Madagascar*

BEST TIME:	May to June, September to October			
TROPICAL STORMS:	November to April			
CHARTS:	BA: 4702			
	US: 702			
PILOTS:	BA: 39			
	US: 170, 171			
CRUISING GUIDES:	*East Africa Pilot.*			
WAYPOINTS:				

Departure	Intermediate	Landfall	Destination	Distance (M)
IS371 Egmont 6°38'S, 71°19'E	IS372 Saya 10°00'S, 60°00'E			
	IS373 Malhu 11°30'S, 55°00'E	IS374 Ambre N 11°50'S, 49°15'E	Antseranana *12°16'S, 49°18'E*	1376

Although most cruising boats bound for South Africa continue to sail the traditional route via Mauritius, a route that goes through the Mozambique Channel is gathering popularity, especially as one is able to visit Madagascar on the way. From WP IS371, north of the Egmont Islands, in the SW part of the Chagos archipelago, the direct route to Cap d'Ambre, the northern point of Madagascar, cuts right through Saya de Malha Bank, an area of strong tidal sets and rips. To avoid the worst part of this area, and also to approach Madagascar from a better angle, an initial course should be set for WP IS372 and then WP IS373. The main reason for using the latter waypoint is to sail most of the remaining distance on the latitude of Cap d'Ambre. The purpose of this is that as the SE trade winds hit the mass of Madagascar, their direction becomes more southerly, therefore approaching the island from the east, rather than NE, ensures that the winds are met at a better angle. From WP IS373 a course can be set for WP IS374, 6 miles north of Cap d'Ambre. The nearest port of entry is at Antseranana, on the island's west coast.

IS40 ROUTES IN THE WESTERN INDIAN OCEAN

In spite of its many attractions, the western part of the South Indian Ocean is visited by few cruising boats. The two island groups, the Seychelles and the Comoros, are part of a triangular cruising route between the African mainland and these offshore islands. The area north of Madagascar is peppered with reefs and small islands, which are a diver's paradise, but used to be a navigator's nightmare until satellite navigation took most of those worries away. Nevertheless, the area should still be approached with great caution as the positions of many islands and reefs are incorrectly charted and therefore do not agree with coordinates obtained by GPS.

Weather conditions throughout the area bear a certain similarity. In the Seychelles the SE trade winds prevail from May to the middle of October, although in some years they are not established

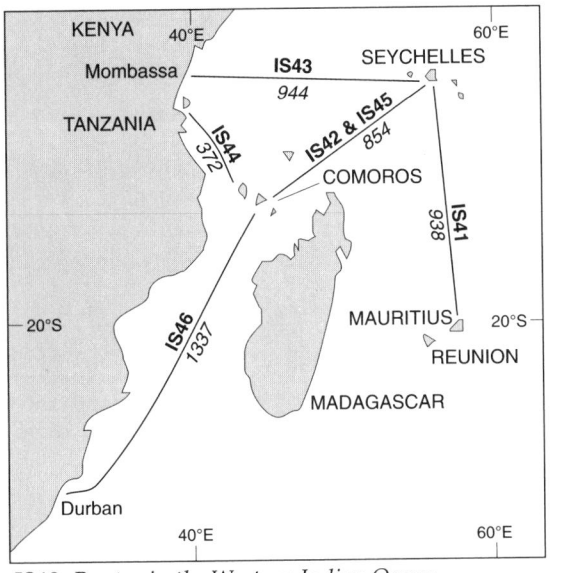

IS40 *Routes in the Western Indian Ocean*

until June or even July. The SE season is the fine weather period, with steady SE winds blowing in July, August, and September. In November the changeover to the NW monsoon is marked by heavy squalls and rain. The NW monsoon is the wet season and lasts until April. During these months winds blow from the NW, W, or WSW. Cyclones are practically unknown and if they do pass through the vicinity it is usually around 200 miles to the south of Mahé.

In the Comoros, the NW monsoon commences at the end of October or early in November and lasts until April. This is the hot and rainy season, which is characterised by irregular winds and squally weather. In the SE season winds blow more regularly, although never too strong, their strength being broken by the mass of neighbouring Madagascar. The changeover between the seasons is marked by calms, variable winds, and squally weather. Occasionally cyclones reach the Comoro Islands, the months with the highest risk being February to April.

IS41 *Seychelles to Mauritius*

BEST TIME:	May to June, October			
TROPICAL STORMS:	November to April			
CHARTS:	BA: 4070	US: 702		
PILOTS:	BA: 39			
	US: 170, 171			
WAYPOINTS:				
Departure	*Intermediate*	*Landfall*	*Destination*	*Distance (M)*
IS411 Mahé SE 4°40'S, 55°33.5'E	IS412 Agalega 10°00'S, 56°10'E IS413 15°00'S, 56°45'E	IS414 Mauritius NW 20°08'S, 57°26'E	Port Louis *20°09'S, 57°29'E*	938

A windward passage for most of the year, the timing of this route offers few alternatives, as the season when northerly winds are more frequent also coincides with the cyclone season. If the passage is made during the SE trade wind season, but outside of the blustery months of July and August, better conditions can be expected in May and early June, or in October, two periods when the winds can be more easterly.

In good light it is possible to use Cerf Passage when leaving Mahé from Port Victoria. Otherwise it is safer to use the main shipping channel. From

WP IS411, at the exit of Cerf Passage, a direct course leads to Mauritius passing close to the west of Coetivy Island, which should be approached with care as it has been reported to lie some 3 miles further west than its charted position. Similar caution should be exercised when passing west of Agalega Island, which is also close to the direct route. To stay clear of all these dangers, on departure from WP IS411 the course should be set to pass through two intermediate waypoints, IS412 and IS413, so as to stay at least 20 miles west of Agalega and surrounding dangers. From WP IS413 the course can be altered for WP IS414 in the approaches to Port Louis, the capital and main port. The Port Authority must be contacted on VHF channel 16 to obtain permission to enter the port. Arriving yachts are normally directed to the customs dock.

Boats occasionally break this passage at the Cargados Carajos Reef, which is close enough to the direct route to warrant the detour. Such a detour is made even more tempting if strong headwinds are encountered, which is often the case. The reef belongs to Mauritius and is visited by fishing boats from that island. Cruising boats are not supposed to stop there unless sheltering from bad weather.

IS42 *Seychelles to Comoros*

BEST TIME:	April to May
TROPICAL STORMS:	November to April
CHARTS:	BA: 4070
	US: 72
PILOTS:	BA: 39
	US: 171
CRUISING GUIDES:	*East Africa Pilot.*
WAYPOINTS:	

Departure	Intermediate	Landfall	Destination	Distance (M)
Route IS42A				
IS420 Mahé N	IS421 Descroches NE			
4°32'S, 55°26'E	5°38'S, 53°44'E			
	IS422 Descroches SW			
	5°42'S, 53°37'E			
	IS423 Boudeuse			
	6°00'S, 52°51'E			
	[IS424 Alphonse]			
	6°30'S, 53°00'E			
	IS425 Cosmoledo	IS426 Comoro N	Moroni	854
	10°00'S, 46°45'E	11°25'S, 43°15'E	*11°42'S, 43°15'E*	
		IS427 Anjouan NW	Mutsamudu	803
		12°08'S, 44°25'E	*12°10'S, 44°24'E*	
Route IS42B				
IS420 Mahé N	IS421 Descroches NE			
	IS422 Descroches SW			
	IS423 Boudeuse			
	IS428 Astrove	IS429 Mayotte NE	Dzaoudzi	853
	10°00'S, 45°20'E	12°44'S, 45°15'E	*12°47'S, 45°15'E*	

Because of the various island groups and numerous reefs encountered on this route, and also the likelihood of strong headwinds at the height of the SE monsoon, when the direction of the wind becomes increasingly southerly as the Comoros are approached, most boats break up this passage into shorter stages by stopping at some of the islands en route. Because winds over 20 knots are the order of the day at the height of the SE trade wind season, the passage should be undertaken at the start of the season, although in April there is still the small risk of a late cyclone.

After leaving Port Victoria on the main island of Mahé, the course goes around the north of the island to WP IS420, north of North Point. From there the course can be set for WP IS421, NE of Descroches Island, one of the Amirante Islands, which has a well protected anchorage on its west side used by boats making this passage. From WP IS422, SW of Descroches Island, the route crosses the Amirante Bank to WP IS423, north of Boudeuse Cay. This section should only be done in good light; under any other conditions it would be safer to make for WP IS424 to pass east of Marie Louise Island and north of Alphonse Island.

Having left behind the last of these islands belonging to the Seychelles, there is a choice of routes to reach either the Comoros or Mayotte. Although the latter belongs geographically to the same group, as a French territory it is separate from the other Comoros. The direct route for the Comoros (IS42A) is sailed by setting course from WP IS423 for WP IS425. This route passes between Cosmoledo Group and Assumption Island before

the course is altered for WP IS426, north of Grand Comoro. The west coast of that island is then followed to the main port at Moroni. The only other official port of entry is Mutsamudu on Anjouan Island. To reach it, from WP IS425 the course should be altered for WP IS427.

A direct route can be sailed to Mayotte (IS42B) by setting a course from WP IS423 for WP IS428. The course can then be altered for WP IS429, in the approaches to Dzaoudzi, the official port of entry into Mayotte. The Port Captain should be contacted on VHF channel 16 for instructions before the perimeter reef is entered.

IS43 *Seychelles to East Africa*

BEST TIME:	May to September				
TROPICAL STORMS:	None				
CHARTS:	BA: 4071				
	US: 70				
PILOTS:	BA: 3, 39				
	US: 170, 171				
CRUISING GUIDES:	*East Africa Pilot.*				
WAYPOINTS:					
Departure	*Intermediate*	*Landfall*	*Destination*		*Distance (M)*
IS431 Mahé N	IS432 Amirante N	IS433 off Mombasa	Mombasa		944
4°32'S, 55°26'E	4°42'S, 53°24'E	4°04'S, 39°45'E	*4°04'S, 39°41'E*		
		IS434 Salaam	Dar es Salaam		973
		6°50'S, 39°24'E	*6°49'S, 39°19'E*		

Favourable winds can be expected on this route throughout the SE trade wind season, from April till October; the most consistent winds are during May to September. During this period the current is also favourable, setting westward, but it turns northward before reaching the African coast.

From WP IS431, north of Mahé's North Point, the route goes due west to pass north of the Amirante Islands through WP IS432, 10 miles north of North Island. At night or in poor visibility the islands should be passed at a safe distance as they are low and the light on North Island is reported to be out of action occasionally. Those who wish to stop can do so by following the directions in IS42.

From WP IS432, the routes split according to their East African destination. Boats bound for Kenya

should set a course for WP IS433, in the approaches to Mombasa. Port Control should be contacted on VHF channels 12 or 16. Other ports of entry into Kenya are Lamu (2°18'S, 40°55'E) and Malindi (3°13'S, 40°07'E).

Boats bound for Tanzania should set a course from WP IS432 for WP IS434, in the approaches to Dar es Salaam. Arriving yachts should anchor in the inner harbour and wait to be visited by the various officials. The other ports of entry into Tanzania are Zanzibar (6°10'S, 39°11'E), Mtwara (10°15'S, 40°12'E), and Tanga (5°04'S, 39°06'E). Formalities in Tanga appear to be the easiest and Tanga Signal Station should be contacted on VHF channel 12 before proceeding to Dhow Wharf for clearance.

IS44 *Comoros to East Africa*

BEST TIME:	May to October			
TROPICAL STORMS:	November to April			
CHARTS:	BA: 4701			
	US: 701			
PILOTS:	BA: 3, 39			
	US: 171			
CRUISING GUIDES:	*East Africa Pilot.*			
WAYPOINTS:				

Departure	Intermediate	Landfall	Destination	Distance (M)
Route IS44A				
IS441 Mayotte NE		IS442 off Mombasa	Mombasa	616
12°44'S, 45°15'E		4°06'S, 39°44'E	*4°04'S, 39°41'E*	
Route IS44B				
IS443 Comoro NW		IS442 off Mombasa	Mombasa	502
11°40'S, 43°12'E				

Favourable winds prevail along this route during the SE monsoon and there is also a north-setting coastal current throughout the year, which can reach as much as 4 knots at the peak of the SE monsoon, but is only slight during the NE monsoon. The most pleasant weather is in July and August, when the temperature is cooler and humidity low.

Whether leaving from Mayotte (IS44A) or Grand Comoro (IS44B), boats bound for Kenya can sail a direct offshore route. From WP441, in the approaches to Dzaoudzi, on Mayotte, a course can be set for WP IS442, in the approaches to Mombasa. Mombasa Port Control should be contacted on VHF channels 12 or 16. Boats leaving from Moroni, on Grand Comoro, can take their departure from WP IS443 and also set a course for WP IS442.

The above offshore routes pass outside Tanzanian waters. The alternative is to take an inshore route inside the reefs that front the Tanzanian coast. If the intention is to cruise most of the Tanzanian coast, clearance formalities should be completed in the southern port of Mtwara (10°15'S, 40°12'E). Other Tanzanian ports of entry are the capital Dar es Salaam (6°49'S, 39°19'E), Zanzibar (6°10'S, 39°11'E), and Tanga (5°04'S, 39°06'E).

The island of Pemba is closed to visitors on security grounds and as there are several sensitive areas in Tanzania skippers are advised to check the situation with the authorities in Dar es Salaam to avoid trouble with local officials.

IS45 *Comoros to Seychelles*

BEST TIME:	May to October
TROPICAL STORMS:	November to April
CHARTS:	BA: 4070
	US: 72
PILOTS:	BA: 39
	US: 171
CRUISING GUIDES:	*Indian Ocean Handbook.*

WAYPOINTS:				
Departure	Intermediate	Landfall	Destination	Distance (M)
IS451 Mayotte NE 12°44'S, 45°15'E	IS452 10°00'S, 48°45'E IS453 9°00'S, 50°00'E IS454 Mahé S 4°49'S, 55°33'E	IS455 Mahé SE 4°40'S, 55°33.5'E	Victoria 4°36.5'S, 55°28'E	791

Because the area around the Comoros is subject to tropical storms, this passage should not be undertaken during the cyclone season. From May to October winds along this route are mostly SSE or SE and there is also a favourable current. There are several island groups north of Madagascar that can be visited en route to the Seychelles, such as Iles Glorieuses or Providence Island, and all of them have protected anchorages.

The direct route from Mayotte passes west of Iles Glorieuses. From WP IS451, in the approaches to Dzaoudzi, a course can be set to pass through two intermediate waypoints, IS452 and IS453. The route continues north of Alphonse Islands to WP IS454, off Mahé's South Point. There the course should be altered to sail due north parallel to the coast to WP IS455, one mile SE of Cerf Passage. In good visibility this pass can be taken to reach Port Victoria, otherwise it may be necessary to carry on past St Anne Island and enter the port through the normal shipping channel. Having contacted the Port Authority on VHF channel 16, yachts must anchor in the quarantine area north of Victoria lighthouse where they will be boarded for clearance.

IS46 Comoros to South Africa

BEST TIME:	October to November			
TROPICAL STORMS:	November to April			
CHARTS:	BA: 4070 US: 72			
PILOTS:	BA: 3, 39 US: 171			
CRUISING GUIDES:	East Africa Pilot, South African Nautical Almanac.			
WAYPOINTS:				
Departure	Intermediate	Landfall	Destination	Distance (M)
IS461 Mayotte SE 13°00'S, 45°12'E	IS462 André 16°00'S, 44°00'E IS463 25°00'S, 40°00'E IS464 28°30'S, 34°00'E	IS465 Richards 28°45'S, 32°10'E IS466 Natal NE 29°51'S, 31°05'E	Richards Bay 28°48'S, 32°06'E Durban 29°52'S, 31°02'E	1264 1337

The direct route to Durban, or other South African ports, leads through the Mozambique Channel, where the north-setting Mozambique Current can create very difficult sailing conditions. Although the winds that blow between Madagascar and the African mainland often come from a favourable direction, strong NE winds blowing against the current produce rough seas. This passage should not be made before the middle of September, when the chances of encountering contrary winds in the Mozambique Channel are greater than later in the year. If necessary the passage south can be interrupted in Madagascar and mainly for this reason the route should follow the eastern side of the Mozambique Channel. South of the Mozambique Channel similar directions apply as for route IS52 which also describes weather conditions in detail.

From WP IS461, off the SE extremity of Mayotte, the offshore route goes SW to WP IS462 off Cape St André. From there the route runs parallel to the west coast of Madagascar passing between Chesterfield and Juan de Nova islands all the way to WP IS463, also passing to the east of Europa Island. From WP IS463 the course should be altered for WP IS464. Depending on weather conditions, from that point one can close with the South African coast, especially if intending to stop first

at Richards Bay, in which case landfall will be made at WP IS465. If bound for Durban a course should be set for WP IS466, in the approaches to Durban. Durban Harbour Radio can be contacted before entering the port, but this is not compulsory. Yachts should proceed to the international jetty before formalities are completed ashore.

Few boats make this passage nonstop when the large island of Madagascar lies so conveniently close to the route. If a stop in Madagascar is envisaged, the best place to clear in is at Hell Ville (13°24'S, 48°17'E). Although Madagascar is now visited by many cruising boats, formalities are not too clear nor are the fees charged consistent. For southbound boats a good port for last provisions is Majunga or Mahajanga (15°43'S, 46°19'E). Boats that have stopped in the French administered Juan de Nova have been well received.

IS50 ROUTES FROM THE MASCARENE ISLANDS

Mauritius has always been a popular stopover from where to prepare for the long and difficult leg to South Africa. This passage can be a rough trip and there are few other areas in the world that have such a bad reputation among cruising boats as the southwestern part of the Indian Ocean. The strong south flowing Agulhas Current can create extremely rough conditions when hit by a SW gale, similar to conditions encountered off Cape Hatteras when the Gulf Stream is hit by a violent northerly wind. Several boats have got themselves into serious trouble on this passage, being knocked down or rolled over and dismasted, between Mauritius and Durban or on the next leg to Cape Town.

Boats heading north from Mauritius sail into a much more benign region where the weather is mostly fine. Although the entire area is prone to tropical cyclones, the really dangerous period is December to April. From April to November the SE trades blow almost continuously, usually freshening by mid-morning and

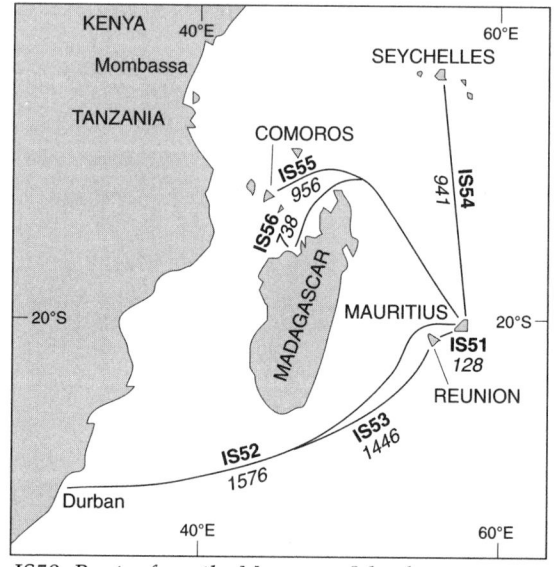

IS50 *Routes from the Mascarene Islands*

getting lighter by mid-afternoon. The wind often dies away at night under the influence of the land, and if it does not go calm at night, it will normally blow hard the following morning. The SE trade winds are at their strongest in June, July, and August. In the cyclone season, which is the most inclement time of year, SE winds are still the most common wind, but they are more moderate in strength and are subject to interruptions by winds from W or NW, or by calms.

IS51 *Mauritius to Réunion*

BEST TIME:	October to November				
TROPICAL STORMS:	November to April				
CHARTS:	BA: 4070				
	US: 700				
PILOTS:	BA: 39				
	US: 170, 171				
WAYPOINTS:					
Departure	*Intermediate*	*Landfall*	*Destination*	*Distance (M)*	
IS511 Mauritius SW 20°10'S, 57°25'E		IS512 Réunion 20°50'S, 55°23'E	Pointe des Galets *20°55'S, 55°18'E*	128	

This short passage between the largest two of the Mascarene Islands can be made at any time outside the cyclone season. Most boats stop at the French overseas territory of Réunion on their way to South Africa in October or early November. Many of those who stop in Réunion do so to stock up with French goods and to obtain a South African visa, as there is a South African Consulate in the capital St Dénis. Although such visas are not compulsory for sailors who do not leave their boats while in South Africa, they are recommended for those who intend to travel inland.

From WP IS511, off Port Louis, a direct route passing north of Réunion leads to WP IS512 in the approaches to Pointe des Galets.

Entry formalities for Réunion are completed at Pointe des Galets. The Port Captain should be contacted on VHF channel 16 before proceeding to the fishermen's dock. The other port of entry is Saint Pierre (21°20'S, 55°29'E).

IS52 *Mauritius to South Africa*

BEST TIME:	October to November				
TROPICAL STORMS:	November to April				
CHARTS:	BA: 4070				
	US: 700				
PILOTS:	BA: 3, 39				
	US: 170, 171				
CRUISING GUIDES:	*East Africa Pilot, South Africa Nautical Almanac.*				
WAYPOINTS:					
Departure	*Intermediate*	*Landfall*	*Destination*	*Distance (M)*	
IS521 Mauritius SW 20°10'S, 57°25'E	IS522 Réunion E 21°25'S, 56°00'E				
	IS523 27°00'S, 47°00'E				
	IS524 28°30'S, 34°00'E	IS525 Richards 28°45'S, 32°10'E	Richards Bay *28°48'S, 32°06'E*	1502	
		IS526 Natal NE 29°51'S, 31°05'E	Durban *29°52'S, 31°02'E*	1576	

The best time to leave Mauritius is early in November when the frequency of spring gales around latitude 30°S is getting less and the chances of an early cyclone are remote. The recommended procedure is to try and keep about 150 miles off the southern tip of Madagascar as the weather in the vicinity of this island is often unsettled. Sailing at this distance from land it is also possible to heave-to if a front arrives with contrary winds. This course also avoids a reputed freak wave area on the extended continental shelf off Madagascar. Yet another reason why it is recommended to stay at least 150 miles south of Madagascar is because the South Equatorial Current splits here, half of it merging with the south flowing Agulhas Current, the other half flowing north into the Mozambique Channel. By closing too early with the African coast several boats have been pushed north by the northern branch of the current, while hoping for a southerly boost from the Agulhas Current. The winds up to this point can be expected to be favourable, although not necessarily trade wind conditions as encountered earlier on.

The weather of the entire area between Madagascar and the Cape of Good Hope is dominated by the frontal systems which are created by Antarctic lows moving eastward. The approach of a cold front is usually heralded by a gradual change in the appearance of the sky, with cirrus clouds marching in from the west. These are replaced by dense banks of cumulus, while the wind backs slowly from E to NW, freshening all the time. After a brief interlude the gale arrives from the SW, its severity and duration depending on the nature and extent of the front. During the passing of a front, when the wind shifts suddenly from E or NE to SW, conditions in the Agulhas Current can become hazardous, especially around the 100 fathom line. In such a situation it is best to head immediately for the coast as the waves are smaller in the shallower water near the coast. Alternatively one should try and keep well offshore in deeper water and only approach the coast when close to the destination.

Although it is difficult to predict the kind of weather to expect when closing with the South African coast, one should keep an eye on the barometer. A local method of forecasting the approach of a SW buster is to watch the barometer. As it starts falling the winds will probably be NE. Once the barometer stops falling, the wind becomes light and then ceases altogether. The moment the barometer starts rising, one has between half an hour and one hour before the arrival of the SW gale, which may be enough warning to leave quickly the 100 fathom line.

Most boats have encountered very mixed weather on this route, with winds blowing at anything from 0 to 50 knots. However, very few are spared the SW gales that occur south of Madagascar and which succeed each other at two to three day intervals. After the area south of Madagascar has been passed a new course should be set to a point 200 miles ENE of Durban. Depending on wind and weather a direct course can be steered from there to Durban. A common mistake is to allow too much for leeway, trying to make landfall north of Durban, expecting to be taken south by the current. However, should a SW gale arrive while close to the coast, one would be pushed even further north and in that case the alternative is to seek shelter in Richards Bay. This port is also recommended if landfall is made too far north of Durban. The subsequent 90 mile leg from Richards Bay to Durban can be made later with a favourable weather forecast.

As the main consideration is to avoid crossing the Agulhas Current when the winds are from SW, up to date weather reports are essential. Useful weather reports are broadcast at 1303 GMT on 17655, 4376, 8740.8 kHz, and VHF channel 26. These are reports from the various lighthouses along the South African coast and so give details of wind strength and direction, as well as barometric pressure, going from south to north. One can therefore assess if a low system is coming up the coast and take appropriate action.

Although it has been suggested that boats bound for South Africa should sail directly to Port Elizabeth in order to avoid the worst of the Agulhas Current, rather than stop at Richards Bay or Durban, experienced local sailors strongly advise against such a course of action. The Agulhas Current reaches its maximum width and strength close to the latitude of Port Elizabeth making this the most dangerous area during bad weather. Furthermore, the chances of encountering the centre of the lows which are moving parallel with the coast are much greater in these latitudes than if the coast is approached north of Richards Bay, where the Agulhas Current is also narrower. It is therefore better to make landfall in about latitude 28°S and continue south only with a favourable weather forecast.

From WP IS521, off Port Louis, the recommended

route to avoid the dangerous area south of Madagascar passes east of Réunion through WP IS522. From there a course can be set for WP IS523 and thence for WP IS524. Depending on the port of destination as well as weather conditions, the course can then be altered to close with the coast. A convenient port of entry is Richards Bay, where a boat may be sent out to guide a yacht into the port. Boats bound for Richards Bay should make landfall at WP IS525. Those wishing to proceed directly to Durban should set course for WP IS526, in the approaches to Durban. Durban Harbour Radio can be contacted before entering the port, but this is not compulsory. Yachts are normally directed to the international jetty and formalities are completed ashore.

IS53 *Réunion to South Africa*

BEST TIME:	October to November			
TROPICAL STORMS:	November to April			
CHARTS:	BA: 4070			
	US: 700			
PILOTS:	BA: 3, 39			
	US: 170, 171			
CRUISING GUIDES:	*East Africa Pilot, South Africa Nautical Almanac.*			
WAYPOINTS:				
Departure	*Intermediate*	*Landfall*	*Destination*	*Distance (M)*
IS531 Réunion SW 21°20'S, 55°28'E	IS532 27°00'S, 47°00'E			
	IS533 28°30'S, 34°00'E	IS534 Richards 28°45'S, 32°10'E	Richards Bay *28°48'S, 32°06'E*	1373
		IS535 Natal NE 29°51'S, 31°05'E	Durban *29°52'S, 31°02'E*	1446

Similar directions apply as for route IS52 from Mauritius. Several of those who have made this passage described it as the toughest leg of their entire voyage. It is therefore essential to prepare the boat thoroughly for this passage.

The small port of St Pierre, on the SW coast of Réunion, is a convenient point of departure. From WP IS531, outside St Pierre, an initial course can be set for WP IS532, so as to keep well outside the dangerous area south of Madagascar as described in the previous route. From WP IS532, the same directions apply as those described for route IS52.

IS54 *Mauritius to Seychelles*

BEST TIME:	June to September
TROPICAL STORMS:	November to April
CHARTS:	BA: 4071
	US: 702
PILOTS:	BA: 39
	US: 170, 171
CRUISING GUIDES:	*Indian Ocean Handbook.*

| WAYPOINTS: | | | | |
Departure	Intermediate	Landfall	Destination	Distance (M)
IS541 Mauritius NW 20°08'S, 57°26'E	IS542 Agalega 15°00'S, 56°45'E IS543 10°00'S, 56°10'E IS544 Mahé S 4°49'S, 55°33'E	IS545 Mahé SE 4°40'S, 55°33.5'E	Victoria 4°36.5'S, 55°28'E	941

The SE trade winds provide fair winds on this route from May to October, although the weather tends to be occasionally squally. Cyclones affect the area around Mauritius from the middle of November until the end of April or even beginning of May, during which time it is best to avoid being in this area. As the route passes fairly close to the Cargados Carajos Reefs, some boats take the opportunity to stop at one of these small islands. They belong to Mauritius and permission to stop there should be obtained from the Fisheries Department of Mauritius before leaving Port Louis.

A direct course can be sailed all the way from Mauritius to Mahé, the main island of the Seychelles. Starting off from WP IS541, in the approaches to Port Louis, a course can be set first for WP IS542 so as to sail at least 20 miles west of Agalega Island and surrounding dangers. The route then passes through WP IS543 and continues towards Mahé passing close to the west of Coetivy Island, which should be approached with care as it has been reported to lie some 3 miles further west than its charted position. Landfall should be made at WP IS544, off Mahé's South Point. The course should be altered there to sail due north parallel to the coast to WP IS545, one mile SE of Cerf Passage. In good visibility this pass can be used to reach Port Victoria, otherwise it may be necessary to carry on past St Anne Island and enter the island's main port through the beaconed shipping channel. Having contacted the Port Authority on VHF channel 16, arriving yachts must anchor in the quarantine area north of Victoria lighthouse where they will be boarded for clearance.

IS55 *Mauritius to Comoros*

BEST TIME:	May to October			
TROPICAL STORMS:	November to April			
CHARTS:	BA: 4070	US: 72		
PILOTS:	BA: 39	US: 170, 171		
CRUISING GUIDES:	*East Africa Pilot.*			
WAYPOINTS:				
Departure	Intermediate	Landfall	Destination	Distance (M)
Route IS55A IS551 Mauritius NW 20°08'S, 57°26'E	IS552 Ambre E 11°50'S, 50°30'E IS553 Ambre N 11°50'S, 49°15'E	IS554 Mayotte NE 12°44'S, 45°15'E	Dzaoudzi 12°47'S, 45°15'E	956
Route IS55B IS551 Mauritius NW	IS552 Ambre E IS553 Ambre N	IS555 Anjouan NE 12°02'S, 44°30'E IS556 Comoro SE 12°00'S, 43°45'E	Mutsamudu 12°10'S, 44°24'E Moroni 11°42'S, 43°15'E	1203 1070

During the SE trade wind season, from May to October, this is a downwind run to the northern tip of Madagascar. The favourable winds should continue all the way to the Comoros, the group of small islands spread out between Madagascar and the African coast. Mayotte belongs geographically to the Comoros, but as it is a French territory it is separate from the independent Comoros.

From WP IS551, off Port Louis, a direct route leads to WP IS552, east of Cap d'Ambre, the northern extremity of Madagascar. As the route passes very close to Tromelin Island, a tiny French possession lying halfway between Mauritius and the northern tip of Madagascar, the passage can be interrupted there. Having passed Cap d'Ambre at a reasonable distance to avoid the rough seas in its vicinity, the course can be altered for either Mayotte or one of the islands in the Comoros. The route to Mayotte (IS55A) passes close by the Geyser Bank, which should be avoided. From WP IS553,

north of Cap d'Ambre, the course should be altered for WP IS554, in the approaches to Dzaoudzi, the official port of entry into Mayotte. The Port Captain should be contacted on VHF channel 16 for instructions before the perimeter reef is entered.

Boats bound for the Comoros (route IS55B) may stop at Iles Glorieuses, two small islands surrounded by a reef. From there, or if a stop in the Glorieuses is not intended, from WP IS553, north of Cap d'Ambre, a direct course can be sailed to the nearest of the Comoros, which is Anjouan. The landfall point for that island is IS555, off its north point. From there the course is altered to reach the port of Mutsamudu. Because the prevailing winds are from the south, boats bound for Grand Comoro should approach that island from the SE, rather than the north. To do this, from WP IS553 a course should be set for WP IS556, off Grand Comoro's SE point. From there, the south and west coasts of the island are followed to Moroni.

IS56 *Mauritius to Madagascar*

BEST TIME:	May to October			
TROPICAL STORMS:	November to April			
CHARTS:	BA: 4702	US: 702		
PILOTS:	BA: 39	US: 171		
CRUISING GUIDES:	*East Africa Pilot.*			
WAYPOINTS:				
Departure	*Intermediate*	*Landfall*	*Destination*	*Distance (M)*
IS561 Mauritius NW 20°08'S, 57°26'E	IS562 Ambre E 11°50'S, 50°30'E	IS563 Ambre N 11°50'S, 49°15'E	Antseranana *12°16'S, 49°18'E*	738

More cruising boats are visiting this large island off the coast of Africa which receives the full force of the SE trade winds blowing across the Indian Ocean. The strongest SE winds are in July, August, and September. Madagascar is under the influence of these winds all year, although the southern limit of the SE trade winds moves up the coast from August to November. During this period variable winds are experienced in the southern half of the island, although most winds are from an easterly or northeasterly direction. Winds from these directions can blow quite strongly. In March, when the ITCZ is further south, the northern tip of the island loses the SE winds to NE and NW winds. Madagascar lies within the cyclone belt, although cyclones are not as frequent as in the Mauritius

area. The South Equatorial Current splits at the centre of the island and runs north and south along the east coast. The current along the west coast is mostly south-setting.

As better sailing conditions will be encountered by sailing from Mauritius around the northern tip of Madagascar, directions as far as Cap d'Ambre are similar to those given for route IS55. Rather than sail a direct course to Cap d'Ambre, better conditions will be found if the northern tip of Madagascar is approached from the east. Therefore an initial course should be sailed for WP IS562 from where the route continues west along the same latitude to WP IS563 before altering course for the NW coast of the island. The nearest port of entry is at Antseranana.

IS60 ROUTES FROM AFRICA

The gradual easing of restrictions in some African countries has resulted in an increase in the number of cruising boats visiting various countries in East Africa, although the majority continue to limit their cruising to the offlying islands. Some boats reach East Africa by sailing south through the Red Sea and along the African coast during the NE monsoon. Others reach the area by making a detour via the islands of the South Indian Ocean before continuing towards the Red Sea. The best weather conditions for boats northbound from East Africa are encountered during the SW monsoon, particularly in September when the winds are less boisterous than at the height of the season, between June and August. The islands of the South Indian Ocean are occasionally visited by boats coming from South Africa, a tough trip against the prevailing winds and current. No less tough is the passage to Australia in the Roaring Forties, in an area of strong westerly winds which at least blow from a favourable direction.

Along the coast of East Africa, the SE trade winds blow steadily from April to October and rarely exceed 20 knots. The wide band of northbound current runs close to the shore and can be augmented by these SE winds so as to reach 4 knots, which makes it difficult if not impossible to sail south during the wrong season. For this reason, voyages along the East African coast should start at the most southerly point and follow the coast in a northerly direction. During the NE monsoon, when winds from the NE and E prevail, this current is slacker. Along the Tanzanian coast it is possible to take an inshore route which stays inside the reefs and islands. East Africa is not affected by the tropical cyclones that occur further south and east. Weather conditions around South Africa are described on page 503.

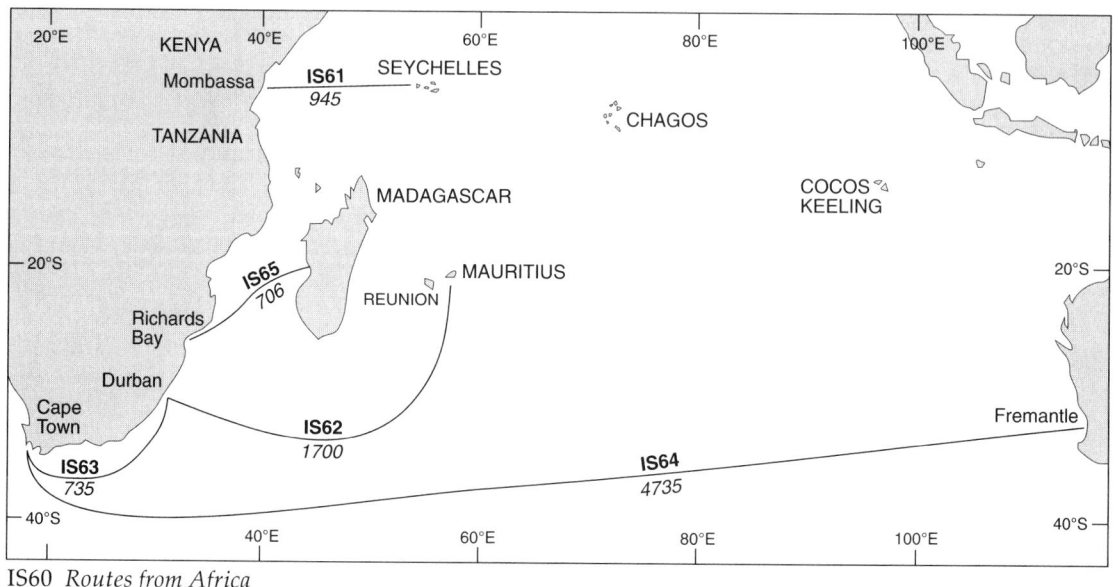

IS60 *Routes from Africa*

IS61 *East Africa to Seychelles*

BEST TIME:	January to March			
TROPICAL STORMS:	None			
CHARTS:	BA: 4071			
	US: 70			
PILOTS:	BA: 3, 39			
	US: 170, 171			
CRUISING GUIDES:	*Indian Ocean Handbook.*			
WAYPOINTS:				

Departure	Intermediate	Landfall	Destination	Distance (M)
IS611 Mombasa 4°04'S, 39°45'E	IS612 Amirante N 4°42'S, 53°24'E	IS613 Mahé N 4°32'N, 55°26'E	Victoria *4°36.5'S, 55°28'E*	945
IS614 Dar es Salaam 6°50'S, 39°24'E	IS612 Amirante N	IS613 Mahé N	Victoria	973

The NE monsoon makes itself felt along this route between January and March, when conditions for an eastbound passage are favourable, even if the winds are often light. Between December and April the current along this route is also favourable. Although this is the cyclone season in other parts of the South Indian Ocean, cyclones very rarely reach the latitude of the Seychelles. Should a cyclone threaten to come this way, with adequate warning boats on passage from Africa could turn north at the first sign of an approaching storm and move quickly out of its way into an area not affected by tropical storms.

A direct route leads outside all dangers from the Kenyan coast to Mahé, the main island in the Seychelles. From WP IS611, in the approaches to Mombasa, a direct course can be set for WP IS612, 10 miles north of North Island, the northernmost of the Amirante Islands. At night or in poor visibility the islands should be passed at a safe distance as they are low and the light on North Island is sometimes out of action. The course can then be altered for WP IS613, north of Mahé's North Point, in the approaches to Port Victoria. This is entered through the main shipping channel.

Boats leaving from a Tanzanian port, such as Dar es Salaam, follow a similar route. From WP IS614, in the approaches to Dar es Salaam, a direct course can be set for WP IS612. The rest of the route is similar to the one described above.

IS62 *Durban to Mauritius*

BEST TIME:	May			
TROPICAL STORMS:	November to April			
CHARTS:	BA: 4070			
	US: 70, 700			
PILOTS:	BA: 3, 39			
	US: 170, 171			
WAYPOINTS:				

Departure	Intermediate	Landfall	Destination	Distance (M)
IS621 Natal E 29°52'S, 31°05'E	IS622 30°00'S, 50°00'E			
	IS623 Brabant 20°25'S, 57°15'E	IS624 Mauritius S 20°12'S, 57°24'E	Port Louis *20°09'S, 57°29'E*	1700

Few boats attempt to sail a rhumb line between these two points because of the strong south-flowing Agulhas current and the high probability of encountering contrary winds. The recommended tactic is to make easting with the help of the prevailing westerly winds of higher latitudes. On leaving Durban, from WP IS621 a SE route is taken so that, depending on weather conditions, easting is made between latitudes 30°S and 35°S. However, one should be prepared to go even further south in search of westerly winds, possibly as far as 40°S. Strong westerlies should be encountered in those latitudes and also frequent squalls. Having sailed at least 800 miles in a SE direction, a point will be reached where the course can be altered for a more direct route to Mauritius. The NE course will lead first into an area of variable winds and calms. The SE trade winds can sometimes be found as far south as 30°S and, once found, they should ensure a fast passage for the rest of the voyage. The best month for this passage is May when the cyclone season has come to an end in the South Indian Ocean and the winter gales of higher latitudes are only about to begin.

Mauritius will be approached from the south by a route which will pass east of Réunion Island. Landfall will be made at WP IS623, off Cape Brabant, the SW extremity of Mauritius. From there the course can be altered for WP IS624, in the approaches to Port Louis.

IS63 *Durban to Cape Town*

Best time:	January to March
Tropical storms:	None
Charts:	BA: 4204
	US: 61003, 61000
Pilots:	BA: 2, 3
	US: 123, 171
Cruising guides:	*South Africa Nautical Almanac.*

The best time to make this passage along the South African coast is between January and March, when weather conditions can be expected to be the most benign. Few people attempt to make this passage in one go without seeking shelter in one of the few good ports en route. In fact the lack of sheltered anchorages is only one of three factors that make sailing along this section particularly difficult, the other two being the Agulhas Current and the unpredictable weather pattern. The Agulhas Current runs in a SW direction following the 100 fathom (200 metres) contour of the continental shelf and can attain up to 6 knots in places. The weather around the southern extremity of the African continent is greatly influenced by pressure systems moving NE from the Southern Ocean. As mentioned in route IS52, a SW gale combined with the strong south-flowing current can create giant waves up to 60 ft in height and even higher.

It has been established from research carried out into the formation of these freak waves that in all cases the dominant waves came from the SW. This always appears to coincide with a specific weather pattern, when areas of low pressure move along the coast in a NE direction. It is not uncommon during such conditions for the wind to suddenly change from a near NE gale to a full SW gale, the wind reinforcing the existing wave pattern which acts against the Agulhas Current. Usually the largest waves occur between the edge of the continental shelf and an area 20 miles to seaward and this is the reason why mariners are advised to move inshore inside the 100 fathom line as soon as there is a sign of an approaching SW gale. Although coastal passages are outside the scope of this book, the area under discussion has caused so many nightmares to small boat voyagers that the Durban to Cape Town route has been considered in sections.

Durban to East London (250 m)
As there is absolutely no safe shelter along this stretch of coast, it is essential to leave Durban with a good forecast. It is recommended to leave Durban at the end of a SW gale when the barometer has topped out above 1020 millibars. On leaving Durban one should head straight for the 100 fathom line to take full advantage of the strong south-setting current. If the weather deteriorate unexpectedly, one must close with the shore immediately so as to avoid the worst of the waves.

East London to Port Elizabeth (120 m)

The same rules for leaving apply as for the run from Durban south with the proviso that if the weather is still favourable when level with East London and the barometer is not falling dramatically, it is better to continue to Port Elizabeth rather than stop at East London. In case of a sudden deterioration of the weather, the same kind of avoiding action should be taken as described earlier. It must be stressed that the Agulhas Current is very strong between these two ports and also that there are inshore setting currents into some of the bays en route.

Port Elizabeth to Mossel Bay (170 m)

This section presents less problems than the previous ones as there are several places en route where one can shelter from a gale. One of the first of these ports is Knysna, although the entrance is quite difficult because of the strong tidal currents and can become hazardous during a SW gale when heavy swells break across the entrance. As one of the most scenic areas in the whole of South Africa, a stop in Knysna should not be missed. Advice on how to negotiate the tricky entrance can be obtained from the National Sea Rescue Institute who monitor channel 16. Shelter can also be found in Mossel Bay, near Cape Seal in Plettenberg Bay, and close to Cape St Francis, where one should beware of uncharted reefs. The anchorage at Cape St Francis should be avoided in a SW blow when the large swell makes it untenable unless one is prepared to anchor in deep water. Swell is also a major problem in the inner harbour at Mossel Bay, and therefore one of the outer moorings should be used.

Mossel Bay to Cape Town (195 m)

There are several places where one can anchor safely during unfavourable weather and on no account should Cape Agulhas be rounded in bad weather. There are onshore setting currents near all headlands on this route, which are also fronted by reefs, making navigation very difficult, especially in poor visibility. The Royal Cape Yacht Club continues to be most accommodating towards visiting boats and has excellent facilities. Docking facilities are also available at the Victoria and Alfred waterfront development, which is nearer to the city centre.

IS64 *Cape Town to West Australia*

BEST TIME:	December to February			
TROPICAL STORMS:	November to April			
CHARTS:	BA: 4204, 4070			
	US: 70, 204			
PILOTS:	BA: 2, 3, 17, 39			
	US: 123, 170, 175			
CRUISING GUIDES:	*Circumnavigating Australia's Coastline.*			
WAYPOINTS:				
Departure	*Intermediate*	*Landfall*	*Destination*	*Distance (M)*
IS641 Table S	IS642 Agulhas			
34°05'S, 18°12'E	37°00'S, 20°00'E			
	IS643			
	39°00'S, 30°00'E			
	IS644	IS645 Garden	Fremantle	4735
	39°00'S, 100°00'E	32°06'S, 115°38'E	*32°00'S, 115°45'E*	

As most of this passage will be made in the Roaring Forties, or even higher latitudes, it is recommended to sail in the southern summer when the frequency of gales is lowest, the weather warmer and there is little risk of encountering icebergs. Although the recommended time coincides with the season of tropical storms, these very rarely reach high latitudes and the only area where they might be encountered is close to Western Australia.

On leaving Cape Town, from WP IS641, a SSE course can be set for WP IS642 to avoid the area of the Agulhas Bank, which has a high frequency of gales and also a contrary current. Even if the course made good is SSW because of SE winds, the lost ground can be made up later when the area of westerly winds has been reached. In October and November the northern limit of icebergs extends to latitude 39°S in the area comprised between longitudes 20° and 30°E, so the course should turn east before this area is reached.

For vessels going to Western Australia the route runs between latitudes 39°S and 40°S, where the proportion of westerly winds is relatively high during the summer months and the weather considerably warmer than if one went south to about latitude 50°S, where the predominance of westerly winds, and gales, is indeed higher. It must be stressed that a reluctance to go far enough south in search of westerly winds and staying around latitude 35°S usually means a higher proportion of SE winds, and therefore a much slower passage. The course should be altered for Fremantle, or any other West Australian destination, only after meridian 100°E has been crossed. Taking as a point of reference WP IS644, boats bound for Fremantle can set a course from that point for WP IS645, NW of Garden Island in the approaches to Fremantle. The continuation of the route towards Bass Strait is described in route IS17 (page 485).

IS65 *Northbound from South Africa*

BEST TIME:	May to October
TROPICAL STORMS:	November to April
CHARTS:	BA: 4700, 4701
	US: 700, 701
PILOTS:	BA: 3
	US: 171
CRUISING GUIDES:	*East Africa Pilot.*
WAYPOINTS:	

Departure	Intermediate	Landfall	Destination	Distance (M)
AS650 Richards Bay *28°48'S, 32°06'E*	AS651 Richards *28°45'S, 32°10'E*	AS652 Inhaca *26°00'S, 33°01'E*	Maputo *25°59'S, 32°35'E*	197
AS650 Richards Bay	AS651 Richards	AS653 Augustine *12°30'S, 43°20'E*	Toleara *23°22'S, 43°40'E*	706

In spite of the unfavourable current, lack of yachting facilities and other difficulties, boats setting off from South Africa with the intention of visiting places on the east side of the continent have little choice but to make the best of what is available. Good planning will help in finding a weather window with favourable conditions at least for the start of the northbound passage, although strong SW winds will have to be avoided because of the dangerous conditions created when they collide with the south-flowing Agulhas Current. Route IS52 has more weather information.

Prevailing winds as far as the Mozambique Channel are SE or SW and, especially in the vicinity of land, are light in the morning but can reach gale force by the afternoon. A spell of light to moderate SE winds is the best and Richards Bay, north of Durban, makes a perfect departure port. The welcoming Zululand Yacht Club, with its small marina and range of facilities, has made this into one of the best sailing centres on the east coast of Africa, and is therefore the ideal place to wait for favourable weather conditions.

As most northbound boats are heading for destinations beyond neighbouring Mozambique, the choice is between staying close to the African coast or sailing across to Madagascar. Those who wish to stop in Mozambique should follow the African coast and make landfall off Cape Inhaca at the entrance into the Bay of Maputo. The former port of Lourenço Marques, now the capital of Mozambique, lies on the north bank of the Espirito Santo river and is reached through one of two channels, the northern one being recommended for those who do not know the area as it is simpler and used by large ships. The Port

Authority should be contacted on channel 16, and will advise where to berth to complete formalities.

The other alternative is to sail directly to Madagascar and complete entry formalities at Toleara, in the Bay of St Augustine. Madagascar, and especially its NW coast, is now the main cruising destination in the area.

19

WINDS AND CURRENTS
IN THE RED SEA

Winds

The distinctive long shape of the Red Sea, bordered by low arid coasts with high mountains rising some twenty miles inland, dictates in some measure the direction of winds, which tend to blow parallel to these coasts, either from a NW or SE direction. These winds differ significantly in the southern and northern areas of the Red Sea, and in the south show a seasonal variation due to the movement of the convergence zone between the wind systems of the northern and southern hemispheres.

Although the Red Sea is well to the north of the equator, the ITCZ moves into this area to reach its farthest position north in July, around 12°N. At this time of year the ITCZ marks the boundary between the SW monsoon of the Indian Ocean and the prevailing NW winds of the northern Red Sea. During these summer months NW winds blow down the entire length of the Red Sea merging into the SW monsoon in the Gulf of Aden.

In winter the ITCZ lies well to the south of this region, but there is another unrelated convergence zone which lies around 18°N from October to May and marks the boundary between the SE winds in the southern part of the Red Sea and the NW winds of the northern section. This convergence zone is usually marked by cloudy skies in contrast to the ubiquitous sunshine prevailing in the region as a whole. This convergence zone is associated with rain and drizzle.

SE winds predominate from October to January in all areas south of the convergence zone. From January to May the SE winds may not penetrate quite as far as the zone itself, but still predominate in the most southerly areas and in the Strait of Bab el Mandeb. These winds are strongest from November to February, averaging around 20

knots, but gale force winds of 30 knots and over occur fairly frequently. September and May are transitional months with lighter winds. In the Strait of Bab el Mandeb, a funnelling effect occurs which increases the wind speed at all times of the year, but especially in the winter months November to March, when it is frequently 25 knots or more.

In the northern part of the Red Sea from around 20°N, winds from the N to NW predominate in all months of the year, being stronger in winter than in summer. However, in the most northerly part, the Gulf of Suez, winds are more frequently over 20 knots from April to October with the highest frequency of gale force winds during this time. The Gulf of Suez is the only part of the Red Sea to be affected by depressions moving east across the Mediterranean.

Although the Red Sea winds are on average light to moderate, periods of complete calm do occur, sometimes for several days at a time. No tropical storms have been recorded in any part of the Red Sea. There are, however, two strong winds occurring in this region. The *haboob* is a short squall of over 35 knots blowing off the coast of Sudan between S and W, raising lots of sand and dust. *Haboobs* occur particularly in the Port Sudan area and are most common between July and September. The other wind is the *khamsin*, a strong dry S to SE wind, which blows off the land in Egypt and causes sandstorms. It occurs most commonly between February and May.

All of these winds, which bring sand and dust, reduce visibility considerably, often to less than 100 feet, especially near the coast. On the other hand, due to the special refraction conditions prevailing in the Red Sea, land and lights are often visible for much greater distances than normal, up to 100 miles away. This effect can also affect the horizon, raising or lowering it, which can produce errors in astronavigational observations, up to 20′ error in longitude and 10′ error in latitude. This phenomenon can affect observations taken before and after noon in different ways and can produce the impression of an apparent cross-current. It is thought that refraction is less at twilight and in the early morning, so therefore the taking of star sights has been recommended in this region. A brilliant luminescence sometimes occurs in the Red Sea making the water appear shallower. With the presence of unlit reefs extending far offshore in several places, these conditions may explain why so many yachts came to grief in this region in the past. Satellite navigation has improved safety considerably, but navigation should still be treated with due caution as most charts do not agree with satellite observations and the positions of most dangers are therefore approximate.

The Red Sea area is a hot arid region with a low rainfall. The average temperature is very high, around 30°C, but often reaches over 40°C in the day and even temperatures exceeding 50°C are not uncommon. Temperatures are lowest in winter in the more northerly part, dropping to 18°C in the Gulf of Suez on a winter night. This contrasts with the southern areas of the Red Sea, where in August the temperature is over 40°C by day and does not drop below 32°C even at night, which can easily lead to heat exhaustion in unclimatised people. Care must be exercised in this area, especially on metal yachts, because the temperature of a steel deck can easily rise to a blistering 70°C.

Currents

The overall direction of the currents in the Red Sea is influenced by the monsoons in the Indian Ocean. From November until April, while the NE monsoon is blowing, water is pushed into the Red Sea and there is a predominantly N to NW setting current along the axis of the Red Sea. From May until October, when the SW monsoon prevails over the Indian Ocean, water is drawn out of the Red Sea and a S to SE setting current prevails. Due to the narrowness and shape of the Red Sea, there is a great variability in the currents and many lateral currents run in and out from the main stream, particularly near islands and reefs. These cross-currents occur in all months and are very variable. They are not as strong as was first believed, because many apparent cross-currents were found to be due to errors in astronavigation produced by the refraction effect on the horizon. The strongest current is experienced in the Strait of Bab el Mandeb, reaching 2 knots in the NE monsoon season. In the transitional months between monsoons, April and May, or October, there is little or no current.

20

ROUTES IN THE
RED SEA

In spite of its many attractions, good anchorages, excellent fishing, and magnificent diving, the Red Sea has just as many disadvantages from the cruising point of view and therefore most people try and pass through it as quickly as possible. In most cases the problems are of a political nature and countries such as Saudi Arabia and Yemen do not encourage yachts to visit them, while Sudan and Jordan only tolerate them. The reception in Egypt depends entirely on the current situation, which can change from day to day, although the transit of the Suez Canal itself is normally dealt with efficiently.

An area worth exploring by those with time on their hands is the Gulf of Aquaba. Three of the four countries bordering this narrow stretch of water, Egypt, Jordan, and Israel, have ports of entry at Sharm el Sheik (27°51'N, 34°17'E), Aquaba (29°31'N, 35°00'E), and Eilat (29°33'N, 34°57'E). The notable exception is Saudi Arabia, which positively discourages visits by yachts, not just in the Gulf of Aquaba, but anywhere on its coasts. Cruising boats that have strayed into Saudi waters in the past have been turned firmly away. So while this situation continues Saudi ports should be avoided.

A significant change has occurred in Eritrea, where the coming of peace after the prolonged war with Ethiopia has made it again possible to include this area into one's cruising plans. For all the above reasons, the political situation in the bordering countries should be followed carefully before arriving in the Red Sea to know if there are any areas which should be avoided. As the Middle East is one of the most volatile regions of the world, the current situation should be monitored continuously by listening regularly to the

international news on a reputable station such as the BBC World Service.

For those who may be put off by too much paperwork and dealings with officials, the drastic alternative is to undertake a nonstop passage up or down the middle of the Red Sea. Unfortunately such a solution may be just as unattractive because of the large amount of shipping and often unfavourable wind. Because of all these factors, most sailing boats that pass through the Red Sea compromise by alternating offshore legs with coastal cruising in daily hops. The method has much to commend it as it is less trying for the crew than a nonstop passage and is also safer, because many of the numerous navigational hazards can be avoided in this way. The average time in which the entire length of the Red Sea can be navigated in this manner is between three and four weeks.

Because coastal cruising is outside the scope of this book, only the offshore passages are described in detail. However, as some of the distances may be covered in shorter stages all relevant charts should be carried on board. Reefs and other dangers are well marked, particularly on British Admiralty charts, and navigation among the reefs is not difficult in good light. Eyeball navigation is not as difficult as it would appear, and provided the time of arrival is planned carefully, so as to have good light when entering a reef anchorage, navigating among the coastal reefs should present no great problem. When seeking an anchorage for the night it is advisable not to leave this until too late in the afternoon because the lower sun casts a sheen over the water obscuring dangers which otherwise are easily seen.

RN Northbound Routes

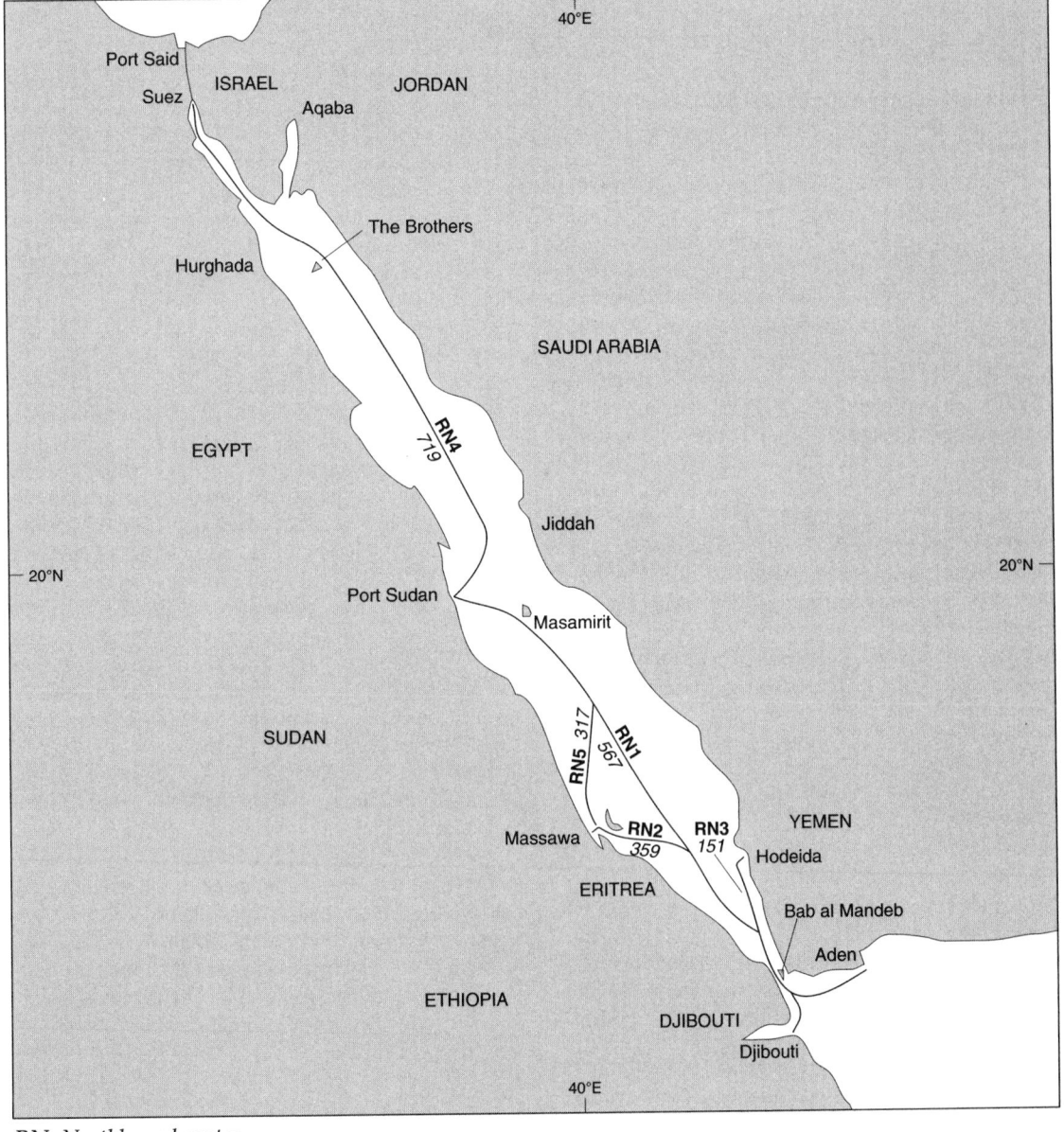

RN *Northbound routes*

Regardless of the time of year, northbound boats usually have to contend with contrary winds for at least half their passage up the Red Sea. Therefore it is difficult to recommend a preferred time of year, especially as the Red Sea passage is usually a continuation of a voyage, the timing of which has been decided by other factors. Most boats undertake their northbound voyage at the end of winter, between February and April, usually after having crossed the North Indian Ocean during the NE monsoon. Although NW winds prevail in the northern half of the Red Sea throughout the year, these tend to be lighter in spring than in winter, making April one of the best months for the northbound voyage. Another advantage of a late March or April passage is that the Mediterranean is reached as the weather starts getting warmer and the cruising season begins. Although the headwinds of the Red Sea have become something of a legend among sailors, it must be pointed out that winds do not always follow the axis of the sea and, although forced to tack, boats can usually choose a more favourable tack. Another observation worth bearing in mind is that the wind tends to shift with the sun, being more NNE in the morning and NW in the afternoon. During the EUROPA Round the World Rally, in March 1992, all boats in the Racing Division managed to sail the entire distance between Port Sudan and Suez, some of the boats with good windward performance having to tack very little by using the slant of the winds to best advantage and covering the distance in remarkably fast times. Even some of the boats in the Cruising Division coped with the contrary winds well and, as they were allowed to use their engines, good times were recorded by motorsailing at the most efficient angle whenever possible.

Apart from having to cope with the inclement weather, northbound boats have also run into difficulties with overzealous local officials, often military. It is therefore strongly recommended not to stop in any country before having cleared in correctly, avoid any military area and, if anchoring in remote places, to do it in company of other boats. Among the sensitive areas to be avoided are the following: the small strait on the east side of Perim Island, as well as the neighbouring anchorage on the Yemeni side; anchoring in Zubair and Hanish Islands; and the border area between Eritrea and Sudan where an offshore distance of at least 12 miles should be observed.

RN1 *Bab el Mandeb to Port Sudan*

BEST TIME: October to January
CHARTS: BA: 6, 138, 141, 143
US: 62090, 62290, 62270
PILOTS: BA: 64
US: 172
CRUISING GUIDES: *Red Sea Pilot.*
WAYPOINTS:

Departure	*Intermediate*	*Landfall*	*Destination*	*Distance (M)*
RN10 Perim W 12°38'N, 43°21'E	RN11 Umari 13°00'N, 43°15'E RN12 Zuqar E 14°00'N, 42°51'E RN13 Zubair SW 15°00'N, 42°00'E RN14 Jabal at Tair 15°30'N, 41°40'E			
	RN15 Farasan 17°00'N, 40°40'E	[RN19 Dohrat Abid] 18°15'N, 38°45'E		441
	RN16 Masamirit E 18°50'N, 38°55'E			
	RN17 Hindi Gider 19°30'N, 38°00'E	RN18 Sudan NE 19°36'N, 37°17'E	Port Sudan *19°37'N, 37°14'E*	567

Very few boats choose to continue their voyage from the Indian Ocean into the Red Sea without stopping and the distinctly narrow choice is between Aden and Djibouti. Because of the uncertain situation in Aden, and the limited range of facilities there, Djibouti has become the more popular port of call. Djibouti has reasonable repair facilities, good provisioning, and an active yacht club. It also has regular flights to Paris, which makes it a good port for crew changes.

The weather at the recommended time is usually favourable with a north-setting current in the Strait of Bab el Mandeb and southerly winds possibly as far as the latitude of Port Sudan.

Boats leaving Djibouti for the Red Sea should pass to the east of the Musha Islands and clear the headland of Ras Bir by at least 10 miles before altering course for the Strait of Bab el Mandeb (Gates of Sorrow). The Djibouti coast to the west of the Musha Islands, as well the area facing Bab el Mandeb, should not be approached too closely as vessels have been molested by rebels during disputes with the central Djibouti government. Boats leaving from Aden have a clear run to the strait. Whether coming from Djibouti or Aden, boats passing through the strait should do so west of Perim Island. A traffic separation zone is in operation in the strait and northbound vessels must keep to the starboard side. Perim Island should not be passed unnecessarily close because it is a restricted area. For the same reason, Small Strait east of Perim Island should only be used in an emergency. An anchorage used occasionally by boats waiting for either daylight or favourable winds to pass through Bab el Mandeb is located in a small bay off the Yemeni coast, NE of Bab el Mandeb in approximate position 12°43'N, 43°35'E. In principle, the anchorage should only be used by boats that have cleared into Yemen at Aden.

The 200 miles from Bab el Mandeb to Jabal at Tair Island, which has a powerful light on it, can be made either nonstop or in shorter stages by anchoring at one of the two island groups en route. If the winds are favourable it is advisable to make as much northing as possible while they last, rather than stop in the islands. Both Hanish and Zubair Islands belong to Yemen, and although anchoring by yachts in transit is usually tolerated, landing is prohibited. In poor visibility or heavy weather it is better to pass to the east of the Hanish Islands, where clearer landmarks make it easier to avoid the various dangers. On the other hand, Zubair

Islands should be passed on their west side where there are no offlying dangers.

From WP RN10, west of Perim Island, in the Strait of Bab el Mandeb, a course should be set for WP RN11, to stay with the northbound traffic. From that point it is easier to set a course which stays east of the Hanish Islands by making for WP RN12, east of Zuqar Island. The route passes through Abu Ail Channel, between the rock of that name and Zuqar Island, and heads for WP RN13, WSW of Zubair Island. It is close to this point that the main route is left by boats bound for either Massawa in Eritrea (route RN2), or Hodaida in Yemen (route RN3).

From the Zubair Islands the trunk route continues in a NW direction past Jabal at Tair, whose powerful light is an excellent reference while negotiating a safe course between the various dangers that front both shores of the Red Sea, the width of the fairway being about 60 miles in this area. From WP RN14, west of Jabal at Tair, a new course is set for WP RN15 so as to avoid both the Farasan Islands on the Saudi side and the Dahlach Bank off the Eritrean coast. For those who do not wish to take the inshore route to Port Sudan, the route continues to WP RN16, east of the light on Masamirit Islet, which should be approached from the SE and passed on its east side because of the dangerous area south of it. The course can then be altered for WP RN17, north of Hindi Gider light, so as to pass outside the numerous reefs that litter this area. There follows a final course alteration for WP RN18, south of Wingate Reef, at the entrance into Port Sudan. Boats which do not intend to stop in Port Sudan should continue on their offshore route by setting a course from WP RN16, off Masamirit Light, for WP RN43. The continuation of the route to Suez is described in RN4.

Before entering Port Sudan, Port Sudan Radio should be contacted on VHF channel 16 to advise the boat's name, nationality, and ETA. Having entered the port, the boat should proceed to the yacht anchorage in the NW part of the harbour (19°36.5'N, 37°13.4'E), and wait to be visited by quarantine and security officials. Other formalities will have to be completed in East Town, where the Port Authority's offices are located.

For those who prefer to cover some of the distances south of Port Sudan in shorter stages by sailing inside the reefs, there are two ways of approaching the Sudanese coast. The first option is to make for Khor Nawarat, an anchorage lying very close to the border between Eritrea and Sudan.

Because of the dangerous reefs and islets in the Suakin Group and the reportedly unpredictable currents, Khor Nawarat should be approached with extreme caution and only if the vessel's position has been confidently established. To reach the area, the main route described above is left at WP RN15 from where a course should be set for WP RN19, south of Dohrat Abid, at the start of the channel passing between the reefs in the Suakin Group.

An alternative way to reach the Sudanese coast is to pass close to the south of Masamirit Islet and make for Trinkitat harbour by threading one's way carefully through the various reefs. An inshore passage, reasonably well beaconed, leads both from Khor Nawarat and Trinkitat to Port Sudan. An interesting stop on this inshore route is the abandoned city of Suakin. Although not a port of entry, cruising boats will be allowed to stop by contacting Port Control on channel 14. Shore passes will be issued to those arriving without Sudanese visas.

RN2 *Bab el Mandeb to Massawa*

Best time:	October to January			
Charts:	BA: 6, 141, 171			
	US: 62090, 62290, 62130			
Pilots:	BA: 64			
	US: 172			
Cruising guides:	*Red Sea Pilot.*			
Waypoints:				
Departure	*Intermediate*	*Landfall*	*Destination*	*Distance (M)*
RN20 Perim W	RN21 Umari			
12°38'N, 43°21'E	13°00'N, 43°15'E			
	RN22 Zuqar E			
	14°00'N, 42°51'E			
	RN23 Zuqar N			
	14°06'N, 42°41'E			
	RN24 Midir	RN25 Sahrig	Massawa	359
	15°10'N, 40°35'E	15°00'N, 41°00'E	*15°37'N, 39°29'E*	

Similar directions apply as for route RN1 as far as Zuqar Island. Having negotiated Abu Ail Channel, on the NE side of Zuqar, a course is set first for WP RN24 and then RN25, at the entrance into South Massawa Channel. This channel, between the African mainland and Dahlach Island, leads into Massawa (Mits'iwa), Eritrea's main port.

As a result of the cessation of hostilities with Ethiopia and the declaration of independence by Eritrea, the Eritrean authorities are encouraging tourism and cruising boats are welcome to call there. Northbound boats can regain the offshore route either by using the same South Channel, or they can take the longer North Massawa Channel, which runs parallel to the coast in a northerly direction.

Massawa Port Control must be contacted on channel 16 before entering the outer harbour. Formalities will be completed there and all fees paid in US dollars before permission is given to move to the better shelter found in the inner harbour, although the entrance, protected by a reef, is difficult. Fuel is available there.

Boats proceeding to Massawa must not stop anywhere in Eritrea before having cleared in. To avoid any problems, northbound boats may clear in at Assab (13°00'N, 42°44'E), which is also an official port of entry.

RN3 *Bab el Mandeb to Hodaida*

BEST TIME:	October to January				
CHARTS:	BA: 6, 143				
	US: 62090, 62290				
PILOTS:	BA: 64				
	US: 172				
CRUISING GUIDES:	*Red Sea Pilot.*				
WAYPOINTS:					

Departure	Intermediate	Landfall	Destination	Distance (M)
RN30 Perim W 12°38'N, 43°21'E	RN31 Umari 13°00'N, 43°15'E RN32 Zuqar E 14°00'N, 42°51'E	RN33 Kathib W 14°53'N, 42°48'E	Hodaida *14°47'N, 42°57'E*	151

Boats bound for Hodaida should follow the same directions as for route RN1 until level with Zuqar Island. From WP RN32 a course can be sailed which passes to the east of Abu Ail rock. To avoid the various dangers, from WP RN32 the course should be altered for WP RN33, so that landfall is made off Ras Kathib. This is the northern point of a long and narrow peninsula that has created a perfectly shel-

tered natural harbour in which the port of Hodaida occupies the southern extremity. A 10 mile long buoyed channel leads into Hodaida, whose Port Control should be contacted on VHF channel 16 to advise ETA, name of vessel, and other details before permission is given to proceed into the port. The Yemeni capital Sanaa is easily reached overland from Hodaida.

RN4 *Port Sudan to Suez*

BEST TIME:	March to April				
CHARTS:	BA: 8, 63, 138				
	US: 62250, 62230, 62195				
PILOTS:	BA: 64	US: 172			
CRUISING GUIDES:	*Red Sea Pilot.*				
WAYPOINTS:					

Departure	Intermediate	Landfall	Destination	Distance (M)
RN40 Sudan NE 19°36'N, 37°17'E	RN41 Sanganeb 19°45'N, 37°35'E RN42 Abington 21°00'N, 38°00'E RN43 Zabargad 23°40'N, 36°30'E RN44 Daedalus 24°55'N, 35°40'E RN45 Brothers 26°20'N, 35°00'E RN46 Shaker E 27°30'N, 34°15'E RN47 Gubal NE 27°43'N, 33°50'E RN48 Shukeir E 28°10'N, 33°25'E	RN49 Suez S 29°34'N, 32°35'E	Port Suez *29°58'N, 32°33'E*	719

North from Port Sudan, boats bound for Egypt and the Suez Canal have the same choice as before and can either stay inside the reefs or sail offshore. The best area for day sailing starts immediately to the north of Port Sudan, with several well protected inlets among the reefs. Compared to the southern half of the Red Sea, the north has fewer offshore dangers and the direct route has a clear run all the way to Daedalus Reef (24°56'N, 35°52'E). The recommended route runs roughly parallel to the axis of the Red Sea, although it favours the Sudanese side in case the decision is taken to head for the coast and seek temporary shelter in one of the many inlets.

Having left Port Sudan, from WP RN40, south of Wingate Reef, an initial course is set to WP RN41, east of Sanganeb Reef. The course is then altered for WP RN42, east of Abington Reef, where the offshore route coming up from Masamirit Light is joined. A useful landmark on this offshore route is Gezirat Zabargad, a high rocky islet off Foul Bay, an area which is best avoided even by those who have been coastal sailing to this point. The route passes east of Zabargad.

North of Foul Bay, longer offshore legs become increasingly necessary as there are fewer safe anchorages along the Egyptian coast. From WP RN44, west of Daedalus Reef, the route continues in a NW direction towards the Brothers, which are passed on their east side. A safe all weather anchorage can be found at nearby Hurghada (27°13.8'N, 33°50.7'E), where it is also possible to clear into Egypt. From Hurghada the Gulf of Suez can be reached via Tawila Channel, which avoids a detour past Shaker Island and the Strait of Gubal.

From WP RN45, east of the Brothers, the offshore route heads for the Strait of Gubal, which is entered at WP RN46, east of Shaker Island. From WP RN47 the route runs down the middle of the Gulf of Suez passing through an intermediate WP RN48, off Ras Shukeir. Landfall is finally made at WP RN49, in the approaches to Suez. Navigation through the narrow Gulf of Suez can be daunting, due to the numerous oil rigs, heavy shipping, and the usually contrary wind. The problem is exacerbated by the presence of many disused oil platforms, some of which are not marked by lights. Traffic separation lanes are in operation for the entire length of the Gulf of Suez, with northbound traffic using the right hand lane. Sailing boats, especially if they need to tack, or if motorsailing to windward, normally fare better by favouring the eastern side of the narrow Gulf. It must also be stressed that the waypoints listed for the Gulf of Suez are only meant as guidelines.

The Suez Canal Authority should be contacted on VHF channel 16 to give an ETA. If Suez Bay is reached during the night it is recommended to anchor either off the main channel or in the waiting area in Port Ibrahim and wait for daylight before passing through the heavy traffic to the Suez Canal Yacht Club. As the yacht club is in the Suez Canal area, yachts should not proceeed there without permission from the Canal Authority. If not using the yacht club the recommended anchorage for yachts intending to transit the Canal is just inside the southern breakwater in Port Ibrahim. The breakwater can be passed either west or east and the anchorage is at its eastern end, close to the entrance into the North Basin.

A shipping agent or his representative will arrive in his launch soon after Suez Bay has been entered offering to make arrangements for transiting the Suez Canal. Agency fees are extremely competitive and skippers are advised not to accept an offer before a fee has been agreed. Agents normally deal with all formalities, both for entry into Egypt and for transiting the Canal. See also page 585 concerning the transit through the Suez Canal.

RN5 *Massawa to Port Sudan*

BEST TIME:	March to May
CHARTS:	BA: 138, 141
	US: 62120, 62270
PILOTS:	BA: 64
	US: 172
CRUISING GUIDES:	*Red Sea Pilot.*

WAYPOINTS:				
Departure	*Intermediate*	*Landfall*	*Destination*	*Distance (M)*
RN50 Massawa *15°37'N, 39°29'E*	RN51 North 15°40'N, 39°30'E			
	RN52 Abu 16°00'N, 39°20.5'E			
	RN53 Harat N 16°15'N, 39°20'E			
	RN54 Difnein 16°38'N, 39°15'E			
	RN55 Offshore 18°00'N, 39°30'E			
	RN56 Masamirit E 18°50'N, 38°55'E			
	RN57 Hindi Gider 19°30'N, 38°00'E	RN58 Sudan NE 19°36'N, 37°17'E	Port Sudan *19°36'N, 37°14'E*	317

With the gradual opening of Eritrea to cruising, more boats stop in Massawa on their way north. Although the continuation of the northbound voyage can be made in coastal stages, by staying in sheltered waters, the offshore route can be rejoined by leaving Massawa through the North Channel. The recommended route follows a clear channel between the mainland and Harat Island. The route passes west of Sheikh el Abu, a rocky islet marked by a light that is reported not to be oper-ational. A deep channel leads to the next light at Difnein, also reported to be out of action like most lights in Eritrean waters, from where, with due caution, the offshore route may be rejoined. An inshore route may be sailed all the way to Sudan, but because of reported tensions in the border area between the two countries, staying in international waters and therefore following the offshore route is recommended. Route RN1 details the offshore route, as well as the approaches to Port Sudan.

RS SOUTHBOUND ROUTES

The best time for a southbound passage through the Red Sea depends on just as many factors as a northbound voyage, although weather conditions are invariably better. The most pleasant time to head south is probably during the spring months, from February to April, when the weather is becoming warmer in the northern areas and it is not too hot in the southern section. At this time favourable winds can be expected to last at least as far as the latitude of Port Sudan. From May onwards winds from the NW should be carried the entire length of the Red Sea. The timing of this passage usually depends on the destination after the Red Sea, and the weather in the North Indian Ocean must be taken into account. For an east-bound passage across the North Indian Ocean the SW monsoon, which blows from May to October, ensures the most favourable winds, although these may be too strong at the height of the monsoon in July and August when a high proportion reach gale force. For this reason, and also the unbearable heat, the summer months in the Red Sea are best avoided. Therefore, if a southbound passage cannot be undertaken towards the end of the NE monsoon, the only alternative is to do it during the autumn transitional period. However, due attention must be paid to the risk of cyclones in the Arabian Sea, as their highest frequency coincides with the same transitional periods. See routes IN33, IN34, IT22, and IT23 (pages 457, 471 and 472).

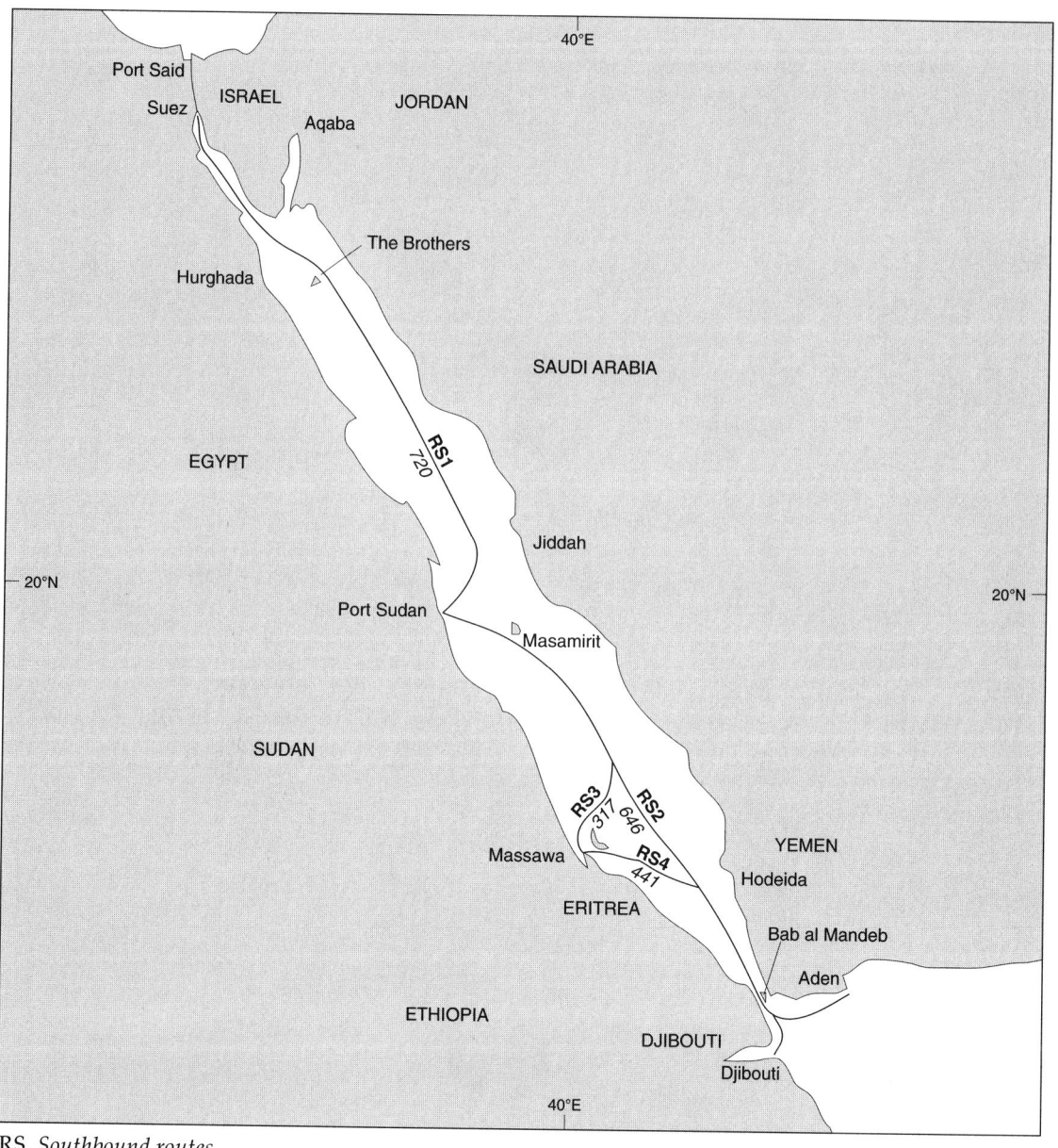

RS *Southbound routes*

RS1 *Suez to Port Sudan*

BEST TIME:	February to April			
CHARTS:	BA: 8, 63, 138			
	US: 62195, 62230, 62250			
PILOTS:	BA: 64			
	US: 172			
CRUISING GUIDES:	*Red Sea Pilot.*			
WAYPOINTS:				
Departure	*Intermediate*	*Landfall*	*Destination*	*Distance (M)*
RS10 Suez S	RS11 Shukeir W			
29°34'N, 32°35'E	28°10'N, 33°15'E			
	RS12 Gubal NW			
	27°47'N, 33°44'E			
	RS13 Shaker W			
	27°28'N, 34°06'E			
	RS14 Brothers			
	26°20'N, 35°00'E			
	RS15 Daedalus			
	24°55'N, 35°40'E			
	RS16 Zabargad			
	23°40'N, 36°30'E			
	RS17 Abington			
	21°00'N, 38°00'E			
	RS18 Sanganeb	RS19 Sudan NE	Port Sudan	720
	19°45'N, 37°35'E	19°36'N, 37°17'E	*19°36'N, 37°14'E*	

Because favourable winds are much more likely to be encountered on southbound passages, most boats cover as much as possible of the Red Sea in long offshore legs and, in contrast to northbound boats, coastal hopping is less common. Because traffic separation lanes are in operation for the entire length of the Gulf of Suez, the intermediate waypoints listed above are only meant as a guideline. Sailing boats normally fare much better by keeping away from the traffic by favouring the east side of the narrow Gulf. At the southern end of the Gulf of Suez, several miles can be saved by sailing through either Zeit or Tawila Channels which lead to the anchorage at Hurghada. If an inshore passage is preferred south of Foul Bay, a convenient place to go behind the reefs is at Ras Hadarba, close to the border between Egypt and Sudan. The entire distance from there to Port Sudan can be covered mostly in sheltered waters where safe anchorages are easily found every night.

Taking WP RS10, south of Suez Bay, as a point of departure, the offshore route runs along the axis of the Gulf of Suez as far as WP RS11, off Ras Shukeir.

This first section is the most difficult because of the heavy traffic and also the oil platforms that are to be found everywhere in the Gulf of Suez, many of those no longer in use not being marked by lights. Having reached WP RS12, at the northern entrance into the Strait of Gubal, the course is altered for WP RS13, east of Shaker Island. From there a course is set to pass east of the Brothers through WP RS14 and on to WP RS15, west of Daedalus Reef. The route then crosses the mouth of Foul Bay where an intermediate WP RS16 is used to pass at a safe distance west of Gezirat Zabargad, a high rocky islet. From the Strait of Gubal to WP RS16 the route favours the western shore where an anchorage can be found in many sheltered bays or inlets.

Having passed Foul Bay, the offshore route heads for WP RS17, east of Abington Reef. From this point, boats bound for Port Sudan leave the offshore route and head in a SW direction. Boats continuing nonstop on an offshore route should alter course for WP RS22, east of Masamirit Light (see route RS2).

To reach Port Sudan, from WP RS17, the course

is altered for WP RS18, east of Sanganeb Reef and finally to WP RS19, south of Wingate Reef, at the entrance into Port Sudan. Before entering the harbour, Port Sudan Radio should be contacted on VHF channel 16 to advise the boat's name, nationality, and ETA. Having entered the port the boat should proceed to the yacht anchorage in the NW part of the harbour (19°36.5'N, 37°13.4'E), and wait to be visited by quarantine and security officials. Other formalities will have to be completed in East Town, where the Port Authority's offices are located.

RS2 *Port Sudan to Gulf of Aden*

BEST TIME:	February to April			
CHARTS:	BA: 6, 138, 141, 143			
	US: 62270, 62290, 62090			
PILOTS:	BA: 64			
	US: 172			
CRUISING GUIDES:	*Red Sea Pilot.*			
WAYPOINTS:				
Departure	*Intermediate*	*Landfall*	*Destination*	*Distance (M)*
RS20 Sudan SE 19°35'N, 37°16'E	RS21 Hindi Gider 19°30'N, 38°00'E			
	RS22 Masamirit E 18°50'N, 38°55'E			
	RS23 Farasan 17°00'N, 40°40'E			
	RS24 Jabal at Tair 15°30'N, 41°40'E	[RS293 Kathib N] [14°58'N, 42°50'E]	[Hodaida] [*14°47'N, 42°57'E*]	452
	RS25 Zubair SW 15°00'N, 42°00'E			
	RS26 Zuqar E 14°00'N, 42°51'E			
	RS27 Umari 13°00'N, 43°15'E			
	RS28 Mandeb W 12°34'N, 43°19'E			
	RS29 Mandeb S 12°25'N, 43°35'E			
	RS290 Ras Bir 12°00'N, 43°32'E	RS291 Musha 11°42'N, 43°18'E	Djibouti *11°36.5'N, 43°07.5'E*	646
		RS292 Yemen W 12°42'N, 44°54'E	Aden *12°48'N, 44°58'E*	673

Boats leaving Port Sudan bound for Bab el Mandeb and the Indian Ocean may take an inshore route as far as either Trinkitat or Khor Nawarat. From Trinkitat the open sea is reached via a pass which leads due east through the reefs and islets of the Suakin Group. From Khor Nawarat, all dangers of the Suakin Group are left to port and a safe course is set as soon as open water is reached. Since the cessation of hostilities between Eritrea and Ethiopia, and the subsequent independence declaration by Eritrea, it is once again possible to sail through the waters south of Sudan. Those interested in continuing on an inshore route should use North Massawa Channel to reach the Eritrean port of Massawa and complete entry formalities in that country. The open sea is then reached through the South Channel, leading SE from Massawa between the African coast and Dahlach Island.

If the winds are favourable on leaving Port Sudan, the offshore route should be preferred. In this case, from WP RS20, outside Port Sudan, the initial course should go to WP RS21, so as to pass to NE of Hindi Gider light and the various dangers to SW of it. The route then goes to WP RS22, east of Masamirit light to join the offshore route down the middle of the Red Sea. From this point the route follows the axis of the Red Sea passing through WP RS23, halfway between Dahlach Bank, on the Eritrean side, and Farasan Islands, on the Saudi side. The route continues in a SE direction to pass through WP RS24, west of Jabal at Tair, a conspicuous island with a powerful light, which provides a useful point of reference. Two groups of islands lying south of it, Zubair and Hanish Islands, offer shelter in heavy weather. Both island groups should be approached with caution as there are some offlying dangers. Zubair Islands are best passed on their west side, while Jabal Zuqar and the Hanish Islands should be passed to the east paying careful attention to the various rocks in their vicinity.

Boats intending to call at Hodaida, in Yemen, should leave the offshore route at Jubair at Tair and from WP RS24 set a course for WP RS293, at the landfall buoy north of Ras Kathib. This is the northern point of a long and narrow peninsula that has created a perfectly sheltered natural harbour in which the port of Hodaida occupies the southern extremity. A 10 mile long buoyed channel leads into Hodaida, whose Port Control should be contacted on VHF channel 16 to advise ETA, name of vessel, and other details before permission is given to proceed into the port. The Yemeni capital Sanaa is

easily reached overland from Hodaida.

Those who do not wish to interrupt their voyage should stay with the offshore route south of WP RS24. From WP RS25, west of Zubair, a course is set to pass through Abu Ail Channel, NE of Jabal Zuqar, to WP RS26. From there the course is altered to pass through WP RS27 and on to the northern approaches of the Strait of Bab el Mandeb. Because of a traffic separation zone in the strait, southbound boats should keep to the west side and make for WP RS28. Having passed through Bab el Mandeb into the Gulf of Aden, the course continues to WP RS29. From that point boats bound for Djibouti should alter course for WP RS290 so as to pass well clear of Ras Bir, on the African side. Rebel forces have molested vessels in this area in the past and this is the reason why it is recommended to stay well off this coast and pass east of the Musha Islands. One more course alteration for WP RS291 is needed to pass east of the Musha Islands and approach the port of Djibouti from the NE. The recommended yacht anchorage (11°36.5'N, 43°07.5'E) is off the Djibouti Yacht Club whose facilities may be used by visiting boats. The various authorities are in the nearby commercial harbour and must be visited to complete entry formalities.

From WP RS290 boats bound for Aden should alter course for WP RS292, SW of the entrance into the port of Aden. A marked channel leads into the Inner Harbour, where yachts anchor off the customs dock. Boats are normally met on arrival by a port control launch and then directed to the anchorage.

RS3 *Port Sudan to Massawa*

BEST TIME:	February to April
CHARTS:	BA: 138, 141
	US: 62120, 62270
PILOTS:	BA: 64
	US: 172
CRUISING GUIDES:	*Red Sea Pilot.*

WAYPOINTS:				
Departure	*Intermediate*	*Landfall*	*Destination*	*Distance (M)*
RS30 Port Sudan *19°37'N, 37°14'E*	RS31 Sudan NE 19°36'N, 37°17'E RS32 Hindi Gider 19°30'N, 38°00'E RS33 Masamirit E 18°50'N, 38°55'E RS34 Offshore 18°00'N, 39°30'E RN35 Difnein 16°38'N, 39°15'E RN36 Harat N 16°15'N, 39°20'E RN37 Abu 16°00'N, 39°20.5'E	RN38 North 15°40'N, 39°30'E	Massawa *15°37'N, 39°29'E*	317

The long passage to Djibouti or Aden can now be interrupted in Eritrea, where cruising boats are welcome. The main port of Massawa has reasonable facilities and visiting boats must proceed there immediately for clearance. A sheltered inshore route can be sailed from Port Sudan, but as stopping anywhere in Eritrea is prohibited unless one has cleared in, the offshore route is preferable. Another reason why the offshore route is recommended is because of tensions reported in the border area between the two countries where cruising boats have been harassed for passing through military sensitive areas.

Massawa is reached through the North Channel, which winds its way between a number of islands and reefs. Having left the offshore route, a course should be steered towards Difnein islet which is marked by a light, but, like most navigational aids in Eritrean waters, it was reported to be unoperational. The inshore route follows a deep channel between the mainland and Harat Island. Having passed west of Sheikh el Abu islet, landfall is made in the outer approaches to Massawa. Skippers are reminded not to stop anywhere in Eritrea before having cleared in at Massawa and therefore the inshore route should be timed to be sailed in daylight.

Massawa Port Control should be contacted on channel 16 before entering the harbour. Boats are normally directed to the quay on Massawa (Mitsiwa) Island to be boarded by various officials. Fuel and water is arranged through the immigration official. Provisioning and repair facilities are reasonably good.

RS4 *Southbound from Massawa*

BEST TIME:	February to April
CHARTS:	BA: 6, 141, 171
	US: 62090, 62290, 62130
PILOTS:	BA: 64
	US: 172
CRUISING GUIDES:	*Red Sea Pilot.*

WAYPOINTS:				
Departure	*Intermediate*	*Landfall*	*Destination*	*Distance (M)*
RS40 Massawa	RS41 Sharig			
15°37'N, 39°29'E	15°00'N, 41°00'E			
	RS42 Midir			
	15°10'N, 40°35'E			
	RS43 Zuqar N			
	14°06'N, 42°41'E			
	RS44 Zuqar E			
	14°00'N, 42°51'E			
	RS45 Umari			
	13°00'N, 43°15'E			
	RS46 Mandeb W			
	12°34'N, 43°19'E			
	RS47 Mandeb S			
	12°25'N, 43°35'E			
	RS48 Ras Bir	RS49 Musha	Djibouti	441
	12°00'N, 43°32'E	11°42'N, 43°18'E	*11°36.5'N, 43°07.5'E*	
		RS491 Yemen W	Aden	504
		12°42'N, 44°54'E	*12°48'N, 44°58'E*	

The port of Massawa is left through the South Channel, which should be negotiated in good light as all beacons and leading lights have been reported as missing. The offshore route is joined near Jabal Zuqar Island, from where the south-bound route follows as closely as possible the axis of the Red Sea as far as Bab el Mandeb. The two destinations beyond Bab el Mandeb, Aden or Djibouti, are described in detail in RS2.

21
WINDS AND CURRENTS OF THE MEDITERRANEAN SEA

The Mediterranean climate is on the whole extremely pleasant, marked by long hot summers and mild winters. Most gales and rain occur in winter months, few storms interrupting the long summer. Local conditions vary considerably, stronger winds and squalls often resulting from local phenomena and not due to the overall weather pattern. Tropical storms do not affect this region.

The Mediterranean can be divided into two halves, Western and Eastern, corresponding to the two deeper basins which are separated by a ridge, running through Italy, Sicily, and Malta to the African coast. In the summer the Western Mediterranean comes under the influence of the Atlantic high pressure area centred near the Azores, while the Eastern Mediterranean is influenced by the low pressure area east of the Mediterranean, which is an extension of the Indian Ocean monsoon. As a rule weather systems move across the Mediterranean from west to east and this is particularly true of depressions in the winter months. The commonest winds over the entire area are from the northerly sector, more from the NW in the western basin, N in the Aegean and NE in the eastern part. Well chronicled down the centuries are the various regional winds, which are a notable feature of Mediterranean weather.

Close to the coast the weather is greatly affected by the height of the land and other topographical features. Local conditions vary enormously, any prevailing wind usually being lighter near the coast, while land and sea breezes have a strong effect. The land and sea breezes are particularly marked in summer months and reach 20 to 30 knots in some places. The direction of the wind changes not only with the time of day, but also with the orientation of the coast. A reversal in the direction of the wind usually occurs between early morning and late afternoon. Local squalls are more frequent where the coast is mountainous and the wind is frequently accelerated down valleys or between islands. These effects are particularly true for high islands and should be borne in mind when anchoring in the lee of such valleys, particularly in Greece in the meltemi season.

Mistral

'Magistralis' meaning 'masterful' was the name originally given to the cold dry NW wind which holds masterly sway over the Western Mediterranean in both frequency and strength. Now corrupted to 'mistral' or 'maestral', these NW winds are formed when cold air flowing down over France is blocked by the heights of the Alps and is diverted to pour into the Mediterranean via the Rhone valley. The mistral blows strongly in the Gulf of Lions and the Gulf of Genoa, while the Rhone delta area and Marseille receive the full force of the mistral on almost 100 days a year. On average 20 knots, the mistral is frequently stronger and can reach 50–60 knots on occasion. The mistral often reaches the Balearics and Sardinia and on occasion can be felt as far as Malta and North Africa. The French Riviera east of Marseille is sheltered by the mountains behind the coast and the mistral is felt less there.

The mistral blows at intervals throughout the

year, although it is commonest in winter, normally lasting from three to six days and is typified by clear skies. Along the Spanish coast this NW wind is called the *tramontana*, being strong, cold, and dry with many local variations.

Vendavales

These are strong SW winds which blow between North Africa and the Spanish coast, especially in the late autumn and early spring. These winds, which do not last long, can reach gale force and are associated with depressions moving across Spain and Southern France. The *vendavales* are associated with squalls and thunderstorms, but are less strong near the African coast and the NE coast of Spain. They are much stronger when funnelled through the Strait of Gibraltar. Hitting the west coast of Sardinia and the Gulf of Genoa, these strong SW winds are called *libeccio* in Italian.

Sirocco

In general usage, this name is used to describe any winds from the south bringing hot air off the continent of Africa. Due to depressions moving east across the Sahara Desert, the sirocco blows off the north coast of Africa very hot and dry, often laden with sand and dust, thus reducing visibility. As these winds pass across the sea, they pick up some moisture, and so in Spain, Malta, Sicily, Sardinia, and Southern Italy the sirocco arrives at a lower temperature and with a higher humidity than off the African coast. In those places it is a warm hazy wind associated with a low layer of continuous cloud. Rain falling through the dust carried by these winds can sometimes be red or brown.

A similar wind blows off the Arabian peninsula to affect Israel, Lebanon, Cyprus, Crete, and other southern islands in the Eastern Mediterranean, particularly in the transitional periods between seasons, from April to June, September, to October. In Egypt the sirocco is called the *khamsin*, which means 50 in Arabic, because it occurs most frequently in the 50 days following the Coptic Easter. It usually blows at gale force for about one day and is most common from February to April. Later in May and June the *khamsin* is less frequent but can last longer.

Levante

These NE winds blow near the Spanish coast, reaching gale force in spring (February to May) and autumn (October to December). In summer months from June to September, the *levante* is shorter and has less strength. The *levante* is formed when a depression is situated between the Balearics and North Africa, usually when there is a high pressure area over the European landmass to the north.

The *levante* is most common along the central Spanish coast and can continue into the Strait of Gibraltar, where it is funnelled to become easterly and is known as *levanter*. The *levante* brings lower temperatures and rain, which is often heavy near the coast, while the long fetch produces heavy seas.

Gregale

These strong winds also from the NE are felt in the Central Mediterranean, on the coasts of Sicily and Malta and especially in the Ionian Sea. They flow out of high pressure areas situated over the Balkans and are common in the winter months, especially in February. These winds usually blow at gale force, are cold, and produce a heavy swell. The NE coast of Malta is particularly vulnerable as the main harbours are open to the NE. It was a *gregale* that wrecked St Paul on the Maltese coast in the first century AD.

Meltemi

This wind is more commonly known by its Turkish name 'meltemi' than as the etesian wind, which is taken from the Greek word meaning 'annual'. These regular winds blow steadily over the eastern basin of the Mediterranean all summer, commencing in May or early June and continuing until September or even October. The meltemi is at its strongest and steadiest in July and August. Even when the meltemi is not blowing, or while it is being established in the earlier months, it is rare to get winds from any other direction during this time. Periods of calm can often occur at the beginning of the season. The meltemi has many similarities with a monsoon and can be regarded as an extension of the Indian monsoon caused by the low pressure area east of the Mediterranean.

The meltemi blows from the north in the central Aegean, tending to be more NE in the northern Aegean and NW in the southern areas, extending across the whole eastern basin, although it peters out before reaching the southern shores. The meltemi is a fresh wind on average 15–20 knots, and associated with fine clear weather. Often it reaches up to 30 knots, especially in the afternoons and occasionally it reaches 40 knots. It is less strong in the most northerly areas and strongest in the S and SW Aegean. The meltemi tends to decrease at night.

Western Mediterranean

The summers are fine with few storms. Gale force winds do occur, but these are often generated by local depressions over a limited area. Because of this they are difficult to predict and give little warning of their onset, as an impending gale is rarely preceded by a meaningful change in barometric pressure. Strong winds such as *vendavales*, sirocco, or *levante* are more common in the transitional months of spring and autumn. The mistral can blow in summer but is much less frequent than at other times of the year. The commonest wind over this area is from the NW, except in the most southerly areas near the African coast, where winds from the E and NE are more frequent. There can be calm periods for several days at a time. There is little rain over this area in summer, except for occasional thunderstorms near some of the coasts.

In winter winds are much more variable and gales more frequent. Depressions from the Atlantic track in from the west, either across France or Spain or through the Strait of Gibraltar. Also some local depressions form in the Gulf of Lions or the Gulf of Genoa and track to the south, bringing strong winds and squally weather. The mistral gales are more frequent in winter months and NW winds predominate over this area. *Vendavales* and *libeccio* blow especially in late autumn and early spring. In spite of the increased frequency of gales in winter, there are also some quiet periods. Although most rain falls during winter as showers, temperatures are mild and there are frequent sunny days.

Eastern Mediterranean

The summers are dominated by the seasonal winds from the northern quarter, which blow strongly but are associated with clear skies and fine weather. Rainfall is scant and almost non-existent on the southern shores. The climate of the eastern basin is a little more continental than the western or central areas, which means fewer fronts, less rain, and a lower humidity. It is noted for long hot summers and short winters. Most of the rain falls in winter.

In winter depressions track in an easterly direction either SE towards Cyprus or NE towards the Black Sea. Although small in size, these depres-

sions can be very violent as they develop rapidly and with little warning. Some violent storms in this area are dangerous as they are local in character, arriving quickly out of a clear sky. Although winds from the northerly sector are commonest in winter too, winds from all directions do occur and there are strong gale force winds particularly from the south. Both S and N winds are more prolonged than E or W winds. November to February are the worst months with cold dry N to NE gales and warm moist SE to SW gales which bring dust. When a depression passes there can be a change from S to N within a few hours. At the transitional period between seasons, such as in April and May, calms can occur for several days.

Currents

The Mediterranean loses more water by evaporation than it receives from rivers emptying into it, but there is a general inflow of water from the Atlantic Ocean at all times of the year. This east-setting current is strongest through the Strait of Gibraltar and along the North African coast, where it averages around 2 knots. After passing through the channel between Sicily and Tunisia it gradually loses its strength as it flows eastward. There is a weaker counterclockwise circulation in both of the two basins of the Mediterranean joined by an east-setting current in the Malta channel between the two areas. In the western basin this current flows north up the west coast of Italy. It turns west along the south coast of France and continues south down the Spanish coast. In the eastern basin, the east-setting current turns north along the coast of Israel and Lebanon, west along the Turkish coast, and completes the circle along the northern coast of Crete. A branch makes a counterclockwise circulation of the Aegean Sea, being joined in its southward movement by water flowing out of the Black Sea and into the Mediterranean via the Bosporus and Dardanelles. Another branch makes a counterclockwise circulation of the Adriatic.

Excepting the steady current along the North African coast, the actual currents are very variable and are affected considerably both by the direction and force of the wind and local conditions. For example, when the meltemi is blowing, a S to SW setting current predominates in the Central and Western Aegean. The strongest currents are experienced in the Strait of Gibraltar, the Bosporus, and Dardanelles. Other straits, such as the Strait of Messina, are strongly affected by tidal currents.

22

ROUTES IN THE MEDITERRANEAN SEA

Sailing conditions in the Mediterranean have been reviled and ridiculed by modern sailors more than in any other part of the world and the most repeated saying is that 'in the Mediterranean one either gets too much wind or none at all, and what one gets is on the nose'. Fortunately this is not always true and although the winds encountered in this inland sea cannot be compared in constancy to the trade winds of the Caribbean or Indian Ocean, most offshore passages can be made under sail. The Mediterranean has been plied for many centuries by all kinds of wind driven craft and some of the voyages of ancient time have become legend. Being aware of the capricious nature of Mediterranean winds, ships used to be provided with a set of sturdy oars and although slaves have gone out of fashion, diesel engines can replace them perfectly well.

Because of its long maritime history, the weather of the Mediterranean is well known and this simplifies the task for those intending to do some forward planning. As the sailing season stretches over almost nine months of the year, from early March to the end of November, a lot of ground can be covered if an early start is made. This is recommended especially for those planning to make west to east passages as westerly winds are more common during early spring and late autumn. However, because weather patterns in the Mediterranean are less clearly defined than in other parts of the world, a 'best time' to make a particular passage is far less accurate than elsewhere. With a few exceptions, the weather can rarely be regarded as dangerous in the Mediterranean and the most violent storms mostly occur in winter, January and February being the worst months.

The Mediterranean is crisscrossed by innumerable routes, far too many to be dealt with in this book. Also, most of these routes involve a certain amount of coastal cruising and so can hardly be described as offshore routes. Finally, the multitude of good harbours throughout the Mediterranean coupled with the unparalleled richness and variety of places to visit ashore means that most people prefer coastal cruising. In consequence, this chapter deals primarily with the most frequented offshore routes.

In the Mediterranean, perhaps more than anywhere else, forward planning is of crucial importance and as this book is aimed primarily at offshore sailors the routes described and suggestions made are meant for sailors who are not normally based in the Mediterranean and for whom the Mediterranean is only part of a longer voyage.

There are two principal gateways into the Mediterranean, Gibraltar being used mainly by sailors arriving from Northern Europe and America, while Port Said witnesses the arrival of sailors who have reached the Mediterranean through the Red Sea and Suez Canal. The latter may be European sailors returning home at the completion of a world voyage, or sailors from other continents, from North America, Australia, New Zealand, or the Far East, in the midst of a circumnavigation. Most of these sailors arrive in the Mediterranean determined to see and do as much as possible in the shortest time possible, which may not be as easy as it first appears. The Mediterranean has been described as the 'cradle of civilisation' and, whether one agrees with that description or not, there is certainly no other region of the world which offers so much to see in such a concentrated area, from archaeological sites to historic cities, beautiful islands and stunning scenery. So the main danger is in trying to cover too much ground in one season and ending up by seeing much less than planned. Also, the Mediterranean is not the small lake it appears and the distance between Gibraltar and the Suez Canal is twice that between Miami and the Panama Canal!

Because many sailors arrive in the Mediterranean planning to spend only one season there the following suggestions are aimed primarily at them. Those starting off from Gibraltar, especially if they have had to cross the Atlantic to get there, are at a certain disadvantage as the sailing season will be well advanced by the time they arrive. For such late starters it is important to get to the furthest point as quickly as possible. As one can never be completely sure what kind of winds to expect, it is wise to cover as many miles as possible early on so as to have time in hand for the rest of the cruise. Such a tactic is particularly important if one wishes to cruise in the Eastern Mediterranean, in which case one should attempt to sail with as few stops as possible to Northern Greece so as to arrive there before the onset of the strong northerly winds of summer. These winds will then ensure favourable sailing conditions while exploring the delights of the Aegean Sea, whether among the Greek islands or on the Turkish mainland.

Gibraltar is an excellent port in which to prepare for an eastbound passage and, although the current is always favourable, it is worth waiting for a spell of westerly winds before leaving. The Eastern Mediterranean can be reached by either going north or south of Sicily. If the destination is the Ionian Sea, or parts of Greece which are easier reached through the Corinth Canal, it is better to sail north of Sicily and through the Strait of Messina. Otherwise, a southern route, which possibly calls at Malta, is to be favoured if the destination is in Crete, Cyprus, or Port Said. A logical decision is to start a cruise in the northern part of the Aegean in late spring or early summer, after which the summer can be spent exploring the Eastern Mediterranean. By August one should start moving westward and, if neither Malta nor the Balearics were visited on the outward voyage, they can easily be included on the return route to Gibraltar.

In the Eastern Mediterranean favourable northerly winds are common throughout the summer, but by early autumn the winds become more variable, and prolonged calms are frequent, especially on passages to Malta. Because westbound passages have fewer chances of favourable winds than passages in the opposite direction, one should allow

more time for such passages and also be prepared to motor through the unavoidable calms. A stop in Malta is only recommended for boats coming from Port Said, Cyprus, or Crete. Those coming from mainland Turkey or the Greek islands would do better to sail through the Strait of Messina and continue north of Sicily.

Those planning to continue across the Atlantic should attempt to be in Gibraltar not much later than the end of September so as to have sufficient time for the subsequent passage to the Canaries. Those intending to sail to Northern Europe will find that weather conditions in autumn are rarely favourable and, rather than fight the elements, it is probably wiser to leave the boat in the Mediterranean for the coming winter. There are indeed plenty of good ports and marinas where this can be done at a competitive price. Similarly, American sailors should seriously consider leaving their boat in the Mediterranean between seasons, sailing their boats across the Atlantic during one summer, then finding a suitable place to leave the boat for the coming winter. This then leaves them free to return early the following season and be poised to start cruising as early as April. They then have nearly six months of Mediterranean cruising before preparing for a return voyage via the Canaries and Caribbean.

Sailors reaching the Mediterranean by way of the Red Sea are in a much better position as they normally transit the Suez Canal in March or April, thus arriving in the Eastern Mediterranean at the best possible time. Having reached that area so early, they can visit first Cyprus and Eastern Turkey, and possibly Israel as well, before following the earlier suggestion and make for the Northern Aegean by June. From there on, the same itinerary will be followed as the one sailed by boats that have come from the Atlantic.

With more time at one's disposal, and this normally means more than one year, unless one is able to move very fast, other areas of the Mediterranean can be explored, from the French Riviera to North Africa, or the increasingly popular Black Sea, where the gradual easing of restrictions in the former Communist countries has opened new cruising areas to those ambitious enough to reach them.

The Adriatic Sea

CRUISING GUIDES: *Adriatic Pilot.*
The war in former Yugoslavia put out of bounds

one of the most attractive cruising areas in Europe. While hostilities appear to have spared most of the offshore islands, it will be many years before this coastline returns to normality. The small coastline of Slovenia has been largely unaffected by the war waged by its neighbours, while Croatia is making determined efforts to attract cruising boats once again to its attractive coastline. Foreign boats have started trickling back but nowhere in the huge numbers seen in the past. While the present situation continues no one should enter that area before having obtained confirmation that it is safe to do so. Albania itself is also slowly coming out of the cold and yachts which have stopped in one of the Albanian ports have been allowed to spend a short time there. Compared to the diversity of Croatia, the east coast of Italy has very little to offer and there is only a limited number of safe harbours along the entire coast.

Because of its narrowness and other specific factors, weather conditions in the Adriatic tend to be very localised. The most dangerous wind is the *bora*, a violent northerly wind that occurs mostly in winter. There is a north-setting current along the eastern shore which can be used to advantage when making northbound passages. It is generally advisable to favour the eastern shore when bound in either direction, because of the availability of sheltered anchorages.

The Aegean Sea

CRUISING GUIDES: *Greek Waters Pilot, Saronic, Turkish Waters Pilot.*
The islands of the Grecian archipelago and the Turkish coast of Asia Minor offer a great variety of cruising opportunities and this is reflected in the large number of sailing boats that ply the Aegean each summer. Navigation rarely presents any real problems, there are countless safe harbours and anchorages, all dangers are clearly marked on charts and even the traditional rivalry between Greece and Turkey affects visiting sailors only in a tangential way.

Ideally, the Aegean should be cruised from north to south, and because of the prevailing northerly winds of summer it is recommended to arrive in the Northern Aegean before the end of May so as to benefit from a favourable wind for the following three months. The ever increasing popularity of these cruising grounds makes most ports very crowded during the peak holiday months of July

and August, when more secluded anchorages should be sought out. As the safe cruising season extends from March to November it is possible to visit most harbours either before or after the great summer invasion. This may be also the time to visit some of the adjacent areas, such as Istanbul or the Black Sea.

When the meltemi is blowing strongly offshore, violent gusts often occur in the lee of high ground. Accelerated down the land, this can produce 40–50 knots of wind very suddenly in an area previously calm. This effect occurs particularly on steep southern coasts, both of islands and the mainland. The meltemi is also funnelled through straits, ravines, and between islands. When sheltering on a southerly coast during a northerly gale this squally effect must be allowed for.

The Marmara and Black Sea

CRUISING GUIDES: *Black Sea Cruising Guide.*
Most boats reach this area from the SW, island hopping through the Aegean, although a few boats arrive in the Black Sea by way of the Danube. The passage through the Aegean should be undertaken in spring, before the onset of the meltemi, when winds are either light or non-existent and one must be prepared to motor. Because of the strong outflowing current in the Dardanelles, tacking against a NE wind is almost impossible, the task made even more difficult by the large amount of shipping. A weak counter-current is usually felt on the European side of the strait, which should be favoured as far as Chanakkale, where it is compulsory to cross to the Asian side to clear into Turkey. The rest of the Dardanelles and the crossing of the Sea of Marmara is best done in daily stages, both because of the amount of shipping and the usual lack of wind at night.

Passing through the Bosporus should only be attempted in daylight and the European side of the strait should be favoured where a weaker counter-current will be found. A thick haze often occurs on summer mornings, which makes navigation very difficult in the strait due to the large number of ships.

Until not so long ago, cruising in the Black Sea used to be limited to a few Turkish ports and the designated ports of entry of the other countries: Bulgaria, Romania, and the Soviet Union. The fall of Communism has certainly brought about an opening up of all those countries, but unfortunately foreign cruising boats are still submitted to endless formalities. Bulgaria and Romania are now welcoming cruising yachts openly but in both Russia and the Ukraine foreign yachts are supposed to arrive only after having received an official invitation by either a yacht club or a shipping agency. In all these countries tourist visas should be obtained in advance for every crew member. One of the most attractive Black Sea countries is Georgia, but civil war in this former Soviet republic has made it into a no-go area for foreigners.

The Black Sea enjoys a climate very similar to the Mediterranean in summer, being mainly fine and sunny, with winds predominantly from the NW or W formed by the same system which generates the meltemi. In winter the weather is much colder, especially in more northerly parts where ice can occur. Very variable conditions prevail in the transition months, April–May and September–October, the winds changing quickly both in force and direction. Local effects as well as land and sea breezes are well marked. In the Dardanelles and Bosporus NE winds are the most frequent as there is a general airflow from the Black Sea into the Aegean. If the wind is not blowing from the NE in these narrows it is usually from the opposite SW direction.

M10 MEDITERRANEAN ROUTES FROM GIBRALTAR

With the Strait of Gibraltar safely behind them, eastbound boats have a much easier task when leaving Gibraltar than boats setting off in the opposite direction. The only time when one should not consider leaving Gibraltar is during strong easterly winds. Generally, winds tend to be funnelled either west or east in the strait. At Gibraltar westerly winds predominate in winter and easterly in

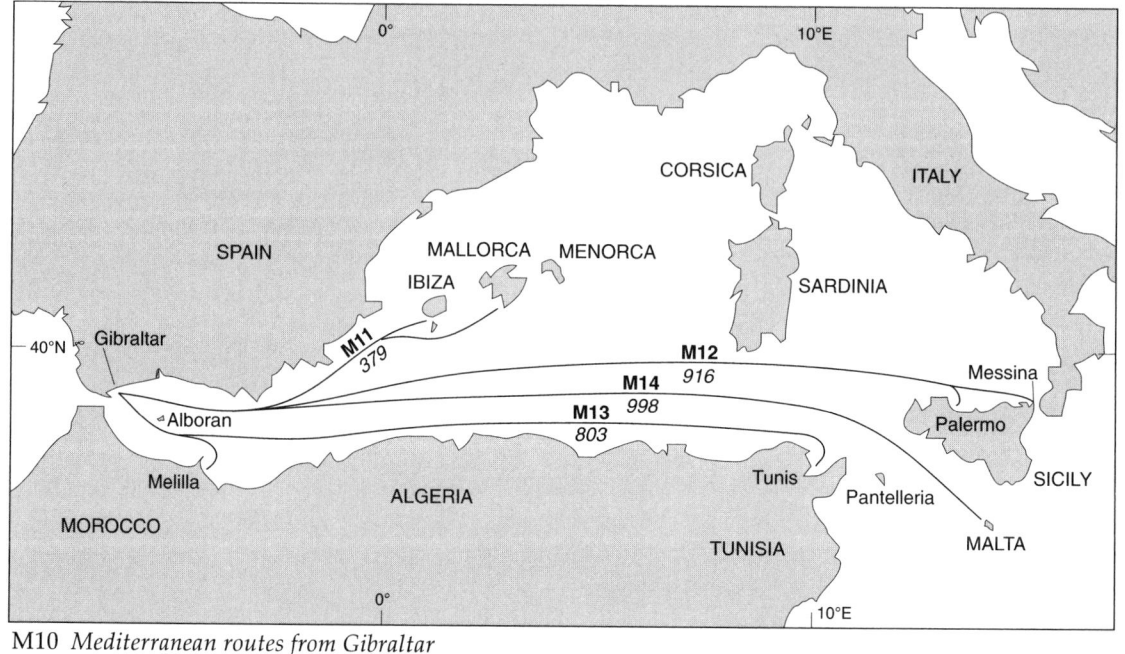

M10 *Mediterranean routes from Gibraltar*

summer. *Levanters* are more frequent from July to October and can blow for up to 15 days at a time, although not always too strongly, their average strength being around 15 knots. In winter the *levanter* is shorter but stronger, bringing rain, clouds,

and haze. *Vendavales* also occur most frequently in the winter from November to March. In the lee of the Rock the wind causes eddies blowing strongly from different directions only a short distance apart.

M11 *Gibraltar to the Balearics*

BEST TIME:	May to June			
CHARTS:	BA: 2717 US: 301			
PILOTS:	BA: 45 US: 130, 131			
CRUISING GUIDES:	*East Spain Pilot (Islas Baleares), Spanish Mediterranean Yachtsman's Directory.*			
WAYPOINTS:				

Departure	Intermediate	Landfall	Destination	Distance (M)
M111 Europa 36°04'N,5°20'W	M112 Gata S 36°35'N, 2°10'W M113 Palos 37°35'N, 0°30'W	M114 Espalmador 38°48'N, 1°25'E	Ibiza *38°54'N, 1°28'E*	379
M111 Europa	M112 Gata S M113 Palos M115 Formentera E 38°40'N, 1°40'E	M116 Ibiza S 38°51'N, 1°28'E M117 Mallorca SW 39°28'N, 2°37'E	Ibiza Palma *39°33'N, 2°38'E*	395 454

From any of the marinas or the anchorage near Gibraltar airport, boats should make their way to Europa Point and WP M111, south of that remarkable landmark. From that point the recommended route runs parallel to the Spanish coast keeping at least 20 miles offshore where steadier winds will be found. Along the entire length of the Spanish coast there are several good harbours in which shelter can be sought in bad weather. A favourable east-setting current is felt at least as far as Cabo de Gata, which is passed at a distance of approximately 10 miles to the south through WP M112. From this point the route turns NE passing close to Cabo de Palos through WP M113. It is at this point that boats bound for ports further up the Spanish coast should continue on a route parallel with that coast, whereas boats bound for the Balearics head offshore for WP M114, if the intention is to call first at Ibiza, in which case the recommended route passes west of Formentera. WP M114 is 5 miles west of Espalmador Islet and there are several deep channels between the southern extremity of Ibiza

and Espalmador Islet. The currents in the channels are strong and often set against the prevailing wind, which can result in rough seas in strong winds. Under such circumstances it is better to pass east of Formentera, which is also the recommended procedure if one is bound directly for Palma de Mallorca. In this case, from WP113 a course is set for WP M115, off the SE point of Formentera. From there, boats bound for Ibiza should alter course for WP M116, outside Ibiza harbour, whereas those bound for Mallorca should set a course for WP M117, in the Bay of Palma in the approaches to Palma de Mallorca.

There are several marinas in Palma and the most convenient, nearest to the town centre, is run by the Real Club Nautico, located in Darsena San Pedro, in the eastern part of the port. The club monitors VHF channel 9 permanently. Arriving yachts should go to the reception dock to be assigned a berth. Club de Mar, located inside Porto Pi, in the western part of the harbour, is a much larger marina but further from town.

M12 *Gibraltar to Sicily*

BEST TIME:	May to June			
CHARTS:	BA: 4301			
	US: 301			
PILOTS:	BA: 45			
	US: 130, 131			
CRUISING GUIDES:	*Italian Waters Pilot.*			
WAYPOINTS:				

Departure	Intermediate	Landfall	Destination	Distance (M)
M121 Europa 36°04'N,5°20'W	M122 Gata S 36°35'N, 2°10'W			
	M123 Sardinia S 38°30'N, 8°00'E	M124 Gallo 38°17'N, 13°20'E	Palermo *38°07'N, 13°22'E*	916
M121 Europa	M122 Gata S			
	M123 Sardinia S			
	M125 Vulcan 38°20'N, 15°00'E	M126 Peloro 38°19'N, 15°39'E		1016

The same route, and similar directions as for route M11 should be followed as far as Cabo de Gata. From there the route continues in an easterly direction to WP M123, some 35 miles SW of Sardinia. At that point, boats bound for the Sicilian capital should alter course for WP M124, off Cape Gallo, in the approaches to Palermo. Boats bound for the Strait of Messina should continue almost due east to WP M125, to pass south of Vulcan Island, and make landfall at WP M126, off Cape Peloro, in the northern approaches to the Strait of Messina.

Having reached the legendary narrows separating Sicily from mainland Italy, those intending to stop have a choice of ports on the east coast of Sicily, although the busy port of Messina should be avoided because of the continuous ferry traffic.

In the Strait of Messina the wind tends to blow either in a northerly or southerly direction along the axis of the strait. Sometimes the wind will be NE on the eastern side, NW on the western side, and very light in the middle. Alternatively it can be S to SE in the southern approaches, changing abruptly to NW in the northern approaches, which creates a heavy sea. Violent gusts come off the high ground, which together with strong tidal currents and a number of small whirlpools and eddies contribute to the strait retaining the flavour of Scylla and Charybdis of the time of Odysseus. A line of bores called *tagli* can occur at the change of tide. It is therefore essential to time one's transit of the strait with a favourable tide.

M13 *Gibraltar to North Africa*

BEST TIME:	May to October
CHARTS:	BA: 4301
	US: 301
PILOTS:	BA: 45
	US: 131
CRUISING GUIDES:	*North Africa.*

WAYPOINTS:				
Departure	Intermediate	Landfall	Destination	Distance (M)
M130 Europa 36°04'N, 5°20'W	M131 Forcas 35°33'N, 3°00'W		Melilla 35°17'N, 2°56'W	135
			Sidi Fredj 36°46'N, 2°51'W	192
M130 Europa	M132 Alboran S 35°50'N, 3°00'W			
	M133 Tenes 36°45'N, 1°20'E			
	M134 Bengut 37°20'N, 4°00'E			
	M135 Bougaroni 37°20'N, 6°25'E			
	M136 Sorelles 37°20'N, 8°35'E			
	M137 Enghela 37°30'N, 9°45'E		Bizerte 37°16'N, 9°53'E	755
	M138 Plane 37°12'N, 10°23'E	M139 Cartage 36°53'N, 10°23'E	Sidi bou Said 36°52'N, 10°21'E	803

There is a large choice of destinations on the North African shore, from the small Spanish possessions of Ceuta and Melilla all the way to the east coast of Tunisia. The latter has become the favourite cruising destination in North Africa, mainly as a result of the opening of a number of good marinas. Few boats stop in Algeria, where yachting facilities continue to be very basic.

From WP M130, south of Europa Point, the route goes south of Alboran Island and stays close to the North African coast to benefit from the favourable east-setting current. If the intention is to call at either Melilla or Sidi Fredj, in Algeria, the initial course goes to WP M131, off Cape Tres Forcas, from where the course can be altered for the intended port of destination. Sidi Fredj has a marina and is reported to have the best yachting facilities in Algeria.

Boats bound for ports further east on the Algerian coast or ports in Tunisia should also take a route that goes south of Alboran Island. Their first WP will be M132, some ten miles south of that island, from where the course is altered for WP M133, off Cape Tenes. From that point, the route follows the North African coast closely to take advantage of the favourable current, passing through a number of intermediate waypoints, all of which avoid sailing into territorial waters. Staying a prudent distance off the coast is also advisable to avoid the areas frequented by local fishing boats, especially at night, as some of the smaller boats do not show lights. One of the dangers to be avoided along this route are the Sorelles rocks, SW of Galite Island. From WP M136, south of those rocks, the course is altered for WP M137, North of Cape Enghela. Having reached this point, boats intending to call at Bizerte should alter course for the coast, whereas those bound for Tunis should set a SE course for WP M138 so as to pass SE of Cani Island. From WP M138, east of Plane Island, the course turns due south and makes landfall at WP M139, off Cape Cartage, in the approaches to the Tunisian capital. The nearest marina is at Sidi bou Said and arriving boats should make their way there to complete entry formalities.

M14 *Gibraltar to Malta*

BEST TIME:	May to June, November			
CHARTS:	BA: 4301			
	US: 301			
PILOTS:	BA: 45			
	US: 130, 131			
CRUISING GUIDES:	*North Africa, Yachtsman's Handbook to Malta.*			
WAYPOINTS:				

Departure	Intermediate	Landfall	Destination	Distance (M)
M141 Europa	M142 Gata SE			
36°04'N, 5°20'W	36°25'N, 2°00'W			
	M143 Sentinelle S			
	38°00'N, 9°40'E			
	M144 Pantelleria			
	36°55'N, 12°00'E			
	M145 Gozo	Malta NE	Valletta	998
	36°05'N, 14°27'E	35°56'N, 14°32'E	*35°54'N, 14°31'E*	

A more offshore route than M13 can be sailed by boats bound for Malta, unless one is determined to take full advantage of the favourable east-setting current along the African coast, in which case the same directions apply as far as WP M137, at the entrance into the Skerki Channel at the NE extremity of Tunisia.

During the summer months, from May to September, the recommended route does not follow the African shore so closely and passes north of Alboran Island as the advantages to be gained by sailing an inshore route are probably cancelled out by the disadvantages. Along the entire North African coast, vessels should keep outside of territorial waters and also pay attention to local fishing boats, especially at night as many do not show lights. Westerly winds are more likely to be encountered along this route during the remaining months of the year, from October to April, and therefore this passage is best planned either at the beginning or end of the season. During summer, if consistent easterly winds are met, it is usually better to make the voyage in stages, stopping either in Spain and the Balearics, or along the African coast. The African coast should be avoided in winter when strong northerly gales make it a dangerous lee shore. If easterly winds persist after leaving Gibraltar, either in summer or winter, better conditions will be experienced by staying closer to the Spanish coast than North Africa. Such a route continues eastwards as far as the south of Sardinia before tacking across the channel between Cape Bon and Sicily.

The direct route takes its departure from WP M141, south of Europa Point, from where an initial course is set for WP M142, 20 miles SE of Cabo de Gata. From there a long offshore leg goes all the way to WP M143 passing halfway between North Africa and Sardinia. From that point, the course become SE and passes through the Skerki Channel to pass close to the north of the island of Pantelleria. The course continues in almost the same direction to WP M145, east of Gozo. From there the course is altered for WP M146 so that landfall is made north of the Maltese capital. Arriving boats should contact Valletta Port Control on VHF channels 12 or 16 before proceeding to one of the reception docks at Msida Marina or Lazaretto Creek. The Yachting Centre can be contacted on VHF channel 9 to request docking information.

M20 Routes from the Balearic Islands

M20 *Routes from the Balearic Islands*

The Balearic Islands, and especially Mallorca, are now one of the top yachting centres in the world and both docking and repair facilities are of the highest standard. Very few cruising boats visiting the Mediterranean miss calling at the Balearics and indeed they are an attractive place to explore and also an excellent place at which to prepare the boat for a long passage. This can be of particular inter-est to those planning to cross the Atlantic to the Caribbean and for whom a stop in the Balearics at the end of summer has a great attraction.

Summers are hot, but winters are mild, the main reason for the Balearics also being one of the main tourist centres in the Mediterranean. Northerly winds predominate in summer and gale force winds are confined to the winter season.

M21 *Balearics to French Riviera*

Best time:	May to October	
Charts:	BA: 4301	
	US: 301	
Pilots:	BA: 45, 46	
	US: 131	
Cruising guides:	*South France Pilot, Mediterranean France and Corsica, Guide to French Mediterranean Ports.*	

WAYPOINTS:				
Departure	*Intermediate*	*Landfall*	*Destination*	*Distance (M)*
M211 Dragonera 39°35'N, 2°17'E		M212 Pomègues 43°10'N, 5°20'E	Marseille *43°21'N, 5°19'E*	266

During the summer months the prevailing wind on this route is NW. The worst thing that can affect a vessel bound for the French coast is to encounter a mistral, which can be very violent in the Gulf of Lions. The mistral affects mainly the western parts of the French Riviera, ports lying east of St Raphael being less affected. A direct course can be sailed from the Balearics to practically every port on the French Riviera. If a mistral is forecast it is better to close with the coast immediately and then reach the intended destination by sailing under the protection of the coast, or go into one of the many ports to seek shelter should the weather deteriorate.

Depending on the subsequent destination, one should start cruising at one or the other end of the Riviera. Generally it is better to make landfall at a western port, such as Marseille, and then sail east along the coast as far as Nice or even beyond before taking off for Corsica or Italy. Such a route is also attractive for those planning to return to the

Balearics, as a complete circle can be accomplished by sailing from the French Riviera to Corsica and from there back to the Balearics. Such a route also uses the prevailing winds to best advantage.

Boats leaving from Palma de Mallorca have to reach the open sea before a course can be set for a French port. Because of the prevailing summer winds it is better to leave from the west of Mallorca by making one's way to Isla Dragonera, the small island lying off the western extremity of Mallorca. Having reached WP M211, boats bound for Marseille can set a direct course for WP M212, in the SE part of the Bay of Marseille, south of Pomègues Island. There are several marinas in or around Marseille, but for short term visitors the most convenient is the one inside the old port (Vieux Port), which is located in the centre of Marseille. This is entered between the two ancient forts, the reception dock for visitors being immediately on the starboard side.

M22 *Balearics to Messina Strait*

BEST TIME:	April to October			
CHARTS:	BA: 4301			
	US: 301			
PILOTS:	BA: 45			
	US: 131			
CRUISING GUIDES:	*Italian Waters Pilot.*			
WAYPOINTS:				
Departure	*Intermediate*	*Landfall*	*Destination*	*Distance (M)*
M221 Menorca 39°52'N, 4°19'E	M222 Sardinia S 38°30'N, 8°00'E	M224 Gallo 38°17'N, 13°20'E	Palermo *38°07'N, 13°22'E*	451
	M223 Vulcan 38°20'N, 15°00'E	M225 Peloro 38°19'N, 15°39'E		550

The route from either Mallorca or Menorca passes so close to Sardinia that most boats make a small detour to visit at least the southern part of this island. Because of its location at the SE extremity of the Balearics, Puerto Mahon on Menorca is a good place to leave from. From WP M221, outside Mahon, an initial course is set for WP M222, SW of

Sardinia. Boats intending to stop first at Palermo should alter course for WP M223, off Cape Gallo, in the approaches to the Sicilian capital. Boats bound for the Strait of Messina nonstop should continue almost due east from WP M223 to WP M224, south of Vulcan Island, and make landfall at WP M225, off Cape Peloro, in the northern approaches to the Strait of Messina.

Having reached these narrows separating Sicily from mainland Italy, those intending to stop have a choice of ports on the east coast of Sicily. A port to be avoided is the busy port of Messina because of the continuous ferry traffic. For more details on

weather conditions in the Strait of Messina see route M12. Boats bound for the Eastern Mediterranean and wishing to avoid Messina Strait, can do so by passing south of Sicily and possibly calling at Malta (see route M23).

M23 *Balearics to Malta*

BEST TIME:	April to October				
CHARTS:	BA: 4301				
	US: 301				
PILOTS:	BA: 45				
	US: 131				
CRUISING GUIDES:	*Yachtsman's Handbook to Malta, North Africa.*				
WAYPOINTS:					
Departure	*Intermediate*	*Landfall*	*Destination*		*Distance (M)*
M231 Menorca 39°52'N, 4°19'E	M232 Sentinelle E 38°00'N, 9°20'E M233 Pantelleria 36°55'N, 12°00'E M234 Gozo 36°05'N, 14°27'E	M235 Malta NE 35°56'N, 14°32'E	Valletta *35°54'N, 14°31'E*		543

Similar directions apply for this route as far as the south of Sardinia as those described in route M22. Having reached WP M232, between North Africa and Sardinia, the course continues in a SE direction and passes through the Skerki Channel, then WP M233, NE of the island of Pantelleria and on to WP M234, east of Gozo. From there the course can be altered for WP M235 so that landfall is made north

of the Maltese capital. Valletta Port Control should be contacted on arrival on VHF channels 12 or 16 before proceeding to one of the reception docks at Msida Marina or Lazaretto Creek. The Yachting Centre, which administers the various marinas in the Maltese capital, can be contacted on VHF channel 9 to request docking information.

M24 *Balearics to Gibraltar*

BEST TIME:	May to September				
CHARTS:	BA: 2717				
	US: 301				
PILOTS:	BA: 45				
	US: 130, 131				
CRUISING GUIDES:	*Yacht Scene, East Spain Pilot.*				
WAYPOINTS:					
Departure	*Intermediate*	*Landfall*	*Destination*		*Distance (M)*
Route M24A M241 Mallorca SW 39°28'N, 2°37'E	M243 Formentera E 38°40'N, 1°40'E M244 Gata SE 36°25'N, 2°00'W	M245 Europa 36°04'N, 5°20'W	Gibraltar *36°08'N, 5°21'W*		453

Departure	Intermediate	Landfall	Destination	Distance (M)
Route M24B				
M242 Ibiza S	M243 Formentera E			
38°51'N, 1°28'E	M244 Gata SE	M245 Europa	Gibraltar	402

This route should have favourable winds at least as far as Cabo de Gata. It is at that point that a contrary east-setting current becomes most noticeable, and so the mainland coast should not be approached too soon. Boats leaving from Palma de Mallorca, from WP M241 should set an intial course which passes south of Ibiza and east of Formentera. From WP M243 a new course is set to pass through WP M244, well to the south of Cabo de Gata. The Spanish coast should be approached only after Cabo de Gata has been passed as the east-going current is strongest in the vicinity of this cape. The route then follows the coast of Spain closely so as to avoid the stronger current offshore. If strong westerly winds are encountered when approaching Gibraltar it is better to seek shelter in a Spanish port along the Costa del Sol to wait for a change rather than try to make headway against both contrary wind and current. See also route AN16 (page 46) for details on weather conditions in the Strait of Gibraltar as well as directions for negotiating the strait.

Having made landfall south of the light on Europa Point, arriving boats should proceed to the customs dock, in Marina Bay, south of the runway, to complete formalities.

M25 *Balearics to Corsica*

BEST TIME:	May to October			
CHARTS:	BA: 4301			
	US: 301			
PILOTS:	BA: 45, 46			
	US: 131			
CRUISING GUIDES:	*Islas Baleares, Mediterranean France and Corsica Pilot.*			
WAYPOINTS:				

Departure	Intermediate	Landfall	Destination	Distance (M)
M250 Mahon	M251 Menorca E			
39°52'N, 4°19'E	*39°52'N, 4°22'E*			
	M252 Scorno	M253 Corse S	Bonifacio	242
	41°12'N, 8°15'E	*41°20'N, 9°05'E*	*41°23'N, 9°08.8'E*	

The picturesque Menorcan port of Mahon is the best departure point for this passage and should be used as an intermediate port even if leaving from one of the other Balearic Islands. Taking one's leave off Cape Negro, in the approaches to Mahon, the direct route to Corsica passes close to the small island of Asinara, off the NW tip of Sardinia. A most convenient, as well as attractive, Corsican port is Bonifacio at the southern extremity of that island. Having made landfall off Cape Pertusato, a fjord-like sound leads to the perfectly sheltered port of Bonifacio. This has been identified as the home of the Laestrygonians in the *Odyssey* and one cannot fail to be reminded of Homer's description as one follows the wake of Ulysses into that magnificent natural harbour.

M26 *Balearics to Tunisia*

BEST TIME:	May to October			
CHARTS:	BA: 4301			
	US: 301			
PILOTS:	BA: 45			
	US: 131			
CRUISING GUIDES:	*Islas Baleares, North Africa.*			
WAYPOINTS:				

Departure	Intermediate	Landfall	Destination	Distance (M)
M260 Palma *39°33'N, 2°38'E*	M261 Mallorca S 39°26'N, 2°40'E M262 Cabrera 39°15'N, 3°02'E M263 Cani 37°23'N, 10°05'E M264 Plane 37°12'N, 10°23'E	M265 Cartage 36°53'N, 10°23'E	Sidi bou Said *36°52'N, 10°21'E*	418
M266 Mahon *39°52'N, 4°19'E*	M267 Menorca SE 39°50'N, 4°21'E M263 Cani M264 Plane	M265 Cartage	Sidi bou Said	348

Whether leaving from Mallorca or Menorca, it is worth waiting for a spell of northerly winds before setting off on this passage. Boats leaving from Palma should set a course that runs parallel to the SW coast of Mallorca to pass through the Cabrera Passage. Having passed Cape Salinas, a direct course can be sailed for the Cani Islands, a cluster of rocky islets close to the northern coast of Tunisia. If leaving from Menorca landfall will be made also close to the Cani light. From there the route turns south towards Cape Cartage and the approaches to Tunis. Although some of the better marinas are on Tunisia's east coast, Sidi bou Said has the advantage of being close both to the capital of Tunis, and its airport, and also the ruins of Cartage, Tunisia's main tourist attraction. Facilities at Sidi bou Said are the best in the area.

M30 ROUTES FROM MEDITERRANEAN FRANCE

The French Riviera, and particularly the Côte d'Azur, from Marseille to the Italian border, has one of the highest concentrations of marinas in the world. As to be expected, yachting facilities are of the highest standard. Sailors hailing from other parts of the world are somewhat at a loss when a decision has to be made concerning cruising along this coast. One important suggestion is to avoid

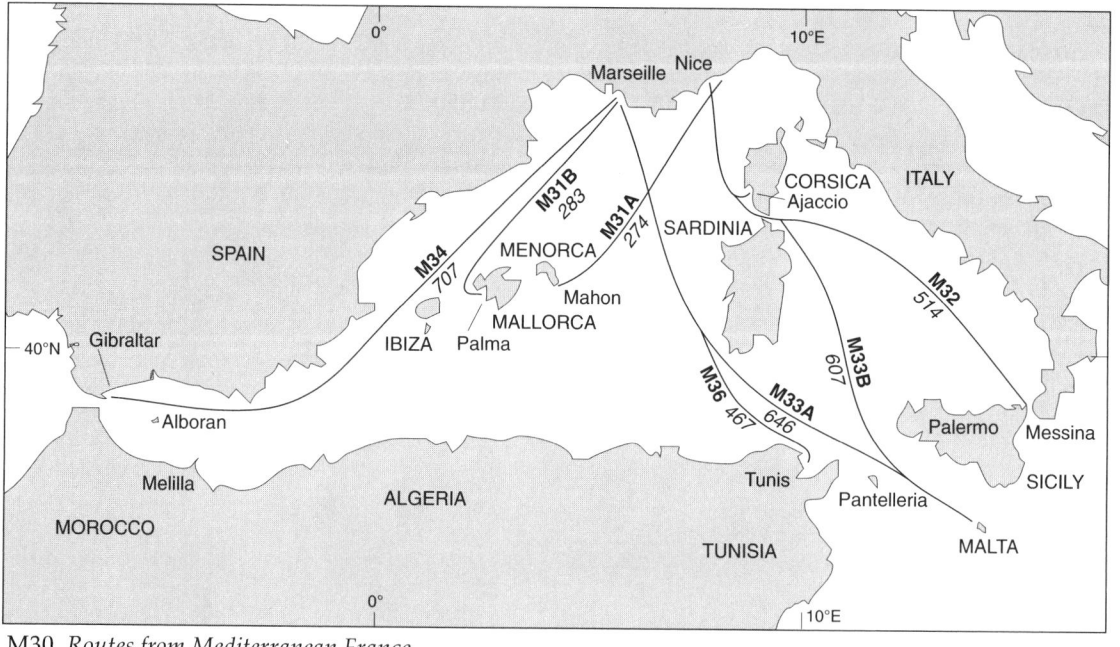

M30 *Routes from Mediterranean France*

arriving at the height of summer, in July and August, when all ports and marinas are full and in most places it is impossible to find docking space. A much better time is either late spring or early autumn, when the weather is pleasant and neither the ports nor the resorts are so crowded.

The weather is pleasant for most of the year, although summers tend to be hot. The Gulf of Lions is especially noted for sudden changes in wind and weather, with very different conditions in places near together. The strongest wind is the mistral, which can produce unpleasant conditions. After the mistral, the next common wind is the *marin*, which blows warm and moist, SE to SW off the sea, and although not as strong as the mistral it raises a heavy sea.

M31 *French Riviera to Balearics*

BEST TIME:	April to October
CHARTS:	BA: 4301
	US: 301
PILOTS:	BA: 45, 46
	US: 131
CRUISING GUIDES:	*Islas Baleares.*
WAYPOINTS:	

Departure	Intermediate	Landfall	Destination	Distance (M)
Route M31A				
M311 Menton		M312 Menorca E	Mahon	274
43°45'N, 7°30'E		39°52'N,4°22'E	*39°52'N, 4°19'E*	
Route M31B				
Marseille	M313 Pomègues	M314 Dragonera	Palma	283
43°21'N, 5°19'E	*43°10'N, 5°20'E*	*39°35'N, 2°17'E*	*39°33'N, 2°38'E*	

Marseille, or one of the ports in its vicinity, is a good point of departure for boats that have cruised along the French Riviera coast in a westerly direction. Those who may have cruised in the opposite direction will take their departure from a port further east, possibly as far as Menton, near the Italian border. For those starting that far east, a detour to Corsica has certain attractions. If sailing nonstop, a convenient port of arrival in the Balearics is Mahon, on Menorca (route M31A). Landfall is made at WP M312, off Cabo Negro, from where the narrow channel is followed into the port of Mahon.

Boats leaving the Riviera from further west (route M31B), such as Marseille, should take their

departure from WP M313, east of the small island of Pomègues, in the SE part of the Bay of Marseille. From that point a direct course can be sailed across to Mallorca. Boats bound for Palma de Mallorca, should make their landfall on the NW coast of the island and then follow Mallorca's west coast into Palma. There are a number of marinas in the Bay of Palma, while in Palma itself the most convenient, as it is nearest to the town centre, is the marina run by the Real Club Nautico, located in Darsena San Pedro, in the eastern part of the port. The club monitors VHF channel 9 permanently. Arriving yachts should go to the reception dock to be assigned a berth.

M32 *French Riviera to Messina Strait*

BEST TIME:	May to October				
CHARTS:	BA: 4301				
	US: 301				
PILOTS:	BA: 45, 46				
	US: 130, 131				
CRUISING GUIDES:	*Italian Waters Pilot.*				
WAYPOINTS:					
Departure	*Intermediate*	*Landfall*	*Destination*		*Distance (M)*
M321 Ferrat	M322 Sanguinaire		Ajaccio		127
43°40'N, 7°17'E	41°54'N, 8°35'E		*41°55'N, 8°44'E*		
	Bonifacio				
	41°23'N, 9°06'E				
	M323 Maddalena NE				
	41°16'N, 9°27'E				
	M324 Panaria	M325 Peloro			514
	38°35'N, 15°00'E	38°19'N, 15°39'E			

Most boats bound for the Strait of Messina and beyond will probably stop in Corsica on their way south as the island straddles the direct route south. Because the west coast of Corsica is more attractive and has a number of good harbours, most boats leaving the Riviera make straight for Calvi or Ajaccio. Favourable winds can be expected during the summer months and even the mistral blows from the right direction, although it is usually associated with rough seas. From WP M321, off Cap Ferrat, in the approaches to the port of Nice, a direct course can be sailed to WP M322, off Ajaccio. A first suggested stop is at this attractive Corsican port.

From Ajaccio the route continues around the SW coast of Corsica and reaches the Tyrrhenian Sea through the Bonifacio Strait. Another suggested

stop is at the small port of Bonifacio, on the north side of the strait. This strait, separating Corsica from Sardinia, is an intricate waterway dotted with rocks and islets, although navigation through the channels that traverse it is not too difficult. Having passed through the strait and regained the open sea, from WP M323, NE of the Italian island of Maddalena, a direct course can be set for WP M324, between Panaria and Salina, in the Aeolian Islands. A slight course alteration is needed to reach WP M325, off Cape Peloro, in the northern approaches to the Messina Strait.

The timing of the passage through this strait separating Sicily from mainland Italy should be calculated in relation to the state of the tide. The currents through the Messina Strait depend on the tide and can attain over 4 knots at springs. The southgoing stream has a longer duration and this can be further increased by a northerly wind. Each turn of the tide is accompanied by one or more tidal bores. These waves are only dangerous to small craft if a strong wind is blowing against the tide.

M33 *French Riviera to Malta*

BEST TIME:	May to September
CHARTS:	BA: 4301
	US: 301
PILOTS:	BA: 45, 46
	US: 130, 131
CRUISING GUIDES:	*Yachtsman's Handbook to Malta, North Africa.*
WAYPOINTS:	

Departure	Intermediate	Landfall	Destination	Distance (M)
Route M33A				
M331 Pomègues	M332 Toro		Valletta	646
43°10'N, 5°20'E	38°50'N, 8°10'E			
	M333 Pantelleria			
	36°55'N, 12°00'E			
	M334 Gozo	M335 Malta NE	*35°54'N, 14°31'E*	
	36°05'N, 14°27'E	35°56'N, 14°32'E		
Route M33B				
M336 Ferrat	M337 Sanguinaire		Ajaccio	127
43°40'N, 7°17'E	41°54'N, 8°35'E		*41°55'N, 8°44'E*	
	Bonifacio			
	41°23'N, 9°06'E			
	M338 Maddalena E			
	41°15'N, 9°36'E			
	M333 Pantelleria			
	M334 Gozo	M335 Malta NE	Valletta	607

Favourable winds can be expected for most of this passage during the summer months. Depending on the port of departure, there is a choice of routes, as one can go either east or west of Corsica. The more direct route (M33A) stays west of both Corsica and Sardinia, and is recommended especially if leaving from one of the more western ports on the French Riviera. If leaving from a port such as Marseille, from WP M331, east of the small island of Pomègues, in the SE part of the Bay of Marseille, a direct course can be set for WP M332, off Sardinia's SW point. From there, the route runs through Skerki Channel to WP M333, north of the island of Pantelleria.

Boats leaving from one of the more eastern ports,

such as Nice, may prefer to sail first to Corsica, and from there take a more indirect route (M33B) by going through the Strait of Bonifacio and then east of Sardinia. On this route, from WP M338, east of Maddalena, a direct course can be set for WP M333, north of Pantelleria. The two routes join at that point and continue towards WP M334, off Gozo, before the course is altered for WP M335, north of La Valletta.

Valletta Port Control should be contacted on arrival on VHF channels 12 or 16 before proceeding to one of the reception docks at Msida Marina or Lazaretto Creek. The Yachting Centre can be contacted on VHF channel 9 to request docking information.

M34 *French Riviera to Gibraltar*

BEST TIME:	April to May, October			
CHARTS:	BA: 4301			
	US: 301			
PILOTS:	BA: 45, 46			
	US: 130, 131			
CRUISING GUIDES:	*Yacht Scene, Mediterranean Spain.*			
WAYPOINTS:				
Departure	*Intermediate*	*Landfall*	*Destination*	*Distance (M)*
Marseille	M341 Pomègues			
43°21'N, 5°19'E	*43°10'N, 5°20'E*			
	M342 Antonio			
	38°50'N, 0°40'E			
	M343 Palos			
	37°35'N, 0°30'W			
	M344 Gata SE	M345 Europa	Gibraltar	707
	36°25'N, 2°00'W	*36°04'N, 5°20'W*	*36°08'N, 5°21'W*	

The number of boats which sail this entire route without stopping is very small, especially as the Balearics, which straddle the direct course, are a very tempting stop. Boats leaving from ports in the eastern part of the French Mediterranean coast may sail a course which passes to the east of the Balearics. The direct route from more western ports, such as Marseille, passes to the west of the Balearics and stays close to the Spanish coast for most of its length.

As far as the Balearics favourable winds are to be expected throughout the summer months. The chances of easterly winds in the second half of the passage are higher in late spring and autumn. There is also a higher proportion of easterly winds along the North African coast, so it may pay to take a course which runs closer to that shore, but not close enough to be affected by the east-setting current.

Boats leaving from Marseille and WP M341, east of the small island of Pomègues, in the SE part of the Bay of Marseille, should set an initial course for WP M342, to pass halfway betwen Ibiza and Cabo

San Antonio, on the Spanish mainland. The course continues parallel with the Spanish coast to WP M343, off Cabo Palos, before the course is altered for WP M344, so as to pass well to the south of Cabo de Gata and avoid the strong current that sets to the east around that cape. The Spanish coast should be approached only after Cabo de Gata has been passed as the eastgoing current is strongest in the vicinity of the cape. The route then follows the coast of Spain closely so as to avoid the stronger current offshore. The alternative, as explained above, is to seek better winds by favouring the African coast.

Having made landfall south of the light on Europa Point, boats intending to stop in Gibraltar should make their way to the customs dock, in Marina Bay, to complete formalities. The dock is located south of the runway and is reached by going past North Mole.

Those continuing into the Atlantic without stopping should consult route AN16 (page 46) for details on weather conditions in the Strait of Gibraltar as well as directions for negotiating the strait.

M35 *French Riviera to Corsica*

BEST TIME:	April to October			
CHARTS:	BA: 1780			
	US: 53100			
PILOTS:	BA: 46			
	US: 131			
CRUISING GUIDES:	*Mediterranean France and Corsica Pilot, La Corse.*			
WAYPOINTS:				

Departure	Intermediate	Landfall	Destination	Distance (M)
M350 Nice	M351 Ferrat	M352 Corse W	Ajaccio	126
43°42'N, 7°17'E	*43°40'N, 7°17'E*	*41°56'N, 8°39'E*	*41°55'N, 8°44'E*	
M350 Nice	M351 Ferrat	M353 Corse N		
		43°03'N, 9°28'E		
		M354 Corse E	Bastia	127
		42°43'N, 9°29'E	*42°42'N, 9°27'E*	

This favourite offshore destination for yachts based on the French Riviera gets very crowded during the period of French summer vacations (15 July to 15 August), and finding a place to dock is often impossible. Corsica should therefore be visited in early or late summer, when the weather is perfect and the movement of yachts is still at a tolerable level. The worst weather conditions in the area are created by a strong mistral, and although the NW winds blow from a favourable direction, a strong mistral should be avoided not so much because of the strength of the winds but because of the sea conditions that it produces. In a threatening mistral it is best to head for one of the ports on the east coast of Corsica, such as Bastia. The most popular destination on the west coast is the capital Ajaccio, which also has the best yachting facilities on the island.

M36 *French Riviera to Tunisia*

BEST TIME:	May to October			
CHARTS:	BA: 4301			
	US: 301			
PILOTS:	BA: 45			
	US: 131			
CRUISING GUIDES:	*South France Pilot, North Africa.*			
WAYPOINTS:				

Departure	Intermediate	Landfall	Destination	Distance (M)
M360 Marseille	M361 Pomègues			
43°21'N, 5°19'E	*43°10'N, 5°20'E*			
	M362 Sardinia SW			
	39°00'N, 7°55'E			
	M363 Cani			
	37°23'N, 10°05'E			
	M364 Plane	M365 Cartage	Sidi bou Said	467
	37°12'N, 10°23'E	*36°53'N, 10°23'E*	*36°52'N, 10°21'E*	

The area around Marseille is prone to spells of mistral throughout the year and although the NW wind blows from a favourable direction, this passage should not be started if a mistral is predicted as the rough seas produce extremely unpleasant sailing conditions. The direct route passes close to Sardinia, where shelter can be sought in deteriorating weather. Landfall will be made north of the light marking the Cani Islands, a group of rocky islets close to the North African shore. From there the route turns south towards the large Bay of Tunis, where the marina at Sidi bou Said provides the best facilities in the area and is also an official port of entry. It is also conveniently located close to the ruins of Cartage and the international airport.

M40 ROUTES FROM SICILY

Most boats on a transmediterranean passage call at a Sicilian port or at least sail through the Messina Strait on their way to their destination. Situated at the crossroads of several offshore routes, Sicily has plenty of good ports in which to make a longer or shorter stop. For boats preparing to leave on a passage to Greece or beyond, there are several ports south of the Messina Strait. The small port at Taormina has the advantage of not only being close to the strait, but also convenient for visiting Mount Etna.

In summer a strong sea breeze blows onshore in the daytime in Sicily, being NE at Palermo, NE to S at Syracuse, and S to SW at Agrigento, on the

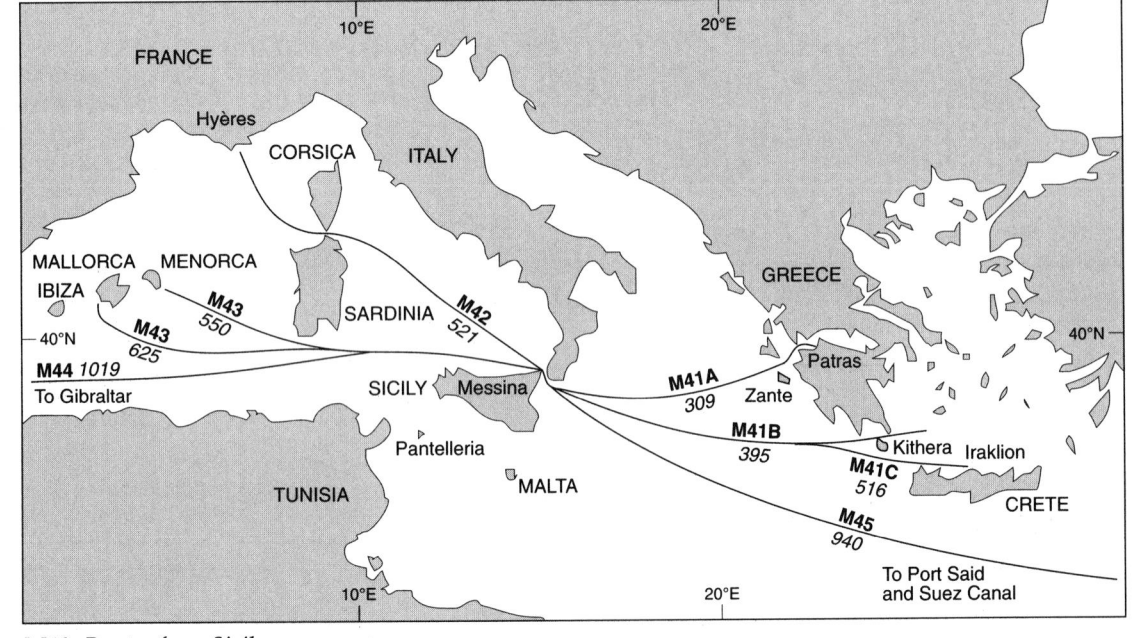

M40 *Routes from Sicily*

south coast. In the Strait of Messina the wind tends to blow either in a N or S direction along the strait, depending on the prevailing conditions. Sometimes the wind will be NE on the eastern side, NW on the western side, and very light in the middle. Alternatively it can be S to SE in the southern approaches, changing abruptly to NW in the northern approaches, which creates a heavy sea. Violent gusts come off the high ground, which together with strong tidal currents and a number of small whirlpools and eddies contribute to the strait retaining the flavour of Scylla and Charybdis as

experienced by Odysseus. Mirages of a multiple image type are sometimes seen in the strait. The currents through the Messina Strait depend on the tide and can attain over 4 knots at springs. The southgoing stream has a longer duration and this can be further increased by a northerly wind. Each turn of the tide is accompanied by several tidal bores. These waves are only dangerous to small craft if a strong wind is blowing against the tide. The state of the tide should be assessed correctly so as to transit the strait with a fair tide.

M41 *Sicily to Greece*

BEST TIME:	May to October			
CHARTS:	BA: 1439			
	US: 302			
PILOTS:	BA: 45, 47, 48			
	US: 131, 132			
CRUISING GUIDES:	*Greek Waters Pilot, Saronic.*			
WAYPOINTS:				
Departure	*Intermediate*	*Landfall*	*Destination*	*Distance (M)*
Route M41A				
M410 Messina	M411 Armi			
38°11'N, 15°37'E	37°54'N, 15°37'E			
	M412 Spartivento	M413 Zante	Patras	309
	37°55'N, 16°06'E	38°00'N, 20°30'E	*38°15'N, 21°44'E*	
Route M41B				
M410 Messina	M411 Armi			
	M414 Sapientza			
	36°45'N, 21°35'E			
	M415 Tainaron			
	36°22'N, 22°30'E			
	M416 Kithera	M417 Malea		395
	36°26'N, 22°56'E	36°23'N, 23°12'E		
Route M41C				
M410 Messina	M411 Armi			
	M414 Sapientza			
	M415 Tainaron			
	M418 Antikithera	M419 Dhia	Iraklion	516
	35°49'N, 23°20'E	35°30'N, 25°08'E	*35°16'N, 25°09'E*	

Having passed through the Strait of Messina, boats bound for the Aegean can reach it either through the Corinth Canal (route M41A), or by rounding the southern tip of the Peloponnese (route M41B). The northern route has the advantage of reaching ports

in the Saronic Gulf as well as the central islands of the Aegean more directly. This is important in summer, when the meltemi is blowing strongly and contrary winds can make it very difficult to reach the same islands if coming from the SW. In spring and autumn the southern route is an acceptable alternative. The latter is also to be preferred if bound for Crete, Rhodes, or points further east.

Once the strait has been left safely behind, from WP M410, off the port of Messina, the initial course goes due south to WP M411, off Capo dell' Armi. Boats sailing the northern route should alter course for WP M412, south of Cape Spartivento. From that point a direct course can be set across the Ionian Sea for WP M413, north of Zante Island in the approaches to the Gulf of Patras. Those who wish to clear into Greece can do so in the port of Zante, on the east coast of the island of the same name. Those who prefer to continue towards the Corinth Canal may clear into Greece further east, such as in the port of Patras, close to the western entrance to the canal.

From WP M411, south of the Messina Strait, boats sailing the southern route can set a direct course for WP M414, SW of Sapientza Island. From this point, the route goes around the three fingers of the Peloponnese by passing through WPs M415, M416, and finally reaching M417. The last way-point, off Cape Malea, is at the SW extremity of the Aegean Sea, with its multitude of destinations.

Boats bound for Crete (route M41C) should leave the above route at WP M415 and set a new course for WP M418, south of Antikithera Island. From there, the route runs parallel to the north coast of Crete to WP M419, west of Dhia Island, in the approaches to Iraklion, the main port and capital of Crete. Boats should proceed into the old Venetian harbour, where there are a number of pontoons for yachts. If there is no free space cruising boats may use the quay immediately to the east of the small boat harbour.

M42 *Sicily to French Riviera*

BEST TIME:	May to June, September, October				
CHARTS:	BA: 4301				
	US: 301				
PILOTS:	BA: 45, 46				
	US: 130, 131				
CRUISING GUIDES:	*Mediterranean France and Corsica, South France Pilot.*				
WAYPOINTS:					
Departure	*Intermediate*	*Landfall*	*Destination*		*Distance (M)*
M421 Peloro 38°19'N, 15°39'E	M422 Panaria 38°35'N, 15°00'E M423 Maddalena NE 41°16'N, 9°27'E M424 Pertusato *41°20'N, 9°05'E*	M425 Porquerolles 43°00'N, 6°20'E	Hyères *43°05'N, 6°10'E*		521

The direct route from the Strait of Messina to Corsica passes through the Aeolian Islands and traverses the Tyrrhenian Sea to the Strait of Bonifacio. There are several channels leading through these narrows, the main passage (Boca Grande) being the easiest to negotiate. This route is often taken by boats heading for the Canal du Midi at the end of their Mediterranean cruise. With persistent NW winds it is better to sail from Corsica to the nearest port on the mainland French coast and make westing by sailing along the coast. This is also the recommended practice to avoid a strong mistral, when conditions can be become very rough

in the Gulf of Lions and it is better to wait for an improvement in one of the many harbours along this coast.

Having negotiated the Strait of Messina, from WP M421, in the northern approaches to the strait, an initial course is set for WP422, west of Panaria Island. From there, the route continues to WP423, off the island of Maddalena in the approaches to Bonifacio Strait. This strait, separating Corsica and Sardinia, is dotted with rocks and islets, although the channels are clearly marked and it is not difficult to traverse it. If a stop in Corsica is not intended and having regained the open sea, from

WP424, west of Cape Pertusato, a direct course can be sailed for the French mainland and WP M425. A good landfall is east of the island of Porquerolles at the entrance into the Bay of Hyères. A first stop can be made on Porquerolles itself, where there is a small harbour (43°00'N, 6°12'E). Hyères itself has a large marina and is one of the biggest sailing centres on the Riviera.

An alternative route for those who wish to visit ports at the eastern extremity of the French Riviera is to stay east of Corsica and cross to the mainland from its northern point. In this way the NW winds of summer will be met at a better angle and the worst of a possible mistral may also be avoided.

Because of the difficulties associated with a passage through the Strait of Messina from south to north, an alternative route for boats sailing from Greece to Corsica and Southern France is to pass south of Sicily, thus avoiding the Messina Strait altogether.

M43 *Sicily to Balearics*

BEST TIME:	May to June, September to October			
CHARTS:	BA: 165, 2717			
	US: 301			
PILOTS:	BA: 45			
	US: 131			
CRUISING GUIDES:	*East Spain Pilot (Balearics), Spanish Mediterranean Yachtsman's Directory.*			
WAYPOINTS:				

Departure	Intermediate	Landfall	Destination	Distance (M)
M431 Peloro 38°19'N, 15°39'E	M432 Vulcan 38°20'N, 15°00'E			
	M433 Sardinia S 38°30'N, 8°00'E	M434 Menorca E 39°52'N, 4°22'E	Mahon *39°52'N, 4°19'E*	550
	M435 Salinas 39°13'N, 3°05'E	M436 Mallorca S 39°26'N, 2°40'E	Palma *39°33'N, 2°38'E*	625

Most boats bound for the Balearics from Sicily take their departure from the Messina Strait. From WP M431, north of the strait, the route runs west parallel to the north coast of Sicily, to WP M432, south of Vulcan Island. The course is altered there for WP M433, south of Sardinia. From that point, boats bound for Menorca can set a direct course for WP M434, off Cabo Negro, from where the narrow channel is followed into the port of Mahon.

Boats bound for Palma de Mallorca should set a course from WP M433 for WP M435, off Cape Salinas, at the SE extremity of Mallorca. From there the course is altered for WP M436, in the Bay of Palma. There are several marinas in the Bay of Palma, while in Palma itself the most convenient, as it is nearest to the town centre, is the marina run by the Real Club Nautico, located in Darsena San Pedro, in the eastern part of the harbour. The club monitors VHF channel 9 permanently. Arriving yachts should go to the reception dock to be assigned a berth.

M44 *Sicily to Gibraltar*

BEST TIME:	May to June, October			
CHARTS:	BA: 4301			
	US: 301			
PILOTS:	BA: 45			
	US: 130, 131			
CRUISING GUIDES:	*Yacht Scene, East Spain Pilot (Costa del Sol).*			
WAYPOINTS:				

Departure	Intermediate	Landfall	Destination	Distance (M)
M441 Peloro 38°19'N, 15°39'E	M442 Vulcan 38°20'N, 15°00'E			
	M443 Sardinia S 38°30'N, 8°00'E			
	M444 Gata SE 36°25'N, 2°00'W	M445 Europa 36°04'N, 5°20'W	Gibraltar *36°08'N, 5°21'W*	1019

Boats that have passed through the Messina Strait should follow a course which runs parallel to the north coast of Sicily. From WP M441, off Cape Peloro, north of Messina Strait, an initial course can be set for WP M442, south of Vulcan Island. The route continues almost due west to WP M443, south of Sardinia. There follows a long offshore leg to WP M444, which has been set well to the south of Cabo de Gata in order to avoid the strong current that sets to the east around that cape. The offshore route may be left after Cabo de Gata has been passed to close with the Spanish coast to avoid the stronger current offshore.

The chances of easterly winds on this route are higher in late spring and autumn. The proportion of easterly winds is higher along the North African coast, so if one has access to weather information it may be better to sail a route which stays closer to that shore, but not close enough to be affected by the prevailing east-setting current.

Having made landfall at WP M445, south of the light on Europa Point, boats should make their way to the customs dock, in Marina Bay, to complete formalities. The dock is located south of the runway and is reached by going past North Mole.

Those continuing into the Atlantic without stopping should consult route AN16 (page 46) for details on weather conditions in the Strait of Gibraltar as well as directions for negotiating the strait.

M45 *Sicily to Port Said*

BEST TIME:	June to August			
CHARTS:	BA: 4302			
	US: 302			
PILOTS:	BA: 45, 49			
	US: 130, 131, 132			
CRUISING GUIDES:	*Mediterranean Cruising Handbook, Red Sea Pilot.*			
WAYPOINTS:				

Departure	Intermediate	Landfall	Destination	Distance (M)
M451 Messina 38°11'N, 15°37'E	M452 Armi 37°54'N, 15°37'E			
	M453 Damietta 32°00'N, 31°50'E	M454 Said 31°25'N, 32°18'E	Port Said *31°15'N, 32°18'E*	940

Favourable winds can be expected along this route for most of the year. Because the current normally sets eastward along the Egyptian coast, and the current is augmented by the waters of the Nile, especially when the river is in flood, landfall should be made to the west of Port Said. As the water is shallow throughout the area, the coast should not be approached beyond the 20 fathom line which can be followed as far as Damietta. Boats undertaking this passage are usually bound for the Red Sea and are only calling in Egypt because of the Suez Canal. Those who wish to stop in an Egyptian port before Port Said can do so at Alexandria. However, yachting facilities for visitors are limited in that port and the only ones available belong to the Alexandria Yacht Club, which is one of the most unwelcoming clubs in the world. Those who wish to visit the interior of Egypt would do better to do it from either Port Said or Suez, whose yacht clubs are much more helpful.

Having transited Messina Strait, an initial course is set from WP M451 for WP M452, off Capo dell'Armi. From that point a direct course can be set from WP M453, off the Damietta mouth in the Nile delta. From there the course is altered for WP M454, in the northern approaches to Port Said and the Suez Canal. Because of the low, featureless Egyptian coast and the shallow depths which extend several miles offshore, the position of Port Said is very difficult to ascertain if landfall is made either too far east or west. The situation is further complicated by the occasionally strong currents in the area, which can be influenced by the state of the Nile waters.

The cluster of ships at anchor is usually the best indication of the approaches to Port Said. The approach channel to Port Said extends several miles to the north and is well marked by buoys. It should be entered at its northern extremity and no shortcuts taken because of a number of wrecks lying outside this channel. Small vessels are allowed to proceed into the harbour without a pilot and all formalities can be completed after the vessel has berthed at Fouad Yacht Club. This is situated on the eastern side of the harbour. See page 585 for details on transiting the Suez Canal.

M50 ROUTES FROM MALTA

Malta's position in the centre of the Mediterranean makes it an ideal jumping off point for ports in either the Western or Eastern Mediterranean. Yachting facilities are among the best in the Mediterranean as Malta was an important yachting centre long before the Balearics, Costa del Sol, Greece, and Turkey became such popular cruising destinations. Its convenient location, excellent repair facilities, and pleasant climate make it a good wintering spot.

The summers are hot, while the winters are mild. Being so close to the African coast, the weather is very much under the influence of that large landmass. The sirocco can be strong and there is also a daily change in wind direction due to strong land and sea breezes.

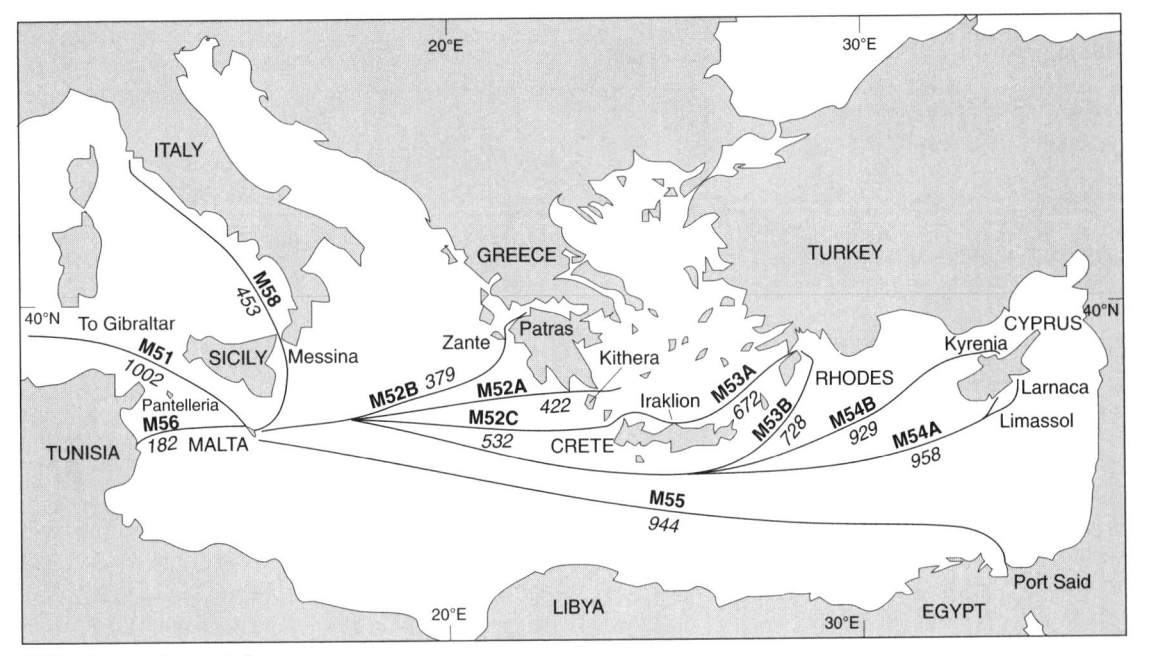

M50 *Routes from Malta*

M51 *Malta to Gibraltar*

BEST TIME:	April to May, October			
CHARTS:	BA: 4301			
	US: 301			
PILOTS:	BA: 45			
	US: 130, 131			
CRUISING GUIDES:	*Yacht Scene, East Spain Pilot (Costa del Sol).*			
WAYPOINTS:				

Departure	Intermediate	Landfall	Destination	Distance (M)
M511 Malta NE 35°56'N, 14°32'E	M512 Gozo 36°05'N, 14°27'E M513 Pantelleria 36°55'N, 12°00'E M514 Sentinelle S 38°00'N, 9°40'E M515 Gata SE 36°25'N, 2°00'W	M516 Europa 36°04'N, 5°20'W	Gibraltar *36°08'N, 5°21'W*	1002

The autumn is when most passages are made on this route as boats that have spent the summer in the Eastern Mediterranean are rushing west to join the annual exodus to the Caribbean. Depending on the direction of the wind, the route after leaving Malta can pass either north or south of Pantelleria Island. If strong NW winds are encountered SW of Sicily, shelter should be sought in the lee of

Pantelleria. With persistent contrary winds it is better to head from Malta across to Tunisia and stay close to that coast as far as Cape Bon. After Cape Bon, the route should stay offshore to avoid east-setting currents on the coast of Africa.

In late summer, early autumn northerly winds can be expected for the first half of this passage, while the second half has a better chance of favourable easterly winds in spring and late autumn. During late summer calms are frequent on this route, especially in the vicinity of Malta.

Unless one has access to reliable weather information, the shortest route should be sailed. From WP M511, outside Valletta harbour, an initial course is set to pass east of Gozo. From that point (M512), the route turns north and passes north of Pantelleria Island through WP M513 and on to WP M514, south of Sardinia. From there the course becomes westerly and passes well to the south of Cabo de Gata, at the SE extremity of the Iberian peninsula. The Spanish coast should be approached only after the

above cape has been passed as there is a strong easterly current in its immediate vicinity.

Having made landfall south of the light on Europa Point, arriving boats should proceed to the customs dock in Marina Bay, south of the runway, to complete formalities. The two older marinas are in that bay, whereas the new Queensway Marina is inside the commercial harbour, which will be passed on the way to the customs dock. Boats sailing through the Strait of Gibraltar without stopping, should consult route AN16 (page 46) for details on weather conditions in the Strait of Gibraltar as well as directions for negotiating the strait.

M52 *Malta to Greece*

Best time:	April to May, October			
Charts:	BA: 1439			
	US: 302			
Pilots:	BA: 45, 47, 48			
	US: 130, 131, 132			
Cruising guides:	*Greek Waters Pilot, Saronic.*			
Waypoints:				

Departure	Intermediate	Landfall	Destination	Distance (M)
Route M52A				
M521 Malta E	M522 Tainaron			
35°54.5'N, 14°31.5'E	36°20'N, 22°28'E			
	M523 Kithera	M524 Malea		422
	36°26'N, 22°56'E	36°23'N, 23°12'E		
Route M52B				
M521 Malta E		M525 Zante S	Patras	379
		37°32'N, 20°50'E	38°15'N, 21°44'E	
Route M52C				
M521 Malta E	M526 Gramvousa			
	35°45'N, 23°35'E			
	M527 Spathi	M528 Dhia	Iraklion	532
	35°46'N, 23°45'E	35°30'N, 25°08'E	35°16'N, 25°09'E	

Winds on this eastbound route across the Ionian Sea are variable throughout the year with the highest frequency of westerly winds in winter. There is a preponderance of northerly winds in summer, with light winds and calms being more common at the beginning and end of summer. The most direct route to the Aegean (M52A) passes south of the Peloponnese and approaches the Cyclades from the SW. Any of the three channels separating Cape Malea from Crete can be used, although the northernmost Elafonisos Channel, between Kithera Island and Cape Malea, is usually favoured as it is the most sheltered from the prevailing winds. Boats

taking this most direct route to the Aegean can sail a direct course from WP M521, outside Valletta Harbour, to WP M522, off Cape Tainaron, on the middle finger of the Peloponnese. The course is then altered for WP M523 to pass clear of the northern extremity of Kithera Island. The Aegean Sea is entered at the last waypoint (M524), off Cape Malea, from where one has the choice of a multitude of destinations.

Because of the constancy of the northerly winds in the Aegean during summer, between the middle of June and the end of August it is more convenient to approach the Cyclades from the NW rather than SW, as described above, and therefore route M52B is recommended in summer. Taking WP M521, outside Valletta, as the departure point from Malta, a direct course can be sailed to WP M525, south of Zante. The south coast of that island is followed around to pass through the channel separating it from the Peloponnese coast. Those who wish to clear into Greece at the earliest opportunity can do so in the port of Zante. For those who do not wish to stop, from Zante the route continues into the gulfs of Patras and Corinth and reaches the Aegean through the Corinth Canal.

Boats bound for Crete (M52C) should sail a more southern route than M52A and use the Antikithera

Channel, south of the small island of the same name and then continue parallel to the north coast of Crete. Landfall can be made at WP M526, off Cape Gramvousa, at the NW extremity of Crete. From there the course can be altered for WP M527 to pass north of Cape Spathi. Boats bound for Iraklion should continue as far as WP M528, west of Dhia Island, in the approaches to the Cretan capital. Boats should proceed into the old Venetian harbour, where there are a number of pontoons for yachts. If there is no free space cruising boats may use the quay immediately to the east of the small boat harbour.

M53 *Malta to Rhodes*

BEST TIME:	June to August			
CHARTS:	BA: 1439			
	US: 302			
PILOTS:	BA: 45, 48			
	US: 130, 131, 132			
CRUISING GUIDES:	*Greek Waters Pilot.*			
WAYPOINTS:				

Departure	Intermediate	Landfall	Destination	Distance (M)
Route M53A				
M531 Malta E	M532 Crete NW	M533 Rhodes NW	Mandraki	672
35°54.5'N, 14°31.5'E	35°45'N, 23°30'E	36°25'N, 28°12'E	*36°27'N, 28°14'E*	
Route M53B				
M531 Malta E	M534 Crete S			
	34°45'N, 24°07'E			
	M535 Koufonisi			
	34°45'N, 26°10'E			
	M536 Rhodes E	M537 Rhodes NE	Mandraki	728
	36°00'N, 28°10'E	36°26'N, 28°16'E		

The island of Rhodes is a useful starting point for cruises in Eastern Turkey and this passage from Malta is usually made at the start of summer when winds on this route are variable. Better winds are experienced in summer when northerly winds prevail for most of the distance. There are two routes that can be sailed from Malta to Rhodes, and each has its own attraction. The route which goes around the north coast of Crete (M53A) will appeal to those who prefer to make some stops en route. From WP M531, outside Valletta harbour, a direct course can be set for WP M532, in the Antikithera Channel,

between the island of that name and the NW coast of Crete. From that point the route cuts across the Southern Aegean all the way to WP M533, NW of Mandraki harbour, on the NW coast of Rhodes. The route passes a number of dangers north of Crete, all of which are marked by lights.

Those who wish to reach Rhodes by an offshore route, which stays south of Crete (M53B), may find better conditions on this slightly longer route. Such a route will avoid the swell encountered in the Southern Aegean during summer, but may lose the winds in the lee of Crete. When sailing in the lee of that island, especially during July and August, when the meltemi is blowing strongly in the Aegean, violent gusts occasionally blow down the steep slopes on the south coast of Crete.

Boats taking route M53B, from WP M531, outside La Valleta, should set an initial course for WP M534, south of Gavdhos Island. From that point the route continues due east, parallel to the south coast of Crete, to WP M535. At that point, the course turns NE and makes for WP M536, off the SE extremity of Rhodes, before a final course alteration is made for WP M537, in the eastern approaches to the port of Mandraki. The port is reached by rounding the northern tip of Rhodes. Mandraki (Limin Rhodou) is always crowded and visiting boats may find it difficult to secure a free berth. Additional docking space was planned for 1994.

M54 *Malta to Cyprus*

BEST TIME:	June to August			
CHARTS:	BA: 1439 US: 302			
PILOTS:	BA: 45, 49 US: 130, 131, 132			
CRUISING GUIDES:	*Turkish Waters and Cyprus Pilot.*			
WAYPOINTS:				
Departure	*Intermediate*	*Landfall*	*Destination*	*Distance (M)*
Route M54A				
M541 Malta E	M542 Crete S			
35°54.5'N, 14°31.5'E	34°45'N, 24°07'E			
	M543 Zevgari			
	34°33'N, 32°55'E			
	M544 Akrotiri SW	M545 Akrotiri NW	Limassol	923
	34°34'N, 33°03'E	34°39'N, 33°03'E	*34°39'N, 33°03'E*	
	M546 Kiti	M547 Dades	Larnaca	958
	34°47'N, 33°39'E	34°52'N, 33°39'E	*34°55'N, 33°38'E*	
Route M54B				
M541 Malta E	M542 Crete S			
	M548 Cyprus NW	M549 Snake	Kyrenia	929
	35°26'N, 32°55'E	35°22'N, 33°15'E	*35°20'N, 33°19'E*	

The route to Cyprus passes immediately to the south of Crete and in strong northerly winds it is possible to close with the Cretan coast to benefit from the lee provided by the high island. However, when sailing close to the coast, attention must be paid to the strong gusts which occasionally blow with great force down the steep mountain slopes towards the sea.

Because of the declaration of independence by the Turkish side of Cyprus and the still unresolved dispute over partition, the authorities in the Greek side do not welcome boats that have called first in Northern Cyprus and then visit the south. For this reason, those intending to call in Northern Cyprus should perhaps do so after having visited Southern Cyprus. Northern Cyprus, and especially the attractive port of Kyrenia, is a good starting point for visits to the southern coast of neighbouring Turkey.

Boats bound for Southern Cyprus (route M54A), should set an initial course from WP M541, outside Valletta harbour, for WP M542, south of Gavdhos Island, a small island off the SW point of Crete. The route then continues parallel to Crete and crosses over to WP M543, SW of Cape Zevgari, on the south coast of Cyprus. The course continues to WP M544, off Cape Gata, from where boats bound for Limassol should alter course for WP M545, in the NW corner of Akrotiri Bay. Yachts either anchor in the commercial harbour or in the fishing harbour nearby. Limassol Marina is a further six miles to the NE (34°42.5'N, 33°09.5'E). The marina uses the callsign Sheraton Harbour and monitors VHF channels 9 and 16.

Boats bound for Larnaca should continue across Akrotiri Bay to WP M546, off Cape Kiti. A course alteration will be needed for WP M547, off Cape Dades, south of the port of Larnaca. Larnaca Marina monitors VHF channel 16. Occasionally yachts are asked to anchor in the outer harbour while a berth is found for them.

Boats sailing route M54B to Northern Cyprus should follow the same route as far as WP M542, SW of Crete. The route then passes close to

Gaidhouronisi, another small island off the Cretan coast and continues to WP M548, off Cape Kormakiti, at the NW extremity of Cyprus. The course is altered there for WP M549, off Snake Island, west of Kyrenia (Girne). The capital of Northern Cyprus has a small harbour and yachting facilities are much below those available in the south. Yachts usually go into Kyrenia's inner harbour, which is very attractive but also very small. As the approaches to this older harbour are not lit, night arrivals should be avoided. The new commercial port is located NE of the town.

M55 *Malta to Port Said*

BEST TIME:	June to August			
CHARTS:	BA: 4302			
	US: 302			
PILOTS:	BA: 45, 49			
	US: 130, 131, 132			
CRUISING GUIDES:	*Mediterranean Cruising Handbook.*			
WAYPOINTS:				
Departure	*Intermediate*	*Landfall*	*Destination*	*Distance (M)*
M551 Malta E	M552 Damietta	M553 Said	Port Said	944
35°54.5'N, 14°31.5'E	32°00'N, 31°50'E	31°25'N, 32°18'E	*31°15'N, 32°18'E*	

Favourable northerly winds prevail along this route during summer. If the passage is made in winter or in strong northerly winds it may be advisable to pass closer to Crete, as there are several harbours along its south coast where shelter can be found in bad weather. However, when sailing close to Crete, attention must be paid to the strong gusts which occasionally blow with great force down the steep mountain slopes towards the sea.

Boats undertaking this passage are usually bound for the Red Sea and are only calling in Egypt because of the Suez Canal. Those who wish to stop in an Egyptian port before Port Said can do so at Alexandria. However, yachting facilities for visitors are limited in that port and the only ones available belong to the Alexandria Yacht Club, which is one of the most unwelcoming clubs in the world. Those who wish to visit the interior of Egypt would do better to do it from either Port Said or Suez, whose yacht clubs are much more helpful.

A direct course can be sailed all the way from Malta and WP M551 to WP M552, north of the Damietta mouth of the Nile river, in the approach-

es to Port Said. At that point the course should be altered for WP M553, north of Port Said and the entrance into the shipping channel leading to the Suez Canal. Because of the low, featureless coast and the shallow depths which extend several miles offshore, the position of Port Said is very difficult to ascertain if landfall has been made either too far east or west. The situation is further complicated by the occasionally strong currents in the area, which are also influenced by the state of the Nile waters.

The cluster of ships at anchor is usually the first indication of the approaches to Port Said. The approach channel to Port Said extends far offshore and is well marked by buoys. It should be entered at its northern extremity and no shortcuts taken because of a number of wrecks lying outside this channel. Small vessels are allowed to proceed into the harbour without a pilot and all formalities can be completed after the vessel has berthed at Fouad Yacht Club. This is situated on the eastern side of the harbour. See page 585 for details on transiting the Suez Canal.

M56 *Malta to Tunisia*

BEST TIME:	May to October			
CHARTS:	BA: 165			
	US: 301			
PILOTS:	BA: 45			
	US: 131			
CRUISING GUIDES:	*North Africa.*			
WAYPOINTS:				

Departure	*Intermediate*	*Landfall*	*Destination*	*Distance (M)*
M560 Valletta *35°54'N, 14°31'E*	M561 Comino 36°00'N, 14°18'E			
	M562 Linosa 35°55'N, 12°53'E	M563 Kuriate 35°50'N, 11°04'E	Monastir *35°46'N, 10°50'E*	182
M560 Valletta	M564 Malta NE 35°56'N, 14°32'E			
	M565 Gozo 36°05'N, 14°27'E			
	M566 Pantelleria 36°55'N, 12°00'E			
	M567 Bon 37°08'N, 11°03'E	M568 Cartage 36°53'N, 10°23'E	Sidi bou Said *36°52'N, 10°21'E*	225

There are two route options on leaving Malta and the choice will be dictated by subsequent cruising plans. If only an intermediate stop is sought to break a longer passage to Gibraltar, Balearics or even the French Riviera, a stop in one of the marinas close to Tunis is probably the best solution. Otherwise, one of the marinas on the east coast, such as Monastir, is more attractive. In the latter case, on leaving La Valletta, depending on wind conditions, one has the choice of leaving the main island on Malta to either port or starboard. If decid-

ing to sail through the straits separating Malta from Gozo, the point of departure will be close to the small island of Comino. The route then passes close to the north of Linosa and makes landfall north of the light on Kuriate.

The more northern route leaves both Malta and Gozo to port and makes landfall close to Cape Bon. From there the route turns SW towards Cape Cartage and the approaches to the Tunisian capital, where the marina at Sidi bou Said has the best facilities.

M57 *Malta to Balearics*

BEST TIME:	May to October
CHARTS:	BA: 4301
	US: 301
PILOTS:	BA: 45
	US: 131
CRUISING GUIDES:	*Islas Baleares.*

WAYPOINTS:				
Departure	*Intermediate*	*Landfall*	*Destination*	*Distance (M)*
M570 Valletta *35°54'N, 14°31'E*	M571 Malta NE 35°56'N, 14°32'E M572 Gozo 36°05'N, 14°27'E M573 Pantelleria 36°55'N, 12°00'E M574 Cabrera 39°15'N, 3°02'E	M575 Mallorca S 39°26'N, 2°40'E	Palma *39°33'N, 2°38'E*	625

Leaving both Malta and Gozo to port, the recommended route tends NW and passes close to Pantelleria Island, which may be visited in settled weather. Strong northerly winds will produce short steep seas in the channel between Sicily and the African mainland. Even in moderate northerly winds a route should be sailed that passes through the Skerki Channel and avoids the Skerki Bank, where the shallow waters produce rough seas. Landfall will be made off Cape Salinas, at the SE extremity of Mallorca. The route passes through the Cabrera Passage, between the island of that name and Mallorca, from where it runs parallel to the island's SW coast to reach Palma de Mallorca. There are a number of marinas in the well sheltered Bay of Palma and the most conveniently located is run by Real Club Nautico, in the eastern part of the port. The club monitors channel 9. Club de Mar, located inside Puerto Pi, in the western part of the harbour, also has good facilities but is further from the city.

M58 *Malta to Italy*

BEST TIME:	April to October			
CHARTS:	BA: 4301 US: 301			
PILOTS:	BA: 45, 46 US: 131			
CRUISING GUIDES:	*Italian Waters Pilot.*			
WAYPOINTS:				
Departure	*Intermediate*	*Landfall*	*Destination*	*Distance (M)*
M580 Valletta *35°54'N, 14°31'E*	M581 Malta NE 35°56'N, 14°32'E M582 Passero 36°37'N, 15°20'E M583 Armi 37°54'N, 15°37'E M584 Messina 38°11'N, 15°37'E M585 Peloro 38°19'N, 15°39'E M586 Pontine 40°50'N, 12°40'E	PN587 Linaro 42°00'N, 11°50'E	Civitavecchia *42°04'N, 11°48'E*	453
M580 Valletta	M588 Gozo 36°05'N, 14°27'E M589 Egadi 37°55'N, 12°08'E	M589 Elia 39°00'N, 9°30'E	Marina del Poetto *39°11.6'N, 9°09.8'E*	328

With the bulk of Sicily lying astride any direct route to ports on the west coast of Italy, one has the choice of sailing through the Messian Strait to southern ports, such as Naples, or to pass to the west of Sicily if bound for more northern ports in mainland Italy or any port in Sardinia.

The classic route through Messina calls for careful timing and navigation so as to pass through the strait at the most favourable time. Having left the Maltese capital, a direct course leads to the SE extremity of Sicily, where the ancient port of Syracuse makes an interesting stop. An alternative stop can be made at Taormina, which is close enough to the Messian Strait to allow for better timing for the passage through the narrows. Having left the strait behind, the route passes west of Stromboli and also west of the Pontine Islands. There are many opportunities to stop along this route, but if bound for Rome the most convenient marina will be Riva di Traiano at Civitavecchia.

Boats bound for ports in Sardinia, or even destinations in Northern Italy, will find a route that passes west of Sicily both easier and shorter. From Gozo, the route passes between the Egadi Islands. An attractive destination within walking distance of Cagliari is Marina Piccola del Poetto, located on the sheltered north side of a small peninsula NE of Cagliari.

M60 ROUTES FROM GREECE

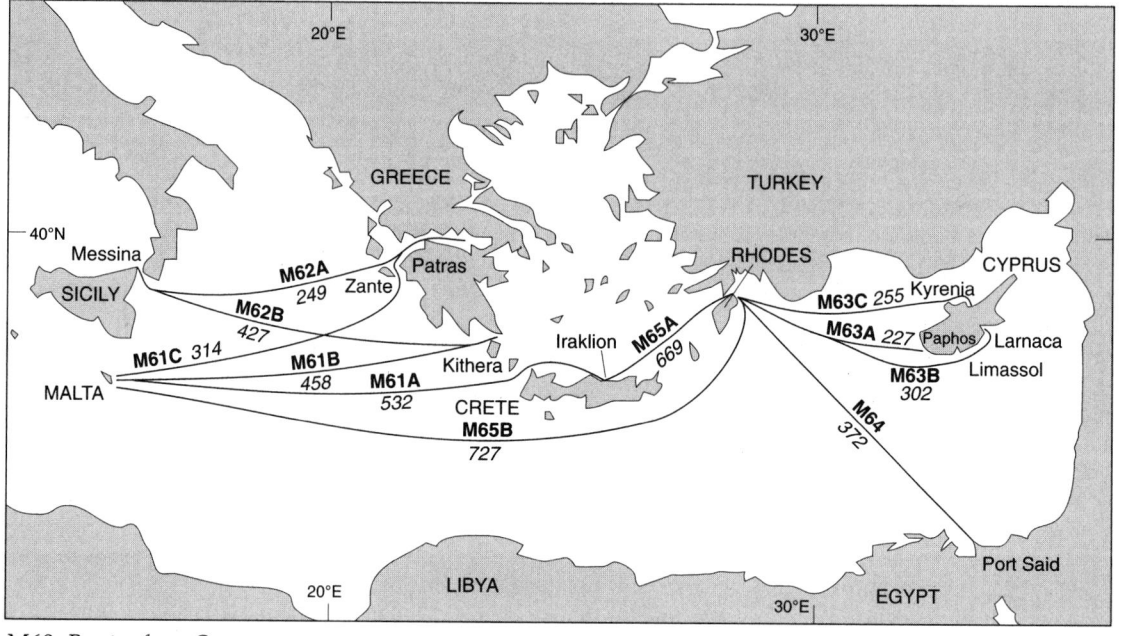

M60 *Routes from Greece*

The Greek islands continue to be one of the most popular cruising grounds in the world and very few long distance cruising boats pass through the Mediterranean without visiting them. The main feature of the Aegean, from where all of the above routes originate, are the strong northerly winds of summer. These winds prevail from June until August and they must be taken into account when drawing up any cruising plans which include that part of the world. The best strategy is to try to arrive in the Northern Aegean by the end of May and then sail slowly south with the help of the meltemi. By the end of summer one is then ready to embark on one of the following routes.

M61 *Greece to Malta*

BEST TIME:	June to August				
CHARTS:	BA: 1439				
	US: 302				
PILOTS:	BA: 45, 47, 48				
	US: 130, 131, 132				
CRUISING GUIDES:	*North Africa, Yachtsman's Handbook to Malta.*				
WAYPOINTS:					
Departure	*Intermediate*	*Landfall*	*Destination*		*Distance (M)*
Route M61A					
M611 Crete NW		M612 Malta E	Valletta		438
35°45'N, 23°30'E		35°54.5'N, 14°31.5'E	*35°54'N, 14°30.5'E*		
Route M61B					
M613 Malea	M614 Tainaron				
36°20'N, 22°28'E	36°23'N, 23°12'E				
	M615 Kithera	M612 Malta E	Valletta		458
	36°26'N, 22°56'E				
Route M61C					
M616 Zante N		M612 Malta E	Valletta		314
38°00'N, 20°30'E					

Whereas boats on the opposite route have to contend with the strong northerly winds of summer and therefore have a choice of route to reach the Aegean, the same winds make the passage to Malta much easier. To leave the Aegean one can use any of the channels between the Peloponnese and Crete, although the closest channel to Crete, which goes SE of Antikithera, is probably the simplest. Boats which have included Crete on their itinerary can join the offshore route at the same point (route M61A). A route which passes close to Cape Malea (M61B) benefits from the shelter provided by the Peloponnese by staying longer in the lee of the land before reaching the open sea. Boats which have used the Corinth Canal, or are leaving from one of the Ionian islands, will join route M61C.

From WP M611, in Antikithera Channel, a direct course can be set by boats on route M61A for WP M612, off Valletta harbour. Boats leaving the Aegean closer to the Peloponnese and joining route M61B should take their departure from WP M613, off Cape Malea. The route passes through an intermediate waypoint before a direct course for Malta can be set from WP M615, north of Kithera Island. On route M61C, a suggested point of departure is WP M616 north of Zante Island, from where a direct course can be set for WP M612, in the approaches to the Maltese capital.

On arrival in Malta, boats should contact Valletta Port Control on VHF channels 12 or 16 before proceeding to one of the reception docks at Msida Marina or Lazaretto Creek. The Yachting Centre can be contacted on VHF channel 9 to request docking information.

M62 *Greece to Messina Strait*

BEST TIME:	May to August			
CHARTS:	BA: 1439			
	US: 302			
PILOTS:	BA: 45, 48, 49			
	US: 130, 131, 132			
CRUISING GUIDES:	*Italian Waters Pilot.*			
WAYPOINTS:				

Departure	Intermediate	Landfall	Destination	Distance (M)
Route M62A				
M621 Zante N	M622 Spartivento			
38°00'N, 20°30'E	37°55'N, 16°06'E			
	M623 Armi	M624 Messina		249
	37°54'N, 15°37'E	38°11'N, 15°37'E		
Route M62B				
M625 Malea	M626 Tainaron			
36°20'N, 22°28'E	36°23'N, 23°12'E			
	M627 Kithera			
	36°26'N, 22°56'E			
	M628 Sapientza			
	36°45'N, 21°35'E			
	M623 Armi	M624 Messina		427

There are two main routes reaching the Messina Strait from Greece. Boats leaving from the Central Aegean may prefer to use the Corinth Canal and pass north of the Peloponnese (route M62A), whereas boats which are in the Southern Aegean should join route M62B.

Route M62A takes its departure from Greece at WP M621, in the channel between the islands of Cephalonia and Zante. The route goes right across the Ionian Sea to WP M622, off Cape Spartivento at the toe of Italy. The coast is followed around the next cape to WP M623 to approach the Messina Strait from the south.

Boats taking the more southern route should start off from WP M625, off Cape Malea. The three fingers of the Peloponnese are followed around to WP M628, situated off Sapientza Island, from where a direct course can be set for WP M623 off

Capo dell'Armi, in the southern approaches to Messina Strait.

The narrow strait separating mainland Italy from Sicily has its own weather peculiarities. Usually the wind tends to blow either in a northerly or southerly direction along the axis of the strait. Sometimes the wind will be NE on the eastern side, NW on the western side, and very light in the middle. Alternatively it can be S to SE in the southern approaches, changing abruptly to NW in the northern approaches, which creates a heavy sea. Violent gusts come off the high ground, which together with strong tidal currents and a number of small whirlpools and eddies remind one of why this is the presumed location of the Scylla and Charybdis of the *Odyssey*. A line of bores called *tagli* can occur at the change of tide. It is therefore essential to time one's transit of the strait with a favourable tide.

M63 *Rhodes to Cyprus*

BEST TIME:	April to October			
CHARTS:	BA: 183	US: 302		
PILOTS:	BA: 48, 49			
	US: 130, 132			
CRUISING GUIDES:	*Turkish Waters & Cyprus Pilot.*			
WAYPOINTS:				

Departure	Intermediate	Landfall	Destination	Distance (M)
Route M63A				
M630 Rhodes NE		M631 Paphos W	Paphos	227
36°26'N, 28°16'E		34°45'N, 32°22'E	*34°45'N, 32°25'E*	
Route M63B				
M630 Rhodes NE	M632 Cyprus W			
	34°40'N, 32°20'E			
	M633 Zevgari			
	34°33'N, 32°55'E			
	M634 Akrotiri SW	M635 Akrotiri NW	Limassol	267
	34°34'N, 33°03'E	34°39'N, 33°03'E	*34°39'N, 33°03'E*	
	M636 Kiti	M637 Dades	Larnaca	302
	34°47'N, 33°39'E	34°52'N, 33°39'E	*34°55'N, 33°38'E*	
Route M63C				
M630 Rhodes NE	M638 Strongili			
	36°05'N, 29°37'E			
	M639 Cyprus NW	M6310 Snake	Kyrenia	255
	35°26'N, 32°55'E	35°22'N, 33°15'E	*35°20'N, 33°19'E*	

The most direct route from Rhodes (M63A) leads to Paphos, a small port on the SW coast of Cyprus, from where it is easy to reach the two major ports in Southern Cyprus, Limassol and Larnaca. Because of the unresolved dispute between the two sides of the island, caused by the declaration of independence by the Turkish side, the alternative route (M63C) should only be used if the intention is to visit Northern Cyprus. The authorities in Greek Cyprus do not approve of boats stopping in Northern Cyprus first, so for the time being it is better to visit the south before the north. An easterly current sets along the coast of Cyprus, and because of this current Cape Andreas, at the NE extremity of the island, should be approached with caution.

Boats bound for Southern Cyprus (route M63A) and intending to stop first at Paphos, which is an official port of entry, can set a direct course from WP M630, off Mandraki harbour, for WP M631, west of Cape Paphos. The small harbour is reached by passing south of this cape.

Boats bound for Limassol or Larnaca (route

M63B) should set a course from WP M630 for WP632, SW of Cyprus. From there the course is altered for WP M633, SW of Cape Zevgari, on the south coast of Cyprus. The course continues to WP M634, off Cape Gata, from where boats bound for Limassol should alter course for WP M635, in the NW corner of Akrotiri Bay. Yachts either anchor in the commercial harbour off the town of Limassol or in the fishing harbour nearby. Limassol Marina is a further six miles to the NE (34°42.5'N, 33°09.5'E). The marina uses the callsign Sheraton Harbour and monitors VHF channels 9 and 16. Boats bound for Larnaca should continue across Akrotiri Bay to WP M636, off Cape Kiti. A course alteration will be needed for WP M637, off Cape Dades, south of the port of Larnaca. Larnaca Marina monitors VHF channel 16 and will give berthing instructions. Occasionally yachts are asked to anchor in the outer harbour while a vacant berth is found for them.

Boats sailing route M63C to Northern Cyprus will pass close to the south coast of Turkey. From

WP M630, off the NE tip of Rhodes, an initial course should be set for WP M638, off Strongili Island. From there the course can be altered to make landfall at WP M639, off Cape Kormakiti, at the NW extremity of Cyprus. The course is altered there for WP M6310, off Snake Island, west of Kyrenia, the capital of Northern Cyprus.

M64 *Rhodes to Port Said*

BEST TIME:	April to October				
CHARTS:	BA: 183				
	US: 302				
PILOTS:	BA: 48, 49				
	US: 130, 132				
CRUISING GUIDES:	*Mediterranean Cruising Handbook, Red Sea Pilot.*				
WAYPOINTS:					
Departure	*Intermediate*	*Landfall*	*Destination*		*Distance (M)*
M641 Rhodes NE 36°26'N, 28°16'E	M642 Damietta 32°00'N, 31°50'E	M643 Said 31°25'N, 32°18'E	Port Said *31°15'N, 32°18'E*		372

Favourable winds can be expected along this route for most of the year. Because the current normally sets eastward along the Egyptian coast, and the current is augmented by the waters of the Nile, especially when the latter is in flood, landfall should be made to the west of Port Said. As the water is shallow throughout the area, the coast should not be approached beyond the 20 fathom line, which can be followed as far as Damietta.

A direct course can be set from WP M641, off the NE point of Rhodes, for WP M642, off the Damietta mouth of the Nile. From there the course is altered for WP M643, in the northern approaches to Port Said and the Suez Canal. Boats are normally met by a pilot launch and directed to the Fouad Yacht Club on the eastern side of the harbour. See page 585 for details on transiting the Suez Canal.

M65 *Rhodes to Malta*

BEST TIME:	June to August				
CHARTS:	BA: 1439				
	US: 302				
PILOTS:	BA: 45, 48				
	US: 130, 131, 132				
CRUISING GUIDES:	*North Africa, Yachtsman's Handbook to Malta.*				
WAYPOINTS:					
Departure	*Intermediate*	*Landfall*	*Destination*		*Distance (M)*
Route M65A					
M651 Rhodes NW 36°25'N, 28°12'E	M652 Crete NW 35°45'N, 23°30'E	M653 Malta E 35°54.5'N, 14°31.5'E	Valletta *35°54'N, 14°30.5'E*		669
Route M65B					
M654 Rhodes NE 36°26'N, 28°16'E	M655 Rhodes E 36°00'N, 28°10'E				
	M656 Koufonisi 34°45'N, 26°10'E				
	M657 Crete S 34°45'N, 24°07'E	M653 Malta E	Valletta		727

There are two routes that can be sailed to Malta, one passing north of Crete, the other passing south. The northern route should appeal to those who intend to stop on the way as there are several convenient ports on the north coast of Crete. Both routes can be sailed nonstop and the waypoints listed above are for direct passages. The northern route, although slightly shorter, has the disadvantage of stronger winds and relatively high swell during the months when the meltemi is in force in the Aegean. At such times the southern route, although longer, may be preferable.

Boats sailing the northern route (M65A), should take their departure from WP M651, west of Mandraki, from where a direct course can be sailed all the way to WP M652, in the Antikithera Channel, NW of Crete. This route passes a number of dangers, such as the Sofrana Rocks, which are well marked by lights. From WP M652 a direct course can then be sailed to WP M653, east of Valletta.

Boats sailing the southern route (M65B) should take their departure from WP M654, NE of Rhodes, from where an initial course can be set to WP M655, off the east coast of the island. From that point the course can be altered for WP M656, off Koufonisi Island, SE of Crete. The route then runs parallel to the south coast of Crete to WP M657, south of Gavdhos Island. From there a direct route leads to WP M653, off the Maltese capital. Arriving boats should contact Valletta Port Control on VHF channels 12 or 16 before proceeding to one of the reception docks at Msida Marina or Lazaretto Creek. The Yachting Centre, which manages all marinas in the Maltese capital, can be contacted on VHF channel 9 to request docking information.

M70 ROUTES FROM PORT SAID

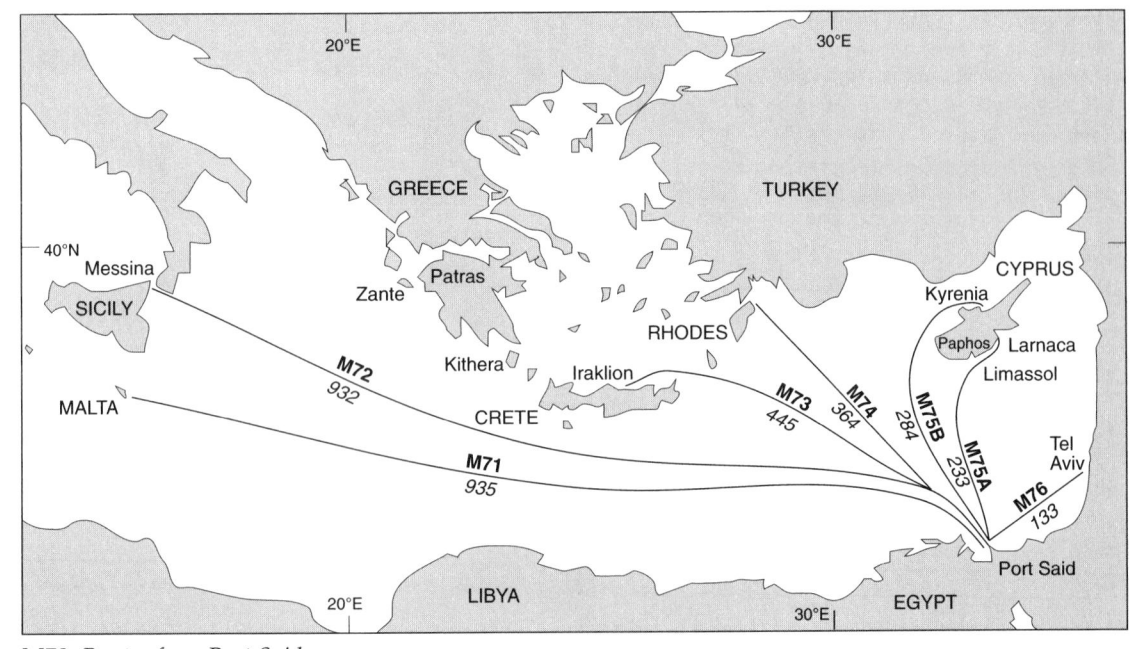

M70 *Routes from Port Said*

Having transited the Suez Canal and arrived in Port Said, suddenly the entire Mediterranean lies before one. Routes from Port Said fan out in all directions and, because of its convenient location, most destinations are within easy reach. The exception is for routes heading in a NW direction, as contrary winds are likely to be encountered, particularly in summer. This is a good reason for timing an arrival in Port Said for late spring if one is headed in that direction.

M71 *Port Said to Malta*

BEST TIME:	April to May, September to October				
CHARTS:	BA: 4302				
	US: 302				
PILOTS:	BA: 45, 49				
	US: 130, 131, 132				
CRUISING GUIDES:	*North Africa, Yachtsman's Handbook to Malta.*				
WAYPOINTS:					

Departure	Intermediate	Landfall	Destination	Distance (M)
M711 Said	M712 Damietta	M713 Malta E	Valletta	935
31°25'N, 32°18'E	32°00'N, 31°50'E	35°54.5'N, 14°31.5'E	*35°54'N, 14°30.5'E*	

On leaving Port Said, an initial course can be set for WP M712, north of the Damietta mouth of the Nile, in order to reach deeper water. From that point a direct course can be set for WP M713, just outside the Maltese capital. Contrary winds are predominant on this route and every shift of wind should therefore be used to advantage. A good supply of fuel should also be loaded in Port Said to be able to motor if necessary in calms or light winds. Preferably the route should pass close to the south coast of Crete, where shelter can be sought in strong W or NW winds. If shelter is sought in the lee of Crete, or if passing close to the island, attention must be paid to the strong gusts blowing down the steep mountains.

On arrival in Malta, boats should contact Valletta Port Control on VHF channels 12 or 16 before proceeding to one of the reception docks at Msida Marina or Lazaretto Creek. The Yachting Centre can be contacted on VHF channel 9 to request docking information.

M72 *Port Said to Messina Strait*

BEST TIME:	April to May, September to October				
CHARTS:	BA: 4302				
	US: 302				
PILOTS:	BA: 45, 49				
	US: 130, 131, 132				
CRUISING GUIDES:	*Italian Waters Pilot.*				
WAYPOINTS:					

Departure	Intermediate	Landfall	Destination	Distance (M)
M721 Said	M722 Damietta			
31°25'N, 32°18'E	32°00'N, 31°50'E			
	M723 Crete SW			
	34°40'N, 24°00'E			
	M724 Armi	M725 Messina		932
	37°54'N, 15°37'E	38°11'N, 15°37'E		

The recommended route to the Messina Strait passes close to Crete, where a waypoint (M723) has been set SW of the island of Gavdhos. If necessary, the route can be altered earlier, so as to pass between Gavdhos and Crete. From WP M723 a direct course can be set to WP M724 off Capo dell'Armi, in the southern approaches to Messina Strait.

The narrow strait separating mainland Italy from Sicily has its own weather peculiarities. Usually the wind tends to blow either in a northerly or southerly direction along the axis of the strait. Sometimes the wind will be NE on the eastern side, NW on the western side, and very light in the middle. Alternatively it can be S to SE in the southern approaches, changing abruptly to NW in the northern approaches, which creates a heavy sea. Violent gusts come off the high ground, which together with strong tidal currents and a number of small whirlpools and eddies make it easier to see why the Scylla and Charybdis of the *Odyssey* are reputed to have been located in this strait. A line of bores called *tagli* can occur at the change of tide. It is therefore essential to time one's transit of the strait with a favourable tide.

M73 *Port Said to Crete*

BEST TIME:	April to May, September to October			
CHARTS:	BA: 183			
	US: 302			
PILOTS:	BA: 49			
	US: 132			
CRUISING GUIDES:	*Greek Waters Pilot.*			
WAYPOINTS:				
Departure	*Intermediate*	*Landfall*	*Destination*	*Distance (M)*
M731 Said	M732 Damietta			
31°25'N, 32°18'E	32°00'N, 31°50'E			
	M733 Sidheros			
	35°20'N, 26°21'E			
	M734 Crete NE	M735 Crete N	Iraklion	445
	35°25'N, 26°10'E	35°23'N, 25°20'E	*35°16'N, 25°09'E*	

Strong northerly winds make this a difficult passage in summer, but better conditions are normally experienced in either spring or autumn, when most boats sail this route. Boats bound for islands in the Aegean will fare better by taking route M74 and enter the Aegean from the SE. Sailing north from Crete is difficult throughout the summer, so a stop there is better left for the end rather than the start of an Aegean cruise.

From WP M732, north of the Damietta mouth of the Nile, a course can be set for WP M733, east of Cape Sidheros, the NE point of Crete. There are several attractive ports on the north coast of Crete and these can be reached by rounding Cape Sidheros and closing with the coast. Boats bound for Iraklion should alter course for WP M734. From there the route runs parallel to the north coast of Crete to WP M735, NE of Iraklion. Boats should proceed into the old Venetian harbour, where there are a number of pontoons for yachts. If there is no free space cruising boats may use the quay immediately east of the small boat harbour.

M74 *Port Said to Rhodes*

BEST TIME:	April to May, September to October			
CHARTS:	BA: 183			
	US: 302			
PILOTS:	BA: 48, 49			
	US: 130, 132			
CRUISING GUIDES:	*Greek Waters Pilot.*			
WAYPOINTS:				

Departure	Intermediate	Landfall	Destination	Distance (M)
M741 Said	M742 Damietta	M743 Rhodes NE	Mandraki	364
31°25'N, 32°18'E	32°00'N, 31°50'E	36°26'N, 28°16'E	*36°27'N, 28°14'E*	

Having left Port Said and its busy approaches, from WP M742, north of the Damietta mouth in the Nile delta, a direct course can be set for the NE point of Rhodes and WP M743. The port of Mandraki is reached by rounding the NE extremity of the island. Mandraki (Limin Rhodou), the main port of Rhodes, is always crowded and cruising boats may find it difficult to secure a free berth, especially in the summer.

Because of the preponderance of contrary winds along this route, it may be necessary to motor in calm or light winds. If strong NW winds persist while in Port Said, it is better to make a detour via Cyprus and follow directions as for route M83 (page 575).

M75 *Port Said to Cyprus*

BEST TIME:	April to October			
CHARTS:	BA: 183			
	US: 302			
PILOTS:	BA: 49			
	US: 132			
CRUISING GUIDES:	*Turkish Waters & Cyprus Pilot.*			
WAYPOINTS:				

Departure	Intermediate	Landfall	Destination	Distance (M)
Route M75A				
M751 Said	M752 Akrotiri SW	M753 Akrotiri NW	Limassol	198
31°25'N, 32°18'E	34°34'N, 33°03'E	34°39'N, 33°03'E	*34°40'N, 33°03'E*	
	M754 Kiti	M755 Dades	Larnaca	233
	34°47'N, 33°39'E	34°52'N, 33°39'E	*34°55'N, 33°38'E*	
Route M75B				
M751 Said	M756 Cyprus SW		Paphos	202
	34°40'N, 32°20'E		*34°45'N, 32°25'E*	
	M757 Arnauti			
	35°07'N, 32°12'E			
	M758 Cyprus NW	M759 Snake	Kyrenia	284
	35°26'N, 32°55'E	35°22'N, 33°15'E	*35°20'N, 33°19'E*	

Cyprus is a popular destination for boats that have transited the Suez Canal as it provides a convenient springboard for subsequent visits to neighbouring Middle Eastern countries. Unfortunately the continuing disagreement between the two parts of Cyprus make it difficult to cruise between North and South Cyprus. As the authorities in Northern Cyprus do not seem to mind boats having called first in the South, that part of Cyprus should be visited first. The small port of Paphos, on the SW coast of Cyprus, is a convenient point of departure for boats bound for either Rhodes or Southern Turkey and can also be used for shelter should the weather deteriorate suddenly.

A direct route for any port on the south coast of Cyprus can be set as soon as the long entrance channel of Port Said has been left behind. Boats bound for Limassol should set a course for WP M752, off Cape Gata from where the course can be altered for WP M753, in the NW corner of Akrotiri Bay. The marina at Larnaca, in Larnaca Bay, is a favourite refitting and wintering spot among long distance voyagers. To reach it an initial course should be set for WP M754, off Cape Kiti, from where the route turns north into Larnaca Bay.

Boats bound for Northern Cyprus (route M75B) will find it much more convenient to round Cyprus from the west as a strong east-setting current makes it more difficult to go around Cape Andreas, the NE extremity of the island. If sailing this route, which leaves Cyprus to starboard, a first recommended waypoint (M756) is off Paphos. From there a small detour can be made into this official port of entry into Cyprus, or one can continue to WP M757, off Cape Arnauti, at the NW extremity of Cyprus. From there the course can be altered for WP M758, off Cape Kormakiti and finally landfall can be made at WP M759, near Snake Island, in the approaches to Kyrenia (Girne), the capital of Northern Cyprus. Cruising boats usually go into the inner harbour, which is very small. As the approaches to this older harbour are not lit night arrivals should be avoided. A new commercial port is located NE of the town.

M76 *Port Said to Israel*

BEST TIME:	April to October			
CHARTS:	BA: 183			
	US: 302			
PILOTS:	BA: 49			
	US: 132			
CRUISING GUIDES:	*Mediterranean Cruising Handbook.*			
WAYPOINTS:				
Departure	*Intermediate*	*Landfall*	*Destination*	*Distance (M)*
M761 Said		M762 Aviv S	Tel Aviv	133
31°25'N, 32°18'E		32°04'N, 34°43'E	*32°05'N, 34°46'E*	

This is a route taken by those who wish to start their cruising in the very east of the Mediterranean. From Port Said boats bound for Tel Aviv can set a direct course for WP M762, off Tel Aviv Marina. A big swell makes itself felt in the Eastern Mediterranean throughout the year and the seas breaking in the shallow waters off the Israel coast occasionally make it difficult to enter some ports. Boats approaching the Israeli coast are supposed to contact the authorities when 40 miles off to give details of vessel and ETA. On approaching the coast yachts are met and occasionally boarded by a patrol boat, which then accompanies the vessel to the port of entry. Tel Aviv Marina monitors VHF channel 16, but because of the difficult entrance night arrivals should be avoided. A guide boat is occasionally sent out by the marina to assist those not familiar with the entrance. There is a better marina at Ashkelon (31°40'N, 34°32'E), south of Tel Aviv, which is a port of entry and therefore recommended.

M80 ROUTES FROM CYPRUS

The strategic position of Cyprus in the Eastern Mediterranean makes it an excellent starting point for voyages in any direction. The one major problem is the continuing dispute between the authorities of the divided island, those in Southern Cyprus not welcoming yachts that have called first in Turkish speaking Northern Cyprus. Occasionally yachts which had stopped in Northern Cyprus first have not been permitted to call at a port in Southern Cyprus. The authorities in Northern Cyprus do not seem so particular about boats that have called in the south first. If this situation persists, these facts should be taken into account when drawing up cruising plans for that part of the world.

The weather is generally pleasant with northerly winds prevailing in summer, especially along the north coast. Variable winds are more common along the south coast, where day breezes are also a phenomenon that contributes to a complicated weather picture. An easterly current sets along the northern coast, which is particularly noticeable in the vicinity of Cape Andreas, the NE extremity of the island.

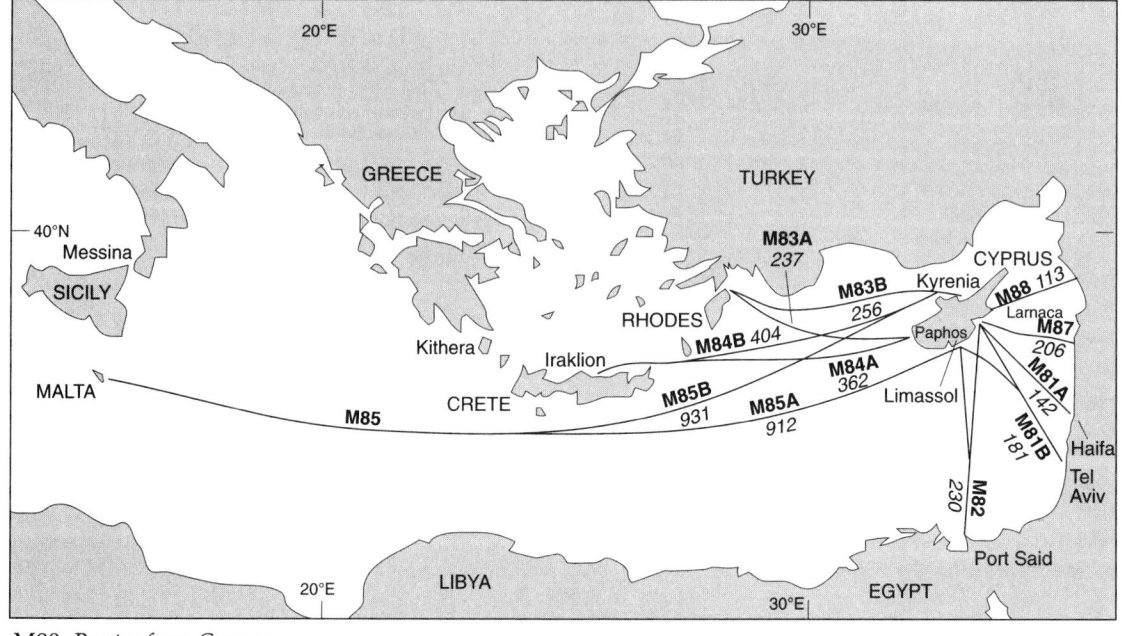

M80 *Routes from Cyprus*

M81 *Cyprus to Israel*

BEST TIME:	April to October
CHARTS:	BA: 183
	US: 302
PILOTS:	BA: 49
	US: 132
CRUISING GUIDES:	*Mediterranean Cruising Handbook.*
WAYPOINTS:	

Departure	Intermediate	Landfall	Destination	Distance (M)
Route M81A				
M811 Larnaca Bay		M813 Akko	Haifa	142
34°54'N, 33°39'E		32°52'N, 34°56'E	*32°49'N, 35°00'E*	
M812 Akrotiri W		M813 Akko	Haifa	147
34°39'N, 33°04'E				
Route M81B				
M811 Larnaca Bay		M814 Aviv N	Tel Aviv	181
		32°06'N, 34°44'E	*32°05'N, 34°46'E*	
M812 Akrotiri W		M814 Aviv	Tel Aviv	178

The best point of departure for the short passage to Israel is Larnaca, where up to date information should be obtained from the port authorities concerning sensitive areas to be avoided. There is a choice of destinations on the Israeli coast, with most boats making either for Haifa or for Tel Aviv. The former is a busy commercial port with little attraction for cruising boats. Tel Aviv has a good marina and is also a better place for visits into the interior, such as Jerusalem. Boats approaching the Israeli coast are supposed to contact the authorities when 40 miles off to give details of vessel and ETA. On approaching the coast yachts are met and occasionally boarded by a patrol boat, which then accompanies the vessel to the port of entry.

Whether leaving from Larnaca and WP M811, in Larnaca Bay, or from Limassol and WP M812, in Akrotiri Bay, a direct course can be sailed to WP M813, NW of Cape Carmel, in the approaches to Haifa, before the course can be altered for the port of Haifa. Spartan Reef, in the NW part of the Bay of Akko (Acre) should be avoided as the swell normally breaks over it. There is a small marina at Akko, north of Haifa, and there are plans to increase its capacity. In Haifa itself, the Carmel Yacht Club occasionally has room for visitors at their facility at the mouth of Kishon River.

Boats sailing to Tel Aviv (route M81B) should use the same departure points and set a course for WP M814, NW of Tel Aviv. Tel Aviv Marina monitors VHF channel 16, but because of the difficult entrance night arrivals should be avoided. Tel Aviv Marina is usually full and is therefore no longer recommended, but there are two new and larger marinas north and south of Tel Aviv. Close to the north of the city is Herzliya Marina (32°10'N, 34°47.6'E), while some 20 miles to the south is Ashkelon (31°40'N, 34°32'E). Both marinas have good facilities but only Ashkelon is an official port of entry.

M82 *Cyprus to Port Said*

BEST TIME:	April to October	
CHARTS:	BA: 183	US: 302
PILOTS:	BA: 49	
	US: 132	
CRUISING GUIDES:	*Mediterranean Cruising Handbook, Red Sea Pilot.*	

WAYPOINTS:				
Departure	*Intermediate*	*Landfall*	*Destination*	*Distance (M)*
M821 Larnaca Bay 34°54'N, 33°39'E	M822 Kiti 34°47'N, 33°39'E	M825 Said 31°25'N, 32°18'E	Port Said *31°15'N, 32°18'E*	230
M823 Akrotiri W 34°39'N, 33°04'E	M834 Akrotiri SW 34°34'N, 33°03'E	M825 Said	Port Said	224

This route benefits from favourable winds for most of the summer. From most ports on the south coast of Cyprus there is a clear run to a point 10 miles north of the entrance into Port Said, which is the recommended anchorage for commercial shipping waiting to transit the Suez Canal. Because of the low, featureless coast and the shallow depths which extend several miles offshore, the position of Port Said is very difficult to ascertain if landfall is made either too far east or west. The situation is further complicated by the unpredictability of the currents in the area, which are also influenced by the state of the Nile waters. The cluster of ships at anchor is usually the first indication of the approaches to Port Said.

Boats leaving from Larnaca and WP M821 should set an initial course to WP M822, to clear Cape Kiti. From WP M822 a direct course can be set for WP M825, at the northern entrance into the shipping channel leading into Port Said. Boats leaving from Limassol, in the NW part of Akrotiri Bay, should set an initial course from WP M823 for WP M824, off Cape Gata. From that point, a direct course can be sailed to WP M825, off Port Said.

The approach channel to Port Said extends far offshore and is well marked by buoys. It should be entered at its northern extremity and no shortcuts taken because of a number of wrecks lying outside this channel. Small vessels are allowed to proceed into the harbour without a pilot and all formalities can be completed after the vessel has berthed at the Fouad Yacht Club. This is situated on the eastern side of the harbour.

M83 *Cyprus to Rhodes*

BEST TIME:	April to May, September to October			
CHARTS:	BA: 183			
	US: 302			
PILOTS:	BA: 48, 49			
	US: 130, 132			
CRUISING GUIDES:	*Greek Waters Pilot.*			
WAYPOINTS:				
Departure	*Intermediate*	*Landfall*	*Destination*	*Distance (M)*
Route M83A M831 Paphos W 34°45'N, 32°22'E		M835 Rhodes NE 36°26'N, 28°16'E	Mandraki *36°27'N, 28°14'E*	237
Route M83B M832 Kyrenia N 35°21'N, 33°18'E	M833 Cyprus NW 35°26'N, 32°55'E			
	M834 Strongili 36°05'N, 29°37'E	M835 Rhodes NE	Mandraki	256

It is generally recommended to wait for a spell of E or SE winds before making this passage, which can be hampered by strong northerly winds in summer. If persistently strong W or NW winds occur after the start of this passage, it is preferable to go on the port tack and head for the Turkish coast where either a change in the weather can be awaited or shorter tacks taken along the coast.

A convenient port to wait for favourable conditions for boats sailing route M83A is Paphos, on the SW coast of Cyprus. Boats coming from ports on the south coast of the island can join the offshore route close to that point. From WP M831, outside Paphos harbour, a direct course can then be set for

WP M835, situated off the NE tip of Rhodes.

Boats leaving from Kyrenia, in Northern Cyprus (route M83B), should set an initial course from WP M832 for WP M833, off Cape Kormakiti. The subsequent offshore route passes close to a group of islands off the south coast of Turkey. Those who wish, may clear into Greece at Kastellorizon. Otherwise, from WP M834, off the small island of Strongili, the course is altered for WP M835, in the approaches to Mandraki, the main port on the island of Rhodes. Mandraki (Limin Rhodou) is always crowded and cruising boats may find it difficult to secure a free berth. Additional docking space was planned for 1994.

M84 *Cyprus to Crete*

BEST TIME:	April to May, September to October				
CHARTS:	BA: 1439				
	US: 302				
PILOTS:	BA: 48, 49				
	US: 132				
CRUISING GUIDES:	*Greek Waters Pilot.*				
WAYPOINTS:					
Departure	*Intermediate*	*Landfall*	*Destination*		*Distance (M)*
Route M84A					
M841 Paphos W	M842 Sidheros				
34°45'N, 32°22'E	35°20'N, 26°21'E				
	M843 Crete NE	M844 Crete N	Iraklion		362
	35°25'N, 26°10'E	35°23'N, 25°20'E	*35°16'N, 25°09'E*		
Route M84B					
M845 Kyrenia N	M846 Cyprus NW				
35°21'N, 33°18'E	35°26'N, 32°55'E				
	M847 Kasos				
	35°18'N, 26°52'E				
	M843 Crete NE	M844 Crete N	Iraklion		404

Directions are similar to those for route M83, with the advantage that the prevailing northerly winds of summer will be met at a better angle. However, boats bound for islands in the Aegean would do better to sail to Rhodes, as described in route M83, and enter the Aegean from the SE. Because of the strong meltemi, sailing north from Crete is difficult throughout the summer, so when making plans for an Aegean cruise it is better to visit the islands to the north of Crete first and leave Crete for later.

Whether leaving from the south or north of Cyprus, the routes to the north coast of Crete con-

verge in Dhiavlos Kasou, the channel separating Crete from the island of Kasos. Boats leaving from Southern Cyprus (route M84A) will find it convenient to take their departure from Cyprus at Paphos, on the SW coast of the island. From WP M841 a direct course can be set for WP M842, east of Cape Sidheros, at the NE extremity of Crete.

Boats leaving from Northern Cyprus on route M84B, will sail a course to pass clear of Cape Kormakiti, the NW extremity of Cyprus, before being able to set a course for WP M847, south of Kasos Island. At that point the course can be altered for WP M843, NE of Crete, and joins the route from Southern Cyprus. The route for Iraklion runs parallel to the north coast of Crete to WP M844, NE of the Cretan capital. Boats should proceed into the

old Venetian harbour, in the SW corner of the large commercial harbour. If there is no free space at one of the pontoons, cruising boats may use the quay immediately east of the small boat harbour.

M85 *Cyprus to Malta*

BEST TIME:	June to August				
CHARTS:	BA: 4302				
	US: 302				
PILOTS:	BA: 45, 49				
	US: 130, 131, 132				
CRUISING GUIDES:	*North Africa, Yachtsman's Handbook to Malta.*				
WAYPOINTS:					
Departure	*Intermediate*	*Landfall*	*Destination*		*Distance (M)*
Route M85A					
M851 Cyprus S	M852 Crete S	M853 Malta E	Valletta		912
34°33'N, 32°55'E	34°45'N, 24°07'E	35°54.5'N, 14°31.5'E	*35°54'N, 14°30.5'E*		
Route M85B					
M854 Kyrenia N	M855 Cyprus NW				
35°21'N, 33°18'E	35°26'N, 32°55'E				
	M852 Crete S	M853 Malta E	Valletta		931

Reasonable conditions can be expected on this route throughout the summer, with best chances of favourable winds between the middle of June and the middle of August. Calms become more frequent with the approach of autumn.

Boats leaving from one of the ports in Southern Cyprus, such as Larnaca or Limassol, should take their departure from Cyprus at WP M851, SW of Cape Zevgari (route M85A). From this point the route then passes south of Crete through WP M852, south of Gavdhos Island. From there a direct course can be set for WP M853, at the

entrance into Marsamxett Harbour.

Boats sailing route M85B from Kyrenia, in Northern Cyprus, should take their leave from the island at WP M855, off Cape Kormakiti, from where a course can be set to pass south of Crete through WP M852 and on to WP M853, in the approaches to the Maltese capital. On arrival in Malta boats should contact Valletta Port Control on VHF channels 12 or 16 before proceeding to one of the reception docks at Msida Marina or Lazaretto Creek. The Yachting Centre can be contacted on VHF channel 9 to request docking information.

M86 *Cyprus to Southern Turkey*

BEST TIME:	April to May, September to October
CHARTS:	BA: 183
	US: 302
PILOTS:	BA: 49
	US: 132
CRUISING GUIDES:	*Turkish Waters & Cyprus Pilot, Cruising Guide to the Turquoise Coasts of Turkey.*

WAYPOINTS:				
Departure	*Intermediate*	*Landfall*	*Destination*	*Distance (M)*
Route M86A				
M861 Kyrenia N	M862 Dildarde	M863 Alanya S	Alanya	96
35°21'N, 33°18'E	36°20'N, 32°07'E	36°30'N, 32°02'E	*36°32'N, 32°01'E*	
Route M86B				
M864 Paphos W	M865 Yeranisou	M863 Alanya S	Alanya	110
34°45'N, 32°22'E	35°00'N, 32°12'E			

Northern Cyprus, and especially the port of Kyrenia, is a perfect departure point for the south coast of Turkey. Boats coming from Southern Cyprus (route M86B) will fare better by starting from a western port, such as Paphos. Rounding Cyprus from the east is not recommended because of the east-setting current along the north coast and in the vicinity of Cape Andreas.

If leaving from Kyrenia, boats sailing route M86A have a choice of destinations, from Anamur on the east side of the Gulf of Antalya, to Antalya itself, or Finike, further west. If the intention is to cruise the Turkish coast from east to west, it is advisable to sail first to Alanya, which is the nearest port of entry coming from this direction, and complete entry formalities there. From WP M861, north of Kyrenia, a course is set for WP M862. From there the course can be altered for WP M863, south of Alanya. Because the small port is always crowded with local boats, visiting yachts normally anchor north of the pier, where protection from the prevailing wind is good.

Boats leaving from one of the ports in Southern Cyprus (route M86B), such as Paphos, should set an initial course for WP M865. From that point, the course can be altered for WP M863, south of the port of Alanya.

M87 *Cyprus to Lebanon*

BEST TIME:	May to October			
CHARTS:	BA: 183			
	US: 54440, 54480			
PILOTS:	BA: 49			
	US: 132			
CRUISING GUIDES:	*Mediterranean Cruising Handbook, Turkish Waters and Cyprus Pilot.*			
WAYPOINTS:				
Departure	*Intermediate*	*Landfall*	*Destination*	*Distance (M)*
M870 Larnaca	M871 Cyprus E	M872 Tair	Jounieh	206
34°55'N, 33°38'E	34°55'N, 33°40'E	33°59'N, 35°33'E	*33°59'N, 35°39'E*	
M873 Kyrenia	M874 Cyprus N			
35°20'N, 33°19'E	35°25'N, 33°21'E			
	M875 Kidhes	M876 Ramkin	Tripoli	163
	35°45'N, 34°37'E	34°30'N, 35°42'E	*34°28'N, 35°50'E*	

For boats leaving from any port in Southern Cyprus the best port of arrival in Lebanon is Jounieh. Lebanon's only marina is located there and facilities are also of a good standard. The Lebanese Navy must be contacted when still in international waters. The callsign for Jounieh and Beirut is Oscar Charlie, for Tripoli it is Oscar November, and Oscar Sierra for Sidon and Tyre. The other four ports are all commercial harbours and this is why Jounieh is recommended. The movement of boats between ports is subject to severe restrictions and coastal sailing should therefore be avoided if possible.

Boats leaving from Northern Cyprus may also sail directly to Jounieh, but if the intention is to visit other Lebanese ports then landfall should be made at Tripoli and then sail southward from there. From the NE extremity of Cyprus at Cape Andreas a direct course can be sailed to make landfall off Ramkin light in the approaches to Tripoli. The Lebanese Navy (callsign Oscar November) should be contacted on channel 16 while still outside the 12 mile limit to request pratique.

M88 *Cyprus to Syria*

BEST TIME:	May to October				
CHARTS:	BA: 183				
	US: 54440, 54480				
PILOTS:	BA: 49	US: 132			
CRUISING GUIDES:	*Mediterranean Cruising Handbook.*				
WAYPOINTS:					
Departure	*Intermediate*	*Landfall*	*Destination*		*Distance (M)*
M880 Larnaca	M881 Cyprus E				
34°55'N, 33°38'E	*34°55'N, 33°40'E*				
	M882 Greco	M883 Syria SW	Latakia		113
	34°55'N, 34°05'E	*35°30'N, 35°43'E*	*35°31'N, 35°46'E*		
M884 Kyrenia	M885 Cyprus N				
35°20'N, 33°19'E	*35°25'N, 33°21'E*				
	M886 Kidhes	M887 Syria W	Latakia		129
	35°45'N, 34°37'E	*35°32'N, 35°43'E*			

Whether leaving from a port in Southern or Northern Cyprus, the best place to arrive in Syria is Latakia. Boats leaving from Larnaca will have a clear run once Cape Greco is left behind. The same applies to boats that left from Kyrenia and have cleared the Kidhes Islets off Cape Andreas at the NE extremity of the island.

Port Control should be contacted at the 12 mile limit and, if bound for Latakia, permission should be requested to proceed to the southern basin to complete formalities. Boats may be asked to take a pilot at the harbour entrance. The pilotage fee is included in the general harbour fee. Those who arrive without visas will be issued shore passes. Coastal sailing is discouraged and subject to restrictions. If going to one of the other two ports open to foreign flagged vessels, at Banias (35°14'N, 35°56'E) and Tartous (34°54'N, 35°52'E), clearing in and out formalities will have to be repeated.

M90 ROUTES FROM ISRAEL

M91 *Israel to Cyprus*	*580*
M92 *Israel to Port Said*	*581*
M93 *Israel to Malta*	*581*
M94 *Israel to Crete*	*582*

Only a few routes set out from the easternmost country in the Mediterranean and most boats that sail them usually make a first stop in Cyprus. As most of the eastern shores of the Mediterranean lack natural harbours, boat movement is confined to a few ports. Yachting facilities in Israel itself have seen a great improvement and there are now several marinas dotted about at convenient intervals along the Mediterranean coast, the two largest and with best facilities being the marinas at Herzliya, situated north of Tel Aviv, and Ashkelon, south of that city.

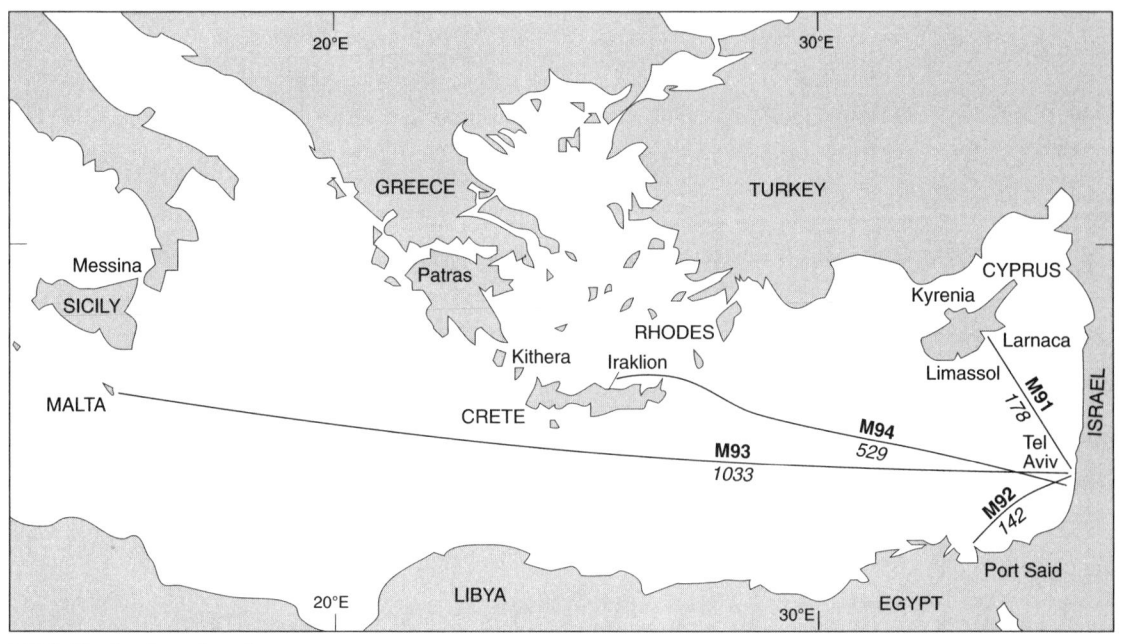

M90 *Routes from Israel*

M91 *Israel to Cyprus*

Best time:	April to June, September to October			
Charts:	BA: 183			
	US: 302			
Pilots:	BA: 49			
	US: 132			
Cruising guides:	*Turkish Waters & Cyprus Pilot.*			
Waypoints:				

Departure	*Intermediate*	*Landfall*	*Destination*	*Distance (M)*
M911 Akko		M913	Larnaca	139
32°52'N, 34°56'E		34°54'N, 33°39'E	*34°55'N, 33°38'E*	
M912 Aviv N		M913	Larnaca	178
32°06' N, 34°44'E				

Contrary winds are common on this route and therefore a more northerly starting port, such as Haifa, is recommended. Most boats sailing this route usually head for Larnaca before continuing around the south or north of Cyprus. Larnaca Marina (34°55'N, 33°38.5'E) monitors VHF channel 16. Occasionally yachts are asked to anchor in the outer harbour while a berth is found for them.

Boats leaving from Haifa should make their way past Spartan Reef, north of Cape Carmel, to WP M911, from where a direct route leads to WP M913, in the Bay of Larnaca. Boats leaving from Tel Aviv and WP M912 can set a course for the same WP M913.

M92 *Israel to Port Said*

BEST TIME:	April to October			
CHARTS:	BA: 183			
	US: 302			
PILOTS:	BA: 49			
	US: 132			
CRUISING GUIDES:	*Mediterranean Cruising Handbook.*			
WAYPOINTS:				
Departure	*Intermediate*	*Landfall*	*Destination*	*Distance (M)*
M921 Aviv S		M922 Said	Port Said	142
32°04'N, 34°45'E		31°25'N, 32°18'E	*31°15'N, 32°18'E*	

A contrary current usually makes itself felt along this route and it is therefore preferable not to follow the coast too closely, where the current is strongest. If landfall is made too far east of Port Said, it is often difficult to identify any coastal features and the approaches to Port Said will only be indicated by the large number of ships lying at anchor in the recommended waiting area.

From WP M921, outside Tel Aviv marina, a direct course can be set for WP M922, in the northern approaches to Port Said. The approach channel into Port Said is taken from this point. The channel should be entered at its northern extremity and no shortcuts taken because of a number of wrecks lying outside this channel. Small vessels are allowed to proceed into the harbour without a pilot and all formalities can be completed after the vessel has berthed at the Fouad Yacht Club. This is situated on the eastern side of the harbour.

M93 *Israel to Malta*

BEST TIME:	June to September			
CHARTS:	BA: 4302			
	US: 302			
PILOTS:	BA: 45, 49			
	US: 131, 132			
CRUISING GUIDES:	*North Africa, Yachtsman's Handbook to Malta.*			
WAYPOINTS:				
Departure	*Intermediate*	*Landfall*	*Destination*	*Distance (M)*
M931 Aviv N	M932 Crete S	M933 Malta E	Valletta	1033
32°06'N, 34°44'E	34°45'N, 24°07'E	35°54.5'N, 14°31.5'E	*35°54'N, 14°30.5'E*	

This passage can be undertaken at any time during summer when mostly northerly winds can be expected. From WP M931, outside Tel Aviv marina, a direct course can be set for WP M932 to pass south of Crete and Gavdhos Island. From there a new course can be set for WP M933, east of the entrance into Marsamxett harbour. On arrival in Malta boats should contact Valletta Port Control on VHF channels 12 or 16 before proceeding to one of the reception docks at Msida Marina or Lazaretto Creek. The Yachting Centre can be contacted on VHF channel 9 to request docking information.

M94 *Israel to Crete*

BEST TIME:	May to October
CHARTS:	BA: 183
	US: 302
PILOTS:	BA: 48, 49
	US: 132
CRUISING GUIDES:	*Greek Waters Pilot.*
WAYPOINTS:	

Departure	Intermediate	Landfall	Destination	Distance (M)
M940 Ashkelon	M941 Crete NE	M942 Crete N	Iraklion	529
31°40'N, 34°32'E	*35°25'N, 26°10'E*	*35°23'N, 25°20'E*	*35°16'N, 25°09'E*	

Inaugurated by the Millennium Odyssey as a non-stop leg, boats sailing the direct route from Israel to Crete have a choice of marinas in the proximity of Tel Aviv from where to take their departure from Israel. Close to the north of Tel Aviv is the well endowed marina at Herzliya, while to the south is Ashkelon Marina, which is given as a recommended point of departure from Israel as it is also an official port of entry.

The direct route leads to a point off Cape Sidheros, the NE extremity of Crete. Although there are a number of ports on Crete's north coast, the best facilities are at Iraklion. The recommended route runs parallel to the coast to make landfall close to the entrance into the commercial harbour. The old Venetian port is where cruising boats normally dock, but if there is no space one should come alongside the quay immediately to the east of the small boat harbour, near the Iraklion Sailing Club.

23
PANAMA AND
SUEZ CANALS

PANAMA CANAL

The gradual handing over of the Panama Canal to the Panamanian authorities by the United States does not appear to have affected the actual operation of the Canal, and transiting procedures are just as straightforward and easy to accomplish as before. By the year 2000 the Canal will be operated entirely by Panama.

Atlantic side

Cristobal Signal Station should be contacted on VHF channel 12 when 3 miles from the harbour entrance and again when passing between the breakwaters. Traffic lights control the movement of vessels between the breakwaters, but small yachts may enter at any time provided they do so close to the sides. Having entered the large harbour, yachts should proceed in a southerly direction to the recommended anchorage, which is located to the east of Channel buoy no. 4 and to the south of Cristobal Mole. The yacht anchorage, called the Flats, is marked by red and amber buoys. Alternatively, one may ask permission to proceed directly to the Panama Canal Yacht Club, which can be contacted on VHF channel 64. Clearance instructions can be requested on VHF channel 16. Both at Cristobal and Balboa, on the Pacific side, yachts may be boarded by a Panamanian boarding officer, who has many functions and will perform customs, quarantine, and immigration duties. Those who prefer to remain at anchor can come to the club by dinghy and use its facilities, provided permission has been obtained beforehand.

Pacific side

Yachts arriving at the Pacific side of the Canal should contact Flamenco Signal Station on VHF channel 12 and will be directed to either anchor off the Balboa Yacht Club or pick up one of its moorings. The club office is open all day on weekdays and until noon on Saturday and monitors VHF channel 63. Clearance formalities can be arranged at the club.

When clearance formalities are completed on arrival, the Port Authority will issue a cruising permit, which is needed whether transiting the Canal or not. This also applies to those wishing to visit the San Blas Islands on the Atlantic side for which an additional permit has to be obtained at Porvenir, where all boats are required to stop and check in before proceeding to the islands.

Those wishing to transit the Canal must follow the following steps once clearance formalities have been completed:

1 The skipper must call the Admeasurer's office (tel. 46 7293 on the Atlantic side, 52 4570 on the Pacific side) to make arrangements for a Panama Canal Tonnage Certificate to be issued. In Cristobal, the Admeasurer's office is on the first floor of the Administration Building no.1105. In Balboa, the office is on the first floor of Building 729, Marine Bureau Building. The offices are open 0700–1600 Monday to Saturday. Payment must be made in cash in US dollars. Neither travellers cheques nor any other currency than dollars are accepted. On top of the actual transit fee, a flat admeasurement fee of $350 was introduced in 1996 and the fees are expected to rise again in 1998 so that a cruising boat will be expected to pay around $1000 for the transit.

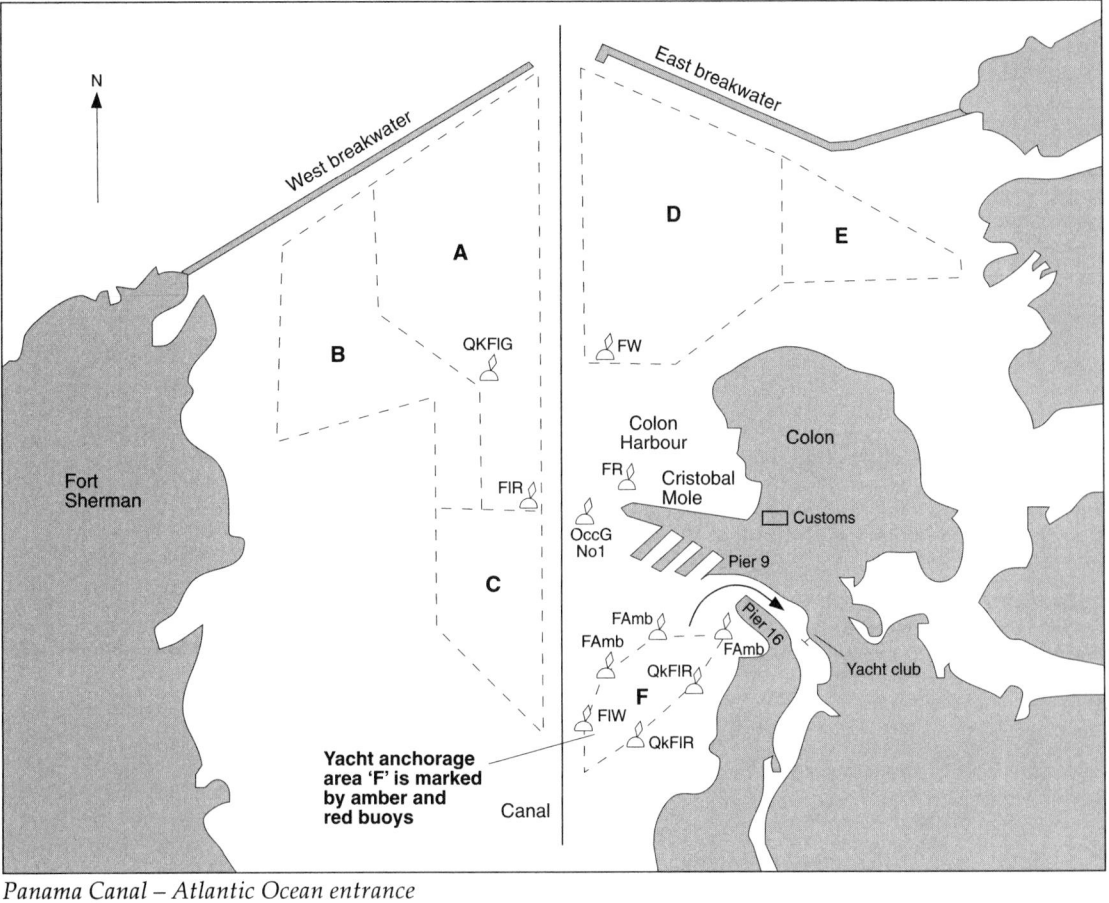

Panama Canal – Atlantic Ocean entrance

2 After admeasurement, the captain has to report to the Marine Traffic Control Office (Building 1105, second floor, Cristobal or Building 910, La Bola, on the Pacific side). An officer will explain the requirements for the transit, such as four mooring lines not less than 100 ft long and not less than 22 mm (7/8 inch) in diameter, four linehandlers in addition to the helmsman and adequate fenders. The vessel must be able to maintain a speed of 5 knots under her own power. Inspect all lines and cleats to ensure that they are in good order as they will be put under heavy strain during the transit. If in need of additional linehandlers, contact Panama Transit Services on tel. 28 8056.

3 The captain is then given a provisional pilot time for his scheduled transit, prior to which he will be required to call Marine Traffic Control (tel. 52 4202 or VHF channel 12) to confirm the time. Yacht transits take place every day of the week and depend on shipping movement, but on average yachts have to wait three days before transiting. Yachts normally make the transit in two days, spending the night anchored off Gamboa. The pilot arrives early in the morning and leaves for the night, returning the following morning to complete the transit. Yachts must maintain their schedule regardless of weather conditions. Yachts that cannot maintain a speed of 5 knots will need a change of pilot at Gamboa, halfway through the Canal. However, if one has indicated that a speed of 5 knots could be maintained and this was not achieved, the yacht will be delayed at Gamboa until a second pilot becomes available the following day. All additional expenses for this will be paid by the owner. Yachts that cannot maintain more than 4 knots have to be towed through the Canal by a Commission launch, for which a fee is charged.

There are three types of lockage for yachts under 125 ft (38 m) LOA when transiting the Canal:

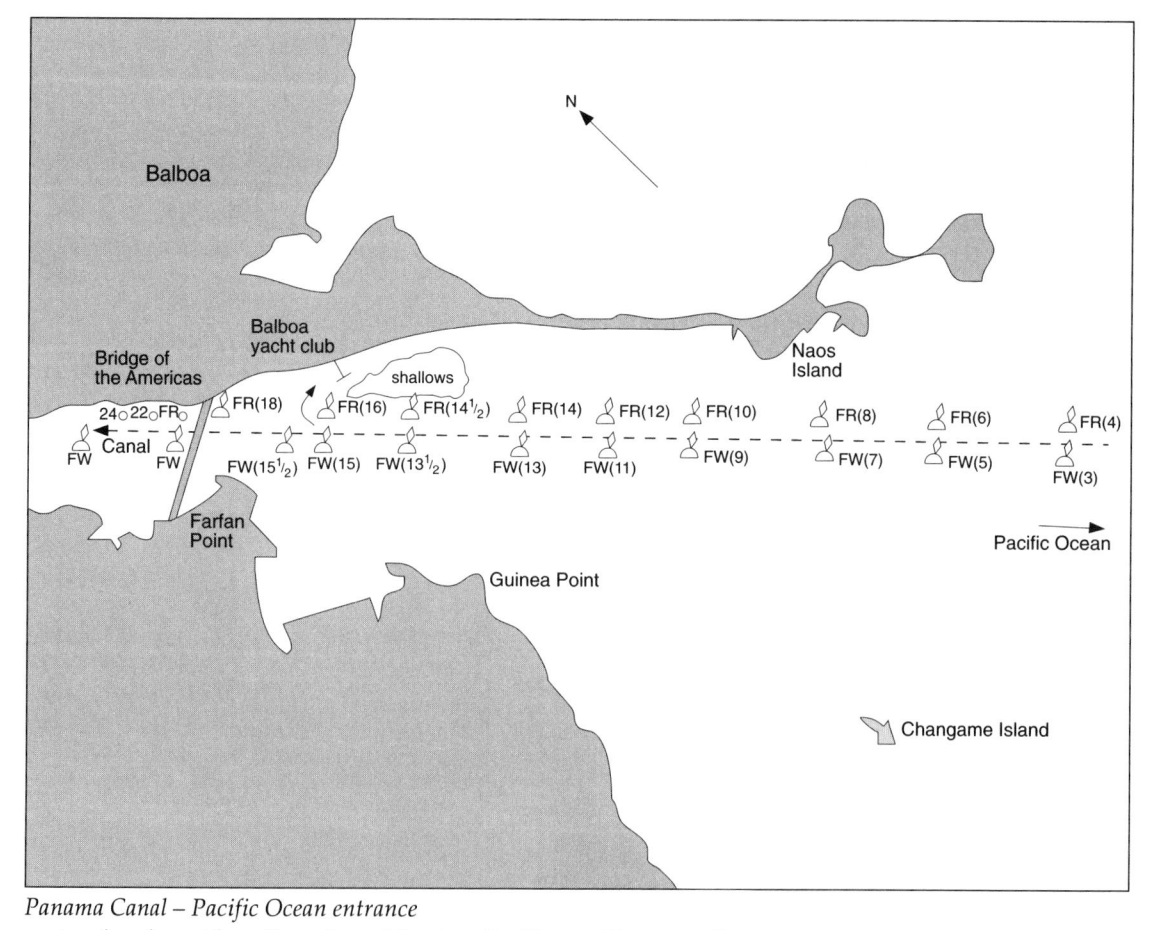

Panama Canal – Pacific Ocean entrance

centre chamber, sidewall, or alongside a tug. Traffic Control decides on the type of lockage for each yacht. Because of the roughness of the walls and the turbulence created during the filling of the chambers, yachts usually transit centre chamber or alongside a Commission tug, but each yacht must be capable of centre lockage.

Centre chamber lockage: The vessel is held in the centre of the chamber by two bow and two stern lines. Yachts are sometimes rafted together in which case only those on the outside will handle two mooring lines each.

Sidewall lockage: Only two 100 ft lines are required but plenty of fenders as the walls are rough concrete. Care should be taken of the rigging and spreaders which may hit the walls as the water is lowered in the chamber. This type of lockage is not recommended for yachts of less than 70 ft LOA.

Alongside a tug: Two 50 ft lines are required and also two springs, as well as adequate fenders. This is the best type of lockage for small yachts and it is the preferred lockage used by the Canal pilots.

SUEZ CANAL

The 87.5 mile long Suez Canal links the Mediterranean and the Red Sea by way of several lakes and without any locks. Its opening in 1869 had a tremendous impact on international shipping as it halved the distance between Europe and the Far East. In its long history, the Canal has been closed twice as a result of war, in 1956 for a year and in 1967 for seven years. It is now used regularly by about 100 ships per day and its recent upgrading has made it possible for the Canal to be transited by vessels of up to 200 000 tons.

Vessels under 300 tons are allowed to use the canal free of charge, although there are some additional fees that have to be paid by all users, including the smallest yacht. The captains of small vessels intending to transit the canal are allowed by the Suez Canal Authority to complete the formalities on their own, but as they are very complicated, the

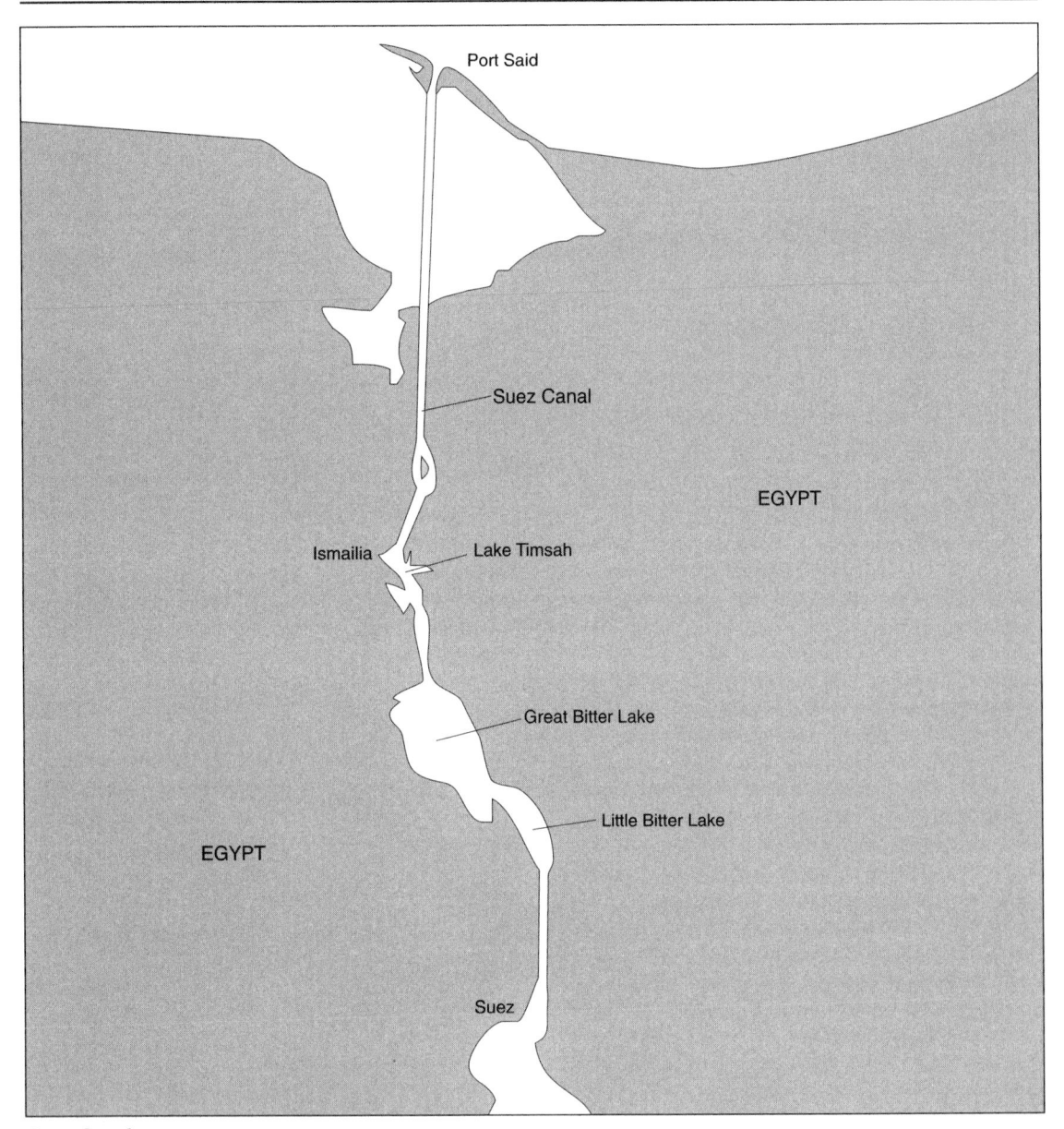

Suez Canal

use of a shipping agent is strongly recommended. Both in Port Said and Suez there are firms which specialise in handling small boats and their representatives are usually on station in the approaches to the Canal offering their services, sometimes rather forcefully. If the services of a local agent are employed, all additional costs must be specified by the agent and fees agreed in advance. Agent fees and transit costs all have to be paid in US dollars, therefore it is advisable to carry some funds in

notes, including smaller denominations.

Those who do not wish to be delayed after the transit of the Canal is completed, can request outward clearance from either Port Said or Suez while completing formalities for their transit. They can proceed on their way as soon as they have dropped the pilot at the end of the Canal. Those wishing to visit inland areas of Egypt either before or after passing through the Canal need a tourist visa, which can be obtained on arrival. During a

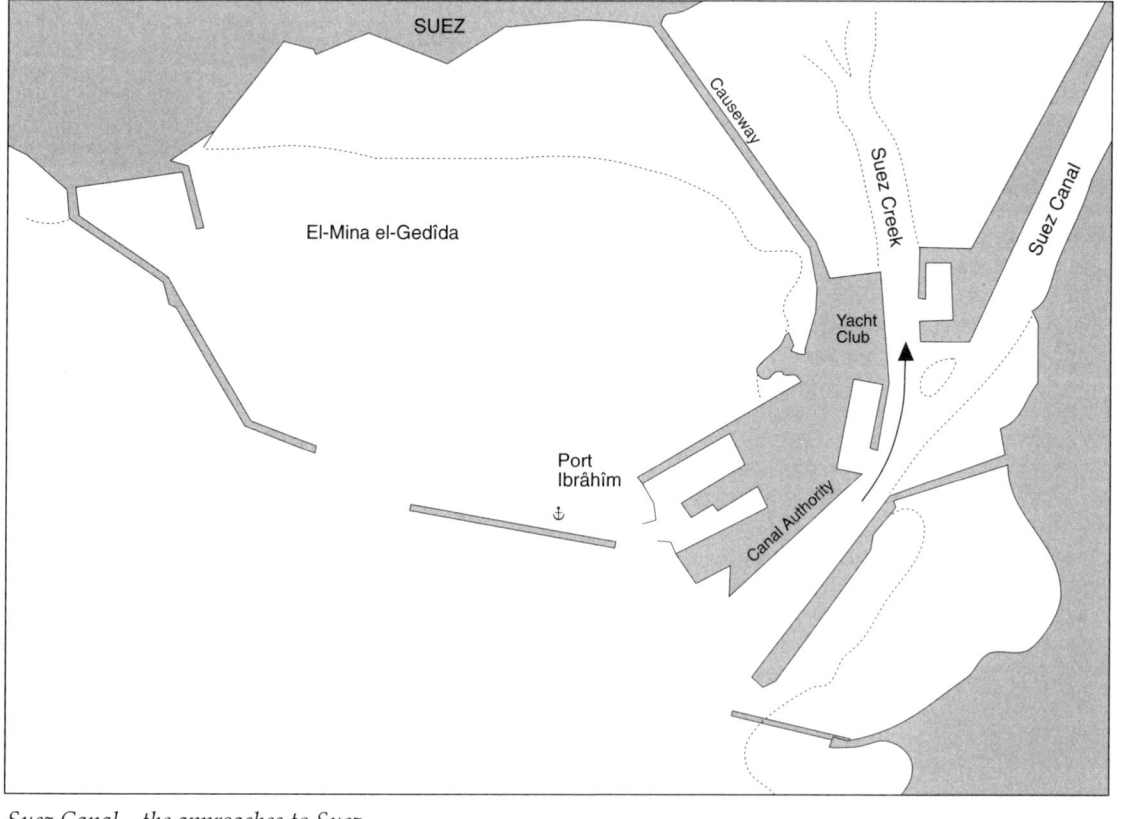

Suez Canal – the approaches to Suez

trip inland, the boat can be left in the care of either yacht club.

Because of the length of the Canal, very few yachts are able to transit the Canal in one day. Small vessels are not permitted to use the Canal at night and for this reason it is necessary to anchor overnight at Ismailia, in the NW corner of Lake Timsah. The crew are normally allowed to use the local yacht club but must not leave the premises. Usually the same pilot will rejoin the yacht at dawn to complete the transit.

Yachts must be capable of maintaining a speed of 5 knots under power. The speed limit in the Canal is 9 knots. The use of sails is not permitted in the Canal, although with the pilot's permission the mainsail may be run up while crossing the Bitter Lakes if the weather warrants this. If the vessel is delayed for any reason and Ismailia cannot be reached before nightfall, the captain may be required to anchor for the night in a place where the yacht does not impede the passage of larger vessels. The transit procedure is as follows:

Southbound

Small vessels arriving at the Mediterranean entrance to the Canal in Port Said must berth at the Fouad Yacht Club, which is situated on the east side of the harbour. Because of the high density of traffic and intricate approaches, Port Said harbour should not be entered at night. On the morning of the transit, a pilot will board the vessel at a place agreed with the agent. The pilot will take the vessel as far as Ismailia, where the night will be spent at anchor in Lake Timsah. The pilot will be collected by launch and either the same pilot or a replacement will join the yacht the following morning to complete the transit. On arrival in Suez, yachts usually moor at the Suez Yacht Club, situated in a creek on the west bank, very close to the southern end of the Canal. The pilot will give instructions how to reach the club and he can be dropped there.

Northbound

Vessels approaching the Canal from the Red Sea must anchor in Port Ibrahim, in the NE corner of Suez Bay, close to the north of the Canal entrance. After formalities have been completed, the boat can move to the Suez Yacht Club, or remain at anchor. Whether completing formalities alone or with the help of an agent, a pilot appointed by the Canal Authority will join the yacht on the morning of the agreed day, either at the yacht club or more likely at the customs wharf close to the entrance to the Canal, on the west side of the harbour. Yachts normally transit just after the morning convoy has left Suez, between 0900 and 1100. Usually on the first day of the transit yachts only manage to go as far as Ismailia, where the night is spent at anchor in Lake Timsah. The pilot will be collected by a launch and either the same pilot or a replacement pilot will join the yacht the following morning to complete the transit. Occasionally, if the morning convoy is late leaving Port Said, the yacht is delayed leaving Ismailia and may have to spend a second night in the Canal. On arrival in Port Said, the pilot will be picked up by a launch and the yacht is free to proceed on her way. Those who have obtained onward clearance can put to sea immediately. Those who wish to stay should proceed to the Fouad Yacht Club, on the east side of the harbour.

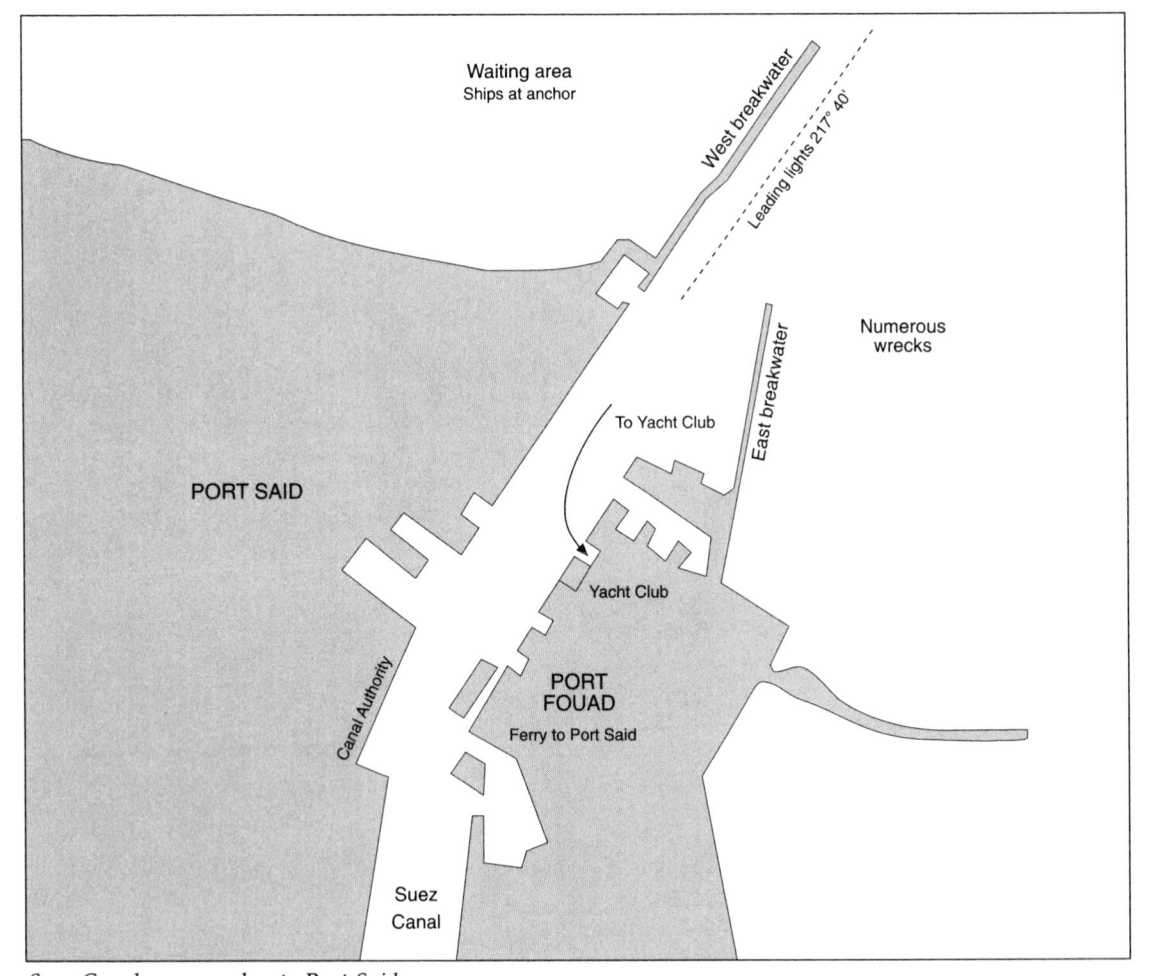

Suez Canal – approaches to Port Said

Cruising Guides

Adriatic Pilot; Trevor & Dinah Thompson, Imray, Great Britain
Atlantic Crossing Guide; RCC Pilotage Foundation, Adlard Coles Nautical, Great Britain and International Marine, USA
Atlantic Islands; RCC Pilotage Foundation, Imray, Great Britain
Atlantic Pilot Atlas, James Clarke, Adlard Coles Nautical, Great Britain
Atlantic Spain and Portugal; RCC Pilotage Foundation, Imray, Great Britain
Azores Cruising Guide; ed Gwenda Cornell, World Cruising Publications, Great Britain
Baltic Southwest Pilot; Mark Brackenbury, Adlard Coles Nautical, Great Britain
Black Sea Cruising Guide; Rick & Sheila Nelson
Brittany and Channel Islands Cruising Guide; David Jefferson, Adlard Coles Nautical, Great Britain
Canary Islands Cruising Guide; ed Jimmy Cornell, World Cruising Publications, Great Britain
Channel Islands Pilot; Malcolm Robson, Adlard Coles Nautical, Great Britain
Charlie's Charts of Costa Rica; Margo Wood, Charlie's Charts, Canada
Charlie's Charts of Polynesia (The South Pacific east of 165°W Longitude); Charles Wood, Charlie's Charts, Canada
Charlie's Charts of the Hawaiian Islands; Charles Wood, Charlie's Charts, Canada
Charlie's Charts of the US Pacific Coast; Charles & Margo Wood, Charlie's Charts, Canada
Charlie's Charts of the Western Coast of Mexico; Charles Wood & Janet Steele, Charlie's Charts, Canada
Charlie's Charts, North to Alaska; Charles Wood, Charlie's Charts, Canada
Circumnavigating Australia's Coastline; Jeff Toghill
Coastal Cruising Guide to the Atlantic Coast; Embassy Marine, USA
Coastal Cruising Handbook of the Royal Akarana Yacht Club; Mary Hamilton & D'arcy Whiting, New Zealand
Complete Boating Guide to Florida's East Coast; Embassy Marine, USA
Cruising Association Handbook, Yachting Guide for Southwest Baltic to Gibraltar; Cruising Association, Great Britain
Cruising Beyond Desolation Sound; John Chappell
Cruising Guide Acapulco to the Panama Canal; Charles & Nancy Goodman
Cruising Guide San Francisco to Ensenada; Brian Fagan
Cruising Guide to Abaco; Steve Dodge
Cruising Guide to Belize and Mexico's Caribbean Coast; Freya Rauscher
Cruising Guide to British Columbia; Bill Wolferstan, Whitecap Books, Canada
Cruising Guide to California's Offshore Islands; Brian Fagan
Cruising Guide to Cuba; Simon Charles
Cruising Guide to Eastern Florida; Claiborne Young
Cruising Guide to Germany and Denmark; Brian Navin
Cruising Guide to Narrangasett Bay and the South Coast of Massachusetts; Lynde Morris Childress, Patrick Childress and Tink Martin, International Marine, USA
Cruising Guide to New Caledonia; Joel Marc
Cruising Guide to Newfoundland; ed. Sandy Weld
Cruising Guide to Nova Scotia; Peter Loveridge, International Marine, USA
Cruising Guide to Puget Sound; M Scherer, International Marine, USA
Cruising Guide to Southeast Asia; Stephen Davies and Elaine Morgan, Imray, Great Britain
  1. *South China Sea, Philippines, Thailand and Singapore*
  2. *Papua New Guinea, Indonesia, Malacca Strait*
Cruising Guide to Trinidad and Tobago; Chris Doyle, Cruising Guide Publications, USA
Cruising Guide to Venezuela and Bonaire; Chris Doyle and Jeff Fisher, Cruising Guide Publications, USA
Cruising Guide to West Africa; RCC Pilotage Foundation, Great Britain
Cruising Guide to the Abacos and Northern Bahamas; Darrell Wyatt, Westcott Cove Publishing, USA

Cruising Guide to the Caribbean; William Stone & Ann Hays

Cruising Guide to the Exuma Cays Land and Sea Park; Stephen Pavlidis

Cruising Guide to the Kingdom of Tonga in the Vava'u Group; The Moorings, Cruising Guide Publications, USA

Cruising Guide to the Leeward Islands; Chris Doyle, Cruising Guide Publications, USA

Cruising Guide to the Netherlands; Brian Navin, Imray, Great Britain

Cruising Guide to the New England Coast; Roger Duncan

Cruising Guide to the Northwest Caribbean; Nigel Calder, International Marine, USA

Cruising Guide to the Nova Scotia Coast; ed. John McKelvy Jr.

Cruising Guide to the Sea of Cortez; ed. Simon and Nancy Scott

Cruising Guide to the Turquoise Coasts of Turkey; Marcia Davock

Cruising Guide to the Virgin Islands; Nancy & Simon Scott

Cruising Ports: Florida to California; John Rains

Cruising the Chesapeake; William Shellenberger, International Marine, USA

Cruising the Coral Coast; Alan Lucas, Horwitz Grahame, Australia

Cuba: A Cruising Guide; Nigel Calder

Den Norske Los Sailing Directions (Arctic Pilot)

Destination NZ, Bluewater Cruisers' Guide to New Zealand's Northern Waters; Graham Brice and Christopher Carey

East Africa Pilot; Delwyn McPhun, Imray, Great Britain

East and North Coasts of Ireland Sailing Directions; Irish Cruising Club

East Spain Pilot; Robin Brandon, Imray, Great Britain

    Costas del Azahar; Dorada & Brava

    Costas del Sol and Blanca

Faeroe, Iceland & Greenland; RCC Pilotage Foundation, Great Britain

Falkland Island Shores; Ewen Southby-Tailyour, Adlard Coles Nautical, Great Britain

Gentleman's Guide to Passages South; Bruce van Sant, Cruising Guide Publications, USA

Greek Waters Pilot; Rod Heikell, Imray, Great Britain

Guide to Cruising the Chesapeake Bay; Chesapeake Bay Communications, USA

Guide to French Mediterranean Ports, including Corsica; Derek Bowskill, Adlard Coles Nautical, Great Britain

Indian Ocean Handbook; Rod Heikell, Imray, Great Britain

Ionian; Rod Heikell, Imray, Great Britain

Islas Baleares; ed. Anne Hammick, Imray, Great Britain

Italian Waters Pilot; Rod Heikel, Imray, Great Britain

Landfalls of Paradise, Cruising Guide to the Pacific Islands; Earl Hinz, Western Marine Enterprise, USA

Madeira Cruising Guide; World Cruising Publications, Great Britain

Mediterranean Cruising Handbook; Rod Heikel, Imray, Great Britain

Mediterranean France and Corsica Pilot; Rod Heikell, Imray, Great Britain

Normandy and Channel Islands Pilot; Mark Brackenbury, Adlard Coles Nautical, Great Britain

North Africa, Gibraltar to Morocco, Algeria, Tunisia & Malta; RCC Pilotage Foundation, Imray, Great Britain

North Biscay Pilot; ed. Nicholas Heath, Imray, Great Britain

North Brittany and Channel Islands Cruising; Peter Cumberlidge

Northern Territory Coast; John Knight, Australia

Norwegian Cruising Guide; John Armitage and Mark Brackenbury, Adlard Coles Nautical, Great Britain

Panama Canal Pilot's Handbook; The Panama Canal Commission

Red Sea Pilot; E Morgan and S Davies, Imray, Great Britain

Reed's Nautical Alamanac, Caribbean; ed. John & Leslie Kettlewell

Reed's Nautical Almanac, North American East Coast; ed. John & Leslie Kettlewell

Sail Thailand; ed. Collin Piprell

Sailor's Guide to the Windward Islands; Chris Doyle, Cruising Guide Publications, USA

Saronic, the Saronic and Argolic Gulfs including the Peloponnese; Rod Heikel

South Africa Nautical Almanac; Tom Morgan

South Atlantic Coasts of South America; Pete and Annie Hill, RCC Pilotage Foundation, Great Britain

South Biscay Pilot; Robin Brandon, Adlard Coles Nautical, Great Britain

South and West Coasts of Ireland Sailing Directions; Irish Cruising Club

South France Pilot; Robin Brandon, Imray, Great Britain
  East Cote d'Azur
  The Riviera
  Golf du Lion
  La Corse

Southern Ocean Cruising; Sally and Jerome Poncet, Government Printing Office, Falkland Islands

South Pacific Anchorages; Warwick Clay, Imray, Great Britain

Street's Cruising Guide to the Eastern Caribbean; Donald Street, Norton, USA

Texas & Louisiana Cruising Guide; ed. Bob Heller

The Bahamas Cruising Guide; Mathew Wilson, International Marine, USA

The Baltic Sea; RCC Pilotage Foundation, Great Britain

The Forgotten Middle; *Cruiser's Guide to the Pacific Coasts of Guatemala, El Salvador, Honduras and Nicaragua*; Roy and Carol Roberts

The Insider's Cruising Guide to the Rio Dulce; Frank Schooley

The Lesser Antilles; ed. Oz Robinson, Imray, Great Britain

The Pacific Crossing Guide; ed. Michael Pocock, Adlard Coles Nautical, Great Britain

The Panama Guide; Nancy and Tom Zydler

The Shell Channel Pilot; Tom Cunliffe

The Yachtsman's Guide to Jamaica

Turkish Waters & Cyprus Pilot; Rod Heikell, Imray, Great Britain

Turks & Caicos Charts; Bob Gascoine

World Cruising Guide; ed. Gwenda Cornell, World Cruising Publications, Great Britain

Yachting Guide to the ABC Islands; Gerard van Erp

Yachting Guide to Bermuda; ed. Edward Harris

Yachting Guide to the ABC Islands; Gerard van Erp

Yachting Guide to the South Shore of Nova Scotia; Arthur Dechman

Yachtsman's Fiji; Michael Calder

Yachtsman's Guide to the Virgin Islands; ed. Meredith Fields, Tropic Isle Publishers, USA

Yachtsman's Guide to the Windward Islands; Julius Wilensky

Yachtsman's Handbook and Cruising Guide to Malta; CAS Services, Malta

Yachtsman's Navigator Guide to the Chilean Channels; Alberto Mantellero

LIST OF ROUTES (in numerical order)

AN11	*Europe to North America (northern routes)*
AN12	*Europe to North America (southern routes)*
AN13	*Southbound from Northern Europe*
AN14	*Routes across the Bay of Biscay*
AN15	*Northern Europe to Portugal*
AN16	*Northern Europe to Mediterranean*
AN17	*Northern Europe to Madeira*
AN18	*Northern Europe to Canary Islands*
AN19	*Northern Europe to Azores*
AN21	*Portugal to Gibraltar*
AN22	*Portugal to Canary Islands*
AN23	*Portugal to Madeira*
AN24	*Portugal to Azores*
AN25	*Portugal to Northern Europe*
AN31	*Gibraltar to Madeira*
AN32	*Gibraltar to Canary Islands*
AN33	*Gibraltar to Lesser Antilles*
AN34	*Gibraltar to Northern Europe*
AN35	*Gibraltar to Portugal*
AN36	*Gibraltar to Azores*
AN37	*Gibraltar to North America*
AN38	*Gibraltar to Atlantic Morocco*
AN41	*Madeira to Canary Islands*
AN42	*Madeira to Lesser Antilles*
AN43	*Madeira to Azores*
AN44	*Madeira to Northern Europe*
AN45	*Madeira to Portugal*
AN46	*Madeira to Gibraltar*
AN51	*Canary Islands to Lesser Antilles*
AN52	*Canary Islands to Cape Verde Islands*
AN53	*Canary Islands to West Africa*
AN54	*Canary Islands to Bahamas*
AN55	*Canary Islands to Bermuda*
AN56	*Canary Islands to Azores*
AN57	*Canary Islands to Madeira*
AN58	*Canary Islands to Gibraltar*
AN61	*Cape Verde Islands to Azores*
AN62	*Cape Verde Islands to Lesser Antilles*
AN63	*West Africa to Azores*
AN64	*West Africa to Lesser Antilles*
AN65	*West Africa to Northern Brazil and Guyanas*
AN71	*Lesser Antilles to Venezuela*
AN72	*Lesser Antilles to ABC Islands*
AN73	*Lesser Antilles to Colombia*
AN74	*Lesser Antilles to Panama*
AN75	*Lesser Antilles to Greater Antilles*
AN76	*Lesser Antilles to Bahamas*
AN77	*Lesser Antilles to North America*
AN78	*Lesser Antilles to Bermuda*
AN79	*Lesser Antilles to Azores*
AN81	*Virgin Islands to Panama*
AN82	*Virgin Islands to Jamaica*
AN83	*Virgin Islands to the Gulf of Mexico*
AN84	*Virgin Islands to Turks & Caicos*
AN85	*Virgin Islands to Bahamas*
AN86	*Virgin Islands to Florida*
AN87	*Virgin Islands to North America*
AN88	*Virgin Islands to Bermuda*
AN89	*Virgin Islands to Azores*
AN91	*Panama to Central America*
AN92	*Panama to the Gulf of Mexico and Florida*
AN93	*Panama to Jamaica*
AN94	*Panama to Hispaniola*
AN95	*Panama to Virgin Islands*
AN96	*Panama to Lesser Antilles*
AN97	*Panama to Colombia*
AN98	*Panama to Venezuela and the ABC Islands*
AN99	*Panama to Bahamas and USA*
AN101	*ABC Islands and Venezuela to Lesser Antilles*
AN102	*ABC Islands and Venezuela to Virgin Islands*
AN103	*Northbound from Venezuela and the ABC Islands*
AN104	*ABC Islands and Venezuela to Panama*
AN105	*ABC Islands and Venezuela to Colombia*
AN106	*Colombia to Panama*
AN107	*Jamaica to Panama*
AN108	*Jamaica to Central America and Mexico*
AN111	*Northbound from the Bahamas and Florida*
AN112	*Bahamas to Bermuda*
AN113	*Bahamas to the Eastern Caribbean*
AN114	*Bahamas to Panama*
AN115	*Florida to Bermuda*
AN116	*Florida to the Eastern Caribbean*
AN117	*Southbound from Florida*
AN118	*Southern Bahamas to the Western Caribbean*
AN121	*Bermuda to USA*
AN122	*Bermuda to Canada*
AN123	*Bermuda to Northern Europe*
AN124	*Bermuda to Gibraltar*
AN125	*Bermuda to Azores*
AN126	*Bermuda to Lesser Antilles*
AN127	*Bermuda to Virgin Islands*
AN131	*Azores to Ireland*
AN132	*Azores to English Channel*
AN133	*Azores to Portugal*
AN134	*Azores to Gibraltar*
AN135	*Azores to Madeira*
AN136	*Azores to Canary Islands*
AN137	*Azores to Bermuda*
AN138	*Azores to USA*
AN139	*Azores to Canada*
AN141	*North America to Northern Europe*
AN142	*North America to Mediterranean*
AN143	*North America to Bermuda*
AN144	*North America to Azores*
AN145	*North America to the Eastern Caribbean*
AN146	*North America to Bahamas*
AN147	*North America to Panama*
AN148	*North America to the Western Caribbean*
AN151	*English Channel to the Baltic*
AN152	*England to Scandinavia*
AN153	*Scotland to Norway*
AN154	*Scotland to Spitsbergen*
AN155	*Scotland to Iceland*
AN156	*Ireland to Iceland*
AN157	*Scotland to Greenland*
AN158	*Ireland to Greenland*

AN161	*Southbound from the Baltic*		**PN25**	*Panama to Hawaii*
AN162	*Scandinavia to England*		**PN26**	*Central America and Mexico to Hawaii*
AN163	*Scandinavia to Scotland*		**PN27**	*Mexico and Central America to Panama*
AN164	*Norway to Spitsbergen*		**PN31**	*Hawaii to Alaska*
AN165	*Norway to Iceland*		**PN32**	*Hawaii to the Pacific Northwest*
AN166	*Norway to Greenland*		**PN33**	*Hawaii to California*
AN171	*Northbound from North America*		**PN34**	*Hawaii to Central America and Mexico*
AN172	*Greenland to Iceland*		**PN35**	*Hawaii to Line Islands*
AN173	*Iceland to Spitsbergen*		**PN36**	*Hawaii to Marshall Islands*
AN174	*Iceland to Norway*		**PN37**	*Hawaii to Japan*
AN175	*Iceland to Scotland*		**PN38**	*Hawaii to Guam*
AN176	*Iceland to Ireland*		**PN41**	*Singapore to the Gulf of Siam*
AN177	*Iceland to Greenland*		**PN42**	*Singapore to Vietnam*
AN178	*Iceland to Canada and Bermuda*		**PN43**	*Singapore to Hong Kong*
AN179	*Southbound from Greenland*		**PN44**	*Singapore to the Philippines*
AT11	*Europe to South Africa*		**PN45**	*Singapore to North Borneo*
AT12	*Canary Islands to South Africa*		**PN51**	*Philippines to Singapore*
AT13	*North America to South Africa*		**PN52**	*Philippines to Hong Kong*
AT14	*Canary Islands to Brazil*		**PN53**	*Philippines to Japan*
AT15	*Cape Verde Islands to Brazil*		**PN54**	*Philippines to Guam*
AT16	*West Africa to Brazil*		**PN55**	*Philippines to Palau*
AT17	*Lesser Antilles to Brazil*		**PN61**	*Hong Kong to Singapore*
AT21	*Brazil to Lesser Antilles*		**PN62**	*Hong Kong to Philippines*
AT22	*Brazil to Europe*		**PN63**	*Hong Kong to Japan*
AT23	*South Africa to Azores*		**PN64**	*Hong Kong to Guam*
AT24	*South Africa to Lesser Antilles*		**PN65**	*Taiwan to Guam*
AT25	*South Africa to North America*		**PN66**	*Hong Kong to Vietnam*
AT26	*Cape Horn to Europe*		**PN71**	*Japan to Alaska*
AT27	*Cape Horn to North America*		**PN72**	*Japan to Pacific Northwest*
AS11	*Cape Town to St Helena*		**PN73**	*Japan to California*
AS12	*St Helena to Ascension*		**PN74**	*Japan to Hawaii*
AS13	*St Helena to Brazil*		**PN75**	*Japan to Marshall Islands*
AS14	*Cape Town to Brazil*		**PN76**	*Japan to Guam*
AS21	*South America to South Africa*		**PN77**	*Japan to Hong Kong*
AS22	*Brazil to Tristan da Cunha*		**PN78**	*Japan to China*
AS23	*Tristan da Cunha to Cape Town*		**PN79**	*Japan to Philippines*
AS24	*South America to Falkland Islands*		**PN81**	*Guam to Palau*
AS25	*South America to Tierra del Fuego*		**PN82**	*Guam to Carolines*
AS26	*Southbound from Brazil*		**PN83**	*Guam to Japan*
AS27	*Northbound from Falkland Islands*		**PN84**	*Palau to Guam*
AS28	*Northbound from Tierra del Fuego*		**PN85**	*Guam to Philippines*
AS29	*Northbound from Argentina and Brazil*		**PN86**	*Palau to Philippines*
AS31	*Falklands to Tristan da Cunha*		**PN91**	*Kiribati to Hawaii*
AS32	*Falklands to South Georgia*		**PN92**	*Marshall Islands to Hawaii*
AS33	*Falklands to Antarctica*		**PN93**	*Line Islands to Hawaii*
AS34	*Falklands to Tierra del Fuego*		**PN94**	*Marshall Islands to Kiribati*
AS35	*Tierra del Fuego to Falkland Islands*		**PN95**	*Marshall Islands to the Carolines*
AS36	*Tierra del Fuego to Antarctica*		**PN96**	*Kiribati to the Carolines*
AS37	*Antarctica to Tierra del Fuego*		**PT11**	*Southbound from Panama*
AS38	*Antarctica to Falkland Islands*		**PT12**	*Panama to Galapagos*
PN11	*California to Hawaii*		**PT13**	*Panama to Marquesas*
PN12	*Southbound from California*		**PT14**	*California and Mexico to Galapagos*
PN13	*Northbound from California*		**PT15**	*California to Marquesas*
PN14	*California to British Columbia*		**PT16**	*California to Tahiti*
PN15	*Alaska to British Columbia*		**PT17**	*Pacific Northwest to Marquesas*
PN16	*British Columbia to California*		**PT18**	*Mexico and Central America to Marquesas*
PN17	*Pacific Northwest to Hawaii*		**PT19**	*Central America to Galapagos and Easter Island*
PN18	*California to Alaska*		**PT21**	*Marquesas to Hawaii*
PN19	*Pacific Northwest to Alaska*		**PT22**	*Tahiti to Hawaii*
PN21	*Panama to Central America and Mexico*		**PT23**	*Tahiti to Panama*
PN22	*Central America and Mexico to California*		**PT24**	*Cook Islands to Hawaii*
PN23	*Panama to British Columbia*		**PT25**	*Hawaii to Tahiti*
PN24	*Panama to Alaska*		**PT26**	*Hawaii to Marquesas*

PT31	*Tuvalu to Kiribati*		**PS78**	*Vanuatu to Torres Strait*
PT32	*Kiribati to Tuvalu*		**PS79**	*Vanuatu to Solomon Islands*
PT33	*New Guinea to Philippines*		**PS81**	*Solomon Islands to Papua New Guinea*
PT34	*New Guinea to Micronesia*		**PS82**	*Solomon Islands to Torres Strait*
PT35	*Palau to New Guinea*		**PS83**	*Solomon Islands to Queensland*
PT36	*Micronesia to Southern Melanesia*		**PS84**	*Papua New Guinea to Queensland*
PT37	*Melanesia to Micronesia*		**PS85**	*Papua New Guinea to Torres Strait*
PS11	*Galapagos to Marquesas*		**PS86**	*Papua New Guinea to Indonesia*
PS12	*Galapagos to Easter Island*		**PS91**	*New South Wales to New Zealand*
PS13	*Galapagos to Gambier Islands*		**PS92**	*New South Wales to New Caledonia*
PS14	*South America to Easter Island*		**PS93**	*New South Wales to Fiji*
PS15	*Easter Island to Pitcairn*		**PS94**	*New South Wales to Vanuatu*
PS16	*Pitcairn to Gambier Islands*		**PS101**	*Queensland to New Zealand*
PS17	*Easter Island to Magellan Strait or Cape Horn*		**PS102**	*Queensland to New Caledonia*
PS18	*Ecuador and Peru to Chile*		**PS103**	*Queensland to Vanuatu*
PS21	*Gambier to Marquesas*		**PS104**	*Queensland to Fiji*
PS22	*Marquesas to Tuamotus*		**PS105**	*Queensland to Solomon Islands*
PS23	*Marquesas to Tahiti*		**PS106**	*Queensland to Papua New Guinea*
PS24	*Marquesas to Northern Cooks*		**PS107**	*North Queensland to Darwin*
PS25	*Tahiti to Austral Islands*		**IN11**	*Singapore to Western Malaysia*
PS26	*Tahiti to Cape Horn or Magellan Strait*		**IN12**	*Western Malaysia to Thailand*
PS31	*Society Islands to Cook Islands*		**IN13**	*Western Malaysia to Sri Lanka*
PS32	*Society Islands to Tonga*		**IN14**	*Thailand to Sri Lanka*
PS33	*Society Islands to Samoa*		**IN15**	*Thailand to Singapore*
PS34	*Society Islands to New Zealand*		**IN21**	*Sri Lanka to Red Sea*
PS35	*Southern Cook Islands to Samoa*		**IN22**	*Sri Lanka to Oman*
PS36	*Southern Cook Islands to Tonga*		**IN23**	*Sri Lanka to India*
PS37	*Cook Islands to New Zealand*		**IN24**	*Sri Lanka to Maldives*
PS38	*Northern Cook Islands to Samoa*		**IN25**	*Sri Lanka to Singapore*
PS39	*Northern Cook Islands to Tonga*		**IN26**	*Maldives to India*
PS41	*Samoa to Tonga*		**IN27**	*Maldives to Oman*
PS42	*Samoa to Fiji*		**IN28**	*Maldives to Red Sea*
PS43	*Samoa to Wallis*		**IN31**	*India to Red Sea*
PS44	*Samoa to Society Islands*		**IN32**	*Oman to Red Sea*
PS45	*Tonga to Society Islands*		**IN33**	*Red Sea to Sri Lanka*
PS46	*Tonga to Samoa*		**IN34**	*Red Sea to Maldives*
PS47	*Tonga to Fiji*		**IN35**	*India to Oman*
PS48	*Tonga to New Zealand*		**IT11**	*Bali to Singapore*
PS49	*Northbound from Samoa*		**IT12**	*Bali to Sri Lanka*
PS51	*Fiji to Samoa*		**IT13**	*Cocos Keeling to Sri Lanka*
PS52	*Fiji to Tonga*		**IT14**	*Chagos to Sri Lanka*
PS53	*Fiji to New Zealand*		**IT15**	*Chagos to Maldives*
PS54	*Fiji to New Caledonia*		**IT16**	*Seychelles to Red Sea*
PS55	*Fiji to Vanuatu*		**IT17**	*Kenya to Red Sea*
PS56	*Wallis to Fiji*		**IT18**	*Kenya to Sri Lanka*
PS57	*Tuvalu to Fiji*		**IT21**	*Maldives to Chagos*
PS58	*Tuvalu to Wallis*		**IT22**	*Red Sea to East Africa*
PS59	*Wallis to Tuvalu*		**IT23**	*Red Sea to South Indian Ocean*
PS61	*New Zealand to New South Wales*		**IT24**	*Sri Lanka to Chagos*
PS62	*New Zealand to Queensland*		**IT25**	*Sri Lanka to Mauritius*
PS63	*New Zealand to New Caledonia*		**IS11**	*Torres Strait to Darwin*
PS64	*New Zealand to Fiji*		**IS12**	*Torres Strait to Bali*
PS65	*New Zealand to Tonga*		**IS13**	*Darwin to Ambon*
PS66	*New Zealand to Cook Islands*		**IS14**	*Darwin to Bali*
PS67	*New Zealand to Tahiti*		**IS15**	*Darwin to Christmas Island*
PS68	*New Zealand to Cape Horn or Magellan Strait*		**IS16**	*West Australia to Cocos Keeling*
PS71	*New Caledonia to Fiji*		**IS17**	*West Australia to Bass Strait*
PS72	*New Caledonia to New Zealand*		**IS21**	*Bali to Christmas Island*
PS73	*New Caledonia to New South Wales*		**IS22**	*Bali to Chagos*
PS74	*New Caledonia to Queensland*		**IS23**	*Bali to Cocos Keeling*
PS75	*New Caledonia to Torres Strait*		**IS24**	*Bali to Mauritius*
PS76	*Vanuatu to New Caledonia*		**IS25**	*Bali to Darwin*
PS77	*Vanuatu to North Queensland*		**IS31**	*Christmas Island to Cocos Keeling*

IS32	*Cocos Keeling to Mauritius*		**M31**	*French Riviera to Balearics*
IS33	*Cocos Keeling to Chagos*		**M32**	*French Riviera to Messina Strait*
IS34	*Christmas Island to Chagos*		**M33**	*French Riviera to Malta*
IS35	*Chagos to Seychelles*		**M34**	*French Riviera to Gibraltar*
IS36	*Chagos to Mauritius*		**M35**	*French Riviera to Corsica*
IS37	*Chagos to Madagascar*		**M36**	*French Riviera to Tunisia*
IS41	*Seychelles to Mauritius*		**M41**	*Sicily to Greece*
IS42	*Seychelles to Comoros*		**M42**	*Sicily to French Riviera*
IS43	*Seychelles to East Africa*		**M43**	*Sicily to Balearics*
IS44	*Comoros to East Africa*		**M44**	*Sicily to Gibraltar*
IS45	*Comoros to Seychelles*		**M45**	*Sicily to Port Said*
IS46	*Comoros to South Africa*		**M51**	*Malta to Gibraltar*
IS51	*Mauritius to Réunion*		**M52**	*Malta to Greece*
IS52	*Mauritius to South Africa*		**M53**	*Malta to Rhodes*
IS53	*Réunion to South Africa*		**M54**	*Malta to Cyprus*
IS54	*Mauritius to Seychelles*		**M55**	*Malta to Port Said*
IS55	*Mauritius to Comoros*		**M56**	*Malta to Tunisia*
IS56	*Mauritius to Madagascar*		**M57**	*Malta to Balearics*
IS61	*East Africa to Seychelles*		**M58**	*Malta to Italy*
IS62	*Durban to Mauritius*		**M61**	*Greece to Malta*
IS63	*Durban to Cape Town*		**M62**	*Greece to Messina Strait*
IS64	*Cape Town to West Australia*		**M63**	*Rhodes to Cyprus*
IS65	*Northbound from South Africa*		**M64**	*Rhodes to Port Said*
RN1	*Bab el Mandeb to Port Sudan*		**M65**	*Rhodes to Malta*
RN2	*Bab el Mandeb to Massawa*		**M71**	*Port Said to Malta*
RN3	*Bab el Mandeb to Hodaida*		**M72**	*Port Said to Messina Strait*
RN4	*Port Sudan to Suez*		**M73**	*Port Said to Crete*
RN5	*Massawa to Port Sudan*		**M74**	*Port Said to Rhodes*
RS1	*Suez to Port Sudan*		**M75**	*Port Said to Cyprus*
RS2	*Port Sudan to Gulf of Aden*		**M76**	*Port Said to Israel*
RS3	*Port Sudan to Massawa*		**M81**	*Cyprus to Israel*
RS4	*Southbound from Massawa*		**M82**	*Cyprus to Port Said*
M11	*Gibraltar to the Balearics*		**M83**	*Cyprus to Rhodes*
M12	*Gibraltar to Sicily*		**M84**	*Cyprus to Crete*
M13	*Gibraltar to North Africa*		**M85**	*Cyprus to Malta*
M14	*Gibraltar to Malta*		**M86**	*Cyprus to Southern Turkey*
M21	*Balearics to French Riviera*		**M87**	*Cyprus to Lebanon*
M22	*Balearics to Messina Strait*		**M88**	*Cyprus to Syria*
M23	*Balearics to Malta*		**M91**	*Israel to Cyprus*
M24	*Balearics to Gibraltar*		**M92**	*Israel to Port Said*
M25	*Balearics to Corsica*		**M93**	*Israel to Malta*
M26	*Balearics to Tunisia*		**M94**	*Israel to Crete*

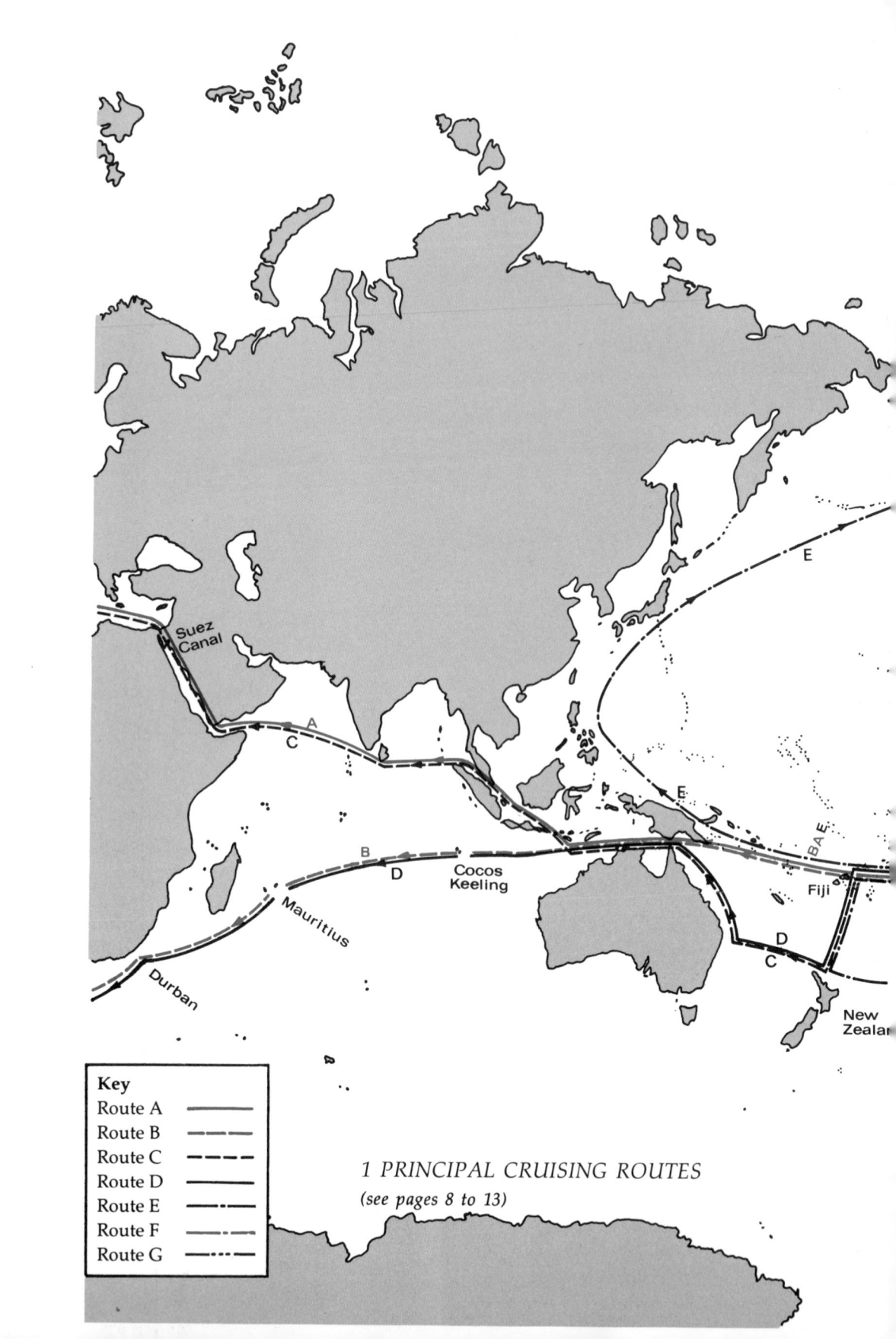

Suez
Canal

A

C

B

D

Cocos
Keeling

Mauritius

Durban

E

E

B A E

Fiji

D

C

New
Zealand

Key

Route A	———
Route B	— — —
Route C	- - - -
Route D	———
Route E	—·—·—
Route F	—·—·—
Route G	—··—··—

1 PRINCIPAL CRUISING ROUTES
(see pages 8 to 13)